T0330419

THE HANDBOOK OF
ECONOMIC
DEVELOPMENT
AND
INSTITUTIONS

THE HANDBOOK OF
ECONOMIC
DEVELOPMENT
AND
INSTITUTIONS

EDITED BY

Jean-Marie Baland,
François Bourguignon,
Jean-Philippe Platteau,
and Thierry Verdier

PRINCETON UNIVERSITY PRESS
PRINCETON AND OXFORD

Jacket art courtesy of Shutterstock

Library of Congress Cataloging-in-Publication Data

Names: Bourguignon, François, author. | Platteau, J. P. (Jean-Philippe), 1947– author. |
Baland, Jean-Marie, author.
Title: The handbook of economic development and institutions / François Bourguignon,
Jean-Philippe Platteau, Jean-Marie Baland.
Description: Princeton : Princeton University Press, [2020]
Identifiers: LCCN 2019020148 | ISBN 9780691191218 (hardcover)
Subjects: LCSH: Economic development—Political aspects. |
Economics—Sociological aspects. | Economic policy.
Classification: LCC HD87 .B687 2020 | DDC 338.9—dc23
LC record available at https://lccn.loc.gov/2019020148

British Library Cataloging-in-Publication Data is available

This Handbook is the result of work funded under the Economic Development and Institutions
research programme. Oxford Policy Management (OPM) was appointed by the UK Department
for International Development to deliver this programme, which aims to "produce a body of
evidence and insights into what practicable actions produce institutional changes that improve
economic outcomes and increase growth." The consortium is led by OPM and includes the
Paris School of Economics, University of Namur, and Aide à la Décision Économique.

This project was funded with UK aid from the UK government.

CONTENTS

PART 4   FAMILIES, GENDER, AND CULTURE

PART 5   SECTORAL APPROACHES

CONTRIBUTORS

Meghana Ayyagari
   George Washington University, School of Business

Jean-Marie Baland
   Center for Research in Economic Development
   University of Namur, Department of Economics

Pranab Bardhan
   University of California, Berkeley, Department of Economics

Thorsten Beck
   Cass Business School, City, University of London

Tessa Bold
   Stockholm University, Institute for International Economic Studies

François Bourguignon
   Paris School of Economics

Ernesto Dal Bó
   University of California, Berkeley, Department of Economics

Jaime de Melo
   International Centre for Trade and Sustainable Development
   University of Geneva, School of Economics and Management

Asli Demirgüç-Kunt
   The World Bank

Steven N. Durlauf
   Harris School of Public Policy
   University of Chicago, Department of Economics

Antonio Estache
   ECARES, Université libre de Bruxelles

Joan Esteban
   Insitut d'Analisi Economica
   Barcelona GSE
   International Economic Association

Marcel Fafchamps
   Stanford University, Department of Economics

Frederico Finan
   University of California, Berkeley, Department of Economics

Catherine Guirkinger
   Centre for Research in Economic Development
   University of Namur, Department of Economics

Jan Willem Gunning
Vrije Universiteit Amsterdam, Department of Economics

Stephan Klasen
University of Göttingen, Department of Economics

Eliana La Ferrara
Bocconi University, Department of Economics
Laboratory for Effective Anti-Poverty Policies

Vojislav Maksimovic
Robert H. Smith School of Business

Dilip Mookherjee
Boston University, Department of Economics

Kaivan Munshi
University of Cambridge, Department of Economics

Marcelo Olarreaga
University of Geneva, School of Economics and Management
World Trade Institute

Jean-Philippe Platteau
Centre for Research in Economic Development
University of Namur, Department of Economics

Imran Rasul
University College London, Department of Economics
Centre for the Microeconomic Analysis of Public Policy at the
Institute for Fiscal Studies
International Growth Centre

Debraj Ray
New York University, Department of Economics

Gerard Roland
University of California, Berkeley, Department of Econmics
Centre for Economic Policy Research
National Bureau of Economic Research

E. Somanathan
Indian Statistical Institute, the Economics and Planning Unit

Rohini Somanathan
Delhi School of Economics, Department of Economics

Jakob Svensson
Stockholm University, Institute for International Economic Studies
Centre for Economic Policy Research

Ragnar Torvik
Norwegian University of Science and Technology, Department of Economics

Thierry Verdier
Paris School of Economics

THE HANDBOOK OF
ECONOMIC
DEVELOPMENT
AND
INSTITUTIONS

ECONOMIC DEVELOPMENT AND INSTITUTIONS

An Introduction

Jean-Marie Baland, François Bourguignon, Jean-Philippe Platteau, and Thierry Verdier

In recent decades, economists have increasingly emphasized the importance of institutions as a fundamental factor for economic growth and development. Starting with the influential work of Acemoglu et al. (2001, 2005), an abundant literature in economic and political sciences has investigated theoretically and empirically the impact of institutions on some aggregate developmental outcomes (mostly GDP per capita or growth, but sometimes other outcomes such as health, education, or political rights). The findings of this literature have been of critical importance for development economists and policy practitioners because they suggest that institutional quality may be an important determinant of the persistence of poverty and low developmental outcomes in the world.

At the same time, aggregate cross-country analyses have fundamental limits in properly identifying the causality link from institutions to development (Pande and Udry 2005). This calls for a need to provide precise descriptions of the mechanisms through which institutions play a role in determining various development outcomes as well as to move beyond aggregate studies to explore the heterogeneity of institutions in different settings. Moreover, we must emphasize the importance of informal institutions in developing countries and their significant role in shaping socioeconomic outcomes. They are, however, much harder to "measure."[1] We also need to better understand their interactions with formal institutions and how they jointly affect the actions and interactions of various members of society.

These issues are not new and they have long attracted the attention of social scientists, including economists. A deep-rooted view among the latter is that changes in traditional values, attitudes, and institutions were necessary for long-run development (for an overview of sociologists' contributions, see Yousfi 2011). Arthur Lewis (1955) certainly shared this view when, commenting on the historical failure of Spain to exploit the economic opportunities presented by the discovery of the New World, he concluded that "It is possible for a nation to stifle its economic growth by adopting passionately and intolerantly religious doctrines of a kind which are incompatible with growth" (Lewis 1955: 107).

On the other hand, Lewis was inclined to think that religious beliefs, for example, may evolve and be re-interpreted depending on the economic environment confronting societies. In Lewis's framework, these two views can be reconciled: traditional values and attitudes, whenever they are hostile to economic advancement, will eventually adapt themselves to new economic opportunities, yet as this adaptation process may take time, traditional culture is likely to slow down the rate of change and also distort its effects (Lewis 1955: 106).

> Other authors also thought that institutions and the economy co-evolve: Not only must economic organization be transformed, but social organization . . . must also be modified so that the basic complex of values and motivations may be more favorable for development. (Meier and Baldwin 1957: 356, 359)

> Generally, a slow but steady development is likely to create fewer political, social and economic tensions; and it is likely that an attempt to force the pace too strenuously may also be economically wasteful because the social and personal changes may not take place which are necessary to enable individuals or the society to profit from the development and to sustain it. (Bauer and Yamey 1957: 71)

This raises the question, to what extent are some institutions themselves transformed by economic development. We need to better understand the process of institutional change and its interaction with the dynamics of economic development. In fact, it may well be the case that some institutions have to change or be changed rather significantly before economic growth can take place, as in the case of extractive institutions analyzed by Acemoglu et al. (2001).[2] Others need not and may be viewed as "spontaneously" evolving with economic development. One of the issues is then to determine which institutions belong to the former "fundamental" category and which fit within the latter "adaptative" category. In addition, adaptive processes and their interactions with growth and development are presumably highly nonlinear (see Durlauf, this Handbook). Thus, it is possible that very few institutions need to change before growth starts, yet until some critical institutions have sufficiently evolved, growth will remain rather slow.

This approach to the role of institution seems to us much more fruitful and relevant than the sort of grand approach that purports to discover the institutional determinants of growth and development conceived as fundamental prerequisites for growth. It echoes the "adaptative" perspective suggested by Joseph Schumpeter in his critique of Max Weber Ideal Types:

> So soon as we realize that pure Feudalism and pure Capitalism are equally unrealistic creations of our own mind, the problem of what it was that turned the one into the other vanishes completely. The society of the feudal ages contained all the germs of the society of the capitalist age. These germs developed by slow degrees, each step teaching its lesson and producing another increment of capitalist methods and of capitalist "spirit." (Schumpeter 1954: 80–82)

In the following sections, we will first propose some definitions of the key concepts, then present the various chapters of this Handbook and their global focus, before discussing open avenues that we feel are in need of further research.

I.1. DEFINITION OF KEY CONCEPTS

We conceive of institutions as rules, procedures, or other human devices that constrain individual behavior, either explicitly or implicitly, with a view to making individual expectations about others' behavior converge and allowing individual actions to become coordinated (North 1990). By definition, they are not exclusively determined by the technological environment but also depend upon the local culture, for instance, in the selection of a particular focal point in a multiplicity of possible equilibria (Aoki 2001). These focal points can themselves get progressively "institutionalized" as a norm of behavior.

Contracts constitute a very good example of our conception of an institution. Indeed, a contract is a procedure that, properly implemented, constrains individual behaviors and consequently frames actors' expectations on the likely outcome. A contract involves the following features. First, it specifies a set of actions to be implemented (how, where, when, and by whom). Second, it involves the specification of the various consequences when these actions are not undertaken (conditional on the degree of verifiability and enforcement capacity of the parties involved). As such, these elements create constraints on actors' behaviors and expectations on outcomes within and outside the limits of the contract.

Contracts are typically incomplete. As a result, they may be subject to culturally embedded local interpretations and converging expectations. For instance, standard incentive compatibility conditions would predict the observation of a considerable variety of contracts with terms varying according to the characteristics of the parties involved (e.g., their degree of risk aversion). The fact that some contract terms—for example, the shares in sharecropping contracts, or the interest rates in loan contracts—tend to be uniform in particular areas suggests that focal point representations may be present (Stiglitz 1996).[3]

We conceive of an institution as formal when the rules that it embodies are made explicit, most typically when they are written, and when they are enforced through channels widely accepted as official (Helmke and Levitsky 2004). Regarding the first feature, the requirement is that the rules are stated in a sufficiently clear and articulated manner that the people involved have little uncertainty about how they are expected to behave in given circumstances. Regarding the second feature, it is to the extent that the rules are effectively enforced that people also know the likely consequences of their actions.[4] If rule violation is imperfectly detected, enforcement is itself imperfect and these consequences are uncertain.

An important implication is that, because they are written, formal rules contain information that is perfectly transferable to an individual who does not belong to the community or group in which they have been laid down. They thus resemble blueprints in the field of technology: both are codified statements and prescriptions that can be understood by anyone who has learned the language in which they are written. Also, a well-functioning formal institution specifies not only the actions required in specific circumstances but also the sanctions that follow violations of the prescriptions. To put it another way, it is a codified mechanism that determines the allocation of decision responsibilities (it thus delimits a domain of individual freedom) and its implementation inside a particular social group and in well-defined circumstances. To illustrate, a political constitution under a presidential regime states the conditions and frequency of presidential elections. The expectations of citizens and political actors are shaped by this constitution, and they act accordingly. The very fact that a president tempted by authoritarian rule and unlimited mandate knows that he must first amend the constitution, and that there are rules organizing a constitutional change, is evidence that it is an institution in the formal sense. Many private contracts, such as a loan contract, share the same characteristics.

There are three important qualifying remarks that must accompany the preceding way of defining a formal institution. First, it does not imply that the rule is mechanically followed. The most obvious reason is that the identification of the circumstances that apply leaves room for interpretation by the actors or the law enforcers. Hence the unavoidable subjectivity of the judges dealing with cases where a rule is invoked. In particular, whether attenuating circumstances can be called for is a matter for the judge or the jury (in a court of appeal) to decide. In addition, the prescriptions of the law themselves may be stated in rather vague or incomplete terms, thereby requiring the judge to exercise his own judgmental capacity. For example, in the divorce legislation of some advanced countries, the alimony to be regularly paid by a man to his ex-spouse may not exceed a certain proportion of his income (one-third in Belgium) while the precise amount should be calculated in such a way that the level of living of the ex-spouse does not fall. All judges nevertheless know that this requirement is impossible to meet because divorce has the general effect of impoverishing both parties (owing to the loss of scale economies). Even granting the maximum proportion to the ex-wife is typically insufficient to allow her to maintain her previous standard of living. The subjective appreciation of the law by the judges is again necessary to make a decision about the proportion eventually set by the court. There are thus numerous cases in which "even when institutions are formally codified, their guiding expectations often remain ambiguous and always are subject to interpretation, debate, and contestation" (Mahoney and Thelen 2010: 10–11).

Second, the rules themselves may comprise ambiguous or contradictory statements about the appropriate behavior. For example, it is well known that the Sharia, which is the written sacred foundation of Islam, comprises normative statements that are not easily compatible with each other (e.g., those defining the appropriate dress code for women or the obligation of married women to go to the mosque for prayer).[5] In another example, when laws are subject to innumerable amendments by the parliament, as is the case in present-day France, they are susceptible to containing inner contradictions that make the task of the enforcing agencies especially difficult.

The third qualification relates to the nature of the enforcement mechanism. A formal institution has to be implemented through a channel widely accepted as official. In most cases it goes directly through the operation of the rule of law with sanctions that are backed by a central authority. Formal institutions, however, may also involve self-imposed official rules that govern local organizations such as corporations, political parties, and interest groups. In such cases, the direct enforcer seems to be the organization itself (i.e., the board of the corporation, the committee of the political party, or the council of the association), and not necessarily the state. The state is still likely to be the last recourse and backing enforcement power, while the rules and the specifics of the implementation mechanism are decided by the organization itself. In any case, directly or indirectly, a well-functioning state seems to be necessary to make formal institutions credible.

It should be observed that even under an effective state, judges or bureaucrats may decide to refrain from implementing the law or the formal rules. For example, in West

Africa, judges dealing with inheritance cases may opt for a settlement that rests on a compromise between the formal law and the custom. Thus, when one son and one daughter disagree about their entitled shares of the wealth of their deceased father, there are cases where the judge persuades the defendant (the son who asks for the enforcement of the custom according to which he should inherit the entire wealth of the father) and the claimant (the daughter who asks for the enforcement of the statutory law that has established the principle of gender equality in matters of inheritance) to accept a verdict based on the Islamic law (the daughter receives one-half of the brother's share). In this manner, the authority of Islam is invoked (the claimant and the defendant are both Muslims) with a view to avoiding a confrontational approach that is likely to disrupt family relations. The example attests that judges may be confronted with a trade-off between their preference for doing their duty, which is to apply the statutory law strictly, and their own intrinsic preference for the outcome (Aldashev et al. 2012b). Incidentally, this example also shows that the stark opposition between French colonial countries relying on written codes and British colonial countries relying on the common law, a distinction that is routinely used to identify the role of institutions behind long-term growth performances, may not be as relevant as initially thought.

It is tempting to consider informal rules as the strict complement of formal rules, that is, as unwritten rules that are enforced through non-official punishment mechanisms. Regarding the first aspect, they resemble routines, i.e., unwritten ways of doing things that are learned through direct concrete experience rather than through abstract knowledge acquisition (Nelson and Winter 1982). As a result, they are genuinely understood only by members of the group that has generated them. An associated feature of informal rules is that they are typically loose and somewhat flexible. This is, in particular, because the circumstances under which they apply are not precisely spelled out. In fact, the way they apply may vary depending not only upon circumstances but also upon the social status or the bargaining strength of the parties involved.

Regarding the enforcement aspect, there may be three types of sanctions against violations. First, they may correspond to a punishment (e.g., an indemnity to be paid to the aggrieved party by way of compensation for the damage inflicted) meted out by an informal authority in the sense of an authority that does not possess an official status or is not officially recognized (Wade 1988; Putnam 1993; Baland and Platteau 1996, chs. 8 and 12). Second, other members of the community or social group may impose sanctions in a decentralized manner, such as when ostracization or reputation mechanisms are brought into play (Ellickson 1991; Ostrom 1990; Greif 1989). Finally, sanctions can be internalized through a psychological mechanism (social learning and cultural transmission), anchoring the prescriptions in the agents' preferences (Weber 1978; Frank 1988; Coleman 1990; Elster 1989; Bisin and Verdier 2000).

The first punishment method tends to dominate in vertically structured societies, while the second one is more typical of relatively egalitarian and close-knit communities with dense social networks. As for the third mechanism, it is generally found in both types of societies. Moreover, where the first method is implemented, a "mini-state" must exist to enforce the informal rules. The difference between informal and formal institutions then follows from one of the aforementioned characteristics of the latter: formal rules are enacted and enforced by a central official state over a well-defined area (e.g., national) while informal rules are enforced by a local authority (typically of a traditional kind) recognized only over the restricted space of a community, clan, kinship network, or extended family.

The distinction matters because, when the environment changes, informal rules may be more difficult to enforce than formal rules, especially if their enforcement goes through decentralized punishment. This is because the former are less strictly encoded and more dependent upon expectations that tend to evolve as the environment changes. For example, an informal rule that guides which procedure to follow when starting a strike is more easily violated when the surrounding circumstances change than would a formal rule (Knight 1992).

The third punishment mechanism associated with internalization differs from the other two for the following reasons. First, it does not require as much information (observation by others) to be effective. Second, it cheaply solves the problem of free rider of second degree (who punishes the failure to punish) and indirect reciprocity. Finally, it dynamically evolves differently through a cultural transmission based on different principles (conformism, paternalism, comparison with peers, social learning) that do not necessarily react the same way to environmental changes as the two other mechanisms (a "mini-state" authority for the first method, and a reputation mechanism associated with the repetition of the relationship for the second method). Note also that the various sanctioning mechanisms may interact with each other (positively or negatively).

As is often the case with typologies, there is nevertheless a grey zone in which the difference between formal and informal rules is not as clear-cut as suggested above, at least regarding the first feature. In fact, informal rules may sometimes be provided in the form of written customs, for example. It is nevertheless noteworthy that, albeit written, they remain limited to local areas or communities. Thus, for instance, English customs or the French "coutumes" varied considerably from one region to another, whether written or not, hence the difficulty of codifying and standardizing them over a large territory. On the other hand, some customs spread in an evolutionary manner through vast territories so that they can no longer be considered local. A striking example is the code of driving on the right side of the road that began as a formal prescription imposed by Napoleon in the French empire but later spread to contiguous areas in a gradual and informal way, as analyzed by Peyton Young (1998). Another example that pertains to developing countries is the system of marriage payments: the widespread existence of bride prices in Sub-Saharan Africa and dowries in India.

The second "mirror" feature of informal institutions is not subject to the ambiguity that the first feature potentially presents. In other words, it is always true that informal rules are not enforced through a modern legal system. We can therefore adopt two different definitions of informal institutions or rules: rules are informal *stricto sensu* (*ss*) when they share the two aforementioned features—they are unwritten rules applying to a restricted social group or community and enforceable through nonlegal mechanisms at work inside that group or community, while rules are informal *lato sensu* (*ls*) when they only display the second feature—they are written rules applying to large populations yet enforceable through nonlegal mechanisms at work inside small groups or communities.

To reach substantive meaning, it is also important not to define informal institutions as a residual category, in the sense that it can be applied to virtually any behavior that departs from, or is not accounted for by, the written rules. To avoid such a problem, one must say more about what an informal institution is not. First, informal institutions are, of course, not synonymous with weak institutions. Empirically, a potential major asymmetry between formal and informal institutions is the degree of observability of the effective functioning of these institutions. It is easier to observe weak formal institutions and to treat informal institutions as a residual. However, observing formal institutions with some dysfunction does not necessarily mean that there is an underlying informal institution that matters underneath. In other words, many formal institutions are ineffective, yet such weakness does not necessarily imply the presence of (effective) informal institutions. Second, informal institutions must be distinguished from other informal behavioral regularities. Not all regular informal behavior is rule-bound or rooted in shared expectations about others' behavior. For instance, removing one's hat in a church is an informal institution or social norm, whereas removing one's coat in a restaurant is simply a behavioral regularity (Brinks 2003). Third, informal institutions should be distinguished from informal organizations. Although blurred by the fact that informal rules are often embedded within organizations, the game theoretical distinction between "players" and rules of the game is analytically convenient. By the same token, one can make a distinction between informal institutions and the broader concept of culture (or shared values). Embedded in people, culture may help to shape informal institutions and facilitate the construction and maintenance of shared expectations. However, shared expectations may or may not be rooted in broader societal values.[6]

As is evident from the preceding discussion, societies may differ institutionally in many respects. A first source of variation lies in the relative importance of formal versus informal institutions (as stressed by Polanyi 1957). A second source lies in the type of dominant punishment mechanisms undergirding informal institutions. Third, from a dynamic perspective, there are societies, typically Anglo-Saxon societies, in which formal institutions emerge as the result of a codification of informal rules that have been implemented informally over a rather long period of time. In other societies, those influenced by the Roman tradition, for example, formalization often comes about as the expression of a hierarchical centralized power that decides to establish a clear rule defining appropriate behavior.

I.2. PRESENTATION OF THE CONTRIBUTIONS

The chapters contained within this Handbook follow the above definition of institutions in an explicit or an implicit manner. In the latter instance, a particular institutional structure may be embedded or concealed behind the mechanism described. Changes in mechanisms typically entail institutional changes that are then explicitly addressed.

This Handbook is divided into five different parts. Part 1 deals with political institutions, clientelism, and the role of inequality. The first chapter, written by Ernesto Dal Bó and Fred Finan, presents an in-depth survey of the experimental evidence available on political institutions and focuses on three main dimensions: (i) political accountability, which includes electoral rules, information, and political norms; (ii) state capacity, which includes taxation, bureaucratic incentives, or the design of a monitoring system; and (iii) the quality of enforcement, including the awareness of one's rights, the selection of judges, or the design of the enforcement scheme. The second chapter, by Pranab Bardhan and Dilip Mookherjee, focuses on clientelism and the mechanisms used by political actors to deliver benefits selectively to voters in return for their votes. As they argue, clientelistic practices are not specific to poor countries and persist along the process of development. Their nature changes as they move from pure clientelism, which involves discretionary allocation of benefits to particular individuals, to programmatic (pork-barrel) politics, which covers a group of citizens with designated characteristics. They review the literature and investigate the consequences of these two types of clientelism. They argue that programmatic politics arises with property right reforms and, in turn, by generating public goods, it fosters economic development. As a result, the relationship between clientelism and development should be viewed as a two-way dynamic interaction.

After investigating the "institutional economy" of the natural resource curse, Ragnar Torvik, in chapter 3, reviews the literature relating resource endowment, political power, and institutions, arguing that it is the initial interplay between these three components that determines the evolution of the economy and of its institutions. He then discusses the design of institutional reforms in a politically constrained context, so that the reform is politically feasible and acceptable. In chapter 4, Rohini Somanathan investigates the persistence of group inequality in democracies, where groups consist of citizens who are given a socially recognized marker, such as race, caste, color, or language. In this context, she discusses the relative merits of affirmative action policies as compared to public policies that are not based on those group identifiers. The dearth of real evidence comparing the relative effectiveness of these different policies in the short run and in the long run is unfortunate. Somanathan ultimately questions group classification on the grounds that it conceals large intra-group differences and, more fundamentally, shapes social identity. Finally, Joan Esteban and Debraj Ray present a panoramic view of the literature on social conflict and economic development, organized around three widely shared views: higher standards of living reduce the probability of conflict; inequality nurtures conflict; and most conflicts in developing countries are ethnic in nature. An important line for further research is based on the fact that a substantial share of social conflict can be attributed to economically similar groups. The dividing cleavage is then noneconomic (though the conflict can still be over economic resources) and manifests itself along ethnic lines. For this reason, the interaction between ethnic identity and economic characteristics, and how such interaction might result in ethnic conflict, is a research topic of the highest importance. A related question raised by the review involves the role of institutions in framing economic divergence or competition into ethnic rivalry and stronger ethnic identities.

Part 2 of this Handbook reviews the literature on growth, economic development, and institutions. In chapter 6, Steven Durlauf introduces this part by reviewing the empirical evidence relating "institutions" and "growth." Cross-country evidence is limited, given its general inability to identify a particular mechanism as well as massive uncertainty about the appropriate "model" (i.e., specification). The few existing structural approaches combining theory with data suffer from the multiplicity of the possible interpretations of the same empirical regularities. Historical analyses, based on a deep understanding of the context, probably provide strong, albeit specific, evidence on institutions. The most promising research strategy integrates knowledge emerging from those three different approaches into a consistent interpretational framework. Relatedly, while "institutions matter," a key challenge is to translate broad institutional categories such as those used to compare national experiences, into operational and, hence, context-specific institutional configurations. The author concludes in favor of more work on the policy implications of the institution and growth literature, with a focus on context-specific institutional portfolios. In chapter 7, Thorsten Beck takes stock of the literature on financial development and the role of institutions, and highlights the possible trade-offs between financial development, economic growth, and stability. Given its intertemporal nature, the financial sector is one of the most intensive in institutions, and its outreach critically depends on governance and trust. Also, by increasing competition in the real sector, financial development fosters demands by the society for institutional change. Policywise, it is critical to identify the institutional and political constraints on the development of the financial sector. The optimal sequencing of institutional change for financial development remains an open issue.

Part 3 investigates the role of institutions in international economic exchanges, in particular trade, aid, and migration. In chapter 8, Jaime de Melo and Marcelo Olarreaga focus on the role played by trade agreements, trade promotion organizations, and private labeling or trading platforms in shaping trade flows and their impact in developing economies. An important issue raised there is the gradual shift from an exchange of access rights to markets to deeper reforms which typically involve social, environmental, and investment norms and policies, the consequences of which we need to assess and understand better, particularly in the South. François Bourguignon and Jan Willem Gunning, in chapter 9, investigate the two-way relationship between foreign aid and local institutions and the resulting trade-offs. Direct aid may encourage rent-seeking and discourage the institutional reforms needed, while conditionality may promote governance and institutional improvements. On the other hand, the quality of governance and institutions in a country plays a key role in attracting foreign aid and in making it more effective. The authors propose a simple model aimed at organizing the discussion around these issues, illustrating the major trade-offs and providing key analytical distinctions between different types of aid. The refined taxonomy proposed, combined with relevant measures of institutional quality, provides clear avenues for future empirical research. In chapter 10, Kaivan Munshi reviews the literature on migration, focusing on the role of community networks, which facilitate migration in the short run but can have detrimental consequences on the migrant in the long run, typically by restricting spatial or occupational mobility. The review raises two important questions: first, what are the circumstances under which such networks form and, second, what are the static and dynamic inefficiencies associated with these networks?

Part 4 of this Handbook focuses on the role of culture, gender, and families and, more generally, on the role of informal institutions. In a thought-provoking chapter, Marcel Fafchamps studies contract enforcement in market exchange and rejects the widespread notion that formal institutions simply displace informal ones. On the basis of experimental and anthropologic evidence, he develops instead the central idea that formal institutions should be thought of as reinforcing informal arrangements, which are themselves based on norms, emotions, and thought processes. He then explores the role of families and communities in the transmission and perpetuation of these norms, and how, in many instances, they fit market institutions well. In chapter 12, Gerard Roland provides an exhaustive survey of the economic literature on culture, institutions, and economic development, and particularly examines the different dimensions of culture. He also investigates the determinants of cultural change and the origins of cultural diversity. A central question in this chapter is the tension between a notion of cultural inertia, which may be related to its transmission mechanisms, and the numerous instances of fast-moving cultural traits and attitudes. Relatedly, the sources of cultural diversity remain an open issue, and more research is needed to identify the fundamental pillars of different cultures, as well as their commonalities, and to understand their determinants.

Catherine Guirkinger and Jean-Philippe Platteau, in chapter 13, discuss families as a fundamental informal institution. Drawing from scattered empirical works as well as historical studies, they focus on the dynamics of households and families in response to change in the economic environment: division of family land, household splits, inheritance rules. The various roles families play implies that adaptation to change in one dimension often implies increased inefficiencies in other dimensions. In this respect, some of the critical functions of families (for instance, judiciary or political) and the existence of authority structures within families are typically ignored in most economic approaches. The authors call for more work on the evolution of households and families, the determinants of household's organizational structure, as well as a better understanding of the impact of family laws on family structure and their members' welfare. Moreover, they illustrate and emphasize the possibility of non-monotonous transformations of family structures such as when collective forms give rise to more individualized forms that in turn can become re-collectivized under circumstances that they elucidate. In chapter 14, Stephan Klasen investigates gender relations as resulting from formal and informal institutions, highlighting large differences in the magnitude and evolution of gender gaps. After reviewing the extensive literature on the impact of gender gaps on economic development, he investigates the differential evolution of these gaps, for instance in comparing the rapidly changing access to education to the much more stable norms governing segregation and restrictions in occupation. He also discusses the possibility of backlash effects through which resistance to gender-equalizing trends develops. He concludes by reviewing the scant literature on the determinants of gender gaps and their evolution, and calls for more research on this issue.

Part 5 investigates the interconnections between institutions and economic development in a number of different sectors. In chapter 15, Imran Rasul presents what is known about the impact of institutions and the state on worker outcomes, firm behavior, and the labor market in developing economies, presenting new descriptive evidence from various surveys. His survey covers issues such as the institutional constraints on firm expansion, job matching, entrepreneurial skills, and the role of unions, and suggests the need to better understand the effects of changes in institutional packages on labor market outcomes, instead of singling out particular reforms. In chapter 16, Meghana Ayyagari, Asli Demirgüç-Kunt, and Vojislav Maksimovic review the literature on the role of institutions in the financing of firms. Firm financing in developing countries suffers from poor protection of the investors' rights as well as information barriers arising from poor accounting practices and inadequate public recordings of credit or bankruptcies. However, in their overview of a firm's life cycle at the micro level, there is little evidence of a long-term impact of institutions on firms. This may be because institutions matter for the entry of new firms, or because institutions change frequently over a firm's life, so that one needs to better understand the short-run effect of institutional changes on firms' evolutions at different points of their life cycles. Little is known about those two issues.

In chapter 17, Antonio Estache provides a comprehensive survey of the extensive literature on infrastructure services and discusses various institutional and policy alternatives. Poor project selection, poor maintenance, and poor ability to improve access are all linked to institutional choices. In practice, the latter involve privatization and partnerships, deregulation, independent regulation, decentralization, or shared mandates. The pro-market orientation of many recent reforms did not improve the situation. More research is needed to understand, both theoretically and empirically, the role institutions can play in improving the performance of the sector, taking into account the specificities of particular infrastructures as well as the structural characteristics of the economy. In their review of education, institutions, and economic development, provided in chapter 18, Tessa Bold and Jakob Svensson identify teachers' effort, knowledge, and skills as the main bottlenecks in improving educational performance in developing countries. They then discuss the question of scaling up successful micro-interventions, focusing on local implementability and wider political economy constraints. Two key research issues, at the local level, are how to design appropriate performance contracts for teachers and how to improve the knowledge content and the pedagogical skills of the teachers. At a higher level, we need to better understand how to scale up interventions, given the political and institutional constraints in place, and the possible impact of private educational subsidies for the poor.

Chapter 19, by Eliana La Ferrara, investigates the role of the media as a tool for institutional change. She addresses three main issues. The first one, which has been well explored by economists, is the role of media in providing information that impacts political accountability, typically through voter participation and voting outcomes. The second one deals with media bias and media capture, which relates to the degree of political control and ideological biases in the information released by the media. While the evidence comes in large part from high-income countries, the importance of media bias and capture in the weaker institutional setting of many developing countries clearly calls for more research in the latter context. The third issue is the role of media in inducing social change, through their impact on norms, preferences, beliefs, and attitudes. An important gap there is how entertainment media can be used to foster civic values and political participation. In chapter 20, E. Somanathan surveys the role of institutions in addressing environmental issues. At the level of local resources, such as forests, we need to develop a clearer understanding of the economic and political determinants of decentralization, given the overall success of local-level management schemes compared to more centralized ones. At the national or subnational level, for issues such as waste disposal, traffic congestion, or access to clean water, we still know very little about the performance of alternative regulatory institutions. (Estache, in this Handbook, makes an essentially similar point when discussing the closely related theme of infrastructures.) The possibility of low-level equilibrium traps and how to solve them also requires more investigation.

I.3. BROAD RESEARCH AVENUES

From the collection of surveys described above, it appears that two broad research avenues are of particular interest. The first one is the interaction between institutions, in particular those between formal and informal institutions. As discussed by Fafchamps and Somanathan (this Handbook), one question is the extent to which these two types of institutions are complements or substitutes. Additionally, many contributors to this Handbook share the view that institutions are essentially changing and endogenous. The second research issue pertains to institutional change, and the importance of not limiting our attention to abrupt changes induced by ambitious policy reforms. Gradual changes may play a more important role and it is therefore essential that economists pay them much more attention than they have done in the past.

I.3.1. Substitution and Complementarity Effects between Formal and Informal Institutions

Formal and informal institutions interact in a variety of ways. A useful starting point for a typology of interactions between formal and informal institutions is the two-dimensional typology of Helmke and Levitsky (2004) that was developed in the context of comparative politics, but can be extended to other socioeconomic contexts as well. This is illustrated in table I.1.

Table I.1.

Outcomes	Effective Formal Institutions	Ineffective Formal Institutions
Convergent	Complementarity	Substitution
Divergent	Accommodation	Competition

The first dimension concerns the degree to which formal and informal institutional outcomes converge. The distinction here is whether informal rules produce substantively similar or different results from those expected from a strict and exclusive adherence to formal rules. Where there exists substantial discrepancy or contradiction across outcomes emanating from informal and formal rules, formal and informal institutions diverge. Where outcomes are not substantively different, formal and informal institutions converge.

The second dimension refers to the effectiveness of the relevant formal institutions, that is, the extent to which formal rules and procedures are enforced and complied with in practice. Effective formal institutions actually constrain or enable individuals' choices and there is a high probability of official sanctions in case of rule violation. Where formal institutions are ineffective, agents expect a low probability of enforcement (and hence a low expected cost of violation).

According to the table, four different types of institutional interaction patterns can arise. The upper left column combines effective formal rules and convergent outcomes, producing *complementarity* between informal and formal institutions. In such cases, informal institutions either address contingencies not dealt with in the formal rules or facilitate the pursuit of individual goals within the formal institutional framework. They may also serve as pillars for the functioning of formal institutions, creating or strengthening incentives to comply with formal rules that might otherwise exist merely on paper. A typical example relates to the effectiveness of a political constitution such as the US Constitution that clearly depends on a complementary set of shared beliefs and expectations among citizens, or the efficiency of Singapore's postcolonial bureaucracy (the formal organization of which resembled those of Indonesia and the Philippines), which has been attributed to underlying norms of meritocracy and discipline. The discussion of "embeddedness" by Marcel Fafchamps (this Handbook) is a clear example of powerful complementarity between formal contract institutions and social norms.

The lower left column of the table combines effective formal institutions and divergent outcomes. This corresponds to a situation of *accommodation* between informal and formal institutions. In such a case, informal institutions create incentives to behave in ways that alter the substantive effects of formal rules, but without directly violating them. They contradict the spirit, but not the letter, of the formal rules. Accommodation occurs when a contradiction emerges between outcomes generated by the formal rules and prescriptions emanating from customary or informal rules. The effectiveness of formal rules, however, impedes an outright change or open violation of the rules. Accommodation helps to reconcile conflicting dimensions within the existing formal institutional arrangements and results from the implementation and interpretation of formal rules by actors subject to informal prescriptions (see the earlier example of succession laws in West Africa and the discussion and examples in Guirkinger and Platteau, this Handbook).

The cell in the lower right column of the table combines ineffective formal rules and divergent outcomes, producing *competition* between informal and formal institutions. In such cases, informal institutions structure incentives in ways that are incompatible with the formal rules: to follow one rule, actors must violate another. Typical examples of such situations occur, for instance, when particularistic informal institutions like clientelism and nepotism occur in various contexts of weak formal political or economic institutions (Hoff and Sen 2005; Mookherjee and Bardhan, this Handbook). Thus, competing informal institutions are often found in postcolonial contexts in which formal institutions were imposed on indigenous rules and authority structures. In postcolonial Ghana and India, for instance, civil servants were officially instructed to follow the rules of the public bureaucracy, but most believed they would pay a significant social cost (such as a loss of standing in the community) if they ignored kinship group norms that obliged them to provide jobs and other favors to their families and villages (Price 1975; Kakar 1978).

Finally, the upper right column of the table considers the combination of ineffective formal institutions and converging outcomes, thus corresponding to a situation of *substitution* between formal and informal institutions. In such cases, informal institutions are employed by agents who seek outcomes compatible with formal rules and procedures but in environments where formal rules are not routinely enforced. Hence, in substitution situations, informal institutions achieve what formal institutions were designed, but failed, to achieve. For instance, traditional and informal norms of income sharing within communities substitute for formal insurance markets as they tend to achieve the same type of insurance mechanisms as these formal markets which remain incomplete because of lack of verifiability and/or asymmetric information between contracting parties.

The previous typology allows us to classify the nature of the interactions between informal and formal institutions at a given point in time. It should be clear that the sign of such links may evolve dynamically depending on the institutional path followed by society. In this respect, it should also be emphasized that informal and formal institutions influence each other along a dynamic two-way process. Specific formal rules and institutions may be inspired by (or simply formally reflect) already well diffused and practiced social norms of behaviors. In return, such a formalization process may as well modify dynamically the structure of the informal interactions that inspired the design of these formal rules. The inclusion of informal practices into formal law, and in return the constraints effectively imposed by formal law rulings on informal codes of behaviors, are clear examples of such a two-way dynamic interactive process.

I.3.2. Gradual Institutional Change

We still know very little about institutional change. When institutions are conceptualized as Nash equilibria and are therefore considered as stable outcomes, the only manner in which they can possibly change is as a result of exogenous shocks that modify some key parameters of the game considered. The shocks can consist of technological or other changes that end up modifying the payoffs accruing to some or all of the agents, changes that bring new actors onto the scene and/or remove old ones from it, changes that allow for new individual actions or alter the agents' expectations regarding others' actions. New Nash equilibria then emerge while old equilibria stopped displaying this property.

Just think of the distinction between inclusive and extractive political equilibria described by Acemoglu and Robinson (2012). Once a country has attained one or the other equilibrium, it gets trapped into it. Therefore, an exogenous shock or a chance event is required to move a country from the vicious (extractive) to the virtuous (inclusive) equilibrium. In the words of Greif and Laitin (2004, 633): "A self-enforcing institution is one in which each player's behaviour is a best response. The inescapable conclusion is that a change in self-enforcing institutions must have an exogenous origin." The same authors nevertheless stress indirect institutional effects (so-called feedback effects) that either expand or reduce the set of situations in which an institution is self-enforcing. By redefining some of the exogenous parameters as endogenous variables (that they call "quasi-parameters"), they are able to account for the stability or the breakdown of different institutional equilibria. As illustrations, they propose the decline versus the resiliency of social order in Venice and Genoa and the decline versus persistence of ethnic cleavages in Estonia and Nigeria.

On the other hand, it is evident that, in a static framework, we are not told anything about the pathway that leads from the old to the new equilibrium, and how the latter is influenced by the former (bear in mind that an equilibrium selection problem arises in the new situation created by the shock). Precisely because it is based on a dynamic framework, the evolutionary approach to institutions avoids the last aforementioned difficulty. Nonetheless, the problem of explaining institutional change remains. According to a central theorem of evolutionary game theory, evolutionary equilibria have the properties of strategic equilibria: for a large class of evolutionary games, if the dynamics converge, they converge toward a steady state in which the limiting distributions are in equilibrium in the same sense as in classical game theory. The population seems to learn the rational equilibrium as its distribution evolves, and this is true despite the fact that limited rationality of the actors is assumed. An institution thus exists as a set of stable individual behaviors given what the other agents are doing. As a result, it answers the definition of a coordination mechanism of some sort (Montet and Serra 2003: 8–9; Bowles 2004).

In explaining institutional change, the attention of economists inspired by an equilibrium approach is naturally directed to major events deemed to be significant enough to disturb an existing equilibrium. Radically different is the approach proposed by a group of social scientists who are more interested in gradual and piecemeal changes based on endogenous developments that often unfold incrementally and only "show up" or "register" as change if a somewhat long time frame is considered (Mahoney and Thelen 2010: 2). In this perspective, the sources of institutional change are not simply exogenous shocks or environmental shifts, and path-dependent lock-in effects are considered to be rare in real societies.

For the sake of illustration, we can cite the transformation of land tenure rules in Sub-Saharan Africa during the last century. This transformation can be described as an incremental individualization process whereby rules of corporate ownership of land gradually gave way to freehold rights. To identify the successive steps in the process, one must reckon that, far from being a monolithic concept, private property in land involves a continuum of attributes: the rights to use the land, to make decisions about its current exploitation and about its improvement through investment, to bequeath it, to lend it, to rent it out (against a cash payment), to donate it and, finally, to sell it. Even the latest right may not be availed of in a single move: in the beginning, the right to sell may be granted only on the condition that the sale has been approved by designated members of the family or community. On the other hand, the right of the purchaser to keep the land may be limited by the right of the seller to retake possession of it as soon as he has the required wherewithal.

Mahoney and Thelen distinguish between four modal types of institutional change: displacement, layering, drift, and conversion. *Displacement* means the removal of existing rules and the introduction of new ones. *Layering* refers to the introduction of new rules on top of or alongside existing ones. *Drift* is the changed impact of existing rules due to shifts in the environment. Finally, *Conversion* is the changed enactment of existing rules due to their strategic redeployment. Note that displacement can be a slow-moving process when new institutions are introduced and directly compete with an older set of institutions. Layering changes the ways in which the original rules structure behavior. Drift occurs when rules remain formally the same but their impact changes as a result of shifts in external conditions: institutional change can then be said to grow out of the neglect of an institution or, more precisely, the failure to adapt and update it to maintain its traditional impact in a changed environment. By contrast, conversion occurs when rules remain formally the same but are interpreted and enacted in new ways thanks to the intervention of actors who exploit the inherent ambiguities of the existing institutions (Mahoney and Thelen 2010: 15–17).

The authors then suggest that differences in the character of existing institutions as well as in the prevailing political context affect the likelihood of specific types of change. The role of these two key dimensions revolves around the following two questions:

- Does the political context afford defenders of the status quo strong or weak veto possibilities?
- Does the targeted institution afford actors opportunities for exercising discretion in interpretation or enforcement?

Table I.2 provides a way to think about how these two dimensions interact and determine the type of expected institutional change.

Our example of gradual institutional change in land rights in Sub-Saharan Africa appears to belong to the case labeled "weak veto possibilities," so that transformation has

Table I.2.

Characteristics of the Political Context	Characteristics of the Targeted Institution	
	Low level of discretion in interpretation/enforcement	High level of discretion in interpretation/enforcement
Strong veto possibilities	Layering	Drift
Weak veto possibilities	Displacement	Conversion

been incremental and rather smooth. What is less clear, however, is whether it falls under the high or the low level of discretion in interpretation/enforcement, that is, whether we are dealing with a case of displacement or a case of conversion. Evidence tends to indicate that conversion is probably the best way to describe the type of change involved, implying that customary rules are characterized by a rather high level of discretion in interpretation/enforcement.

Viewed through the lens of the economics profession, the gradual change approach suffers from a major disadvantage: it does not allow clear identification with the consequence that causal relationships cannot be established. On the contrary, the approach centered on exogenous changes in equilibria, because it uses the comparative-static method to study change, is able to solve the identification problem by exploiting exogenous shocks. The fact remains that, as the aforementioned example attests, it may be unreasonable to dismiss the gradual change approach and to thus deprive ourselves of the promising bridge that it puts up between the works of historians and the works of economic historians and development economists.

It is desirable to go beyond the broad characterizations of change types proposed by Mahoney and Thelen with a view to better understanding the way gradual change possibly articulates with abrupt change. More precisely, we would like to have a better theory in support of their claim that "gradually unfolding changes may be hugely consequential as causes of other outcomes" (Mahoney and Thelen 2010: 3).

To what extent and under which circumstances can an apparently discontinuous change be considered as the outcome of a slow-moving process of gradual institutional change that prepared the ground for the institutional break? An insightful example is the demise of serfdom in Tokugawa, Japan, as described by T. C. Smith (1959). This demise is depicted as the end outcome of a sustained process of gradual emancipation of the serfs (the *nago*) as a result of the development of rural (silk-producing) industries which created an acute competition for local labor. Despite the calls issued by the landlords (the *oyakata*), the state did not use its repressive force to bring runaway serfs back to their masters. As a consequence, the implicit labor contracts ruling within the feudal estates were progressively modified to allow more freedom and better terms for the tenants. The Japanese experience is in striking contrast to the experience of Russia, for instance, where serfs became emancipated (in 1861) as a result of a top-down, state-directed reform abolishing serfdom. Even here, however, some caution is required: in some estates, gradual reforms had been introduced before 1861 under the initiative of enlightened landlords (Zuravskaya and Markevich 2015).[7]

Relatedly, institutional change, although continuous in its essential dynamics, may actually appear as fragmented and discrete from the point of view of an external observer. This is related to Timur Kuran's (1995) idea of "private truth and public lies" inspired by the Iranian revolution, namely the fact that some latent institutional change may occur in a continuous way in the private or informal sphere of the society, and only appear publicly or formally once these hidden changes have crossed a specific threshold. Such processes may then be viewed as mechanisms of "neutral" institutional developments, which up to certain threshold effects do not seem to matter much in terms of societal outcomes, but which in complement to other changes or shocks to the system may trigger punctuated and discrete relevant institutional dynamics afterward. Developing models of such institutional dynamics and identifying historical situations for such phenomena may help reconcile in an innovative way the two views describing institutional changes (discontinuous versus gradual) that have been discussed so far.

As emphasized by Ragnar Torvik (this Handbook), the analysis of endogenous change immediately raises the issue of the role of different actors with a stake in that change, calling for a political economy approach that features the relative power weights of the various actors, the negotiating arenas existing in the society, and the motives of the state. Why is it, for example, that the Tokugawa state refrained from meeting the landlords' demand for strict enforcement of the feudal type of labor relations? In the case of land tenure in Africa, the relatively smooth process of incremental change that has been described can only occur if the central state does not interfere awkwardly, for example by appropriating valuable customary lands for the purpose of promoting the interests of the ruling elite, by imposing land titling measures "ex abrupto" when the individualization process is still in its infancy, or by imposing private property rights when scale economies and externalities work in favor of traditional corporate ownership. On the other hand, the local customary authorities may have a vested interest in maintaining a traditional system of land tenure rules from which they derive ample benefits, such as the right to adjudicate competing claims and to settle land conflicts. What are their motives for not resisting the ongoing changes?

Recent economic literature proposes a number of theories of gradual change that do not rely on evolutionary mechanisms and the associated assumptions of limited rationality, nor on discrete equilibrium shifts. For example, Acemoglu and Jackson (2015) have written a model of interactions between the law and prevailing social norms in which agents meet in pairwise encounters and are allowed to denounce violators of the law. They show that in this setup the law may gradually evolve to adapt to the social norm. Conversely, Aldashev et al. (2012a) have developed a dynamic model that shows how the custom may gradually evolve in the direction of the law in a world where customary authorities pronounce judgments referring to the custom. Interestingly, expanding economic opportunities have the same effect as a statutory law when both circumstances afford weaker groups new exit possibilities and, hence, confer greater bargaining power upon them (see Guirkinger and Platteau, this Handbook). But these gradual changes may be disrupted and even overturned if political power changes hands and progressive laws are rescinded or cease to be enforced. Another application of economic theory of gradual change to institutions is the paper by Bidner and François (2013) on the emergence of political accountability. They focus on the role played by *political norms*—specifically, the extent to which leaders abuse office for personal gain and the extent to which citizens punish such transgressions. They show how qualitatively distinct political norms can coexist because of a dynamic complementarity in which citizens' willingness to punish transgressions is raised when they expect such punishments to be used in the future. Their analysis also highlights the role of leaders, offering an account of how their actions can instigate enduring change, within a fixed set of formal institutions, by disrupting prevailing political norms. A key finding is that such changes are asymmetric in effect—a series of good leaders can (and eventually will) improve norms, whereas bad leaders cannot damage them.[8] If there is a small yet growing number of works dedicated to the theory of gradual change applied to some institutional issues, empirical studies by economists remain very rare.

NOTES

1. As noted by many contributors to this Handbook (for instance Estache, Durlauf, or Bourguignon and Gunning), our measurement of institutions remains rudimentary and approximate. More detailed research to define relevant measures of institutions in specific contexts is clearly needed.
2. Extractive institutions are defined by the authors as institutions allowing a "small" group of individuals to exploit the rest of the population, as opposed to "inclusive" institutions in which "many" people are included in the process of governing and sharing the benefits of development.
3. For another, more orthodox interpretation, however, see Allen and Lueck (2002: 88–92).
4. For Aoki (2001), effective enforcement is an inherent attribute of an institution: a representation is an institution only if it is deemed credible, and it is deemed credible only if it is properly enforced.
5. The advice of the Prophet to the faithful is thus: "Do not prevent your wives from going to the mosque even though they are better off in their homes" (cited from Platteau 2017: 95–96).
6. It should be mentioned that certain types of organizations such as corporations and firms are actually clusters of institutional interactions including both formalized aspects (internal governance structures and self-imposed rules of functioning) as well as informal dimensions (corporate culture). They may coexist in complementary or substitutive ways. As such, although they are not stricto-sensu institutional rules in the sense of North, one may obviously consider them as important institutional clusters that in some analyses can be analyzed as institutions.
7. Interestingly, the main factor driving the change in Japan is market development in response to growing demand for silk. In the individualization of land tenure in Africa, the engine consists of both population growth and market integration, the latter force being itself influenced partly by the development of transport infrastructure.
8. Acemoglu and Jackson (2015) also study the emergence and dynamic evolution of social norms in response to individual behavior and actions by leaders. In their model, leaders are agents endowed with visibility of acts who are part of a sequence of players through time. This visibility allows leaders to play a coordinating role that can induce a sequence of good play from immediate followers. They also show that social norms can be shaped by a pattern of mean-reverting dynamics of expectations and behavior.

REFERENCES

Acemoglu, D., and M. O. Jackson. 2015. "Social Norms and the Enforcement of Laws." Technical Report, National Bureau of Economic Research, Washington, DC.
Acemoglu, Daron, and James Robinson. 2012. *Why Nations Fail—The Origins of Power, Prosperity and Poverty.* London: Profile Books.
Acemoglu, Daron, Simon Johnson, and James A. Robinson. 2001. "The Colonial Origins of Comparative Development: An Empirical Investigation." *American Economic Review* 91, no. 5 (December): 1369–1401.
Acemoglu, Daron, Simon Johnson, and James A. Robinson. 2005. "Institutions as the Fundamental Cause of Long-Run Growth." In *Handbook of Economic Growth*, Vol. 1, Part A, edited by Philippe Aghion and Steve Durlauf, pp. 385–472. Amsterdam: Elsevier.

Aldashev, Gani, Imane Chaara, Jean-Philippe Platteau, and Zaki Wahhaj. 2012a. "Using the Law to Change the Custom." *Journal of Development Economics* 97(1): 182–200.

Aldashev, Gani, Imane Chaara, Jean-Philippe Platteau, and Zaki Wahhaj. 2012b. "Formal Law as a Magnet to Reform the Custom." *Economic Development and Cultural Change* 60(4): 795–828.

Allen, D. W., and D. Lueck. 2002. *The Nature of the Farm—Contracts, Risk, and Organization in Agriculture.* Cambridge, MA and London: MIT Press.

Alston, L., T. Eggertsson, and D. North. 1996. *Empirical Studies in Institutional Change.* Cambridge: Cambridge University Press.

Aoki, Masahiko. 2001. *Toward a Comparative Institutional Analysis.* Cambridge, MA: MIT Press.

Baland, Jean-Marie, and Jean-Philippe Platteau. 1996. *Halting Degradation of Natural Resources: Is There a Role for Rural Communities?* Oxford: Oxford University Press.

Bauer, Peter T., and Basil S. Yamey. 1957. *The Economics of Under-developed Countries.* Cambridge: Cambridge University Press.

Bidner, Chris, and Patrick François. 2011. "Cultivating Trust: Norms, Institutions and the Implications of Scale." *Economic Journal* 121(555): 1097–1129.

Bidner, Chris, and Patrick François. 2013. "The Emergence of Political Accountability." *Quarterly Journal of Economics* 128(3): 1397–1448.

Bisin, Alberto, and Thierry Verdier. 2000. "Beyond the Melting Pot: Cultural Transmission, Marriage and the Evolution of Ethnic and Religious Traits." *Quarterly Journal of Economics* 115(3): 955–988.

Bowles, Sam. 2004. *Microeconomics—Behavior, Institutions, and Evolution.* New York: Russell Sage Foundation and Princeton, NJ: Princeton University Press.

Brinks, Daniel. 2003. "Informal Institutions and the Rule of Law: The Judicial Response to State Killings in Buenos Aires and São Paulo in the 1990s." *Comparative Politics* 36(1): 1–19.

Coleman, James S. 1990. *Foundations of Social Theory.* Cambridge, MA and London: Belknap Press of Harvard University Press.

Ellickson, Robert. 1991. *Order without Law: How Neighbors Settle Disputes.* Cambridge, MA and London: Harvard University Press.

Elster, Jon. 1989. *The Cement of Society: A Study of Social Order.* Cambridge: Cambridge University Press.

Frank, Robert. 1988. *Passions within Reason: The Strategic Role of Emotions.* New York: Norton.

Greif, Avner. 1989. "Reputation and Coalitions in Medieval Trade: Evidence on the Maghribi Traders." *Journal of Economic History* 49(4): 857–882.

Greif, Avner, and D. Laitin. 2004. "A Theory of Endogenous Institutional Change." *American Political Science Review* 98(4): 633–652.

Helmke, Gretchen, and Steven Levitsky. 2004. "Informal Institutions and Comparative Politics: A Research Agenda." *Perspectives on Politics* 2(4): 725–740.

Hoff, Karla, and Arijit Sen. 2005. "The Kin System as a Poverty Trap?" *Policy Research Working Paper,* series no. 3575, World Bank.

Kakar, S. 1978. *The Inner World, a Psychoanalysis Study of Childhood and Society in India.* Oxford: Oxford University Press.

Knight, Jack. 1992. *Institutions and Social Conflict.* Cambridge: Cambridge University Press.

Kuran, Timur. 1995. *Private Truths, Public Lies—The Social Consequences of Preference Falsification.* Cambridge, MA: Harvard University Press.

Lewis, W. A. 1955. *Theory of Economic Growth.* London: George Allen and Unwin.

Mahoney, James, and Kathleen Thelen (eds.). 2010. *Explaining Institutional Change—Ambiguity, Agency, and Power.* Cambridge: Cambridge University Press.

Meier, Gerald M., and Robert E. Baldwin. 1957. *Economic Development: Theory, History, Policy.* New York: Wiley.

Montet, C., and D. Serra. 2003. *Game Theory and Economics.* London: Palgrave Macmillan.

Nelson, Richard R., and Sydney Winter. 1982. *An Evolutionary Theory of Economic Change.* New Haven, CT: Yale University Press.

North, Douglass C. 1990. *Institutions, Institutional Change and Economic Performance.* Cambridge: Cambridge University Press.

Ostrom, Elinor. 1990. *Governing the Commons: The Evolution of Institutions for Collective Action.* Cambridge: Cambridge University Press.

Pande, Rohini, and Christopher Udry. 2005. "Institutions and Development: A View from Below." Economic Growth Center, discussion paper no. 928, Yale University.

Platteau, Jean-Philippe. 2017. *Islam Instrumentalized: Religion and Politics in Historical Perspective.* Cambridge: Cambridge University Press.

Polanyi, Karl. 1957. *The Great Transformation.* New York: Rineholt.

Price, Robert M. 1975. *Society and Bureaucracy in Contemporary Ghana.* Berkeley: University of California Press.

Putnam, Robert. 1993. *Making Democracy Work: Civic Traditions in Modern Italy.* Princeton, NJ: Princeton University Press.

Schumpeter, Joseph A. 1954. *History of Economic Analysis.* New York: Oxford University Press.

Smith, T. C. 1959. *The Agrarian Origins of Modern Japan.* Stanford, CA: Stanford University Press.

Stiglitz, Joseph. 1996. "Theories of Sharecropping." In *The Economic Theory of Agrarian Institutions*, edited by Pranab Bardhan, ch. 1. Oxford University Press.

Wade, Robert. 1988. *Village Republics: Economic Conditions for Collective Action in South India.* Cambridge: Cambridge University Press.

Weber, Max. 1978. *Economy and Society.* Berkeley: University of California Press.

Young, Peter. 1998. *Individual Strategy and Social Structure.* Princeton, NJ: Princeton University Press.

Yousfi, Hélam. 2011. "Culture and Development: The Continuing Tension between Modern Standards and Local Contexts." In *Culture, Institutions and Development: New Insights into an Old Debate*, edited by Jean-Philippe Platteau and Robert Peccoud, pp. 20–64. London: Routledge.

Zuravskaya, Ekaterina, and Andreï Markevich. 2015. "The Economic Impact of the Abolition of Russian Serfdom." Working Paper, New Economic School (Moscow) and Paris School of Economics.

PART 1

POLITICAL INSTITUTIONS, CLIENTELISM, AND INEQUALITY

1

AT THE INTERSECTION

A Review of Institutions in Economic Development

Ernesto Dal Bó and Frederico Finan

1.1. INTRODUCTION

The driving question throughout this chapter is as follows: What do we know about how legal and political institutions (and reforms thereof) can successfully improve development outcomes? To answer this question, we review pertinent evidence from the fields of economics and political science and draw from studies of a range of economies worldwide. When useful, we include evidence based on observational data, and whenever possible we emphasize evidence stemming from the literature exploiting quasi-experimental and experimental variation. This review is inclusive of nearly 200 publications and identifies 40 "open" research questions.

1.1.1. What Do We Mean by "Institutions"?

In this chapter, we define institutions according to North's (1991) "rules of the game." This admittedly broad definition comprises a wide range of social and economic, legal and political, and normative and procedural rules, incentive structures, and organizations.

To put this definition in context, consider the basic economic institutions in common across high-income and lower-income countries, including a variety of firms, contracts, and wage labor schemes that all tend to exist everywhere. However, the details of their functioning and the results of these ubiquitous economic institutions differ markedly across contexts. The starting point for this chapter is to understand that such differences are largely due to different legal regimes (whether in conception or de facto application), and in turn due to different political institutions and performance. In fact, many of the legal institutions of interest function as economic institutions.

1.1.2. Why Examine Institutions for Economic Development?

Many writers in economics and political science have emphasized the connection between institutions and the economic performance of societies. Some of these institutions

Table 1.1.

Thematic Areas	Political Institutions	Legal Institutions
Analytical areas		
Information diffusion	X	X
Incentives and selection	X	X

are directly economic in nature and include social constructions as basic as firms, the wage relationship, and long-term contracts (Williamson 1985). These economic institutions owe much of their profile to the legal regimes that regulate individual and business person-hood, the ability to hold and dispose of property, or to enter contracts. Therefore, legal regimes have consequences for what economic activities can take place, for how they take place, and for who may undertake them. Not surprisingly, economic agents can have strong preferences with regard to the definition of legal rules and their enforcement, as attested by the large literature on lobbying and corruption. This implies that legal re-gimes are endogenous to political forces, which are themselves shaped by existing po-litical institutions. Thus, the political framework of a society acts as a meta-institution from which the others derive (Rodrik 2000). Both the legal and political performances of societies introduce improvements through policy or institutional innovations.

1.1.3. Our Approach

This chapter contains two main sections, respectively dealing with political and legal institutions. These constitute the two main substantive themes to be taken up by the Cen-ter for Effective Global Action (CEGA) and its partners as part of EDI. As will be seen, research along these two themes repeatedly involves two broad classes of processes or mechanisms. One is the operation of incentives and selection forces, and the other is the diffusion of information. These are the two broad "analytic categories" that tend to cross-cut the substantive themes. This is in keeping with one of the priorities of EDI, namely, to illuminate the mechanisms through which institutions affect development. The cells that result from the intersection of substantive themes and analytic categories constitute the main areas of research to be reviewed and where we expect work done under the auspices of EDI. The matrix shown in table 1.1 allows a quick visualization of the research space.

The extent to which formal institutions operate is limited in real life: people's recog-nition of those institutions, conflicts with custom-based arrangements, enforcement costs, and corruption can all get in the way. Thus, an important topic within both legal and political institutions is the connection between formal institutions and informal arrange-ments, as well as the forces that drive changes in that connection. In the context of legal institutions, we will consider work on the use of formal property rights, titles, and the challenges involved in expanding business formalization. In the context of political in-stitutions, we will review work on the topics of political practices and norms that either reinforce or undermine the spirit of constitutional arrangements. In other words, the sometimes complex relationship between formal and informal institutions will be taken up within the respective chapters wherever pertinent.

The plan for this chapter is as follows. In the next section, we offer a quick summary of key findings and open questions. In section 1.3, we review evidence on political institutions, broadly understood. In section 1.4, we review work in the area of legal institutions. After reviewing the available evidence, in each of these sections we highlight what we believe to be important open questions. Section 1.5 offers a brief conclusion.

1.2. SUMMARY OF FINDINGS AND OPEN QUESTIONS

Here, we offer a short summary of the key findings of our review, as well as a selective highlight of open questions. To facilitate absorption of this information, we present these in bullet point format. More detailed versions of these findings and related discussions are presented in the respective chapters.

In the section on political institutions, we offer a review of work in two main areas: representation and accountability and state capacity. The rationale for covering these two areas is that political forces impact outcomes depending on two elements: (i) the will to shape outcomes in a particular way; and (ii) the means to do so. Political will depends on institutions shaping representation and accountability, and political means depend on state capacity. Within the topic of representation and accountability, we deal with electoral rules, information and transparency, and political norms.

The key findings on electoral rules are as follows:

- Electoral rules affect the composition of the electorate and, ultimately, policy.
  » There is evidence of effects on voter turnout and policy; evidence is both observational (Miller 2008; Cascio and Washington 2014) and from quasi-/natural/controlled experiments (Pande 2003; Chattopadhyay and Duflo 2004; Fujiwara 2015).
  » There is evidence of effects on political selection (e.g., quality and moderation of candidates; Beath et al. 2014).
  » Re-election, term limits, and term length impact incentives, with effects on fiscal policy (Besley and Case 1995), corruption (Ferraz and Finan 2008), and effort (Dal Bó and Rossi 2011).

Open questions on electoral rules are:

- Which electoral rules most affect corruption?
- What is the optimal term length?
- Should there be term limits (in the extreme, should there be re-election at all)?
- Are rules that broaden representation inimical to accountability and competence?
- Endogenous institutions: how do institutions originate, and does their origin affect performance?

Key findings on information and transparency:

- Information matters for political behavior, in terms of:
  » Turnout and preferences (Gentzkow 2006; DellaVigna and Kaplan 2007; Gerber et al. 2009; Giné and Mansuri 2014; Bidwell et al. 2015; Kendall et al. 2015).
  » Electoral accountability (Ferraz and Finan 2008).
  » Political strategy (see Bidwell et al. 2015, where more information led to more gift-giving and vote-buying).

Open questions on information and transparency:

- Does transparency, by heightening accountability, improve public good provision?
- What makes information credible and usable to citizens?
- When does transparency lead to better political selection versus a reinforcement of harmful political strategies?

Key findings on political norms:

- Civic education campaigns on voting process and against violence and vote-buying increase perceptions of security (Collier and Vicente 2014) and trust in electoral authorities (Aker et al. 2015).
- Social capital may drive voters' standards of accountability (Nannicini et al. 2013).
- Political attitudes are shaped by education curricula (Cantoni et al. 2015) and by gender representation institutions (Beaman et al. 2009).

Open questions on political norms:

- What are the drivers and consequences of government legitimacy?
- How do political norms interact with formal institutions?
- What institutions can limit clientelism, patronage, and dynastic politics?
- What are the effects on political participation and accountability of specific cultural traits, such as trust, respect for others, and individualism versus collectivism?

The quality of policy and of its implementation depends largely on state capacity, which in turn depends on three key elements: state personnel, state resources, and state procedures. We covered work in each of these areas.

Key findings on state capacity—personnel:

- Selection
  - » Key theoretical trade-off in state hiring: competence versus motivation—this supposed trade-off does not seem acute empirically (Dal Bó et al. 2013).
  - » Wages help attract better people, especially in difficult areas (Dal Bó et al. 2013).
- Incentives: pay for performance tends to improve service delivery (Banerjee et al. 2008; Basinga et al. 2011) and tax collection (Khan et al. 2014).
- Monitoring: can help reduce corruption through either community involvement or information (Reinikka and Svensson 2005; Björkman and Svensson 2009; Björkman et al. 2014; Banerjee et al. 2011; Olken 2007).

Open questions on state capacity—personnel:

- What are the effects of nonfinancial incentives?
- When does performance pay lead to multitasking distortions?
- Do extrinsic incentives crowd out intrinsic motivation?
- When do top-down audit-based approaches work better than community monitoring?
- Can citizen feedback platforms promote political accountability and improve service delivery?

Key findings on state capacity—financial resources:

- Windfalls may weaken accountability and public goods-to-resource ratios (Brollo et al. 2013; Caselli and Michaels 2013).
- Good tax design helps—particularly a VAT paper trail (Pomeranz 2015) and third-party reporting (Kleven et al. 2011).
- Campaigns toward taxpayers: exhortative messages work less well than threats of audits (McGraw and Scholz 1991; Blumenthal et al. 2001; Castro and Scartascini 2015).

Open questions on state capacity—financial resources:

- What areas of taxation are most affected by corruption?
- How much of the revenue gap in developing countries can be closed by incentivizing tax collectors?
- When do windfalls strengthen accountability and public sector productivity?
- Is third-party reporting more or less effective under weak legal institutions?

The second main theme we reviewed involves legal institutions, many of which are economic in nature. For legal institutions to function well requires four elements. First, it must specify a legally sanctioned right. Second, the beneficiaries or holders of such a right must be aware of their entitlement and be able to access the means to have their rights upheld. Third, there must be an enforcement machinery available to uphold those rights, comprising, for example, courts. Fourth, conditions must exist so that court rulings can be enforced. Here, we review the key findings in the literature for each of these components and specify open questions.

Key findings on rights—emphasis on property and titling:

- Effects of titling: varying results; best evidence shows property rights increase investment (Field 2005; Ali et al. 2014).
- Impacts stemming strictly from titling allowing for collateralization (De Soto 2000) are still looking for support.
- Encouragements to formalize business (by lowering costs, offering information) are often ineffective (McKenzie and Woodruff 2008; McKenzie and Sakho 2010) and inconsequential for productivity and growth.
- Dual economy: informal firms likely lack the "quality" to compete in the formal sector (La Porta and Shleifer 2014):
  » Efforts to unleash their potential by formalizing are likely to have limited effects; and
  » Prosecution may be counterproductive if the informal sector acts as an informal safety net.

Open questions on rights—emphasis on property and titling:

- Are there instances where titling/formalization relaxes credit constraints?
- If complementary reforms are needed, what are the key complementary reforms?
- There is a great deal of literature on small firm informality, registration, and tax regulations, but what are the regulatory barriers for firm growth from land titling and zoning?

- What are the social costs of formalizing informal firms?
- Is the informal economy a complement or a hindrance to its formal counterpart?

Key findings on awareness and access:

- Presence of paralegals in treated villages helps promote knowledge of the rights of women (Mueller et al. 2018).
- Pro bono legal assistance tends to improve outcomes for beneficiaries:
  » Eviction is less likely (Frankel et al. 2001; Greiner et al. 2012), there are better justice and welfare outcomes (Sandefur and Siddiqi 2013), and there is better conflict resolution (Blattman et al. 2014).

Open questions on awareness and access:

- How do improved legal outcomes translate into improved welfare?
- Does broader legal access affect productive activities?
- Does a more extensive "rule of law" create aggregate (i.e., General Equilibrium) effects?
  » Methodological challenge: separating effects on preferences versus expectations.

Key findings on courts:
The evidence so far stems from observational studies, some relying on structural estimation approaches.

- Incentives and selection matter for the decisions judges make (Lim 2013; Iaryczower et al. 2013)
  » Elections different from appointments;
  » Media coverage matters (Lim and Snyder 2015).
- Political pressures (re-election incentives) affect sentencing (Berdejó and Yuchtman 2013).

Open questions on courts:

- How do career concerns affect incentives for judges?
- Beyond judges, what is the role of staff and organizational support in producing timely outcomes, and how can they be improved?
- What is the impact of judicial quality on economic activity?
- Would the extant results survive randomized controlled trial (RCT) study?

Key findings on quality of enforcement:

- Only a subset of interventions work at improving policing (Banerjee et al. 2014), and how interventions affect the power of implementing bureaucrats is key.
- Higher inspections affect regulated behavior by firms (Duflo et al. 2014), and who pays inspectors (regulator versus regulated firm) matters in terms of what they report (Duflo et al. 2013). This confirms the basic notions from hierarchical agency models.

Open questions on quality of enforcement:

- How much do improvements in enforcement generate displacement in wrongdoing?

- Is there an interactive effect of incentives to monitors and the monitored?
- What reforms can improve the political economy of implementation across reforms pursuing a similar objective (specifically taking into account the incentive compatibility of public middle management, their discretion, and information)?

1.3. POLITICAL INSTITUTIONS

There are vast differences across the world in the way political life is organized. As fundamental as political organization is for a society, these differences are far from immutable. If one were to classify countries based on their 1980 Polity scores, only 26% of countries would have appeared democratic and more than 53% would have appeared autocratic. However, less than 40 years later, the world looks decidedly different: 54% of countries appear democratic and only 12% are autocracies.

Understanding why countries adopt different political institutions and the impact of these choices on economic development and well-being has been an active area of research over the last 20 years. Thus far, some basic patterns have emerged. In general, countries with "better" political institutions also adopt more "inclusive" economic institutions that allow for broader participation, secure property rights more effectively, erect fewer barriers to entry, and offer wider ranges of formal contracts. More specifically, there is an association between economic performance and the political regime that is in place. As shown in figure 1.1, countries that are better off economically also tend to have political systems that are more open and democratic.

While these correlations have been documented in various studies, they do not imply causal links between political institutions and economic development. Indeed, the connection between democracy and income has been of interest to social scientists for a long time, and arguments for causality have been made in both directions. Lipset (1959) famously offered his "modernization" hypothesis according to which rising levels of income would lead to democratization. More recently, Acemoglu et al. (2015) have argued that democratization leads to growth. Figure 1.2 shows the association estimated in their paper on the evolution of GDP per capita around democratization events.

These empirical associations, and the arguments around them, suggest that something of fundamental importance is at stake in the connection between political institutions and development; however, they do not determine directions of causality, nor unbundle the broad connections into the many component parts that are likely in operation. This observation suggests a path forward for where research should proceed: to understand the links between political institutions and growth, both in terms of causal effects and the details of which institutions matter and how. The task at hand is to elucidate specific mediating links between political institutions and economic performance.

The analysis of political institutions can make progress by asking about the determinants of a basic political failure: when and why do important demands from large social groups remain unanswered? In virtually every political system, social demands are largely met by a policy machine that has the state at its center. Those administering the state have both specific motives to act and the means to do so. Thus, political failures can typically be mapped into any combination of two types of problems: a lack of will

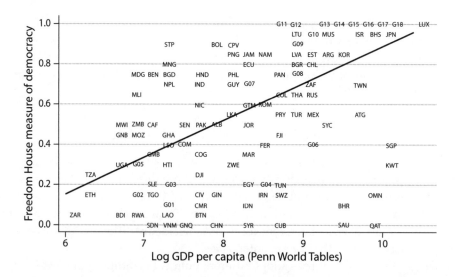

FIGURE 1.1. Association between GDP per capita (Penn Tables, average 1990–1999, PPP) and democracy (Freedom House). *Source*: Acemoglu et al. (2008).

or a lack of capacity to respond to demands. A lack of will to respond relates to issues of representation and accountability. These are critically affected by incentives and selection in the political arena, in turn, are shaped by, among other things, information and transparency, electoral rules, and political norms. These themes are taken up in our first subsection on representation and accountability. The lack of capacity to respond to demands relates typically to state capacity. It may include issues of information about problems, or the means to resolve them. This is taken up in our second subsection.

As may already be clear, we define political institutions broadly; that is, not only as the set of rules and norms that organize political activities, but also the organizations that shape actions within the political systems, such as government, political parties, trade unions, and so on.

1.3.1. Representation and Accountability

Political institutions matter for the ways power is distributed and utilized. They determine how preferences are aggregated and whose preferences end up counting in decisions on the provision of public goods and the choice of legal institutions. This is the "representation" dimension of political institutions. In addition, political institutions affect the accountability regime facing elected officials. Thus, political institutions may affect policies and welfare through both the representation and the accountability channels. In this review, we will focus on three elements that matter for representation and accountability:

- Electoral rules;
- Information and transparency; and
- Political norms and culture.

For each of these elements, we review the pertinent empirical evidence to ascertain how they affect the policies that get enacted.

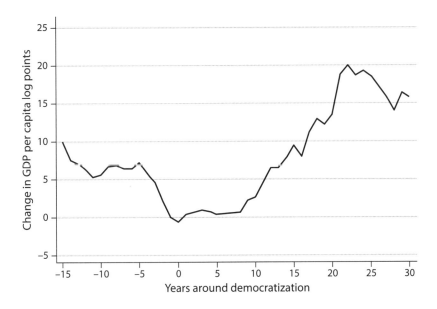

FIGURE 1.2. GDP per capita around a democratization. *Source*: Acemoglu et al. (2015).

1.3.1.1. Electoral Rules

Electoral rules affect both who can participate in public affairs (whether as a voter or a representative), how electoral competition is regulated, and what type of accountability regime will be in place over representatives. We focus on how electoral rules affect three sets of outcomes, namely: citizen behavior and participation, political selection, and politician behavior.

Effects on Citizen Behavior and Participation

At a basic level, electoral rules determine who can vote. As Lizzeri and Persico (2004) remarked, at the beginning of the nineteenth century most countries, including those that are fully democratic today, restricted electoral participation, if any, to a small subset of the male population. A century later, several countries had expanded suffrage to most males. In the next few decades, women would be included as well.

The most basic question is about verifying that such extensions are followed by a rapid increase in voter participation. A large strand of the literature has examined the effects of suffrage laws on voter turnout. For instance, Lott and Kenny (1999) showed that state-level voter participation among adults age 21 and older increased by 44% the year after women were enfranchised in the United States. Similarly, after the passage of the Voting Rights Act of 1965 in the United States, which outlawed hurdles to voter registration such as literacy tests, voter registration among blacks increased by much larger margins in those states that had retained such hurdles up to that point (Cascio and Washington 2014).

Electoral rules also affect the way in which candidates can compete for office and this, in turn, can also affect turnout. For example, Sanz (2015) uses a regression discontinuity design to compare turnout under closed-list proportional representation against an open-list, plurality-at-large system where voters can vote for individual candidates from the same or different party lists. He finds that the open-list system increases turnout by between one and two percentage points.

Barone and De Blasio (2013) take advantage of a natural experiment in Italy to identify the effect of electoral rules on turnout. For municipalities with fewer than 15,000 residents, the mayor and city council are elected under a single-ballot system by which the candidate receiving a plurality of votes wins the election and his or her party is guaranteed two-thirds of the seats on the council. At 15,000 residents and above, municipalities use a dual-ballot runoff system to select the mayor, and seats on the council are awarded proportionally. The authors show that the dual-ballot system increases turnout by one percentage point, which they attribute to the positive effects on fiscal discipline, broad representation, and politician quality induced by the dual-ballot system.

A natural question is whether rules affecting turnout matter for who gets elected, and for which policies are implemented. These questions are tackled next.

Effects on Political Selection

Electoral rules can affect political selection both directly and indirectly. Several countries have adopted political reservations, which directly determine who can hold office. These selection effects are mechanical and follow directly from the enforcement of the reservation system, as attested in several studies. To avoid duplication, we review studies of the effects of reservations in the following subsection, when examining policy effects.

However, it should be noted that electoral rules can also impact selection indirectly, by determining how votes are aggregated. Besley et al. (2011) use a dataset on 1,400 world leaders between 1848 and 2004 and find that, compared to autocracies, democracies select more educated leaders. Controlling for country and year fixed effects, they find that democracies are 20% more likely to select a highly educated leader.

While the possibility of experimenting with electoral rules has been elusive, some work has made just this type of contribution. Beath et al. (2016) performed a field experiment in Afghanistan to examine voters' trade-off between candidate quality and policy alignment. They randomly assigned regions either multiple single-member districts or an at-large, multiple-member district for the election of village council members. Their results suggest that an at-large district produces council members who are better educated and less extreme. The empirical pattern is explained through a formal model where, under multiple-single member districts, the anticipation of policy bargaining by representatives of the different districts leads voters to value candidates with more extreme positions, even if they are less competent. The adversarial aspect is muted in an at-large district, leading voters to prioritize competence.

Effects on Political Behavior and Policy

Electoral rules can affect political behavior and policies through a variety of channels. One is by simply affecting the composition of the electorate directly (e.g., franchise extent); the other is indirectly, by affecting the costs of participation. In a world in which the median voter determines policy, any changes to the composition of the electorate via suffrage laws or the relaxation of voter capacity constraints can result in policy shifts.

A large component of policy is redistributive. As highlighted by Bowles (forthcoming),[1] a key driver of inequality differentials across societies is not the pretax inequality generated by economic activity, but rather the amount of redistribution that takes place through the mediation of the political process. This motivates the need to interrogate the record on whether institutional changes that affect the composition of the electorate affect behavior and policy.

Miller (2008) examines the effect of women's suffrage in the United States. Using state-level variation in when women were given the right to vote, he demonstrates that the sudden increase in women voters led to large increases in public health spending. Miller's conclusion is that politicians responded to the demands of a new constituency that systematically places higher priority on children's welfare and the provision of public goods.

Fujiwara (2015) examined the effect of introducing electronic voting in Brazil. In the 1998 election, only municipalities with more than 40,500 registered voters adopted electronic voting, while the rest adopted the technology before 2002. A regression discontinuity design demonstrates that electronic voting reduced spoiled ballots and enfranchised the less-educated. An alternative design gaining identification from the phase-in across time suggests that the shift in voting patterns led to increased spending on healthcare, as well as increased prenatal visits and increased newborn birth weight for infants of less-educated mothers.

The study by Cascio and Washington (2014), which we referred to earlier, proceeds by exploiting the removal of literacy tests at registration after the 1965 Voting Rights Act. The authors study whether the increase in the effective voting rights of African Americans was accompanied by an increase in the share of public spending benefiting them. Employing a triple-difference framework over a 20-year period, they find that counties with higher black population shares in former literacy test states saw greater increases in both voter turnout and state transfers than comparison counties in non-literacy test states.

A stark example of institutional changes that affect the composition of the electorate is political reservations in India. Chattopadhyay and Duflo (2004) use political reservations for women in India to study the impact of women's leadership on policy decisions. Since the mid-1990s, one-third of village council head positions have been randomly reserved for women, which allows for causal interpretation of the results. Based on a household survey, which elicited the public goods preferences of women in sample villages, the authors found that female representation led to policy decisions better reflecting the preferences of women. In West Bengal, this implied more investment in drinking water and roads.

Pande (2003) uses political reservations in India to examine the role of mandated political representation in providing disadvantaged groups a level of influence over policymaking. The variation used in Pande's paper is at the state level, and it exploits the fact that the extent of state-level political reservation enjoyed by a minority group varies by its population share, which is only revised during census population estimates. This creates discrete changes in representation even though the underlying population share is continuous. The author finds that political reservations favoring disadvantaged groups in Indian states have increased the redistribution of resources in favor of those groups. An example is increases in spending on education programs.

Chin and Prakash (2011) examine the impact of political reservations for disadvantaged minority groups on poverty. The analysis is basically a reproduction of Pande's (2003) study but with a different dependent variable. The paper finds that increasing the share of seats reserved for scheduled tribes significantly reduces poverty, while increasing the share of seats reserved for scheduled castes has no impact on poverty. A political reservation for scheduled tribes has a greater effect on rural poverty than urban poverty, and appears to benefit people near the poverty line as well as those far below it.

Every policy has its winners and losers, and electoral rules help to aggregate—and to some extent adjudicate—such conflicts of interest. However, different electoral rules will weigh specific groups differently, and if preferences are heterogeneous then this can lead to differences in political behavior. Hinnerich and Pettersson-Lidbom (2014) compare the effects of representative and direct democracy on the redistribution of resources toward the poor. The authors use a regression discontinuity in Swedish municipalities between 1919 and 1938, exploiting a population threshold that determined whether representative government must be adopted. They demonstrate that direct democracies spend about half as much on public welfare programs, noting that "direct democracy may be more prone to elite capture." They suggest that in direct democracies, citizens might face greater difficulty in solving their collective action problems; the chairman of the town meeting was often a member of the elite and held a large amount of agenda-setting power; and open votes allowed opportunities for intimidation. Furthermore, the authors show that additional transfers in representative democracies were only directed toward organized groups of citizens.

Olken (2010) randomly assigned 49 Indonesian villages to choose development projects either through electing representatives or through direct plebiscites. With respect to the project, villages with plebiscites reported much higher satisfaction, knowledge, perceived benefits, and willingness to contribute. The authors suggest that this effect is largely attributable to a legitimizing effect of the plebiscite process rather than a change in the nature of the projects selected, noting that the latter was mostly limited to projects chosen by women being located in poorer areas.

Electoral institutions affect policy not only through their impact on representation, but also through accountability. Some work has investigated the differences between majoritarian and proportional representation systems. Persson and Tabellini (2003) argue that majoritarian systems enhance accountability, while Persson et al. (2003) offer cross-country evidence in support of that claim.

A key lever of accountability in a democratic system is the re-election incentive. A body of evidence uses the institutional variation in term limits across the states of the United States to examine the effects of re-election incentives. Besley and Case (1995) pioneered this literature, showing that term limits affect the fiscal policy of US governors. In the American states between 1950 and 1986, per capita spending and taxes were higher under term-limited governors. List and Sturm (2006) build upon Besley and Case (1995) to provide evidence that electoral incentives influence other policies in the United States, including environmental policy.

Ferraz and Finan (2011) show that re-election incentives reduce corruption. Comparing mayors who are in their first term with those who are in their second term and can no longer be re-elected, they find that second-term mayors have greater indicators of corruption. Second-term corruption is more pronounced among municipalities with less access to information and where the likelihood of judicial punishment is lower.

In a related paper, de Janvry et al. (2012) examine whether re-election incentives affect the performance of a decentralized conditional cash transfer program in Brazil. They too exploit the variation in re-election incentives induced by term limits. They show that while this federal program successfully reduced school dropout rates by 8 percentage points, the program's impact was 36% greater in municipalities governed by mayors who could be re-elected compared to those with lame-duck mayors. Moreover, first-term mayors with good program performance were much more likely to get re-elected. These mayors adopted program implementation practices that were not only more transparent but also were associated with better program outcomes.

While re-election incentives have been shown to motivate politician effort, as predicted by classic agency models (e.g., Barro 1973; Ferejohn 1986), the possibility of "too much accountability" has been raised as potentially undermining some minimally necessary job stability. Dal Bó and Rossi (2011) exploit two natural experiments in the Argentine legislature to assess the causal effect of term length on various measures of politicians' legislative effort. Results for separate measures as well as an aggregate index of legislative effort show that longer terms increase effort. Shorter terms appear to discourage effort not because of campaign distractions but because of an investment payback logic: when effort yields returns over multiple periods, longer terms yield a higher chance of capturing those returns and therefore incentivizing effort. This suggests that some stability over time horizons may be desirable, and that too frequently occurring electoral uncertainty can get in the way of adequately conducting state business.

Thus far, when asking whether electoral institutions affect behavior, we have focused on the behavior of representatives. But a comparable question can be asked about the behavior of voters, who make decisions on political participation, on policy, and on how to interact with each other.

Some work has examined whether local participatory institutions encourage cooperation. Fearon et al. (2009) analyze the impact of a community development project in Liberia that was paired with organizing local democratic institutions for decisions on the project. The authors find evidence that villages randomized into treatment subsequently cooperated more (i.e., raised more resources) in a public goods game. Some natural subsequent questions are whether an unbundled treatment that did not simultaneously affect resources would have had a similar effect. Another is whether this pattern would extend to other, at scale, community projects. Casey et al. (2012) conducted an RCT in Sierra Leone that also involved a community development project based on local participation. They studied a broad variety of outcomes and found effects on local public goods provisions and some economic outcomes, but no lasting effects on decision-making, the inclusion of marginalized groups, or collective action.

One particularly intriguing question is whether some political institutions may affect the behavior of citizens not through the policies they induce but through a "legitimacy effect." Dal Bó et al. (2010) used a lab experiment to show that a policy with the potential to increase cooperation is more effective when the policy is chosen democratically by subjects rather than being exogenously imposed. A clever experimental design circumvents the selection bias inherent in democratic selection of policy, allowing the authors to conclude that the mere fact that a policy was selected democratically can have an effect separate from the policy's inherent content and merits. This suggests that merely allowing individuals to participate in the political process can have a legitimizing effect on the policy that is produced, regardless of whether it changes the content of policy output.

Political institutions that affect the composition of the electorate may also have effects not through the policy that is selected but through the way in which policies are implemented. The political economy of policy implementation is an area that has received limited attention. Work analyzing how the political regime affects the impact of a given intervention, for example aid, offers one line of attack.[2]

Open Research Questions

- Do electoral rules affect political selection, and if so along which dimensions of candidate quality?
- Do electoral rules affect corruption?
- What is the optimal term length for officials?
- Are term limits optimal?
- Are rules that broaden representation inimical to accountability and competence?
- Are optimal rules different depending on the level of political development?

1.3.1.2. Information and Transparency
The asymmetry of information between voters and politicians lies at the heart of most models of political accountability. The presumption is that politicians enjoy an information advantage over voters about either the state of the world, their true level of competence, their motives for holding office, the effects of a policy, or all of the above. Because the incentives of politicians do not always align with those of voters, the asymmetry of information may then allow politicians to act opportunistically at the expense of voters' welfare. If this class of models approximates reality, then the potential for information and transparency to affect the political equilibrium and improve welfare cannot be understated.

But even if one were to assume that information matters, a series of practical questions remains unanswered. What type of information matters? How should this information be presented? How do we reduce the cost of acquiring this information? Are there trade-offs to be mindful of, and is there such a thing as providing too much information?

In this section we review some of the empirical evidence on the effects of information on political behavior. As in the previous section, we focus on three sets of outcomes, namely: citizen behavior and participation, political selection, and politician behavior. Here, however, we categorize the contributions to this literature depending on whether the information provided was about the actions (and/or performance) of the politicians, the politician's type, or the state of the world.

Information about the Actions and/or Performance of Politicians
There is a large body of literature that examines the effects on political accountability of providing voters with information about their politicians' performance.[3] While studies

vary in the content of the information provided to voters, several studies have shown that providing information about how corrupt the politician is can be quite effective in promoting political accountability. For example, Ferraz and Finan (2008) exploit variation in the timing of disclosure of information on corruption involving mayors in Brazil. The exogenous timing variation stems from the lottery-based timing of audits by the federal government. They find that, conditional on the number of irregularities detected, audit findings disclosed before elections were taken into account by voters. Corrupt mayors were punished at the polls while mayors who had committed no irregularities were rewarded. These effects are stronger in municipalities in which local radio is present to diffuse this information. Several findings have been uncovered in the disclosure of audit reports in other countries such as Puerto Rico (Bobonis et al. 2015) and Mexico (Larreguy et al. 2015).

Other studies, however, have documented that voters may not always react to information about the corruption of incumbent politicians. Chong et al. (2015) worked with an NGO to implement a door-to-door campaign and found that providing information about misuse of public funds had no effects on incumbent vote shares. Humphreys and Weinstein (2012) also implemented a large field experiment in Uganda to evaluate the impact of providing information to voters based on a detailed scorecard that reports the performance of MPs. They find that voters are sensitive to the information provided in the scorecard and update their beliefs. Ultimately though, the information had no impact on the vote shares of politicians.

What accounts for these contrasting findings? There are several possibilities, many of which have yet to be explored. One reason might pertain to voters' perception of the credibility of the source of the information and how it is conveyed. In the case of the audit studies, the information is usually being provided by an independent federal body via media outlets. On the other hand, in some of the other studies, NGOs or the researchers themselves gather and distribute the information. Who the originator of the information is and how the information is communicated to voters might be one explanation for why these effects seem to vary by context.

Some of these issues are explored in Alt et al. (2016), who rely on variation within the same institutional context to examine how beliefs are updated based on new information. They run a survey experiment in Denmark and find that an unemployment projection from the Danish Central Bank, which is highly credible among citizens, causes voters to update their beliefs more readily than does receiving information from government or opposition political parties.

Voters are not the only actors who are potentially affected by an information campaign. The politicians themselves might also respond in ways that can dampen the effects of negative coverage. For instance, Cruz et al. (2015) find evidence that politicians respond to information disclosure by engaging in more vote-buying. They implemented a field experiment in which they provided information to voters in the Philippines about the existence and importance of a large infrastructure public spending program one week before a municipal election. They show that the intervention led to changes in voter knowledge about the program and incumbent politicians, and that incumbent politicians responded by increasing resources targeted at voters through vote-buying. That said, when looking at turnout or voting patterns, Cruz et al. (2015) found no significant effects.

Similar effects were found by Bidwell et al. (2015), who used political debates in Sierra Leone as a vehicle through which to provide information to voters. Large groups of voters were exposed to films featuring debates among candidates for Congress. The intervention relied on a mobile cinema that visited 112 of 224 randomly selected voting locations in the five weeks before the election. The authors document that politicians who participated in policy debates and had this information randomly shown across localities increased campaigning effort, as measured by gift-giving, the monetary value of gifts, and the number of in-person visits.

Malesky et al. (2012) examine the impact of a randomized broadcast of information through an online newspaper on legislative debates, query transcripts, and scorecards of individual politicians in a non-democratic regime (Vietnam). They find insignificant effects on performance and voting, but lower re-election rates for delegates affected by the information, as they were less likely to be reappointed by the party elites. Furthermore, the results suggest delegates whose actions are publicized are more likely to shift their positions to conform to party guidelines, and that those who fail to adopt conformist positions are the most likely to be removed from office in the next elections.

Information about the "Type" of Politicians

Information on the characteristics of politicians and what they stand for can also affect political outcomes. The impact of transparency interventions of this type has been studied across highly diverse contexts, such as those in Sierra Leone, India, Benin, Mali, Indonesia, and São Tomé e Príncipe (STP).

Banerjee et al. (2010) conducted an RCT involving the distribution of report cards to citizens living in slums in India. The information covered not only the performance of legislators but also their personal background and that of the main challengers for office. The information was provided through local newspapers. The result was an increase of two percentage points on turnout (from a baseline slightly above 57%), a decrease in cash-based vote-buying, and a decrease in the vote shares of incumbents that were low-performing or faced high-quality challengers.

As mentioned earlier, Bidwell et al. (2015) used political debates in Sierra Leone as a vehicle through which to provide information to voters. Exposure to the debates affected voter knowledge and shifted voting toward the candidates who fared better during the debates. This suggests that higher transparency in general, and more policy discussion in particular, creates a "flight to quality." As also mentioned earlier, however, increases were observed in gift-giving and other, potentially vicious, political strategies as well.

Fujiwara and Wantchekon (2013) implemented a field experiment in collaboration with leading candidates of the 2006 presidential election in Benin. Their design had candidates adopt different strategies across villages. In some randomly selected villages the campaign strategy was "non-clientelist," while in other, control, villages the strategy was the traditional one, which tends to contain clientelistic elements. The intervention in treated villages was a bundle that also included public deliberation in the form of town hall meetings. Voters reported a higher perception that the campaign informed voters about candidate characteristics and reduced support for the dominant candidate in the village. However, the bundled intervention did not appreciably impact reported turnout, vote-buying, or support for candidates running the town meetings.

The role of information is not restricted to negative information that tightens accountability by inducing punishment at the polls. Kendall et al. (2015) show that positive information about the quality of politicians can also impact political selection. They implemented a field experiment on the occasion of the mayor of the Italian city of Arezzo seeking re-election. The intervention provided information signaling the high quality of a mayoral policy. (In particular, a city development plan developed by the mayor had been ranked first by the regional government and received extra funding because of its quality.) The authors show that voters update their beliefs and change their voting when provided with this positive information, but display much weaker reactions when information is provided solely on ideological policy positions.

Information about the State of the World

Gathering information is costly. Thus, even if we abstract from the information that politicians may actively want to hide (e.g., information about negative aspects of their background or record), limitations remain in terms of the information available to voters about the policies that are implemented and their effects on welfare. Several studies have shown that providing voters with more or less access to political news can influence both their level of political engagement and their political beliefs. For instance, Gentzkow (2006) documents that turnout in the United States decreased with the introduction of television. Because TV crowded out other sources of news with more political content, he argues that the primary explanation for these findings is a reduction in political knowledge.

DellaVigna and Kaplan (2007) investigate the effects of the expansion of the conservative-leaning Fox television network on partisan vote shares (Fox's presence helps Republicans). Using a difference-in-differences approach, they found that exposure to Fox News increased Republican vote share by 4 percentage points in the 2000 presidential elections. Other US-based studies focus on political choices, like Gerber et al. (2009), who offered free subscriptions to households to either a conservative-leaning or a liberal-leaning newspaper in the US state of Virginia and found that a newspaper subscription does not affect turnout (as reflected in voting self-reports), but the leanings of the newspaper that is received did affect self-reported support for a Democratic candidate. Moreover, subscription to either newspaper tended to decrease support for the incumbent (Republican) presidential candidate. This suggests that higher exposure of news of any kind makes voters less supportive of an embattled incumbent, as President George W. Bush was at the end of his second term, but by the same token might strengthen an incumbent who is doing well. However, there are challenges in comparing the context and findings in the United States to those in other countries.

More recently, experiments manipulating information in political settings have been implemented in countries as diverse as India, China, Denmark, Mozambique, and Pakistan. For example, some studies have measured positive effects on voter turnout by creating exogenous variation in the information available on the voting process.

Giné and Mansuri (2014) conducted an RCT treating rural women in Pakistan and detected large effects on female turnout as well as strong spillover effects on neighboring, untreated women. Aker et al. (2015) conducted an intervention with several treatments and delivery tools, including newspapers and text messages via mobile phones, as well as the distribution of leaflets and the creation of a hotline for reporting electoral problems.

The intervention offered information on the voting procedures as well as encouragement to participate. The authors detected an increase in turnout of nearly 5 percentage
points as well as a reduction in electoral problems under the newspaper treatment.

The evidence reviewed so far indicates that, compatible with the agency view of delegation and accountability, transparency and information matter to how citizens engage
with the political system and how well that system serves them. Two issues loom large
at this point. The first is what creates incentives for the media to contribute to transparency by publishing useful information. As highlighted by La Ferrara (2016, an RA1 paper
for EDI), this question has not been adequately investigated. The second issue is that the
study of information and transparency typically takes as given the preferences and norms
that shape individual behavior—partly because these elements are likely slow-changing
relative to the drivers of preferences and norms. However, this raises the question of
whether particular interventions can affect elements such as preferences and norms and
whether this matters to political and socioeconomic outcomes. We turn to this issue in
the following subsection.

Open Research Questions

- Does information disclosure, by affecting accountability, improve public good
  provision?
- Does the credibility of information affect political outcomes?
- What makes information usable to citizens?
- What creates incentives for the media to provide politically valuable information?
- What determines whether higher transparency leads to better political selection
  versus a reinforcement of vicious political strategies by incumbents?
- Does more transparency lead to changes in political institutions and norms?

1.3.1.3. Political Norms

Non-experimental work has shown that societal outcomes depend both on formal institutions and on equilibrium behavior that, while shaped by institutions, is further affected
by values and mutual expectations ("culture" and "norms"). In fact, these "soft" elements,
which are often thought to be transmitted within the family (Bisin and Verdier 2001;
Tabellini 2008), may greatly amplify or mitigate the effects of formal institutions (whether
political or economic in nature). For example, studies have shown that cultural traits
linked to national origin can affect the choice of family living arrangements and female
labor participation (Giuliano 2007; Fernández et al. 2004) and that political traditions in
the pre-industrial era correlate with contemporaneous political attitudes (Giuliano and
Nunn 2013). In addition, cultural traits and political preferences appear to be impacted
by particular shocks to technology and human experience. Alesina et al. (2013) explore
the origins of gender roles in relation to the introduction of the plow, while Giuliano
and Spilimbergo (2014) show evidence consistent with the notion that the Great Depression shaped the political preferences of cohorts going through their formative teenage
years at the time (in a more liberal-leaning direction).

An additional aspect of culture that can affect economic and political outcomes, as
indicated by Roland (2016), is the contrast between individualist and collectivist mind-
sets. In the case of politics the connection is direct, since so much of political life depends

on resolving collective action problems. In other words, political norms and culture may affect the way citizens engage with the political system. For example, political norms may be one reason why practices like clientelism take root against more programmatic forms of democracy.[4]

A common conceptual distinction links values and culture to drivers of the preferences of individuals, and norms to individuals' expectations of mutual behavior that drive equilibrium selection. It is very difficult to empirically identify expectation effects that act through equilibrium shifting versus equilibrium switching, and even to distinguish between changes in preferences and changes in expectations. Therefore, in this section we will organize evidence as pertaining to culture when it *likely* involves changes in preferences or attitudes, and to norms when it *likely* involves changes in aspirations or expectations, including trust. Such changes may be brought about by any number of interventions, such as education campaigns, institutional reforms, and interventions that alter the patterns of social interaction.

We begin by asking whether civic education campaigns can alter modalities of political engagement and political outcomes. Some of the interventions reviewed earlier in this chapter offered voters information about candidates and government performance. Some of those interventions also included treatments that aimed at changing the way citizens engaged with the political system.

For example, Vicente (2014) implemented a randomized door-to-door campaign against vote-buying during a presidential election in São Tomé e Príncipe. This campaign, sponsored by the National Electoral Commission, emphasized the importance of voting not according to vote-buying transactions but according to one's conscience. The campaign decreased the reported perception of voting decisions being affected by money and increased the perception that voting was conducted in good conscience. More materially, it decreased turnout (which may reflect the presence of turnout buying) and helped the incumbent politician obtain a larger vote share by 4 percentage points. Accordingly, the author's interpretation was that challengers must rely more heavily on vote-buying than incumbents.

The intervention by Aker et al. (2015), which relied on various vehicles for educating voters on voting procedures as well as enabling a hotline for reporting electoral problems, affected self-reported trust in the electoral commission (although puzzlingly the increase in the perception of the commission's neutrality was far weaker).

An extreme form of electoral problem is violence, which is often present in developing countries with unconsolidated democracies. Collier and Vicente (2013) studied the effects of a randomized anti-violence campaign conducted by the NGO Action Aid before the 2007 elections in Nigeria. They found evidence that the campaign increased perceptions of security and reduced actual events of violence as reflected in journalistic accounts.

Political participation, and resisting vote-buying and violence, all have in common that they entail incurring a private cost to provide a public benefit. In other words, they are at the heart of the collective action problem (Olson 1965). This suggests that an important component of political culture and norms might be the inclination of citizens to mitigate the collective action problem by behaving cooperatively.

This has led to a small but growing literature on measuring the effects of social capital on political behavior, where social capital is defined as engaging in societal norms of cooperation that are individually costly but socially beneficial. For example, Nannicini et al. (2013) examine the effects of social capital on political selection and accountability. Building on the work of Guiso et al. (2004, 2008), they use average per capita blood donations in the Italian provinces as their main proxy for social capital. Based on this variation, they examine whether members of the Italian parliament are more likely to have a criminal investigation against them or are more likely to be absent from the legislature in electoral districts with less social capital. They find that this is indeed the case, and that voters in districts with more social capital are more likely to punish misbehaving incumbents.

Padró i Miquel et al. (2015) also provide evidence of the interaction between social and political norms for village elections in China. They examine whether the impact of local elections on political accountability varies depending on a village's level of social capital, as measured by the presence of village temples, which play an important role in organizing local collective action. Using a difference-in-differences strategy, the authors find that the introduction of elections had only a minimal impact on public goods provision in villages with low social capital, but a large effect in villages with high social capital.

Finan and Schechter (2012) provide evidence from a field experiment in Paraguay to show how norms of reciprocity can affect political behavior. In Paraguay, local politicians hire community leaders as election brokers in order to promote their candidacy and offer them money and other forms of aid in exchange for the promise of their vote. The authors conduct a survey with the actual middlemen who broker the vote-buying exchanges between voters and politicians. They combine survey information on vote-buying experienced in a 2006 municipal election with experimental data on individual intrinsic reciprocity. They find that political brokers target vote-buying offers to individuals who have strong norms of reciprocity.

Changes to social and political norms might also be one reason why the effects of historical institutions tend to persist over time.[5] For example, Banerjee and Iyer (2005) show that variation in the colonial land revenue institutions set up by the British in India during the 1800s led to sustained differences in local economic outcomes. Part of this persistence, they argue, had to do with the lack of social cohesion in ex-landlord controlled districts, which relied on an oppressive revenue system. These conflictual environments thus limited the possibility of collective action, which contributed to the persistent effects of these formal institutions even after they ceased to exist.

Some of the research reviewed here sought to affect political attitudes through interventions that contained not only information but also exhortative components. These components often involve invoking civic duty or even values. A body of literature, mostly on tax compliance, has examined the effect of direct exhortations that contain normative standards (e.g., "this action constitutes a duty"), a positive norm description (e.g., "most people behave this way"), or even information about the potential penalties that could follow from no payment.

The evidence is mixed. In various studies, normative exhortations were not found to be effective at improving compliance, while threats of closer scrutiny or emphasis on penalties were effective (McGraw and Scholz 1991; Blumenthal et al. 2001; Fellner et al. 2013; Castro and Scartascini 2015). In one other study, however, appeals to the norm of payment and its public good consequences were effective (Hallsworth et al. 2017).

More closely related to political behavior, Guan and Green (2006) conducted a canvassing experiment with Chinese students and showed that encouragement to vote emphasizing civic duty increases turnout by more than 12 percentage points. Gerber and Rogers (2009) conducted a survey field experiment before two different elections (in New Jersey and California) in which they exposed registered voters to two different "positive norm descriptions," one emphasizing that the vast majority of people do vote, and one emphasizing the opposite. They found this to have an effect on subsequent self-reports of intention to vote. Whether interventions appealing to descriptive social norms can affect actual turnout remains an open question.

Interventions that offer information may lead an actor to change behavior, although the information may only be relevant to a temporary situation (e.g., a specific election) so the effect may be by definition short-lived. Interventions aimed at altering attitudes may also be short-lived, even though the attitude change could in principle persist. An open question is the extent to which attitudinal changes are persistent depending on the type of intervention that is performed. One type of treatment that is thought to have long-lasting effects is school-based education, since this intense exposure presumably inculcates values that are internalized.

Education has been thought to be effective in shaping political attitudes, although rigorous evidence on this has been lacking. It has been proposed that education can be an instrument of government-led nation-building (Alesina and Reich 2015), and there is evidence that US states differentially introduced compulsory education requirements when they were most in need of instilling civic values to the population in compositional flux due to immigration (Bandiera et al. 2019). But can the content of education truly affect political attitudes? Cantoni et al. (2015) exploit the staggered introduction of a new curriculum in Chinese high schools to evaluate the effect of a change in school curriculum on political attitudes. They find that the curriculum change led to a higher appreciation of Chinese governance and of the value of local democracy, and a skepticism toward free markets. In particular, students exposed to the new curriculum have greater trust in government officials, view government officials as more civic-minded, and see bribery as less prevalent and effective. In addition, students exposed to the new curriculum see China as more democratic but are more skeptical of unconstrained democracy—which matches the message of the new textbooks. Finally, "treated" students convey more skeptical views of unconstrained free markets, which is also in line with the content of the new curriculum. Working from official documents that convey the official intent behind the reform, the authors establish that the realized outcomes were broadly in line with the intended outcomes.

Beath et al. (2013) examine a development program that mandated women's community participation. The community development program was part of a RCT in 500 villages in Afghanistan. As part of a community-driven development program, the village had to establish a development council with equal participation of men and women in the election of the council and in the selection of development projects. While the study finds increased female participation in various activities, it found no effects on the division of intra-family decision-making or on attitudes toward the general role of women in society.

A way in which norms may affect the operation of the political system is by shaping attitudes toward, and preferences for, certain types of leaders. Interventions that can affect baseline expectations of and attitudes toward different types of leaders could alter the patterns of representation. Beaman et al. (2009) exploit random variation in mandated exposure to female leaders across village councils in the Indian state of West Bengal to investigate the extent to which such exposure reduces a bias against female leadership at the village level. One possibility is that exposure to female leaders may affect statistical discrimination, by showing males that females perform well. Another possibility is that it may affect deep-seated tastes. The authors use various measures of attitudes toward female leadership, including statements by subjects of perceived effectiveness and implicit association tests (IATs). The latter likely help capture changes in tastes as opposed to statistical discrimination. The evidence shows no changes in IAT-reflected tastes (except when it comes to occupational associations) but significant changes in the perception of female effectiveness. The authors conclude that while exposure to female leadership may not easily change deep-seated tastes, it may affect perceptions of female effectiveness. Thus, exposure to female leadership may still translate into shifted future support for female leaders.

An additional way in which "norms" may play a role is by affecting the standards that voters use to evaluate government. Gottlieb (2016) evaluates a civics course intervention that educated voters on the capacity and responsibilities of government, as well as on the comparative performance of local politicians. A posterior survey experiment reflected a higher predisposition of treated citizens to sanction badly performing government and vote on performance. In addition, challenges to authority in town hall meetings become more likely. Ideally, future work will look to identify effects on actual behavior at the polls.

The extent to which temporary interventions may affect baseline tastes and attitudes remains an important question for future research, as is understanding the mechanisms by which changes take place. One basic distinction is between effects driven by changes in factual information that may affect judgment (including statistical discrimination), changes in expectations about the behavior of others that lead to adjustments in behavior, and changes in tastes. Identifying the separate mechanisms is not easy, but the creative use of measurement (as exemplified by the use of IATs) and experimental design can help. The experimental manipulation of treatment content can aid in either introducing or eliminating pure informational effects such as statistical discrimination; the variation in the share of treated subjects can help shift (or eliminate) effects that operate via expectations about the behavior of others. The latter approach has been exploited in laboratory studies that succeed in isolating both taste-driven and expectation-driven effects (e.g., Dal Bó and Dal Bó 2014 show that exposure to moral messages triggers taste-driven effects as well as expectation-driven effects; the latter give rise to a "moral social multiplier" that amplifies the power of moral statements at sustaining cooperation). Progress has also been made using variation in observational data to identify the presence of a tax evasion social multiplier driven by audit congestion costs (Galbiati and Zanella 2012).

Open Research Questions

- What are the drivers and consequence of government legitimacy?
- What are the main drivers of political attitudes leading to cleaner political practices and tighter political accountability?
- What mechanisms reduce or eliminate bias and stereotypes in political attitudes?

- When attempting to resolve collective action problems, how important is it to shift norms (understood as expectations about mutual behavior) relative to transforming preferences?
- How do political norms help to overcome political failures?
- What are the effects on political participation and accountability of specific cultural traits, such as trust, respect for others, and individualism versus collectivism?
- How do political norms interact with formal institutions? Do specific norms promote more political accountability?

1.3.2. State Capacity

The state is a fundamental institution underlying the production of both order and prosperity. The state typically involves a complex organization manned by full-time, specialized personnel. In democratic countries, the state relies on two main types of personnel. One is politicians, who occupy elected positions and carry out the functions of government. Elected officials hold office with a term length that is typically a few years, and have no default path of office progression. The other type of personnel is bureaucrats, who are appointed rather than elected and who can typically expect to develop a career progressing along clearly specified ranks. The bureaucracy supports the government but can in principle be quite free of government interference. Of course these characterizations depend at least in part on how well-functioning a state is. As it turns out, states function in very different ways across and within countries, and can display surprisingly disparate levels of effectiveness. Understanding what can help governments work better at all levels is a central part of a pro-growth, institutions-centered research agenda.

If one conceptualizes the state as operating a production function of public goods, the inputs can be divided into three parts: personnel, resources, and procedures. We cover work dealing with each of these in what follows. These themes align well with priority topics in other EDI research exercises, which include the bureaucracy and management practices in the state as priority areas (e.g., Mookherjee, forthcoming).

1.3.2.1. Personnel Selection

The most basic aspect in personnel policy is selecting the individuals who will become public employees. Two fundamental questions in the area of selection of state personnel concern the type of individuals that should be selected into government and what instruments can help with recruiting those types.[6]

It has long been debated in the field of public administration whether public sector employees have a different vocational profile compared to private sector employees. More specifically, are the motives of public employees different? Because the public sector involves public service, it is possible that individuals with high levels of prosocial motivation may be differentially attracted to public sector jobs. This argument has also been made in relation to other mission-driven organizations, such as NGOs. The literature on public administration and economics tends to find support for this idea. One type of evidence stems from patterns in survey data. Using data from the World Values Survey for 52 countries, Cowley and Smith (2014) found that public sector workers on average display higher intrinsic motivation than workers in the private sector, even after controlling for differences in basic socioeconomic characteristics. Another approach is to perform lab-in-the-field interventions, where different types of employees play experimental games. Banuri and Keefer (2013) find that, compared to those in the private sector, employees from the public sector of Indonesia are much more prosocial in their playing of the dictator game. A third approach is to explore experimental variation among individuals and simultaneously explore their vocational inclination before they choose a career. Serra et al. (2011) rely on both survey and experimental data to show that prosocial inclination correlates with a preference for public sector jobs in Ethiopia. Kolstad and Lindkvist (2013) document a similar relationship in Tanzania.

Cowley and Smith (2014) find that, although public sector workers tend to be more intrinsically motivated than private sector workers on average, this difference depends on the corruption level of the country. In countries with high levels of corruption, intrinsically motivated individuals are not more likely to join the public sector. This suggests that the level of development in the country, and the level of integrity of government, may affect the preference of those self-selecting into careers. This is also a reminder that prosociality is of course only one characteristic out of many that could be relevant for public sector selection. Personal integrity may also vary across individuals and affect career choices.

Some studies have measured integrity through lab-experimental types of games. Hanna and Wang (2015) conduct an experimental study with students from a university in India. In the experiment, students play a series of games designed to measure various personality traits, including integrity (a propensity to refrain from cheating) and prosocial behavior. The authors find that students who cheated in a dice game are more likely to express interest in a public sector job. Banerjee et al. (2015) examine embezzlement of resources in an experiment in which "supervisors" evaluate the performance of "workers," then claim a budget to compensate the workers, and finally hand out the compensation. Thus, there are two margins of corruption: over-reporting the worker's performance to claim a larger budget, and then underpaying the worker. Both types of subjects are "corrupt" in that they tend to over-claim resources and underpay workers. However, aspiring bureaucrats, they find, are more corrupt than aspiring private sector employees in the sense that they over-claim resources by a significantly larger amount, but do not underpay workers by a significantly larger amount.

Barfort et al. (2015) also conduct a cheating experiment, but among students in Denmark, one of the least corrupt countries in the world. They show that Danish students who plan to enter the public sector behave with more integrity in experimental games where it is possible to cheat. This is related to a lower concern for financial compensation. One interpretation of these findings is that the intensity of financial motivation may affect both integrity and self-selection, leading those who highly value financial compensation to self-select into the sector where that compensation is most prominent, be it legal (in the private sector) or illegal (in the public sector in more corrupt countries). Substantiating this exact interpretation is a matter for future research.

Workers differ not only in terms of their prosociality and preference for financial rewards but also in terms of their quality. In addition to the honest and intrinsically motivated, governments also value individuals of high quality; however, if higher-quality candidates demand more compensation, higher wages may be needed to attract these individuals. A problem with higher compensation is that it may attract individuals with higher valuation of financial rewards, who in light of the evidence above may also be less honest or prosocial. This danger is studied in a small theoretical literature in economics (e.g., Delfgaauw and Dur 2008; Francois 2000; Prendergast 2007). This work explains how offering higher wages may create a cost by attracting individuals who are more corruptible or care less about the mission. Whether a trade-off between quality and motivation/integrity exists is ultimately an empirical question. Recently, some scholars have explored the extent to which financial incentives can affect a government's ability to recruit publicly motivated and high-quality individuals.

Dal Bó et al. (2013) implemented a field experiment as part of an official Mexican federal government program called the Regional Development Program (RDP), which sought to enhance state presence in 167 of Mexico's most marginalized municipalities. As part of the recruitment drive to hire 350 development agents, two different wage offers were randomly assigned across 106 recruitment sites. In one set of recruitment sites, the program offered MXN 5,000 per month, while in the other sites the program offered a wage of MXN 3,750. Based on this random variation, the study finds that higher wages do help attract a higher-quality candidate pool. In the places that announced a higher salary, the average applicant was smarter, had better personality traits, had higher earnings, and had a better occupational profile (e.g., more experience and white-collar background). Moreover, contrary to theoretical concerns, these effects do not come at the cost of attracting less publicly motivated candidates, as measured by their performance in the Perry (1996) public service motivation inventory.

The power of wages is not limited to attracting a larger and better applicant pool. Higher wages also increase an organization's ability to fill vacancies. In the Dal Bó et al. (2013) study, the authors found that the Mexican government was 35.2% more likely to fill the vacancy when offering the higher wage, which corresponds to a short-run labor supply elasticity of 2.15.

Part of the reason why higher wages lead to higher recruitment rates is because they help to compensate for aspects of the job that a candidate dislikes. This mechanism was on clear display in Dal Bó et al. (2013). Although the applicants for the RDP position were all applying for the same job, the jobs were located in different municipalities throughout the country. At the time of the application, the candidates did not know where the job was located and were only told this information during the offer stage. As a result, jobs that were ex ante quite similar became quite different ex post depending on where the job was located and the characteristics of the municipality. The authors show that distance to the municipality (from their current residence) and attributes such as the level of drug violence and the lack of public goods in the municipality were all important hurdles to filling the vacancies. Fortunately, however, higher wages proved to be an effective instrument in clearing these hurdles.

A complementary approach to making public sector employment attractive can be to offer favorable career prospects. This can also have positive selection effects, as shown by Ashraf et al. (2015). These authors partnered with the government of Zambia to hire approximately 330 community healthcare workers, and introduced experimental variation in the way the position was advertised. In 24 of the 48 districts, potential candidates saw a job advert that highlighted the job's promotion prospects and the opportunity for career advancement. In the other districts, applicants saw an ad that emphasized the service dimension as well as the social importance of the job. In the districts where the job ads stressed career incentives, applicants were much more qualified (as measured by their high school test scores and past performance in their natural science courses). These applicants also displayed a high degree of prosocial motivation, with levels that were similar to the applicants that applied under the social incentive treatment. While the applicants who applied under the career incentives treatment did place a higher weight on career benefits, the authors conclude that making career versus social incentives salient did not induce a trade-off between a higher-quality applicant pool and a prosocially motivated one.

In contrast to these two studies, Deserranno (2015) finds that stronger financial incentives can lead to an applicant pool that is less socially motivated. She conducted a field experiment in collaboration with the NGO BRAC in rural villages of Uganda. The experiment involved a recruitment drive for health promoters. Because the job was new to the villages, the experiment was able to introduce variation in how the financial aspects of the job were advertised. In one treatment, the job advertisement mentioned the minimum amount that a health promoter was expected to earn. In another treatment, the ads communicated the maximum amount a health promoter was expected to earn. A third treatment advertised the mean earnings that could be expected.

The study found that announcing the maximum amount attracted 30% more candidates relative to announcing the minimum amount, but those candidates had less experience as health volunteers and were much more likely to state "earning money" as the most important feature of the job. In the context of a dictator game, candidates in the medium- and high-pay treatments were also 24 percentage points less likely to donate to a public health NGO. Despite detecting these large effects on measures of intrinsic motivation, the author did not find treatment effects on candidate quality, as measured by the applicant's education and income.

In sum, a scant experimental literature has studied the role of compensation and career prospects on the quality and motivation of employees that are attracted. The evidence is mixed, both on the quality effects and on the possibility of a trade-off between quality and motivation. This is not surprising. There are treatment and context differences across the studies; however, the existence of a trade-off between quality and motivation, for example, depends on how these personal traits are correlated within the broader population, as shown theoretically by Dal Bó et al. (2013). These three studies, which were conducted in very different contexts, represent a step forward in the literature—but without more information on how personality traits vary across broader populations, it is difficult to make general conclusions about the exact trade-offs that financial incentives induce.

We have reviewed evidence on how different recruitment instruments can have selection effects along two broad families of personal traits, namely quality and intrinsic motivation. But do personal traits matter? It is conceivable that quality characteristics (typically associated with cognitive capacity and education) affect performance. But whether intrinsic motivation (typically related to vocational profile and prosociality) should matter is less clear.

One argument as to why motivation should matter is that it affects match quality between employer and employee. If employers and employees have shared objectives, then the tension between organizational goals and the provision of incentives is relaxed

(Besley and Ghatak 2005). For governments, who are responsible for providing public goods that are difficult to price in the market, the ability to recruit public service–motivated individuals might be especially beneficial. If individuals have high levels of intrinsic motivation, then they are less likely to shirk in an environment where incentives are low-powered and/or when there are important non-contractible elements in the provision of a service (Francois 2000).

A large empirical literature in public administration has explored correlations that are in line with these theoretical arguments. It has been shown that intrinsic motivation—and specifically public service motivation—is associated with higher levels of performance in government (Perry and Hondeghem 2008). Naff and Crum (1999), in turn, explore a large sample of more than 8,000 US federal employees and find that public sector motivation correlates with individuals' last performance evaluations. Using data from 22 federal agencies in the United States, Park and Rainey (2008) find that public service motivation is positively correlated with self-reported measures of job productivity and quality of work. Similar results are found using government data from Switzerland (Ritz 2009) and the Netherlands (Steijn 2008). These patterns are confirmed by a meta-study indicating that public service motivation is positively correlated with job performance in the public sector, broadly defined (Petrovsky 2009).

Economics is making a slow entry into this literature through RCTs. For example, as part of an experiment monitoring health clinics in the district of Punjab, Callen et al. (2015) examined the job performance of clinic doctors. They found that doctors who scored higher on the Perry public service motivation index were less likely to shirk and falsify health reports. Deserranno (2015), who as discussed earlier investigates the case of Ugandan health promoters, found that prosocial motivation strongly predicts job performance. Specifically, those health promoters who had donated a greater share of their endowment to a local NGO visited a larger number of households and provided more prenatal checks. In the context of an audit study on bednet distribution programs, Dizon-Ross et al. (2015) conduct a survey on nurses at antenatal care centers in Uganda, Ghana, and Kenya. They find that nurses tend to exhibit high levels of prosocial motivation, and that this level is predictive of job performance.

The mounting evidence connecting public service motivation and performance on the job is highly indicative, but remains short of proving a causal link. Even in the context of experiments, it remains difficult to manipulate motivation to generate exogenous variation in it. However, some indirect approaches have been tried recently that induce variation in the characteristics of applicants to a given position while holding some important factors constant, like potential incentive effects. Both the studies by Ashraf et al. (2015) and Deserranno (2015) are examples of this approach. Ashraf et al. (2015) used their two different recruitment strategies (one career-oriented, one socially oriented) to create variation in the type of health promoters that were recruited. After recruitment, all the health workers were given the same responsibilities and placed under the same incentives. Based on this design, they find health workers attracted by career incentives to be much more effective at delivering health services. For example, they carried out 29% more household visits over an 18-month period, and triggered higher use of health facilities and tracking of children's health care. The treatment group included candidates who scored better during training (so are more capable) but did not score differently in terms of prosocial motivation. The impact of these health workers appears to owe much to unobservable characteristics, although those who prioritize career advancement over social impact tend to perform worse. This indicates that it is quite possible that prosocial inclinations play a positive role in performance.

The study by Deserranno (2015) provides stronger evidence in support of the relationship between prosociality and job performance. She finds that agents recruited under the low-pay condition, who were measured to be more prosocial, perform better during the first year of work than those who were recruited under the high-pay condition: they visited more households and provided more pre- and postnatal checks. She also finds that they were more likely to target the most vulnerable households.

These studies support the view that there are important "selection" effects that affect job performance. But it remains to be investigated further what might be involved in such effects. As was argued at the start of this section, prosocial motivation is frequently found to be correlated with job performance, and some of the experimental studies have found that wage and career prospects can affect the prosocial inclination of candidates. However, prosocial motivation correlates with other personal traits, including psychological characteristics such as the "Big Five."[7] Short of randomly offering jobs to individuals based on a specific personal trait, it is difficult to separate the effects of intrinsic motivation from other positive personality traits. Even that approach would encounter the hurdle that there may be unobservable personality correlates that drive performance.

An alternative way of investigating the role of personality traits is to examine the heterogeneous treatment effects of some interventions along those traits. A good illustration of such an approach is the study by Callen et al. (2015). The intervention they studied aimed at curbing absenteeism by doctors and staff in clinics in Punjab. One reason why absenteeism was high is that controls were lax, and if inspections took place then the doctors and inspectors would collude. The authors collaborated with officials of the Department of Health to introduce a new monitoring program in 18 of the 35 districts that made up the experimental sample. The intervention involved replacing the traditional paper-based monitoring system for clinic utilization and worker absence with a smartphone application. The new system allowed health system inspectors to upload the results of their assigned visit to a central dashboard that instantly updated reports at different levels of aggregation. The data, which included geotagged, time-stamped facility staff photos, made it difficult for inspectors to collude and falsify their reports. The study did find that the monitoring technology increased the number of inspections, but interestingly there was significant heterogeneity in the treatment effects depending on the personality characteristics of the inspector. Higher-quality inspectors responded much more positively to the treatment. A one standard deviation increase in the Big Five index measure of a healthcare professional is associated with a differential 35 percentage point treatment effect in terms of health inspections.

The overall takeaway of these studies is that individual traits—be they about competence or about personality traits and motivation—matter both for job performance and for the way workers respond to interventions. A corollary is that the development of state capacity may require well-thought-out recruitment drives in order to shape the labor supply available to the state, as well as screening policies in order to choose well among available candidates. However, the particular way in which governments may want to adjust recruitment and screening may depend on country characteristics. This is suggested by the contrasting link between honesty and preference for the public sector across countries, and by the fact that the trade-off between competence and public service motivation often may not be present. Understanding what are the key correlates that would indicate how best to recruit and screen appears to be an important direction for future research.

Once the state's personnel are in place, two more aspects of the employment relationship become key: incentives and monitoring. We tackle these next.

Incentives

The study of incentives has been one of the most active areas of research in economics in the last few decades, both theoretically and empirically. But the intersection of the sphere of incentive studies with that of empirical and experimental work is less well populated. Nonetheless, some interesting studies provide valuable findings and a review can offer directions for future research.

There are three important questions surrounding incentive schemes in the state administration. The first is whether incentive schemes such as pay for performance can improve performance along the intended dimension. The second is whether using more high-powered incentive schemes triggers distortions along dimensions that are not incentivized. The third is whether principals tend to design schemes optimally given the trade-offs facing them when attempting to provide incentives. A fourth question is whether extrinsic incentives crowd out intrinsic incentives. As will be seen, there is some experimental evidence on the first and second questions, while the third and fourth remain open.

Some of the initial investigations of pay for performance took place in the context of front-line service delivery. Olken et al. (2014) conducted a field experiment in Indonesia in which villages were given a block grant each year to use for any purpose related to health or education. In treatment villages, 20% of the total amount set aside for block grants in a subdistrict was allocated based on performance on the targeted health and education indicators; in control villages, the block grant was allocated based only on population. The incentive was offered to the whole community and was generally not passed on to service providers but was instead used for carrying out program-related activities (e.g., nutritional supplements, subsidies for childbirth, etc.). The authors found that the incentivized areas performed better on the targeted health indicators (on average, the eight targeted health indicators were about 0.04 standard deviations higher in the incentivized than non-incentivized villages). There were no detectable differences between incentivized and non-incentivized areas on educational outcomes.

Most of the studies investigating pay for performance, however, have focused on programs where incentives are directly given to providers. For example, in the context of healthcare, Banerjee et al. (2008) studied financial incentives for nurses' attendance in India. In that experiment, the nurses who were recorded absent more than half of the days in a month would get their pay reduced by the number of days they were recorded absent, and nurses who were absent more than half of the days in two consecutive months would be suspended from government service. Nurses used a protected time/date stamp machine to verify attendance. The authors detected a substantial treatment effect in the short run, but the effect diminished over time and was zero by the end of their study. Although they do not have the data to confirm this, anecdotal evidence suggests the decline was due to nurses learning how to exploit loopholes in the systems and recording more exempt absences over time.

Basinga et al. (2011) (see also Gertler and Vermeersch 2012) studied a pay-for-performance intervention in Rwanda that provided incentives to primary care facilities equal to a 38% increase in total compensation for facility personnel. The incentives were based on the quantity of visits to the facility, as well as the content of services provided during the visits. The authors found that the incentives led to a substantial increase in productivity (around 20%), which translated into increases in pre- and postnatal services, as well as improved infant health. Circling back to the previous emphasis on individual characteristics, an important complementarity was detected between treatment and provider skill at baseline.

Combining a healthcare focus in an education environment, Miller et al. (2012) conducted a field experiment in 72 Chinese primary schools in which school principals were incentivized to reduce anemia among their students. Principals were paid RMB 150 per student who changed from anemic to non-anemic over the course of the intervention. A 50% reduction in anemia resulted in a two-month salary increase for principals. Control groups did not receive financial incentives, but did receive the same information and subsidies as the treatment group. The incentives reduced anemia by about 5 percentage points (23%) compared to the control group.

Schools are another front-line service delivery area where incentive studies have been performed. Duflo et al. (2012) report on an experiment designed to improve teacher attendance in 60 treated schools in India (out of 120), by relying on cameras and a payment scheme that rewarded attendance. Teachers were paid a base wage for 20 days of work, penalized for showing up less, and rewarded with a bonus for showing up more than 20 days. The effect of the treatment was a reduction in absenteeism of 21 percentage points. The authors then estimated a structural model that permits counterfactual simulations indicating that a cost-minimizing policy should have considered a higher threshold and larger bonus.

Front-line service delivery by the state must be funded with fiscal revenue. Thus, a natural question is whether incentives can help the state obtain the resources it needs to finance public goods. Khan et al. (2014) conducted a large-scale field experiment in Punjab, Pakistan, where they allocated 482 property tax units into either one of three performance-related pay schemes or a control. Two years later, incentivized units had revenues that were higher than the control units by 9.3 log points, which implied a 46% higher growth rate. The scheme that rewarded tax collectors purely on revenue did best, increasing revenue by 12.8 log points (62% higher growth rate), with little penalty for customer satisfaction and assessment accuracy compared to the two other schemes that explicitly also rewarded these dimensions. The study offers evidence compatible with the idea that one consequence of higher-powered incentives was an increase in the size of bribes that were exchanged whenever collusion took place, with lower frequency of corruption. This is consistent with many simple models of bribery, which predict a negative correlation between bribe levels and frequency of corruption.

While less frequent corruption should be a desirable outcome, a higher volume of bribes may still be seen as problematic. There are other types of undesirable outcome predicted by theory when high-powered incentives are introduced, for example multi-tasking distortions. These occur when rewarding performance along one specific activity leads to reductions in performance along other, unincentivized activities. An illustration of this type of effect is offered by Baicker and Jacobson (2007), who documented that, when allowed to keep the revenue from assets seized in drug arrests, police agencies in the United States increased drug arrests but simultaneously reduced enforcement on other crimes, like burglary. The police thus displayed a revenue-seeking attitude, in that arrests go up more strongly in connection with drugs like cocaine and heroin that yield more lucrative seizures than marijuana.

Besides policing, other areas where multitasking effects are expected are education and health. In education, the typical concern is that incentivizing teachers to improve student test scores on a few subjects may lead to underinvestment in other areas. Muralidharan and Sundararaman (2011) evaluated a large-scale teacher incentive program in the state of Andhra Pradesh in India. They studied a school-level randomized trial in which, based on test scores, public school teachers were paid incentives at both the group and individual levels. The incentives at play were calibrated to be around 3% of a typical teacher's annual salary. The researchers found that the incentives promoted learning. Two years later, students in incentivized schools had test scores 0.27 standard deviations higher in math and 0.17 standard deviations higher in language. Despite these sizeable effects, they found no evidence of multitasking: students also did better in subjects (like social studies and science) that were not placed under the incentive scheme. These effects also increased over time: after five years, students in treatment schools had test scores 0.54 standard deviations higher in math and 0.35 standard deviations higher in language, and still had higher test scores in non-incentivized subjects (Muralidharan 2012).

Glewwe et al. (2010) evaluated a randomized trial of teacher incentives in Kenya, where an NGO provided in-kind prizes to teachers in Kenyan public schools on the basis of school-level performance on district exams. In contrast to the previous study, they found that, while incentivized schools performed better on the government exam used to compute the incentives, there was no evidence of improved scores on an exam covering non-incentivized areas, suggesting that in their context multitasking was a real issue. Teachers may have responded to incentives by devoting more effort to developing test-taking skills than to general instruction. In sum, incentives led to improvement in the incentivized areas in both studies, but while in India there were positive spillovers to non-incentivized ones, this did not take place in Kenya.

In the Miller et al. (2012) study reported earlier, they document that incentivized school principals were more likely to use subsidies for iron-focused supplements, whereas non-incentivized school principals used subsidies for supplements that could affect both iron *and* overall calorie intake. To the extent that both types of supplementation are considered valuable health policy objectives, this result would reflect a multitasking distortion.

One important issue is understanding why certain interventions have long-lasting effects and others do not. The schools in the Duflo et al. (2012) study were run by an NGO, which may have had more independence in enforcing the incentives than the government sometimes does. It remains to be established which of these effects is more likely to generalize: the positive long-run effects found in Duflo et al. (2012) or the rapid decline in effectiveness found in Banerjee et al. (2008).

Monitoring

A key question in governmental organizations, where a pay-for-performance approach is often impractical, is whether the adoption of new monitoring approaches can induce higher employee effort and more successful public service delivery.

One way in which accountability may be enhanced is by involving the community in the monitoring of public service delivery. Olken (2007) studied the random assignment of top-down monitoring of public works projects as well as an approach relying on community involvement. He showed that audits significantly reduce corruption (i.e., a discrepancy between official costs and an independent assessment of cost) while community involvement in monitoring has little impact.

Björkman and Svensson (2009) evaluated an intervention that involved mobilizing community-based monitoring, as well as providing report cards on the performance of the local health clinic compared to those in other places and against the national standard for primary healthcare provision. The community-based aspect relied on having citizens and health workers meet to discuss the state of health services and elaborate a plan to monitor and improve those services. The authors found that the intervention caused a significant improvement in the performance of health workers. One result of that improvement was a reduction in child mortality. The authors' interpretation is that the intervention helped people resolve the collective action problem, thereby holding providers accountable. In subsequent work, Björkman et al. (2014) tried to disentangle the effects of information provision from the effects of collective mobilization through community participation in meetings. To this effect, the new intervention, while still involving information provision, did not include comparison information vis-à-vis other health clinics. The evidence suggests that, without information on relative performance, participation in community meetings had little impact on outcomes. Two lingering questions are whether the results obtained with the provision of benchmarking information could have been obtained in the absence of the mobilization component, and whether similar interventions have been tried in other services.

Answers to these questions are suggested by Banerjee et al. (2010), who studied an initiative aimed at improving the education services through citizen participation in village education committees (VECs). The VECs in India, while existent at baseline, were not active, and most members of the community did not know about their existence. Subsequently, an NGO-led intervention was rolled out in order to raise awareness about the VECs. This can be equated to an "information only" intervention. The result was that the VECs continued not to function, which was not due to circumstances that would have precluded any intervention from having an effect. Alternative interventions that included training did trigger improvements in educational outcomes.

While valuable, monitoring by the community must overcome important collective action problems. Interventions based on information may have even stronger effects when some lower-level agent can be active in monitoring upper levels. Reinikka and Svensson (2005) evaluated a newspaper campaign in Uganda that helped parents and head teachers in schools reduce the amount of leakage affecting the resources schools were supposed to receive. According to their evidence, head teachers that were geographically closer to a newspaper outlet had better knowledge about the program that made funds available, and as a result managed to capture a substantially larger share of the resources intended for them.

A potentially important complement to community involvement in the monitoring of public service delivery is technology. In fact, as e-governance becomes more widespread, countries have increased their investment in, and use of, e-monitoring systems. Several studies described in our discussion of incentives based on provider attendance utilize such systems. The Duflo et al. (2012) study reviewed earlier based incentives on information obtained via time-stamped photographs. However, as highlighted by Banerjee et al. (2008), the robustness of such monitoring systems is sensitive to how tamper-proof the overall monitoring mechanism is. If nurses can get away with disabling the monitoring system, then to the extent that they act as self motivated, rational agents, they will do so. Perhaps even more important, the existence of loopholes in the monitoring regime, or a lack of capacity in utilizing its data, may render virtually useless the extra information created by the monitoring system.

Two studies, by Dhaliwal and Hanna (2014) and Callen et al. (2015), expand our understanding about the potential of technological innovations to assist monitoring and hence the administration of service provision. Dhaliwal and Hanna (2014) studied the rollout of biometric devices used to monitor staff (nurses and pharmacists) and doctors at primary health centers in southern India. In centers with the new monitoring technology, worker attendance increased by 14.7%, an effect that was driven by staff rather than by doctors. Improved monitoring impacted health. Underweight births decreased by 26% and births attended by a doctor increased by 16%. One (perhaps obvious) aspect of improved monitoring is that it holds workers more accountable and can reduce their rents. This could lead to lower job satisfaction. In line with this, the authors detect lower satisfaction among members of staff as well as attempts to circumvent the system. Overall, these results indicate that improved monitoring can enhance service delivery but can also affect personnel rents in a way that generates a backlash against the newly deployed technology. This suggests that a larger capacity than that minimally required to deploy the technology might be needed, namely the capacity to deal with the personnel resistance that the technology may trigger. This study also highlights the importance of measuring impact. Without the measured improvements in health outcomes, the evidence on staff resistance could have led to the monitoring system being judged a failure.

We discussed earlier the importance of personality traits and how they may affect the response to interventions. If monitoring gets in the way of shirking and more generally rent extraction, and these activities hold different value to individuals with different types of motivation, then we may expect the impacts of monitoring to vary with the personality of the service provider. As discussed above, Callen et al. (2015) reported on a monitoring experiment wherein the traditional paper-based monitoring system for absenteeism, resource availability, and clinic utilization was replaced by a smartphone application. A mobile data connection transmitted the data generated by health inspectors to a central data center in real time. The data were then aggregated and processed to generate decision-relevant charts and summary statistics. Callen et al. (2015) found that senior health inspectors who score higher on the Big Five personality inventory are more likely to respond to a report of an underperforming facility by compelling better subsequent staff attendance. They also find that inspectors who score higher on personality tests are more likely to reduce absenteeism when dashboards summarizing decision-relevant data are implemented. In short, this chapter offers evidence in support of the idea that individual personality characteristics explain heterogeneity in responses to improved monitoring.

Callen and Long (2015) introduced monitoring into the electoral machine, by randomly announcing the presence of a photo quick count—photography of preliminary vote counts at the station level—before electoral results were aggregated at higher levels. Announcing this to election officials reduces fraud, both in terms of distortions in the aggregation of votes as well as in terms of the theft of election materials. The treatment also reduced votes for politically powerful candidates and candidates connected to election officials.

Overall, some basic aspects of principal–agent theories are borne out by the evidence, namely that agents respond to incentives and monitoring, and that selecting agents carefully pays off. One issue that remains open is to what extent principals optimize contracts or other arrangements depending on the nature, incentives, and means available to lower-level officials. Baicker and Jacobson (2007) showed that counties offset nearly 80% of each dollar seized by police forces during arrests by reducing budgets. Another aspect that remains understudied is the relative power of intrinsic motivation versus extrinsic incentives, and whether the latter may crowd out the former.

Open Research Questions

- What types of personality traits affect job performance in the public sector?
- What are the effects of nonfinancial incentives on job performance?
- What are the conditions under which performance-related pay can lead to multitasking concerns?
- Can citizen feedback platforms promote political accountability and improve service delivery?
- What are the costs and benefits of rotation schemes with the public sector?
- Do principals optimize contracts or organizational arrangements given the trade-offs present in incentivizing personnel?
- Do extrinsic incentives crowd out intrinsic motivation?

1.3.2.2. Financial Resources

The resources available to the state may come from two broad sources: taxes and rents. The first are typically raised from income, trade, and assets owned by economic agents. The second come from resources exploited by the state. Natural resources are an important source.

Whether states rely more on one source or another may matter, since it is conceivable that institutions affect the way states obtain their revenue, and that the way states obtain their revenue may further affect economic and even institutional outcomes.

Social scientists have long been concerned with the potential negative effects of natural resource wealth, due to its likely leading to less growth and bureaucratic quality (Sachs and Warner 1995), more rent-seeking (Lane and Tornell 1996), and slacker political accountability when existing institutions are weak (Robinson et al. 2006). It has also been feared that dependence on natural resources may be inimical to democracy (Ross 2001; but see Downing 1992 for a contrasting historical view). Although a more comprehensive data panel analysis across several countries does not seem to confirm these fears (Haber and Menaldo 2011; Caselli and Tesei 2015), there are some indications that windfalls may weaken accountability and the extent to which resources are channeled into public goods (Brollo et al. 2013; Caselli and Michaels 2013). In contrast, it has been hypothesized that taxation pressure goes hand in hand with increased oversight and tighter accountability. This of course could comprise causal effects going both ways.

One possibility is that taxation creates a demand for accountability. Paler (2013) conducted a lab-in-the-field experiment exposing subjects to different frames in terms of whether a decision maker would extract rents from a windfall budget versus a tax originated budget, and measured the stated willingness of subjects to demand further information or make a complaint against government by sending a postcard. The taxation frame increased the demand for information and the use of the postcard complaint, offering some support for the idea that taxation enhances taxpayer scrutiny. If taxation begets a demand for control, this might be enhanced when having clearer information about behavior is conditional on poor performance. However, an interaction of the taxation frame with the provision of actual information did not enhance complaints, although this study did not control for citizen priors, making it unclear what the information treatment effect should be hypothesized to be. Further work on the link between tax pressure and the demand for accountability is sorely needed.

The other direction of causation is that stronger institutions and capabilities allow the government to raise revenue. This point is prominently made by North and Weingast (1989) in relation to government debt. In their interpretation, stronger ability to commit helps the government issue debt. Another way in which stronger institutions may help the government is through enhanced legitimacy and tax compliance. Tax compliance may also increase due to governmental capabilities to detect taxable activity.

A very specific form of institutional advantage is a judicious choice of tax instruments. It is widely believed that adopting a form of VAT increases tax compliance due to the paper trail it generates. Pomeranz (2015) examines this notion through a randomized trial on a large sample of Chilean firms. Letters were mailed to those in the treatment group to increase the salience of the threat of an audit. If the paper trail already had a deterrent effect, the letters should have a smaller effect on transactions subject to a paper trail, and this is what Pomeranz finds. She also shows that increased tax compliance spills over to firms' trading partners. Linkages between taxpayers may be exploited to improve compliance. One of them is who reports income. Kleven et al. (2011) conducted a large tax enforcement field experiment in Denmark, and showed that tax evasion is near zero for third-party reported income but considerable for self-reported income. This suggests that governments with weak enforcement capabilities may want to "max out" their use of mechanisms that involve as much self-enforcement as possible.

Tax compliance may depend on various other aspects of the tax regime. Of course, given institutions and tax instruments, tax levels are also relevant for compliance. Kleven et al. (2011) showed that higher marginal tax rates lead to more evasion but even more (legal) avoidance. However, in addition to tax levels, the salience of tax penalties and the likelihood of audits may also be relevant. A significant literature has utilized randomized interventions based on messages to taxpayers to investigate what type of communication can improve tax compliance. We reviewed several of these when commenting on the role of norms and the potential use of exhortative messages; the literature tends to find support for using messages that increased the salience of audits and penalties (McGraw and Scholz 1991; Blumenthal et al. 2001; Fellner et al. 2013; Castro and Scartascini 2015). Kleven et al. (2011) demonstrated in the context of their experiment in Denmark that audits and letters threatening audits affect self-reported income but not third-party reported income.

An additional resource is to manipulate the shame felt by those who do not comply. Perez-Truglia and Troiano (2016) conducted an experiment in the United States showing that receiving letters increasing the salience of financial penalties and shaming among neighbors increased compliance (the shaming condition involved appearing on a list of tax delinquents mailed to the neighborhood).

Open Research Questions

- Is third-party reporting effective in the context of weak legal institutions?
- When do financial windfalls strengthen political accountability and public sector productivity?
- What are the effects of fiscal audits on public service delivery?
- When is it convenient to decentralize tax collection, given political and capacity constraints at the local level?
- What areas of tax collection are most affected by corruption?

1.3.2.3. Procedures

Management practices encompass a broad category of the procedures used in government. Informed by the survey and interview methods employed by Bloom and Van Reenen (2007; 2010), Rasul and Rogger (2018) evaluated the management practices employed by bureaucrats in Nigeria across different ministerial units. The authors studied how management practices relate to the quantity and quality of public services, measured for instance through the completion rate of projects. They find that bureaucratic autonomy is positively associated with delivery of public services and that incentive schemes actually decrease public project completion rates. They conjecture that this decrease occurs because "bureaucrats are engaged in complex tasks, the relationship between bureaucratic inputs to outputs is uncertain, and there is considerable ambiguity in the design and implementation process for many public projects." They suggest, then, that incentive schemes might create an excessive regulatory burden or encourage perverse behaviors to manipulate the system. One might also imagine a standard multitasking model in which some behaviors are observable while others are not. The incentive scheme could result in an inefficient allocation away from unobservable tasks that nevertheless are important to the delivery of public services (as theorized by Holmstrom and Milgrom 1991). The findings by Rasul and Rogger highlight the need for RCTs to validate their observational results. The area of management practices and bureaucratic procedures is generally in great need of further study.

An additional relevant aspect to government procedures involves legal requirements and rules to govern dispute resolution, the protection of property rights, and the regulation of economic activity. We briefly cover these issues in section 1.4 on legal institutions.

Open Research Questions

- To what extent do changes in managerial practices affect the provision of public goods?
- What are the effects of decentralization on public service delivery and accountability?
- What are the factors that affect a government's decision to outsource public goods?
- Are privately provided public goods produced at lower cost? Is there a quality trade-off?
- What are the benefits and costs of public–private partnerships?

1.4. LEGAL INSTITUTIONS

Personal security and the security of claims to property are thought to be a basic driver of investment and development (see, for example, Haggard et al. 2008). Reviewing the theoretical and empirical literature on the rule of law and economic development, Haggard et al. point to substantial evidence that rule-of-law indicators correlate with growth. For instance, it is well known that indices that capture the degree of protection of property rights correlate with income per capita, as shown in figure 1.3.

The protection of property rights and the rule of law can be seen as a function of legal institutions, broadly understood. Therefore, attention to legal institutions is warranted, given their potential role in fostering economic growth. In order to make progress in reviewing pertinent work, it is beneficial to unbundle legal institutions and specify their main components. The easiest way to perform such decomposition is to ask what it takes to have a legal right to bind. First, it must be legally sanctioned. Second, its beneficiaries/holders must be aware of their entitlement and be able to access the means to have their rights upheld.

Third, there must be an enforcement machinery available to uphold those rights, comprising, for example, courts. Fourth, conditions must exist so that court rulings can be enforced. This simple description yields the following elements as relevant to the functioning of legal institutions:

1. A legally sanctioned right (such as personal identity, a title of property, etc.)
2. Awareness and access:
   a. Awareness of legal rights
   b. Access to legal advice and representation. Access to dispute resolution mechanisms
3. Courts
4. Enforcement

These factors are likely to have multiple effects. As emphasized by Besley and Ghatak (2010) and Ghatak (2016, RA4), insecure property rights create a risk of expropriation that depresses incentives to invest and promotes protective measures that are socially wasteful, as well as prevents the realization of gains from trade. In addition, the factors listed above are likely to be strongly complementary. In this section, we examine studies analyzing the effects of changes in one of these factors, and highlight the need for work in most of these areas.

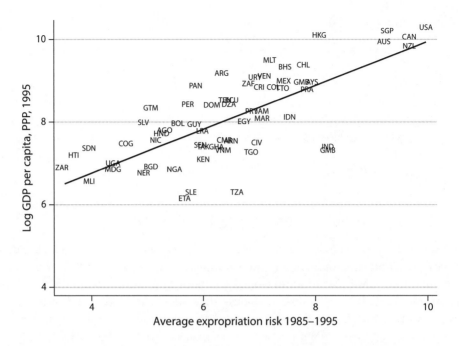

FIGURE 1.3. OLS relationship between expropriation risk and income. *Source*: Acemoglu et al. (2001).

The performance of a legal system—and therefore its impact on the economy—depends on the elements just highlighted being both present and functional. But performance may also respond to aspects of legal conception and design. We take these up in the last subsection.

1.4.1. Legally Sanctioned Rights: Property Titles

The starting point of a regime that protects property rights in any shape or form is the legal sanctioning of those rights, be it at the individual or collective level.

A basic right is that of the individual as a legal person, but even this basic right can be challenged in the developing world. Beqiraj and McNamara (2014) point out that birth registrations are difficult for the poor in many parts of the world. While some countries place impediments to registration, others have had success with inducements. Herbert (2015) observes that lack of legal identity can interfere with individuals' ability to obtain many vital public services, including access to the justice system. In fact, some institutional variation has been used to show that whether certain groups can benefit from the recognition of a property right can affect the distribution of resources. Nagarajan et al. (2010) use a natural experiment in India to show that changing inheritance laws increased women's likelihood of inheriting property. The age of women at marriage increased, and there was a positive effect on women's educational attainment.[8] Indeed, an important instrument in the economic performance of a person is that of property rights over assets. In this connection, a legally sanctioned property right over land and other assets can be important, for instance in the collateralization of loans (De Soto 2000). But what is the pattern of evidence about the effects of sanctioning formal legal rights?

Some authors have relied on observational data to study the effects of the formalization of property rights, including urban and rural land titling. Cox (2008) reviews some of this early literature. The overall picture is mixed. Some of these studies find a positive impact on investment and land value (Alston et al. 1996) and positive effects on output and crop choices reflecting a longer-term orientation (World Bank 2004). However, other studies report non-existent or even negative effects. Several of these were done in the context of African nations (see Davis and Trebilcock 1999). One paradoxical aspect of the sanctioning of formal property rights is that while it reduces the uncertainty of some groups, it may increase that of others, who relied on custom based rights that are then deniable under the new regime. In addition, the sanctioning of formal property rights introduces a new set of interactions that may be more prone to elite manipulation (Platteau 1995).

These studies, while valuable, tend to focus on fairly complex processes that are quite distant from a clean experiment. Closer to the experimental ideal, Galiani and Schargrodsky (2010) used a natural experiment in Buenos Aires to identify the effect of land titling on investment, household size, and education. The variation of interest originated in a law from 1984 that expropriated a piece of land from its owners to formally entitle the squatters that had occupied the land. While some owners accepted a government settlement, others fought in court, significantly delaying titling of some squatters. Surveys conducted in 2003 and 2007 demonstrate that families who received early titles showed increased housing investment, decreased household size, and better-educated children. The authors show that these effects are likely due to increased investment, since titling did not improve access to credit. A paradoxical aspect of this study is that the expropriation of owners led to entitling squatters but de-entitling original owners. This may have had an impact on the incentives of those and other owners—presumably in a different direction, since they had been expropriated. The question that lingers, then, is what may have been the net overall effects of an intervention that, rather than creating property rights, redistributed them. To explore this, one would want to examine cases where there is an unambiguous creation of property rights.

Field (2005) offers an example of such a study, examining the effects of titling on investment in Peru. The program under study significantly reduced the cost and bureaucratic hurdles involved in obtaining a title. She relies on a difference-in-differences design, and compares the change in investment before and after implementation of titling to the change operated in households the program had not yet reached (alternatively, she also compares against households that already held titles). Titling appears to have economically large and statistically significant effects: housing renovations increase by two-thirds and are largely financed without credit, implying that tenure security rather than access to credit tends to drive the effects.[9]

Ali et al. (2014) rely on quasi-experimental methods (a geographic regression discontinuity) to evaluate a land tenure regularization program in Rwanda. This program had the objective of clarifying land ownership and reducing disputes in the post-genocide era. An evaluation of a pilot of the program showed improved land access for married women, less gender bias in the recording of inheritance rights, and, importantly for the preservation of the productive potential of land, a doubling of investments in soil conservation. No effects on relaxation of credit constraints were detected (although this is perhaps due to the short-term span of the evaluation).

The literature to date seems to provide little support for the notion that titling re-laxes credit constraints, leaving open the question of whether De Soto's hypothesis on the value of mobilizing the savings of the indigent as collateral can really alter the development picture. Constraints other than credit may be binding and arrest the economic development potential of the poor. The evidence on the credit-relaxing effects of titling appears even more modest than that on the effects of microcredit, as as-sessed by Banerjee et al. (2015) and Beck (2016, RA1): while a consistent pattern of modest positive effects has been documented, the effects are far from transformative. Clearly, more experimental-grade research is needed to map out the effects of titling on various outcomes, as well as the interaction of formal property rights with custom-based ar-rangements. This leads us straight into the topic of the links between formality and informality.

1.4.1.1. Formality vs. Informality
The existence of a large informal sector is seen as both a symptom and a contributing factor to underdevelopment. La Porta and Shleifer (2008) view informality as a result and not a cause of low economic productivity, and they suggest that the tax implications of formalization could simply bankrupt previously informal businesses. Others, like Besley and Persson (2011), highlight informality as limiting the ability of government to raise taxes and provide public goods. That tension can be cast in terms of what the drivers and the consequences of formality are.

1.4.1.2. Drivers of Formality
The key question is whether interventions can affect the choice of existing firms to go formal or encourage the formation of new formal firms. Next we review literature that is pertinent to that question, and do so following our two cross-cutting analytic categories—incentives (mainly in relation to the costs of formalizing or the threat of in-spections) and information.

De Andrade et al. (2013) conducted a field experiment in Brazil to evaluate the effec-tiveness of incentives and inducements for firms to formalize. Firms were randomized into one of five groups; the first was a control, the second received information about how to formalize, the third received this information as well as free registration costs and the services of an accountant for a year, the fourth received an enforcement visit from an inspector, and the fifth had a neighboring firm receive an enforcement visit. Results suggest that only inspections have positive effects and that the effect increases the like-lihood of formalization by about 24%. The authors conclude that many informal firms will not formalize unless coerced, implying that formalization might offer them little benefit. However, increased tax revenues more than offset the cost of increasing inspec-tions, implying a benefit to state capacity.

One of the hurdles in formalizing business may be the costs related to formalizing. Some studies have manipulated those costs in order to determine whether and to what extent costs matter. Bruhn (2011) examined the effect of "one-stop-shop" business regis-tration in urban areas of Mexico. This reform allowed businesses to satisfy municipal, state, and federal registrations all at once in a single process. Gaining identification from the staggered implementation of the program, Bruhn shows that the number of regis-tered businesses increased by 5% and that this was to the result of former wage earners starting new businesses. However, the reform did not make existing businesses more likely to register. Also, wage employment increased by 2.2% and the income of incumbent businesses declined by 3%.

De Mel et al. (2013) performed a field experiment in Sri Lanka that attempted to induce registration by providing information, reimbursing direct costs, and paying large one-time sums. Information and reimbursement had no effect, while a payment of one-half to one month's worth of median profits induced one-fifth of firms to register. A payment of two months' worth of profits induced half of firms. The authors note that the most common reason for not registering is that firms often operate under informal land arrangements and cannot prove their tenancy of the land on which they operate. With respect to the effects of formalization, they find increased advertising and use of receipt books but no increase in government contracts, use of bank loans or accounts, or participation in government programs.

Mullainathan and Schnabl (2010) studied the effect of a municipal licensing reform in Lima, Peru, which decreased the cost and time of obtaining a license. Using a pre-post design, they find that the number of provisional licenses issued to informal firms increased sharply. Still, many businesses failed to renew these licenses after one year; as the authors explain, "many business owners think there is a high probability that the business will not survive for more than one year."

Bruhn and Loeprick (2014) examined the effect of preferential tax regimes for "micro" and small businesses in Georgia. Micro businesses (falling under a certain revenue threshold) were exempted from taxation entirely, while small businesses (falling under a higher threshold) were given the option of being taxed on revenue instead of profits (which decreases compliance costs). The authors use a regression discontinuity design to show that the new tax regime increased micro business registration propensity by a large amount, but only in the first year following the reform. There was no such effect on small businesses. Finally, they find reduced tax compliance around the micro threshold in the first year but not subsequently.

Branstetter et al. (2014) evaluated the effects of a reform in Portugal that reduced the cost of firm entry. The authors show that firm formation and employment increased but mainly among "marginal" firms that were low-technology, small, operated by poorly educated owners, and less likely to survive after two years.

De Giorgi and Rahman (2013) distributed brochures in Bangladesh offering information on the procedures and benefits of registration. Although this treatment increased the knowledge available to those making decisions at firms, it had no impact on registration. The authors conjecture that low benefits, such as access to markets, and high indirect costs, such as taxation and regulations, could serve as barriers to formality.

To sum up, the emerging picture on the drivers of formalization is mixed. Only a subset of interventions that incentivized formalization have yielded positive effects. Moreover, the studies that offered information that could encourage formality have shown little to no effect.

1.4.1.3. Consequences of Formalization
One of the promises of formalization, as with titling more generally, is a potential effect on credit, and ultimately on firm performance to the extent that the relaxed credit constraint makes available better productive strategies to the firm. A review of the literature on

this relationship tends to yield some positive results, although the positive picture is far from uniform.

McKenzie and Woodruff (2008) performed an RCT that provided cash and grants to small, informal retail firms in Mexico. In that way, they relaxed credit constraints. The intervention led to strongly positive effects. The authors estimate a monthly return to capital of about 20–33%, which as they note is three to five times higher than market interest rates.

McKenzie and Sakho (2010) use proximity to the local tax office as an instrument for formalization in Bolivia, demonstrating that it significantly increases profits. On the other hand, they detect heterogeneous treatment effects: the gains are concentrated among mid- size firms and marginal small or large firms see a decrease in profits. They also find that owners of large, informal firms are of higher ability than large, formal firm owners, which contrasts with the usual result among smaller firms that informal firm owners are of lower ability. However, they find no effect overall on the use of trade credit, the receipt of working capital from suppliers or customers, and the likelihood of having a bank loan.

The study by de Mel et al. (2013) that we reviewed earlier shows that formalization had no effect on the use of bank loans or accounts.

1.4.1.4. Assessment

Overall, interventions to foster business formalization have met with little success in terms of increased formalization, and the consequences for the firms that formalize are heterogeneous. While not yet conclusive, at the broadest level this evidence challenges the view that informal firms are deep reservoirs of economic potential. According to La Porta and Shleifer (2014), growth is driven by higher-quality firms that tend to be formal, and as countries grow in tandem with their formal firms, the relative and absolute weight of informality tends to decrease. In this view, it makes sense for informal firms to remain informal simply because they do not have the quality level to survive in the formal economy.

While formalization of existing firms may do little to drive national growth, or directly help growth in modern industrial sectors, the regularization of titles and property rights could potentially have nontrivial effects on local economies, for example when it interacts with traditional systems of management of land property and tenure. In addition, an informal sector that absorbs employment, by contributing to social peace, may paradoxically help the social environment in which the modern formal sector operates. That said, whether this positive externality exists and if so outweighs any negative externalities is still far from clear.

Open Research Questions

- Are there instances where formal property rights relax credit constraints?
- What are the effects of land titling on access to credit and investment in local economies?
- With much of the existing literature on the informality of small-scale enterprises focused on registration and tax regulations, what is the importance of other regulatory barriers for firm growth, such as land titling and zoning?
- What are the social costs of formalizing informal firms?
- Is the informal economy a help or a hindrance for its formal counterpart?

1.4.2. Access and Awareness

In keeping with the central role of information in this review, we will cover work that attempts to make individuals aware of their rights and the means at their disposal to have their rights respected. However, it is important to recall that actual access can be expanded by increasing the supply of services and by connecting people to services that exist but had not traditionally been available to certain groups. We cover work affecting either of those margins in this section.

Some natural ways of expanding legal access are through pro bono representation and through the deployment of legal clinics. Frankel et al. (2001) randomly assigned low-income tenants to receive free legal representation at the housing court in New York. Only 22% of represented tenants had final judgments against them, in comparison to 51% of the control group. Furthermore, represented tenants were less likely to face eviction and their landlords were more likely to face an order to abate the rent or provide repairs.

Another margin for intervention is the extent of legal assistance, as investigated by Greiner et al. (2012). In their study, individuals facing cases in the housing court of Massachusetts were randomly assigned to receive either full legal assistance (in accordance with the traditional attorney–client relationship) or only limited "lawyer-for-the-day" assistance. The study found no significant effect of full versus limited assistance on any legal outcomes. The authors alternatingly conjecture that this implies either the high quality of limited service or the low quality of the full assistance provided in this specific experiment. In a very similar study, Pattanayak et al. (2013) performed an experiment with individuals facing eviction at the Massachusetts District Court rather than the housing court. The authors found that two-thirds of participants receiving full representation retained possession of their housing unit following the proceeding, while only one-third of the limited assistance group did. Furthermore, the treatment group was mandated to pay less rent compared to the control group (about 7.5 months' worth of rent).

In the final study of legal assistance in the United States that we will highlight, Greiner and Pattanayak (2012) randomized the offer of legal assistance in administrative appeals of unemployment benefit eligibility decisions. The authors find that representation had no statistically significant effect on the outcome of the case but that it delayed proceedings by two weeks on average.

Thus, on the whole, there are ambiguous results from studies providing free legal assistance in the United States. There seems to be little evidence of the type we have just reviewed in developing countries, where legal institutions tend to be weaker. However, using experimental or quasi-experimental methods, three studies examine the provision of legal assistance by trained community members.

Sandefur and Siddiqi (2013) conducted an RCT of a legal empowerment intervention in Liberia. The experiment involved the provision of pro bono mediation and advocacy services through community paralegals trained in the formal law. The authors found strong and robust impacts on justice outcomes and significant downstream welfare benefits, including increases in household and child food security of 0.24 and 0.38 standard deviations, respectively. They found no impact on attitudes or behavior, but strong impacts associated with taking a case to the paralegals, suggesting that at least in the short term, paralegals provide a directly redistributive role.

Barendrecht et al. (2013) evaluated the staggered (not randomized) rollout of the *Facilitadores Judiciales* (Judicial Facilitators) program in Nicaragua. In this program, communities nominated facilitators to receive treatment to provide fellow community members with legal assistance. The authors find fewer reports of legal problems, decreased costs of justice, and higher social cohesion in treated regions following treatment. One issue with the study findings, unfortunately, is that the data make it clear that treated and control regions differ systematically.

Mueller et al. (2015) evaluated a similar program in Tanzania that did rely on experimental variation in the presence of paralegals in different villages that were part of a program of community-based legal aid with a focus on gender. They find small to moderate effects of paralegal presence on the propensity of women to attend legal seminars and on their resulting knowledge about the rights of women to own land.

An important aspect of legal institutions concerns dispute resolution. Blattman et al. (2014) studied the short-term effects of a mass education campaign to promote alternative dispute resolution (ADR) in Liberia. Eighty-six out of 246 municipalities were randomly assigned to receive ADR training, which ultimately reached 15% of adults in the treated municipalities. After one year, the authors observed higher rates of resolution of land disputes, lower rates of violence, spillovers to untreated residents, more extrajudicial punishment, and weakly more nonviolent disagreements. The authors conclude that "mass education can change high-stakes behaviors, and improving informal bargaining and enforcement behavior can promote order in weak states."

Promoting order in weakly institutionalized environments represents a large challenge. Blattman and Annan (2016) evaluate a program that randomly offered assistance in the form of agricultural training and capital to ex-fighters in Liberia. While the treatment in this intervention was not legal in nature, it had a concern with legal outcomes, namely involvement in illicit activities. Fourteen months later, treated individuals had more intensively substituted farming activities for illicit ones and displayed less propensity to engage in mercenary activity. Ray and Esteban (2016, RA1) reviewed theories and evidence on common perceptions surrounding the logic of conflict. Their analysis of the literature, and the paucity of work in this White Paper reporting on institutional innovations that can lower the likelihood of conflict, both suggest that further experimental work on institutions and conflict is sorely needed.

Open Research Questions

- What are the effects on conflict resolution of legal assistance in weakly institutionalized polities? How do these effects interact with traditional norms and customs?
- How does access to legal assistance affect economic performance?
- What institutions can promote law and order and diminish the likelihood of conflict?

1.4.3. Courts

There are several important aspects to the functioning of courts. Two aspects that have received attention in the literature are among those we have emphasized in other sections, namely, incentives and selection. In keeping with that emphasis, we quickly review work on those themes as they pertain to the judiciary. Although experimental evidence is scant, a handful of scholars have used observational data and formal models to examine the incentives and selection effects of judges.

The (perhaps somewhat naïve) benchmark for evaluating the behavior of judges is that of neutrality and independence from pressures, whether they be pressures originating in interested parties or in the judges' own interests. In the context of political institutions, we earlier asked whether institutions that shape accountability and the career prospects of politicians affect their behavior. Here we ask the same question regarding judges. Berdejó and Yuchtman (2013) examined political cycles in the behavior of Washington State judges. The authors analyze observational data on the electoral time line and sentencing decisions, showing that judges hand out sentences that are on average 10% higher near the end of their electoral cycles and that a sharp increase in discretionary deviations beyond the sentencing guidelines largely account for this effect. Based on this evidence, the authors argue that judges respond to political pressure by seeking to appear tough and that a system based on appointment rather than election would produce more moderate sentencing patterns.

The implicit idea in the paper by Berdejó and Yuchtman is that sentencing is visible to constituents. The natural way in which sentencing may become visible is through the media. Lim et al. (2015) examine the behavior of state trial court judges in the United States between 1986 and 2006 to investigate whether information provided by the media affects sentencing. These judges attain office in various ways: some are appointed by the governor, some are elected in partisan elections following nomination by political parties, and the largest share are elected in nonpartisan elections. The authors take advantage of the varying overlap of judicial districts and media markets to investigate the effect of media coverage on sentence length by judges. The effects of coverage are positive on judges elected in nonpartisan elections and not for the others. The authors interpret this as reflecting the fact that judges elected through partisan elections are already known quantities for the electorate, and those who were appointed do not face an accountability pressure. The emerging picture is one in which the media makes for harsher sentencing, although the institutional details regarding judicial nominations and appointments are crucial in modulating that effect.

Lim (2015) investigated the level of damages awarded in civil adjudication cases in US state courts. She shows that in areas in which the news media frequently covers court decisions, liberal and conservative courts grant similar damage awards. In contrast, liberal courts tend to award larger damages than conservative courts in areas that see little such coverage. Lim concludes that "the presence of active media coverage may enhance consistency in the civil justice system."

Lim and Snyder (2015) examined judicial elections across 39 US states. They show that candidate quality (as reflected in bar association ratings) affects election outcomes in nonpartisan elections but does not in partisan ones. The authors conclude that "to the extent that partisan voting behavior crowds out the influence of candidate quality on voting outcomes, the desirability of the partisan election system should be carefully assessed." While the literature on political behavior has highlighted the information-economizing role of parties, it is conceivable that in some settings partisanship could have negative effects. Understanding when and where partisanship works to improve selection is an open question.

Selection effects in the judiciary are important, and constituency preferences may play a role even for appointed judges. Lim (2013) specified and estimated a dynamic structural model that she then applied to the data on judicial districts in Kansas. The evidence indicates that while elected judges face the discipline of re-election incentives, this does not mean that a system of appointments will eliminate a link between constituency preferences and judge performance. Under an appointment system, voter preferences are expressed at the time of judge selection.

The idea that judge selection is important has been substantiated outside of the United States as well. Grossman et al. (2016) analyzed rulings in Israeli courts and showed that the verdicts on Arab defendants vary significantly depending on whether there is at least one Arab member in the panel of judges.

Iaryczower et al. (2013) developed a structural estimation approach by which to examine state supreme courts' decisions in criminal cases in the United States. They showed that justices who do not face voters have better information, are more likely to change their preconceived opinions on a case, and are more effective.

We have considered whether electoral pressure and media coverage affect judicial rulings. Iaryczower and Shum (2013) extended attention to the role of campaign contributions. They showed evidence compatible with the idea that the voting of individual judges in various state supreme courts in the United States is affected by campaign contributions, although the effects move different individuals in opposing directions and ultimately tend to cancel out.

The papers reviewed in this section provide evidence that incentives and selection forces are important in determining the functioning of the judiciary. But the judiciary involves other types of personnel, including staff, as well as organizational choices on how to deal with the sometimes heavy burden of caseload. It would be valuable to have evidence on whether, and to what extent, improvements on these alternative margins can help enhance the effectiveness of the judiciary.

Open Research Questions

- Can improvements in the efficiency of courts reduce crime and fraud and encourage investment?
- How do career concerns affect judges' sentencing decisions?
- What is the extent of judicial corruption and how does it impact economic development?

1.4.4. The Quality of Enforcement

What are the causes and consequences of quality of enforcement? The quality of enforcement is tightly related to the functioning of the police, judiciary, inspector, and auditor cadres, as well as regulatory authorities. Some of the differences in the performance of a legal system may be related to matters of legal design, which we take up in the last subsection; here, we focus on the role of incentives and accountability, selection, monitoring, and information.

Banerjee et al. (2014) report on two RCTs designed to study the determinants of police performance in Rajasthan, India. They focused on the role of various levers affecting incentives and monitoring, such as limitation of arbitrary transfers, rotation of duty assignments and days off, increased community involvement, training, decoy visits, and incentives tied to station performance. The authors found robust effects for the last three interventions. A noteworthy point is that the reforms that do not work fail due to poor implementation, and this might be tied to the fact that they reduce middle management–level authority. The outcomes were registering cases brought up through decoy visits, satisfaction with police service, public perceptions, and performance in terms of testing for driver sobriety.

García et al. (2013) examined the randomly staggered rollout of a police patrolling program in Colombia that encouraged community involvement and introduced incentives tied to the crime levels in officers' assigned districts. The authors found a significant reduction in brawls and homicides, arguing that the interventions may have strengthened motivation and a sense of accountability. One possibility, however, is that the lower crime statistics may have arisen as a result of manipulation of reporting rates.

Duflo et al. (2013) performed an RCT in the Indian state of Gujarat to evaluate how auditors of pollutant firms report differently depending on whether they are selected and paid by the firms themselves or the regulator. The authors report three main results: first, the existing system of firms hiring auditors was rife with corruption, with auditors misrepresenting actual emissions as often just below the limit. Second, regulator-hired auditors were more truthful and sharply reduced the share of plants reported to be in compliance. Third, the treatment induced monitored plants to reduce emissions. The authors conclude that "reformed incentives for third-party auditors can improve their reporting and make regulation more effective."

In another study involving inspections and regulatory oversight, Duflo et al. (2014) used an RCT to study an increase in the frequency of plant inspections by environmental regulators in India. Although treated plants were more likely to be inspected and cited for pollution violations, they only marginally reduced emissions. Furthermore, the regulators were not more likely to identify the worst violators, defined by emissions of five times the standard or more. The authors observe that, while treatment inspections were assigned randomly, discretionary inspections often specifically target those plants likely to be extreme polluters.

While there are RCTs varying either the monitoring or incentives of private agents like firms and those of law enforcers, we do not have studies (that we have identified in this review) varying monitoring or incentives on both sets of agents at the same time, to determine whether they are complements or substitutes.

Most of the studies reviewed focus on determinants of enforcement. Some of them (e.g., Duflo et al. 2014 on pollution) also study effects on the type of behavior that the enforced regulation seeks to curb. But most studies do not do this, and an open area of inquiry is how improved enforcement can be brought about and how it may affect outcomes. There are many open questions in this area.

Open Research Questions

- What are the political and administrative determinants of regulatory independence and effectiveness?
- To what extent do improvements in enforcement cause net social gains as opposed to displacement? For example, increased pollution monitoring on some

firms could lead them to have higher costs, but their losing market share would displace activity to other firms who pollute more. In long-run equilibrium, the impact of inspections on pollution could be smaller unless all firms are treated.

- Does increased monitoring, through ICT, reduce police corruption and police brutality?
- Do third-party verification schemes help to reduce collusion between regulators and can pay-for-performance schemes improve the quality of policing?
- What are the determinants of the independence of regulatory authorities?

1.4.5. Legal Design: Its Role and Regulatory Effects

Legal systems differ by design, both in terms of regulatory implications (e.g., in determining the rights of minority shareholders or of labor organizations) and in terms of pure legal procedure. In connection with the latter, legal systems differ, for example, in terms of the role they assign to judges, the standards used for collecting and admitting evidence to be used in court, the role played by trials, and the procedures involved in litigation. These design "details" may affect outcomes directly even when holding constant the incentives, selection, information, and monitoring issues analyzed earlier (and perhaps also indirectly by affecting these very issues as well).

Djankov et al. (2003) argue that procedural formalism is a relevant metric that encompasses many of those legal "details," and they show that metric to be strongly associated—in a detrimental way—with legal outcomes, such as the ability to evict a tenant for failure to pay rent or to collect a bounced check. The degree of procedural formalism by the year 2000 is in turn strongly affected by the legal origin of a country's legal system, e.g., whether it is civil law or common law. One view could be that legal procedures are on trend toward convergence and that given enough time all legal systems will approximate some optimum. However, in newer work, Balas et al. (2009) showed that procedural formalism across countries with different legal origins has if anything diverged since 1950, suggesting important forces prevent convergence even if procedural formalism is associated with worse outcomes.

Several legal differences across countries have regulatory implications, because they affect the way economic activity is organized. One example of this is the extent to which legal rules and procedures affect the ease with which new business can be authorized to operate. As shown by Djankov et al. (2002), the time and cost involved in starting a new business varies widely across countries and is associated with economic outcomes such as the size of the informal economy. In addition, and compatible with the idea that legal and regulatory regimes are endogenous to political institutions, the burden of regulatory entry is positively associated with deviations from democracy and limited government. The potential role of political institutions driving legal variation that impacts regulatory outcomes is also present in the case of labor relations—dominance by political parties is associated across countries with more generous social security, but also with more stringent labor regulation (Botero et al. 2004). Heavier regulation tends to correlate with lower labor force participation and youth unemployment.

Another way in which legal aspects can affect economic activity is through the regulation of conflicts of interest in economic organizations. One example is the degree to which controlling interests in a firm can exploit their power to the detriment of other interests (e.g., minority shareholders, creditors, etc.). To measure that degree, Djankov et al. (2008) compile an index of "self-dealing" for more than 70 countries, which reflects aspects such as the need for approval of business decisions made by controlling interests and the scope for litigation to seek redress. The authors show that this index is associated with important measures, such as stock market capitalization as a share of GDP, ownership concentration, and the number of firms over GDP ratio.

An important challenge in concluding that countries should actively reduce procedural formalism or other type of legal design aspects in order to improve legal performance is the possibility that the choice of legal procedure could be endogenous to other perceived distortions that those procedures are supposed to mitigate or guard against. We are not aware of empirical work at the micro level that relies on exogenous variation to investigate the effect of reductions in procedural formalism or regulatory burden. The experiments that have been performed on the costs of business formalization are one way of addressing issues of regulatory burden, but do not operate through deep changes in legal aspects. Work that can illuminate deeper legal and regulatory changes would be valuable. One possible avenue for progress is to focus on legal and regulatory institutions that can be affected at the local level, be it geographic, or project-based. There are many institutional complexities in the design of regulation—e.g., as it pertains to the development and maintenance of infrastructure—that await evaluation with stronger empirical methods. This is evident from Estache's (forthcoming) detailed review of theoretical and empirical contributions in the area of infrastructure regulation.

Open Research Questions

- How does the enforcement of bankruptcy laws affect firm behavior?
- How does the deregulation of labor laws impact labor relations?
- Do reductions in procedural formalism increase judicial performance and does this translate into changes in the incentives and behavior of economic agents?

1.5. CONCLUSIONS

Legal and political institutions are fundamental drivers of economic development. In this review, we highlight the need for rigorous research to better understand the causes and consequences of these institutions for the developing world. While this call for research stands upon a large extant empirical literature, from which several important lessons have emerged, few studies have been able to overcome the endogeneity concerns associated with institutions. As a result, our understanding of the causal pathways by which these institutions operate remains incomplete.

RCTs offer a powerful methodology with which to push this research agenda forward. In contrast with other approaches, RCTs can assure us that the factors that determine the adoption of a particular set of institutions are not biasing our comparison of places that have adopted to those that have not. Institutions can also affect outcomes through various channels. Well-designed RCTs will often allow researchers to separately identify the possible mechanisms.

While RCTs offer many benefits over alternative methodologies, they are not without limitations. The main concern that often arises is whether the results of a study can be generalized either to other settings (i.e., *external validity*) or at a different scale (i.e., *scalability*). Although issues of external validity are not unique to RCTs, the opportunities to conduct experiments can often be limited to specific settings or with special implementation partners. Issues of scalability arise because randomized evaluations compare the difference between treatment and comparison populations in a given area. If the effects of the treatment depend on the scale of the intervention (e.g., due to general equilibrium effects, or even in who implements the broader program), then the effects of the treatment can be quite different if it were to be adopted more broadly.

Generalizability is a serious challenge, but some substantial progress can be made through linked RCTs. By conducting RCTs in different countries that are linked in the sense that they investigate similar mechanisms (e.g., a particular type of disseminating information on corruption) that are expected to lead to institutional change, we can overcome the issues of external validity. A good analogy is provided by the recent multi-country RCT study by Banerjee et al. (2015). In this study, the authors describe results from a set of pilot projects in Ethiopia, Ghana, Honduras, India, Pakistan, and Peru encompassing 11,000 households. Each project provided short-term aid and longer-term support to help participants graduate to a sustainable level of existence. In each country, the program was adjusted to suit different contexts and cultures, while staying true to the same overall principles. This multi-pronged approach is relatively expensive, but the theory of change is that the combination of these activities is necessary and sufficient to obtain a persistent impact. At the end of the intervention, they found statistically significant impacts on all 10 key outcomes or indices. One year after the end of the intervention, 36 months after the productive asset transfer, eight out of 10 indices still showed statistically significant gains, and there was very little or no decline in the impact of the program on the key variables (consumption, household assets, and food security).

Another approach to resolving issues of external validity and scalability is to allow for multi-arm treatments and to conduct the experiment at scale. With multi-armed treatments, experimenters can separate out the mechanisms by which institutional changes may take place. Thus, the point is not only to show that some specific intervention produces a particular change but also to understand how this change takes place, what other interventions could have the same effect, and to what extent the interventions can be scaled up. The study by Gertler et al. (2015) is an illustration of such an approach. It investigates the effects and mechanisms (behavioral change versus investment) of health promotion campaigns designed to eliminate open defecation in at-scale randomized field experiments from four countries: India, Indonesia, Mali, and Tanzania. The field experiments are at-scale in the sense that the interventions were designed and implemented by governments as part of their national environmental health strategies, and randomly rolled out geographically over time. The combination of at-scale cluster randomized field experiments with common measurement of outcomes in four countries provides not only strong internal validity but also a degree of external validity not seen in most studies.

A third approach to create more robust knowledge is to accumulate findings that are strongly complementary and connected through the measures that are used. For example, we reviewed work showing that financial incentives attract workers with better individual characteristics such as intelligence and personality traits (Dal Bó et al. 2013). However, it would be natural to wonder whether other inducements could have similar effects and whether those individual characteristics matter for performance. Studies by

Ashraf et al. (2015) and Callen et al. (2015) answered just these questions; we therefore have a body of work showing that a specific set of individual characteristics matters for performance and there are multiple ways of recruiting personnel with those features. While these research complementarities can arise spontaneously, work attempting to incorporate them by design would be valuable.

NOTES

This chapter has been written with generous support from the United Kingdom's Department of International Development, through the Economic Development & Institutions (EDI) program at the Center for Effective Global Action (CEGA). Oxford Policy Management leads EDI in partnership with Paris School of Economics, University of Namur, Aide a la Decision Economique, and CEGA. The authors would also like to acknowledge the diligent research support that David Foster, PhD student in the Department of Political Science at the University of California, Berkeley, provided throughout the development of this work. The authors similarly value the support and contributions of Leah Bridle and Andrew Westbury, as well as Temina Madon and Edward Miguel.

1. Several papers are cited throughout this document as "forthcoming." In most cases, these references are to a series of *path-finding papers* soon to be released under the EDI program. For more information about these documents, please contact edi@opml.co.uk.
2. See Bourguignon and Gunning (forthcoming) for a review of work on foreign aid and development.
3. We have reviewed some of the related work as part of a recent World Bank Policy Research Report (World Bank 2016). On the specific theme of media and politics, see the excellent review by Prat and Strömberg (2013).
4. Bardhan and Mookherjee (forthcoming) review work both theoretical and empirical on clientelism. In this section, we also comment on some of the empirical work in the area.
5. World Bank (2016) provides a thoughtful discussion of this point.
6. Some of the themes in this section are covered in the recent review by Finan et al. (forthcoming).
7. The Big Five personality traits originated in a psychology model put forward by Ernest Tupes and Raymond Christal in 1961; the traits have been defined as: openness to experience, conscientiousness, extraversion, agreeableness, and neuroticism.
8. Guirkinger and Platteau (forthcoming) survey further evidence on the impact of inheritance laws and discuss how legal reforms that interact with household processes can have different effects depending on norms and customs.
9. Bardhan (forthcoming) reviews work on the topic of land tenure systems, which tends to confirm the idea that security of tenure leads to investment and productivity gains.

REFERENCES

Acemoglu, Daron, Simon Johnson, and James A. Robinson. 2001. "The Colonial Origins of Comparative Development: An Empirical Investigation." *American Economic Review* 91, no. 5 (December): 1369–1401. doi:10.1257/aer.91.5.1369.

Acemoglu, Daron, Simon Johnson, James A. Robinson, and Pierre Yared. 2008. "Income and Democracy." *American Economic Review* 98, no. 3 (June): 808–42. doi:10.1257/aer.98.3.808.

Acemoglu, Daron, Suresh Naidu, Pascual Restrepo, and James A. Robinson. 2015. "Democracy Does Cause Growth." Working Paper, December. http://economics.mit.edu/files/11227.

Aker, Jenny C., Rachid Boumnijel, Amanda McClelland, and Niall Tierney. 2015. "Payment Mechanisms and Anti-Poverty Programs: Evidence from a Mobile Money Cash Transfer Experiment in Niger," July. https://sites.tufts.edu/jennyaker/files/2010/02/Zap_- 29july2015.pdf.

Aker, Jenny C., Paul Collier, and Pedro C. Vicente. 2015. "Is Information Power? Using Mobile Phones and Free Newspapers during an Election in Mozambique." Working Paper, January. https://sites.tufts.edu/jennyaker/files/2010/02/cell79.pdf.

Alesina, Alberto, Paola Giuliano, and Nathan Nunn. 2013. "On the Origins of Gender Roles: Women and the Plough." *Quarterly Journal of Economics* 128, no. 2 (May): 469–530. doi:10.1093/qje/qjt005.

Alesina, Alberto, and Bryony Reich. 2013. "Nation Building." Working Paper. National Bureau of Economic Research, February. www.nber.org/papers/w18839.

Ali, Daniel Ayalew, Klaus Deininger, and Markus Goldstein. 2014. "Environmental and Gender Impacts of Land Tenure Regularization in Africa: Pilot Evidence from Rwanda." *Journal of Development Economics* 110(C): 262–75.

Alonso, Pablo, and Gregory B. Lewis. 2001. "Public Service Motivation and Job Performance Evidence from the Federal Sector." *American Review of Public Administration* 31, no. 4 (December): 363–80. doi:10.1177/02750740122064992.

Alston, Lee J., Thráinn Eggertsson, and Douglass C. North (eds.) 1996. *Empirical Studies in Institutional Change. Political Economy of Institutions and Decisions.* Cambridge; New York: Cambridge University Press.

Alston, Lee J., Gary D. Libecap, and Robert Schneider. 1996. "The Determinants and Impact of Property Rights: Land Titles on the Brazilian Frontier." *Journal of Law, Economics, and Organization* 12, no. 1 (April): 25–61.

Alt, James E., David D. Lassen, and John Marshall. 2016. "Credible Sources and Sophisticated Voters: When Does New Information Induce Economic Voting?" *Journal of Politics* 78, no. 2 (April): 327–42. doi:10.1086/683832.

Ashraf, Nava, Oriana Bandiera, and Scott S. Lee. 2015. "Do-Gooders and Go-Getters: Career Incentives, Selection, and Performance in Public Service Delivery." Working Paper, March. www.hbs.edu/faculty/Pages/item.aspx?num=46043.

Baicker, Katherine, and Mireille Jacobson. 2007. "Finders Keepers: Forfeiture Laws, Policing Incentives, and Local Budgets." *Journal of Public Economics* 91, no. 11–12 (December): 2113–36. doi:10.1016/j.jpubeco.2007.03.009.

Balas, Aron, Rafael La Porta, Florencio Lopez-de-Silanes, and Andrei Shleifer. 2009. "The Divergence of Legal Procedures." *American Economic Journal: Economic Policy* 1, no. 2 (August): 138–62. doi:10.1257/pol.1.2.138.

Bandiera, Oriana, Myra Mohnen, Imran Rasul, and Martina Viarengo. 2019. "Nation-Building Through Compulsory Schooling During the Age of Mass Migration." Forthcoming in *Economic Journal*. doi:10.1111/ecoj.12624.

Banerjee, Abhijit, Raghabendra Chattopadhyay, Esther Duflo, Daniel Keniston, and Nina Singh. 2014. "Improving Police Performance in Rajasthan, India: Experimental Evidence on Incentives, Managerial Autonomy and Training." Working Paper, October. http://economics.mit.edu/files/10192.

Banerjee, Abhijit, and Lakshmi Iyer. 2005. "History, Institutions, and Economic Performance: The Legacy of Colonial Land Tenure Systems in India." *American Economic Review* 95, no. 4 (September): 1190–1213. doi:10.1257/0002828054825574.

Banerjee, Abhijit, Lakshmi Iyer, and Rohini Somanathan. 2008. "Public Action for Public Goods." In *Handbook of Development Economics*, vol. 4, edited by T. Paul Schultz and John Strauss, 1st edition. Amsterdam; New York: North Holland.

Banerjee, Abhijit, Selvan Kumar, Rohini Pande, and Felix Su. 2011. "Do Informed Voters Make Better Choices? Experimental Evidence from Urban India." Working Paper, November. www.povertyactionlab.org/node/2764.

Banerjee, Abhijit V., Rukmini Banerji, Esther Duflo, Rachel Glennerster, and Stuti Khemani. 2010. "Pitfalls of Participatory Programs: Evidence from a Randomized Evaluation in Education in India." *American Economic Journal: Economic Policy* 2, no. 1 (February): 1–30. doi:10.1257/pol.2.1.1.

Banerjee, Abhijit V., Esther Duflo, and Rachel Glennerster. 2008. "Putting a Band-Aid on a Corpse: Incentives for Nurses in the Indian Public Health Care System." *Journal of the European Economic Association* 6, no. 2–3 (May): 487–500. doi:10.1162/JEEA.2008.6.2–3.487.

Banerjee, Abhijit V., Dean Karlan, and Jonathan Zinman. 2015. "Six Randomized Evaluations of Microcredit: Introduction and Further Steps." *American Economic Journal: Applied Economics* 7, 1–21.

Banerjee, Ritwik, Tushi Baul, and Tanya Rosenblat. 2015. "On Self Selection of the Corrupt into the Public Sector." *Economics Letters* 127 (February): 43–46. doi:10.1016/j.econlet.2014.12.020.

Banuri, Sheheryar, and Philip Keefer. 2013. "Intrinsic Motivation, Effort and the Call to Public Service." Policy Research Working Paper, No. 6729. World Bank, Washington DC.

Bardhan, Pranab. 2016. "Institutions and Development: An Overview of Case Studies (Culled from the Literature on China and India)." EDI-RA1 Working Paper.

Bardhan, Pranab, and Dilip Mookherjee. 2016. "Clientelistic Politics and Economic Development: An Overview." EDI-RA1 Working Paper.

Barendrecht, Maurits, Margot Kokke, Martin Gramatikov, Robert Porter, Morly Frishman, and Andrea Morales. 2013. "Impact Assessment of the Facilitadores Judiciales Programme in Nicaragua." Working Paper. Helsinki, Finland: United Nations University World Institute for Development Economics Research, October. www.wider.unu.edu/publication/impact-assessment-facilitadores-judiciales-programme-nicaragua.

Barfort, Sebastian, Nikolaj Harmon, Frederik Hjorth, and Asmus Leth Olsen. 2015. "Dishonesty and Selection into Public Service in Denmark: Who Runs the World's Least Corrupt Public Sector?" Discussion Paper. University of Copenhagen. Department of Economics, September 4. http://econpapers.repec.org/paper/kudkuiedp/1512.htm.

Barone, Guglielmo, and Guido de Blasio. 2013. "Electoral Rules and Voter Turnout." *International Review of Law and Economics* 36 (October): 25–35. doi:10.1016/j.irle.2013.04.001.

Barro, Robert J. 1973. "The Control of Politicians: An Economic Model." *Public Choice* 14, no. 1 (March): 19–42. doi:10.1007/BF01718440.

Basinga, Paulin, Paul J. Gertler, Agnes Binagwaho, Agnes L. B. Soucat, Jennifer Sturdy, and Christel M. J. Vermeersch. 2011. "Effect on Maternal and Child Health Services in Rwanda of Payment to Primary Health-Care Providers for Performance: An Impact Evaluation." *The Lancet* (London) 377, no. 9775 (April 23): 1421–28. doi:10.1016/S0140–6736(11)60177–3.

Beaman, Lori, Raghabendra Chattopadhyay, Esther Duflo, Rohini Pande, and Petia Topalova. 2009. "Powerful Women: Does Exposure Reduce Bias?" *Quarterly Journal of Economics* 124, no. 4 (November): 1497–1540. doi:10.1162/qjec.2009.124.4.1497.

Beaman, Lori, Esther Duflo, Rohini Pande, and Petia Topalova. 2012. "Female Leadership Raises Aspirations and Educational Attainment for Girls: A Policy Experiment in India." *Science* 335, no. 6068 (February 3): 582–86. doi:10.1126/science.1212382.

Beath, Andrew, Fotini Christia, Georgy Egorov, and Ruben Enikolopov. 2016. "Electoral Rules and Political Selection: Theory and Evidence from a Field Experiment in Afghanistan." *Review of Economic Studies* 83(3): 932–68.

Beath, Andrew, Fotini Christia, and Ruben Enikolopov. 2013. "Empowering Women through Development Aid: Evidence from a Field Experiment in Afghanistan." *American Political Science Review* 107, no. 3 (August): 540–57. doi:10.1017/S0003055413000270.

Beck, Thorsten. 2016. "Finance, Institutions and Development: Literature Survey and Research Agenda." EDI-RA1 Working Paper.

Beqiraj, Julinda, and Lawrence McNamara. 2014. "The Rule of Law and Access to Justice in the Post-2015 Development Agenda: Moving Forward But Stepping Back." Working Paper. London: Bingham Centre for the Rule of Law, BIICL, August. www.biicl.org/documents/289_post-2015_bingham_centre_paper_2014–04.pdf.

Berdejó, Carlos, and Noam Yuchtman. 2013. "Crime, Punishment, and Politics: An Analysis of Political Cycles in Criminal Sentencing." *Review of Economics and Statistics* 95, no. 3 (July 2): 741–56. doi:10.1162/REST_a_00296.

Besley, Timothy, and Anne Case. 1995. "Incumbent Behavior: Vote-Seeking, Tax-Setting, and Yardstick Competition." *American Economic Review* 85(1): 25–45.

Besley, Timothy, and Maitreesh Ghatak. 2005. "Competition and Incentives with Motivated Agents." *American Economic Review* 95(3): 616–36.

Besley, Timothy, and Maitreesh Ghatak. 2010. "Property Rights and Economic Development." In *Handbook of Development Economics*, Vol. 5, edited by Dani Rodrik and Mark Rosenzweig: 4525–95. The Netherlands: North-Holland.

Besley, Timothy, Jose G. Montalvo, and Marta Reynal-Querol. 2011. "Do Educated Leaders Matter?" *Economic Journal* 121, no. 554 (August 1): F205–27. doi:10.1111/j.1468–0297.2011.02448.x.

Besley, Timothy, and Torsten Persson. 2011. "Pillars of Prosperity: The Political Economics of Development Clusters." The Yrjö Jahnsson Lectures. Princeton, NJ: Princeton University Press.

Bidwell, Kelly, Katherine E. Casey, and Rachel Glennerster. 2015. "DEBATES: Voter and Political Response to Political Communication in Sierra Leone." SSRN Scholarly Paper. Rochester, NY: Social Science Research Network, August 24. http://papers.ssrn.com/abstract=2658750.

Bisin, Alberto, and Thierry Verdier. 2001. "The Economics of Cultural Transmission and the Dynamics of Preferences." *Journal of Economic Theory* 97, no. 2 (April): 298–319. doi:10.1006/jeth.2000.2678.

Björkman, Martina, and Jakob Svensson. 2009. "Power to the People: Evidence from a Randomized Field Experiment on Community-Based Monitoring in Uganda." *Quarterly Journal of Economics* 124, no. 2 (May 2009): 735–69. doi:10.1162/qjec.2009.124.2.735.

Björkman Nyqvist, Martina, Damien de Walque, and Jakob Svensson. 2014. "Information Is Power: Experimental Evidence on the Long-Run Impact of Community-Based Monitoring." Policy Research Working Paper, World Bank. https://ideas.repec.org/p/wbk/wbrwps/7015.html.

Blattman, Christopher, and Jeannie Annan. 2016. "Can Employment Reduce Lawlessness and Rebellion? A Field Experiment with High-Risk Men in a Fragile State." *American Political Science Review* 110, no. 1 (February): 1–17.

Blattman, Christopher, Alexandra C. Hartman, and Robert A. Blair. 2014. "How to Promote Order and Property Rights under Weak Rule of Law? An Experiment in Changing Dispute Resolution

Behavior through Community Education." *American Political Science Review* 108, no. 1 (February): 100–120. doi:10.1017/S0003055413000543.

Bloom, Nicholas, and John Van Reenen. 2007. "Measuring and Explaining Management Practices Across Firms and Countries." *Quarterly Journal of Economics* 122, no. 4 (November): 1351–1408. doi:10.1162/qjec.2007.122.4.1351.

Bloom, Nicholas, and John Van Reenen. 2010. "Why Do Management Practices Differ across Firms and Countries?" *Journal of Economic Perspectives* 24, no. 1 (March): 203–24. doi:10.1257/jep.24.1.203.

Blumenthal, Marsha, Charles Christian, and Joel Slemrod. 2001. "Do Normative Appeals Affect Tax Compliance? Evidence from a Controlled Experiment in Minnesota." *National Tax Journal* 54, no. 1 (March): 125–38.

Bobonis, Gustavo J., Luis R. Cámara Fuertes, and Rainer Schwabe. 2015. "Monitoring Corruptible Politicians." Working Paper, December. http://homes.chass.utoronto.ca/~bobonis/BCS_PRAudit_15-12.pdf.

Botero, Juan C., Simeon Djankov, Rafael La Porta, Florencio Lopez-de-Silanes, and Andrei Shleifer. 2004. "The Regulation of Labor." *Quarterly Journal of Economics* 119, no. 4 (November): 1339–82. doi:10.1162/0033553042476215.

Bourguignon, François, and Jan Gunning. 2016. "Foreign Aid and Governance: A Survey." EDI-RA1 Working Paper.

Bowles, Samuel. 2016. "Institutions and Economic Inequality: Some Unanswered Questions." EDI-RA1 Working Paper.

Branstetter, Lee, Francisco Lima, Lowell J. Taylor, and Ana Venâncio. 2014. "Do Entry Regulations Deter Entrepreneurship and Job Creation? Evidence from Recent Reforms in Portugal." *Economic Journal* 124, no. 577 (June): 805–32. doi:10.1111/ecoj.12044.

Brollo, Fernanda, Tommaso Nannicini, Roberto Perotti, and Guido Tabellini. 2013. "The Political Resource Curse." *American Economic Review* 103, no. 5 (August): 1759–96. doi:10.1257/aer.103.5.1759.

Bruhn, Miriam. 2011. "License to Sell: The Effect of Business Registration Reform on Entrepreneurial Activity in Mexico." *Review of Economics and Statistics* 93, no. 1 (February): 382–86. doi:10.1162/REST_a_00059.

Bruhn, Miriam, and Jan Loeprick. 2014. "Small Business Tax Policy, Informality, and Tax Evasion—Evidence from Georgia." SSRN Scholarly Paper. Rochester, NY: Social Science Research Network. http://papers.ssrn.com/abstract=2500783.

Callen, Michael, Saad Gulzar, Ali Hasanain, Yasir Khan, and Arman Rezaee. 2015. "Personalities and Public Sector Performance: Evidence from a Health Experiment in Pakistan." Working Paper. National Bureau of Economic Research, May. www.nber.org/papers/w21180.

Callen, Michael, and James D. Long. 2015. "Institutional Corruption and Election Fraud: Evidence from a Field Experiment in Afghanistan." *American Economic Review* 105, no. 1 (January): 354–81. doi:10.1257/aer.20120427.

Cantoni, Davide, Yuyu Chen, David Y. Yang, Noam Yuchtman, and Y. Jane Zhang. 2015. "Curriculum and Ideology." Working Paper, July 15. www.barcelona-ipeg.eu/wp-content/uploads/2015/09/curriculum_draft_20150715.pdf.

Cascio, Elizabeth U., and Ebonya Washington. 2014. "Valuing the Vote: The Redistribution of Voting Rights and State Funds Following the Voting Rights Act of 1965." *Quarterly Journal of Economics* 129, no. 1 (February): 379–433. doi:10.1093/qje/qjt028.

Caselli, Francesco, and Guy Michaels. 2013. "Do Oil Windfalls Improve Living Standards? Evidence from Brazil." *American Economic Journal: Applied Economics* 5, no. 1 (January): 208–38. doi:10.1257/app.5.1.208.

Caselli, Francesco, and Andrea Tesei. 2015. "Resource Windfalls, Political Regimes, and Political Stability." *Review of Economics and Statistics*, August 12. doi:10.1162/REST_a_00538.

Casey, Katherine, Rachel Glennerster, and Edward Miguel. 2012. "Reshaping Institutions: Evidence on Aid Impacts Using a Preanalysis Plan." *Quarterly Journal of Economics* 127, no. 4 (November 1): 1755–1812. doi:10.1093/qje/qje027.

Castro, Lucio, and Carlos Scartascini. 2015. "Tax Compliance and Enforcement in the Pampas: Evidence from a Field Experiment." *Journal of Economic Behavior & Organization* 116 (August): 65–82. doi:10.1016/j.jebo.2015.04.002.

Chattopadhyay, Raghabendra, and Esther Duflo. 2004. "Women as Policy Makers: Evidence from a Randomized Policy Experiment in India." *Econometrica* 72, no. 5 (September 1): 1409–43. doi:10.1111/j.1468-0262.2004.00539.x.

Chin, Aimee, and Nishith Prakash. 2011. "The Redistributive Effects of Political Reservation for Minorities: Evidence from India." *Journal of Development Economics* 96, no. 2: 265–77.

Chong, Alberto, L. Ana, Dean Karlan, and Leonard Wantchekon. 2015. "Does Corruption Information Inspire the Fight or Quash the Hope? A Field Experiment in Mexico on Voter Turnout, Choice, and Party Identification." *Journal of Politics* 77, no. 1: 55–71.

Collier, Paul, and Pedro C. Vicente. 2014. "Votes and Violence: Evidence from a Field Experiment in Nigeria." *Economic Journal* 124, no. 574 (February 1): F327–55. doi:10.1111/ecoj.12109.

Cowley, Edd, and Sarah Smith. 2014. "Motivation and Mission in the Public Sector: Evidence from the World Values Survey." *Theory and Decision* 76, no. 2 (February): 241–63. doi:10.1007/s11238-013-9371-6.

Cox, Marcus. 2008. "Security and Justice: Measuring the Development Returns—A Review of Knowledge." Report prepared for DFID. London: Agulhas Development Consultants Ltd., August. www.gsdrc.org/document-library/security-and-justice-measuring-the-development-returns-a-review-of-knowledge/.

Cruz, Cesi, Philip Keefer, and Julien Labonne. 2015."Incumbent Advantage, Voter Information and Vote Buying." Working Paper, April 26. http://lacer.lacea.org/handle/123456789/53087.

Dal Bó, Ernesto, and Pedro Dal Bó. 2014. "'Do the Right Thing': The Effects of Moral Suasion on Cooperation." *Journal of Public Economics* 117 (September): 28–38. doi:10.1016/j.jpubeco.2014.05.002.

Dal Bó, Ernesto, Frederico Finan, and Martín A. Rossi. 2013. "Strengthening State Capabilities: The Role of Financial Incentives in the Call to Public Service." *Quarterly Journal of Economics* 128, no. 3 (August): 1169–1218. doi:10.1093/qje/qjt008.

Dal Bó, Ernesto, and Martín A. Rossi. 2011. "Term Length and the Effort of Politicians." *Review of Economic Studies* 78, no. 4 (October 1): 1237–63. doi:10.1093/restud/rdr010.

Dal Bó, Pedro, Andrew Foster, and Louis Putterman. 2010. "Institutions and Behavior: Experimental Evidence on the Effects of Democracy." *American Economic Review* 100, no. 5 (December): 2205–29. doi:10.1257/aer.100.5.2205.

Davis, Kevin, and Michael J. Trebilcock. 1999. "What Role Do Legal Institutions Play in Development?" Draft prepared for the International Monetary Fund's Conference on Second Generation Reforms, November 8–9. University of Toronto, October 20. www.ppge.ufrgs.br/GIACOMO/arquivos/diremp/david-trebilcock-1999.pdf.

De Andrade, Gustavo Henrique, Miriam Bruhn, and David McKenzie. 2013. "A Helping Hand or the Long Arm of the Law? Experimental Evidence on What Governments Can Do to Formalize Firms." Discussion Paper. Bonn, Germany: IZA, May. http://ftp.iza.org/dp7402.pdf.

De Giorgi, Giacomo, and Aminur Rahman. 2013. "SME Registration Evidence from a Randomized Controlled Trial in Bangladesh." Policy Research Working Paper. World Bank, March. http://elibrary.worldbank.org/doi/abs/10.1596/1813-9450-6382.

De Janvry, Alain, Frederico Finan, and Elisabeth Sadoulet. 2012. "Local Electoral Incentives and Decentralized Program Performance." *Review of Economics and Statistics* 94, no. 3 (August): 672–85. doi:10.1162/REST_a_00182.

Delfgaauw, Josse, and Robert Dur. 2008. "Incentives and Workers' Motivation in the Public Sector." *Economic Journal* 118, no. 525 (January): 171–91. doi:10.1111/j.1468–0297.2007.02108.x.

DellaVigna, Stefano, and Ethan Kaplan. 2007. "The Fox News Effect: Media Bias and Voting." *Quarterly Journal of Economics* 122, no. 3 (August 1): 1187–1234. doi:10.1162/qjec.122.3.1187.

De Mel, Suresh, David McKenzie, and Christopher Woodruff. 2013. "The Demand For, and Consequences Of, Formalization among Informal Firms in Sri Lanka." *American Economic Journal: Applied Economics* 5, no. 2 (April): 122–50. doi:10.1257/app.5.2.122.

Deserranno, Erika. 2015. "Financial Incentives as Signals: Experimental Evidence from the Recruitment of Health Workers." Working Paper, October. http://economics.mit.edu/files/10968.

De Soto, Hernando. 2000. *The Mystery of Capital: Why Capitalism Triumphs in the West and Fails Everywhere Else.* New York: Basic Books.

Dhaliwal, Iqbal, and Rema Hanna. 2014. "Deal with the Devil: The Successes and Limitations of Bureaucratic Reform in India." Working Paper. National Bureau of Economic Research, September. www.nber.org/papers/w20482.

Dizon-Ross, Rebecca, Pascaline Dupas, and Jonathan Robinson. 2015. "Governance and the Effectiveness of Public Health Subsidies." Working Paper. National Bureau of Economic Research, July. www.nber.org/papers/w21324.

Djankov, Simeon, Rafael La Porta, Florencio Lopez-de-Silanes, and Andrei Shleifer. 2002. "The Regulation of Entry." *Quarterly Journal of Economics* 117, no. 1 (February): 1–37. doi:10.1162/003355302753399436.

Djankov, Simeon, Rafael La Porta, Florencio Lopez-de-Silanes, and Andrei Shleifer. 2003. "Courts." *Quarterly Journal of Economics* 118, no. 2 (May): 453–517. doi:10.1162/003355303321675437.

Djankov, Simeon, Rafael La Porta, Florencio Lopez-de-Silanes, and Andrei Shleifer. 2008. "The Law and Economics of Self-Dealing." *Journal of Financial Economics*, Darden—JFE Conference Volume: Capital Raising in Emerging Economies, 88, no. 3 (June): 430–65. doi:10.1016/j.jfineco.2007.02.007.

Downing, Brian M. 1992. *The Military Revolution and Political Change: Origins of Democracy and Autocracy in Early Modern Europe*. Princeton, NJ: Princeton University Press.

Duflo, Esther, Michael Greenstone, Rohini Pande, and Nicholas Ryan. 2013. "Truth-Telling by Third-Party Auditors and the Response of Polluting Firms: Experimental Evidence from India." *Quarterly Journal of Economics* 128, no. 4 (November): 1499–1545. doi:10.1093/qje/qjt024.

Duflo, Esther, Michael Greenstone, Rohini Pande, and Nicholas Ryan. 2014. "The Value of Regulatory Discretion: Estimates from Environmental Inspections in India." Working Paper. National Bureau of Economic Research, October. www.nber.org/papers/w20590.

Duflo, Esther, Rema Hanna, and Stephen P. Ryan. 2012. "Incentives Work: Getting Teachers to Come to School." *American Economic Review* 102, no. 4 (June): 1241–78. doi:10.1257/aer.102.4.1241.

Estache, Antonio. 2016. "Institutions for Infrastructure in Developing Countries: What We Know . . . and the Lot We Still Need to Know." EDI-RA1 Working Paper.

Fearon, James D., Macartan Humphreys, and Jeremy M. Weinstein. 2009. "Can Development Aid Contribute to Social Cohesion after Civil War? Evidence from a Field Experiment in Post-Conflict Liberia." *American Economic Review* 99, no. 2 (May): 287–91. doi:10.1257/aer.99.2.287.

Fellner, Gerlinde, Rupert Sausgruber, and Christian Traxler. 2013. "Testing Enforcement Strategies in the Field: Threat, Moral Appeal and Social Information." *Journal of the European Economic Association* 11, no. 3 (1 June): 634–60. doi:10.1111/jeea.12013.

Ferejohn, John. 1986. "Incumbent Performance and Electoral Control." *Public Choice* 50, no. 1/3: 5–25.

Fernández, Raquel, Alessandra Fogli, and Claudia Olivetti. 2004. "Mothers and Sons: Preference Formation and Female Labor Force Dynamics." *Quarterly Journal of Economics* 119, no. 4 (1 November): 1249–99. doi:10.1162/0033553042476224.

Ferraz, Claudio, and Frederico Finan. 2008. "Exposing Corrupt Politicians: The Effects of Brazil's Publicly Released Audits on Electoral Outcomes." *Quarterly Journal of Economics* 123, no. 2 (1 May): 703–45. doi:10.1162/qjec.2008.123.2.703.

Ferraz, Claudio, and Frederico Finan. 2011. "Electoral Accountability and Corruption: Evidence from the Audits of Local Governments." *American Economic Review* 101, no. 4 (June): 1274–1311. doi:10.1257/aer.101.4.1274.

Field, Erica. 2005. "Property Rights and Investment in Urban Slums." *Journal of the European Economic Association* 3, no. 2–3 (May): 279–90. doi:10.1162/jeea.2005.3.2–3.279.

Finan, Frederico, Benjamin Olken, and Rohini Pande. 2017. "The Personnel Economics of the State." In *The Handbook of Field Experiments*, Vol. 2, pp. 467–514.

Finan, Frederico, and Laura Schechter. 2012. "Vote-Buying and Reciprocity." *Econometrica* 80, no. 2 (March 1): 863–81. doi:10.3982/ECTA9035.

Francois, Patrick. 2000. "'Public Service Motivation' as an Argument for Government Provision." *Journal of Public Economics* 78, no. 3 (November): 275–99. doi:10.1016/S0047-2727(00)00075-X.

Frankel, Martin, Carroll Seron, Gregg Van Ryzin, and Jean Frankel. 2001. "Impact of Legal Counsel in Outcomes for Poor Tenants in New York City's Housing Court: Results of a Randomized Experiment." *Law & Society Review* 35, no. 2: 419–34.

Fujiwara, Thomas. 2015. "Voting Technology, Political Responsiveness, and Infant Health: Evidence from Brazil." *Econometrica* 83, no. 2 (1 March): 423–64. doi:10.3982/ECTA11520.

Fujiwara, Thomas, and Leonard Wantchekon. 2013. "Can Informed Public Deliberation Overcome Clientelism? Experimental Evidence from Benin." *American Economic Journal: Applied Economics* 5, no. 4 (October): 241–55. doi:10.1257/app.5.4.241.

Galbiati, Roberto, and Giulio Zanella. 2012. "The Tax Evasion Social Multiplier: Evidence from Italy." *Journal of Public Economics* 96, no. 5–6 (June): 485–94. doi:10.1016/j.jpubeco.2012.01.003.

Galiani, Sebastian, and Ernesto Schargrodsky. 2010. "Property Rights for the Poor: Effects of Land Titling." *Journal of Public Economics* 94, no. 9–10 (October): 700–729. doi:10.1016/j.jpubeco.2010.06.002.

García, Juan Felipe, Daniel Mejia, and Daniel Ortega. 2013. "Police Reform, Training and Crime: Experimental Evidence from Colombia's Plan Cuadrantes." Working Paper. Caracas, Venezuela: CAF, January. https://ideas.repec.org/p/col/000089/010497.html.

Gentzkow, Matthew. 2006. "Television and Voter Turnout." *Quarterly Journal of Economics* 121, no. 3 (August): 931–72. doi:10.1162/qjec.121.3.931.

Gerber, Alan S., Dean Karlan, and Daniel Bergan. 2009. "Does the Media Matter? A Field Experiment Measuring the Effect of Newspapers on Voting Behavior and Political Opinions." *American Economic Journal: Applied Economics* 1, no. 2 (April): 35–52. doi:10.1257/app.1.2.35.

Gerber, Alan S., and Todd Rogers. 2009. "Descriptive Social Norms and Motivation to Vote: Everybody's Voting and So Should You." *Journal of Politics* 71, no. 1 (January 1): 178–91. doi:10.1017/S0022381608090117.

Gertler, Paul J., and Christel Vermeersch. 2012. "Using Performance Incentives to Improve Health Outcomes." SSRN Scholarly Paper. Rochester, NY: Social Science Research Network, June 1. http://papers.ssrn.com/abstract=2089240.

Gertler, P., M. Shah, M. Alzua, L. Cameron, S. Martinez, and S. Patil. 2015. "How Does Health Promotion Work? Evidence from the Dirty Business of Eliminating Dirty Defecation." UC Berkeley: Center for Effective Global Action. https://escholarship.org/uc/item/8b17z49c.

Ghatak, Maitreesh. 2016. "Property Rights and Development: A Brief Overview." EDI-RA4 Presentation.

Giné, Xavier, and Ghazala Mansuri. 2014. "Money or Ideas? A Field Experiment on Constraints to Entrepreneurship in Rural Pakistan." SSRN Scholarly Paper. Rochester, NY: Social Science Research Network, June 1. http://papers.ssrn.com/abstract=2461015.

Giuliano, Paola. 2007. "Living Arrangements in Western Europe: Does Cultural Origin Matter?" *Journal of the European Economic Association* 5, no. 5 (September): 927–52. doi:10.1162/JEEA.2007.5.5.927.

Giuliano, Paola, and Nathan Nunn. 2013. "The Transmission of Democracy: From the Village to the Nation-State." *American Economic Review* 103, no. 3 (May): 86–92. doi:10.1257/aer.103.3.86.

Giuliano, Paola, and Antonio Spilimbergo. 2014. "Growing Up in a Recession." *Review of Economic Studies* 81, no. 2 (April): 787–817. doi:10.1093/restud/rdt040.

Glewwe, Paul, Nauman Ilias, and Michael Kremer. 2010. "Teacher Incentives." *American Economic Journal: Applied Economics* 2, no. 3 (July): 205–27. doi:10.1257/app.2.3.205.

Gottlieb, Jessica. 2016. "Greater Expectations: A Field Experiment to Improve Accountability in Mali." *American Journal of Political Science* 60, no. 1: 143–57. doi:10.1111/ajps.12186.

Greiner, D. James, and Cassandra Wolos Pattanayak. 2012. "Randomized Evaluation in Legal Assistance: What Difference Does Representation (Offer and Actual Use) Make?" *Yale Law Journal* 121, no. 8: 2118–2214.

Greiner, D. James, Cassandra Wolos Pattanayak, and Jonathan Hennessy. 2012. "How Effective Are Limited Legal Assistance Programs? A Randomized Experiment in a Massachusetts Housing Court." Working Paper. Washington, DC: National Legal Aid & Defender Association, March 12. http://legalaidresearch.org/?p=1664.

Grossman, Guy, Oren Gazal-Ayal, Samuel D. Pimentel, and Jeremy M. Weinstein. 2016. "Descriptive Representation and Judicial Outcomes in Multiethnic Societies." *American Journal of Political Science* 60, no. 1 (January): 44–69. doi:10.1111/ajps.12187.

Guan, Mei, and Donald P. Green. 2006. "Noncoercive Mobilization in State-Controlled Elections: An Experimental Study in Beijing." *Comparative Political Studies* 39, no. 10 (December): 1175–93. doi:10.1177/0010414005284377.

Guirkinger, Catherine, and Jean-Philippe Platteau. 2016. "The Dynamics of Family Systems: Lessons from Past and Present Times." EDI-RA1 Working Paper.

Guiso, Luigi, Paola Sapienza, and Luigi Zingales. 2004. "The Role of Social Capital in Financial Development." *American Economic Review* 94, no. 3 (June): 526–56. doi:10.1257/0002828041464498.

Guiso, Luigi, Paola Sapienza, and Luigi Zingales. 2008. "Alfred Marshall Lecture: Social Capital as Good Culture." *Journal of the European Economic Association* 6, no. 2–3 (May): 295–320.

Haber, Stephen, and Victor Menaldo. 2011. "Do Natural Resources Fuel Authoritarianism? A Reappraisal of the Resource Curse." *American Political Science Review* 105, no. 1 (February): 1–26. doi:10.1017/S0003055410000584.

Haggard, Stephan, Andrew MacIntyre, and Lydia Tiede. 2008. "The Rule of Law and Economic Development." *Annual Review of Political Science* 11, no. 1: 205–34. doi:10.1146/annurev.polisci.10.081205.100244.

Hallsworth, Michael, John List, Robert Metcalfe, and Ivo Vlaev. 2017. "The Behavioralist as Tax Collector: Using Natural Field Experiments to Enhance Tax Compliance." *Journal of Public Economics* 148 (April): 14–31.

Hanna, Rema, and Shing-Yi Wang. 2015. "Dishonesty and Selection into Public Service: Evidence from India." Working Paper, October. http://assets.wharton.upenn.edu/~was/corruption_selection_paper.pdf.

Herbert, Siân. 2015. "Improving Access to Justice through Information and Communication Technologies." Research Report. GSDRC, February. www.gsdrc.org/publications/improving-access-to-justice-through-information-and- communication-technologies/.

Hinnerich, Björn Tyrefors, and Per Pettersson-Lidbom. 2014. "Democracy, Redistribution, and Political Participation: Evidence from Sweden 1919–1938." *Econometrica* 82, no. 3 (May 1): 961–93. doi:10.3982/ECTA9607.

Holmstrom, Bengt, and Paul Milgrom. 1991. "Multitask Principal–Agent Analyses: Incentive Contracts, Asset Ownership, and Job Design." *Journal of Law, Economics, and Organization* 7, special issue: 24–52. doi:10.1093/jleo/7.special_issue.24.

Humphreys, Macartan, and Jeremy Weinstein. 2012. "Policing Politicians: Citizen Empowerment and Political Accountability in Uganda Preliminary Analysis." Working Paper, April 19. http://cu-csds .org/wp-content/uploads/2009/10/ABCDE-paper.pdf.

Iaryczower, Matias, Garrett Lewis, and Matthew Shum. 2013. "To Elect or to Appoint? Bias, Information, and Responsiveness of Bureaucrats and Politicians." *Journal of Public Economics* 97 (January): 230–44. doi:10.1016/j.jpubeco.2012.08.007.

Iaryczower, Matias, and Matthew Shum. 2013. "Money in Judicial Politics: Individual Contributions and Collective Decisions." Working Paper, October 3. http://scholar.princeton.edu/sites/default /files/miaryc/files/judmoney.pdf.

Kendall, Chad, Tommaso Nannicini, and Francesco Trebbi. 2015. "How Do Voters Respond to Information? Evidence from a Randomized Campaign." *American Economic Review* 105, no. 1 (January): 322–53. doi:10.1257/aer.20131063.

Khan, Adnan Q., Asim I. Khwaja, and Benjamin A. Olken. 2014. "Tax Farming Redux: Experimental Evidence on Performance Pay for Tax Collectors." Working Paper. National Bureau of Economic Research, October. www.nber.org/papers/w20627.

Khemani, Stuti. 2015. "Buying Votes versus Supplying Public Services: Political Incentives to Under-Invest in pro-Poor Policies." *Journal of Development Economics* 117 (November): 84–93. doi:10.1016/j .jdeveco.2015.07.002.

Kleven, Henrik Jacobsen, Martin B. Knudsen, Claus Thustrup Kreiner, Søren Pedersen, and Emmanuel Saez. 2011. "Unwilling or Unable to Cheat? Evidence from a Tax Audit Experiment in Denmark." *Econometrica* 79, no. 3 (May): 651–92. doi:10.3982/ECTA9113.

Kolstad, Julie Riise and Ida K. Lindkvist. 2013. "Pro-Social Preferences and Self-Selection into the Public Health Sector: Evidence From an Economic Experiment." *Health Policy and Planning* 28(3): 320–27.

La Ferrara, Eliana. 2016. "The Media as a Tool for Institutional Change in Development." EDI-RA1 presentation.

Lane, Philip R., and Aaron Tornell. 1996. "Power, Growth, and the Voracity Effect." *Journal of Economic Growth* 1, no. 2 (June): 213–41. doi:10.1007/BF00138863.

La Porta, Rafael, and Andrei Shleifer. 2008. "The Unofficial Economy and Economic Development." Working Paper. National Bureau of Economic Research, December. www.nber.org/papers/w14520.

———. 2014. "Informality and Development." *Journal of Economic Perspectives* 28, no. 3 (August): 109–26. doi:10.1257/jep.28.3.109.

Larreguy, Horacio A., John Marshall, and James M. Snyder Jr. 2015. "Publicizing Malfeasance: When Media Facilitates Electoral Accountability in Mexico." https://bfi.uchicago.edu/sites/default/files /research/Local_Media_Mexico_v_9.pdf.

Leisink, Peter, and Bram Steijn. 2009. "Public Service Motivation and Job Performance of Public Sector Employees in the Netherlands." *International Review of Administrative Sciences* 75, no. 1 (March): 35–52. doi:10.1177/0020852308099505.

Lim, Claire S. H. 2013. "Preferences and Incentives of Appointed and Elected Public Officials: Evidence from State Trial Court Judges." *American Economic Review* 103, no. 4 (June): 1360–97. doi:10.1257/ aer.103.4.1360.

———. 2015. "Media Influence on Courts: Evidence from Civil Case Adjudication." *American Law and Economics Review* 17, no. 1 (Spring): 87–126. doi:10.1093/aler/ahv005.

Lim, Claire S. H., and James M. Snyder Jr. 2015. "Is More Information Always Better? Party Cues and Candidate Quality in U.S. Judicial Elections." *Journal of Public Economics* 128 (August): 107–23. doi:10.1016/j.jpubeco.2015.04.006.

Lim, Claire S. H., James M. Snyder Jr., and David Strömberg. 2015. "The Judge, the Politician, and the Press: Newspaper Coverage and Criminal Sentencing across Electoral Systems." *American Economic Journal: Applied Economics* 7, no. 4 (October): 103–35. doi:10.1257/app.20140111.

Lipset, Seymour Martin. 1959. "Some Social Requisites of Democracy: Economic Development and Political Legitimacy." *American Political Science Review* 53, no. 1: 69–105. doi:10.2307/1951731.

List, John A., and Daniel M. Sturm. 2006. "How Elections Matter: Theory and Evidence from Environmental Policy." *Quarterly Journal of Economics* 121, no. 4 (November 1): 1249–81. doi:10.1093 /qje/121.4.1249.

Lizzeri, Alessandro, and Nicola Persico. 2004. "Why Did the Elites Extend the Suffrage? Democracy and the Scope of Government, with an Application to Britain's 'Age of Reform,'" *Quarterly Journal of Economics* 119, no. 2 (May 1): 707–65. doi:10.1162/0033553041382175.

Lott, John R., Jr., and Lawrence Kenny. 1999. "Did Women's Suffrage Change the Size and Scope of Government?" *Journal of Political Economy* 107, no. 6: 1163–98.

Malesky, Edmund, Paul Schuler, and Anh Tran. 2012. "The Adverse Effects of Sunshine: A Field Experiment on Legislative Transparency in an Authoritarian Assembly." *American Political Science Review* 106, no. 4 (November): 762–86. doi:10.1017/S0003055412000408.

McGraw, Kathleen M., and John T. Scholz. 1991. "Appeals to Civic Virtue versus Attention to Self-Interest: Effects on Tax Compliance." *Law & Society Review* 25, no. 3: 471–98. doi:10.2307/3053724.

McKenzie, David, and Yaye Seynabou Sakho. 2010. "Does It Pay Firms to Register for Taxes? The Impact of Formality on Firm Profitability." *Journal of Development Economics* 91, no. 1 (January): 15–24. doi:10.1016/j.jdeveco.2009.02.003.

McKenzie, David, and Christopher Woodruff. 2008. "Experimental Evidence on Returns to Capital and Access to Finance in Mexico." *World Bank Economic Review* 22, no. 3 (December): 457–82. doi:10.1093/wber/lhn017.

Miller, Grant. 2008. "Women's Suffrage, Political Responsiveness, and Child Survival in American History." *Quarterly Journal of Economics* 123, no. 3 (August 1): 1287–1327. doi:10.1162/qjec.2008.123.3.1287.

Miller, Grant, Renfu Luo, Linxiu Zhang, Sean Sylvia, Yaojiang Shi, Patricia Foo, Qiran Zhao, Reynaldo Martorell, Alexis Medina, and Scott Rozelle. 2012. "Effectiveness of Provider Incentives for Anaemia Reduction in Rural China: A Cluster Randomised Trial." *BMJ* 345 (July 27): e4809. doi:10.1136/bmj.e4809.

Miller, J. Mitchell, and Lance H. Selva. 1994. "Drug Enforcement's Double-edged Sword: An Assessment of Asset Forfeiture Programs." *Justice Quarterly* 11, no. 2 (June): 313–35. doi:10.1080/07418829400092271.

Mookherjee, Dilip. 2016. "State Bureaucracy and Economic Development: A Research Agenda." EDI RA4 Presentation.

Mueller, Valerie, Lucy Billings, Tewodaj Mogues, Amber Peterman, and Ayala Wineman. 2015. "Filling the Legal Void? Impacts of a Community-Based Legal Aid Program on Women's Land-Related Knowledge, Attitudes, and Practices." *Oxford Development Studies* 46(8): 453–69.

Mullainathan, Sendhil, and Philipp Schnabl. 2010. "Does Less Market Entry Regulation Generate More Entrepreneurs? Evidence from a Regulatory Reform in Peru." In *International Differences in Entrepreneurship*, edited by Josh Lerner and Antoinette Schoar: 159–77. Chicago: University of Chicago Press. www.nber.org/chapters/c8225.

Muralidharan, Karthik. 2012. "Long-Term Effects of Teacher Performance Pay: Experimental Evidence from India." Working Paper, April 10. http://sticerd.lse.ac.uk/presentations/Long%20Term%20Effects%20of%20Teacher%20P erformance%20Pay%20-%2010%20April%202012.pdf.

Muralidharan, Karthik, and Venkatesh Sundararaman. 2011. "Teacher Performance Pay: Experimental Evidence from India." *Journal of Political Economy* 119, no. 1 (February): 39–77. doi:10.1086/659655.

Naff, Katherine C., and John Crum. 1999. "Working for America: Does Public Service Motivation Make a Difference?" *Review of Public Personnel Administration* 19, no. 4 (October): 5–16. doi:10.1177/0734371X9901900402.

Nagarajan, Hari, Aparajita Goyal, and Klaus Deininger. 2010. "Inheritance Law Reform and Women's Access to Capital: Evidence from India's Hindu Succession Act." World Bank, June 1. http://documents.worldbank.org/curated/en/2010/06/12414709/inheritance-law-reform-womens-access-capital-evidence-indias-hindu-succession-act.

Nannicini, Tommaso, Andrea Stella, Guido Tabellini, and Ugo Troiano. 2013. "Social Capital and Political Accountability." *American Economic Journal: Economic Policy* 5, no. 2 (May): 222–50. doi:10.1257/pol.5.2.222.

North, Douglass C. 1991. "Institutions." *Journal of Economic Perspectives* 5(1). American Economic Association: 97–112.

North, Douglass C., and Barry R. Weingast. 1989. "Constitutions and Commitment: The Evolution of Institutions Governing Public Choice in Seventeenth-Century England." *Journal of Economic History* 49(4): 803–32. http://www.jstor.org/stable/2122739.

Olken, Benjamin A. 2007. "Monitoring Corruption: Evidence from a Field Experiment in Indonesia." *Journal of Political Economy* 115, no. 2 (April): 200–249. doi:10.1086/517935.

Olken, Benjamin A. 2010. "Direct Democracy and Local Public Goods: Evidence from a Field Experiment in Indonesia." *American Political Science Review* 104, no. 2 (May): 243–267. doi:10.1017/S0003055410000079.

Olken, Benjamin A., Junko Onishi, and Susan Wong. 2014. "Should Aid Reward Performance? Evidence from a Field Experiment on Health and Education in Indonesia." *American Economic Journal: Applied Economics* 6, no. 4 (October): 1–34. doi:10.1257/app.6.4.1.

Olson, Mancur. 1965. "The Logic of Collective Action: Public Goods and the Theory of Groups." *Harvard Economic Studies*, v. 124. Cambridge, MA: Harvard University Press.

Padró i Miquel, Gerard, Nancy Qian, and Yang Yao. 2014. "Social Fragmentation, Public Goods and Elections: Evidence from China." Working Paper, August 14. http://personal.lse.ac.uk/padro /working-papers/Hetero_20140814.pdf.

Paler, Laura. 2013. "Keeping the Public Purse: An Experiment in Windfalls, Taxes, and the Incentives to Restrain Government." *American Political Science Review* 107, no. 4 (November): 706–725. doi:10.1017/S0003055413000415.

Pande, Rohini. 2003. "Can Mandated Political Representation Increase Policy Influence for Disadvantaged Minorities? Theory and Evidence from India." *American Economic Review* 93, no. 4 (September): 1132–51. doi:10.1257/000282803769206232.

Park, Sung Min, and Hal G. Rainey. 2008. "Leadership and Public Service Motivation in U.S. Federal Agencies." *International Public Management Journal* 11, no. 1: 109–42. doi:10.1080/10967490801887954.

Pattanayak, Cassandra Wolos, D. James Greiner, and Jonathan Hennessy. 2013. "The Limits of Unbundled Legal Assistance: A Randomized Study in a Massachusetts District Court and Prospects for the Future." *Harvard Law Review* 126, no. 4 (February): 901–89.

Perez-Truglia, Ricardo, and Ugo Troiano. 2016. "Shaming Tax Delinquents: Evidence from a Field Experiment in the United States." SSRN Scholarly Paper. Rochester, NY: Social Science Research Network, April 1. http://papers.ssrn.com/abstract=2558115.

Perry, James L. 1996. "Measuring Public Service Motivation: An Assessment of Construct Reliability and Validity." *Journal of Public Administration Research and Theory* 6, no. 1 (January): 5–22.

Perry, James L., and Annie Hondeghem. 2008. "Building Theory and Empirical Evidence about Public Service Motivation." *International Public Management Journal* 11, no. 1: 3–12. doi:10.1080 /10967490801887673.

Persson, Torsten, and Guido Enrico Tabellini. 2003. *The Economic Effects of Constitutions*. Munich Lectures in Economics. Cambridge, MA: MIT Press.

Persson, Torsten, Guido Tabellini, and Francesco Trebbi. 2003. "Electoral Rules and Corruption." *Journal of the European Economic Association* 1, no. 4 (June 1): 958–89. doi:10.1162/154247603322493203.

Petrovsky, Nicolai. 2009. "Does Public Service Motivation Predict Higher Public Service Performance? A Research Synthesis." Working Paper, September 24. http://www2.ku.edu/~pmranet/conferences /OSU2009/papers/Petrovsky,%20Nicolai.%20Does%20Public%20Service%20Motivation% 20Predict%20Higher%20Public%20Service%20Performance%20-%20A%20Research%20Synthesis .pdf.

Platteau, Jean-Philippe. 1995. "Reforming Land Rights in Sub-Saharan Africa: Issues of Efficiency and Equity." Discussion Paper. Geneva, Switzerland: United Nations Research Institute for Social Development.

Pomeranz, Dina. 2015. "No Taxation without Information: Deterrence and Self-Enforcement in the Value Added Tax." *American Economic Review* 105, no. 8 (August): 2539–69. doi:10.1257/aer.20130393.

Prat, Andrea, and David Strömberg. 2013. "The Political Economy of Mass Media," in *Advances in Economics and Econometrics: Theory and Applications*, Proceedings of the Tenth World Congress of the Econometric Society.

Prendergast, Canice. 2007. "The Motivation and Bias of Bureaucrats." *American Economic Review* 97, no. 1 (March): 180–96. doi:10.1257/aer.97.1.180.

Rasul, Imran, and Daniel Rogger. 2018. "Management of Bureaucrats and Public Service Delivery: Evidence from the Nigerian Civil Service." *Economic Journal* 128: 413–46. doi:10.1111/ecoj.12418.

Ray, Debraj, and Joan Esteban. 2016. "Conflict and Development." EDI-RA1 Working Paper.

Reinikka, Ritva, and Jakob Svensson. 2005. "Fighting Corruption to Improve Schooling: Evidence from a Newspaper Campaign in Uganda." *Journal of the European Economic Association* 3, no. 2–3 (May): 259–67. doi:10.1162/jeea.2005.3.2–3.259.

Ritz, Adrian. 2009. "Public Service Motivation and Organizational Performance in Swiss Federal Government." *International Review of Administrative Sciences* 75, no. 1 (March): 53–78. doi:10.1177/0020852308099506.

Robinson, James A., Ragnar Torvik, and Thierry Verdier. 2006. "Political Foundations of the Resource Curse." *Journal of Development Economics*, Special Issue in honor of Pranab Bardhan, 79, no. 2 (April 6): 447–68. doi:10.1016/j.jdeveco.2006.01.008.

Rodrik, Dani. 2000. "Institutions for High-Quality Growth: What They Are and How to Acquire Them." *Studies in Comparative International Development* 35, no. 3 (September): 3–31. doi:10.1007 /BF02699764.

Roland, Gerard. 2016. "Culture, Institutions, and Development." EDI-RA1 Working Paper.

Ross, Michael L. 2001. "Does Oil Hinder Democracy?" *World Politics* 53, no. 3 (April): 325–361. doi:10.1353/wp.2001.0011.

Sachs, Jeffrey D., and Andrew M. Warner. 1995. "Natural Resource Abundance and Economic Growth." Working Paper. National Bureau of Economic Research, December. www.nber.org/papers/w5398.

Sandefur, Justin, and Bilal Siddiqi. 2013. "Delivering Justice to the Poor: Theory and Experimental Evidence from Liberia." Working Paper, November 15. http://cega.berkeley.edu/assets/cega_events /61/5D_Political_Economy-_Violence.pdf.

Sanz, Carlos. 2015. "The Effect of Electoral Systems on Voter Turnout: Evidence from a Natural Experiment." *Political Science Research and Methods FirstView* (October): 1–22. doi:10.1017/psrm.2015.54.

Serra, Danila, Pieter Serneels, and Abigail Barr. 2011. "Intrinsic Motivations and the Non-Profit Health Sector: Evidence from Ethiopia." *Personality and Individual Differences* Volume 51(3): 309–14.

Steijn, Bram. 2008. "Person-Environment Fit and Public Service Motivation." *International Public Management Journal* 11(1): 13–27. doi:10.1080/10967490801887863.

Tabellini, Guido. 2008. "The Scope of Cooperation: Values and Incentives." *Quarterly Journal of Economics* 123, no. 3 (August): 905–50. doi:10.1162/qjec.2008.123.3.905.

Verdier, Thierry, and Jean-Philippe Platteau. 2016. "Interactions Between Formal and Informal Institutions." EDI-RA4 Approach Paper.

Vicente, Pedro. 2014. "Is Vote-buying Effective? Evidence from a Field Experiment in West Africa." *Economic Journal* 124(574): 356–87.

Williamson, Oliver E. 1985. *The Economic Institutions of Capitalism: Firms, Markets, Relational Contracting.* New York; London: Free Press; Collier Macmillan.

World Bank. 2004. *World Development Report 2005: A Better Investment Climate for Everyone.* Washington, DC: World Bank, September 28. http://web.worldbank.org/WBSITE/EXTERNAL/EXTDEC /EXTRESEARCH/EXTWDRS/0,,contentMDK:23062314~pagePK:478093~piPK:477627~theSitePK :477624,00.html.

World Bank. 2016. "Making Politics Work for Development: Harnessing Transparency and Citizen Engagement." Policy Research Report. May. www.worldbank.org/en/research/publication /making-politics-work-for-development

2

CLIENTELISTIC POLITICS AND ECONOMIC DEVELOPMENT

An Overview

Pranab Bardhan and Dilip Mookherjee

2.1. INTRODUCTION

Political clientelism represents a classic instance of an informal political institution that plays an important role in political economy of underdevelopment. The pervasiveness of vote-buying and clientelistic "machine" politics in traditional societies has been extensively documented in various case studies and political ethnographies.[1] Besides studies from nineteenth- and early twentieth-century United States and United Kingdom, and Italy in the mid-twentieth century (Kitschelt and Wilkinson 2007; Chubb 1982; Golden 2000), they include contemporary practices in many middle- and low-income countries, such as vote-buying in Argentina (Stokes 2005), practices followed by PRI operatives in Mexico (Rizzo 2015), or political brokers in a Mumbai municipal ward election (Björkman 2013).

While clientelism has sometimes been hailed for its redistributive impact and filling in gaps in social services provided by the state, most writers believe the broader systemic consequences undermine democracy and development in a variety of ways: lowering public goods, effective political competition, and accountability of elected officials. Some writers have additionally argued broader pernicious effects of clientelism, such as induced incentives for elected politicians to selectively enforce regulations, enlarge informalization, and perpetuate insecurity of property rights in order to keep constituents poor and dependent. The descriptive literature has highlighted the following features of clientelistic politics:

- Monitoring voters and time lags between voting and service delivery creates enforcement problems on both (voter and party) sides. Hence clientelism requires a political culture involving long-term relationships, reciprocity, and trust between party operatives and voters.

- Political brokers or intermediaries (social patrons) play an important role in overcoming these monitoring and enforcement problems. This generates hierarchical interlinkage between political patronage and social patronage mechanisms, wherein social patrons act as brokers, delivering votes of their clients to parties in exchange for payments or post-election delivery promises by political parties.
- Clientelistic relationships tend to be directed to poor voters as their votes are cheaper to buy, thereby enhancing vertical equity.
- Political parties are motivated to target clientelistic transfers to narrow "swing" constituencies, resulting in horizontal inequity.
- Clientelistic benefits are excludable by their very nature in order to be used to incentivize voters to lend political support, thereby generating an inherent bias in favor of private benefits or local (versus national) public goods.
- Among private benefits, some forms are better suited than others to overcome enforcement problems, resulting in biases in favor of short-term public employment rather than cash transfers and recurring rather than one-time benefits.
- Clientelism creates political incentives for weakening enforcement of property rights and regulations to permit selectiveness in their application: the phenomenon of *forbearance* (Holland 2016), thereby creating a large informal sector, insecure property rights, and an impression of weak state capacity.[2]

A systematic analysis requires a precise definition of clientelism that identifies its distinctive features, which helps derive analytical propositions that can be empirically tested and allow inferences concerning its normative consequences. The Wikipedia definition of clientelism states: "exchange systems where voters trade political support for various outputs of the public decision-making process." In other words, it refers to discretionary provision of private benefits by government officials and political parties selectively to particular groups of citizens, in exchange for their votes. Hicken (2011) argues that the key element is the contingent and reciprocal nature of the exchange.

However, descriptive accounts often include both vote purchases via upfront pre-election payments (which are unconditional), as well as post-election delivery promises conditional on political support: the preceding definition would include only the latter. Vicente and Wantchekon (2009) refer to these as "vote-buying" and "clientelism" respectively. The theoretical analysis of Dekel, Jackson, and Wolinsky (2008) shows the two forms generate distinct implications for equilibrium bribes and policies chosen. Hence it is necessary to distinguish the narrow definition (focusing on selective delivery of benefits by parties to those it believes supported them recently) from a broader definition which includes both.[3] In a multi-period setting, it is hard to draw a relevant distinction between pre-election and post-election delivery of benefits. As we elaborate below, the critical issue is not the timing of benefits, but whether delivery of public services to citizens can be conditioned by politicians on their political support.

Political clientelism needs to be distinguished from social "patron-client" relationships. The latter refers to hierarchical social networks such as nexuses between landlords and tenants, employers and workers, community leaders and members, or brokers and their clients. Political clientelism by contrast involves exchanges between specific voter constituencies (or brokers representing them) and political parties, sometimes in a

competitive market setting (where a constituency could choose between different political parties to sell their votes). However, there is often a close symbiosis between the
two forms of patronage: social patrons are frequently appointed as brokers by political
parties to mediate their transactions with individual citizens.

This chapter focuses particularly on how clientelistic politics differs from programmatic politics, where delivery of public services to citizens is not conditioned on their
political support. This distinction has often been blurred in the literature. Policy platforms in programmatic politics may be designed by political contestants to influence
(future) political support from specific constituencies via pork-barrel programs. The line
that divides pork-barrel politics from the wider definition of clientelism therefore seems
rather thin. Partly for this reason we think it is helpful to focus on the narrower definition of clientelism: it enables a conceptually clearer contrast between the two forms of
politics. Specifically, the key issue is whether the receipt of benefits by individual citizens is at the discretion of elected officials, or described by (well-defined) rules and (well-
enforced) citizen entitlements. The hallmark of clientelism is the discretionary and informal nature of the decision made by a political agent to deliver a benefit to any given
citizen. Indeed, there is a natural connection between clientelism and the informal sector, which can be defined as the set of citizens who lack clear entitlements to state benefits. This enables political agents to incentivize those in the informal sector to support
them politically. Section 2.2 describes a range of mechanisms used by party operatives
to monitor votes of individual voters in elections based on secret ballots.

By contrast, programmatic politics caters to citizens in the formal sector with secure
entitlements defined on the basis of publicly observable characteristics such as location,
age, gender, ethnicity, occupation, or asset ownership, enforced by an independent judiciary and media oversight. It is the formal institution counterpart of clientelism, with
codified rules of citizen entitlement enshrined in legislation and enforced by judicial institutions. Examples are social security and tax laws, or formula-bound transfers to specific groups of citizens (e.g., local governments). Entitlements of those in the formal sector (who have adequate documentation to establish their citizenship and criteria necessary
to qualify for entitlements) are not subject to discretion exercised by political agents or
elected officials. Political competition within programmatic politics therefore takes the
form of rival contestants presenting policy platforms represented by explicit and enforceable rules defining citizen entitlements. When formal institutions such as citizen identification and courts are weak, rules defining entitlements are not transparent or clear; even
if citizens may be aware of their entitlements, it may be hard for them to seek redress
when these are denied. With a large informal sector, the space then emerges for clientelistic practices to appear: de jure formal entitlements can be selectively honored by elected
officials for their clients and denied to others. As we explain in section 2.3, this can have
profound consequences for the outcomes of electoral competition: clientelism thrives
when the informal sector is sufficiently large relative to the formal sector, resulting in bias
in favor of private benefit transfers particularly to poorer citizens, undersupply of public
goods, pro-incumbency advantages, and low political turnover. Section 2.4 reviews a
growing literature using econometric analysis of large datasets testing these predictions.

We then turn to issues concerning institutional dynamics between clientelism and
program politics in section 2.5. Various authors have noted a tendency for clientelism to
decline and be replaced by programmatic politics as countries develop, as seen in UK and

US political history over the nineteenth and early twentieth centuries (Cox 1987; Mitgang 2000; Acemoglu and Robinson 2000; Lizzeri and Persico 2004). Contemporary middle-income countries such as Mexico and Brazil have recently initiated programs to provide secure land titles and conditional cash transfers which have expanded the scope of programmatic politics. Development could be both a cause and effect of this institutional transformation. But such dynamics are not inevitable: countries such as Italy or Japan still exhibit clientelistic patterns, or local politics in various parts of the United States (see for example Stanton 2003 for a vivid account of the state of Rhode Island between 1970 and 2000 under Providence mayor Buddy Cianci).[4] The nature and determinants of the transition of political institutions are less well understood than the static attributes and consequences. We review related theoretical models and empirical examinations of this institutional dynamic.

Finally, section 2.6 concludes with a summary of what has been learned so far and open questions that deserve attention in future research.

2.2. ENFORCEMENT MECHANISMS AND POLITICAL CULTURE

Any description of political clientelism has to explain how votes can be bought in democracies with secret ballots. In the narrower definition of clientelism, benefits are delivered conditional on their voting behavior; hence party operatives need to verify how a client voted. The broader definition includes vote-buying via unconditional pre-election transfers: how do these affect incentives of recipients to vote subsequently? The literature has provided a number of answers to this question, with interesting implications for the distinctive "political culture" of societies with pervasive clientelism.

In the context of vote-buying, one answer is provided by social norms of reciprocity based on gift exchange and loyalty. Finan and Schechter (2012) provide supportive evidence from Paraguay, where recipients of political favors demonstrated greater tendency for reciprocity in experimental "trust" games. In some contexts, (marked) ballots are handed out by party operatives; this is still legal in Argentina, Uruguay, and Panama (Stokes 2007). Modern technology can sometimes be harnessed creatively: there are informal accounts from southern Italy of how voters are required to take a picture of their cast ballot on their cell phones and show these to party operatives in order to claim clientelistic benefits.

Group sanctions are sometimes brought into play: neighborhoods that vote against a party or candidate as revealed in constituency vote counts could be discriminated against collectively with respect to supply of local public or private goods. For this reason electoral authorities in India stopped providing public reports of vote counts at the booth level (Kitschelt and Wilkinson 2007). More sophisticated mechanisms rely on public signals of political support to their patrons by individual voters (e.g., in the form of participation in election rallies), as in theoretical models of Bardhan-Mookherjee (2018) and Sarkar (2014). Each citizen is required to choose one party or candidate to declare public support for. In turn, parties would restrict benefit delivery among those expressing support. Citizens would then have a private incentive to vote for their chosen patrons, thereby obviating the need for any monitoring of their vote by the parties.

The most common accounts of clientelism assign a key role to intermediaries that act as brokers for the political transaction, in a hierarchical arrangement between political parties, brokers, and voter groups. Parties deliver a given stock of benefits to brokers in exchange for delivery of votes from a specific group of voters. The broker distributes these benefits within the group on the basis of fine-tuned relationships with individual voters, which enables them to establish their credibility and identify specific needs and preferences of individual citizens. In-depth interviews with political operatives and citizens, by Björkman (2013) in the context of an Indian city and Rizzo (2015) in the context of Mexican elections, reveal how brokers develop bonds of reciprocity with citizens and a reputation for providing them help and access to government services. As Rizzo argues, "brokers are not only instrumental in helping parties win elections, but in helping governments govern."

Marcolongo (2017) develops a theoretical model of political brokerage that formalizes this. Politicians have an incentive to hire brokers in order to capitalize on the latter's fine-grained information concerning specific needs and preferences of individual citizens, and reputation for honoring pre-election delivery promises ex post. They enter into a "deal" with a local broker in which they promise to transfer a block of services (besides private rents or cash payments) for the broker to allocate within the group that the broker represents, if they happen to be elected in exchange for votes from this group. Brokers "shop" on behalf of the voter group they represent across alternative candidates and "deliver" the votes of this group on the basis of assessment of credibility/reputation of each candidate and the magnitude of promised benefits. Having selected a politician, the broker recommends to the voter group in question that they vote in favor of this politician. Following this recommendation is incentive compatible for the broker's clients, since the benefits will only be delivered in the event that the politician with whom the broker has made a deal succeeds in winning the election. Consistent with Rizzo's assessment, Marcolongo's model illustrates that clientelism improves targeting by bringing better information to bear on allocating services among voters in the relevant jurisdiction. On the other hand, it creates a policy bias in favor of private transfers at the expense of low public goods and allows elected officials and brokers to appropriate higher rents.

Some empirical evidence consistent with these accounts of political brokerage is provided by Larreguy, Marshall, and Querubín (2016), who argue that politicians need to monitor the performance of brokers in delivering promised votes by examining vote outcomes in the most closely matched constituency. They provide detailed evidence from Mexico that the PRI achieved greater political support in rural communal land areas with a better match between the jurisdictions of the communal areas controlled by brokers and electoral constituencies.

2.3. STATIC THEORETICAL MODELS

2.3.1. Abstract Models

Dal Bó (2007) provides a theoretical analysis of a specific form of vote-buying by an external party or principal (such as an interest group) who bribes members of a committee to manipulate their votes on a specific decision. Outcomes preferred by the principal can be induced at arbitrarily low cost via offer strategies where payments to each member are conditioned on the vector of votes cast. Payments are promised only to pivotal voters; these ensure voting for the outcome desired by the principal is a weakly dominant strategy for every member. Hence, every member votes for this outcome. No one ends up being pivotal, so no payments actually need be made. This form of manipulation requires that all votes be observable. When payments can be conditioned only on individual votes, in conjunction with or alternately on the total vote count, costs of manipulation rise but may still permit manipulation to take place. Observing individual votes need not allow greater manipulation when the total vote count is observable. Collusion among voters (e.g., when they are organized into disciplined parties) can substantially lower costs of manipulation.

Dekel, Jackson, and Wolinsky (2008) study a vote buying contest between two parties where parties and voters have exogenous stakes over the election outcome. Two specific forms of vote-buying are compared: upfront unconditional payments and campaign promises (conditional on winning). These correspond respectively to all-pay versus winner-only-pay auctions. Either form of vote-buying results in outcomes that weight party preferences at the expense of voter preferences. Conditional payments result in higher vote payments to voters and decisions that are partially based on voter preferences. Upfront payments result in negligible payments and election outcomes determined entirely on the basis of party preferences. Hence conditionality of voter payments matters and may be valuable to voters.

A common theme of these two papers is that vote-buying induces outcomes that weight party preferences more than voter preferences. They also explain how the efficiency implications of vote-buying are ambiguous, where efficiency is measured by aggregate surplus of parties and voters. If parties reflect narrow interest groups, then efficiency falls. But if party stakes simply reflect an aggregate of voter stakes, the opposite is true. Another feature of these models is that policies or collective decisions are made directly by voters, rather than by parties that seek to manipulate them. Hence they do not pertain to indirect democracies where voters delegate policy choices to elected politicians.

2.3.2. More Structured Models

Stokes (2005) presents a model of repeated interaction between voters and a single party "machine" that faces a single passive challenger. Policies vary on a single dimension; each citizen has quadratic preferences over the policy with an ideal point. The policy positions of the two parties differ exogenously. In the absence of any vote-buying, citizens will vote for the party whose policy is closer to their ideal point. The party machine can manipulate votes by offering upfront payments to voters with specific ideal points in exchange for their promise to vote for them. Such fine-tuned targeting is possible as machine party operatives (or their appointed brokers) can identify the ideal point of every voter and monitor their voting behavior stochastically. Those voters receiving payments and subsequently discovered to have deviated by voting for the challenger instead are punished by being forever denied any opportunity to sell their votes. The machine will then have an incentive to buy votes only from "swing" voters, those with ideal points in an intermediate range. Purchasing the support of core supporters is unnecessary, while purchasing support of loyal supporters of the challenger is either infeasible or too expensive. It is worthwhile for the incumbent to target poor voters who have a mild intrinsic inclination to vote for the challenger, since they are less likely to deviate from the promise to vote for the incumbent, and their votes are relatively cheap to buy. The potential scope of such vote-buying is higher the narrower the policy gap between the two parties, the higher the probability of monitoring, and the higher the value of the private reward to voters relative to their ideological values. Stokes concludes that clientelism involving upfront payments will be more common with poorer voters located in low population communities with strong social networks that are weakly opposed to the machine party. She tests these predictions using survey data from an Argentinian province. However, the model focuses only on upfront vote-buying rather than the narrower definition of clientelism. By fixing policies exogenously, it does not examine implications of clientelism for policy choices of elected politicians. Nor does it allow for the challenger to behave strategically in response.

Robinson and Verdier (2013) examine consequences of clientelism for policy choices. They construct a model in which clientelism takes the form of promises to provide public sector jobs by an incumbent patron, conditional on winning the next election. Public sector job offers are credible because public enterprises generate rents for politicians; by contrast, cash payments are not credible since these are costly ex post. Similar to Stokes (2005), their model is based on an asymmetry between the incumbent and the challenger: the latter is passive and unable to offer public sector job offers conditional on being elected. The model delivers over-employment in the public sector (as this enables the incumbent to garner more votes), as well as under-investment in activities that raise private sector productivity (as this helps relax incentive constraints for voters who are offered public sector jobs). These phenomena also appear in a version of the model where votes are unobservable—the incumbent credibly provides jobs only to a specific voter group conditional on winning; these voters are then incentivized to vote for the incumbent.

Politician credibility also plays a key role in the theory of Keefer and Vlaicu (2008), in which clientelism appears as an alternative to programmatic politics which is rendered infeasible when politicians are unable to credibly commit to deliver on promises expressed in electoral platforms. They argue this is an important problem in "young" democracies, where politicians have yet to develop nationwide reputations. Consequently they are forced into strategies of entering into clientelistic deals with brokers or patrons of specific voter groups that have sufficient credibility to deliver their votes in exchange for supplies of private benefits. This results in overprovision of private benefits and underprovision of public goods.

Bardhan and Mookherjee (2012) and Sarkar (2014), on the other hand, construct models of clientelistic electoral competition that abstract from the problem of credibility of politicians. They focus instead on voter incentives and implications for policy outcomes and political competition. In the Bardhan-Mookherjee model, votes are monitored stochastically by party operatives; those (among expressed supporters) discovered to have deviated to voting for the opposition party are denied the benefits. Effects of clientelism are contrasted with those of elite capture: a bias in favor of transfers of private benefits to poor voters in the former, in contrast to elites in the latter. In the Sarkar model, pre-election expression of support is observed by both parties (as it takes the form of public signals such as attendance in political rallies), whence voting for the party whose rally he attends is incentive-compatible even in the absence of any party monitoring. Both models have the feature that (a) there is underprovision of public goods and overprovision of private benefits; (b) more private transfers are provided to poor voters as the marginal utility of these transfers is larger for them, making their votes cheaper to buy; and (c) vote shares depend on voter beliefs concerning which party will win the election (which Sarkar refers to as "contagious voting"). The latter feature implies the possibility of multiple "sunspot" equilibria, with different sets of self-fulfilling beliefs. A party that is more favored to win can buy votes more cheaply, as voters are more willing to enter into deals with them, and the favorite then does win with higher probability. Hence clientelist politics can give rise to reversals of fortune among competing political parties driven by fluctuating voter beliefs rather than changes in any fundamental characteristics. While such phenomena are known to be possible in models of strategic voting with three or more contesting parties, clientelism renders it possible even with two contestants.

Bardhan and Mookherjee (2018) present a theoretical model comparing effects of clientelistic politics with programmatic politics, which embeds the Dixit-Londregan (1996) theory of programmatic politics and clientelistic politics as special cases. Clientelistic practices are rendered possible owing to the existence of a large informal sector, comprising households whose access to state services is at the discretion of elected politicians. This enables electoral contestants to threaten to withhold service delivery to informal sector citizens that do not extend their political support. Such strategies can be implemented by organizing pre-election rallies where attendance of citizens is publicly observable (or other means of public expression of support such as waving election banners in the streets or in one's house); post-election service deliveries to individual citizens are conditioned on such public expressions of support. This dispenses with the need for candidates to monitor votes cast, since those attending the rally of a given candidate have a natural incentive to subsequently vote for that candidate. Decisions of informal sector citizens regarding which candidate to support has instrumental consequences for their own access to state services, as the latter is jeopardized if the candidate they backed loses the election.

This generates two distinctive implications for the way citizens in the informal sector vote, compared to those in the formal sector. First, informal sector votes are unaffected by public good components of electoral platforms, or their perceptions of corruption of rival candidates. Second, they generate the phenomenon of "contagious voting" described above. The first feature implies that politicians have low incentives to provide public goods or engage in less corruption. The second feature implies inherent lopsidedness of electoral competition resulting in large asymmetries in vote shares driven by voter beliefs rather than substantive differences among candidates. Equilibrium policy platforms diverge, with the favored candidate relying more on directed private transfers at the expense of public goods to mobilize voter support. Natural dynamic extensions of this model yield pro-incumbency advantages and low political turnover. In contrast, societies with a large formal sector are more likely to exhibit policy convergence even if one party has an advantage in terms of popularity on non-policy grounds; both parties select platforms involving higher supplies of public goods.

The model shows that welfare comparison between resulting outcomes of clientelistic politics and programmatic politics is ambiguous in general. Directed private benefits are biased in favor of poorer citizens, unless they are substantially less amenable to switch votes on the basis of material inducements. At the same time, clientelism is associated with lower supplies of public goods which tend to benefit all citizens in a similar way.

Hence clientelistic politics can result in greater redistribution. On the other hand, this can be offset by adverse welfare effects of lower supply of public goods. To the extent that growth rates are related more to public goods such as investment in infrastructure, public health, or general education rather than private transfers, clientelistic societies can exhibit lower growth rates. The likelihood of a low-level societal trap is accentuated by reluctance of political incumbents to reduce the size of the informal sector, since this could mean jeopardizing an important component of their political support.

2.4. EMPIRICAL EVIDENCE

2.4.1. Association of Clientelism Measures with Targeted versus Non-Targeted Program Delivery

Keefer (2007) tests the Keefer-Vlaicu theory of differences between young and mature democracies with respect to measures of targeted transfers (proportion of GDP accounted for by wage bill and public investment) and non-targeted benefits (rule of law, bureaucratic quality, low corruption, government share of newspapers, secondary school enrollment rates). In a cross-section of nearly a hundred countries, these are shown to be significantly related to number of years of competitive elections as predicted by the theory, after controlling for population, GDP per capita, land area, age structure, percentage of rural population. The cross-country regression raises obvious concerns regarding omitted variables/alternative explanations and reverse causality (whereby non-targeted benefits enhance persistence of democracy). The author shows the results are unaffected by additionally controlling for a number of omitted variables such as political institutions, fractionalization, conflict, and voter information.

These identification concerns are overcome in an RCT experiment in Benin by Wantchekon (2003), in which presidential candidates were persuaded to alter their campaign speech in randomly selected villages. In one out of six villages per district they delivered a speech focusing only on transfers targeted to village residents (in the form of jobs, subsidies, and local public goods); in another they focused on national goals (national unity, poverty reduction, growth, improving the judicial system, protection of environment, and women/child rights). In the remaining four control villages, the campaigns focused on both sets of goals. Villages promised targeted benefits scored on average 10% higher votes than the control, while those promised non-targeted benefits scored 5% less than the control. However, this experiment pertains mainly to relative popularity of targeted versus non-targeted policy goals. It does not say much about voter support for clientelistic politics relative to programmatic politics, both of which are compatible with targeted transfers.

2.4.2. Household Survey–Based Evidence on Benefit Distribution

Stokes (2005) uses a survey of 1,920 voters from three Argentina provinces during 2001–2002 to test some of the predictions of her theoretical model. Across these voters, political patronage in the form of material goods received from political parties in a recent campaign, or promises of help and jobs when needed, were negatively correlated with voter income, education, housing quality, and village population. They were positively correlated with receipt of ballots from party operatives and expression of support for the Peronist party (the main source of benefits). With the exception of the correlation with ballots received, all the other correlations are also consistent with programmatic politics. Hence while the results are suggestive, they do not provide definitive evidence of the existence of clientelistic politics rather than programmatic politics.

Bardhan et al. (2009, 2015a) conducted household surveys for 2,400 households in 89 villages of West Bengal, India, to examine how receipt of different kinds of benefits from local governments and political parties were correlated with expressions of support for alternative parties. They distinguish between recurring and one-time benefits. The former include employment in food for work programs, subsidized loans, agricultural inputs, and help during personal emergencies, for which every household is eligible every year, irrespective of past receipt patterns. These are all private, directed transfers. One-time benefits include local public goods, such as access to roads and drinking water, and private benefits, such as provision of land titles, low-income houses, toilets, or certificates that entitle recipients to food and fuel subsidies. Recurring benefits are more conducive to sustaining clientelistic relationships involving repeated interaction between parties and voters; a recipient of a one-time benefit has no incentive to continue to vote for the party that provided the benefit since continued provision of the benefit is not feasible. They find a significant positive correlation between receipt of recurring benefits and political support for the incumbent, while the corresponding correlation with receipt of one-time benefits is statistically indistinguishable from zero. These results obtain after controlling for village dummies and a large range of household characteristics.

However, these results are subject to two sets of concerns. First, while the correlations are consistent with clientelistic politics, they are also consistent with programmatic politics. In the latter, citizens may respond more favorably to electoral platforms promising delivery of recurring benefits, as anticipated future benefits could be larger for recurring benefits in terms of their expected present value, even if the flows of these benefits are less significant than one-time benefits in any given period. Second, there could be concerns about omitted variables or endogeneity, as the studies did not attempt to isolate effects of exogenous sources of variation in benefit distribution. For instance, it is possible that incumbents distribute more recurring benefits to their supporters for ideological reasons, as in a citizen candidate model. In that case voter support would be positively correlated with benefits received, and one might erroneously infer the presence of clientelism.

One possible response to this concern is that under the alternative hypothesis, one would expect the incumbent party to also distribute more one-time benefits to its supporters. Hence assuming that one-time benefits are valued at least as much as recurring benefits by recipients, one would expect at least a similar correlation between one-time benefits and voter support. Recent papers by Bardhan et al. (2015b) and Dey and Sen (2016) directly address these endogeneity concerns in the context of services delivered by local governments in the Indian state of West Bengal. The former authors use a political redistricting shock as an instrument for variation in different kinds of benefits (interacted with household characteristics) by local governments. Local government jurisdictions that were redistricted into more competitive constituencies in state and national elections, and controlled by the same party at upper and lower levels, received larger budgetary allotments for recurring benefit programs than one-time benefit programs. Such redistricting was created by an impartial judicial commission in response to past demographic shifts, and was thus plausibly exogenous. Using the combination of redistricting to more competitive constituencies and political alignment as an instrument, this permits the authors to examine the implications of resulting flows of different benefit programs on political support expressed by residents. Both the least squares and instrumental variable double difference estimates show a significant positive coefficient of recurring benefits received on political support expressed, unlike one-time benefits and local public goods. Dey and Sen (2016) use a regression discontinuity approach based on outcomes of close elections in 2008 which changed political alignment between village councils and the next higher tier of local governments. They show that aligned constituencies received larger allotment of benefits from employment-generating schemes; this raised the vote share of the incumbent by 2% in the subsequent (2013) election.

Direct evidence concerning vote-buying is provided by Khemani (2015) using household surveys in a province in the Philippines. Thirty-eight percent of respondents were aware of vote-buying in their village, and 18% reported receiving offers personally. She shows that the village average proportion of reported vote-buying was significantly negatively correlated with health workers, projects, and proportion of children with normal weight, across a sample of 60 villages. Controls included village poverty, population, location, road quality, as well as measures of electoral competition, mayoral power within the village, municipal fiscal capacity, and distance to municipal center. Similar results obtain from a cross-country study of 33 African states using Afro-barometer data. While the direct use of vote-buying prevalence represents an advance, the study is vulnerable to obvious concerns regarding interpretation, such as whether the vote-buying is a cause of low health service provision. In particular, there is no indication of sources of variation of vote-buying across villages, a question of interest in its own right.

Larreguy, Marshall, and Querubín (2016) provide evidence concerning one plausibly exogenous determinant of variation in vote-buying across different parts of rural Mexico: the fit or overlap between rural communal land areas or ejidos and electoral constituencies. A closer fit permits political parties to more precisely evaluate vote delivery efforts of local brokers, rendering clientelistic contracts more effective as instruments of vote mobilization. Using data from local municipal elections between 1994 and 2010, they show that PRI votes are positively correlated with fit interacted with PRI incumbency at the state level, while provisions of schools and teachers per capita are negatively correlated. Controls include overlap, PRI state incumbency, municipality fixed effects, and state-year dummies. Consistent with the identification assumption, fit by itself had an insignificant effect. While the sources of variation of fit are not explained, it is hard to establish plausible alternative explanations for the results on the basis of programmatic politics hypotheses.

In summary, empirical work has shown evidence consistent with hypotheses of clientelistic politics both across countries as well as within developing and middle-income countries such as Argentina, Benin, India, Mexico, and Philippines. However, many of these studies are vulnerable to econometric concerns, besides the criticism that many of these patterns could be exhibited by programmatic politics as well. The literature has been progressing lately in various directions to address these concerns.

A number of recent experimental papers provide interesting insights into the political culture of clientelism, e.g., citizen normative assessments of vote-buying practices and the role they play in measurement and incidence of the phenomenon. Under-reporting of vote buying is highlighted by Gonzalez-Ocantos et al. (2012) in the context of Nicaraguan household surveys following the 2008 municipal elections. They design a "list experiment" in which households are asked to report the total number of activities carried out by party operatives in their respective neighborhoods, from among a pre-specified list. The experiment contrasts responses between randomly chosen treatment and control groups who differ only with regard to vote-buying solicitations as a listed activity among others that do not raise significant moral concerns. Comparisons of the number of activities reported provides an estimate of vote-buying that is less likely to be biased, compared with direct questions inquiring about vote buying. Comparisons of the list estimate with direct household surveys provide a measure of under-reporting in the latter. The list estimate they obtain is 25% of the population who report having received vote-buying offers, as against only 2% in direct household surveys. Somewhat in contrast to most other studies, reported vote-buying is not higher for poorer or less educated voters.

Gonzalez-Ocantos, de Jonge, and Nickerson (2014) provide evidence concerning normative evaluations of vote-buying by citizens of five Latin American countries, as expressed by responses to hypothetical questions. On average more than three out of four respondents consider the practice unacceptable, and 5–10% consider it acceptable. Practices wherein parties reward loyal supporters are considered less objectionable than when they use benefits as bribes to purchase the loyalty of swing voters. In Uruguay and Bolivia, more educated respondents were more approving of low-income citizens selling their votes, suggesting they trade off concrete redistributive benefits with adverse systemic consequences.

Leight, Pande, and Ralston (2016) conduct laboratory experiments in the United States and Kenya, which show that vote-buying reduces voters' willingness to punish politicians for corrupt rent-seeking; politicians in turn respond by appropriating more rents. Vicente and Wantchekon (2009) provide an overview of a number of RCT experiments in Benin and São Tomé e Príncipe which examine the effect of treatments varying with respect to campaign promises by electoral candidates, the role of citizen town meetings, and voter awareness programs. These experiments suggest the role of policies that empower women (who are less responsive to clientelist platforms than men) and voter education initiatives to reduce vote-buying.

2.5. INSTITUTIONAL DYNAMICS AND ECONOMIC DEVELOPMENT

Many scholars (Cox 1987; Mitgang 2000; Lizzeri and Persico 2004; Kitschelt and Wilkinson 2007; Camp, Dixit, and Stokes 2014) have noted that clientelistic political practices tend to decline along the process of development, e.g., in the context of nineteenth- and early twentieth-century history of the United Kingdom and the United States. However, clientelistic practices tend to persist in some countries and contexts (especially at the municipal or provincial level even within developed countries). The typical pattern is for clientelistic politics to be replaced by programmatic politics.

There is likely to be a two-way interaction between such institutional changes and economic development. There has been considerably greater discussion of why development may undermine clientelistic practices: these are elaborated below. Effects going in the opposite direction are also likely, given the arguments and evidence for how sub-stitution of clientelistic by programmatic politics is likely to improve governance, raise spending on health and education, and generate public goods rather than directed private transfers.

Stokes (2005, 2007) and Kitschelt and Wilkinson (2007) describe a variety of reasons why development would cause clientelistic practices to erode:

- As voter incomes rise, their price goes up, rendering vote-buying more expensive for parties.
- As areas become better connected and societies become more mobile, social networks in traditional rural societies become less effective, thereby lowering the ability of brokers to monitor voters and mediate clientelist transactions.
- Expansion of the formal sector reduces dependence of citizens on elected officials for favors.
- Voters become less dependent on local community or party leaders for their livelihoods as opportunities to out-migrate rise.
- As income and risk-bearing capacity increase, people are less dependent on the insurance functions provided by local patrons or caste/clan network.
- Citizen demand for public, non-targeted benefits (such as public health, education, infrastructure, low corruption, better governance quality) relative to targeted benefits increases as they escape extreme poverty and graduate from manual farm employment to self-employment, particularly in non-agricultural enterprises.
- Citizens become more aware of mis-governance or social costs of vote-buying owing to spread of media and information through various sources.
- Costs of programmatic political advertising decline, owing to development of technology of mass media.

In the context of nineteenth-century Britain, Cox (1987) and Lizzeri and Persico (2004) argue that the extension of the franchise was an important cause of the decline in vote-buying: it made it progressively more difficult for legislators to win elections by purchasing small swing constituencies. This however gives rise to the question of what motivated the franchise extension, an issue that has been the subject of a considerable debate (Acemoglu and Robinson 2000; Lizzeri and Persico 2004). Cox (1987) also stresses other changes in political institutions, such as the growing power of the executive branch of government over the legislative branch.

While these are all plausible reasons, there is little solid empirical evidence on either of them, or assessment of their relative strength. An exception is Vicente (2014), who uses an experiment involving randomized rollout of an education/awareness campaign concerning the ill effects of vote-buying in the West African islands of São Tomé e Príncipe, which succeeded in lowering reported levels of vote-buying.

An important factor contributing to the decline of clientelism is the growth of non-discretionary entitlement programs: growth of programmatic politics crowds out clientelistic politics. For instance, a popular account for the decline of clientelistic practices in local New York or Boston politics during the middle of the twentieth century was the creation of Social Security in the 1930s, which delivered financial benefits directly to poorer sections of the population, rendering them less dependent on local party machines.

A number of recent papers provide evidence from Mexico and Brazil of similar effects resulting from land reforms and CCT programs. De Janvry, Gonzalez-Navarro, and Sadoulet (2014) and Dower and Pfutze (2015) provide evidence that PROCEDE, a program that created individual property rights in land in rural Mexico between 1993 and 2006, caused a shift in votes toward PAN, a more right-wing party compared to the PRI, which tended to be the incumbent party in most areas. They use a difference-of-difference regression utilizing the program's rollout across different parts of Mexico. De Janvry et al. ascribe this to two possible reasons: those receiving titles became more market-oriented, and a decline in clientelism as local party officials could no longer allocate use rights on a discretionary basis depending on political support. The possible role of the former is suggested by the fact that the rightward shift was more pronounced in areas where the land was more valuable. Dower and Pfutze argue in contrast that most of the change can be ascribed to a decline in clientelism, as the effect appeared only in areas where the PRI had been traditionally entrenched. Moreover, the effect was symmetric irrespective of whether the main opponent of the PRI was to the right or the left of the PRI, and the same mechanism with opposite results occurred in municipalities where some non-PRI party was traditionally entrenched.

Similar results have been observed in Brazil as a consequence of the recent growth of Bolsa Familia (BF), a large CCT program covering 12 million households. BF was designed to be a nationwide formula-driven entitlement program administered by the federal government, with cash transfers deposited directly into beneficiary bank accounts. Fried (2012) provides evidence that BF delivery was politically neutral: program coverage deviations from planned targets exhibited quantitatively small correlations of the "wrong" sign with various political criteria such as local vote share of the federal incumbent party PT, measures of local political competition, and swing characteristics. Frey (2015) examines the impact of BF coverage using an instrumental variable regression discontinuity design. He estimates that a 10% increase in BF coverage reduced the incumbency advantage of local mayors by 8%, increased political competition (lowering victory margins by 6%, raising the number of candidates by 0.6, and educational qualifications of candidates), lowered private campaign contributions to incumbents by 40%, and increased healthcare and education spending shares by 2–3%.

These studies give rise to the question of what drove the political motivation for incumbents benefiting from clientelistic practices to implement entitlement programs that would undermine those practices. One possible explanation is an intent to promote economic development, as a result of some external shocks, combined with a lack of concern or awareness for political consequences. De Janvry et al. (2014) ascribe the motivation for PROCEDE as appearing from suggestions of technocratic economists within the PRI administration that were concerned to implement land reforms that would raise productivity of Mexican farmers and allow them to compete better with North American farmers as NAFTA came into effect from the mid-'90s onward.

Another explanation may lie in political incentives at the federal versus local levels. Mitgang (2000) describes Franklin D. Roosevelt's decision as governor of New York State to institute anti-corruption inquiries against Jimmy Walker, charismatic mayor of New York in the early 1930s and head of the Democratic party machine from which Roosevelt had himself emerged. These inquiries led to the political downfall of Walker and the party machine. Mitgang's account suggests that Roosevelt's motive was to raise his national reputation and credibility as a presidential candidate. In a similar vein, Larreguy, Marshall, and Trucco (2015) provide evidence that CORETT, an urban land titling program in Mexico for squatters, generated political gains for the party that was incumbent at the federal level, while resulting in political losses for the same party where it was the incumbent at the municipal level (and even larger losses for other parties that were local incumbents). These losses owed presumably to a decline in scope for clientelistic practices which tend to arise mainly at the municipality level.

2.6. CONCLUSION

In this overview of the existing literature, we focused mainly on political clientelism: how it differs from programmatic politics, and how development may be accompanied and aided by a transition from the former to the latter. There is a large literature in comparative politics on clientelistic politics in developing and middle-income countries which is primarily descriptive, with limited formalization in terms of theoretical modeling and econometric analysis. More formal quantitative analyses have begun to emerge recently. We argued the key analytical distinction between clientelism and programmatic pork-barrel politics in terms of discretion exercised by elected officials in the targeting of public benefits. Such discretion is facilitated in countries with a large informal sector, where property rights are not well-defined and judicial institutions are weak, leaving room for political favoritism in law enforcement. The models explain how clientelism generates lopsided political competition, pro-incumbency, and political hysteresis, greater biases in favor of directed private transfers to swing constituencies at the expense of public goods, and in favor of public sector employment and other recurring benefits at the expense of one-time benefits. In terms of welfare consequences, the models predict that clientelism is likely to generate static redistribution in favor of the poor, at the expense of growth and long-term poverty reduction. It may also create a vested interest among political incumbents to perpetuate weakness of institutions that permit clientelism to thrive and their own grip on power to be maintained.

Empirical research has been plagued with difficulties in measurement and identification, similar to most research on corruption. Most of the available evidence is indirect, but there are recent studies based on direct evidence and on plausible identification strategies. There are a few historical studies regarding the dynamics of clientelism along the process of economic and institutional development, which largely confirm theoretical expectations that a rise in programmatic politics (at the federal level) in the form of nationwide entitlement programs and property right reforms cause clientelistic practices (at the local level) to erode.

Future research is expected to provide more detailed and credible empirical evidence concerning prevalence of clientelism, its static and dynamic consequences. In addition, the following questions could also receive more attention:

- Are there any welfare or redistributive benefits from clientelism? The fact that clientelistic programs tend to be directed to the poor has been pointed out by many scholars and verified in a number of empirical studies. Holland (2016) argues that the related phenomenon of forbearance allows elected politicians greater opportunities to redistribute benefits to the poor, free from legislative or judicial oversight. Programmatic redistributive programs are bound by layers of bureaucracy and red tape because of their need to cope with such oversight. Munshi and Rosenzweig (2015) argue that ethnic politics in India where caste groups play an important role has the virtue of generating higher club goods to members of those groups based on threats of community sanctions. These overcome problems of free-riding and the tendency of elected politicians to not honor pre-election promises. On the other hand, caste leaders tend to favor their own caste members at the expense of other castes in the targeting of redistributive private goods. To the extent that there are clientelistic elements in caste based politics, this suggests there are both welfare benefits and costs of such practices. In particular, the threat of informal community-based sanctions in political clientelism may provide some disciplinary role for elected leaders. Incorporation of such factors in the theoretical model developed so far would render ambiguous the implications of clientelism for public good delivery. This implies the need for further empirical studies on this issue.[5]

- The theoretical models and empirical evidence suggest that clientelism may induce greater static redistribution to poorer and more vulnerable groups, as their votes are "cheaper to buy." But this could come at the expense of supply of public goods, which include infrastructure and better governance, which thereby ends up lowering growth. Is there any evidence that clientelism is a possible source of such a trade-off between static redistribution and growth? What are the consequences for the dynamics of poverty?

- How does the presence of clientelism affect the trade-off between political centralization and decentralization? Are regional parties or local governments more prone to clientelistic practices than national parties or the federal government? If so, decentralization may be associated with higher clientelism. This may provide an additional element to consider in debates concerning fiscal federalism, as argued in Mookherjee (2015).

- The welfare implications of political reservations on the basis of ethnicity or gender may depend on the prevalence of clientelism. For example, caste-based reservations of political office may generate greater clientelism, which may provide an explanation for the effectiveness of such reservations in promoting targeting to disadvantaged groups (as argued by Bardhan and Mookherjee 2012). However, it may also aggravate the welfare distortions associated with clientelism, such as bias in favor of recurring private benefits, lowered political competition, and supply of public goods.

- Theoretical models predict that clientelism enhances a tendency toward strategic voting and multiple equilibria, even in a two-party system, besides lowering political competition. It may also provide a source of incumbency advantages. These propositions could be tested empirically. There may also be deleterious effects of clientelism on incentives for political participation of citizens in the middle class who belong to the formal sector, because of the induced incentives to politicians to "pander" to poorer citizens in the informal sector.

- What are the implications of clientelism for selection of political leaders, or for the allocation of talent between the private and public sectors?

- Is there evidence concerning "forbearance": might political incumbents have an incentive to deliberately prevent formalization of agents in the informal sector, secure (e.g., legally guaranteed) property rights, or rule of law, in order to preserve their incumbency via clientelistic means? More generally, might clientelism be a source of endogenous perpetuation of informalization and insecurity, and weak state capacity more generally?
- Much more work is needed on questions concerning the institutional dynamics of political clientelism. Why does clientelism tend to erode more in some countries than in others along the process of development? Is there evidence of the role of increased incomes, mobility, communications, literacy, citizen awareness in the decline of clientelism? To what extent does declining clientelism contribute to economic development, and what are the specific channels (e.g., greater spending on health and education, other public goods, lowered forbearance)?

NOTES

Survey article prepared for the Economic Development and Institutions (EDI) research network. The chapter has benefited from comments of a referee and EDI conference participants.
1. See Hicken (2011) for an extensive survey of these studies.
2. Holland therefore argues that weaknesses in state capacity may owe partly to the unwillingness of elected politicians to enforce regulations rather than an inherent lack of capacity, with examples from a number of Latin American countries.
3. The broader definition could be phrased as follows: "where political agents deliver benefits selectively to voters in return for their votes, or in a manner calculated to induce them to reciprocate with their votes."
4. In some contexts a reverse pattern has been manifested: e.g., in Argentina, Levitsky (2001, 2003) argues that the decline in labor unions in the wake of globalization, privatization, and technical change in the late twentieth century witnessed the metamorphosis of the Peronist party from labor politics to machine politics.
5. In this connection, greater care should be taken to identify which publicly provided benefits are truly public and which are more in the nature of private transfers. For instance, how would one classify education, when a large part of government educational spending takes the form of high teacher salaries which may actually constitute private transfers?

REFERENCES

Acemoglu, D., and J. Robinson. 2000. "Why Did the West Extend the Franchise?" *Quarterly Journal of Economics* 115: 1167–1199.

Bardhan, P., S. Mitra, D. Mookherjee, and A. Nath. 2014. "Changing Voting Patterns in Rural West Bengal: Role of Clientelism and Local Public Goods." *Economic and Political Weekly*, March 15, 54–62.

Bardhan, P., S. Mitra, D. Mookherjee, and A. Sarkar. 2009. "Local Democracy and Clientelism: Implications for Political Stability in Rural West Bengal." *Economic and Political Weekly* 44, no. 9 (February 28): 46–58.

Bardhan, P., S. Mitra, D. Mookherjee, and A. Sarkar. 2015a. "Political Participation, Clientelism and Targeting of Local Government Programs: Analysis of Survey Results from Rural West Bengal, India." In *Is Decentralization Good for Development?* edited by J. P. Faguet and C. Poschl. New York: Oxford University Press.

———. 2015b. "Resource Transfers to Local Governments: Political Manipulation and Voting Patterns in West Bengal." Working Paper, Boston University.

Bardhan, P., and D. Mookherjee. 2012. "Political Clientelism-cum-Capture: Theory and Evidence from West Bengal." Working Paper, Institute for Economic Development, Boston University.

———. 2018. "A Theory of Clientelistic Politics versus Programmatic Politics." Working Paper, Department of Economics, Boston University.

Björkman, L. 2013. "You Can't Buy a Vote: Cash and Community in a Mumbai Election." MMG working paper 13–01, Max Planck Institute for Ethnicity and Religion.

Camp, E., A. Dixit, and S. Stokes. 2014. "Catalyst or Cause? Legislation and the Demise of Machine Politics in Britain and the US." *Legislative Studies Quarterly* 39(4): 559–592.

Chubb, J. 1982. *Patronage, Power and Poverty in Southern Italy*. Cambridge: Cambridge University Press.

Cox, G. 1987. *The Efficient Secret*. Cambridge: Cambridge University Press.

Dal Bó, E. 2007. "Bribing Voters." *American Journal of Political Science* 51(4): 789–903.

Dekel, E., M. O. Jackson, and A.Wolinsky. 2008. "Vote-Buying: General Elections." *Journal of Political Economy* 116(2): 351–380.

de Janvry, A., M. Gonzalez-Navarro, and E. Sadoulet. 2014. "Are Land Reforms Granting Complete Property Rights Politically Risky? Electoral Outcomes of Mexico's Certification Program." *Journal of Development Economics* 110: 216–225.

Dey, S., and K. Sen. 2016. "Is Partisan Alignment Electorally Rewarding? Evidence from Village Council Elections in India." IZA Working Paper No. 9994.

Dixit, A., and J. Londregan. 1996."The Determinants of Success of Special Interests in Redistributive Politics." *Journal of Politics* 58, no. 4 (November): 1132–1155.

Dower, P. C., and T. Pfutze. 2015. "Vote Suppression and Insecure Property Rights." *Journal of Development Economics* 114(C): 1–19.

Finan, F., and L. Schechter. 2012."Vote-Buying and Reciprocity." *Econometrica* 80(2): 863–882.

Frey, A. 2015. "Cash Transfers, Clientelism and Political Enfranchisement: Evidence from Brazil." Working Paper, University of British Columbia.

Fried, B. 2012. "Distributive Politics and Conditional Cash Transfers." *World Development* 40(5): 1042–1053.

Golden, M. A. 2000. "Political Patronage, Bureaucracy and Corruption in Postwar Italy." Russell Sage Foundation working paper.

Gonzalez Ocantos, E., C. K. de Jonge, C. Melendez, J. Osorio, and D. W. Nickerson. 2012. "Vote-Buying and Social Desirability Bias: Experimental Evidence from Nicaragua." *American Journal of Political Science* 56(1): 202–217.

Gonzalez Ocantos, E., C. K. de Jonge, and D. W. Nickerson. 2014. "The Conditionality of Vote-Buying Norms: Experimental Evidence from Latin America." *American Journal of Political Science* 58(1): 197–211.

Graziano, L. 1976. "A Conceptual Framework for the Study of Clientelistic Behavior." *European Journal of Political Research* 4(2): 149–174.

Hicken, A. 2011. "Clientelism." *Annual Review of Political Science* 14: 289–310.

Holland, A. 2016. "Forbearance." *American Political Science Review* 110(2): 232–246.

Keefer, P. 2007. "Clientelism, Credibility and Policy Choices of Young Democracies." *American Journal of Political Science* 51(4): 804–821.

Keefer, P., and R. Vlaicu. 2008. "Democracy, Credibility and Clientelism." *Journal of Law, Economics and Organization* 24(2): 371–406.

Khemani, S. 2015. "Buying Votes versus Supplying Public Services." *Journal of Development Economics* 117: 84–93.

Kitschelt, H., and S. Wilkinson. 2007. *Patrons, Clients and Policies: Patterns of Democratic Accountability and Political Competition*. Cambridge and New York: Cambridge University Press.

Larreguy, H., J. Marshall, and P. Querubín. 2016. "Parties, Brokers and Voter Mobilization." *American Political Science Review* 110(1): 160–179.

Larreguy, H., J. Marshall, and L. Trucco. 2015. "Breaking Clientelism or Rewarding Incumbents? Evidence from the Urban Titling Program in Mexico." Working Paper, Department of Government, Harvard University.

Leight, J., R. Pande, and L. Ralston. 2016. "Value for Money? Vote-Buying and Politician Accountability in the Laboratory." Working Paper, Department of Economics, Williams College.

Levitsky, S. 2001. "Transforming Labor-Based Parties in Latin America." Working Paper no. 288, Department of Government, Harvard University.

———. 2003. "From Labor Politics to Machine Politics." *Latin American Research Review* 38(3): 3–35.

Lizzeri, A., and N. Persico. 2004. "Why Did the Elites Extend the Suffrage?" *Quarterly Journal of Economics*, 707–765.

Marcolongo, G. 2017. "Vote-Buying: When the Broker Observes the Voters' Needs." Working Paper, Department of Economics, Boston University.

Mitgang, H. 2000. *Once Upon a Time in New York*. New York: Simon & Schuster.

Mookherjee, D. 2015. "Political Decentralization." *Annual Reviews of Economics* 7: 231–249.

Munshi, K., and M. Rosenzweig. 2015. "Insiders and Outsiders: Local Ethnic Politics and Public Good Provision." Working Paper, Yale University.

Rizzo, T. 2015. "Motivated Brokers." SSRN id 2619843, Working Paper, MIT.

Robinson, J., and T. Verdier. 2013. "The Political Economy of Clientelism." *Scandivanian Journal of Economics* 115(2): 260–291.

Sarkar, A. 2014. "Clientelism, Contagious Voting and Quality of Electoral Institutions." Working Paper, Economics Research Unit, Indian Statistical Institute, Kolkata.

Stanton, M. 2003. *The Prince of Providence.* New York: Random House.

Stokes, S. 2005. "Perverse Accountability: A Formal Model of Machine Politics with Evidence from Argentina." *American Political Science Review* 99(3): 315–325.

———. 2007. "Is Vote-Buying Undemocratic?" In *Vote-Buying: Who What When and How?*, edited by F. Schaffer. Boulder, CO: Lynne Rienner.

Vicente, P. 2014. "Is Vote-Buying Effective?' *Economic Journal* 124: 356–387.

Vicente, P., and L. Wantchekon. 2009. "Clientelism and Vote-Buying: Lessons from Field Experiments in African Elections." *Oxford Review of Economic Policy* 25(2): 292–305.

Wantchekon, L. 2003. "Clientelism and Voting Behavior." *World Politics* 55: 399–422.

3

FORMAL INSTITUTIONS AND DEVELOPMENT IN LOW-INCOME COUNTRIES

Positive and Normative Theory

Ragnar Torvik

3.1. INTRODUCTION

Institutions have emerged as a main, and possibly the main, explanation for income differences between countries. In this chapter, I aim to give an overview of parts of the literature on institutions, point out lessons and shortcomings, discuss policy implications, identify what questions the literature has not yet addressed, and propose future directions for this literature.

The chapter has three main parts. In the first part, section 3.2, the effect of formal institutions on economic development is discussed. There seems to be a broad agreement that institutions are first-order determinants of growth. There is more disagreement on how natural resource abundance affects growth—is it abundance in itself that affects growth, or is it the interaction with institutions that is crucial? Proponents of the so-called resource curse argue that natural resources lower economic growth, retard democracy, and cause civil conflict. Opponents argue that there are no such robust effects. The disagreement exists largely because neither the proponents nor the opponents have convincing empirical evidence to back their claims. Those who argue that natural resources are likely to have adverse economic and political effects use measures of resource abundance that are likely to bias results in favor of a resource curse. Likewise, those who claim there is no curse use measures of resource abundance that likely bias the results in their direction. To date, no one has established a convincing exogenous cross-country measure of resource abundance.

However, in any case the resource curse is not a "curse." For every Nigeria or Venezuela, there is a Norway or a Botswana. In some countries, natural resources have induced prosperity. In others, they have induced poverty. It can be argued that the literature has asked the least relevant question. Oil probably induces poverty in Nigeria but prosperity in Norway. Is the most interesting question then to measure the average effect of oil on growth in Nigeria and Norway? Furthermore, if the average effect of oil on growth in Nigeria and Norway is negative, does this really mean that oil is a curse?

The second main part of the chapter, section 3.3, discusses what forces shape institutions and how institutions evolve. Historically, institutions have developed under the influence of the interplay between resource endowments and political power. For example, the income divergence between North America and Latin America is seen as a result of divergence in institutions, again traced back to different factor endowments interacted with the initial distribution of political power. Natural resources may thus influence institutions, and it may even be that those with current political power have an incentive to erode institutions when such resources are discovered, or when their value increases. Moreover, it seems that institutions often change in a direction that is in the interest of politicians, but not of the society at large. In particular, presidentialism seems an equilibrium constitution in many weakly institutionalized countries, while parliamentarism does not.

This section also discusses recent literature that argues that institutions endogenously cluster, and that development failures in different dimensions typically go hand in hand.

The third main part of the chapter, section 3.4, takes a normative view of endogenous institutions, asking first how institutions *should* be designed, and puts emphasis on how this depends on the initial equilibrium in society. I term this context-dependent institutional design. This seems to be a main area where the payoff from policy advice is high, but the literature thin.

Second, section 3.4 examines the political economy of institutional reform, studying how reform can be designed under the additional constraint that reform is on the political equilibrium path. I discuss some previous studies that have examined this issue, but a main shortcoming of the literature so far is that it contains few guidelines on how reform should be designed and implemented when those with political power see it in their own interest to block it. This is, it is argued, a main question to which researchers should turn.

3.2. INSTITUTIONS AND ECONOMIC PERFORMANCE

Following North and Thomas (1973), Hall and Jones (1999), and Acemoglu, Johnson, and Robinson (2001, 2002, 2005a, 2005b), the literature on institutions has become one of the most influential in the social sciences in recent decades. The main message in this literature is that institutions are main driving forces in explaining cross-country income differences.

North (1991: 97) asserts that "Institutions are the humanly devised constraints that structure political, economic and social interaction. They consist of both informal constraints (sanctions, taboos, customs, traditions, and codes of conduct), and formal rules (constitutions, laws, property rights)." This is a very broad definition of institutions, in that it encompasses dimensions of institutions one would often label as norms, such as taboos and codes of conduct. The definition is fully consistent with the understanding of institutions in Baland, Bourguignon, Platteau, and Verdier (this volume), however, and to explain the coevolution of economic interaction and institutional development over time, it seems clear that such informal constraints are important. In particular, in early small-scale societies such constraints may be the only institutions that structure inter-action. Formal rules became important at much later stages of development, when socie-ties had expanded from bands, groups, and tribes into cities, states, and nations. Bowles and Gintis (2013) provide an overview of the long-term endogenous coevolution of human cooperation, culture, and institutions. They emphasize that "The distinctive human ca-pacity for institution-building and cultural transmission of learned behaviour allowed social preferences to proliferate. Our ancestors used their capacities to learn from one another and to transmit information to create distinctive social environments. The re-sulting institutional and cultural niches reduced the costs borne by altruistic co operators and increased the costs of free-riding" (p. 197). In this view, therefore, institutions are key not only in explaining why some nations are much richer than others, but in explain-ing the very evolution of humans themselves, as well as why they are so successful compared with other species.

Greif (1993) shows another example of the historical importance of institutions, dis-cussing how eleventh-century Maghribi traders developed institutions to support im-personal exchange relations. Traders needed agents to organize and operate trade in the Mediterranean, and because of uncertainty and imperfect information, these traders had the potential to pocket part of the income. The Maghribi traders developed a network with information exchange and punishment to avoid this, and these interactions with the agents were not based on legal contracts, but were an "institution that might be called a coalition" (p. 526) with "constraints that supported the operation of a reputation mech-anism that enabled the Maghribi traders to overcome the commitment problem. In turn, the reputation mechanism reinforced the coalition on which the coalition was based."

In discussing present-day income differences between countries, the importance of institutions also as formal rules increases. In the remainder of this chapter, institutions as informal constraints such as taboos and customs will not be discussed. This is not to say that they are unimportant. Nevertheless, it seems useful to limit the scope of our discussion: other chapters in this volume have, as a main emphasis, the study and evo-lution of informal institutions. Thus, in this chapter, only formal institutions in the defi-nition of Baland, Bourguignon, Platteau, and Verdier (this volume) will be discussed.

Even when leaving out a discussion of institutions as informal constraints, there are additional key issues on which one must take a stand. In particular, one may have the view that institutions exist because they are efficient from the point of view of society—and if not, they would be changed; an equilibrium institution is an efficient institution. In this view, it is challenging to argue that a main cause for cross-country income differ-ences is institutions. An alternative view is that institutions may be, and are often likely to be, inefficient. Different actors may have different preferences over which institutions they prefer, and these preferences reflect their power. Those with substantial political power may prefer very different institutions compared with those with little power. Those who are economically privileged may prefer very different institutions from those who are not, and so on. Institutions allocate power, including the power to shape insti-tutions themselves, as I will revisit later in the chapter. In this view, there is little or noth-ing that guarantees that, from the point of view of society, equilibrium institutions are efficient. Different agents have different preferences over institutions, and it is unlikely that all of these preferences coincide with the institutions that are the most desirable from the point of view of society.

Formal institutions allocate political power to some actors in society. In reality, however, the political power of actors can also be highly dependent on their connections, their resources, their standing in society, and so on. Acemoglu et al. (2005a) distinguish between de jure and de facto power to separate the two. The equilibrium outcome with regard to political and economic power (and, as I will discuss, the evolution of institutions) is to be found in the interaction of de jure and de facto power.

Why do institutions affect economic outcomes? According to North (1991: 97), "Throughout history, institutions have been devised by human beings to create order and reduce uncertainty in exchange. Together with the standard constraints of economics they define the choice set and therefore determine transaction and production costs and hence the profitability and feasibility of engaging in economic activity."

Several influential econometric studies, and in particular Hall and Jones (1999), Acemoglu et al. (2001), Easterly and Levine (2003), and Rodrik, Subramanian, and Trebbi (2004), have been decisive in promoting the view that a main driver of international income differences is the quality of institutions. A common denominator in these studies is that they acknowledge that it is not sufficient to simply look at the correlation between income and some measure of institutional quality. First, countries with high income may more easily adopt, afford, or prefer some types of institutions. In such cases of reverse causality, one cannot interpret the correlation between institutions and income as causal. Second, there may be omitted variables that are correlated with both income and institutions, in which case a correlation between institutions and income cannot be interpreted as the causal effect from institutions to income.

3.2.1. Which Institutions Matter?

The influential contributions noted above use measures of institutions that are closely related to the security of property rights (these property rights being secure both against expropriation from other private actors and from the government). According to Bardhan (2005: 500), "This preoccupation of the literature with the institution of security of property rights, often to the exclusion of other important institutions, severely limits our understanding of the development process." The strength of this critique, however, can be questioned. First, authors such as Acemoglu et al. (2001) perform robustness tests where they show that their results also hold using other measures of institutions. Second, and possibly more important, is that what matters is probably a cluster of institutions. In the interpretation of Acemoglu (2005: 1041), "In Acemoglu, Johnson and Robinson (2001), we defined a broad cluster of institutions as a combination of economic, political, social, and legal institutions that are mutually reinforcing." One implication of this is that searching for which particular institutional dimension matters may be futile. Another implication, little studied in the literature so far, is what this means for the normative question regarding institutional design and reform implementation. I return to this issue at the end of the chapter, when I discuss endogenous institutions and reform.

Nevertheless, although one may hold the view that clusters of institutions are most important, it should also be of interest to shed light on which particular parts of such clusters are the most important. Here I briefly review two important institutional characteristics in the existing literature: democracy and forms of government.

3.2.1.1. Democracy

A long-standing controversy is whether democracy promotes economic growth. Barro (1996) investigates how growth rates are affected by democracy, and finds that when controlling for other explanatory variables such as education, rule of law, and investment, "the overall effect of democracy on growth is weakly negative" (p. 23). There are, however, several issues with Barro's analysis, in addition to it having the well-known challenges of standard cross-country regressions. In particular, one could argue that democracy stimulates growth exactly by promoting education, rule of law, and investment. Thus, it is not obvious that controlling for these when investigating the effects of democracy is the best way to proceed. Tavares and Wacziarg (2001) investigate this issue further, arguing that, "In theory, if a comprehensive institution such as democracy matters, it should matter indirectly through its effect on variables that in turn determine economic growth" (p. 1342). They aim to identify the channels by which democracy affects growth, finding that it increases growth through the accumulation of human capital and, to some extent, by lowering income inequality, whereas it decreases growth by lowering the rate of physical capital accumulation.

Rigobon and Rodrik (2005) compare democracy and rule of law and find that the rule of law is more important in explaining income differences than democracy, but that both have a positive effect on income. Gerring et al. (2005) review the literature on democracy and growth, and conclude that democracy has a small negative or zero effect on growth. This literature is challenged by Acemoglu et al. (2018), who point out many weaknesses with previous studies and then use democratizations in countries in the same region to instrument for democratization in a country. Thus, compared to previous studies, they obtain exogenous variation in democratizations that can be used to identify the causal effect of democracy on growth. They find that democratization increases GDP per capita by 20% in the 25 years after democratization. Moreover, they investigate the mechanisms, finding support for democracy increasing income through higher investment, economic reforms, increased provision of public goods, and by reduced social unrest. An interesting interaction is that democracy seems to be more growth-enhancing the higher the educational level of the population.

3.2.1.2. Form of Government

All countries in Latin America, and most countries in Africa, have presidential systems. Linz (1978) suggests that presidential democracies tend to be less stable and more prone to coups. If this assertion holds true, then, because a typical result in many studies is that political instability reduces growth, a likely implication is that presidentialism is an obstacle to growth. Persson, Roland, and Tabellini (2000) argue that presidential systems have lower levels of taxation, less public spending, and less rents than parliamentary systems. Persson and Tabellini (2003) find empirical support for smaller governments in presidential countries, while there seems to be no robust empirical evidence that presidentialism is associated with less rents. Robinson and Torvik (2016) develop a theory of presidentialism and parliamentarism that contains the opposite result of Persson et al. (1997, 2000), in that presidentialism is associated with worse policy outcomes: less of the public income is used to provide public goods, and more is transferred to the political elite. The reason for this difference is that in Robinson and Torvik (2016), presidentialism is not about strengthening checks and balances as in Persson et al. (1997, 2000), but is rather a vehicle to monopolize economic and political power. Thus, the economic outcome becomes less efficient. One way to view these results is that presidentialism works better when other institutions are strong in the first place, while in many countries in Latin America, Africa, and Asia, presidentialism concentrates power rather than spreads it. Thus, presidentialism may be particularly damaging to growth in weakly institutionalized countries.

Another main difference in electoral systems is between proportional representation systems and majoritarian systems. Again Persson et al. (1997, 2000) have been influential, developing theories where proportional representation systems have larger governments and more redistribution than majoritarian systems: a prediction that receives empirical support in Persson and Tabellini (2003). There may also be a tendency for more pork-barrel projects in majoritarian regimes. One assertion is that the size of government is smaller in majoritarian systems and that policy is less efficient. The implications for growth, however, are unclear.

A problematic feature with the literature investigating whether specific dimensions of institutions matter is that if it is a cluster of institutions that is important, then the literature may present highly biased estimates. Assume, for instance, a simplified example where two types of institutional characteristics mattered; say democracy and the independence of the legal system. Assume that to have democracy we need some independence of the legal system, and to have independence of the legal system we need to have some degree of democracy. Then, two alternative studies that instrument democracy and independence of the legal system with the same instrument would both conclude that the institutional characteristic they focused on was highly important, although in reality it was the cluster of the two that was important. To address this issue, we would need separate instruments for democracy and for the independence of the legal system. For more on the empirical challenges when clusters of institutions are crucial, see Acemoglu (2005).

Unfortunately, few studies allow for "horse races" between different institutions. An exception is Acemoglu and Johnson (2005), who compare institutions that ensure private property rights with institutions that regulate interactions between private actors. The first type of institution is hypothesized to be dependent on settler mortality and population density in countries being colonized, as in Acemoglu et al. (2001, 2002), while the second is related to the type of legal system and thus hypothesized to depend on the identity of the colonizing country, as in La Porta et al. (1998). Thus, one can establish one instrument for each type of institution. The conclusion is that of the two types of institutions, the only relevant institutions for growth are those related to property rights.

A critique of the macro-data used in the analysis of institutions and growth is presented by Pande and Udry (2005), who find that "The instruments that dominate the literature are based on geography and on colonial and precolonial history. These variables exploit long-term persistent institutional features of a country. The IV strategy purges the estimates of the effect of any institution that change on the path of development, because these are clearly endogenous to the growth process. This, however, implies that the IV strategy by design is not able to identify the consequences of institutional change for growth" (p. 6). Pande and Udry (2005) also have a number of other critiques of the literature, and argue that an empirical strategy that relies more on micro-data and within-country variation is the best way to proceed.

A main challenge in the literature is that to date, we have limited knowledge on which particular institutions are the most important ones in the cluster of institutions that affect growth. Or, and even more challenging—is it a fruitful research avenue to attempt to identify which part of the institutional cluster is the most important?

Moreover, not only do different parts of institutions interact, but institutions also interact with other variables. A main interaction is between institutions and the resource endowments of a country. A huge literature has emerged under the label "the resource curse," initially arguing that richness in natural resources is a curse, and later focusing on whether it is the interaction of natural resources and institutions that may produce low growth (as well as other bad economic and political outcomes). This literature has particular relevance for developing countries not only because many of these are resource abundant and have weak institutions, but also because the results from this literature have implications for the effects of foreign aid, which may sometimes be seen as a close analogy to foreign exchange received from the sale of natural resources. Thus, in the next subsections I review this literature in some detail, starting with the initial literature and then turning attention to more recent contributions that focus on the interaction between natural resources and institutions.

3.2.2. The Resource Curse

Since the 1950s, conventional wisdom has been that countries specializing in resource exports would be growth losers. Due to elasticity pessimism and technology optimism, the price of natural resources would fall relative to those of industrial goods. Engel effects meant that the demand for natural resources would not keep up with income, low price elasticities would lead to increased supply that depressed prices, and technological development would result in products that relied less on raw materials. Paradoxically, today some economists argue that specialization in resource exports may be unattractive for exactly the opposite reason: it is so profitable that it may in fact turn into a curse.

Initial theoretical models by van Wijnbergen (1984) and Krugman (1987), and initial case studies by Gelb (1988) and Karl (1997), showed that petroleum resources could have negative economic as well as political effects. Interest in this topic accelerated, however, with the claim by Sachs and Warner (1995) that these were not only isolated examples, but in fact a pattern that could be generalized: resource abundance is bad for economic growth.

The initial empirical literature starting with Sachs and Warner (1995) can be divided into two parts. The first part of the literature finds that resources are bad for outcomes such as growth, democracy, and violent conflict. The second part of the literature finds that there is no such connection, or even that resources are good for such outcomes. Unfortunately, both strands of the literature use measures of resource abundance that are likely to drive their conclusions.

3.2.2.1. Measures of Resource Abundance

The seminal cross-country study on the resource curse by Sachs and Warner (1995) measures resource abundance by natural resource exports as a share of GDP, and finds a negative correlation between resource abundance and growth rates in the period 1965–1990. In their study, Sachs and Warner also control for variables such as initial income level, openness of the economy, institutional quality, education, etc. Their measure of resource abundance is likely to overestimate the negative influence of natural resources on growth. An often-used argument for this, however, is an unconvincing one: because resources are measured as a share of GDP, rich countries will, other things being equal, be measured as resource poor, while poor countries will be measured as resource rich. Although this is correct when the measure is viewed in isolation, the studies that use this measure in growth regressions control for initial GDP. Thus, this potential problem is, at least to some degree, dealt with.

Nevertheless, the cross-country regressions are likely to contain biases because of omitted variables. Consider two hypothetical societies. Assume that the culture, the institutions, or some unknown characteristic, makes the incentives for undertaking production better in one of the societies than in the other. In the "good" society, the incentive to undertake production relative to extracting natural resources is then high. In the "bad" society, however, the incentive to extract natural resources relative to undertaking production is high. If the initial income is the same, the "bad" society will derive more income from the extraction of natural resources than the "good" society. It is also likely that the "good" society will have higher growth than the "bad" one. However, the lower growth in the "bad" society is not due to a high natural resource intensity in income. Neither is the high natural resource intensity in income due to low growth. It is the factor that we cannot fully account for that explains both.

Other influential papers that find evidence of a resource curse, but that use different measures, may also overestimate the negative influences of resource abundance. Gylfason (2001) uses a stock measure, rather than a flow measure, of resource abundance. He calculates natural capital as a share of a country's total capital and finds a negative correlation between this measure and variables such as growth, level of GNP, and educational variables. Again, these correlations are interesting, but must be interpreted with caution. In particular, because human capital makes up large parts of a country's total capital, and human capital in turn is calculated as a present value of wages, countries with a high wage level will be measured as resource poor.

Brunnschweiler and Bulte (2008) criticize the use of flow measures such as the ratio of natural resource exports to GDP. In their view, such variables are more likely to measure resource dependence and not resource abundance. They argue that a better measure of resource abundance would reflect resource stocks, but unlike Gylfason (2001) they do not measure resource stocks as a percentage of total capital. Using resource stocks, they find no evidence of a resource curse. Rather, they find that resource abundance positively affects both growth and institutional quality. Their data and method have been challenged by van der Ploeg and Poelhekke (2010), however, who point out that the stock measures used by Brunnschweiler and Bulte (2008) are derived from flow measures.

In a similar spirit to Brunnschweiler and Bulte (2008), Alexeev and Conrad (2009) argue that the findings of a resource curse "are due mostly to misinterpretation of the available data" (p. 598). Alexeev and Conrad (2009) use variables such as hydrocarbon deposits per capita and value of oil output per capita. They conclude that "high endowments of oil and other minerals have a positive impact on per capita GDP" (p. 592), and that "natural resource endowments positively affect long-term growth rates of countries."

Using oil reserves or oil production as a measure of resource abundance, however, is likely to introduce biases that portray oil as having more favorable effects than what is the reality. Well-functioning countries that have long been industrialized may have discovered more of their subsoil assets, leading to such successful countries being measured as resource abundant. For instance, Collier (2010) compares the value of known subsoil assets per square kilometer in countries with high GDP to those with low GDP. In the former, the value of known subsoil assets is four times the value in the latter. It is reasonable to assert that at least part of this difference is because more of the existing reserves have been discovered in successful countries than in unsuccessful countries. Cust and Harding (2017), using a regression discontinuity design, find that at national borders, exploration companies drill on the side with the best institutions two times out of three. Thus, the studies that use (known) resource wealth or resource production as a measure of resource abundance are likely to overestimate the eventual positive effects of natural resource abundance.

3.2.2.2. GDP Growth and GDP Level

Obviously, in the long run the countries with high GDP growth rates will be equivalent to those with a high level of GDP. Still, these two measures of economic success are not equivalent. The initial literature arguing for a resource curse uses growth rates over a period of a few recent decades, controlling for initial income. Alexeev and Conrad (2009) argue that this may bias the results in favor of a resource curse because "it is possible that a large oil endowment results in high growth rates in the early stages of extraction and slower rates when oil deposits mature" (p. 586). In this way, slow growth in mature oil economies may be a natural, and even an optimal, response. Alexeev and Conrad (2009) argue that using GDP levels is preferable.

A common problem with GDP measures—whether growth rates or levels—is a flaw in the calculation of GDP for countries that extract nonrenewable resources. When oil is extracted and sold, this is calculated as income. It is not. To see the logic, consider another type of public wealth; say the government owns some financial assets that it then sells off and buys some other assets. The sales of these financial assets should not be considered income in GDP. The government has simply changed its allocation of wealth. In the same way, the sale of a barrel of oil is not income. It is exchanging natural resource wealth for another type of wealth. However, in the GDP accounts, selling off oil wealth is included as income. The GDP estimates of oil economies are therefore inflated. Using GDP levels to argue that oil is beneficial to a country, therefore, may suggest that oil economies are wealthier than they are (for GDP growth rates, the bias may go both ways).

It is likely that the effect of natural resources has changed over time. In the countries with strong institutions, which industrialized first, natural resources contributed to this industrialization. In the countries with weak institutions, that did not industrialize, natural resources may have been exploited later and had a different impact, as I discuss below. Using GDP levels hides the historical heterogeneity, averaging those who did well and those who did badly.

3.2.3. Institutions and the Resource Curse

Sachs and Warner (1995) resorted to a Dutch disease explanation for their finding of a resource curse. They assumed that the spending of resource income crowds out activities that generate learning and growth. Investigating whether the curse operates through institutions (which they measure with bureaucratic efficiency), they ask if institutions are endogenous to resources. They do not find that resources influence institutions, and conclude that the curse "does **not** appear to work through the bureaucracy effect" (p. 19; bold in original). However, as argued by Mehlum, Moene, and Torvik (2006), even if institutions are not endogenous to resources, the resource curse may operate through institutions. Resource abundance may simply have different effects depending on the initial institutions in place. Indeed, this is the result obtained by Mehlum et al. (2006). When institutions are grabber friendly, that is, when they provide weak protection of property rights, have ill-functioning legal systems, and are not able to control corruption, then resource abundance correlates with lower growth. In contrast, when institutions are producer friendly, resource abundance correlates with higher growth. Countries with institutional quality in the top 20% escape the resource curse.

Boschini, Pettersson, and Roine (2007) use instruments for institutional quality and obtain similar results, while Collier and Goderis (2012) obtain similar results using panel data. These findings do not imply that the Dutch disease literature is irrelevant. However, overspending and Dutch disease are more likely an outcome of the resource curse than a cause. As emphasized by Robinson and Torvik (2005) and Robinson, Torvik, and Verdier (2006, 2014), when institutions invite patronage to secure political support, countries are especially prone to overspending, bad quality investments, and low growth. Matsen, Natvik, and Torvik (2016) develop a theory to explain why voters may, even when they are fully rational, reward politicians with stronger political support when they choose a less efficient oil extraction path.

Andersen and Aslaksen (2008) find that resources lower growth in presidential democracies, but not in parliamentary democracies. A likely explanation for this is that, with the exception of the US presidential system, most presidential systems concentrate substantial power in the hands of the president. This makes institutions in such countries less inclusive than in those with parliamentary institutions, where the prime minister depends on the continuous support of the legislature.

Bulte and Damania (2008) find that resource abundance is more likely to cause negative outcomes in autocracies than in democracies. Arezki and Brückner (2012) find that increased export prices lead to a reduction of external debt in democracies, but not in autocracies. Cabrales and Hauk (2010) develop a political economy model where resource abundance crowds in human capital accumulation when institutions are good, but crowds it out when they are bad, and they find empirical support for such an effect. Boschini et al. (2007) find that lootable resources, in combination with weak institutions, have the worst growth effects. A combination of diamonds and grabber-friendly institutions puts a country at the bottom of the list. Van der Ploeg and Poelhekke (2009) argue that the resource curse is less pronounced in countries with well-developed financial institutions. Arezki, Hamilton, and Kazimov (2011) conclude that negative effects "of resource windfalls on macroeconomic stability and economic growth are moderated by the quality of political institutions" (p. 14).

Robinson and Torvik (2013) develop a simple theory of the conditional resource curse, showing how the comparative statics of the equilibrium depend on institutions. With strong checks and balances, a resource discovery increases income by more than the value of the discovery. The reason is that the resources crowd in other productive activity. With checks and balances absent, however, a resource discovery decreases total income. The reason is that, in such a case, resources crowd in destructive activity. In turn, this makes productive activity even less profitable, crowding in destructive activity further. With weak institutions, a resource discovery has a multiplier effect. However, the bad news is that the multiplier is negative.

The resource curse literature has been too occupied with studying the average effect of resource abundance. The more interesting question is why oil induces prosperity in some places but poverty in others. The recent literature has identified several dimensions in which the countries where resources have contributed to prosperity differ from the countries where resources have contributed to poverty. This literature suggests that the key differences arise because of differences in political and private incentives. These differences, in turn, can be traced back to differences in institutions. For a review of the literature on institutions and the conditional resource curse, see Torvik (2009).

Institutions may also themselves be endogenous to resource abundance. They are equilibrium outcomes. Historically, there is little doubt that resource endowments, be they represented by the availability of slaves, silver and gold, or arable land, have been fundamental in shaping institutions. However, the impact of resource abundance on institutions seems not only to be of historical interest. Why did voters in Venezuela allow President Hugo Chávez to monopolize power by dismantling checks and balances? Why did dictators in Egypt and Tunisia leave power when the demand for democracy increased, while in Saudi Arabia and Bahrain they did not? Why did the civil war end in Mozambique when resources dried up after the cold war, while in Angola, where UNITA controlled diamonds and MPLA oil, it went on for another 10 years? It is difficult to argue that the answers to these questions are unrelated to natural resources. However, they are not *only* related to natural resources; they are also related to initial institutions.

Institutional quality is, in several dimensions, the common denominator in the literature on the conditional resource curse. Much of the empirical literature to date, however, concentrates on correlations. As with the cross-country literature that focuses on the average effect of resource abundance discussed above, this raises obvious concerns related to omitted variables and endogenous measures of resource abundance.

To date, a main problem with the resource curse literature is that no one has been able to develop a truly exogenous cross-country measure of resource abundance. Another shortcoming of the literature is, as I discuss below, its normative implications: what does it imply for the design of policy and of institutions?

3.3. ENDOGENOUS INSTITUTIONS: POSITIVE APPROACHES

In the previous sections, institutions were seen as exogenous features of the economy. If institutions affect growth, either by themselves or through interaction with other country characteristics, the obvious next question is: what determines institutions?

I consider this question in the remainder of the chapter, and I discuss positive as well as normative approaches to endogenous institutions. Moreover, the normative design of institutions involves both how this design should depend on initial institutions, and also which institutional designs represent a political equilibrium.

Institutions allocate power. Those with economic and political power have the opportunity, and the incentives, to choose institutions that preserve their power. Therefore, institutions tend to reproduce. This implies that institutions are shaped by history, and, through this channel, by variables such as natural resource endowments. However, at the same time it also means that institutions may change when, for instance, resource endowments, or their value, change. The discovery of new natural resources, or a price increase that makes existing resources more valuable, may demand new types of institutions to utilize the new opportunities.

North (1991: 97) points out that institutions "evolve incrementally, connecting the past with the present and the future; history in consequence is largely a story of institutional evolution in which the historical performance of economies can only be understood as a part of a sequential story. Institutions provide the incentive structure of an economy; as that structure evolves, it shapes the direction of economic change towards growth, stagnation, or decline."

I start by discussing several dimensions of the broad question of positive institutional development, before I turn to the normative question of how institutions and institutional reform should be designed in the next section.

3.3.1. Does Growth Produce Democratic Institutions?

A key policy question is if one should insist on developing countries being democratic. Most social scientists would probably subscribe to the view that democratic values are, by themselves and by the rights they imply, of first-order importance for the well-being of citizens. However, an alternative view may hold that for developing countries, democracy may follow growth and that for this reason, if one succeeds in achieving growth, then a by-product of that will be democratization. A possible consequence of such a view is that for developing countries it is more important to achieve growth than democracy. However, to be able to discuss this normative question one must first clarify whether economic growth produces democratic institutions.

The view that economic growth leads to democracy is most famously associated with the modernization hypothesis of Lipset (1959). It is a well-documented fact that income and democracy are strongly correlated, and many authors, such as Barro (1996), interpret this relationship as causal, running from income to democracy. Barro (1999) also finds that if democracy occurs at low levels of development, then it is unstable. The causal interpretation of the literature is challenged by Acemoglu et al. (2008), who argue that the previous literature is troubled by reverse causality in that democracy may produce high income levels, and it is also troubled by omitted variable bias in that there are common factors not controlled for that explain the simultaneous existence of both high growth and democracy. They show that with country-fixed effects, and also with instruments for income, there is no causal effect of income on democracy. Their interpretation is that economic and political development are interwoven, in that some countries followed a path of dictatorship, repression, and low growth, whereas others followed a path of democracy and economic growth. This view is broadly consistent with the main thesis in Besley and Persson (2011) that development typically clusters, which I will return to below.

Cervellati et al. (2014) revisit the study of Acemoglu et al. (2008) and find that there are important and significant heterogeneous effects of income on democracy. In particular, among former colonies, higher income retards democracy, while in noncolonies, it promotes it. This is a very important extension for many developing countries, showing that the view that income growth can be achieved first and democracy later is even less relevant than what the results in Acemoglu et al. (2008) suggest.

In modernization theory, causality runs from income to democracy. However, a large body of recent research argues that causality mainly runs in the opposite direction. It is the presence of inclusive institutions that produces growth, and the presence of extractive institutions that retards it. In turn, a main variable explaining the evolution of extractive versus inclusive institutions is the interplay between resource endowments and initial political power. In these theories, which I review next, the causality can be seen as running from resource endowments to institutions, and then to growth.

3.3.2. Human Capital and Institutions

The modernization hypothesis of Lipset (1959) asserts that one mechanism by which modernization affects institutions is through education, which lays the foundation for democracy. Bourguignon and Verdier (2000) develop a model where political participation depends on the educational level of the population, and where a better-educated population may endogenously crowd in democracy.

Glaeser et al. (2004) argue that Europeans primarily brought human capital to the colonies and not institutions. Based on this, they are critical of the approach of Acemoglu et al. (2001). Institutions may be the result of human capital. The issue of human capital and institutions is discussed at some length in Acemoglu, Gallego, and Robinson (2014), who argue that, in fact, Europeans brought more human capital to their extractive colonies than to their settler colonies. Moreover, based on econometric results, they argue that there is no causal impact of human capital on institutions.

A related possible hypothesis is that education has an interaction effect with the stability of institutions. One could hypothesize, for instance, that the stability of democracy, or of the degree of checks and balances in the constitution, depends on how educated the population is at large. Conditional on democratizing, or conditional on having checks and balances in the constitution, an educated population can more clearly voice opposition when those with political power aim to change institutions back so that they become less inclusive. Furthermore, it may be easier to recruit able opposition leaders in an educated population.

3.3.3. The Evolution of Inclusive and Extractive Institutions

Several influential papers, in particular Sokoloff and Engerman (2000) and Acemoglu et al. (2001), argue that resource endowments have historically been decisive for the emergence and persistence of institutions. Sokoloff and Engerman (2000) discuss colonization of the New World of North and South America, where initially, "most knowledgeable observers regarded the North American mainland to be of relatively marginal economic interest, when compared with the extraordinary opportunities available in the Caribbean and Latin America" (p. 217). Factor endowments were far more lucrative in the latter, resulting in specialized production of sugar and other highly valued crops with the help of slave labor. Income per capita (including slaves) was higher than in the North. However, the lucrative factor endowments and resulting large-scale specialization also meant the establishment of societies with a very unequal distribution of wealth and political power. In turn, this "contributed to the evolution of institutions that protected the privileges of the elites and restricted opportunities for the broad mass of the population to participate fully in the commercial economy even after the abolition of slavery" (p. 221). In contrast, the economies in the North "were not endowed with substantial populations of natives able to provide labor, nor with climate and soils that gave them a comparative advantage in the production of crops characterized by major economies using slave labor" (p. 223). The result was that in the North, production was based on more homogenous laborers in terms of human capital and wealth. Because of the limited economies of scale, they operated as independent proprietors. Thus, economic and political power was less monopolized, in turn opening up for the development of institutions that, according to Acemoglu and Robinson (2012), were more inclusive.

Acemoglu et al. (2001), the authors of one of the most influential papers in economics in recent decades, investigate different colonization strategies, how they depend on factor allocations and diseases in the surrounding environment, and how they shape institutions. Some societies, in particular those where conditions for European settlement are unfavorable, invite a colonial "hit and exploit" strategy. To grab resources, existing institutions must be dismantled and replaced by extractive institutions. The more resources there are to be grabbed, the higher the profitability of extractive institutions. In other societies, where the conditions for European settlement are more favorable, institutions that protect the property rights of those who settle are installed. When settlement is attractive, resources do not attract institutions that favor predatory behavior. If anything, it can be argued that resources here crowd in institutions that secure investment, entrepreneurship, and growth.

Related to this, Acemoglu, Johnson, and Robinson (2002) discuss in detail the effect of population density and urbanization rates on the evolution of extractive institutions. Countries with a high population density and urbanization rate were relatively prosperous, making it tempting for colonizing powers to install extractive institutions. In addition, in such countries it was easier to force the population to work in mines and plantations, which also required extractive institutions. With the industrial revolution, those places where extractive institutions had been introduced failed to be able to invest to take advantage of the new income opportunities.[1]

As shown by Acemoglu, Johnson, and Robinson (2005b), colonization did not only affect institutions in the colonized countries differently, it also had different impacts on institutions in the colonizing powers. The resources in the New World provided increased potential for trade. In Portugal and Spain there were few checks on the monarchy and thus, "it was the monarchy and groups allied with it that were the main beneficiaries of the early profits from Atlantic trade and plunder, and groups favouring changes in political institutions did not become powerful enough to induce them" (p. 551). This view is consistent with North and Thomas (1973), who point out that the incomes from silver and gold from the American colonies freed the Spanish monarchy from the constraints of the parliament. Atlantic trade made institutions less inclusive. In the Netherlands and Britain, however, there were more checks on royal power, and "the rise in Atlantic trade enriched and strengthened commercial interests outside the royal circle and enabled them to demand and obtain the institutional changes necessary for economic growth" (Acemoglu et al. 2005b). In particular, "Checks on royal power and prerogatives emerged only when groups that favoured them, that is commercial interests outside the royal circle, became sufficiently powerful politically" (p. 550). In the Netherlands and Britain, therefore, the number and political strength of private entrepreneurs grew, in turn demanding institutions where the monarchy was weakened and opportunities for private businesses improved. Institutions in Spain and Portugal diverged from those in the

Netherlands and Britain. The different political development, in turn, contributed to divergence in economic outcomes.

3.3.4. Endogenous Institutions and the Resource Curse

Examples of how resource abundance may have shaped institutions more recently are given in Ross (2001a). Ross shows that in several Southeast Asian countries, timber booms resulted in politicians demolishing institutions deliberately. The timber gave politicians a way to earn big money—but to do so, they had to dismantle the institutions that were set up to protect the forests. Rather than institution-building, politicians were incentivized to engage in institution destruction. Resource abundance makes it more attractive for politicians to have fewer checks on their power, and if there are weak checks on their power in the first place, then such a further weakening is feasible.

It is perhaps not surprising that political leaders find fewer checks and balances attractive when natural resources are plentiful. Indeed, the conventional wisdom in the literature, such as Persson et al. (2000), is that when there are few checks and balances, politicians are able to grab more rents. In this way checks and balances are bad for politicians, but good for the citizens. According to the standard paradigm, therefore, voters should be highly in favor of checks and balances in the political system. As pointed out by Acemoglu et al. (2013), however, voters in several resource-abundant Latin American countries have willingly, sometimes enthusiastically, removed checks and balances on their presidents. In Venezuela, shortly after his election in 1998, President Hugo Chávez rewrote the constitution and in 1999, 72% of the people who voted supported his move to a unicameral legislature, reallocating powers to himself. Later, several additional changes, for instance the removal of term limits, weakened checks and balances further, again with the approval of voters. Similarly, after winning the 2006 election in Ecuador, President Rafael Correa rewrote the constitution, moving to a unicameral legislature and increasing his powers, taking control of monetary policy back from the central bank and gaining the power to suspend the legislature. In 2008, 64% of voters supported the new constitution. In 2009, 61% of Bolivian voters similarly supported a new constitution, significantly increasing Evo Morales's powers.

These examples show that the most widely used paradigm for understanding checks and balances is, by itself, insufficient to understand why voters would dismantle such checks and balances, because it would suggest that voters should prefer maximal checks on presidents. Acemoglu et al. (2013) develop a theory to explain why, in particular in countries with vast natural resources, high income inequality, and/or a rich elite that may influence policy through non-electoral means such as bribing and lobbying, poor voters may find it in their own interest to dismantle checks and balances. Political rents are lower with checks and balances. But this is a double-edged sword, because this also means that politicians are cheaper to bribe. In turn, the rich elite can then buy politicians to obtain a policy more consistent with their own self-interest, in particular a policy with less income redistribution. The more costly this is to the poor, the more there is to gain from income redistribution. Thus, when income inequality is high and the state receives substantial income from natural resources, poor voters may prefer to dismantle checks and balances. By doing so, they realize that they increase the powers of the president, allowing him to grab more rents, but at the same time they insulate him from the influences of the rich. By making President Hugo Chávez strong, they made the rich elite weak.

3.3.5. Democracy and the Resource Curse

We have already seen that with resource abundance, political elites may find it particularly attractive to monopolize economic and political power. A possible way to achieve this is to avoid democracy. Resource income not only provides the incentive to prevent, or delay, a transition to democracy; it also provides the means. The means, in turn, can be a combination of sticks and carrots. The Arab Spring is a particularly interesting recent example. After December 2010, the demand for democracy increased in all countries in the region, but the political outcomes were very different. In oil-poor Egypt and Tunisia, the previous dictators quickly gave in to protests and left power. In oil-rich Libya, by contrast, Muammar Gaddafi decided to use his oil-fueled military machine to fend off the demand for democracy. Had it not been for foreign intervention, he would most likely have succeeded. In Saudi Arabia, the political elite responded in yet a different way, with the king announcing major increases in income transfers to citizens. It seems, at least so far, that he succeeded in paying his way out of democracy.[2] Although the Arab Spring illustrates that political elites have different means to fight democracy, and that the strategy and success may depend on oil abundance, a remaining question is whether, in general, oil retards democracy. The empirical literature suggests that it may.

Ross (2001b) finds that countries rich in oil are, on average, less democratic than other countries, after controlling for income, geography, religion, and so on. Three channels through which this may arise are discussed. The first is through what is termed the rentier effect; oil income can be used to buy off demands for accountability and provide patronage in exchange for political support. This channel relies on carrots. The second relies on sticks and is termed the repression effect. Ross notes that in resource-rich states, "resource wealth may allow the government to spend more on internal security and so block the population's democratic aspirations" (p. 335). The third, termed the modernization effect, states that if resource-based growth implies an economy with less education and fewer high-skill occupations, then the social forces that demand democracy will be weakened.

Haber and Menaldo (2011) rightly criticize the literature for being plagued with omitted variables and reverse causality and ask, "Do natural resources fuel authoritarianism, or is it the other way around? Might it be the case that the only economic sectors that yield rates of return high enough to compensate for expropriation risk in authoritarian states are oil, gas, and minerals, thereby engendering resource reliance?" (p. 3). Using panel data that follow countries over long periods of time, they observe countries prior to becoming resource reliant, and include country-fixed effects. They conclude that "Our results indicate that oil and mineral reliance does not promote dictatorship over the long run. If anything, the opposite is true" (p. 25). It should be noted, however, that this conclusion is not as robust as it may seem. When a country becomes more democratic, it normally becomes more transparent. Increased transparency, in turn, means that data on oil wealth and revenues that were previously hidden become more publicly available. Thus, in a regression with country-fixed effects, a positive correlation between democracy and the proceeds from the oil sector does not imply that oil is good for democracy. It may be that measured oil income or oil wealth increases as a result of countries becoming more democratic. Also using a panel dataset with country-fixed effect, Aslaksen (2010) finds results that are different from those of Haber and Menaldo (2011).[3]

Tsui (2011) argues that the timing and size of oil discoveries are more exogenous than oil production or exports, and finds "that larger oil discoveries are causally linked to slower transitions to democracy" (p. 90). Interestingly, Tsui also finds that "oil discovery has almost no effect for democratic countries" (p. 90). This supports an assertion that it is particularly when institutions are nonrepresentative in the first place that resource abundance may endogenously push them into becoming even less representative. Dunning (2008) discusses several ways in which the effect of resource abundance on democracy is conditional.

A related empirical literature investigates whether politicians in resource-abundant countries succeed in using their resource wealth to secure political support and hold on to their power. According to the leader in *The Economist* of September 29, 2012, "Had it not been for the oil boom, Mr. Chávez would surely have long since become a footnote in Venezuelan history." Although less vocal, the scientific literature on the topic, for instance Andersen and Aslaksen (2013), does find that political leaders in oil-rich countries remain in office longer. Monteiro and Ferraz (2010) find the same for municipalities with oil windfalls in Brazil. Matsen, Natvik, and Torvik (2016) develop a theory model of petro populism.

3.3.6. Installing Weak Property Rights

Another institutional evolution that seems, unfortunately, to have gained increased importance in developing and transition countries in recent decades is that politicians find it in their own interest to introduce weak property rights. This may seem counterintuitive at first, because in many countries they control large amounts of economic resources, and thus they should have an interest in securing property rights. This view, of course, stops short of asking why the politicians became so economically powerful in the first place. Sonin (2003) develops a theory of inequality and the institutional dynamics following transition, motivated by the experience in Russia where "the oligarchs' success at rent-seeking led them to prefer relatively weak protection of property rights and forced other economic agents to invest in private protection from expropriation. Due to the oligarchs' political power, the Russian state has failed to establish and to enforce a system of clearly defined property rights" (p. 716). Thus, given that some narrow but powerful groups have been able to capture the political and economic systems, they may have a strong incentive to make sure institutions are not made more inclusive, as this erodes their economic and political power.

The development of Zimbabwe after independence in 1980 provides another example of the political attractiveness of weak property rights. After monopolizing power and rewarding allies with political patronage, the economy in the 1990s deteriorated at a rapid pace. As a result, receiving patronage became even more important, and at some point, the only economic resources left to hand over were those grabbed from others. To do so, the protection of private property was actively dismantled with the help of the state. This was an effective strategy to maintain political support despite the economy performing poorly. The handing out of patronage in the form of grabbing the assets of others necessitated the dismantling of effective private property rights. In turn, the dismantling of property rights meant that the only option was to rely on political patronage. The Mugabe regime succeeded in making entrepreneurs dependent on the regime, rather than the regime dependent on the entrepreneurs. But how was the Mugabe regime able to monopolize political power in the first place?

3.3.7. Endogenous Presidentialism

The evolution from parliamentarism to presidentialism in Africa shows a remarkable pattern (Robinson and Torvik 2016). When African countries became independent, parliamentary constitutions outnumbered presidential constitutions by 4 to 1. Thereafter, country after country switched from parliamentarism to presidentialism. Currently only three countries that started out with a parliamentary constitution have retained it: Botswana, Mauritius, and South Africa. Interestingly, two of these three, Botswana and Mauritius, are the most economically successful countries in Africa since independence. None of the countries that started out with a presidential constitution have replaced it with a parliamentary one.

The most influential theory comparing parliamentarism and presidentialism in economics is the work of Persson et al. (1997, 2000) discussed above. Their theory is heavily inspired by the US presidential system, viewing presidentialism as a way of introducing strong checks and balances, and thereby preventing the political system from transferring rents from the population to the politicians. It seems, however, that such a view is not representative for presidential regimes in most other countries, be they in Latin America (in which all countries are presidential), in Eastern Europe or the former Soviet Union, or in Africa. Clearly, the desire of Joseph Mobutu to make himself president in 1967, rather than remain prime minister of Congo, represented a reduction in checks and balances. The same can be said for Robert Mugabe in Zimbabwe in 1987, Siaka Stevens in Sierra Leone in 1978, Hastings Banda in Malawi in 1966, and Kwame Nkrumah in Ghana in 1960. In these regimes, the introduction of presidentialism monopolized the political power around the president and his allies. Later changes to the regimes, such as the dismantling of term limits on the presidents, concentrated the power further.

A likely explanation for prime ministers preferring a transformation to presidents, emphasized by Robinson and Torvik (2016), is that it makes them politically stronger in that they do not need continuous political support in the legislature as a prime minister does. This monopolization of power, in turn, makes them grab more rents and provide fewer public goods to the population. Presidents may be supported by their allies even if these allies realize that a president will make himself stronger, because an advantage of a president for the allies is the monopolization of political power within a narrower group. For presidents and their allies this is thus attractive, in particular when there is strong polarization between different groups. For the provision of public goods and economic growth, however, it is disastrous.

A number of institutional characteristics may persist, change, or evolve in line with the interests of a narrow group, because those with the political power also have the power to determine institutional design. Interestingly, there is a strong correlation between different dimensions of institutions, and recent studies examine such institutional clusters and why they emerge.

3.3.8. Endogenous Clustering of Institutions

Besley and Persson (2011) document that different dimensions of institutional quality are highly correlated and are clustered with low levels of development and income. Countries that typically have weak fiscal capacity also have weak legal institutions, nonpeaceful resolution of conflicts, and low levels of income. Development failures in different dimensions occur together. Besley and Persson (2011) develop models of such development clusters, where different dimensions of institutions are complements. For instance, a higher fiscal capacity makes it more attractive to invest in legal capacity that increases income, because then there is more income to tax. Higher legal capacity, which makes income higher, makes it more attractive to invest in fiscal capacity. The clustering of institutions is endogenous. Now consider an incumbent in a country where tax revenues will be narrowly spent to favor the group that happens to be in power. An incumbent in such a regime will have weak incentives to invest in legal and fiscal capacity, because if he loses power, the system will turn against his own interests. If, however, the incumbent has power in a country where tax revenues are spent in a way that has common interests, then even if he loses power he will enjoy the benefits of high fiscal and legal capacity. Such an incumbent will thus have an incentive to invest in institutions with better legal and fiscal capacity.

Besley and Persson (2011) develop a theory of state capacity, which is a cluster of institutions in which the state has the monopoly of violence, the authority and the capacity to enforce laws and raise tax incomes, and the ability to provide public goods. State capacity can be seen as a necessary, although far from sufficient, condition for good institutions. It can be argued that countries such as China, and even North Korea, have high state capacity. But nondemocratic societies lack the mechanisms by which the population ensures that the state capacity is used in a way that is consistent with the interests of the broad segments of the population. As observed by Acemoglu and Robinson (2016: 31) in the context of Rwanda, "If it suits the regime, this state capacity can be used to some extent to provide public goods and promote development. But as Rwandan history so vividly shows, it can also be used to repress and terrorize its people."

According to the paradigm in Acemoglu and Robinson (2012), state capacity must be combined with political power broadly distributed in society if what one may think of as the cluster of inclusive political institutions is to emerge. Acemoglu and Robinson (2016: 2) further argue that state capacity and the broad distribution of political power are interrelated: "In fact, we claim, once one looks closer at how states are built and how power is spread there is a basin of attraction in which these two processes are highly complementary."

Acemoglu et al. (2016) show how state capacity may not be created exactly when it may be most needed. In a system where political power is held by the elite, creating a centralized state induces citizens of different backgrounds, interests, regions, or ethnicities to coordinate their demands in the direction of general-interest public goods, rather than narrow issues that only concern themselves. This change in the political agenda that endogenously follows state centralization, as has been historically documented for instance in Tilly (1995) for the British case, implies that the creation of a central state induces citizens to find a common voice. This makes them stronger against those with political power, and in particular this political agenda effect is powerful when the gain in having general-interest public goods provided is high. Thus, from the view of those with political power, this may be exactly the situation in which they will not find it in their interest to build a centralized state.

3.4. ENDOGENOUS INSTITUTIONS: NORMATIVE APPROACHES

Up until this point, my discussion of endogenous institutions has focused mainly on how and why institutions may take the particular forms they do. In doing so, I have also touched upon normative issues, in that some particular characteristics of institutions have been seen to produce more favorable economic outcomes than others.

I now take the normative dimension one step further and discuss more explicitly how institutions *should* be designed. I divide this discussion into two main parts. First, I discuss what I will term context-dependent institutional design. That is, how should institutions be designed dependent on the initial economic and political equilibrium. Second, I discuss what I will term the political economy of institutional design. That is, how should institutional reform be designed to ensure that it is on the political equilibrium path?

3.4.1. Context-Dependent Institutional Design

Economists often implicitly, or even explicitly, recommend policy based on what standard economic theory suggests is first best, and moreover that this first best is independent of the initial political or economic equilibrium. One example of such a view on policy advice is what the Washington institutions for some time subscribed to, namely that a main, or maybe even the main policy challenge, was "getting prices right." Introduce a market economy, and then prices will be right, and development follows. In this view, there is also scope for institutional design, but the design of institutions has as its main emphasis to make sure market forces are allowed to operate. Most economists today would probably agree that this view is too simplistic, and that unfortunately there are more complicated and challenging forces at work; this implies that one-size-fits-all types of policy advice are not guaranteed to produce favorable outcomes. In the theory of institutions and growth I have discussed so far, institutions have much more important and fundamental roles than ensuring market prices are at correct levels.

This raises the natural question of how institutions should be designed. Rodrik (2004: 2) finds that "the empirical literature on institutions and growth has pointed us in the right direction, but that much more needs to be done before it can be operationalized in any meaningful way. Many of the policy implications drawn from this literature are at best irrelevant and at worst misleading." Although Rodrik does not explain in depth why such policy implications may be misleading, one interpretation is that different forces are at work when institutions are strong compared with when they are weak. It follows that the design of policy or of institutions has different outcome effects in different contexts. This raises the question of how policy and institutional designs should depend on the initial state of society. It seems that this is a field of research that has received little attention, and where it is important to gain additional knowledge.

In particular, Laffont (2005: 245–246) argues that

> a given developing country is characterized by specific values of some crucial parameters such as the cost of public funds (which reflects the quality of the tax system), or the propensity to corruption (which reflects the lack of education, among other things), but also by the quality of institutions such as the quality of democ-

racy, the quality of the judiciary, or the quality of auditing. Policy recommendations for such a country should be based on a model which incorporates all these features. The work needed to obtain the mapping from the characteristics of the country to the policy recommendations is daunting, and probably beyond the capacity of the few researchers in this area.

Laffont nevertheless undertakes a pioneering effort in starting to develop such a view to reform. He concludes, for instance, that

> We have shown that the institution "separation of powers" which can be useful to mitigate the costs created by the opportunism of regulators, is even more valuable in developing countries. This is because these countries suffer from high costs of public funds (due to inefficient tax systems), from low transaction costs of collusion (due to poor auditing and monitoring), and from less efficient technologies. However, the implementation of this institution is more difficult and more costly for the same reasons, leaving us with an ambiguous result if the various weaknesses of these countries are not addressed simultaneously. (p. 242)

Unfortunately, the normative design of policy and the institutions to undertake them has not progressed far since Laffont's contribution. In this subsection of the chapter I aim to shed light on one possible way forward by investigating how policy, and the institutions to undertake it, may be designed to combat the resource curse, and most important why the answer to this may depend on the quality of initial institutions. Arguably, this part of the chapter (along with much of what will be discussed in the subsection on the political economy of institutional design below) is more speculative that the other parts, in that a very simple, and maybe overly simplistic, framework to investigate the issue is set out. This example is drawn from Torvik (2018), which discusses a very simple model of the establishment of a petroleum fund.

3.4.1.1. Example: Petroleum Funds

The setting up of a petroleum fund can contribute to the long-term income potential from resources from oil and gas being achieved, but it can also have the opposite effect. A key determinant is the initial institutions in place. Unfortunately, much policy advice seems to neglect this.

There are several reasons why a petroleum fund may help alleviate the challenges associated with an abundance of oil and gas. A petroleum fund makes policy more based on rules and less the object of day-to-day political decisions. This has the potential to ensure a more long-term perspective on policy. Such a long-term view on the petroleum assets is important for several reasons. First, as what is often termed oil income is not really income in the conventional sense, but selling off one type of asset (nonrenewable assets) and replacing it with another (dollars), a petroleum fund is wealth management. Continuously using the proceeds from the sale of petroleum for consumption is not like using regular income; rather, it involves reducing the stock of assets of a country. Second, consuming too much of the petroleum proceeds in the short run induces a structural shift away from traded and toward (public and private) nontraded sectors, which is not sustainable. It must, at some point, be reversed. The traded industries lost today must be developed again in the future. Given that such redevelopment of industries is more difficult than the original structural shift that caused their demise, such reversals are costly and likely to induce considerable unemployment. Third, a petroleum fund may contribute to investment decisions being based on long-term economic criteria and not day-to-day political decisions. Investment decisions based on political criteria that involve clientelism, patronage, corruption and nepotism has been identified as a main challenge in petroleum-abundant countries (Robinson, Torvik, and Verdier, 2006). Fourth, a petroleum fund ensures the decoupling of resource spending and resource income. Oil prices and production levels are volatile, and a petroleum fund can transform volatile income streams into a stable use of the proceeds from natural resource wealth. This has a stabilization effect on the economy, ensuring that the cycles in the resource sector are not magnified by the use of resource income, and also allows for the provision of public services to be more stable. In conclusion, there are many potential benefits associated with establishing a petroleum fund.

Several petroleum funds, such as the Alaska Permanent Fund and the Government Pension Fund Global in Norway, are widely seen as contributing positively to the management of natural resource wealth. Many countries have drawn inspiration from these institutional designs of petroleum funds. Recently, additional important lessons arose from the petroleum funds operating in Africa. A challenge with the establishment of these funds has been that the initial institutions in place have often been weaker than the institutions that were in place when similar funds were established in North America or Norway. On the one hand, one could argue that this makes the establishment of a petroleum fund more important, as the quality of political decisions on how to spend resource income may be worse, and thus the potential payoffs from establishing a new institution such as a petroleum fund are more important. On the other hand, one could argue that a weak initial institutional and democratic infrastructure makes the establishment of such a fund more risky, as the probability the fund is not managed and used as intended increases. Furthermore, one could argue that the need for public investments is typically higher in African countries than in mature industrialized countries, meaning that the optimal trade-off between current and future spending is shifted toward the present. Then, a petroleum fund, which has as one of its main objectives to save resource income for the future, is less relevant.

Some of the initial experiences with petroleum funds in Africa have not been favorable. One particular example is Chad, which—assisted by the World Bank—established a "future generations fund" where petroleum revenues were set aside. The fund was set up as part of an agreement with the World Bank which involved financing of the pipeline from Chad to the port in Cameroon. However, when political tensions erupted, the fund was raided by the president and spent on the military, and as a response the World Bank aborted their relations with the regime. Another example is Angola, which established its petroleum fund in 2008. In 2013, the son of President Dos Santos became the head of its board. This questions whether or not the petroleum fund is in reality a new way to manage the country's resource wealth, and whether the fund is independent from the current political elite holding power.

The establishment of a petroleum fund means that financial resources should be available for the future. A challenge with such financial resources is that they are lootable. Thus, if institutions are not sufficiently strong to prevent looting, these financial assets may invite rent-seeking, corruption, or grabbing. Thus, more resources may be devoted to such activities, which has negative externalities on the rest of the economy. In addition, it may even be that politicians have incentives to undermine institutions further, if this is what it takes to be able to use the petroleum fund in a way that is of personal benefit to the political elite. This has further negative externalities on the economy, which in turn may worsen if investors today see that in the future, the institutions that were designed to protect them are even less aligned to their interests. In this way, the future institutional and economic equilibrium may be adversely affected by the establishment of a petroleum fund exactly when initial institutions are not sufficiently strong.

Consider an alternative to designing a petroleum fund with financial assets, namely to instead use the proceeds to invest in, for instance, human capital. Such capital is considerably less lootable than financial assets. In fact, to gain income from such capital, politicians must develop tax systems and state capacity. Thus, if anything, the incentives may be aligned with better, rather than worse, institutions. The negative externalities from predatory behavior present under a petroleum fund may thus be mitigated by the presence of a higher level of human capital. In addition, the payoffs of such investments may be high exactly when the level of human capital is low initially.

What constitutes good institutional design, therefore, in this example of whether or not to establish a petroleum fund, may depend heavily on the initial institutional equilibrium. Failing to take this into account may result in policy advice where one assumes that what has worked well in some institutional settings also works well in others. This may have the implication that resource abundance, which works favorably in some institutional settings but not in others, makes resource-abundant countries diverge even more. The same institutional design in these countries in fact has opposite effects.

Glaeser and Shleifer (2003) present an ambitious theory of institutional design to secure property rights, where, "In our theory, whatever law enforcement strategy the society chooses, private individuals will seek to subvert its workings to benefit themselves. The efficiency of alternative institutional arrangements depends in part on their vulnerability to such subversion. The theory leads to predictions as to what institutions are appropriate under what circumstances" (p. 401). In particular, in discussing the relevance for transition and developing economies, they discuss the mapping from the cost of subverting justice—which they term X—to institutional design, to be that "The first, and arguably most important, message of our model is that in situations of extremely low X, the optimal government policy is to do nothing. When the administrative capacity of the government is severely limited, and both its judges and regulators are vulnerable to pressure and corruption, it might be better to accept the existing market failures and externalities than to deal with them through either the administrative or judicial process. For if a country does attempt to correct market failures, justice will be subverted, and resources will be wasted on subversion without successfully controlling market failures" (p. 420). Thus, in this case, the best thing to do is simply give up. Another interpretation is that in such circumstances, the important thing to focus on is to increase the cost of subversion before trying to combat the consequences of low costs of subversion.

Unfortunately, to date, too little knowledge has been obtained on context-dependent institutional design. It is thus hoped that this field will expand in the future, as it seems to be of huge importance for providing advice on policy and institutional design in countries where the initial equilibrium is unfavorable.

3.4.2. Political Economy of Institutional Design

At one level, one could argue that the normative implications obtained from the theory of institutions and economic growth are perhaps obvious: implement the institutional designs that have been shown to promote growth. This, however, does not represent substantial progress on this issue, partly for the reasons discussed in the previous subsection on context-dependent institutional design, but also for an additional main reason: even in cases where it may be clear how institutions should be designed, and how this design should depend on the initial state of institutions, those with the political power may have an interest inconsistent with changing institutions in this direction. Indeed, if the institutional changes that produce a better economic outcome for society are obvious, then why have these institutional changes not already been undertaken? A likely answer is that those with political power see it in their interest to block such reforms. For example: democracy is better for society at large than dictatorship, yet the same may not hold true for the dictator.

Even when all political power rests with the dictator, however, this argument does not fully explain why a change from dictatorship to democracy does not occur. If democracy produces a better outcome for society at large, then the winners from institutional reform can compensate the losers and still be better off. In this way, the institutions we observe are observed precisely because they are efficient. This view probably has few supporters today, and for an obvious reason: promises of such future compensation are not credible. Those that stand to lose political power from institutional change will not be compensated in the future, precisely because they lost political power. Thus, they see it in their interest to block institutional reform, even if such reforms benefit society at large.

Rodrik (1996) discussed the political economy approach to policy reform and institutional design and pointed out that "the normative implications of these models for policy and institutional design have to be worked out" (p. 25). In this section, I review the literature on the political economy of institutional design, and the question that concerns us throughout is: How should reform packages be designed to ensure that they are on the political equilibrium path?

Obviously, the answer to this question depends on the distribution of political power between groups in society, as well as the policy preferences of these groups. Below, I simplify and specify three groups that may have different political power and different preferences with regard to institutional reform: politicians, citizens, and international organizations. Many of the differences between the different contributions in the literature (or the lack of such contributions) can be traced back to how much political power each of these groups has and to differences in their preferences for reform.

3.4.2.1. Economics of Transition: How to Convince Citizens to Support Reform
In the early 1990s, following the collapse of the Soviet Union and the transition from centrally planned to market economies in Eastern Europe, a debate emerged around the political economy of reform. A key topic in this debate was how a democracy might block or reverse reform and what implications such political economy constraints might have for reform design. In this literature, politicians and international organizations were typically assumed to be interested in reform, while, for various reasons, voters might have

incentives to block it. Starting with the assumption that politicians and international organizations wanted reform, the key issue was how to make citizens support it.

In one class of models, the population at large must support reform for it to be undertaken. In these models, the political economy constraint is thus that the reform must be designed so that a majority of citizens support it.

In Fernandez and Rodrik (1991), the voters may block reform because of uncertainty, even if the reform is welfare-improving and voters are risk-neutral. The intuition is that even if a majority of voters gain from reform, it is, ex ante, uncertain who these are. Thus, assume that there are two sectors of the economy, and that those in the state sector lose from the reform but those in the private sector gain from the reform. Prior to the reform, 40% of the voters are in the private sector, while 60% are in the state sector. After the reform, 40% will remain in the state sector, while 60% of the voters will be in the private sector. Let the gain per individual be the same in the private sector as the loss per individual in the state sector. Thus, in this case a majority of individuals gain from reform, and because the individual gain for winners equals the individual gain for losers, reform is also welfare-improving (because there are more winners than losers). Yet in this case, reform will not be undertaken. The 40% in the private sector will support it, while the 60% in the state sector will not. The reason for the latter is that each of the state employees has a probability of one-third of being a winner from the reform, but a probability of two-thirds of being a loser.

Should the reform be undertaken, however, it will not be reversed. After the reform, when uncertainty is revealed, 60% of voters gain and will support it. This shows a rather general feature of institutional reform: it changes not only the economic, but also the political, equilibrium. This is what makes it so challenging to undertake. Those with political power today realize reform will change their equilibrium political power.

A normative implication from this approach is that the revelation of individual uncertainty ahead of reform will make it politically feasible. If the majority gains from reform and the identities of the winners are known, then reform will have majority political support. Another possible solution is to promise that those who lose will be compensated. The obvious problem with this, however, is again that those who lose will be in the future minority, and thus promises that they will receive future compensation are not credible.

In Dewatripont and Roland (1992), the government can either adopt a one-stage reform or let the reform be imposed gradually. When the government can commit to future reforms, those who are losers from the reforms implemented tomorrow may support a reform today, to avoid being losers tomorrow. Thus, the political equilibrium may be reform implementation if it is gradual, but no reform implementation if it is not gradual. In Dewatripont and Roland (1995), there is aggregate uncertainty as to what the effects of reforms are. In this case, they show that there are several arguments for gradual reform. In particular, when there is uncertainty and there are high reversal costs, a big bang reform might be politically infeasible. A gradual reform allows for the possibility of early reversal after some uncertainty has been revealed and thus may attract sufficient political support for it to be launched. Furthermore, when there is strong complementarity among the different elements of the reform package, this may be an argument in favor of gradualism, as launching one part of the reform package may create future political support for another.

One possibility, stressed by Lau, Qian, and Roland (2000), is to ensure that reform is Pareto-improving by designing a policy where the agents that obtain rents under the existing system maintain those under the reform. In particular, they discuss the dual-track system of reforms in China, where "The introduction of the market track provides the opportunity for economic agents who participate in it to be better off, whereas the maintenance of the plan track provides implicit transfers to compensate potential losers from the market liberalization by protecting the status quo rents under the preexisting plan. Thus the dual approach is, by design, Pareto-improving" (p. 122). A crucial element in such a policy package is the commitment to adhere to it. While this may have been possible to achieve at that time in China, it might in many cases be difficult to enact. This is particularly so when those who stand to lose if reforms are changed at a later stage overlap with those who lose political power as a result of the reforms.

It is interesting to note, as does Roland (2002: 42), that the experiences from countries in transition is that, "The sequence of reforms in transition economies are roughly in line with political economy theory, which suggests that reforms expected to be more popular should start first. For example, in all of Central and Eastern Europe, democratic reforms preceded economic reforms. Aspirations for democracy were very strong throughout the region, and support for economic reform was less strong than support for democracy."

In many transition countries today, it seems that we have moved to a situation where it is not the population as such but the economic and political elites that resist institutional change. In this sense, many of the obstacles for institutional reform in the former communist countries have today resulted in the transition ending with a concentration of economic and political power in the hands of a few, who in turn use their political power to maintain the status quo. This leads us to another part of the literature, which in many cases seems more relevant, but unfortunately is also more difficult to develop.

3.4.2.2. Economics of Preserving Power: How to Convince Politicians to Support Reform

The most tricky, but unfortunately most relevant, situation seems to be when citizens support reform but politicians oppose it and have at the same time monopolized power to a sufficient extent that they can block it. This situation indicates that political power and efficiency cannot be studied as separate phenomena. Furthermore, because political power in many cases originates from economic power, arguments that efficiency can be studied separately from income and wealth distribution are too narrow and may even lead to very bad policy advice. Acemoglu and Robinson (2013: 189) stress that

> though much work still remains to be done in clarifying the linkages between economic policies and future political equilibria, our approach does not simply point out that any economic reform might adversely affect future political equilibria. Rather, building on basic political economy insights, it highlights that one should be particularly careful about the political impacts of economic reforms that change the distribution of income or rents in a society in a direction benefiting already powerful groups. In such cases, well intentioned economic policies might tilt the balance of political power even further in favor of dominant groups, creating significant adverse consequences for future political equilibria.

Dixit (1997: 225) also discusses the role of economists as advisors and argues that "The advice must be based on reasoning that includes the political process; it must use game theory and political analysis as well as conventional economic analysis." Dixit uses the example of free trade and finds that "Good advice in this game will tell the politician how to manipulate the game in the ultimate interest of freer trade; 'If we are to succeed, we must understand the motives and strategies of the other players in the game. Here is my judgement of how the various interests will line up and how they will try to counter our moves. To the extent that we can move first and quickly, here is my advice on how we should try to devise the rules of the game — set the agenda or the procedures — to deflect or defeat or hijack their strategies'" (p. 228).

Although these authors pinpoint a main challenge with institutional reform, remaining questions about how to undertake institutional reform when it is welfare-improving but those with political power resist it is an area that has received little attention. The question of how we, in such cases, can design institutional reform in general, and democratization in particular, should receive attention from researchers. As the literature stands today, we recognize the challenge, but how to best deal with it remains largely unknown. For instance, starting with an autocracy, how could those holding political power currently, who stand to lose if democracy is adopted, be convinced that they should still support such a transition? How should reform be designed so that such an outcome constitutes a political equilibrium?

3.4.2.3. Conditionality

Rather than implementing reform using only domestic support, another possibility is to meet domestic political force with foreign political force—which is one way to think about what "conditionality" aims to do. Here, some external actors, international organizations that are donors, demand that if assistance is to be given it should be met with some type of institutional reforms or particular policies. Drazen discusses the role of international organizations and whether they should impose conditionality: "To put it simply, *why is conditionality needed if it is in a country's best interests to undertake the program in question?* This, to my opinion, is a question which IMF documents struggle and often talk around. I will argue that it is basically impossible to justify conditionality in the absence of a conflict of interest of some sort" (2002: 36; italics in original). Drazen shows how, in a case where there is a conflict between a reformist government and domestic interest groups opposing reform, conditionality may affect the political equilibrium so that the reform is undertaken.

A standard way to impose conditionality, previously used frequently by Washington organizations, is to trade assistance for policy. For instance, if assistance is to be given, then the currency shall be devalued, free trade adopted, or some subsidies cut. A problem with this form of conditionality is that it attacks the consequence rather than the cause. Why was the policy in place to start with? Presumably, this is because it favors the politically powerful. Using conditionality to make a change in policy might therefore be an equilibrium in the short run, but is unlikely to be an equilibrium in the long run, unless assistance and conditionality are made permanent. Moreover, specifying a change in one type of policy, which in isolation reduces rents for the politically powerful, might result in compensating behavior in another policy area to avoid rents being reduced.

One possible, and perhaps natural, consequence of this view is that conditionality should be placed on institutional reform, rather than directly on policy. Institutional reforms that change the distribution of political power, say to introduce democracy, might have more permanent effects than placing conditionality directly on policy. Democratic reform changes the political equilibrium, and therefore may be more difficult to reverse. Conditionality that is able to produce permanent changes in the institutional equilibrium will also produce more permanent changes in policy, compared with if conditionality is put on the policy itself.

A counterargument against this view, however, is that it shortcuts the challenge we started with, namely how to make autocracies democratize if it is not in the interest of the current politically powerful. One could argue, therefore, that this type of conditionality is difficult to implement.

In the political economy literature on reform in Eastern Europe, a main argument for those who proposed a big bang approach, in particular associated with Jeffrey Sachs, was the complementarity of reforms. Another argument related to complementarity that may be important to consider is that those with political power who resist institutional reform may not have the power to block all institutional reforms. In such a case, when there is complementarity, inducing reform in one institutional dimension may make it easier to achieve reforms in others. Thus, a possible strategy is to opt for reform in some areas in the hope that it could endogenously result in reforms in others. The literature on the endogenous clustering of institutions suggests that the institutional equilibrium in one dimension depends on the institutional equilibrium in another. Therefore, if one has a better possibility of changing institutions in one dimension than in another, the new equilibrium might also involve a new institutional equilibrium in those institutions one cannot change directly.

Let us briefly consider some possible examples from the literature on how such institutional interdependencies may provide opportunity for institutional change. Admittedly, this is again speculative, as this is not a topic that has been considered in any of the contributions discussed below. Nevertheless, it might be interesting to start developing some possible normative implications from the literature on the endogenous clustering of institutions, by asking how changes in one type of institution may induce change in another.

In Besley and Persson (2011), the higher is the investment in fiscal capacity, the better is the legal capacity. Thus, reforming the legal system may crowd in better state capacity in other dimensions as well. Furthermore, the legal system may be easier to reform than institutions that are more closely under the direct control of politicians. The crowding in effect of legal institutions on other favorable equilibrium institutions is also present in Acemoglu et al. (2013), although for a different reason. Consider a case where, when the quality of the judicial system is poor, the voters respond by removing checks and balances from the constitution because the legal system is not able to prevent politicians being bribed, and the voters therefore want to remove checks and balances to make the president stronger. In this case, a reform to install checks and balances will backfire: it does not constitute a political equilibrium. However, if a reform in the judicial system is undertaken, then a constitution that involves checks and balances is on the political equilibrium path. The intuition for this is that when the legal system is of higher quality, then it is more difficult to bribe politicians, and in turn this removes the incentive for voters to make the president stronger. Thus, as in Besley and Persson (2011), a reform in one institutional dimension induces an equilibrium shift in another institutional dimension.

In Besley and Persson (2011), equilibrium state capacity will be better the more common interest is politics, because then the current political regime need not fear that state capacity will be turned against it should it lose power. Therefore, making policy more common interest crowds in state capacity. Thus, if one is able to achieve this, either through democratization, support for free media, or support for civil organizations, it may increase the equilibrium state capacity. The same comparative statics hold in Acemoglu et al. (2016), albeit again for a different reason. Citizens who organize themselves change the political agenda endogenously in favor of more general-interest public goods and away from parochial transfers. In turn, this removes the incentive of political elites not to centralize the state; an incentive that was present to avoid citizens organizing in the first place. Acemoglu et al. (2016) argue that the emergence of social democratic parties in Scandinavia had such a favorable effect, where

> in countries such as Sweden, Norway and Denmark, social democratic parties formed the nexus of citizen organizations in the first half of the 20th century, and managed to coordinate several aspects of citizen-firm negotiations and other citizen demands. The literature on Scandinavian social democracy emphasizes that it was successful precisely because it built multi-class and multi-sectoral coalitions uniting rural and urban interests . . . Moene and Wallerstein (2006) have suggested that the creation of social democracy in the 1930s, rather than following it, preceded many of the features of Scandinavian societies commonly argued to undergird social democratic politics, such as social harmony. Like our approach, this argument emphasizes how various societal and state institutions respond to the formation of a powerful social democratic party. (p. 28)

3.4.2.4. Windows of Opportunity and Lock-In of Institutions
The strength of political power fluctuates. Institutions are persistent. A possible policy implication of this is that, when a window of opportunity opens, it is important to reform institutions because these may permanently alter the institutional equilibrium, so that when the situation returns to normal this does not imply that the institutional equilibrium is the same as it was before. Using windows of opportunity to change politics rather than institutions may turn out to be less durable.

A related argument is made in Roland (2002: 46), who notes that "One important variable that has not been studied seriously so far by economists is the strength of the noncommunist elites at the beginning of the transition. A closely related point that was made earlier is discussing the strength of civil society in different transition countries. There is a striking difference between Poland, where the Catholic Church and the Solidarity trade union counterbalanced the communist elites, and Russia, where little counterbalance existed to the former members of the communist ruling class who engaged in a frenzy of asset grabbing once it was clear that the communist regime was dead." A lesson for donors and international organizations may again be that, in nondemocratic countries, support for civil society that counterbalances the existing ruling elites may improve the prospects for political and economic development with institutional reform.

However, if institutions are nondemocratic, should one insist on democracy being installed before assistance is given, or should one accept the regime and give support in any case? This is a fundamental question where more research is needed, and for which there are many issues that will not be discussed here. For instance, by giving assistance, is one in danger of reducing the probability of a transition to democracy?

There are some arguments that follow from the literature review above, which imply that pushing for democratization is better than waiting and hoping that growth will come first, and that democracy will follow endogenously. First, as seen in the discussion on whether democracy follows growth, the causal connection here is, at best, unclear. Cervellati et al. (2014) strengthen the argument against the "income first democracy later view" in that in former colonies higher income actually lowers the probability that democracy will arise. An additional argument can be found in Acemoglu et al. (2018), namely that there is an interaction effect of democracy and education on growth, implying that democratization with support for education may give particularly favorable growth effects.

Using strong pressure to encourage early democratization is also an argument in the situation where it is the current holders of power that resist institutional change. With democracy, their future political power is more uncertain and moreover may depend positively on the utility they are able to generate for voters. In this sense, democracy may crowd in other good institutions both because those that currently hold power put increased weight on what happens when they lose power (which now happens with a higher probability than under autocracy), and because the decrease in the survival probability may be smaller if institutions are reformed in a way that produces better outcomes for the population.

Nevertheless, as pointed out by Acemoglu and Robinson (2016), some authors such as Huntington (1968) and Fukuyama (2011, 2014) see democracy as a final step in the creation of good institutions, arguing that if democracy comes ahead of state capacity, there is increased danger that a movement toward good institutions will derail. A counterargument against this view, however, is that if state capacity develops before democracy, then it is always tempting for the powerful to monopolize their political and economic power by using the state capacity in their own self-interest.

3.5. CONCLUDING REMARKS

Few areas have been more influential within economics over the last 15 years than the literature on institutions and economic growth. This literature has opened new avenues of research and has integrated important topics from other social sciences into economics, allowing for a better understanding of development. Two parts of the literature, namely the one on the mapping from institutions to growth, and the positive literature on endogenous institutions, have in particular delivered important new knowledge.

It seems uncontroversial today that institutions are a first-order determinant of prosperity. Moreover, many of the mechanisms by which institutions affect growth are well understood, although a possible area where more research may be needed is to unravel in greater detail which institutions are the most important, as well as how institutions of prosperity cluster and why. Furthermore, the evolution of institutions has benefited from a substantial amount of influential high-quality research, where the political economy approach pioneered in several papers of Acemoglu, Johnson, and Robinson stands out as the most impressive. The terms *extractive* and *inclusive* institutions from Acemoglu and Robinson (2012) are so influential that they have become part of our everyday vocabulary.

With regard to the literature on institutions and growth, Pande and Udry (2005: 3) find that "this literature has served its purpose and is essentially complete." Although this may not be correct, it does suggest that the most important future research challenges are in other areas.

Another part of the literature, namely that on normative endogenous institutions, has to date not progressed significantly. Too much policy advice fails to acknowledge that policy implications are context dependent and implicitly assumes that policies that have been beneficial in some institutional environments, such as petroleum funds, will be equally successful in others. Such policy advice may be very damaging. Economists are partly to blame by failing to develop normative approaches that delineate how policy should depend on the initial context.

Even more challenging is how necessary institutional reform can be implemented when those currently in power see such reforms as being against their own interests. Reforms that work well if they are implemented, but that do not constitute a political equilibrium, have limited usefulness. General equilibrium is a key concept in economics, but must also include political equilibrium. If not, what one refers to as general equilibrium is in fact only a very narrow form of partial equilibrium. A main challenge for the economics profession is to develop approaches that design institutional reforms that are stable after the window of opportunity has closed, or that shift the political incentives of those with political power in a direction to ensure that their interests are more consistent with those of the citizens more generally.

NOTES

This chapter is based on presentations in Namur, Belgium, in January 2016 and in Paris in June 2016. I am grateful for the feedback from the participants and in particular for detailed comments from Jean-Marie Baland and Denis Cogneau.
1. Nunn (2008) and Dell (2010) also document long-run effects on outcomes from historically determined institutions. Dell (2010) finds, for instance, that inside *mita* districts (districts with forced labor), household consumption is 25% lower and stunting in children is about six percentage points higher. An alternative view to the institutions hypotheses of Sokoloff and Engerman (2000) and Acemoglu, Johnson, and Robinson (2001) is advanced by Allen, Murphy, and Schneider (2012), who argue that the initial income differences between North America and Latin America were in fact not as substantial, and that "two streams of migrations in the colonial period—one emanating from North-Western Europe at high wages and the other from Iberia at lower wages—created an early difference in income levels in British and Spanish America. These initial differences were compounded by differences in human capital accumulation and differences in the incentives to mechanize production, which accelerated divergence after independence. Thus, these initial wage differences led to the Great Divergence in the Americas" (p. 829). Williamson (2009) is skeptical about the statement that Latin America has always been unequal compared with other regions, and on the basis of this, he questions the theories that argue that the initial inequality in Latin America is to blame for the disappointing development.
2. Hodler (2018) develops a model to explain the variations in political strategies across the Arab world in response to the Arab Spring.
3. Andersen and Ross (2014) present a critique of Haber and Menaldo (2011).

REFERENCES

Acemoglu, Daron. 2005. "Constitutions, politics, and economics: a review essay on Persson and Tabellini The economic effects of constitutions." *Journal of Economic Literature* 43, 1025–1048.

Acemoglu, Daron, Francisco A. Gallego, and James A. Robinson. 2014. "Institutions, human capital, and development." *Annual Review of Economics* 6, 875–912.

Acemoglu, Daron, and Simon Johnson. 2005. "Unbundling institutions." *Journal of Political Economy* 113, 949–995.

Acemoglu, Daron, Simon Johnson, and James A. Robinson. 2001. "The colonial origins of comparative development: An empirical investigation." *American Economic Review* 91, 1369–1401.

———. 2002. "Reversal of fortune: geography and institutions in the making of the modern world income distribution." *Quarterly Journal of Economics* 117, 1231–1294.

———. 2005a. "Institutions as a fundamental cause of long-run growth." In *Handbook of Economic Growth*, edited by Philippe Aghion and Steven N. Durlauf, ch. 6. Amsterdam: Elsevier.

———. 2005b. "The rise of Europe: Atlantic trade, institutional change, and economic growth." *American Economic Review* 95, 546–679.

Acemoglu, Daron, Simon Johnson, James A. Robinson, and Pierre Yared. 2008. "Income and democracy." *American Economic Review* 98, 808–842.

Acemoglu, Daron, Suresh Naidu, Pascual Restrepo, and James A. Robinson. 2018. "Democracy does cause growth." *Journal of Political Economy*, forthcoming.

Acemoglu, Daron, and James A. Robinson. 2012. *Why Nations Fail: The Origins of Power, Prosperity, and Poverty*. New York: Crown.

———. 2013. "Economics versus politics: pitfalls of policy advice." *Journal of Economic Perspectives* 27, 173–192.

———. 2016. "Paths to inclusive political institutions." Working paper, MIT.

Acemoglu, Daron, James A. Robinson, and Ragnar Torvik. 2013. "Why do voters dismantle checks and balances?" *Review of Economic Studies* 80, 845–875.

———. 2016. "The political agenda effect and state centralization." NBER Working Paper No. 22250.

Alexeev, Michael, and Robert Conrad. 2009. "The elusive curse of oil." *Review of Economics and Statistics* 91, 586–598.

Allen, Robert C., Tommy E. Murphy, and Eric B. Schneider. 2012. "The colonial origins of divergence in the Americas: a labor market approach." *Journal of Economic History* 72, 863–894.

Andersen, Jørgen J., and Silje Aslaksen. 2008. "Constitutions and the resource curse." *Journal of Development Economics* 87, 227–246.

———. 2013. "Oil and political survival." *Journal of Development Economics* 100, 89–106.

Andersen, Jørgen J., and Michael L. Ross. 2014. "The big oil change: a closer look at the Haber-Menaldo analysis." *Comparative Political Studies* 47, 993–1021.

Arezki, Rabah, and Markus Brückner. 2012. "Commodity windfalls, democracy and external debt." *Economic Journal* 122, 848–866.

Arezki, Rabah, Kirk Hamilton, and Kazim Kazimov. 2011. "Resource windfalls, macroeconomic stability and growth: the role of political institutions." IMF Working Paper 11/142.

Aslaksen, Silje. 2010. "Oil and democracy: more than a cross-country correlation." *Journal of Peace Research* 47, 421–431.

Bardhan, Pranab. 2005. "Institutions matter, but which ones?" *Economics of Transition* 13, 499–532.

Barro, Robert J. 1996. "Democracy and growth." *Journal of Economic Growth* 1, 1–27.

Besley, Timothy, and Torsten Persson. 2011. *Pillars of Prosperity*. Princeton, NJ: Princeton University Press.

Boschini, Anne D., Jan Pettersson, and Jesper Roine. 2007. "Resource curse or not: A question of appropriability." *Scandinavian Journal of Economics* 109, 593–617.

Bourguignon, Francois, and Thierry Verdier. 2000. "Oligarchy, democracy, inequality and growth." *Journal of Development Economics* 62, 285–313.

Bowles, Samuel, and Herbert Gintis. 2013. *A Cooperative Species: Human Reciprocity and Its Evolution*. Princeton, NJ: Princeton University Press.

Brunnschweiler, Christa N., and Erwin Bulte. 2008. "The resource curse revisited and revised: A tale of paradoxes and red herrings." *Journal of Environmental Economics and Management* 55, 248–264.

Bulte, Erwin, and Richard Damania. 2008. "Resources for sale: corruption, democracy and the natural resource curse." *The B.E. Journal of Economic Analysis & Policy* 8(1): article 5.

Cabrales, Antonio, and Esther Hauk. 2010. "The quality of political institutions and the curse of natural resources." *Economic Journal* 121, 58–88.

Cervellati, Matteo, Florian Jung, Uwe Sunde, and Thomas Vischer. 2014. "Income and democracy: comment." *American Economic Review* 104, 707–719.

Collier, Paul. 2010. *The Plundered Planet*. New York: Oxford University Press.

Collier, Paul, and Benedikt Goderis. 2012. "Commodity prices and growth: an empirical investigation." *European Economic Review* 56, 1241–1260.

Cust, James, and Torfinn Harding. 2017. "Institutions and the location of oil exploration." Unpublished, Norwegian School of Economics.

Dell, Melissa. 2010. "The persistent effects of Peru's mining mita." *Econometrica* 78, 1863–1903.

Dewatripont, Mathias, and Gerard Roland. 1992. "Economic reform and dynamic political constraints." *Review of Economic Studies* 59, 703–730.

———. 1995. "The design of reform packages under uncertainty." *American Economic Review* 85, 1207–1223.

Dixit, Avinash. 1997. "Economists as advisors to politicians and to society." *Economics and Politics* 9, 225–230.

Drazen, Allan. 2002. "Conditionality and ownership in IMF lending: a political economy approach." *IMF Staff Papers* 49, 36–67.

Dunning, Thad. 2008. *Crude Democracy: Natural Resource Wealth and Political Regimes*. New York: Cambridge University Press.

Easterly, William, and Ross Levine. 2003. "Tropics, germs and crops: how endowments influence economic development." *Journal of Monetary Economics* 50, 3–39.

Fernandez, Raquel, and Dani Rodrik. 1991. "Resistance to reform: status quo bias in the presence of individual-specific uncertainty." *American Economic Review* 81, 1146–1155.

Fukuyama, Francis. 2011. *The Origins of Political Order: From Prehuman Times to the French Revolution*. New York: Farrar, Straus and Giroux.

———. 2014. *Political Order and Political Decay: From the Industrial Revolution to the Globalization of Democracy*. New York: Farrar, Straus and Giroux.

Gelb, Alan. 1988. *Oil Windfalls: Blessing or Curse?* New York: Oxford University Press.

Gerring, John, Philip Bond, William Barndt, and Carola Morene. 2005. "Democracy and growth: a historical perspective." *World Politics* 57, 323–364.

Glaeser, Edward L., Rafael La Porta, Florenzio Lopez-de-Silanes, and Andrei Shleifer. 2004. "Do institutions cause growth?" *Journal of Economic Growth* 9, 271–303.

Glaeser, Edward L., and Andrei Shleifer. 2003. "The rise of the regulatory state." *Journal of Economic Literature* 41, 401–425.

Greif, Avner. 1993. "Contract enforceability and economic institutions in early trade: the Maghribi traders coalition." *American Economic Review* 83, 525–548.

Gylfason, Thorvaldur. 2001. "Natural resources, education, and economic development." *European Economic Review* 45, 847–859.

Haber, Stephen, and Victor Menaldo. 2011. "Do natural resources fuel authoritarianism? A reappraisal of the resource curse." *American Political Science Review* 105, 1–26.

Hall, Robert E., and Charles I. Jones. 1999. "Why do some countries produce so much more output per worker that others?" *Quarterly Journal of Economics* 114, 83–116.

Hodler, Roland. 2018. "The political economics of the Arab spring." *Economic Inquiry* 56, 821–836.

Huntington, Samuel. 1968. *Political Order in Changing Societies*. New Haven, CT: Yale University Press.

Karl, Terry Lynn. 1997. *The Paradox of Plenty: Oil Booms and Petro-States*. Berkeley: University of California Press.

Krugman, Paul. 1987. "The narrow moving band, the Dutch disease, and the competitive consequences of Mrs. Thatcher: notes on trade in the presence of dynamic scale economies." *Journal of Development Economics* 27, 41–55.

Laffont, Jean-Jacques. 2005. *Regulation and Development*. Cambridge: Cambridge University Press.

La Porta, Rafael, Florencio Lopez-de-Silanes, Andrei Schleifer, and Robert W. Vishny. 1998. "Law and finance." *Journal of Political Economy* 106, 1113–1155.

Lau, Lawrence J., Yingyi Qian, and Gerard Roland. 2000. "Reform without losers: an interpretation of China's dual track approach to reform." *Journal of Political Economy* 108, 120–143.

Linz, Juan. 1978. *The Breakdown of Democratic Regimes. Crisis, Breakdown, and Reequilibration*. Baltimore, MD: Johns Hopkins University Press.

Lipset, Seymour. 1959. "Some social requisites of democracy: economic development and political legitimacy." *American Political Science Review* 53, 69–105.

Matsen, Egil, Gisle J. Natvik, and Ragnar Torvik. 2016. "Petro populism." *Journal of Development Economics* 118, 1–12.

Mehlum, Halvor, Karl Moene, and Ragnar Torvik. 2006. "Institutions and the resource curse." *Economic Journal* 116, 1–20.

Moene, Karl, and Michael Wallerstein. 2006. "Social democracy as a development strategy." In *Globalisation and Egalitarian Redistribution*, edited by Pranab Bardhan, Samuel Bowles, and Michael Wallerstein. New York: Russell Sage Foundation.

Monteiro, Joana, and Claudio Ferraz. 2010. "Does oil make leaders unaccountable? Evidence from Brazil's offshore oil boom." Unpublished manuscript, PUC-Rio.

North, Douglass C. 1991. "Institutions." *Journal of Economic Perspectives* 5, 97–112.

North, Douglass C., and Robert P. Thomas. 1973. *The Rise of the Western World: A New Economic History*. New York: Cambridge University Press.

Nunn, Nathan. 2008. "The long term effects of Africa's slave trades." *Quarterly Journal of Economics* 123, 139–176.

Pande, Rohini, and Christopher Udry. 2005. "Institutions and development: a view from below." Economic Growth Center Discussion Paper No. 928, Yale University.

Persson, Torsten, Gerard Roland, and Guido Tabellini. 1997. "Separation of powers and political accountability." *Quarterly Journal of Economics* 112, 1163–1202.

———. 2000. "Comparative politics and public finance." *Journal of Political Economy* 108, 1121–1161.

Persson, Torsten, and Guido Tabellini. 2003. *The Economic Effects of Constitutions*. Cambridge, MA: MIT Press.

Rigobon, Roberto, and Dani Rodrik. 2005. "Rule of law, democracy, openness and income." *Economics of Transition* 13, 533–564.

Robinson, James A., and Ragnar Torvik. 2005. "White elephants." *Journal of Public Economics* 89, 197–210.

———. 2013. "Institutional comparative statics." In *Advances in Economics and Econometrics*, edited by Daron Acemoglu, Manuel Arellano, and Eddie Dekel. New York: Cambridge University Press.

———. 2016. "Endogenous presidentialism." *Journal of the European Economic Association* 14, 907–942.

Robinson, James A., Ragnar Torvik, and Thierry Verdier. 2006. "Political foundations of the resource curse." *Journal of Development Economics* 79, 447–468.

———. 2014. "Political foundations of the resource curse: a simplification and a comment." *Journal of Development Economics* 106, 194–198.

Rodrik, Dani. 1996. "Understanding economic policy reform." *Journal of Economic Literature* 34, 9–41.

———. 2004. "Getting institutions right." *CESifo DICE Report* 2, 10–15.

Rodrik, Dani, Arvind Subramanian, and Francesco Trebbi. 2004. "Institutions rule: the primacy of institutions over geography and integration in economic development." *Journal of Economic Growth* 8, 131–165.

Roland, Gerard. 2002. "The political economy of transition." *Journal of Economic Perspectives* 16, 29–50.

Ross, Michael L. 2001a. *Timber Booms and Institutional Breakdown in Southeast Asia*. New York: Cambridge University Press.

———. 2001b. "Does oil hinder democracy?" *World Politics* 53, 325–361.

Sachs, Jeffrey D., and Andrew M. Warner. 1995. "Natural resource abundance and economic growth." NBER Working Paper No. 5398.

Sokoloff, Kenneth L., and Stanley L. Engerman. 2000. "Institutions, factor endowments, and paths of development in the New World." *Journal of Economic Perspectives* 14, 217–232.

Sonin, Konstantin. 2003. "Why the rich may favour poor protection of property rights." *Journal of Comparative Economics* 31, 715–773.

Tavares, Jose, and Romain Wacziarg. 2001. "How democracy affects growth." *European Economic Review* 45, 1341–1378.

Tilly, Charles. 1995. *Popular Contention in Great Britain, 1758–1834*. Cambridge, MA: Harvard University Press.

Torvik, Ragnar. 2009. "Why do some resource abundant countries succeed while others do not?" *Oxford Review of Economic Policy* 25, 241–256.

———. 2018. "Should developing countries establish petroleum funds?" *Energy Journal* 39(4): 85–101.

Tsui, Kevin K. 2011. "More oil, les democracy: evidence from worldwide crude oil discoveries." *Economic Journal* 121, 89–115.

van der Ploeg, Frederick, and Steven Poelhekke. 2009. "Volatility and the natural resource curse." *Oxford Economic Papers* 61, 727–760.

———. 2010. "The pungent smell of 'red herrings': subsoil assets, rents volatility and the resource curse." *Journal of Environmental Economics and Management* 60, 44–55.

van Wijnbergen, Sweder. 1984. "The Dutch disease: a disease after all?" *Economic Journal* 94, 41–55.

Williamson, Jeffrey G. 2009. "Five centuries of Latin American inequality." NBER Working Paper No. 15305.

4

GROUP INEQUALITY IN DEMOCRACIES

Lessons from Cross-National Experiences

Rohini Somanthan

4.1. INTRODUCTION

Group inequalities in well-being are a prominent feature of many modern democracies. Some of these, such as those between black and white populations in the United States and South Africa, or between upper and lower castes in India, have emerged from a history of feudalism and discrimination. Others are the result of more recent political and economic events such as civil and transnational wars, refugee movements, financial crises, and labor mobility.

State policies that address group inequalities have also followed many different trajectories. An especially controversial policy divide relates to group-based affirmative action. The positions taken by the two largest democracies, India and the United States, are diametrically opposed. India has ardently pursued quotas for historically disadvantaged groups in universities, public employment, and politics, while the United States has systematically eliminated such preference in recent years and focused on improving access to public schooling.

This chapter takes stock of what we know about the ways in which major democracies have viewed social groups and addressed inequalities between them. The survey is conceptually divided into three parts. The first of these is descriptive and outlines the ways in which individuals have been classified into groups in different countries and the types of data that allow us to track changes in group outcomes. Race, color, birthplace, language, and occupation are used in different combinations across space and time. I examine the determinants and implications of these alternative classifications. The second part discusses the theoretical and empirical literature on the most important mechanisms that generate inequality and govern its transmission. A summary of theoretical models is followed by the empirical approaches used to test them. Preference-based and statistical discrimination, intergenerational transmission of wealth, failures in credit and housing markets, neighborhood sorting, and social networks have all been put forward as explanations. The third part of the survey focuses on research gaps that can form the basis for future inquiry into the types of institutions that effectively contribute to greater societal equality.

I argue that our understanding of social inequalities is greatly constrained by state decisions on how to categorize a population into groups. We need to better understand how differences in social classification affect our perceptions of inequality between and within countries and the ways in which state policy can create new notions of individual identity. Research in sociology and in social psychology has discussed these questions of categorization, but they remain outside the realm of mainstream research in economics. Crossing disciplinary lines can help us relate the deprivation faced by individuals to status differences across groups. Research on group inequalities is also disproportionately concentrated in the United States, and this is reflected in the survey. This is partly because European countries have restricted the collection of social data and there is limited research capacity in poorer regions of the world where social inequalities and ethnic conflict are most prevalent. Comparative research that focuses on how redistributive institutions operate in particular social and regional contexts can help guide effective policy.

4.2. GROUP BOUNDARIES

Measuring group inequality requires defining groups. This process is more complex and controversial than commonly perceived. The major sources for statistics on group incomes and well-being are national censuses and labor force surveys. While most countries collect social data, they are quite different with regard to the coarseness and nature of categories used, the methods of enumeration, and the ways in which their citizens respond to questions on social background. Some idea of the variation in race and ethnic classification is useful in order to interpret differences and trends in group inequality.

Morning (2008) studies 138 census questionnaires around the year 2000 and finds about two-thirds collect some type of ethnic information such as race, religion, caste, ancestry, nationality, and color. The number of categories used often depends more on the nature of political power and national ideologies than on any fundamental differences in population demographics. This makes aggregate measures of social distance time- and context-specific.

The United States, with its long history of census enumeration, is a good example. Early censuses were designed to determine political representation and the tax base. Native Americans, who were not taxed, were not enumerated. The first census of 1790 distinguished white males and females, all other free persons, and slaves. *Color* appeared in 1850 with the distinctions of White, Black, and Mulatto; *race* appeared in 1870. Starting in 1890 until the early twentieth century, mixtures of Black, White, and American Indian blood were recorded under numerous heads. New categories such as Chinese, Japanese, Korean, Mexican, Hindu, Cuban, Vietnamese, and Asian Indian were slowly added after these groups entered the country. Starting in 1970, racial and ethnic categories were self-reported. After millions of Americans reported themselves as *Other* in both 1980 and 1990, and multiracial populations complained about being unable to properly self-classify, a federal directive in 1997 expanded the number of categories and allowed multiple responses in the census of 2000.[1]

Canada, in spite of its geographical proximity to the United States and many demographic similarities, allowed its residents more flexibility in how they report ethnicity. The census allows them to self-identify using multiple categories which include ancestry, nationality, language, and ethnicity. It has also experimented with changing the order in which different options are listed, with French before English in some years and not in others. The responses reveal a strong national identity, with *Canadian* being the most popular response to the ethnic question. Brazil and South Africa also provide interesting contrasts to the United States. While the US census defined Black in terms of the "one drop rule" for most of its history and did not admit multiracial identities until recently, South African censuses recorded the four categories of African, Colored, European, and Asian throughout the twentieth century and thereby officially recognized a mixed blood group even though there were strict laws that governed interactions between whites and non-whites. Interestingly, these categories remained unchanged with the dismantling of apartheid (Khalfani and Zuberi 2001; Davis 2001). Brazilian censuses have historically recorded color because mixtures of European, African, and indigenous people were very much a part of the nation's identity. More recently, and partly as a result of social activism, census questions on African and indigenous descent have been added (Nobles 2000).

The Latin American countries have all had fairly similar histories with regard to census enumeration. In the colonial period most countries enumerated race. After gaining their independence from Spain and Portugal, racial distinctions were condemned by most national leaders, and many of these countries prided themselves on their racially mixed populations. In fact, after the Mexican Revolution of 1910, to emphasize the new balance of power, the order in which racial data was tabulated also changed. Indigenous populations were listed first, followed by Mixed and then White. After 1950, most countries in Latin America stopped recording race, and some replaced this with language. By 1970, no country other than Cuba recorded race. Since then, race has re-appeared in various databases in response to local and international pressures to actively bridge racial gaps in income and opportunities. Almost all censuses now have questions on indigenous and African ancestry. Responses to these have generated new data on inequality by race. These data form the basis of a large affirmative action program in public universities in Brazil.[2]

In contrast with the Americas, many European countries have historically taken the position that national identity is best promoted by ignoring ethnicity. France has been especially vehement in this regard. Between 1891 and 1999, official statistics used only three categories of citizenship—the French, "French by acquisition," and foreigners. British censuses recorded the birthplace of individuals since 1841 but discontinued recording nationality beginning with the 1961 census. Both these countries have changed the categories they use since the 1990s, Britain more than France. In France, the Histoire Familiale (Family History) survey, in collaboration with the census, asked survey respondents about the birthplace of their parents, so "descendants of immigrants turned into a statistical category" (Simon 2008: 12). In Britain, although the Census Act of 1920 had permitted the census to inquire about "nationality, race and language," this was not done until 1991, when an ethnic group question was asked for the first time in British history. The 1991 census asked respondents to assign themselves to one of nine categories, which distinguished, for example, "Black-other" from "Any-other" and within Black, those of Caribbean and African descent. Asians could be Indian, Pakistani, Bangladeshi, or Chinese (Fenton 1996). Recording ethnicity appears to be becoming more acceptable.

In many cases, official categories were designed to hide important differences in identity. Israel records religion and birthplace but not ethnicities such as Arab.[3] Rwanda, in its attempt at nation-building after the genocide in 1994, outlawed the use of ethnic labels such as Hutu and Tutsi which were in any case occupations turned into ethnicities by Belgian colonists.[4]

Social classification in India is particularly complex and is based on both religion and caste. Caste enumeration began under colonial rule in the late eighteenth century. Caste was always self-reported, and the populations of individual castes often changed in response to incentives or favors granted to particular groups. The caste structure was therefore fluid, especially as it appeared in reported statistics (Cassan 2015; Sharan 2003). After independence, the many thousands of castes and communities were grouped into four categories: the Scheduled Castes (SCs), Scheduled Tribes (STs), Other Backward Classes (OBCs), and a residual category with all others. These were created to administer the country's affirmative action program (Galanter 1984). The SCs and STs were given proportional representation in parliament in 1950. There are now quotas for each of the first three categories in state and federal employment and in public universities, and they are collectively known as the *Backward Classes*. Because the gains from affirmative action are so substantial, there have been many petitions by caste groups to be classified as "backward," making categories even more ambiguous (Somanathan 2011). Moreover, inequalities within each of these official categories are substantial (Kumar and Somanathan 2016).

The purpose of this historical narrative on the official categorization of identity is to emphasize that data on groups are influenced by ideological and political forces. Measured group inequality is the result of both fundamental differences in the well-being of groups and changes in how group boundaries are perceived by individual and state actors.

4.3. MECHANISMS: THEORY

This section discusses theoretical contributions to the study of group inequality, and section 4.4 examines whether the empirical evidence allows us to distinguish between alternative theories.

4.3.1. Discrimination

Preference-based discrimination is perhaps the most straightforward explanation for persistent group inequality. Becker (1957) formalized this as the disutility to employers and consumers from interacting with a discriminated group. He used the term *discrimination coefficient* to represent the percentage by which money costs and returns are different from net payoffs, which include the psychic and other nonpecuniary costs of interaction. In Becker's formulation, if discrimination against a factor k is measured by a discrimination coefficient d_k, an employer dealing with this factor and paying a money wage π is assumed to act as if the wage is $\pi(1+d_k)$, an employee offered π by this factor, acts as if the wage rate is $\pi(1-d_k)$, and a consumer buying from such a factor at the price p acts as if he is paying $p(1+d_k)$.

These preferences generate differences in market outcomes across groups. Market discrimination exists if the ratio of wages of workers in the two groups is different from what would exist in the absence of discrimination. The market discrimination coefficient (MDC) is the percentage difference in net wages of the nondiscriminated and the discriminated groups. Becker acknowledged that the relationship between wages, segregation in transactions, and the individual discrimination coefficients was mediated by a number of factors such as the organizational structure of the labor market and the degree of substitutability between labor from different social groups. But he did not formalize the connections between residential segregation, labor market outcomes, and individual preferences.

The emergence of information economics in the 1970s focused attention on the effects of asymmetric beliefs in markets (Akerlof 1970). It led to new models of statistical discrimination in which prior beliefs on the lower productivity of minorities or women could be self-fulfilling because they lower expected returns from investments in education and training for these groups (Arrow 1972; Phelps 1972; Spence 1973).

The distinction between preference-based and statistical discrimination is important because in the case of statistical discrimination, policies that change beliefs can set in motion hiring processes that lead to greater group equality. For preference-based discrimination, one might imagine that greater contact in residential and employment spaces may lead to more empathetic relations across groups. Until that happens, constitutional protections and legal structures that ensure their application may be the only recourse. In the next section, I discuss why it is empirically difficult to distinguish between these two very different explanations for group inequality.

4.3.2. Intergenerational Transmission

Group inequalities can also persist through the intergenerational transmission of income and wealth. If labor market returns for all groups are the same for a given level of skill, but credit markets do not function smoothly, groups that are initially poorer may remain so. These circumstances provide the strongest case for redistributive transfers that equalize incomes and opportunities across groups.

Loury (1981) has an early model of intergenerational transmission in the face of dysfunctional credit markets. Individual earnings are assumed to depend on ability and education. No borrowing is possible, so parents can only invest in the education of their offspring by sacrificing current consumption. Diminishing marginal utility of consumption results in poorer parents investing less in educating a child of given ability. This makes children of initially poor ethnic groups, poorer on average.

Loury's paper provides two important insights into the evolution of group inequality. First, if ability is distributed identically across groups, poverty traps are unlikely. This is because even dynasties that are initially poor have high incomes whenever they have children of sufficiently high ability. One such generation can lift families out of perpetual poverty. Formally, the paper shows that under reasonable technical conditions, there is a unique distribution of income to which the economy converges, and this does not depend on the initial distribution of income. The second main result of the paper is that redistribution can improve efficiency by strengthening the correlation between ability and investments in training. From the perspective of group inequality, the paper shows that while poorer groups will not remain poor forever, redistribution can improve aggregate incomes while also reducing inequality.

4.3.3. Neighborhoods and Networks

Neighborhoods and social networks are an important determinant of earnings. This area of research has traditionally been the domain of sociologists, most of whom have focused on cities in the United States. The urban landscape in the United States exhibits extreme residential segregation by race and ethnicity, in spite of well-functioning land markets and laws that prohibit discrimination in housing. This is especially true of the older cities in the Northeast and Midwest. The United States also has a relatively mobile population and schools traditionally have been locally financed. The geographical distribution of the population therefore has direct implications for the quality of schooling.

Within economics, models have focused on how neighborhood sorting influences earnings. Tiebout (1956) first emphasized the difference between pure public goods like defense and locally financed goods such as schooling. In the case of local public goods, households can move to neighborhoods where tax rates and public good quality matches their preferences. This sorting improves the efficiency of public good provision but also generates inequality in earnings. Later work has shown that neighborhood sorting can create inequalities even with no preference differences. Moreover, in the presence of peer effects, this sorting may have considerable efficiency costs. Benabou (1993) shows that even with initially identical individuals, peer effects in local public goods such as education can lead to the ghettoization of certain parts of a city.

Once we incorporate race into models of sorting, there are direct implications for group inequality. The nuanced relationship between race-based preferences and segregation was studied by Thomas Schelling in the late 1960s. Schelling showed that segregated neighborhoods need not reflect strong in-group biases and a preference for some integration by all groups is consistent with equilibria with complete neighborhood segregation (Schelling 1969, 1978). Segregation, in turn, is related to group inequalities in education and skills. Sethi and Somanathan (2004) extend Shelling's ideas by incorporating both race and public goods into preferences. They show that even when the ideal neighborhood for all individuals is partially integrated, segregation occurs if income disparities between groups or races are either very large or very small. A unique integrated equilibrium only exists for intermediate racial income disparities. Group inequalities thus depend on the joint distribution of race and income in society. If, for example, black populations are on average poorer than whites, then high-income black households will live in poorer neighborhoods than high-income whites, and if neighborhood effects are important, this could be a source of persistent inequality by race. I will come back to the evidence on this in section 4.4.

The link between residential segregation and group inequality is strongest when there is local financing of public goods and labor mobility across localities. Many countries have limited mobility or centrally administered education systems. South Africa enforced segregation by race until the end of apartheid in 1994, so residential choices were limited.[5] In other countries, such as India, rigidities in land markets resulted in immobile populations. Although there is a great deal of segregation by caste in India, it typically happens within villages. Lower castes often reside in secluded hamlets within villages, and informal norms may limit their access to other groups. They are also concentrated in menial and low-paid occupations and in particular hamlets within larger villages. Discrimination in such cases operates directly rather than through housing markets, taxes, and spending on public goods. In most European countries public education is centrally administered and finances are not determined to the same extent by residential segregation.

Neighborhoods are one setting in which social interactions influence inequality. Jobs are another. Seminal work by Mark Granovetter in the early 1970s revealed the importance of networks in labor markets. Using detailed interviews with 100 people who had changed jobs in the Boston suburb of Newton between 1968 and 1969, Granovetter (1974) shows that more than half of all new jobs were obtained through personal contacts. Many of these were not advertised, but rather, created upon finding promising potential candidates. Granovetter also found that jobs obtained through contacts had, on average, higher pay and prestige and were more satisfying than those obtained through other means. The sample used consisted of white-collar jobs in professional, managerial, and technical fields. Previous research had already established the importance of referrals in blue-collar jobs. The accumulated evidence from these studies shows that models of research in economics that ignore social relations miss important features of labor markets. Granovetter (1985) elaborates on the more general problem of models in neoclassical economics not being sufficiently embedded in the realities of social structure.

Economists have recently begun to formalize the ways in which social networks influence the operation of labor markets. Calvo-Armengol and Jackson (2004) present an elegant model of information transmission that can explain divergent unemployment rates across social networks. Since many networks operate along ethnic lines, this type of model speaks directly to the different labor market outcomes we observe across groups. In each period, all individuals receive a signal about a job opportunity with some probability. If unemployed, the person takes the job. If already employed, the signal is passed on to a randomly chosen unemployed person in their network. If everyone in a network is employed, the information is lost. The probability of finding a job is therefore increasing in the number of connections to employed people in a network, and contagion effects can result in polarized outcomes across groups. If there is a given cost to staying in the network, those with low prospects of finding a job drop out, making it less likely that others formally in their network would find a job. Conversely, each additional job for someone in a network increases the probability of the unemployed in the network finding jobs.

Apart from information, networks may help trade through reputation-building (Greif 1993). They may also help enforce norms for repayment in credit markets and encourage participation in new markets (Jackson 2014). Bowles et al. (2014) illustrate how peer effects that operate through social networks can amplify inequality in human capital investments over time. The features of networks that lead to the fastest dissemination of stimuli is an area of active research. For mobility, there seems to be some support for Granovetter's claim that there is "strength in weak ties." Being loosely connected to multiple networks may be more beneficial than being in the midst of a dense but isolated set of connections (Granovetter 2005). Social networks could also reduce the chances of individual success through the spread of negative stimuli or behaviors. Disease, crime, smoking, substance abuse, and fertility are all profoundly influenced by social interactions.

Network effects on group inequality is a particularly promising area for collaborative research between economists, sociologists, and anthropologists, and there are many open questions in this area that remain under-explored (Geertz 1978).

4.3.4. Group Heterogeneity and Collective Action

The final set of formal models I consider are those relating to the effects of social heterogeneity on collective action and conflict. There are two distinct approaches in this literature. The first focuses on how the demographic composition of an area (village, town, district, or city) affects the propensity of its residents to engage in collective action for public goods. The second relates to the potential for conflict in heterogeneous societies.

Alesina et al. (1999) is an early and influential paper in the literature on social divisions and public goods. It contains a two-stage voting game in which citizens first vote on the public budget and then on the type of public good that the budget is used to finance. Diverse communities vote for lower taxes because the public good preferred by the median voter is far from the optimal choice of most voters. In contrast, homogeneous communities agree on how taxes are spent and therefore support higher taxation. The model is tested using the classification of race in the 1990 US Census. Counties and cities that are more ethnically fractionalized have lower fractions of their budgets spent on education, roads, and trash services. Later work recognizes that some diverse communities may do quite well, but only because a varied set of skills in production compensates for divergent preferences.[6]

There are several channels other than voting through which collective action could operate. Banerjee et al. (2008) provide a general theoretical framework that incorporates many of the theoretical ideas in this field. The collective action game is non-cooperative in that benefits from a public good depend on group membership but costs are privately incurred. Each individual decides on a level of collective effort based on these common benefits and private costs. In equilibrium, the probability of a region getting a public good (this could also be interpreted as the share of the public budget that it receives) depends on the share of total collective effort it exercises. Social groups may differ along many dimensions: their preferences for public goods, their political influence in getting them, and their costs of engaging in collective action. All of these affect the relationship between the social composition of a region and the type and quality of public goods within it.

The literature on social conflict and ethnic divisions is huge and includes contributions from many social science disciplines. Among economists, Joan Esteban and Debraj Ray have focused on why group conflict is organized along ethnic rather than class lines even though the benefits of state policy are often class-based. The poor, for example, benefit from employment guarantee schemes and the rich from lower tax rates. They argue that organizing a conflict requires both resources and time. The rich within ethnic groups are best suited to provide the former and the poor the latter. The economic gains from conflict along ethnic lines are therefore greater than those along class lines (Esteban and Ray 2008). Caselli and Coleman (2013) provide an alternative explanation for the same phenomenon. They argue that winners and losers in an ethnic conflict are easily distinguished because ethnic markers are hard to change. With class conflict, losers can pretend to be part of the winning group, and this dilutes the gains to winners. This weakens incentives to engage in class conflict.

To operationalize any theory based on social divisions, we need to ask how these divisions should be measured. There are two questions related to measurement that must be resolved. How should social boundaries be demarcated? How should we construct measures as a function of the shares of population in demarcated groups? Research in economics has focused on how to construct measures based on divisions but not on which divisions matter. Political scientists and sociologists have more readily acknowledged the difficulty in thinking of divisions as exogenously determined. Brubaker (2009) and Fearon and Laitin (2000) are surveys of the literature on the construction of identity and good introductions to this field with its many complexities and unresolved questions.

4.4. MECHANISMS: EVIDENCE

The survey of evidence in this section is provided in order of the theoretical mechanisms discussed above.

4.4.1. Tests for Discrimination

Early studies of discrimination in the labor market used cross-sectional data and regression methods to test whether race and ethnicity affected labor market outcomes such as wages and employment. An indicator variable for race or ethnicity that was negative and statistically significant from zero after controlling for education, region of residence, age, experience, occupation and other such characteristics suggested labor market discrimination. Cain (1986) summarizes this approach and points out obvious difficulties. Most important, if discrimination does exist, very few variables that are used as controls in these empirical models are exogenously determined. Race, caste, and ethnicity determine where families live, the type of schooling they receive, and the occupations they enter. Any effects we find in addition to those that influence these choices are just a small part of the discrimination effect. Also, the use of aggregate datasets can hide segregation at a more disaggregate level. It is possible that neighborhoods and firms are completely segregated within a city, yet city aggregates would not reveal this segregation.

Recognizing that discrimination in labor markets could influence individual investments in education and the assignment of employees to jobs, Blinder (1973) and Oaxaca (1973) independently presented a variant of the regression model to decompose wage differentials by race and gender into those attributable to differences in endowments and those resulting from differential returns to given qualifications. This is now popularly referred to as the Oaxaca-Blinder decomposition. Blinder (1973) attributed about one-third of the black-white wage gap in the United States in the late 1960s to endowments and the rest to discrimination.

A decomposition of this kind provides a useful summary of sources of wage differences but cannot establish causality unless we are able to convincingly isolate individual background characteristics that are not affected by racial attitudes. We are most interested in group inequality when race and ethnicity are truly salient. In such cases most aspects of life are affected by social identity, including residence, health, and parental endowments. These are the types of variables that are often treated as exogenous in wage regressions.

Arrow (1998) points to some limitations of economic models in understanding the sources of discrimination. Becker's taste for the discrimination model is plausible in a world in which repeated and voluntary transactions occur among employers and employees, customers and firms. It is less appropriate for transactions within large corporations or those in housing or credit markets. Employers in big companies have very little contact with employees, and those selling houses have no future contact with their buyers. Arrow points out that if we have reasonably accurate measures of individual productivity, they can help us distinguish between preference-based and statistical discrimination, since the former predicts wage differences for equally productive workers while the latter does not. Such productivity data are not often available. Neal and Johnson (1996) use pre-market test score data from the Armed Forces Qualification Test (AFQT) as a proxy for productivity and find that much of the black-white wage gap of workers in their twenties is explained by this measure. All these approaches are severely limited if discrimination, segregation, and social networks cause selective attrition of potential black workers from specific occupations or from the labor force altogether.

Partly in response to the difficulties in identifying the presence of discrimination with secondary datasets, there has been an increased interest in correspondence and audit studies, especially in labor and housing markets. Audit studies use actual individuals who are trained to act alike while correspondence studies use fictitious ones, created by researchers to be identical except for characteristics such as race, caste, ethnicity, or gender, often indicated through names that are typical for these groups. Differences in call-back rates provide evidence of discrimination. In the United States, employers are only entitled to base their decisions on observable characteristics other than race and gender, and the difference in call-back rates therefore measures discrimination in the legal sense. If the characteristics presented to employers are only a subset of those that employers perceive as affecting productivity, these studies do not provide unbiased estimates of taste-based discrimination as defined by Becker. Only under the implausible assumption that unobservable characteristics have the same distribution across groups of workers do we identify taste-based discrimination from these studies. Heckman and Siegelman (1993) show that even if the expected value of these unobservables is the same across black and white workers, differences in their variances can lead to audit studies either underestimating or overestimating the taste-based discrimination coefficient. Neumark (2012) provides a method for adjusting audit estimates to obtain a discrimination coefficient under a set of plausible assumptions, summarizes data from audit studies, and suggests that these studies provide more limited evidence of labor market discrimination than is often claimed. He argues that skills and social environments are central to explanations of differences in well-being by race in the United States.

4.4.2. Intergenerational Mobility

The extent of intergenerational mobility in income and wealth has been estimated for several countries. For the United States, the Panel Study of Income Dynamics (PSID) provides a particularly rich source of longitudinal data on earnings for about 5,000 families starting in 1968. Solon (1992) uses 348 father-son pairs of earnings for sons born between 1951 and 1959 in the United States and finds that the elasticity of sons' earnings with respect to fathers' earnings is roughly 0.4. Estimated elasticities for other OECD countries are typically much lower. Corak and Heisz (1999) use Canadian tax data for 400,000 father-son pairs and find an elasticity of 0.2. The higher mobility relative to the United

States is concentrated in the tails of the income distribution. Not surprisingly, Scandinavian countries exhibit mobility at or below the level for Canada. Britain is similar to the United States (Solon 2002; Atkinson et al. 1978).

There is less evidence on transmission for particular racial and ethnic groups. Altonji and Doraszelski (2005) use the PSID and find that the explanatory power of income and demographics is much greater for white than for black households in the United States. The racial gap is hard to explain using individual characteristics. George Borjas, in his recent book (Borjas 2011, ch. 8), summarizes accumulated evidence from his own research on the social mobility of immigrants to the United States and finds that although there is limited persistence between generations of a single family, ethnic differences persist due to the importance of what he terms *ethnic capital*. Groups that are disadvantaged on the labor market are more likely to segregate into ethnic ghettos, and adequate explanations for long-run group inequality therefore require us to look beyond families to neighborhoods.

4.4.3. Segregation and Networks

Following the Civil Rights Act of 1964, the sociologist James Coleman was commissioned by the US Department of Health, Education and Welfare to study whether children of different racial and ethnic backgrounds had similar levels of access to resources in public schools. The report also investigated the sources of differences in achievement across social groups. The Coleman Report of 1966 found extreme levels of racial segregation across schools resulting largely from the segregation of neighborhoods. Although the goal of the report was to suggest ways in which resources could be equalized across school environments in order to equalize opportunity, the data showed that equalization in funding alone was unlikely to equalize outcomes because of the influence of neighborhoods and families.

Since the Coleman report, residential segregation in the United States has been intensively studied. These studies show that racial income disparities explain a very small fraction of black-white residential segregation (Denton and Massey 1988; Farley and Frey 1994; Massey and Denton 1987; Sethi and Somanathan 2009) and that segregation has profound effects on well-being. Cutler and Glaeser (1997) find that segregation is associated with systematically lower education and employment outcomes for black households and higher fractions of unmarried mothers. Gaskin et al. (2012) finds evidence of poorer access to healthcare. African American zip codes have much higher odds of facing a shortage of primary care physicians. Collins and Margo (2000) show that many of the negative effects of racial concentration did not manifest themselves until the 1970s.

Cross-country studies of segregation are complicated by the absence of a standard classification of groups, as discussed in section 4.2. Most European countries do not record race. Group inequalities in these countries are therefore based on categories of skill, education, or birthplace (Bachmann et al. 2014). Inequalities by race are therefore hidden. There are many studies of racial segregation in the United States, South Africa, and Brazil because these censuses record race or color. In an interesting study of segregation and racial inequality, Hunter (2007) shows how the rise of AIDS in South Africa was partly an outcome of the patterns of segregation and migration of the African population.

4.5. LESSONS FOR POLICY AND INSTITUTIONAL DESIGN

We have seen that major democracies have conceptualized and addressed the issue of group inequalities in quite different ways. Many of the OECD countries in Western Europe have focused on individuals, while others, such as India, South Africa and, more recently, Brazil, have used affirmative action to directly tackle income disparities across social groups. This has resulted in very different types of redistributive institutions across countries. Constitutions that have focused on the individual have stressed universal rather than group rights, and public policies have focused on expanding public education.

Public education seems to have been effective in bringing about a convergence of group incomes, even though groups were not directly targeted. Goldin and Katz (2009) study the evolution of wage inequality in historical and cross-national perspective. The United States was a pioneer in extending public education to the masses in the nineteenth and twentieth centuries, a time when school systems in most countries served only the elite. This substantially reduced racial inequality in the United States relative to, for example, England. Some of these equalizing effects have been undone since the last quarter of the twentieth century because new technology has favored workers in the upper tail of the wage distribution. Card and Krueger (1996) use micro-data from the US Census for two southern states in the United States and show that the equalization of school resources across black and white students over the twentieth century did contribute to narrower racial wage gaps when these students entered the labor market.

For India, we find that education was an important driver of mobility for historically disadvantaged groups, yet was politically less popular than targeted policies such as affirmative action in government jobs. Kumar and Somanathan (2016) present data from the Indian census over the period 1961–2001 which suggests that disadvantaged castes had the largest gains in educational attainment in states that emphasized public schooling rather than those in which these groups had political influence. As the returns to education increased in the liberalized economy of of the 1990s, Munshi and Rosenzweig (2006) show that families from the lower ranked castes that invested in education had high returns in the labor market. In spite of this, Indian states that had more legislators from among these castes had lower budgetary spending on public education (Pande 2003). Drèze and Sen (2013) provide a historical and comparative account of development for the various regions in India. In their assessment, education spending and quality have been central to effective development in India, and states that have followed universalist rather than targeted policies have been the most successful.[7] Kjelsrud and Somanathan (2017) also find that spending on primary education is more progressive than many targeted transfers in India because poor households have larger families and rely heavily on public schools, while the middle and upper classes have increased their use of private schools.

Universal healthcare policies have also influenced group disparities. Andrews (2014) compares racial inequalities in the United States and Brazil. Racial differences have historically been larger in Brazil, mainly due to the expansion of education in the United States. However, social programs that address class differences in Brazil gained momentum in the 1990s and have dramatically reduced racial disparities in life expectancy, infant mortality, and educational attainment.

In contrast to public education and healthcare spending, affirmative action policies have been very controversial. Affirmative action probably constitutes the most significant ideological divide on policies relating to group inequality. The political economy of India has led to an ever-expanding role for caste-based affirmative action, yet disparities across castes remain very large and the way that castes are classified combined with the low levels of educational attainment of the most disadvantaged makes it unlikely that they can benefit from these policies (Somanathan 2006). Loury (2016) argues that the condition of African Americans in the United States must be understood in terms of the two fundamental processes of *categorization* and *signification*, and it is unclear that affirmative action policies that attempt to equalize particular outcomes rather than status will do much for the problem of race in the United States.

To the extent that intergenerational transmission of wealth and quality of peers influences the ability of poorer groups to acquire skills, policies that improve access to credit and those that allow racial integration in neighborhoods are likely to be effective. Most countries, however, have had very little success with racial integration. In spite of the rise of an African American middle class in the United States in the second half of the twentieth century, neighborhoods remain extremely segregated. The ill effects of such segregation on labor market outcomes by race have become stark since the 1980s, and racial differences in crime rates are now astounding (Collins and Margo 2000; O'Flaherty and Sethi 2015). In South Africa, even many of the universities that were at the forefront of the struggle to end apartheid have re-segregated (Vergnani 2000). Indian villages have traditionally been segregated by caste and castes themselves have been endogamous. There is no evidence that 65 years of affirmative action have had any significant impact on such segregation.

What then have we learned from the literature on group inequality on the types of institutions that foster a common experience of citizenship for individuals from different social backgrounds? And what are important areas of future inquiry?

I believe that one important takeaway from this survey of the literature is that countries classify their populations into social groups in many ways, and differences in categorization have profound implications for the measurement of inequality. We can only study the effects of what we measure and although neoliberal movements in many European countries have heightened racial conflict and inequality, these have been little studied because most of these countries do not record race in their official data. In countries such as India, with large affirmative action programs, the classification of caste is coarse and hides many inequalities across groups. In the United States, race has always been recorded but the number of categories has multiplied over the years, so measures of inequality over time are not comparable. Our study of institutions must therefore include the institutions that classify and collect social data. These are often ignored by social scientists.

Second, and related, classification itself changes identity. This has been demonstrated powerfully in the case of both Brazil and India. In Brazil, some of the changes in inequality between groups distinguished by color can be attributed to the willingness of individuals to classify themselves as *Negro* or Black following the introduction of affirmative action (Marteleto 2012). In India too, the introduction of affirmative action increased the fractions listed among the *backward classes*. Institutions designed to reduce inequalities therefore change the demographics of the population.

Finally, the large number of studies on policies relating to group inequality have estimated the effects of particular policies, but we do not have enough work that can compare the relative effectiveness of alternatives. This is ultimately the type of information that policy makers need in order to design institutions that will effectively achieve their goals of greater equality.

NOTES

1. See Yanow (2015: ch. 2–4).
2. See Loveman (2014) for detailed histories of enumeration in Latin America.
3. See Goldscheider (2002).
4. See Wimmer (2013: 53–54) for the colonial period and Eramian (2014) for changes after 1994.
5. Restrictions on the location and movement of Africans in South Africa are detailed in the United Nations booklet of Public Information (1969).
6. See Alesina and Ferrara (2005) for an elaboration of this idea and a survey of the literature.
7. See chapter 5, and the discussion at the end of chapter 3.

REFERENCES

Akerlof, G. 1970. The market for lemons: qualitative uncertainty and market mechanism. *Quarterly Journal of Economics* 84(3): 488–500.

Alesina, A., Baqir, R., and Easterly, W. 1999. Public goods and ethnic divisions. *Quarterly Journal of Economics* 114(4): 1243–1284.

Alesina, A. and Ferrara, E. L. 2005. Ethnic diversity and economic performance. *Journal of Economic Literature* 43(3): 762–800.

Altonji, J. G. and Doraszelski, U. 2005. The role of permanent income and demographics in black/white differences in wealth. *Journal of Human Resources* 40(1): 1–30.

Andrews, G. R. 1992. Racial inequality in Brazil and the United States: 1990–2010. *Journal of Social History* 47(4): 829–954.

Arrow, K. J. 1972. Models of job discrimination. In *Racial Discrimination in Economic Life*, vol. 83, edited by A. H. Pascal. Lexington, MA: Lexington Books.

———. 1998. What has economics to say about racial discrimination? *Journal of Economic Perspectives* 12(2): 91–100.

Atkinson, A. B., Trinder, C., and Maynard, A. 1978. Evidence on intergenerational income mobility in Britain. *Economics Letters* 1(4): 383–388.

Bachmann, R., Bechara, P., and Schaffner, S. 2014. Wage inequality and wage mobility in Europe. *Review of Income and Wealth* 62(1): 181–197.

Banerjee, A., Iyer, L., and Somanathan, R. 2008. Public action for public goods. *Handbook of Development Economics* 4: 3117–3154.

Becker, G. S. 1957. *The Economics of Discrimination*. Chicago: University of Chicago Press.

Benabou, R. 1993. Workings of a city: location, education, and production. *Quarterly Journal of Economics* 108(3): 619–652.

Blinder, A. S. 1973. Wage discrimination: reduced form and structural estimates. *Journal of Human Resources* 8(4): 436–455.

Borjas, G. J. 2011. *Heaven's Door: Immigration Policy and the American Economy*. Princeton, NJ: Princeton University Press.

Bowles, S., Loury, G. C., and Sethi, R. 2014. Group inequality. *Journal of the European Economic Association* 12(1): 129–152.

Brubaker, R. 2009. Ethnicity, race, and nationalism. *Annual Review of Sociology* 35: 21–42.

Cain, G. G. 1986. The economic analysis of labor market discrimination: A survey. *Handbook of Labor Economics* 1: 693–785.

Calvo-Armengol, A. and Jackson, M. O. 2004. The effects of social networks on employment and inequality. *American Economic Review* 94(3): 426–454.

Card, D. and Krueger, A. 1996. School resources and student outcomes: an overview of the literature and new evidence from North and South Carolina. *Journal of Economic Perspectives* 10(6): 31–50.

Caselli, F., and Coleman, W. J. 2013. On the theory of ethnic conflict. *Journal of the European Economic Association* 11(s1): 161–192.

Cassan, G. 2015. Identity-based policies and identity manipulation: evidence from Colonial Punjab. *American Economic Journal: Economic Policy* 7(4): 103–131.

Collins, W. J. and Margo, R. A. (0000. When did ghettos go bad? Residential segregation and socio-economic outcomes. *Economics Letters* 69: 239–243.

Corak, M. 2013. Income inequality, equality of opportunity, and intergenerational mobility. *Journal of Economic Perspectives* 27(3): 79–102.

Corak, M. and Heisz, A. 1999. The intergenerational earnings and income mobility of Canadian men: evidence from longitudinal income tax data. *Journal of Human Resources* 34(3): 504–533.

Cutler, D. M. and Glaeser, E. L. 1997. Are ghettos good or bad? *Quarterly Journal of Economics* 112(3): 827–872.

Davis, F. J. 2001. *Who Is Black?: One Nation's Definition*. University Park, PA: Penn State Press.

Denton, N. A. and Massey, D. S. 1988. Residential segregation of Blacks, Hispanics, and Asians by socioeconomic status and generation. *Social Science Quarterly* 69(4): 797.

Drèze, J. and Sen, A. 2013. *An Uncertain Glory: India and Its Contradictions*. Princeton, NJ: Princeton University Press.

Epple, D. and Romano, R. E. 1998. Competition between private and public schools, vouchers, and peer-group effects. *American Economic Review* 88(1): 33–62.

Eramian, L. 2014. Ethnicity without labels? Ambiguity and excess in "post-ethnic" Rwanda. *Focaal* 2014(70): 96–109.

Esteban, J. and Ray, D. 2008. On the salience of ethnic conflict. *American Economic Review* 98(5): 2185–2202.

Farley, R. and Frey, W. H. 1994. Changes in the segregation of Whites from Blacks during the 1980s: Small steps toward a more integrated society. *American Sociological Review* 59(1): 23–45.

Fearon, J. D. and Laitin, D. D. 2000. Violence and the social construction of ethnic identity. *International Organization* 54(04): 845–877.

Fenton, S. 1996. Counting ethnicity: social groups and official categories. In *Interpreting Official Statistics*, edited by R. Levitas and W. Guy, 143–165. London: Routledge.

Galanter, M. 1984. *Competing Equalities: Law and the Backward Classes in India*. Berkeley: University of California Press.

Gaskin, D. J., Dinwiddie, G. Y., Chan, K. S., and McCleary, R. R. 2012. Residential segregation and the availability of primary care physicians. *Health Services Research* 47(6): 2353–2376.

Geertz, C. 1978. The bazaar economy: Information and search in peasant marketing. *American Economic Review* 68(2): 28–32.

Goldin, C. and Katz, L. 2009. *The Race between Education and Technology*. Cambridge, MA: Harvard University Press.

Goldscheider, C. 2002. Ethnic categorizations in censuses: comparative observations from Israel, Canada, and the United States. In *Census and Identity: The Politics of Race, Ethnicity, and Language in National Censuses*, 71–91. Cambridge: Cambridge University Press.

Granovetter, M. 1974. *Getting a Job: A Study of Contacts and Careers*. Chicago: University of Chicago Press.

———. 1985. Economic action and social structure: The problem of embeddedness. *American Journal of Sociology* 91(3): 481–510.

———. 2005. The impact of social structure on economic outcomes. *Journal of Economic Perspectives* 19(1): 33–50.

Greif, A. 1993. Contract enforceability and economic institutions in early trade: the Maghribi traders' coalition. *American Economic Review* 83(3): 525–548.

Heckman, J. J. 1998. Detecting discrimination. *Journal of Economic Perspectives* 12(2): 101–116.

Heckman, J. J. and Siegelman, P. 1993. The urban institute audit studies: their methods and findings. In *Clear and Convincing Evidence: Measurement of Discrimination in America*. Urban Institute, Washington, DC.

Hunter, M. 2007. The changing political economy of sex in South Africa: The significance of unemployment and inequalities to the scale of the aids pandemic. *Social Science & Medicine* 64(3): 689–700.

Jackson, M. O. 2014. Networks in the understanding of economic behaviors. *Journal of Economic Perspectives* 28(4): 3–22.

Khalfani, A. K. and Zuberi, T. 2001. Racial classification and the modern census in South Africa, 1911–1996. *Race and Society* 4(2): 161–176.

Kjelsrud, A. and Somanathan, R. 2017. Poverty targeting through public goods. In *Poverty and Income Distribution in India*, edited by Banerjee et al. New Delhi: Juggernaut.

Kumar, H. and Somanathan, R. 2016. Affirmative action and long-run changes in group inequality in India. Technical report, Working Paper, UNU WIDER.

Loury, G. C. 1981. Intergenerational transfers and the distribution of earnings. *Econometrica: Journal of the Econometric Society* 49(4): 843–867.

———. 2016. When black lives matter: The ethics of race, crime and punishment in America. The Lee Lecture on Politics and Government, All Souls College, Oxford University. Delivered on May 25.

Loveman, M. 2014. *National Colors: Racial Classification and the State in Latin America.* New York: Oxford University Press.

Marteleto, L. J. 2012. Educational inequality by race in Brazil, 1982–2007: structural changes and shifts in racial classification. *Demography* 49(1): 337–358.

Massey, D. S. and Denton, N. A. 1987. Trends in the residential segregation of Blacks, Hispanics, and Asians: 1970–1980. *American Sociological Review* 52(6): 802–825.

Morning, A. 2008. Ethnic classification in global perspective: a cross-national survey of the 2000 census round. *Population Research and Policy Review* 27(2): 239–272.

Munshi, K. and Rosenzweig, M. 2006. Traditional institutions meet the modern world: caste, gender, and schooling choice in a globalizing economy. *American Economic Review* 96(4): 1225–1252.

Neal, D. A. and Johnson, W. R. 1996. The role of pre-market factors in Black-White wage differences. *Journal of Political Economy* 104(5): 869–895.

Neumark, D. 2012. Detecting discrimination in audit and correspondence studies. *Journal of Human Resources* 47(4): 1128–1157.

Nobles, M. 2000. *Shades of Citizenship: Race and the Census in Modern Politics.* Palo Alto, CA: Stanford University Press.

Oaxaca, R. 1973. Male-female wage differentials in urban labor markets. *International Economic Review* 14(3): 693–709.

O'Flaherty, B. and Sethi, R. 2015. Urban crime. *Handbook of Regional and Urban Economics* 5: 1519–1621.

Pande, R. 2003. Can mandated political representation increase policy influence for disadvantaged minorities? Theory and evidence from India. *American Economic Review* 93(4): 1132–1151.

Phelps, E. S. 1972. The statistical theory of racism and sexism. *American Economic Review* 62(4): 659–661.

Schelling, T. C. 1969. Models of segregation. *American Economic Review* 59(2): 488–493.

———. 1978. *Micromotives and Macrobehavior.* New York: Norton.

Sethi, R. and Somanathan, R. 2004. Inequality and segregation. *Journal of Political Economy* 112(6): 1296–1321.

———. 2009. Racial inequality and segregation measures: some evidence from the 2000 census. *Review of Black Political Economy* 36(2): 79–91.

Sharan, A. 2003. From caste to category: colonial knowledge practices and the depressed/scheduled castes of Bihar. *Indian Economic & Social History Review* 40(3): 279–310.

Simon, P. 2008. The choice of ignorance: the debate on ethnic and racial statistics in France. *French Politics, Culture & Society* 26(1): 7–31.

Solon, G. 1992. Intergenerational income mobility in the United States. *American Economic Review* 82(3): 393–408.

———. 2002. Cross-country differences in intergenerational earnings mobility. *Journal of Economic Perspectives* 16(3): 59–66.

Somanathan, R. 2006. Assumptions and arithmetic of caste-based reservations. *Economic and Political Weekly* 41(24): 2436–2438.

———. 2011. The demand for disadvantage. In *Culture, Institutions, and Development: New Insights Into an Old Debate*, pages 125–140. New York: Routledge.

Spence, M. 1973. Job market signaling. *Quarterly Journal of Economics* 87(3): 355–374.

Tiebout, C. M. 1956. A pure theory of local expenditures. *Journal of Political Economy* 64(5): 416–424.

United Nations Booklet of Public Information, U. N. O. 1969. Segregation in South Africa: Questions and answers on the policy of apartheid. New York.

Vergnani, L. 2000. Racial segregation is revived in South Africa's dormitories. *Chronicle of Higher Education* 46: A57–A59.

Wimmer, A. 2013. *Ethnic Boundary Making: Institutions, Power, Networks.* New York: Oxford University Press.

Yanow, D. 2015. *Constructing "Race" and "Ethnicity" in America: Category-Making in Public Policy and Administration.* New York: Routledge.

5

CONFLICT AND DEVELOPMENT

Debraj Ray and Joan Esteban

No society is immune from the darkest impulses of man.
—Barack Obama, New Delhi, India, January 27, 2015

5.1. INTRODUCTION

In this review, we examine the links between economic development and social conflict. By *economic development*, we refer broadly to aggregate changes in per capita income and wealth or in the distribution of that wealth. By *social conflict*, we refer to within-country unrest, ranging from peaceful demonstrations, processions, and strikes to violent riots and civil war. In whatever form it might take, the key feature of social conflict is that it is *organized*: It involves groups and is rooted—in some way or form—in within-group identity and cross-group antagonism.[1]

Our review is organized around the critical examination of three common perceptions: that conflict declines with ongoing economic growth; that conflict is principally organized along economic differences rather than similarities; and that conflict, most especially in developing countries, is driven by ethnic motives. Although these perceptions are not necessarily wrong, they are often held too closely for comfort; hence the qualification "critical" in our examination.

Within-country conflicts account for an enormous share of the deaths and hardships in the world today. Since World War II, there have been 22 interstate conflicts with more than 25 battle-related deaths per year; 9 of these conflicts have killed at least 1,000 people over the entire history of the conflict (Gleditsch et al. 2002). The total number of attendant battle deaths in these conflicts is estimated to be around 3–8 million (Bethany and Gleditsch 2005). The very same period has witnessed 240 civil conflicts with more than 25 battle-related deaths per year, and almost half of these conflicts killed more than 1,000 people (Gleditsch et al. 2002). Estimates of the total number of battle deaths in these conflicts are in the range of 5–10 million (Bethany and Gleditsch 2005). To the direct count of battle deaths, one would do well to add the mass assassination of up to 25 million noncombatant civilians (during the same time period; Center for Systemic Peace) and

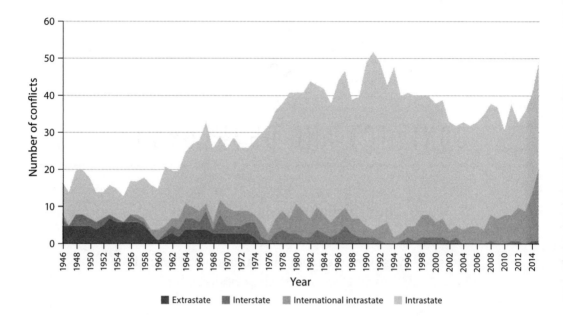

FIGURE 5.1. Armed conflicts by type, 1946–2015. Conflicts include cases with at least 25 battle deaths in a single year. Figure taken from Melander et al. (2016).

indirect deaths due to disease and malnutrition, which have been estimated to be at least four times as high as violent deaths, not to mention the forced displacements of 60 million individuals by 2015 (UNHCR 2015).[2] In 2015, there were 29 ongoing conflicts that had killed 100 or more people in 2014, with cumulative deaths for many of them climbing into the tens of thousands. Figure 5.1 depicts global trends in inter- and intrastate conflict, and figure 5.2 shows the distribution of these conflicts over the world regions.

Of course, things were probably worse in the past. For instance, Steven Pinker's book *The Better Angels of Our Nature* (Pinker 2011) is a delightfully gruesome romp through the centuries in an effort to show that violence of all forms has been on the decline. And he is undoubtedly correct: Compared to the utter mayhem that prevailed in the Middle Ages and certainly earlier, we are surely constrained—at least relatively speaking—by mutual tolerance, the institutionalized respect for cultures and religions, and the increased economic interactions within and across societies. To this one must add the growth of states that seek to foster those interactions for the benefit of their citizens and that internalize the understanding that violence—especially across symmetric participants—ultimately leads nowhere.

And yet, it is not hard to understand why this sort of long-run celebration seemingly flies in the face of the facts. We appear to live in an incredibly violent world. Not a day goes by, it seems, when we do not hear of some new atrocity: individuals beheaded, planes shot from the sky, suicide bombings of all descriptions, mass killings, and calls to even more escalated violence. True, perspective is important: We did not live a century ago, nor in the Middle Ages, nor in the early days of Christendom. Nor did those eras have access to the Internet, where each act of savagery can be played on YouTube or by media outlets specializing in breaking news. With the calm afforded by a longer historical view,

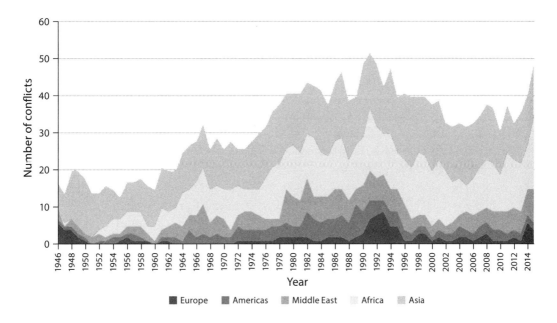

FIGURE 5.2. Armed conflicts by region, 1946–2015. Conflicts include cases with at least 25 battle deaths in a single year. Figure taken from Melander et al. (2016).

a perspective that Pinker correctly brings to the table, we can place our tumultuous present into context.

What today's violence does show, however, is that there are limits to peace and civility as long as there are enormous perceived inequities in the world, and, as we try to argue in this review, high on that list of perceived inequities are economic considerations. Even the most horrific conflicts, those that seem entirely motivated by religious or ethnic intolerance or hatred, have that undercurrent of economic gain or loss that flows along with the violence, sometimes obscured by the more gruesome aspects of that violence but never entirely absent. From the great religious struggles of the past to modern civil wars and ethnic conflicts, we can see—if we look hard enough—a battle for resources or economic gain: oil, land, business opportunities, or political power (and political power is, in the end, a question of control over economic resources).

This sort of economic determinism is unnecessarily narrow to some sensibilities, and perhaps it is. Perhaps conflict, in the end, is a "clash of civilizations" (Huntington 1996), an outcome of simple ethnic hatred, or the unfortunate corollary of a religious or ideological dogma. Perhaps, but that sort of reasoning is incomplete. Is anti-Semitism a fundamental construct; or is racism just a primitive abhorrence of the Other; or is the caste system born from some primeval, intrinsic desire to segregate human beings? In all of these queries, there is a grain of truth: Anti-Semitism, racism, or ethnic hatred is deeply ingrained in many people, perhaps by upbringing or social conditioning. Often, we can get quite far by simply using these attitudes as working explanations to predict the impact of a particular policy or change (and we do so in section 5.5). But stopping there prevents us from seeing a deeper common thread that, by creating and fostering such attitudes, there are gains to be made, and those gains are often economic. By following the economic trail and asking *cui bono?*, we can obtain further insights into the origins of prejudice and violence that will—at the very least—supplement any non-economic understanding of conflict.

This review, therefore, asks the following questions:

1. How is economic prosperity (or its absence) related to conflict? What is the connection between economic development and conflict? Does economic growth dampen violence or provoke it?
2. Is the main form of economic violence between the haves and the have-nots? Is conflict born of economic similarity or difference?
3. Is there evidence for the hypothesis that "ethnic divisions"—broadly defined to include racial, linguistic, and religious differences—are a potential driver of conflict? And if so, does this rule out economic motives as a central correlate of conflict?

5.2. THREE COMMON PERCEPTIONS ABOUT CONFLICT

We organize the themes of this review around three common perceptions.

Perception 1: Conflict Declines with Per Capita Income. Perhaps the most important finding of the literature on the economics of conflict is that per capita income is systematically and *negatively* correlated with civil war, whether one studies "incidence" or "onset." This is a result that appears and reappears in the literature, especially in large-scale cross-country studies of conflict (see, e.g., Collier and Hoeffler 1998, 2004a, 2004b; Fearon and Laitin 2003a; Hegre and Sambanis 2006).

Yet even this seemingly robust finding is fraught with difficulties of interpretation. Although there is no doubting the correlation between these two variables, there is also little doubt that countries with a history of active conflict are likely to be poor or that there are omitted variables, such as the propping up of a dictatorship by international intervention or support, that lead to both conflict and poverty. There are also issues of conceptual interpretation that we discuss in section 5.3.

The argument we make in this review is that economic development is intrinsically uneven. That tranquil paradigm on which generations of economists have been nurtured—balanced growth—must be replaced by one in which progress occurs in fits and starts via processes in which one sector and then another takes off, to be followed by the remaining sectors in a never-ending game of catch-up. Thus, it is often the case that overall growth is made up of two kinds of changes: one that creates a larger pot to fight over, and therefore increases conflict, and another that raises the opportunity cost to fighting, and therefore decreases conflict. Whether conflict is positively or negatively related to growth will therefore depend on the type of growth, specifically, how uneven it is across sectors or groups. Cross-country studies are too blunt to pick up these effects in any detail.

Perception 2: Conflict Is Created by Economic Difference, Rather Than Similarity. The great revolutions of the twentieth century were born of economic difference and of the realization that a relatively small elite reaped most of the rewards while a large, struggling proletariat suffered under a disproportionately small share of the pie. The traditional literature on crisis and revolution, in which the contributions of Karl Marx are central, focuses nearly exclusively on class conflicts. More recently, Piketty (2014) documents the rise of economic inequality in the second half of the twentieth century. Movements such as Occupy have rehighlighted the awareness of economic differences and the connections between those differences and social unrest.

And yet, there are eerie lines along which conflict occurs across economically *similar*, rather than different, groups. This conflict is over resources that are explicitly and directly contested: a limited pool of jobs (e.g., natives versus immigrants), the same customers (business rivalries across organized groups), or scarce land. Because the conflict is over the direct use of a resource, the groups are often remarkably similar in their economic characteristics, although there are exceptions to this rule.[3] The gains from conflict are immediate: The losing group can be excluded from the sector in which it directly competes with the winners.

This is the second theme of this chapter. It leads naturally to the view that ethnicity is perhaps a marker for organizing similar individuals along opposing lines, which takes us to our third and final perception.

Perception 3: Conflicts in Developing Countries Are Based on Ethnic Differences. Conflicts in postcolonial developing countries, although certainly not immune to the gravitational pull of class, have often been organized along *ethnic* lines. Specifically, many conflicts appear to be largely ethnic, geographical, and religious in nature, whereas outright economic class struggle is relatively rare. Indeed, as noted by Fearon (2006), 100 of the 700 known ethnic groups participated in rebellions over the period 1945–1998. Observations such as these led Horowitz (1985: 92), a leading researcher in the area of conflict, to remark that "in much of Asia and Africa, it is only modest hyperbole to assert that the Marxian prophecy has had an ethnic fulfillment."

This perception is the subtlest of all to analyze. The facts, as laid down by Horowitz and others, are certainly correct. But there are two puzzles to confront. First, if conflicts are ethnic, then "ethnic divisions" must somehow bear a strong statistical relationship to conflict. It turns out that the answer to this question is somewhat involved and, in part, fundamentally rests on a proper conceptualization of what "ethnic divisions" entail. Second, if such a result were to be true, how would one interpret it? One approach is based on the primordialist position that at the heart of all conflicts is intrinsic hatred and that conflict is a Huntingtonian "clash of civilizations." A second approach is instrumentalist: Non-economic divisions can be and frequently are used to obtain economic or political gains by violent means, often through exclusion.

And this takes us back to Perception 2. Nothing dictates that the groups in conflict must be *economically* distinct. Indeed, we have argued the contrary. If two groups are very similar economically, it is more likely that they will intrude on each other's turf: The motives for exclusion and resource grabbing—and therefore for violence—may be even higher. In such situations, organized violence will *necessitate* the instrumental use of markers based on kin, religion, geography, and other possibly observable differences—in a word, on ethnicity. In short, there is no contradiction between the use of non-economic markers in conflict and the view that conflict may be driven by economic forces.[4]

5.3. ECONOMIC DEVELOPMENT AND CONFLICT

Systematic empirical studies of conflict begin with the work of Collier and Hoeffler (1998, 2004a) and Fearon and Laitin (2003a). These are cross-sectional studies (presumably) aimed at establishing the correlates of civil war, though causal interpretations have all too readily been advanced. Perhaps the most important finding from this literature is that conflict is negatively related to per capita income. In this section, we discuss alternative interpretations of this finding, but we also critically examine the finding itself.

5.3.1. The Empirical Finding

Collier and Hoeffler (1998, 2004a) and Fearon and Laitin (2003a) observe that per capita income and conflict are significantly and negatively correlated. Table 5.1 reproduces the central table used by Fearon and Laitin (2003a). They study the onset of "civil war," which they define as (*a*) "fighting between agents of (or claimants to) a state and organized, non-state groups," having (*b*) a yearly average of at least 100 deaths, with a cumulative total of at least 1,000 deaths, and (*c*) at least 100 deaths on both sides (to rule out genocides or one-sided massacres) (76). These criteria are similar though not identical to other criteria used in the literature, which principally vary in the size of the thresholds and generally lack the third criterion.

They conclude that

> Per capita income . . . is strongly significant in both a statistical and a substantive sense: $1,000 less in per capita income is associated with 41% greater annual odds of civil war onset, on average . . . The income variable is not just a proxy for "the West," whose states might have low rates of civil war for reasons of culture or history that have little to do with income. The estimated coefficient . . . remains strongly significant. (Fearon and Laitin 2003a: 83)

One can discuss this finding on a number of levels, and we do so next.

5.3.1.1. The Definition of Conflict

We get an obvious preliminary consideration out of the way: There are conflicts, and there are conflicts. Whether threshold-like criteria involving substantial numbers of deaths are adequate depends on the type of question the analyst has in mind. Many types of organized unrest can lead to relatively low levels of deadly violence: demonstrations, strikes, coups, the detaining of political prisoners, or even the growth of organized crime come to mind. Their costs might even exceed the costs imputed to civil wars. Indeed, one might argue that this type of social unrest corresponds more clearly to the Marxian notion of "class struggle" rather than a recurring state of armed civil war.[5] The problem, of course, is that we do not have comprehensive data of this sort.

When violence is involved, it could have potent and long-lasting consequences for social tension and yet have low numbers of fatalities attached to it. Think of the Irish Republican Army (IRA) movement in the United Kingdom; the Red Army Faction in West Germany in the late 1970s; the Black Panther movement in the United States; the permanent situation of turmoil in Italy, with either real or fabricated extreme left terrorist actions; the military coups in Greece and Turkey; the failed coups in France in 1958 and in Spain in 1981; and the Euskadi Ta Askatasuna (ETA) movement (again in Spain) since

Table 5.1. Logit analyses of determinants of civil war onset, 1945–1999

Variable	[1] Civil War	[2] Ethnic War	[3] Civil War	[4] Civil War (COW)
Prior war	**−0.954 (0.314)	*−0.849 (0.388)	**−0.916 (0.312)	−0.551 (0.374)
Per capita income	***−0.344 (0.072)	***−0.379 (0.100)	***−0.318 (0.071)	***−0.309 (0.079)
log(Population)	***0.263 (0.073)	***0.389 (0.110)	***0.272 (0.074)	**0.233 (0.079)
log(% mountain)	**0.219 (0.085)	0.120 (0.106)	*0.199 (0.085)	***0.418 (0.103)
Noncontiguous state	0.443 (0.274)	0.481 (0.398)	0.426 (0.272)	−0.171 (0.328)
Oil Exporter	**0.858 (0.279)	*0.809 (0.352)	**0.751 (0.278)	***1.269 (0.297)
New state	***1.709 (0.339)	***1.777 (0.415)	***1.658 (0.342)	**1.147 (0.413)
Instability	**0.618 (0.235)	0.385 (0.316)	*0.513 (0.242)	*0.584 (0.268)
Democracy [Polity IV]	0.021 (0.017)	0.013 (0.022)		
Ethnic Fractionalization	0.166 (0.373)	0.146 (0.584)	0.164 (0.368)	−0.119 (0.396)
Religious Fractionalization	0.285 (0.509)	*1.533 (0.724)	0.326 (0.506)	*1.176 (0.563)
Anocracy			*0.521 (0.237)	*0.597 (0.261)
Democracy [Dichotomous]			0.127 (0.304)	0.219 (0.354)
Constant	***−6.731 (0.736)	***−8.450 (1.092)	***−7.019 (0.751)	***−7.503 (0.854)
Observations	6327	5186	6327	5378

Note: The dependent variable is coded as "1" for country years in which a civil war began and as "0" in all others. Columns 1, 2, and 3 use conflict onset data as described by Fearon and Laitin (2003a), and column 4 uses conflict data from the Correlates of War (COW) project. Per capita income and population are in thousands and lagged 1 year. For all variable definitions, see Fearon and Laitin (2003a). Standard errors are in parentheses, with *, **, and *** representing associated p-values lower than 0.05, 0.01, and 0.001, respectively. Adapted from Fearon and Laitin (2003a, table 1).

the early 1970s. One could add the many revolutionary movements and bloody military coups in Latin America in countries with per capita incomes well above those of many Asian or African countries. How can it be that this does not sufficiently show up in the empirical results? Is this because the number of deaths did not go beyond some arbitrary threshold of 50 or 100 yearly casualties?

More generally, we cannot discard the possibility that the empirical results capture more the explicit outbreaks of civil war, whereas, in reality, there could be active sources of discontent that do not always come to fruition in the form of multiple deaths and overt conflict. That is, the reasons for conflict could well be active at all economic levels, but poverty allows that conflict to fully express itself. A hypothesis compatible with this alternative interpretation is that richer countries have better state capacity to contain insurgencies than poor countries, a line of reasoning to which we return below (section 5.3.2.2).

We do not wish to dwell excessively on this specific issue. There is not much more that can be done with the data we currently have. Our only point is that developed countries may have relatively more of the "quieter conflicts," leading to a bias in the observed correlation between per capita income and conflict.

5.3.1.2. Endogeneity

The negative relationship between per capita income and conflict clearly must be interpreted with a great deal of caution, rife as it is with endogeneity. Ongoing conflict will destroy productive capacity, leading to lower per capita income. For instance, Hess (2003) estimates the cost of all civil wars to be 8% of the world's GDP, and de Groot (2009) finds that global GDP in 2007 would have been 14.3% higher if there had not been any conflict since 1960. Using geolocalized data for Africa with a 1-degree grid, Mueller (2016) finds that for every year that a cell in that grid experiences more than 50 fatalities, growth is reduced by about 4.4 percentage points.[6]

There are also important omitted variables to contend with. Both low per capita income and conflict could be the joint outcome of weak political institutions, as mentioned above. Djankov and Reynal-Querol (2010) argue that country-specific historical factors are highly significant in explaining both conflict and weak institutions and that they render nonsignificant the role of low per capita income. Besley and Reynal-Querol (2014) find that local conflicts over the past few centuries are highly significant in explaining today's civil wars, as well as today's development outcomes. Ashraf and Galor (2013) and Arbath et al. (2015) argue that genetic diversity explains both the level of development and social conflict.

A good instrument for per capita income would alleviate some of these concerns. Rainfall is potentially such an instrument, and this connection is exploited by Miguel et al. (2004). Their analysis must rely, however, on regions in which rainfall significantly affects output, which explains their focus on Sub-Saharan Africa. Specifically, a large fraction of output is agricultural, and irrigation is far from being widespread. Indeed, a first-stage regression of income growth on weather shock works very well for Sub-Saharan Africa. Yet this strategy is obviously limited. Rainfall shocks do not work well outside the Sub-Saharan sample or, indeed, even over more recent time periods for Sub-Saharan Africa.

Miguel et al. (2004) work with a conflict database developed by the Peace Research Institute of Oslo (PRIO) in conjunction with the University of Uppsala. (We return to this database in section 5.5.2.) The specification they use is somewhat different from that employed by Collier and Hoeffler (1998, 2004a, 2004b) and Fearon and Laitin (2003a): They relate the incidence of civil conflict in Sub-Saharan Africa (over the period from 1981 to 1999) to the *growth rate* of per capita GDP (rather than its level). The relationship Miguel et al. (2004: 727) uncover is strong: "A five-percentage-point drop in annual economic growth increases the likelihood of a civil conflict (at least 25 deaths per year) in the following year by over 12 percentage points, which amounts to an increase of more than one-half in the likelihood of civil war."

Table 5.2 reproduces the main results found by Miguel et al. (2004). Of particular interest are columns 3–5, which report the instrumental variables specifications and show

Table 5.2. Economic growth and civil conflict in Sub-Saharan Africa

| | Conflict Deaths ≥25 | | | | ≥1000 |
| | [1] | [2] | [3] | [4] | [5] |
Variable	OLS	OLS	IV-2SLS	IV-2SLS	IV-2SLS
Economic Growth t	-0.210 (0.200)	-0.210 (0.160)	-0.410 (1.480)	-1.130 (1.400)	*-1.48 (0.82)
Economic Growth $t-1$	0.010 (0.200)	0.070 (0.160)	**-2.250 (1.070)	**-2.550 (1.100)	-0.77 (0.70)
log(GDPpc 1979)	0.085 (0.084)		0.053 (0.098)		
Democracy [Polity IV $t-1$]	0.003 (0.006)		0.004 (0.006)		
Ethnolinguistic Fractionalization	0.510 (0.400)		0.510 (0.390)		
Religious Fractionalization	0.100 (0.420)		0.220 (0.440)		
Oil Exporter	-0.160 (0.200)		-0.100 (0.220)		
Log Mountainous	0.057 (0.060)		0.060 (0.058)		
Log Population $t-1$	*0.182 (0.086)		*0.159 (0.093)		
Country FE	no	yes	no	yes	yes
R^2	0.53	0.71	–	–	–
Root Mean Square Error	0.31	0.25	0.36	0.32	0.24
Observations	743	743	743	743	743

Note: Dependent variable: civil conflict ≥25 deaths (and ≥1,000 deaths in column 4). For detailed variable definitions, see Miguel et al. (2004). Huber robust standard errors are in parentheses, with *, **, and *** representing associated confidence levels higher than 90%, 95%, and 99%, respectively. Regression disturbance terms are clustered at the country level. The instrumental variables for economic growth in regressions 3–5 are growth in rainfall, t and growth in rainfall, $t-1$. A country-specific year time trend is included in all specifications (coefficient estimates not reported). Adapted from Miguel et al. (2004, table 4).

the negative association between growth and conflict. It is also noteworthy that the *level* of per capita income plays no role once growth rates are included in the picture.[7] This is not to say that the previous cross-sectional correlations are necessarily suspect but rather that the exact nature of the relationship between income and conflict—questions of correlation and causation aside—is far from cast in stone. We return to this issue in section 5.3.3, after we discuss matters of interpretation.

5.3.2. Questions of Interpretation

If we tentatively buy the causal link from low income (or negative shocks to income) to conflict, there are two main interpretations to consider:

1. *Opportunity cost.* Individuals allocate their time between productive work and conflictual activity to obtain resources. When the society is poor, the opportunity cost of engaging in conflict is lower.
2. *Weak institutions.* States in poor societies are ill-equipped to handle the demands and pressures of conflicting groups and succumb more easily to open conflict.

The first of these interpretations is favored by Collier and Hoeffler (1998, 2004a) and the second by Fearon and Laitin (2003a).

5.3.2.1. Opportunity Cost

The opportunity cost argument, going back to Becker (1968) and Ehrlich (1973) and echoed in Skaperdas (1992), Hirshleifer (1995), Grossman and Kim (1995), Dal Bó and Dal Bó (2011), and Miguel et al. (2004),[8] emphasizes the fact that conflict and production are often alternative choices. In poorer societies, engaging in the alternative of productive labor has a low payoff. So there could be a greater incentive to participate in conflict.

The opportunity cost argument is prima facie reasonable, and we return to it in a more nuanced way below (section 5.3.3). But it is obviously inadequate as an explanation for the income–conflict correlation. True, the opportunity cost of conflict is lower in a poorer society, but so, presumably, are the gains from conflict: There is less to seize. The argument must connect the opportunity costs of conflict *relative* to the potential gains from conflict. But the movement of per capita income up or down does not immediately affect this relative magnitude in any particular way.

So even if considerations of opportunity cost are appropriate—and we believe that they are—once nested into the context at hand, the explanation leaves something to be desired. It is this schizophrenic nature of economic change that generates really interesting predictions about conflict and development, but those predictions will need to be examined under a finer lens and not through considerations of aggregate income alone. We return to this question below (section 5.3.3).

We note in passing that it is easier to buy the opportunity cost argument in the case of short-term income *shocks*, which is the leading case examined by Miguel et al. (2004). For instance, if the potential conflict is over oil resources held by a state, then a sudden change in, say, agricultural employment opportunities may well lead to more of the conflict.

5.3.2.2. Weak Institutions

A second explanation for the prevalence of social conflict in poorer countries is one favored by Fearon and Laitin (2003a): The state is too weak either to adequately solve the competing claims of different groups or to effectively prevent conflict when it does break out. Their empirical findings, while similar to those of Collier and Hoeffler, are interpreted thus:

> [T]he civil wars of the period have structural roots, in the combination of a simple, robust military technology and decolonization, which created an international system numerically dominated by fragile states with limited administrative control of their peripheries . . . [O]ur analysis suggests that while economic growth may correlate with fewer civil wars, the causal mechanism is more likely a well-financed and administratively competent government. (Fearon and Laitin 2003a: 88)

Just as in the case of the opportunity cost argument, the effect of a weak state on the likelihood of conflict must balance two forces in opposite directions. Weak states are easier to confront, but the payoff from victory is equally modest, if for no other reason than the fact that victory can in turn be challenged (Mehlum and Moene 2011). On the other hand, not *all* prizes naturally scale up and down with per capita income and state weakness. For instance, the discovery of natural resources, by suddenly increasing the rent controlled by a weak state, can become a destabilizing factor, a "curse." Likewise, if there is intrinsic value (over and beyond economics) attached by a group to religious, cultural, or political dominance, weak states can contribute to conflict.

So "state capacity" certainly matters. As defined by Skocpol (1985), state capacity refers to the ability of a government to administer its territory effectively through four basic state capacities: the capacity to mobilize financial resources (extractive capacity), the capacity to guide national socioeconomic development (steering capacity), the capacity to dominate by using symbols and creating consensus (legitimation capacity), and the capacity to dominate by the use or threat of force (coercive capacity). Snider (1990), who, like Fearon and Laitin (2003a), links state capacity (or the lack thereof) to the likelihood of violent conflict, proposes to measure such capacity by the share of the government budget in aggregate GDP. This measure is now standard in the literature, and, indeed, there are dramatic differences in this measure across rich and poor countries. Germany, France, and the United Kingdom have a budget/GDP ratio more than twice that of many African countries.

While we have already touched on issues of endogeneity, it bears reiteration that state capacity and conflict can jointly evolve in a self-reinforcing manner. For instance, countries that have undergone civil war experience a loss in capacity (see, e.g., Chowdhury and Mansoob 2013), which makes the government less able to manage public affairs, to effectively confront future uprisings, or to generate growth. The recent contributions by Besley and Persson (2008, 2009, 2010, 2011) and McBride et al. (2011) have not only popularized among economists the notion of "state capacity" but have also developed a more nuanced theoretical basis for thinking about the intertwined connections between capacity and conflict.

5.3.3. Development and Conflict Reconsidered

So far, we have been somewhat skeptical about the observed cross-sectional relationship between per capita income and social conflict. At the same time, we believe that the core conceptual arguments—based on opportunity cost or weak state capacity—have great merit and are capable of extension to more nuanced contexts. Such extensions may not yield a straightforward connection between development and conflict, but that does not make the exercise any less useful.

Consider the opportunity cost argument applied to societies that experience uneven growth. Ongoing structural change, rapid technical progress, and globalization all lead to situations in which economic growth is not uniform across the entire economy. Sometimes that growth can spur conflict if the gains are viewed as loot to be seized. Or it can decrease conflict by increasing the opportunity costs of engaging in unproductive, violent activity. Both outcomes are possible in principle.

Dal Bó and Dal Bó (2011) formalize this idea in the context of a simple general equilibrium model. They consider an economy with several sectors: The productive sectors differ (as in the Heckscher-Ohlin framework) in the capital intensity of production, and there is, in addition, a sector that generates unproductive "appropriation" or conflict, with its participants essentially preying on the output of the productive sectors. Individuals freely sort themselves into the sectors; the equilibrium size of the "appropriation sector" is used as a measure of overall conflict.

Consider such an equilibrium and suppose that the capital-intensive sector receives a positive shock. Then wealth increases all around, but because the sector that benefits is relatively capital-intensive, the *relative* prices move against labor. The resulting lowering of wages (relative to other prices) permits the opportunity cost argument to come into its own: More labor flows into the appropriation sector, and conflict rises. (It can even be shown by example that the increase in conflict might overpower the positive shock that generated it in the first place, resulting in a negative outcome in the net.) Conversely, positive shocks to the labor-intensive sector (or policies that subsidize employment) will raise relative wages, implying this time that conflict declines. As for the net effect when the economy grows overall: Who knows? It would depend on whether that growth is balanced or not and, if not, on the technological profile of the sectors that benefit from growth.

The findings of Miguel et al. (2004) fit well within this framework. A weather shock impinges on agriculture, which is labor-intensive. Thus, conflict is expected to rise with adverse shocks. This argument, while in no way negating the finding itself, calls into question the conceptual validity of the instrument as one that affects "overall growth." With a disaggregated view in mind, weather shocks can be seen as affecting particular segments of that economy—the labor-intensive agricultural sector, to be precise. Whether there is an overall negative causal relationship running from per capita income to conflict is not, therefore, established by this particular choice of instrument.

Dube and Vargas (2013) explicitly cast their empirical study within the Dal Bó–Dal Bó model. They study how internal conflicts in Colombia are affected by the movements of world prices for two commodities that are particularly pertinent to that country: oil and coffee. (Colombia is a major exporter of both products.) For each of these commodities, they interact its international price with the amount of that good produced in each municipality. When coffee prices rise, conflict falls more in coffee-producing municipalities. In sharp contrast, when oil prices rise, conflict *increases* in oil-producing municipalities. These observations are in line with the Dal Bó–Dal Bó model. Coffee production is a relatively labor-intensive activity, so that a rise in coffee prices is likely to lead to an increase in wages relative to the overall price index. The opportunity cost argument then kicks in, reducing conflict. In contrast, oil extraction and processing are capital-intensive, so that the opportunity cost argument runs in the opposite direction, with positive shocks generating conflict.

In fact, coffee prices fell by 68% over the period 1997–2003, and oil prices rose by 137% over the period 1998–2005. The estimates of Dube and Vargas (2013) suggest that the former led to 18% more guerrilla attacks and 31% more paramilitary attacks in the average coffee-producing municipality relative to non-coffee-producing municipalities. There is also evidence for the channel explored by Dal Bó and Dal Bó (2011): Wages and hours of work fall to a greater extent in the average coffee municipality. In contrast, the rise in oil prices appears to induce an additional increase of 14% in paramilitary attacks in the average oil-producing municipality. Again, there is evidence of the channel: Oil municipality tax revenue increases differentially, and so do the kidnappings of politicians and leaders.

In summary, theories of uneven growth demand that we keep track of the opportunity cost of engaging in conflict *relative* to the expected payoff from conflict. It may be that the latter rises while the former increases less so, thereby making rebellion a more likely outcome.

5.4. CONFLICT DRIVERS: DIFFERENCE OR SIMILARITY

Karl Marx justifiably stands at the apex of all studies of within-country conflict, and research on the subject has been dominated by the Marxist view that *class* is the only relevant social cleavage and *class conflict* the fundamental source of social unrest. For Marx, social conflict would pave the road to the ultimate downfall of capitalism, with workers seizing control of the means of production from the capitalists. So the struggle across economic classes has been viewed as focal, often correctly so. Quite apart from the great revolutions of the early and mid-twentieth century, "class consciousness" continues in some shape or form to the present day: Witness, for instance, the explicit awareness of and discontent over high inequality that followed on the heels of the financial crisis of 2008.[9] Class conflict, or the fear of it, is also at the heart of all taxation systems, which invariably display some degree of progressivity. The recent contribution by Piketty (2014) has played an important role in publicizing the remarkable increase in income inequality in all the Organization for Economic Cooperation and Development (OECD) countries. Is such an intuitive link between inequality and conflict backed by the data?

5.4.1. Empirical Evidence on Social Conflict and Inequality

On the whole, though, the relationship between inequality and social conflict appears to be far more nuanced than what is suggested by a simple argument based on class alone and, in the stark form posited by Marx, tenuous at best. Researchers, mostly in political science, have tried for decades to find a convincing empirical connection (see, e.g., Nagel 1974; Midlarski 1988, Muller et al. 1989). Lichbach (1989) mentions 43 papers on the subject—some, according to him, "best forgotten." He concludes that the overall evidence obtained by all these works is thoroughly mixed. Some studies support each possible relationship between inequality and conflict, and others show no relationship at all. A recurrent observation is that under several measures of inequality, including the Gini index, conflict appears to be low both for low and for high values of inequality. Midlarsky (1988: 491) remarks on the "fairly typical finding of a weak, barely significant relationship between inequality and political violence . . . rarely is there a robust relationship discovered between the two variables."

While in the previous section we critically questioned the validity and interpretation of an empirically robust correlation between income and conflict, in the next section we must confront the lack of confirmatory empirical evidence on the inequality–conflict nexus.

5.4.2. Why We Do Not Find a Clear Link Between Inequality and Conflict

In the introduction to his book *On Economic Inequality*, Amartya Sen (1973: 1) asserts that "the relation between inequality and rebellion is indeed a close one." Why, then, can we not see this relationship in the data? In this section, we discuss a number of reasons for this failure.

First, all recent empirical exercises have tried to link income inequality with civil war, with the same conceptual problems of defining conflict that we describe above. Indeed, it is plausible that the dominant form taken by the class struggle envisioned by Marx is social unrest—strikes, demonstrations, etc.—rather than armed civil war. Therefore, empirical work on this nexus should pay special attention to indicators of "lower voltage" social unrest.

Second, all the contributions to this literature that we are aware of lack a well-defined model that informs and shapes the empirical test. The Gini index may not be suited to adequately capture social tensions, and the notion of polarization (Esteban and Ray 1994; Wolfson 1994) should be employed instead. We may also be missing very relevant interactions that a model would help us identify. We think that adequately modeling potential social conflict triggered by income differences is a priority for future research. In section 5.5, we develop just such a model for ethnic conflict.

Third, class conflict is often latent and inadequately expressed because, in a word, the rich have the means but not the motive to express this conflict, while the poor have the motive but lack the means. The experience of grassroots movements such as Occupy show how difficult it is to sustain a conflict on the basis of energy, enthusiasm, and anger alone. Where class conflict has emerged into the open, it has been dependent on sustained financing as well as labor. Money and finance are synergistic in conflict. This is a line of argument that Esteban and Ray (2008, 2011b) employ to explain the salience of nonclass conflict, perhaps along religious or ethnic lines.[10]

Finally, the fundamental tenets of the Marxian position could, in turn, be challenged. There are reasons to believe that economic similarity may be just as conflictual as economic inequality and, what is more, that a fight between two economically similar groups could be bitter and prolonged. This is the topic we turn to next.

5.4.3. Social Conflict and Similarity

Even if we could obtain empirical support for the argument that income inequality can generate social conflict, it is also undeniable that a situation of economic *similarity* can be conflictual in a direct way that no class confrontation can emulate. When employment, land, or business resources are scarce, like is often pitted against like, invariably to the great disappointment of conventional Marxists. The self-described socialist candidate in the 2016 US presidential race, Bernie Sanders, recently stated in an interview (Klein 2015) that open borders posed a threat:

Bring in all kinds of people, work for $2 or $3 an hour, that would be great for them. I don't believe in that. . . . You know what youth unemployment is in the United States of America today? . . . You think we should open the borders and bring in a lot of low-wage workers, or do you think maybe we should try to get jobs for those kids?

While the immigrant–native schism is the best-known example of conflict caused by economic similarity, it is by no means the only one. For instance, in developing countries, and at the heart of all ostensibly ethnic or religious conflicts, the land grab often plays a central role. A leading example is the Rwandan conflict, where economic desperation was clearly seen to play a major role in what appeared to be unreasoning ethnic hatred:

> [E]conomic desperation, blighting individuals' presents and their perceived futures, was a contributor to the willingness of many thousands of poor farmers and urban dwellers (a) to fear the possibility of a Tutsi land-and-jobs grab under a victorious RPF [Rwandan Patriotic Front] regime, (b) to be tempted by more specific hopes for land and jobs, or, more crudely still, to participate in order to grab a share of the victims' property. (Austin 1996: 10; quoted in Andre and Platteau 1998: 38–39)

Austin's observations for Rwanda find supportive echoes in the studies of Prunier (1996), Andre and Platteau (1998), and many others, as well as in other contexts. After all, Rwanda is far from being the only example of land conflicts disguised as ethnic hatred. Finally, labor and land do not exhaust the similarity interface: There are also business interests. For instance, ostensibly religious conflicts in India are laden with sinister economic undertones; witness, for instance, the systematic decimation of rival businesses during the anti-Sikh pogroms of 1984. Likewise, Hindu–Muslim conflicts are inextricably linked with economic motives. As Asghar Ali Engineer (1987: 969) writes of one of these episodes (in Meerut, India),

> If [religious zeal] is coupled with economic prosperity, as has happened in Meerut, it has a multiplying effect on the Hindu psyche. The ferocity with which business establishments have been destroyed in Meerut bears testimony to this observation. Entire rows of shops belonging to Muslims . . . were reduced to ashes.

Mitra and Ray (2014) study the determinants of the different waves of Hindu–Muslim violence. Accordingly, in their work, a clear pattern emerges: Conflict appears to react significantly and positively to an increase in Muslim per capita income, while the opposite reaction, a decline in conflict, occurs with an increase in Hindu per capita income. The very fact of a connection between changes in group relative incomes and subsequent conflict is of interest, as it suggests a clear instrumental basis for conflict.

Figure 5.3 summarizes the findings of Mitra and Ray (2014). Each panel contains lines that connect a particular region of India over three rounds of the National Sample Survey, ordered by the (logarithm of) Hindu and Muslim per capita expenditure in those rounds. (The Survey uses expenditure as a proxy for income.) The vertical axis records the logarithm of total "casualties"—killed plus injured—in the 5-year period starting immediately after the rounds. Region-specific and time-specific effects on conflict have been eliminated from the latter number; only the residuals are plotted. The line segments are generally upward sloping in figure 5.3a and downward sloping in figure 5.3b, showing that, indeed, conflict follows an increase in Muslim per capita income, while a decline in

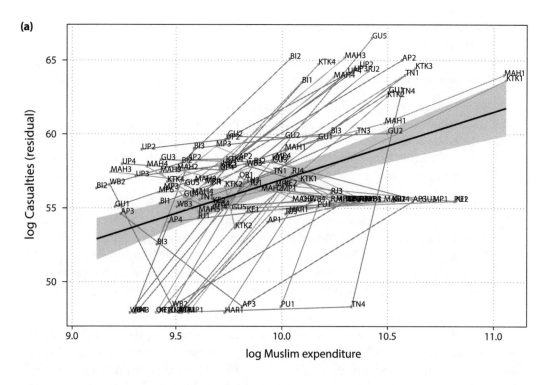

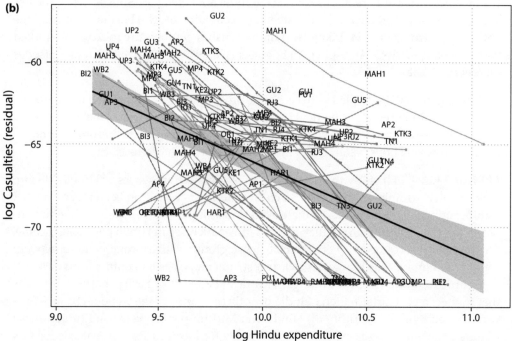

FIGURE 5.3. Conflict and per capita expenditure in India for (*a*) Muslims and (*b*) Hindus. Each panel plots the residual of casualties in the 5-year period following expenditures, after region and time effects have been removed. Each line segment connects three data points for a region. *Source*: Figure taken from Mitra and Ray (2014, fig. 4).

conflict occurs after an increase in Hindu per capita income. Mitra and Ray argue that the rise in Hindu income represents an opportunity cost effect, much like the change in coffee prices in Colombia in the study by Dube and Vargas (2013). Hindu income increases serve to reduce Hindu–Muslim violence. The rise in Muslim incomes, on the other hand, is analogous to the change in oil revenues in the work of Dube and Vargas: It aggravates the desire to loot or to seek retribution against an upstart community.

The work of Mitra and Ray (2014) illustrates the story of ethnic conflict that we have in mind. It is an instrumentalist view and is quite opposed in spirit to the notion espoused by Samuel Huntington (1996) that such violence is a "clash of civilizations." (The instrumentalist view, incidentally, is far from being our creation (see, e.g., Brubaker and Laitin 1998).) The argument runs in two steps. First, economic *similarity*, not difference, can breed tensions; such tensions, involving as they do the direct contestation of resources, can be extremely acute. Second, the resolution of such tensions involves the use of existing ethnic divisions or categories to create a sense of us versus them, thereby accentuating the salience in those divisions. We recognize that such an instrumentalist view cannot survive entirely on its own: There must be some exploitable historical animosity embedded in those ethnic divisions. Nevertheless, on the surface, a conflict across economically similar groups that differ in caste, ethnicity, or geography can be a profoundly economic conflict!

It is entirely reasonable to assume that, with uneven growth or globalization, some social or economic groups will benefit more than others, possibly because of their fortuitous positioning.[11] This is certainly true of income groups, because higher income or wealth may permit individuals to incur the threshold costs that are needed for training for and entry into a new occupation or to incur the setup costs for entering a new business. But it is also true of ethnic groups whenever such groups exhibit some degree of geographical or sectoral specificity. Returning to the Hindu–Muslim example, we observe that the Gulf boom led to differential gains between Hindus and Muslims. Rising oil prices resulted in a sizable increase in the demand for labor in the Gulf countries. Indian Muslims were more likely to emigrate there than Indian Hindus. In turn, this flow resulted in remittances back to India from the Gulf, affecting Muslim incomes and expenditures in India, often generating highly visible real estate improvements, and presumably improving the ability of Indian Muslims to enter new business sectors.

These changes in group-specific relative incomes can have deep effects on individual aspirations and possibly on resulting frustrations (see Ray 1998, 2006; Appadurai 2004; Genicot and Ray 2014). Albert Hirschman's parable (see Hirschman and Rothschild 1973; Gurr 1968) of a multilane traffic jam comes to mind: You are in one of the lanes and stationary, like all the cars around you. Now the cars in the other lane begin to move. Do you feel better or worse? Presumably, that depends on how long the other lane has been moving. Unevenness can be tolerated or even welcomed as it raises aspirations across the board, but it will be tolerated for only so long. On the flip side of this parable, uneven growth can be frustrating rather than inspiring, and economic development may be threatened by violent means.

Note that such frustration may not necessarily be tied to intergroup *inequality*. The improvement in the economic fortunes of a rival group may be viewed as a threat (or a source of frustration) even when that rival group is poorer than your group. In the latter case, an increase in cross-group *equality* can be conflictual. The key word is *unevenness*, not inequality.[12] If two groups have disparate incomes, as in a caste-based or feudal society, cross-group interaction may be limited and pose little threat. But as the fortunes of the deprived group improve, the previously advantaged groups may feel threatened and react with violence (see, e.g., Olzak and Shanahan 1996). This argument echoes de Tocqueville's (1955) study of the French Revolution, in which he repeatedly stressed the apparent paradox that the Revolution was the outcome of improvement, not impoverishment. It was precisely because the middle classes were becoming richer that they were more conscious of where they felt they *should* stand. In that new light, the privileges of aristocracy were unacceptable. And so it was that "[t]he French found their position insupportable, just where it had become better" (de Tocqueville 1955: 186). In summary, "[i]t is not always that from going from bad to worse that a society falls into revolution" (222).

Observe that, in the argument of Olzak and Shanahan (1996), it is the advantaged groups that have the upper hand in igniting a conflict—perhaps the disadvantaged groups are too poor or in a numerical minority. In the de Tocqueville (1955) argument, it is the rising frustration of the relatively disadvantaged groups that leads to the proverbial storming of the Bastille (though not proverbial in his case). Just *which* group has this power to ignite a conflict may be deeply rooted in the history of the society.

5.4.4. Difference and Similarity: A Summary

The traditional economic view of conflict is that it is driven by large inequalities in income and wealth. Oddly enough, the empirical support for this assertion is mixed. In the previous sections, we discussed why this might be so. We need good theory to precipitate the form of the relationship, followed by empirical research that takes serious advantage of the theory. While there is little doubt—as can be seen simply by looking at the world around us—that large inequalities create social tension and unrest, it is entirely unclear what the specific structure of that relationship should be, for instance, whether a measure of inequality or polarization should be used as an explanatory variable. The technology of conflict, such as the synergistic use of labor and financing, also requires careful study. It is only with such building blocks in place that we can begin to conjecture the particular relationship to be examined. We believe that this is a significant area for future research.

Our second point is that the possibility of class-driven conflict does not preclude the existence of other sources of social discontent. In the next section, we examine the case of ethnic conflict. But the more basic observation is that similarity can be directly conflictual when resources are limited and economic change is unevenly distributed. This is possibly relevant even for developed countries, but it is a first-order consideration in developing countries. Nonclass conflict is the outcome, and ethnicity is a convenient marker to categorize individuals on either side of some quasi-artificial divide. It is not that the marker is not real: It is certainly as real as or more real than the dividing line between, say, the viciously competitive supporters of rival soccer teams. It does not take much for people to fight. But additionally, more than a soccer match is at stake: It is the division of economic gains. From this point of view, conflict is more about the *change* in the relative income status of two similar groups rather than the overall level of inequality, a consideration that also appears in Stewart (2002). How group-based aspirations are formed and how certain groups might react to frustrated aspirations remain important and open research directions.

5.5. CONFLICT AND ETHNIC DIVISIONS

We now turn to a particularly pernicious non-economic marker: ethnicity, broadly defined to include religious or ethnolinguistic differences. Suppose that we use the criterion, employed by the PRIO, that a conflict is "ethnic" if it involves a clash against the state on behalf of some ethnic or religious group (see Fearon 2006). Under this criterion, more than half of the civil conflicts recorded since the end of World War II have been classified as ethnic by the Political Instability Task Force dataset (see also Fearon and Laitin 2003a, 2003b). Such conflicts involved 14% of the 709 ethnic groups categorized worldwide (see Fearon 2003). Brubaker and Laitin (1998), examining the history of internal conflicts in the second half of the twentieth century, are led to remark on "the eclipse of the left-right ideological axis" (424) and the "marked ethnicization of violent challenger-incumbent contests" (425). Horowitz (1985: 92), in a monumental treatise on the subject of ethnic conflict, observes that "[t]he Marxian concept of class as an inherited and determinative affiliation finds no support in [the] data. Marx's conception applies with far less distortion to ethnic groups."

While we do not mean to suggest that *all* conflicts between ethnic groups are those between economically similar groups, they often are. Ethnicity might serve as a convenient rallying cry to include and exclude. Of course, for that to happen, the society in question must have ethnic divisions to draw upon to begin with. That leads to the following hypothesis: "Ethnically divided" societies are more likely to engage in conflict. Do we have evidence to support this view?

5.5.1. Fractionalization, Polarization, and Ethnic Conflict

The first question to be answered is: Just what does "ethnically divided" mean? There is a classical measure that attempts to get at this concept, and it was first introduced in the 1964 edition of the Soviet *Atlas Narodov Mira* (Bruk and Apenchenko 1964). If $\{n_1, n_2, \ldots, n_m\}$ stand for the population shares of m ethnic groups, then the *fractionalization index* is given by

$$F = \sum_{i=1}^{m} n_i(1 - n_i), \tag{5.1}$$

which can be interpreted as the probability that two individuals drawn at random from the society will belong to different groups.

Fractionalization is a famous index that has been put to work on several occasions. It has been connected to low per capita GDP (Alesina et al. 1999), slow economic growth (Easterly and Levine 1997), underprovision of public goods (Alesina and La Ferrara 2005), or poor governance (Mauro 1995). It is also closely connected to the Gini coefficient of economic inequality.[13]

Unsurprisingly, this is the measure that leading scholars initially used as a possible correlate of conflict (see Collier and Hoeffler 1998, 2004a; Collier 2001; Fearon and Laitin 2003a). Yet, the verdict is surprisingly murky: There does not appear to be a strong relationship between conflict and ethnic fractionalization. Look again at the Fearon and Laitin (2003a) regression, reproduced in table 5.1. Ethnic fractionalization is marginally significant, and only in some specifications. The same lack of significance can be observed in the results of Miguel et al. (2004), reproduced in table 5.2, or in the studies by Collier and Hoeffler (1998, 2004a). Fearon and Laitin (2003a: 82) conclude that the observed "pattern is thus inconsistent with . . . the common expectation that ethnic diversity is a major and direct cause of civil violence."

And yet, these statistical findings remain strangely at odds with the frightening ubiquity of within-country ethnic conflicts. We reiterate a now-familiar complaint below: This is in part because we are not using theory to inform the empirical specification at hand. The fact that fractionalization is an easily available index is not a good enough reason to conclude that if *that* measure is uncorrelated with conflict, then ethnic divisions are not conflictual. We need a theory that connects conflict to "ethnic divisions," and we must exploit that connection in the empirics.

The problem is (as is true of empirical research more generally) that, often, little discipline is imposed on the specification of a conflict regression. Much of that research involves the kitchen sink approach of including all variables that could possibly play a role in ethnic conflict. Such an approach is problematic on at least three counts. First, the number of plausible variables is unbounded, not just in principle but apparently also in practice: 85 different variables have been used in the literature (Hegre and Sambanis 2006). Trying them out in various hopeful combinations smacks uncomfortably of data mining. Second, even if we could narrow down the set of contenders, there are many ways to specify the empirical equation that links those variables to conflict. Finally, the absence of a theory hinders the interpretation of the results.

Motivated by the need to capture how conflictual a society is, Esteban and Ray (1994) introduce a measure of *polarization* based on the intergroup perceived distances d_{ij} as well as on their size.[14] They derive the central index

$$P = \sum_{i=1}^{m}\sum_{j=1}^{m} n_i^2 n_j d_{ij}. \tag{5.2}$$

The polarization index P speaks to the existence of deep cleavages, not a "fractionalization" of society into many small and possibly inconsequential fissures. Polarization differs deeply from fractionalization. For instance, P attains its maximum when the population is divided into two equally sized groups at some maximum distance from each other, while F attains its maximum when every individual is his own group, different from the rest. For a detailed discussion of the differences between polarization and fractionalization, readers are referred to Esteban and Ray (2011a).

We will, of course, need to think about how to implement d empirically. But there is a noteworthy special case in which d is "binary": $d_{ij} = 1$ if $i \neq j$, and 0 otherwise. That reduces P to the measure

$$R = \sum_{i=1}^{m}\sum_{j=1}^{m} n_i^2 (1 - n_i). \tag{5.3}$$

This is the index used by Montalvo and Reynal-Querol (2005) in their study of the determinants of intermediate- and high-intensity civil war, as defined by the PRIO. We discuss their results in section 5.5.2.2. Before we do so, we describe how a theory of conflict can highlight the role of polarization and fractionalization in capturing "ethnic divisions."

5.5.2. Are Ethnic Divisions Conflictual?

If ethnicity is indeed salient, conflict should be related to the existence of "ethnic divisions" in society. How do we conceive of that connection?

5.5.2.1. Theory

From a statistical perspective, fractionalization and polarization are just two seemingly equally reasonable ways of measuring ethnic divisions. Which (if any) of these should matter in connecting ethnic "divisions" to conflict? This is the issue studied by Esteban and Ray (1999, 2011a), who introduce an explicit game-theoretic model of conflict. (The informal exposition in this section draws heavily on the work of Esteban et al. 2012b.)

Consider m groups engaged in conflict. Think of two types of prizes at stake. One type is "public," the individual payoff from which is undiluted by the recipient's own group size. Examples include a norm or culture, a religious state, the abolition of certain rights or privileges, the repression of a language, the banning of certain organizations, the seizing of political power, or the satisfaction of seeing one's own group vindicated or previous defeats avenged. Let u_{ij} be the payoff experienced by an individual member of group i in the case in which group j wins and imposes its preferred policy; $u_{ii} > u_{ij}$ is true almost by definition. This induces a notion of "distance" across groups i and j : $d_{ij} \equiv u_{ii} - u_{ij}$, which can be interpreted as the loss to i of living under the policy implemented by j.

The other type of prize is "private." Examples include access to oil or other mineral deposits (or the revenue from them), specific material benefits obtained from administrative or political positions, or just plain loot. In contrast to public prizes, private prizes are diluted by group size: The larger the group, the smaller is the return per capita. Moreover, there is no fine-tuned notion of intergroup distance with private prizes: Either your group seizes the loot, or it does not.

Individuals in each group expend costly resources (time, effort, risk) to influence the probability of success. The winners get to make the decisions and enjoy the prize(s); the losers have to live with the policies chosen by the winners. A *conflict equilibrium* is just the induced Nash equilibrium of this game with an extended payoff structure that includes both individual and group concerns (see Esteban and Ray 2011a for a detailed discussion of this point). Briefly, we assume that an individual will act selfishly, and to some extent, will act in the interest of the ethnic group.

Let us measure the intensity of conflict—call this C—by the money value of the average, per capita level of resources expended in conflict. Esteban and Ray (2011a) argue that the population-normalized C is described by the approximate formula

$$C \sim [\lambda P + (1 - \lambda)F], \tag{5.4}$$

for large populations, where λ is the relative degree to which the prize is public, and F and P are the polarization and fractionalization indices described earlier in equations (5.1) and (5.2), the former constructed using binary distances and the latter using intergroup distances d_{ij} derived from "public" payoff losses $u_{ii} - u_{ij}$. The constant of proportionality (not explicitly stated in equation 5.4) will depend on the scale of the prize(s) as well as the extent to which a typical individual places payoff weight on his group.

Note how the theory informs empirical specification. In particular, the publicness of the prize is naturally connected to polarization. With public payoffs, group size counts twice: once because the payoffs accrue to a larger number and again because a larger number of individuals internalize that accrual and therefore contribute more to the conflict. Intergroup distances matter, too: The precise policies interpreted by the eventual winner continue to be a cause of concern for the loser. Both these features—the "double emphasis" on group size and the use of distances—are captured by the polarization measure P. On the other hand, when groups fight for a private payoff—say, money—one winner is as bad as another to an individual whose group does not win, and measures based on varying intergroup "distances" become irrelevant. Moreover, with private payoffs, group identification counts for less than it does with public payoffs, as group size erodes the per capita gain from the prize.

In short, the theory tells us to obtain data on P and F and combine them in a particular way. It informs us, moreover, that F alone is unlikely to be significant in explaining conflict, as the resulting omitted variable P would confound the effects laid bare in equation (5.4).

5.5.2.2. Empirics

Esteban et al. (2012a, 2012b) study 138 countries in 5-year intervals over the period 1960–2008. They measure conflict intensity in two ways. The first is by using the death toll. In this review, we consider one such example, which is the index PRIO-C in table 5.3. For every 5-year period and every country, set conflict equal to 1 if that country has experienced more than 25 but less than 1,000 battle-related deaths in any of these years; to 2 if the country has experienced more than 1,000 battle-related casualties in any of those years; and to 0 otherwise.[15] The second approach is to use a nondeath measure; they employ the Index of Social Conflict (ISC, in table 5.3) computed by the Cross-National Time-Series Data Archive (Banks 2008), which embodies eight different manifestations of internal conflict, such as politically motivated assassinations, riots, guerrilla warfare, etc.

To compute P and F, Esteban et al. (2012a, 2012b) rely on Fearon (2003), who identifies more than 800 "ethnic and ethno-religious" groups in 160 countries. For intergroup distances, Laitin (2000), Fearon (2003), and Desmet et al. (2012) employ the *linguistic distance* between two groups as a proxy for group "cultural" distances in the space of public policy (see Esteban et al. 2012a, 2012b for details). Such a proxy undoubtedly takes Esteban et al. (2012a, 2012b) out on a limb, but reflects a common trade-off. On the negative side, linguistic distances are at best an imperfect proxy for the unobserved "true distances." But factors that are closer to the unobserved truth—say, answers to survey questions about the degree of intergroup antagonism or, perhaps, a history of conflict—are deeply endogenous to the problem at hand. Whether the trade-off is worth it is something that only a mixture of good intuition and final results can judge.

To obtain a relative publicness index by country, Esteban et al. (2012a, 2012b) use the value of oil reserves per capita as a a proxy for privateness. They create an index of "publicness" by measuring the degree of power afforded to those who run the country, "more democratic" being regarded as correlated with "less power" and, consequently, a lower valuation of the public payoff to conflict. The latter indicator is multiplied by per capita GDP to convert the "poor governance" variables into monetary equivalents. (The results are robust to the precise choice of this conversion factor; see Esteban et al. 2012a, 2012b.) To obtain relative publicness, Esteban et al. (2012a, 2012b) convert the two indices into a single ratio A, used in table 5.3.

Table 5.3. Ethnicity and Conflict

Variable	[1] PRIO-C	[2] ISC	[3] PRIO-C	[4] ISC
P	***5.16 (0.001)	***19.50 (0.002)	−1.48 (0.606)	−16.33 (0.227)
F	*0.93 (0.070)	*3.56 (0.061)	0.76 (0.196)	0.31 (0.878)
$P\Lambda$			***11.174 (0.003)	***61.89 (0.001)
$F(1-\Lambda)$			*1.19 (0.097)	***10.40 (0.000)
GDPPC	**−0.34 (0.047)	***−2.26 (0.004)	*−0.36 (0.080)	***−3.02 (0.001)
POP	***0.24 (0.000)	***1.14 (0.000)	***0.21 (0.001)	***1.30 (0.000)
NR	−0.27 (0.178)	−0.53 (0.497)	−0.00 (0.570)	0.00 (0.432)
MOUNT	0.00 (0.537)	0.02 (0.186)	0.00 (0.362)	*0.03 (0.061)
NCONT	***1.06 (0.001)	***4.55 (0.001)	**0.77 (0.026)	***4.28 (0.001)
POLITICS	0.18 (0.498)	0.29 (0.789)	−0.00 (0.328)	**−0.00 (0.026)
LAG	***1.99 (0.000)	***0.46 (0.000)	***1.94 (0.000)	***0.44 (0.000)
CONST	−	0.90 (0.915)	−	9.19 (0.398)
(Pseudo)-R^2	0.35	0.43	0.36	0.44
Observations	1125	1111	1104	1090
Countries	138	138	138	138

Note: 138 countries over 1960–2008, with the time period divided into 5-year intervals. Dependent variables PRIO-C and ISC are indices of conflict described in the text. Variables P and F are measures of polarization and fractionalization described in text. Variable A is an index of relative publicness described in text. All specifications employ region and time fixed effects, not shown explicitly. *p*-values are in parentheses, with *, **, and *** representing associated *p*-values lower than 0.05, 0.01, and 0.001, respectively. Robust standard errors adjusted for clustering have been employed to compute *z*-statistics. Columns 1 and 3 are estimated by maximum likelihood in an ordered logit specification, and columns 2 and 4 by OLS. For detailed descriptions of these and all control variables, see Esteban et al. (2012b). Adapted from Esteban et al. (2012b, table 1).

Columns 1 and 2 of table 5.3 record the results for each specification of the conflict intensity variable—the death-based outcome PRIO-C and the aggregated indicator of several conflict dimensions ISC. Ethnicity turns out to be a significant correlate of conflict, in sharp contrast to the findings of the previous studies mentioned above. Throughout, P is highly significant and positively related to conflict. F also has a positive and significant coefficient.

Quite apart from statistical significance, the effect of these variables is quantitatively important. Taking column 1 of table 5.3 as a reference, if we move from the median polarized country (Germany) to the country in the 90th percentile of polarization (Niger) while changing no other institutional or economic variable in the process and evaluating those variables at their means, the predicted probability of experiencing conflict (i.e., the probability of observing strictly positive values of PRIO-C) rises from approximately 16% to 27%, which implies an increase of 69%. Performing the same exercise for F (countries at the median and at the 90th percentile of F are Morocco and Cameroon, respectively) takes us from 0.19% to 0.25% (an increase of 31%).

In columns 3 and 4 of table 5.3, the main independent variables are $P^*\Lambda$ and $F^*(1 - \Lambda)$, just as specified by the theory, where Λ is our estimated degree of relative publicness. Polarization interacted with Λ is positive and highly significant, and the same is true of fractionalization interacted with $1 - \Lambda$. These results confirm the relevance of both polarization and fractionalization in predicting conflict once the variables are interacted with relative publicness in the way suggested by the theory.

Indeed, the level terms P and F are no longer significant on their own once entered in interacted form with Λ. Assuming that the proxy for relative publicness accurately captures all the issues at stake, this is precisely what the model would predict. For instance, polarization should have no further effect over and beyond the "λ-channel": Its influence should dip to zero when there are no public goods at stake. The fact that the measure Λ happens to generate exactly this outcome is of interest. But the public component of that estimate is built solely on the basis of governance variables. If that construction wipes out all extraneous effects of polarization (as it appears to do), it may suggest that primordial factors such as pure ethnic differences per se have little to do with ethnic conflict.

Esteban et al. (2012a, 2012b) present a large number of variations on these regressions. We refer the reader to those papers for more details.

Esteban et al. (2012a, 2012b) are not the first to take polarization to the data. In an earlier contribution, Montalvo and Reynal-Querol (2005) study the determinants of intermediate- and high-intensity civil war, as defined by the PRIO. (Montalvo and Reynal-Querol do not relate polarization to public prizes or fractionalization to private prizes.) To measure ethnic divisions, they use the measure of ethnic polarization in equation (5.3). We summarize their main result by quoting them (Montalvo and Reynal-Querol 2005: 805):

> The first column [in a multicolumn table of regressions] shows that the index of ethnolinguistic fractionalization . . . has no statistically significant effect on the incidence of civil wars. This result is consistent with Fearon and Laitin (2003a) and Collier and Hoeffler (1998). If we substitute the index of ethnic fractionalization by the RQ index of ethnic polarization [which is the measure in equation (5.3)] . . . we find (column 2) a positive and statistically significant effect on the incidence of civil wars. . . . Column 3 checks the relative strength of the index of ethnic polarization versus fractionalization, and shows that the coefficient on ethnic fractionalization is not significantly different from zero, while the one on polarization is positive and significant.

5.5.3. Ethnic Salience: A Summary and Research Directions

A society has several potential cleavages, most of which lie dormant at any one point in time. After all, the term "ethnicity" covers a variety of traits that can be invoked to substantiate a division: religion, language, regional identity, gender, and so forth. And overlying all these traits, though sometimes obscured, is the deep difference that comes from economic inequality. Just how these various factors interact and exactly which cleavage is ignited in any given situation are research topics of first-order importance. In particular, we need to understand why an ethnic division often acquires salience over an economic division.

From this perspective, the results on ethnic divisions and violence that we have summarized represent the tip of the iceberg. For instance, the fact that an ethnic division exists is not enough reason for it to be invoked. We also need to study the economic characteristics of each ethnic group, along with its demographics. The theoretical framework has to be enriched to allow for a far more nuanced interaction of economics and ethnicity. It is only such a framework that can suggest the right specification to take to the data. Such a research project seems indispensable if we are to truly understand the fundamental connections between inequality, ethnicity, development, and conflict.

In this section, we discuss some specific arguments that bear on the salience of nonclass markers in conflict, as well as the interaction between economic and ethnic characteristics. We have already touched briefly on some of these issues in sections 5.4.2 and 5.4.3, but they are worth additional elucidation in the specific context of ethnic conflict.

In the first place, economic demarcation across classes is a two-edged sword: While it breeds resentment, the very poverty of the have-nots separates them from the means for a successful insurrection. Conflict is not always an outpouring of individuals onto the streets, though in times of extreme stress it may well be. Yet even such movements that are explicitly based on class—Occupy being a recent and visible example—require sustained organization and financing so as not to die out. That requires, in turn, a commitment to class struggle by some socially aware subsegment of the wealthy, so that a large rebellion by the proletariat or the peasantry can be sustained in a viable way. This is rare, and in developing countries, where the problem of poverty is so endemic, it is rarer still.

In contrast, in conflicts across groups that are not demarcated by pure economic considerations, each group will have both poor and rich members, with the former supplying conflict labor and the latter supplying conflict finances. Esteban and Ray (2008) use this line of reasoning to argue for the salience of ethnic conflict. As an example, suppose that individuals can be rich or poor and of either of two ethnic identities. The issue is, then, whether individuals will prefer to form alliances using class or ethnicity. When effective activism requires both labor and finance, this will happen more easily with ethnic alliances. Therefore, controlling for the size of the prize, the poor of the majoritarian ethnic group will prefer an ethnic to a class alliance.

This argument suggests an interesting interaction between inequality and ethnicity, in which ethnic groups with a higher degree of within-group inequality will be more effective in conflict (Esteban and Ray 2011b). Such a hypothesis is entirely distinct from—though complementary with—the notion of "horizontal inequality" across ethnic groups, in which economic differentials *across* ethnic groups are an important correlate of conflict (Stewart 2002; Østby 2008; Cederman et al. 2011). Both hypotheses are worth testing. As an example, Huber and Mayoral (2014) compute the Gini index of the income distribution within ethnic groups, as well as across groups, for a number of countries. In their study, within-group inequality is highly significant in explaining violent conflict. Between-group horizontal inequality is not. Here, again, is an echo of similarity–differences theme discussed above (section 5.4). More research on this theme is surely needed.

Second, the use of ethnicity (in a broad sense, including caste and religion) is related to the ease of identification and policing. Color and language are, of course, among the most commonly used identifiers. But there are others—among them geography, clothing, and (not entirely accurately) bodily identifiers such as circumcision.[16] As several researchers have observed, these markers can be used not just as a way of identifying the enemy during a conflict but also to deny a losing group any share of the spoils after a conflict (see, e.g., Fearon 1999; Chandra 2004; Caselli and Coleman 2013). In particular, Fearon (1999); Caselli and Coleman (2013); and Bhattacharya et al. (2015) use the ease (or absence) of group-member identification as a starting point for theories of ethnic conflict.

Third, the possibility of conflict across ethnic lines—while conceivably economic—presumes that there is some reason for there to be conflict across groups to begin with. There are two broad views on the ethnicity–conflict nexus (see, e.g., Brubaker and Laitin 1998; Fearon 2006). The "primordialist" view (e.g., Ignatieff 1993; Huntington 1996) takes the position that ethnic differences are ancestral, deep, and irreconcilable and, for these reasons, invariably salient. In contrast, the "instrumental" approach pioneered by Bates (1983) and discussed by Brubaker and Laitin (1998) sees ethnicity as a strategic basis for coalitions that seek a larger share of economic or political power. Under this view, ethnicity is a device for restricting the spoils to a smaller set of individuals. Certainly, the two views interact. Strategic ethnic conflict could be exacerbated by hatreds and resentments—perhaps ancestral or perhaps owing to a recent clash of interests—that are attached to the markers themselves. And there could also be factors at play other than economic considerations or hatreds: For instance, exclusion might be easier if ethnic groups are geographically concentrated (see, e.g., Matuszeski and Schneider 2006; Weidmann et al. 2010).

Fourth, it is worth taking note of the possible inadequacy of political institutions to solve the competing claims of the main social groups in developing countries. Developing countries were born from a process of often sudden or hasty decolonization that left newborn governments especially vulnerable to a host of competing claims. As Mayoral and Ray (2015) argue, postcolonial societies inherited certain institutions—e.g., progressive taxation, land reform, public provision of education or healthcare—that were designed to temper class conflict. That focus finds its echo even in scholarship. Noteworthy contributions such as those of Acemoglu et al. (2001) or Glaeser (2002) often invoke the implicit viewpoint of class to evaluate institutions. For instance, the differential effect of civil and common law is often viewed through the different treatment of private ownership. Our concern is different: Ethnically divided countries (which are correlated with poorer countries) may be less equipped to make transfers across ethnic groups than across income classes. Such class-sensitive arrangements are no coincidence, as the colonizing countries from which these newcomers separated have had centuries of experience in developing those very institutions. But the divisions in the newly born countries are often *ethnic*, and there are few analogous institutions for the differing fiscal treatment of ethnic groups. Such countries are therefore more prone to conflictual challenges on ethnic fronts.

Thus, economic policy in developing countries must often adapt to the realities of ethnicity, religion, or caste. After all, ethnic differences are often a (noisy) proxy for economic differences. The reason developing countries hone in on those ethnic differences—rather than on class per se—is that individual income is far harder to observe and can be an inadequate basis for policy.[17]

And as already noted, ethnicity, while imperfect, is often observable and therefore frequently used as a second-best solution to identify economic differences.

Particularly in Sub-Saharan Africa, but also in many other developing countries, income inequality is closely attached to ethnic identity. As an illustration, the Gini index of incomes can be decomposed into the inequality between ethnic groups, the inequality within groups, and a residual overlap term. In Sub-Saharan Africa, between-group inequality accounts for a large part of recorded inequality: It is more than three times as large as in the OECD countries and 50% larger than in other developing countries (data on ethnic inequality come from Huber and Mayoral 2014). In addition, between-group inequality is the component of the Gini decomposition that co-moves most with the Gini, with a correlation of almost 0.7. Hence, explaining income inequality in Sub-Saharan Africa often goes hand in hand with explaining between-group inequality.[18]

Given these correlations with economics, and given the general difficulty of observing individual incomes, it is hardly any surprise that public discourse often focuses on ethnicity. But it is not just discourse, it is also public action. For instance, government expenditures are often biased toward group-specific investments or transfers rather than universal public investment. This bias is especially remarkable in Sub-Saharan African countries, where ethnic divisions are deeper. Public investments often have a strong ethnic undertone (see, e.g., the study of road-building in Kenya by Burgess et al. 2015). Even explicit and formal policies have been formulated on the basis of non-economic markers. India has possibly the largest affirmative action program in the world, based on a massive reservation of jobs, college admissions, and political positions *by caste*. While that reservation has been historically justified on the basis of past inequities perpetuated on the so-called scheduled castes, there is little doubt that it has served as a proxy for *economic* redistribution. Such policies, even when well-intentioned, create an enormous salience for claims that are ethnically based and generate ethnic violence when those claims are not acceded to. A particularly recent example comes from Gujarat, where the influential and generally well-heeled Patel community has demanded "their share" of quotas in government jobs. In August 2015, violence broke out in Ahmedabad, leaving several dead.

At one level, such violence is reminiscent of an absurdist drama. How does an economically better-off community ask for quotas? The answer becomes clear when one recognizes that such ethnic divisions generally correlate with income, but do not correlate perfectly. Therefore, there are always grievances that can be justified: A rich person from a scheduled caste may get a government-sanctioned advantage relative to a poor Patel. And yet, ethnicity—including caste, in this case—needs to be retained because it is observable whereas, all too often, income is not.

5.6. CONCLUDING REMARKS

We have presented a panoramic view of the literature on social conflict and economic development organized around three widely shared views: Higher standards of living reduce the probability of conflict; inequality nurtures conflict; and most conflicts in developing countries are ethnic in nature. On the way, we have also described a number of research questions still open in each of these three broad fields. To briefly conclude, we divide these research suggestions into three major lines of potential progress in our understanding of economic development and social conflict.

The first line of research takes into serious consideration the idea that economic growth is unbalanced by nature. The uneven impact of sector- or group-specific economic fortune upsets traditional social and economic rankings. We must think not just of high aspirations that serve to inspire but also of high aspirations that can serve to frustrate. These considerations seem particularly relevant when differential economic growth takes place among previously similar groups.

The second line of research is to better explain the link between income inequality and social conflict. The one thing we know is that that connection is far from straight-forward, and, at many points in this chapter, we have emphasized both this fact and the possible reasons for it. There is much to be gained from a closer marriage between the-ory and empirics, similar to—but going well beyond—the analysis of the determinants of ethnic conflict summarized in the previous section. The discipline imposed by the-ory will tell us which are the relevant independent variables and how they interact.

The third line of research is related to the second, but goes beyond it. We have a long and distinguished tradition in theories of social conflict based on economic *distance*. But a substantial share of social conflict can be attributed to economically *similar* groups. The dividing cleavage is then non-economic (though the conflict can still be over economic resources). Typically, that cleavage manifests itself along ethnic lines. For this reason, the interaction between ethnic identity and economic characteristics and how such interac-tion might result in ethnic conflict are research topics of the highest importance.

In short, we need to broaden our horizons beyond economics, even for conflicts that are intrinsically economic in nature. We must explore more fully the interdependence between income distribution, ethnic identity, economic development, and social conflict.

NOTES

We are extremely grateful to the EDI Project, which sponsored and supported this research; in par-ticular, we thank Jean-Marie Baland, Anne Michels, Jean-Philippe Platteau, and members of the Sci-entific Committee of the EDI Project, who provided useful comments and guidance. D. R. acknowl-edges support from the National Science Foundation under grants SES-1261560 and SES-1629370. J. E. acknowledges support from the Spanish Ministerio de Economía e Innovación under grant ECO2015-66883-P. This chapter originally appeared in the *Annual Review of Economics, Annu. Rev. Econ.* 2017. 9:263–93.

1. That is not to argue that individual instances of violence, such as (unorganized) homicide, rape, or theft, are unimportant, and indeed, some of the considerations discussed in this chapter po-tentially apply to individual violence as well. But social conflict has its own particularities, spe-cifically, its need to appeal to and build on some form of group identity: religion, caste, kin, or occupational or economic class. In short, social conflict lives off of both identity and alienation.
2. Such displacements also have a high cost in lives due to endemic sicknesses to which the newly settled population is not immune to (see Cervellati and Sunde 2005; Montalvo and Reynal-Querol 2007).
3. For instance, the land acquisition debates in India feature very different groups because buyers and (potential) sellers see the land as being put to very different uses.
4. Economic similarity across groups is just one of many possible arguments for the salience of eth-nic violence. See section 5.5.3 for a more detailed discussion.
5. However, note that the Marxian view is that conflict is precipitated by the development of the "productive forces," whereas what we observe is that higher GDP reduces the likelihood of conflict.
6. Collier and Hoeffler (2004a, 2004b) estimate the typical cost of a civil war to be around $50 billion and argue that this reduces the future growth rate by 2 percentage points. The recent computa-tions by Gates et al. (2012) indicate that a medium-sized conflict with 2,500 battle deaths increases undernutrition by an additional 3.3%, reduces life expectancy by about 1 year, increases infant mortality by 10%, and deprives an additional 1.8% of the population from access to potable water. Undoubtedly, that in turn affects per capita income. For a rigorous methodology for com-puting the costs of conflict, see Abadie and Gardeazabal (2010). For an overview of the different quantitative cost estimates, see Lindgren (2004), de Groot (2009), and Mueller (2013).

7. This observation is related to Ciccone's (2011) critique of Miguel et al.'s (2004) exercise. Effectively, their specification connects conflict at date t to the growth of rainfall between periods $t-2$ and $t-1$. Ciccone argues that this connection says very little about the level–level relationship or indeed about whether conflict levels are affected by rainfall shocks, in the sense of a downward departure from "normal" rainfall levels, as opposed to a reduction in rainfall over two successive years. The latter could be a shock but could also be a mean reversion (if period $t-2$ had supernormal rainfall). Indeed, Ciccone (2011) finds no robust link between rainfall levels (or shocks) and civil conflict.

8. For instance, Hirshleifer (1991: 187) writes, "[R]ational behavior in a conflict interaction . . . is for the poorer side to specialize more in fighting, the richer side more in production."

9. Inequality made it to the headlines of articles in the popular press (see, e.g., Anthony 2014, titled "Class war is back again—and British politicians are running scared," or Schuman 2014, titled "There's a class war going on and the poor are getting their butts kicked"). In 2015, Cartier boss Johann Rupert declared he could not sleep because of the fear that "rising inequality will spark class war" (Petroff 2015). Earlier, in 2006, the bosses were a bit more bullish: In an interview with the *New York Times*, Warren Buffett said, "There's class warfare, all right . . . but it's my class, the rich class, that's making war, and we're winning" (Stein 2006).

10. There is also a literature that argues, both theoretically and empirically, that more unequal countries appear to carry out less redistributive policies, when a standard median voter argument would perhaps have suggested the opposite (see, e.g., Perotti 1996; Bénabou 2003). The main argument in this literature is that the poor may be less active politically.

11. This is in line with the argument of Bates (1983), who emphasizes the impact of uneven growth facilitating the emergence of an economic and cultural elite. This elite provides the leadership and the means for the escalation.

12. There is little evidence for the argument that the relative deprivation of a group or, indeed, overall economic inequality is conflictual. See, for instance, Lichbach (1989) for cross-country studies and Spilerman (1970, 1971, 1976); Wilson (1978); and Olzak and Shanahan (1996) for studies on race riots in the urban United States.

13. The Gini coefficient is proportional to $\sum_{i=1}^{m}\sum_{j=1}^{m} n_i n_j d_{ij}$, where d_{ij} is a measure of intergroup distance between i and j, usually absolute income differences. The fractionalization measure F corresponds precisely to the case in which d is "binary": $d_{ij}=1$ if $i\neq j$, and 0 otherwise.

14. Esteban and Ray (1994, 1999, 2011a); Wolfson (1994); and Duclos et al. (2004) all develop related measures of polarization that attempt to incorporate deep cleavages.

15. This index uses data from the jointly maintained database under the Uppsala Conflict Data Program and the PRIO, which gives the index its name.

16. Horowitz (1985: 41–51) provides many examples of the use of these and other markers to identify ethnic differences.

17. That is not to say that discourse in developed countries is immune to playing the ethnic card. Perhaps the most visible recent example is Ta-Nehisi Coates's (2016) call for direct transfers (reparations) to African Americans.

18. Alesina et al. (2016) show that what matters most for development are economic differences between ethnic groups coexisting in the same country rather than ethnic diversity per se or income inequality as conventionally measured (i.e., independent of ethnicity). Easterly and Levine (1997) were the first to stress the key role of ethnic identity (see also Stewart 2002 and, more recently, Cederman et al. 2011).

REFERENCES

Abadie, A., and Gardeazabal J. 2010. *Methods for Measuring the Costs of Conflict*. Unpublished manuscript, DIW Berlin. https://www.diw.de/documents/dokumentenarchiv/17/diw1.c.346916.de/gardeazabalonflictecc. pdf.

Acemoglu, D., Johnson, S., and Robinson, J. A. 2001. The colonial origins of comparative development: an empirical investigation. *Am. Econ. Rev.* 91:1369–1401.

Alesina, A., Baqir, R., and Easterly, W. 1999. Public goods and ethnic divisions. *Q. J. Econ.* 114:1243–84.

Alesina A., and La Ferrara E. 2005. Ethnic diversity and economic performance. *J. Econ. Lit.* 43:721–761.

Alesina, A., Michalopoulos, S., and Papaioannou, E. 2016. Ethnic inequality. *J. Polit. Econ.* 124:428–488.

Andre, C., and Platteau, J.-P. 1998. Land relations under unbearable stress: Rwanda caught in the Malthusian trap. *J. Econ. Behav. Organ.* 34:1–47.

Anthony A. 2014. Class war is back again—and British politicians are running scared. *The Guardian*, November 30. https://www.theguardian.com/society/2014/nov/30/class-war-is-back-again.

Appadurai, A. 2004. The capacity to aspire: culture and the terms of recognition. In *Culture and Public Action*, edited by V. Rao and M. Walton, 59–84. Palo Alto, CA: Stanford University Press.

Arbatli, C. E., Ashraf, Q. H., and Galor, O. 2015. *The Nature of Conflict.* CESifo Working Paper 5486, CESifo Group, Munich. http://www.cesifo-group.de/portal/page/portal/DocBaseontent/WP/WP -CESifoorkingapers/ wp-cesifo-2015/wp-cesifo-2015–08/cesifo1p5486.pdf.

Ashraf, Q., and Galor, O. 2013. The "Out of Africa" hypothesis, human genetic diversity, and comparative economic development. *Am. Econ. Rev.* 103:1–46.

Austin, G. 1996. *The effects of government policy on the ethnic distribution of income and wealth in Rwanda: a review of published sources.* Consult. Rep., World Bank, Washington, DC.

Banks, A. 2008. *The 2016 Edition of the Cross-National Time-Series Data Archive.* Jerusalem: Databanks Int. http://www.cntsdata.com.

Bates, R. H. 1983. Modernization, ethnic competition, and the rationality of politics in contemporary Africa. In *State versus Ethnic Claims: African Policy Dilemmas*, edited by D. Rothchild and V. A. Olunsorola, 152–171. Boulder, CO: Westview Press.

Becker, G. 1968. Crime and punishment: an economic approach. *J. Polit. Econ.* 76:169–217.

Bénabou, R. 2003. Human capital, technical change, and the welfare state. *J. Eur. Econ. Assoc.* 1:522–532.

Besley, T., and Persson, T. 2008. Wars and state capacity. *J. Eur. Econ. Assoc.* 6:522–530.

———. 2009. The origins of state capacity: property rights, taxation, and politics. *Am. Econ. Rev.* 99:1218–1244.

———. 2010. State capacity, conflict, and development. *Econometrica* 78:1–34.

———. 2011. Fragile states and development policy. *J. Eur. Econ. Assoc.* 9:371–398.

Besley, T., and Reynal-Querol, M. 2014. The legacy of historical conflict. Evidence from Africa. *Am. Polit. Sci. Rev.*108:319–336.

Bethany, L., and Gleditsch, N. P. 2005. Monitoring trends in global combat: a new dataset of battle deaths. *Eur. J. Popul.* 21:145–166.

Bhattacharya, S., Joyee, D., and Kundu, T. 2015. Mobility and conflict. *Am. Econ. J. Microecon.* 7(1):281–319.

Brubaker, R., and Laitin, D. D. 1998. Ethnic and nationalist violence. *Annu. Rev. Sociol.* 24:423–452.

Bruk, S. I., and Apenchenko, V. S., eds. 1964. *Atlas Narodov Mira [Atlas of the Peoples of the World].* Moscow: Main Adm. Geod. Cartogr. (GUGK).

Burgess, R., Jedwab, R., Miguel, E., Morjaria, A., and Padró, Miquel G. 2015. The value of democracy: evidence from road building in Kenya. *Am. Econ. Rev.* 105:1817–1851.

Caselli, F., and Coleman, J. 2013. On the theory of ethnic conflict. *J. Eur. Econ. Assoc.* 11:161–192.

Cederman, L.-E., Weidmann, N. B., and Gleditsch, K. S. 2011. Horizontal inequalities and ethno-nationalist civil war: a global comparison. *Am. Polit. Sci. Rev.* 105:478–495.

Center for Systemic Peace. http://www.systemicpeace.org/inscrdata.html.

Cervellati, M., and Sunde, U. 2005. Human capital formation, life expectancy, and the process of development. *Am. Econ. Rev.* 95:1653–1672.

Chandra, K. 2004. *Why Ethnic Parties Succeed: Patronage and Ethnic Headcounts in India.* Cambridge: Cambridge University Press

Chowdhury, A. R., and Mansoob, M. S. 2013. A note on war and fiscal capacity in developing countries. *Peace Econ. Peace Sci. Public Policy* 19:431–435.

Ciccone, A. 2011. Economic shocks and civil conflict: a comment. *Am. Econ. J. Appl. Econ.* 3(4):215–227.

Coates, T-N. 2016. The case for considering reparations. *The Atlantic*, January 27. http://www.theatlantic .com/politics/archive/2016/01/tanehisi-coates-reparations/427041/.

Collier, P. 2001. Economic causes of civil war and their implications for policy. In *Turbulent Peace: The Challenges of Managing International Conflict*, edited by C. A. Crocker, F. O. Hampson, and P. Aall, 143–162. Washington, DC: US Institute of Peace.

Collier, P., and Hoeffler, A. 1998. On economic causes of civil war. *Oxf. Econ. Pap.* 50:563–573.

———. 2004a. Greed and grievance in civil war. *Oxf. Econ. Pap.* 56:563–595.

———. 2004b. Conflicts. In *Global Crises, Global Solutions*, edited by B. Lomberg, 129–155. Cambridge: Cambridge University Press.

Dal Bó, E., and Dal Bó, P. 2011. Workers, warriors, and criminals: social conflict in general equilibrium. *J. Eur. Econ. Assoc.* 9:646–677.

de Groot, O. 2009. *A methodology for the calculation of the global economic costs of conflict.* Project Paper 2, Dtsch. Inst. Wirtsch, Berlin. https://www.diw.de/documents/dokumentenarchiv/17/diw1.c.345864 .de/degroot_gecc_project_paper.pdf.

de Tocqueville, A. 1955. *The Old Regime and the French Revolution*. New York: Anchor Books.

Desmet, K., Ortuño-Ortin, I., and Wacziarg, R. 2012. The political economy of ethnolinguistic cleavages. *J. Dev. Econ.* 97:322–332.

Djankov, S., and Reynal-Querol, M. 2010. Poverty and civil wars: revisiting the evidence. *Rev. Econ. Stat.* 92:1035–1041.

Dube, O., and Vargas, J. F. 2013. Commodity price shocks and civil conflict: evidence from Colombia. *Rev. Econ. Stud.* 80:1384–421.

Duclos, J.-Y., Esteban, J., and Ray, D. 2004. Polarization: concepts, measurement, estimation. *Econometrica* 72:1737–1772.

Easterly, W., and Levine, R. 1997. Africa's growth tragedy: policies and ethnic divisions. *Q. J. Econ.* 112:1203–1250.

Ehrlich, I. 1973. Participation in illegitimate activities: a theoretical and empirical investigation. *J. Polit. Econ.* 81:521–565.

Engineer, A. A. 1987. Ethnic conflict in South Asia. *Econ. Polit. Wkly* 22(25):969–971.

Esteban, J., Mayoral, L., and Ray, D. 2012a. Ethnicity and conflict: an empirical study? *Am. Econ. Rev.* 102:1310–1342.

———. 2012b. Ethnicity and conflict: theory and facts? *Science* 336:858–865.

Esteban, J., and Ray, D. 1994. On the measurement of polarization. *Econometrica* 62:819–852.

———. 1999. Conflict and distribution. *J. Econ. Theory* 87:379–415.

———. 2008. On the salience of ethnic conflict. *Am. Econ. Rev.* 98:2185–2202.

———. 2011a. Linking conflict to inequality and polarization. *Am. Econ. Rev.* 101:1345–1374.

———. 2011b. A model of ethnic conflict. *J. Eur. Econ. Assoc.* 9:496–521.

Fearon, J. D. 1999. Why ethnic politics and "pork" tend to go together. Unpublished manuscript, Department of Political Science, Stanford University.

———. 2003. Ethnic and cultural diversity by country. *J. Econ. Growth* 8:195–222.

———. 2006. Ethnic mobilization and ethnic violence. In *The Oxford Handbook of Political Economy*, edited by B. R. Weingast and D. A. Wittman, 852–868. Oxford: Oxford University Press.

Fearon, J. D., and Laitin, D. D. 2003a. Ethnicity, insurgency, and civil war. *Am. Polit. Sci. Rev.* 97(1):75–90.

———. 2003b. *Ethnicity, insurgency, and civil war: dataset*. http://www.stanford.edu/ group/ethnic /publicdata/publicdata.html.

Gates, S., Hegre, H., Nygård, H. M, and Strand, H. 2012. Development consequences of armed conflict. *World Dev.* 40:1713–1722.

Genicot, G., and Ray, D. 2014. *Aspirations and inequality*. Unpublished manuscript, Department of Economics, New York University, New York. http://www.econ.nyu.edu/user/debraj/Papers /GenicotRayAsp.pdf.

Glaeser, E. L. 2002. Legal origins. *Q. J. Econ.* 117:1193–1229.

Gleditsch, N. P., Wallensteen, P., Eriksson, M., Sollenber, M., and Strand, H. 2002. Armed conflict 1946–2001: a new dataset. *J. Peace Res.* 39:615–637.

Grossman, H. I., and Kim, M. 1995. Swords or plowshares? A theory of the security of claims to property. *J. Polit. Econ.* 103:1275–1288.

Gurr, T. 1968. Psychological factors in civil violence. *World Polit.* 20:245–278.

Hegre, H., and Sambanis, N. 2006. Sensitivity analysis of empirical results on civil war onset. *J. Confl. Resolut.* 50:508–535.

Hess, G. D. 2003. The economic welfare cost of conflict: an empirical assessment. Working Paper 852, CESifo Group, Munich.

Hirschman, A. O., and Rothschild, M. 1973. The changing tolerance for income inequality in the course of economic development, with a mathematical appendix. *Q. J. Econ.* 87:544–566.

Hirshleifer, J. 1991. The paradox of power. *Econ. Polit.* 3:177–199.

———. 1995. Anarchy and its breakdown. *J. Polit. Econ.* 103:26–52.

Horowitz, D. 1985. *Ethnic Groups in Conflict*. Berkeley: University of California Press.

Huber, J., and Mayoral, L. 2014. Inequality, ethnicity and conflict. Unpublished manuscript, Department of Political Science, Columbia University, New York. http://polisci.columbia.edu/files/polisci /u86/huber%20mayoral_0.pdf.

Huntington, S. P. 1996. *The Clash of Civilizations and the Remaking of World Order*. New York: Simon & Schuster.

Ignatieff, M. 1993. *Blood and Belonging*. London: Noonday Press.

Klein, E. 2015. Bernie Sanders: the Vox conversation. Vox, July 28. http://www.vox.com/2015/7/28 /9014491/bernie-sanders-vox-conversation.

Laitin, D. D. 2000. What is a language community? *Am. J. Polit. Sci.* 44(1):142–155.

Lichbach, M. I. 1989. An evaluation of "does economic inequality breed political conflict?" studies. *World Polit.* 41(4):431–470.

Lindgren, G. 2004. Measuring the economic costs of internal armed conflict: a review of empirical estimates. Unpublished manuscript, Department of Peace and Conflict Resolution, Uppsala University, Uppsala, Sweden.

Matuszeski, J., and Schneider, F. 2006. Patterns of ethnic group segregation and civil conflict. Unpublished manuscript, Harvard University, Cambridge, MA. http://www.cgdev.org/doc/events/02.09 .07/Matuszeski-JMP.pdf.

Mauro, P. 1995. Corruption and growth. *Q. J. Econ.* 110:681–712.

Mayoral, L., and Ray, D. 2015. Groups in conflict: size matters, but not in the way you think. Unpublished manuscript, Institute for Analytical Economics, Barcelona, Spain. http://mayoral.iae-csic .org/research/15Size10.pdf.

McBride, M., Milante, G., and Skaperdas, S. 2011. Peace and war with endogenous state capacity. *J. Confl. Resolut.* 55:446–468.

Mehlum, H., and Moene, K. O. 2011. The battle of regimes. Unpublished manuscript, Centre of Equality, Social Organization, and Performance, Department of Economics, University of Oslo, Norway. http://www.sv.uio.no/esop/english/research/ unpublished-works/working-papers/2011/The%20 battle%20of%20regimes.pdf.

Melander, E., Pettersson, T., and Themnér, L. 2016. Organized violence, 1989–2015. *J. Peace Res.* 53:727–42.

Midlarski, M. I. 1988. Rulers and the ruled: patterned inequality and the onset of mass political violence. *Am. Polit. Sci. Rev.* 82(2):491–509.

Miguel, E., Satyanath, S., and Sergenti, E. 2004. Economic shocks and civil conflict: an instrumental variables approach. *J. Polit. Econ.* 112:725–753.

Mitra, A., and Ray, D. 2014. Implications of an economic theory of conflict: Hindu-Muslim violence in India. *J. Polit. Econ.* 122:719–765.

Montalvo, J. G., and Reynal-Querol, M. 2005. Ethnic polarization, potential conflict and civil war. *Am. Econ. Rev.* 95:796–816.

———. 2007. Fighting against malaria: prevent wars while waiting for the miraculous vaccines. *Rev. Econ. Stat.* 89:165–177.

Mueller, H. 2013. The economic cost of conflict. Working Paper, International Growth Centre, London.

———. 2016. Growth and violence: argument for a per capita measure of civil war. *Economica* 83:473–497.

Muller, E. N., Seligson, M. A., and Fu, H. 1989. Land inequality and political violence. *Am. Polit. Sci. Rev.* 83:577–586.

Nagel, J. 1974. Inequality and discontent: a non-linear hypothesis. *World Polit.* 26:453–472.

Olzak, S., and Shanahan, S. 1996. Deprivation and race riots: an extension of Spilerman's analysis. *Soc. Forces* 74:931–961.

Østby, G. 2008. Polarization, horizontal inequalities and violent civil conflict. *J. Peace Res.* 45:143–162.

Perotti, R. 1996. Growth, income distribution, and democracy: what the data say. *J. Econ. Growth* 1:149–187.

Petroff, A. 2015. Cartier boss says rising inequality will spark class war. CNN Money, June 11. http:// money.cnn.com/2015/06/10/luxury/cartier-inequality-class-war/.

Piketty, T. 2014. *Capital in the Twenty-First Century.* Cambridge, MA: Harvard University Press.

Pinker, S. 2011. *The Better Angels of Our Nature: Why Violence Has Declined.* London: Penguin Books.

Prunier, G. 1996. *The Rwanda Crisis: History of a Genocide.* New York: Columbia University Press.

Ray, D. 1998. *Development Economics.* Princeton, NJ: Princeton University Press.

———. 2006. Aspirations, poverty and economic change. In *What Have We Learnt About Poverty,* ed. A. Banerjee, R. Bénabou, and D. Mookherjee, 409–422. Oxford: Oxford University Press.

Schuman, M. 2014. There's a class war going on and the poor are getting their butts kicked. *Time,* April 1. http://time.com/44917/income-inequality-karl-marx-class-war-poverty/.

Sen, A. K. 1973. *On Economic Inequality.* Oxford: Clarendon Press.

Skaperdas, S. 1992. Cooperation, conflict, and power in the absence of property rights. *Am. Econ. Rev.* 82:720–739.

Skocpol, T. 1985. Bringing the state back in: strategies of analysis in current research. In *Bringing the State Back In,* edited by P. B. Evans, D. Rueschemeyer, and T. Skocpol, 3–42. Cambridge: Cambridge University Press.

Snider, L. W. 1990. The political performance of governments, external debt service, and domestic political violence. *Int. Polit. Sci. Rev.* 11:403–422.

Spilerman, S. 1970. The causes of racial disturbances: a comparison of alternative explanations. *Am. Sociol. Rev.* 35:627–649.

———. 1971. The causes of racial disturbances: test of an explanation. *Am. Sociol. Rev.* 36:427–443.

———. 1976. Structural characteristics of cities and the severity of racial disorders. *Am. Sociol. Rev.* 41:771–793.

Stein, B. 2006. In class warfare, guess which class is winning. *New York Times*, November 26. http://www. nytimes.com/2006/11/26/business/yourmoney/26every.html.

Stewart, F. 2002. Horizontal inequalities: a neglected dimension of development. Working Paper, World Institute for Development Economic and Research, UN University, Helsinki. http://www .wider.unu.edu/publications/annual-lectures/enB/AL5/.

United Nations High Commissioner for Refugees (UNHCR). 2015. Worldwide displacement hits all-time high as war and persecution increase. UNHCR, Geneva. http://www.unhcr.org/558193896 .html.

Weidmann, N. B., Rød, J. K., and Cederman, L.-E. 2010. Representing ethnic groups in space: a new dataset. *J. Peace Res.* 47:491–499.

Wilson, W. J. 1978. *The Declining Significance of Race: Blacks and Changing American Institutions*. Chicago: University of Chicago Press.

Wolfson, M. C. 1994. When inequalities diverge. *Am. Econ. Rev.* 84:353–358.

PART 2

INSTITUTIONS AND GROWTH

6

INSTITUTIONS, DEVELOPMENT, AND GROWTH

Where Does Evidence Stand?

Steven N. Durlauf

6.1. INTRODUCTION

Arguments on the relationship between institutions and growth have appeared throughout the history of economics. Nevertheless, the last two decades have seen institutions emerge as the touchstone of thinking on growth and economic development. The contemporary prominence of institutional explanations of economic success and failure has three interrelated sources.

1. Economic historians have provided detailed studies of the interactions of institutions and economic development in a wide range of historical episodes. These episodes vary widely in time and in scale, with studies ranging from details of microeconomic relations to claims about the long-term effects of particular institutions on macroeconomic development (see Nunn 2009 for an overview).

2. Development economists have linked relative successes and failures in environments where the institutions of advanced economies are either attenuated or absent. The types of institutions under study encompass a broad array of fields. One side of the literature studies politics and governance in developing societies, while another focuses on the ways that informal institutions such as social networks substitute for weaknesses in financial markets or legal systems. Surveys by Baland, Moene, and Robinson (2008) and Cox and Fafchamps (2007) provide a useful counterpoint.

3. Growth economists have applied formal econometric and statistical models to cross-country datasets and identified general patterns linking empirical proxies for institutions types and quality with economic outcomes. Within this enterprise, a number of institutional measures have been argued to have marginal explanatory power in predicting cross-country growth differences. Institutions have been further argued to represent the most robust fundamental growth

determinant in empirical exercises that center on such determinants (see for example Rodrik, Subramanian, and Trebbi 2004).

While distinct sources of evidence, these different dimensions of empirical research have built upon one another and have undergirded modern growth theory in a synergistic fashion. Historical episodes and evidence from development studies are ubiquitous in growth economics just as general claims in growth economics have informed economic history and development economics. One impressive feature of the institutions and growth literature is the way that these different evidentiary bases have been integrated in making the empirical case for the importance of institutions (see for example of the argumentation that underlies Acemoglu and Robinson 2005).

This chapter is designed to present a concise overview of the state of evidence on institutions and growth. There is no serious disagreement with the proposition that "institutions matter." Disagreements have to do with specifics, how and to what extent particular institutions matter in particular contexts. Suppose one argues that the failures of centrally planned economies or the travails of post-Soviet Russia are evidence that "institutions matter." While I think it is indisputably the case that this abstract proposition is true, this fact does not by itself directly entail much in terms of understanding the importance of institutions in other episodes, nor does it say much about the specifics of policy reform of the type under contemporary discussion. My focus is on this more precise type of knowledge about the effects of institutions on growth and development. This chapter does not pretend to be exhaustive; a comprehensive overview would require a book-length treatment. My goal here is to communicate a sense of the state of the literature, both successes and limitations.

Section 6.2 discusses definitions and measurement. I address conceptual issues in defining institutions as well as the transition from concepts to quantitative measures. Section 6.3 examines statistical evidence on growth and institutions. My conclusions for this class of studies will be largely negative, for reasons that involve the general limits in the ability of the main types of statistical models that are employed, cross-country growth regressions, to credibly identify particular growth mechanisms. Section 6.4 discusses structural analyses. These analyses, I argue, are useful in illustrating the potential extent to which a particular type of institution may be able to explain some aggregate outcomes. However, these types of studies provide, at best, very limited evidence on institutions per se. Section 6.5 considers historical studies. I argue that these studies are the strongest source of evidence on institutions. This strength, however, derives from a specificity of contextual knowledge that leads to questions about general conclusions. Section 6.6 gives an interpretation of evidence from these three sources. I argue that the state of knowledge in the institutions and growth literature is a successful example of abductive reasoning, also known as *inference to the best explanation* in the philosophy of science literature. Abduction/inference to the best explanation refers to the process by which evidence is integrated across available sources and conclusions drawn on which explanation of a given phenomenon best fits the evidence. I claim that abduction provides the appropriate conceptual framework for understanding how evidence has led to a consensus emerging for the salience of institutions in explaining cross-country heterogeneity and intra-country dynamics. Section 6.7 concludes with some thoughts on potential new directions for research on the institutions, growth, and development relationship.

I note one omission from the survey: laboratory studies. Interesting evidence has emerged, in a range of controlled experiments, for how different rules affect behaviors. Well-known examples include Frey and Bohnet (1995) on institutions and preferences for fairness and Dal Bó, Foster, and Putterman (2010) on democratic choices and cooperation. I omit this work because its implications for the institution/economics relationship are so remote from the large-scale contexts of the latter. As such, the experimental literature helps buttress the other sources of evidence but, unlike those sources, cannot stand on its own with reference to the sorts of questions the institutional literature addresses

6.2. DEFINITIONS AND MEASUREMENT

Empirical analyses of the institutions/economic outcomes relationship naturally require specification of institutions. A first question concerns the meaning of the rubric "institutions."[1] North (1990: 3) provides one classic definition of institutions as

> the rules of the game in a society or, more formally, humanly devised constraints that shape interaction. In consequence, they structure incentives in human exchange, whether, political, social, or economic.

By way of comparison, Greif (2006: 39) states that institutions constitute

> a system of rules, beliefs, and norms, and organizations that together generate a regularity of (social) behavior (italics removed).

Baland, Bourguignon, Platteau, and Verdier (this volume) describe institutions as

> rules, procedures, or other human devices that constrain individual behavior, with a view to making individual expectations about others' behavior converge and to allowing individual actions to become more coordinated.

There are dimensions along which these definitions differ. For example, while Greif treats beliefs as an institution, Baland et al. argue that institutions matter *because* they shape beliefs. And neither conception requires that beliefs be thought of as constraints in the sense of North. That said, there is clearly much overlap, most obviously in terms of the emphasis on "rules."

Broad definitions, such as those proposed by North, Greif, and Baland et al., are an important background for empirical work because they emphasize the varied and rich range of social relationships and interactions that should be considered in studying. The range of the institutions and economics literature is well reflected in them. However, definitions of this type do not provide much guidance for empirical work since they can include so many distinct forms of political and social structures. The breadth of these definitions also raises questions of whether other general categories, such as culture, can be meaningfully distinguished from institutions; I return to this in the conclusion of this chapter.

Such a broad conceptualization of institutions also runs the danger of defining institutions functionally. One example is social capital which, as discussed in Knowles (2007), is closely linked to North's conceptualization. Some treatments of social capital equate it with solidarity, others with trust. In my view, functional definitions should be avoided in empirical research because they undermine a clear strategy for meaningful empirical evaluation. Solidarity and trust are endogenous outcomes, and so to equate them with social capital is to miss the factors that create and shape social capital. Portes (1998) and Durlauf (2002) discuss how functional social capital definitions end up ascribing success-ful social outcomes to its presence without a distinct social capital measure.[2]

To elaborate a simple example of the limits of overly broad definitions, consider a so-ciety in which individuals are all devout Kantians. Rational agents would exhibit high degrees of trust because of the trustworthiness of the individuals in the society. Hence the social capital as trust definition would be uninformative since trust is derivative from ethical behaviors. Further, if the process of transmission of ethics occurs at the family level, then there is no dimension along which the common norm should be thought of as collectively devised (North) or as a system (Greif). This example indicates how a func-tional definition, trust constitutes an institution, may be misleading. Further, even if institutions shape levels of trust, treating trust as an institution begs the question of how it is produced.

With reference to empirical work, the upshot of this discussion is that general defini-tions of institutions underdetermine what does or does not appropriately constitute an institution. Put differently, these types of broad definitions may embrace a superset of the union of different conceptions of institutions, but are not sufficiently precise to pro-vide clear guides to empirical research.

While conceptual definitions may be elusive for institutions, this does not necessar-ily entail a fundamental impediment to empirical work. Both the New Institutional Eco-nomics and the growth and development literatures have addressed the definitional challenge by focusing on subsets of institutions. These subsets can involve extremely spe-cific institutions, or larger classes. The first column of table 6.1 provides a representative sample of the literature. This strategy is perfectly consistent with the absence of defini-tional precision for institutions; the boundaries of a category, set, or concept may be ill-defined while some members are unambiguously members of it. By analogy, ambiguity about the definition of money does not preclude analysis of the Federal Reserve interest rate or money supply rules. Some institutions are very precisely defined, such as a spe-cific forced labor system in the Andes studied by Dell (2010). In other cases, empirical work is predicated on indices that aggregate disparate features of complex institutions such as democracy (Tavares and Wacziarg 2001 among others).

In the empirical institutions literature, one basic empirical strategy has emerged around the analysis of classes of institutions characterized by certain general character-istics. A classic distinction divides institutions between formal and informal ones. Legal systems are very different institutions from social norms. Platteau (1994a: 535) defines institutions as

> conscious coordination efforts; or by resorting to external sanction systems (which presuppose the existence of an authority structure).

This allows for both formal and informal institutions, an example of the latter being a community in which ostracism punishes wrongdoers. Platteau (1994a, 1994b) argues that his definition appropriately distinguishes institutions from cases in which rules of conduct can be "established and sustained in a completely spontaneous way" (535). This distinction means that moral norms interact with institutions to, for example, facilitate

Table 6.1. Regression analyses linking institutions,
economic development, and growth

Institution	Study	Respective Claims (effect, significance)
Competitiveness in executive recruitment	Coyne and Tan (2012)	(+,*)
Democracy	Acemoglu, Naidu, Restrepo, and Robinson (2013), Barro (1996), Helliwell (1994), Papaioannou and Siourounis (2008), Persson and Tabellini (2006), Persson and Tabellini (2009), Tavares and Wacziarg (2001)	(+,*), (+/−,*), (−,0), (+,*), (+,*), (+,*), (−,*)
Economic, political, civic freedom	Dawson (1998)	(+,*)
Executive constraints	Acemoglu, Johnson, and Robinson (2002), Acemoglu, Johnson, and Robinson (2005)	(+,*), (+,*)
Financial development	Benhabib and Spiegel (2000)	(+,*)
Forced mining labor (*mita*)	Dell (2010)	(−,*)
Government consumption share of GDP	Barro (1991)	(−,*)
Institutional quality index	Collins and Bosworth (2003), Easterly and Levine (2003), Glaeser, La Porta, Lopez-de-Silanes, and Shleifer (2004), Tan (2010)	(+,*), (+,*), (0,0), (+,*)
Meta-study, various		(+,*)
Political instability	Alesina, Özler, Roubini, and Swagel (1996)	(−,*)
Property rights	Dawson (2003)	(+,*)
Protection against expropriation risk	Acemoglu, Johnson, and Robinson (2001), Acemoglu, Johnson, and Robinson (2002), Gorodnichenko and Roland (2010)	(+,*), (+,*), (+,*)
Public investment share of GDP	Barro (1991)	(+,0)
Religion	Acemoglu, Johnson, and Robinson (2001, 2005)	(0,0)
Rule of law	Dollar and Kraay (2003), Mehlum, Moene, and Torvik (2006), Rodrik, Subramanian, and Trebbi (2004)	(+,*), (+,*), (+,*)
Social infrastructure (government anti-diversion policies, trade openness)	Hall and Jones (1999)	(+,*)
Use of markets	Dawson (2003)	(+,*)

Note: (,*) : significance. (, 0) : not significant. (+,) : positive finding. (−,− : negative finding. (+/−,*) : not linear significant effects. (0,0) : evidence of a zero effect.

the solution of coordination problems. This is a useful approach from the measurement perspective because it equates formal institutions to collective action processes, which are presumably identifiable given observability of the process itself or its direct consequences—what Platteau calls an authority structure. Platteau emphasizes how informal institutions interact with formal ones in the development process. A complementary division is proposed by Voigt (2010) between de jure and de facto institutions, a division that focuses on the interplay of formal and informal institutions as well as on the roles of different types of institutions in determining equilibrium outcomes. Hence, whether the Stalin Constitution of 1936 was or was not, in its written provisions, the most free in the world, is irrelevant, since the existence of the institution called the security organs determined actual levels of liberty.

A distinct strategy to defining sets of institutions is via their common effects. The most prominent example of this strategy is the research program defined by Acemoglu, Johnson, and Robinson (2001, 2002), Acemoglu and Johnson (2005), and Acemoglu and Robinson (2005), which studies institutions and their relationship to broadly defined property rights. Following Acemoglu et al. (2002: 1262):

> we take a good organization of society to correspond to a cluster of (political, economic, and social) institutions ensuring that a broad cross section of society has effective property rights. We refer to this cluster as institutions of private property, and contrast them with extractive institutions, where the majority of the population faces a high risk of expropriation and holdup by the government, the ruling elite, or other agents. Two requirements are implicit in this definition of institutions of private property. First, institutions should provide secure property rights, so that those with productive opportunities expect to receive returns from their investments, and are encouraged to undertake such investments. The second requirement is embedded in the emphasis on "a broad cross section of the society."

This approach defines institutions by the way they influence individual decision-making, i.e., how they shape incentives. Acemoglu et al. go on to say (2002: 1262–3):

> A society in which a very small fraction of the population, for example, a class of landowners, holds all the wealth and political power may not be the ideal environment for investment, even if the property rights of this elite are secure. In such a society, many of the agents with the entrepreneurial human capital and investment opportunities may be those without effective property rights protection. In particular, the concentration of political and social power in the hands of a small elite implies that the majority of the population risks being held up by the powerful elite after they undertake investments.

The discussion makes it clear why the Acemoglu, Johnson, and Robinson approach is not a functional definition. Institutions are not directly defined by their effects on growth and development, but on how they alter individual decisions.

Other approaches complement the focus on property rights by considering the broad range of ways that institutions interact with economic life. Rodrik (2005) divides institutions into those that are (1) market-creating (e.g., property rights); (2) market-regulating (rules for addressing market failures); (3) market-stabilizing (macro-level monetary fiscal and financial policies); (4) market-legitimizing (political inclusiveness via democratic rules and social insurance). This approach, which focuses on institutions and governance, is not designed to be exhaustive but to be policy relevant. The approach is also focused on complementing property rights with other dimensions along which institutions matter. Bardhan (2005, 2016) makes parallel arguments of this type, with an emphasis on the effects of institutions on resolving coordination problems and creating democratic resolutions of disagreements.

The plethora of possible ways to characterize classes of institutions, in my judgment, actually enriches empirical work. Choices on how to organize institutions into distinct categories need not be invariant across studies and in fact should be tailored to the questions that need to be addressed. Typologies of institutions matter for a given study, of course, because a typology defines the institutional features of interest. But the multiplicity of typologies does not necessarily entail an identification problem since conclusions about institutions organized in one fashion are substantively consistent with conclusions derived from a different organization. Put differently, institutional definitions do not "carve nature at its joints." Each division provides a perspective on how institutions matter, and these perspectives are not incompatible with one another. This is not a claim that "anything goes." A study of the treatment effect of a given institution is well defined to the extent that the institution under study is well defined in the context of the study, not whether the definition is portable across studies. The same argument would apply to more structural analyses.

While I conclude that conceptual difficulties in institutional definition have been successfully addressed, in contrast, there are measurement issues involved in the transition from a conceptually precise set of institutions to associated empirical measures for them. Here I highlight two major impediments to empirical work.

A first measurement problem is the relationship between the concepts by which institutions are understood and the statistical measures that have been constructed for empirical work. As discussed in Shirley (2005) and Voigt (2013), for example, variables measuring institutional quality are indices that aggregate very different dimensions of a political system. Consider the institution "democracy." The democracy indices that are employed in empirical work create a scalar measure of the level of democracy based on elections, civil liberties, and other conceptually distinct aspects of a polity.[3] Similar concerns may be raised for corruption indices and the like. Concepts such as democracy and corruption constitute umbrellas for many different facets of socioeconomic and political structures. These different facets do not naturally allow for a meaningful scalar measure of the underlying concept. This limit can matter. For example, as shown in Tavares and Wacziarg (2001), greater democracy can reduce growth via associated reductions in income inequality and increases in educational investment but can inhibit growth via greater government consumption and lower physical capital accumulation.

Difficulties in measurement differ across institutional types. While measuring legal systems is complicated because of the plethora of facets of a system, the challenges involve judgments based on dimension reduction, which in turn is based on the observables of the system. In contrast, measurement of social norms is necessarily indirect, requiring either survey data on beliefs and attitudes or the embedding of norms in a structural model of outcomes, which involve quite different judgments. This needs to be remembered when "horse races" are run to compare the explanatory power of alternative institutions.

A second measurement issue concerns the distinction between institutions and equilibrium outcomes associated with institutions, a distinction that is the basis of a famous critique of institutional measurement by Glaeser et al. (2004). These authors argue that three standard measures of institutional quality—expropriation probability, government effectiveness, and limits to executive power—do not measure institutions per se. Rather, these are equilibrium outcomes, reflecting the interplay of institutions with the state of the economy and society. As such, they are not measures of "durable rules, procedures or norms that the word 'institutions' refers to" (274). Glaeser et al. conclude that cross-country growth heterogeneity is better explained by human capital accumulation, and that economic development leads to better institutions. The distinction between equilibrium outcomes and underlying institutions is not simply an issue of endogeneity of institutions but rather is a question of timescale. This means that one cannot instrument the institutional measures with any set of "predetermined" variables. Valid instruments need to exhibit similar durability as the underlying institutions one wishes to capture.[4] This concern has led these authors to focus on legal origins, itself a type of institution, as a source of long-run differences between countries.

The importance of these measurement limitations differs across the two sources of empirical evidence on institutional effects: statistical models based on cross-country regressions, and historical studies.

6.3. CROSS-COUNTRY REGRESSIONS

Much empirical growth evidence, in particular in the 1990–2010 period, relied on various formulations of cross-country growth regressions.[5] Table 6.1 provides a survey of representative studies. Given concerns over the endogeneity of institutions, there is a cognate literature based on various instrumental variables. These are summarized in table 6.2a.

The strength of the evidence from cross-country studies of course depends on the credibility of inferences using this methodology. As a source of substantive information on the mechanisms underlying growth and development, cross-country regressions have been subjected to very severe criticism (see Durlauf, Johnson, and Temple (2005) for a delineation of a host of problems). For purposes of this discussion, I would emphasize that cross-country regression evidence has often proven to be fragile because of the sensitivity of findings to the choice of control variables. Different papers come to different conclusions on institutions because of the choice of control variables. And this set of control variables is massive. Durlauf and Quah (1998) argue that there are virtually as many growth variables that have been proposed as countries, while Durlauf et al. (2005) further argue that more than 40 distinct growth theories are proxied for by these variables. Further, growth theory is open-ended in the sense discussed in Brock and Durlauf (2001): one growth theory typically does not logically entail that another theory is either false or empirically irrelevant. In other words, specific growth theories are specific mechanisms that do not rule out other mechanisms in the overall growth process. Hence, the alternative specifications of growth regression controls are limited only by the number of combinations of growth determinants and associated measures that are available. Conceptually, each growth regression is a model and the cross-country growth literature faces massive model uncertainty, by which I mean each choice of control variables determines a distinct growth model.

In order to constructively address the sensitivity of growth regression evidence to model choice, Fernandez, Ley, and Steel (2001) and Sala-i-Martin, Doppelhofer, and Miller (2004) proposed the use of model averaging techniques to be applied to growth regressions. Model averaging, in essence, aggregates model-specific evidence across specifications, using weights that reflect relative goodness of fit of the individual models as well as any prior plausibility differences an analyst wishes to assign to the models. A relatively recent example is Durlauf, Kourtellos, and Tan (2008). From the perspective of understanding the effects of institutions on growth, this approach allows one to measure the effects accounting for the fact that the "true" growth regression specification is not known to the analyst. As such, the methodology is appropriate for identifying robust evidence concerning a given growth determinant. When done in a formal Bayesian fashion, one can compare the posterior probability that a given growth regressor appears in the true model, assuming the true model is an element of the space of models studied.

In the context of cross-country growth differences, model averaging exercises have not produced much evidence that institutions matter. For example, Fernandez et al. (2001) assign a posterior probability of 0.516 to the presence of a rule of law measure (their empirical proxy for legal institutions) in the true growth model; the prior probability in the analysis was 0.5. Among variables with posterior probability of 0.9, the fraction of the population that is Confucian is the only non-Solow growth determinant that is plausibly a proxy for institutions that survives this standard. By this, I mean that these averaging exercises assign sufficiently large standard errors to growth variable coefficients that one cannot conclude anything about their relationship to growth. Sala-i-Martin et al. (2004) find that the posterior inclusion probabilities for various institutional variables are very small, using somewhat different institutional measures. Durlauf, Kourtellos, and Tan (2008) search for robust determinants of the aggregate growth as well as decomposition of the aggregate into components driven by human capital growth, physical capital growth, and total factor productivity growth. This study also fails to find much evidence of an institution/growth link, except for some effect of one institutional measure, constraints on the executive and on physical capital accumulation. This chapter draws distinctions between deep growth determinants and proximate growth determinants, in particular macroeconomic policy, and concludes that proximate growth determinants are more robust predictors of cross-country growth differences than fundamental ones, with the exception of regional fixed effects.

What should one make of the failure of growth regressions literature to produce robust evidence for the role of institutions? The reasons why the evidence has proven to be weak are more likely due to limitations of the methodology as opposed to the lack of importance of institutions. Recall the discussion of Glaeser et al. (2004) on institutions as durable objects and the suggestion made earlier that institutions function on a slower timescale than the time intervals over which growth regressions are estimated. From this perspective, institutions represent a background context against which proximate growth determinants, e.g., savings or macroeconomic policy, function. Relative to this formulation, aggregate growth is not well approximated by a linear model. A better formulation is one in which the coefficients that link proximate determinants to growth are themselves functions of longer timescale variables such as institutions. Such a model is nonlinear as institutional determinants and proximate determinants interact. This can matter empirically, i.e., linear models can fail to reveal underlying nonlinear

Table 6.2a. Instrumental variables used in cross-country studies

Instrumental Variable	Study
Agricultural crops that have higher production economies of scale than others, like sugar, coffee, rice, and cotton	Easterly (2007), Engerman and Sokoloff (1997, 2000, 2002), Isham, Woolcock, Pritchett, and Busby (2005), Laeven and Woodruff (2007)
Distance from equator	Ahlerup, Olsson, and Yanagizawa (2009), Bockstette, Chanda, and Putterman (2002), Burnside and Dollar (2004), Edison, Levine, Ricci, and Słok (2002), Eicher and Leukert (2009), Hall and Jones (1999), Kögel (2005), Masters and Macmillan (2001)
English speakers	Bockstette, Chanda, and Putterman (2002), Burnside and Dollar (2004), Dollar and Kraay (2003), Kögel (2005), Masters and Macmillan (2001)
Ethnolinguistic fractionalization	Aidt (2009), Clague, Keefer, Knack, and Olson (1999), Easterly and Levine (1997), Easterly, Ritzen, and Woolcock (2006), Knack and Keefer (1997), Mauro (1995)
European-language speakers	Alcalá and Ciccone (2004), Bocksette, Chanda, and Putterman (2002), Burnside and Dollar (2004), Dollar and Kraay (2003), Eicher and Leukert (2009), Hall and Jones (1999), Kögel (2005), Masters and Macmillan (2001), Rodrik (1999), Rodrik, Subramanian, and Trebbi (2004)
Gravity equation for bilateral trade flows	Alcalá and Ciccone (2004), Dollar and Kraay (2003), Frankel and Romer (1999), Rodrik, Subramanian, and Trebbi (2004)
Initial inequality	Easterly, Ritzen, and Woolcock (2006)
Latitude	Diamond (1997)
Legal origin	Acemoglu and Johnson (2005), Aghion, Howitt, and Mayer-Foulkes (2005), Ahlerup, Olsson, and Yanagizawa (2009), Claessens and Laeven (2003), Clague, Keefer, Knack, and Olson (1999), Edison, Levine, Ricci, and Słok (2002), Glaeser, La Porta, Lopez-de-Silanes, and Shleifer (2004), La Porta, Lopez-de Silanes, and Shleifer (2008), Levine (1998), Levine, Loayza, and Beck (2000), Papaioannou (2009)
Log of indigenous population density in 1500	Acemoglu, Gallego, and Robinson (2014), Acemoglu and Johnson (2005), Burnside and Dollar (2004), Glaeser, La Porta, Lopez-de-Silanes, and Shleifer (2004), Papaioannou (2009)
Malaria index	Gooch, Martinez-Vazquez, and Yedgenov (2016)
Mean distance from the ocean or a navigable river	Ahlerup, Olsson, and Yanagizawa (2009)

Natural resources like oil and minerals	Isham, Woolcock, Pritchett, and Busby (2005), Sala-i-Martin and Subramanian (2013)
Percentage of law students in 1963	Knack and Keefer (1997)
Predicted trade share	Alcalá and Ciccone (2004), Bockstette, Chanda, and Putterman (2002), Kögel (2005), Masters and Macmillan (2001), Rodrik (1999), Rodrik, Subramanian, and Trebbi (2004)
Settler mortality	Acemoglu, Gallego, and Robinson (2014), Acemoglu and Johnson (2005), Acemoglu, Johnson, and Robinson (2001), Acemoglu, Johnson, and Robinson (2002), Acemoglu, Johnson, Robinson, and Thaicharoen (2003), Aghion, Howitt, and Mayer-Foulkes (2005), Alcalá and Ciccone (2004), Alfaro, Kalemli-Ozkan, and Volosovych (2008), Claessens and Laeven (2003), Dollar and Kraay (2003), Easterly and Levine (2003), Glaeser, La Porta, Lopez-de-Silanes, and Shleifer (2004), Rodrik (1999), Rodrik, Subramanian, and Trebbi (2004)
State antiquity	Bardhan (2005), Bockstette, Chanda, and Putterman (2002), Kögel (2005)
Tropics, germs, and crops	Easterly and Levine (2003)
Variability in rainfall	Haber and Menaldo (2011), Nugent and Sanchez (1999)
Voice and Accountability Index	Aidt (2009)

relationships in the growth process (Bernard and Durlauf 1996) such as those that produce poverty traps.

A different approach to evaluating the empirical importance of institutions was initiated by Rodrik et al. (2004), who compare three "deep" or "fundamental" growth determinants: institutions, integration in the world economy, and geography. Using instruments for geography due to Frankel and Romer (1999) and instruments for institutions from Acemoglu et al. (2001), they find little evidence that either integration or geography matter for growth, once institutions are controlled for. Geography does affect institutions and so does have indirect consequences.

Additional evidence on the salience of institutions among fundamental variables is due to Tan (2010), who considers interactions between institutions and other variables. In this analysis, measures of institutions, geography, and fractionalization are used to identify subsets of countries that obey a common linear growth model. Tan finds that there are multiple growth regimes indexed by institutional quality. While finding little evidence of a distinct role for geography, he does find a distinct role for ethnic fractionalization, so that if institutional quality is below a certain threshold, greater ethnic fractionalization can produce a low growth regime.

6.3.1. Instrumental Variables

Much of the empirical growth/institutions literature has properly been concerned with the identification of causal effects of institutions in the light of endogeneity. For regression analysis, this has involved a search for instrumental variables. Table 6.2a describes some of the instruments that have appeared in the institutions/growth regressions. Of course, some form of an instrument is required for any study when institutions are codetermined with the outcomes of interest. Table 6.2b presents instruments that have appeared in various case studies.

Arguments on behalf of instrumental variables have, to a large extent, focused on whether they are predetermined relative to the time period over which institutions and growth are being studied. Thus, there is either an implicit or an explicit set of assumptions being made about the timescale at which variables are determined. One example of implicit assumptions involves the use of ethnolinguistic fractionalization as an instrument for ethnic conflict or social cohesion, e.g., Easterly and Levine (1997) and Easterly, Ritzen, and Woolcock (2006), or corruption, e.g., Aidt (2009) and Mauro (1995). The logic of these exercises is to treat exogenous border determination (typically by a combination of a stable post–World War II world order in the West and borders determined by the vagaries of decolonization by various European powers). Use of an ethnolinguistic heterogeneity measure as an instrument for ethnic violence thus presupposes that migration patterns are slow relative to the time period under study. A famous example of an explicit assumption on timescales is the use, in Acemoglu, Johnson, and Robinson (2005), of settler mortality as an instrument for migration to colonies. In this analysis, the migration of institutions from the colonial power, i.e., institutions that support private property rather than extraction of rents, was exogenously influenced by whether settlers could endure in a given colony. While there has been some controversy over the measurement of the instrument (see Albouy 2012 and the response of Acemoglu, Johnson, and Robinson 2012), the logic of the instrument is clear.

Table 6.2b. Instrumental variables used in case studies

Instrument	Study
Agricultural tenancy reform	Banerjee, Gertler, and Ghatak (2002)
Being conquered by the British between 1820 and 1856	Banerjee and Iyer (2005)
Ethnolinguistic fractionalization	Miguel and Gugerty (2005)
Implementation of the Trade-Related Intellectual Property Rights Agreement	Chaudhuri, Goldberg, and Jia (2006)
Industry-location averages of bribery and taxation	Fisman and Svensson (2007)
Land reform	Do and Iyer (2003)
Political connections	Fisman (2001)
Reforms that are related to market liberalization, an innovative ownership form of firms, and large-scale state-owned enterprises	Qian (2003)
Variation across regions induced by the timing of the national tilting program and differences across target populations in level of preprogram ownership rights	Field (2007)
Variation in mandated political representation for disadvantaged groups	Pande (2003)
Variation in privatization of water services	Galiani, Gertler, and Schargrodsky (2005)
Variation in rural bank branch expansion	Burgess and Pande (2005)
Variation in spread of debt relief tribunals	Visaria (2009)
Variation in states which amended the Industrial Disputes Act in a pro-worker direction	Besley and Burgess (2004)

The search of instruments that evolve at lower timescales than the phenomena under study has led to much interest in geographic instruments, for which it is trivial to argue that the instrument is, in any relevant sense, predetermined. As illustrated in tables 6.2a and 6.2b, examples include distance from the equator, latitude, and distance from an ocean or navigable river.

In my judgment, the focus on predetermined instruments has often been misguided because it has directed attention away from the requirement for instrument validity that instruments are orthogonal to model errors. These errors include all growth determinants that are omitted in a given econometric model. This is a very difficult assumption to defend because of theory's open-endedness. Focusing on geography, there are a plethora of channels by which geography affects growth, ranging from effects on the distribution of disease to the effects on political institutions. Relative to institutions, this general criticism also has force. Any cross-country regression is a parsimonious low-dimension approximation of the true growth process, one that omits theoretically valid and known growth determinants.[6] A valid instrument has to be uncorrelated with the entire set of omitted growth determinants. This is the necessary standard for instruments for institutions to pass, and argumentation in the empirical literature all too often falls short. The complexities and richness of the growth process make the search for instrumental variables problematic.

The difficulties with drawing conclusions about mechanisms from instruments are illustrated by the ways in which ethnolinguistic heterogeneity and geography have been used. As noted, ethnolinguistic heterogeneity is used as an instrument for both ethnic conflict and social cohesion, as well as for corruption. Conflict and cohesion are distinct mechanisms determining social and political equilibria, and both differ from corruption. The fact that one instrument is plausibly linked to three separate mechanisms implies that any study that does not simultaneously include all three factors suffers from the critique I have described, i.e., the instrument will be correlated with omitted growth determinants. Similarly, geographic instruments are linked to multiple (more proximate) factors. If one considers an instrument for malaria prevalence, this can be associated with settler mortality or labor productivity in a given location.

While my overall assessment is that the cross-country regression literature has not established a decisive case for the empirical importance of institutions in general, let alone for the roles of particular institutions, that does not mean that they are without value. First, these studies establish data patterns and thus stylized facts about the interplay of growth/development and institutional measures. The analyses therefore matter in the sense of providing ways to allow interaction with data to update prior beliefs.

6.4. STRUCTURAL ANALYSES

A distinct, albeit small, set of empirical studies has constructed formal structural models to assess how particular institutions can affect aggregate outcomes. Table 6.3 provides examples of studies of this type. The studies are typically based on model calibration rather than estimation. Thus, these types of studies represent explicit examinations of the quantitative role of an institution in a fully delineated economic environment in contrast to cross-country growth regressions which are essentially reduced form exercises, even if theory is used ex post to interpret coefficients. In these papers, institutions are given mathematically precise formulations.

The state of financial development has been a primary focus of structural analyses. The reason for this is that the modeling of the level of financial development has drawn on ideas in the macroeconomics and finance literatures on market frictions. For example, Azariadis and de la Croix (2006) focus on financial market liberalization, which is modeled as the lifting of credit constraints for individual consumers from an initial condition in which borrowing is not allowed. This paper focuses on how both human and physical capital accumulation are affected and shows that deregulation can exacerbate inequality, when the relatively poor are not affected by the introduction of a market to allow for human capital loans. An important feature of this study is that it distinguishes between transition effects, where lower physical capital accumulation (in response to human capital opportunities) can hurt the disadvantaged, versus steady-state effects. These theoretical possibilities are shown to be quantitatively important. Greenwood, Sanchez, and Wang (2013) interpret financial development as improvements in the ability of lender to monitor borrowers and link this capacity to reduction in interest rate spreads between types of assets. A calibration based on the US and Taiwanese financial and output data is used to demonstrate the quantitative importance of these improve-

Table 6.3. Calibration studies

Variable of Interest	Study	Claim
Democracy	Seim and Parente (2013)	+
Entrepreneurs	Dias and McDermott (2006)	+
Epidemic shocks	Lagerlof (2003)	−
Financial development	Greenwood, Sanchez, and Wang (2013)	+
Financial frictions	Buera, Kaboski, and Shin (2011), Buera and Shin (2017)	−, −
Financial market liberalization	Azariadis and de la Croix (2006), Gine and Townsend (2004)	+
Limited enforcement	Amaral and Quintin (2010)	−
Quality of legal institutions	Castro, Clementi, and Macdonald (2009)	+
Religious affiliation	de la Croix and Delavallade (2015)	−
Thai Million Baht Village Fund program	Kaboski and Townsend (2011)	−

ments and, in turn, to argue that a country such as Uganda could more than double per capita output if financial "best practices" were implemented.

Structural analyses have also focused on political and social institutions. Seim and Parente (2013) develop a positive analysis of the coevolution of industrialization and democracy, in which an elite chooses to shift a society from autocracy to democracy, essentially because of the levels of taxes and expropriation that exist under different political regimes. De la Croix and Delavallade (2015) argue that differences in southeast Asian economic development can be understood by different religious beliefs, as they affect attitudes toward children. Here religious heterogeneity is interpreted as preference heterogeneity.

These papers are useful in corroborating that various theoretical relationships between institutions and aggregate output can be quantitatively important. In this sense, these studies demonstrate that empirical evidence on the role of certain institutions *may* conclude that their effects are first order. The limitation of these studies is the standard limitation of calibration exercises. While the extent to which the model matches data moments can give an indication of whether the model can approximate the phenomenon under study, it does not address the question of whether it does. This does not mean that these exercises do not have empirical value. It is important to understand whether a particular low-dimensional approximation is or is not close to the complicated reality that is approximated. Again, the value of these exercises is that they can update prior theoretical beliefs by interaction with data.

6.5. HISTORICAL STUDIES

The most compelling evidence on institutions, in my judgment, comes from the study of institutions in historical context. This approach has combined rigorous economic theory with deep understanding of context. There are both microeconomic and macroeconomic versions of such work.

Table 6.4. Effects of various historical events on variables plausibly related to growth

Institution	Study	Claim
Atlantic trade with the New World, Africa, and Asia	Acemoglu, Johnson, and Robinson (2005)	+
Credit markets	Azariadis and de la Croix (2006)	+
Culture	Tabellini (2010)	+
External trade in slaves	Nunn (2008)	−
Investor rights protection	La Porta, Lopez-de-Silanes, Shleifer, and Vishny (1997)	+
Laissez-faire autocratic rulers (vs. kleptocrats)	Seim and Parente (2013)	+
Mita-forced labor system	Dell (2010)	−
Non-landlord revenue collection institutions (vs. landlord)	Banerjee and Iyer (2005)	+
Podesteria (vs. consulate)	Greif (1997)	+
Promoting industrial policies before opening up to trade	Akerman, Nghavi, and Seim (2016)	+
Property rights	Acemoglu, Johnson, and Robinson (2001)	+
Protestantism (literacy)	Becker and Woessmann (2009)	+
State antiquity	Bockstette, Chanda, and Putterman (2002)	+
Terrorist activity	Abadie and Gardeazabal (2003)	−
The indirect form of the British rule (vs. direct)	Iyer (2010), Lange (2004)	+, +
The length of colonial rule	Feyrer and Sacerdote (2009)	+

On the microeconomics side, a pioneering analysis is due to Greif (1989, 1993, 1994) who in a series of papers argued that reputation mechanisms emerged among Maghribi traders to enforce contracts. This work was based on detailed archival analyses and remains an exemplar. The claims have not gone unchallenged. Edwards and Ogilvie (2012) argue that formal legal rules were essential; see Greif (2008) for an unpublished response to the working paper version of Edwards and Ogilvie. This dispute does not question the role of institutions in facilitating Maghribi trading relations, but rather whether informal or formal institutions are key.

Other uses of history have involved the identification of long-run effects of particular institutions. Rather than focus on institutions in a particular time period, these studies focus on how particular institutions have created path dependence in socioeconomic outcomes. Table 6.4 gives examples of these types of studies and indicates the breadth of this literature.

An impressive example of using a given historical context to identify long-run institutional effects is Dell (2010), who explores the effects of a particular forced labor mining system, called mita, that operated in parts of Bolivia and Peru between 1573 and 1812.

The system applied to a particular region, which allows Dell to compare developmental differences between adjacent mita and non-mita locations in an Andean area of Peru where population observables such as ethnicity are identical. This allows for application of regression discontinuity methods. Dell identified a substantial negative effect of the mita system on contemporary household consumption and child health. The success of this empirical strategy derives from the use of a sufficiently narrow context where one can plausibly argue that the plethora of "other" reasons for economic development heterogeneity are not present. This justifies the use of the regression discontinuity approach. Put differently, Dell identifies a context where the open endedness of growth theory does not impede credible inference.

This analysis is also powerful because Dell is able to move beyond a credible identification argument to uncover the effects of the mita system and explore the channels that led to the consumption and health effects described above. This second-stage exercise identifies lower levels of market participation, i.e., prevalence of subsistence farming as a proximate cause, and adverse effects of the mita system on provision of public goods such as roads and education as well as the adverse effects of mita on large landholding formation. The paper is an exemplar of integrating different sources of information into a comprehensive analysis.

The strengths of microeconomic studies, which derive from the specificity of the environments studied, naturally delimit the extent to which the empirical work can be extrapolated to other contexts or to general policy conclusions. Other studies focus on more macroeconomic contexts and have, in turn, led to more general claims about the institutions/growth nexus. To be clear, there is no clean dichotomy between microeconomic and macroeconomic studies. But, in my view, the distinction is important because it is suggestive of the identification problems involved in a given exercise.

The most visible example of macroeconomic studies are the pioneering studies by Acemoglu and Robinson, who have developed a broad theory of institutional differences to explain cross-country per capita income differences; Acemoglu and Robinson (2012) is a popular summary. This work has important predecessors in the economic history literature, notably North (1990), as well as relatively contemporary work such as Engerman and Sokoloff (2008). That said, the Acemoglu and Robinson program has been transformative by the integration of theoretical and historical analysis; more on this below.

Another dimension of this work has been driven to an important extent by the development of new datasets. As such, the success of these studies is an exemplar for what Caplin (2016) has called economic data engineering. Following Caplin, datasets have been, in the institutional literature, constructed in order to answer particular questions. Notice that this empirical strategy overcomes identification problems and complements the use of economic theory. The strategy is distinct from the search for natural experiments. While the choice of contexts for which to construct data is analogous to the search for a natural experiment, in the case of historical contexts, choosing one is only the start of a data construction process.

One important and well-known example of this type of research is Nunn (2008), which studies the long-term effects of the African slave trade on economic development. Nunn finds that the intensity of the slave trade that occurred in a contemporary nation (measured by the ratio of slaves exported to area of the country) is negatively associated with per capita GDP, a finding that is robust when one uses geographic instruments relevant to slave trade profitability to account for endogeneity of slave trade intensity.

A general issue in historical studies is the uniqueness of the institution studied relative to the overall developmental history of a country. To see why this needs to be done, consider the question of identifying how serfdom affected Russian economic development, which has been studied recently by, among others,[7] using cross-regional variation in the number of serfs and other measures of the extent of that institution. In order for long-run data to identify a causal effect of spatial variations in serfdom intensity, it is necessary that the various momentous events in Russia, be it the famine of 1893 or the civil or world wars, did not generate spatial effects that are correlated with serfdom intensity. The general problem is that if one relies on variations in a particular "large" event that occurs at one point in time, its influence will be preserved only if subsequent events are uncorrelated with it. Even if the individual events are, in isolation, ex ante independent of the one under study, a researcher has to be able to argue that none of them is ex post correlated with the initial event. Returning to the serfdom example, if spatial variation from famines and wars occurred independently from serfdom variability, that does not mean that none of them are ex post correlated. And once one considers how geographic or other factors operating at a lower timescale interact with the locations of events such as prevalence of serfdom or intensity of famine or locations of battles, it becomes evident that the independence assumption is itself extremely difficult to defend as plausible.

Returning to Nunn, one might argue that in order to demonstrate contemporary effects in Africa from the slave trade, one needs to account for any correlations between the patterns of enslavement and the effects of ethnic conflict induced by arbitrary borders, which has been argued by Easterly and Levine (1997) among others, as an explanation. Nunn does not directly address this issue, but argues (to be fair, tentatively) that higher levels of slave trade damaged the capacity for identities to emerge at higher levels of aggregation than ethnicity and so are causal with respect to the Easterly and Levine findings. This may well be the case, but in my judgment this indicates the importance of bringing more theoretical structure to such econometric exercises if one is interested in coevolution of factors at different timescales.

While obvious in the abstract, it is important to recognize that successful use of historical episodes requires deep immersion in the details of the relevant history. Ogilvie and Carus (2015) argue that a number of the standard lessons of the historical literature for the role of institutions in growth are overstated. At one level, these authors challenge the conclusions of particular episodes; I have discussed the example of the Maghribi traders above. At another level, they challenge monocausal approaches to institutions. For example, Ogilvie and Carus argue that contracting institutions, which involve private relationships, should be understood as functioning on the same plane as property rights and that the two interact, rather than being separate spheres. As such, Ogilvie and Carus make a persuasive argument that one should focus on portfolios of institutions as levers of development and growth, both because of interaction effects and because different configurations of institutions can produce similar effects. These are issues to which I will return below.

6.6. ABDUCTION AND THE STATE OF KNOWLEDGE ON INSTITUTIONS AND GROWTH

Where does the empirical literature on institutions and growth stand? There is much empirical evidence, ranging from reduced form regressions to historical studies that support a role for institutions in growth and development. There is no general disagreement on this proposition from any field of economics, be it economic history, development, or growth economics. But does the now-banal claim that institutions matter translate into a first-order conception of the determinants of economic prosperity or failure? Put differently, while a study such as Rodrik, Subramanian, and Trebbi (2004) evaluates whether institutions belong in the "true" model of fundamental determinants to growth, it is not designed to measure empirical salience.

Acemoglu and Robinson (2005, 2012), and the background research that underlies these, is arguably the most prominent exception to this claim as they integrate evidence from many contexts to draw very broad conclusions that institutions are fundamental to understanding historical patterns of development and growth.[8] Combining evidence from stark comparisons such as North versus South Korea, historical examples such as the Mayan and Roman Empires, as well as evidence from formal econometric methods, these authors have developed general propositions that the institutions that protect private property while simultaneously ensuring that the benefits of economic development and growth are inclusive, constitute a powerful way to understand why nations prosper or stagnate. Further, they argue that institutional differences with respect to these features provide insights for contexts ranging from capitalist to socialist/centrally planned economies, advanced industrialized nations versus Sub-Saharan Africa, and within-region variation in development.

While their work is not presented using this language, the Acemoglu and Robinson research program should be understood as an example of abduction (Heckman and Singer 2017), also known as inference to the best explanation. Abduction is the stuff of science, i.e., the drawing of conclusions from a host of evidentiary sources. Such inferences are neither deductive nor inductive. They involve complex judgments in integrating evidence from different sources. Abduction underlies much of the best empirical social science. Why? Because each type of evidence that can bring to bear on a topic such as the role of institutions in development and growth has important limitations. Formal econometric exercises identify general patterns, but they either are correlative in nature or contingent on assumptions of questionable validity. Historical examples may resemble experiments, but the heterogeneity of contexts makes it difficult to extrapolate. Structural modeling approaches are similarly contingent on assumptions that are questionable. For each approach, theory open-endedness delimits the evidentiary value of models. The point is not that each source of evidence is worthless, but that each is limited. Acemoglu and Robinson develop their generalizations from a variety of empirical approaches.

The abductive nature of the Acemoglu and Robinson research program also involves the rich interplay of theory and empirics. Again, this process underpins abduction. For example, consider how one accounts for endogeneity of institutions in assessing the effects of institutions. I have criticized instrumental variables approaches to endogeneity. The constructive approach is to explicitly examine the determinants of institutional quality, and to use theory to structure how one draws inferences about institutions as mechanisms, for example from historical data.

Abduction is useful in interpreting critiques that have been made of the work, notably the Acemoglu and Robinson (2012) book *Why Nations Fail*. MacLeod (2013) argues that the absence of counterfactuals in historical examples means that the role of institutions is not identified from them. This view equates the substantive question of the role of institutions in development and growth with the statistical question of whether historical evidence maps into a particular model of causality. They are not equivalent. In contrast, Sachs (2012), who argues against the conceptual framework on the ground it oversimplifies the process of development and prosperity at the expense of other factors, notably geography, can be placed in a comparison with Acemoglu and Robinson using abductive arguments. Subramanian (2012) focuses on the utility of their general framework for understanding India and China. Here I only note that adjudication of these critiques itself requires abduction, which involves specifying explicit alternative theories to Acemoglu and Robinson (a theory of growth based on geography, a theory of growth based on interplay of geography and growth, etc.) and evaluating a range of qualitatively different types of evidence. One can do this as well in terms of evaluating Chinese exceptionalism as an alternative to the general Acemoglu and Robinson theory. Here abduction will involve assessment of the extent to which the broad theory addresses evidence from specific cases in sufficient depth and to what extent generalization across cases is warranted.

To be clear, the use of qualitative and quantitative evidence is a hallmark of the new institutional economics. Kuran (2018) is a recent deep example of abduction with reference to understanding the effects of Islam.

6.7. CONCLUSIONS

The summary of my arguments is simple: institutions have been established to matter both in general and in a host of interesting specific contexts. This is true whether one considers a particular institution as broad as democracy or as pathological as slavery. It is also true when the objective is to explain why different regions of the world, or countries within regions, exhibit substantial heterogeneity.

As rich, and in my judgment persuasive, as the current literature is, there are areas where I would recommend fruitful research directions.

First, I believe that the emerging literature on the interplay of culture and institutions is an especially important development. Alesina and Giuliano (2015) surveys the state of this literature, while Bisin and Verdier (2017) is an important recent example of the formal modeling of culture/institutions coevolution. By culture, I follow a commonly used definition from Guiso, Sapienza, and Zingales (2006: 23) who interpret culture as

> those customary beliefs and values that ethnic, religious, and social groups transmit fairly unchanged from generation to generation.

In this respect, I disagree with definitions of institutions that include values and beliefs. This is because institutions are intrinsically involved with interactions between individuals and rules that direct these interactions, and so it is appropriate to define them at a level of populations beyond an individual. The cultural economics literature, as surveyed by Guiso, Sapienza, and Zingales, or Alesina and Giuliano, also matters for understanding the endogeneity of institutions.

In this spirit, there is much value in expanding the understanding of the interplay of institutions with the emergence of ethics. As formalized by Roemer (2010) among others, ethical conduct represents a path to the solution of collective action problems that is conceptually distinct from institutions per se. As demonstrated by Alger and Weibull (2013), for example, "homo moralis" can emerge via repeated interactions. It has long been understood that market activity presupposes behaviors that move beyond self-interest (Arrow 1974). In my judgment, the usual study of norms as outcomes of repeated games with sanctions is usefully complemented by a recognition that there are normative influences on choice that are better understood as constraints as opposed to arguments of the utility function per se; this view is found in Baland and Platteau (2000), who (chapter 6) refer to "norms and constraints on self-interest." The importance of ethics in development is elaborated in Platteau (1994a, 1994b, 2000), who draws an important distinction between social and moral norms, where the latter involve internalized senses of guilt and shame. Bardhan (2000) is one empirical example of how ethics affects collective actions problems in irrigation. Further, a number of authors have shown how institutions can affect ethics. One example is Bardhan's (2005) emphasis on democratic participation, which has much salience, if one wishes to understand how the ethical underpinnings needed for a constitution to function can be created. In contrast, Falk and Szech (2013) have shown how markets, whose behavior is one key objective of institutional design, can diminish the impact of certain ethical values on choices. Systematic development of the ethics/institutions relationship seems very promising.

Second, I believe the successes of the institutions and growth literature in terms of producing de facto abductive analyses would be enhanced by the development and use of explicit tools for abduction. This recommendation, of course, does not just apply to the subject of this chapter, but to any social science context in which multiple sources of evidence are available. Heckman and Singer (2017) provide a general conceptualization of abduction in economic analysis. In the institutions context, one area where there is a need for formal methods is suggested by my discussion of the identification problem for the persistent effects of large historical episodes. I argued that there are two problems with work of this type: ex post correlation of historical events that are ex ante independent as well as correlation in the events. These problems are not, I believe, amenable to standard econometric methods. I do not pretend to have suggestions on how to resolve these problems for historical studies, but their resolution is critical for credible identification. More generally, the explanation of major historical events is a key objective of the institutions literature, and so naturally requires abduction. Beyond formal tools, there are gains from trade in considering successful de facto examples of abduction outside of an institutions framework, e.g., Donohue and Heckman (1991), to see how the weighing of evidence compares to examples in the institutions literature.

Formal tools for abduction are still in their infancy. Such tools amount to the creation of rules by which different sorts of evidence, in the current context, historical studies, regression analysis, random controlled trials, and the like, are quantitatively integrated to evaluate propositions. Katz and Singer (2007) is a rare example of such an endeavor. Their work, however, involves a concrete question, whether yellow rain observed in Southeast Asia was due to a biological weapon. The question of whether institutions constitute a successful monocausal theory of development is profoundly different as it involves assessing the theory as an approximation against more complicated alternatives. It is a commonplace that successful social science theories are low-dimension approximations of a complex reality. What is needed are more systematic ways of drawing such judgments.

Third, I see a need for more work on the translation of evidence on institutions into policy recommendations. It is relatively straightforward to identify institutions to be avoided. Further, there now exist a number of well-established general policy conclusions that may be drawn from the extant empirical literature. There is much consensus with respect to the Acemoglu and Robinson view that institutions which (1) secure property rights so that there are incentives for productive economic activity and (2) are inclusive across broad parts of populations, appear ubiquitous when one considers sustained economic success. North, Wallis, and Weingast (2009) and North et al. (2012) have made a very compelling case for violence reduction as fundamental to how institutions facilitate development. Similarly, there is no serious disagreement about the importance of the rule of law, be it in terms of formal governance a la La Porta, Lopez-de-Silanes, and Shleifer (2008) or private rules that Dixit (2004) defines as the areas of "lawlessness and economics." However, the evidence for these and other very broad claims, persuasive in terms of general theory, does not lead to obvious policy conclusions, once egregious institutions are avoided. Each of these perspectives identifies how institutions can incentivize productive individual activities in ways that are simultaneously socially desirable in the presence of market frictions. These theories are not tautological as they provide reasons why these individual and aggregate effects occur. But the mapping of general propositions to microeconomic specifics requires much additional argumentation. This also has implications for the experimental side of development economics. Pande and Udry (2005) make this argument in the context of the class of decentralized interventions that are the hallmark of randomized controlled studies. While some policy interventions may be efficacious regardless of institutional environment (Banerjee and Duflo 2011), to conclude from those successes that one should delimit policy interventions to those that are "institutions-robust" is not tenable from any decision-theoretic perspective of which I am aware.

Concretely, the policy side of the institutions and growth literature would benefit from more attention to decision theory. This is so in several respects. First, policy recommendations should be thought of in terms of portfolios. The desirable incentive effects for sustained growth can be produced by multiple configurations of institutions. The Asian tigers differ along many institutional dimensions from the United Kingdom, United States, and Australasia. And policies are of course synergistic. In general, the sorts of questions that define positive research on institutions and economics usually focus on whether particular institutions matter. My claim is a corollary of the Ogilvie and Carus (2015) critique of historical studies of institutions and growth. The one addendum I would make is to emphasize the contextual specificity of portfolio weights, whose determination requires the "thick" description that Ogilvie and Carus argue is needed in historical work.

Second, there are always questions of the second best. Are institutions that reduce corruption always growth-enhancing? Presumably not, if the corruption mitigates expropriation or bureaucratic barriers to innovation. This is a variant of the standard problem of external validity: does evidence that corruption hurts growth in one context apply to another?

Third, the issues of model uncertainty, for example possible nonlinearity, that have mattered for the institutions and regression literature need to be integrated into policy assessment. Here I really am doing no more than suggesting that explicit decision-theoretic formulations be used when policy recommendations are made.

In conclusion, there are many empirical successes for the institutions, development, and growth literature and at the same time many important unanswered questions. Hence this literature should continue to be vibrant.

NOTES

I thank Arik Roginsky, Aiday Sikhova, and Nicholas for superb research assistance. Jean-Marie Baland and Jean-Philippe Platteau have provided invaluable feedback on earlier drafts.

1. While other general categories such as markets also require specificity for empirical work, institutions constitute an especially elastic category, as discussed below.
2. Some social capital definitions invoke specific phenomena, e.g., networks. But these definitions beg the question of what distinguishes social capital as a natural kind from the phenomena, which can themselves be defined as institutions.
3. Other limits to the indices involve the distinctions between formal and informal or de jure and de facto institutions. Democracy indices are constructed using procedural measures which may not characterize either the operational aspects of a system (e.g., voting restrictions, corruption) or the extent to which polarization in a country means that minority preferences are ever reflected in policy choices.
4. I am not aware of any analyses of timescale and instrumental variable validity in the institutions literature.
5. Some studies look at intra-country regional heterogeneity in institutions.
6. The difficulty of identifying valid instruments for institutions in the context of growth regressions may be contrasted with the way instruments are identified in a simultaneous equations model (SEM), where exclusion restrictions generate instruments. A given SEM is a closed system that allows a researcher, via exclusion restrictions or restrictions on the relationships between parameters, to use theory to generate instruments in a way precluded by theory open-endedness in a growth regression.
7. To be clear, I discuss identification issues for these papers because they are significant research contributions.
8. The work of the school of economic history associated with Douglass North is a fundamental predecessor.

REFERENCES

Abadie, A. and J. Gardeazabal. 2003. "The Economic Costs of Conflict: A Case Study of the Basque Country." *American Economic Review* 93: 113–132.

Acemoglu, D., F. Gallego, and J. Robinson. 2014. "Institutions, Human Capital, and Development." *Annual Review of Economics* 6: 875–912.

Acemoglu, D. and S. Johnson. 2005. "Unbundling Institutions." *Journal of Political Economy* 113: 949–995.

Acemoglu, D., S. Johnson, and J. Robinson. 2001. "The Colonial Origins of Comparative Development." *American Economic Review* 91: 1369–1401.

———. 2002. "Reversal of Fortune: Geography and Institutions in the Making of the Modern World Income Distribution." *Quarterly Journal of Economics* 117: 1231–1294.

———. 2003. "An African Success Story: Botswana." In *In Search of Prosperity: Analytical Narratives on Economic Growth*, edited by D. Rodrik. Princeton, NJ: Princeton University Press.

———. 2005. "The Rise of Europe: Atlantic Trade, Institutional Change, and Economic Growth." *American Economic Review* 95: 546–579.

———. 2012. "The Colonial Origins of Comparative Development: An Empirical Investigation: Reply." *American Economic Review* 102: 3077–3110.

Acemoglu, D., S. Johnson, J. Robinson, and Y. Thaicharoen. 2003. "Institutional Causes, Macroeco-
    nomic Symptoms: Volatility, Crises and Growth." *Journal of Monetary Economics* 50: 49–123.
Acemoglu, D., S. Naidu, P. Restrepo, and J. Robinson. 2013. "Democracy, Redistribution and Inequality."
    National Bureau of Economic Research Working Paper no. 19746.
Acemoglu, D. and J. Robinson. 2000. "Democratization or Repression?" *European Economic Review* 4:
    683–693
———. 2005. "Institutions as a Fundamental Cause of Long-Run Growth." In *Handbook of Economic
    Growth* 1, edited by P. Aghion and S. Durlauf. Amsterdam: North Holland.
———. 2006. "De Facto Political Power and Institutional Persistence." *American Economic Review* 96:
    325–330.
———. 2012. *Why Nations Fail: The Origins of Power, Prosperity, and Poverty*. New York: Crown
    Publishing.
Acemoglu, D. and M. Ucer. 2015. "The Ups and Downs of Turkish Growth, 2002–2015: Political Dy-
    namics, the European Union and the Institutional Slide." *National Bureau of Economic Research* 21608.
Aghion, P., P. Howitt, and D. Mayer-Foulkes. 2005. "The Effect of Financial Development on Conver-
    gence: Theory and Evidence." *Quarterly Journal of Economics* 120: 173–222.
Ahlerup, P., O. Olsson, and D. Yanagizawa. 2009. "Social Capital vs Institutions in the Growth Pro-
    cess." *European Journal of Political Economy* 25: 1–14.
Aidt, T. 2009. "Corruption, Institutions, and Economic Development." *Oxford Review of Economic Pol-
    icy* 25: 271–291.
Akerman, A., A. Naghavi, and A. Seim. 2016. "Oligarchies and Development in a Global Economy: A
    Tale of Two Elites." *Economic Inquiry* 54: 229–246.
Albouy, D. 2012. "The Colonial Origins of Comparative Development: An Empirical Investigation:
    Comment." *American Economic Review* 102: 3059–3076.
Alcalá, F. and A. Ciccone. 2004. "Trade and Productivity." *Quarterly Journal of Economics* 119: 613–646.
Alesina, A. and P. Giuliano. 2015. "Culture and Institutions." *Journal of Economic Literature* 53: 898–944.
Alesina, A., S. Özler, N. Roubini, and P. Swagel. 1996. "Political Instability and Economic Growth."
    Journal of Economic Growth 1: 189–211.
Alfaro, L., S. Kalemli-Ozcan, and V. Volosovych. 2008. "Why Doesn't Capital Flow from Rich to Poor
    Countries? An Empirical Investigation." *Review of Economics and Statistics* 90: 347–368.
Alger, I. and J. Weibull. 2013. "Homo Moralis—Preference Evolution Under Incomplete Information
    and Assortative Matching." *Econometrica* 81: 2269–2302.
Amaral, P. and E. Quintin. 2010. "Limited Enforcement, Financial Intermediation, and Economic De-
    velopment: A Quantitative Assessment." *International Economic Review* 51: 785–811.
Arrow, K. 1974. *The Limits of Organization*. New York: Norton.
Azariadis, C. and D. de la Croix. 2006. "Financial Institutional Reform, Growth, and Equality." In *In-
    stitutions, Development, and Economic Growth*, edited by T. Eicher and C. Garcia Peñalosa. Cam-
    bridge, MA: MIT Press.
Baland, J.-M., F. Bourguignon, J.-P. Platteau, and T. Verdier (this volume). "Economic Development
    and Institutions: An Introduction."
Baland, J.-M., K. Moene, and J. Robinson. 2008. "Governance and Development." In *Handbook of De-
    velopment Economics* 5, edited by D. Rodrik and M. Rosenzwieg. Amsterdam: Elsevier.
Baland, J.-M. and J.-P. Platteau. 1996. *Halting Degradation of Natural Resources: Is There a Role for Rural
    Communities?* Oxford: Oxford University Press.
Banerjee, A. and E. Duflo. 2011. *Poor Economics: A Radical Rethinking of the Way to Fight Global Poverty*.
    New York: Public Affairs.
———. 2014. "Do Firms Want to Borrow More? Testing Credit Constraints Using a Directed Lending
    Program." *Review of Economic Studies* 81: 572–607.
Banerjee, A., P. Gertler, and M. Ghatak. 2002. "Empowerment and Efficiency: Tenancy Reform in West
    Bengal." *Journal of Political Economy* 2: 239–280.
Banerjee, A. and L. Iyer. 2005. "History, Institutions, and Economic Performance: The Legacy of Co-
    lonial Land Tenure Systems in India." *American Economic Review* 95: 1190–1213.
Bardhan, P. 2000. "Irrigation and Cooperation: An Empirical Analysis of 48 Irrigation Communities
    in South India." *Economic Development and Cultural Change* 48: 847–865.
———. 2005. "Institutions Matter, But Which Ones?" *Economics of Transition* 13: 499–532.
———. 2016. "State and Development: The Need for a Reappraisal of the Current Literature." *Journal
    of Economic Literature* 54: 862–892.
Barro, R. 1991. "Economic Growth in a Cross Section of Countries." *Quarterly Journal of Economics* 106:
    407–443.

———. 1996. "Democracy and Growth." *Journal of Economic Growth* 1: 1–27.

Becker, S. and L. Woessmann. 2009. "Was Weber Wrong? A Human Capital Theory of Protestant Economic History." *Quarterly Journal of Economics* 124: 531–596.

Benhabib, J. and M. Spiegel. 2000. "The Role of Financial Development in Growth and Investment." *Journal of Economic Growth* 5: 341–360.

Bernard, A. and S. Durlauf. 1996. "Interpreting Tests of the Convergence Hypothesis." *Journal of Econometrics* 71.1: 161–173.

Besley, T. and R. Burgess. 2004. "Can Labor Regulation Hinder Economic Performance? Evidence from India." *Quarterly Journal of Economics* 119: 91–134.

Bisin, A. and T. Verdier. 2017. "On the Joint Evolution of Culture and Institutions." *National Bureau of Economic Research Working Paper* 23375.

Bockstette, V., A. Chanda, and L. Putterman. 2002. "States and Markets: The Advantage of an Early Start." *Journal of Economic Growth* 7: 347–369.

Brock, W. and S. Durlauf. 2001. "Growth Empirics and Reality." *World Bank Economic Review* 15: 229–272.

Buera, F., J. Kaboski, and Y. Shin. 2011. "Finance and Development: A Tale of Two Sectors." *American Economic Review* 101: 1964–2002.

Buera, F. and Y. Shin. 2017. "Productivity Growth and Capital Flows: The Dynamics of Reforms." *American Economic Journal: Macroeconomics* 9: 147–185.

Burgess, R. and R. Pande. 2005. "Do Rural Banks Matter? Evidence from the Indian Social Banking Experiment." *American Economic Review* 95: 780–795.

Burnside, A. C. and D. Dollar. 2004. "Aid, Policies, and Growth: Revisiting the Evidence." *World Bank Policy Research Working Paper* 3251.

Caplin, A. 2016. "Economic Data Engineering." Mimeo, New York University.

Careaga, M. and B. Weingast. 2003. "Fiscal Federalism, Good Governance, and Economic Growth in Mexico." In *In Search of Prosperity: Analytic Narratives On Economic Growth*, edited by D. Rodrik. Princeton, NJ: Princeton University Press.

Carlsson, F. and S. Lundström. 2002. "Economic Freedom and Growth: Decomposing the Effects." *Public Choice* 112: 335–344.

Castro, R., G. Clementi, and G. MacDonald. 2009. "Legal Institutions, Sectoral Heterogeneity, and Economic Development." *Review of Economic Studies* 76: 529–561.

Chaudhuri, S., P. Goldberg, and P. Jia. 2006. "Estimating the Effects of Global Patent Protection in Pharmaceuticals: A Case Study of Quinolones in India." *American Economic Review* 96: 1477–1514.

Claessens, S. and L. Laeven. 2003. "Financial Development, Property Rights, and Growth." *Journal of Finance* 58: 2401–2436.

Clague, C., P. Keefer, S. Knack, and M. Olson. 1999. "Contract-Intensive Money: Contract Enforcement, Property Rights, and Economic Performance." *Journal of Economic Growth* 4: 185–211.

Clark, G. and S. Wolcott. 2003. "One Polity, Many Countries: Economic Growth in India, 1873–2000." In *In Search of Prosperity: Analytic Narratives on Economic Growth*, edited by D. Rodrik. Princeton, NJ: Princeton University Press.

Collins, S. and B. Bosworth. 2003. "The Empirics of Growth: An Update." *Brookings Papers on Economic Activity* 2: 113–206.

Cox, D. and M. Fafchamps. 2007. "Extended Family and Kinship Networks: Economic Insights and Evolutionary Directions." In *Handbook of Development Economics* 4: 3711–3784, edited by T. P. Schultz and J. Strauss. Amsterdam: Elsevier.

Coyne, D. and C. Tan. 2012. "Do Political Institutions Yield Multiple Growth Regimes?" *Economics Bulletin* 32: 1442–1454.

Dal Bó, P., A. Foster, and L. Putterman. 2010. "Institutions and Behavior: Experimental Evidence on the Effects of Democracy." *American Economic Review* 100: 2205–2229.

Dawson, J. 1998. "Institutions, Investment, and Growth: New Cross-Country and Panel Data Evidence." *Economic Inquiry* 36: 603–619.

———. 2003. "Causality in the Freedom–Growth Relationship." *European Journal of Political Economy* 19.3: 479–495.

de la Croix, D. and C. Delavallade. 2015. "Religions, Fertility and Growth in South-East Asia." *IRES Discussion Papers* 201502.

de la Croix, D., M. Doepke, and J. Mokyr. 2016. "Clans, Guilds, and Markets: Apprenticeship Institutions and Growth in the Pre-Industrial Economy." *National Bureau of Economic Research* 22131.

DeLong, J. B. 2003. "India since Independence: An Analytic Growth Narrative." In *In Search of Prosperity: Analytic Narratives On Economic Growth*, edited by D. Rodrik. Princeton, NJ: Princeton University Press.

de Silanes, F., R. La Porta, A. Shleifer, and R. Vishny. 1998. "Law and Finance." *Journal of Political Economy* 106: 1113–1155.

Dell, M. 2010. "The Persistent Effects of Peru's Mining Mita." *Econometrica* 78: 1863–1903.

Diamond, J. 1997. *Guns, Germs, and Steel: The Fates of Human Societies*. New York: Norton.

Dias, J. and J. McDermott. 2006. "Institutions, Education, and Development: The Role of Entrepreneurs." *Journal of Development Economics* 80: 299–328.

Dixit, A. 2004. *Lawlessness and Economics*. Princeton, NJ: Princeton University Press.

Do, Q. and L. Iyer. 2003. "Land Rights and Economic Development: Evidence from Vietnam." *World Bank Policy Research Working Paper* 3120.

Dollar, D. and A. Kraay. 2003. "Institutions, Trade, and Growth." *Journal of Monetary Economics* 50: 133–162.

Donohue, J. and J. Heckman. 1991. "Continuous Versus Episodic Change: The Impact of Civil Rights Policy on the Economic Status of Blacks." *Journal of Economic Literature* 26: 1603–1643.

Durlauf, S. 2002. "On the Empirics of Social Capital." *Economic Journal* 112: F459–F479.

Durlauf, S., P. Johnson, and J. Temple. 2005. "Growth Econometrics." *Handbook of Economic Growth* 1, edited by P. Aghion and S. Durlauf, 555–677. Amsterdam: Elsevier.

Durlauf, S., A. Kourtellos, and C. Tan. 2008. "Are Any Growth Theories Robust?" *Economic Journal* 118: 329–346.

Durlauf, S. and D. Quah. 1998. "The New Empirics of Economic Growth." In *Handbook of Macroeconomics* 1, edited by J. Taylor and M. Woodford. Amsterdam: Elsevier.

Easterly, W. 2007. "Inequality Does Cause Underdevelopment: Insights from a New Instrument." *Journal of Development Economics* 84: 755–776.

Easterly, W. and R. Levine. 1997. "Africa's Growth Tragedy." *Quarterly Journal of Economics* 112: 1203–1250.

———. 2003. "Tropics, Germs, and Crops: How Endowments Influence Economic Development." *Journal of Monetary Economics* 50: 3–39.

Easterly, W., J. Ritzen, and M. Woolcock. 2006. "Social Cohesion, Institutions, and Growth." *Economics & Politics* 18: 103–120.

Edison, H., R. Levine, L. Ricci, and T. Sløk. 2002. "International Financial Integration and Economic Growth." *Journal of International Money and Finance* 21: 749–776.

Edwards, J. and S. Ogilvie. 2012. "Contract Enforcement, Institutions, and Social Capital: The Maghribi Traders Reappraised." *Economic History Review* 65: 421–444.

Efendic, A., G. Pugh, and N. Adnett. 2011. "Institutions and Economic Performance: A Meta-Regression Analysis." *European Journal of Political Economy* 27: 586–599.

Eicher, T. and A. Leukert. 2009. "Institutions and Economic Performance: Endogeneity and Parameter Heterogeneity." *Journal of Money, Credit and Banking* 41: 197–219.

Engerman, S. and K. Sokoloff. 1997. "Factor Endowments, Institutions, and Differential Paths of Growth Among New World Economies." In *How Latin America Fell Behind*, edited by S. Haber, 260–304. Stanford, CA: Stanford University Press.

———. 2000. "History Lessons: Institutions, Factors Endowments, and Paths of Development in the New World." *Journal of Economic Perspectives* 14: 217–232.

———. 2002. "Factor Endowments, Inequality, and Paths of Development Among New World Economies." *Economía* 3: 41–109.

———. 2008. "Debating the Role of Institutions in Political and Economic Development: Theory, History, and Findings." *Annual Review of Political Science* 11: 119–135.

Esfahani, H. and M. Ramirez. 2003. "Institutions, Infrastructure, and Economic Growth." *Journal of Development Economics* 70: 443–477.

Falk, A. and N. Szech. 2013. "Morals and Markets." *Science* 10: 707–711.

Fernandez, C., E. Ley, and M. Steel. 2001. "Model Uncertainty in Cross-Country Growth Regressions." *Journal of Applied Econometrics* 16: 563–576.

Feyrer, J. and B. Sacerdote. 2009. "Colonialism and Modern Income: Islands as Natural Experiments." *Review of Economics and Statistics* 91: 245–262.

Field, E. 2007. "Entitled to Work: Urban Property Rights and Labor Supply in Peru." *Quarterly Journal of Economics* 122: 1561–1602.

Fischer, S., R. Sahay, and C. Vegh. 1996. "Economies in Transition: The Beginnings of Growth." *American Economic Review* 86: 229–233.

Fisman, R. 2001. "Estimating the Value of Political Connections." *American Economic Review* 91: 1095–1102.

Fisman, R. and J. Svensson. 2007. "Are Corruption and Taxation Really Harmful to Growth? Firm Level Evidence." *Journal of Development Economics* 83: 63–75.

Francisco, A. and A. Ciccone. 2004. "Trade and Productivity." *Quarterly Journal of Economics* 119: 613–646.

Frankel, J. and D. Romer. 1999. "Does Trade Cause Growth?" *American Economic Review* 89: 379–399.

Frey, B. and I. Bohnet. 1995. "Institutions Affect Fairness: Experimental Investigations." *Journal of Institutional and Theoretical Economics* 151: 286–303.

Galiani, S., P. Gertler, and E. Schargrodsky. 2005. "Water for Life: The Impact of the Privatization of Water Services on Child Mortality." *Journal of Political Economy* 113: 83–120.

Gine, X. and R. Townsend. 2004. "Evaluation of Financial Liberalization: A General Equilibrium Model with Constrained Occupation Choice." *Journal of Development Economics* 74: 269–307.

Glaeser, E., R. La Porta, F. Lopez-de-Silanes, and A. Shleifer. 2004. "Do Institutions Cause Growth?" *Journal of Economic Growth* 9: 271–303.

Gooch, E., J. Martinez-Vazquez, and B. Yedgenov. 2016. "A Superior Instrument for the Role of Institutional Quality on Economic Development." Working Paper, Georgia State University.

Gorodnichenko, Y. and G. Roland. 2010. "Culture, Institutions and the Wealth of Nations." *Center for Economic Policy Research Discussion Paper* 8013.

Greenwood, J., J. Sanchez, and C. Wang. 2013. "Quantifying the Impact of Financial Development on Economic Development." *Review of Economic Dynamics* 16: 194–215.

Greif, A. 1989. "Reputation and Coalitions in Medieval Trade: Evidence on the Maghribi Traders." *Journal of Economic History* 49: 857–882.

———. 1993. "Contract Enforceability and Economic Institutions in Early Trade: The Maghribi Traders' Coalition." *American Economic Review* 83: 525–548.

———. 1994. "Cultural Beliefs and the Organization of Society: A Historical and Theoretical Reflection on Collectivist and Individualist Societies." *Journal of Political Economy* 102.5: 912–950.

———. 1997. "Self-Enforcing Political System and Economic Growth: Late Medieval Genoa." *Social Science Research Network* 97–037.

———. 2006. *Institutions and the Path to the Modern Economy: Lessons from Medieval Trade.* Cambridge: Cambridge University Press.

———. 2008. "Contract Enforcement and Institutions Among the Maghribi Traders: Refuting Edwards and Ogilvie." *CESifo Working Paper* 2350.

Greif, A., P. Milgrom, and B. Weingast. 1994. "Coordination, Commitment, and Enforcement: The Case of the Merchant Guild." *Journal of Political Economy* 102: 745–776.

Guiso, L., P. Sapienza, and L. Zingales. 2006. "Does Culture Affect Economic Outcomes?" *Journal of Economic Perspectives* 20: 23–48.

Haber, S. and V. Menaldo. 2011. "Rainfall, Human Capital, and Democracy." Available at SSRN 1667332. 2011 Apr 2.

Haggard, S. 2004. "Institutions and Growth in East Asia." *Studies in Comparative International Development* 38: 53–81.

Haggard, S. and C. Moon. 1990. "Institutions and Economic Policy: Theory and a Korean Case Study." *World Politics* 42: 210–237.

Hall, R. and C. Jones. 1999. "Why Do Some Countries Produce So Much More Output Per Worker Than Others?" *Quarterly Journal of Economics* 114: 83–116.

Heckman, J. and B. Singer. 2017. "Abducting Economics." *American Economic Review* 107: 298–302.

Helliwell, J. 1994. "Empirical Linkages between Democracy and Economic Growth." *British Journal of Political Science* 24: 225–248.

Isham, J., M. Woolcock, L. Pritchett, and G. Busby. 2005. "The Varieties of Resource Experience: Natural Resource Export Structures and the Political Economy of Economic Growth." *World Bank Economic Review* 19: 141–174.

Iyer, L. 2010. "Direct Versus Indirect Colonial Rule in India: Long-Term Consequences." *Review of Economics and Statistics* 92: 693–713.

Jones, C. and P. Romer. 2010. "The New Kaldor Facts: Ideas, Institutions, Population, and Human Capital." *American Economic Journal: Macroeconomics* 2: 224–245.

Kaboski, J. and R. Townsend. 2011. "A Structural Evaluation of a Large-Scale Quasi-Experimental Microfinance Initiative." *Econometrica* 79: 1357–1406.

Katz, R. and B. Singer. 2007. "Can an Attribution Assessment Be Made for Yellow Rain?" *Politics and the Life Sciences* 26: 24–42.

Kaufmann, D., M. Mastruzzi, and D. Zavaleta. 2003. "Sustained Macroeconomic Reforms, Tepid Growth: A Governance Puzzle in Bolivia?" In *In Search of Prosperity: Analytic Narratives on Economic Growth*, edited by D. Rodrik. Princeton, NJ: Princeton University Press.

Knack, S. and P. Keefer. 1997. "Does Social Capital Have an Economic Payoff? A Cross-Country Investigation." *Quarterly Journal of Economics* 112: 1251–1288.

Knowles, S. 2007. "Is Social Capital Part of the Institutions Continuum and Is It a Deep Determinant of Development?" In *Advancing Development*, edited by G. Mavrotas and A. Shorrocks. London: Palgrave Macmillan.

Kuran, T. 2018. "Islam and Economic Performance: Historical and Contemporary Links." *Journal of Economic Literature* 56: 1292–1359.

Laeven, L. and C. Woodruff. 2007. "The Quality of the Legal System, Firm Ownership, and Firm Size." *Review of Economics and Statistics* 89: 601–614.

Lagerlof, N. 2003. "From Malthus to Modern Growth: Can Epidemics Explain the Three Regimes?" *International Economic Review* 44: 755–777.

La Porta, R., F. Lopez-de-Silanes, and A. Shleifer. 2008. "The Economic Consequences of Legal Origins." *Journal of Economic Literature* 46: 285–332.

La Porta, R., F. Lopez-de-Silanes, A. Shleifer, and R. Vishny. 1997. "Legal Determinants of External Finance." *Journal of Finance* 52: 1131–1150.

Lange, M. 2004. "British Colonial Legacies and Political Development." *World Development* 32: 905–922.

Levine, R. 1998. "The Legal Environment, Banks, and Long-Run Economic Growth." *Journal of Money, Credit and Banking* 30: 596–613.

Levine, R., N. Loayza, and T. Beck. 2000. "Financial Intermediation and Growth: Causality and Causes." *Journal of Monetary Economics* 46: 31–77.

Lipton, P. 2004. *Inference to the Best Explanation*, second edition. London: Routledge.

Mauro, P. 1995. "Corruption and Growth." *Quarterly Journal of Economics* 110: 681–712.

Macleod, W. B. 2013. "On Economics: A Review of 'Why Nations Fail' by D. Acemoglu and J. Robinson and 'Pillars of Prosperity' by T. Besley and T. Persson." *Journal of Economic Literature* 51: 116–143.

McLean, I. and A. Taylor. 2003. "Australian Growth: A California Perspective." *National Bureau of Economic Research* 8408.

Mehlum, H., K. Moene, and R. Torvik. 2006. "Institutions and the Resource Curse." *Economic Journal* 116: 1–20.

Miguel, E. and M. Gugerty. 2005. "Ethnic Diversity, Social Sanctions, and Public Goods in Kenya." *Journal of Public Economics* 89: 2325–2368.

Navas, A. 2013. "Trade Openness, Institutional Change and Economic Growth." *Sheffield Economic Research Paper Series* 2013018.

North, D. 1990. *Institutions, Institutional Change and Economic Performance*. Cambridge: Cambridge University Press.

North, D., J. Wallis, S. Webb, and B. Weingast. 2012. *In the Shadow of Violence: Politics, Economics, and the Problems of Development*. Cambridge: Cambridge University Press.

North, D., J. Wallis, and B. Weingast. 2009. *Violence and Social Orders: A Conceptual Framework for Interpreting Recorded Human History*. Cambridge: Cambridge University Press.

Nugent, J. and N. Sanchez. 1999. "The Local Variability of Rainfall and Tribal Institutions: The Case of Sudan." *Journal of Economic Behavior & Organization* 39: 263–291.

Nunn, N. 2008. "The Long-Term Effects of Africa's Slave Trades." *Quarterly Journal of Economics* 123: 139–176.

———. 2009. "The Importance of History for Economic Development." *Annual Review of Economics* 1: 65–92.

Ogilvie, S. and A. Carus. 2015. "Institutions and Economic Growth in Historical Perspective." *Handbook of Economic Growth* 2, edited by P. Aghion and S. Durlauf. Amsterdam: Elsevier.

Olivier, B. and A. Shleifer. 2001. "Federalism With and Without Political Centralization: China versus Russia." *International Monetary Fund Staff Papers* 48: 171–179.

Pande, R. 2003. "Can Mandated Political Representation Increase Policy Influence for Disadvantaged Minorities? Theory and Evidence from India." *American Economic Review* 93: 1132–1151.

Pande, R. and C. Udry. 2005. "Institutions and Development: A View from Below." Working Paper, Economic Growth Center, Yale University.

Papaioannou, E. 2009. "What Drives International Financial Flows? Politics, Institutions and Other Determinants." *Journal of Development Economics* 88: 269–281.

Papaioannou, E. and G. Siourounis. 2008. "Democratisation and Growth." *Economic Journal* 118: 1520–1551.

Persson, T. and G. Tabellini. 2006. "Democracy and Development: The Devil in the Details." *American Economic Review* 96: 319–324.

———. 2009. "Democratic Capital: The Nexus of Political and Economic Change." *American Economic Journal: Macroeconomics* 1: 88–126.

Platteau, J.-P. 1994a. "Behind the Market Stage Where Real Societies Exist—Part I: The Role of Public and Private Order Institutions." *Journal of Development Studies* 30: 533–577.

———. 1994b. "Behind the Market Stage Where Real Societies Exist—Part II: The Role of Moral Norms." *Journal of Development Studies* 30: 753–817.

———. 2000. *Institutions, Social Norms, and Economic Development.* Amsterdam: Harwood Academic.

Portes, A. 1998. "Social Capital: Its Origins and Applications in Modern Sociology." *Annual Review of Sociology* 24: 1–24.

Qian, Y. 2003. "How Reform Worked in China." In *In Search of Prosperity: Analytic Narratives on Economic Growth*, edited by D. Rodrik. Princeton, NJ: Princeton University Press.

Ranis, G. 1989. "The Role of Institutions in Transition Growth: The East Asian Newly Industrializing Countries." *World Development* 17: 1443–1453.

Rodrik, D. 1999. "Where Did All the Growth Go? External Shocks, Social Conflict, and Growth Collapses." *Journal of Economic Growth* 4: 385–412.

———. 2005. "Growth Strategies." In *Handbook of Economic Growth* 1, edited by P. Aghion and S. Durlauf. Amsterdam: North Holland.

Rodrik, D., A. Subramanian, and F. Trebbi. 2004. "Institutions Rule: The Primacy of Institutions over Geography and Integration in Economic Development." *Journal Of Economic Growth* 9: 131–165.

Roemer, J. 2010. "Kantian Equilibrium." *Scandinavian Journal of Economics* 112: 1–24.

Romer, P. 1992. "Two Strategies for Economic Development: Using Ideas and Producing Ideas." *World Bank Economic Review* 6: 63–91.

Sachs, J. 2012. "Government, Geography, and Growth: The True Drivers of Economic Development." *Foreign Affairs* 91: 142–150.

Sala-i-Martin, X., G. Doppelhofer, and R. Miller. 2004. "Determinants of Long-Term Growth: A Bayesian Averaging of Classical Estimates Approach." *American Economic Review* 94: 813–835.

Sala-i-Martin, X. and A. Subramanian. 2013. "Addressing the Natural Resource Curse: An Illustration from Nigeria." *Journal of African Economies* 22: 570–615.

Seim, A. and S. Parente. 2013. "Democracy as a Middle Ground: A Unified Theory of Development and Political Regimes." *European Economic Review* 64: 35–56.

Shirley, M. 2005. "Institutions and Development." In *Handbook of New Institutional Economics*, edited by Claude Menard and Mary M. Shirley, 611–638. New York: Springer.

Sokoloff, K. and S. Engerman. 2000. "History Lessons: Institutions, Factors, Endowments, and Paths of Development in the New World." *Journal of Economic Perspectives* 14: 217–232.

Subramanian, A. 2012. "Which Nations Failed?" *American Interest* 30: 1–4.

Subramanian, A. and S. Satyanath. 2004. "What Determines Long-Run Macroeconomic Stability? Democratic Institutions." *International Monetary Fund* 4–215.

Tabellini, G. 2010. "Culture and Institutions: Economic Development in the Regions of Europe." *Journal of the European Economic Association* 8: 677–716.

Tan, C. 2010. "No One True Path: Uncovering the Interplay Between Geography, Institutions, and Fractionalization in Economic Development." *Journal of Applied Econometrics* 25: 1100–1127.

Tavares, J. and R. Wacziarg. 2001. "How Democracy Affects Growth." *European Economic Review* 45: 1341–1378.

Temple, J. 2003. "Growing into Trouble: Indonesia after 1966." In *In Search of Prosperity: Analytic Narratives on Economic Growth*, edited by D. Rodrik. Princeton, NJ: Princeton University Press.

Visaria, S. 2009. "Legal Reform and Loan Repayment: The Microeconomic Impact of Debt Recovery Tribunals in India." *American Economic Journal: Applied Economics* 1: 59–81.

Voigt, S. 2013. "How (Not) to Measure Institutions." *Journal of Institutional Economics* 9.01: 1–26.

Young, A. 1992. "A Tale of Two Cities: Factor Accumulation and Technical Change in Hong Kong and Singapore." In *Research Macroeconomics Annual 1992*, edited by O. Blanchard and S. Fischer. Cambridge, MA: MIT Press.

7

FINANCE, INSTITUTIONS, AND DEVELOPMENT

Literature Survey and Research Agenda

Thorsten Beck

7.1. INTRODUCTION

For better or worse, the financial sector has a critical role in modern market economies. While it can be a force for development, by providing basic payment and transaction services, intermediating society's savings to its best uses, and offering households, enterprises, and governments risk management tools, it can also be a source of fragility, as we have been reminded during the recent global financial crisis and the ongoing Eurozone crisis, but also by numerous banking crises in emerging and developing markets. At the same time, the financial sector is critically connected to the overall institutional framework in a country. Given that the intertemporal nature of financial transactions makes it one of the most "institution-sensitive" sectors, a financial system can only thrive in an environment with effective institutions that reduce agency conflicts between contract parties. There might also be reverse influences from a thriving financial sector to institutional strengthening of a country.

This chapter summarizes the current state of knowledge across different literatures relevant for economic development. Specifically, it discusses the evidence on the relationship between financial sector deepening and economic development, the different channels and mechanisms through which finance and development interact, but also the open questions and challenges. The main section of the chapter discusses the role of institutions in the relationship of finance with economic development, including possible bidirectional causality, but also important complementarity in their respective impact on development. The chapter looks at the interaction between financial sector development and institutional development, how they influence each other, and how their respective impact on economic development is conditioned on the quality of the other.

An extensive empirical literature has shown a positive relationship between financial development and economic growth for developing and emerging markets, though with important nonlinearities. A more recent literature has explored the relationship between access to financial services and individual welfare and firm growth. A separate, equally extensive literature has shown a positive relationship between rapid credit growth and systemic banking distress and economic crises. Several recent papers have shown an important trade-off between the growth benefits of financial deepening and fragility risks. This trade-off is not surprising but can be directly explained by theoretical models of financial intermediation.

Financial deepening does not happen in an institutional vacuum. Theory and empirical research have shown the importance of the institutional framework for financial deepening, but also financial stability, including the contractual framework, the informational environment, and private property right protection. These same elements of the institutional framework, however, are also important factors for overall economic development, so that the question arises to what extent financial sector development is simply a by-product of institutional development or a driver. Financial sector development in turn can also contribute to institutional deepening, by breaking up entrenched relationships and fostering competition.

There is also an important question on the role of public versus private institutions as well as formal versus informal institutions in their relationship with financial sector deepening. This question has recently arisen in the context of the rapid development of the Chinese financial system, mostly in the absence of formal Western institutions. This debate also has critical policy repercussions for financial sector policymakers in low-income countries tasked with financial sector development.

The question of how to foster efficient and stable financial systems is critical and will be discussed extensively. One can broadly distinguish between three different strands of the literature, where the first focuses on specific policies and institutions. The second strand focuses on the interest of different stakeholders and links (the lack of) institutional reforms conducive to financial sector deepening back to the political structure of the society. A third strand sees these political constraints in a historical context, where only outside shocks can change the equilibrium and thus lead to reforms. In terms of policy messages, it is important to see these three strands as complementary.

A final word of caution. This survey is related to and builds on a large number of already existing surveys in the different areas that are being covered. Rather than being comprehensive, it tries to be selective but consistent in linking the different literatures to each other.

The remainder of the chapter is structured as follows. The next section provides a critical overview of the finance and growth literature, with an emphasis on low-income countries. Section 7.3, the main part of the chapter, examines the relationship between the institutional framework of a country and financial sector deepening. Section 7.4 concludes with policy implications and a forward-looking research agenda.

7.2. FINANCE AND GROWTH

There is large variation in the development and efficiency of financial systems around the world. On average, low-income countries have the shallowest financial markets, with few providers, few and costly products, and short maturities. Consequently, volumes and the number of transactions are low, and only a small share of the population has access to the formal financial system. As I will discuss in the following, an extensive theoretical and empirical literature has considered the importance of underdeveloped financial markets for economic development, especially economic growth and poverty alleviation.

7.2.1. Finance and Growth—Toward a Consensus View?

Before discussing the empirical literature, it is important to note that the theoretical literature does not predict an unambiguously positive relationship between financial and economic development. On the one hand, efficient financial systems might enhance economic development by (i) providing payment services, reducing transaction costs and thus enabling the efficient exchange of goods and services; (ii) pooling savings from many individual savers, and thus helping overcome investment indivisibilities and allowing exploitation of scale economies;[1] (iii) economizing on screening and monitoring costs and thus increasing overall investment and improving resource allocation; (iv) helping monitor enterprises and reduce agency problems within firms between management and majority and minority shareholders, again improving resource allocation; and (v) helping reduce liquidity risk and thus enable long-term investment, as shown by Diamond and Dybvig (1983). On the other hand, better resource allocation may depress saving rates enough such that overall growth rates actually drop with enhanced financial development.[2] This can happen if the income effect of higher interest rates is larger than the substitution effect. Recent research has pointed to other growth-reducing effects of financial sector deepening, as the financial sector might also attract too many resources relative to the real sector, with negative repercussions for growth.[3] A priori, it is thus not clear whether financial sector development contributes to economic development or not. And even if we find a positive impact, the importance of financial sector development relative to other policy areas is not clear either.

An extensive empirical literature has tested these theoretical predictions and has, to a large extent, shown a positive relationship between financial sector development and economic growth. What started with simple cross-country regressions, as used by King and Levine (1993a, 1993b), has developed into a large literature using an array of different techniques to look beyond correlation and controlling for biases arising from endogeneity and omitted variables. Specifically, using instrumental variable approaches, difference-in-difference approaches that consider the differential impact of finance on specific sectors and thus point to a smoking gun, explorations of specific regulatory changes that led to financial deepening in individual countries, and micro-level approaches using firm-level data have provided the same result: financial deepening is a critical part of the overall development process of a country (see Levine 2005 for an overview of the literature). While each methodology is subject to specific criticisms, the overwhelming evidence across different methodologies and aggregation levels provides robust reassurance that financial sector development should be on policymakers' priority list for economic development. This literature has also provided insights into the channels through which finance fosters economic growth. Overall, the evidence has shown that finance has a more important impact on growth through fostering productivity growth and resource allocation than through pure capital accumulation (Beck, Levine, and Loayza 2000).[4]

Financial sector development is important not only for fostering the economic growth process, but also for dampening the volatility of the growth process. Financial systems can alleviate the liquidity constraints on firms and facilitate long-term investment, which ultimately reduces the volatility of investment and growth (Aghion et al. 2010). Similarly, well-developed financial markets and institutions can help dampen the negative impact that exchange rate volatility has on firm liquidity and thus investment capacity (Aghion et al. 2009). This is especially important in economies that depend heavily on natural resources and are thus subject to high terms of trade and real exchange rate volatility, as is the case for many low-income countries. It is important to note, however, the important difference between real and financial/monetary shocks, whereby the latter can be exacerbated by deeper financial systems (Beck, Lundberg, and Majnoni 2006). Finally, financial development increases the effectiveness of monetary policy, widens the fiscal policy space, and allows a greater choice of exchange rate regimes (IMF 2012).

More recent evidence has also established favorable effects of financial deepening on income distribution. Similarly, as in the case of the effect of finance on growth, theory does not make unambiguous predictions for the relationship between financial sector development and poverty alleviation. On the one hand, theory predicts that due to entry barriers, only richer population segments will benefit from financial sector development, thus widening income inequality.[5] On the other hand, theory predicts that barriers of indivisibilities and information asymmetries are more binding for the poor, so that they stand to benefit most from financial sector development.[6]

Cross-country evidence has shown that countries with higher levels of financial development see faster drops in income inequality and poverty rates, results that are confirmed with in-depth studies for individual countries, including the United States, Thailand, and India.[7] Tentative evidence also suggests that this poverty-reducing effect of financial deepening comes again more through resource allocation and indirect effects through labor and product markets, rather than through expanding access to credit to a larger share of population. I will return to this topic in section 7.2.5.

7.2.2. Finance and Growth—Post-2008 Divergence

While most of the finance and growth literature has focused on the average effect of financial development on economic growth, nonlinearities were taken into account early on, such as by including financial sector indicators in logs rather than levels and by dropping specific country groups (such as commodity exporters) for which many of the standard predictions of growth theory are not assumed to hold. More recent research, however, has focused more closely on these nonlinearities in the relationship between finance and growth. Specifically, there is evidence that the effect of financial development is strongest among middle-income countries, whereas other work finds a declining effect of finance and growth as countries grow richer. Rioja and Valev (2004a, 2004b) show that the effect of finance on growth is strongest for middle-income countries. These findings are consistent with Rousseau and D'Onofrio (2013), who show that it is monetization rather than financial intermediation that seems to matter for growth across Sub-Saharan Africa. Aghion, Howitt, and Mayer-Foulkes (2005) argue that the impact of finance on growth is strongest among low- and middle-income countries that are catching up to high-income countries in their productivity levels and fades away as countries approach the global productivity frontier.[8]

There are several, not exclusive, explanations for such nonlinearities, as put forward by the recent literature and partly informed by the recent crisis, though most of these relate more to middle- and high-income than low-income countries. First, the measures of financial depth and intermediation the literature has been using might simply be too crude to capture quality improvements at high levels of financial development. In addition, the financial sector has gradually extended its scope beyond the traditional activity of intermediation toward non-intermediation financial activities (Demirgüç-Kunt and Huizinga 2010). As a result, the usual measures of intermediation services have become less and less congruent with the reality of modern financial systems. In low-income countries, on the other hand, financial development indicators might capture mostly short-term transactions that have little impact on long-term growth. A second reason for non-linearities might be the beneficiary of the credit as argued by Beck et al. (2012), who explore the differential growth effects of enterprise and household credit. Consistent with theory, they find that the growth effect of financial deepening comes through enterprise rather than household credit. Most of the financial deepening in high-income countries has come through additional household lending, which might explain the insignificant finance-growth relationship across high-income countries.[9] Third, the financial system might actually grow too large relative to the real economy if it extracts excessively high informational rents and, in this way, attracts too much young talent to the financial industry (Bolton et al. 2011; Philippon 2010). Finally, and related, the financial system can grow too large due to the safety net subsidy we will discuss below that results in too aggressive risk-taking and overextending of the financial system.

One important and rather under-researched group of countries concerns the natural resource–rich countries and the question whether financial development is as important for this group of countries as for other developing and emerging markets. Beck (2011) shows that the importance of financial sector development for economic growth is as important in commodity-based economies, but that there is evidence for a Dutch disease phenomenon in financial sectors in these countries, crowded by the natural resource–related activities. On the other hand, the natural resource curse might expand to the financial sector; Beck and Poelhekke (2016) show that natural resource windfall gains are not intermediated through the financial sector, but rather through other, less effective channels. This ultimately has negative repercussions for long-term growth.

7.2.3. Stability vs. Growth

As much as financial sector development can contribute to economic development, credit boom and bust cycles can exacerbate economic volatility. The same mechanism through which finance helps growth also makes finance susceptible to shocks and, ultimately, fragility. Specifically, the maturity and liquidity transformation from short-term savings and deposit facilities into long-term investments is at the core of the positive impact of a financial system on the real economy, but also renders the system susceptible to shocks, with the possibilities of bank and liquidity runs. The information asymmetries and ensuing agency problems between savers and entrepreneurs that banks help to alleviate can also become a source of fragility given agency conflicts between depositors/creditors and banks. The opacity of banks' financial statement and the large number of creditors (compared to a real sector company) undermine market discipline and encourage banks to take too much risk, ultimately resulting in fragility.[10]

Systemic financial fragility is often associated with asset price cycles, as documented, for example, by Rajan and Ramcharan (2015) for land prices in the United States in the

1920s. They show that the commodity price boom between 1917 and 1920 resulted in rapid credit expansion across the United States linked to land price inflation, while the subsequent bust particularly affected areas with higher credit availability, where the land price fall was more pronounced, and more banks subsequently failed.

The role that finance has as a lubricant for the real economy thus likewise exacerbates the effect of financial fragility on the real economy. The failure of financial institutions can result in significant negative externalities beyond the private costs of failure; it imposes external costs on other financial institutions through different contagion effects and the economy at large. The costs of systemic banking distress can be substantial, as reported by Laeven and Valencia (2013), reaching over 50 percent of GDP in some cases in fiscal costs and over 100 percent in output loss. Cross-country comparisons have shown that during banking crises, industries that depend more on external finance are hurt disproportionately more, an effect that is stronger in countries with better developed financial systems.[11]

The external costs of bank failures have made banking one of the most regulated sectors and have led to the introduction of explicit or implicit safety nets across most countries of the modern world that—at a minimum—protect depositors, in many cases, especially during the recent crisis, as well as non-deposit creditors or even equity holders. It is this safety net subsidy, in turn, that induces aggressive risk-taking by banks as shown by multiple country-level and cross-country studies and that might also explain the overextension of the financial system (see, e.g., Demirgüç-Kunt and Kane 2002). It is important to note that this safety net subsidy does not have to be explicit, but can be very much an implicit one, as seen in the recent crisis. Until recently, most senior creditors and uninsured depositors were made whole in Europe, a tendency only broken with the Cyprus crisis resolution. It can also extend beyond banking, as seen during the recent crisis; several segments of the financial system outside the regulatory perimeter, including investment banks and money market funds, became the subject of government guarantees in the United States.

It is important to note, however, that most banking crises in low-income countries are not associated with credit boom-and-bust cycles, but rather with governance problems, including corruption and theft, and also outright incompetence. Maturity mismatches are rarely at the core of banking distress in low-income countries, while deficiencies in bank regulation and supervision and government and political interference loom large (Honohan and Beck 2007).

Ultimately, both theory and empirical work document an important stability-growth trade-off in financial sector deepening, with a positive impact on competition, resource allocation, and growth, and a negative impact through a higher crisis probability. Ranciere, Tornell, and Westermann (2008) show that the first moment of credit growth is positively associated with GDP growth in a large cross-country panel, while the third moment (skewness) is negatively associated, suggesting a positive relationship between systemic fragility and growth. While this is not an endorsement that crises are good for growth, it implies that systemic banking crises as a result of faster credit growth are not growth-constraining. In line with this finding, Ranciere, Tornell, and Westermann (2006) show that the positive growth effect of financial liberalization outweighs the negative growth effect through a higher crisis probability for emerging and developing markets. This does not necessarily suggest that systemic banking crises are growth-enhancing—to the contrary; it rather makes the important point that systemic risk-taking and consequently fragility associated with financial deepening has overall positive growth repercussions.

7.2.4. Finance and Growth—Caveat Medida

One important caveat across the finance and growth literature—though often ignored—is that we have only very crude indicators of the development of financial institutions and market and the efficiency with which financial services are provided to households, enterprises, and governments. Specifically, there is not a clear mapping between the functions of finance as spelled out by theory and the empirical gauges of financial sector development, which capture mostly the size, activity, or efficiency of different financial institutions or markets.[12] Consequently, one has to be careful in interpreting the empirical relationship between standard indicators of financial sector development, such as Private Credit to GDP, and economic growth. Specifically, this variable indicates the quantity, not the quality, and focuses only on regulated financial institutions. It does not capture the maturity structure. It does not capture how widespread the use of credit services is among enterprises and households and the ease with which enterprises and households can access credit. Importantly, it is not clear that there is a linear mapping from higher levels of Private Credit to GDP into more efficient and developed financial markets. Credit provision in an economy fluctuates substantially with the business cycle (Bernanke and Gertler 1989), so that short-term variations in Private Credit to GDP for a given country are thus unlikely to reflect changes in the efficiency and development of financial markets and institutions. More important and as already discussed, credit cycles are often related to asset price cycles, so that rapid increases in Private Credit to GDP might reflect credit bubbles rather than rapid improvements in the efficiency and development of financial systems. In this context, it is important to point out that the theoretical models mentioned in section 7.2.1 relate to the long-term relationship between financial development and growth and not short-term fluctuations, reflected also in the empirical literature that has typically focused on longer time period (at least five years, preferably ten or even more).

While the measurement error has long been recognized as one of the biases in cross-country regressions, there has been less focus on it than on reverse causation or omitted variable biases. While there are ongoing attempts to develop more accurate gauges, capturing specific dimensions of financial sector development, it seems unlikely that we will ever get to the perfect measure.

7.2.5. Finance and Growth—Individual vs. Aggregate Effects

There is a critical difference between effects of financial development on the household-/firm-level and the aggregate effects. This is important especially in the debate on the role of finance in poverty alleviation. On the one hand, an extensive empirical literature, using both observational data and randomized control trials, has explored the impact of improved access to specific financial services, including credit, savings, and insurance, on firm growth or household welfare. On the other hand, the aggregate finance and development literature has focused on the role of financial sector development in allocating resources to their most productive uses, fostering innovation and competition and improving governance across the economy. Not only is this contrast academically important, but the relative importance of effects on the individual vs. aggregate levels has important policy repercussions. To give one example, in order to maximize the impact of financial sector development on poverty reduction, should the focus be on financial inclusion policies (and if yes, which type of services) or on making the financial system more efficient (Ayyagari, Beck, and Hoseini 2013)?

An extensive literature has gauged the effect of access to credit on households' welfare and growth of micro-enterprises.[13] As summarized by Banerjee, Karlan, and Zinman (2015) in their introductory paper on a special issue of the AEJ: Applied Economics with six microcredit assessments, there is "a consistent pattern of modestly positive, but not transformative, effects." There are several reasons why the impact of microcredit is so limited and why the impact is heterogeneous.[14] First, micro-entrepreneurs might not be credit constrained and/or other constraints within the business environment might be more binding, which might also explain the limited take-up of microcredit in many circumstances. Second, there might be rapidly diminishing returns, in the form of an S-shaped production. Initial returns might be high, but rapidly decreasing (Banerjee and Duflo 2007). Micro-enterprises' capacity to grow might thus be limited. Third, a large number of borrowers use credit for consumption rather than investment purposes, as documented for example by Johnston and Morduch (2008) in Indonesia, Attanasio et al. (2015) in rural Mongolia, and Karlan and Zinman (2010) in the Philippines. In addition, there is a fragility risk to donor or political efforts to expand microcredit rapidly; most prominently, following a rapid expansion of the microcredit industry, India's Andhra Pradesh saw a major crisis in the sector in 2010. Some of the characteristics resemble those of a classical banking boom and bust cycle that we described above.

On the other hand, as already discussed, there is some tentative evidence that financial deepening can reduce income inequality and poverty alleviation through indirect channels. On the aggregate cross-country level, Beck et al. (2012) find that the negative relationship between financial depth and changes in income inequality goes through enterprise and not household credit. Assuming that access to formal credit by microenterprises is more likely to be captured by household credit, this suggests that the pro-poor nature of financial deepening is primarily linked through indirect effects. However, this study is subject to the important caveats on cross-country comparisons. In addition, recent evidence also suggests that financial deepening can contribute to employment growth, especially in developing countries (Pagano and Pica 2012), consistent with the studies for Thailand and the United States. Giné and Townsend (2004) compare the evolution of growth and inequality in a dynamic general equilibrium model with the actual development in the Thai economy and show that financial liberalization and the consequent increase in access to credit services can explain the fast GDP per capita growth, rapid poverty reduction, and initially increasing but then decreasing income inequality. Underlying these developments are occupational shifts from the subsistence sector into the intermediated sector and accompanying changes in wages. Net welfare benefits of increased access are found to be substantial, and, though they are concentrated disproportionately on a small group of talented, low-wealth individuals who without credit could not become entrepreneurs, there are also benefits to a wider class of workers because eventually wage rates increase as a result of the enhanced access to credit by potential entrepreneurs. Ayyagari et al. (2013) find a strong negative relationship between financial deepening, rather than financial inclusion, and rural poverty, following financial liberalization in the 1990s in India. They also find that financial deepening reduced poverty rates among the self-employed and supported an interstate migration from rural areas into the tertiary sector in urban areas.

These findings are also consistent with evidence that a large share of micro-entrepreneurs are lifestyle entrepreneurs in the absence of better opportunities as salaried wage earners in formal businesses (e.g., Bruhn 2013, for Mexico). This in turn can explain the limited growth opportunities (or ambitions) mentioned above. In addition, such entrepreneurs are less likely to benefit the broader economy by creating jobs.

Taken together, the empirical evidence so far suggests an important difference between two concepts—*Finance and Poverty Alleviation* and *Finance for the Poor*. By changing the structure of the economy and allowing more entry into the labor market by previously unemployed or underemployed segments of the population, financial deepening (more efficient financial institutions and markets) helps reduce income inequality and poverty, as discussed above. By doing so, financial deepening can help achieve more inclusive growth and also help overcome spatial inequality in growth benefits. It is thus important to understand that the effects of financial deepening on employment and poverty alleviation do not necessarily come through the widespread "democratization of credit" but rather a credit allocation, which might relax financing constraints of some though not necessarily all firms. This also implies that microcredit is not necessarily the most important policy area to reap the benefits of financial deepening for poverty alleviation.

For the poor to benefit directly from financial sector deepening and broadening (*Finance for the Poor* concept) it is important to look beyond credit to other financial services that are needed by the poor, such as simple transaction or savings services. There is increasing evidence from randomized control trials (RCTs) on the positive effects of access to formal savings services, tailored to the poor, on firm growth and household welfare. To give just a few examples: Dupas and Robinson (2013a) show that the expansion of savings accounts in rural Kenya leads to higher investment among female micro-entrepreneurs, though not male entrepreneurs. Dupas and Robinson (2013b) show that the use of different commitment devices, including lockboxes with and without keys, individual health savings accounts, and joint health pots, leads to higher preventive healthcare spending. And providing access to formal savings does not seem to undermine the role of informal safety nets, as documented by Dupas, Keats, and Robinson (2018) who show that households with such access rely less on their extended family but are more likely to be supportive of friends and family.

Similarly, Brune et al. (2015) find in their study for Malawian cash crop farmers that using a commitment savings product increases investment and crop output by 21%, with an increase of 11% in consumption. Ashraf, Karlan, and Yin (2006) show that the introduction of a commitment savings product in the Philippines led to a shift toward female-oriented durable good consumption. Finally, Prina (2015) finds in her experimental study for Nepal that access to savings accounts appears to help households to manage their resources better, prioritizing on expenditure categories, such as education and food consumption, and to feel more in control of their financial situation.

While even more recent, there is a small literature that documents the positive effect that access to more efficient payment systems—most notably digital finance or mobile money—can have for welcoming the poor. The quick take-up of the mobile money transfer service M-Pesa in Kenya to send remittances across the country—crowding out informal channels—as documented in household surveys, shows the rapid take-up of this payment method. Jack and Suri (2014) examine the impact of reduced transaction costs after the introduction of M-Pesa in Kenya on risk-sharing and find that M-Pesa users are more likely to absorb negative income shocks, especially among lower income households. Blumenstock, Eagle, and Fafchamps (2016) use mobile phone transfers over four years in Rwanda and show that these transfers are used to help people affected by natural disasters, such as an earthquake near Lake Kivu. Beck et al. (2018) show an important interaction between access to more efficient payment services and access to trade credit by small entrepreneurs in Kenya.

In summary, the tentative policy conclusions that arise from this literature are that while it should be a goal to achieve access to basic transaction and savings services for as large a share of the population as possible to enable them to participate in the modern market economy, the agenda in boosting access to credit should focus on improving the efficiency of this process, replacing access through political connection and wealth as it still happens in many developing countries with access through competition. By channeling society's resources to the most promising project, both growth-increasing and poverty-reducing effects can be achieved.

7.3. WHAT DRIVES FINANCIAL DEVELOPMENT?

It is important to note that financial development is not a policy variable in itself, but rather the result of market forces and an array of policies and institutions. In this section, I will discuss different policy areas and institutional arrangements that the literature has shown to foster financial sector development. In this context it is important to distinguish between the deep-seated institutional framework and very specific policies. Finally, I will link financial sector and institutional development to the concept of the financial possibility frontier, a concept that takes us back to the trade-off between the growth and fragility effects of financial sector deepening.

In the following I will discuss both policies and institutions. While a detailed discussion on the difference between the two would go beyond the scope of this chapter, I will refer to policies as government actions to introduce certain reforms (e.g., regulatory reforms, liberalization of prices, privatization, etc.) or build or reform institutions, such as credit registries, court systems, etc. Institutions, on the other hand, can be the result of policy action but can also develop over time.[15] Critically, and as discussed below, institutions can be both formal and informal, public and private. One can also distinguish between the institutional framework in the broader sense and very specific institutions.

The interaction of finance with institutions is present on at least three levels. First, given its intertemporal nature, finance is one of the most "institutions-intensive" sectors, and its development has been shown to depend critically on a conducive institutional framework, including effective contractual framework and transparency. Second, the outreach of the financial system and, ultimately, its impact on economic development, increases in governance and trust, as this will allow expansion of the financial system to lower-income population segments and small and medium-sized enterprises. Third, an effective and competitive financial system can also improve institutions; by increasing competition in the real sector, it can allow new entry and foster entrepreneurship, which can increase demand for effective and accessible institutions, with ultimate positive repercussions for economic development.

7.3.1. What Drives Financial Sector Development?

One can broadly distinguish between three different responses to this question, which are also linked to three different literatures.[16] The first approach is to identify policies and institutions related to deeper and safer financial systems. This literature has identified macroeconomic stability, effective contractual and information frameworks, and incentive-compatible financial safety nets as preconditions for sound and sustainable financial deepening. These policies are also often at the core of financial sector reform programs developed by the IMF and World Bank for developing countries.

A second approach argues that the level and structure of financial development and the underlying institutional infrastructure are a function of political decision processes. The decisions do not necessarily maximize aggregate social welfare, but reflect the interests of the incumbent elites or coalitions of interest groups. Financial sector reform programs that do not take into account the distribution of political power and interests are set to fail, according to this view.

A third approach focuses on historic determinants. A recent literature has shown significant differences in financial sector depth between countries with Common Law tradition and countries with Civil Code tradition, especially the Napoleonic type Civil Code tradition. Colonial history and religious differences have also been cited as decisive factors for different development paths of financial systems across the world.

In the following, I will discuss each of these views in turn. As will become clear, these three views are not exclusive, but they imply very different views on the nature and role of government within the financial system.

7.3.1.1. The Policy View

The literature has identified very specific policies and institutions that are conducive to financial sector development. Macroeconomic stability has often been stressed as *conditio sine qua non* for financial sector development, given the intertemporal character of many financial transactions. Cross-country comparisons suggest that macroeconomic stability is critical for financial deepening (Boyd, Levine, and Smith 2001), while country experiences suggest that macroeconomic stability is a necessary condition for unlocking the financial deepening process. For instance, deposit mobilization and credit expansion in transition economies only took off when disinflation became entrenched (IMF 2012).

A second important area is the contractual and informational framework, which encompasses the rights of secured and unsecured creditors, the efficiency of credit registries and bureaus, the quality of court systems and the efficiency of contract enforcement, the existence and quality of collateral registries and accounting standards. This also includes effective corporate governance rules for the relationship between management and shareholders and minority and majority shareholders. I will discuss each in turn.

First, La Porta et al. (1997), Levine, Loayza, and Beck (2000), and Djankov, McLiesh, and Shleifer (2007) demonstrate the importance of contractual institutions, such as creditor rights, for financial sector development. Using firm-level data, Qian and Strahan (2007) show that, on average, firms in countries with stronger secured creditor rights have longer-maturity loans and more secured debt. Also using firm-level data, Love, Martínez Pería, and Singh (2016) find that introducing collateral registries for movable assets increases firms' access to bank finance, with the effect larger among smaller firms, while using loan-level data, Calomiris et al. (2017) show loan-to-values of loans collateralized with movable assets are lower in countries with weak collateral laws, relative to immovable assets, and that lending is biased toward the use of immovable assets. These cross-country studies have been complemented by country-specific studies, including Jappelli, Pagano, and Bianco (2005) on Italy and Laeven and Woodruff (2007) on Mexico.

In addition, several papers have explored the implementation of specific reforms. For example, Visaria (2009) exploits the staggered introduction of debt recovery tribunals for claims above a certain threshold across states in India in the 1990s, which made contract enforcement much speedier and more efficient. She finds that this reform reduced loan delinquency and the cost of credit. However, there were also distributional repercussions from this reform, as documented by Von Lilienfeld-Toal, Mookherjee, and Visaria (2012); total credit increased for larger borrowers, while it decreased for smaller borrowers, consistent with an inelastic aggregate supply of credit and additional demand by larger borrowers more easily satisfied. They also document a reallocation of lending away from rural areas toward urban and metropolitan areas. Chemin (2009, 2012) focuses on the role of the court system and uses the geographic variation in the procedural handling of court cases in India following a reform in 2002 and shows that a more efficient court procedure resulted in a reduction in case backlog in courts, lower contract breach, and higher investment by firms in fixed assets; the positive effect of court reform fell mostly on farmers whose access to credit was eased and contract-intensive sectors, such as formal manufacturing companies. Ponticelli and Alencar (2016) gauge the interaction of legal reform and the efficiency of court systems, exploiting municipality-level variation in Brazil, and show that the introduction of a bankruptcy reform in 2005 resulted in a higher increase in secured lending to manufacturing firms and a higher increase in firm investment in municipalities with less congested courts. Assunção, Benmelech, and Silva (2014) show that the 2004 reform in Brazil that facilitated the repossession of cars used as collateral for car loans, increased access to credit by riskier and self-employed borrowers and resulted in larger loans with lower interest rates and longer maturities. However, by expanding the borrower population toward riskier clientele, the reform also led to higher default rates. Finally, Campello and Larrain (2016) show that a legal reform in Romania enlarging the menu of assets that could be used as possible collateral resulted in firms operating in sectors intensive in movable assets increasing their ability to borrow.

However, the positive supply-side effects might be countered by negative demand-side effects of legal reform, as documented by Vig (2013). Specifically, he finds that following the strengthening of secured creditor rights in 2002 in India, there was actually a 5.2% decrease in the use of secured debt by firms, which might be due to the threat of premature liquidation faced by borrowers under stronger creditor rights.

One important debate in this context is the distinction between coercion-constraining institutions, which govern the relationship between governments and private citizens, and contract enforcement institutions, which govern the relationship between private citizens. Most of the reforms discussed above refer to the latter rather than the former. And while the contract-enforcing institutions seem of more immediate concern for financial transactions, coercion-constraining institutions are as important, as trust in private property right protection is critical for investors afraid of expropriation risk. The broader question—beyond the scope of this chapter—arises on whether effective contract enforcement institutions are feasible in a weak coercion-constraining institutional framework. Finally, some studies have explored differential effects between these two types of institutions, with stronger effects from coercion-constraining effects than contract enforcement institutions (Acemoglu and Johnson 2005), though questions on the measurement of these two concepts arise (Woodruff 2006). Cull and Xu (2005) find for China that both types of institutions, influencing access to credit and expropriation risk, matter for the reinvestment decisions of Chinese entrepreneurs.

Second, the establishment of credit registries that allow the sharing of information among lenders can help overcome information asymmetries in banking markets. Theory suggests positive effects of credit information sharing on screening accuracy and thus profitability of banks, but also—in case that positive information is being shared—for the possibility of borrowers to build up reputation capital and for competition to increase among lenders (Pagano and Jappelli 1993; Padilla and Pagano 1997). Cross-country studies have confirmed the positive relationship between effective credit information sharing and financial sector development and firms' access to credit (Pagano and Jappelli 1993; Djankov, McLiesh, and Shleifer 2007; Brown, Jappelli, and Pagano 2009). The cross-country literature has been complemented by specific country studies, such as by De Janvry, McIntosh, and Sadoulet (2010), who use the entry of a credit registry for microfinance institutions to gauge the effect on both adverse selection and moral hazard by gauging the effect of the announcement on the behavior of existing borrower groups in this joint-liability institution and subsequent changes in the composition of groups. The authors find lower default rates due to both effects. There might also be offsetting effects on expanding the borrower population and fragility; Gonzalez-Uribe and Osorio (2014) document that the decision in 2008 to erase past default information from the Colombian credit bureau resulted in new borrowing opportunities for blacklisted borrowers with banks with whom they had no prior relationship, but also higher default among these loans.

As an alternative to formal contractual and informational institutions, peer monitoring and social capital have been stressed, especially for smaller, less formal borrowers. The success of the cooperative movement in Continental Europe in the nineteenth and twentieth centuries has relied on personal guarantors and group-based peer monitoring (Banerjee, Besley, and Guinnane 1994). Related to this concept is the embedment of such financial institutions in a local community with repeated interactions. This also points to the importance of context-specific design elements for such institutions, as the comparison of the successful German cooperatives with the failed experiment of cooperatives in Ireland shows.

The idea of peer monitoring based on group liability and local social capital has also been at the core of the microcredit movement. Ghatak and Guinanne (1999) provide a theoretical basis for the way joint-liability lending enhances the screening and monitoring process of borrowers and improves on the enforcement of contract in the absence of formal judiciary processes (either because of their complete lack, their inefficiency, or their high costs). An expansive empirical literature—beyond the brief purview of this chapter—has assessed the effectiveness of these mechanisms.

A third area concerns competition and market structure. Competition has an ambiguous relationship with financial sector deepening and financial stability. On the one hand, competitive markets can increase efficiency and ultimately outreach and depth of financial markets. On the other hand, private information acquisition by financial institutions relies on the availability of rents, counter to the idea of perfectly competitive markets. Similarly, in the area of stability, different theories make different predictions on the relationship between competition and bank fragility, with empirical evidence not clear-cut either. In terms of market structure, there is overwhelming evidence across the developing (and developed) world of a negative impact of government ownership and management of commercial banks on the efficiency and stability of financial systems. Somewhat more ambiguous is the impact of foreign bank ownership, where theory and empirical work have not reached a final conclusion.

The competition of the banking market also has important repercussions for the effect of institutional reforms. Credit supply will be more elastic in a more competitive financial system, so that the negative distributional repercussions discussed above for India might not be as prevalent. Besley, Burchardi, and Ghatak (2012) show theoretically and empirically that improving property rights has a stronger effect in more competitive banking systems. The same argument, however, also applies to the fragility risks of competition, where higher competition might exacerbate a lending boom and therefore the negative implications of the subsequent bust (Rajan and Ramcharan 2015).

Competition can also have important effects on the structure of microfinance markets, as documented by De Quidt, Fetzer, and Ghatak (2018a, 2018b). Specifically, in the absence of credit information sharing, higher competition among microfinance providers results in lower repayment incentives; similarly, higher competition and the increasing entry of for-profit microfinance providers will result in a shift from the joint-liability to the individual lending model.

One important question is the sequencing of policy reforms. Many developing, especially low-income countries face implementation constraints beyond political constraints. This raises the question, which reforms have the highest benefit-cost ratio, as well as which reforms have the quickest impact (which then in turn might crowd in demand for further reforms). There is a small literature that has explored these issues. Most prominently, Djankov et al. (2007) document in cross-country comparison the relative importance of information frameworks vis-à-vis contractual frameworks for developing countries, with the reverse holding for developed countries. In the area of contractual institutions, Haselmann, Pistor, and Vig (2010) have distinguished between those that chiefly enable the individual lender to recover on a debt (by, e.g., recovering collateral) and those that are mainly concerned with resolving conflicts between different claimants (such as, e.g., bankruptcy codes). Using data from the transition economies of Central and Eastern Europe—which adopted relevant legal reforms at different times after the collapse of the planned economy system—they show that bank lending is more sensitive to the institutions that govern individual claims than to those that resolve conflicts between multiple claimants. Given their heavier reliance on secured lending, it is not surprising that foreign bank lending increases by even more.

While this so far provides some evidence that reforms directed at simple contractual relationships and reforms directed at the information rather than enforcement environment might be more promising in economically and institutionally less developed economies, more research is needed in this area. Ultimately, what is needed is a binding-constraints-cum-reform-feasibility analysis on the country level. In summary, the policy view sees the problem of financial deepening as one of choosing the right policies. It emphasizes that this mix might differ across countries at different levels of economic and financial development and with different needs. It explicitly recognizes the trade-off in some of these policies, including competition. As has become clear, the policy view starts from the existence of market failures and assumes competent and well-meaning political and regulatory authorities. We will come back to this important point in the next section.

7.3.1.2. Finance and Politics

If the empirical literature has identified the necessary conditions for financial sector deepening, why are these policies not put into place? This is where the second view, the finance and politics view, comes in. The policy view of financial deepening argues that government acts in the best interests of society, ultimately maximizing the social planner's problem, though possibly with less information available. This public interest view also argues that the market failures inherent in financial markets require a strong government involvement in the financial system beyond regulation and supervision. The private interest view, on the other hand, which is at the core of the politics and finance approach to financial sector deepening, argues that policymakers, including regulators, act in their own interest, maximizing private rather than public welfare. Politicians thus do not intervene in the financial system to further public welfare but to divert the flow of credit to politically connected firms (Becker and Stigler 1974). The private interest view is at the core of the political economy view of financial deepening. It stipulates that financial sector policies and regulations are the outcome of political processes.

Let me mention a few examples that illustrate the political economy view of financial deepening, in line with the policies mentioned in the previous section. While cross-country comparisons have shown the importance of credit information sharing for financial deepening, especially in developing countries, there are both winners and losers of effective systems of credit information sharing. Specifically, a wider sharing of information about borrowers, which allows these borrowers in turn to build up reputation capital, undermines information rents of incumbent banks. Bruhn, Farazi, and Kanz (2013) show that countries with lower entry barriers into the banking market and thus a greater degree of contestability in the banking system are less likely to adopt a privately run credit bureau, as are countries characterized by a high degree of bank concentration. In these countries, incumbent banks stand to lose more monopoly rents from sharing their extensive information with smaller and new players. Interestingly, these relationships do not hold for public credit registries (mostly at central banks), which underlines the limitations of purely private institutions and the positive role of governments.

On a broader level, Perotti and Volpin (2010), for example, show that in countries with lower political accountability and diffusion of information and thus more dominant elites, corporate governance is less effective and there is lower entry of new firms into industries more reliant on external finance. Biais and Mariotti (2009) show that the distribution of political power can influence whether a society adopts debtor- or creditor-friendly bankruptcy regimes, where the latter is more likely to lead to financial deepening. As incumbent and wealthy entrepreneurs do not rely on external funding, they are more interested in soft bankruptcy laws to prevent the entry of new, less wealthy entrepreneurs that can contest their market position. Similarly, Aney, Ghatak, and Morelli (2016) show that if the median voter is a worker, she will not necessarily support the surplus-maximizing legal reforms but rather reforms that are beneficial for wage earners, which might prevent a general property right protection reform. On the other hand, Caselli and Gennaioli (2008) show that financial sector reforms in the presence of a market for control (i.e., where ownership stakes in enterprises can easily be acquired and sold) will face less political resistance from the incumbents than deregulation that results in open entry, as the incumbents are able to "cash in" on their rents with outsiders acquiring their firms, using external finance.

A third example relates to the regulatory framework. A large literature has pointed to the risk of both regulatory capture—regulators representing the interests of the regulated, i.e., banks—and political capture—regulators representing short-term political interests. Regulatory capture biases regulators toward liquidity support; similarly, political capture makes regulators care more about today's economic and political consequences of failure resolution than the dynamic effect of the moral hazard risk created by these actions. Given the short-term horizon of politicians, captured regulators would thus heavily discount the future moral hazard repercussions of today's resolution actions. Empirical evidence supports the bias in resolution decisions if supervisors are subject to political capture (Brown and Dinc 2005; Bongini, Claessens, and Ferri 2001; Imai 2009). Political economy constraints can also play an important role in crisis resolution, as documented by Ardagna and Caselli (2014) for the case of the two bailouts of the Greek government in 2010 and 2011. Specifically, they argue that communication frictions between governments and their voters and the time limitation on negotiation rounds between different parties led to decisions in 2010 and 2011 that were individually but not collectively rational, i.e., not the optimal outcome available.

It is important to note that the same financial sector policy can be interpreted under the public interest and the private interest view. Take the expansion of housing finance in the United States in the 1990s and 2000s. The public interest view would interpret the expansion of access to mortgage finance as expanding the bankable population by financial innovation, including credit scoring and securitization techniques. In hindsight, it very much seems that access to housing might have overshot the frontier of sustainable access, which therefore led to a bubble and subsequent bust. However, both the ex ante and the ex post interpretations of the housing boom and bust cycle are so far consistent with the public interest view. Mistakes made during the crisis can be explained with misconceptions of where the frontier really was, and honest policy mistakes.[17] The private interest view would rather focus on political interests pushing for housing credit and higher home ownership, with policies such as the Community Reinvestment Act and guarantees provided by government-sponsored financial institutions, such as Fannie Mae and Freddie Mac. As laid out convincingly by Rajan (2010), in the absence of easy solutions to reduce income inequality, there was a political focus on reducing consumption inequality, which included boosting access to credit.

7.3.1.3. The Historical Determinants of Financial Development

A third view, directly related to the finance and politics view, sees today's level and structure of financial systems as a result of historical processes and thus reflections of historic political conflicts. The historical view of financial deepening sees strong persistence in financial systems. In the following, I will mention a few theories that focus on historical determinants of financial deepening.

One set of theories views historical events in Europe more than 200 years ago as shaping the legal and regulatory frameworks across the globe today through their influence on political and institutional structures in these countries. Specifically, the legal origin theory sees political conflicts in England and France in the Medieval Age and during the Glorious and French Revolutions shaping the role and independence of judiciaries in these countries. Different points on the trade-off between centralized power to avoid civil unrest and freedom to allow economic activity in England and France during medieval times influenced the government's approach to the judiciary, with France taking a much more centralized approach than England (Glaeser and Shleifer 2002). Alternatively, one can consider the role of the judiciary during the Glorious Revolution, where the judges sided with the winning Parliament, and the French Revolution, where the judges were on the losing side. This resulted in a strengthening of the judiciary's independence but also their role in lawmaking in England, while it reduced the judiciary to an executing role in France, with law- and rule-making concentrated in the legislative and executive branches of government. However, this also resulted in a different degree of flexibility and adaptability of the legal systems in England and France. England's legal system was more adaptable due to a stronger role for jurisprudence and reliance on past decisions and the ability of judges to base decisions on principles of fairness and justice, whereas France's legal system was more rigid, based on bright-line rules and little if any role for jurisprudence and previous decisions.[18]

Through the Napoleonic Wars in the early nineteenth century, the Napoleonic legal tradition was spread throughout continental Europe. Subsequently, legal traditions were spread throughout the rest of the world, mostly in the form of colonization, with the British common law tradition adopted in all British colonies and the Napoleonic civil code tradition transplanted to Belgian, Dutch, Portuguese, Spanish, and French colonies. The legal structures originating in these different traditions have proven to be very persistent, especially in developing countries. Take the example of the Napoleonic legal tradition. First, while the European nations overcame the rigidities of the Napoleonic code, they exported its antagonism toward jurisprudence and its reliance on judicial formalism to minimize the role of judges. This comes with the tradition of avoiding open disputes about legal interpretation and the aversion against jurisprudence. Second, given that the Napoleonic doctrine sees judges as purely executing civil servants, judges frequently "are at the bottom of the scale of prestige among the legal professions in France and in many nations that adopted the French Revolutionary reforms, and the best people in those nations accordingly seek other legal careers" (Merryman 1996: 116). Third, and as a consequence of the previous point, there is a stronger reliance on bright-line laws to limit the role of the courts. Once a country adopts the bright-line approach to lawmaking, this can lead into a trap, as courts will not be challenged to develop legal procedures and methods to deal with new circumstances, thus retarding the development of efficiently adaptive legal systems (Pistor et al. 2002, 2003). By the same token, Common Law systems can be persistent, given the high social reputation of judges attracting talent to this profession and the role of jurisprudence allowing for a vibrant legal debate fostering legal innovation.

Empirical evidence has shown that countries with a Napoleonic legal tradition have fewer independent judiciaries and fewer adaptable legal systems.[19] Countries with a Napoleonic legal tradition also have—on average—weaker property rights protection and contractual institutions that are less conducive to external finance, including weaker protection for minority shareholders and secured and unsecured creditors. Enforcement of contracts is costlier and slower in civil code countries, as is the registration of property and collateral. This has the overall effect of smaller and less effective financial markets in civil code countries (La Porta et al. 1998; Beck, Demirgüç-Kunt, and Levine 2003a). In sum, deep-seated historically determined legal institutions have shaped political structures (relative power of different player and importance of private property rights vis-à-vis governments) and specific contractual institutions, such as court systems and collateral registries.[20]

There has also been countervailing evidence. Berkowitz, Pistor, and Richard (2003) stress that the transplant process—not just whether countries are classified as having British, French, German, or Scandinavian legal origins—is important for establishing well-functioning legal systems. Pistor et al. (2002) describe the significant differences in the transplant process in Colombia and Chile, which resulted in the latter adopting more appropriate and efficient legal institutions than the former. There is also evidence on time variation in legal institutions, which is not compatible with time-invariant legal traditions, and it has been suggested that it is changing political conditions that determine institutions (e.g., Pagano and Volpin 2005). Brunt (2007) analyzes the transition of South Africa from a Dutch to an English colony and shows that it is the definition of property rights and thus coercion-constraining institutions rather than changes in contract enforcement institutions that resulted in improvements in agricultural productivity and output in the early nineteenth century.

An alternative explanation refers not to the identity of the colonizing power but the mode of colonization, also referred to as endowment view. Distinguishing between settler and extractive colonies, Acemoglu, Johnson, and Robinson (2001, 2002) show that the former developed stronger property rights protection than the latter, given the political and societal structures that natural resource extraction in the latter implied. The initial colonization mode, in turn, was determined by the disease environment that European colonizers encountered as well as the incidence of native population in the colonized areas. Areas with more hostile disease environments and/or large native population concentrations were more likely to be settled in an extractive mode. The political structures developed during the colonization period endured after independence, therefore also making the weak property rights and contract enforcement institutions persistently weak beyond independence. This hypothesis is part of the broader social conflict theory, most clearly and eloquently formulated by Acemoglu, Johnson, and Robinson (2005), which posits that de jure political institutions reflect de facto political institutions that in turn are driven by resource distribution in a society. Political institutions are persistent, as the ruling group will fortify its de facto political power with the structure of de jure political power. The institutional framework is therefore not necessarily the most efficient, but rather the reflection of the economic and political distribution of power, which makes it inflexible when new opportunities or technologies arise. Changes in political institutions and thus the institutional framework are most likely with technological or other exogenous shocks.

Empirical evidence shows the importance of the colonization mode for the development of financial markets today (Beck et al. 2003a). Countries that were initially colonized in an extractive mode have less developed financial markets today. This effect is in addition to that of the legal tradition discussed above.

Beyond using the colonization experience to document the importance of initial political structures and resource distribution, the legal tradition and endowment views show the importance of political structures and persistence in financial system development. These hypotheses suggest that changes in the legal institutions that underpin thriving financial markets are only possible under outside pressure or exogenous shocks, such as new technologies, dramatic sociopolitical change, or globalization. Similarly, changes in financial sector policies are more likely under exogenous pressure. Let me give a few examples.

In the 1990s, the transition economies of Central Europe faced the challenge to build market-based financial systems from scratch, while the continuing relationships between banks and incumbent but insolvent enterprises and the resulting fragility had severe negative macroeconomic repercussions. The need for recapitalization of banks due to nonperforming loans resulted in rising fiscal deficits, monetary overhang, and thus inflation. The solution to this continuous cycle of repayment problems, accumulation of nonperforming assets, recapitalization, and inflation was the adoption of a disciplining tool to impose a hard budget constraint on enterprises and banks alike. Credibly committing to monetary stability in turn forced the necessary reforms in the financial sector to avoid future recapitalization. In many countries, banks were therefore not only privatized but sold to foreign banks, which helped sever the links between state-owned enterprises and banks.[21] What essentially was needed was a straitjacket that tied policymakers' hands and prevented them from bailing out financial and nonfinancial institutions. Foreign bank entry as well as the perspective of EU accession thus provided the necessary outside discipline to transform financial systems.

Similarly, in Brazil the introduction of the Real Plan in 1994 that terminated the long-running inflationary tradition prevented the government from bailing out banks owned by individual states, as it had done several times before, and thus forced a complete restructuring of these institutions (Beck, Crivelli, and Summerhill 2005). In Argentina, the establishment of a currency board in 1991 started the restructuring process of provincial banks (Clarke and Cull 2002). Technological innovation was critical in driving branch deregulation in the United States in the 1970s and 1980s.

Technology can also play an important role. As shown by Kroszner and Strahan (1999), the invention of automated teller machines (ATMs), in conjunction with court rulings that ATMs are not bank branches, weakened the geographical bond between customers and banks, and improvements in communications technology lowered the costs of using distant banks. These innovations reduced the monopoly power of local banks, weakening their ability and desire to fight against deregulation, ultimately leading to branch deregulation. The timing of this deregulation across states, in turn, was very much a function of initial conditions, ranging from party politics to the importance and independence of insurance companies.

Beyond influencing political and thus institutional structures, history can also have an impact on today's financial systems by creating social capital and trust. Guiso, Sapienza, and Zingales (2004) exploit the large variation within Italy to show the importance of social capital—historically predetermined—for financial sector development. Using data on immigrants in the United States, Osili and Paulson (2008a, 2008b) show the persistence of institutional constraints, as immigrants from countries with worse institutions are less likely to use formal financial services in the United States, and if they do so, they do so less extensively.

The influence of religious beliefs and institutions might also have an important impact on financial sector development (Stulz and Williamson 2003). In particular, the Catholic Church has historically taken a negative stance toward charging interest and creditor rights, and the Quran prohibits the charging of interest. In contrast, the Protestant Reformation advanced a different religious attitude toward finance, whereby the payment of interest was considered a normal part of commerce, so that the rights of creditors were more naturally emphasized in countries dominated by Protestant religions. As shown by Stulz and Williamson (2003), countries with a predominantly Catholic religious heritage tend to have less developed credit markets and more poorly developed financial institutions. Grosjean (2011) uses micro-data for six South Eastern countries, part of which used to be part of the Ottoman Empire and shows that former Islamic rule is associated with lower financial development today, even within countries. Moreover, localities with Armenian, Jewish, or Greek minorities, who were allowed to practice interest lending under Ottoman rule, have higher levels of bank penetration. By contrast, Islamic religion and trust in the financial system play no role in explaining such long-term persistence.

Finally, specific historic events might turn into a traumatic experience for nations, with long-ranging implications for institutions. Murphy (2005) sees the 1720s Mississippi bubble, with its subsequent banking crisis and hyperinflation, as critical for the negative French attitude toward the financial sector. Similarly, the hyperinflationary experience in Germany has resulted in a hawkish approach toward monetary policy deeply entrenched for the following 80 years. Malmendier and Nagel (2010) show that "depression babies," that is, individuals growing up during the Depression era in the United States, are less likely to invest in equity and have overall more risk-averse investment strategies.

7.3.2. Financial Development and Institutional Constraints

The previous section has shown that financial sector development depends critically on the institutional framework of a country, where the latter is often driven by historic experiences. This interrelationship between financial and institutional development can be conceptualized using the financial possibility frontier, as, for example, developed in Barajas et al. (2013).

Specifically, this concept starts from the premise that financial systems are constrained by two major market frictions, transaction costs and risks, which can constrain the deepening and broadening of financial systems in developing countries. Financial intermediaries and markets arise exactly because these market frictions prevent direct intermediation between savers and borrowers. However, the efficiency with which financial institutions and markets can overcome market frictions is critically influenced by a number of state variables—factors that are invariant in the short term (often lying outside the purview of policymakers)—that affect provision of financial services on the supply side and can constrain participation on the demand side. State variables thus impose an upper limit on sustainable financial deepening in an economy at a given point in time. These variables are either directly related to the financial sector (for, e.g., macroeconomic fundamentals, the available technology, contractual and information frameworks underpinning the financial system, prudential oversight) or related to the broader sociopolitical and structural environment in which the financial system operates. Among the state variables is the institutional framework, including contractual framework and transparency, as discussed above.

Using the concept of state variables allows us to define the financial possibility frontier as a rationed equilibrium of supply and demand. In other words, this is the maximum sustainable depth (e.g., credit or deposit volumes), outreach (e.g., share of population reached), or breadth of a financial system (e.g., diversity of domestic sources of long-term finance) that can be realistically achieved at a given point in time. The financial possibility frontier can move over time, as income levels change, the international environment adjusts, new technologies arise, and—most important—the overall sociopolitical environment in which financial institutions work changes. Critically, policy levers including the macroeconomic environment and contractual and information frameworks can be used to push out the frontier, although such benefits can rarely be reaped in the short term.

Figure 7.1 illustrates the concept in a stylized way. I graph the frontier in a three-dimensional space, where the x- and z-axes denote structural and policy state variables, respectively, while the y-axis denotes financial development. All three axes are one-dimensional representations of an array of variables. A movement outward on the x-axis indicates improvement in the structural state variables—e.g., size, demographic structure, sociopolitical situation—conducive to financial deepening. Similarly, movements outward on the z-axis indicate improvements in long-term policies and institutions—e.g., macroeconomic stability, contractual framework—that are conducive for financial deepening.

The plane in figure 7.1 indicates the financial possibility frontier, i.e., the level of financial development sustainable in the long term for a given combination of structural and policy state variables. The frontier allows us to distinguish between several challenges to deepen and broaden financial systems in developing countries and the corresponding policies. Depending on where a financial system stands relative to the frontier and where the frontier stands in comparison to other countries with similar characteristics, different policy priorities apply and thus different functions for government. In the following, I will discuss situations, where (i) a financial system is below the frontier, (ii) a financial system is above the frontier, and (iii) the frontier is too low.

First, the financial possibility frontier may be low relative to countries at similar levels of economic development due to deficiencies in state variables. Here we can distinguish between the role played by structural and policy variables. Among structural variables, low population density and small market size increase the costs and risks for financial institutions, excluding large segments of the population from formal financial services. In addition, economic informality of large parts of the population lowers demand for as well as supply of financial services. Among policy variables, absence of an

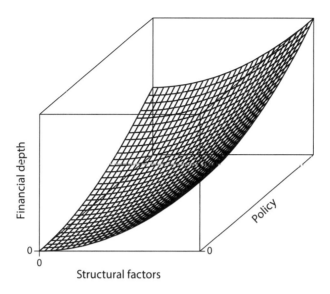

FIGURE 7.1. Stylized financial possibility frontier. *Source*: Beck and Feijen (2014).

adequate legal, contractual, and institutional environment or persistent macroeconomic instability can explain a low frontier. Focusing on the role of institutions in this context, a low financial possibility frontier thus illustrates the importance of institution-building for sustainable financial deepening.

Second, there is the possibility that a financial system lies below the frontier, i.e., below the constrained maximum defined by state variables, due to demand- and/or supply-side constraints. Demand-side constraints can arise if, for instance, the number of loan applicants is too low due to self-exclusion (e.g., due to lack of financial literacy) or because of a lack of viable investment projects in the economy (e.g., as a result of short-term macroeconomic uncertainty). Supply-side constraints influencing idiosyncratic risks or those artificially pushing up costs of financial service provision might also serve to hold the financial system below the frontier. For instance, lack of competition or regulatory restrictions might prevent financial institutions and market players from reaching out to new clientele or introducing new products and services. Similarly, regulatory barriers could prevent deepening of certain market segments, as can weak systems of credit information sharing or opacity of financial information about firms. Importantly, this situation points to options for policymakers for sustainable financial sector deepening within the existing institutional framework.

Finally, the financial system can move beyond the frontier, indicating an unsustainable expansion of the financial system beyond its fundamentals. For instance, boom-bust cycles in economies can occur in the wake of excessive investment and risk taking (often facilitated by loose monetary policy) by market participants. Experience from past banking crises suggests that credit booms and subsequent busts typically occur in environments characterized by poorly defined regulatory and supervisory frameworks. As underscored by the global financial crisis, financial innovation and regulatory ease can foster rapid deepening, but also pose challenges for financial stability. Finally, fragility in many developing countries is often linked to governance problems, so that an over-shooting of the financial possibility frontier may also be related to limited supervisory and market discipline.

The concept of the financial possibility frontier has been partially operationalized in empirical exercises by Barajas et al. (2013) in the form of a benchmarking exercise. This exercise relates the actual level of financial development indicators to values predicted from a cross-country panel regression analysis including different socioeconomic characteristics. This benchmarking exercise can be interpreted both in the cross-section, i.e., comparing the gap between actual and predicted values across countries as over time within a given country. The latter in particular can also serve as a gauge for the buildup of fragilities.

7.3.3. Institutions and Financial Structure

The institutional framework is not only important for the development but also the structure of financial systems. In broad terms, economists have distinguished between bank- and market-based financial systems. While both financial institutions and markets can help overcome information asymmetries and agency problems, they do so in different ways. Financial institutions create private information, which helps them reduce information asymmetries. Financial markets, on the other hand, create public information, aggregated into prices. Similarly, there are differences in the mechanisms through which financial institutions and markets exercise corporate governance. Banks can help improve corporate governance directly through loan covenants and direct influence on firm policy and indirectly through reducing the amount of free cash flows senior management has available. Financial markets can help improve corporate governance by linking payment of senior management to performance, through voting structures and the threat of takeover if the stock price falls below a value that is seen below fair value. Finally, there are different ways financial institutions and markets help diversify risks. Banks offer better intertemporal risk diversification tools, whereas markets are better in diversifying risk cross-sectionally. Markets are better in offering standardized products, and banks are better in offering customized solutions. However, banks and markets can also be complementary through instruments such as securitization, allowing exit strategies for venture capitalists, and by providing competition to each other.[22]

The importance of financial institutions or markets can be interpreted in a broader sense as the predominance of relationship-based financial transactions or arms-length-based financial transactions. In the absence of easily available information and easily enforceable contracts, reliance on close relationships and thus repeated interactions between borrowers and lenders, which allows the collection of proprietary and soft (i.e., not quantifiable) information and direct governance tools, might be the only option. However, this means broader repercussions for the economy, as this limits the share of entrepreneurs with access to credit and might result in entrenched lending relationships undermining competition.

The predominance of relationship versus arms-length financial transactions in an economy can be related back to the institutional framework. While the weak institutional development thus limits financial institutions to rely on private information and thus relationship-based financial transactions (and ultimately explains the bank-based nature of financial systems in many developing countries), it also prevents the development of public capital markets.

However, the dominance of institutions supporting arms-length financial transactions has been questioned, also related to the discussion on private versus public institutions. Allen, Qian, and Qian (2005) and Allen et al. (2012) argue that recent financial sector development in both India and China is built on private if not informal institutional frameworks rather than the European-style contractual institutions, discussed above. This is a relevant debate also in the context of fostering financial sector development in many low-income countries lacking effective public institutions.

An alternative to using the local institutional framework is to use foreign institutional and macroeconomic frameworks. One characteristic of many developing and emerging markets is the tendency to focus on foreign currency rather than local currency loans and even on financial contracts subject to foreign rather than local jurisdictions, which is the result of lack of trust in domestic macroeconomic management and contractual institution. As discussed by de la Torre and Schmukler (2004) based on observations across Latin America, it is important to understand that these are shortcuts that result in risk reallocation rather than risk reduction, most notably from price risk (against volatile real interest and real exchange rate changes) to price-induced default risk. It has contributed to the high degree of dollarization in many financial systems of the developing world and has thus made macroeconomic management even more difficult in these countries (as foreign exchange policy has a direct impact on financial stability). Outsourcing contract enforcement outside domestic borders can also undermine local institution-building.

7.3.4. From Financial Deepening to Institution-Building

As much as thriving financial markets depend on institutions, there might be a feedback loop from financial deepening to institution-building, although this reverse link has not been quite rigorously documented yet in the literature. On the one hand, thriving financial markets can foster competition in the real economy. Evidence from the United States has shown that financial liberalization has contributed to higher entry and exit of enterprises (Kerr and Nanda 2009). Giannetti and Ongena (2009) show for Central and Eastern Europe that foreign bank entry helped reduce the importance of entrenched lending relationships and thus foster entrepreneurship and competition. Financial liberalization can also contribute to lower discrimination, as shown by Black and Strahan (2001) and Levine, Levkov, and Rubinstein (2014) using the US branch deregulation in the 1970s and '80s as identification strategy.

One important question in this context is whether financial deepening can happen in societies that lack institutional support. Low-income countries often suffer from a lack of accountability and transparency in political institutions and policymaking processes, which puts them in a catch-22 situation—on the one hand, they do not have the necessary institutional framework to support efficient and sustainable financial systems; on the other hand, the development of financial markets can contribute to institution-building.[23] In this context, questions such as the substitutability of private and public institutions come up, as well as whether contract enforcement institutions can be improved even in the absence of coercion-constraining institutions (Greif 2005). However, the role of technology in expanding financial services and the role of nongovernment entities, including cross-border banks, and regional integration can also be critical in overcoming this catch-22 by working around these institutional constraints.

7.4. CONCLUSIONS

The primary purpose of this chapter is to take stock of the existing theoretical and empirical literature on the interaction of financial systems and institutional quality in their importance for economic development, especially where relevant for low-income countries. In this concluding section, the chapter will discuss policy implications of the literature as it currently stands as well as avenues for future research.

In terms of policy implications for developing countries, the different literatures discussed in this chapter and their interactions suggest that it is critical to identify the binding constraints that hold back sustainable financial sector development, but also the political constraints that might prevent addressing these policy constraints. In the absence of external pressures, institutional reform fostering financial sector development cannot happen against the interests of the ruling elite, as the experience of the transition economies has clearly shown. In countries with more entrenched communist elites, and where these elites had higher surplus stakes in the form of natural resource rents, there was slower or no development of the necessary legal institutions for a functioning market economy (Beck and Laeven 2006).

Finally, any policy reform has to happen within a given historically predetermined institutional framework. Trying to impose institutions out of a different legal tradition is not helpful, as Russia found out the hard way; the short flirtation with the Common Law tradition did not bear fruit. Take the example of court reform. In spite of their shortcomings and deficiencies, court systems in the former British colonies still have a reasonable reputation. They can rely on a large body of case law and precedents, from London and other parts of the former British Empire. What courts in many common-law countries in Africa are lacking are capacity and specific skills. The introduction of commercial courts might be helpful in this context. The situation in most Civil Code countries in Africa is different, as courts in these countries have deficiencies along many dimensions and suffer from a very low reputation. In these countries, establishing alternative dispute resolution systems might be more helpful.

The survey also poses numerous research questions going forward. First, in the area of institution-building, what are the institutions and policies that are most relevant for financial sector deepening in developing countries, and is there an optimal sequencing? Related to these issues is the over-arching question on the role of government in financial service provision, caricatured by Honohan and Beck (2007) in the contrast of the modernist and activist approaches, i.e., an exclusive focus on institution-building and maintaining macro-stability versus a more interventionist approach, which focuses on market frictions and government institutions and policies to overcome them. While an extensive literature has documented the limited success (if not failure in most cases) of direct government provision of financial services, especially on the lending side, an array of market-activist policies that address market frictions, while providing proper governance structures and sunset clauses, have been suggested. Also, the success of several East Asian countries in providing the necessary external finance for rapid development has often been associated, not with market-based financial systems, but rather with strong government intervention if not outright financial repression (World Bank 1993). Most East Asian economies relied on development finance institutions as a catalyst for funding investment projects. To which extent can the East Asian experience be transferred to other developing regions of the world, including Sub-Saharan Africa?

Second, what is the relative importance of different segments of the financial system, including banks, capital markets, and contractual savings institutions? With rising incomes and structural changes in the real economy, the need for specific financial services changes over time, to the same extent that the possibilities to sustain specific institutions and markets change. What is the optimal structure of financial systems for different economic structures and income level? What financial structures are optimal for agriculturally dominated economies and natural resource–based countries? What kind of financial system allows economies to move from low- to middle-income and middle- to high-income status? How does a financial system move from a relationship-based system to an arms-length system, and is there an optimal stage of economic development and structure to do so? How strong is path dependence and is leapfrogging possible in financial structures, and what policies and interventions can help?

While previous work has mostly focused on banks versus markets, a more granular view might be necessary, including distinguishing between different types and sizes of financial institutions (e.g., nonbank financing companies, specialized vs. universal banks, focused local grassroots financial institutions vs. large institutions, contractual savings institutions, such as insurance companies, pension funds, and mutual funds) and financial markets (e.g., bonds vs. equity, short-term money vs. long-term capital markets). While research has often focused on banks versus public capital markets, there might also be an important role for private equity, more suitable for countries whose enterprise population cannot sustain a public stock exchange. One recent hypothesis suggests that economies relying on industries with many small enterprises require financial systems relying on smaller financial institutions with local roots (Lin, Sun, and Jiang 2009), although this has not been empirically confirmed (Beck, Demirgüç-Kunt, and Singer 2013).

Related to this issue is the question of whether there is a specific sequence with which different segments of the financial system (banks, capital markets, contractual savings institutions) arise and specific policies that can support their emergence. The experience in Europe and the United States has shown that different development paths are possible; can we learn from these for today's developing countries? Finally, what is the relative importance of informal and formal finance for long-term growth? As discussed above, recent papers have pointed to the importance of informal financial sources for firm growth as part of the Indian and Chinese success stories (Allen et al. 2005; Allen, Chakrabarti, et al. 2012). Can we learn from these experiences for other developing countries, including those in Africa, which are characterized not only by deficiencies in the formal institutional framework, but also by a lack of private institutions (Fafchamps 2004)?

Finally, what is the optimal degree of competition and rents in the financial system? An extensive literature shows that limited competition can help provide incentives to establish long-term lender-borrower relationships (see, e.g., Petersen and Rajan 1995), and the success of M-Pesa in Kenya has often been associated with the dominant market position of Safaricom, which allowed the provider to reach scale economies rapidly. So, rents are an integral part of the financial system, providing incentives for long-term relationships and innovation. On the other hand, contestability is important, as new entrants can bring new technologies and products, thus increasing efficiency with positive repercussions for depth and inclusion. The case of M-Pesa can also be interpreted as a story of competition, as Safaricom was allowed as a new entrant to compete against banks in the area of payment services. However, a high degree of competition might also undermine long-term relationships between lenders and borrowers, thus having important distributional repercussions across firms. In the area of stability, there is an ongoing discussion about the benefits and risks of competition (see, e.g., Beck, de Jonghe, and Schepens 2013). More research is required in this area, including to explore whether the optimal degree of rents and competition varies across countries with different levels of economic, financial, and institutional development and structure.

In closing, a few remarks on methodology. The agenda discussed above implies a multitude of different methodologies and data sources, using both observational data and experimental settings, such as RCTs. Different research questions demand different methodologies and data. Historical and longer-period analyses might be more appropriate to gauge structural and institutional questions, while RCTs and other experimental approaches might be more adequate to assess interventions with expected results in the short-term horizon. However, the same question can be gauged with different methodologies and using data on different aggregation levels. The role of theory is critical in terms of showing different hypothetical channels and mechanisms for empirically established relationships. Finally, for research to succeed in obtaining the necessary data, asking relevant questions but also maximizing its impact, a close interaction is necessary between researchers and donors, practitioners and policymakers. This relationship can often be critical for obtaining micro-level data, such as from credit registries or specific financial institutions, or for undertaking experiments or RCTs. However, these links are also critical for disseminating research findings and having an impact on practice and policy in the financial sector.

NOTES

Cass Business School, City University, and CEPR. Comments by participants at a workshop in Namur are gratefully acknowledged.
1. See, for example, McKinnon (1973) and Acemoglu and Zilibotti (1997).
2. See, for example, Bencivenga and Smith (1991) and King and Levine (1993b).
3. See, for example, Philippon (2010) and Bolton, Santos, and Scheinkman (2011).
4. See also the extensive firm-level literature, discussed in the chapter by Ayyagari, Demirgüç-Kunt, and Maksimovic.
5. Greenwood and Jovanovic (1990).
6. Galor and Zeira (1993); Aghion and Bolton (1997); Galor and Moav (2004).
7. See Beck, Demirgüç-Kunt, and Levine (2007); Beck, Levine, and Levkov (2010); and Ayyagari, Beck, and Hoseini (2013).
8. More recently, Arcand, Berkes, and Panizza (2015) find that the finance and growth relationship turns negative for high-income countries, identifying a value of 110% private credit to GDP as an approximate turning point, with the negative relationship between finance and growth turning significant at around 150% private credit to GDP, levels reached by some high-income countries in the 2000s.
9. These findings are confirmed in recent studies by Mian, Sufi, and Verner (2017), who show in a cross-country study that an increase in the household debt-to-GDP ratio predicts lower output growth and a higher unemployment rate over the medium run, and Chakraborty, Goldstein, and MacKinlay (2014) who show for the United States that banks that are active in strong housing markets increase mortgage lending and decrease commercial lending, with consequently lower investment by firms that borrow from these banks.

10. See Carletti (2008) for an overview.
11. Dell'Ariccia, Detragiache, and Rajan (2008) and Kroszner, Laeven, and Klingebiel (2007).
12. See Beck, Demirgüç-Kunt, and Levine (2000) for an extensive discussion of different indicators.
13. Ghatak (2015) presents a theoretical framework that documents the important role that lack of access to credit can have for poverty traps on the individual level, but also stresses income- and behaviour-related constraints.
14. See Banerjee (2013) for an in-depth discussion.
15. Following North (1990) and as also defined in the introduction to this Handbook, institutions can be understood as institutions as "rules, procedures or other human devices that constrain individual behaviour, either explicitly or implicitly, with a view to making individual expectations about others' behaviour converge and to allowing individual actions to become coordinated."
16. This section is partly based on Beck (2018).
17. See, however, Levine (2010), which details the intentional "looking the other way" by US regulators as new sources of risk arose.
18. Other important groups constitute the German and the Scandinavian legal systems, which are based on similar political structures as the French civil code tradition but have a more flexible and adaptable structure.
19. La Porta et al. (2004) and Beck, Demirgüç-Kunt, and Levine (2003b).
20. This is also confirmed by within-country studies, as for example by Berkowitz and Clay (2005, 2006), who show the persistent effects of Common Law and Civil Law experience in the former British colonies compared to former French and Spanish colonies across the United States for judicial structures and independence today.
21. See Giannetti and Ongena (2009).
22. See Stulz (2001) for an overview.
23. This is parallel to a similar situation in international financial liberalization as discussed by Kose et al. (2009).

REFERENCES

Acemoglu, Daron, and Simon Johnson. 2005. "Unbundling Institutions." *Journal of Political Economy* 113: 949–995.

Acemoglu, Daron, Simon Johnson, and James A. Robinson. 2001. "The Colonial Origins of Comparative Development: An Empirical Investigation." *American Economic Review* 91: 1369–1401.

———. 2002. "Reversal of Fortunes: Geography and Institutions in the Making of the Modern World Income Distribution." *Quarterly Journal of Economics* 117: 1133–1192.

———. 2005. "Institutions as the Fundamental Cause of Long-Run Growth." In *Handbook of Economic Growth*, edited by Philippe Aghion and Steven N. Durlauf. Amsterdam: Elsevier.

Acemoglu, Daron, and Fabrizio Zilibotti. 1997. "Was Prometheus Unbound by Chance? Risk, Diversification, and Growth." *Journal of Political Economy* 105: 709–751.

Aghion, Philippe, George-Marios Angeletos, Abhijit Banerjee, and Kalina Manova. 2010. "Volatility and Growth: Credit Constraints and the Composition of Growth." *Journal of Monetary Economics* 57: 246–265.

Aghion, Philippe, Philippe Bacchetta, Romain Rancière, and Kenneth Rogoff. 2009. "Exchange Rate Volatility and Productivity Growth: The Role of Financial Development." *Journal of Monetary Economics* 56: 494–513.

Aghion, Philippe, and Patrick Bolton. 1997. "A Theory of Trickle-Down Growth and Development." *Review of Economic Studies* 64: 151–72.

Aghion, Philippe, Peter Howitt, and David Mayer-Foulkes. 2005. "The Effect of Financial Development on Convergence: Theory and Evidence." *Quarterly Journal of Economics* 120: 173–222.

Allen, Franklin, R. Chakrabarti, S. De, J. Qian, and M. Qian. 2012. "Financing Firms in India," *Journal of Financial Intermediation* 21: 409–445.

Allen, Franklin, J. Qian, and M. Qian. 2005. "Law, Finance and Economic Growth in China," *Journal of Financial Economics* 77, 57–116.

Aney, Madhav, Maitreesh Ghatak, and Massimo Morelli. 2016. "Credit Market Frictions and Political Failure." *Journal of Monetary Economics* 81: 48–64.

Arcand, Jean Louis, Enrico Berkes, and Ugo Panizza. 2015. "Too Much Finance?" *Journal of Economic Growth* 20: 105–148.

Ardagna, Silvia, and Francesco Caselli. 2014. "The Political-Economy of the Greek Debt Crisis: A Tale of Two Bailouts." *American Economic Journal: Macroeconomics* 6: 291–323.

Ashraf, Nava, Dean Karlan, and Wesley Yin. 2006. "Tying Odysseus to the Mast: Evidence from a Commitment Savings Product in the Philippines." *Quarterly Journal of Economics* 121: 673–697.

Assunção, Juliano, Efraim Benmelech, and Fernando Silva. 2014. "Repossession and the Democratization of Credit." *Review of Financial Studies* 27: 2661–2689.

Attanasio, Orazio, Britta Augsburg, Ralph de Haas, Emla Fitzsimons, and Heike Harmgart. 2015. "The Impacts of Microfinance: Evidence from Joint-liability Lending in Mongolia." *American Economic Journal: Applied Economics* 7: 90–122.

Ayyagari, Meghana, Thorsten Beck, and Mohamad Hoseini. 2013. "Finance and Poverty: Evidence from India." CEPR Discussion Paper 9497.

Banerjee, Abhijit. 2013. "Microcredit Under the Microscope: What Have We Learned in the Past Two Decades, and What Do We Need to Know?" *Annual Review of Economics* 5: 487–519.

Banerjee, Abhijit, Timoty Besley, and Timothy Guinnane. 1994. "The Neighbor's Keeper: The Design of a Credit Cooperative with Theory and a Test." *Quarterly Journal of Economics* 109: 491–515.

Banerjee, Abhijit, and Ester Duflo. 2007. "The Economic Lives of the Poor." *Journal of Economic Perspectives* 21: 141–67.

Banerjee, Abhijit, Dean Karlan, and Jonathan Zinman. 2015. "Six Randomized Evaluations of Microcredit: Introduction and Further Steps." *American Economic Journal: Applied Economics* 7: 1–21.

Barajas, Adolfo, Thorsten Beck, Era Dabla-Norris, and Seyed Reza Yousefi. 2013. "Too Cold, Too Hot, Or Just Right? Assessing Financial Sector Development Across the Globe." IMF Working Paper 13/81.

Beck, Thorsten. 2011. "Finance and Oil: Is There a Natural Resource Curse in Financial Development?" In *Beyond the Curse: Policies to Harness the Power of Natural Resources*, edited by Rabah Arezki, Thorvaldur Gylfason, and Amadou Sy, 81–106. Washington, DC: IMF.

———. 2018. "What Drives Financial Sector Development? Policies, Politics and History." In *Handbook of Finance and Development*, edited by Thorsten Beck and Ross Levine. Cheltenham and Camberley, UK, and Northampton, MA: Edward Elgar.

Beck, Thorsten, Berrak Büyükkarabacak, Felix K. Rioja, and Neven T. Valev. 2012. "Who Gets the Credit? And Does It Matter? Household vs. Firm Lending across Countries." *B.E. Journal of Macroeconomics: Contributions* 12.

Beck, Thorsten, Juan Miguel Crivelli, and William Summerhill. 2005. "State Bank Transformation in Brazil, Choices and Consequence." *Journal of Banking and Finance* 29: 2223–2257.

Beck, Thorsten, Olivier de Jonghe, and Glenn Schepens. 2013. "Bank Competition and Stability: Cross-country Heterogeneity." *Journal of Financial Intermediation* 22: 218–244.

Beck, Thorsten, Asli Demirgüç-Kunt, Luc Laeven, and Ross Levine. 2008. "Finance, Firm Size, and Growth." *Journal of Money, Banking and Credit* 40: 1379–1405.

Beck, Thorsten, Asli Demirgüç-Kunt, Luc Laeven, and Vojislav Maksimovic. 2006. "The Determinants of Financing Obstacles." *Journal of International Money and Finance* 25: 932–952.

Beck, Thorsten, Asli Demirgüç-Kunt, and Ross Levine. 2000. "A New Database on Financial Development and Structure." *World Bank Economic Review* 14: 597–605.

———. 2003a. "Law, Endowments, and Finance." *Journal of Financial Economics* 70, 137–181.

———. 2003b. "Law and Finance: Why Does Legal Origin Matter?" *Journal of Comparative Economics* 31: 653–675.

———. 2007. "Finance, Inequality and the Poor." *Journal of Economic Growth* 12: 27–49.

Beck, Thorsten, Asli Demirgüç-Kunt, and Vojislav Maksimovic. 2005. "Financial and Legal Constraints to Firm Growth: Does Size Matter?" *Journal of Finance* 60: 137–177.

Beck, Thorsten, Asli Demirgüç-Kunt, and Dorothe Singer. 2013. "Is Small Beautiful? Financial Structure, Size and Access to Finance." *World Development* 52: 19–33.

Beck, Thorsten and Erik Feijen. 2014. "Benchmarking Financial Systems: Introducing the Financial Possibility Frontier." World Bank Policy Research Working Paper 6615.

Beck, Thorsten, and Luc Laeven. 2006. "Institution Building and Growth in Transition Economies." *Journal of Economic Growth* 11: 157–186.

Beck, Thorsten, Ross Levine, and Alexey Levkov. 2010. "Big Bad Banks? The Winners and Losers from Bank Deregulation in the United States." *Journal of Finance* 65: 1637–1667.

Beck, Thorsten, Ross Levine, and Norman Loayza. 2000. "Finance and the Sources of Growth." *Journal of Financial Economics*: 261–300.

Beck, Thorsten, Chen Lin, and Yue Ma. 2014. "Why Do Firms Evade Taxes? The Role of Credit Information Sharing and Banking Sector Outreach." *Journal of Finance* 69: 763–817.

Beck, Thorsten, Mattias Lundberg, and Giovanni Majnoni. 2006. "Financial Intermediary Development and Growth Volatility: Do Intermediaries Dampen or Magnify Shocks." *Journal of International Money and Finance* 25: 1146–1167.

Beck, Thorsten, and Steven Poelhekke. 2016. "Follow the Money: Does the Financial Sector Intermediate Natural Resource Windfalls?" Mimeo.

Beck, Thorsten, Haki Pumak, Ravindra Ramrattan, and Burak Uras. 2018. "Payment Instruments, Finance and Development." *Journal of Development Economics* 133: 162–188.

Becker, Gary, and George Stigler. 1974. "Law Enforcement, Malfeasance, and Compensation of Enforcers." *Journal of Legal Studies* 3: 1–18.

Bencivenga, Valerie R., and Bruce D. Smith. 1991. "Financial Intermediation and Endogenous Growth." *Review of Economics Studies* 58: 195–209.

Berkowitz, Daniel, and Karen Clay. 2005. "American Civil Law Origins: Implications for State Constitutions." *American Law and Economics Review* 7: 62–84.

———. 2006. "The Effect of Judicial Independence on Courts: Evidence from the American States." *Journal of Legal Studies* 35: 399–440.

Berkowitz, Daniel, Katharina Pistor, and Jean-François Richard. 2003. "Economic Development, Legality, and the Transplant Effect." *European Economic Review* 47: 165–195.

Bernanke, B. S., and M. Gertler. 1989. "Agency Costs, Net Worth, and Business Fluctuations." *American Economic Review* 79: 14–31.

Besley, Timothy, Konrad Burchardi, and Maitreesh Ghatak. 2012. "Incentives and the De Soto Effect." *Quarterly Journal of Economics* 127: 237–282.

Biais, Bruno, and Thomas Mariotti. 2009. "Credit, Wages and Bankruptcy Laws." *Journal of European Economic Association* 7.

Black, Sandra, and Philip Strahan. 2001. "The Division of Spoils: Rent-Sharing and Discrimination in a Regulated Industry." *American Economic Review* 91: 814–831.

Blumenstock, Joshua, Nathan Eagle, and Marcel Fafchamps. 2016. "Air Time Transfers and Mobile Communications: Evidence in the Aftermath of Natural Disasters." *Journal of Development Economics* 120: 157–181.

Bolton, Patrick, Tano Santos, and Jose Scheinkman. 2011. "Cream Skimming in Financial Markets." *Journal of Finance* 71: 709–736.

Bongini, Paola, Stijn Claessens, and Giovanni Ferri. 2001. "The Political Economy of Distress in East Asian Financial Institutions." *Journal of Financial Services Research* 19: 5–25.

Boyd, John H., Ross Levine, and Bruce D. Smith. 2001. "The Impact of Inflation on Financial Sector Performance." *Journal of Monetary Economics* 47: 221–248.

Brown, Craig, and Serdar Dinc. 2005. "The Politics of Bank Failures: Evidence from Emerging Markets." *Quarterly Journal of Economics* 120: 1413–1444.

Brown, Martin, Tullio Jappelli, and Marco Pagano. 2009. "Information Sharing and Credit: Firm-Level Evidence from Transition Countries." *Journal of Financial Intermediation* 18: 151–172.

Bruhn, Miriam. 2013. "A Tale of Two Species: Revisiting the Effect of Registration Reform on Informal Business Owners in Mexico." *Journal of Development Economics* 103: 275–283.

Bruhn, Miriam, Subika Farazi, and Martin Kanz. 2013. "Bank Competition, Concentration and Credit Reporting." World Bank Policy Research Working Paper 6442.

Brune, Lasse, Xavier Giné, Jessica Goldberg, and Dean Yang. 2015. "Facilitating Savings for Agriculture: Field Experimental Evidence from Malawi." *Economic Development and Cultural Change* 64(2): 187–220.

Brunt, Liam. 2007. "Property Rights and Economic Growth: Evidence from a Natural Experiment." CEPR Discussion Paper 6404.

Calomiris, Charles, Mauricio Larrain, Jose Liberti, and Jason Sturgess. 2017. "How Collateral Laws Shape Lending and Sectoral Activity." *Journal of Financial Economics* 123: 163–188.

Campello, Murillo, and Mauricio Larrain. 2016. "Enlarging the Contract Space: Collateral Menus, Access to Credit and Economic Activity." *Review of Financial Studies* 29: 349–383.

Carletti, Elena. 2008. "Competition and Regulation in Banking." In *Handbook of Financial Intermediation and Banking*, edited by Anjan Thakor and Arnoud Boot, 449–482. Amsterdam: Elsevier.

Caselli, Francesco, and Nicola Gennaioli. 2008. "Economics and Politics of Alternative Institutional Reforms." *Quarterly Journal of Economics* 123: 1197–1250.

Chakraborty, Indraneel, Itay Goldstein, and Andrew MacKinlay. 2014. "Do Asset Prices Have Negative Real Effects?" Mimeo.

Chemin, Matthieu. 2009. "Do Judiciaries Matter for Development? Evidence from India." *Journal of Comparative Economics* 37: 230–250.

———. 2012. "Does the Quality of the Judiciary Shape Economic Activity? Evidence from a Judicial Reform in India." *Journal Law, Economic and Organization* 28: 460–485.

Clarke, George R. G., and Robert Cull. 2002. "Political and Economic Determinants of the Likelihood of Privatizing Argentine Public Banks." *Journal of Law and Economics* 45: 165–197.

Cull, Robert, and Lixin C. Xu. 2005. "Institutions, Ownership, and Finance: The Determinants of Profit Reinvestment among Chinese Firms." *Journal of Financial Economics* 77: 117–146.

De Janvry, Alain, Craig McIntosh, and Elisabeth Sadoulet. 2010. "The Demand and Supply Side Impacts of Credit Market Information." *Journal of Development Economics* 93: 173–188.

De la Torre, Augusto, and Sergio L. Schmukler. 2004. "Coping with Risks through Mismatches: Domestic and International Financial Contracts for Emerging Economies." *International Finance* 7: 349–390.

Dell'Ariccia, Giovanni, Enrica Detragiache, and Raghuram Rajan. 2008. "The Real Effect of Banking Crises." *Journal of Financial Intermediation* 17: 89–112.

Demirgüç-Kunt, Asli, and Harry Huizinga. 2010. "Bank Activity and Funding Strategies: The Impact on Risk and Returns." *Journal of Financial Economics* 98: 626–650.

Demirgüç-Kunt, Asli, and Edward Kane. 2002. "Deposit Insurance around the Globe? Where Does It Work?" *Journal of Economic Perspectives* 16: 175–195.

Demirgüç-Kunt, Asli, Inessa Love, and Vojislav Maksimovic. 2006. "Business Environment and the Incorporation Decision." *Journal of Banking and Finance* 30: 2967–2993.

Demirgüç-Kunt, Asli, and Vojislav Maksimovic. 2002. "Funding Growth in Bank-Based and Market-Based Financial Systems: Evidence from Firm-Level Data." *Journal of Financial Economics* 65: 337–363.

De Quidt, Jonathan, Thiemo Fetzer, and Maitreesh Ghatak. 2018a. "Commericalization and the Decline of Joint Liability Microcredit." *Journal of Development Economics* 134: 209–225.

———. 2018b. "Market Structure and Borrower Welfare in Microfinance." *Economic Journal* 128: 1019–1046.

Diamond, Douglas W., and Philip H. Dybvig. 1983. "Bank Runs, Deposit Insurance and Liquidity." *Journal of Political Economy* 91: 401–419.

Djankov, Simeon, Caralee McLiesh, and Andrei Shleifer. 2007. "Private Credit in 129 Countries." *Journal of Financial Economics* 84: 299–329.

Dupas, Pascaline, Anthony Keats, and Jonathan Robinson. 2018. "The Effects of Savings Accounts on Interpersonal Financial Relationships: Evidence from a Field Experiment in Rural Kenya." *Economic Journal*, forthcoming.

Dupas, Pascaline, and Jonathan Robinson. 2013a. "Savings Constraints and Microenterprise Development: Evidence from a Field Experiment in Kenya." *American Economic Journal: Applied Economics* 5: 163–192.

———. 2013b. "Why Don't the Poor Save More? Evidence from Health Savings Experiments." *American Economic Review* 103: 1138–1171.

Fafchamps, Marcel. 2004. *Market Institutions in Sub-Saharan Africa: Theory and Evidence.* Cambridge, MA: MIT Press.

Galor, Oded, and Omer Moav. 2004. "From Physical to Human Capital Accumulation: Inequality and the Process of Development." *Review of Economic Studies* 71: 1001–1026.

Galor, Oded, and Joseph Zeira. 1993. "Income Distribution and Macroeconomics." *Review of Economic Studies* 60: 35–52.

Ghatak, Maitreesh. 2015. "Theories of Poverty Traps and Anti-Poverty Policies." *World Bank Economic Review* 29: S77–S105.

Ghatak, Maitreesh, and Timothy Guinanne. 1999. "The Economics of Lending with Joint Liability: Theory and Practice." *Journal of Development Economics* 60: 195–228.

Giannetti, Mariassunta, and Steven Ongena. 2009. "Financial Integration and Firm Performance: Evidence from Foreign Bank Entry in Emerging Markets." *Review of Finance* 13: 181–223.

Giné, Xavier, and Robert M. Townsend. 2004. "Evaluation of Financial Liberalization: A General Equilibrium Model with Constrained Occupation Choice." *Journal of Development Economics* 74: 269–307.

Glaeser, Edward L., and Andrei Shleifer. 2002. "Legal Origins." *Quarterly Journal of Economics* 117: 1193–1229.

Gonzalez-Uribe, Juanita, and Daniel Osorio. 2014. "Information Sharing and Credit Outcomes: Evidence from a Natural Experiment." Working Paper.

Greenwood, J., and B. Jovanovic. 1990. "Financial Development, Growth, and the Distribution of Income." *Journal of Political Economy* 98: 1076–1107.

Greif, Avner. 2005. "Commitment, Coercion and Markets: The Nature and Dynamics of Institutions Supporting Exchange." In *Handbook of New Institutional Economics*, edited by Claude Ménard and Mary M. Shirley, 727–788. Dordrecht: Springer.

Grosjean, Pauline. 2011. "The Institutional Legacy of the Ottoman Empire: Islamic Rule and Financial Development in South Eastern Europe." *Journal of Comparative Economics* 39: 1–16.

Guiso, Luigi, Paola Sapienza, and Luigi Zingales. 2004. "Does Local Financial Development Matter?" *Quarterly Journal of Economics* 119: 929–969.

Haselmann, Rainer, Katharina Pistor, and Vikrant Vig. 2010. "How Law Affects Lending." *Review of Financial Studies* 23: 549–580.

Honohan, Patrick, and Thorsten Beck. 2007. *Making Finance Work for Africa*. Washington, DC: World Bank.

Imai, Masami. 2009. "Political Influence and Declarations of Bank Insolvency in Japan." *Journal of Money, Credit and Banking* 41: 131–158.

International Monetary Fund. 2012. Enhancing Financial Sector Surveillance in Low-Income Countries—Financial Deepening and Macro-Stability. Washington, DC.

Jack, William, and Tanveer Suri. 2014. "Risk Sharing and Transaction Costs: Evidence from Kenya's Mobile Money Revolution." *American Economic Review* 104: 183–223.

Jappelli, Tullio, and Marco Pagano. 1994. "Saving, Growth, and Liquidity Constraints." *Quarterly Journal of Economics* 109: 83–109.

Jappelli, Tullio, Marco Pagano, and Magda Bianco. 2005. "Courts and Banks: Effects of Judicial Enforcement on Credit Markets." *Journal of Money, Credit and Banking* 37: 223–244.

Johnston, Don, and Jonathan Morduch. 2008. "The Unbanked: Evidence from Indonesia." *World Bank Economic Review* 22: 517–537.

Karlan, Dean, and Jonathan Zinman. 2010. "Expanding Credit Access: Using Randomized Supply Decisions to Estimate the Impacts." *Review of Financial Studies* 23: 433–464.

Kerr, William R., and Ramana Nanda. 2009. "Democratizing Entry: Banking Deregulations, Financing Constraints, and Entrepreneurship." *Journal of Financial Economics* 94: 124–149.

King, Robert G., and Ross Levine. 1993a. "Finance and Growth: Schumpeter Might Be Right." *Quarterly Journal of Economics* 108: 717–738.

———. 1993b. "Finance, Entrepreneurship, and Growth: Theory and Evidence." *Journal of Monetary Economics* 32: 513–542.

Kose, Ayan, Eswar Prasad, Kenneth Rogoff, and Shang-Jin Wei. 2009. "Financial Globalization: A Reappraisal." *IMF Staff Papers* 56: 8–62.

Kroszner, Randall S., Luc Laeven, and Daniela Klingebiel. 2007. "Banking Crises, Financial Dependence, and Growth." *Journal of Financial Economics* 84: 187–228.

Kroszner, Randall S., and Philip E. Strahan. 1999. "What Drives Deregulation? Economics and Politics of the Relaxation of Bank Branching Deregulation." *Quarterly Journal of Economics* 114: 1437–1467.

Laeven, Luc, and Chris Woodruff. 2007. "The Quality of the Legal System, Firm Ownership, and Firm Size." *Review of Economics and Statistics* 89: 601–614.

La Porta, Rafael, Florencio Lopez-de-Silanes, Christian Pop-Eleches, and Andrei Shleifer. 2004. "Judicial Checks and Balances." *Journal of Political Economy* 112: 445–470.

La Porta, Rafael, Florencio Lopez-de-Silanes, Andrei Shleifer, and Robert W. Vishny. 1997. "Legal Determinants of External Finance." *Journal of Finance* 52: 1131–1150.

———. 1998. Law and Finance. *Journal of Political Economics* 106: 1113–1155.

Laeven, Luc, and Fabian Valencia. 2013. "Systemic Banking Crises Database." *IMF Economic Review* 61: 225–270.

Levine, Ross. 2005. "Finance and Growth: Theory and Evidence." In *Handbook of Economic Growth*, edited by Philippe Aghion and Steven N. Durlauf, 865–934. Amsterdam: Elsevier.

———. 2010. "An Autopsy of the U.S. Financial System: Accident, Suicide or Negligent Homicide?" *Journal of Financial Economic Policy* 2: 196–213.

Levine, Ross, Alexey Levkov, and Yona Rubinstein. 2014. "Bank Deregulation and Racial Deregulation." *Critical Finance Review* 3: 1–48.

Levine, Ross, Norman Loayza, and Thorsten Beck. 2000. "Financial Intermediation and Growth: Causality and Causes." *Journal of Monetary Economics* 46: 31–77.

Lin, Justin, Xifang Sun, and Ye Jiang. 2009. "Toward a Theory of Optimal Financial Structure." World Bank Policy Research Working Paper 5038.

Loayza, Norman V., and Romain Rancière. 2006. "Financial Development, Financial Fragility, and Growth." *Journal of Money, Credit and Banking* 28: 1051–1076.

Love, Inessa, María Soledad Martínez Pería, and Sandeep Singh. 2016. "Collateral Registries for Movable Assets: Does Their Introduction Spur Firms' Access to Bank Finance?" *Journal of Financial Services Research* 49: 1–37.

Malmendier, Ulrike, and Stefan Nagel. 2010."Depression Babies: Do Macroeconomic Experiences Affect Risk-Taking?" *Quarterly Journal of Economics* 126: 373–416.

McKinnon, Ronald I. 1973. *Money and Capital in Economic Development.* Washington, DC: Brookings Institution.

Merryman, John Henry. 1996. "The French Deviation." *American Journal of Comparative Law* 44: 109–119.

Mian, Atif, Amir Sufi, and Emil Verner. 2017. "Household Debt and Business Cycles Worldwide." *Quarterly Journal of Economics* 132: 1755–1817.

Murphy, Antoin. 2005. "Corporate Ownership in France: The Importance of History." In *A History of Corporate Governance around the World*, edited by Randall Morck, 185–219. Chicago: University of Chicago Press.

North, Douglass. 1990. *Institutions, Institutional Change, and Economic Performance.* Cambridge: Cambridge University Press.

Osili, Una Okonkwo, and Anna Paulson. 2008a. "What Can We Learn About Financial Access from U.S. Immigrants? The Role of Country of Origin Institutions and Immigrant Beliefs." *World Bank Economic Review* 22: 431–455.

———. 2008b. "Institutions and Financial Development: Evidence from International Migrants in the United States." *Review of Economics and Statistics* 90: 498–517.

Padilla, Jorge, and Marco Pagano. 1997. "Endogenous Communication Among Lenders and Entrepreneurial Incentives." *Review of Financial Studies* 10: 205–236.

Pagano, Marco, and Tulio Jappelli. 1993. "Information Sharing in Credit Markets." *Journal of Finance* 48: 1693–1718.

Pagano, Marco, and Giovanni Pica. 2012. "Finance and Employment." *Economic Policy* 69: 5–55.

Pagano, Marco, and Paolo Volpin. 2005. "Managers, Workers and Corporate Control." *Journal of Finance* 60: 841–868.

Perotti, Enrico, and Paolo Volpin. 2010. "Politics, Investor Protection and Competition." Working Paper.

Petersen, Mitchell, and Raghuram Rajan. 1995. "The Effect of Credit Market Competition on Lending Relationships." *Quarterly Journal of Economics* 110: 407–443.

Phillipon, Thomas. 2010. "Financiers vs. Engineers: Should the Financial Sector be Taxed or Subsidized?" *American Economic Journal: Macroeconomics* 2: 158–182.

Pistor, Katharina, Yoram Keinan, Jan Kleinheisterkamp, and Mark D. West. 2002. "The Evolution of Corporate Law: A Cross-Country Comparison." *University of Pennsylvania Journal of International Economic Law* 23: 791–871.

———. 2003. "Innovation in Corporate Law." *Journal of Comparative Economics* 31: 676–694.

Ponticelli, Jacopo, and Leonardo Alencar. 2016. "Court Enforcement, Bank Loans and Firm Investment: Evidence from a Bankruptcy Reform in Brazil." *Quarterly Journal of Economics* 131: 1365–1413.

Prina, Silvia. 2015. "Banking the Poor via Savings Accounts: Evidence from a Field Experiment." *Journal of Development Economics* 115: 16–31.

Qian, Jun, and Philip Strahan. 2007. "How Law and Institutions Shape Financial Contracts: The Case of Bank Loans." *Journal of Finance* 62: 2803–2834.

Rajan, Raghuram. 2010. *Fault Lines: How Hidden Fractures Still Threaten the World Economy.* Princeton, NJ: Princeton University Press.

Rajan, Raghuram, and Rodney Ramcharan. 2015. "The Anatomy of a Credit Crisis: The Boom and Bust in Farm Land Prices in the United States in the 1920s." *American Economic Review* 105: 1439–1477.

Rajan, Raghuram G., and Luigi Zingales. 1998. "Financial Dependence and Growth." *American Economic Review* 88: 559–586.

Rancière, Romain, Aaron Tornell, and Frank Westermann. 2006. "Decomposing the Effects of Financial Liberalization: Crises vs. Growth." *Journal of Banking and Finance* 30: 3331–3348.

———. 2008. "Systemic Crises and Growth." *Quarterly Journal of Economics* 123: 359–406.

Rioja, Felix, and Neven Valev. 2004a. "Finance and the Sources of Growth at Various Stages of Economic Development." *Economic Inquiry* 42: 127–140.

———. 2004b. "Does One Size Fit All? A Reexamination of the Finance and Growth Relationship." *Journal of Development Economics* 74: 429–447.

Rousseau, Peter, and Alexandra D'Onofrio. 2013. "Monetization, Financial Development, and Growth: Time Series Evidence from 22 Countries in Sub-Saharan Africa." *World Development* 51: 132–153.

Straub, S. 2005. "Informal Sector: The Credit Market Channel." *Journal of Development Economics* 78: 299–321.

Stulz, R. M. 2001. "Financial Structure, Corporate Finance, and Economic Growth." In *Financial Structure and Economic Growth: Cross-Country Comparisons of Banks, Markets, and Development*, edited by A. Demirgüç-Kunt and R. Levine. Cambridge, MA: MIT Press.

Stulz, Rene, and Rohan Williamson. 2003. "Culture, Openness, and Finance." *Journal of Financial Economics* 70: 313–349.

Vig, Vikrant. 2013. "Access to Collateral and Corporate Debt Structure: Evidence from a Natural Experiment." *Journal of Finance* 68: 881–928.

Visaria, Sujata. 2009. "Legal Reform and Loan Repayment: The Microeconomic Impact of Debt Recovery Tribunals in India." *American Economic Journal: Applied Economics* 1: 59–81.

von Lilienfeld-Toal, Ulf, Dilip Mookherjee, and Sujata Visaria. 2012. "The Distributive Impact of Reforms in Credit Enforcement: Evidence from India Debt Recovery Tribunals." *Econometrica* 80: 497–558.

Woodruff, Christopher. 2006. "Measuring Institutions." In *International Handbook on the Economics of Corruption*, edited by Susan Rose-Ackerman, 105–125. Cheltenham: Edward Elgar.

World Bank. 1993. *The East Asian Miracle. Economic Growth and Public Policy*. Washington, DC.

PART 3

TRADE, AID, AND MIGRATION

8

TRADE-RELATED INSTITUTIONS AND DEVELOPMENT

Jaime de Melo and Marcelo Olarreaga

8.1. INTRODUCTION

It is only a slight exaggeration to say that until the publication of two papers in 1995, trade economists were comfortable saying that international trade was largely governed by differences in endowments and productivity, especially since the ongoing worldwide reductions in barriers to trade were erasing borders. Trefler (1995) convincingly showed that accommodating home market bias in consumption and differences in technology trump differences in factor endowment as determinants of trade patterns. McCallum (1995) showed that borders matter considerably more than predicted, even for highly integrated countries like the United States and Canada. Since then trade economists have turned their attention to the role of institutions in explaining the pattern of trade. Inspired by the work on institutions and development by North and colleagues (Milgrom et al. 1990) and by the institutions-and-growth literature (Acemoglu et al. 2005), Nunn (2007), Levchenko (2007), Chor (2010), and others have argued and given evidence that current-day trade is largely codetermined by the quality of contracting institutions and the traditional technology and endowments environments. Nunn and Trefler (2015) survey this literature historically and, more narrowly, on the sources of manufacturing comparative advantage.

From a developing-country perspective, the takeaway is that domestic institutions are needed to solve contract problems to get the economy to diversify toward the production of more sophisticated productivity-raising goods but also that initial conditions, some deeply rooted in history, have been determinant in the pattern of trade and subsequent path of domestic institutions. While market failure due to the lack of contract enforcement is no doubt important for low-income countries, other obstacles are equally important. These include those associated with externalities, information asymmetries, and coordination failures and are the subject of this chapter.

This chapter focuses on trade-related institutions (TRI) as they affect trade (and are affected by trade) in developing countries. In an attempt to limit institutions to those that are more directly targeted to traded activities, we focus on "new" market failures that may appear as firms and consumers reach international markets. Domestically these may be related to the changing nature of the relation of transactions (e.g., related to arm's-length transactions like reputation, contractibility) or existing market failures that may be exacerbated by trade (e.g., regional public goods, property rights for common pool resources may be exacerbated by the opportunity to trade).

To set this focus in perspective, section 8.2 recalls very briefly the deep long-run factors that have been identified as having an influence on the contemporary trade institutions relation as captured by macro-performance indicators. The extensive cross-country literature on growth, trade, and institutions has been unable to bring convincing evidence to confirm three often-cited anecdotal conjectures: that countries with better "institutions" and countries that trade more grow faster; and that countries with better institutions tend to trade more.

The survey then concentrates on three categories of TRIs. Section 8.3 starts with trade agreements—regional and multilateral agreements—that shape the developing countries' position in the World Trading System. Section 8.4 surveys what we know about Trade Promotion Organizations (TPOs) that have been set up to help firms participate in international markets by confronting the widespread externalities they face (lack of information about foreign markets, discoveries by pioneer exporters, coordination failures, or the absence of private insurance schemes). Section 8.5 examines private TRIs: labeling, fair trade, consumer boycotts, and trading platforms as transmitters of reputation mechanisms. The issue here is the extent to which private sector interests can be aligned with broader development objectives since in the presence of not only market failures, but also government failures, private sector institutions may provide an alternative to public institutions.

Each section is organized into two subsections. In the first subsection, the focus is on what we have learned about each of these selected issues in the existing literature, focusing where possible on low-income countries. In the second subsection, we suggest areas and we then turn to what we would like to know about each of these issues and their impact on development in the literature ahead. Throughout, the focus is on lessons from empirical contributions. Section 8.6 concludes.

8.2. TRADE, GROWTH, AND INSTITUTIONS: FROM DEEP TO SHALLOW DETERMINANTS

A growing literature on the deep determinants of development has explored the role of biological and cultural factors in long-term development outcomes. Long-term historical factors, as captured by relative genetic distance and cultural differences, have been found to predict population levels around 1500, and more recently, income per capita. In Africa, Michalopoulos and Papaioannou (2013, 2014) show that national institutions have little effect on economic performance of homogenous ethnic groups separated by national borders, and "dual" economic-institutional infrastructures coexist with customary rules being dominant in the countryside and colonial-national institutions becoming relevant for regions closer to the capitals. Long-term differences in technology and productivity hold at the level of populations rather than locations. Spolaore and Wacziarg (2009) find that the persistence in comparative development outcomes across populations is strongly correlated with the relative genetic distance to the technological frontier so that popula-tions that are historically farther from the innovators tend to face higher costs to imitate and adopt new technologies. The implication is that to understand differences in trade outcomes, one must not only consider differences in geography, policies, and institutions (e.g., relation-based or rule-based institutions) but also the transmission of biological and cultural factors. The findings of this literature, summarized in Spolaore and Wacziarg (2014), are beyond the scope of this work but should be kept in mind when studying the trade-institution nexus in low-income countries.[1]

Initial conditions and comparative advantage have also been found to play an impor-tant role in the historical development literature on domestic institutions reviewed by Nunn and Trefler (2015). The rise of the three-corner Atlantic trade (exports of slaves from Africa, commodities from the Americas, and manufactures from Europe) following the discovery of America supports the view that endowments and initial conditions deter-mined comparative advantage. In turn, the resulting distribution of income subsequently shaped long-lasting institutions. To this day, less trust pervades societies involved in transatlantic slave trade that required insecurity of property rights and disrespect of human rights. Likewise, specialization in plantations in South America resulted in com-parative advantage that generated a very unequal distribution of income that allowed the elites to establish growth-retarding institutions to protect their dominant position (Engerman and Solokoff 2000; Dell 2010).[2] In those environments, positive terms-of-trade shocks in coercive societies led to increased coercion rather than to wage increases. Con-temporary evidence on oil discoveries suggests they causally move regimes away from democracy (Tsui 2011). Nunn and Trefler (2015) conclude "conjecturing that the impact of international trade on domestic institutions is the simple most important source of the long-run gains from trade."

Moving to the contemporary trade-growth-institution link, for a long time, trade econ-omists have been confounded by the trade-income link: is trade an engine of growth or a handmaiden of growth? In an early influential contribution that addressed the two-way causality between export growth and GDP, Feder (1982) set up a model in which the marginal productivity of capital could be higher in export sectors. He found support for this conjecture in a sample of semi-industrialized countries over the period 1964–1973. But the subsequent extensive cross-country literature on growth, trade, and institutions has been unable to bring convincing evidence to confirm three often-cited anecdotal conjectures: that countries with better "institutions" and countries that trade more grow faster; and that countries with better institutions also tend to trade more.[3]

Two studies leading to contrasting conclusions illustrate the difficulties confronting cross-country macro-level studies. Using an event analysis in which they identified sig-nificant breaks in the trade regime by inspection of trade policy reports, Wacziarg and Welch (2008) found that countries liberalizing trade for at least eight years experienced an increase in investment rates and growth accelerations following the trade liberaliza-tion. These results are subject to confounding influences, as trade liberalization was usu-ally part of broader reform packages and subject to reverse causality. Using tariff data for a cross-section of 63 countries over the 1972–2000 period, Nunn and Trefler (2010) un-cover a strong correlation between aggregate growth and a country's tariff structure that protects disproportionately skill-intensive sectors (a proxy for R&D spending) where a cut-off was used to separate high- and low-skill intensive sectors. To get at causality,

they add an industry dimension (18 sectors) and find that a skill-biased tariff distribution causes a differential expansion of skill-intensive industries that is beneficial for
growth. But this mechanism only explains 25% of the correlation between growth and
the skill bias of tariffs. They then add six standard indicators of governance from the
World Bank to control for the omission of the institution channel on the grounds that it
is countries with better institutions that protect skill-intensive sectors. Adding these variables nibbles another 35–40% of the correlation, still leaving 40% of the correlation to be
explained. Remarking that these governance indicators supposedly focus only on corruption and illegal rent-seeking, on the basis of correlations of the skill bias of tariffs
with new measures of political connections and diplomatic tickets, Nunn and Trefler
(2010) stretch their argument to say that the remaining correlation can be explained by
purely legal and socially acceptable rent-seeking activities (see their fig. 3) that enter
prominently into the political economy models of trade policy to conclude that the skill
bias of protection might be an improved measure of rent-seeking activity.

Much work has also been carried out on trade costs for macro studies. Exploiting the
closing of the Suez Canal for 8 years—a truly exogenous shock—Feyrer (2009) estimates
an elasticity of trade to distance about half the typical value of cross-section estimates,
suggesting that the typical cross-country estimates are capturing the effects of omitted
variables. He then uses the predicted trade volumes to identify the effect of trade on income, obtaining plausible estimates of the effects of trade in goods on income that are
not subject to the omitted variable bias of the Frankel and Romer (1999) study. Also, in
spite of progress, this literature still has to solve the "distance puzzle" for low-income
countries first uncovered by Leamer and Levinsohn (1995).[4] Bergstrand et al. (2015) do
find evidence of decreasing international trade costs relative to internal trade costs for
40 (mostly developed) countries and 8 manufacturing sectors. Persisting high internal
trade costs in low-income countries are likely to hamper their participation in international trade in spite of falling international trade costs. As an example, based on micro
consumer price data, Atkin and Donaldson (2015) estimate that the log of distance on
internal trade costs is about four times higher in Ethiopia and Nigeria than in the United
States and that all the benefits from a reduction in price go to intermediaries rather than
to the final consumers. For low-income countries, more reliable estimates of trade costs
may be obtained by disaggregated estimates at the sectoral level, as in Bergstrand et al.
(2015), but further insights on trade costs from gravity-based estimates of trade will have
to wait until we have better estimates of internal versus external trade costs.

In sum, macro evaluations of trade costs, most based on the gravity model, cannot
escape the problem of attribution as they generally lack a convincing counterfactual
macro evaluation of trade costs. The studies have also had difficulty disentangling the
different components of trade costs (hard or soft infrastructure, at or behind-the-border
policies) and the links with the institutional environment. Reviewing the evidence,
Goldberg and Pavcnik (2016) conclude that the growing perception that trade policy is no
longer relevant is largely due to our inability to measure the various forms of nontariff
barriers that have replaced tariffs as the primary tools of policy, including in many developing countries.

Finally, more directly linked to our preoccupations, a large literature establishes that
domestic contracting institutions have a strong impact on the current pattern of comparative advantage across manufacturing sectors. As an indication of the overall importance of

contracting institutions on the pattern of comparative advantage, Nunn and Trefler report results on the correlates of bilateral trade in manufactures at the two-digit ISIC level for a group of 83 countries. The regressors include the traditional Hecksher-Ohlin determinants of bilateral trade along with indicators of the contract intensity (product market, labor market, and financial markets) of sectoral production. When entered interactively with indicators of governance as captured by the rule of law of Kaufmann et al. (2003), these indicators of contract intensity all enter significantly. Several indicators of contract intensity are as important quantitatively as the traditional indicators of comparative advantage (see table 4 in Kaufmann et al. 2003).[5] One would also expect that the quality of contracting institutions matters for the observed concentration of exports in low-income countries and probably also matters for the short life of their exports.[6]

8.3. TRADE AGREEMENTS

Trade agreements are the most common TRI. When the General Agreement on Tariffs and Trade (GATT) started multilaterally regulating international trade relations in 1947, it only had 23 members. A large majority were high-income countries with a few middle-income countries and no low-income country. Today GATT's successor, the World Trade Organization (WTO), has 164 members (as of July 2016) with another 16 countries currently negotiating accession. This leaves only 17 countries outside the WTO system, of which the largest are Ethiopia, Eritrea, North Korea, Somalia, and Turkmenistan. Figure 8.1(a) shows that trade openness has grown equally among members and non-members and figure 8.1(b) shows a growth in membership following the creation of the WTO.

Preferential Trade Agreements (PTAs) have also proliferated since the early 1990s.[7] Table 8.1 shows the current landscape of PTAs. One sees a very large number of PTAs among developing countries (henceforth South-South) in both goods and services. Interestingly, membership has expanded beyond regional or "natural" partners.[8] Since the signing of NAFTA in 1994, PTAs between developed and developing countries (henceforth North-South) have also become more common, as can be seen in table 8.1.

The rapid increase in WTO membership by developing countries and their rapidly growing participation in South-South and North-South PTAs are likely to have affected their development prospects through the insertion of their economies in global markets. Development prospects probably also evolved through the change in domestic institutions imposed by trade agreements, in particular after the creation of the WTO at the end of the Uruguay Round and the rapid growth in North-South trade agreements.

Indeed, until the completion of the Uruguay Round in 1994, international trade relations were largely governed by the GATT in a "live and let live" environment where disputes were resolved through diplomacy rather than rules-based dispute settlements. Low-income members in particular did not participate in the negotiations and could opt out of agreements.[9] Then, the primary function of the GATT was a forum to bring members to negotiate reciprocal tariff reductions (i.e., "shallow" integration) among members.

The advent of the WTO brought the single undertaking (i.e., all members including those wanting to gain membership had to sign all disciplines) and with it the obligation to grant not only trade concessions in goods (GATT), but also services (GATS), trade-related investment measures (TRIMS), intellectual property (TRIPS), customs procedures,

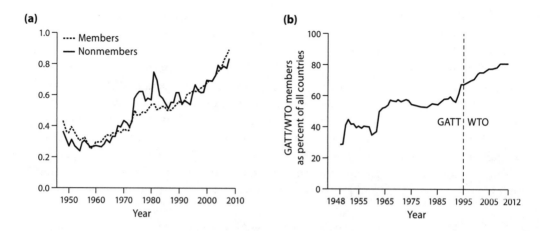

FIGURE 8.1. (a) Openness and (b) Membership Growth in the GATT/WTO. *Source*: Johns and Peritz (2015).

sanitary and phito-sanitary measures (SPS), and a dispute settlement understanding (DSU). The objective was to bring greater transparency in measures affecting trade and to house a forum to help resolve trade disputes among members. This new environment implies a much deeper integration among WTO members which imposes a new set of rules and institutions, particularly among developing countries. The fact that the number of developing country members kept growing is an indication of the applicants' perceived gains of membership in this new environment, and this in spite of the more stringent accession requirements.[10]

This growing application for membership could also reflect a "domino effect" first conjectured by Baldwin (1995) in the case of the successive enlargements of the EC. Being left out could result in less advantageous market access (i.e., facing a more elastic demand curve) or more difficulty in obtaining the required unanimity approval for WTO membership.

Similarly, in their review of regionalism at the time, Melo and Panagariya (1992) conjectured that, as opposed to the first wave of North-North and South-South RTAs (where most South-South RTAs were not implemented) during the 1960s and '70s, the new wave of RTAs, many of the North-South type, were likely to be welfare-improving. Drawing on the stylized outcomes of multilateralism under the GATT, Ethier (1998) sketches a theory confirming this conjecture. According to Ethier (1998), the second wave of North-South RTAs has allowed the reform-minded developing countries to buy deep links with large countries and has been complementary to multilateralism. On the other hand, several authors have raised concerns about the possibility that the institutional changes and regulations imposed by the Northern on their Southern partners may not be adequate to their level of development (Disdier et al. 2015; Wade 2003).

In the next subsection we look at what we know about the impact that both the WTO and RTAs have had on the development prospects of low-income countries: both directly on their trade flows with other countries, but also indirectly through changes in rules, institutions, and rent-seeking in low-income countries. We then turn to what we would like to know about the impact of the WTO and RTAs on the development prospects of these countries.

Table 8.1. Number of active PTAs, goods, goods and services, and regional type, 2010

	Goods	Goods & Services
Developed-Developed	13	9
Developed-Developing	36	40
Developing-Developing	145	41
Bilateral	104	64
Plurilateral	38	11
Plurilateral (At least 1 party is a PTA)	52	15
Intra-regional	110	33
Cross-regional	84	57

Source: WTO (2011, table B5). Active PTAs.

8.3.1. Trade Agreements (TA): What Do We Know?

Interdependence in the trading system implies that a government's actions affect outcomes abroad and each government would like others to take into account its concerns when setting policy. Such an outcome can only occur if there is all-around willingness to cooperate. The dominant literature about TAs, especially when it comes to empirical support, is that they are about correcting the damage (externalities) that countries inflict on their partners; call it terms-of-trade (TOT) manipulation or denial of market access.[11] Developed by Bagwell and Staiger (1999, 2002, 2010), it delivers two important results. First it shows that absent cooperation, countries will be caught in a prisoner's dilemma as they will seek to maximize their TOT. Second, reciprocity and MFN (most favored nation status), the two pillars of the GATT/WTO, are sufficient to remove this externality, even if countries have other motives than maximizing welfare as would be the case if the government's objective includes a certain distribution of income. In that case, by removing the terms-of-trade externality, reciprocity and MFN will deliver the politically optimum trade policy for each country.[12]

The TOT rationale for trade agreements has been confronted to the data and has found empirical support. Broda, Limão, and Weinstein (2008) find that over the period 1993–2000, non-GATT members impose higher tariffs where they have market power confirming the first result above. Simulations by Ossa (2014) also suggest that the observed tariff reductions under GATT/WTO are compatible with the TOT rationale for trade agreements. Indeed, Ossa (2014) calculates that the median Nash equilibrium in a multisector seven-region model would be as high as 58%, which corresponds to the magnitudes observed during the tariff wars of the 1930s when there was clearly no cooperation in tariff setting. Bagwell and Staiger (2011) provide evidence that the use of market power is neutralized upon WTO accession, which lends support for the second result above.

One could conclude from this literature that the WTO has been successful at internalizing TOT externalities. Two recent papers, however, suggest that TOT may not yet be fully internalized in the WTO, leaving room for further cooperation. Using a model with many exporters to a given market, Ludema and Mayda (2013) show that WTO importers may still be able to use their market power when setting tariffs. Free-riding by some exporters in tariff negotiations will result in MFN tariffs not being fully internalized.

Table 8.2. Tariff water in the WTO

	All goods	Agriculture	Manufacturing
All countries	0.11	0.26	0.09
High-income countries	0.07	0.25	0.05
Middle-income countries	0.16	0.23	0.16
Low-income countries	0.36	0.72	0.33

Source: Foletti et al. (2011).

They empirically show that WTO members with MFN tariffs exhibit their market power, particularly when they are facing exporters that are not heavily concentrated. Nicita, Olarreaga, and Silva (2018) use the fact that WTO members negotiate maximum tariffs (called tariff bindings) above which they cannot set their applied tariffs to show that whenever there is a difference between the tariff binding and the applied tariff (labeled tariff water), WTO members set their tariffs non-cooperatively. Given that tariff water exists in more than three-quarters of WTO members' tariff lines, this suggests that tariffs are rarely set cooperatively in the WTO. Bown (2015) further shows that future WTO accessions also lead to a reduction in applied tariffs for acceding and WTO members. These three papers tend to suggest that there is significant room for further internalizing TOT among WTO members. This is the view adopted by Bagwell, Bown, and Staiger (2016) in their survey of the TA literature.

The potential for low-income countries to further internalize their TOT is particularly large since the extent of tariff water in their WTO schedule is much larger. As table 8.2 illustrates, the amount of tariff water in low-income countries is on average five times larger than in high-income countries. For manufacturing goods, it is seven times larger and tariff water is 72% for agricultural goods in low-income countries. So, in principle, there is still significant scope for bringing low-income countries closer to a more cooperative behavior within the rules set by the WTO.

The problem with this view is that it implicitly assumes that low-income countries have market power. The empirical literature reviewed earlier tends to show that when low-income countries have market power, they will use it to set tariffs non-cooperatively if they are outside the WTO or if there is water in their tariff schedules. But using the estimates of export supply elasticity of the rest of the world, Nicita, Olarreaga, and Silva estimate that for the 12 low-income countries in their sample, the average optimal non-cooperative tariff is 0.9%—much smaller than the 53% estimated for major trading partners by Ossa (2014).[13] The internalization of the externalities caused by the use of such small market power is unlikely to provide a rationale for low-income countries to participate in trade agreements. So, to a large extent the mainstream theoretical and empirical literature for the existence of TAs seems orthogonal to the rationale for low-income countries to participate in TAs. Indeed, much of the growing evidence in testing the TOT theory of TAs reviewed by Bown (2015) relates to developed countries.

Among the other rationales for a TA, the commitment theory appears most applicable to developing countries. Initiated by Staiger and Tabellini (1987), the main contribution is by Maggi and Rodríguez-Clare (1998), who view TAs as a commitment device for governments vis-à-vis domestic lobbies. In a model where governments cannot credibly commit to the socially optimal policy, over-investment by producers in import-competing sectors will lead in equilibrium to overprotection of import-competing sectors. A TA then provides a credible commitment device through which governments tie their hands when facing import-competing lobbies.

To our knowledge, there is little empirical evidence supporting these predictions—a reflection that the predictions have not been confronted to the data so far.[14] There is, however, indirect evidence suggesting that the commitment theory may be the driving force. From an examination of data for all developing countries between 1980 and 2001, Tang and Wei (2009) find that GATT/WTO accession tends to raise income temporarily (growth and investment accelerate for 5 years, leading to an economy permanently larger by 20%), but only for those countries with poor governance, results supportive of the commitment explanation of TAs.

Extending the results of Tang and Wei (2009), Allee and Scalera (2012) examine the effects of different types of GATT/WTO accession negotiations on trade flows after classifying countries into three groups: early accession (33 members), automatic accession under the GATT for former colonies (65 members), and rigorous accessions (50 members) over the period 1950–2006.[15] In a panel in which exports are correlated with per capita GDP and other controls, they find robustly that countries that engaged in the greatest amount of accession-driven trade liberalization experience the greatest amount of trade increases after joining, while those that made little commitment to liberalization experience no trade increase. In all cases, trade gains decline over time. While the identification strategy deserves further scrutiny (endogeneity of GDP, omitted variable bias), their robustness to the measures of stringency of accession suggests that the modalities of GATT/WTO membership may be evidence of the importance of institutions on trade outcomes.

There is a conceptual problem with the theory that sees TA exclusively as a commitment device. It is not clear what would be the incentives for the trading partner to enforce the agreement. This is partly solved in Maggi and Rodríguez-Clare (2007), who put together the two rationales for TA: the TOT and the commitment device.[16] Yet a puzzle remains: what about low-income countries with very little market power? The credibility problem clearly gives this type of country incentives to sign TA with partners that have large market power and that would sanction them if they were to deviate from their commitments. But it is difficult to see the incentives for the large trading partner to enforce these agreements if the low-income country has no market power. And, without credible enforcement by the large trading partner, there is no credibility gain for the low-income country from the TA.[17]

However, it is possible that the Northern partner in a North-South TA would have an incentive to enforce the agreement with a low-income partner if the Northern partner wishes to build up a reputation with a view to establish future TAs with other Southern partners that also look for a TA as a commitment device. The Northern partner may then have an incentive to build such a reputation because it would allow it to build a "hub-and-spoke" network of TAs from which it could extract trade rents from the collection of smaller Southern partners. The many FTAs signed by the United States, each with its different set of rules of origin, and to a lesser extent with the EU FTAs, may fit this description.[18]

Note that this puzzle is stronger for multilateral TAs than for PTAs, which can explain why the WTO's Doha Round has made little progress, with developing countries often blocking progress or the negotiation of new agreements. In the case of PTAs, countries that have little market power in global markets may have stronger market power in regional markets. Broda et al. (2008) provide indirect evidence for this, showing that market power increases with the remoteness of the importer. More remote countries may trade in more segmented regional markets, which may give them some regional market power even though at the global level they do not enjoy much market power. The proliferation of South-South and North-South PTAs could then be explained by the combination of credibility and TOT arguments, as in Maggi and Rodríguez-Clare (2007).

Other factors have been important in the proliferation of South-South PTAs. In the first wave of PTAs in the 1960s and 1970s, the rationale for exploiting economies of scale through an exchange of market access to overcome the very small domestic market was important.[19] These early attempts at exchanges of market access through PTAs failed to fulfill expectations because of the lack of complementarities across partners and the lack of compensation funds at the regional level for adjustment among partners with very different levels of development (Foroutan 1992).[20] And for Sub-Saharan Africa, newly acquired political independence and the quest for consolidating national sovereignty were also strong.[21]

Table 8.3 describes the main RTAs currently active in Africa along with the membership and objectives stated in the treaties. As pointed out by skeptics of the main theories of TAs discussed above, none of the economic rationales discussed above (TOT or market access, enhanced credibility) are mentioned. Rather, political motives and "deep integration" appear among the most cited motives.[22] The membership shows a sharp heterogeneity in geographical and economic characteristics (resource-rich and resource-poor, landlocked and coastal, large and small).

In principle these sharp geographical disparities signal a potential for large benefits from economic integration. At the same time, with a very heterogeneous membership, there is a trade-off between the benefits of common policies which depend on the extent of cross-border policy spillovers and their costs, which depends on the extent of policy preference differences across member countries. Common decision-making internalizes the spillovers, but it moves the common policy away from its preferred national policy (i.e., a loss of national sovereignty). In Africa, spillovers are important as transport and communications infrastructure are under-provided, but the ethnolinguistic diversity across "artificial" borders suggests strong differences in policy preferences hindering the supply of public goods through the adoption of common regional policies.

The new South-South and North-South PTAs launched since the Uruguay Round have gone deeper and have tried to address the lack of complementarities and lack of compensation funds of the early South-South PTAs of the 1970s and 1980s. They also seem to have been somewhat more successful at promoting intra-regional trade than the early PTAs.

Table 8.4 classifies South-South PTAs along two dimensions: depth and breadth, following the lines in Horn, Mavroidis, and Sapir (2010), who distinguish between provisions covered by the WTO (called WTO+) and undertakings that extend beyond WTO provisions (called WTO-X). For both, they distinguish if the coverage is likely to be legally enforceable or not, which they call "legal inflation." Whereas their classifications cover EU and US PTAs and lead them to conjecture that these PTAs are a way to impose their regulatory standards on Southern partners (see below), table 8.4 only reports measures for PTAs involving a small sample of 21 South-South PTAs.

Table 8.3. Main Preferential Trade Agreements in Africa

Abbreviation	Name of RTA	Type of Agreement	Members	Year Originated	Year Agreement Signed	Objective
AMU (11.56)	Arab Maghreb Union	Free Trade Area	Algeria, Libya, Mauritania, Morocco, Tunisia	1988	1989	- Economic and political unity among Maghreb countries.
Agadir (21.66)	Agadir Agreement	Free Trade Area	Egypt, Jordan, Morocco, Tunisia	2001	2004	- Establish an FTA among members prior to a Euro-Mediterranean FTA as envisaged in the Barcelona Process. - Boost competitiveness of their products into European Union (EU) markets; expand cooperation, commercial exchange, and free trade between members. - Agadir Agreement spectrum includes customs, services, certificates of origin, government purchases, financial dealings, preventive measures, intellectual property, standards and specifications, dumping, and mechanisms to resolve conflicts.
EMCC/ CEMAC (6.24)	Economic and Monetary Community of Central Africa	Customs & Monetary Union	Cameroon, Central African Republic (L), Chad (L), Congo, Equatorial Guinea, Gabon	1959[1]	1994	- Create a common market based on the free movement of people, goods, capital, and services. - Ensure a stable management of the common currency. - Secure environment for economic activities and business in general. - Harmonize regulations of national sectoral policies

Table 8.3. (*continued*)

Abbreviation	Name of RTA	Type of Agreement	Members	Year Originated	Year Agreement Signed	Objective
COMESA (8.04)	Common Market for Eastern and Southern Africa	Customs Union	Burundi (L), Comoros, DR Congo, Djibouti, Egypt, Eritrea, Ethiopia (L), Kenya, Libya, Madagascar, Malawi (L), Mauritius, Rwanda (L), Seychelles, Sudan, Swaziland (L), Uganda (L), Zambia (L), Zimbabwe (L)	1965[2]	1993	- Achieve sustainable economic and social progress in all Member States through increased cooperation and integration in all fields of development, particularly in trade, customs, and monetary affairs, transport, communication and information, technology, industry and energy, gender, agriculture, environment and natural resources.
EAC (12.07)	East Africa Community	Customs Union	Burundi (L), Kenya, Rwanda (L), Tanzania, Uganda (L)		1999	- Widen and deepen cooperation among Partner States in, among others, political, economic, and social fields for their mutual benefit. To this extent the EAC countries established a Customs Union in 2005 and a Common Market in 2010. Enter into a Monetary Union and ultimately become a Political Federation of the East African States.
ECOWAS (7.23)	Economic Community of West African States	Trade, Currency, Political Union	Benin, Burkina Faso (L), Cape Verde, Côte d'Ivoire, Gambia, Ghana, Guinea, Guinea Bissau, Liberia, Mali (L), Niger (L), Nigeria, Senegal, Sierra Leone, Togo	1965[3]	1975/1993	- Achieve a common market and a single currency. Provide for a West African parliament, an economic and social council, and an ECOWAS court of justice to replace the existing Tribunal and enforce Community decisions. The treaty also formally assigned the Community with the responsibility of preventing and settling regional conflicts.

Organization	Type	Year	Members	Objectives
PAFTA (9.45) Pan-Arab Free Trade Area	Free Trade Area	1997	Bahrain, Egypt, Iraq, Jordon, Kuwait, Lebanon, Libya, Morocco, Oman, Palestine, Qatar, Saudi Arabia, Sudan, Syria, Tunisia, United Arab Emirates, Yemen	- Elimination of customs duties and other fees and duties having similar effects. - Eliminate all non-tariff barriers, including Administrative, Monetary, Financial, and Technical barriers. - Preferential treatment for least developed member states.
SACU (21.07) Southern African Customs Union	Customs & Monetary Union	1910[3]	Botswana (L), Lesotho (L), Namibia, South Africa, Swaziland (L)	- Facilitate the cross-border movement of goods between the territories of the Member States. - Create effective, transparent and democratic institutions to ensure equitable trade benefits to Member States. - Promote conditions of fair competition in the Common Customs Area and investment opportunities.
SADC (11.45) Southern African Development Community	Free Trade Area	1996	Angola, Botswana (L), Lesotho (L), Malawi (L), Mauritius, Mozambique, Namibia, South Africa, Swaziland (L), Tanzania, Zambia (L), Zimbabwe (L)	- Enhance growth and poverty alleviation; support the socially disadvantaged through Regional Integration. - Evolve common political values, systems, and institutions; promote and defend peace and security. - Promote self-sustaining development on the basis of collective self-reliance and the inter-dependence of Member States. - Achieve complementarity between national and regional strategies and programs.

(continued)

Table 8.3. (continued)

Abbreviation	Name of RTA	Type of Agreement	Members	Year Originated	Year Agreement Signed	Objective
SADC (11.45) (continued)						- Achieve sustainable utilization of natural resources and effective protection of the environment. - Strengthen and consolidate historical, social, and cultural affinities.
WAEMU / UEMOA (10.33)	West African Economic and Monetary Union	Customs & Monetary Union	Benin, Burkina Faso (L), Côte d'Ivoire, Guinea-Bissau, Mali (L), Niger (L), Senegal, Togo		1994	- Increase competitiveness through open markets; rationalize and harmonize the legal environment. - Convergence of macroeconomic policies and coordination of sectoral policies; create a Common Market. - The coordination of sectoral policies.
GCC (8.92)	Gulf Cooperation Council	Political & Economic Union	Bahrain, Kuwait, Oman, Qatar, Saudi Arabia, United Arab Emirates		1981	- Formulate similar regulations in religious, finance, trade, customs, tourism, legislation, and administration. Establish a common currency.

Source: WTO RTA database. Melo and Tsikata (2015, table 1).

Note: 1. Creation of Equatorial Customs Union; 2. Creation of Preferential Trade Area for Eastern and Southern Africa; 3. First agreement signed; 4. Creation of Southern African Development Community; (L) for landlocked members. Figures in parentheses are the Trade Complementarity Index of the respective RTAs at the year of agreement signed. In comparison, European Common Market has a TCI of 41.71 in 1962; Mercosur 24.21 in 1994; NAFTA 58.02 in 1994.

Table 8.4. Depth and breadth of measures in a selection of developing-country RTAs

		Breadth						
		Type of trade		Technology	Factors of production			
		Goods	Goods & Services	Innovation & IPR	Investment & Capital	Labor	All
Depth	Tariffs (τ)	1.00	0.48	0.57	0.62	0.38	0.33
	τ & NTBs	1.00	0.48	0.57	0.62	0.38	0.33
	τ & BTB policies	0.90	0.47	0.58	0.63	0.37	0.32
	τ & other policies	0.38	0.75	0.88	0.88	0.88	0.75
	All	0.33	0.71	0.86	0.86	0.86	0.71

Source: Authors calculations from data in the WTO Trade Report (2011).
Notes: Share of Agreements that cover different combinations of depth (columns) and breadth (rows) measures. An RTA covers a type of measure if at least one of the measures in that category is covered. NTB = Non-tariff barriers (export taxes, SPS, TBT, STE, AD, CVM); BTB = Behind-the-border (state aid, government procurement, TRIMs, TRIPs, competition policy). Technology (TRIPs, IPR, Innovation policies, Research and Technology). Labor (Labor Market regulation, Social matters, illegal immigration, visa, and asylum) Other policies: see Maggi (2016, table A1). Sample: 21 South-South trade agreements selected on the basis of per capita income.

The table shows that, on paper at least, objectives extend beyond the "shallow" integration objectives of removing tariffs, with half including market access in Services markets as well.[23] An interesting issue is whether this taxonomy can inform on how breadth and depth interact and if those interactions are different across different types (North-North, North-South, and South-South) of PTAs. Is the depth of policy cooperation deeper when the agreement is broader? The sample is too small to answer such a question, but there is a need for a better understanding of the interaction between depth and breadth in the design of South-South and North-South TAs as well as their development impact.

The rapid increase in PTAs since the 1990s has led to an extensive literature on the impact that their growth has on the GATT and WTO. At a time when the Uruguay Round negotiations were stalled and the United States had just begun entering the fray of Regional Trade Agreements (RTAs), Bhagwati (1992) launched a "stumbling block vs building block" literature. For developing countries that are the main beneficiaries of an open trading system, so far at least, if the proliferation of (successful?) RTAs may have slowed down (halted?) multilateral negotiations, they have not led to an increase in protection against non-members (Freund and Ornelas 2010; Baldwin 2014). Most studies have concluded that RTAs have not been a stumbling block.[24]

The issue, however, is what role is left for multilateralism and the WTO in this new environment. Baldwin (2014) suggests that there is a need for new rules for cooperation in the WTS that will lead to deeper constraints on national policies (and hence on national sovereignty) than those under the WTO. PTAs or issue-oriented plurilaterals would then be the best avenue for carrying out this task, as agreement on these deeper constraints is more likely to be reached among a smaller number of negotiating members.[25] The risk with the development of PTAs and issue-oriented plurilaterals to tackle deeper issues such as investment, labor, social, and environmental clauses that are outside the WTO system is that they may leave low-income countries on the sidelines, which may hurt their development prospects or lead them to upgrade their regulatory standards to the Northern partners' at the expense of trade with non-bloc Southern partners (see below).

8.3.1.1. The Development Impact of TAs

With the Single Undertaking, the creation of the WTO signaled a clear break from the "live and let live" days of the GATT, a kind of natural experiment on institutional development for developing countries as they acquired rights and had to take on obligations, although they usually did not have to reduce tariffs substantially upon joining the WTO. A large literature has tried to detect a GATT/WTO effect in gravity models, and of participation in PTAs mostly using a dummy for participation in the TA (GATT/WTO or PTA) often yielding mixed results. We review the main findings below, referring to Limão (2016) for more detailed discussion.[26]

Using a panel gravity specification with multilateral resistance terms, Subramanian and Wei (2007) looked for breaks in the data upon membership to the WTO. They found that the WTO resulted in a large but uneven impact on world trade with the developed countries that participated more actively in reciprocal negotiations than developing countries gaining the most. Not surprisingly, manufacturing exporters were also found to benefit more than agricultural exporters as import barriers in agriculture were subject to "dirty" tarification resulting in very little actual liberalization for agricultural goods during the Uruguay Round.[27] Eicher and Henn (2011) reclassified the dummy variables to distinguish WTO membership from PTAs, both among WTO members and among non-members. They also found heterogeneity in the WTO effects, with modest effects of WTO accession for countries that had higher imports and thus higher potential market power and initial tariffs. Limão extends the data to 2010, also separating WTO and PTA membership. In all estimates reported in his table 2, the WTO effect remains positive, though it is reduced when controlling for bilateral PTAs. He also obtains that the estimated effects of all PTAs and WTO membership are significantly larger after 10 years (about twice as large). So the latest theory-consistent gravity model estimates that belonging to GATT/WTO reduces trade costs.[28]

Turning to PTA membership, Maggi (2014, table 2) reports high average trade cost reduction estimates of 15% given that WTO (2011) estimates average preferential margins at 2.1%. Taking into account the AVE of Non-tariff Barriers (NTBs), he shows that the estimates are still on the high side and sees a trade elasticity puzzle. He then convincingly argues and gives evidence that this puzzle can be partially accounted for once we take into account the uncertainty that PTAs (or WTO's tariff bindings) solve. Handley and Limão (2015) provide evidence of the quantitatively large impact associated with the reduction of the uncertainty brought by PTAs and tariff bindings in the case of Portugal's and Spain's accession to the EC. Interestingly, when they distinguish between reciprocal and non-reciprocal PTAs like the GSP, they find no effect for the non-reciprocal PTAs that are typically shrouded by uncertainty.[29] So the conclusion of these gravity results is that the estimated increases in trade reflect other PTA-related effects like a reduction in trade policy uncertainty that go beyond reduction in tariffs and NTBs.

As discussed above, the creation of the WTO and the new South-South and North-South PTAs since the mid-1990s have also gone much deeper in terms of commitments, which imply not only changes in trade policies (e.g., removal of NTBs like voluntary export restraints), but also a costly-to-implement change in domestic institutions for low-income countries since the agreements under the Single Undertaking of the WTO were largely at the insistence of developed countries (see estimates in Finger 1999 and Finger and Shuler 2000). Deep PTAs also imply institutional changes. We review both, starting first with the WTO agreements.

The multilateral Customs Valuation Agreement (CVA) is an institutional development that aims at curbing tax evasion and corruption at customs. The links between trade policy and customs corruption have been studied extensively, though no general conclusion emerges from the studies reviewed here. Gatti (1999) and Fisman and Wei (2004) show how tariff dispersion helps corruption. Using answers on bribes from a random sample of shipments to ports in South Africa (Durban) and Mozambique (Maputo), Djankov and Sequeira (2014) show that the probability (and amount) of bribes is higher in Maputo, where there is interaction between clearing agents and customs officials, than in Durban where there isn't any. They distinguish between cost-reducing "collusive" bribes that reduce uncertainty and cost-raising "coercive" bribes resulting from having to pay for access to a port service. In a follow-up study drawing on Mozambique's tariff reform, Sequeira (2016) shows that the reform reduced the probability of collusive bribes relative to coercive bribes that were still possible because of the monopsonistic position of clearing agents. Jong and Bogmans (2011) show that general corruption reduces trade, but that corruption at customs helps trade (greasing wheel effect). Dutt and Traça (2010) show that corruption helps trade when tariffs are high. Anson, Cadot, and Olarreaga (2006) show that pre-shipment inspections may increase corruption as it provides information to corrupt customs officials (also see Yang 2008). Javorcik and Narciso (2017) show how the CVA led to a shift in tax evasion and corruption from under-invoicing to a reclassification of goods. Thus, the general conclusion from the literature suggests that, while the CVA has addressed some of the problems associated with customs corruption, it may have created others.

Other WTO agreements, such as the Trade-Related Investment Measures (TRIMS) or Trade-Related Intellectual Property (TRIPS), have put constraints in terms of the type of industrial and protection policies countries can use to protect intellectual property. In the case of TRIMS, local content requirements are banned where some may argue that in some industries (renewable energies), some degree of local content can help with technology transfers. The TRIPS agreement has also aimed at enforcing more stringent intellectual property laws in developing countries, and an important literature has explored the impact of TRIPS signing and how these new WTO agreements have shrunk the "development space" of developing countries as countries are faced with a smaller number of policies to choose from (Wade 2003; Fink and Maskus 2005; Finger and Schuler 2004).

Another important development of the WTO is the creation of a strong dispute-settlement mechanism that could, in principle, be favorable to developing countries as the trading system is moving away from a power-based resolution of conflicts toward a rule-based regime. Bown (2009) reviews bilateral trade disputes over the period 1995–2011. Compliance with rulings has been very high. The WTO has thus "established itself as one of the most, if not the most, successful international organizations in terms of enforcement and dispute settlement" (Maggi 2014). This is important because, if credibility is the motive for low-income countries to join the WTO, a strong enforcement mechanism is necessary. At the same time, it is noteworthy that in their review of the trade dispute settlements over 1995–2009, Bown and Reynolds (2017) find that they concur with the TOT theory for high-income countries, leading them to ponder "what specific purposes developing countries have in mind when they sign onto Trade Agreements like the WTO."

Labor, social, and environmental clauses in TAs can also have consequences on the development prospects of low-income countries. Developing countries have historically been hostile to the introduction of labor and environmental standards in the WTO because of the induced reduction in competitiveness for their exports, and the risk of labor, social, or environmental clauses being used as a protectionist instrument by more advanced members. This line of reasoning is based on a static view of comparative advantage and institutions that ignores the two-way causality between comparative advantage and institutions. More stringent labor, social, and environmental regulation in low-income countries "imposed" by a TA can help shift their comparative advantage toward sectors with higher growth potential.

If developing countries have been reluctant to embrace labor, social, and environmental regulations at the multilateral level, they have been introduced in North-South PTAs. Since NAFTA, many PTAs involving the QUAD (i.e., Canada, the EU, Japan, and the United States) have included labor, social, and environmental clauses as well as investment and sometimes competition agreements.[30] As documented by Horn, Mavroidis, and Sapir (2010), the depth of integration in the EU and US PTAs has extended well beyond negotiations at the WTO, often on North-South basis. South-South PTAs have also grown rapidly, but the delegation of authority necessary to support "deep" integration that would contribute to institution-building has not occurred.[31]

Beyond the potentially positive impact that these clauses may have on the shift of comparative advantage of low-income countries, they can also help unblock the political equilibria imposed by a strong political minority. Polaski (2004) provides an interesting example of how the labor clause in the US-Cambodia Trade and Investment Framework Agreement was used by the government of Cambodia to introduce more labor-friendly legislation in terms of working conditions and minimum wages against lobbying by owners of large Cambodian firms in the apparel sector. Interestingly, the US-Cambodia agreement offered stronger tariff preferences into the US market for Cambodian firms that satisfy social and labor regulations. Thus, instead of sanctioning Cambodian apparel exporters for not complying with the social and labor clauses, it provided more generous preferences to those who complied. Whether to rely on carrots or sticks to enforce institutional decisions is a topic that deserves further attention. The issue of whether sectoral or economy-wide regulations should be imposed should also be further investigated. It is unclear which is preferable. In the presence of sectoral social and labor clauses, there is a risk of worsening labor conditions in other sectors. In the presence of economy-wide labor and social clauses, there is the risk of sanctioning firms and sectors with adequate work conditions for the exploitation of workers in other firms or sectors.

In the last 50 years, environmental issues have emerged globally to the point that the original Bretton Woods architecture (GATT/IMF/World Bank) and environmental issues are now inextricably linked. In a linked climate-trade-finance global policy coordination structure, climate and more generally the sustainability of the environment (e.g., biodiversity, deforestation) now need to be added to the global policy bargaining set. A shift at the WTO from a negative contract to a positive contract offers the prospect of potentially stronger trade disciplines (for instance through the setting up of plurilateral trade agreements).[32] These institutional challenges are beyond the scope of this chapter but deserve attention.

Differences in property rights regimes are an externality that can be a source of comparative advantage. The opportunity to trade can also influence the quality of institutions and, as in all cases of second-best, the opportunity to trade can be welfare-reducing. Along the lines of Chichilnisky (1994), in a model where property rights are endogenously determined and depend on enforcement policies, Copeland and Taylor (2009) show that the opportunity to trade can alleviate or worsen the tragedy of the commons. They show that in general an opening to trade will lead to an enforcement of property rights as the opportunity cost of labor engaged in the extraction of natural resources goes up. Depending on the pattern of technological progress in resources extraction and in the technology for monitoring illegal harvesters, resource depletion may increase or fall. They give several examples of both instances.[33]

Environmental degradation and conflict are clearly linked to trade in weak institutional environments and with the opportunity to trade, a topic that will presumably be covered in other contributions to this project (see Collier 2010; Berman et al. 2017). Collier and Venables (2010) and Ruta and Venables (2013) review the institutional reforms at the multilateral level that would improve the protection of natural resource assets in weak institutional environments.

Finally, there is growing literature on the impact of TAs on conflict and war. It is well-known that the original motives behind the creation of the European Community after World War II were to diffuse the threat of future military conflicts. Low-income countries, many abundant in natural resources, are prone to conflicts, and political cooperation has also been high among the objectives of these regional trade blocs (see table 8.3).[34] The experience of RTAs around the world supports the view that economics and politics are complements (rather than substitutes, as argued by the defenders of multilateralism). RTAs reduce the probability of war through two channels. First, trade-creating exchange takes place, increasing the opportunity cost of war. Second, as political scientists have argued, sufficiently "deep" RTAs reduce information asymmetries as partners know each other better. Then incentives for countries not to report their true options in an attempt to extract concessions are reduced. Discussions among members spill over to political issues, diffusing political disputes that could escalate into political conflicts. These two channels reduce the probability of costly conflicts. By the same token, globalization that involves a shift of trade toward distant partners reduces this opportunity cost, increasing the likelihood of conflicts.

Martin et al. (2008) build these insights into a bargaining model where rational states will enter into an RTA if the expected economic gains from trade creation and the security gains resulting from the decrease in the probability of disputes degenerating into war exceed the political costs of entering the RTA. Using data covering the 1950–2000 period, they find support for the hypothesis that increased bilateral trade deters bilateral war because it increases the opportunity cost of war, while multilateral openness has the opposite effect. In subsequent work based on the same data, Martin et al. (2012) find support for their theory of PTA formation: country pairs with large economic gains from RTAs and high probability of conflict are more likely to sign an RTA.

8.3.2. Trade Agreements and Development: What Would We Like to Know?

The survey of the literature on TAs and development in the previous section suggests at least five avenues for future research. First, with border protection levels having fallen worldwide, regional integration is no longer about an exchange of market access (at the expense of outsiders) but about "deep" behind-the-border reforms leading to increased integration. Labor, social, and environmental standards, competition and investment policies, and institutions are increasingly at stake, in particular when looking at North-South trade agreements where the potential for external enforcement is probably larger. A better understanding and assessment of the trade and development implications of these deeper agreements is needed. Are labor, social, and environmental clauses "imposed" for protectionist reasons in North-South agreements? How do they impact domestic institutions in low-income countries? And do they help the development prospects of low-income countries by shifting their comparative advantage toward sectors with higher growth potential?

Second, with a stalled Doha Round of trade negotiations in the WTO, it is clear that RTAs have become the more dynamic institution regulating international trade, even though the dispute settlement mechanisms of the WTO have also been very active. A first issue of interest is whether or not, as questioned by Bagwell, Bown, and Staiger (2016), the WTO is "passé" and, if not, what can the WTO do for low-income countries that they cannot get (or get better than) through their membership in PTAs. Another is a finer knowledge of the landscape of these PTAs, extending the methodology of Horn, Mavroidis, and Sapir (2010) to the large sample of South-South PTAs. How does the depth and breadth trade-off affect the impact of PTAs in low-income countries?[35] In their review of the bilateral PTAs of the EU and the United States with Southern partners, after controlling for "legal inflation" in the EU PTAs, Horn, Mavroidis, and Sapir (2010) conjecture that the ground-breaking provisions (i.e., their WTO-X provisions not included in the agenda of the WTO negotiations) related to regulatory issues suggests that these agreements are about exporting their regulatory approaches to their PTA partners.[36] Disdier et al. (2015) provide evidence that the harmonization of technical barriers to trade by the Southern partner to the Northern partner's standards increases its exports to the North and leads to trade deflection with the South. We need to know more about whether harmonization to less costly to implement international (rather than to Northern regional) standards would likely be preferable for Southern partners, who would then avoid getting trapped in a hub-and-spoke structure with the Northern partner. An in-depth analysis of the consequences of dispute settlement bodies in bilateral and regional TAs is also missing. In particular the proliferation of State-Investor arbitration courts, where foreign firms can challenge governments outside the national judicial system, need to be examined. They clearly protect foreign investors, and provide a clear legal framework, but there is anecdotal evidence that these arbitrators associated with bilateral trade or investment agreements have often overruled national regulators and legislators (Estache and Phillippe 2016).[37] The extent to which these arbitration courts provide an opportunity for legal forum shopping and an associated increase in judiciary uncertainty deserves further study.

Third, while we have a relatively good handle on the motivations for trade agreements among large developed countries, it is less so for small developing countries. The credibility and commitment channel of Maggi and Rodríguez-Clare provides a promising avenue for understanding their participation in TAs, but we have little empirical support for its predictions that would help us assess the importance of this channel, and in which type of countries/situations/institutions they are more likely to play a more important role. Also, while the theory explains why the developing country wants to commit to a TA, it is unclear why the developed country participates at all in the agreement. Other papers have explored this issue through linkage (Limão 2007) where the North has non-economic objectives (fight against terrorism or drugs), but it still does not explain why the North may want to enforce the agreements for other trade-related policies. Without any credible enforcement from the North, the South will not solve its time-inconsistency problems with a TA. This sits at odds with the rapid growth in low-income country membership in the WTO in spite of accession requirements becoming tougher. Signaling, fear of domino effects, and the role that uncertainty may play in the decision to join a TA are probably interesting research avenues in this area.

Fourth, if most of the evidence on PTAs and trade policies toward non-members seems to support the view that PTAs are complementary to multilateralism, this evidence hardly covers low-income countries. Thus, in Africa, when ECOWAS recently moved to a CU, at the insistence of Nigeria, a five-band tariff-structure was adopted, suggesting a protectionist stance especially in view of the tariff overhang among members. Studies on the consequences of integration on trade policy toward non-members along the lines of those reviewed above are needed for low-income countries.

Fifth, we now have more than two decades of experience with reciprocal North-South PTAs and only a few evaluations.[38] None are on reciprocal PTAs with low-income countries. The EU's current negotiations go beyond the Deep and Comprehensive FTAs (DCF-TAs) currently under negotiation between the EU and Southern and Eastern neighbors: they also include the Economic Partnership Agreements (EPAs) with ACPs. For most members, the EPA partnerships apparently bring little. There is no market access for LDCs, rules of origin are still complex and they include some "deep" provisions beyond multilateral negotiations, and it is unclear whether these provisions are legally enforceable, or whether they mostly reflect "legal inflation." Is institution-building really among the motivations for these agreements as often claimed? Did the costs associated with negotiating the deep African RTAs (SACU, CEMAC, and UEMOA), which were borne by colonizers, lay the foundations for more intensive trade later on? Increased trade among members would have raised the opportunity cost of future wars among members by increasing their interdependence along the lines suggested by Martin et al. (2008, 2012) and by Mayer and Thoenig (2016). At the same time, much trade in Africa involves insecure goods that require resource-using protection, altering the usual calculus of the gains from trade. In that environment, as shown by Garfinkel et al. (2015), autarky may be preferred to free trade.

8.4. TRADE PROMOTION ORGANIZATIONS

Important externalities are associated with the gathering of foreign market information related to consumer preferences, business opportunities, quality and technical requirements, etc. Private firms alone will not provide sufficient foreign market information, as companies hesitate to incur research and marketing costs that can also benefit competitors. The same logic applies to pioneer exporters, who make a considerable investment in attempts to discover what works in foreign markets, cultivating contacts, establishing distribution chains, and other costly activities that can be directly or indirectly used by their rivals (Hausmann and Rodrik 2003). The uncertainty associated with trading across markets with different regulations, weak institutions, and the overall lack of familiarity with foreign markets hurt exporters (Araujo, Mion, and Ornelas 2016). Trade promotion Organizations (TPOs) can provide this information without having each firm paying the cost of acquiring the necessary information.[39] In small developing countries, being able to fulfill the large and diversified demand of importers in world markets will require some form of coordination across firms. Especially in low-income countries where credit constraints are significant, TPOs can help small and medium-size firms cooperate to satisfy large demands in world markets.[40]

Whether market failures come from externalities associated with foreign market information, discoveries by pioneer exporters, the absence of private insurance schemes, or coordination failures, they all support the case for government intervention to help domestic firms fully participate in international markets (Copeland 2008). Since the beginning of the twentieth century, governments have addressed this type of market failure with TPOs that mainly aim at internalizing information spillovers and solving coordination failures.

While some of these market failures could be privately addressed through intermediaries or privately funded agencies, the presence of positive externalities that can go beyond the group of firms that directly benefit from their programs implies that, if left to the private sector, the type of services offered by these TPOs will be underprovided. A private association of exporting firms will address the market failure associated with information spillovers for firms within the association, but when spillovers affect firms outside the association it will again be the source of inefficiencies. Here we focus on government sponsored TPOs. Section 8.5 addresses the role of private TRIs.

The early literature in the late 1980s and early 1990s was quite critical of TPOs. Kedia and Chhokar (1986), for example, found that export promotion programs in the United States have little impact, largely because of a lack of awareness in the private sector of the services that were offered by these government agencies. Keesing and Singer (1991) conducted a series of extensive interviews with senior officials at the ITC, European Commission, the Export Marketing Development Division of the Commonwealth Secretariat, and numerous TPOs in developing and developed countries. The conclusion was that TPOs had failed in promoting exports, except in a few East Asian countries (Singapore, Hong Kong, Korea, and Taiwan). The main reasons for this failure according to those interviewed by Keesing and Singer were the strong anti-trade bias embedded in most countries' trade regimes, the bureaucratic nature of these agencies that lacked client orientation and that were staffed with civil servants who were out of touch with their clients in the private sector, as well as their lack of leadership and adequate funding. The few successful cases of trade promotion (Singapore, Hong Kong, Korea, and Taiwan) all adopted more supply and enterprise-oriented strategies, as well as a more overall open trade regime.[41]

By the late 1990s, the strong bias against exports had vanished for most developing countries as trade reforms were put in place. This led many prominent development economists to adopt a more benign view of TPOs. In a study of how governments can promote nontraditional exports in Africa, one of Helleiner's main recommendations was to create an adequately funded TPO to help exporters overcome the costs and risks of entering unfamiliar and demanding international markets (Helleiner 2002). We now survey the more recent studies highlighting what we know before turning to knowledge gaps to be filled.

8.4.1. Trade Promotion: What Do We Know?

The recent literature on the impact of trade promotion can be divided into studies that use country-level information and studies that use firm-level data. We review both, starting with the macro-level studies.

8.4.1.1. Macro-econometric Studies

Rose (2005) uses a gravity framework where exports are explained by the traditional geographic determinants as well as by the presence of a diplomatic representation in the destination market. He convincingly argues that over the last decades, diplomatic representation has had a strong commercial component as other motives decline due to falling communication costs. Whereas before many political decisions were made by embassies, nowadays the speed of communication leads to a much more centralized decision-making process where the most important decisions are made in capitals and less politically oriented work is undertaken in embassies. Using an IV estimator where the presence of a diplomatic representation is instrumented using the country's importance as measured by proven oil reserves and its diplomatic attraction measured by the number of nice restaurants and sights, Rose finds that a consulate can increase bilateral exports by 6–10%.[42]

Following Rose (2005), several papers have tried to focus more directly on export promotion rather than embassies and look at the impact of export promotion agencies' representation abroad on exports. Volpe et al. (2012) use information on the location of branches of TPOs for several Latin American and Caribbean countries over the period 1995–2004 and find that the presence of these branches is associated with higher exports of differentiated goods. Hayakawa, Lee, and Park (2014) also find large effects for export promotion branches of Japan's and South Korea's TPOs.

But export promotion goes beyond office representation abroad. In fact only a fraction of TPOs have offices abroad. A World Bank TPO survey of 2010 reveals that only 41% of TPOs have offices abroad, and among low-income countries the share drops to 21%. There are many other large differences between low- and high-income countries' TPOs. In high-income countries, the median TPO budget represents 0.037% of GDP, and 0.021% in the median low-income country. The median TPO employs 191 workers in high-income countries and only 50 in the median low-income country.[43] In both income groups, the lion's share of funding comes from the government, with a small share from bilateral and multilateral donors in the low-income group.

Spending patterns are similar across both income groups, the largest share going to marketing (trade fairs and missions) with 10–25% of the budget allocated to export support services, country image, and market research. TPO budgets are also allocated to the same type of firms across both groups, with a greater focus on small and medium-size firms relative to large firms. In both groups of countries, TPOs also tend to spend a larger share of their budget on established exporters rather than on non-exporters or new exporters, and the relative importance given to established exporters is slightly higher in low-income countries.

Using the survey implemented by the World Bank in 2005, Lederman, Olarreaga, and Payton (2010) estimate an export equation with TPO's characteristics as explanatory variables. After instrumenting the export promotion budget with the number of years until the next election and the number of years since the TPO was created, and controlling for GDP per capita, trade restrictiveness at home and abroad, exchange rate volatility, and geographic determinants of exports, they estimate that the marginal impact of the export promotion budget on exports is around 0.04. Thus, in this cross-section, a 1% increase in export promotion budgets leads to a 0.04% increase in exports. At the sample mean, $1 spent on export promotion leads to $40 of additional exports. Interestingly, export promotion delivers larger gains where most needed, i.e., when facing stronger market access barriers abroad (tariff and nontariff barriers) or when exporting differentiated products rather than homogeneous goods.

In a panel from a follow-up survey conducted by the World Bank and by the European Trade Promotion Organization in 2010 and 2015, Olarreaga, Sperlich, and Trachsel (2016) control for unobserved heterogeneity by using country and year fixed effects. They estimate that, on average, a 1% increase in export promotion budgets results in an increase in exports of 0.074%, which is higher than the returns estimated by Lederman et al. (2010). At the sample mean, an additional dollar spent on export promotion yields $87 of exports.[44]

Next, they use a semi-parametric model where the coefficient measuring the returns to export promotion budgets depends on TPO characteristics to estimate which among the observable TPO characteristics yield larger returns. They found that having a larger share of private sector seats in the executive board, and a focus on established exporters and large and medium-size (rather than small) firms tend to raise export returns. A larger share of the budget funded by the government also tends to increase returns, except when it is getting close to being fully publicly funded. These results would suggest that for programs to be visible and generate externalities, they should probably be targeted to large established exporters, even if these may be the firms that least need assistance. As noted below, these exploratory results call for a better understanding of the trade-off between helping firms' needs and maximizing spillovers from TPO programs and are an avenue for future research if we want to understand how TPO programs should work.

Since the ultimate objective of export promotion is not to increase exports per se, but rather to increase economic and social well-being by addressing market failures associated with export activities, are the returns to export promotion in terms of GDP as large as the returns in terms of exports? Extending their semi-parametric model, Olarreaga et al. (2016) estimate the returns in terms of GDP per capita rather than exports. They find that on average a 1% increase in export promotion budgets generates a 0.065% increase in GDP per capita. These are very large returns.[45] At the sample mean, $1 spent on export promotion generates $384 in terms of GDP.

To explain such large returns one probably needs to move beyond learning-by-doing or learning-by-exporting for firms benefiting from the export promotion programs. Some sort of externality is needed where the benefits from export promotion are not limited to treated firms, but also affect firms that do not directly benefit from the program. Learning from the experiences of successful and unsuccessful exporters that benefit from export promotion programs can be one important mechanism through which non-exporters or exporters to other markets (or exporters of other products) can indirectly benefit from export promotion. In this case, small amounts in export promotion can have a large impact in terms of export growth. The even larger returns in terms of GDP could also partly reflect learning-by-doing. Firms benefiting from the program become more productive, and their growth does not only translate into larger exports, but also larger domestic sales.

Learning-by-doing or by-observing is not necessarily specific to the supply side: it can also occur on the demand side. As exporting firms become more successful in the export market, in the presence of asymmetric information about the quality of products, observing provides valuable information to domestic consumers regarding the quality and reputation of the firm and therefore increases the domestic demand for the products of exporting firms as shown by Shy (2000). Note that, as underlined by Copeland (2008), it is not clear that in such a setup, export promotion is welfare-increasing as there is probably too much exporting in the asymmetric information equilibrium. Therefore, understanding whether learning-by-observing occurs on the demand or supply side in the domestic economy has important welfare implications for export promotion that so far have not been explored.

To find out if the very large returns could be driven by very large returns in high-income countries, we run the same specification as in Olarreaga et al. (2016) but in a sample of low- and middle-income countries (with a GNP per capita in 2005 dollars below $12,736). Results are reported in table 8.5. We obtain returns as large as in the full sample if

Table 8.5. Returns to export promotion in low-income countries

	Log of Exports of Goods and Services					Log of GDP				
	(1)	(2)	(3)	(4)	(5)	(6)	(7)	(8)	(9)	(10)
Log of TPO Budget	0.051*	0.072**	0.061**	0.101**	0.086**	0.057**	0.056**	0.061**	0.051*	0.066**
	(0.022)	(0.027)	(0.022)	(0.031)	(0.020)	(0.014)	(0.017)	(0.013)	(0.023)	(0.028)
Log of Population	2.119**	1.666**	2.392**	1.780**	2.496**		0.223	0.853**	0.027	0.753**
	(0.507)	(0.503)	(0.507)	(0.434)	(0.441)		(0.342)	(0.284)	(0.299)	(0.241)
Log of TPO Budget*LIC			-.013**		-.014**			-.007**		-.007**
			(0.004)		(0.004)			(0.002)		(0.001)
# obs.	530	326	530	302	505	549	340	549	316	524
R^2	0.997	0.996	0.997	0.995	0.994	0.997	0.993	0.997	0.993	0.997

Source: Author's estimations.

Note: All regressions have country and year FE. Columns (1) to (3) and (6) to (9) are estimated using ordinary least squares. Columns (4) to (5) and (9) to (10) are estimated using the share of the executive board seats in the hands of the private sector and the share of public funding, as well as their interaction as instruments. Columns (1), (3), (5), (6), (8) and (10) used the entire sample. All other columns include only low- and middle-income countries (LIC) with a income per capita below USD 12,736. Robust standard errors are in parenthesis; * stands for significance at the 5 percent level and ** for significance at the 10 percent level.

not larger. Indeed, the export returns in the low- and middle-income sample in column (2) are larger than those in column (1), and the GDP per capita returns are very similar in the two samples when comparing columns (7) and (6). However, when we test for difference in returns by interacting a low- and middle-income country dummy with the TPO budget in the full sample, we tend to obtain smaller returns in low- and middle-income countries regardless of whether or not we instrument the TPO budget with TPO characteristics (share of public funding and share of seats in the executive board held by the private sector) as can be seen in columns (3), (5), (8), and (10).

Thus, returns to export promotion are on average lower in low- and middle-income countries, although the differences in average returns between high-income, and low- and middle-income countries is not very large. According to the IV estimates in columns (5) and (10), GDP per capita returns are on average 11% smaller, and export returns 16% smaller in low- and middle-income countries. One would expect higher returns in low-income countries. Attenuation bias, different characteristics of the export bundle resulting from weaker domestic institutions could explain these results. It could be that the returns to TPO funding are highest for middle-income countries with more contract-intensive export bundles. Note that these results are also limited by the sample size for low-income countries, so that one cannot label this a "TPO puzzle," but rather view these results as a call for further work before suggesting that there is room for improvement in TPO activities in low-income countries.[46]

It is also possible that low-income countries' TPO programs are not as efficient as their high-income countries' counterparts. Figure 8.2 contrasts the performance indicators used in the two groups of countries. In low-income countries, performance is evaluated in terms of the number of exporters and the value of exports, while in high-income countries the number of clients and client satisfaction surveys are used more frequently. Note that 96% of TPOs in high-income countries have formal client follow-up routines, whereas this is the case in only 72% of TPOs in low-income countries. Given that, as discussed above, a focus on exporters and export growth may be misleading when the ultimate objective of export promotion is income growth, a shift in low-income countries to the performance evaluation methods used in high-income countries may be desirable.

While the evidence of macro studies suggests that there may be large gains from export promotion in terms of both exports and real income, they clearly face the problem of omitted confounding factors which must certainly contribute to the large estimates reported in these studies. Moreover, it is almost impossible for these studies to identify the mechanisms through which these gains and externalities operate. Studies using firm-level data can deal better with confounding factors than macro studies and can provide greater internal validity.

8.4.1.2. Micro-econometric Studies

With greater internal validity, micro-econometric studies are complements to the macro studies. They help identify the externalities suggested by the large return estimates from the macro studies reviewed above and, more generally, identify the mechanisms through which different programs operate. They can also (at least sometimes) allow for a clearer identification strategy of the causal links between export promotion and exports or income growth. Most literature at the firm level has also found a positive impact of export promotion on exports. The early firm-level literature has used customs data and has

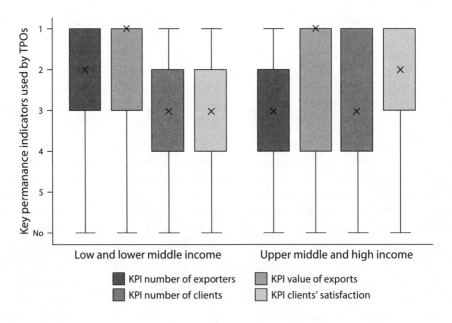

FIGURE 8.2. Distribution ofTPO measures of performance by Key Performance Indicator. *Note:*The median is indicated by x.The top of the box provides the 75th percentile of the distribution and the bottom of the box, the 25th percentile. The top and bottom whiskers provide the adjacent values to the 75th and 25th percentiles. *Source:* World Bank Survey ofTPO 2010.

found that firms that benefit from export promotion programs see improvements in their extensive margins as they export a larger number of products to a larger number of countries.

Volpe and Carballo (2008) use a matching difference-in-difference estimator in a sample of Peruvian exporting firms (customs data) and find that export promotion affects exports mainly through a firm's extensive margin in terms of both new export markets and new products, but has little impact on the intensive margin.

Volpe and Carballo (2010a) go beyond average effects of export promotion programs on exports and disentangle the impact of Prochile's programs on exports of Chilean exporting firms across their size distribution. They found that small firms benefit more than large firms. Among small firms, the effect is driven by the intensive rather than extensive margins. This result is also confirmed in a sample of Argentinean exporting firms in Volpe, Carballo, and Garcia (2012).

Van Biesebroeck, Konings, and Volpe-Martincus (2015) show that export promotion has helped Belgian and Peruvian firms survive in export markets that were more hard hit by the great recession, leading also to higher sales along the intensive margin as sales were 20% higher for firms that benefited from the program. Note that, as pointed out by the authors, this does not mean that programs need to be scaled up, as it is not clear what will be the effect of these programs if they were to be provided to all firms. Note also that the fact that there is a large impact on exports does not justify the use of these instruments from an economic point of view. One would need to identify the externalities associated with these programs before deciding to scale them up.

Cadot et al. (2015) focus on the impact of a Tunisian export promotion program on exporting firms' behavior and found using a difference-in-difference estimator that firms benefiting from the program increase their exports along the extensive and intensive margins, but that the impact disappears after three years. Their result is very interesting for at least two reasons. First, the fact that the impact disappears can be due to the uncertainty associated with the institutional environment in Tunisia, which raises interesting questions regarding the effectiveness of export promotion programs similar to the critiques addressed in the early literature to programs that were operating in an environment with a strong anti-export bias. Second, and perhaps more interesting, the economic case for export promotion relies on the existence of spillovers from firms benefiting from the program to firms that are not directly benefiting from the program. Yet, all of the literature surveyed so far assumes that there are no externalities and looks at the impact on exporting firms. The fact that after three years the impact vanishes in Tunisia could be due to the presence of strong externalities, which supports the case for export promotion.[47]

Another problem with the microeconomic studies surveyed so far is that they rely on customs data, rather than on firm-level data, so they cannot examine the firm-extensive margin, i.e., the decision for firms to start exporting. In order to address this type of question and the externalities that may exist between exporting and non-exporting firms, one must match customs-level data with firm-level data. This has been done in the studies surveyed below.

Cruz (2014) matches firm and customs data in Brazil and provides evidence of export promotion services helping Brazilian medium-size firms enter the export market. So, combining this result with the results of Volpe and Carballo (2010a) and Volpe et al. (2012) suggests that export promotion helps medium-size firms enter export markets and small exporting firms diversify across products and markets.

Lederman et al. (2016) show in a sample of Latin American firms that export promotion helps firms enter into and survive in export markets, but participation in export promotion programs has little impact on the intensive margin. Broocks and van Biesebroeck (2017) also show that export promotion works mainly through the extensive margin in a sample of Belgian firms, but in the case of experienced exporters they also observe increases in their intensive margin. Drawing on firms' individual export flows at a very disaggregated level, Koenig et al. (2010) detect export spillovers on the extensive margin but not on the intensive margin, a result that they interpret as suggesting that spillovers operate mostly via fixed costs. The spillovers on the decision to start exporting are strongest when they are specific, by product and destination, and are not significant when considered on all products-all destinations.

More recently, randomized experiments at the firm level have shown that the returns to export promotion can be large. Atkin, Khandelwal, and Osman (2017) conduct an experiment where they offer to a random set of firms the opportunity to export high-quality carpets to retailers in the United States and Europe. They found that treated firms had an increase in profits of around 20% and larger increases in the quality of goods they produced, which is consistent with learning-by-exporting.

Breinlich et al. (2017) also conduct a controlled trial by providing targeted information to a randomly selected set of firms regarding the benefits and costs of exporting. Their objective is to assess the role that information plays on the perceptions that firms have about costs and benefits of selling in international markets. They found that treated non-exporters become less likely to export, whereas treated exporters become more likely to export, suggesting that the provision of information can have an impact on firms' behavior.

Using data for Colombian firms, Volpe and Carballo (2010b) show that the bundling of TPO services provides larger returns. Through difference-in-difference and propensity matching methods, they identify that a combination of counseling, trade agenda, and trade missions and fairs provides larger returns for targeted firms than the sum of actions in isolation. Much more of this type of work is needed to guide TPOs in their interventions. For example, are trade fairs as effective as trade missions? Which fair? Which type of trade mission? Is Colombia special? We do not know the answers to these questions.

A growing literature is focusing on the identification of positive externalities from exporting to non-exporting firms suggested by the macro results described above. Using an employer-employee dataset for Portugal, Mion and Opromolla (2014) find that there is a wage premium for managers associated with their previous experience as managers in firms that were exporting to similar markets. This wage premium is as large as the one associated with the firm's productivity. Similarly, Fernandes and Tang (2014) show that Chinese firms learn from the export experience of their neighbors and that this is particularly helpful in entering export markets. Wei, Wei, and Xu (2014), using a structural model of incentives to export and become a "pioneer," found that there are spillovers associated with the discovery of new export markets (export "pioneers") as well as important costs, but that their size may not necessarily justify government intervention because of the importance of first-mover advantages, and the fact that as long as "pioneer" profits are larger than the discovery costs, there is no market failure even in the presence of positive spillovers across firms.[48]

8.4.2. Trade Promotion and Development: What We Would Like to Know?

We have surveyed the literature on the impact of TPO on exports and development and have identified several areas for future research.

First, and perhaps most important, we need more evidence on the extent of information and other spillovers associated with trade promotion. Their existence is an important precondition for export promotion.[49] The pure economic case for export promotion relies on the presence of information externalities from firms being treated by the program to other firms who benefit indirectly from the program. The evidence on this type of learning-by-observing is small and ambiguous. Clerides at al. (1998) find that the probability of becoming an exporter is positively affected by the share of exporters in the local industry. Greenaway and Kneller (2004) find similar results in a sample of UK firms. On the other hand, Bernard and Jensen (2004) found no impact in a sample of US firms, and Aitken et al. (1997) find that there exist spillovers but only from foreign multinationals (MNEs) and not from general export activity. To our knowledge the only study that looks at how export promotion spills over to other firms is Cruz (2014) (and to some extent Cadot et al. 2015) who explores how the share of treated firms in a region and industry affects the export behavior of non-treated firms. This implicitly assumes that externalities happen within and not across regions and industries. This may be a strong assumption. As an alternative and using matched employer-employee data, Cruz is able to track the movement of workers from exporting to non-exporting firms and observes the impact on the export behavior of non-exporting firms.

The recent literature on identifying export externalities (Fernandes and Tang 2014; Mion and Opromolla 2014; Wei et al. 2014) can provide a good starting point to examine the impact of export promotion on firms that are not directly targeted by the program. Importantly, when spillovers are present, the methodologies used to measure the impact of TPO programs must be adapted to control for these negative or positive externalities. To understand how TPO programs should be designed, we need a better understanding of the trade-off between helping firms' needs and maximizing spillovers from TPOs' programs.

Second, and as argued earlier, learning-by-doing or learning-by-exporting does not provide a justification for export promotion by itself. It may explain the large returns and the larger GDP than export returns, but it does not provide a justification for intervention without some other market failure. For example, there may be a case for intervention in the presence of learning-by-doing if access to credit is limited which does not allow firms to invest in learning-by-doing (Copeland 2008). Note that this is more likely to be the case in low-income countries with weak market institutions.

The literature on learning-by-exporting tends to suggest that there is very little learning-by-exporting in developed countries and that the fact that more productive firms tend to export is due to selection rather than learning-by-exporting. However, recent evidence tends to suggest that this may not be so in a developing-country context. Blalock and Gertler (2004) provide evidence for Indonesia, Van Biesebroeck (2005) for nine Sub-Sahara African countries,[50] and Foster et al. (2014) for half of Sub-Sahara African countries. Thus, more studies that look at the extent to which credit constraints (and other market failures) are preventing low-income countries' firms to benefit from learning-by-exporting are needed. Identification is needed of which type of firms suffers the most from credit constraints (or other market failures) and simultaneously which types have the largest potential for learning-by-exporting. This set may be empty, but one could conjecture that small firms are precisely those that meet the two conditions (stronger credit constraints and larger potential for learning-by-exporting). But if, as argued earlier, learning occurs when products are sold in the domestic market, then there may be too much exporting, and export promotion could be counterproductive. Sorting out the source of these learning externalities is crucial to improve our understanding of how TPO activities work.

Third, the literature on which are the best instruments available to TPOs to address different types of market failures is scant, although the theory delivers clear messages on the question of in-kind assistance versus subsidies. Blackorby and Donaldson (1988) show that the latter will affect firm behavior and lead to inefficient outcomes, where firms would show interest in exporting only to benefit from the subsidy, whereas a training program has no commercial value. However, when firms are credit constrained, the more efficient instrument may indeed be financial assistance. Likewise, we know very little about the employment effects of TPOs, an issue of importance in low-income countries.[51] More generally, the link between the market failure justifying intervention and the instruments being used has not been explored empirically. This would help get closer to the elusive welfare implications of TPO programs.

8.5. PRIVATE TRADE INSTITUTIONS

Market failures across international markets can sometimes be corrected by private institutions, and in the area of environmental economics, particularly climate change, it is increasingly recognized that private authority—both delegated and entrepreneurial—is taking on the role of regulation to implement and enforce rules to manage global environmental problems (Green 2013). Whether it is information externalities that are corrected by private certification schemes rather than by government setting of standards, or excessive market power that is corrected by "fair trade" type mechanisms rather than (domestic or international) competition policy, or Walmart deciding to go green, there is a crucial distinction between public and private trade institutions that makes the study of the latter more complex. By definition, private institutions set voluntary schemes, and participation by foreign or domestic firms is often conditional on satisfying a set of requirements either in terms of product characteristics or of the production process itself.

We restrict our review of the literature on private institutions in two dimensions. First, we only review the literature on private trade institutions, i.e., those that affect international trade flows across countries. Second, we focus on the impact of private trade institutions on social and economic outcomes in low-income countries. Do "fair trade" mechanisms help poor farmers in low-income countries? Do consumer boycotts in the North help improve workers' conditions or the environment in the South? As we will see, sometimes apparently well-designed private institutions may give rise to unexpected outcomes.[52]

8.5.1. Private Trade Institutions: What Do We Know?

Missing domestic institutions may be the most important hurdle for producers (especially small producers) in low-income countries wishing to export. Negri and Porto (2016) study burley tobacco that accounts for close to 60% of Malawi's export earnings. Using household survey data, they compare the performance of producers belonging to burley tobacco clubs with non-members. The clubs have written documents that define rights and rules. These clubs perform collective action, ease access to auction floors, and provide other services, all of which contribute to lower transaction costs. Negri and Porto establish that club membership causes a significant increase in output per acre and in sales per acre, and that the difference in yields and sales generated by club membership is equivalent to increases in tobacco prices of between 37% and 54%. One cannot generalize from this case study, though it suggests that in the low-income environment of the majority of LDCs where the bulk of activity is in rural areas, local nonmarket institutions can play a major role in facilitating crop production associated with exports. In effect, the lack of domestic institutions is a significant barrier for agricultural producers to get goods to local markets and intermediaries and, from there, to export.

Asymmetric information regarding product, seller, or production processes characteristics can jeopardize markets with high-cost characteristics. As in the classic lemons market problem that focuses on product characteristics, the markets for environmentally safe or socially responsible products may not exist if producers cannot credibly convey to consumers who care about the production processes they employ that they satisfy certain requirements. These information asymmetries tend to be exacerbated by borders, ethnolinguistic diversity that becomes larger with differences in regulations and their enforcement across countries. Labeling and third-party certification schemes are the private sector response to these potential market failures.

Another related important objective of labeling schemes is to introduce economic incentives for firms in domestic and foreign countries to adopt production processes that are more respectful of workers, the environment, and other socioeconomic objectives. This idea is not new and can be traced back to at least the slave abolitionist in the United States and the "free produce" movement, which in the early nineteenth century introduced "free labor" stores in the United States. As discussed by Glickman (2004), these stores only sold goods that were produced without slavery. While the movement was not economically very successful, it did introduce the idea that this type of scheme can help consumers have a more responsible consumption, but also can help change the way goods are produced. Labeling has a dual role, as certification of products through tests and as a setter of standards. First, it ensures that the market for products that may be more costly to produce is able to exist and therefore ensures consumer gains. Second, it creates incentives to produce goods in a more socially or environmentally responsible manner.

The theory of labeling tends to suggest that it is welfare-improving as the provision of information in a world with asymmetric information will increase welfare. Podhorsky (2013) develops a two-country model with differentiated products and imperfectly informed consumers. Consumers in both countries value the quality (think production process) of goods, but cannot discern across different types of goods without certification. Firms in each country differ in their abilities to produce quality, and the distribution of technological ability is superior in the home country. Podhorsky shows that even in the case where the certification program is partly set for protectionist purposes (to improve the home-country terms of trade), welfare is higher both at home and abroad because of the gains associated with the information provided to consumers.[53]

But assuming that global demand for certified products is large enough is not a sufficient condition for these certification schemes to achieve their economic and social outcomes in the South. The most studied certification schemes are Fairtrade programs. Fairtrade programs ensure that the price paid to certified producers (p^{FT}) is always above the world price (p^{W}) and never below a certain minimum price ($\bar{p}$):

$$p^{FT} = \max(p^{W}; \bar{p}) + \text{social premium.}$$

In the case of coffee, the Fairtrade minimum price ($\bar{p}$) is USD1.40 per pound of washed Arabica, and the social premium is USD0.20, which ensures a minimum Fairtrade price of USD1.60 per pound.[54] This also ensures that Fairtrade farmers always receive a price that is higher than the world price by the equivalent of the social premium.[55]

There is a large empirical literature suggesting that the price received by farmers participating in Fairtrade certification schemes is indeed higher, and that the quality of products and production processes is improved. However, most existing studies suffer from identification problems as they compare before and after outcomes for certified farmers only without any control group, or they compare certified and noncertified farmers in a cross-section.

There are a few noteworthy exceptions. Dragusanu and Nunn (2018) provide evidence for coffee producers in Costa Rica using a difference-in-difference estimator. Balineau (2013), using panel data, shows that Fairtrade had a significant impact on the quality of cotton produced by certified Malian growers and that the quality produced by non-certified but geographically close producers also increased via spillover effects, while also controlling for selection bias and the possibility of a mean reversion process. As with export promotion, the importance and size of spillovers from certified producers deserves more attention to better establish causality since, in the presence of contagion between the treated and the control group, it becomes trickier to measure the impact of treatment.[56]

Learning externalities as in Balineau (2013) are one reason why there may be contagion. But simpler market forces can also lead to biased estimates. In a theoretical analysis of Fairtrade programs, Podhorsky (2015) introduces monopsonistic intermediaries in these markets. The introduction of the Fairtrade scheme creates an alternative distribution channel that bypasses intermediaries. Podhorsky shows that the Fairtrade program reduces the market power of oligopsonistic intermediaries, which not only makes farmers benefiting from the program better off, but also farmers excluded from the program who now face less powerful intermediaries and benefit from higher prices. On the other hand, Baland and Duprez (2007b) show that the introduction of this type of scheme in the presence of insufficient demand for certified products will lead to winners and losers. This suggests that any attempt at measuring the impact of Fairtrade certification on prices received by farmers needs to take into account the impact of the introduction of the scheme on the degree of competition in the market for noncertified products.[57]

There is also an important literature suggesting that labeling, and in particular Fair Trade programs, may not necessarily be welfare-increasing. Fairtrade mechanisms that aim at improving the livelihood of poor workers in a sustainable manner may end up bringing little gains to participating farmers in the presence of free entry, as rents get dissipated in a system where higher prices are set but quantities are fixed (de Janvry et al. 2015). Indeed, certified Fairtrade farmers are not allowed to sell all their production at the higher price offered by the label. They can only sell the share of their production that is required by the Freetrade buyer. As more farmers enter the Fairtrade program attracted by higher prices, the quantity that each farmer is allowed to sell at the Fairtrade price is reduced, and the benefit of participation in the program for the certified farmer is reduced. De Janvry et al. show that expected profits from participation in a Fairtrade coffee cooperative in Central America are close to zero when taking into account farmers' output that is certified but not sold at Fairtrade prices. The realized profits for participating farmers are even negative when the world price is above $\bar{p}$.

There are also critiques regarding the long-term incentives that these types of schemes create in low-income countries. Collier (2007) questions the dynamic benefits of Freetrade certification which provides benefits to farmers only as long as they keep producing the same products that left them in poverty and that world prices for these products remain low. In such a setup, there are probably more efficient ways of addressing poverty concerns that do not create incentives to keep producing the "wrong" bundle of goods.

On eco-labeling, Fischer and Lyon (2014) study the impact on environmental quality of competition between NGO-sponsored labels and industry-sponsored labels in a model of credence goods (where the consumer cannot assess if the product is environmentally friendly). When labeling is multi-tiered, deterioration in environmental quality is unambiguous.

Another source of private external enforcement is consumer boycotts in the North that respond to environmental, labor, or human rights violations in developing countries, and may help developing countries engage in institutional reforms. The literature has highlighted that these types of initiatives can backfire as they address distortions only indirectly. For example, Basu and Zarghamee (2009) have shown that consumer boycotts based on child labor violations in the South can lead to more, not less, child labor, as it hurts not only firms using child labor, but also the families of working children. Baland and Duprez (2007a) also illustrate how replacement of child workers by adult workers in the export sector and the shift of child workers to the nontraded sector due to boycotts in the North can result in lower levels of welfare in the South as well as increases in child labor. Targeting poverty and increasing the incentives to attend school with conditional cash transfer programs may be a more efficient way of addressing child labor issues than restrictions on international trade.[58]

Shifting consumer preferences in the North under globalization are also a source for the growth of private institutions. Consumers in Northern countries care increasingly about the ethical implications of their consumption decisions which often cannot be inferred from the characteristics of the goods they consume ("credence goods"). If the goods were produced in Northern countries, regulation could correct the information asymmetry between firms and consumers. With globalization triggering delocalization to the South where production is cheaper and regulation is weak, consumers in the North will be ready to finance NGOs that will help correct "the governance deficit" emerging under globalization (Gereffi and Mayer 2006). Krautheim and Verdier (2016) develop a two-country model that broadens our perspective on global production chains and international NGO activism which has an impact on both the socioeconomic environment of international corporations and the incentives for governments in the South to invest in regulatory capacity. Further research is needed to better understand the role of international advocacy by NGOs and their effects on offshoring patterns between the North and the South.

8.5.1.1. Trading Platforms and Reputation Mechanisms

The literature on intermediaries in low-income countries focuses on their market power, often at the expense of small farmers—notably for marketing boards and stabilization funds, although predatory pricing may also have other causes.[59] Small producers face relatively high costs of entering international markets, and when they enter them they will often face much larger intermediaries that will exploit their market power. The advent of the Internet and online markets such as eBay, Amazon, and Alibaba is changing the landscape for both manufacturing and agricultural firms. Their presence drastically reduces the costs of entering international markets and helps bypass large intermediaries altogether to directly reach international consumers in very distant markets.

Lendle et al. (2015) show how online markets help match buyers and sellers far apart through a reduction in search costs. They estimate that the effect of distance on international trade flows is 65% smaller on eBay than on offline markets. This means that transactions that would have never taken place in offline markets because buyers and sellers were too far apart are made possible in online markets. Interestingly, the distance-reduction effect of online platforms is stronger where most needed. Indeed, the reduction is larger in low-income countries that import differentiated goods (with more

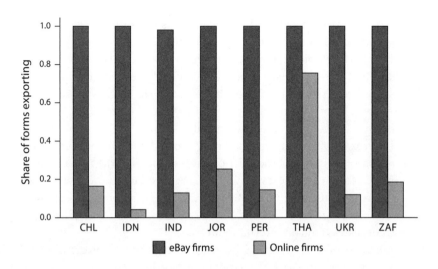

FIGURE 8.3. Online platforms and the cost of entering export markets. *Source*: Lendle and Vézina (2015).

information requirements), when trading partners speak a different language, and when corruption, income inequality, and uncertainty avoidance are high in the importing country.

Access to international markets has also been made more democratic by online platforms. Lendle et al. (2013) show that contrary to what is observed offline, almost all US firms selling on eBay in the domestic US market also sell in international markets. The share of exporters is 84% among US firms selling on the eBay platform, which is several orders of magnitude larger than what is generally observed offline for US firms (see Bernard et al. 2012). Among low-income countries this is even more striking, with almost all firms in low-income countries selling on eBay in the domestic market also exporting (see figure 8.3). They also tend to export to many more markets than their offline counterparts (Lendle and Vézina 2015).

Interestingly these exporting firms also tend to be much smaller than their offline counterparts, suggesting that the fixed costs necessary to access international markets via online platforms are much smaller than offline. This is important because tackling growing within-country income inequality is a challenge facing policymakers. Large reductions in trade costs through the development of online platforms can help democratize access to global markets and therefore contribute to reductions in income inequality through better access to international larger markets for small and less productive firms (see Helpman et al. 2010, and Helpman et al. 2015). Thus, instead of having only large firms benefiting from access to thick international markets, online platforms allow small and low-productivity firms in low-income countries to also benefit from being able to sell in these thick international markets, and also to access niche markets that may be a better match for some small firms.

A reason why entry costs are particularly small in online platforms is that they provide a relatively costless means for establishing reputation as a reliable seller of good products, even when located in a region or country with a bad reputation or institutions.

This is because the feedback mechanisms of both buyers and sellers provided by most online platforms may provide sufficient trust for trading relationships that would not have occurred otherwise (Lendle et al. 2015).

Interestingly, the feedback provided by online platforms is more useful when it is most needed. Agrawal, Lacetera, and Lyons (2016), using data from o-Desk, an online job platform, show that the information provided by the worker's previous experience on the platform disproportionately helps workers from developing countries find new contracts at higher wages. The prospects (and limitations) for the Internet to overcome institutional and government failures, and perhaps foster institutional improvements, is intriguing. It deserves further attention.

8.5.2. Private Trade Institutions and Development: What Would We Like to Know?

The review of private TRI and development above identifies several research avenues. First, the existence of private trade institutions such as labeling and certification schemes is justified by the presence of information asymmetries. Addressing these market failures and allowing markets that would not have otherwise existed to prevail through labeling and certification is a desirable answer by the private sector from a global perspective. From the perspective of small producers in low-income countries, the evidence so far suggests this may not always be the case. More work is needed to better understand which schemes are more likely to achieve their development objectives (for example Fairtrade schemes with fixed quantities are unlikely to do so). Also, the consequences of industry-driven versus NGO-driven labeling whose objectives are orthogonal deserve further exploration.

Second, in their review of the Faitrade literature, Dragusanu, Giovannucci, and Nunn (2014) call for a tightening of the methodologies used so as to control for contagion through learning by nonparticipating farmers and general equilibrium effects in local markets (stronger or weaker monopsony power for intermediaries, for example). The impact evaluations should also compare the characteristics of farmers that participate in these schemes with those that remain outside, as nonparticipants may be poorer as they might be unable to pay rapidly rising certification costs.

Third, some initiatives may also be too small to matter. Fairtrade labeling that aims at reducing poverty by providing minimum prices to farmers as well as a social premium evaluated represents only 0.005% of world trade, as indicated in table 8.6. Even for coffee, which represents 55% of total Fairtrade sales, the share of Fairtrade products in total world trade is barely 1.4%.[60] For all other products it is significantly below 1%. For these initiatives to have an impact in working conditions and promote environmentally friendlier production processes in developing countries, it is necessary to scale them up. The extent to which they can be scaled up, and the desirability of scaling up some of these initiatives, have been challenged by the work of de Janvry et al. (2015) and others. These are areas that need to be further explored.

Fourth, an important related issue on which more work is needed is the proliferation of Fairtrade labels, but also other types of labeling. Differing interests lead to competition between labeling groups. Ibanez and Grolleau (2008), Mason (2013), and Fischer and Lyon (2014) develop the theory. Balineau (2013) and de Janvry et al. (2015) give evidence on cotton and coffee respectively. It seems that agency problems may grow as the number

Table 8.6. Importance of fair trade exports in total world trade, 2013

Product	HS codes	FT sales (million EUR)	FT sales (million USD)	Share in Total FT	World Trade (million USD)	Share of FT in world trade
Coffee	0901	519	692	55%	38453	1.3497%
Bananas	0803	137	183	15%	17552	0.7805%
Cocoa	1801	96	128	10%	11333	0.8471%
Sugar	1701	62	83	7%	29595	0.2095%
Flowers and plants	0602; 0603	47	63	5%	17293	0.2718%
Fresh and dried fruit, and nuts	08 ex 0803	26	35	3%	121532	0.0214%
Tea, herbs, and spices	09 ex 0901; 0910	24	32	3%	38175	0.0629%
Cotton and quinoa	5201; 121299	14	19	1%	18260	0.0767%
Honey	0409	6	8	1%	2435	0.2464%
Other	Other codes	13	17	1%	19985372	0.0001%
Total Sales		944	1259	100%	20280000	0.0047%

Source: Author's calculations using UN's Comtrade for world trade data (available through wits.worldbank .org), Fairtrade (2014), Fair Trade Monitoring Trade and Benefits for fair trade sales, and FAO (2014), International Quinoa trade (http://www.fao.org/3/a-i4042e/i4042e20.pdf). Data are for year 2013 (except world trade in quinoa, which is for 2012).

of Fairtrade labels increases. It may not be in the interest of private certifying agencies to fully enforce certification requirements. This in turn creates problems for the consumer, who does not know whether to trust the certification, and the value of the schemes may dissipate. One common critique is that there is not much more than a bit of marketing behind some of these certifying schemes which benefit from the willingness to clear the conscience of consumers in more developed countries. There is also a need for a better understanding of the financing of many of these certification institutions. Many are financed by the fees collected from the firms they are supposed to certify (e.g., Fair Trade or Fair Labor Association). This can lead to conflict of interests, which can jeopardize their effectiveness and can lead to deterioration in the trust put by consumers in these schemes.

Fifth, another problem raised by Dragusanu et al. (2014) in their survey of the economics of fair trade is that in certified cooperatives, the trust that farmers have on the cooperative and its leader is smaller than in noncertified cooperatives. This is apparently largely due to the use of the social premium that gets paid to the cooperative by the buyer and whose allocation is not always clear to the individual farmer who is a member of the cooperative.

Sixth, regarding online platforms, the extent to which online platforms have helped small producers circumvent monopsony power by offline intermediaries is an area that remains largely unexplored.[61] Doing so would require the matching of online and offline sales at the firm level which has proven difficult to do so far, though technically it is not impossible if statistical offices and firms are willing to lift the confidentiality of the name of each firm. Otherwise pseudo-panel techniques could be used.

More generally, the matching of online and offline data at the firm level will help address concerns regarding self-selection biases. Indeed, firms participating on online markets may be very different from firms not participating in online markets, which may explain part of the existing results in the literature. For example, distance may matter less online not because it reduces search costs, but because of the preferences of owners and managers of online firms that are more open to remote international markets.

Last, but not least, providing access to online platforms can also be an efficient tool to promote exports, as almost all firms participating in online markets also export. An impact evaluation of programs providing access to online markets on the export behavior of treated firms and the extent to which there are spillovers to other firms seems an interesting research avenue for understanding how export promotion can help small firms. The role of hard and soft infrastructure (roads, transport, and postal services) in making these schemes efficient should also be carefully evaluated.

8.6. CONCLUDING REMARKS

The relationship between domestic institutions—mostly contracting institutions—and trade has been recently covered and surveyed by Nunn and Trefler (2015). Here we have concentrated on less-covered trade-related institutions (TRIs). We have surveyed the literature on Trade Agreements (TAs), Trade Promotion Organizations (TPOs), and private Trade Related Institutions (TRIs) to suggest what type of TRI is more likely to help the development prospects of low-income countries. Throughout the chapter, we highlight the tension between the more micro-focused contributions that are closest to dealing with the attribution problem at the cost of external validity and the more macro cross-country studies that face the problem of confounding influences. Sections 8.3.2, 8.4.2, and 8.5.2 discuss the specific areas we believe need more work to ascertain the impact of TAs, TPOs, and private TRIs on development in low-income countries. Below we recapitulate the research areas that appear the most promising.

Regarding TAs, many issues require further work and are discussed in section 8.3.2. Some research avenues are long overdue. We need a better understanding of the rationales behind the participation of low-income countries in TAs. Time inconsistency in government policies is probably a good candidate, but the existing models cannot really explain why there is enforcement if low-income countries have no market power. Combining the time-inconsistency rationale with models of profits-shifting as in Mrázová (2015) or production relocation as in Ossa (2011) could provide a way out.

Second, with PTA agreements covering greater provisions (e.g., labor and environmental clauses, regulatory measures), we need to understand how the increase in breadth affects the depth of these agreements (i.e., full elimination of NTBs) and how domestic supporting institutions are impacted.

Third, are PTAs complementary to multilateralism when it comes to PTAs among low-income countries? Almost all existing evidence is on developed countries or Latin America and East Asia. Do results extend to Sub-Saharan Africa and South Asia?

The second type of TRI we examine are TPOs. They should have a leading role to address the multiple market failures faced by firms in low-income countries. Research from macro and micro studies suggests that they have a large and positive impact on exports and GDP. However, from a welfare perspective the case for export promotion relies on the existence of spillovers from firms benefiting from the programs to other firms. There is little direct evidence on how widespread these spillovers are, and what are their determinants. We need more evidence on how externalities spread across firms.

Second, learning-by-doing or learning-by-exporting can also provide a justification for export promotion, but only in the presence of some market failure like a credit constraint. This is more likely to be observed in low-income countries. A better understanding of the profile of firms that are more likely to be simultaneously subject to learning-by-exporting and the likelihood that they are negatively affected by market failures would help clarify the welfare implications of export promotion programs.

A better understanding of what types of export promotion program are more effective in low-income countries (in-kind assistance versus subsidies, participation in fairs versus technical assistance, etc.) is also needed. More generally, the link between the market failure justifying intervention and the instruments used has not been explored empirically.

As to the literature labeling and certification, causal impacts of adoption need to be identified more carefully. As with export promotion programs, externalities from participation in the program are likely to be very large. Identifying these externalities is important to correctly evaluate the impact of different programs. This raises the important question of the need for scaling up some of these programs that are too small to matter.

Last, but not least, the extent to which online platforms may help small producers circumvent monopsony power by offline intermediaries is a promising research area. An impact evaluation or randomized control trial of programs providing access to online markets on domestic and foreign sales of treated firms and the extent to which there are spillovers to other firms would deserve attention. Understanding the heterogeneity of the impact in different geographic, institutional, and infrastructure environments is also deserving of further investigation.

NOTES

1. Genetic distance refers to differences across populations and genetic diversity to heterogeneity within populations. Genetic diversity (highest among African and lowest among Amerindian populations) should be productivity-enhancing and costly because it may reduce trust and coordination among individuals. Cultural diversity and patterns of cultural transmission are also important for long-term development outcomes. Spolaore and Wacziarg (2014) summarize this large literature that points to the persistence of culture traits through intergenerational transmission. Guiso et al. (2009) find that somatic distance between European populations is negatively correlated with bilateral trust and, in turn, with bilateral trade. Felbermayr and Toubal (2010) find that one-third of the trade-cost channel in bilateral European trade is attributable to cultural distance. Maystre et al. (2014) find that cultural values, as captured by the World Value Surveys, exhibit high-frequency variation in response to trade shocks.
2. In Europe, the growth of long-distance medieval trade triggered a shift from relation-based to rule-based trade with higher fixed costs but lower marginal costs. The long history of Venice's Republic saw the rise of a merchant class that pushed for modern innovations in contracting institutions (i.e., the commenda) while shifting power in their favor that they then used to set up a coercive apparatus to suppress opposition (Puga and Trefler 2014). In their review of the historical literature, Nunn and Trefler (2015, sec. 5) report more evidence that, historically, trade and comparative advantage have been key in the development of domestic institutions.

3. Dollar and Kraay (2003) is an example of that literature. See Pritchett's (2013) comments on how the authors are unsuccessful in their "torture test" causality. François and Manchin (2013) also deal with 5-year panel data in a gravity model. They try to disentangle the effects of differences in the quality of infrastructure and institutions on bilateral trade using a structural gravity model. Their two-stage estimations take zero trade flows into account, but their attempt to account for the endogeneity of infrastructure and institutional quality had to resort to lagged principal components of various measures of infrastructure and institutional quality.

4. Leamer and Levinsohn (1995) noted that contrary to expectations from a "death of distance" (in which international trade costs fall more rapidly than internal trade costs), in repeated estimates of the gravity equation, the estimate of the distance coefficient usually failed to fall (and sometimes increased) in value. Many explanations have been put forward, none fully satisfactory since the puzzle seems to persist for low-income countries (see Carrère et al. 2013). Calibrations of the gravity equation à la Novy (2013) by Arvis et al. (2016) also find that the gap in trade costs between low-income countries and other country groupings have not fallen over the 1995–2012 period. An exception is Yotov (2012), who finds that the estimate of the coefficient of distance falls over the period 1965–2005 when external trade costs are correctly measured relative to internal trade costs.

5. The quality-of-institutions indicators are: product-markets (relationship specificity of inputs, Herfindhal index of concentration of inputs, job complexity all multiplied by an indicator of rule of law); labor-market (sales volatility × labor-market flexibility); and financial market (external finance dependence × financial dependence). Industry measures are taken from the US Regressions and include country and industry fixed effects. See Kaufmann et al. 2003, table 5.4. Nunn and Trefler discuss reverse causality, omitted variable bias, and benchmarking bias using US data for all countries. The robust conclusion is that contracting institutions matter for comparative advantage.

6. Hausmann, Hwang, and Rodrik (2007) develop an indicator of the income level of a country's exports that could be correlated with the indices of the contract intensity of production. In a sample covering 1985–2005 that includes 22 low-income countries, Brenton et al. (2010) find a lot of heterogeneity in survival rates at the HS-4 level and that regional and product-specific experience count most for export survival for low-income countries.

7. This surge in PTAs largely coincided with the launch of a continental FTA across the Americas in 1991 as the United States was turning away from multilateralism for fear that the Uruguay Round negotiations would not conclude. For the EC, the spread was ongoing anyway. In his review of the political economy of EC regionalism, Sapir (1998) notes that regionalism, especially trade preferences, have always been the principal instrument of foreign policy of the EC. The proliferation also might have been reinforced by the fact that the portfolio for foreign relations was divided among four EC commissioners. He also notes that the United States opposed the EC having reciprocal FTAs with ACP countries until it also moved away from championing multilateralism.

8. A literature has developed that because proximity supposedly results in lower transport costs, regional PTAs are more likely to be welfare increasing. The debate is unsettled, though for the United States over the period 1965–1995, Krishna (2003) finds no evidence to support the thesis that the welfare effects of preferential trade with geographically close partners is welfare increasing.

9. Historically, until they gained in importance in world trade and their import-substitution-led development strategies were shown to be dominated by the export-led strategies of some Asian countries, developing countries—especially the low-income countries—were either outside the GATT or they were bystanders throughout the GATT rounds. Developing countries were peripheral to the WTS, relying on nonreciprocal preferences from industrial countries (the Generalized System of Preferences—GSP) and on a first wave of South-South reciprocal Regional Trade Agreements (RTAs). First in 1971, then in 1979, the LDC category (set up in 1971) established the "enabling clause" providing the legal basis for Special and Differential Treatment (SDT) and the very lenient treatment until the establishment of the WTO (see Ornelas 2016).

10. Under the GATT, article 33 on accession required a two-thirds majority to accept the applicant and was usually left to a working party with few votes taking place in practice. However, article 26 granted membership automatically on the basis of sponsorship that was usually obtained by the former colonial power. Under the current WTO accession process (now article 12 of the WTO Agreement), all applicants have to go through the process that includes a longer list of required agreements to negotiate (GATS, TRIMS, TRIPS . . .) as well as the prevalence of

WTO+ requirements that go beyond the obligations of established WTO members that do not have to change their commitments.

11. Other reasons for a TA beyond those examined below include profit-shifting via firm deloca-tion which could be another beggar-thy-neighbor motive for trade policy that could be internal-ized by a TA. Ossa (2011) develops a monopolistic competition where protection attracts foreign firms to the home country, resulting in a welfare loss (gain) for the (foreign) home country. A TA would then internalize this externality. In a model with fragmentation of production and offshoring with trade in intermediate inputs where prices are determined by bilateral bargain-ing between buyers and sellers, Antràs and Staiger (2012) show that a hold-up problem occurs when relationship-specific investments are required when contracts between buyers and sellers are incomplete. Then a TA will help raise an inefficiently low level of investment under free trade. Using the value-added content of exports for 14 major economies over 1995–2009, Blanchard et al. (2016) find that final goods tariffs are decreasing in the foreign content of domestically produced final goods and also when domestic content of foreign goods is high. Grossman (2016) reviews these theoretical contributions on the rationale for trade agreements as well as international agreements to protect intellectual property.

12. The third result is the "subsidy puzzle," i.e., that the GATT should encourage countries to use subsidies to reduce the externality they inflict on partners. Since subsidies are prohibited by the GATT, this result sits poorly in the dominant theory. Maggi (2014) and Grossman (2016) discuss the subsidy puzzle and conditions needed to solve it.

13. The optimal noncooperative tariff is simply given by the inverse of the export supply elasticity faced by each importer. The larger is the elasticity (i.e., the more elastic is the supply of the rest of the world), the smaller is the optimal tariff. The 12 countries are Benin, Burkina Faso, Burundi, Central African Republic, Côte d'Ivoire, Madagascar, Malawi, Mali, Niger, Rwanda, Uganda, and Togo. See table 1 in Nicita et al. (2018).

14. Maggi (2014) reviews the evidence of the commitment theory. See also Liu and Ornelas's (2014) study of TA commitment devices for fragile democracies. An exception is Arcand, Olarreaga, and Zoratto (2015), who show that trade agreements are more likely to be signed by governments that do not give either too much or too little weight to social welfare in their objective function, which is one of the predictions in Maggi and Rodríguez-Clare (1998). This is because govern-ments that give a lot of weight to social welfare will not be sensitive to lobbying by import-competing producers, and those that give too little weight to social welfare and put all their weight on the lobbying rents will have no incentive to pre-commit to free trade through a TA.

15. Indicators of rigor of accession include the number of working party members, the number of years, the number of rounds of questions, the change in applied tariff from the year of applica-tion to the year of accession.

16. Fiorini and Lebrand (2016) also develop a commitment motive for a TA in services through com-mercial presence because of the complementarity between services and non-services inputs in downstream production of goods.

17. Schiff and Winters (2003: ch. 4) expressed reservations along these lines, pointing out that in North-South agreements, the Northern partner often lacks the incentive to enforce. More recently, this can be seen in the Economic Partnership Agreements (EPAs) signed by the EU with ACP countries which have not lived up to the initial intention of the agreements at their launch (see Melo and Régolo 2014).

18. We thank Thierry Verdier for this suggestion.

19. Melo, Panagariya, and Rodrik (1992) review the theory at the time, emphasizing that economies of scale could be a reason for integrating but that this gain would also be available on a multi-lateral basis. From a cross-section of 101 countries with 78 developing countries, by two subpe-riods (1960–72 and 1973–85), Melo, Montenegro, and Panagariya (1992) failed to find any effect on growth for dummy variables capturing North-North and South-South PTAs.

20. Moncarz, Olarreaga, and Vaillant (2016) provide evidence that tariff preference within Merco-sur and its common external tariff were used by its larger member (Brazil) to move its produc-tion bundle toward more sophisticated products.

21. Fernandez and Portes (1998) and Schiff and Winters (2003) review the "non-traditional" motives for RTAs among developing countries. Non-traditional refers to effects other than exchange of market access and concerns about the trade diversion and trade creation effects discussed by Viner.

22. Regan (2015) and Ethier (2013) argue that the TOT theory of PTAs does not correspond to what politicians have in mind when they negotiate TAs and argue that trade prospects could trigger

participation of export interests. Grossman (2016) reviews their critiques, concluding that research is needed to see if PTAs might bring dormant export interests into the political process.

23. The linear integration model (goods markets followed by factor markets) has often been criticized as failing to exploit the high integration benefits from integration in services markets (see Melo and Tsikata 2015 for further discussion).

24. Freund and Ornelas (2010) review the literature. Krishna (2013), Limão (2006), and Karacaovali and Limaõ (2008) find evidence that PTAs may still be a stumbling bloc for the EU and the United States.

25. In the context of climate-related negotiations, Victor (2015) suggests six tasks that climate clubs could perform better than the multilateral system in coordinating measures to deal with climate change. See also Nordhaus (2015) and Mavroidis and Melo (2015).

26. Limão (2016) reviews the shortcomings of what Head and Mayer (2014) refer to as the "naïve" gravity model estimates that fail to take into account multilateral resistance terms. Theory-consistent gravity models still face three problems: small sample size in a cross-section, choice of controls (multiple atheoretical controls), and omitted variable bias as countries could be simultaneously pursuing unilateral trade liberalization. Up until the 1990s, no data are available on bilateral tariffs, so the models capture the WTO/PTA effect by a dummy variable so these models have the properties of an average treatment effect in which the control group shares all of the same characteristics for all covariates except membership. Among others, this implies that members and non-members share the same trade cost elasticity, ε, usually estimated in the range $3 < \varepsilon < 7$. Using Limão's notation, this implies that the average estimated ad valorem trade cost reduction from the PTA/WTO membership is given by $PTA^{ave} \equiv \varphi/\varepsilon$ where φ is the fixed-effect coefficient estimate. In this regard, reviewing carefully the evidence on North-South and South-South reciprocal PTAs up until the mid-1990s, Foroutan (1998) documents that during the 1980s and 1990s, much reduction in protection in developing countries took place among countries that were not members of a PTA and that, in Latin America, trade liberalization was taking place simultaneously with PTA membership, so the gravity estimates suffer from a time-varying omitted variable bias in addition to time-invariant unobserved variables that can be handled by FEs (see Baier and Bergstrand 2007). Limão (2016: table 2) reports estimates covering the period 1960–2010 that show that the PTA coefficient estimates, φ, are reduced by half when controlling for all FE.

27. Dirty tarification was defined as the transformation of non-tariff barriers into tariff barriers as decided during the Uruguay Round, but at levels of protection much higher than those imposed by the non-tariff barriers.

28. All these estimates are "average treatment effects" raising the issue of the appropriate control group. See Egger and Tarlea (2017).

29. Qualification for US AGOA preferences is contingent on governance indicators, as is qualification for GSP+ preferences of the EU. GSP preferences can be terminated at the discretion of the grantor. Unilateral trade preferences may also be counterproductive for exporters who will not wish to incur lobbying costs to get access to foreign markets, as argued by Ozden and Reinhardt (2005) and Conconi and Perroni (2012, 2015). See the discussion in Ornelas (2016).

30. GSP programs also now provide additional preferential access to developed country markets conditional on labor and environmental standards.

31. In their review of the challenges facing regional trade agreements in Africa, Melo and Tsikata (2015) note that the great disparities across partners (resource-rich and resource-poor, coastal and land-locked, large and small) combined with the lack of compensation hamper progress. On delegation of authority versus representation of national interests in regional institutions, see Melo, Panagariya, and Rodrik (1992) and Spolaore (2013).

32. Victor (2015) calls these "climate clubs," noting six tasks they could perform from designing smart border measures to deal with carbon leakage to crafting conditional commitments. Using a calibrated world trade model with CO_2 emissions, Nordhaus (2015) shows that across-the-board tariffs in a 5%–20% range to nonparticipants in a carbon club is incentive-compatible and could avoid free-riding. Required changes in the GATT rules to deal with the climate change problem are discussed in Mavroidis and Melo (2015).

33. As evidence of the interaction of trade and property regimes, Xu (2015) studies trade in virtual water via its embodiment in agricultural products. She finds support for the hypothesis that countries with weak property rights regimes have greater volumes of embodied water in their exports. Evidence of the importance of environmental policies on comparative advantage is also strong for trade in virtual carbon (the pollution-haven hypothesis) and for trade in products that

degrade the environment from countries with lax environmental policies toward countries with more stringent standards. Fischer (2010) surveys the literature.

34. Melo and Tsikata (2015: table 1) lists the objectives of RTAs in Africa. Cooperation and security matters are almost always cited among the main objectives.

35. With an extended codification of the depth of PTAs, will the larger estimates of the ATE effect of FTA participation for deep FTAs in Maggi (2014: table 2) carry over to this dataset?

36. In the EU, "ground-breaking" provisions relate to competition policy and in the United States, to environmental and labor standards.

37. The Uruguay-Philip Morris dispute over the legislation banning smoking in enclosed public spaces that passed in 2006 in Uruguay is an example of such a case. The international arbitration under the Uruguay-Switerzland bilateral investment agreement has decided to go ahead with the multi-million-dollar claim by Philip Morris that such a ban has hurt the company's value in Uruguay where it had previously invested.

38. NAFTA has been the subject of tenth and twentieth anniversary assessments. The EU has also recently concluded DCFTAs with its Eastern neighbors (Ukraine, Georgia, Moldova) and is currently negotiating DCFTAs with its Southern Mediterranean neighbors.

39. The literature also refers to Export Promotion Agencies (EPAs). TPOs and EPAs will be used interchangeably.

40. There is also an important literature that examines how the sophistication of the export bundle can help export growth. Hausman, Hwang, and Rodrik (2007) originally provide evidence of this across countries, whereas Jarreau and Poncet (2012) and Poncet and Starosta (2013) provide evidence within China and show that the sophistication of the export bundle matters for growth, but only when considering the export bundle of domestic (not foreign) firms that do not participate in export processing programs. This hints at the limits of these programs in helping spur growth.

41. This is an example of the two-way causality between policies and institutions.

42. These results are subject to the criticisms of Baier and Bergstrand (2007) mentioned above who show that panel data methods control better for omitted (time-invariant) endogeneity bias.

43. The institutional structure of TPOs tends to be more similar across income groups (about 50% are either an autonomous or semi-autonomous government agency, and the executive board seats in the hands of the private sector number around 50% in both income groups).

44. At the sample mean, in an early cross-section on a smaller sample, Lederman et al. (2010) estimate that $1 spent on export promotion leads to $40 of additional exports. Interestingly, export promotion delivers larger gains where most needed, i.e., when facing stronger market access barriers abroad (tariff and non-tariff barriers) or when exporting differentiated products rather than homogeneous goods. One reason why the returns may be higher in the panel when endogeneity is better addressed could be reverse causality: countries with larger export promotion agencies are those that tend to have lower exports.

45. They also explored the heterogeneity of impact across different agency characteristics and found that agencies that tend to spend a larger share of their budget on marketing activities tend to generate larger gains in terms of GDP. Note that interestingly, they do not find that the determinant of export returns are the same as the determinants of GDP returns, which suggest that programs and agencies' characteristics need to clearly define their objectives.

46. Olarreaga et al. (2016) found that the TPO characteristics that matter for export returns do not necessarily matter for GDP per capita return. For example, a focus on a few targeted sectors rather than all sectors yields larger export returns, but it does not affect the returns in terms of GDP per capita. And some characteristics that tended to yield larger returns in terms of exports yield lower returns in terms of GDP per capita. This is the case for example of the share of funding coming from public sources, which tends to increase export returns but reduces GDP per capita returns. These results are important, because they suggest that what may matter for export returns may not work if the TPO objective is to increase income per capita. Thus, putting objectives and evaluating the performance of TPOs in terms of export growth may be counterproductive when the ultimate objective is to increase economic well-being.

47. Cadot et al. (2015) do not find evidence of spillovers in their paper, although they recognize that not finding some type of spillover precludes the absence of other types of spillovers. Cruz (2014) finds strong evidence of spillovers from export promotion programs in Brazil.

48. Indeed, the presence of externalities is not a sufficient condition for a market failure. For a market failure to occur, one would need to know that the cost of entering new markets is smaller than the profits for the discoverer, and the latter become larger in the presence of strong first-mover advantages.

49. One could think justifying export promotion along the lines of a club is good, where there is non-rivalry in the consumption of information and knowledge obtained in foreign markets. However, the way this information is generated by TPOs implies externalities, as the information is obtained with the help of successful and not so successful exporting firms in different markets.

50. The nine countries are Burundi, Cameroon, Côte d'Ivoire, Ethiopia, Ghana, Kenya, Tanzania, Zambia, and Zimbabwe.

51. Using firm-level data, Munch and Schaur (2018) find that export promotion positively affects employment in small firms.

52. For some, the development of "private authority" is essential, especially in the design of public good policies like climate policies (see Green 2013). This is perhaps tangential to this project except insofar as it relates to SDGs in developing countries.

53. This result relies on the assumption that preferences are identical in both countries, i.e., consumers care in the same way about the "quality" of the products being certified, an assumption that is unlikely to hold when considering standard setting between the North and the South. Also, a labeling scheme on socially responsible products may end up having no impact at all if at the existing equilibrium price without information the demand for socially responsible products is smaller than the existing supply of socially responsible products. In this case, the (disequilibrium) price of socially responsible products would be smaller after certification, which implies that the new and old equilibrium price will be identical for all goods (Mattoo and Singh 1994).

54. See http://www.fairtrade.net/products/coffee.html for up-to-date information on minimum prices and social premiums. Note also that since 2014, the world price for mild Arabica coffee has been above the minimum price of USD1.40 per pound.

55. To benefit from these higher prices, farmers need to comply with some minimum standards for workers' conditions (no forced or child labor, no gender discrimination, and wages that respect labor laws), environmental standards, and be an organization in producer cooperatives where decisions are made democratically and the benefits from the social premium are invested in socially and environmentally desirably projects. The cost of certification is around USD1500–USD2000.

56. On the basis of an examination of 92 randomized control trials published in top journals over 2009–2014, Peters et al. (2016) warn that the papers do not discuss the hazards of external validity, nor do they provide information to assess potential problems.

57. Note that it is not clear that the result in Podhorsky (2015) is robust to the introduction of intermediaries facing downward sloping demand curves. In her paper, intermediaries are price takers. It seems that the introduction of downward sloping demand curves may actually lead to lower prices for noncertified producers. In any case, what matters for identifying the impact of certification is to account for the externality regardless of whether the externality is positive or negative.

58. See also the Bharadwaj, Lakdawala, and Li (2014) study of the child labor ban legislation passed in India in the 1980s that provides evidence that poor families were worse off after the ban.

59. Case studies on cash crops by McMillan et al. (2003) on cashew nuts in Mozambique, and Melo et al. (2000) on vanilla in Madagascar, give support to Olson's logic of collective action, i.e., a case of exploitation of the many (small farmers) by the few (intermediaries). Melo (2010) compares the two case studies, providing counterfactual simulations of the distributional impact of raising the number of traders. From a sample of six cash crops in Africa, McMillan (2001) provides evidence that predatory taxation and the inability of governments to commit to low taxes is due to sunk costs and low discount factors rather than to marketing boards. The political economy literature on trade policy is not reviewed here.

60. Note that we are only taking the sales under the Fairtrade label. This is the main fair trade certification mechanism, but there are others, which account for a smaller portion of fair trade sales.

61. Access to mobile phones has also been shown to encourage political mobilization during economic downturns in Africa (Manacorda and Tesi 2016).

REFERENCES

Acemoglu, D., S. Johnson, and J. Robinson. 2005. The Rise of Atlantic Trade, Institutional Change and Economic Growth. *American Economic Review* 95: 546–579.

Agrawal, Ajay, Nicola Lacetera, and Elizabeth Lyons. 2016. Does Standardized Information in On-line Markets Disproportionately Benefit Job Applicants from Less Developed Countries? *Journal of International Economics* 103: 1–12.

Aitken, Brian, Gordon Hanson, Ann Harrison. 1997. Spillovers, Foreign Investment and Export Behavior. *Journal of International Economics* 43(1–2): 103–132.

Albornoz, Fernando, Hector Calvo-Pardo, G. Corcos, and Emanuel Ornelas. 2012. Sequential Exporting. *Journal of International Economics* 88(1): 17–31.

Allee, Todd, and Jamie Scalera. 2012. The Divergent Effects of Joining International Organizations: Trade Gains and the Rigors of WTO Accession. *International Organization* (66): 243–276.

Anderson, James, and Yoto Yotov. 2016. Terms of Trade and Global Efficiency Effects of Free Trade Agreements, 1990–2002. *Journal of International Economics* 99: 276–298.

Anson, José, Olivier Cadot, and Marcelo Olarreaga. 2006. Tariff Evasion and Customs Corruption: Does PSI Help? *BE Journal of Economic Analysis & Policy* 5 (1). https://www.degruyter.com/view/j/bejeap.2005.5.issue-1/issue-files/bejeap.2005.5.issue-1.xml.

Antràs, Pol, and Robert Staiger. 2012. Offshoring and the Role of Trade Agreements. *American Economic Review* 102(7): 3140–3183.

Araujo, Luis, Giordano Mion, and Emanuel Ornelas. 2016. Institutions and Export Dynamics. *Journal of International Economics* 98: 2–20.

Arcand, Jean-Louis, Marcelo Olarreaga, and Laura Zoratto. 2015. Weak Governments and Trade Agreements. In *The Purpose, Design and Effects of Preferential Trade Agreements*, edited by Andreas Dür and Manfred Elsig, 82–112. Cambridge: Cambridge University Press.

Arvis, Jean-François, Yves Duval, Ben Shepherd, and C. Utoktham. 2016. Trade Costs in the Developing World: 1996–2010. *World Trade Review* 15(3): 451–474.

Atkin, David, and Dave Donaldson. 2015. Who Is Getting Globalized? The Size and Implications of Intra-National Trade Costs. NBER No. 21439.

Atkin, David, Amit Khandelwal, and Adam Osman. 2017. Exporting and Firm Performance: Evidence from a Randomized Experiment. *Quarterly Journal of Economics* 132(2): 551–615.

Bagwell, K., C. Bown, and R. Staiger. 2016. Is the WTO Passé? *Journal of Economic Literature* 54(4): 1125–1231.

Bagwell, Kyle, and Robert W. Staiger. 1999. An Economic Theory of GATT. *American Economic Review* 89(1): 215–248.

———. 2002. *The Economics of the World Trading System*. Cambridge, MA: MIT Press.

———. 2010. The WTO: Theory and Practice. *Annual Review of Economics* 2: 223–256.

———. 2011. What Do Trade Negotiators Negotiate About? Empirical Evidence from the World Trade Organization. *American Economic Review* 101(4): 1238–1273.

———. 2016. *Handbook of Commercial Policy*, vols. 1A and 1B. Amsterdam: North-Holland.

Baier, Scott L., and Jeffrey H. Bergstrand. 2007. Do Free Trade Agreements Actually Increase Members' International Trade? *Journal of International Economics* 71(1): 72–95.

Baier, Scott, Jeffrey Bergstrand, and Ronald Mariuto. 2014. Economic Determinants of PTAs Revisited. *Review of International Economics* 22(1): 31–58.

Baland, Jean-Marie, and Cédric Duprez. 2007a. Made in Dignity: The Impact of Social Labels. Working Papers 1001, University of Namur.

———. 2007b. Are Fair Trade Labels Effective Against Child Labour? CEPR discussion paper 6259.

Baldwin, R. E. 1995. A Domino Theory of Regionalism. In *Expanding European Regionalism: The EU's New Members*, edited by R. Baldwin, P. Haaparanta, and J. Kiander. Cambridge: Cambridge University Press.

———. 2014. WTO 2.0: Governance of 21st Century Trade. *Review of International Organizations*. 9(2): 261–283. (Also Trade, Policy Insight No. 64 CEPR.)

Balineau, Gaëlle. 2013. Disentangling the Effects of Fair Trade on the Quality of Malian Cotton. *World Development* 44(C): 241–255.

Bardhan, Pranab. 2006. Institutions, Trade and Development, mimeo, Berkeley.

Basu, Kaushik, and Homa Zarghamee. 2009. Is Product Boycott a Good Idea for Controlling Child Labor? A Theoretical Investigation. *Journal of Development Economics* 88: 217–220.

Bergstrand, Jeffrey, Mario Larch, and Yoto Yotov. 2015. Economic Integration Agreements, Border Effects and Distance Elasticities in the Gravity Equation. *European Economic Review* 78: 307–327.

Berman, Nicolas, Mathieu Couttenier, Dominic Rohner, and Mathias Thoenig. 2017. This Mine Is Mine! How Minerals Fuel Conflict in Africa. *American Economic Review* 107(6): 1564–1610.

Bernard, Andrew, and Bradford Jensen. 2004. Exporting and Productivity in the USA. *Oxford Review of Economic Policy* 20(3): 343–357.

Bernard, Andrew, Bradford Jensen, Stephen Redding, and Peter Schott. 2012. The Empirics of Firms Heterogeneity and International Trade. *Annual Review of Economics* 4(1): 283–313.

Bhagwati, J. 1992. Regionalism and Multilateralism: An Overview. In *New Dimensions in Regional Integration*, edited by Melo and Panagariya. Cambridge: Cambridge University Press.

Bharadwaj, Prashant, Leah Lakdawala, and Nicholas Li. 2014. Perverse Consequences of Well-Intended Regulations: Evidence from India's Child Labor Ban. NBER Working Paper 19602.

Biesebroeck, Johannes Van. 2005. Exporting Raises Productivity in Sub-Saharan African Manufacturing Firms. *Journal of International Economics* 67(2): 373–391.

Biesebroeck, Johannes van, Jozef Konings, and Christian Volpe-Martincus. 2015. Did Export Promotion Help Firms Weather the Crisis? *Economic Policy* 31 (88): 653–702.

Bigsten, Arne, Paul Collier, Stefan Dercon et al. 2000. Contract Flexibility, and Dispute Resolution in African Manufacturing. *Journal of Development Studies* 36(4): 1–17.

Blackorby, Charles, and David Donaldson. 1988. Cash versus Kind, Self-Selection, and Efficient Transfers. *American Economic Review* 78(4): 691–700.

Blalock, Garrick, and Paul Gertler. 2004. Learning from Exporting Revisited in a Less Developed Setting. *Journal of Development Economics* 75: 397–416.

Blanchard, Emily, Chad Bown, and Robert Johnson. 2016. Global Supply Chains and Trade Policy, CEPR DP No.11044.

Bohara, A., K. Gawande, and P. Sanguinetti. 2004. Trade Diversion and Declining Tariffs: Evidence from Mercosur. *Journal of International Economics* 64: 65–88.

Bown, Chad. 2009. *Self-Enforcing Trade: Developing Countries and the WTO Dispute Settlement.* Washington, DC: Brookings Institution.

———. 2015. What's Left for the WTO? World Bank DP No. 7502.

Bown, Chad, and Kara Reynolds. 2017. Trade Agreements and Enforcement: Evidence from WTO Dispute Settlement. *American Economic Journal: Economic Policy* 9(4): 64–100.

Brecher, Richard. 1974. Minimum Wage Rates and the Pure Theory of International Trade. *Quarterly Journal of Economics* 88(1): 98–116.

Breinlich, Holger, David Donaldson, Patrick Nolen, and Greg Wright. 2017. Information, Perceptions and Exporting—Evidence from a Randomized Control Trial. Working Paper, University of Essex.

Brenton, Paul, Christian Saborowski, and Erik Von Uexkull. 2010. What Explains the Low Survival of Developing Country Exports? *World Bank Economic Review* 24(3): 474–499.

Broda, Christian, Nuno Limão, and David Weinstein. 2008. Optimal Tariffs and Market Power: The Evidence. *American Economic Review* 98(5): 2032–2065.

Broocks, Annette, and Johannes Van Biesebroeck. 2017. The Impact of Export Promotion on Export Market Entry. *Journal of International Economics* 107: 19–33.

Cadot, Olivier, Ana Fernandes, Julien Gourdon, and Aadiyta Mattoo. 2015. Are the Benefits from Export Support Durable? *Journal of International Economics* 97(2): 310–324.

Cadot, Olivier, Ana Fernandes, Julien Gourdon, Aaditya Mattoo, and Jaime de Melo. 2014. Evaluating Aid for Trade: A Survey of Recent Studies. *World Economy* 37(4): 516–529.

Calvo-Pardo, Hector, Caroline Freund, and Emmanuel Ornelas. 2009. *The Asean Free Trade Agreement: Impact on Trade Flows and External Trade Barriers in Costs and Benefits of Regional Economic Integration.* Oxford: Oxford University Press.

Carrère, Céline, Jaime de Melo, and John Wilson. 2013. The Distance Puzzle and Low-Income Countries: An Update. *Journal of Economic Surveys* 27(4): 717–742.

Chichilnisky, Graciela. 1994. North-South Trade and the Global Environment. *American Economic Review* 84(4): 851–874.

Chor, Davin. 2010. Unpacking Sources of Comparative Advantage: A Quantitative Approach. *Journal of International Economics* 82(2): 152–167.

Clerides, Sofronis, Saul Lach, and James Tybout. 1998. Is "learning by exporting" Important? Micro-dynamic Evidence from Colombia, Mexico and Morocco. *Quarterly Journal of Economics* 113(3): 903–947.

Collier, Paul. 2007. *The Bottom Billion.* Oxford: Oxford University Press.

———. 2010. *The Plundered Planet: How to Reconcile Prosperity with Nature.* Oxford: Oxford University Press.

Collier, Paul, and Anthony J. Venables. 2010. International Rules for Trade in Natural Resources. *Journal of Globalisation and Development* 1(1)- ISS1. Art1. 1–19.

Conconi, Paola, and Carlo Perroni. 2012. Conditional versus Unconditional Trade Concessions for Developing Countries. *Canadian Journal of Economics* 45: 613–631.

———. 2015. Special and Differential Treatment of Developing Countries in the WTO. *World Trade Review* 14: 67–86.

Copeland, Brian R. 2008. Is There a Case for Trade and Investment Promotion Policy? In *Trade Policy Research 2007*, edited by Dan Ciuriak. Ottawa: Foreign Affairs and International Trade Canada.

Copeland, Brian R., and M. Scott Taylor. 2009. Trade, Tragedy, and the Commons. *American Economic Review* 99(3): 725–749.

Cruz, Marcio. 2014. Essays in Trade and Development Economics. Phd dissertation: Graduate Institute of International and Development Studies, Geneva.

Davis, Christina, and Meredith Wilf. 2016. WTO Membership. In *The Oxford Handbook of the Political Economy of International Trade* edited by Lisa Martin, ch. 20. Oxford: Oxford University Press.

Dell, Melissa. 2010. The Persistent Effect of Peru's Mining Mita. *Econometrica* 78(6): 1863–1903.

Disdier, Anne-Célia, Lionel Fontagné, and Olivier Cadot. 2015. North-South Standards Harmonization and International Trade. *World Bank Economic Review* 29(2): 327–352.

Djankov, Simeon, and Sandra Sequeira. 2014. Corruption and Firm Behaviour: Evidence from African Ports. *Journal of International Economics* 94(2): 277–329.

Dollar, David, and Aart Kraay. 2003. Institutions, Trade and Growth. *Journal of Monetary Economics* 50: 133–162.

Dragusanu, Raluca, Daniele Giovannucci, and Nathan Nunn. 2014. The Economics of Fair Trade. *Journal of Economics Perspectives* 28(3): 217–236.

Dragusanu, Raluca, and Nathaniel Nunn. 2018. The Impacts of Fair Trade Certification: Evidence from Coffee Producers in Costa Rica. NBER working paper 24260.

Dutt, Pushan, and Daniel Traça. 2010. Corruption and Bilateral Trade Flows: Extortion or Evasion? *Review of Economics and Statistics* 92(4): 843–860.

Egger, P., and F. Tarlea. 2017. Comparing Apples to Apples: Estimating Consistent Partial Effects of Preferential Economic Integration Agreements. CEPR DP No. 11894.

Ehrlich, S. 2007. Access to Protection: Domestic Institutions and Trade Policies in Democracies. *International Organization* 61(3): 571–605.

Eicher, Theo, and Christian Henn. 2011. In Search of WTO Trade Effects: Preferential Trade Agreements Promote Trade Strongly but Unevenly. *Journal of International Economics* 83(2): 137–153.

Engerman, Stanley, and Kenneth Solokoff. 2000. Paths of Development in the New World. *Journal of Economic Perspectives* 76: 166–176.

———. 2012. *Economic Development in the Americas since 1500: Endowments and Institutions*. Cambridge: Cambridge University Press.

Estache, Antonio, and Caroline Philippe. 2016. What If the TTIP Changed the Regulation of Public Services? Lessons for Europe from Developing Countries. ECARES working paper 2016–26.

Estevadeordal, Antoni, Caroline Freund, and Emmanuel Ornelas. 2008. Does Regionalism Affect Trade Regionalism Towards Non-Members? *Quarterly Journal of Economics* 123: 1531–1575.

Ethier, Wilfred, J. 1998. Regionalism in a Multilateral World. *Journal of Political Economy* 106(6): 1214–1245.

———. 2013. The Trade-Agreement Embarassement. *Journal of East Asian Economic Integration* 17: 243–260.

Feder, Gershon. 1982. On Exports and Economic Growth. *Journal of Development Economics* 12: 59–73.

Felbermayr, Gabriel, and Farid Toubal. 2010. Cultural Proximity and Trade. *European Economic Review* 54(2): 279–293.

Fernandez, Ana, and Heiwai Tang. 2014. Learning to Export from Neighbors. *Journal of International Economics* 94: 67–84.

Fernandez, R., and J. Portes. 1998. Returns to Regionalism: An Analysis of Nontraditional Gains from Regional Trade Agreements. *World Bank Economic Review* 12(2): 197–220.

Feyrer, James. 2009. Distance, Trade and Income: The 1967 to 1975 Closing of the Suez Canal as a Natural Experiment. NBER working paper 15557.

Finger, J. Michael. 1999. The WTO's Special Burden on Less Developed Countries. *Cato Journal* 19(3): 425–437.

Finger, J. Michael, and P. Schuler. 2000. Implementation of the Uruguay Round: The Development Challenge. *World Economy* 23(4): 511–525.

———, eds. 2004. *Poor Peoples Knowledge: Promoting Intellectual Property in Developing Countries*. Oxford: Oxford University Press for the World Bank.

Fink, Carsten, and Keith Maskus. 2005. *Intellectual Property And Development: Lessons From Economic Research*. Oxford: Oxford University Press for the World Bank.

Fiorini, M., and M. Lebrand. 2016. The Political Economy of Services Trade Agreements. CESIFO No. 5927.

Fischer, Carolyn. 2010. Does Trade Help or Hinder the Conservation of Natural Resources? *Review of Environmental Economics and Policy* 4(1): 103–121.

Fischer, Carolyn, and Thomas P. Lyon. 2014. Competing Environmental Labels. *Journal of Economics & Management Strategy* 23(3): 692–716.

Fisman, R., and S. Wei. 2004. Tax Rates and Tax Evasion: Evidence from Missing Imports in China. *Journal of Political Economy* 112(2): 471–496.

Foletti, Liliana, Marco Fugazza, Alessandro Nicita, and Marcelo Olarreaga. 2011. Smoke in the (Tariff) Water. *World Economy* 34(2): 248–264.

Foroutan, Faezeh. 1992. Regional Integration in Sub-Saharan Africa. In *New Dimensions in Regional Integration*, edited by Melo and Panagariya. Cambridge: Cambridge University Press.

———. 1998. Does Membership in a Regional Preferential Trade Arrangement Make a Country More or Less Protectionist? *World Economy* 21(3): 305–355.

Foster-McGregor, Neil, Anders Isaksson, and Florian Kaulich. 2014. Learning by Exporting Versus Self-Selection: New Evidence from 19 Sub-Saharan African Countries. *Economic Letters* 125(2): 212–214.

François, Joseph, and Miriam Manchin. 2013. Institutions, Infrastructure and Trade. *World Development* 46: 165–175.

Frankel, Jeffrey, and David Romer. 1999. Does Trade Cause Growth? *American Economic Review* 89(3): 379–399.

Freund, Caroline, and Emanuel Ornelas. 2010. Regional Trade Agreements, Annual Review of Economics. *Annual Reviews* 2(1): 139–166.

Garfinkel, Michelle R., Stergios Skaperdas, and Constantinos Syropoulos. 2015. Trade and Insecure Resources. *Journal of International Economics* 95(1): 98–114.

Gatti, Roberta. 1999. Corruption and Trade Tariffs, or A Case for Uniform Tariffs. Policy Research Working Paper Series 2216, World Bank.

Gereffi, G., and F. Mayer. 2006. Globalization and the Demand for Governance. In *The New Offshoring of Jobs and Global Development*, edited by G. Gereffi, 39–58. ILO Social Policy Lectures. International Institute for Labor Studies, Geneva.

Glickman, Lawrence. 2004. Buy for the Sake of the Slave: Abolitionism and the Origins of American Consumer Activism. *American Quarterly* 56(4): 889–912.

Goldberg, Pinelopi, and Nina Pavcnik. 2016. The Effects of Trade Policy. In *Handbook of Commercial Policy*, vol. 1, part A, edited by Bagwell and Staiger, 161–206.

Gopinath, Gita, Elhanan Helpman, and Kenneth Rogoff, eds. 2014. *Handbook of International Economics*. Amsterdam: North-Holland.

Green, Jessica. 2013. *Rethinking Private Authority: Agents and Entrepreneurs in Global Environmental Governance*. Princeton, NJ: Princeton University Press.

Greenaway, David, and Richard Kneller. 2004. Exporting and Productivity in the United Kingdom. *Oxford Review of Economic Policy* 20(3): 358–371.

Grether, J. M., N. Mathys, and J. de Melo. 2012. Unravelling the World-Wide Pollution Haven Effect. *Journal of International Trade and Development* 21(1): 131–162.

Grossman, Gene. 2016. The Purpose of Trade Agreements. In Bagwell and Staiger eds., *Handbook of Commercial Policy*, vol. 1, part A, 379–434.

Guiso, Luigi, Paolo Sapienza, and Luigi Zingales. 2009. Cultural Biases in Economic Exchange. *Quarterly Journal of Economics* 124(3): 1095–1131.

Hainmueller, J., M. Hiscox, and S. Sequeira. 2015. Consumer Demand for the Fair Trade Label: Evidence from a Multi-Store Field Experiment. *Review of Economics and Statistics* 97(2): 242–256.

Handley, Kyle. 2014. Exporting under Trade Policy Uncertainty: Theory and Evidence. *Journal of International Economics* 94(1): 50–66.

Handley, Kyle, and Nuno Limão. 2015. Trade and Investment under Policy Uncertainty: Theory and Firm Evidence. *American Economic Journal: Economic Policy* 7(4): 189–222.

Hausmann, Ricardo, Jason Hwang, and Dani Rodrik. 2007. What You Export Matters. *Journal of Economic Growth* 12(1): 1–25.

Hausmann, Ricardo, and Dani Rodrik. 2003. Economic Development As Self-Discovery. *Journal of Development Economics* 72(2): 603–633.

Hayakawa, Kazunobu, Hyun-Hoon Lee, and Donghyun Park. 2014. Do Export Promotion Agencies Increase Exports? *Developing Economies* 52(3): 241–261.

Head, Keith, and Thierry Mayer. 2014. Gravity Equations: Workhorse, Toolkit and Cookbook. In *Handbook of International Economics*, edited by Gopinath et al., ch 4.

Helleiner, Gerald K. 2002. *Non-traditional Export Promotion in Africa: Experience and Issues*. United Kingdom: Palgrave MacMillan.

Helpman, Elhanan, Oleg Itskhoki, Marc-Andreas Muendler, and Stephen Redding. 2015. Trade and Income Inequality: from theory to estimation. Mimeo. Princeton University.

Helpman, Elhanan, Oleg Itskhoki, and Stephen Redding. 2010. Inequality and Unemployment in a Global Economy. *Econometrica* 78(4): 1239–1283.

Hogan, Paul, Donald Keesing, and Andrew Singer. 1991. The Role of Support Services in Expanding Manufactured Exports in Developing Countries. Mimeo, World Bank.

Horn, Henrik, Giovanni Maggi, and Robert Staiger. 2010. Trade Agreements as Endogenously Incomplete Contracts. *American Economic Review* 100(1): 394–419.

Horn, Henrik, Petros Mavroidis, and André Sapir. 2010. Beyond the WTO: An Anatomy of EU and US Preferential Trade Agreements. *World Economy* 33(11): 1565–1588.

Ibanez, L., and G. Grolleau. 2008. Can Ecolabeling Schemes Preserve the Environment? *Environmental and Resource Economics* 40: 233–249.

Janvry, Alain de, Craig McIntosh, and Elisabeth Sadoulet. 2015. Fair Trade and Free Entry: Can a Disequilibrium Market Serve as a Development Tool? *Review of Economics and Statistics* 97(3): 567–573.

Jarreau, Joachim, and Sandra Poncet. 2012. Export Sophistication and Economic Growth: Evidence from China. *Journal of Development Economics* 97: 281–292.

Javorcik, Beata, W. Keller, and J. Tybout. 2008. Openness and Industrial Response in a Wal-Mart World: A Case Study of Mexican Soaps, Detergents and Surfactant Producers. *World Economy* 31(12): 1558–1580.

Javorcik, B., and G. Narciso. 2017. Accession to the World Trade Organization and Tariff Evasion. *Journal of Development Economics* 125: 59–71.

Johns, Leslie, and Lauren Peritz. 2015. The Design of Trade Agreements. In *The Oxford Handbook of the Political Economy of International Trade,* edited by Lisa Martin, ch 18. Oxford: Oxford University Press.

Jong, Eelke de, and Christian Bogmans. 2011. Does Corruption Discourage International Trade? *European Journal of Political Economy* 27(2): 385–398.

Karacaovali, Baybars, and Nuno Limão. 2008. The Clash Of Liberalizations: Preferential vs. Multilateral Trade Liberalization in the European Union. *Journal of International Economics* 74(2): 299–327.

Kaufmann, D., A. Kraay, and M. Mastruzzi. 2003. Governance Matters III: Governance Indicators for 1996–2002. World Bank Policy Research working paper 3106.

Kedia, Ben, and Jagdeep Chhokar. 1986. An Empirical Investigation of Export Promotion Programs. *Columbia Journal of World Business* 21: 13–20.

Keesing, Donald, and Andrew Singer. 1991. *Development Assistance Gone Wrong: Failures in Services to Promote and Support Manufactured Exports.* Economic Development Institute, World Bank.

Keller, W., and C. Shiue. 2008. Institutions, Technology and Trade. NBER working paper No. 13913.

Khandelwal, Amit K., Peter K. Schott, and Shang-Jin Wei. 2013. Trade Liberalization and Embedded Institutional Reform: Evidence from Chinese Exporters. *American Economic Review* 103(6): 2169–2195.

Koenig, Pamina, Florian Mayneris, and Sandra Poncet. 2010. Local Export Spillovers in France. *European Economic Review* 54(4): 622–641.

Kotabe, Massaki, and Michael R. Czinkota. 1992. State Government Promotion of Manufacturing Exports: A Gap Analysis. *Journal of International Business Studies* 23(4): 637–658.

Krautheim, Sebastian, and Thierry Verdier. 2016. Offshoring with Endogenous NGO Activism. *Journal of International Economics,* Elsevier, vol. 101(C): 22–41.

Krishna, Pravin. 2003. Are Regional Trade Partners Natural? *Journal of Political Economy* 111(1): 202–26.

———. 2013. Preferential Trade Agreements in the World Trading System: A Multilateralist View. In *Globalization in an Age of Crisis: Multilateral Economic Cooperation in the Twenty-First Century,* edited by R. Feenstra and A. Taylor. Chicago: University of Chicago Press.

Leamer, Edward, and James Levinsohn. 1995. International Trade: The Evidence. In *Handbook of International Economics* vol. 3, edited by Gene Grossman and Kenneth Rogoff, 1339–1394. Amsterdam: Elsevier North-Holland.

Lederman, Daniel, Marcelo Olarreaga, and Lucy Payton. 2010. Export Promotion Agencies: Do They Work? *Journal of Development Economics* 91: 257–265.

Lederman, Daniel, Marcelo Olarreaga, and Lucas Zavala. 2016. Export Promotion and Firm Entry into and Survival in Export Markets. *Canadian Journal of Development Economics* 37(2): 142–158.

Lendle, Andreas, Marcelo Olarreaga, Simon Schropp, and Pierre-Louis Vézina. 2013. eBay Anatomy. *Economics Letters* 121: 115–120.

———. 2015. There Goes Gravity: How eBay Reduces Trade Costs. *Economic Journal* 126: 401–441.

Lendle, Andreas, and Pierre-Louis Vézina. 2015. Internet Technology and the Extensive Margin of Trade: Evidence from eBay in Emerging Economies. *Review of Development Economics* 19(2): 375–386.

Levchenko, Andrei. 2007. Institutional Quality and International Trade. *Review of Economic Studies* 74(3): 791–819.

———. 2012. International Trade and Institutional Change. *Journal of Law, Economics and Organization* 29(5): 1145–1181.

Limão, Nuno. 2006. Preferential Trade Agreements as Stumbling Blocs for Multilateral Trade Liberalization: Evidence from the US. *American Economic Review* 96(3): 896–914.

———. 2007. Are Preferential Trade Agreements with Non-Trade Objectives a Stumbling Block for Multilateral Liberalization? *Review of Economic Studies* 74(3): 821–855.

———. 2016. Preferential Trade Agreements. In *Handbook of Commercial Policy*, edited by Bagwell and Staiger, ch 5. Also NBER working paper 22138.

Liu, Xuepeng, and Emmanuel Ornelas. 2014. Free Trade Agreements and the Consolidation of Democracy. *American Economic Journal: Macroeconomics* 6(2): 29–70.

Ludema, Ronald, and Anna-Maria Mayda. 2013. Do Terms of Trade Effects Matter for Trade Agreements. *Quarterly Journal of Economics* 128(4): 1837–1893.

Maggi, Giovanni. 2014. International Trade Agreements. In *Handbook of International Economics*, edited by Gopinath, ch 6. Also Cowles Discussion paper no. 1417.

Maggi, Giovanni, and Andrés Rodríguez-Clare. 1998. The Value of Trade Agreements in the Presence of Political Pressures. *Journal of Political Economy* 106(3): 574–601.

———. 2007. A Political-Economy Theory of Trade Agreements. *American Economic Review* 97(4): 1374–1406.

Manacorda, Marco, and Andrea Tesi. 2016. Liberation Technology: Mobile Phones and Political Mobilization in Africa. CEPR No. 11278.

Mansfield, E., and E. Reinhardt. 2007. International Institutions and the Volatility of International Trade. *International Organization* 62(4): 621–652.

Martin, Lisa, ed. 2015. *The Oxford Handbook of the Political Economy of International Trade*. Oxford: Oxford University Press.

Martin, P., T. Mayer, and M. Thoenig. 2008. Make Trade, Not War. *Review of Economic Studies* 75(3): 865–900.

———. 2012. The Geography of Conflicts and Regional Trade Agreements. *American Journal: Macroeconomics* 4(4): 1–35.

Mason, Charles. 2013. The Economics of Eco-Labeling: Theory and Empirical Implications. *International Review of Environmental and Resource Economics* 6: 341–372.

Mattoo, Aaditya, and Harsha Singh. 1994. Eco-Labeling: Policy Considerations. *Kyklos* 47(1): 53–65.

Mavroidis, P., and J. de Melo. 2015. Climate Change Policies and the WTO: Greening the GATT Revisited. In *Towards a Workable and Effective Climate Regime*, edited by S. Barrett, C. Carraro, and J. de Melo, 225–239. CEPR and FERDI.

Mayer, Thierry, and Mathias Thoenig. 2016. Regional Trade Agreements and the Pacification of Eastern Africa. IGC working paper.

Maystre, Nicolas, Jacques Olivier, Mathias Thoenig, and Thierry Verdier. 2014. Product-Based Cultural Change: Is the Village Global. *Journal of International Economics* 92(2): 212–230.

McCallum, John. 1995. National Borders Matter: Canada-US Regional Trade Patterns. *American Economic Review* 85(3): 615–623.

McMillan, M. 2001. Why Kill the Golden Goose? A Political Economy Model of Export Taxation. *Review of Economics and Statistics* 83(1): 170–184.

McMillan, M., K. Horn, and D. Rodrik. 2003. When Economic Reform Goes Wrong: Cashews in Mozambique. Brookings Trade Forum, 97–151.

Melo, J. de. 2010. Trade Reforms in Natural-Resource-Abundant Economies. In *Trade Adjustment Costs in Developing Countries: Impacts, Determinants and Policy Responses*, edited by G. Porto and B. Hoekman. CEPR and World Bank.

Melo, Jaime de, Claudio Montenegro, and Arvind Panagariya. 1992. Regional Integration, Old and New. WBSP No. 985.

Melo, J. de, M. Olarreaga, and W. Takacs. 2000. Pricing Under Double Market Power: Madagascar and the International Vanilla Market. *Review of Development Economics* 4(1): 1–20.

Melo, Jaime de, and Arvind Panagariya, eds. 1992. *New Dimensions in Regional Integration*. Cambridge University Press and CEPR.

Melo, Jaime de, and Arvind Panagariya. 1992. Introduction. In Melo and Panagariya, eds., *New Dimensions in Regional Integration*, 3–21.

Melo, Jaime de, Arvind Panagariya, and Dani Rodrik. 1992. Regionalism: A Country Perspective. In Melo and Panagariya eds., *New Dimensions in Regional Integration*, 159–201.

Melo, Jaime de, and Julie Régolo. 2014. The African Economic Partnership Agreements with the EU: Reflections Inspired by the Case of the East African Community. *Journal of African Trade* 1(1): 15–24.

Melo, Jaime de, and Yvonne Tsikata. 2015. Regional Integration in Africa: Challenges and Prospects. In *The Oxford Handbook of African Economics: vol. 2: Practices and Policies*, edited by C. Monga and J. Lin. Oxford: Oxford University Press.

Michalopoulos, Stelios, and Elias Papaioannou. 2013. Pre-colonial Ethnic Institutions and Contemporary African Development. *Econometrica* 81(1): 113–152.

———. 2014. National Institutions and Subnational Development in Africa. *Quarterly Journal of Economics* 126(1): 115–213.

Milgrom, Paul, Douglas North, and Barry Weingast. 1990. The Role of Institutions in the Revival of Trade: The Law Merchant, Private Judges, and the Champagne Fairs. *Economics and Politics* 2(1): 1–23.

Mion, Giordano, and Luca Opromolla. 2014. Managers' Mobility, Trade Performance and Wages. *Journal of International Economics* 94: 85–101.

Moncarz, Pedro, Marcelo Olarreaga, and Marcel Vaillant. 2016. Regionalism as Industrial Policy: Evidence from Mercosur. *Review of Development Economics* 20(1): 359–373.

Mrázová, Monika. 2015. Trade Agreements When Profits Matter. Mimeo, University of Geneva.

Munch, Jacob, and Georg Schaur. 2018. The Effect of Export Promotion on Firm-Level Performance. *American Economic Journal: Economic Policy* 10(1): 357–387.

Negri, Mariano, and Guido Porto. 2016. Burley Tobacco Clubs in Malawi: Non-Market Institutions for Exports. *International Economics* 146: 85–107.

Nicita, Alessandro, Marcelo Olarreaga, and Peri Silva. 2018. Cooperation in WTO's Tariff Waters? *Journal of Political Economy* 126(3): 1302–1338.

Nordhaus, William. 2015. Climate Clubs: Overcoming Free Riding in International Climate Policy. *American Economic Review* 105: 1–32.

Novy, Dennis. 2013. Gravity Redux: Measuring International Trade Costs with Panel Data. *Economic Inquiry* 51(1): 101–121.

Nunn, Nathaniel. 2007. Relationship-Specificity, Incomplete Contracts, and the Pattern of Trade. *Quarterly Journal of Economics* 122(2): 569–600.

Nunn, Nathaniel, and Daniel Trefler. 2010. The Structure of Tariffs and Long-run Growth. *American Economic Journal: Macroeconomics* 2(4): 158–194.

———. 2015. Domestic Institutions as a Source of Comparative Advantage. In *Handbook of International Economics*, vol. 4, edited by Gopinath et al., ch 5.

Olarreaga, Marcelo, Stefan Sperlich, and Virginie Trachsel. 2019. Exploring the Heterogeneous Effects of Export Promotion. *World Bank Economic Review,* forthcoming.

Ornelas, Emmanuel. 2016. Special and Differential Treatment for Developing Countries. In *Handbook of Commercial Policy*, vol. 1, part A, edited by Bagwell and Staiger, 369–342.

Ossa, Ralph. 2011. A New Trade Theory of the GATT/WTO Negotiations. *Journal of Political Economy* 119(1): 122–152.

———. 2014. Trade Wars and Trade Talks with Data. *American Economic Review* 104(12): 4104–4146.

Ozden, Caglar, and Eric Reinhardt. 2005. The Perversity of Preferences: GSP and Developing Country Trade Policies. *Journal of Development Economics* 78: 1–21.

Peters, Jorg, Jorg Langbein, and Gareth Roberts. 2016. Policy Evaluation, Randomized Controlled Trials, and External Validity—A Systematic Review. *Economic Letters* 147: 51–54.

Podhorsky, Andrea. 2013. Certification Programs and North–South Trade. *Journal of Public Economics* 108: 90–104.

———. 2015. A Positive Analysis of Fair Trade Certification. *Journal of Development Economics* 116: 169–185.

Polaski, Sandra. 2004. Cambodia Blazes a New Path to Economic Growth and Job Creation. Carnegie Paper.

Poncet, Sandra, and Felipe Starosta. 2013. Export Upgrading and Growth: The Prerequisite of Domestic Embeddedness. *World Development* 51: 104–118.

Pritchett, Lant. 2013. Comments on Institutions, Trade and Growth. *Journal of Monetary Economics* 50: 163–166.

Puga, D., and D. Trefler. 2014. International Trade and Institutional Change: Medieval Venice's Response to Globalization. *Quarterly Journal of Economics* 129(2): 753–821.

Regan, D. H. 2006. What Are Trade Agreements For? Two Conflicting Stories Told by Economists with a Lesson for Lawyers. *Journal of International Economic Law* 9: 951–988.

———. 2015. Explaining Trade Agreements: The Practioners' Story and the Standard Model. *World Trade Review* 14(3): 391–417.

Rose, Andrew. 2005. Does the WTO Make Trade More Stable? *Open Economies Review* 16(1): 7–22.

———. 2007. The Foreign Service and Foreign Trade: Embassies as Export Promotion. *World Economy* 30(1): 22–38.

Ruta, Michele, and Anthony J. Venables. 2013. International Trade in Natural Resources: Practice and Policy. *Annual Review of Resource Economics* 4(1): 331–352.

Sapir, Andre. 1998. The Political Economy of EC Regionalism. *European Economic Review* 42: 717–732.

Schiff, M., and A. Winters. 2003. Regional Integration and Development, World Bank.

Sequeira, Sandra. 2016. Corruption, Trade Costs and Gains from Tariff Liberalization: Evidence from Southern Africa. *American Economic Review* 106(10): 3029–3063.

Shy, Oz. 2000. Exporting as a Signal for Product Quality. *Economica* 67(265): 79–90.

Spolaore, Enrico. 2013. What Is European Integration Really About? A Political Guide for Economists. *Journal of Economic Perspectives* 27(3): 125–144.

Spolaore, Enrico, and Romain Wacziarg. 2009. The Diffusion of Development. *Quarterly Journal of Economics* 124(2): 469–529.

———. 2014. How Deep Are the Roots of Economic Development. *Journal of Economic Literature* 51(2): 1–45.

Staiger, Robert, and Guido Tabellini. 1987. Discretionary Trade Policy and Excessive Protection. *American Economic Review* 77(5): 823–837.

Subramanian, Arvind, and Shang-Jin Wei. 2007. The WTO Promotes Trade, Strongly But Unevenly. *Journal of International Economics* 72(1): 151–175.

Tang, M.-K., and S.-J. Wei. 2009. The Value of Making Commitments Externally: Evidence from WTO Accessions. *Journal of International Economics* 78(1): 216–229.

Trefler, Daniel. 1995. The Case of Missing Trade and Other Mysteries. *American Economic Review* 85(5): 1029–1046.

Tsui, Kevin. 2011. More Oil, Less Democracy: Evidence from Worldwide Crude Oil Discoveries. *Economic Journal* 121(89): 115–122.

Vezina, Pierre-Louis. 2014. Race to the Bottom Tariff Cutting. *Review of International Economics* 22(3): 444–458.

Victor, David. 2015. The Case for Climate Clubs. E-15 Initiative, ICSTD.

Volpe, Christian, and Jerónimo Carballo. 2008. Is Export Promotion Effective in Developing Countries? Firm-Level Evidence on the Intensive and the Extensive Margins of Exports. *Journal of International Economics* 76: 89–106.

———. 2010a. Beyond the Average Effects: The Distributional Impacts of Export Promotion Programs in Developing Countries. *Journal of Development Economics* 92: 201–214.

———. 2010b. Export Promotion: Bundled Services Work Better. *World Economy* 33: 1718–1756.

Volpe, Christian, Jerónimo Carballo, and Pablo M. Garcia. 2012. Public Programs to Promote Firms' Exports in Developing Countries: Are There Heterogeneous Effects by Size Categories? *Applied Economics* 44(4): 471–491.

Wacziarg, Romain, and Karen Welch. 2008. Trade Liberalization and Growth: The Evidence. *World Bank Economic Review* 22(2): 187–231.

Wade, Robert. 2003. What Strategies Are Viable for Developing Countries Today? The World Trade Organization and the Shrinking of "Development Space." *Review of International Political Economy* 10(4): 621–644.

Wei, Shangjin, Ziru Wei, and Jianhuan Xu. 2014. Assessing Market Failures in Export Pioneering Activities: Evidence from Chinese Exporters. CEPR Discussion paper 10187.

Whalley, John. 2011. What Role for Trade in a Post 2012 Global Climate Policy Regime. *World Economy* 34(11): 1844–1862.

World Trade Organization. 2011. World Trade Report: The WTO and Preferential Trade Agreements: From Co-existence to Coherence.

Xu, Ankai. 2015. The Trade of Virtual Water: Do Property Rights Matter? Mimeo. IHEID, Geneva.

Yang, Dean. 2008. Can Enforcement Backfire? Crime Displacement in the Context of Customs Reform in the Philippines. *Review of Economics and Statistics* 90(1): 1–14

Yotov, Y. 2012. A Simple Solution to the Distance Puzzle. *Economics Letters* 117: 794–798.

9

FOREIGN AID AND GOVERNANCE

A Survey

François Bourguignon and Jan Willem Gunning

9.1. INTRODUCTION

The volume of foreign aid that a country receives, its effectiveness in promoting development, and the quality of its governance and institutions are intimately linked. A low level of governance inevitably reduces the impact of aid on development and discourages donors, who worry that only a small part of aid will actually reach its intended goal. At the same time, through conditioning aid on institutional reforms, donors may also try to promote key governance improvements favorable to development. Failing this, however, foreign aid may actually be a disincentive, rather than an incentive, to institutional reforms and may even be responsible for a deterioration of the quality of governance in recipient countries.

Donors could enhance the effectiveness of aid if they could condition their contribution upon how it would be used or the observed development results in recipient countries. In doing so, however, they face four major types of constraint, most of which are essentially institutional:

1. the ability of the government of the recipient country to change the effects of aid from what the donor intended, either directly, by exploiting fungibility, or indirectly, by changing (or not changing!) policies;
2. the limited credibility of the threat of sanctions by donors if conditionality is not met, i.e., the so-called Samaritan dilemma;
3. the competition among donors, which may trap individual donors in some inefficient non-cooperative equilibrium;
4. the cost of effectively monitoring aid programs.

There is also a possibility that the conditionality sought by donors may not fit the needs or the reality of the recipient country.

Even though effectiveness may be enhanced through progress in alleviating the preceding constraints, thus reducing the leakage of aid toward non-developmental uses, the risk exists that "free" public resources undermine the quality of the governance and political institutions in the recipient country. The case most often made concerns the limited need to resort to taxation to finance public activity and public goods, which diminishes the accountability of the State to citizens and facilitates the persistence of corrupt authoritarian regimes.

This two-way negative relationship between foreign aid, its development effectiveness, and the weakness of institutions in developing countries has triggered severe critiques of foreign aid, and even suggestions that it should be eliminated (Easterly 2006; Moyo 2009; Deaton 2013). On the side of the donors, it has made the allocation of aid more selective, favoring countries with better governance and leaving aside worse governed, and most often poorer countries. In both cases, a major consequence is to reduce and/or misallocate the resources potentially available to foster the reduction of global poverty.

The main goal of this survey is to review the economic theory and the evidence underlying the preceding arguments, with a view toward identifying ways of minimizing the potentially negative spillovers of foreign aid on the governance of recipient countries and improving the overall institutional apparatus of aid delivery in donor and recipient countries, as well as in international organizations.

The literature on foreign aid is voluminous, especially on the issue of the effectiveness of aid or the aid-growth relationship. This chapter intends to be selective, with an emphasis on the institutional factors that determine the volume, the allocation, and the effectiveness of aid, and on its institutional consequences in recipient countries.

The chapter first offers a short synthesis of the theoretical literature on the aid donor–recipient relationship based on a main model that covers several dimensions of that relationship. The first part of the chapter (section 9.2) thus provides a general theoretical reference for the review of the policy-oriented literature on the two-way relationship between governance and aid in the rest of the chapter. The following two parts deal with the more applied literature considering in turn the way aid can affect development outcomes.

One way is by relaxing the budget constraint of the recipient country. In this view, aid enables the government to finance activities that it would not have funded without it. What matters in this case is the size of the increase, not its source: if government revenue had increased by the same amount in some other way (for example as a result of an oil boom), then it would have been spent in exactly the same way. In this case, therefore, aid is assumed to have no effect on the way the government spends additional revenue or on institutional arrangements in the economy. Aid has an effect solely by providing additional revenue and thereby enabling an increase in government spending. This is the case of *aid as finance* handled in section 9.3. Such a view seems to closely resemble the way foreign aid was initially perceived and the famous "two-gap model."[1] In the spirit of a survey that deals with aid and institutions, however, that section will essentially deal with the way governance and other institutional factors affect how much a given country receives or how donors allocate their aid among countries.

Alternatively, aid is seen as an instrument for changing policies and institutions in a way favorable to achieving donor objectives, first of all poverty reduction. In this view, such reform would not have taken place without the aid; in particular, it would not have taken place if the government had received the same amount of additional revenue from another source. This implies that donor and government objectives differ: the aid is needed to convince the government to undertake a reform which it would not have implemented otherwise, even if it had the resources.[2] This is the case of *aid as reform*.

This taxonomy is useful. For example, some critics of conditionality consider it an illusion to think that aid can be used to change policies or institutions. In effect they argue that aid can be effective only as finance. (This amounts to a return of what was the conventional wisdom half a century ago.) In practice, aid can play both roles, but conceptually they are clearly quite different. The distinction between aid as finance and aid as reform is therefore often illuminating and we will use it frequently.

The discussion of "aid for reform" is organized into two parts. Section 9.4 discusses the various channels through which aid can possibly affect the institutions of recipient countries, several of them in the line of the arguments developed in the first part of this survey but within a more pragmatic perspective. Section 9.5 concentrates on the evidence available regarding the actual impact of aid on institutions. This literature extends the voluminous body of work on the effectiveness of aid, effectiveness being considered almost exclusively under the angle of GDP growth, which is also briefly summarized in that part of the chapter.

Section 9.6 is devoted to the issues that remain largely unanswered in the aid-governance literature and possible directions for future research.

9.2. GOVERNANCE AND CONDITIONALITY IN CANONICAL MODELS OF THE DONOR-RECIPIENT RELATIONSHIP

Despite the importance of the subject for development and despite the intensity of the debate on the effectiveness of aid, there are relatively few fully elaborated theoretical models of the relationship between donors of aid and governments in recipient countries. It is true that the principal-agent model and the theory of optimal contracts may be far from the practice of aid. Yet, a sound theoretical framework seems a prerequisite for an in-depth analysis of the way aid and recipient countries' institutions do interact in affecting development.

A synthetic review of the theoretical aid literature emphasizing the role of institutions and governance in recipient countries was undertaken for this chapter through a simplified model meant to incorporate the main features of existing models. The full model is presented in the appendix to this chapter. It is summarized in what follows.

As a starting point, we consider the simple case of one donor and one recipient country, aid being viewed by the donor as a transfer to the government of the recipient country aimed at alleviating poverty in that country. In other words, the donor is considered as perfectly altruistic, and possible strategic motives for aid are ignored. The government of the recipient country is assumed to use the aid flow of resources as it pleases if aid is unconditional, so that the part of aid that will reach the poor depends on the objective function and the domestic constraints it faces. However, the donor may wish to make its aid conditional on part of it reaching the poor either directly or through policies that will affect them favorably. A simple model that borrows from two key models of the donor-recipient relationship, Adam and O'Connell (1999) and Azam and Laffont (2003), is used to discuss the role of the recipient country's institutions and governance in this framework. An alternative framework relying on Bourguignon and Platteau (2018a) is then briefly discussed, which seems particularly adequate to handle the case of a single donor facing various recipients as analyzed later in this chapter. Finally, a few remarks will be made on the case of several donors.

9.2.1. Aid, Governance, and Conditionality in a Simple Model of the Donor-Recipient Country Relationship

As in the rest of this chapter, aid is seen here as a transfer by the donor to the recipient country, the finality of which is to reduce poverty. However, because aid takes place between sovereigns, the government of the recipient country will ultimately have the responsibility of channeling the resources provided by the donor to the poor people in its population, either directly or under the form of some policy that benefits them. This is where the governance in the recipient country matters. In a country ruled by some egocentric autocrats—i.e., an "extractive" regime, in the words of Acemoglu and Robinson (2012)—only a small part, if any, of the donor's transfer will reach the poor. The opposite would hold with more "inclusive" institutions. The main issue in the donor-recipient relationship is how a donor should handle this potential "leakage" in the aid flow away from its target. Most of the literature focuses on the case of an autocratic regime in the recipient country. The following model takes a more general perspective in the sense that the well-being of the poor may weigh positively in the objective function of the recipient country's government.

9.2.1.1. A Simple Model of Distortive (and Regressive) Redistribution

The preceding general argument may be formalized in the following elementary way along the lines of a model due to Adam and O'Connell (1999).

Let the population of a recipient country be partitioned into two groups, the elite with weight n in the population, and the rest of the population, deemed to be poor, with weight $1-n$. Note, however, that the model can easily be extended to the case where there is a middle class in between.[3] Let y stand for the standard of living of the elite, and x $(<y)$ for that of the poor. Both include an after-tax market income part and a cash transfer. The market income part depends on a distortive policy instrument, say a proportional tax rate, t, with the income accruing to the elite being a fixed multiple, c (>1), of the income of the poor. The after-tax market income of both groups is denoted $h(t)$ for the poor and $c.h(t)$ for the elite, with $h(t)$ being a decreasing and a concave function of t. If z and s are respectively the cash transfers made by the government to the elite and to the poor, the net income per capita of the two groups is given by:

$$y = c.h(t) + z \qquad\qquad (9.1.1.a)$$

$$x = h(t) + s. \qquad\qquad (9.1.1.b)$$

The cash transfers must satisfy the following budget constraints:

$$n.z + (1-n).s + G \leq H(t) = (nc + 1 - n)t.h(t) \;/\; (1-t); z \geq 0, s \geq 0 \qquad (9.1.2)$$

where $H(t)$ stands for the tax revenue and G for exogenous public expenditures. $H(t)$ actually is the well-known Laffer curve and is assumed to be inverted-U shaped.

An important institutional constraint in this model, but not really specific of low-income countries, is that the existing institutions do not allow for lump-sum negative transfers, as made clear by the last part of (9.1.2). Indeed, if this were possible then there would be no need for a distortive instrument like a tax to fund public expenditures and redistribution between the two groups.

The policy instruments in this model consist of t, z, and s. They are assumed to be chosen by a government that maximizes the following objective function:

$$Max\ u(y) + \theta v(x) \tag{9.1.3}$$

under the constraints (9.1.1) and (9.1.2). This function, in particular the parameter θ, is meant to encapsulate the effect of those institutional features in the recipient country that determine the poverty alleviation inclination of its government. It is often absent from the theoretical models of aid, which rely on the assumption that $\theta = 0$, as in Adam and O'Connell (1999), or on the assumption that (9.1.3) is quasi-linear in y, as in Azam and Laffont (2003), which will be seen to be almost equivalent. Yet, there is no reason to believe that recipient countries are all run by pure autocrats or that autocrats do not have to care about the poor population in their country. In what follows, we give several alternative interpretations of the objective function (9.1.3) depending on the institutional context in the recipient country.

Before doing so, it may be noted that in the preceding framework, foreign aid, a, may be introduced as a shift parameter in the budget constraint. It is equivalent to replacing G by $G-a$ in (9.1.2), which becomes:

$$n.z + (1-n).s + G - a \le H(t); z \ge 0, s \ge 0. \tag{9.1.4}$$

This budget constraint is valid as long as aid is unconditional. If the donor imposes some condition on the use of aid, the preceding budget constraint remains valid but some additional condition has to be added to the maximization of (9.1.3).

9.2.1.2. The Implicit Institutional Framework of the Model

A first interpretation of the preceding framework would be that institutions work in the recipient country in a way equivalent to a benevolent social planner with (9.1.3) as a social welfare function, $u(\ )$ and $v(\ )$ being standard increasing and concave utility functions and θ being the weight given to the poor.

In a more politically realistic way, a second interpretation is that (9.1.3) stands for some bargaining between political representatives of the two population groups, θ being then the relative bargaining power of the poor group. It may also stand for a government in a semi-democratic setting maximizing votes in its favor in the next election, the vote of the elite depending positively on y and that of the poor people on x, while θ would represent the relative weight of their vote at the election—i.e., the differential turnout rate. Note that this argument would be reinforced if a middle class with more political power than the poor had been introduced in the model, which could be hurt as much as the poor by an increase in the distortive tax rate without cash transfer compensation.

In a fully democratic society and assuming reasonably that $n < 1/2$, θ would be infinitely large as the majority would decide about the tax rate and redistribution, as in the well-known model by Meltzer and Richard (1981). Symmetrically, θ would be zero in a country where an egotistic elite would hold full political power without any risk of losing it. Note that the first case is equivalent to assuming $u(y) = 0$ and $v(x) = x$ in (9.1.3) and symmetrically in the second case.

Intermediate cases may be interpreted in various ways. As in other papers in the theoretical aid literature, the recipient country may be assumed to be ruled by an elite that cares about the poor, θ then representing the degree of its altruism, as in Besley (1997). Alternatively, θ may also be interpreted as a penalty that the elite would incur under one form or another if they pressured the poorest part of the population too much. For instance, if the probability of a rebellion were a decreasing function of the level of living of the poor, say $\pi(x)$ with $\pi'(\ )<0$, and θ the utility cost of subduing the rebellion, as in Acemoglu and Robinson (2001), or being overwhelmed by it, the expected utility of the elite would be depend on:

$$y - \theta\pi(x),$$

which is of the same form as (9.1.3) above but with a different interpretation of $v(x)$ $(=-\pi(x))$ and most importantly a quasi-linear specification with respect to y.

This quasi-linear specification has strong implications. In particular, it leads to results very close to the autocratic elite with $\theta=0$. To see this, consider the simple problem of allocating a given amount B among the two groups. The maximization of (9.1.3) with $\theta=0$, the pure autocracy case, leads obviously to $x=0$, whereas the solution with a quasi-linear specification in y leads to a constant value for x, given by $v'(x)=(1-n)\ /\ n\theta$, so that any change in B, for instance through aid, is fully appropriated by the elite and has no impact whatsoever on the poor. In reference to the case above where the elite fears for its future, this could be referred to as the "constrained autocracy."

With such references, it is tempting to consider the general case (9.1.3) with $\theta>0$ and $u''(y)<0$ as a "non-autocratic" regime, which does not mean full democracy ($\theta=\infty$) and is consistent with a political regime that may be dominated by the elite. In that sense the present model is more general than the earlier theoretical literature on aid based on the assumption of autocratic regimes.

In summary, the weight θ assigned to poor people in the objective function (9.1.3) as well as the shape of the functions $u(\ )$ and $v(\ )$ may result from very different institutional settings. As far as the donor-recipient country relationship is concerned, however, which setting is ultimately responsible for θ being high or low or for the functions $u(\ )$ and $v(\ )$ being more or less concave does not really matter. What matters is how much weight the decision process in the government sphere is, in one way or another, giving to the poor.

Institutions are also implicit in other parts of the model. In particular, it was assumed above that the distortion in the economy was due to a tax that could finance, inter alia, a transfer, z, to the elite. Actually, this rent may be generated unofficially and in a distortive manner in many different ways, through holding monopolistic positions or through high-level corruption, for instance. Representing such rent-seeking distorting behavior through the tax system and a fully transparent budget constraint in (9.1.1) and (9.1.2) is over-simplifying. Yet this specification captures the essential fact that there are instruments in the hands of the government of the recipient country to extract rents in favor of the elite—or possibly of the poor—at the cost of reducing the efficiency of the economy.[4]

The interesting question, therefore, is how aid may affect that behavior and, ultimately, how its benefits will be shared by the elite and the poor people.

9.2.1.3. The Basic Properties of the Model with Respect to Aid and Governance

We present here the main properties of the model sketched above, which seem important for the analysis of the aid and governance issue. The proof is sketched in the appendix.

The Case of Unconditional Aid

If unconditional, aid is equivalent to reducing the need to finance public expenditures—see (9.1.4) above.[5] Analyzing the effect of aid is thus like letting G vary. The following properties are easily derived.

Property 1. There cannot be cash transfers simultaneously in favor of the poor and the elite due to the presence of a deadweight loss in redistribution, or the assumed convexity of the function $h(t)$. It is thus the case that either the rent of the elite, z, or the transfer to the poor, s, or possibly both are equal to zero. If this were not the case, it would be possible to improve the lot of the two groups by financing part of the public expenditures through reducing both cash transfers, the loss being compensated by less tax distortion.

Thus there are three regimes in that economy corresponding to whether part of the tax revenue is spent on cash transfers or not, and in the former case, whether the transfer goes to the elite or to the poor. For a given aid flow, or public expenditures, a cash transfer in favor of the elite will take place for low values of θ and in favor of the poor for θ above some threshold. In between, there is an interval where the government makes no cash transfer and uses all the tax revenues and the aid flow to cover public expenditures. We concentrate in what follows on the case where θ is below the threshold where cash is transferred to the poor or, in other words, where the government has no pro-poor bias, which somehow justifies the intervention of the donor.

Under this assumption, we now examine the effect of a small increase in the aid flow on the tax rate and the amount, possibly nil, transferred to the elite.

Property 2. In the case of an autocratic regime ($\theta = 0$ or $u(y) = y$), an increase in the aid flow increases the rent z going to the elite if the rent was initially positive, the most likely case, whereas the tax rate remains constant.

Property 3. If θ is strictly positive but relatively small—and $u(\ )$ strictly concave—an increase in aid is spent partly on reducing the tax rate so that the income of both the elite and the poor rise. Yet, the effect on the rent going to the elite depends on the value of θ in an ambiguous way. The increase in aid is spent exclusively on reducing the tax rate if the rent going to the elite is initially zero, thus for middle values of the governance parameter, θ.

The latter property is important since it suggests that as the society moves away from strict autocracy, aid becomes *effective* in the sense that it increases the efficiency of the economy by reducing distortions, thus benefiting the poor as well as the elite. The present model is specified in a purely static way, but it could be interpreted in a dynamic way with personal incomes x and y being defined as a discounted flow over some period and the tax rate negatively affecting the growth rate.[6] This is an effect rarely alluded to in the literature on the effectiveness of aid in promoting growth.[7] Likewise, it is important to stress that the positive effect of an increase in aid on the standard of living of the poor goes through this efficiency effect.

Another implication of the preceding property is the justification it gives to aid selectivity. If the aid flow is endogenous or if the donor has a fixed amount of aid to allocate among various recipients, the aid received by a country should rely on variables representing the quality of the governance and the level of public expenditures of a country, excluding the transfer to the elite. Thus, the size of aid might not have to depend on a complex combination of policies and institutions. It should simply rely on the pro-elite bias in the recipient country, which may be described in different ways, but in particular by the size of the rent going to the elite, if it can be measured, or the inequality of incomes.

The Case of Conditional Aid

Instead of transferring unconditionally a flow of resources that depends, inter alia, on the governance of the country and its exogenous expenditures, the donor can make the volume of its aid conditional on the *policy* pursued in the recipient country, namely, here the tax rate or possibly a cash transfer to the poor. Yet, such a conditionality will be accepted only if the objective function of the government of the recipient country is at least equal to its level in the absence of aid, $W^1(\theta, G)$.

The optimal conditional aid is then given by the solution of:

$$Max_{x,a}\ V(x) - Ca\ s.t\ (9.1.1),\ (9.1.2),\ (9.1.4)\ and\ u(y) + \theta v(x) \geq W^1\ (\theta, G);\ z,s \geq 0 \quad (9.1.5)$$

where $V(x)$ is the utility that the donor derives from the standard of living of the poor in the recipient country and C the unit cost of aid. The solution of this maximization problem may lead to three regimes according to whether one of the cash transfers, z or s, is strictly positive or not and which transfer is positive in the first case.

Two cases must be considered, depending on whether the rent going to the elite is zero or strictly positive in the absence of aid.

Property 4. If the rent of the elite is nil in the absence of aid, the optimal conditional aid involves a lower tax rate and possibly a cash transfer to the poor.

Property 5. If the rent of the elite is strictly positive in the absence of aid, the optimal conditional aid always reduces the distortive tax rate and the rent going to the elite. Depending on the preferences of the donor and the governance parameter, θ, the rent of the elite may be driven to zero and even replaced by a cash transfer to the poor.

Property 6. When the objective function of the recipient country's government is quasi-linear—as in the case of the "constrained autocracy"—the flow of optimal aid and the income of the poor are increasing in the governance parameter θ, although the latter has no effect with unconditional aid.

Property 7. The optimal conditional aid is "supported" by a contract imposed upon the recipient country's government that relates the aid flow to be received to the tax rate

$$a = A + B.t \quad (9.1.6)$$

where the constants A and B are appropriately chosen.

In other words, left free to choose t under the preceding constraint and the budget constraint, the government of the recipient country would choose the value that is optimal from the donor's point of view.

The Crucial Issue of Time Consistency in Conditional Aid

The preceding decentralized contract could also be set ex post, in the (a,x) space, rather than ex ante, in the (a,t) space. Yet, from the point of view of the implementation of the conditionality, and that of the optimal contract itself, there is a major difference between both approaches.[8] In the latter case, the contract is about the policy to be implemented, something that, in certain circumstances, the donor might be able to observe, whereas in the former case the contract is in terms of the outcome of the policy. There is a time dimension in that case that is absent from the optimal aid contract on policy. If there is some unobserved randomness in the actual outcome, i.e., the income of the poor, a crucial issue of *time consistency* then arises, which may ultimately make conditionality ineffective.

Assume some random shock is affecting the economy, and in particular the income of the poor. This has two implications. First, the optimal contract in the (a,x) space must take into account that randomness. Second, assume that the observed outcome is extremely low, so that the aid flow corresponding to the optimal contract is itself very small. How would the donor react to a demand by the recipient country not to comply with the contract and provide more aid than in the contract? If the donor is expected to do as requested, actually in agreement with its utility function in (9.1.5), thus being time inconsistent in following its altruistic inclination, then a key credibility problem arises. If the government in the recipient country anticipates such behavior by the donor, it will simply ignore the conditionality rule (9.1.6) expressed as a function of the outcome x. This problem is known in the aid literature as the "Samaritan" dilemma—see Svensson (2000, 2003) and the survey by Kumar (2015). From a theoretical point of view, this really is the heart of the aid conditionality issue. It is this issue of credibility that led Torsvik (2005: 506) to conclude that "it is more realistic to model the interaction between the parties (i.e. the donors and recipient countries' governments) as a non-contractible relationship."

This issue of time consistency would also arise in a multi-period framework with the conditionality aid contract labeled in terms of the policy. If at the end of the first period, the donor discovers that the recipient country's government did not hold on its policy, it should not renew the contract and stop aid. Yet, its utility function in (9.1.5) will lead the donor not to hold on that threat and the recipient country to ignore the contract.

An important point to stress in connection with this issue of the time consistency of a conditional aid contract is that it arises with a great deal of strength in the case of a single recipient country. If several recipient countries compete for a fixed amount of aid, then the credibility of a conditional aid contract is much stronger since failure to apply the penalty to one low-performing recipient—i.e., to give more aid than actually stipulated in the contract—would penalize the others. This argument is made in Svensson (2003), who also suggests that, as the donor might be tempted to increase its total aid budget in such a circumstance, it would be better to delegate the management of aid to an agency without this kind of flexibility. Quite clearly, this is a strong argument in favor of multilateral development agencies like the multilateral development banks managing the aid budget provided by national donors.

9.2.1.4. Summary of the Implications of the Preceding Model and Extensions

Despite its simplicity, the model analyzed in this section has several important implications for the role played by institutions in the aid donor-recipient relationship when the donor is assumed to exclusively care about the welfare of the poor in the recipient country. First, of course, the way the recipient country's government weighs the interest of the poor and non-poor is crucial in determining the impact of unconditional aid on the efficiency of the economy—i.e., its degree of distortion—and the income of the poor. Second, the fact that any redistribution of domestic income is costly in terms of economic efficiency makes aid a factor of economic efficiency and/or costless redistribution, the more so the more inefficient the institutions achieving domestic redistribution in one direction or another, i.e., the tax system in the model but, more generally, all rent-generating institutions. Third, conditional aid is necessarily more efficient and more pro-poor than unconditional aid for the same volume of aid. This is the case in all institutional contexts, provided that aid conditionality may be defined ex ante in terms of observable and irreversible policy instruments or reform decisions. If conditionality is defined ex post on outcomes, i.e., the income of the poor, or if policies and reforms are reversible, then time consistency and credibility issues make conditional aid actually equivalent to unconditional aid. Even in that case, the problem is probably less serious when there are several recipient countries competing for a given amount of aid.

Two extensions of the preceding model are mentioned in the appendix to this chapter which do not lead to drastically revising the preceding properties and conclusions. The first one consists of endogenizing the public expenditures assuming the latter enter separately the objective function (9.1.3) of the government. The second extension introduces an additional distortion in the model which is under the control of the government and generates a rent to the elite—e.g., monopoly power or import license—so that the rent does not consist exclusively of a cash transfer as in the model above.

9.2.2. Optimizing Aid Delivery as an Alternative View at the Conditionality of Aid

For further use in the next section of this survey and also as an alternative to the preceding model, it is worth mentioning the recent work by Bourguignon and Platteau (2018a), who revisited the one-donor-one-recipient country relationship in a somewhat different framework. Their approach focuses on the way aid is delivered and the implicit conditionality in the mode of delivery rather than on the volume of aid and quantitative conditional goals. It also deals with the institutions in the recipient country in a slightly different way than in other models in the literature, emphasizing the substitutability between internal and external ways of disciplining the leadership in the recipient country.

The volume of aid is assumed to be exogenous, and the main issue is how it is to be delivered: what monitoring and what penalty in case the leadership in the recipient country appears to be confiscating too much of the aid flow instead of channeling it, in one way or another, to the poor? The behavior of the recipient country's leadership, assimilated to the elite of the previous model, is expressed in terms of the share of aid, y, which it keeps for itself and is represented by the following objective function:

$$Max_y \; y - \theta y^2 - \gamma \pi(by) \; s.t. y \in [0,1] \tag{9.1.7}$$

where θy^2 is meant to represent the "internal discipline" that the population of the recipient country may impose on its leader in case it diverts too high a share of the foreign aid.[9] γ is the penalty inflicted by the donor if the leader may be convicted of embezzling some part of the foreign aid, $\pi()$ being an increasing function that describes the probability this would happen. For a given y, that probability is higher the more closely the donor monitors the use being made of its aid, b being the intensity of the monitoring. The $\gamma\pi()$ term thus represents the "external discipline" exerted by the donor on the government of the recipient country.

The internal discipline, θy^2, in (9.1.7) plays the same role as θ in the preceding model and may describe various institutional settings. It may correspond to the political system with the leadership losing electoral power if seen as diverting too much of the aid flow that would benefit the middle class as well as poor people. For a given aid flow and if the diverted resources are used to buy political capital, this term may stand for the declining marginal return of that political investment. More simply, it may also correspond to a falling marginal utility of the leadership for additional resources.

The donor wishes to maximize the share of aid, $1-y$, that will reach the poor people, but incurs a cost, that of the monitoring of aid and that of the penalty if needed. The latter may correspond to the fact that the penalty may affect the poor people in the recipient country—as when the penalty consists of reducing future aid—as well as the reputation of the government of the donor country with respect to its constituency or the donor community—e.g., donor agencies do not like publicizing their failures. The donor's objective function thus is:

$$D = V\left[w + a(1 - y^*)\right] - C(b) - D(\gamma).\pi(by^*) \tag{9.1.8}$$

where $V(\ )$ is the utility the donor derives from alleviating poverty in the recipient country—w being the income of the poor without aid and a being the flow of aid per capita—whereas $C(\ )$ and $D(\ )$ are the cost functions incurred by the donor. The latter are increasing and convex whereas the welfare function is increasing and concave. Finally, y^* is the solution of the leader's maximization problem (9.1.7) and is thus a function of the aid delivery parameters b and γ and of the internal discipline, or governance parameter, θ.

"Conditional" aid in this setting does not refer to the volume of aid, which is exogenous, but to the way it is delivered. The intensity of the monitoring and the size of the penalty ultimately determine the share of aid that will reach the poor. Note that the way this outcome is obtained is not explicit. It may consist of lump-sum transfers if existing institutions allow for this or involve some policy instruments as in section 9.2.1.

Using a standard principal-agent framework, the optimal aid delivery (b^*, γ^*) is given by the solution of the following program:

$$Max_{b,\gamma} \, V[w + a(1 - y^*)] \; s.t. y^* - \theta y^{*2} - \gamma\pi\,(by^*) \geq U$$

where U is the reservation utility level of the leader in the recipient country.

The question is then to know how the optimal aid delivery (b^*, γ^*) and the associated level of fraud, y^*, vary with the quality of the internal governance, θ. Roughly speaking, it can be shown that: (a) the internal discipline θ and the external discipline (b^*, γ^*) are substitutes in the sense that the latter falls when the former rises; (b) somewhat paradoxically, there may be "over-substitution" in the sense that the extent of the fraud, y^*, may increase despite the fact that the internal governance θ has improved. This is because the donor may reduce the external discipline by more than the increase in the internal discipline. This second result depends on the shape of the various functions in the model, and in particular the cost functions, but it is shown in Bourguignon and Platteau (2018a) that it holds under very standard assumptions on these functions.

These results are important because they show that the delivery of aid—monitoring and punishing in case of fraud detection—may be used to counteract the negative effects of bad governance on the effectiveness of aid in reaching the poor or some other predetermined goal. The logic of the conditionality here differs from what was seen earlier in the sense that no contract is signed according to which aid is provided if some assigned reform is put in place. A close monitoring with an explicit penalty in case of no completion is what replaces the conditionality contract. Unlike in the preceding canonical model, the quality of the domestic institutions and the attitude of the leadership with respect to poverty does not determine the volume of aid. It determines the intensity of the monitoring of aid.

As in the preceding model, one may also doubt that donor will activate the penalty γ in the presence of evidence of embezzlement by the leadership of the recipient country. Time consistency is as much an issue here since there is a lag between the disbursement of aid and the time evidence on the use made of it becomes available and a new aid tranche must be disbursed—or not disbursed if this is the penalty. This issue is less likely to be a problem if the donor faces several recipient countries, as will be seen below.

9.2.3. A Recipient Country Facing Various Donors

Part of the theoretical aid relationship literature focuses on the case where a single country receives aid from several donors. Various issues arise in such a framework. They essentially refer to whether donors need to cooperate rather than to compete should they all want to actually be present in the recipient country, which then acts as a kind of discriminatory monopsonist, or to act independently, in which case they may be giving too much or too little in a more or less efficient way.[10] The institutional issue in such a framework has a great deal to do with donors and their capacity to coordinate or not (Bourguignon and Platteau 2015a). Interestingly enough, this has to do with the nature of the institutions in the recipient country.

If donor countries coordinate, the role of domestic institutions in affecting the volume and the delivery of aid is the same as in the analysis above. The interesting issue then is whether the quality of institutions in the developing countries may trigger more or less cooperation among donors. The framework proposed by Torsvik (2005) with two altruistic donors and a fully autocratic government in the recipient country sheds light on this issue.

If the recipient country's government were channeling all the aid received to the poor, donors would face a typical public good situation asking for some coordination among them. As they both care about the standard of living of the poor in the recipient country, the non-cooperative Nash equilibrium would lead to too little aid being provided, as each donor would consider his flow of aid independently from that of the other. On the contrary, if they coordinate, each donor knows his contribution will be topped up by the other donor, which increases the marginal utility of his own contribution. The overall aid flow is therefore larger. Donor coordination is thus a good thing if the recipient country's government can be trusted in channeling aid, or at least a good part of it, to the poor. However, it makes matters worse if this is not the case, as the recipient country is actually facing a single donor with the negative consequences seen above for the effectiveness of aid. In this very simple example, the pro-poor bias of the recipient country's government matters for whether donors should coordinate or not.

It turns out that this kind of result also depends on the way aid is delivered, and the preceding result can be reverted if the aid relationship is viewed from a different, dynamic angle. Consider a sequential game where the recipient country's government would first decide about a policy leading to some standard of living of the poor and then donors would transfer aid directly to the poor, or possibly to the government with a fully enforceable contract according to which all the aid will be channeled to the poor. In such a situation, coordination among the donors is necessarily a good thing, even though the government of the recipient country may not have been pro-poor in the first stage of the game, anticipating that the donors would compensate what was implicitly taken away from the poor. More generally, Platteau (2003) has shown how the recipient country's leadership could take advantage of the competition among donors when the latter have to prove to their own constituency that they provided aid to that specific country.

In summary, this short argument shows that the nature of institutions in the recipient country may determine not only the volume and the type of delivery of foreign aid but also the way in which multiple donors would organize themselves to be as effective as possible.

This part of the chapter has reviewed the theoretical underpinnings of the aid–donor relationship and the way the quality of the governance was affecting the nature of the aid contract and its effectiveness in making aid actually contribute to the alleviation of poverty. We now consider more pragmatic aspects of it, starting with the way the governance of recipient countries may affect the geographic allocation of aid by donors, thus considering governance as given and aid as essentially providing additional financing to recipient countries rather than helping them to reform.

9.3. AID AS "FINANCE": GOVERNANCE CRITERIA IN AID ALLOCATION

The first part of this chapter showed how a single donor would take into account the quality of the governance of a single recipient country to determine the volume of the aid flow and whether aid should be delivered unconditionally or conditionally on some action by the recipient country's government. In this section we expand this basic framework by considering the case of a single donor facing various recipient countries and having to allocate its aid among these countries. In line with the general objective of this survey, we want to analyze the way the allocation of aid across various recipient countries may depend on the relative quality of institutions and governance in these countries, along with their relative needs, i.e., their degree of poverty.

As before, we start from a simple vision of unconditional aid, taking the behavior of leaders in recipient countries and therefore the institutions behind them as given. Using a framework similar to the one presented earlier, it turns out that some simple allocation rules can be derived. Those rules are then compared to the actual allocation implemented by donors and explicit allocation rules posted by multilateral donors. The final section addresses some additional issues concerned with the implications of aid conditionality and the multiplicity of donors for the selectivity of aid.

9.3.1. Optimal Unconditional Allocation of Aid by a
Single Donor with Several Recipient Countries

The issue of allocating a given volume of aid among a set of recipient countries and, in the first place, of selecting those countries that would receive aid, has been studied rather early in the aid literature, although most often empirically and more with the objective of identifying the motivation of donors than the role of recipient countries' institutions. As a matter of fact, early theoretical models like those of Dudley and Montmarquette (1976) and Trumbull and Wall (1994), interestingly and symptomatically enough, largely ignored the issue of aid effectiveness and the role of recipient countries' governance. The same is true of the early empirical literature.

The first papers to explicitly tackle the issue of aid effectiveness in allocating aid are probably the influential papers by Collier and Dollar (2001, 2002), which explored the country allocation of aid that would have the maximum impact on global poverty, given the policy and the institutions in recipient countries and their positive impact on growth and poverty reduction.[11]

The model below expands on both the early models of aid selectivity and the Collier-Dollar approach by introducing the quality of institutions in the former and providing a more general theoretical framework to the latter. It is based on a simple framework proposed by Bourguignon and Platteau (2018b).

A single donor is assumed to have an exogenous amount of aid, A, to allocate among two countries ($i = 1, 2$). A generalization to any number of countries will be given later. Both the size, n_i, and the mean income, w_i, of the poor population before taking into account the effect of aid are exogenous in the two countries. Note that w_i differs from the standard GNI per capita commonly used in the aid allocation literature. The knowledge of the proportion of poor people in the population, the share of household income in GNI, and the distribution of household income within the population or some measure of inequality would be necessary to infer both w_i and n_i from the knowledge of the GNI per capita and the size of the population. We shall assume in what follows that both w_i and n_i are observed by the donor, but all the analysis could be conducted in terms of the GNI per capita and the size of the total population, provided that the preceding information is available.

As in one of the models in the first part of this chapter, it is assumed that, out of a given aid flow to country i, only a percentage x_i reaches directly or indirectly the poor, the rest being appropriated by the elite.[12] Unlike in the previous section, however, it is assumed that this effectiveness ratio is exogenous. Assuming that the utility, V, the donor derives from providing aid to a country depends on the living standard of the poor in that country, given the impact of aid, the objective function of the donor may be denoted:

$$\text{Max}_{s_1+s_2 \leq 1}\ n_1 V\left(w_1, \frac{s_1 A x_1}{n_1}\right) + n_2 V\left(w_2, \frac{s_2 A x_2}{n_2}\right) \qquad (9.2.1)$$

where s_i is the share of total aid going to country i. To simplify, the analysis is momentarily restricted to the case where the function $V(\ )$ is additive and takes the following logarithmic form:

$$V(w_i, s_i A x_i / n_i) = \text{Log}[w_i + s_i x_i A / n_i]. \qquad (9.2.2)$$

Note that this specification assumes that the donor is essentially altruistic and does not provide aid for other motives than poverty reduction in the countries that receive it.

The solution of (9.2.1) with the specification (9.2.2) leads to the following first-order condition for an interior solution:

$$\frac{w_1 + s_1 x_1 A / n_1}{x_1} = \frac{r w_2 + s_2 x_2 A / n_2}{x_2}$$

and, using $s_1 + s_2 = 1$, to:

$$s_1 = \frac{n_1}{n_1 + n_2}\left[1 + \frac{n_2}{A}\left(\frac{w_2}{x_2} - \frac{w_1}{x_1}\right)\right] \qquad (9.2.3)$$

and symmetrically for s_2.

In other words, the share of country i in the aid granted by the donor is its share in the total population (or the population of poor people) corrected by a term that describes its advantage in terms of *governance adjusted needs (GAN)*, x_i/w_i. In this expression the "needs" is logically represented by the inverse of the initial income and governance by the share of aid that reaches the poor. If the two countries have the same initial income, then the country with the better governance, i.e., the higher x, will get more than its demographic share. If the two countries have the same governance, the country with the highest needs, i.e., the lowest w_i, will get more than its population share. If the poorest country is at the same time the less well governed, it may end up at an advantage or a disadvantage with respect to the other country, depending on the two GAN ratios x_i/w_i.

It can be seen in the preceding expression that the optimal allocation of aid depends on the total amount of aid being granted. Corner solutions may arise depending on the total aid available. If the GAN ratio of country 1 is larger than that of country 2, then all the aid available will go to country 1 if the total amount available is small enough.

A more general case is obtained by replacing the logarithmic form in (9.2.2) by the familiar power function:

$$V(w_i, s_i A x_i / n_i) = \frac{1}{1-\varepsilon}\left[w_i + s_i x_i A / n_i\right]^{1-\varepsilon} \qquad (9.2.4)$$

where $\varepsilon \in [0,\infty]$ can be interpreted as the aversion of the donor to poverty—or inequality among the poor. In that case, the share of country 1 is given by:

$$s_1 = \frac{n_1 x_1^{1/\varepsilon - 1}}{n_1 x_1^{1/\varepsilon - 1} + n_2 x_2^{1/\varepsilon - 1}}\left[1 + \frac{n_2 x_2^{1/\varepsilon - 1}}{A}\left(\frac{w_2}{x_2^{1/\varepsilon}} - \frac{w_1}{x_1^{1/\varepsilon}}\right)\right]. \qquad (9.2.5)$$

Two changes are readily apparent when comparing this formula with (9.2.3) above. On the one hand, the GAN ratio is now $w_2 / x_2^{1/\varepsilon}$, which takes into account the aversion of the donor to poverty. On the other hand, even in the case where both countries have the same GAN ratio, the allocation of aid still depends on the relative governance of the two countries, as can be seen in the term before the square bracket. In the extreme cases, it can be seen in (9.2.5) that only governance matters and all the aid is allocated to the country with the best governance when the donor has no poverty aversion ($\varepsilon = 0$). On the contrary, only needs—i.e., w_i—and population size matter when poverty aversion is infinite.

A somewhat paradoxical property of this more general specification is that the share of aid going to a country can fall when its governance, x_i, improves. This is easily understood. An improvement in the governance of country i makes the aid of the donor more efficient, but it also increases the income of the country's poor, thus making aid less needed. It is easily proven that the second effect dominates the first if the aversion of the donor to poverty is high enough—see Bourguignon and Platteau (2018b).

This simple two-country model can generalize easily to any number of countries—Bourguignon and Platteau (2018b: appendix B).

9.3.2. Aid Selectivity and Governance in Practice

The preceding discussion was largely theoretical, but the literature on aid allocation is mostly empirical. Two types of approach may be distinguished in that literature. The first is essentially descriptive, seeking to identify the implicit criteria, including self-interested ones, used by donors in selecting aid recipients and allocating aid among them. Concerning recipient countries, donors' allocation criteria included almost exclusively income per capita and population in a first stage. However, following the influential World Bank report *Assessing Aid* in 1998 and its focus on policy and institutional factors as aid effectiveness factors, the emphasis shifted toward governance factors. The second approach to aid allocation is prescriptive.[13] It explores the allocations that would be optimal in view of some explicit social welfare function or global development objective and incorporates factors that are thought to make aid more effective in reaching development goals, including of course some institutional and policy features of the recipient countries. Somewhere between these two approaches lies another one that consists of formal aid allocation rules used by multilateral donors, in particular the so-called Performance Based Allocation (PBA) rule in the aid management arm of the World Bank (IDA) and other multilateral development banks.

We review these three perspectives on aid allocation and the corresponding role of institutional factors in turn.

9.3.2.1. Donors' Aid Allocation Criteria

Most of the early descriptive econometric models of the geographical allocation of aid bore upon the motivation of the donors, and in particular political motives. The characteristics of the recipient countries were restricted to the GDP per capita and population. The attention of the analysts focused on the elasticity of aid with respect to these two indicators alongside other variables standing for non-developmental motivations of donors, for instance the strategic importance of recipient countries, their economic potential (for the donor country), cultural and ideological similarity, and the like.[14] Such an approach was quite understandable at a time when the behavior of the donors was much influenced by geopolitics and the Cold War and not just by purely developmental goals.

Things did change during the 1990s, in particular with the reassessment of the developmental role of foreign aid—e.g., World Bank (1998)—and, most important, the starting debate on the effectiveness of aid in promoting economic growth and development. In this respect, the paper by Burnside and Dollar (2000), a draft of which circulated some years before its publication, had a powerful influence by suggesting that the quality of policies and institutions in a country was a major factor in making foreign aid development effective. Based on this, it was then logical to ask whether such factors influenced the allocation behavior of donors.

An influential paper in this endeavor was Alesina and Dollar (2000), where regressions on the geographical allocation of aid included as an explanatory variable the democratic nature of the recipient countries and their openness to trade—with the finding that more open and more democratic countries were indeed receiving more aid. In another influential paper, Alesina and Weder (2002) tested whether, other things equal, available corruption indicators were affecting the aid share of recipient countries. Their general answer was negative, even though differences were found across donors—with Scandinavian donors allocating relatively less to countries with the reputation of being corrupt. More recent estimates by Dreher et al. (2011) confirm the non-significant role of corruption when analyzing which countries receive aid, but find a significant effect when focusing on how much aid countries do receive.

The impact of other aspects of recipient countries' policy or institutional features on donors' aid allocation behavior was analyzed, with varying results depending on available data. In a comprehensive analysis of bilateral donor-recipient aid flow time series, Berthélemy and Tichit (2004) found a significant impact of past economic growth, the FDI flow, primary school enrollment, and progress in infant mortality in recipient countries. Yet, it was not really clear whether all these variables actually reflected policies or institutions in recipient countries or some other factor. Restricting the analysis to aid flows from various donors to Sub-Saharan countries between 1977 and 1998, Birdsall et al. (2003) found no significant effect of the Country Policy and Institutional Assessment (CPIA), an indicator elaborated by the World Bank that summarizes the quality of policies and institutions in a given country. However, working on a cross-section of donor and recipient countries annually between 1999 and 2002, Dollar and Levin (2006) found a significant elasticity of aid flows with respect to the CPIA index in a majority of donor countries and in multilateral organizations. This may be evidence of the broadly shared intuition that aid determinants have changed over time, donors having become more selective over the last 10 or 15 years in terms of the quality of policies and institutions in recipient countries.[15]

Dollar and Levin's (2006) analysis, as well as several papers by Easterly on the weight of corrupt countries in the portfolio of DAC donors—in particular Easterly and Pfutze (2008)—may be considered more prescriptive than descriptive. In both cases, the objective was to rank donor countries in terms of their higher or lower sensitivity to corruption, or, more generally, institutions and policies' quality, than to simply estimate the importance of these features in aid allocation among other factors.

9.3.2.2. Prescriptive Empirical Models of Aid Allocation

Assuming donors are essentially motivated by altruistic rather than strategic or other non-developmental objectives, the theoretical model developed in the previous section should lend itself rather easily to empirical implementation, provided that the right data are available to proxy its parameters and variables.

Collier and Dollar (2002) applied a model of this type to analyze the allocation of aid that would maximize global poverty reduction. Let the poverty headcount ratio in country i, h_i, depend on GDP per capita, Y_i according to $h_i = \varphi_i Y_i^{\eta_i}$, where φ_i is some income distribution parameter and η_i the growth elasticity of the poverty headcount, and then let the objective function be:

$$Max \sum_{i=1}^{m} N_i \Delta h_i \qquad\qquad (9.2.6)$$

where N_i is the total population in country i. Assuming in addition that the growth rate of the economy is a function $F(p_i, \alpha_i)$ of a parameter p_i representing the quality of policies and institutions and the GDP share of aid, $\alpha_i (= s_i A / N_i Y_i$ with the same notations as before for total aid, A, and the share, s_i, going to country i),[16] the objective function (9.2.6) becomes:

$$Max \sum_{i=1}^{m} N_i F(p_i, s_i A / N_i Y_i) \eta_i h_i \; s.t \sum_{i=1}^{m} s_i \leq 1 . \qquad (9.2.7)$$

Assuming $F( )$ is increasing and concave with respect to the aid share, α_i, this problem is similar to the optimal aid allocation model in the previous section, with some changes in the nature of the variables taken into account. In particular, the policy/institution parameter p_i plays a role opposite to x_i.

The function $F(p_i, \alpha_i)$ used by Collier and Dollar is a re-estimation of the growth-aid-policy relationship in Burnside and Dollar (2000). That relationship is specified as:

$$G(p_i, \alpha_i) = B_{0i} + \alpha_i . (B_1 + B_2 p_i - B_3 \alpha_i) \qquad (9.2.8)$$

where the B's are coefficients estimated econometrically on panel recipient country data, B_2 and B_3 being strictly positive.

With these specifications, the first-order condition of the maximization problem (9.2.7) is:

$$B_1 + B_2 p_i - 2 B_3 s_i A / N_i Y_i - \lambda Y_i / h_i \eta_i \leq 0 \qquad (9.2.9)$$

where λ is the Lagrange multiplier associated with the constraint in (9.2.7).

It then follows that countries that will receive no aid are the countries with the lowest value of the following expression:

$$(B_1 + B_2 p_i) h_i \eta_i / Y_i \qquad\qquad (9.2.10)$$

which may be considered as the equivalent of the "governance-adjusted need" (GAN) ratio in the preceding section. The countries most likely to receive aid have a better governance (p_i) and/or more poverty (h_i) and/or low GDP per capita (Y_i) than the others. Note that this expression is more intricate than n_i and $w_i / x_i^{1/\varepsilon}$ in (9.2.5) above because poverty in the previous model was directly represented by w_i and n_i, whereas these magnitudes are now implicit behind h_i and Y_i.

It is easy to show from (9.2.10) that the number of countries receiving aid increases with the overall size of the aid budget, as with the generalization of (9.2.5) to more than two countries. In the Collier-Dollar benchmark calculation for 1996, approximately 20 out of a set of 60 developing countries considered in their analysis were receiving positive aid. Most of them were in Sub-Saharan Africa, but still a third were in other regions. This did not prevent some Sub-Saharan countries like Guinea or Zimbabwe from receiving aid because the quality of their governance was too low.

Interestingly enough, countries not receiving aid in the poverty-efficient aid allocation in Collier-Dollar turned out to be countries actually receiving the least aid, as a proportion of GDP, in the official aid statistics (DAC), suggesting that, taken altogether, donors' motivation was not too distant from the global poverty reduction objective. On the opposite side, a major problem arose with India, which, according to the first-order condition (9.2.9) above should have received a very substantial part of total aid, essentially because of its size.[17] In order to get results less distant from reality, the authors had to constrain the aid given to India. Their exercise is thus evidence of a "small country" bias in the actual allocation of aid. Clearly, something is missing in the specification of the optimal aid allocation model based on some kind of utilitarian framework to explain that distance between the optimal and the actual aid allocation.

Beynon (2003) undertook some extensive sensitivity analysis of the Collier-Dollar results, especially with respect to the coefficients of the Burnside-Dollar type growth-aid equation (9.2.8), the robustness of which has been subject to a rather hot debate.[18] The result is that the set of countries not receiving aid is rather robust, but the allocation of aid among countries receiving positive aid is not.

A more fundamental weakness of the Collier-Dollar's objective function is its focus on instantaneous poverty reduction, as opposed to poverty reduction over some longer time horizon. This is a difference with the general specification (9.2.2) used in the preceding section, which is consistent with any time period, as what really matters is the standard of living of poor people in the recipient country with and without aid over some arbitrary time period. On the contrary, the objective function (9.2.6) is short term–oriented, unless it is assumed that the decline in the number of poor will be constant over time. Wood (2008) showed how the optimal allocation of aid in the Collier-Dollar framework should depend on the donors' time horizon.

An interesting but rather different approach to the optimal allocation of aid was taken by Cogneau and Naudet (2007), even though it also indirectly relied on the Collier-Dollar growth-aid-policy framework. Instead of adopting a kind of welfarist objective function based on global poverty, they explored the implications of pursuing an equal opportunities approach, in the sense of Roemer (1998), to the optimal allocation of aid.[19] In other words, instead of taking aid as an adjuvant to poverty reduction, they considered it essentially as a way of compensating countries for adverse *circumstances* beyond their control and the reach of their policies and institutional reforms. This meant two key departures from the Collier-Dollar approach. On the one hand, a distinction was made in projecting poverty reduction between the impact of circumstances beyond the control of recipient countries and that of policy efforts, as described by the CPIA indicator, in favor of economic growth and poverty reduction. In using the growth equation (9.2.8), Cogneau and Naudet thus replaced the policy/institution variable p_i by the value predicted in a regression of the CPIA indicator on initial country characteristics, as a proxy for "circumstances."[20] On the other hand, they replaced the global poverty minimization objective used in Collier-Dollar by a Rawlsian criterion, minimizing the projected poverty in the country with the highest projected poverty headcount ratio at the time horizon of the exercise.

The difference with the Collier-Dollar aid allocation was substantial. This is not really surprising since the Cogneau-Naudet approach is equivalent to ignoring the positive impact on the effectiveness of aid of those policies and institutions in recipient countries not directly dictated by their "circumstances." In their approach, aid is thus compensating ex ante differences across countries in pursuing poverty reduction policies, actual policies being under the sole responsibility of recipient countries' governments. On the contrary, the Collier-Dollar approach, and the theoretical model in the previous section, are an ex post approach where the donor takes advantage of the policies implemented in recipient countries to make their aid more effective. Although ethically quite defensible, it is not certain that the compensation approach to aid allocation is an objective that would be seriously considered by actual donors, even purely altruistic ones.

9.3.2.3. The Performance-Based Allocation Rule in Multilateral Organizations

An aid allocation rule among recipient countries is almost unavoidable in multilateral organizations where the multiplicity of partners would make negotiating about a specific allocation recipient country by recipient country an unmanageable task. Negotiating ex ante about the way the allocation must depend on country characteristics is certainly easier.

The International Development Association (IDA), the aid management arm of the World Bank, has been using such a rule for almost 40 years. Other international development banks managing aid funds provided by their members do the same. However, if such a rule has existed for a long time, the formula that governs aid allocation changed several times. Interestingly enough, the formula in use today bears a strong resemblance to the theoretical model in the previous section. The formula in use in IDA is as follows:

$$A_i = CPR_i^4 . (GNI_i / N_i)^{-.125} N_i \qquad\qquad (9.2.11)$$

where A_i is proportional to the aid allocated to country i,[21] CPR_i is the "country performance rating," as defined below, GNI_i/N_i is gross national income per capita (excluding aid), and N_i represents the population. CPR_i is itself an index that is defined as:

$$CPR_i = .24.CPIA1_i + .68.CPIA2_i + 08.PPR_i$$

where *CPIA* is the Country Policy and Institutional Assessment index elaborated by the World Bank staff, which takes into account various aspects of policies and institutions. *CPIA1* stands for the average of the first three clusters of indicators (economic management, structural policies, policies for social inclusion) whereas the *CPIA2* index stands for the fourth, governance, cluster ("public sector management and institutions"). Finally, *PPR* stands for the quality of IDA's project portfolio, or the use of previous aid.

The correspondence between this PBA rule and the theoretical model discussed above is clear but incomplete. The income of the poor, w_i, and their number, n_i, are approximated by the GNI per capita and the total population, as if the distribution of income were the same across countries. However, it is quite possible for two countries to have the same GNI per capita and to have a different proportion of poor people and a different intensity of poverty among them. Concerning governance, the effectiveness ratio, x_i, in the theoretical model is approximated by the country performance rating, CPR, mostly based on the governance cluster of the CPIA index. Yet, the relationship between this indicator, itself a combination of various criteria, from accountability in the public sector to property rights, and poverty reduction is not a direct one.

In light of the theoretical model (9.2.1) in the previous section and in particular the specification (9.2.5), the PBA rule appears very much biased toward governance in comparison with needs. This can be seen from the elasticities 4 and −.125 associated respectively with CPR and GNI/N in (9.2.11). With such elasticities, an improvement by one standard deviation (among low-income countries) of CPIA2 (the governance cluster in the CPIA) would increase the aid flow of a country by roughly 45%, whereas a drop in the GNI per capita by one standard deviation would increase it by only 7%. In terms of (9.2.5) above, this would suggest a rather low value for the poverty aversion parameter ε.

This result may be consistent with the descriptive empirical analyses mentioned above, which find that the actual aid allocation by donors is increasingly sensitive to policy and governance. Note, however, that multilateral donors using the PBA rule also have special programs and procedures for the so-called fragile countries, i.e., less well governed countries that are strongly penalized by the allocation rule.[22] The corresponding budget has increased substantially over the last decade or so, and it is allocated largely on a case-by-case basis. It follows that the actual allocation of aid by multilateral donors may differ from the PBA rule. This also applies to the numerous bilateral donors that implicitly or explicitly apply rules comparable to the PBA.

Another possible explanation for the apparent governance bias of the PBA rule is that it is thought to be an incentive for recipient countries to adopt satisfactory policies and promote good institutions. In other words, the aid allocation rule would include ipso facto a kind of conditionality. Unlike what was discussed earlier, that conditionality may work better, and the Samaritan dilemma might be avoided in the context of several recipient countries. This is because breaking the allocation rule in favor of one recipient country would mean less aid being given to other countries, which would then complain about this special treatment for the others. Yet, whether the PBA rule actually has any positive effect on the governance of receiving countries does not seem to have been thoroughly investigated.

With reference to the PBA rule, Carter's (2014) attempt at optimizing its parameters, i.e., the two exponents in (9.2.11), must be mentioned. He suggested that, instead of being essentially arbitrary, these parameters be chosen so as to maximize social welfare, defined as the sum of the discounted utility of consumption in recipient countries, assuming that the latter follow a Ramsey rule in optimizing growth conditional on aid and under an aid absorption capacity constraint. Unfortunately, Carter's parameter values cannot be compared to the actual PBA rule because of his use of an objective definition of governance—or absorptive capacity constraint—different from the subjective appraisal in the CPIA indicator.

9.3.3. Some Final Remarks on Aid Allocation

The implicit conditionality in the PBA rule is extremely general and by definition homogeneous among recipient countries, whereas it would seem a priori that, to have a chance to be effective, conditionality should be country-specific. However, taking into account such specificity would clearly lead to extraordinarily complex and opaque allocation rules. Think for instance of the Collier-Dollar model above with the growth-aid-policy equation (9.2.8) having different coefficients B_1 and B_2 across countries. Then the selectivity of the allocation of aid would no longer bear on a GAN criterion (9.2.10) that would be the same for all countries. Out of two countries with the same average income, the same poverty rate, and the same quality of governance, one would receive some aid and the other not. By construction, country-specific conditionality is incompatible with the application of general and transparent aid allocation rule.

This conclusion does not necessarily apply if the donor is able to influence the effectiveness of aid through monitoring and sanctioning in the event that too much aid is being diverted from its intended use. In the model above, if the donor can spend some resources in increasing the aid efficiency ratio, x_i, then the optimal allocation of aid will differ from (9.2.3) or (9.2.5). The selectivity associated with the governance parameter, x_i, will be greatly diminished, as, precisely, the donor has the possibility of increasing the effectiveness of aid above x_i, although of course this will cost resources.[23] In terms of an allocation rule like the PBA, this would mean that the rule, and in particular the role of governance, should depend on the monitoring exerted by the donor and the possibility to cut the aid flow to a recipient country on the strong presumption of aid embezzlement. It is not clear that this aspect of aid is taken into account in negotiations leading to the choice of a rule.

A last issue to consider is how the presence of several donors may modify the allocation rule chosen by each donor. This is the same issue as the one discussed in the first part of this chapter, except that in the present framework, what may vary is the share of a fixed amount of aid going to a specific recipient country. This case does not seem to have been studied in the literature, even though it is interesting to know whether the multiplicity of donors is bound to make each donor more or less selective in terms of the governance of recipient countries in comparison to the case where it is isolated and also to what would be optimal if all donors were to coordinate.

To summarize the discussion in this section, it is fair to recognize that both on theoretical and empirical grounds, governance and institutions appear as key factors in the geographical allocation of aid by donors, and therefore in the aid received by a particular country.

The theoretical justification of such dependency relies on the presumption that the quality of institutions improves the effectiveness of aid in promoting development and reducing poverty. There would be little justification for this factor to affect the allocation of aid in the absence of such a relationship. Yet, it must be stressed that, empirically, the mere existence or strength of that relationship are still severely debated.

The evidence shows that bilateral donors do take into account some elements of governance, possibly along other criteria, when allocating their aid among developing countries. This has not always been the case. Multilateral donors have explicit allocation rules that presently give a rather significant weight to governance versus need factors, although special care is taken on a case-by-case basis of these "fragile" countries that would be excluded from aid because of their weak governance. Yet, the emphasis placed by multilateral donors, often imitated by bilateral agencies, on governance factors in their allocation rule raises the issue of the nature of the trade-off they are willing to make between governance and the needs of recipient countries, or more precisely their actual degree of poverty aversion.

In rationalizing the observed aid allocation behavior of donors, three important points should be kept in mind. As far as allocation rules are concerned, first, the approximate nature of the governance and institutional indicators has to be stressed. This is problematic for the allocation itself but also for the estimation of the growth-governance relationship presumably behind this rule. Second, the delivery of aid should matter for its allocation. A donor able to better monitor the projects and programs it finances should rely less on the actual governance in the recipient country. As a matter of fact, the aid provided to the so-called fragile countries is not managed like the aid given to other countries. Third, the argument in this section relies on the implicit assumption that the total aid budget of donors is fixed and what matters is its allocation across recipient countries. But the governance in those countries, or at least the way it is perceived in donor countries, should presumably affect aid budgets. Little evidence is available on this point, though.[24]

9.4. AID AS "REFORM": THE EFFECT OF AID
ON INSTITUTIONS AND GOVERNANCE

9.4.1. Theoretical Arguments

In this section we focus on the channels through which aid can affect institutions. These institutional effects of aid are sometimes intended by donors, as in the case of conditionality, but often are not.

The theoretical literature has identified many ways in which aid can have a negative effect on the welfare of the recipient country. One possibility for such a counterintuitive "aid curse" (e.g., Moss et al. 2006) is the transfer paradox: the direct beneficial effect of the transfer of resources through aid is more than offset by a deterioration in the country's external terms of trade as a result of the transfer (Chichilnisky 1980, 1983; Bhagwati et al. 1983).[25]

The transfer paradox once attracted much interest but has now virtually disappeared from the aid literature. Nowadays the term aid curse is typically used in analogy with the resource curse. The channels identified in the resource curse literature (van der Ploeg 2011) have also become prominent in the aid curse literature as potential explanations for an adverse effect of aid. These channels are relevant in our context since they typically (but not always) involve an adverse effect on institutions. There is, however, an important analytical difference between the two literatures. In the resource curse literature, only the responses of domestic agents (the government, opposition groups, private entrepreneurs, rent seekers, and so on) to a resource boom need to be considered. But in the case of the aid curse there are also external agents to consider: donors can take into account the responses of domestic agents to aid when deciding on the amount of aid and the type of conditionality to be imposed. Hence, the consequences of, for example, elite capture differ between resource and aid curses because a donor will attempt to limit elite capture.

In this section we discuss seven possible channels:

1. Dutch Disease
2. Accountability
3. The Cost of Taxation
4. Government Survival
5. Rent-Seeking and Corruption
6. Conditionality
7. Elite Capture

9.4.1.1. Aid and Dutch Disease
One of the effects of a resource boom (an improvement in the terms of trade or a discovery of a tradable resource such as oil) is Dutch Disease: an increase in the relative price of non-tradables as a result of increased boom-financed domestic spending. Such "real appreciation" is accompanied by an expansion of the production of non-tradables at the expense of tradables. This in itself is not welfare-reducing, and in that sense the Dutch Disease is not a disease. However, if the production of tradables, e.g., manufacturing, involves learning by doing, then a temporary resource boom could lead to a permanent loss of productivity as a result of foregone learning.

The effect of an aid inflow is analytically identical. This Dutch Disease effect of aid has generated an extensive literature (notably Rajan and Subramanian 2005, 2011). Much of this literature is concerned with the negative effect of aid on the production of tradables and thereby on the scope for export-led growth rather than with an effect of aid on institutions. To that extent it is not relevant in our context, but it should be noted that the empirical literature usually cannot make this distinction.

9.4.1.2. Aid and Accountability

Access to aid may induce the recipient government to reduce its reliance on domestic taxation.[26] Government expenditure then increases by less than the amount of aid since part of the aid is used to reduce tax revenue. This has two effects.

The effect that has received most attention in the literature (Jones and Tarp 2016; Moyo 2009; Deaton 2013) is a negative one. The more public expenditure can be financed by aid, the less the recipient will need to "buy" the consent of taxpayers. Accountability to citizens (e.g., through parliaments) over central expenditure is thereby undermined: governments become accountable to donors rather than to their citizens.[27] Aid therefore undermines political institutions and thereby makes collective action difficult (Booth 2011). This will reduce welfare if the government pursues its own objectives rather than taking the interest of its citizens into account. In this case, aid benefits the recipient government and the interest group it represents (a particular class, region, or ethnic group), at the expense of aggregate welfare.

The same argument has been used to explain the resource curse. However, as Frankel (2012) points out, while the need for taxation may indeed lead to democracy ("no taxation without representation"), it is not democracy per se but institutions such as the rule of law and a market economy that promote economic growth. In other words, while aid may promote autocracy by undermining accountability, the effect on development need not be negative.

In addition, note that the analogy of the aid and resource curses may fail: aid is likely to be less fungible than resource rents as a result of conditionality and donor-initiated public expenditure reviews.

9.4.1.3. Aid and the Cost of Taxation

The second effect of an aid-induced reduction in taxation aid is a change in the cost of taxation. This has received much less attention; a notable exception is the Adam and O'Connell (1999) paper, already discussed at some length earlier in this chapter. In their model of clientelism, the sole objective of the government is to use the state to maximize the income of a favored group through transfers, which can be financed either by aid or by tax revenue.

The government sets a tax rate as Stackelberg leader and entrepreneurs subsequently decide how much to invest in a high-return activity that is taxed and in an untaxed, low-return activity. The nature of the equilibrium in this model depends on the relative size of the favored group. If this group is relatively small then it bears only a small part of the cost of the transfer (the increase in the cost of taxation which lowers the income of all groups), whereas the benefits are high since the transfer is divided among a small number of claimants. This gives the government an incentive to set high tax rates. The result will be low growth and high incomes of the favored group.

Conversely, if the relative size of the group exceeds a certain critical level, then the favored group will have to bear so much of the cost of taxation that the costs of a high transfer outweigh its benefits. The result will be an equilibrium that Adam and O'Connell call a developmental state. In that equilibrium tax rates are low, taxation is used only to finance a given level of public expenditure, and there are no transfers. The economy grows rapidly (through investment in the sector that is taxed) and the favored group benefits from this growth through taxes (low rates applied to a high tax base) rather than through transfers.

These two equilibria have radically different implications for the effect of aid. In the former case (when the government has a narrow power base), unconditional aid will, under the assumptions of the model, be used entirely to increase the transfer to the favored group. If the donor is aware of this, it may decide to give no aid. By contrast, in the developmental state, aid will be used to reduce tax rates. This will raise welfare by reducing the cost of taxation.[28]

A change in the tax rate may seem far removed from the institutional development which is our concern here. But in this model it represents a move away from a predatory state toward a more inclusive society (where the inclusion is achieved in spite of the government's total indifference toward the welfare of the non-favored group). This change in the "rules of the game" can be seen as a fundamental institutional change.

Two points should be noted. First, when aid affects institutions by undermining accountability, the effect is unambiguously negative: aid enables the government to deviate from the interests of its citizens by reducing the need to seek their consent for taxation. When, however, the effect works through the cost of taxation channel, then the sign of the effect depends on the nature of the political regime: the effect is negative if the government has a narrow base, but beyond a critical point, in the developmental state, it is positive.[29] Second, aid in this model works by reinforcing preexisting institutional arrangements that affect the distribution of income between the favored group and the rest of the population. In the developmental state, the non-favored group benefits from aid in spite of the government caring only about the welfare of the other group. (This assumption is clearly extreme. If it is relaxed, aid is more likely to be beneficial to the non-favored group.)

9.4.1.4. Aid and Government Survival

Aid can also affect the government's tenure and thereby cause or prevent changes in institutions. In the Adam-O'Connell model the government cannot be challenged and what it spends (other than on transfers) is given. Once this is relaxed, aid can keep the regime in power by financing repression and defense against a coup or secession attempt. The sign of this political survival mechanism is ambiguous since aid may be channeled to the opposition or to civil society groups. Even if such support does not directly threaten the regime's survival, it may force the regime to introduce institutional reforms.

Aid can also affect government survival through political conditionality. In Africa, donors have sometimes made aid conditional on multi-party elections and have on occasion blocked attempts by incumbent presidents to exceed constitutional tenure limits.

9.4.1.5. Aid, Rent-Seeking, and Corruption

As in the case of the resource curse, aid can increase the incentives to engage in rent-seeking. This may explain a negative effect of aid on growth as entrepreneurs shift from production to rent-seeking (Krueger 1974) and can undermine institutional quality through corruption, much like in the case of the resource curse (Djankov et al. 2009). On the other hand, aid can reduce corruption, either directly through institutional reforms or increases in civil service salaries (Menard and Weill 2016) or indirectly through successful conditionality. The indirect effect implies an effect of corruption on aid rather than the other way around. (The possibility of a two way interaction was until recently ignored in much of the empirical literature.)

In modern forms of budget support where conditionality is kept to a minimum, corruption is seen as a "game stopper": while donors have committed themselves to disburse aid with minimal interference, it is understood that aid will be stopped in case of a corruption scandal (Adam and Gunning 2002).

9.4.1.6. Conditionality

In the basic version of the Adam-O'Connell model, the donor has little power: he can allocate aid across countries but has no control over the way it is spent by the recipients. We now relax this by introducing conditionality. Conditionality can play two quite different roles, depending on whether or not the donor and the recipient government fundamentally agree in terms of objectives (Collier et al. 1997).

When there is agreement on objectives, the donor can offer the government a commitment device and thereby make its policies credible in a context of time inconsistency. If the government would reverse its policy (not because it wants to do so but because it could not resist demands to that effect from the opposition), the donor would be committed to cut off aid. This would be sufficiently damaging for those who would otherwise succeed in making the government reverse its policy to desist.

Clearly, this will work only if the donor's action is credible. This has been problematic: donors have been reluctant to commit to cutting off aid even if it was clear that this would help a reforming government (Collier and Gunning 1995; Adam and O'Connell 1999). This reluctance reflects not only the interests of donor bureaucracies but also the political problem of having to explain to citizens in donor countries that aid to a deserving country must be stopped.

Much more common has been the second type of conditionality, where there is a conflict of interest between the donor and the government. Conditionality then does not work as a commitment device but as a means of aligning recipient interests with those of the donor.

In the Adam-O'Connell model the donor can use conditionality to increase the share of the non-favored group in the benefits of aid: aid would then be conditional on a reduction in tax rates. What conditionality can achieve in this model (nothing, gains from aid, or a Pareto-efficient outcome) depends on the nature of the political equilibrium (the size of favored group) and the non-transfer level of government expenditure. Except for a particular intermediate level of expenditure and a large favored group (so that essentially the differences between the principal and the agent do not matter because the government already has an incentive to assist the non-favored group), there is a role for conditionality (proposition 7 in Adam-O'Connell).

In practice, conditionality has been used extensively by donors to effect institutional reform, particularly in the 1980s and 1990s when donor-financed structural adjustment programs in developing countries, notably in Africa, were festooned with conditions on institutional changes.[30] These were often poorly designed. Since structural adjustment aid was supposed to be temporary, a frequent problem was time inconsistency. A government might be induced by the offer of conditional aid to adopt a reform favored by the donors (e.g., trade liberalization) but would have an incentive to reverse the reform once the aid stopped.[31]

This type of conditionality is often called ex ante conditionality: the conditions apply not to the outcomes in which the donor is interested (e.g., poverty reduction) but to policies that are supposed to lead to these outcomes. Since the donor disburses the aid when the recipient promises to implement the desired policy change, this type of conditionality is fundamentally flawed: the recipient may not implement or maintain the reform and the expected outcome may not materialize. (In a repeated game, failure to implement and maintain the reform would be punished by stopping new disbursements. In practice, donor bureaucracies have strong incentives to continue aid in such circumstances so that the threat of stopping aid is not credible.[32])

The theoretical literature usually assumes that conditionality is of the ex post type. Azam and Laffont (2003), for example, assume initially that the donor's commitment is credible and that the contract between the principal (the donor) and the agent (the government) can be written in terms of the outcome of interest to the principal: the consumption level of the poor. When information is incomplete, specifically when the donor does not know to what extent the government cares about the poor, then aid is less effective: as a result of the incomplete information, the optimal aid contract allows the government and information rent. Compared to the full information case, aid is partly "wasted" to pay this rent. However, in this case of informational asymmetry, Azam and Laffont continue to assume that the contract can be written in terms of the consumption of the poor.

The obvious failures of ex ante conditionality have frequently led to proposals to replace it by ex post conditionality (sometimes referred to as payment for results or performance-based aid), that is, by a contract in terms of the donor's ultimate objectives. In this case, aid would be disbursed when proof was submitted of changes in, say, poverty, health, or learning outcomes.[33] Alternatively, the donor would commit to aid for a group of countries with the share of each country determined ex post on the basis of its actual performance (Svensson 2003).

With the notable exception of EU budget support, this type of conditionality has rarely been implemented. This drives a wedge between the theoretical and the empirical literature: the evidence is from a world in which the ex post conditionality of the theoretical literature is the exception rather than the rule.

9.4.1.7. Aid and Elite Capture

Azam and Laffont model the relationship between donor and government in the familiar framework of contract theory. When the full information assumption is dropped, the donor cannot know the type of the government, i.e., the extent to which it cares about the welfare of the poor. The effect of this uncertainty is that a "good" government (one that attaches considerable weight to the consumption of the poor) gets a larger share of the aid than under full information. The difference represents the information rent, compensation for the fact that the government could pretend to be of the "bad" type.

By contrast, Bourguignon and Platteau (2018a) model the government as an agent that would like to appropriate the aid entirely but which faces both internal and external discipline. Internal discipline is reflected in increasing marginal cost to the government of fraud: the larger the share of aid it appropriates for itself, the more it will have to hand over to other groups, possibly as a way to buy their compliance. (Note that this differs fundamentally from an altruistic specification whereby the other groups' welfare is an argument of the government's utility.) This cost function is given and in that sense the quality of governance is exogenous in this model. The donor chooses a degree of monitoring that determines the probability that a given level of fraud will be detected and punished by the donor.[34]

In this model, the optimal level of fraud is an inverse function of total discipline, the sum of the parameters measuring external and internal discipline. The donor (principal) now chooses the optimal level of external discipline, taking into account how the government (agent) will choose its optimal level of fraud. In this model a change in institutional quality (the given strength of internal discipline) affects the amount of aid (the mechanism discussed in section 9.3) but also the level of external discipline. There is therefore a trade-off: greater internal discipline induces the donor to relax external discipline.

The key question is which of these two changes dominates, i.e., what happens to total discipline and hence to the level of fraud. Bourguignon and Platteau show that in particular circumstances (notably when internal discipline is weak), total discipline falls so that better internal discipline leads, somewhat counterintuitively, to *greater* fraud.

In this section the issue is how aid affects institutional quality (rather than the other way around as in section 9.3). If we use elite capture (the fraction of aid that is appropriated by the government) as the measure of institutional quality in the Bourguignon-Platteau model, then the implication is that aid to countries with poor governance (low internal discipline) may increase elite capture and thereby *lower* institutional quality.

9.5. EVIDENCE ON THE EFFECT OF AID ON INSTITUTIONS

Much of the empirical literature investigates the effect of aid on particular measures of institutional quality without identifying the channel. We consider these studies first and then the papers with evidence on the seven channels identified in the previous section.[35]

9.5.1. Evidence Not Limited to Particular Channels: Econometric Studies

The early literature has used cross-country regressions to estimate the effect of aid on macroeconomic outcomes such as the level or growth of GDP (Boone 1996; Burnside and Dollar 2000; Rajan and Subramanian 2008). It is often suggested (e.g., Deaton 2013) that this literature has reached a consensus that this macroeconomic effect is either insignificant or negative.

In fact, recent studies (notably those by Finn Tarp and his co-authors) typically find a positive and significant effect, and in many studies this effect is sizable (Arndt et al. 2010, 2015, 2018; Clemens et al. 2012; Juselius et al. 2014). "The weighted average result from these studies indicates that a sustained inflow of foreign aid equivalent to 10 percent of

GDP is expected to raise growth rates per capita by about one percentage point on average" (Arndt et al. 2018). This implies a 10% rate of return, very much higher than what was suggested in the earlier literature.

There is a vast empirical literature on the effects of aid on the quality of policies and institutions in developing countries and on the reverse effect: of governance in recipient countries on the amount of aid. This literature is plagued by endogeneity issues and many of the results are therefore controversial.

The modern literature starts with Burnside and Dollar (2000), who estimated the effect of aid on economic growth. To take into account the endogeneity of aid in this equation, they estimated a system of two equations (using 2SLS), one for growth, the other for aid. In the growth equation, aid entered twice: as an explanatory variable on its own and also interacted with a variable for the quality of policies. This specification led to the key Burnside-Dollar conclusion: aid has a positive (and significant) impact on growth, but only in an environment of "good" policies. (Only fiscal, monetary, and trade policies were considered; microeconomic policies played no role in the governance indicator.) This conclusion had an obvious policy implication: aid should be "selective," i.e., concentrated on countries with "good" policies. (Under such an aid allocation, better governance leads to higher growth both directly and indirectly, by attracting more aid.) Conversely, aid should not be given to countries that did not yet have the right institutions: without a good policy environment such aid would be wasted. This finding attracted enormous attention, in particular since it deviated so much from donor practice at the time: donors tended to focus aid on countries with poor policies.[36]

The Burnside-Dollar approach was adopted in a large number of subsequent papers. It quickly became clear that the original results were not robust to minor changes in specification or in the period covered and, notably, not to changes in the treatment of outliers. The essential role of the interaction term was questioned: many authors claimed to show that aid was good for growth even in a poor policy environment. If true, there would then be no basis for selectivity in the allocation of aid.

These (somewhat counterintuitive) results themselves came under attack. Rajan and Subramanian (2008) argued that the evidence showed that aid had *no* effect on growth, irrespective of the quality of governance or the type of aid. Their paper quickly acquired a canonical status.[37] This is somewhat surprising since Arndt, Jones, and Tarp (2010) showed that these results were not robust. This important paper remains somewhat in the periphery of the literature, and the Rajan-Subramanian findings continue to be cited by many as the definitive result on aid effectiveness.

Arndt et al. started from a replication of the Rajan-Subramanian analysis. They then introduced a different (better) estimator and some changes in the specification (essentially including more regional fixed effects, some indicators of initial human capital and of geographic conditions). Most important, they used a different set of instruments, correcting a number of errors in the original paper. These changes led to radically different outcomes. Rajan-Subramanian used growth theory to derive an estimate for the effect of aid on growth, concluding that aid of 10% of GDP should raise the growth rate (permanently) by about 1%. Arndt et al. (2010) in fact find an effect that is slightly *higher* than this theoretical prediction, a dramatic reversal of the earlier finding that there was no effect. These results that aid has a substantial impact on growth, in accordance with what theory suggests, have been confirmed in a series of subsequent papers.

9.5.2. Evidence Not Limited to Particular Channels: Case Studies

Aid effectiveness has also been investigated in case studies. These studies (e.g., Collier and Reinikka 2001, for Uganda) confirm that donors practiced selectivity: countries perceived as good policy environments attracted much more aid ("donor darlings"). There is similar evidence for Ghana, Vietnam, and Rwanda. This is important since some of the econometric evidence on this point is methodologically suspect: where the World Bank's CPI was used as an indicator of the quality of governance, reverse causality may well have played a role. The Bank staff who came up with the CPI scores may well have given high scores to countries that performed well in terms of growth, *because* of these outcomes. Obviously, this makes the CPI score endogenous in a growth regression. The case studies are not immune to this problem, but they are probably less vulnerable, giving detailed accounts of institutional arrangements.

There are also numerous case studies on the effect of aid on institutional quality through policy conditionality (e.g., Devarajan et al. 2000; Botchwey et al. 1998; Collier and Reinikka 2001; Gunning 2001). Devarajan et al. studied aid and policy reform in 15 African countries and found that in spite of large amounts of aid, only three (Mali, Ghana, and Uganda) reformed successfully. The key issue in this literature is of course the counterfactual. If a country adopted policies that the donor had made a condition for aid, it does not follow that those policy changes were caused by the aid. The case study evidence is useful since it often describes the way policy changes were arrived at in great detail. In many cases it seems plausible that the domestic political process would have led to the donor-favored changes even in the absence of aid. Uganda and Vietnam are examples of this. In such cases, aid may have been effective because policies were "good," but the good policy environment was not the result of aid. Aid effectiveness then reflects "aid as finance" rather than "aid for reform."

9.5.3. The Paradox of Aid Effectiveness

Intuition suggests that good governance makes aid more effective. The Burnside-Dollar results confirmed this. Not surprisingly, the policy conclusion of aid selectivity therefore survived the early critiques of the Burnside-Dollar econometric procedures: their results were accepted in spite of methodological criticisms because they seemed so very plausible.

This survival was not permanent. The Rajan and Subramanian papers (2005, 2007, 2008, 2011), notably their 2008 paper, came to be accepted as the final proof that aid (at least as practiced) had no effect on growth.

This is sometimes described as a paradox: what seems plausible turns out not to be true and what seems counterintuitive—that aid has no effect—is apparently empirically true. The recent papers, notably those by Finn Tarp and his colleagues (Arndt et al. 2010, 2015, 2018; Jones and Tarp 2016; Juselius et al. 2014) show that there is no paradox: aid in fact has a positive impact of a sizable (and theoretically) plausible magnitude. However, this conclusion is not (yet) widely accepted.

The evidence on the effect of aid on institutions is quite mixed (Jones and Tarp 2016). Djankov et al. (2009) and Busse and Gröning (2009) find a negative effect, but Alesina and Weder (2002) and Knack (2004) find no effect, while Tavares (2003) finds a positive effect: aid reduces corruption (but the effect is quite weak). Menard and Weill (2016) investigate the two-way interaction between aid and corruption with Grange-causality tests. They find no evidence of a significant effect in either direction: there is no clear evidence that changes in aid precede changes in corruption or vice versa. While it has often been suggested that multilateral aid might be more effective than bilateral aid in reducing corruption, the Granger-causality evidence does not support this view: the Menard-Weill result (no significant effect in either direction) is robust to this disaggregation.

While the theoretical view is sharply divided on the sign of the effect of aid on (political) institutions, Dutta et al. (2013) argue that the sign depends on the initial situation: aid makes democracies more democratic and autocracies more autocratic. They find evidence in support of this "amplification" hypothesis. This is reminiscent of the Burnside-Dollar result that aid works, but only in favorable policy environments.

A problem that plagues this literature is the heterogeneity of aid, both in terms of its objectives and its volatility. Clearly, long-term aid in support of democratic reforms will have effects quite different from, say, short-run capacity-building projects. The focus in the empirical literature on the effects of *total* aid is therefore misguided.

We consider the Jones and Tarp (2016) paper in some detail because it explicitly deals with these two types of heterogeneity. This paper uses both a cross-sectional approach and dynamic panel estimators (with panels of different duration: 2, 4, or 6 years): systems GMM, a random effects model, or bias-corrected fixed effects. The authors use five different measures of political institutions as well as a synthetic measure.

Jones and Tarp find a positive effect of aggregate aid on this synthetic measure of institutional quality. This aggregate effect is small, but there is clear evidence of heterogeneity: when aid is given for governance purposes and when aid is relatively stable, it has a substantial positive effect.[38] The difference is enormous, e.g., the effect of stable aid in these estimates is four times as large as that of volatile aid.

In the theory section we noted an ambiguity: aid may affect some aspects of institutional quality (e.g., democracy) but not others (e.g., the rule of law), and it may be the latter which are more important for growth. The Jones-Tarp paper resolves this issue since they find similar positive effects of aid on a wide range of indicators of institutional quality: measures of democracy, "checks" (i.e., the number of players who can veto political decisions), executive constraints, political terror, and judicial independence.

9.5.4. Evidence for Particular Channels

A point to note is that the Jones-Tarp paper provides evidence of a positive effect of aid on governance, but it does not indicate the channels through which this effect runs. This is a general characteristic of the econometric literature. Similarly, the Arndt et al. (2018) study disaggregates the macroeconomic effect of aid in effects due to induced changes in consumption, physical and human capital, and direct changes in productivity. But here again there is no indication of the effect of aid on institutions. In this sense there is a disconnect between the theoretical and the empirical literature. This is a gap which the EDI project aims to fill.

There is, however, some evidence on the seven channels we distinguished in the theoretical section.

9.5.4.1. Aid and Dutch Disease

A large number of developing countries have received very high inflows for very long periods: some three dozen countries received more than 10% of GDP in aid for at least two decades (Moss et al. 2006). This has spawned a series of econometric papers investigating the Dutch Disease effects of aid.

Rajan and Subramanian (2005) find strong evidence of aid-induced Dutch Disease: aid undermines competitiveness by reducing growth, wages, and productivity in the manufacturing and export sectors. This may explain, as the authors suggest, why aid has been less effective in raising growth than expected. (Recall, however, that the recent evidence shows a substantial positive effect of aid on growth contrary to the consensus a decade ago.) The question whether Dutch Disease has detrimental institutional effects is not addressed in the empirical literature. This would be the case, for example, if the aid-induced shift from tradables to non-tradables stifled competition and stimulated rent-seeking.

9.5.4.2. Aid, Accountability, and the Cost of Taxation

In much of the theoretical literature, aid has a negative effect on the government's tax effort. This affects institutional quality through two channels: reduced accountability (a negative effect) and lower cost of taxation (a positive effect). However, there appears to be no clear support for the proposition that aid reduces taxation.

McGillivray and Morrissey (2004) find that expenditure actually increases by *more* than the amount of aid; hence taxes are crowded in rather than out. Where loans and grants are distinguished, the early studies (summarized in Moss et al. 2006) find a clear difference: loans do not affect taxation (presumably because the government has an incentive to raise taxes to service the debt) but grants reduce it.

Clist and Morrissey (2011) revisited this issue. They find that until the mid-1980s loans indeed had a positive effect, but grants had a negative effect on tax effort (as measured by the tax/GDP ratio). However, they find evidence of a structural break in 1985: in the post-1985 period, grants also *increase* tax effort. They suggest that this reflects successful conditionality: donors exhorted the poorest countries (where grants were concentrated) to raise more taxes.[39]

There is case study evidence (Brautigam and Knack 2004; Moss et al. 2006) that aid not only affects tax revenue but the budget process itself. Under aid, budget constraints become weak as governments come to feel that they can appeal to donors to make up any deficit: there are no longer hard budget constraints.

In much of the empirical literature there is a presumption that the effect of aid on institutions through the two tax channels must be negative although, as we have seen, the sign of the effect is ambiguous in the theoretical literature. Jones and Tarp (2016) in fact find a positive effect of aid on political institutions.

9.5.4.3. Aid and Government Survival

Ahmed (2012) presents evidence that aid, as expected, is partly diverted to patronage and through that channel aid reduces government turnover in autocratic regimes.

Anecdotal evidence suggests that donors have been successful in using aid to achieve changes in electoral processes. Whether this contributed to donors' ultimate objectives remains in doubt. In many African countries, multi-party elections appear to have intensified ethnic conflicts (since parties were organized along ethnic or regional lines) while failing to establish democratic control over government spending. Hence, aid brought the appearance of democracy: elections, but not the substance: accountability (Collier 2008). The empirical evidence is devastating. As noted above, Knack (2004) finds no evidence whatsoever of aid on democracy, measured in a number of different ways.

9.5.4.4. Aid, Rent-Seeking, and Corruption

Okada and Samreth (2012) present evidence that aid deters corruption using panel data for 120 developing countries. Asongu (2012), however, using data for 52 African countries, reaches the opposite conclusion: aid increases corruption.

9.5.4.5. Aid and Conditionality

The empirical literature on the effectiveness of conditionality starts with the famous but controversial Burnside and Dollar (2000) paper, which concluded that donors were incapable of changing policies in developing countries through conditionality. While other conclusions of that paper turned out not to be robust, this one has been confirmed in most subsequent econometric work.

Svensson (2003) analyzed data for some 200 structural adjustment efforts and found "no link between a country's reform effort, or fulfillment [sic] of 'conditionality,' and the disbursement rate." In addition, there have been numerous country case studies of the effectiveness of conditionality in effecting policy reform, usually in the context of structural adjustment programs (e.g., Botchwey et al. 1998; Devarajan et al. 2000).

Both types of studies face a serious methodological problem (Gunning 2001). In many cases the failure of conditionality was fairly obvious since the reforms desired by donors were not maintained or even implemented. But in other cases they were, and it is a judgment call whether this reflected successful conditionality or whether the reforms, as has been argued for the case of Vietnam, for example, would also have been implemented in the counterfactual case as a result of a domestic political process (with donors afterward claiming credit for the successful outcome). Devarajan et al. (2000) study conditionality and reform in 15 African countries. Only in three cases (Uganda, Mali, and Ghana) do they conclude that donors were successful in achieving economic reform through conditionality.

Recall that many of the papers in the theoretical literature assume that donors can credibly commit. The empirical literature makes clear that this assumption is not realistic. The resulting time inconsistency has undermined the effectiveness of conditionality (Collier et al. 1997). Kilby (2009) finds evidence that non-enforcement of World Bank conditions reflects politically motivated pressure by powerful donors, notably the United States. Hence, internal bureaucratic incentives (the reason usually given for lack of donor credibility and hence time inconsistency) need not be the only reason for the failure of (ex ante) conditionality.

9.5.4.6. Aid and Elite Capture

Platteau (2004) reports case study evidence of elite capture of aid in Africa. Villagers were well aware of this but continued to support (and even re-elect) the responsible local leader. The reason was that they realized they would be worse off without his giving them access to part of the aid, however small. The fundamental problem in this case was lack of donor coordination. A threat of an individual donor to cut off aid if elite capture continued would not be credible since the leader would be able to continue the aid relationship with another donor.

In a regression study, Bjørnskov (2010) finds evidence that aid changes the distribution of income in favor of the rich in democratic countries, but (somewhat puzzlingly) does not affect the distribution of income in autocracies.

9.6. CONCLUSION

The literature on the effect of aid on institutions constitutes an important subset of the more general literature on the effectiveness of aid. We have emphasized the distinction between two roles of aid: aid as finance and aid as reform. In the former case, aid is simply a resource transfer that enables a government to implement projects or policy reforms it intended to undertake anyway. In the latter case, the way resources are provided changes what the government does, in ways either intended by the donor (as envisaged under conditionality) or not (as when aid induces rent-seeking or keeps a kleptocracy in power).

This literature is enormous but has not arrived at a clear consensus on the way aid (whether as finance or as reform) affects institutions and thereby poverty and other development outcomes. There are at least four reasons for this unsatisfactory state of affairs.

First, to the extent there is empirical evidence on the various channels identified in the theoretical literature (and we have indicated that the coverage is patchy), this is often regression-based and therefore usually subject to endogeneity concerns. There are many studies that use RCTs and natural experiments, but these can address only some components of the effect of aid and institutions; many other aspects do not lend themselves to an experimental approach.

Second, to a surprising extent this is a tale of two literatures: the theoretical and empirical literature are very imperfectly integrated. There is limited evidence on issues that are central in theory (for example the effect of aid on accountability, rent-seeking, or the cost of taxation). Conversely, we have noted that where the two literatures do address the same issues, the empirical evidence sometimes suggests that concerns in the theoretical literature are misplaced.

Third, many studies use measures of aid that aggregate overflows which are likely to have very different effects: emergency assistance versus multiyear programs, tied and untied aid, aid given for political reasons versus development projects. Such aggregate measures are popular in the aid effectiveness literature but, as shown in recent papers, can be quite misleading.

Fourth, empirical papers use measures of governance or policies that may not be appropriate. The indicators used range from the CPIA of the World Bank and the Competitiveness Indicators of the World Economic Forum to the Worldwide Governance Indicators (WGI), themselves ingeniously constructed aggregates of a large number of individual indicators. The number of measures used in empirical papers is bewildering: the largest compilation, that of the University of Gothenburg, comprises as many as 2,067 items. Some of these indicators focus on quite specific aspects of governance, institutions, or policies that may be too detailed to really infer from them the impact of aid. Aggregating them, as done for instance by the WGI, into measures of "control of corruption," "government effectiveness," or the "rule of law" can be problematic: such aggregations are rather arbitrary and do not necessarily capture what is essential in the effect of aid on institutions. As the theoretical analysis in this survey suggests, what really matters is the "pro-poor" stance of the recipient government rather than specific policies or institutions. It might thus be an interesting direction of research to explore new ways of aggregating existing individual indicators along such lines.

The conventional wisdom holds that the effect of aid (through whatever channel) on growth and other outcomes of interest is negative or at best only very weakly positive. The recent literature shows that this is incorrect: the evidence is that aid has a substantial positive effect and that this works through changes in institutions. This is important but probably to some extent simply reflects successful selectivity: when aid is allocated to "pro-poor" governments, then it will have the effect of improving institutions. (Note that this does not invoke conditionality: aid succeeds in the "aid as finance" role rather than "aid as reform.") This is different from the earlier focus on "good policy environments" as the basis for allocating aid:[40] what matters is the nature of the regime (in particular the likelihood of "leakage" or elite capture), rather than the current policy environment.

If it is accepted that, in this sense, the scope for aid to modify institutions is limited, there are in principle two alternative routes: different agents or different policies. In the first case, donors circumvent governments by working with local or international NGOs. While this appears attractive it suffers two obvious major limitations: NGOs are themselves vulnerable to elite capture, and a government that uses the state to serve the interests of narrow factions is unlikely to tolerate NGOs that threaten that objective.

This leaves non-aid policies as instruments for changing institutions. There is much anecdotal evidence that this can work. Examples are the use of trade restrictions to eradicate child labor; transparency and labeling initiatives to expose the sale of "blood diamonds"; media exposure of the use of tax havens; travel and banking restrictions aimed at members of a kleptocratic elite. There is, however, as yet little evidence beyond anecdotes. This seems a promising direction for future research.

The literature on aid effectiveness implicitly classifies aid as either good or bad. In our view this binary approach is not appropriate. In many situations, aid can improve institutions and achieve development objectives while at the same time having adverse effects: elite capture, weakening accountability, and so on. The question is not whether such "taxation" should be eliminated but rather what the maximum rate of such taxation is that is acceptable to the donor.

A Canonical Model of the Donor-Recipient Relationship with a Parametric Representation of the Recipient Country's Governance

François Bourguignon

Several authors have tried to provide a theoretical framework for the analysis of the relationship between donors and recipients of aid. Most important have been in particular the articles by Adam and O'Connell (1999), Svensson (2000, 2003), Azam and Laffont (2003), Torsvik (2005), and more recently, Bourguignon and Platteau (2018a). In the spirit of a survey focusing on institutions and aid, the model presented here generalizes those by Adam and O'Connell and Azam and Laffont by explicitly introducing a varying degree of convergence between the objective function of the donors and that of the decision-makers in the recipient country. The setup of the model is discussed in the main text section 9.2.1. This appendix shows the complete analytics of the model and the proof of the main results mentioned in the chapter text. It also explores some extensions of the basic model to show that its properties are fairly general.

9.A.1. The Model

$$Max_{t,s,z} \; u(y) + \theta v(x) \tag{9.A.1.3}$$

Subject to:

$$x = h(t) + s; \; y = ch(t) + z; \; s, z \geq 0 \tag{9.A.1.1}$$

$$nz + (1-n)s + G \leq H(t) = (nc + 1 - n)h(t) . \frac{t}{1-t}. \tag{9.A.1.2}$$

It is first shown that both transfers s and z cannot be strictly positive at equilibrium. If this were the case, the first-order conditions would lead to:

$$u' = \lambda n; \; \theta v' = \lambda(1-n); \; u'ch' + \theta v'h' + \lambda H' = 0$$

where λ is the Lagrange multiplier associated with the budget constraint (9.A.1.2). Substituting and eliminating λ, it becomes:

$$nch' + (1-n) \, h' + H' = 0.$$

Differentiating $H(t)$ in (9.A.1.2) then leads to:

$$[nc+(1-n)]\frac{1}{(1-t)^2}[(1-t)h'(t)+h(t)]=0.$$

As $h(t)$ is decreasing and concave, this expression is positive for all $t<1$. Indeed, the square bracket is a decreasing function which takes the value zero for $t=1$. It is therefore strictly positive for all values of $t<1$, the same being true for the whole expression. As $t=1$ cannot be an optimum, it follows that z and s cannot be simultaneously strictly positive.

This concludes the proof of Property 1 in the text. From now on, the analysis will focus on the case where the transfer s to the poor is zero and the "rent," z, served to the elite is positive or nil.

9.A.2. Comparative Statics in the Basic Model

In the (x, y), rather than the (z, t) space, the maximization problem with no transfer to the poor writes:

$$Max_{x,y,z}\ u(y)+\theta v(x)\ s.t.\ y=cx+\frac{R(x)-G}{n};z=[R(x)-G]/n\geq0 \qquad \text{(9.A.i)}$$

where $R(x)$ is the government revenue function expressed as a function of x rather than the tax rate t. Optimizing with respect to x is equivalent to optimizing with respect to the tax rate, t, as the two variables are linked through the monotonic declining relationship: $x=h(t)$. This means that $R(x)$ is given by: $R(x)=H(h^{-1}(x))$.

If the last non-negativity constraint on the rent z in (9.A.i) is not binding, the first-order condition writes:

$$\theta v'(x)+[c+R'(x)/n].u'[cx+(R(x)-G)/n]=0. \qquad \text{(9.A.ii)}$$

Note that the first term in square brackets on the left-hand side of this equation must be negative for this condition to hold. In other words, the solution must lie on the decreasing part of the Laffer curve expressed as a function of the income of the poor, x—or the increasing branch of it when expressed as a function of the tax rate. It is easily checked that under the condition that $u(\ )$, $v(\ )$ and $R(\ )$ are concave, the second-order condition is also satisfied. Let $x^*(\theta, G)$ be the solution of that equation and $t^*(\theta, G)=h^{-1}(x^*(\theta, G))$ the associated tax rate.

Differentiating the preceding equation with respect to the key parameters of the model and with respect to x yields the following comparative statics results:

$$\frac{\partial x^*}{\partial\theta}\geq0;\ \frac{\partial x^*}{\partial G}\leq0;\ \frac{\partial x^*}{\partial c}?;\ \frac{\partial x^*}{\partial n}?$$

The comparative statics with respect to c and n are ambiguous. Yet, it can be seen in (9.A.ii) that $\partial x^*/\partial G=0$, $\partial x^*/\partial n\geq0$ and $\partial x^*/\partial c\geq0$ when the utility function $u(\ )$ is linear—the "constrained autocracy," or the pure "autocracy" case $\theta=0$. Any change in public expenditure is then entirely transferred to the rent of the elite, a result found in both Adam and O'Connell and Azam and Laffont and therefore strongly dependent on the institutional context assumed for the recipient country. Also, the larger the demographic size of the elite and the higher the level of inequality, the better it is for the poor. The economy is richer, which leads the government to lower distortive taxes, which benefit both the poor and the elite.

If the non-negative rent constraint is binding, then the solution, $\bar{x}(G)$, of (9.A.i) is given by:

$$R[\bar{x}(G)] = G. \qquad (9.A.iii)$$

Given the inverted-U shape of the Laffer curve, there are two roots to this equation and the solution to (9.A.iii) is the largest one, on the declining part of $R(x)$. The comparative statics are particularly simple in that case since $\partial \bar{x}(G)/\partial G$ is clearly negative. It can also be seen that $\bar{x}(G)$ is increasing with c and n. As before, the size of the economy grows with c and n so that the tax rate needed to fund the expenditures G declines.

The corner solution (9.A.iii) will hold if reducing x, starting from $\bar{x}(G)$ does not improve the objective function of the government. From the derivative of that function in (9.A.ii), this condition writes:

$$\theta v'[\bar{x}(G)] + [c + R'(\bar{x}(G))]. \, u'[c\bar{x}(G)] \geq 0. \qquad (9.A.iv)$$

This condition is more likely to hold, the larger θ, the larger G, and the lower n. In the case where $\theta = 0$ it requires that $c + R'(\bar{x}(G)) \geq 0$, which imposes a lower bound on G.

Figures 9.1a and 9.1b show the two types of equilibrium. The Laffer curve (in terms of x) is the inverted-U shaped curve. On the right-hand side, it reaches the horizontal axis at the zero-tax rate, which is the maximum value for the standard of living of the poor. The budget constraint is the thick solid line, and the dotted line is an indifference curve of the government. Figure 9.1a shows a positive rent equilibrium at E. The rent is given by the segment FE between the $y = cx$ line and the budget constraint. Figure 9.1b shows a zero-rent equilibrium.

9.A.3. Optimal Unconditional Aid

The effect of unconditional aid is equivalent to a drop in exogenous expenditure, G, in the budget constraint (9.A.1.2) or (9.A.i). Figure 9.2 shows the effect of unconditional aid with a strictly positive rent.

It follows that the comparative statics on G in the previous section yield the same result for unconditional aid. Property 2 in the text follows from the case where the government's utility function is quasi-linear in y or when $\theta = 0$. Aid is then completely confiscated by the elite. Property 3 is obtained in the opposite case where the government's utility function is concave in y and θ is strictly positive but sufficiently small to stay in the case where the transfer to the poor is zero. The comparative statics on unconditional aid is shown in figure 9.2. Both the income of the elite and the poor benefit from aid, even though the effect of aid on the rent is ambiguous—it can be seen in figure 9.2 that the distance between the equilibrium and the no-rent line $y = cx$ may increase or decrease. If the initial equilibrium E is close enough to the no-rent equilibrium A, it is also possible that aid drives the rent to 0. In figure 9.2, the equilibrium would move from E to A' if E were close enough to A.

Optimal unconditional aid when the non-negative rent constraint is non-binding is given by the maximization of the donor's objective, $V(x) - C.a$, under the first-order condition (9.A.ii), after substituting $G - a$ for G. It is not possible to represent this in the (x,y)

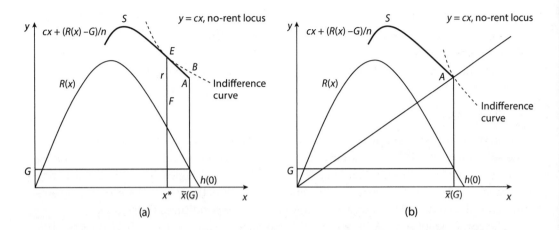

FIGURE 9.1. (*a*) Positive rent equilibrium. (*b*) Zero rent equilibrium.

space. The first-order condition for the optimum level of aid, a^*, with a positive rent is given by:

$$V'[x^*(\theta,G-a)]\frac{\partial x^*}{\partial G}=-C.$$

But the comparative statics yield essentially ambiguous results. In the case of a zero rent, the optimal unconditional aid is given by:

$$V'[\bar{x}(G-a)]=- R'[\bar{x}(G-a)] . \qquad\qquad (9.A.v)$$

The optimal unconditional aid implies a zero rent for the elite if the solution, $\hat{a}$, to the preceding equation and the associated $\bar{x}(G-\hat{a})$ satisfy condition (9.A.iv). Clearly, this depends on the value of the governance parameter, θ, and on the relative shapes of the utility functions $u(\ )$, $v(\ )$, and the Laffer curve, $R(\ )$. The optimal unconditional aid may shift the equilibrium of the economy from the no-rent to the positive rent regime if (9.A.iv) holds for $\bar{x}(G)$ but does not hold for $\bar{x}(G-\hat{a})$. This is because (9.A.iv) is less likely to hold when public expenditures are smaller.

9.A.4. Optimal Conditional Aid
Calling U the reservation level of the objective function of the government, assumed to be equal to the utility of the government in the equilibrium without aid, the optimal conditional aid equilibrium is given by:

$$Max_{a,x} V(x)-Ca \ s.t \ u[cx+(R(x)-G+a) / n]+\theta v(x)\geq U; R(x)\geq G-a. \quad (9.A.vi)$$

The first-order condition writes after isolating a in the first constraint:

$$V'(x)+nC.\{u'^{-1} [U-\theta v(x)] \ \theta v'(x)+nc+R'(x)\} =0 \qquad (9.A.vii)$$

when the rent is strictly positive, and:

$$V'[\bar{x}(G-a)]=- R'[\bar{x}(G-a)] \qquad\qquad (9.A.viii)$$

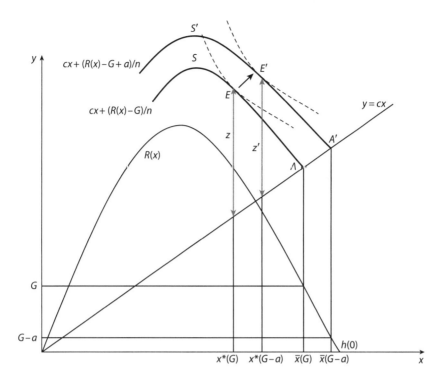

FIGURE 9.2. Effect of unconditional aid.

when the rent is zero. Unsurprisingly, the latter condition is the same as the optimality condition (9.A.vii) for unconditional aid with zero rent. This is because, in both cases, there is no leakage of aid toward the elite of the recipient country. In the case of conditional aid, the zero-rent regime is optimal when the left-hand side of (9.A.vii) is positive for $x = \bar{x}(G - \hat{a})$ where $\hat{a}$ is the solution of (9.A.v).

The comparative statics on θ of (9.A.vi) is ambiguous, even when ignoring the fact that the reservation level U of the recipient country's objective function depends itself on θ in an ambiguous way. The situation is not different from that point of view from the case of unconditional aid. Yet, several simple properties of the optimal conditional aid can be derived.

Consider first the case of a zero-rent regime at point A in figure 9.1 in the absence of aid. As any increase in aid necessarily leads to the government's objective being above its reservation level, the participation constraint in (9.A.vi) is not binding. The optimal conditional aid is somewhere on the $y = cx$ ray beyond point A. If θ is high enough, it may even imply moving to the case where the transfer, s, to the poor is strictly positive, i.e., *below* the $y = cx$ ray.

Property 4. If the rent of the elite is nil in the absence of aid, the optimal conditional aid involves a lower tax rate and, if θ is high enough, a cash transfer to the poor. The objective function of the government is then above its reservation level, U.

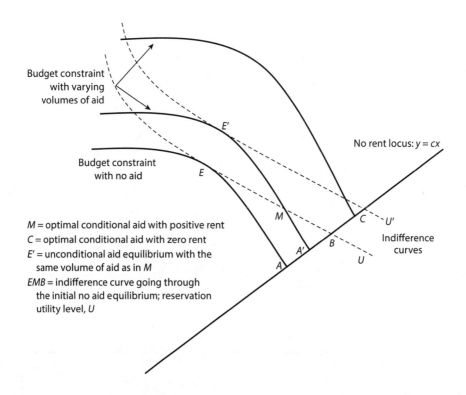

Budget constraint
with varying
volumes of aid

Budget constraint
with no aid

E'

E

No rent locus: $y = cx$

M = optimal conditional aid with positive rent
C = optimal conditional aid with zero rent
E' = unconditional aid equilibrium with the
    same volume of aid as in M
EMB = indifference curve going through
    the initial no aid equilibrium; reservation
    utility level, U

M

C

U'

Indifference
curves

A'

B

A

U

FIGURE 9.3. Optimal conditional aid and unconditional aid.

Consider now the case of a positive rent regime in the absence of aid, i.e., point E in figure 9.3, which is a magnification of the relevant part of figure 9.2. Then the optimal conditional aid will be either at a point on the segment EB along the indifference curve U of the government or along the zero-rent locus, $y = cx$, at point B or beyond it. The participation constraint of the government is binding in the former case but not in the latter. Note also that, although this regime is not represented in figure 9.3, the optimal conditional aid may occur below the $y = cx$ ray with a positive cash transfer to the poor.

Property 5. If the rent of the elite is strictly positive in the absence of aid, the optimal conditional aid always reduces the distortive tax rate and the rent going to the elite. Depending on the preferences of the donor and the governance parameter θ, the rent of the elite may be driven to zero and even replaced by a cash transfer to the poor.

In all cases, the conditionality allows the same volume of aid to achieve a higher level of income for the poor and a more efficient economy than when aid is unconditional. To see this, assume that the optimal conditional aid leads to a point like M on the segment EB in figure 9.3. This point lies on an unconstrained budget curve MA′ for the government of the recipient country. The optimum choice made by the government along that budget curve is at a point like E′ where the budget curve is tangent to an indifference curve of the government's objective function. Clearly, the poor are worse off and the elite better off at E′ than at M. The argument would be the same if the optimal conditional aid led to a point beyond B on the zero-rent line $y = cx$.

The case of the "constrained autocracy," i.e., the quasi-linear objective function of the government with respect to y, leads to stronger comparative results on θ. In that case, the $u'^{-1}[U - \theta v(x)]$ term in (9.A.vii) is constant, so that any increase in θ must be compensated by an increase in x. It follows from the participation constraint that y falls.

Property 6. When the objective function of the recipient country's government is quasi-linear, the income of the poor is increasing and the rent of the elite is decreasing with the governance parameter θ at the optimal conditional aid equilibrium, in stark contrast with the case of unconditional aid.

Under the same conditions, the optimal aid was zero with unconditional aid. This suggests that the governance parameter tends to play a stronger and more positive role with conditional than unconditional aid.

The preceding argument relies on the assumption that the reservation utility of the recipient country's government is the value of its objective function without aid. Yet, a strong case can be made for some bargaining to take place between the donor and the recipient country when conditionality improves the utility function of the donor. This case is ignored here.

9.A.5. The Optimal Conditional Aid Contract

Instead of imposing a target tax rate and a given flow of aid, the optimal conditional aid equilibrium can be reached in a decentralized manner. As in Azam and Laffont (2003), the donor may propose to the government of the recipient country a contract relating the flow of aid to be received to the tax rate to be implemented.

Property 7: The optimal conditional aid is supported by a contract imposed upon the recipient country's government that relates the aid flow to be received to the tax rate

$$a = A + B.t$$

where the constants A and B are appropriately chosen.

If the constants A and B are well chosen, the recipient country's government will choose a point in that constraint that will lead to the tax rate deemed optimal by the donor and a value of its objective function equal to its reservation level. These are the two conditions that allow to determine the values of A and B. Of course, this argument holds in the case of a positive rent regime. If the optimal conditional aid implies a zero rent for the elite, then there is an infinity of schedules of type (A,B) such that the recipient country's government will choose the tax rate targeted by the donor.

The issue of the implementation of such a contract and of optimal conditional aid in general is discussed in the main text.

We now consider various extensions of the basic model and examine whether they can lead to results in contradiction with the previous ones.

9.A.6. Endogenous Public Expenditures

The issue is raised in the text of the implication of assuming that public expenditures are exogenous. It is shown below that the basic message of the model and, in particular, the difference between the positive and zero rent regimes is not modified when public expenditures are endogenous.

Assume the objective function of the government includes an additive term for public expenditures:

$$Max_{x,y,G}\, u(y) + \theta v(x) + s(G) \tag{9.A.ix}$$

with $s(\ )$ increasing and concave. In the (x, y) space, the budget constraint implies that

$$G = R(x) - n(y - cx) + a \tag{9.A.x}$$

whereas the non-negative elite rent requires that

$$y \geq cx. \tag{9.A.xi}$$

Substituting (9.A.ix) in (9.A.viii), the first-order conditions write:

$$cu'(cx) + \theta v'(x) + s'(R(x) + a).R'(x) = 0$$
$$u'(cx) - ns'(R(x) + a) < 0$$

for the zero-rent regime, and

$$u'(y) = ns'(G)$$
$$\theta v'(x) + u'(y).\left(\frac{R'(x)}{n} + c\right) = 0$$

in the case of a positive rent.

It is easily shown that the zero-rent regime will hold for θ high enough for a given level of unconditional aid, or for aid large enough for a given governance parameter, θ. In that regime, the income of the poor is an increasing function of the governance parameter, given aid, which was not the case when public expenditures were exogenous—see (9.A.iii) above. The income of the poor is also an increasing function of aid, given θ. The same two properties hold in the positive rent regime, as it was the case with exogenous expenditures. Also, as with exogenous public expenditures, a change in unconditional aid benefits exclusively the elite when the objective function is quasi-linear in y ("constrained autocracy") or when $\theta = 0$ ("autocracy"), when starting from a positive rent regime.

The main difference with the case where public expenditures are exogenous is the fact that the governance parameter affects the income of the poor and the distribution of aid between the elite and the poor through its impact on public expenditures. Note, however, that the specification of the role of public expenditures in (9.A.ix) is peculiar in the sense that their contribution to the objective function of the government does not depend on the governance parameter, θ. Things would be different, and more intricate, if it depended on θ too, as for instance with:

$$s(G) = p(G) + \theta q(G).$$

The institutional framework behind decisions concerning public goods and access to those public goods by the elite and the poor population would have to be investigated in greater depth to justify such a specification, or still a more complex one. Such a specification would be a particular case of the more general model where public expenditures would be a second argument in the initial functions u(y) and v(x), which is still more intricate.

9.A.7. Sketch of a Model Comprising Two Distortive Instruments

A critique to the model (9.1.1–9.1.3) may be that the tax system is of limited scope in developing countries and the rent of the elite most often consists of other distortive instruments. One could think of extending the original model by adding a second distortive instrument, the revenue of which would only benefit the elite. Let τ be that instrument, for instance through some monopoly situation conceded to the elite by the government, and let's assume it is equivalent to a proportional tax levied by the elite over the whole economy. The original model then writes:

$$x = h(t)(1-\tau)$$
$$y = ch(t)(1-\tau) + (1-b\tau)\tau(1-n+nc).h(t) + z$$

where $(1-b\tau)$ with $b \in [0, 1]$ stands for the distortion linked to instrument τ. The budget constraint writes as before:

$$nz + (1-n)\,s + G \leq (1-\tau)\,H(t)$$

and the objective of the government keeps being given by (9.1.3).

With the same change of variable as before, it is possible to eliminate t so as to stay in the (x, y) space. The budget constraint now writes:

$$y = \left[c + \rho \frac{\tau(1-b\tau)}{(1-\tau)} \right] x + \left[(1-\tau)R\left(\frac{x}{1-\tau} \right) - G + a \right] / n \qquad \text{(9.A.xii)}$$

where $\rho = cn + 1 - n$.

The issue then is that of who decides about the value of τ. If the decision is left to the elite, then τ will be set at the value that maximizes (9.A.xii). The government then solves the maximization program:

$$Max_x\, u(y) + \theta v(x)$$

under the budget constraint (9.A.xiii) where τ is a function of x and under the condition that the rent is going to the elite—i.e., the second square bracket in (9.A.xiii)—is non-negative. Intuitively, the problem is close to the original one. Yet, because of a higher income going to the elite, the government is less likely to grant it a cash rent, and is more likely to transfer cash to the poor except in the "constrained autocracy" or the "autocracy" cases.

An alternative would be the government deciding about the alternative rent, τ. But, the problem is then trivial. The government will always prefer transferring income to the elite under the form of a direct lump-sum transfer, z, rather than through the distorting instrument, τ. This suggests that the presence in an economy of distorting instruments benefiting the elite obeys institutional constraints that somehow prevent conceding lump-sum rents to it. This also suggests that the whole analysis in this model of the aid donor-recipient relationship could have been cast in terms of such a distorting instrument granted by the government to the elite, rather than a cash rent. The implied properties of the relationship would be qualitatively similar, though.

NOTES

1.　Technically, in that model, aid relaxed either the savings or the foreign exchange constraint, whichever was binding in the initial situation.

2. This difference in objectives is the key issue in the literature on conditionality: if the two agents would be in full agreement, conditionality would be pointless. In the extreme case aid acts as a bribe.
3. It will be seen below that it would probably make some of the conclusions stronger.
4. Non-tax distortive redistribution instruments may not be consistent with the budget constraint (2). Yet, the present framework may be extended to two redistribution instruments—see appendix to this chapter.
5. It is assumed reasonably and realistically that $a < G$.
6. This is indeed the specification used by Adam and O'Connell (1999) in a two-period model, under the assumption of an autocratic regime.
7. It might seem that this result depends on G being exogenous. The case of endogenous public expenditures is analyzed in the appendix. The preceding property is not modified.
8. For a more pragmatic discussion of this issue see Gunning (2001) or Adam and Gunning (2002) in the specific case of Uganda. Adam et al. (2004) also discuss the move of European aid toward a "performance-based" criterion.
9. Kilby and Dreher (2010) use a similar framework, the share of embezzled aid being replaced by the distance between actual and intended pro-poor policies and the penalty being the reduction in the volume of aid.
10. See in particular Torsvik (2005), Knack and Rahman (2007), Platteau and Gaspart (2003), Bourguignon and Platteau (2015a), Auriol and Miquel-Forensa (2015).
11. It is interesting to note that despite the emphasis put on the effectiveness of aid since the late 1990s, some authors kept analyzing the allocation of aid without really introducing it in their framework. For instance, Feeny and McGillivray (2008) expands Dudley and Montmarquette (1976) by introducing in their analysis a variable that represents the "bureaucratic expediency of allocating aid in a specific recipient country," which may have something to do with recipient countries' institutions. In their empirical application, however, they proxy this variable by the lagged volume of aid.
12. Note that unlike in the model of section 9A.2, the parameter x_i, which we shall call the "aid effectiveness ratio," is the share of aid actually used to alleviate poverty, rather than the share diverted by the leadership $y_i (= 1- x_i)$.
13. This distinction between descriptive and prescriptive analysis of aid allocation was made by McGillivray (2004).
14. These categorizations of variables are taken from the survey of the literature by Schraeder et al. (1998).
15. For a broader survey of this issue see Peiffer and Boussalis (2015).
16. Collier and Dollar's model is set in terms of α_i rather than s_i. The latter is used here for consistency with the initial theoretical model in the previous section.
17. For countries receiving aid, condition (9.2.9) is binding. It can be seen that this implies that the share of aid increases with population size. As India is considerably bigger than most developing countries, it should have received a substantial share of total aid. This issue does not arise in the case of China, the other giant developing country, because China was among the countries not receiving aid.
18. See the discussion below and of course Easterly et al. (2004) and Burnside and Dollar (2004).
19. A previous attempt at computing a "post-welfarist" optimal aid allocation by Llavador and Roemer (2001), along the lines of Roemer (1998) led to somewhat surprising results, most aid going to East and South-East Asia, and practically nothing to Sub-Saharan Africa.
20. Actually, they simply neutralized that variable by replacing it by its average across recipient countries.
21. The A_i's must be adjusted so that they sum to the total budget available.
22. For further detail, see Guillaumont and Wagner (2015).
23. Bourguignon and Platteau (2015b) explore this case through the simulation of a hypothetical case.
24. Fuchs et al. (2014) find no impact of their proxy for the "quality of aid" on donors' aid budget in a panel regression on 20 DAC donors.
25. The preexisting distortion which causes this immiserizing effect of the transfer is the absence of an optimal tariff.
26. In the simplest specification the amount of government spending is given so that an increase in aid reduces tax revenue one-for-one. If this assumption is relaxed, aid will be used not only to reduce taxation but also to increase public expenditure. The relative size of these effects is the focus of the literature on fungibility. It is worth noting that donors have often insisted that aid

recipients should increase their tax efforts when in fact a reduction of taxation is an optimal response to aid: substituting aid for taxes avoids the cost of taxation.

27. In European history the case of Habsburg Spain (which under Philip II could use Latin American gold rather than taxes to finance the state) can be contrasted with that of England and the Dutch republic, where democratic institutions developed as concessions to taxpayers. See also North and Weingast (1989).

28. This differs from the model of Azam and Laffont (2003) where unconditional aid is always ineffective. In the Adam-O'Connell model this is the case only if the recipient government has a sufficiently narrow base. The reason for the difference is that in the Azam-Laffont model the government of the recipient country directly controls the consumption levels of the rich (the favored group) and the poor, without an intervening taxation technology.

29. This is an obvious case for selectivity in aid allocation.

30. This type of conditionality differs from that considered in section 9.3, which is not aimed at institutional change, but at greater effectiveness of project aid or less leakage of aid to non-intended uses.

31. Clearly, in a two-period model with aid in the first, but not in the second period, the reform will be implemented initially and then reversed in the second period. Actual practice involved multiple structural adjustment aid packages so that the sequence of policy reform and reversal was repeated. A notorious example is the Kenyan experience with trade liberalization, a reform that was repeatedly "sold" to the donors, implemented, and then reversed (Collier et al. 1997).

32. See Collier et al. (1997), Adam and Gunning (2002), and Svensson (2003). Azam and Laffont (2003) acknowledge the problem of lack of donor credibility at the very end of their paper (p. 52), but do not address it.

33. Note that these outcomes need not be the result of the prospect of aid so that there will be type I and II errors in the sense that governments may be rewarded or punished for outcomes that were outside their control.

34. The probability applies to the detection: if fraud is detected, then punishment is certain. The donor's commitment is therefore fully credible in this model, as in Azam-Laffont.

35. In this section we do not consider experimental evidence. This is covered in Chapter 1 of this volume.

36. See, e.g., Collier and Gunning (1999).

37. It is, for example, revealing that Deaton (2013) discusses these results as if they are virtually beyond dispute.

38. Disaggregation by time period shows that the effect is stronger in the post–Cold War period.

39. This is a good thing to the extent it improves accountability, but a bad thing in that it raises the cost of taxation.

40. As in the famous *Assessing Aid* report, World Bank (1998).

REFERENCES

Acemoglu, D. and J. Robinson. 2001. A Theory of Political Transitions. *American Economic Review* 91(4): 938–963.

———. 2012. *Why Nations Fail: The Origins of Power, Prosperity and Poverty*. New York: Crown Business.

Adam, C. S., G. Chambas, P. Guillaumont, S. Guillaumont Jeanneney, and J. W. Gunning. 2004. Performance-Based Conditionality: A European Perspective. *World Development* 32(6): 1059–1070.

Adam, C. S. and J. W. Gunning. 2002. Redesigning the Aid Contract: Donors' Use of Performance Indicators in Uganda. *Word Development* 30(12): 2045–2056.

Adam, C. S. and S. A. O'Connell. 1999. Aid, Taxation and Development in Sub-Saharan Africa. *Economics and Politics* 11(3): 225–253.

Ahmed, F. Z. 2012. The Perils of Unearned Foreign Income: Aid, Remittances, and Government Survival. *American Political Science Review* 106: 146–165.

Alesina A. and D. Dollar. 2000. Who Gives Foreign Aid to Whom and Why? *Journal of Economic Growth* 5(1): 33–63.

Alesina, A. and B. Weder. 2002. Do Corrupt Governments Receive Less Foreign Aid? *American Economic Review* 92: 1126–1137.

Arndt, C., S. Jones, and F. Tarp. 2010. Aid, Growth, and Development: Have We Come Full Circle? *Journal of Globalization and Development* 1(2): article 5.

———. 2015. Assessing Foreign Aid's Long Run Contribution to Growth and Development. *World Development* 69: 6–18.

———. 2018. What Is the Aggregate Economic Rate of Return to Foreign Aid? *World Bank Economic Review* 32: 446–474.

Asongu, S. A. 2012. On the Effects of Foreign Aid on Corruption. AGDI Working Paper 12/031.

Auriol, E. and J. Miquel-Forensa. 2015. Taxing Fragmented Aid to Improve Aid Efficiency. CEPR Discussion Paper No. DP10802.

Azam, J.-P. and J.-J. Laffont. 2003. Contracting for Aid. *Journal of Development Economics* 70(1): 25–58.

Berthélemy, J.-C. and A. Tichit. 2004. Bilateral Donors' Aid Allocation Decisions—A Three-Dimensional Panel Analysis. *International Review of Economics & Finance* 13(3): 253–274.

Besley, T. 1997. Political Economy of Alleviating Poverty: Theory and Institutions. Annual World Bank Conference on Development Economics 1996. World Bank, Washington, DC.

Beynon, J. 2003. Poverty Efficient Aid Allocations—Collier/Dollar Revisited. ESAU Working paper 2, Overseas Development Institute, London.

Bhagwati, J. N., R. A. Brecher, and T. Hatta. 1983. The Generalized Theory of Transfers and Welfare: Bilateral Transfers in a Multilateral World. *American Economic Review* 73: 606–618.

Birdsall, N., S. Claessens, and I. Diwan. 2003. Policy Selectivity Forgone: Debt and Donor Behavior in Africa. *World Bank Economic Review* 17: 409–435.

Bjørnskov, C. 2010. Do Elites Benefit from Democracy and Foreign Aid in Developing Countries? *Journal of Development Economics* 92: 115–124.

Booth, D. 2011. Aid, Institutions And Governance: What Have We Learned? *Development Policy Review* 29(s1): s5–s26.

Botchwey, K., P. Collier, J. W. Gunning, and K. Hamada. 1998. *External Evaluation of the ESAF: Report by a Group of Independent Persons.* Washington, DC: IMF.

Bourguignon, F. and J.-P. Platteau. 2015a. The Hard Challenge of Aid Coordination. *World Development* 69(C): 86–97.

———. 2015b. Aid Effectiveness Revisited: The Trade-Off Between Needs and Governance. Working Paper, Paris School of Economics.

———. 2018a. Optimal Management of Transfers: An Odd Paradox. *Journal of Public Economics* 162: 143–157.

———. 2018b. Should a Poverty-Averse Donor Always Increase the Share of Governance-Improving Countries? CEPR Discussion paper No. 13163.

Brautigam, D. A. and S. Knack. 2004. Foreign Aid and Institutions, and Governance in Sub-Saharan Africa. *Economic Development and Cultural Change* 52: 255–285.

Burnside, C. and D. Dollar. 2000. Aid, Policies and Growth. *American Economic Review* 90: 847–868.

———. 2004. Aid, Policies, and Growth: Reply. *American Economic Review* 94(3): 781–784.

Busse, M. and S. Gröning. 2009. Does Foreign Aid Improve Governance? *Economics Letters* 104: 76–78.

Carter, P. 2014. Aid Allocation Rules. *European Economic Review* 71: 132–151.

Chichilnisky, G. 1980. Basic Goods, the Effects of Commodity Transfers and the International Economic Order. *Journal of Development Economics* 7: 505–519.

———. 1983. The Transfer Problem with Three Agents Once Again: Characterization, Uniqueness and Stability. *Journal of Development Economics* 13: 237–247.

Clemens, M. A., S. Radelet, R. R. Bhavnani, and S. Bazzi. 2012. Counting Chickens When They Hatch: Timing and the Effects of Aid on Growth. *Economic Journal* 122: 590–617.

Clist, P. and O. Morrissey. 2011. Aid and Tax Revenue: Signs of a Positive Effect since the 1980s. *Journal of International Development* 23: 165–180.

Cogneau, D. and J.-D. Naudet. 2007. Who Deserves Aid ? Equality of Opportunity, International Aid, and Poverty Reduction. *World Development.* 35(1): 104–120.

Collier, P. 2008. *The Bottom Billion. Why the Poorest Countries Are Failing and What Can Be Done About It.* Oxford: Oxford University Press.

Collier, P. and D. Dollar. 2001. Can the World Cut Poverty in Half? How Policy Reform and Effective Aid Can Meet International Development Goals. *World Development* 29(11): 1787–1802.

———. 2002. Aid Allocation and Poverty Reduction. *European Economic Review* 46(8): 1475–1500.

Collier, P., P. Guillaumont, S. Guillaumont, and J. W. Gunning. 1997. Redesigning Conditionality. *World Development* 25: 1399–1407.

Collier, P. and J. W. Gunning. 1995. Trade Policy and Regional Integration: Implications for the Relations between Europe and Africa. *World Economy* 18: 387–410.

———. 1999. The IMF's Role in Structural Adjustment. *Economic Journal* 109(459): 634–651.

Collier, P. and R. Reinikka (eds.). 2001. *Uganda's Recovery: The Role of Farms, Firms and Government.* Washington, DC: World Bank.

Deaton, A. 2013. *The Great Escape: Health, Wealth, and the Origins of Inequality*. Princeton, NJ: Princeton University Press.

de la Croix, D. and C. Delavallade. 2014. Why Corrupt Governments May Receive More Foreign Aid. *Oxford Economic Papers* 66: 51–66.

Devarajan, S., D. Dollar, and T. Holmgren (eds.). 2000. *Aid and Reform in Africa*. Washington, DC: World Bank.

Djankov, S., J. G. Montalvo, and M. Reynal-Querol. 2009. "Aid with Multiple Personalities." *Journal of Comparative Economics* 37: 217–229.

Dollar, D. and V. Levin. 2006. The Increasing Selectivity of Foreign Aid, 1994–2003. *World Development* 34(12): 2034–2046.

Dreher, A., P. Nunnenkamp, and R. Thiele. 2011. Are "New" Donors Different? Comparing the Allocation of Bilateral Aid Between Non DAC and DAC Donor Countries. *World Development* 39(11): 1950–1968.

Dudley, L. and C. Montmarquette. 1976. A Model of the Supply of Bilateral Foreign Aid. *American Economic Review* 66(1): 132–142.

Dutta, N., P. T. Leeson, and C. R. Williamson. 2013. The Amplification Effect: Foreign Aid's Impact on Political Institutions. *Kyklos* 66: 208–228.

Easterly, W. 2006. *The White Man's Burden*. New York: Oxford University Press.

Easterly, W., R. Levine, and D. Roodman. 2004. Aid, Policies, and Growth: Comment. *American Economic Review* 94(3): 774–780.

Easterly, W. and T. Pfutze. 2008. Where Does the Money Go? Best and Worst Practices in Foreign Aid. *Journal of Economic Perspectives* 22(2): 29–52.

Feeny, S. and M. McGillivray. 2008. What Determines Bilateral Aid Allocations? Evidence from Time Series Data. *Review of Development Economics* 12(3): 515–529.

Frankel, J. A. 2012. The Natural Resource Curse: A Survey of Diagnoses and Some Prescriptions. Harvard, Kennedy School, Working Paper 12–014.

Fuchs, A., A. Dreher, and P. Nunnenkamp. 2014. Determinants of Donor Generosity: A Survey of the Aid Budget Literature. *World Development* 56: 172–199.

Guillaumont, P. and L. Wagner. 2015. Performance-Based Allocation (PBAZ) of Foreign Aid: Still Alive? In *Handbook on the Economics of Foreign Aid*, edited by B. M. Arvin and B. Lew. Cheltenham: Edward Elgar.

Gunning, J. W. 2001. Rethinking Aid. In *Annual Bank Conference on Development Economics: 2000*, edited by B. Pleskovic and N. Stern. Washington, DC: World Bank.

Hoeffler, A. and V. Outram. 2011. Need, Merit Or Self-Interest—What Determines the Allocation of Aid? *Review of Development Economics* 15: 237–250.

Jones, S. and F. Tarp. 2016. Does Foreign Aid Harm Political Institutions? *Journal of Development Economics* 118: 266–281.

Juselius, K., N. F. Møller, and F. Tarp. 2014. The Long-Run Impact of Foreign Aid in 36 African Countries: Insights from Multivariate Time Series Analysis. *Oxford Bulletin of Economics and Statistics* 76: 153–184.

Kilby, C. 2009. The Political Economy of Conditionality: An Empirical Analysis of World Bank Loan Disbursements. *Journal of Development Economics* 89: 51–61.

Kilby, C. and Dreher, A. 2010. The Impact of Aid on Growth Revisited: Do Donor Motives Matter? *Economics Letters* 107(3): 338–340.

Knack, S. 2004. Does Foreign Aid Promote Democracy? *International Studies Quarterly* 48: 251–266.

Knack, S. and A. Rahman. 2007. Donor Fragmentation and Bureaucratic Quality in Aid Recipients. *Journal of Development Economics* 83(1): 176–197.

Krueger, A. O. 1974. The Political Economy of the Rent-Seeking Society. *American Economic Review* 64: 291–303.

Kumar, A. 2015. Samaritan's Dilemma, Time-Inconsistency and Foreign Aid: A Review of Theoretical Models. In *Handbook on the Economics of Foreign Aid*, edited by B. M. Arvin and B. Lew. Cheltenham: Edward Elgar.

Llavador, H. G. and J. E. Roemer. 2001. An Equal Opportunity Approach to the Allocation of International Aid. *Journal of Development Economics* 64(1): 147–171.

Łukasz, M. 2015. *The Impact of Aid on Total Government Expenditures*. PhD thesis, Tinbergen Institute Amsterdam/Rotterdam.

McGillivray, M. 2004. Descriptive and Prescriptive Analyses of Aid Allocation: Approaches, Issues and Consequences. *International Review of Economics and Finance* 13: 275–292.

McGillavray, M. and O. Morrissey. 2004. Fiscal Effects of Aid. In *Fiscal Policy for Development*, edited by T. Addison and A. Roe, 72–96. Basingstoke, UK: Palgrave Macmillan.

Meltzer, A. and S. Richard. 1981. A Rational Theory of the Size of Government. *Journal of Political Economy* 89(5): 914–927.

Menard, A.-R. and L. Weill. 2016. Understanding the Link between Aid and Corruption: A Causality Analysis. *Economic Systems* 40: 260–272.

Moss, T., G. Pettersson, and N. van de Walle. 2006. An Aid-Institutions Paradox? A Review Essay on Aid Dependency and State Building in Sub-Saharan Africa. Center for Global Development, Working Paper 74.

Moyo, D. 2009. *Dead Aid. Why Aid Is Not Working and How There Is Another Way for Africa*. London: Allen Lane.

North, D. and B. Weingast. 1989. Constitutions and Commitment: The Evolution of Institutions Governing Public Choice in Seventeenth-Century England. *Journal of Economic History* 49(4): 803–832.

Okada, K. and S. Samreth. 2012. The Effect of Foreign Aid on Corruption: A Quantile Regression Approach. *Economic Letters* 11: 240–243.

Peiffer, C. and C. Boussalis. 2015. Determining Aid Allocation Decision-Making: Towards a Comparative Sectored Approach. In *Handbook on the Economics of Foreign Aid*, edited by B. M. Arvin and B. Lew. Cheltenham: Edward Elgar.

Platteau, J.-P. 2003. Decentralized Development as a Strategy to Reduce Poverty? In *Poverty, Inequality and Growth*. Proceedings of the AFD-EUDN Conference, Agence Française de Développement, Paris, pp. 253–330.

Platteau, J.-P. 2004. Monitoring Elite Capture in Community Driven Development. *Development and Change* 35: 243–256.

Platteau, J.-P. and F. Gaspart. 2003. The Risk of Resource Misappropriation in Community Driven Development. CRED, University of Namur.

Rajan, R. and A. Subramanian. 2005. What Undermines Aid's Impact on Growth? NBER Working Paper 11657.

———. 2007. Does Aid Affect Governance? *American Economic Review* 97: 322–327.

———. 2008. Aid and Growth: What Does the Cross-Country Evidence Really Show? *Review of Economics and Statistics* 90: 643–665.

———. 2011. Aid, Dutch Disease, and Manufacturing Growth. *Journal of Development Economics* 94: 106–118.

Roemer, J. 1998. *Equality of Opportunity*. Cambridge, MA: Harvard University Press.

Schraeder, P. J., S. W. Hook, and B. Taylor. 1998. Clarifying the Foreign Aid Puzzle: A Comparison of American, Japanese, French and Swedish Aid Flows. *World Politics* 50(2): 294–323.

Svensson, J. 2000. When Is Foreign Aid Policy Credible? Aid Dependence and Conditionality. *Journal of Development Economics* 61(1): 61–84.

———. 2003. Why Conditional Aid Does Not Work and What Can Be Done About It. *Journal of Development Economics* 70(2): 381–402.

Tavares, J. 2003. Does Foreign Aid Corrupt?, *Economocs Letters* 79: 99–106.

Torsvik, G. 2005. Foreign Economic Aid: Should Donors Cooperate? *Journal of Development Economics* 77: 503–515.

Trumbull, W. and H. Wall. 1994. Estimating Aid-Allocation Criteria with Panel Data. *Economic Journal* 104: 876–882.

van der Ploeg, F. 2011. Natural Resources: Curse or Blessing? *Journal of Economic Literature* 49: 366–420.

Wood, A. 2008. Looking Ahead Optimally in Allocating Aid. *World Development* 36: 1135–1151.

World Bank. 1998. *Assessing Aid: What Works, What Doesn't and Why*. World Bank Policy Research Report.

10

MIGRATION, INSTITUTIONS, AND DEVELOPMENT

Kaivan Munshi

10.1. INTRODUCTION

Mobility is central to the process of development. There is limited occupational and spatial mobility in the premodern economy. The distinguishing feature of a developing economy is that opportunities arise for individuals to move from the village to centers of industrial production. One constraint to mobility is that potential migrants often are unaware of jobs that are available in the city. Urban employers, in turn, are discouraged from hiring migrants with unknown traits and characteristics. Additional constraints to migration include inadequate infrastructure, government safety nets in the city, and private credit.

While much progress has been made in understanding these constraints to mobility, and development more generally, the reality in all developing countries is that migration does occur. However, the bulk of this migration is accounted for by a relatively small number of preexisting communities at the origin, which are defined by kinship (caste, clan, or tribe) or geography (neighborhood, village, or hometown). A wealth of anecdotal evidence from across the world, discussed below, indicates that these communities have historically supported the mobility of their members by solving information and enforcement problems in destination labor markets and by providing them with credit and other forms of mutual assistance. The available evidence indicates that these communities continue to play this supportive role in the contemporary economy when required, and it is thus quite striking that we know so little about the intra-group cooperation that underlies this role.

This is not to say that economists have completely ignored cooperation within preexisting social groups. Greif's (1993) analysis of the Maghribi traders' coalition, and Greif, Milgrom, and Weingast's (1994) investigation of the medieval merchant guild, highlight the role played by non-market institutions in solving commitment problems in the premodern economy. In contemporary economies where private market credit and government safety nets are absent, a voluminous literature documents extremely high levels of risk-sharing in informal community-based mutual insurance arrangements throughout the world; e.g., Townsend 1994; Grimard 1997; Fafchamps and Lund 2003; Angelucci, Di Giorgi, and Rasul 2015. Statistical analyses of the role played by communities in supporting migration, however, are relatively limited. In particular, we know very little about why some population groups or communities were able to cooperate and collectively transform their circumstances in the face of numerous economic and bureaucratic obstacles, while many others were not.

The objective of this chapter is to review the economics literature on migration, with a particular focus on the community aspect of migration, and, based on this review, to highlight areas for future research. Section 10.2 presents a stripped-down version of the Roy model, the workhorse model of individual decision-making in the migration literature. This model does a poor job of predicting bilateral migration flows between countries or regions and in explaining observed patterns of migrant selection. I show in section 10.3 that these deficiencies can be rectified by adding community networks to the Roy model. This section includes a brief review of the voluminous literature in the social sciences on community-based migration, which provides empirical justification for the augmented Roy model. Section 10.4 completes the review of the literature by shifting focus to the long-term consequences of community-based migration; the same networks that support migration initially can restrict occupational and spatial mobility in later generations once they are established at the destination. The augmented Roy model from section 10.3 provides a simple economic explanation for this phenomenon. Section 10.5 lists and discusses unanswered research questions that emerge from the literature review, and section 10.6 concludes.

10.2. THE MIGRATION DECISION

The workhorse model of migration in economics, due to Roy (1951), predicates the individual's location choice on the payoff at the origin, the payoff at the destination, and the cost of moving. This model has been used extensively in empirical studies to predict migration flows between locations and patterns of migrant selection (by education). To incorporate selection, it is necessary to introduce multiple levels of education. For ease of exposition, suppose that there are two education levels: low (L) and high (H). Less educated workers are channeled into low-skill occupations, while more educated workers are channeled into high-skill occupations. The wages at the origin (O) and the destination (D) for the two types of workers are denoted by $W_e^O, W_e^D, e \in \{L, H\}$, respectively. A worker will choose to migrate if $W_e^D - c \geq W_e^O$, where the distribution of the moving cost, c, is independent of education and is characterized by the function $F(c)$.

Within each education category, individuals with moving costs below a threshold $\underline{c}_e$ will migrate, with the fraction of migrants denoted by $F(\underline{c}_e)$. The first prediction of the Roy model is that migration is increasing in $W_e^D - W_e^O$. A large number of studies have tested this prediction, typically with OECD data; e.g., Beine et al. (2011); Bertoli and Fernandez-Huertas Moraga (2012); Docquier et al. (2014). Although wages at the origin and destination do predict bilateral flows between countries, they account for a small part of the variation in these flows. What matters more for the origin-destination flows is the stock of migrants from the origin at the destination. Although other interpretations for this finding are available, one explanation is that the stock of migrants is a measure of the strength of the network at the destination, which, in turn, supports the additional flow of migrants. I will formalize this idea below by adding networks, and network dynamics, to the Roy model.

Because we have assumed that the distribution of moving costs is the same for both types of workers, the second prediction of the Roy model is that there will be positive selection on education if $W_H^D - W_H^O > W_L^D - W_L^O$. Rearranging terms, migrants will be positively selected on education if $W_H^D - W_L^D > W_H^O - W_L^O$; i.e., if there is greater wage inequality at the destination than the origin, as noted by Borjas (1987). As summarized by Abramitzky, Boustan, and Eriksson (2012), empirical tests from across the world find mixed support for this prediction. For example, the nature of migrant selection from Mexico to the United States, a topic of great policy interest that has received much research attention, remains unresolved (Chiquiar and Hanson 2005; Cuecuecha 2005; Orrenius and Zavodny 2005; Mishra 2007; Ibarran and Lubotsky 2007; Fernandez-Huertas Moraga 2011, 2013). The Roy model cannot, in addition, explain the dynamics of migrant selection. As documented by McKenzie and Rapoport (2007), while there is positive selection on education to begin with in the Mexican sending communities that they study, this is replaced by negative selection later on. We will see that the results on migrant selection across different studies can once again be reconciled when community networks are added to the Roy model.

10.3. COMMUNITY-BASED MIGRATION

A natural way to add community networks to the Roy model is to allow them to increase wages at the destination. Labor market networks tend to be concentrated in blue-collar occupations, both in developed and in developing economies. For example, Rees (1966) reports that informal sources accounted for 80% of all hires in blue-collar occupations versus 50% of all hires in white-collar occupations in an early study set in Chicago. This is because educational credentials are a good indicator of competence in white-collar occupations, but not necessarily so in blue-collar occupations. Moreover, production tends to take place in teams in these occupations, making it difficult for the firm to attribute effort or competence to individuals on the job. Networks of socially connected workers can overcome both the information and the enforcement problems that arise with team production. This is incorporated in the theoretical framework by allowing the low-skill wage at the destination, W_L^D, to be increasing in the size of the network, which is organized around migrants from the same origin community.

Suppose that $W_H^D - W_H^O > W_L^D - W_L^O$ to begin with, before migrant networks have had a chance to form. This implies that there will be positive selection on education out of all origin communities. However, if a migrant network does form and grow over time at the destination, then the right-hand side of the preceding inequality will also increase over time, ultimately resulting in a switch in its sign; positive selection is replaced by negative selection, as documented by McKenzie and Rapoport. Note, however, that this dynamic pattern of migrant selection will not be obtained in all communities; we will see momentarily that migrant networks only form when social connectedness in the population from which they are drawn exceeds a threshold level. These networks will also form at different points in time. We could thus obtain positive or negative selection on average in a sample of communities at a given point in time, depending on their population characteristics and when their destination networks formed. The Roy model with networks is thus able to generate the dynamic and the cross-sectional patterns of migrant selection that have been documented in the literature.

To understand why the Roy model, by itself, does a poor job of explaining bilateral migration flows, ignore differences in education and focus instead on the network dynamics. There is a continuum of potential migrants of unit mass from each community in each period. Wages at the origin are denoted by W^O. Wages at the destination in period t are determined by the stock of migrants from the community who are already settled there: $W_t^D = \beta \sum_{\tau=0}^{t-1} \underline{c}_\tau$, where $\underline{c}_\tau$ is the flow of migrants in period τ and β maps network size into wages. β is increasing in the social connectedness of the origin population from which the destination network is drawn; the implicit assumption here is that networks formed from a more connected population will themselves be more connected and, therefore, more effective.

Individuals bear a cost $c \sim U[0, 1]$ when they move. In any period t, individuals with moving costs below a threshold $\underline{c}_t = \beta \sum_{\tau=0}^{t-1} \underline{c}_\tau - W^O$ will thus migrate to the destination. To initiate the network dynamics, $\underline{c}_0$ individuals are moved exogenously to the destination in period 0 from each community. As in Munshi (2011), we can then solve recursively to derive a closed-form solution for the flow of migrants in each period t: $\underline{c}_t = (1+\beta)^{t-1}(\beta \underline{c}_0 - W^O)$. The first point to note from this solution is that the destination network will only grow over time if $\beta \underline{c}_0 > W^O$. There is thus a threshold $\underline{\beta}$ above which migrant networks will form, as documented by Chay and Munshi (2015), separately for black migration from southern counties to northern cities after World War I, and for migration from the Punjab to the United Kingdom after World War II. The second point to note is that the size of the network and, hence, wages is increasing in β above the threshold at any given point in time. Standard datasets do not capture these community-specific differences and so they will do a poor job of explaining bilateral migration flows. The third point to note, once multiple destinations are introduced in the model, is that a small initial advantage at a particular destination will expand rapidly over time due to the compounding network effect. This explains the well-known fact that proximate origin communities with similar characteristics can end up at very different destinations when networks are active; e.g., Carrington, Detragiache, and Vishwanath (1996); Munshi (2003). It is also another reason why the canonical Roy model, without networks, does a poor job of explaining bilateral migration flows.

Based on the preceding discussion, adding networks to the Roy model would reconcile the theory with key stylized facts in the migration literature. This addition has strong empirical support, given the vast literature in the social sciences documenting the important role played by community networks in major migration events. The development of the United States is associated with the first large-scale movement of workers across national boundaries. During the Age of Mass Migration (1850–1913), the United States received 30 million European immigrants. Abramitzky, Boustan, and Eriksson (2014) calculate that this resulted in 38% of workers in northern cities being foreign-born in 1910. Labor markets in the nineteenth century could be divided into three segments: a stable segment with permanent employment, an unstable segment with periodic short-term unemployment, and a marginal but highly flexible segment characterized by spells of long-term and short-term unemployment (Gordon, Edwards, and Reich 1982). Migrants, being newcomers to the US market, typically ended up in the unstable and marginal segments, where the uncertain labor demand and the lack of information about their ability and diligence naturally provided an impetus for the formation of ethnic job networks (Conzen 1976; Hoerder 1991).

Accounts by contemporary observers and an extensive social history literature indicate that friends and kin from the origin community in Europe played an important role in securing jobs for migrants in the US labor market in the nineteenth century and the first quarter of the twentieth century. Early historical studies used census data, which provide occupations and country of birth, to identify ethnic clusters in particular locations and occupations (Hutchinson 1956; Gordon, Edwards, and Reich 1982). Based on the preceding discussion, such clusters arise naturally when networks are active. More recently, social historians have linked parish registers and county data in specific European sending communities to census and church records in the United States to construct the entire chain of migration from those communities as it unfolded over time (Gjerde 1985; Kamphoefner 1987; Bodnar 1985).

Migration from Europe ceased in 1913, but it was soon replaced by the movement of African Americans from the rural South to northern cities. The first major movement of blacks out of the South commenced in 1916. More than 400,000 blacks moved to the North between 1916 and 1918, exceeding the total number who moved in the preceding 40 years. During the first phase of the Great Migration, running from 1916 to 1930, more than one million blacks (one-tenth the black population of the United States) moved to northern cities (Marks 1983). This movement was driven by both pull and push factors. The increased demand for labor in the wartime economy, coupled with the closing of European immigration, gave blacks new labor market opportunities (Mandle 1978; Gottlieb 1987). At the same time, adverse economic conditions in the South, together with segregation and racial violence, encouraged many blacks to leave (Marks 1989; Tolnay and Beck 1990). Although these exogenous forces may have provided the initial impetus for migration, networks linking southern communities to specific northern cities, and to neighborhoods within those cities, soon emerged (Gottlieb 1987; Marks 1991; Grossman 1989; Carrington, Detragiache, and Vishwanath 1996).

The large-scale movement of labor in the United States, supported by migrant networks, was being replicated in other parts of the world as economies industrialized and cities grew in the nineteenth century. For example, Mumbai's industrial economy in the late nineteenth century and through the first half of the twentieth century was characterized by wide fluctuations in the demand for labor (Chandavarkar 1994). As discussed above, frequent job turnover will naturally give rise to labor market networks. The presence of such recruitment networks has indeed been documented by numerous historians studying Mumbai's economy prior to independence in 1947 (Chandavarkar 1994; Morris 1965; Burnett-Hurst 1925). These networks appear to have been organized around the jobber, a foreman who was in charge of a work gang in the mill, factory, dockyard, or construction site, and more important, also in charge of labor recruitment.

Given the information and enforcement problems that are associated with the recruitment of short-term labor, it is not surprising that the "jobber had to lean on social connections outside his workplace such as his kinship and neighborhood connections" (Chandavarkar 1994: 107). Here the endogamous caste, or its non-Hindu equivalent, served as a natural social unit from which to recruit labor. The presence of caste clusters has been documented in Mumbai's mills (Gokhale 1957), docks (Cholia 1941), railway workshops (Burnett-Hurst 1925), and various industries (Chandavarkar 1994). Although most historical accounts of caste-based networking in Indian cities are situated prior to independence in 1947, a few studies conducted over the subsequent decades indicate that these patterns persisted over many generations. For example, Patel (1963) found that 66% of the textile workers he surveyed in Mumbai in 1961–62 got jobs in the mills through the influence of their relatives and friends, many of whom would have belonged to the same caste. Forty years later, Munshi and Rosenzweig (2006) surveyed the parents of school children residing in the same area of the city. Sixty-eight percent of the fathers employed in working-class occupations reported that they received help from a relative or member of their caste in finding their first job, while 44% of fathers in white-collar occupations reported such help.

Labor market networks continue to be active in cities throughout the world, most often among migrant populations. In China, networks of relatives and friends from the same hometown are believed to have played an important role in supporting the largest internal migration in history (Bian 1994; Zhang and Li 2003; Giles, Park, and Cai 2006; Wang 2013). We would expect social ties to play an especially strong role for international migrants in distant and unfamiliar destinations. Indeed, more than 70% of the undocumented Mexicans in the United States, and a slightly higher proportion of the Central Americans, that Chavez (1992) interviewed in 1986 found work through referrals from friends and relatives. Similar patterns have been found in contemporary studies of Salvadoran immigrants (Menjivar 2000), Guatemalan immigrants (Hagan 1994), and Chinese immigrants (Nee and Nee 1972; Zhou 1992) to the United States. Individual respondents in the Mexican Migration Project, which collects information on a sample of individuals from different Mexican origin communities, were asked how they obtained employment on their last visit to the United States; keeping in line with a remarkably consistent pattern across time and space, relatives (35%) and friends or *paisanos* from the origin village in Mexico (35%) account for the bulk of job referrals (Massey et al. 1987).

10.4. LONG-TERM CONSEQUENCES OF COMMUNITY-BASED MIGRATION

Community networks play an important role in destination labor markets by helping new arrivals find jobs. Incumbent workers provide referrals for competent newcomers from their community, who work diligently once they are hired to avoid the social sanctions they would face if they shirked. Social ties thus improve the outcomes of migrants, generating an accompanying increase in migrant flows and improving economic efficiency in the short run. However, the same community networks that support movement from the origin to the destination when they first form can discourage the subsequent occupational and spatial mobility of their members once they are established. This inertia is commonly observed in heavily networked blue-collar communities that were originally established by dynamic migrants but which, over subsequent generations, become especially resistant to change (Gans 1962; Kornblum 1974). The augmented Roy model with community networks that we have developed can be extended to provide a simple explanation for this phenomenon.

Return to the setup with two types of occupations, skilled and unskilled, and two levels of associated education, high (*H*) and low (*L*). We now consider established community networks and the choices of individuals born at the destination, so wages at the origin and moving costs can be ignored. Individuals are heterogeneous in their ability, which determines the cost of education. It costs $\overline{C}$ for low-ability individuals to attain high education, whereas the corresponding cost for high-ability individuals is $\underline{C} < \overline{C}$. We normalize so that the cost of attaining low education is zero.

We continue to assume that the unskilled wage, W_L, is increasing in the (lagged) size of the community network in that occupation, but the dynamics now unfold over multiple generations. In particular, members of the community from the previous generation in the low-skill occupation provide referrals, and increase wages, for the next generation. Let $W_L(0)$ be the unskilled wage when no one from the individual's community selected that occupation in the previous period. Let $W_L(N)$ be the corresponding wage when all N members of the previous generation selected the unskilled occupation. Following Munshi and Rosenzweig (2006), if communities were concentrated entirely in either the skilled or the unskilled occupation in the initial period, then the following conditions ensure that there will be occupational persistence at the level of the community in all subsequent generations:

C1. $W_H - \overline{C} > W_L(0)$

C2. $W_H - \underline{C} < W_L(N)$.

The first condition says that if the low-skill network was not active in the previous generation, then individuals of both types would invest in high education in the current generation and end up in skilled jobs. The second condition says that if everyone in the community selected into the network in the previous generation, then individuals of both types would select low education and end up in the unskilled occupation. If conditions C1 and C2 are satisfied, it follows that communities will stay in the initial equilibrium from one generation to the next, with everyone either investing or not investing in education. The Roy model with networks, where the choice is now about occupation rather than location, can explain why migrant communities can remain locked in their initial occupation for many subsequent generations.

However, economies will restructure over the course of the development process and one consequence of development is that the returns to education, and the skilled wage, will start to grow. When the inequality in condition C2 is just reversed, high-ability individuals from communities that traditionally exclusively selected into the low-skill occupation will invest in high education and earn ε more in the skilled occupation than they would have if the entire community remained in the traditional occupation. If the fraction of high-ability individuals in these communities is non-negligible, then their exit from the network will result in a substantial (first-order) decline in the wage received by low-ability individuals. From a utilitarian perspective, welfare will decline, providing an economic rationale for community-based restrictions on mobility.

Individuals who select out of the traditional low-skill occupation will often move to a new location at the destination. The conventional punishment mechanisms that maintain cooperation within communities will then no longer be effective. Munshi and Rosenzweig argue that an alternative strategy to maintain cooperation in that case would be to instill a strong sense of community identity in childhood, which ensures that individuals remain tied to their community in adulthood. The idea that identity, and values more generally, are purposefully instilled to further community objectives is in line with previous work on this topic in economics; e.g., Bisin and Verdier 2000; Tabellini 2008. It also explains why heavily networked blue-collar communities tend to instill an especially strong sense of identity among their members. Depending on the context, this identity can be instilled centrally by institutions such as the local church or in decentralized fashion by parents, as in Bisin-Verdier and Tabellini.

The community identity described above aligns individual choices more closely with the social optimum. While this identity may thus be welfare enhancing when it is first put in place, it can result in a dynamic inefficiency if it persists in subsequent generations past the point where W_H has grown large enough that it is socially optimal for the high-ability individuals to exit. Cultural norms are persistent by design, which explains why blue-collar communities often appear to stubbornly resist change (despite the fact that the same communities were extremely dynamic when they formed). In general, community networks do a good job of supporting the mobility of groups of individuals, but are less supportive of individual mobility (Munshi and Rosenzweig 2016). A complete characterization of the relationship between community networks and migration requires attention to the tension between individual and group mobility, as well as the dynamic process through which these networks form at the destination, become established over multiple generations, and then serve as the point of departure for further mobility. The discussion that follows covers this and other areas for future research.

10.5. DIRECTIONS FOR FUTURE RESEARCH

There is a wealth of anecdotal evidence that highlights the role played by communities in supporting migration. Adding community networks to the canonical Roy model also allows us to reconcile key stylized facts in the migration literature with the theory. There is evidently a need to incorporate community networks in theoretical models of migration and empirical analyses of this phenomenon. The discussion that follows highlights three areas for future research that would help us better understand the relationship between community-based networks and migration.

10.5.1. Research Question 1. Under What Conditions Do Community-Based Networks Supporting Migration Form?

As discussed above, there is an extensive literature in sociology, anthropology, and social history documenting the role played by ethnic or hometown communities in major migration events. In parallel, the business economics literature provides many examples of the movement of communities from traditional occupations, such as farming and administration, into business; e.g., Gadgil 1959; Nafziger 1978; Damodaran 2008. This occupational mobility was typically accompanied by spatial mobility, from the village to centers of trade and industrial production. Although the literature on community-based migration is rich in detail, a general characterization of the initial conditions that trigger subsequent network growth is missing. Why are some communities, but not others, able to move en masse to distant locations? What forces trigger these group movements?

When deriving the network dynamics above, we simply assumed that a mass c_0 of individuals from each origin community was moved exogenously to the destination in the initial period. We then showed that the network would subsequently take off if $\beta \underline{c}_0$, where β measures social connectedness in the origin community, is sufficiently large. While this simple characterization highlights the importance of the initial shock and relevant community characteristics, network formation in reality is a much more complicated process.

For example, Munshi (2011) describes the process through which a historically disadvantaged caste in India made the transition from agricultural labor to industrial labor, cutting and polishing rough diamonds, and subsequently into the diamond business. Each occupational transition was accompanied by movement to a different location. The caste-community in question, known informally in the industry as the Kathiawaris, made its first move in the mid-1960s, when a change in foreign exchange regulations allowed the Indian diamond industry to take off. Business activity was initially controlled by two wealthy and experienced caste-communities, the Marwaris and the Palanpuris, while the Kathiawaris moved in large numbers from their villages to provincial cities such as Surat and Navsari where cutting and polishing workshops were established.

The second occupational transition (and spatial movement) for the Kathiawaris was precipitated by the discovery of massive diamond deposits in Australia's Argyle mines in 1979. India does not produce rough diamonds, so most exporters travel to Antwerp every month or two, for a few days, to buy rough stones on supplier credit. While each exporter will establish long-term relationships with a small number of suppliers, the community network allows exporters to receive rough stones on credit from a much wider set of suppliers (with community members having long-term relationships with those suppliers standing guarantor for them). An alternative business model for exporters is to establish a branch (and a market reputation) in Antwerp, in which case they operate simultaneously as rough suppliers and (independently of their community network) as exporters. When the supply shock hit the diamond industry in 1979, some Palanpuri businessmen had coincidentally just established branches in Antwerp. These businessmen persuaded their trusted Kathiawari labor contractors to enter business. A sufficiently large number of Kathiawaris entered at that point in time, jump-starting their network. Today there are hundreds of Kathiawari export firms based in Mumbai.

The preceding narrative describes how a confluence of favorable circumstances allowed the Kathiawari network to form and grow: (i) there was a positive shock to the world supply of rough diamonds, (ii) some Palanpuris had established branches in Antwerp and had an incentive to encourage entrants from another community, and (iii) the Palanpuri businessmen and their Kathiawari labor contractors had established long-term bilateral relations by that time. Such a favorable confluence of circumstances only arises rarely, and it is important to characterize general conditions under which networks will form and grow. To achieve this objective, the first step would be to carefully document the forces at work in other such events. Although community networks are constantly forming as new opportunities for mobility arise, much of this activity lies under the surface and is difficult to predict. Opportunities for prospective empirical analyses are thus limited. A more promising approach would be to use retrospective data. This could be historical case studies using archival material or statistical analyses using retrospective survey data or historical administrative records. The key requirements are that there should be sufficient detail on the triggers that resulted in network formation, the theoretically relevant characteristics of the population from which the networks were drawn, e.g., social connectedness, and the subsequent short-run evolution of the networks (reflected in the flow of migrants). The forces that matter will vary with the context. Studies from different contexts are thus needed to provide a comprehensive picture of the conditions under which community-based mobility is initiated, which would lead, in turn, to theoretical modeling of this phenomenon.

10.5.2. Research Question 2. What Is the Magnitude of the Role Played by Community Networks in Historical Migration Events?

There is a wealth of anecdotal evidence pointing to a role for community networks in migration events across the world. In parallel, much progress has also been made in statistically identifying migrant-network effects; e.g., Munshi (2003); Woodruff and Zenteno (2007); McKenzie and Rapoport (2007, 2012); Beaman (2011). The idea that community networks support the occupational and spatial mobility of their members is no longer controversial within economics. However, the argument that these networks should be incorporated in theoretical models and empirical analyses of migration is only justified if the *magnitude* of their role is substantial, and this remains to be determined.

The studies cited above use special research designs to identify network effects. For example, Munshi uses rainfall shocks in Mexican origin communities as statistical instruments for changes in the size of migrant networks at the US destination to estimate the relationship between network size and labor market outcomes. Beaman exploits quasi-random variation in refugee placement and Woodruff-Zenteno and McKenzie-Rapoport use historical variation in access to railroads in origin communities to estimate network effects. Case studies of this sort reveal that networks are active, but they are less useful in quantifying the magnitude of their role. For that, comprehensive data covering a major migration event in its entirety are needed. Administrative data are now becoming increasingly available from countries at different stages of economic development. Major efforts are also underway to digitize historical censuses. If the number of migrants and their destinations and occupations are available for each origin community over the course of an entire migration event, then the data can be used to estimate models of migration with networks and to quantify the role of these networks. The major data challenge here is to obtain community identifiers, and this may require access to information that is not publicly available or has not been previously digitized.

The first step in the quantification exercise is to develop a theoretical model of migration. The augmented Roy model discussed above could serve as an appropriate starting point, although we would want to allow for multiple destinations and an individual-specific payoff at each destination (drawn from an appropriately specified distribution). If there is exogenous variation in the population characteristics of the communities from which the networks are drawn, then the model should generate predictions for clustering at particular destinations or in particular occupations, for example, that allow us to infer with some confidence that networks are active.

The next step in the quantification exercise would be to estimate the structural parameters of the theoretical model that is developed and then predict what migration would have been without networks. This counterfactual experiment will also tell us what the distribution of migrants across space and occupations would have been if networks were absent. The potential limitation of the structural approach is that the magnitude of the network's role will only be estimated accurately if the theoretical structure that is imposed on the data is valid empirically. The validation tests discussed above are especially useful in this regard. Although structural models have been used to study the dynamics of individual migration, the proposed analysis will extend the research frontier on a different and important aspect of migration.

10.5.3. Research Question 3. What Inefficiencies Arise in Economies Where Community Networks Support Mobility?

Communities intervene in developing economies because markets function imperfectly. In this survey, we have focused on their role in supporting the movement of groups of individuals from one location to the other. Although this mobility-enhancing role for the community may increase economic efficiency, there is no substitute for well-functioning markets. Like all non-market interventions, community networks inevitably generate inefficiencies of their own. The discussion that follows lists some of these inefficiencies, but this is just a partial list. A complete characterization of the static and dynamic inefficiencies that accompany community-based migration is an important area for future research.

10.5.3.1. Static Inefficiency

While community identity may sometimes be used to improve outcomes, as discussed above, the conventional mechanism to get self-interested individuals to cooperate within communities is the threat of social punishment. Individuals interact frequently within these communities and, typically, much less frequently across communities. Exclusion from these interactions is thus a severe punishment, which can be used to ensure that community members do not renege on their social obligations.

In the context of migration, frequent interactions between migrants belonging to a common origin community ensure high levels of cooperation at the destination. The inefficiency that arises is that this cooperation does not extend across community lines. Indeed, communities may actively discourage cross-community interactions and trade between individual members because superior options outside the community make social sanctions less effective, resulting in lower internal cooperation. These restrictions on trade can, in turn, result in a misallocation of resources.

For example, Banerjee and Munshi (2004) show that the inability of capital to cross community lines results in a misallocation of resources in Tirupur's production cluster. Local entrepreneurs in Tirupur belong to a wealthy agricultural caste with few alternative uses for its capital. Migrant entrepreneurs, in contrast, are drawn from caste-communities with many generations of business experience; these business communities have many alternative uses for their capital. Using data from a survey of entrepreneurs that collected retrospective information on their capital investment and production, Banerjee and Munshi uncover two facts: (i) that local businessmen hold more capital stock than the outsiders, on average, at all levels of experience; and (ii) that production nevertheless grows faster for the outsiders at all levels of experience; they start with lower levels of production, but outstrip the locals after five years of experience. Banerjee and Munshi develop a simple model in which the entrepreneur's ability and the firm's capital stock are complementary inputs to show that the two stylized facts can only be observed simultaneously if the outsiders have higher ability on average, which is not surprising, given that they are drawn from traditional business communities, but also face a higher cost of capital (interest rate), which is once again not surprising because there are many uses for their capital.

Cheap capital fails to move from the local community to the more competent outsiders, resulting in a misallocation of resources. This misallocation should not be observed within communities, where we expect that well-functioning networks will ensure that all entrepreneurs face the same interest rate; and, Banerjee and Munshi find that firms holding more capital stock do grow faster (and have higher levels of production) within communities. It is only across communities that the negative correlation between capital stock and production is obtained, presumably because the outsiders cannot credibly commit to repaying the locals for the capital they receive.

Anderson (2011) documents similar restrictions on trade in groundwater between castes in North Indian villages. Trade does not occur despite the fact that these castes have been co-residing in these villages for generations, which is indicative of the extremely weak cross-caste social ties in India. The insider-outsider dichotomy is especially pronounced for migrants, as in Tirupur, because they are (by definition) newcomers to the destination market and can only establish social relations with the locals after they have been settled for a sufficient amount of time. In the initial period, they will be forced to rely on their own resources. This strengthens their own networks, accentuating the insider-outsider dichotomy and worsening the misallocation described above. Although numerous historical accounts of migrant labor networks document their efficiency-enhancing role, finding jobs for their members, these accounts do not consider the accompanying misallocation that could arise. While networks help competent members find jobs, even more competent workers from communities with weaker networks could be shut out. This problem is exacerbated by nepotism and collusion—when strong networks enjoy monopoly power in the labor market, they will use this power to recruit relatively incompetent individuals from the community at the margin. More research is needed on this static inefficiency and the wealth inequality across communities, both in the short run and the long run, that arises when community networks are active.

10.5.3.2. Dynamic Inefficiency

When networks are active, individuals will forgo their comparative advantage in particular locations or occupations to move where their community is concentrated. In the short run, there will be too little clustering if individuals do not internalize the positive externality they provide to the rest of the community by joining the network. In the long run, however, there could be too much clustering if individuals' payoffs grow rapidly with experience in those activities where they are best suited, but they select instead into activities where their network is concentrated. In particular, there will be a dynamic inefficiency, with too much clustering, if individual discount factors are lower than the social optimum. The latter is very likely to arise in developing economies where individuals are credit constrained.

Clustering by migrant communities in particular occupations and locations is a commonly observed phenomenon. This clustering, by itself, is not indicative of an economic inefficiency. As the preceding discussion clarifies, inefficiencies will only arise if individuals are too impatient from a social perspective when trading off current gains from the network with the long-term benefits from the activity for which they are most suited. More research, both theoretical and empirical, is needed to better understand the sources of this dynamic inefficiency and to quantify its magnitude. This work around network (group) formation would complement the other dynamic inefficiency that was previously highlighted, which arises when established migrant networks prevent their members from pursuing new opportunities. It would also complement the quantification exercise described above, where the objective was to determine the magnitude of the role played by community networks in major migration events. The quantification of the static and dynamic inefficiencies that these networks generate is an equally important area for future research, which could be implemented using similar data and with suitably modified models of migration that incorporate these inefficiencies.

10.6. CONCLUSION

This chapter surveys the literature on migration, paying special attention to the role that communities play in this process. The canonical Roy model does a poor job of explaining key aspects of migration. This limitation can be remedied by adding networks to the Roy model, with this addition supported by a voluminous literature documenting the role played by communities in migration events throughout the world and over time. One possible reason why networks continue to be ignored in economic analyses of migration is that the *magnitude* of their role remains to be established. This is listed as one of three important areas for future research, based on the survey of the literature. The other areas are (i) a more detailed and comprehensive examination of the conditions under which migrant networks form, and (ii) a systematic assessment of the inefficiencies associated with these networks.

Apart from these gaps in our knowledge of the role played by communities in the process of migration, there are two areas that are related to community-based migration that deserve independent attention. The first has to do with migrant assimilation, a topic of great policy relevance. Despite its importance, we know very little about the assimilation process, both from a theoretical and from an empirical perspective. The discussion on the long-term consequences of community-based migration touched upon this topic, but assimilation is a much more complicated phenomenon. It is also a multigenerational phenomenon that is especially demanding on the data, and this makes empirical research on this topic very challenging. Given how little we know about assimilation, any theoretically grounded research on this topic would be welcome.

The second research area that is related to community-based migration is entrepreneurship. The establishment of firms and the movement of labor to centers of industrial production are key ingredients in the development process. At a fundamental level, the economic models underlying analyses of migration and entrepreneurship are the same; in one case, individuals are moving to a new location (and, typically, a new occupation), whereas in the other case, individuals are moving into a new occupation (often in a different location). Communities play a key role in supporting both migration and entrepreneurship in developing countries, and so ideally these phenomena should be analyzed in a consistent framework, rather than being treated independently, as they currently are in the economics literature.

NOTE

Research support from the National Science Foundation through grants SES-0431827 and SES-0617847 is gratefully acknowledged. I am responsible for any errors that may remain.

REFERENCES

Abramitzky, Ran, Leah Platt Boustan, and Katherine Eriksson. 2012. Europe's Tired, Poor, Huddled Masses: Self-Selection and Economic Outcomes in the Age of Mass Migration. *American Economic Review* 102(5): 1832–1856.

———. 2014. A Nation of Immigrants: Assimilation and Economic Outcomes in the Age of Mass Migration. *Journal of Political Economy* 122(3): 467–506.

Anderson, Siwan. 2011. Caste as an Impediment to Trade. *American Economic Journal: Applied* 3(1): 239–263.

Angelucci, Manuela, Giacomo De Giorgi, and Imran Rasul. 2015. Resource Pooling within Family Networks: Insurance and Investment. University of Michigan, typescript.

Banerjee, Abhijit and Kaivan Munshi. 2004. How Efficiently Is Capital Allocated? Evidence from the Knitted Garment Industry in Tirupur. *Review of Economic Studies* 71(1): 19–42.

Banerjee, Abhijit and Andrew Newman. 1993. Occupational Choice and the Process of Development. *Journal of Political Economy* 101(2): 274–298.

Beaman, Lori A. 2011. Social Networks and the Dynamics of Labor Market Outcomes: Evidence from Refugees Resettled in the U.S. *Review of Economic Studies* 79(1): 128–161.

Beine, Michel, Frederic Docquier, and Caglar Ozden. 2011. Diasporas. *Journal of Development Economics* 95: 30–41.

Bertoli, Simone and Jesus Fernandez-Huertas Moraga. 2012. Visa Policies, Networks and the Cliff at the Border. IZA Discussion Papers 7094, Institute for the Study of Labor (IZA).

Bian, Yanjie. 1994. Guanxi and the Allocation of Urban Jobs in China. *China Quarterly* 140(4): 971–999.

Bisin, Alberto and Thierry Verdier. 2000. "Beyond the Melting Pot": Cultural Transmission, Marriage, and the Evolution of Ethnic and Religious Traits. *Quarterly Journal of Economics* 115 (August): 955–988.

Bodnar, John. 1985. *The Transplanted: A History of Immigrants in Urban America*. Bloomington: Indiana University Press.

Borjas, George. 1987. Self-Selection and the Earnings of Immigrants. *American Economic Review* 77(4): 531–553.

Burnett-Hurst, A. R. 1925. *Labour and Housing in Bombay: A Study in the Economic Conditions of the Wage-Earning Classes of Bombay*. London: P.S. King and Son.

Carrington, William J., Enrica Detriagiache, and Tara Vishwanath. 1996. Migration with Endogenous Moving Costs. *American Economic Review* 86(4): 909–930.

Chandavarkar, Rajnarayan. 1994. *The Origins of Industrial Capitalism in India: Business Strategies and the Working Classes in Bombay, 1900–1940*. Cambridge: Cambridge University Press.

Chavez, Leo. 1992. *Shadowed Lives: Undocumented Immigrants in American Society*. Harcourt Brace Jovanovich College Publishers.

Chay, Kenneth and Kaivan Munshi. 2015. Black Networks After Emancipation: Evidence from Reconstruction and the Great Migration. University of Cambridge, mimeograph.

Chiquiar, Daniel and Gordon H. Hanson. 2005. International Migration, Self-Selection, and the Distribution of Wages: Evidence from Mexico and the United States. *Journal of Political Economy* 113(2): 239–281.

Cholia, R. P. 1941. *Dock Labourers in Bombay*. Bombay.

Conzen, Kathleen Neils. 1976. *Immigrant Milwaukee 1836–1860: Accommodation and Community in a Frontier City*. Cambridge, MA: Harvard University Press.

Cuecuecha, Alfredo. 2005. The Immigration of Educated Mexicans: The Role of Informal Social Insurance and Migration Costs. ITAM mimeograph.

Damodaran, Harish. 2008. *India's New Capitalists: Caste, Business, and Industry in Modern India*. Ranikhet: Permanent Black.

Docquier, Frederic, Giovanni Peri, and Ilse Ruyssen. 2014. The Cross-Country Determinants of Potential and Actual Migration. *International Migration Review* 48(s1): S37–S99.

Fafchamps, Marcel and Susan Lund. 2003. Risk Sharing Networks in Rural Philippines. *Journal of Development Economics* 71: 261–287.

Fernandez-Huertas Moraga, Jesus. 2011. New Evidence on Emigrant Selection. *Review of Economics and Statistics* 93(1): 72–96.

———. 2013. Understanding Different Migrant Selection Patterns in Rural and Urban Mexico. *Journal of Development Economics* 103: 182–201.

Gadgil, D. R. 1959. *Origins of the Modern Indian Business Class*. New York: Institute of Pacific Relations.

Galor, Oded and Joseph Zeira. 1993. Income Distribution and Macroeconomics. *Review of Economic Studies* 60: 35–52.

Gans, Herbert. 1962. *The Urban Villagers: Group and Class in the Life of Italian-Americans.* New York: Free Press of Glencoe.

Giles, John, Albert Park, and Fang Cai. 2006. Reemployment of Dislocated Workers in Urban China: The Roles of Information and Incentives. Michigan State University, Department of Economics, typescript.

Gjerde, Jon. 1985. *From Peasants to Farmers: The Migration from Balestrand, Norway to the Upper Middle West.* Cambridge: Cambridge University Press.

Gokhale, R. G. 1957. *The Bombay Cotton Mill Worker.* Bombay.

Gordon, David M., Richard Edwards, and Michael Reich. 1982. *Segmented Work, Divided Workers: The Historical Transformation of Labor in the United States.* Cambridge: Cambridge University Press.

Gottlieb, Peter. 1987. *Making Their Own Way: Southern Blacks' Migration to Pittsburgh, 1916–30.* Urbana and Chicago: University of Illinois Press.

Greif, Avner. 1993. Contract Enforceability and Economic Institutions in Early Trade: The Maghribi Traders' Coalition, *American Economic Review* 83(3): 525–548.

Greif, Avner, Paul Milgrom, and Barry R. Weingast. 1994. Coordination, Commitment, and Enforcement: The Case of the Merchant Guild. *Journal of Political Economy* 102(4): 745–776.

Grimard, Franque. 1997. Household Consumption Smoothing through Ethnic Ties: Evidence from Cote d'Ivoire. *Journal of Development Economics* 53(3): 319–422.

Grossman, James. 1989. *Land of Hope: Chicago, Black Southerners, and the Great Migration.* Chicago: University of Chicago Press.

Hagan, Jacqueline Maria. 1994. Deciding to Be Legal: A Maya Community in Houston. Philadelphia: Temple University Press.

Hoerder, Dirk. 1991. International Labor Markets and Community Building by Migrant Workers in the Atlantic Economies. In *A Century of European Migrants, 1830–1930*, edited by Rudolph J. Vecoli and Suzanne M. Sinke. Urbana: University of Illinois Press.

Hutchinson, E. P. 1956. *Immigrants and Their Children 1850–1950.* New York: Wiley.

Ibarran, Pablo and Darren Lubotsky. 2007. Mexican Immigration and Self-Selection: New Evidence from the 2000 Mexican Census. In *Mexican Immigration in the United States*, edited by George Borjas. Chicago: University of Chicago Press.

Kamphoefner, Walter D. 1987. *The Westfalians: From Germany to Missouri.* Princeton, NJ: Princeton University Press.

Kornblum, William. 1974. *Blue Collar Community.* Chicago and London: University of Chicago Press.

Mandle, Jay R. 1978. *The Roots of Black Poverty: The Southern Plantation Economy After the Civil War.* Durham, NC: Duke University Press.

Marks, Carole. 1983. Lines of Communication, Recruitment Mechanisms, and the Great Migration of 1916–1918. *Social Problems* 31(1): 73–83.

———. 1989. *Farewell—We're Good and Gone: The Great Black Migration.* Bloomington and Indianapolis: Indiana University Press.

———. 1991. The Social and Economic Life of Southern Blacks During the Migration. In *Black Exodus: The Great Migration from the American South*, edited by Alferdteen Harrison. Jackson and London: University Press of Mississippi.

Massy, Douglas, Rafael Alarcon, Jorge Durand, and Humberto Gonzalez. 1987. *Return to Aztlan: The Social Process of International Migration from Western Mexico.* Berkeley: University of California Press.

McKenzie, David and Hillel Rapoport. 2007. Network Effects and the Dynamics of Migration and Inequality: Theory and Evidence from Mexico. *Journal of Development Economics* 84: 1–24.

———. 2012. Self-Selection Patterns in Mexico-U.S. Migration: The Role of Migration Networks. *Review of Economics and Statistics* 92(4): 811–821.

Menjivar, Cecilia. 2000. *Fragmented Ties: Salvadoran Immigrant Networks in America.* Berkeley: University of California Press.

Mishra, Prachi. 2007. Emigration and Wages in Source Countries: Evidence from Mexico. *Journal of Development Economics* 82(1): 180–199.

Morris, Morris David. 1965. *The Emergence of an Industrial Labor Force in India: A Study of the Bombay Cotton Mills, 1854–1947.* Berkeley: University of California Press.

Munshi, Kaivan. 2003. Networks in the Modern Economy: Mexican Migrants in the U.S. Labor Market. *Quarterly Journal of Economics* 118(2): 549–597.

———. 2011. Strength in Numbers: Networks as a Solution to Occupational Traps. *Review of Economic Studies* 78: 1069–1101.

Munshi, Kaivan and Mark Rosenzweig. 2006. Traditional Institutions Meet the Modern World: Caste, Gender and Schooling Choice in a Globalizing Economy. *American Economic Review* 96(4): 1225–1252.

———. 2016. Networks and Misallocation: Insurance, Migration, and the Rural-Urban Wage Gap. *American Economic Review* 106(1): 46–98.

Nafziger, Wayne. 1978. *Class, Caste, and Entrepreneurship: A Study of Indian Industrialists*. Honolulu: University Press of Hawaii.

Nee, Victor G. and Brett de Bary Nee. 1972. *Longtime Californ': A Documentary Study of an American Chinatown*. New York: Pantheon Books.

Orrenius, Pia M. and Madeline Zavodny. 2005. Self-Selection Among Undocumented Immigrants from Mexico. *Journal of Development Economics* 78(1): 215–240.

Patel, Kunj. 1963. *Rural Labor in Industrial Bombay*. Bombay: Popular Prakashan.

Rees, Albert. 1966. Information Networks in Labor Markets. *American Economic Review (Papers and Proceedings)* 56: 559–566.

Roy, A. D. 1951. Some Thoughts on the Distribution of Earnings. *Oxford Economic Papers* 3(2): 135–146.

Tabellini, Guido. 2008. The Scope of Cooperation: Values and Incentives. *Quarterly Journal of Economics* 123(3): 905–950.

Tolnay, Stewart E. and E. M. Beck. 1990. Lethal Violence and the Great Migration, 1900–1930. *Social Science History* 14(3): 347–370.

Townsend, Robert. 1994. Risk and Insurance in Village India. *Econometrica* 62(3): 171–184.

Wang, Shing-Yi. 2013. Marriage Networks, Nepotism and Labor Market Outcomes in China. *American Economic Journal: Applied Economics* 5(3): 91–112.

Woodruff, Christopher and Renee Zenteno. 2007. Migration Networks and Microenterprises in Mexico. *Journal of Development Economics* 82(2): 509–528.

Zhang, Xiaobo and Guo Li. 2003. Does Guanxi Matter to Nonfarm Employment? *Journal of Comparative Economics* 31: 315–331.

Zhou, Min. 1992. *Chinatown: The Socioeconomic Potential of an Urban Enclave*. Philadelphia: Temple University Press.

PART 4

FAMILIES, GENDER, AND CULTURE

11

FORMAL AND INFORMAL MARKET INSTITUTIONS

Embeddedness Revisited

Marcel Fafchamps

11.1. INTRODUCTION

The development of formal institutions, based on legally enforceable sanctions, is often seen as displacing informal institutions constituted—and having enforcement mechanisms—outside the purview of the law.[1] The logic of the argument is that informal institutions exist because they provide a service, but formal institutions can provide the same service more effectively—either because they are more efficient, more inclusive, or both. When formal institutions are put in place, informal institutions are expected to disappear since they are costly to maintain and are no longer needed. While this argument carries some weight, it fails to recognize that economic exchange takes place between individuals and, as such, is nearly always embedded within a social context. The presence of a social context does not disappear with the introduction of formal institutions. This is the embeddedness hypothesis of Granovetter (1985), which this chapter revisits by combining insights from game theory and behavioral economics.

To motivate my approach, consider the following stylized example. Imagine for a moment a community that does not recognize formal marriage ties. Of course this does not stop couples from cohabitating.[2] In such an environment, we expect couples to stay together as long as they find their relationship beneficial. To this effect they may develop strong interpersonal ties as a form of enforcement mechanism to support their relationship. The logic of the earlier argument predicts that strong interpersonal ties between cohabiting couples should disappear once a formal marriage contract is introduced. After marriage, partners are expected to act toward each other in an impersonal manner, affected only by the terms of their contract and the laws regulating married couples. Yet, as I hope is obvious to anyone, this is not what happens: the simple fact of cohabitation fosters interpersonal ties and triggers strong (good and bad) emotions that are not eliminated by marriage.

What the example illustrates is that it is incorrect or even futile to imagine that the role of formal institutions is to substitute themselves for informal institutions. A more accurate view is to regard formal institutions as enabling informal institutions to perform better. For instance, in the above example, a formal marriage contract may help couples to stay together after a minor quarrel. Since couples invariably quarrel at some point, formal marriage makes their union more durable by introducing sanctions for breach of contract. By making cohabitation more sustainable, marriage protects investments toward household public goods (e.g., raising children), thereby increasing efficiency (e.g., Mnookin and Kornhauser 1979). The formalization of marriage as a contract between two individuals may nonetheless reduce the need for other relation-specific investments, such as the involvement of the spouses' families in arranging the marriage and in exerting social pressure against its dissolution.

A similar reasoning applies to many forms of market exchange. In the absence of formal institutions, trade is often organized around long-term relationships—e.g., between employer and worker, supplier and client, patron and client—often with the support or mediation of other social actors. With repeated exchange comes familiarity and social interaction. These features do not disappear with the introduction of formal market institutions, even if the focus of social exchange may evolve to reflect the different opportunities made possible by formalization. The truth is that trade is a form of social exchange, and any social exchange is embedded in a social context. Interpersonal interaction is not eliminated by formal institutions and contracts. The role of good formal institutions is to reinforce the forms of social interactions that lead to a more efficient, more inclusive outcome, and to discourage those interactions that reduce efficiency and ostracize certain groups and individuals.

The above observations form the organizing principle behind my critical examination of the literature and the derivation of tentative policy implications regarding the introduction of formal market institutions. My emphasis is on how humans perform in markets, especially in a repeated contract setting. The organizing thread is identifying the motivations that people follow when interacting in markets, and what this tells us about the role of formal institutions. To this end, I review and discuss the experimental literature that documents how human behavior responds to changes in contractual design—e.g., material incentives, enforcement mechanism, and ability to coordinate with or punish others. I put particular emphasis on two central themes: how humans interact in environments that resemble a market setting; and how they perform in a repeated contract setting. My ultimate objective is to derive tentative policy implications regarding the interface between formal and informal market institutions.

There already exists a large literature on this topic—notably seminal work by economists such as North (1973, 1990); Cooter and Ulen (1988); Greif (1993, 1994, 2002); Bowles (1998); Platteau (1994a, 1994b); Dixit (2004); and Greif and Tabellini (2010, 2012), but also anthropologists such as Mauss (1973); Polanyi (1944); Sahlins (1972); and Ensminger (1992); historians such as Braudel (1986); and sociologists such as Geertz et al. (1979) and Granovetter (1985). Many of the issues raised here already appear in Smith (1759, 1776). Experimental evidence has also been provided by the cross-cultural project (e.g., Henrich et al. 2005, 2010). While I have benefited immensely from the work of all these authors, my objective here is not to offer a comprehensive summary of their contribution but rather to revisit some of their ideas and insights in the light of recent experimental evidence regarding human behavior. For this reason, I endeavor to keep the references to the literature to what I hope is novel in my presentation.

Market exchange involves many cognitive and non-cognitive processes—e.g., search, inference, prediction, and negotiation. Much attention has already been devoted to these issues both in theory and in experimental economics. I choose to focus on the enforcement of market transactions, with a special emphasis on transactions that entail the possibility of opportunistic behavior. I will organize my presentation primarily around examples of transactions pertaining to goods or labor. As will be clear from the discussion, similar issues arise in other markets, such as those for credit and insurance, where they have typically received more attention. I also do not discuss the protection of property rights against non-contractual violations. This is an interesting topic in its own right, but it would take us too far afield.

The outline of the chapter is as follows. I begin in section 11.2 by introducing different mechanisms that can deter opportunistic breach of contract. Some of these mechanisms rely on rational thought and self-interest; others rely on various forms of intrinsic motivation, including emotions. Implications for institutional design are summarized. In section 11.3 I discuss the different types of social norms that are needed to support different mechanisms for the assignment of individuals to task, either within a family and a hierarchical organization, or by the market. This framework provides useful insights as to the type of normative content that is most conducive to an effective performance of these different assignment mechanisms. Section 11.4 is the heart of the chapter. Starting from the principles derived in sections 11.2 and 11.3, I examine how human behavioral tendencies interact with norms, incentives, and assignment mechanisms to support or undermine market institutions. I start by discussing how altruism and rivalry feed into the competitive process. Next we examine the relationship between mate selection and market matching. This leads me to suggest that humans intuitively understand the operation of markets because it resembles other social processes that evolved beforehand. Breach deterrence is introduced next, first from the point of view of risk attitudes and excusable default. This then leads to a discussion of morality and preferences over process, as distinct from preferences over material outcomes. We end with a brief discussion of individualism and agency, a topic on which more work by economists is needed. In the conclusion, implications are drawn regarding knowledge gaps. In particular, I call for more investigation of how different cultures view different types of incentives and deterrence mechanisms, and I offer some ideas on how this could be achieved.

11.2. BREACH DETERRENCE MECHANISMS

Market transactions are contracts, and most contracts have delayed obligations. This naturally applies to all markets in which the passage of time is of the essence—e.g., credit, insurance, labor, utilities, and services. It also applies to many transactions pertaining to the sale of goods. Examples include: delivery (if a client placed an order); pickup (if a supplier took an order); payment (if client did not pay upon delivery); and warranty (if the item or service was faulty).

It follows that the very first issue that market institutions must address is how to deter opportunistic breach of contract. Without trust, economic performance suffers (e.g., Algan and Cahuc 2010). Several mechanisms to sustain (rational) trust have been identified in the literature. They can be grouped into four broad categories: (1) intrinsic motivation; (2) fear of reprisal; (3) loss of relationship; and (4) loss of reputation (Fafchamps 2010). Much of the economic literature on market institutions and breach deterrence has focused on laws and courts, which fall under the second category.

Intrinsic motivation includes a variety of human emotions that arise in social interactions, such as empathy, altruism, guilt, and shame. With the right upbringing and social norms, these emotions can be harnessed in support of contract performance. Other emotions, however, can also obstruct compliance with contract terms, such as envy, rivalry, and inequality aversion. We revisit several of these issues in section 11.4.

Fear of reprisal encompasses two broad types of punishment: legitimate and illegitimate. Legitimate punishment relies on the use of courts backed by the power of a modern state with a monopoly over legitimate violence. Illegitimate punishment includes a wide range of practices, such as social disapproval, insults, and threats, as well as reliance on thugs, criminal organizations, and corrupt agents of the state.

Much of the economic literature on market institutions and breach deterrence has focused on legitimate punishment by laws and courts—which are equated with "formal market institutions." The dominant paradigm in economics is articulated around the assumption of self-interested rational agents. In this framework, deterrence works if agents anticipate that opportunistic breach will trigger court action and result in a loss larger than the gain from not complying with the contract. This means that, to be an effective deterrent, the threat of court action must be credible (i.e., subgame perfect). In practice, there are many transactions for which this condition is not satisfied. The first possibility is that laws are inadequate and courts ineffective. Much has been written on this important topic, so I need not revisit it here. Even when market-friendly laws and courts are in place, however, there are many reasons why private agents may not use them: going to court is expensive, both in terms of money and time; the defendant may be "judgment-proof," that is, without assets to service the debt; and the plaintiff may be unable to demonstrate contractual breach.

All three conditions are more likely to arise in less developed countries. Economic agents are poor and, as a result, often engage in small transactions for which the cost of going to court far outweighs the possible gain. Being poor, they are also often judgment-proof, making it unlikely that the plaintiff would recover damages. Finally, illiterate buyers and sellers find it difficult to create the paper trail that would document the existence of a contract and its violation by one of the parties. For these reasons, all but the largest transactions among deep-pocket economic agents are beyond the reach of direct enforcement by legal institutions (Fafchamps 2004; Bigsten et al. 2000).

Retaliation also involves strong emotions, such as fear, anger, outrage, self-righteousness, revenge, cunning, lust for power, etc. Much of the economic literature on market institutions has ignored these considerations, focusing instead on rational agents. But emotions can entice agents to engage in legitimate or illegitimate retaliation even when doing so is irrational, i.e., when it generates costs and risks that outweigh material gains. We will discuss in section 11.4 the available evidence on people's willingness to engage in costly punishment for actions that are perceived as breaching a contract, implicit promise, or norm of behavior.

A third category of breach deterrence mechanism is the fear of losing a valuable relationship (e.g., Fafchamps and Minten 2001). This form of breach deterrence mechanism only applies to market exchange that is repeated between two economic agents over time—what the literature sometimes calls "relational contracting." Perhaps the most common form of relational contracting is so-called permanent employment, a labor contract that has no stipulated ending date (other than compulsory retirement wherever applicable). Relational contracting is nonetheless found in many other markets: utilities, banking services, insurance contracts, maintenance contracts, etc. It is also extremely common in markets for goods and commodities: most firms have regular suppliers from whom they purchase the majority of their raw materials and goods for sale. Once a commercial relationship is established, orders are placed over the phone or Internet, goods are delivered, often by a third-party transporter, and an invoice is issued with a set time for payment.

Relational contracting has two main advantages: it economizes on the cost of finding new matches; and it enables agents to deal in a more trusting manner. The two motives are intimately related: it is precisely because relational contracting economizes on search and screening costs that it creates a value to the relationship. The fear of losing this valuable relationship is then what deters opportunistic breach. In economics, this idea has been formalized as a repeated game. A large literature now exists that refines this basic construct—see Fafchamps (2010) for a summary.

The fourth category of breach deterrence mechanism that we consider here is the fear of losing reputation. This concept is distinct from losing a relationship. While a relationship involves only two economic agents, reputation involves a larger set of agents, typically in a given industry, location, or social group. Losing my relationship with a supplier may cut supplies from that source; losing my reputation with all suppliers may cut all sources of supply—and would then mean the end of my business. It follows that economic agents value their reputation and are willing to sacrifice a short-term gain in order to preserve their good name (Tadelis 1999).

Many formal institutions seek to reinforce reputation mechanisms. The first threat to any reputation mechanism is identity theft: someone using my name, brand, or trademark to abuse customers, employers, etc. Formal institutions therefore exist that establish and protect identity—e.g., photo ID, fingerprinting, business registration, trademark protection. They also deter individuals from changing identity in order to evade contractual obligations.

The second threat to any reputation mechanism is the spread of malicious or inaccurate information. Indeed, if reputation is valuable, the temptation is strong for agents to circulate erroneous information to hurt their competitors (e.g., other firms, other employees, or employers). Formal institutions exist that deter libel and defamation. A free press, protected by law, can be a powerful tool to expose defective products, abusive employers, and false advertising. Specific formal institutions may also arise for the sole purpose of circulating accurate information. Examples include private and public agencies dealing with: credit report and credit reference; credit rating; consumer protection; environmental protection; health and safety; auditing of publicly traded corporations; disclosure rules for charities; etc. Many newly created IT service providers similarly seek to protect the identity of their users against misappropriation and offer reputation mechanisms as well (e.g., Amazon, eBay, Expedia). What the Internet has not yet managed to prevent is the circulation of malicious messages (e.g., through reposting and retweeting)—i.e., the industry has not managed to introduce the equivalent of legal protection against libel and defamation.

What this discussion demonstrates is that formal institutions can and do play an important role in the promotion of markets. But they do not primarily achieve this by enforcing contracts directly. Rather, they seek to reinforce informal contract enforcement mechanisms. This observation applies to reputation, as we just saw. But it also applies to other mechanisms. In particular, a number of laws and formal institutions seek to shape the creation and dissolution of contractual relationships in a direction that is seen as socially beneficial. This includes: grades and standards; standardized weights and measures; and rules about the listing of ingredients and other compulsory disclosures. These interventions seek to minimize conflicts due to misrepresentation by one party to a transaction. Rules about bankruptcy and fraud similarly seek to regulate what happens if one agent cannot pay another. Many countries also have laws and norms directing the conditions under which a relational contract may end—think of laws and regulations concerning unfair dismissal, undue termination of a rental or land lease, or the non-renewal of a health or life insurance contract.

Formal institutions also seek to curb certain forms of informal contract enforcement—particularly the reliance on thugs and violence. It has been argued that one of the primary reasons for the establishment of institutions of public order is the reduction of the use of interpersonal violence to adjudicate disputes (e.g., North 1973). By imposing a monopoly over the use of legitimate violence while offering alternative ways of resolving private conflicts, the modern state has singularly reduced recourse to interpersonal violence to resolve contractual disputes. To convince ourselves of the difference this makes, we only need to remember that a high proportion of violent crime is associated with commercial conflict in sectors (e.g., drug trade, prostitution, gambling, human trafficking) that are construed as illegal and hence for which legal redress cannot be sought.

In general, formal institutions do not enforce contracts directly—they only deter opportunistic breach by offering damages and other forms of reparation after the fact. In special cases, however, formal institutions are put in place to directly enforce contracts, without any delay or possibility of default. Examples of such institutions include stock markets, commodity exchanges, and other organized markets in which participants must post a bond before being allowed to contract. Only authorized brokers can place a purchase or sale order in an organized exchange, and this order is guaranteed by a guarantee that the broker has typically put in an escrow account. Public auction floors often follow similar rules, e.g., requiring participants to open a credit line with the house before being allowed to bid.

With the exception of organized exchanges, we have seen that formal institutions deter opportunistic breach primarily in two ways: (1) by offering a strictly organized process for the adjudication of contractual disputes, which economic agents may call upon at their convenience, but which de facto is only relevant for reasonably large transactions among non-poor agents; and (2) by laying down an environment in which an extremely diverse and ever-changing set of public and private agencies support informal mechanisms for the enforcement of contracts, at the exception of interpersonal violence. It is therefore misleading to oppose formal and informal enforcement mechanisms as if the former was a full substitute for the other. The truth is that formal institutions operate primarily by guiding and reinforcing relational contracting and reputation mechanisms.

These observations lead to the key insight behind the rest of this chapter: since formal institutions ultimately rely on informal ones to achieve their objective of fair and efficient exchange, we need a better understanding of informal institutions to make sense of market development.

As we have shown above, market interaction can trigger a wide range of emotions—e.g., guilt, shame, anger, and rivalry. These emotions can help deter opportunistic breach of contract even when, by themselves, they are devoid of strategic purpose. To illustrate, imagine that someone gets angry because I have cheated him in a contract. Telling this person that his anger is calculated to strategically deter breach will only inflame him more: it is equivalent to suggesting that his anger is not "genuine" and he is just pretending—in other words, that he is a liar and a cheat, no better than I am. Anger seems to be morally justified only if it is uncontrollable and non-strategic. As this example illustrates, emotions are not dictated by reason—they represent an instinctive and often irrational response to an action taken by ourselves or someone else.

Although emotions may not follow a reasoned strategic motive, they nonetheless are embedded into a strict logic, and this logic is that of morality: these emotions are ultimately triggered by the transgression of a social norm either by ourselves or by someone else. It follows that the emotions that are mobilized by economic transaction depend on the moral judgment that people pass on their actions and those of others. In order to predict which actions individuals take after a breach of contract, we must therefore be able to predict what moral judgment they will pass on that action. If contract non-compliance is deemed excusable by both parties, for instance, it will trigger no guilt from the breaching party and no anger from the aggrieved party.

The remainder of this chapter is devoted to an exploration of these ideas. We start by developing a way of thinking about social norms not as moral absolutes that must be followed in all circumstances, but rather as sets of internally consistent norm systems that apply to different domains of human activity. At any point in time, individuals may have several such sets of norms that they apply selectively, depending on the domain of activity in which their economic interaction is occurring. We also discuss what happens when individuals apply norms from one domain to another.

We then turn to the experimental evidence regarding the role of emotions and moral judgment in markets and other interpersonal interactions. We find that humans seem naturally attuned to particular aspects of market interaction, and we review what limited evidence is available from economic research on preferences for process and morality more generally.

11.3. SOCIAL NORMS AND DOMAINS OF ACTIVITY

The purpose of this section is to offer a framework to organize social norms into internally consistent sets intended to apply to a specific way of organizing human activity. Our organizing principle is the assignment of people to tasks (Fafchamps 2011, 2012). It is easy to forget that labor markets are not the only way of allocating workers to tasks. Workers can also be allocated to tasks within firms or organizations, typically through command and control. A similar process takes place within the household to assign members to specific chores, while self-employed individuals are assigned to task by market signals.

How much allocation takes place hierarchically within the firm or through the labor market ultimately depends on the duration of labor contracts. If labor contracts are of short duration, workers are allocated to tasks through the labor market: if a task must be undertaken, a worker is hired to undertake it. If a task is no longer required, the worker is laid off—or simply not hired again. If labor contracts are of long duration, workers are allocated to tasks through command and control: if a task must be undertaken, a worker from within the firm is reallocated to undertake it; if a task is no longer required, the worker is reallocated to another task. The allocation role of the labor market thus depends on the duration of employment contracts.

The allocation of workers to tasks can also be organized via the market for goods and services. In the case of microenterprises employing no wage worker, job creation and firm creation coincide. It follows that self-employed workers are "told" what to do by the demand for their products and the supply of raw materials and other inputs. Having clarified how different allocation mechanisms affect who does what, we now discuss each allocation mechanism in greater detail.

11.3.1. Self-Provision, Markets, and Hierarchies

Many goods and services are self-provided within the household (Becker 1965). This is particularly true in poor rural areas where households self-provide a large number of essential commodities. Within the household, the allocation of workers to tasks is based on gift exchange or reciprocal exchange between related individuals. Risk-sharing is the manifestation of reciprocal exchange that has received the most attention from economists (Coate and Ravallion 1993; Ligon, Thomas, and Worrall 2002). Other examples include the exchange of favors (Jackson, Rodriguez-Barraquer, and Tan 2012) and the pooling of land within the lineage (Platteau 2010; Otsuka and Quisumbing 2001).

Within the domain of self-provision, the allocation of workers to tasks is achieved through a combination of intra-household bargaining and social norms. A large literature has looked at the distribution of welfare within households and has identified various determinants of intra-household bargaining (McElroy and Horney 1981; Lundberg and Pollak 1993).

Because the formation of a new household marks the creation of a new production unit, the efficient allocation of workers to tasks therefore depends on how individuals are matched into households (e.g., Fafchamps and Quisumbing 2008). This formation process is largely regulated by the marriage market. The assortative matching of spouses on ethnicity, religion, education, and family background affects not only the intergenerational transmission of skills and wealth but also the productivity of the newly created households in the self-provision of goods and services (e.g., Fafchamps and Quisumbing 2002, 2005a, 2005b). This is well understood by parents who often get involved in the selection of a mate.

The social norms associated with self-provision are specific to that domain of human activity. People are assigned to tasks within a household, either through direct negotiation or, more often than not, by following socially assigned roles (e.g., Fafchamps and Quisumbing 2003; Fafchamps and Wahba 2006). Reciprocity is undefined ex ante. The reward for performing a task is unspecified (i.e., there is no wage or price); it is typically delayed in time; and it is contingent on future shocks. This system allows sharing and redistribution: it is ideal to help the weak, nurture children, and care for less able household members. Decision-making is typically decentralized to the person performing the task, possibly in consultation with others. How much decentralization is possible depends on technology, a point initially made by Boserup (1970) in her pioneering work on the decision power of women. A recent example of this line of work is the evidence that the plow favors a more centralized form of farm management, thereby eroding the decision-making power of women (e.g., Alesina et al. 2013). Social norms are enforced in part through the internalization of norms through upbringing, and through various forms of social pressure (e.g., ostracism, ridicule, bullying, domestic violence, expulsion, honor killing). Formal contracts can also play a role (e.g., marriage), as can externally imposed legal obligations (e.g., child support). Evidence nonetheless suggests that, in many developing countries, the formal legal system has only limited effect on the enforcement of social norms in this domain: customary laws or traditions are often followed even when they violate formal or religious law; participants are reluctant to report norm violations to formal institutions; and there is pressure on individuals not to rely on the legal system. This means that this domain often is largely beyond the reach of formal institutions.

Self-provision means that individuals are not specialized. Gains from specialization can be achieved when workers focus on a smaller range of activities at which they become proficient. For this to be possible, they must provide the good or service not just within the household but to a larger number of people. This essentially means offering these goods and services through the market, typically in or around an urban center (e.g., Fafchamps and Shilpi 2003, 2005). This process manifests itself as the creation of a myriad of micro-enterprises, often known as the "informal sector."

What matters for our purpose is that the social norms required for success as a micro-entrepreneur are not the same as those governing self-provision (Fafchamps 2011). In market exchange, reciprocity in the form of payment is often immediate rather than delayed. Moreover, risk-sharing (e.g., insurance) is separated from compensation for effort (e.g., price). This stands in contrast with gift exchange within the household or extended family, where reciprocity is typically delayed and combined with insurance. These observations were initially made by Polanyi (1944) and Gregory (1982), who call gift-exchange-cum-insurance "generalized reciprocity" and refer to market-style strict reciprocity as "balanced reciprocity." Polanyi was the first to observe that generalized reciprocity is characteristic of exchange within the family, which he regards as the most basic unit of traditional societies, while balanced reciprocity applies outside of the family unit. For our purpose, the implication is that, as individuals begin interacting through the market, they discover hard budget constraints—which is the way the market ensures reciprocity and compensation, but not insurance.

As firms and organizations grow, wage employment develops. By itself, it does not imply a large role for the hierarchical assignment of workers to tasks. If workers are hired for a short period, the allocation of workers to tasks takes place primarily through the labor market. Agricultural laborers, for instance, are often hired by the day or the task.

Large hierarchies cannot function solely with casual labor, however. Size makes it difficult if not impossible for decisions to all be made centrally: the delegation of authority is essential to deal with local problem solving. Delegation of authority to sub-units in turn creates a need to coordinate the activities of the various parts of the organization (e.g., Fafchamps and Soderbom 2006). This coordination cannot be accomplished without trusted management and clerical personnel to process information, e.g., via accounts or reports. This leads to the development of so-called permanent employment contracts. In developed economies these are so pervasive that they are regarded as normal employment.

Workers in permanent employment may be granted a certain amount of autonomy but, ultimately, what task they are assigned to is dictated by what fits the needs of the organization they work for (e.g., Aoki 1984). Given this, workers are expected to comply with their task assignment. Reciprocity is defined ex ante, through the payment of a pre-specified wage at regular intervals. Promotion is based on tenure or past performance. In principle, a permanent employment contract involves no sharing or redistribution other than what is stipulated in the contract: there is no ex post insurance and no consideration for individual circumstances. Roles are defined by the contract or the employer, and so is the level of decision-making devolved to the individual worker—usually in ways strongly influenced by the technology of production. Respect for these norms of behavior is enforced by a combination of loyalty to the employer or firm, guilt for shirking, social pressure from coworkers, harassment by management, threat of job loss, and threat of loss of reputation. There is extensive intervention of the legal system to affect the operation of the assignment process. Interventions are often based on a quid pro quo: more worker loyalty (e.g., no strike) in exchange for better conditions (e.g., wage, health and safety, social insurance, worker autonomy, promotion rules).

11.3.2. Domain Coexistence and Shifting Boundaries

We have seen that different domains of human activity call for social norms with a different content. Yet most individuals operate in multiple domains at the same time. They typically share a household with others, and the life of this household is regulated by self-provision and gift exchange. In addition, they earn a monetary income either from the operation of a farm or small business, or from wage employment—or both. This means that most individuals juggle multiple sets of social norms that apply to different aspects of their economic life. At home they are expected to contribute to household public goods without consideration for immediate reciprocity—i.e., to devote time and resources helping others in a relatively non-strategic manner. But in their business they are expected to insist on unconditional and timely reciprocity in the form of payment, work, or supplies. In their business individuals are expected to take initiative and avail themselves of arbitrage opportunities. But in wage employment they are typically expected to stick to their assigned task and refrain from deriving personal gain from arbitrage opportunities.

Many cases of breach of contract are related in some way to the application of social norms from another domain. An entrepreneur may fail to pay suppliers because enterprise funds were diverted to deal with a family emergency. A worker may fail to report for work because she is taking care of a sick relative. Alternatively, individuals may seek to apply norms from the market realm to transactions normally regulated by the family and handled through gift exchange—e.g., sexual favors. Corrupt workers are those who apply norms from the entrepreneurship domain and take advantage of arbitrage. Alternatively, small entrepreneurs may cluster together, mimic the behavior of each other, and show no initiative at all—as if they were in casual wage employment together. As these examples illustrate, juggling different sets of social norms is fraught with difficulty (e.g., Barr and Serra 2008).

This inherent difficulty is further compounded by the fact that domain boundaries are not constant. The boundaries between the domains of application of the different labor allocation mechanisms tend to shift with economic development. As a result the allocative role of the market changes constantly, on one hand taking over tasks that were previously the realm of self-provision and gift exchange, but on the other hand seeing its allocative rule superseded by command and control within expanding organizations. The domains never disappear—even in the most market-oriented economics, there are still goods and services that are self-provided—but their range of applicability changes over time.

With economic development, individuals learn to rely on the market to obtain goods and services they previously obtained through gift exchange or self-provision. Tasks thus move from one domain, with its rules and obligations, to another domain and another set of rules. Negotiating these changes can be confusing for those involved because to each allocation mechanism is associated a specific set of internally consistent norms and attitudes. For tasks assigned through self-provision and gift exchange, allocation is ultimately based on reciprocity: I help you today because I expect you to help me in a yet-to-be-defined way later. There is no hard budget constraint, which facilitates risk-sharing and redistribution—the needy do not "pay" for the services they require. The kind of social norms that sustain household self-provision and gift exchange nevertheless emphasize the obligation to reciprocate for gifts received, if one is in a position to do so. Self-provision and gift exchange leave much room for altruism and emotions to shape exchange—and thus the assignment of tasks among individuals. Self-provision also encompasses a hierarchical element, with the head of household playing a role similar to that of firm manager, albeit on a smaller scale and with no power to hire or fire workers.

In contrast, market allocation is based on clear—and often instantaneous—reciprocation in the form of money. This leaves little room for risk-sharing and no room for redistribution: money is required to obtain goods and services. Although individuals procure goods and services to each other as they would in a gift exchange economy, the workings of the market do not require moral obligations extending beyond the instantaneous transaction, and the role of altruism is minimized.

In market exchange, hard budget constraints serve as an obstacle to free-riding: individuals cannot consume if they do not contribute to society something that is valuable and worth paying for. In gift exchange, there is no such hard budget constraint so that in principle some people can receive without giving in return. Preventing free-riding is thus more difficult in gift exchange.

Two types of norms can be seen as a way of minimizing free-riding. The first is the moral obligation to reciprocate if possible. This has already been discussed. The second is a sharing norm, or equity norm (e.g., Platteau 2000, 2009, 2014). This basically requires that standards of living remain basically in line with each other: one person cannot rise above all others; if someone has good fortune, she is expected to share this good fortune with others so as to raise the standards of living of the group as a whole. Equity norms of this kind limit free-riding: it is not possible to only take from the group without giving in return. But they do so in a redistributive fashion, i.e., they show no apparent concern for possible discrepancies between someone's standard of living and their economic contribution to society. This is in sharp contrast with the hard budget constraint imposed by the market, which establishes a clear link—i.e., monetary income—between consumption and contribution to society.

The shift from market provision to wage employment calls for another change in norms and attitudes. For people to be efficiently assigned to tasks by the market, they must respond rapidly to arbitrage opportunities. Swift action is needed before someone else seizes the opportunity. In contrast, workers in long-term employment are expected to perform their assigned tasks; they are not expected to set their own tasks in response to arbitrage opportunities. If they do, this is often described as corruption. Hence corruption is equivalent to applying norms from one domain, the market domain, to another domain, the wage employment domain. Nepotism is another form of confusion between the norms applying to different domains: in the realm of gift exchange, reciprocating favors is a social obligation; in wage employment, diverting from one's assigned task to reciprocate favors violates the employment contract.

There can also be cross-subsidization across domains. For instance, a paternalistic employer may act in a fatherly way toward his employees, but expect filial loyalty in return. The putting-out system enables employers to surreptitiously employ unpaid family members whose labor force is under the control of the worker. Unpaid family workers similarly provide an artificial boost to the productivity of small businesses. Employers may also pay their workers on commission, thereby encouraging workers to use their initiative in order to take advantage of arbitrage opportunities—and thereby introducing some of the key elements of self-employment into their labor contract. In all these examples, one domain is seen taking advantage of the social norms applying to another domain.

There is a lot of potential for clashes between the norms applying to different domains. As societies develop and move away from self-subsistence, people have to learn not one but two sets of norms—one regulating interactions through the market, and another regulating hierarchies. It is therefore hardly surprising that the development process is often associated with confusion of norms. Not only do people have to learn new social norms, they also must learn which norms apply when in an environment that is perpetually changing, role models are few, and norms from one domain leak into another domain, or else be taken advantage of.

11.4. BEHAVIORAL CONSIDERATIONS

We have contrasted different types of mechanisms that help enforce market transactions and, more generally, norms of behavior in various domains of economic activity. Norms of behavior in contractual and non-contractual relations of exchange are enforced partly through formal institutions—e.g., courts, contract law, marriage law, labor law, corporate law—and partly through informal means—intrinsic motivations/internalized norms, loss of valuable relationships, loss of reputation, social pressure, illegitimate violence. I have argued in section 11.3 that the respect and violation of social norms trigger a wide range of human emotions, many of which are hard to control or suppress—and thus are not fully rational. Although many of these emotions—e.g., anger at being cheated—serve a de facto deterrence role, they often are not consciously strategic, especially when, as in the case of guilt and shame, they act as a deterrent on the breaching party.

Human emotions are generated through physiological processes (e.g., hormones, reflexes) that are common to all mankind, even if they sometimes vary by gender (e.g., Croson and Gneezy 2009). Furthermore, many of them—e.g., fear, anger, lust, or greed—are fairly primal and involve primitive regions of the brain. We can therefore expect emotions to be widely shared by all members of the human species. This also applies to the emotions most closely associated with our capacity for moral behavior—e.g., guilt, shame, self-righteousness, and moral outrage. However, while the emotions triggered by norm violation are widely shared among humans, the content of the norms that trigger them does differ.

It is widely believed that humans internalize social norms primarily through upbringing while young—what the literature calls primary socialization (e.g., Platteau 1994a)—although new norms can be internalized and old norms abandoned throughout adulthood through secondary socialization, e.g., in schools and churches (e.g., Platteau 1994b). This makes the human mind extremely adept at making moralistic value judgment, but at the same time surprisingly malleable regarding the content of the norms. Anthropologists have documented a number of empirical regularities—all human societies seem to have moral rules regarding incest, homicide, sexual practices, and food. But these rules are astonishingly varied, especially among human groups whose geographic and social isolation helped preserve their original values—the so-called primitive people (e.g., Levi-Strauss 1962, 1966). Social norms also appear capable of varying over a surprisingly short time—and, as we have discussed in section 11.3, conflicting norms manage to co-exist within the same individual at the same point in time.

Taking these observations as a starting point, in this section we examine how behavioral considerations affect our understanding of breach deterrence and markets in general, and how they relate to norms and morality more generally.

So far we have assumed that breach deterrence is achieved by creating a total punishment for breach that yields lower utility than breaching one's contractual or social obligations, and by assuming that people respond rationally to that. This reasoning is based purely on our own outcomes: agents compare the outcomes of breaching and not breaching and pick the outcome that best serves their material interest. There is no consideration for behavioral deviations, including deviations that are triggered by preferences over process, of which morality is a major source.

We begin by discussing the role of altruism and rivalry in the functioning of competition. We then turn to the relationship between markets and mate selection. Next we discuss risk avoidance behavior and how it relates to breach deterrence. We then formally introduce preferences over process and examine the relationship between conditionality and punishment. This leads us to examine the role of individualism and agency. Applications to the violation of norms and contracts are presented at the end.

11.4.1. Comparisons and Competition

Competition is often seen as a hallmark of markets. But competition seems to be fueled by a much more fundamental human urge than anything unleashed by markets. People compare themselves to others when evaluating their life achievements, and this can affect how happy they feel (e.g., Diener et al. 1995, 1999; Kahneman et al. 1999; Layard 2002;

Frey and Stutzer 2002; Blanchflower and Oswald 2004; Luttmer 2005). This explains why happiness is largely insensitive to aggregate growth (e.g., Easterlin 1974, 1995, 2001; Krueger 2009; Clark, Frijters, and Shields 2008) but may vary across cultures or over time (e.g., Runciman 1966; Inglehart et al. 2000).

Interpersonal comparison breeds rivalry, a feature that has been abundantly discussed following the seminal work of Fehr and Schmidt (1999) on inequality aversion (see also Rabin 1993). As shown by Fafchamps and Shilpi (2008), the sensitivity of subjective well-being to the material welfare of others is not limited to urban, market-oriented environments: it is even stronger in isolated areas (see however Ravallion and Lokshin 2005). People do behave altruistically at times, but they do so primarily within the family (e.g., Cox 1987; Ledyard et al. 1995; Hoffman et al. 1996). This may explain why, when they form social attachments, people tend to seek out the company of similar others (e.g., McPherson et al. 2001).

Interpersonal comparisons can also affect savings and consumption choices. The idea of conspicuous consumption, first put forth by Veblen (1899), has found some evidential support in recent papers (e.g., Roth 2014; Bursztyn et al. 2016). The related idea that people overspend in order to keep up with their neighbors (Duesenberry 1949) has similarly been revisited recently (e.g., Di Giorgi et al. 2016). Robson (1992) argues that status considerations affect attitudes to risk. Evidence that people are sensitive to relative status is given by Di Tella et al. (2010).

Competition thus appears to be a natural human behavior, fueled no doubt by the pursuit of self-interest, but also by rivalry based on interpersonal comparisons—even in the absence of material gain (e.g., Curtis and Eswaran 2003). As a result, competition can be harnessed in various types of human interactions, not only through the market. Sibling rivalry is one possible manifestation of competition in the self-provision domain (e.g., Morduch 2000; Leight 2016). Competition in teams has been studied in the context of hierarchical organizations, and there has been considerable theoretical work by economists on competition in teams. Market competition itself has received much attention, and we need not revisit it here.

While competition may often yield an efficient outcome when it is based on pure self-interest in material outcomes, rivalry may generate excess competition whereby agents prefer to destroy each other's material payoff to avoid falling behind (e.g., Macours 2011). Direct evidence can be found in laboratory experiments that give subjects the option to pay in order to destroy (i.e., "burn") the payoff of other subjects. Thankfully most subjects do not make use of this option, but a significant minority does (e.g., Zizzo 2003; Zizzo and Oswald 2001). Furthermore, Fafchamps and Hill (2016) provide experimental evidence from three countries demonstrating that subjects are less likely to join a Pareto-improving team when the option to destroy other subjects' payoff is introduced—and this effect is particularly strong in rural Uganda. Excessive competition has also been documented in auction experiments, where it is known as the "winner's curse." Perhaps the best evidence of this is for second-price auctions for which, under pure self-interest, bidding one's reservation price is optimal—yet many subjects bid more than that, and end up losing money when they win the auction (e.g., Kagel and Levin 1986).

Using case study evidence from Japanese fisheries, Platteau and Seki (2007) offer evidence suggesting how competition can be harnessed for the common good. They argue that people have a social esteem component in their utility function: they derive positive utility from pride when they perform better than their coworkers and, conversely, derive negative utility from shame when their performance is low. By pooling incomes, coworkers with different individual productivities may coexist in the same group: pride compensates those who perform above average for the loss of income they incur from pooling, while shame penalizes those who perform below the group average. The authors show that this mechanism can only work if disparities in productivity are not too large, however. These theoretical predictions are illustrated using a comparison of two fishing cooperatives: one where disparities in performance are not large and where the group has persisted for decades; and one where the cooperative broke down because disparities in performance were too large (see also Fafchamps and La Ferrara 2012 for evidence of self-selection into self-help groups in Kenya).

The observation that competition can be destructive has long been made in history—and is even recorded in the Book of Genesis with the story of Cain and Abel. This probably explains why there are more institutions—formal and informal—to reduce competition than there are to encourage it. Family authorities are called in to arbitrate disputes between siblings or heirs. Customary and tribal authorities are primarily in charge of adjudicating competition between households or lineages over land and other productive assets, and to ensure that rivalry does not break out into tribal warfare (e.g., Scott 1976; Schechter 2007). It has even been argued that a crowning achievement of the modern state has been to reduce the mayhem and wanton destruction of lives and property brought about by competition between groups (e.g., Pinker 2012). Competition for resources is also behind cattle theft and land grabbing (e.g., Andre and Platteau 1998), and many customary and formal institutions exist with the main purpose of ensuring the respect of property rights against the envy and lust for destruction associated with human rivalry.

So far we have emphasized the dark side of other-regarding preferences, namely, rivalry. There is also a bright side, namely, empathy, compassion, and altruism. The fact that people care about others and derive some satisfaction from their well-being is most clearly visible in the self-provision domain. Shared genes and experiences are known to favor group identification and altruism, and these emotions probably are an essential binding agent in nuclear and extended families, helping to sustain gift exchange over long periods of time. It nonetheless remains that social norms in the self-provision domain strongly emphasize the need to share and help others—suggesting that altruism based on shared genes need not be sufficient (see for instance Platteau 2006 and Fehr and Schmidt 2006).

In the market domain, economists typically assume indifference to the material well-being of others. This point is discussed for instance by Bowles (1998), who reflects on the often-heard claim that "markets make people selfish" (see also Arrow et al. 2000 and Bowles et al. 2001). Some evidence on this issue is provided by Belot and Fafchamps (2015). The authors design a dictator-style experiment in which subjects choose between two payoff allocations among themselves and three others. By varying the framing of the game either as a joint allocation decision or a market-like partner selection decision, they find less evidence of altruism—but more evidence of rivalry—in the partner selection frame than in the joint allocation frame. This evidence provides some support to the idea that norms vary across domains and framing affects the choice of norms that people use when deciding what action to take.

How do these observations apply to the hierarchical domain? If workers were truly indifferent to each other's payoffs, we would expect piece-rate wage employment to dominate in many if not most activities, based on observable effort. This is, however, not what is observed. Recent experimental evidence from India shows that performance-based pay and the associated inequality in material outcomes tends to disincentivize low-productivity workers without providing additional incentives for high-productivity ones (Breza et al. 2016). It is also possible to interpret one of the key findings of Bandiera et al. (1999) in the same light: when working side by side in a piece-rate working environment, friends change their relative productivity so as to reduce the disparity in their material payoff. It therefore appears that incentive pay and its associated inequality in material outcomes has a potentially deleterious effect on job performance, a point captured by the inequality aversion hypothesis of Fehr and Schmidt (1999). Recent evidence also suggests that countries differ in the extent of the variation in performance pay that they deem acceptable—see Ockenfels et al. (2010) for a comparison of US and German compensation schemes in the same multinational corporations (see also Bolton and Ockenfels 2000). In practice, hierarchies often promote cooperation instead of competition between workers, especially when the performance of the team depends critically on cooperation, such as in military units, for instance. As a result of the combination of a need to foster cooperation to sustain teamwork, and a resistance to performance pay and the ensuing wage inequality, many hierarchies opt for a relatively flat pay schedule either unconditional on performance or with performance rewards that are far from commensurate with productivity differences between workers. An illustration of this principle is found in Platteau and Nugent (1992), who show that, in small-scale fishing teams where teamwork is a key factor of success, income disparities are not tolerated and labor income is apportioned equally among all coworkers.

11.4.2. Mate Selection, Markets, and Teams

Experimental evidence suggests that for many moderately complicated games, people make systematic mistakes relative to predictions from standard economic models (e.g., Kahneman 2011). Yet there is one moderately complicated game in which they do surprisingly well, even with little or no prior experience—namely, convergence to a single market price for a homogeneous good with different valuations across players. These games were first played by Vernon Smith in the 1950s as part of his teaching of economics to US undergrads. He found that, with very little guidance or framing, students were able to quickly and consistently converge to the competitive supply-equals-demand equilibrium price, and did achieve very high efficiency levels. These findings were subsequently confirmed in a more formal experimental setting (Smith 1962). More recently (e.g., Bulte et al. 2012) they have been shown to hold even in isolated parts of Africa with very little experience of markets. What this suggests is that the human mind finds competitive markets intuitively simple and comes equipped with robust heuristics on how to behave in such a setting. What is unclear from the Smith game is what these heuristics are.

One possible source of insights is the hunting and gathering activities that our ancestors undertook for many generations: within the confines of the family, we share the food we have; but outside that domain, we compete for food. To illustrate this idea with a contemporary example, imagine the following situation. I am at a reception and one pie is left on the buffet. Should I take it, knowing that I have already had plenty of other food, or should I leave it for someone else who hasn't had any of that pie? Many of us would leave the last pie. Now imagine that I am in line at the pastry shop. When my turn comes there is only one pie left. Should I take it, knowing that I have already bought plenty of other food, or should I leave that last pie for someone else? Most of us would simply bless our luck and purchase the pie. The effect of my choice on others is very similar, but in a market frame I am less likely to internalize the negative externality I impose on others by making a particular selection. The social norms people apply therefore seem to depend on the domain in which they operate.

This is an issue I have tried to tackle in my own experimental work. In an already cited dictator-style experiment with Belot (e.g., Belot and Fafchamps 2015), we asked subjects to choose between two payoff allocations involving four players. In one treatment the choice is presented as a choice between two allocation pies. In another treatment, it is presented as selecting a partner among two possible choices. Subjects are also told that if they select one of the available partners, the other two remaining subjects in the group will be automatically matched together. Payoff distributions under the two choices are shown in pie form and are identical to those shown in the first treatment. We also introduce a third treatment in which the link between selecting a partner and affecting others' payoff is less obvious.

We know that in settings similar to the first treatment, subjects often display a preference for equitable distribution of material payoffs (e.g., Fehr and Schmidt 1999; Okada and Riedl 2005; Cooper and Kagel 2013). We find similar evidence. But we observe a significant reduction in altruistic choices in the partner selection treatments—and even an increase in rival choices in treatment 3. This suggests that when individuals select a partner, as they would in a market or a mate selection contest, they act more selfishly or competitively than when they select an allocation, as they would in a household or team environment. The norms that people instinctively apply thus vary depending on whether the frame is reminiscent of the self-provision domain, where sharing norms apply, or of the market domain, where self-regarding behavior is acceptable.

Why are people more competitive and selfish when they select a partner? The hypothesis I propose is that it resembles mate selection, an activity that humans and their primate ancestors have probably been practicing for millions of years. In a marriage market, the handsomest groom does not leave the handsomest bride for his ugly sibling, on the principle that his sibling deserves to be compensated for the bad luck of being ugly.

Competition for partners in the marketplace (e.g., for jobs, employees, suppliers, clients) is similar to competition for mates. Are people good at competing for mates? Comola and Fafchamps (2015) construct an experiment in which people compete for partners in a semi-organized fashion. The game involves many stages and the strategy set is complex—e.g., it is not possible, even for a trained economist, to work out the stable equilibrium of the game without resorting to a computer. Yet, 86% of the games converge to a stable equilibrium, and overall 93% of the formed links belong to one. This shows that subjects are naturally gifted at competing for mates in a market-like competitive setting. Hence outcomes from this decentralized, multi-stage game are very close to those predicted by Becker in the context of marriage markets and generalized as strong pairwise stability in network games. The main source of departure from stable pairings is due to a "once bitten twice shy" effect: we refuse to pair with mates who have been disloyal to us, even if this reduces our payoff.

Rivalry may also affect willingness to form a Pareto-improving team. Once a team is formed, many opportunities arise for redistributive pressures—team members may pressure others to redistribute some of their endowment. Fafchamps and Hill (2015) conduct an experiment in which subjects are invited to form a Pareto-improving team. Once the team is formed, however, subjects can either steal from others (treatment 1), destroy others' payoffs (treatment 2), or give to others (treatment 3). The experiment is conducted in three locations (UK, Kenya, and Uganda) using the same design and protocol. We find that stealing is fairly common in all three populations. Team formation is hindered when the destruction of endowment is feasible (treatment 2), an action that can only be explained by some form of envy or rivalry. Although African participants in the experiment act on average in a more reliable manner than UK subjects, they are much less likely to join a team in treatment 2, suggesting that rivalry is a hindrance to team formation. Kebede and Zizzo (2015) similarly report sizeable destruction of others' payoff in a sample of poor Ethiopian farmers.

11.4.3. Risk Avoidance Behavior

Let us now go back to our main topic of interest, the deterrence of opportunistic breach, which is essential for market exchange to flourish. Deterrence is about convincing people to take actions that reduce the risk that they will breach the contract. It follows that risk attitudes should affect the effectiveness of deterrence. This has long been noted in the literature on crime deterrence. Certain forms of criminality respond to material incentives—e.g., planned types of crime such as burglaries or drug trade. Other forms of criminality arise out of irrational impulses—e.g., jealousy, envy. These are less sensitive to material deterrents.

Based on this analogy, incentive mechanisms based on reason and predictable consequences may be inoperative to deter behavior based on irrational impulses, such as addiction, or on the desire to assist a close relative in need. To the extent that deterrence is effective, however, it will depend on risk preferences. There is much experimental evidence on choices among lotteries. The literature has documented widespread risk aversion, loss aversion, and probability weighting—a set of features summarized under the banner of prospect theory (e.g., Kahneman and Tversky 1979; Tversky and Kahneman 1992; Rabin 2000; Andersen et al. 2008; Andreoni and Sprenger 2011). People also seem to anchor their behavior on reference points (e.g., Camerer et al. 1997; Koszegi and Rabin 2006, 2007) and to suffer from various biases (e.g., Rabin and Thaler 2001; Croson and Sundali 2005; Kahneman 2011). This is well known and need not be discussed in detail here. But risk also generates feelings of fear and apprehension, and these emotions need not lead to rational decisions (e.g., Loewenstein et al. 2001).

More relevant to our purpose are situations in which people seem to misjudge or weight probabilities based on process. One issue of interest is when people underestimate the risk they incur when they undertake an action themselves (e.g., driving) but overestimate the risk they incur when someone else takes an action (e.g., taking a commercial flight). In this case, having individual control over the risk factor seems to affect how acceptable risk is (e.g., Kahneman 2011). This observation applies for instance to the safety of commercially produced food—which corresponds to situations in which consumers incur risk as a result of the actions of others. In these cases, a food scare often results in costly regulation to protect consumers from the risk re-occurring. Often the risk is quite small—and in many cases undocumented by hard evidence, i.e., it could be quite remote. Yet, by supporting the introduction of costly regulation, consumers display a high willingness to pay to reduce a risk that is beyond their control, but may in fact be extremely small relative to the cost (e.g., Kahneman and Ritov 1994).

This is particularly ironic when the food scare or safety scare arises from a consumer taking improper care to ensure their safety. One example of this situation is when a well-known fast-food chain decided to stop selling hot coffee after a consumer burned herself buying one at a drive-through. Other examples include situations when a product is pulled from the market (e.g., unpasteurized apple juice) because a parent fed this product to an infant who then got ill and died. I am not arguing that food safety or consumer safety is irrelevant, only that the total cost imposed on society by the type of health and safety regulation that arises from health scares implies a level of risk aversion that far exceeds the aversion to risk that consumers display in their own everyday actions—e.g., by smoking, drinking too much alcohol or sugary beverages, not exercising enough, having unprotected sex, driving while distracted or intoxicated, engaging in a dangerous sport or hobby, etc.

I have argued that humans have a tendency to overestimate the risk imposed on them by others but to underestimate the risk they represent for themselves. One striking manifestation of this tendency is demand for protection. People often take actions that induce a perception of risk reduction even though logic and evidence tell them it offers little if any protection and may even heighten risk. For instance, some people carry a loaded gun as protection against terrorists. Yet there is little evidence that an average person can repel a terrorist attack because they carry a firearm: most of the time terrorists catch us off guard. The same holds for most criminal attacks. The protection people seek from a loaded weapon thus seems purely symbolic, as if based on magic thinking of the kind nurtured by rumors and pseudo-science circulated on the Internet. The risk, however, is well documented. Most people who die as the result of a homicide are killed in the heat of an argument with a spouse, friend, or relative. Proximity to a weapon increases the likelihood that a brawl turns into homicide. Suicide attempts are also more likely to succeed with a firearm. Keeping a loaded gun is also a significant source of risk to self and loved ones, as a number of recent accidents in the United States have demonstrated. People thus appear to weight the risk caused by others differently from the risk they impose on themselves.

This observation has important bearing on contracting. The borrower—or anyone who incurs a delayed contractual obligation—underestimates the risk arising from his own behavior, while the lender overestimates the risk imposed on him by the borrower. Hence the lender seeks more protection than the borrower finds necessary. One common illustration of this phenomenon is entrepreneurial finance. Aspiring entrepreneurs often are optimistic about their chance of success, even when objective statistics tell them otherwise (e.g., Kahneman 2011). It is then the job of professional lenders to identify those entrepreneurs for whom the objective chance of success exceeds the risk of non-payment (e.g., Lang and Nakamura 1990). Evidence of this can be found in a recent experiment by Augsburg et al. (2015). The authors convinced a lender to offer loans to small entrepreneurs who scored slightly below the lending cutoff. They find that, on average, the lender lost money on those borrowers, while it made a small positive profit on applicants rated above the cutoff.

Optimism about one's own capabilities—and pessimism about others'—is further compounded by regret aversion (e.g., Loomes and Sugden 1982; Gill and Prowse 2012). Making people aware of some future risk often induces them to take costly protective action because they fear that, in the future, they will regret not having taken the action. For instance, when purchasing a small appliance, customers are often induced to purchase an expensive extended warranty. They project themselves into the future and seek to avoid that nagging "told you so!" feeling that may haunt them, should the appliance fail. Regret aversion seems related to the kind of magical thinking we alluded to earlier: mentioning the possibility of a future risk seems to temporarily increase demand for protection against that risk, as if the mere mention of the risk made it more likely—i.e., people behave as if they are superstitious. Having heightened risk by mentioning it, people feel compelled to increase protection because if the risk does materialize, they will feel more responsible: they were given a chance to protect themselves, they chose not to, and they only have themselves to blame for their misfortune.

What is interesting here is that culture and context can affect the kind of risks that people feel liable for, i.e., the risks that they expect to feel responsible for in the future. For instance, for a long time, smokers were told that smoking was a bad habit, but objective evidence of a health risk was missing. A smoker who became ill would have been treated with compassion by all. Now that the health risk associated with smoking has been widely publicized, a smoker is more likely to be held responsible for her ill fortune—i.e., someone is more likely to say "I told you so, it is your fault, etc." To illustrate how perceptions can change, we now live at a time when having a high carb/high sugar diet is beginning to be regarded as a self-imposed health risk. Obesity is seen as lack of discipline, and obese people have to fight stigma and discrimination based on being perceived as responsible for their weight. If an overweight or obese person suffers a heart attack, the individual is much more likely to be on the receiving end of "told-you-so" comments.

What these examples illustrate is that culture and context determine the risk factors that people are regarded as liable for—and for which regret aversion is likely to be strongest. If people are not held responsible for building a house on a friable cliff or on a flood plain, when disaster strikes they will be treated with sympathy by others and regret will be minimized. On the other hand, if they are regarded as partly responsible for their misfortune, sympathy will be reduced and regret heightened—thereby inducing different behavior ex ante. Because of regret aversion and the "told you so" syndrome, willingness to pay for avoiding risk depends on social norms regarding personal responsibility. Of course, legal changes in personal liability also create a material reason for wanting to insure. But even when insurance coverage is guaranteed—as in the case of cancer or heart failure risk in modern welfare states—behavior may still be affected by regret, which is an emotion grounded in morality.

These considerations loom large on the deterrence of contractual breach. People feel responsible only for those actions that, at a particular point in time, others consider they are liable for. Contract law exonerates parties of their contractual obligation in case of force majeure or Act of God. Natural calamities are typically given as examples of Acts of God that exonerate contractual responsibility. Yet we now know that hurricanes, floods, and earthquakes occur with some regularity, and do so more frequently in some places than others. Susceptibility to these natural events can be reduced in various ways—either by reducing the risk directly (e.g., construction standards, avoiding certain locations or routes) or by securing financial protection (e.g., precautionary saving, insurance). Hence, what is regarded as an Act of God may vary with context and circumstance. Failing to report for work because of a sick child may be acceptable in one culture but not in another. Similarly, delaying payment to suppliers because the entrepreneur has a family emergency may be normal in one culture but not in another. In some economies, a buyer who fails to resell a product would not feel exonerated from the obligation to pay suppliers; in others, he would.

What the above discussion suggests is that people seem to have a moral view of risk. They expect to be held responsible for outcomes linked to actions that they see as morally reprehensible. For instance, an entrepreneur may feel accountable if his business goes down after insulting a customer. Taking responsibility for a risk factor makes people want to avoid it. In contrast, people often do not consider themselves as responsible for outcomes that cannot be linked to a morally reprehensible action on their part. For instance, an entrepreneur who borrows from the business to pay his son's hospital bill may feel entitled to delay payment to suppliers, and fail to accept responsibility for subsequent negative consequences on suppliers' credit and business performance.

Economists often share the view that if only contracts could be made complete, information and enforcement problems would disappear. The general sentiment is that complete contracts are impossible because they would be too costly to stipulate and negotiate. Transactions costs are no longer the only possible explanation for incomplete contracts when people regard some risks as exonerating ex post but not ex ante. In the above example, the entrepreneur felt entitled to delay payment because his son happened to have broken a leg. But if the entrepreneur had been obliged by his suppliers to lay out all possible future contingencies, he would no longer be able to pretend that his son's broken leg was an unanticipated event and, as such, an exonerating circumstance. This explains why many legal codes have a concept of force majeure or Act of God, and empower a third party (e.g., a judge or arbiter) to adjudicate ex post whether a particular circumstance was exonerating or not.

A corollary of the above is that the way formal and informal institutions deal with excusable default affects their legitimacy in the eyes of the public. If formal legal institutions do not allow workers to skip work to look after a sick child in a country where healthcare is problematic, these institutions will be held in contempt—and the employers using the law to fire absent workers will be regarded as illegitimate and unworthy of workers' loyalty. Institutions that are illegitimate are not respected and their deterrence effect is lower. Since deterrence is lower, violations are more common, and the likelihood of being caught or punished falls either because the institution's monitoring and punishment capability is overwhelmed, or because law enforcers themselves are reluctant to enforce illegitimate laws (e.g., Kahan 2000; Aldashev et al. 2012a). Furthermore, those who are caught do not feel guilt or shame for their action and are not subject to social pressure.

11.4.4. Preference over Process

Experimental economics has begun to document the fact that human subjects have preferences not just over final outcomes, but also over the process by which final outcomes are reached (e.g., Charness and Rabin 2002). To illustrate, consider the dictator game.

In this game, individual i is endowed with an amount m and asked to share m between another subject i and himself. Many subjects share m equally, others give j somewhat less than half of m. Compare this situation to the reverse dictator game. In this game, it is j who is endowed with m and i who is asked to share m between j and himself. In this case, many subjects are reluctant to take much from j. Yet, from an economist's perspective, the two games should yield the same outcome if subjects only care about material payoffs. The fact that they do not indicates preference over process. Many subjects, for instance, may regard the person endowed with m as being entitled to it and thus may not regard redistributing from j's entitlement as equivalent to redistributing from their own—i.e., j may want to redistribute some of his endowment to i, but that's for j to decide, not i.

The role of morality is to define which processes are acceptable and which are not. For instance, if I give you half my pen, it is okay for you to have it. If I do not give it to you and you take it from me, it is not okay for you to have it—it is called theft. Moral norms determine which processes for generating outcomes are acceptable or fair, and which are not.

Economic reasoning implicitly assumes that the contractual process is morally acceptable because it rests on the mutual agreement of the two parties: if any of them does not find the contract beneficial, he or she can abstain from contracting. As a result, each contract taken in isolation must be Pareto-improving for the parties. Contractual breach, on the other hand, is by definition unilateral and, typically, causes harm to the other party: had the other party known that the contract would be breached, she may not have agreed to it. In other words, breach may undo the Pareto-improving character of the transaction. For this reason it is a priori undesirable.

This reasoning, however, is not shared by everyone. Many people find the contracts they enter in to be unfair and morally reprehensible: the wage they receive may be too low—relative to the wage of others, to their productivity, or to the employer's income; the price they pay may be unfair—relative to their ability to pay or relative to their need of the good or service. Similarly, the distribution of income and wealth that results from the contracts people engage in may be seen as unfair (e.g., Kahneman et al. 1986; Greif and Tadelis 2010). As discussed in section 11.3, markets are not suitable mechanisms to redistribute from the rich to the poor—simply because they rest on voluntary exchange, and the rich typically do not voluntarily want to dispossess themselves of all their wealth. Markets also impose hard budget constraints on people who often are poor and faced with a lot of risk. It follows that markets often lack legitimacy, particularly in countries where self-provision still is an important allocation mechanism and where many people are imbued by gift exchange norms of behavior.

Contracts also have other features that may come into opposition with moral principles (e.g., Fehr and Falk 2002). To explain this point, it is useful to divide moral principles into categories. Many moral precepts are absolute. For instance, "Thou shall not steal" is not conditional on others' behavior—i.e., it does not say "Thou shall not steal from those who are kind to you." Norms can also be conditional on others' behavior. An example of this is "An eye for an eye." This is conditional reciprocity: I am nice to you as long as you are nice to me (e.g., Axelrod 1984). Most incentive systems that economists study are of this kind: wage is paid after completion of the task; the good is delivered after payment is made; warranty is paid if the good is defective. There is some experimental evidence that people condition their willingness to cooperate on what they expect others to do (e.g., Caria and Fafchamps 2014). Conditional reciprocity is typically seen as legitimate by lawyers and economists, but not necessarily so by the general public. People may feel entitled to their wage even if they did not complete the task, if completion was impeded by an event they deem exonerating. They may feel they deserve the good before (or without) payment because they need the good more than the seller needs the money. They may refuse to compensate the buyer for defective supplies if doing so would force them out of a job. People may also reject contracts ex post because the other party exploited their economic or psychological weakness i.e., they may refuse to pay a gambling debt. In all these cases, conditionality is objected to by an absolute moral principle, something along the lines of "Thou shall not hit a man when he is down"—which can be used by the poor to exonerate themselves from contractual obligations that turn out to be too onerous. This creates a link between exoneration from contractual obligations by the poor and the redistributive pressures and sharing norms that we discussed earlier.

Moral principles can also be conditional on type. For instance, norms may dictate that men and women should be treated differently, or that the old should be treated with more respect than the young, or that certain castes or ethnic groups deserve less consideration. Discrimination of this kind is often seen as illegitimate by economists and lawyers, but not necessarily so by the general public. Here too the observations made in section 11.3 help make sense of these realities. In the self-provision domain, allocation to task often follows social roles that are assigned on the basis of gender, age, and other arbitrary social groupings such as ethnicity and caste. In contrast, behavioral norms in a gift economy are absolute, e.g., women cook meals and men work fields. Concerns for reciprocation are present and important, but they are not linked to any particular transaction. Reciprocation is about keeping one's role in the order of things. Norms dictate what contribution each individual is expected to make to the group. Continued membership to the group depends on continued contribution—in that sense it is conditional. But conditionality is not attached to any particular transaction or exchange. In this mental accounting framework, someone may feel entitled to continued support from the group—e.g., to receive a wage—if she has contributed to the group—e.g., by looking after a sick neighbor. This is so even if the neighbor and the employer are two completely different people.

Breach deterrence, being a punishment of a specific action, is conditional on behavior. The economic approach to breach deterrence is to punish breach if it is not excusable (e.g., Hart and Honore 1985). Like all incentive systems, it is an application of conditional reciprocity. Different societies may differ in what types of conditional reciprocity they regard as acceptable (e.g., Fehr and Goette 2007; Fehr et al. 2009; Davies and Fafchamps 2016; Della Vigna et al. 2016). Furthermore, many people do not think of contracts in terms of incentives or conditional reciprocity. For them, a contract creates an absolute moral obligation that has to be respected. In other words, the respect of the contract is an absolute imperative, like the respect of a promise. Breach of contract is the non-respect of a promise and, as such, may trigger moral outrage and result in irrational violence—e.g., insults, blows, etc. The end result of this violence is the same: it serves a deterrence role. But the emotional reaction triggered by breach, and the associated violence, are not seen as planned or anticipated; they are seen as a natural human reaction to having been wronged.

People may fear the violence brought about by outrage triggered by breach of contract, and this may deter opportunistic breach. But should the violence be planned—and advertised as such—it would probably be viewed in a very different light. Imagine that a supplier tells you: "If you do not pay, I will get angry, and I will kill you." This is a threat and will be resented as such. But if it is credible, it will probably have a deterrence effect. The important point, however, is that, should the supplier carry out his threat, it would constitute premeditated murder—and be punished much more harshly than uncontrollable and unplanned violence erupting after the fact, which would probably qualify as manslaughter. What this example illustrates is that, from a moral and even legal point of view, premeditated harm is regarded more negatively, especially if it is materialized by threats, even if it is triggered by a particular action of the victim. To illustrate, imagine a husband who tells his wife, "If I find you again with the neighbor, I will kill you." Clearly the threat is issued to deter behavior, but it would still constitute premeditated murder.

What these examples demonstrate is that premeditated punishment is seen as less morally acceptable than punishment triggered by anger and outrage. This is problematic for optimal deterrence because, in order for a punishment to have a deterrence effect, it must be predictable with high certainty. Yet, announcing up front exactly what punishment will be imposed may weaken the moral legitimacy of the punishment—and thus make it less credible. It follows that it may be optimal for parties to keep the form of punishment unspecified, keeping all their options open in ex post negotiations, including various types of posturing, such as getting angry, or faking it.

By now, it should have become clear that moral judgment, and the many emotions associated with it, need not follow logic (e.g., Sunstein et al. 2002; Sunstein 2005). This point has been demonstrated most clearly by the trolley experiment. In this experiment, the subject is asked to choose between two possible outcomes: the death of four people, or the death of just one. Given this choice, nearly everyone prefers the latter. The same choice is then presented using the following parable. Imagine that a runaway trolley threatens to kill four people, but you can divert it so that it will kill only one. Do you want to activate the switch that will divert the trolley? Most people choose to do nothing. The accepted interpretation—confirmed by other experiments (e.g., Greene 2010, 2012)—is that people do not want to have anything to do with the death of a person. Some have gone as far as claiming that the rules of morality are more akin to those of syntax than those of logic—and that they involve similar or neighboring regions of the brain (e.g., Mikhail 2011). Belot and Fafchamps (2015) find experimental results that are consistent with this interpretation, although much more work is necessary before coming to a definitive conclusion. Di Tella et al. (2015) find evidence suggesting that people conveniently change their beliefs of others' altruism to justify their own antagonism (see also Null 2012).

What is clear, however, is that people have preferences over process: they do not care only about material outcomes, they also care about the process by which outcomes are achieved. Economic reasoning compares outcomes. Welfare analysis, for instance, has as a starting point individual utility defined over outcomes. The nature of the process by which these outcomes are achieved is deemed irrelevant—and attempts to debate policies on the basis of values or principles are often viewed by economists as pretense, that is, as a way of hiding one's "true" motivations, which can only be about material outcomes.

Put differently, many economists see efforts to discuss policies on the basis of anything other than final material outcomes as little more than a ploy to divert attention from true motives and a way to fool the public. The truth is that these efforts are made because the public also cares about values and principles, and these values and principles color the way it sees the process by which a particular policy outcome is achieved.

These observations apply to markets as well. Since markets and incentives are the process by which efficient outcomes are reached, they are implicitly seen as legitimate by economists. Efficiency, of course, is a judgment based solely on material outcomes. To those who also care about process, efficiency is not the sole consideration. To them, the market process need not be seen as legitimate, even when exchange is voluntary. There are many examples of this: the market for sexual favors, illegal drugs, or gambling; the sale of human organs; indenture contracts and the use of bonded labor as collateral; children and women working in coal mines; dangerous and unhealthy wage work; or women working outside of the home. In all these examples, market exchange is or has been legal in some place and time—with frequent legal reversals over time, and exceptions within countries for certain markets or regions. For instance, many forms of dangerous employment are banned and indenture contracts are illegal in many developed economies, but exceptions are made for the military. The point here is that each of these examples triggers strong emotions in most people and provide occasions for endless debate. This alone implies that most people care about process, and market exchange is not always seen as a legitimate process to determine certain outcomes.

Preferences over process also apply to particular practices or incentive structures. Anderson and Simester (2010), for instance, show that consumers are antagonized by illegitimate price changes.

11.4.5. Individualism and Demand for Agency

Economists take it as a starting point that decisions are made by individuals, which justifies using individual utility as the yardstick by which policies and institutions are judged (e.g., Luce 1959, 2010). Perhaps the clearest illustration of this approach is in the literature on intra-household allocation. The household is seen and modeled as a bargaining nexus in which different individuals seek to promote their own utility—possibly augmented to include altruistic or patronizing motives (e.g., Becker 1981). The maintained assumption is that individuals demand agency in order to be able to pursue their own choices. This, for economists, typically means accessing an independent source of income and controlling household expenditures.

This approach to intra-household allocation is in sync with the empowerment agenda, with which it shares an individualistic approach to human welfare and a focus on material outcomes. The two nonetheless differ on the role of process. Economists typically view intra-household allocation from the dual vantage point of efficiency and equity in the allocation of material consumption (e.g., Becker 1973, 1981). Non-economists working on these issues are more interested in the process by which household decisions are made, hence the focus on empowerment, namely: the ability of women to resist decisions imposed upon them by their husband or society at large; and their ability to make their own choices. The first idea refers to the concept of power as defined by Dahl (1957), that is, as the capability that someone has to impose her own choice on someone else. Empowerment is first about changing that for women. The second idea relates to the concept of agency as discussed by Sen, that is, someone's ability to make her own choices (e.g., Afzal et al. 2016).

Behind the apparent simplicity of these concepts lurks an extremely intricate set of issues, which I do not have time to cover in any detail. To illustrate, one distinction that comes to the fore is the distinction between different types of agency: e.g., executive or consultative; complete or partial; positive or negative (veto). Agency is also affected by the process by which collective decisions are taken: is a vote taken; what kind of voting rule is applied; what kind of majority is required for a decision to be accepted; for a decision to be rescinded; what recourse is available for those whose vested interests are threatened. These issues have been the object of much study among economists interested in industrial organizations and mechanism design, but also among political scientists interested in democracy and political processes in general. The same issues arise in many domains of legal study, such as constitutional law, corporate law, and patrimonial law, as well as laws and regulations regarding court proceedings. The bottom line is that there already exists a considerable body of scholarship on issues of process, including a lot of careful thought given to identifying procedural rules that yield equitable and efficient outcomes. Those interested in venturing into this area of inquiry are well advised to avail themselves of the existing literature.

Like economists, the empowerment literature assumes that all individuals demand agency. Since agency is seen as a right, this assumption is never tested or challenged. This has several practical implications. First, it means that people who do not exercise agency are probably oppressed, in the sense that their desire to express agency must be repressed by force or social pressure, otherwise they would naturally express their desire for agency. If this is true, removing oppression should automatically result in a situation in which all individuals exert agency. If this fails to happen, an alternative explanation has to be found, that is, a more insidious form of oppression must be present that does not rely on explicit deterrence. One possibility is that the oppressed have internalized the norms and preferences of their oppressors, i.e., they have been indoctrinated. In this case, granting them agency will not change the nature of the choices that are made: the formally oppressed have internalized that the choices made for them by society are the correct ones. Another possibility is that they lack aspirations or self-respect, and hence either do not wish to exert agency over certain (or all) choices, or they do not believe that certain choices are relevant for them (e.g., Lopes and Oden 1999; Genicot and Ray 2010). In the words of Karl Marx, they have been alienated.

While freedom from oppression fits well with economists' conviction that freedom of exchange leads to mutually beneficial trade and thus higher efficiency, concepts of indoctrination and alienation are hard to reconcile with that of a stable utility function. If individual preferences are malleable, this threatens to undermine the very foundations of welfare analysis, which is the cornerstone of much of economics. Furthermore, it opens up an alternative road into policy, namely, interventions to mold people's preferences so as to match a higher philosophical or moral order. Many development interventions conducted by NGOs are of this nature: they aim to "educate" and "raise awareness" rather than offering people new options for increasing their material welfare.

These interventions, however, remain predicated on the idea that individuals have preferences and are keen to make individual choices based on these preferences. The alternative is decision by consensus. The need for consensus would naturally arise if individuals do not believe they can reach an optimal decision alone. They need the advice of others to make a choice, and thus refrain from making an individual choice. The group has to be involved in their decision-making. This logic can apply within households, or within larger groups such as a kin group, tribe, or religious community.

When collective decision-making is the norm, individual deviations may trigger disapproval, ridicule, or ostracism. As a result, individuals may refrain from making unusual decisions, such as adopting a new crop or consumer product, without first seeking others' approval (e.g., Young and Burke 2001; Zafar 2011). The need for social approval seems to be present in many human endeavors and has been extensively studied in the economic literature on peer effects. Not all peer effects relate to conformism, imitation, or mimicry—some are about information transmission or network externalities. But many aspects of human behavior studied in the peer effect literature are implicitly or explicitly about social reinforcement—e.g., smoking, petty crime, sexual activity, contraception usage, technology adoption, voting, just to name a few (e.g., Kawaguchi 2004; Lundborg 2006; Powell et al. 2005).

Collective decision-making has several advantages: it pools information and insights from multiple individuals; it economizes on individual decision-making—people only have to copy others; it protects less able individuals from making poor decisions; and it provides side benefits such as group identity and a sense of moral vindication of my actions by others. It also has numerous drawbacks: it is complicated to set in motion and thus is slow to respond to new opportunities; it stifles the initiative of creative members of the group; and it often subjects individuals to sustained and overwhelming social pressure (e.g., Hoff and Sen 2006). For these reasons, it is best suited for societies facing a stable environment. It is ill adapted to the market domain and, as a result, tends to become dysfunctional following the onset of the entrepreneurship revolution, that is, the replacement of self-provision by market provision that arises with urbanization. But it may survive in rural areas, and it may even continue to dominate self-provision long after the introduction of market specialization (e.g., Goldstein and Udry 2008; Goldberg 2010). It also may cement group identity among wage workers in large mines or factories, or among masters and apprentices in guilds. The self-help groups promoted in many developing countries are distant contemporary manifestations of the same idea (e.g., Fafchamps and La Ferrara 2012).

An additional upside of replacing individual agency with collective decision-making is collective responsibility: people are not alone facing disapproval for their actions, others share the responsibility with them. By extension, they also incur punishment together (e.g., Greif 2002; Greif and Tabellini 2010, 2012). There are many remaining examples of collective responsibility in contemporary institutions. Arguably the most common is the community regime, according to which the adult members of a household are collectively liable for all the debts incurred by their members. This means that a husband is liable for his wife's debts, and vice versa. Collective responsibility is ultimately predicated on the idea that spouses decide in common. They may not always keep each other informed of their everyday decisions, but they are presumed to have agreed on a common course of action. The alternative is for spouses to keep separate finances, a practice that is found in several parts of Africa practicing hoe agriculture (e.g., coastal West Africa, Cameroon, Congo, etc.). But it is rare in human societies that have historically practiced plow agriculture (e.g., Alesina et al. 2013). Other examples include business partners, who are collectively liable for all the debts of the enterprise. Citizens of a country are similarly collectively liable for all external debts of the country.

Whenever collective responsibility is the rule, individual punishment based on a mutually agreed contract can be seen as illegitimate. The reason is that individuals are not allowed to engage the collective responsibility of the group without getting the group's approval. The logic of this approach is easily illustrated with a contemporary example involving a teenager. Imagine a 15-year-old buys an expensive new car. Since the child is a minor, parents are automatically liable for the contract. Given the impressionable nature of teenagers, society does not fully trust them with making financial decisions of this magnitude. This is why contracts signed by teenagers are regarded as legally invalid unless approved by the parents. This prevents car dealers (and others) from conning teenagers into incurring large contractual obligations.

This collective responsibility logic is often applied to transactions incurred by adult dependents of the household who are regarded as subordinate—i.e., they are assimilated to a minor. In many developing countries today—as in currently developed countries a couple of centuries ago—married women (and other adult dependents) have the same status as a teenager today: they are not allowed to enter into a contract without the approval of the household head (e.g., Afzal et al. 2016). This means that a contract agreed upon by someone's wife can be challenged ex post by her husband. In other words, anyone who contracts with a married woman is taking the risk that the contract will be subsequently challenged. Needless to say, this makes it difficult for a woman to, say, borrow from the bank. The success of microfinance organizations targeting women in South Asia and, increasingly, in Africa may be closely linked to this reality.

Other collective challenges of individual contracts can often be understood as manifestations of collective responsibility. For example, farmers may collectively rebel if a bank threatens to foreclose on the land belonging to one of them. Members of a group may similarly riot following the expulsion of one of their members by a landlord. Some strikes, e.g., following the firing of a worker, can be seen in a similar light, as an action directed to an individual when the group considers itself collectively responsible for the fired worker.

11.5. DISCUSSION

The objective of this chapter is to offer a broad conceptual framework within which the role of formal market institutions is better understood. The starting point of our approach has been that market transactions are embedded in a social context. This includes not just networks, but also social norms, emotions, and thought processes. From this starting point, we have sought to draw lessons regarding the interface between formal institutions (e.g., laws, courts, contracts) and informal institutions.

11.5.1. Summary

We started with an overview of various breach deterrence mechanisms, many of which are often dubbed informal. We saw that there are many enforcement mechanisms other than courts. We also noted that, although breach deterrence seldom rests on direct enforcement by courts, many laws and formal institutions actually seek to reinforce and improve informal enforcement mechanisms rather than enforcing contracts directly.

Formal and informal breach deterrence thus work in tandem, one reinforcing the other. In the next section, we focused on the content of social norms, and we discussed the relationship between norms and assignment to tasks. I argued that there are three main institutional forms of assignment to task: self-provision, markets, and hierarchical assignment. Each has its domain of application and a different set of social norms.

The process of development induces many changes in the coverage of the three domains. This in turn requires changes in the respective importance of norm types. In particular, the self-provision domain must adapt, although it is not entirely clear to what. One possible direction is to encourage entrepreneurship and foster norms favoring arbitrage and initiative—i.e., the seizing of opportunities. Another possible direction is to prepare individuals for wage employment by encouraging discipline and teamwork and discouraging opportunistic behavior. Since the two directions call for largely antagonistic changes in social norms, confusion across domains during the process of development results in pathologies such as corruption, nepotism, and employer paternalism.

Having set the stage for a study of the interface between formal and informal market institutions, we turned to behavioral considerations, drawing largely on the experimental economics literature but also seeking insights and inspiration from other disciplines. We began with a discussion of the close correspondence between market competition and human rivalry. We also noted the similarity between mate selection and the matching processes taking place in markets. These similarities probably explain why, even with little prior experience, humans are strikingly adept at adopting apparently rational behavior in markets, especially regarding understanding prices and competing for market partners.[3]

We then reviewed the more recent evidence on risk avoidance behavior, noting that people's attitude to risk seem to depend on the nature of the risk. For instance, people are more averse to risk imposed by the behavior of others, but less averse to risk generated by their own behavior. One possible explanation is that they are overly optimistic about their own self-control. Another is that people are more willing to accept unfortunate outcomes when they are their own fault. We also discussed regret aversion, a phenomenon suggesting that people do not like to be blamed—or to blame themselves—for bad outcomes. We call this the "told-you-so" syndrome whereby people seek to avoid the guilt associated with a bad action. In other words, the process by which risk arises seems to matter, not just the nature of the risk itself.

We then turned to conditional norms and morality. We first note that many moral precepts are unconditional, i.e., they do not depend on others' actions. This stands in contrast with contractual incentives that always rest on conditional cooperation. We observed that moral behavior involves many different emotions and cannot be relied on to be rational. There is growing evidence that people care deeply about the process by which outcomes are reached and do so in ways that are related to their moral sense. This can generate situations that are a priori strange from the point of view of optimal deterrence, such as when anger driven by moral outrage at a breach of contract is deemed acceptable, but not pointing out that such anger is likely to arise in the future, should the other party not comply with contractual obligations. This feature makes the negotiation of complete contracts fraught with difficulties because of the emotions the process triggers.

We ended with a discussion of collective responsibility and individual agency. We observed that the empowerment literature, like economics, takes individual agency as a right and assumes that people want agency. This literature nonetheless differs from economics in that it recognizes that preference for agency may be malleable. This position leads to contradictions that we did not seek to dispel. Finally, we discussed the logic behind collective decision-making and its corollary, collective responsibility or liability. We provided examples from different cultural environments to illustrate the nature of the process, and how it can come into conflict with the logic of the market and individual decision-making.

11.5.2. What Lessons Can We Draw from This Overview?

The first lesson is the importance of the family. The first normative layer of human societies is probably the family or kinship group. It corresponds to the domain of self-provision and probably has a long evolutionary history. Altruism among family members is based partly on shared genes and partly on shared norms and identity. Assignment to tasks is regulated by social roles and enforced through—sometimes extreme—peer pressure. Reciprocation is delayed and contingent on continued good standing in the group. Agency and autonomy are limited, and collective responsibility and decision-making are the norm.

The second lesson is the role that natural rivalry plays in the functioning of markets. Competition and rivalry seem to be natural human tendencies. When competing for a homogeneous good, convergence to a single price may be because people do not want to pay more—or receive less—than others. This induces them to search until they are secure that information about the price they paid or received will not subsequently subject them to ridicule. Markets for non-homogeneous goods are arguably much more complex. Yet heuristics derived from competition for mates perform reasonably well in ensuring rapid convergence to a stable matching equilibrium. This suggests that people naturally have strong heuristics on how to compete for trading partners. These two observations probably explain why simple markets develop organically with few formation institutions. However, competition and rivalry also predict opportunistic behavior, including a proclivity toward opportunistic breach of contract—either to get ahead of competitors, or to get ahead of the other party to the contract. This is what creates the need for deterrence.

Much thinking on breach deterrence assumes rational thinking: people abide by contract terms if the cost of the combined punishment they will credibly incur exceeds the benefit from breach. This implies that when people make choices that endanger their ability to complete a contract, they must weigh the risk of punishment with the benefit from deviation. Drawing from a large literature on risk avoidance, we made a number of observations that have important implications for market development. We first noted that punishment need not be regarded as legitimate if default is regarded as excusable. Individuals coming from a self-provision world may have a generous definition of what constitutes excusable default, in part because of the leakage of norms from the self-provision domain into the market domain. This tendency combines with lack of asset to create a culture of impunity: people take risks but do not consider themselves liable for the consequences. In particular they divert resources to serve personal or family needs even though this reduces their chance of completing a contract. This impedes market development and results in inefficient forms of market exchange, such as cash-and-carry, when the ability to obtain deliveries and pay upon receipt of an invoice would provide much needed financing. If this obstacle can be overcome, however, regret avoidance and "told-you-so" heuristics can generate strong contractual discipline. This may explain how business groups with strong market ethics can develop rapidly even in environments characterized by widespread opportunism.

Breach deterrence relies on punishment. How is punishment for breach of contract perceived by humans? For a punishment to be effective, it must be legitimate, and to be legitimate it must correspond to a sense of moral duty. Many moral norms are defined in absolute terms, e.g., "Thou shall not kill" or "Thou shall not steal." Punishment for contractual breach, like all contractual incentives, is conditional on behavior. This does not necessarily come naturally to people. Human beings come equipped with an innate punishment mechanism: moral outrage. This is an emotion triggered by the sense of being wronged. Combined with rivalry, it leads people to punish breach of contract as an emotional response, not necessarily because they understand conditional cooperation at a rational, purposive level. When punishment for breach arises out of an emotional response, punishment may go beyond what is reasonable, and may even go against the victim's self-interest. Yet, to the extent that this emotional response is anticipated—and found legitimate—it can serve as an effective deterrent.

11.5.3. Implications for Formal and Informal Institutions

What implications can we draw from these lessons regarding formal institutions? Here is a tentative list:

1. We should recognize that the family, not the individual, is the building block for thinking about contracts. This means integrating collective responsibility and joint agency into the policy thinking about market institutions.
2. While competition and rivalry ensure convergence to the law of one price and motivate people to search for efficient matches, we nonetheless should seek to curb excessive manifestations of rivalry—not only crime and riots, but also cheating and shirking in contracts. Market efficiency requires fair competition.
3. Formal institutions can help clarify what constitutes excusable default in a particular society at a particular point in time. They can also clarify property rights at a time when societies evolve from joint to individual responsibility and ownership (e.g., Aldashev et al. 2011, 2012a).
4. Contract law should be thought of as a model moral code about conditional cooperation in contracts. It must be simple, and it must follow principles that have a clear moral legitimacy, which means that it must adapt to local preferences about process.
5. Contract law should be combined with rules about proportional retaliation in order to tame the excesses driven by moral outrage. Deterrence is good, but excessive retaliation can be counterproductive if it discourages people from entering into contracts.
6. Other formal institutions, such as schools and universities, can also play an important role in fostering the adoption of social norms that are conducive to market exchange and hierarchical organizations (e.g., Cantoni and Yuchtman 2010).

We also draw some implications for informal institutions:

1. The family has to adapt to new methods of assigning people to task, i.e., through self-employment and wage work.
2. Individuals, kinship groups, and tribes have to curb excessive expressions of rivalry, lest they face punishment from the state (assuming the state is strong enough).
3. People have to progressively accept responsibility for the consequences of their actions in contractual situations. In exchange, the market provides much more individual agency. Negotiating the transition from collective responsibility to individual responsibility is part of the transition to markets.
4. People have to internalize contract law as a new moral code. They must learn to act strategically, that is, to follow norms of conditional reciprocity in market situations. Playing strategic games as a child may help develop familiarity with conditional play.
5. People must learn to control their emotions—anger and moral outrage—when confronted with contract breach. This becomes more necessary once formal and informal institutions supersede emotions as the main breach deterrence mechanism.

This requires a long-lasting, multifaceted learning process. There is a role for parents, schools, and churches to play, in addition to the state and international actors. Communities and groups that learn these rules earlier are at an advantage. This means that a successful transition to a full market economy also requires dealing with competition between groups—e.g., ethnic riots; looting of shops and businesses; expulsion or victimization of business communities. Autocrats and populists the world over have too often found it expedient to divert public frustration against business communities instead of themselves. The cost in terms of market development cannot be underestimated. If these rivalries cannot be abated, e.g., through predictable and fair taxation of business income, communities that are successful in business are unable to sustain themselves over time and fail to serve as role models for the rest of the population. This slows down market development and growth.

NOTES

This chapter was written in preparation for the June 5–6, 2016 Paris Conference on Economic Development and Institutions. Financial support from the DfID-funded EDI project is gratefully acknowledged. An early version was presented at the EDI Namur conference in January 2016. I benefited from comments from Avner Greif, Jean-Philippe Platteau, Samuel Bowles, Dilip Mookherjee, Abigail Barr, Joan Esteban, and Jean-Marie Baland.

1. The commonly made distinction between formal and informal suffices to motivate this chapter—since I argue that it is ultimately a misleading characterization of market institutions. The reader is referred to the Introduction in this book for a more detailed and general classification of institutions by degree of formality.
2. For the sake of the example, I assume away common-law marriage, which creates legal obligations from the simple fact of living together.
3. This apparent rationality is surprising given that human subjects are not that good at working out relatively simple strategic games, such as second price auctions. There is also mounting evidence that less educated individuals who are less familiar with markets and strategic games do less well in laboratory experiments involving strategic games than college students from developing countries.

REFERENCES

Afzal, Uzma, Giovanna d'Adda, Marcel Fafchamps, and Farah Said. 2016. "Gender and Agency within the Household: Experimental Evidence from Pakistan." Stanford University, mimeo.

Aldashev, Gani, Imane Chaara, Jean-Philippe Platteau, and Zaki Wahhaj. 2012a. "Using the Law to Change the Custom." *Journal of Development Economics* 97(2): 182–200.

———. 2012b. "Formal Law as a Magnet to Reform the Custom." *Economic Development and Cultural Change* 60(4): 795–828.

Aldashev, Gani, Jean-Philippe Platteau, and Zaki Wahhaj. 2011. "Legal Reform in the Presence of a Living Custom: An Economic Approach." *Proceedings of the National Academy of Sciences (PNAS)*, 108(Supplement 4): 21320 25, December.

Alesina, Alberto, Paola Giuliano, and Nathan Nunn. 2013. "On the Origins of Gender Roles: Women and the Plough." *Quarterly Journal of Economics* 128(2): 469–530.

Algan, Yann and Pierre Cahuc. 2010. "Inherited Trust and Growth." *American Economic Review* 100(5): 2060–2092.

Andersen, Steffen, Glenn W. Harrison, Morten I. Lau, and E. Elisabet Rutstrom. 2008. "Eliciting Risk and Time Preferences." *Econometrica* 76(3): 583–618.

Anderson, Eric T. and Duncan I. Simester. 2010. "Price Stickiness and Customer Antagonism." *Quarterly Journal of Economics* 125: 729–765.

Andre, Catherine and Jean-Philippe Platteau. 1998. "Land Relations Under Unbearable Stress: Rwanda Caught in the Malthusian Trap." *Journal of Economic Behavior and Organization* 34(1): 1–47.

Andreoni, J. and C. Sprenger. 2011. "Uncertainty Equivalents: Testing the Limits of the Independence Axiom." National Bureau of Economic Research (NBER).

Aoki, Masao. 1984. *The Co-operative Game Theory of the Firm.* Oxford: Clarendon Press.

Arrow, Kenneth, Samuel Bowles, and Steven Durlauf. 2000. *Meritocracy and Economic Inequality*, Princeton, NJ: Princeton University Press.

Augsburg, Britta, Ralph De Haas, Heike Harmgart, and Costas Meghir. 2015. "The Impacts of Microcredit: Evidence from Bosnia and Herzegovina." *American Economic Journal: Applied Economics* 7(1): 183–203, January.

Axelrod, Robert. 1984. *The Evolution of Cooperation.* New York: Basic Books.

Bandiera, Oriana, Iwan Barankay, and Imran Rasul. 1999. "Social Connections and Incentives in the Workplace: Evidence from Personnel Data." *Econometrica* 77(4): 1047–1094.

Barr, Abigail and Danila Serra. 2008. "Corruption and Culture: An Experimental Analysis." CSAE Working Paper Series 2008–23, Centre for the Study of African Economies, University of Oxford.

Becker, Gary S. 1965. "A Theory of the Allocation of Time." *Economic Journal* 75(299): 493–517, September.

———. 1973. "A Theory of Marriage: Part I." *Journal of Political Economy* 81(4): 813–846.

———. 1981. *A Treatise on the Family.* Cambridge, MA: Harvard University Press.

Belot, Michele and Marcel Fafchamps. 2015. "Experimental Evidence on Other-Regarding Preferences in Partnership Formation." CEPR Discussion Paper No. 11017, December.

Bigsten, Arne, Paul Collier, Stefan Dercon, Marcel Fafchamps, Bernard Gauthier, Jan Willem Gunning, Anders Isaksson, Abena Oduro, Remco Oostendorp, Cathy Patillo, Mans Söderbom, Francis Teal, and Albert Zeufack. 2000. "Contract Flexibility and Dispute Resolution in African Manufacturing." *Journal of Development Studies* 34(10): 1–37, April.

Blanchflower, D. G. and A. J. Oswald. 2004. "Wellbeing over Time in Britain and the USA." *Journal of Public Economics* 88(7–8), July.

Bolton, G. E. and A. Ockenfels. 2000. "ERC: A Theory of Equity, Reciprocity, and Competition." *American Economic Review* 90(1): 166–193, March.

Boserup, Ester. 1970. *Women's Role in Economic Development.* London: George Allen and Unwin.

Bowles, S. 1998. "Endogenous Preferences: The Cultural Consequences of Markets and Other Economic Institutions." *Journal of Economic Literature* 36(1): 75–111.

Bowles, Samuel, Herbert Gintis, and Melissa Osborne. 2001. "Incentive-Enhancing Preferences: Personality, Behavior, and Earnings." *American Economic Review* 91(2): 155–158.

Braudel, Fernand. 1986. *Civilization and Capitalism.* New York: Harper and Row.

Breza, Emily, Supreet Kaur, and Yogita Shamdasani. 2016. "The Morale Effects of Pay Inequality." Mimeo.

Bulte, Erwin, Andreas Anastasis Kontoleon, John A. List, Ty Turley, and Maarten Voors. 2012. "When Economics Meets Hierarchy: A Field Experiment on the Workings of the Invisible Hand." Mimeo.

Bursztyn, Leonardo, Bruno Ferman, Stefano Fiorin, Martin Kanz, and Gautam Rao. 2016. "Status Goods: Experimental Evidence from Platinum Credit Cards." Mimeo.

Camerer, C. 2003. *Behavioral Game Theory: Experiments in Strategic Interaction*. Princeton, NJ: Princeton University Press.

Camerer, C. and R. H. Thaler. 1995. "Anomalies: Ultimatums, Dictators, and Manners." *Journal of Economic Perspectives* 9(2): 209–219.

Camerer, Colin, Linda Babcock, George Loewenstein, and Richard Thaler. 1997. "Labor Supply of New York City Cabdrivers: One Day at a Time." *Quarterly Journal of Economics* 112: 407–441.

Cantoni, Davide and Noam Yuchtman. 2010. "Educational Institutions and Economic Development." Paper presented at the ADB Conference in London, August.

Caria, A. Stefano and Marcel Fafchamps. 2014. "Cooperation and Expectations in Networks: Evidence from a Network Public Good Experiment in Rural India." CSAE WP 2014–33.

Charness, G. and M. Rabin. 2002. "Understanding Social Preferences with Simple Tests." *Quarterly Journal of Economics* 117(3): 817–869.

Clark, A., P. Frijters, and M. A. Shields. 2008. "Relative Income, Happiness, and Utility: An Explanation for the Easterlin Paradox and Other Puzzles." *Journal of Economic Literature* 46(1): 95–144.

Clark, A. E. and A. J. Oswald. 1998. "Comparison-Concave Utility and Following Behaviour in Social and Economic Settings." *Journal of Public Economics* 70: 133–155.

Coate, Stephen and Martin Ravallion. 1993. "Reciprocity Without Commitment: Characterization and Performance of Informal Insurance Arrangements." *Journal of Development Economics* 40(1): 1–24.

Comola, Margherita and M. Fafchamps. 2015. "An Experimental Study of Decentralized Link Formation with Competition." NBER WP 21768, November.

Cooper, David J. and John H. Kagel. 2013. "Other-Regarding Preferences: A Selective Survey of Experimental Results." *Handbook of Experimental Economics*, vol. 2, edited by J. H. Kagel and A. E. Roth. Princeton, NJ: Princeton University Press.

Cooter, Robert and Thomas Ulen. 1988. *Law and Economics*. Glenview, IL: Scott, Foresman.

Cox, Donald. 1987. "Motives for Private Income Transfers." *Journal of Political Economy* 95(3): 508–543.

Croson, R. and U. Gneezy. 2009. "Gender Differences in Preferences." *Journal of Economic Literature* 47(2): 1–27.

Croson, R. and J. Sundali. 2005. "The Gambler's Fallacy and the Hot Hand: Empirical Data from Casinos." *Journal of Risk and Uncertainty* 30(3): 195–209.

Curtis, Eaton B. and Mukesh Eswaran. 2003. "The Evolution of Preferences and Competition: A Rationalization of Veblen's Theory of Invidious Comparisons." *Canadian Journal of Economics* 36(4): 832–859.

Dahl, Robert A. 1957. "The Concept of Power." *Behavioral Science* 2(3): 201–215.

Davies, Elwyn and Marcel Fafchamps. 2016. "Competition, Enforcement and Reputation in Labor Markets: An Experimental Study in Ghana." Oxford University. Mimeo.

DellaVigna, Stefano, John A. List, Ulrike Malmendier, and Gautam Rao. 2016. "Estimating Social Preferences and Gift Exchange at Work." Mimeo.

Diener, Ed, Marissa Diener, and Carol Diener. 1995. "Factors Predicting the Subjective Wellbeing of Nations." *Journal of Personality Social Psychology* 69(5): 851–864.

Diener, Ed, Eunkook M. Suh, Richard E. Lucas, and Heidi L. Smith. 1999. "Subjective Wellbeing: Three Decades of Progress." *Psychology Bulletin* 125(2): 276–303.

Di Giorgi, Giacomo, A. Frideriksen, and L. Pistaferri. 2016. "Consumption Networks Effects." Mimeo.

Di Tella, Rafael, John Haisken-De New, and Robert MacCulloch. 2010. "Happiness Adaptation to Income and to Status in an Individual Panel." *Journal of Economic Behavior & Organization* 76(3): 834–852, December.

Di Tella, Rafael, Ricardo Perez-Truglia, Andres Babino, Mariano Sigman. 2015. "Conveniently Upset: Avoiding Altruism by Distorting Beliefs about Others' Altruism." *American Economic Review* 105(11): 3416–3142, November.

Dixit, Avinash K. 2004. *Lawlessness and Economics: Alternative Modes of Governance*. Princeton, NJ: Princeton University Press.

Duesenberry, James. 1949. *Income, Savings and the Theory of Consumer Behavior*. Cambridge, MA: Harvard University Press.

Easterlin, Richard A. 1974. "Does Economic Growth Improve the Human Lot? Some Empirical Evidence." In *Nations and Households in Economic Growth: Essays in Honor of Moses Abramowitz*, edited by Paul A. David and Melvin Reder, 89–125. New York: Academic Press.

———. 1995. "Will Raising the Incomes of All Increase the Happiness Of All?" *Journal of Economic Behavior and Organization* 27(1): 35–48.

————. 2001. "Income and Happiness: Towards a Unified Theory." *Economic Journal* 111: 465–484.

Ensminger, Jean. 1992. *Making a Market: The Institutional Transformation of an African Society*. New York: Cambridge University Press.

Fafchamps, Marcel. 2004. *Market Institutions in Sub-Saharan Africa: Theory and Evidence*. Cambridge, MA: MIT Press.

————. 2010. "Spontaneous Markets, Networks, and Social Capital: Lessons from Africa." In *Institutional Microeconomics of Development*, edited by Timothy Besley and Rajshri Jayaraman. CESifo Seminar Series, Cambridge, MA: MIT Press.

————. 2011. "Development, Social Norms, and Assignment to Task." *Proceedings of the National Academy of Sciences (PNAS)*, 108(Supplement 4): 21308–15, December.

————. 2012. "Development, Agglomeration, and the Organization of Work." *Regional Science and Urban Economics* 42(5): 765–770.

Fafchamps, Marcel and Ruth Hill. 2016. "Redistribution and Group Participation: Comparative Experimental Evidence from Africa and the UK." NBER WP 21127, April 2015.

Fafchamps, Marcel and Eliana La Ferrara. 2012. "Self-Help Groups and Mutual Assistance: Evidence from Kenyan Slums." *Economic Development and Cultural Change* 60(4): 707–734, July.

Fafchamps, Marcel and Bart Minten. 2001. "Property Rights in a Flea Market Economy." *Economic Development and Cultural Change* 49(2): 229–268.

Fafchamps, Marcel and Agnes R. Quisumbing. 2002. "Control and Ownership of Assets Within Rural Ethiopian Households." *Journal of Development Studies* 38(2): 47–82.

————. 2003. "Social Roles, Human Capital, and the Intrahousehold Division of Labor: Evidence from Pakistan." *Oxford Economic Papers* 55(1): 36–80.

————. 2005a. "Assets at Marriage in Rural Ethiopia." *Journal of Development Economics* 77(1): 1–25.

————. 2005b. "Marriage, Bequest, and Assortative Matching in Rural Ethiopia." *Economic Development and Cultural Change* 53(2): 347–380.

————. 2008. "Household Formation and Marriage Market." *Handbook of Development Economics* 4 (chapter 51): 3187–3248. Amsterdam: Elsevier.

Fafchamps, Marcel and Forhad Shilpi. 2003. "The Spatial Division of Labor in Nepal." *Journal of Development Studies* 39(6): 23–66.

————. 2005. "Cities and Specialization: Evidence from South Asia." *Economic Journal* 115(503): 477–504.

————. 2008. "Subjective Welfare, Isolation, and Relative Consumption." *Journal of Development Economics* 86(1): 43–60, April.

Fafchamps, Marcel and Mans Soderbom. 2006. "Wages and Labor Management in African Manufacturing." *Journal of Human Resources* 41(2): 346–379.

Fafchamps, Marcel and Jackline Wahba. 2006. "Child Labor, Urban Proximity, and Household Composition." *Journal of Development Economics* 79(2): 374–397.

Fehr, Ernst and Armin Falk. 2002. "Psychological Foundations of Incentives." *European Economic Review* 46(4–5): 687–724.

Fehr, Ernst and Lorenz Goette. 2007. "Do Workers Work More If Wages Are High?" *American Economic Review* 97: 298–317.

Fehr, Ernst, Lorenz Goette, and Christian Zehnder. 2009. "A Behavioral Account of the Labor Market: The Role of Fairness Concerns." *Annual Review of Economics* 1: 355–384.

Fehr, Ernst and Klaus M. Schmidt. 1999. "A Theory of Fairness, Competition and Cooperation." *Quarterly Journal of Economics* 114(3): 817–868.

————. 2006. "The Economics of Fairness, Reciprocity and Altruism: Experimental Evidence and New Theories." In *Handbook on Gift-Giving, Reciprocity and Altruism*, Vol. 1, edited by S.-C. Kolm, J. Mercier-Ythier, and G. Varet, chap. 8, 615–691. Amsterdam: North-Holland and Elsevier.

Frey, Bruno S. and Alois Stutzer. 2002. "What Can Economists Learn from Happiness Research?" *Journal of Economic Literature* 40: 402–435.

Geertz, Clifford, Hildred Geertz, and Lawrence Rosen. 1979. *Meaning and Order in Moroccan Society*. Cambridge: Cambridge University Press.

Genicot, G. and D. Ray. 2010. "Aspirations and Inequality." Georgetown University and New York University working paper.

Gill, D. and V. Prowse. 2012. "A Structural Analysis of Disappointment Aversion in a Real Effort Competition." *American Economic Review* 102(1): 469–503.

Goldberg, Jessica. 2010. "The Lesser of Two Evils: The Roles of Social Pressure and Impatience in Consumption Decisions." Department of Economics, University of Michigan.

Goldstein, Markus and Christopher Udry. 2008. "The Profits of Power: Land Rights and Agricultural Investment in Ghana." *Journal of Political Economy* 116(6): 981–1022.

Granovetter, Mark. 1985. "Economic Action and Social Structure: The Problem of Embeddedness." *American Journal of Sociology* 91(3): 481–510.

Greene, Joshua. 2010. "Of Trolleys and Cheaters: Automatic and Controlled Influence on Moral Judgment." Video available at http://www.santafe.edu/research/videos/play/?id=a768d1f4–06e5 -4533–8ebe-9ba3d3a5c131.

———. 2012. *For the Greater Good: How the Moral Brain Works and How It Can Work Better.* New York: Penguin Press.

Gregory, C. A. 1982. *Gifts and Commodities.* London and New York: Academic Press.

Greif, Avner. 1993. "Contract Enforceability and Economic Institutions in Early Trade: The Maghribi Traders' Coalition." *American Economic Review* 83(3): 525–548.

———. 1994. "Cultural Beliefs and the Organization of Society: A Historical and Theoretical Reflection on Collectivist and Individualist Societies." *Journal of Political Economy* 102(5): 912–950.

———. 2002. "Institutions and Impersonal Exchange: From Communal to Individual Responsibility." *Journal of Institutional and Theoretical Economics (JITE)* 158, no. 1 (March): 168–204.

Greif, Avner and Guido Tabellini. 2010. "Cultural and Institutional Bifurcation: China and Europe Compared." *American Economic Review: Papers & Proceedings* 100(2): 1–10.

———. 2012. "The Clan and the City: Sustaining Cooperation in China and Europe." Stanford and Bocconi Universities. Mimeo.

Greif, Avner and Steven Tadelis (2010). "A Theory of Moral Persistence: Crypto-Morality and Political Legitimacy." *Journal of Comparative Economics* 38(3): 229–244, September.

Hart, Herbert L. A. and Tony Honore. 1985. *Causation in the Law.* New York: Oxford University Press.

Henrich, J., R. Boyd, S. Bowles, C. Camerer, E. Fehr, H. Gintis, R. McElreath, M. Alvard, A. Barr, J. Ensminger, N. Smith Henrich, K. Hill, F. Gil-White, M. Gurven, F. W. Marlowe, J. Q. Patton, and D. Tracer. 2005. "Economic Man in Cross-Cultural Perspective: Behavioral Experiments in 15 Small-Scale Societies." *Behavioral and Brain Sciences* 28(6): 795–815.

Henrich, Joseph, Jean Ensminger, Richard McElreath, Abigail Barr, Clark Barrett, Alexander Bolyanatz, Juan Camilo Cardenas, Michael Gurven, Edwins Gwako, Natalie Henrich, Carolyn Lesorogol, Frank Marlowe, David Tracer, and John Ziker. 2010. "Markets, Religion, Community Size, and the Evolution of Fairness and Punishment." *Science* 327(5972): 1480–1484.

Hoff, Karla and Arijit Sen. 2006. "The Kin System as a Poverty Trap?" In *Poverty Traps*, edited by Samuel Bowles, Steven N. Durlauf, and Karla Hoff, 95–115. New York: Russell Sage Foundation; Princeton, NJ and Oxford: Princeton University Press.

Hoffman, E., K. McCabe, and V. Smith. 1996. "Social Distance and Other-Regarding Behavior in Dictator Games." *American Economic Review* 86: 653–660.

Inglehart, R. and H.-D. Klingemann. 2000. "Genes, Culture, Democracy, And Happiness." In *Subjective Wellbeing Across Cultures*, edited by E. Diener and E. Suh. Cambridge, MA: MIT Press.

Jackson, Matthew O., Tomas Rodriguez-Barraquer, and Xu Tan. 2012. "Social Capital and Social Quilts: Network Patterns of Favor Exchange." *American Economic Review* 102(5): 1857–1897, August.

Kagel, John H. and Dan Levin. 1986. "The Winner's Curse and Public Information in Common Value Auctions." *American Economic Review* 76(5): 894–920, December.

Kahan, D. M. 2000. "Gentle Nudges vs. Hard Shoves: Solving the Sticky Norms Problem." *University of Chicago Law Review* 67: 607–45.

Kahneman, Daniel. 2011. *Thinking Fast and Slow.* London: Penguin Books.

Kahneman, Daniel, Ed Diener, and N. Schwarz. 1999. *Wellbeing: The Foundations of Hedonic Psychology.* New York: Russell Sage Foundation.

Kahneman, Daniel, Jack L. Knetsch, and Richard Thaler. 1986. "Fairness as a Constraint on Profit Seeking: Entitlements in the Market." *American Economic Review* 76(4): 728–741.

Kahneman, Daniel and Ilina Ritov. 1994. "Determinants of Stated Willingness to Pay for Public Goods: A Study of the Headline Method." *Journal of Risk and Uncertainty* 9: 5–38.

Kahneman, D. and A. Tversky. 1979. "Prospect Theory: An Analysis of Decision under Risk." *Econometrica* 47(2): 263–291.

Kawaguchi, D. 2004. "Peer Effects on Substance Use Among American Teenagers." *Journal of Population Economics* 17: 351–367.

Kebede, B. and D. J. Zizzo. 2015. "Social Preferences and Agricultural Innovation: An Experimental Case Study from Ethiopia." *World Development* 67: 267–280.

Koszegi, B. and M. Rabin. 2006. "A Model of Reference-Dependent Preferences." *Quarterly Journal of Economics* 1221(4): 1133–1165, November.

———. 2007. "Reference-Dependent Risk Attitudes." *American Economic Review* 97(4): 1047–1073, September.

Krueger, Alan B. ed. 2009. *Measuring the Subjective Wellbeing of Nations: National Accounts of Time Use and Wellbeing.* Chicago: University of Chicago Press.

Lang, William W. and Leonard I. Nakamura. 1990. "The Dynamics of Credit Markets in a Model with Learning." *Journal of Monetary Economics* 26: 305–318.

Layard, Richard. 2002. "Rethinking Public Economics: Implications of Rivalry and Habit." Mimeo.

Ledyard, John O. 1995. "Public Goods: A Survey of Experimental Research." In *Handbook of Experimental Economics,* edited by J. Kagel and A. E. Roth, 111–194. Princeton, NJ: Princeton University Press.

Leight, Jessica. 2017. "Sibling Rivalry: Endowment and Intrahousehold Allocation in Gansu Province, China." *Economic Development and Cultural Change* 65(3): 457–493.

Levi-Strauss, Claude. 1962. *La Pensee Sauvage.* Paris: Plon.

———. 1966. *Mythologiques I–IV,* vol. 2, Du miel aux cendres. Paris: Plon.

Ligon, Ethan, Jonathan P. Thomas, and Tim Worrall. 2002. "Informal Insurance Arrangements with Limited Commitment: Theory and Evidence from Village Economies." *Review of Economic Studies* 69(1): 209–244.

Loewenstein, George F., Elke U. Weber, Christopher K. Hsee, and Ned Welch. 2001. "Risk as Feelings." *Psychological Bulletin* 127: 267–286.

Loomes, Graham and Robert Sugden. 1982. "Regret Theory: An Alternative to Rational Choice under Uncertainty." *Economic Journal* 92: 805–825.

Lopes, L. L. and G. C. Oden. 1999. "The Role Of Aspiration Level In Risky Choice: A Comparison Of Cumulative Prospect Theory and SP/A Theory." *Journal of Mathematical Psychology* 43(2): 286–313.

Luce, R. D. 1959. *Individual Choice Behavior.* Oxford: Wiley.

Luce, R. Duncan. 2010. "Behavioral Assumptions for a Class of Utility Theories: A Program of Experiments." *Journal of Risk and Uncertainty* 41: 19–27.

Lundberg, Shelly and Robert A. Pollak. 1993. "Separate Spheres Bargaining and the Marriage Market." *Journal of Political Economy* 101(6): 988–1010, December.

Lundborg, P. 2006. "Having the Wrong Friends? Peer Effects in Adolescent Substance Use." *Journal of Health Economics* 25: 214–233.

Luttmer, Erzo F. P. 2005. "Neighbors as Negatives: Relative Earnings and Wellbeing." *Quarterly Journal of Economics* 120(3): 963–1002.

Macours, Karen. 2011. "Increasing Inequality and Civil Conflict in Nepal." *Oxford Economic Papers* 63(1): 1–26, January.

Mauss, Marcel. 1973. "Essai sur le don : Forme et raison de l'echange dans les sociétiés archaïques." In *Sociologie et Anthropologie,* PUF, Collection Quadrige, 149–279.

McElroy, M. B. and J. Horney. 1981. "Nash-Bargained Household Decisions: Toward a Generalization of the Theory of Demand." *International Economic Review* 22(2): 333–349, June.

McPherson, M., L. Smith-Lovin, and J. M. Cook. 2001. "Birds of a Feather: Homophily in Social Networks." *Annual Review of Sociology* 27: 415–444.

Mikhail, John. 2011. *Elements of Moral Cognition: Rawls' Linguistic Analogy and the Cognitive Science of Moral and Legal Judgment.* Cambridge: Cambridge University Press.

Mnookin, Robert and Lewis Kornhauser. 1979. "Bargaining in the Shadow of the Law: The Case of Divorce." *Yale Law Journal* 88: 950–997.

Morduch, Jonathan. 2000. "Sibling Rivalry in Africa." *American Economic Review Papers and Proceedings* 90(2): 405–409.

North, Douglas C. 1973. *The Rise of the Western World* Cambridge: Cambridge University Press.

———. 1990. *Institutions, Institutional Change, and Economic Performance.* Cambridge: Cambridge University Press.

Null, Clair. 2012. "Warm Glow, Information, and Inefficient Charitable Giving." *Journal of Public Economics* 95: 455–465.

Ockenfels, Axel, Dirk Sliwka, and Peter Werner. 2010. "Bonus Payments and Reference Point Violations." IZA Discussion Papers 4795, Institute for the Study of Labor (IZA).

Okada, Akira and Arno Riedl. 2005. "Inefficiency and Social Exclusion in a Coalition Formation Game: Experimental Evidence." *Games and Economic Behavior* 50(2): 278–311, February.

Otsuka, Keijiro and Agnes R. Quisumbing. 2001. "Land Rights and Natural Resource Management in the Transition to Individual Ownership: Case Studies from Ghana and Indonesia." In *Access to Land, Rural Poverty, and Public Action,* edited by Alain de Janvry et al. Oxford: Oxford University Press.

Pinker, Steve. 2012. *The Better Angels of Our Nature: Why Violence Has Declined*. London: Penguin Books.

Platteau, Jean-Philippe. 1994a. "Behind the Market Stage Where Real Societies Exist: Part I—The Role of Public and Private Order Institutions." *Journal of Development Studies* 30(3): 533–577.

———. 1994b. "Behind the Market Stage Where Real Societies Exist: Part II—The Role of Moral Norms." *Journal of Development Studies* 30(4): 753–815.

———. 2000. *Institutions, Social Norms and Economic Development*. London: Routledge, chap. 5.

———. 2006. "Solidarity Norms and Institutions in Agrarian Societies: Static and Dynamic Considerations." In *Handbook on Gift-Giving, Reciprocity and Altruism*, Vol. 1, edited by S.-C. Kolm, J. Mercier-Ythier, and G. Varet, chap. 12, 819–886. Amsterdam: North-Holland and Elsevier.

———. 2009. "Institutional Obstacles to African Economic Development: State, Ethnicity, and Custom." *Journal of Economic Behavior and Organization* 71(3): 669–689.

———. 2010. "Redistributive Pressures in Sub-Saharan Africa: Causes, Consequences, and Coping Strategies." Paper presented at the Conference entitled Understanding African Poverty in the Longue Duree, International Institute for the Advanced Study of Cultures, Institutions, and Economic Enterprise (IIAS), Accra, July 15–17.

———. 2014. "Redistributive Pressures in Sub-Saharan Africa: Causes, Consequences, and Coping Strategies." In *African Development in Historical Perspective*, edited by E. Akyeampong, R. Bates, N. Nunn, and J. Robinson, 153–207. Cambridge: Cambridge University Press.

Platteau, J. P. and J. Nugent. 1992. "Share Contracts and Their Rationale: Lessons from Marine Fishing." *Journal of Development Studies* 28(3): 386–422.

Platteau, J. P. and E. Seki. 2007. "Heterogeneity, Social Esteem and the Feasibility of Collective Action." *Journal of Development Economics* 83(2): 302–325.

Polanyi, Karl. 1944. *The Great Transformation*. New York: Holt, Rinehart, and Winston.

Powell, L. M., J. A. Tauras, and H. Ross. 2005. "The Importance of Peer Effects, Cigarette Prices and Tobacco Control Policies for Youth Smoking Behaviour." *Journal of Health Economics* 24: 950–968.

Rabin, Matthew. 1993. "Incorporating Fairness into Game Theory and Economics." *American Economic Review* 83(5): 1281–1302.

———. 2000. "Risk Aversion and Expected Utility Theory: A Calibration Theorem." *Econometrica* 68: 1281–1292.

Rabin, M. and R. Thaler. 2001. "Anomalies: Risk Aversion." *Journal of Economic Perspectives* 15(1): 219–232, Winter.

Ravallion, Martin and Michael Lokshin. 2005. "Who Cares About Relative Deprivation?" *Journal of Economic Behavior and Organization* 73(2): 171–185, February.

Robson, A. 1992. "Status, the Distribution of Wealth, Private and Social Attitudes to Risk." *Econometrica* 60: 837–857.

Roth, Christopher. 2014. "Conspicuous Consumption and Peer Effects Among the Poor: Evidence from a Field Experiment." CSAE Working Paper WPS/2014–29.

Runciman, W. G. 1966. *Relative Deprivation and Social Justice: A Study of Attitudes to Social Inequality in Twentieth-Century Britain*. London: Routledge.

Sahlins, Marshall. 1972. *Stone Age Economics*. Chicago: Aldine-Atherton.

Schechter, Laura. 2007. "Theft, Gift-Giving, and Trustworthiness: Honesty Is Its Own Reward in Rural Paraguay." *American Economic Review* 97(5): 1560–1582.

Scott, James C. 1976. *The Moral Economy of Peasant: Rebellion and Subsistence in South-East Asia*. New Haven, CT: Yale University Press.

Smith, Adam. [1759] 1976. *The Theory of Moral Sentiments*, Liberty Classics, edited by D. D. Raphael and A. L. Mactie. Indianapolis: Liberty Press.

———. [1776] 1909. *Wealth of Nations*, Harvard Classics, vol. 10, edited by C. J. Bullock. New York: P. F Collier.

Smith,V. L. 1962. "An Experimental Study of Competitive Market Behavior." *Journal of Political Economy* 70(2): 111–137.

Sunstein, Cass R. 2005. *The Laws of Fear: Beyond the Precautionary Principle*. New York: Cambridge University Press.

Sunstein, Cass R., Daniel Kahneman, David Schkade, and Ilana Ritov. 2002. "Predictably Incoherent Judgments." *Stanford Law Review* 54: 1190.

Tadelis, Steven. 1999. "What's in a Name? Reputation as a Tradeable Asset." *American Economic Review* 89(3): 548–563, June.

Tversky, A. and D. Kahneman. 1992. "Advances in Prospect Theory: Cumulative Representation of Uncertainty." *Journal of Risk and Uncertainty* 5(4): 297–323.

Veblen, Thorstein. 1899. *The Theory of the Leisure Class*.

Young, P. and M. A. Burke. 2001. "Competition and Custom in Economic Contracts: A Case Study of Illinois Agriculture." *American Economic Review* 91(3): 559–573.

Zafar, B. 2011. "An Experimental Investigation of Why Individuals Conform." *European Economic Review* 55(6): 774–798.

Zizzo, D. J. 2003. "Money Burning and Rank Egalitarianism with Random Dictators." *Economics Letters* 81: 263–266.

Zizzo, D. J. and A. J. Oswald. 2001. "Are People Willing to Pay to Reduce Others' Incomes?" *Annales d'Economie et de Statistique* 63–64: 39–62.

12

CULTURE, INSTITUTIONS, AND DEVELOPMENT

Gerard Roland

12.1. INTRODUCTION

A very active literature has developed in the last 15 years on the effects of culture on institutions and development. While economists previously abstained from analyzing the economic effects of culture, they increasingly recognize that differences in values and beliefs across the world have many economic implications, be it in influencing attitudes toward thrift, work and effort, innovation, trade, the role of women, openness toward other countries and other cultures, or in affecting political and legal institutions. International databases such as the World Values Survey have made it possible to examine cross-country differences for a large array of cultural values and beliefs.

This chapter exhaustively surveys this recent literature in order to: (1) identify the important themes that emerge from this literature; (2) examine the most important policy implications of those themes for economic development; (3) identify the research gaps and the most fruitful research paths forward for this literature; (4) discuss in particular the most relevant policy issues arising in terms of the interaction between diversity in cultural norms and institutional reforms.

Research on culture in economics started from different angles. The pioneering game-theoretic work of Greif (1994) showed the effects of differences between individualist and collectivist beliefs in the late medieval Mediterranean period by comparing systematically how differences between the collectivist beliefs of the Maghribi traders in the Muslim world and the individualistic beliefs of the Genovese traders affected contract enforcement, social stratification, and openness in trade. The study of belief-induced game-theoretic equilibria leading to self-sustaining beliefs showed powerfully how differences in cultural beliefs can matter and be persistent. The experimental literature early on found stark country differences in outcomes of bargaining games. The pioneering study was that by Roth et al. (1991) documenting differences in outcomes of the ultimatum game in Israel, Japan, Slovenia, and the United States (see also Henrich et al. 2001). Empirical research attempting to understand the determinants of individual preferences, in particular related to trust, led to the finding that national fixed effects tend to play a more important role than individual characteristics (see, e.g., Tabellini 2008b; Algan and Cahuc 2014). This finding led to the suggestion that culture plays an important role in determining people's preferences. Evidence was also produced showing specific effects of culture on people's behavior distinct from institutions. Thus, Fisman and Miguel (2007) showed on the basis of differences in New York parking violations by UN diplomats that there was a strong link between country corruption scores and behavior by UN diplomats in the same institutional setting. Similarly, Miguel et al. (2008) showed that professional soccer players who come from countries with a history of civil conflict in their home country are more likely to behave in a violent way on the soccer field.

Before going any further, we must determine how culture is commonly defined in economics research. A commonly used definition is the following. *Culture is the set of values and beliefs people have about how the world (both nature and society) works as well as the norms of behavior derived from that set of values.*

Let us dwell on the various components of this definition and how it translates in traditional economics jargon. Values are about what gives fundamental meaning to someone in life. Values obviously affect preferences (e.g., the value of effort affects labor-leisure choices) but not only to affect individual choices. Values affect social norms, which strongly affect people's behavior, whether in their fertility choices, savings choices, female labor supply, the extent of peer pressure against behavior that deviates against extant social norms. Beliefs are about how people believe others will behave under particular contingencies, but they are also about nature, the extent of scientific versus superstitious or religious beliefs. Obviously, beliefs affect individual behavior. People who expect others to behave opportunistically will tend to behave opportunistically and vice versa. This definition of culture is a comprehensive definition. It is close to religion in the sense that religion offers a view of how the world works as well as precepts of behavior. Culture is perhaps more inclusive than religion in the sense that it covers all beliefs and values that people have. Culture also evolves somewhat more than religion, at least compared to the fundamental religious texts, even though culture affects the interpretation one makes of religious texts, which obviously varies over time. To avoid any misunderstanding, when economists talk about culture, they do not mean the culinary or clothing habits that are prevalent in a particular country, nor its artistic production, even though the latter are all to a certain extent affected by prevalent values and beliefs. Culture thus only affects a subset of what economists usually understand by preferences. Also, culture is often used in many settings such as "organizational culture," "enterprise culture," or "ghetto culture." Even though these settings are relevant for the analysis of culture, they usually refer to a particular subset of behaviors in the context of their workplace or their neighborhood. When we talk about culture, we will usually not refer to these cultural subsets but instead apply the more comprehensive concept defined above.

Culture is mostly transmitted from parents to children (vertical transmission) but also via peers (horizontal transmission). Bisin and Verdier (2001) have produced the canonical economic model of cultural transmission. It is generally agreed that vertical transmission plays a greater role than horizontal transmission. Therefore, culture tends to be slow-moving over time compared to formal institutions such as political institutions which can change rapidly at times (Roland 2004).

Several methodologies have been used in economic research on culture. The first method is the cross-country approach. It exploits the several large international databases that provide a comprehensive coverage of values. The advantage of the cross-country approach is that it makes it possible to perform a comprehensive and extensive comparison of a very broad set of the values available for a very large set of countries. The disadvantage is that these databases either are not available across time, or if they are, it's only for the last few decades. They thus allow only for a spatial comparison, not for a comparison across time. To the extent that researchers are interested in understanding the effects of culture, this disadvantage could be important. This is less the case if one believes that culture is slow-moving, and thus that recent measures of culture are good proxies for older measures. Nevertheless, in order to convincingly measure the effect of culture on measures that are relevant to understand institutions and development, one needs to have good instrumental variables. This is in general very difficult to find in a macroeconomic context since many variables affect each other mutually in a web of complex interconnections. It is very difficult to find a variable that would affect a particular economic variable only indirectly through a cultural variable, and only through that cultural variable. Because of this difficulty of finding convincing instrumental variables in a macroeconomic context, one often faces a trade-off between the internal validity and the external validity of a particular research endeavor. A smaller spatial scope of research, focusing for example only on within-country, or within-region, heterogeneity makes internal validity easier but at the cost of external validity and vice versa; cross-country studies have a potentially large external validity, but this often comes at the cost of internal validity.

The second method is based on the epidemiological approach pioneered by R. Fernandez (see Fernandez 2011). Based on its similarity with epidemiological research analyzing the spread of diseases, it analyzes the spread of culture based on the country of origin of the migrants. The epidemiological approach to culture has mainly been applied to the United States because it is a country of migrants. It looks at how cultural traits from the county of origin of ancestors influences subsequent generations of US citizens. An advantage of this approach is that individuals coming from different cultural backgrounds will face similar environments in the United States. This makes it easier to isolate the effect of culture on their behavior. The only disadvantage of the epidemiological approach is that it only measures individual actions and behavior, not aggregate effects.

The third method is based on laboratory experiments across countries, or across nationalities, such as foreign students in US universities (see, e.g., Glaeser at al. 2000; Bornthorst et al. 2010). As is usual in laboratory experiments, the subjects are asked to participate in games related to the experiment at hand, and their response is analyzed as a function of their cultural origin. Laboratory experiments on the effects of culture as on other issues have the usual advantages and disadvantages. One creates a controlled environment, which makes it easier to measure particular effects. On the other hand, one can claim that such environments are too artificial to reflect human interactions in the real world.

This is not the first survey on the effects of culture. Algan and Cahuc (2014) focus on the trust component of culture and its effects. Fernandez (2011) surveys the epidemiological approach to culture. Alesina and Giuliano (2015) survey the link between culture and institutions. Compared to these other surveys, this chapter offers a comprehensive survey of the effects of *different* cultural dimensions, and also covers the question of the determinants of cultural change as well as the origins of cultural diversity.

In the first section, we examine exhaustively the literature in terms of (a) which cultural variables are used, and (b) the variable affected by culture. We build on that basis a compact table in matrix form summarizing visually the existing literature. This visual tool is useful to identify existing research concentrations as well as existing holes in the literature. Among the main variables that have been analyzed, the most important one is that of generalized trust. It has been interpreted in various ways: culture of cooperation, culture of active political participation, and generalized morality (as opposed to morality limited to one's ingroup), none of these interpretations necessarily contradicting each other. A second variable for which a literature has developed is the effect of the individualism-collectivism dimension. This literature exploits the data built by Dutch sociologist Hofstede. A large literature exists in cross-cultural psychology, using laboratory experiments to test various aspects of the differences between individualist and collectivist cultures. There is also a literature based on the work of cross-cultural psychologist Shalom Schwartz, which is closely related to the variables identified by Hofstede. Even though we plan to summarize a large part of this literature in matrix form, we need to acknowledge that there is substantial heterogeneity among existing studies. Some studies are only theoretical while most others are only empirical. The quality of existing empirical studies is also quite variable. We will reflect on these issues when mentioning the research.

Next, we discuss some major themes that have emerged in the literature. A first theme is the inertia of culture. Culture, as a whole, usually changes only very slowly, even though some particular, more narrow dimensions of culture (attitudes toward death penalty, attitudes toward women, tolerance for smoking) may change faster. In contrast, while political and legal institutions also exhibit substantial inertia, they may be subject to periods of very radical change (a revolution, a coup). The reason for culture being slow-moving is that cultural transmission is mostly vertical and takes place between parents and children. There is a horizontal component to cultural transmission, based on peers, but it generally plays a much smaller role. Cultural inertia is now well documented, and the chapter will survey the findings from that literature. Cultural inertia has important implications. For one, culture may be a fundamental determinant of institutions, and there is a literature looking at the effects of cultural variables on the quality of institutions but also on democratization. A second implication, which is very important for development policy, is that it is probably counterproductive to want to change cultural attitudes quickly. A better approach might be to build on local cultures and design institutions that are more adapted to these local cultures.

A second theme that needs to be examined is what variables determine cultural change. This is a broad question for which the existing literature is yet rather sparse. A major topic is the effect of economic change as well as social change on cultural values. A related question is why cultural change occurs under some circumstances, but not under others.

A third theme that is important to explain is the origin of particular cultures. This is only partly related to the previous theme. Why is there more trust in some countries than in others? Why did some countries develop an individualistic culture, and why did others develop a collectivist culture? Questions like these have so far mostly remained unanswered, but there is some research examining, for example, the role of particular early agricultural technologies on gender equality and inequality. Some studies have also analyzed the effect of particularly long historical spells, such as the length of time certain territories were under the authority of a specific empire (the Roman or Chinese Empires, the Ottoman Empire, the Austro-Hungarian or the Russian Empire).

12.2. THE ECONOMIC EFFECTS OF CULTURE

In this section, we look at the effect of particular dimensions of culture on economic and institutional variables. We organize this discussion with the help of table 12.1. Columns represent cultural dimensions and rows, the economic variables affected by culture. A particular cell thus contains a reference to a paper (or multiple papers) analyzing the effect of a particular cultural dimension on a variable affected by culture.

As one can see from table 12.1, the cultural dimension that until now has by far been most studied in economics is trust. It is either understood as generalized morality, i.e., norms of morality that are universally valid independent of socioeconomic, family, or ethnic background, as civic culture in society, or as the willingness to cooperate. Arrow famously stated in 1972: "Virtually every commercial transaction has within itself an element of trust, certainly any transaction conducted over a period of time. It can be plausibly argued that much of the economic backwardness in the world can be explained by the lack of mutual confidence."

There is a large experimental literature analyzing trust games played in laboratories. Standard game theory suggests that cooperation is not easy to sustain, especially if people do not face repeated interactions with the same people. This has been contradicted by the result of trust games, showing that people cooperate, even in one-shot games (see, e.g., Boyd et al. 2003; Fehr 2010). Theoretically, cooperation can be sustained by preference for reciprocity (Fehr and Schmidt 2009). Trust has also been linked to social capital (Putnam 1993). Laboratory experiments have been designed to distinguish between altruism, reciprocity, and trust.

In the empirical literature, research on trust is based on answers to the following survey question: "Generally speaking, would you say that most people can be trusted, or that you can't be too careful when dealing with others?" This question is present in a very large number of surveys, thus making it possible to compare the answers: the European Social Survey, the General Social Survey in the United States, the World Values Survey, Latinobarómetro, the Afrobarometer, and the Australian Community Survey. Such surveys form the basis for cross-country studies, as well as within-country studies, on the effects of trust.

As table 12.1 indicates, societies with more trust have been found to be associated with higher income per capita, innovation, financial market development, redistribution, exports, and investment. Higher trust is associated with stronger delegation within organizations, stronger accountability of politicians, and different labor market institutions.

The second cultural dimension that has been studied so far is the individualism/collectivism dimension. The notions of individualism and collectivism are quite widespread but take different meanings in different contexts. Greif (1994) introduced them in his path-breaking comparison of contract enforcement among the Genovese and the Maghribi traders in the late Middle Ages in the Mediterranean. He restricted his

Table 12.1. Economic effects of culture

	Trust	Individualism	Schwartz	Gender roles	Strength of family ties	Culture of honor
Income per capita, TFP, growth	Knack and Keefer (1997), Algan and Cahuc (2010)	Gorodnichenko and Roland (2017)				
Exports and investment	Guiso et al. (2004)	Gorodnichenko et al. (2015)				
Financial market development	Guiso et al. (2004), Cole et al. (2013)					
Innovation (RD/GDP)	Hall and Jones (2009)	Gorodnichenko Roland (2017)				
Firm organization (delegation)	Cingano and Pinotti (2012), Bloom et al. (2012)					
Labor market	Algan and Cahuc (2009)					
Democracy		Gorodnichenko Roland (2015)				
Institutions of regulation	Aghion et al. (2010), Aghion et al. (2011), Pinotti (2012)				Alesina et al. (2010)	
Quality of institutions	Tabellini (2008b)	Klasing (2012), Kyriacou (2016)	Licht et al. (2003)			
Accountability	Nannicini et al. (2013)		Licht et al. (2003)			
Redistribution (includes pensions)	Alesina and Angeletos (2005)				Galasso and Profeta (2018)	

(continued)

Table 12.1. (*continued*)

	Trust	Individualism	Schwartz	Gender roles	Strength of family ties	Culture of honor
LFP of women				Fernandez and Fogli (2009), Fernandez (2007)	Alesina and Giuliano (2007)	
Fertility choices				Fernandez and Fogli (2006), Fernandez and Fogli (2009)	Luke and Munshi (2006)	
Sex ratio				Almond et al. (2019)		
Corruption			Licht et al. (2003)			
Geographical mobility						
Violence						Grosjean (2014)
Efficiency of coordination						Brooks et al. (2015)

comparison then to differences in beliefs about strategies of contract enforcement and hiring practices. Current research on individualism and collectivism is inspired more by the cross-cultural psychology definition of individualism and collectivism that has made substantial use of the data put together by Dutch sociologist Hofstede. He surveyed people with equivalent jobs in different countries in the same company so as to measure cultural differences. To avoid cultural biases in the way questions were framed, the translation of the survey into local languages was done by a team of English and local language speakers. With new waves of surveys and replication studies, Hofstede's measure of individualism has been expanded to almost 80 countries.[1] Hofstede's index, as well as the measure of individualism from other studies, uses a broad array of survey questions to establish cultural values. Factor analysis is used to summarize data and construct indices. In Hofstede's analysis, the index of individualism is the first factor in questions about the value of personal time, freedom, interesting and fulfilling work, etc. This component loads positively on valuing individual freedom, opportunity, achievement, advancement, and recognition, and loads negatively on valuing harmony, cooperation, and relations with superiors. The Hofstede individualism score measures the extent to which it is believed that individuals are supposed to take care of themselves as opposed to being strongly integrated and loyal to a cohesive group. Individuals in countries with a high level of the index value personal freedom and status, while individuals in countries with a low level of the index value harmony and conformity.

Although Hofstede's data were initially collected mostly with the purpose of understanding differences in IBM's corporate culture, the main advantage of this measure of individualism is that it has been validated in a number of studies.[2] For example, across various studies and measures of individualism (see Hofstede 2001 for a review) the United Kingdom, the United States, and the Netherlands are consistently among the most individualist countries, while Pakistan, Nigeria, and Peru are among the most collectivist.

Cross-cultural psychologists consider that the distinction between individualism and collectivism covers many dimensions in order to represent in a comprehensive way cultural differences across the world. Without expanding too much on it (for a recent survey, see Roland 2016), individualism and collectivism have opposed visions of the self, of mode of self-knowledge, of self-consistency and adaptability, of the need for self-enhancement, control strategies, emotional rewards, analytic versus holistic modes of thinking, as well as a number of behavioral and relational differences.

As shown in table 12.1, countries with higher individualism scores are associated with higher levels of innovation and long-run growth, higher quality of institutions, and are more likely to have democratized earlier. Cultural differences along the individualism/collectivism dimension are also associated with lower levels of cross-country vertical integration within multinational firms.

Very closely related to the Hofstede data on individualism/collectivism are the data assembled by cross-cultural psychologist Shalom Schwartz. He developed a core set of values that have common meanings across cultures and can provide a basis for the comparison of cultures across countries. Schwartz's value survey consists of 56–57 value items that ask respondents to indicate the importance of each as "a guiding principle in my life." Between 1998 and 2000, Schwartz gathered survey responses from K–12 schoolteachers and college students, for a total of 195 samples drawn from 67 nations and 70 cultural groups. Each sample generally includes 180–280 respondents, for a total of more than 75,000 surveys. From the data generated by those surveys, he has constructed a "cultural map," which displays the important cultural dimensions he identified. Embeddedness of the individual in the traditional community emphasizes a high degree of respect for tradition and security. At its opposite are autonomy, both intellectual and affective. Intellectual autonomy emphasizes self-direction, whereas affective autonomy emphasizes mostly hedonism and stimulation. Hierarchy is valued in societies where stability of the social order is paramount. It emphasizes power, tradition, and conformity. At its opposite is egalitarianism, which emphasizes universalism. Mastery is about self-assertion and is based on the values of achievement. Harmony is its opposite and also fosters the values of universalism. Note that most of the variation in his data come from the opposition between embeddedness and intellectual and effective autonomy. Empirically, these cultural dimensions strongly correlate with collectivism and individualism in the Hofstede data.

As can be seen from table 12.1, a higher level of autonomy has been found to be associated with higher quality of institutions along a broad number of dimensions.

Let us briefly comment on the other dimensions in table 12.1. An important distinction, when examining cultural values, is to what extent effort versus luck affects individual outcomes. These beliefs obviously affect people's actions, but they also affect their preferences in different ways. Higher beliefs in the role of effort tend to be associated with lower levels of redistribution.

Values and beliefs in gender roles vary a lot across countries and are an important component of cultural differences. While modern Western culture emphasizes equality between men and women, other more traditional cultures confine women to the household and give them fewer rights than to men. Cultural differences on gender roles are a source of cultural clashes in today's world. Very interesting research has been done in this area. The epidemiological method (see above) has been applied intensively here since cultural differences on gender roles affect household choices such as labor force participation of women or fertility choices. Different beliefs in gender roles are associated with differences in labor force participation of women, fertility choices, and sex ratios.

Family values relate to the strength of family ties. In some cultures, family ties are very strong, while they are looser in others. When family ties are strong, the family plays a larger role as an economic unit, whereas when they are looser, there is greater reliance on market relations instead. The strength of family ties can be measured in different ways. The World Value Survey contains many questions about the importance of family, attitudes toward parents, responsibilities of children toward their family, etc. Research has found that the strength of family ties has various economic effects. Stronger family values have been found to be associated with lower geographical labor mobility, more rigid labor market regulations, lower labor force participation of women, and less generous pension systems.

A culture of honor is one where people feel compelled to defend their honor, by violent means usually, if they feel they have been insulted or offended. A culture of honor tends to generate violent behavior, which has been confirmed by empirical studies.

Several observations can be made on the basis of table 12.1. First of all, despite the fact that this literature is very recent, there appear to be comprehensive and diverse effects of cultural differences on a large number of important variables: from growth and innovation to demography, labor markets, political attitudes, and institutions. Causality is difficult to establish completely convincingly in a cross-country context, but it is difficult to deny that culture has important effects and is associated to many variables economists care about.

Second, the effect of culture on institutions (democracy, regulation, corruption, quality of institutions, . . .) seems important. This is not really surprising given the slow-moving character of culture. Culture is bound to shape institutions one way or the other, but the causality is likely to go in both directions. We will examine these topics further below.

Third, the number of different cultural variables does not appear that large compared to the number of outcome variables examined in the literature. This is interesting because culture has many dimensions as it touches all aspects of life. Nevertheless, that does not mean that a large number of cultural dimensions should necessarily have economic effects. When looking at table 12.1, we see that some cultural variables are limited in scope: trust, values on gender roles, family values, culture of honor. Others are more comprehensive. This is the case of individualism and collectivism and of the Schwartz cultural dimensions. As noted above, these are strongly correlated. Individualism is also strongly correlated with trust. This is not surprising since trust has been interpreted as generalized morality, which is what one would expect in a society with an individualist culture where people see each other as citizens with equal rights. It is probably not surprising that the many cultural dimensions are strongly correlated with each other. This means that when we do research on culture, unless we are interested in a particular cultural dimension, it makes sense to use a general index like that of Hofstede or Schwartz.

Two remarks should be made here. First, these general cultural indicators give mostly a ranking of countries. Of course, this ranking is based on an existing set of cultural values, but we cannot exclude the fact that the indicator measures more than what it actually measured. Indeed, if many cultural dimensions are strongly correlated with each other, we do not need to include all cultural measures in a cultural indicator—especially those that have not been measured—since the ranking will be the same with a comprehensive set of measures compared to a more restricted set of measures. The second remark, which is related to the first one, is that cultural psychologists, who have much more experience than economists in researching cultural differences and their effects, consider that the individualism-collectivism cleavage is the most relevant one to understand international cultural differences (see, for example, Heine 2007; in economics, see Klasing 2012). To them, this is not surprising as individualism and collectivism reflect two fundamentally different worldviews with numerous implications that can be traced back conceptually to the distinction between the independent self versus the interdependent self (Markus and Kitayama 1991), as a foundation to individualist and collectivist culture.

It is worth making a final remark about "missing" columns or rows in table 12.1. For example, there are not yet studies on the economic effects of time preferences or risk preferences, even though there is research on the determinants of these cultural differences. These gaps will likely be filled.

12.3. THE INERTIA OF CULTURE

The topic of the inertia of culture came up repeatedly in the previous section. The canonical models used to show the inertia of culture are those by Bisin and Verdier (2000, 2001) and Bisin, Topa, and Verdier (2004). These are models of strategic transmission of values by parents. Standard evolutionary models of cultural transmission in the tradition of Boyd and Richerson (1985) generally predict convergence to the culture of the majority population via simple evolutionary dynamics. In the spirit of Bisin and Verdier, parents may choose to transmit to their children values that will help them fit and thrive in the environment in which they live. This will help accelerate cultural assimilation, but parents from minority groups who care deeply about their culture will want to strongly transmit their values to their children. As a result, one will not observe cultural convergence. Bisin, Patacchini, and Verdier (2016) show that attachment to one's own cultural identity is stronger in mixed rather than segregated neighborhoods in the UK. The Bisin and Verdier framework thus explains quite well the inertia of culture via vertical transmission.

Tabellini (2008a) proposes another model of cultural transmission that involves complementarities between norms and social behavior. The more people exhibit a cooperative behavior, the larger the payoff from cooperation. This in turn makes parents more willing to transmit values of cooperation. Hauk and Saez-Marti (2001) had proposed a similar mechanism to analyze transmission of corruption. Somewhat different is the model by Guiso, Sapienza, and Zingales (2004). It is also related to culture of cooperation and thus to trust. The model proposes to analyze how distrust may persist, but also how it may change in a few generations. In their model, parents transmit conservative priors to their children, biased toward distrust, because they do not want their children to suffer from negative experiences, and thus transmit values that will protect them but prevent them from learning too much about others. Once a positive shock occurs that leads people to experiment more, they may find out that the value of distrust inherited from their parents was unwarranted, and thus transmit values of trust to their offspring. There may be very long periods of persistent distrust, but this may suddenly change in a few generations. The model proposes to rationalize the experience of city-states in Northern Italy in the Renaissance period. That experience did not last that long, as the Counter-Reformation subsequently initiated a dark period, but seems to have had a lasting effect. The model is justified by empirical evidence showing that the gap in trust between older and younger people is smaller in low-trust countries compared to high-trust countries, showing an experience effect (measured by the young-old gap) that is different.

Empirically, the inertia of culture is well established, in particular in the epidemiological literature showing in the United States a persistence of cultural traits people inherited from the country of their ancestors (Fernandez 2011; Tabellini 2008b; Alesina and Giuliano 2011; Guiso et al. 2006). Dohmen et al. (2010, 2011) found strong correlation of values and beliefs between parents and children on *trust and risk* using data from Germany. Ljunge (2014) found similar results on *trust* in a sample of 29 European countries with 87 countries of ancestry. Farre and Vella (2013) present evidence on the inertia in the transmission of *gender values* in the United States; Fong (2001), Luttmer and Singhal (2011), and Eugster et al. (2011) provide evidence on vertical cultural transmission of *preferences for redistribution*.

Some of the research related to the inertia of culture goes further back in time and looks at the historical cultural roots of various kinds of behavior. As already stated above, Grosjean (2014) showed how the significantly higher levels of homicide in the US South relate to a culture of violence inherited from the first European migrants to the United States. In contrast to other regions, migrants to the US South were mostly Scottish-Irish cattle herders. Like in other regions of the world populated mostly by herders (Sardinia, Albania, to mention a few), a culture of violence had developed over time. Cattle can be stolen much more easily than land, and herders developed a culture of honor and violence to deter potential thieves from attacking them to steal their cattle. The fascinating thing is that the effects of this culture can still be seen today in the US South among the descendants of those Scottish-Irish herders, even though the motive (develop an aggressive behavior to protect oneself from potential thieves) disappeared a long time ago. Grosjean also shows that the persistence of the culture of violence can only be found in those locations where the Scottish-Irish migrants and their descendants were in the majority. In other words, the culture of violence persists as a community phenomenon. Wherever the descendants of these herders were in the minority and immersed in another culture, they assimilated and adapted to the values and behavior of the majority in their community.

Related to this research is the earlier work by Fischer (1989) on the long-run effects of the initial cultures of the different waves of migration to the United States and their institutional effects. The first wave, between 1629 and 1641, were the Puritans who settled in Massachusetts. They believed in the importance of education and order and adapted the new institutions to their beliefs. This resulted in relatively high tax rates, a large government, frequent town meetings, and strong and swift justice. The second wave, between 1642 and 1675, were the so-called Cavaliers who migrated to Virginia. Many of them migrated to North America, motivated to find estates as the system of primogeniture gave all land to first-born males. Their beliefs were different from those of the Puritans, with whom they were in conflict in England. They believed that inequality is natural and should not be opposed. They also adopted different institutions from the Puritans: low taxes, low levels of education, and a lack of formal justice. The third wave was formed by the Quakers (1675–1725) who settled mostly in Delaware. Their culture placed a high priority on personal freedom. They introduced institutions of limited government and equal rights, and practiced a less harsh justice. The fourth wave was formed by the Scottish-Irish (1717–1775), mentioned above. They believed in freedom from the law and right to armed resistance, which led to vigilante justice. As we can see, the different waves of migration to the United States were characterized by different cultural backgrounds, resulting in differences in institutions adopted. It is fascinating to realize that these cultural and institutional differences still play a fundamental role in US politics today.

Another interesting piece of evidence related to long-term cultural inertia is that of Voigtländer and Voth (2014) on the persistence of *anti-Semitism* in Germany. In the mid-fourteenth century, in the aftermath of the Black Plague that decimated Europe, Jews were systematically blamed for it and were put to death in pogroms throughout Northern Europe. Voigtländer and Voth found that those towns that killed Jews most after the Black Plague were also more likely to have a higher intensity of anti-Semitic attacks in Interwar Germany, in particular during the Nazi period.

One may wonder which cultural traits show more persistence than others. A paper by Giavazzi, Petkov, and Schiantarelli (2014) addresses that question. They use data from the General Social Survey in the United States to trace cultural evolution over several generations. They found that deep religious values such as family and moral values, but also political orientation (liberal or conservative), vary very little relative to the prevailing US norms. On the other hand, attitudes toward cooperation, redistribution, children's independence, premarital sex, beliefs about the role of effort and frequency of religious practice converge faster toward the US norm. They also found that the speed of convergence varied depending on the country of origin of the ancestors.

12.4. WHAT EXPLAINS CULTURAL CHANGE?

Whereas it is now well established that culture does not change very rapidly, and that cultural inertia is very strong, cultural change does take place. There are periods in time where hardly any change takes place and periods where change takes place much more quickly. Why? What do we know about cultural change? Not much so far, and most of it comes from historical episodes that took place centuries ago. A lot of research on the determinants of cultural values is about the determinants of individual preferences. As much as it is interesting, it is important to distinguish between the determinants of individual preferences and the determinants of how culture changes in a particular community, polity, or country.

At the theoretical level, Doepke and Zilibotti (2008) had analyzed the emergence of bourgeois values of patience and hard work. They look at the dynamic evolution of cultural transmission among artisans, landlords, and workers. They find that artisans end up the most patient and with the highest value for hard work. Industrialization allows for this group to thrive while landlords stay attached to a culture of leisure. Here, preference transmission is dictated by altruistic parents in response to the economic circumstances they are facing. Another theoretical analysis is that by Besley and Ghatak (2016), who analyze how worker motivation (intrinsic or extrinsic) evolves with the reward structures offered on the market place. In a similar vein, Victor Hiller (2011) studies the impact of differences in preferences for autonomy at work on industrialization and the size of the modern industrial sector. Hiller (2014) also examines the effect of female labor supply on gender norms and how the latter reproduce via the gender gap in education.

We already mentioned the work of Guiso et al. (2004) on how the experience of Italian city-states may have led to important cultural change in Northern Italy in the direction of more trust and better civic attitudes. Becker et al. (2016) analyzed the difference between the influence of the Habsburg versus the Ottoman Empire, in terms of the culture of trust and corruption. They found that in the regions that once lay within the boundaries of the Habsburg Empire, public administration is still perceived as more transparent, less corrupt, and better trusted by the population than in areas that used to belong to the Ottoman Empire. Between the eighteenth and the twentieth centuries, the Habsburg Empire employed public administrators with a higher level of education, competence, and integrity. The effects of these reforms are still felt today, a hundred years after the disappearance of the Habsburg Empire. Grosfeld and Zhuravskaya (2015) look at the effects of the Russian Empire, the Habsburg Empire, and the Prussian Empire in contemporary Poland where, before World War I, territories belonged to one of these three empires. They find that territories that belonged to the Habsburg Empire have significantly stronger support for democracy today compared to territories that belonged to the Russian Empire and are also more religious.

Grosfeld et al. (2013) find in the former territory of the "Pale of Settlement" where Jews were allowed to live in the Russian Empire before the Holocaust, that current residents have less support for the market economy, are less entrepreneurial, and more trusting. They find that this is related to the anti-Semitic culture among non-Jews who lived in those territories.

In a similar vein, Grosjean (2011) provides evidence from a gravity model on data from the Life in Transition Survey (LITs) in Eastern and Central Europe showing that the cultural distance between any two localities is reduced by one-third only if these two localities have been in the same empire for more than 100 years.

Using data from the Afrobarometer, Nunn and Wantchekon (2011) show that there is significantly less trust in African countries that suffered more from the slave trade. This is remarkable since slave trade stopped more than 150 years ago.

Tabellini (2010) and Cassar et al. (2013) in different studies found that good institutions may lead to the transmission of values of cooperation. Tabellini (2010) shows that regions of Europe that had institutions with more limited executive power in the past have a higher level of civic attitudes today, and Cassar et al. (2013) report results from experimental market games in Italy and Kosovo showing that a better institutional setup leads to less cheating.

Michau (2013) presents a model where the generosity of unemployment benefits and work ethics coevolve. One result is that high unemployment benefits dull parents' incentive to transmit a strong work ethic to their children. In related research, Lindbeck and Nyberg (2006) found, using data from the World Value Survey and OECD statistics, that the welfare state had negative effects on the transmission of work ethic.

Overall, our understanding of the determinants of cultural change remains very limited. Evolutionary models help us understand the dynamics but say little about initial triggers for change (technology, institutions, climate, war). We know even less about the determinants of cultural change in developing countries.

The most consistent historical evidence that has been put forward concerns the roles played by large empires. Why were large empires successful at cultural change? Think of the spread of Christianity under the Roman Empire, Islam under the Caliphate and the Ottoman Empire, orthodox religion under the Russian Empire, or Confucianism in China. This is all the more paradoxical since in the last 200 years, the world has experienced revolutionary technological and demographic changes. Nevertheless, the modern world has not invented or spread a new, fundamentally different culture. The culture of the modern Western world is fundamentally inherited from the Renaissance period, which was a combination of Christian religion and Greek and Roman culture of the Antiquity. One can even state in a more lapidary way that the culture of the modern world is Judeo-Christian. So, why were these empires so successful at spreading new cultures over centuries while the modern world has not?

We do not have any good answers to that question, only partial ones. Saleh (2018) points to the role of the poll tax in the Caliphate imposed on all non-Muslim inhabitants. In Egypt, poor Copts converted to Islam to avoid paying the tax, so that only a minority of richer Copts did not convert.

I will advance here a hypothesis that seems reasonable to me. In the early empires, the education of elites was usually entirely in the hands of the ruler. Education implied first the ability to read and to write, and this was done in the context of a completely religious education based on the Bible, the Koran, or whatever holy texts are central to that religion. This means several things. First, members of the elite were totally immersed in religion in their formative years. Second, the religious knowledge acquired gave them power over others, which gave them an incentive to want to transmit this religious knowledge. After a while, religious values and beliefs were transmitted vertically from parents to children, but also horizontally through education. Via a trickle-down process, religious knowledge and values were transmitted to ordinary people, and their offspring ended up receiving it both via vertical and horizontal transmission. Thus, by using religious knowledge as the main vehicle for education, religious values became widespread and were transmitted generation after generation in the empires. To a large extent, these values are still transmitted today.

It would be very hard, in a country today, to transmit a new culture that would be radically different from that of the empires, and this for multiple reasons. First of all, in the age of empires, territories were invaded before spreading the empire's religion. Second, that religion was the only path to knowledge and education. After World War II, large-scale invasions have become rare and are ostracized by the international community. Moreover, modern communication has made it possible to access many sources of knowledge. All of this gives an advantage to the cultural status quo, or even if there is some erosion of existing cultures, it prevents big cultural revolutions from taking place. The twentieth century witnessed the attempts to introduce radically new visions of the world compared to those inherited from history: communism and Nazism. Both failed miserably due to economic and/or military defeat. The current spread of radical Islam is mostly restricted to Muslim communities.

12.5. THE ORIGINS OF CULTURAL DIVERSITY

Why are people in Western countries more individualistic and people in Asia more collectivist? Why do we observe differences in trust in different countries and regions? Not only is it important to know why and how culture changes, it is also important to know why particular cultural traits were adopted in some countries while others were adopted in other countries. Understanding the origins of cultural diversity and cultural divergence across the world is probably even more challenging than understanding the determinants of cultural change. This is in part because it requires a comparative perspective, i.e., the same theory or set of mechanisms must explain different outcomes at the same time. Not surprisingly, we know even less about the origins of cultural diversity than about the determinants of cultural change. Most of the research in the area tends to focus on geographical variation as the main reason for cultural differences.

Ostrom (1990) was one of the first to venture into this area. She argued that trust was about norms and that more trust developed in communities in more upland regions because they needed to rely more on coordination to survive. A larger and impressive empirical study with that flavor is the one by Durante (2010), who emphasized the role of climate volatility in shaping values of cooperation. He hypothesized that stronger values of cooperation would evolve in places where people were facing more risks. In an agricultural setting, this means more climate volatility. He found that subregions of Europe that had a larger climate volatility between 1500 and 1700 had higher levels of trust and less strong family ties today.

In a different vein, Alesina et al. (2013) found that soil type affected the choice of use of the plow or the hoe in working the fields. Regions where farming relied heavily on the plow have developed gender roles less favorable to women. Men worked the field because working the plow required a lot of strength and women stayed at home. Many centuries later, countries that had plow-intensive agriculture have more traditional gender roles: lower labor force participation of women and stronger discrimination toward women. This stands in contrast to regions where the hoe was used more frequently. There, women worked on the land as well as men. Those regions developed stronger norms of equality between men and women. The amazing thing is that we still observe these differences today. One can argue that existing gender roles might have encouraged the role of the plow in societies with more discriminating values toward women. However, they argue that the use of the plow is mostly dependent on the type of crop, which itself depends on soil conditions. The plow is more adapted for crops where the land needs to be tilled rather quickly, which is the case for wheat, barley, and rye. Geographical conditions thus led to gender roles that have shaped values on gender roles. The work by Grosjean (2014) cited above is in the same spirit. A culture of violence developed more in those areas where raising cattle is more developed than growing crops.

Another geographical variable that has been argued to affect cultural values is geographical isolation. Ashraf and Galor (2011) developed a model and provided empirical evidence showing that societies that were geographically more isolated benefited from more homogeneity, which was beneficial to economic coordination, but this isolation led to cultural rigidity, which made these societies less ready for the industrialization period. Societies that were less isolated were more exposed to cultural diversity, which made them more adaptable for industrialization. They construct and index geographical isolation, based on the time it would take to travel from each square kilometer to the capital of a country. They construct an indicator of cultural diversity based on answers from the World Values Survey in different countries. They show that geographical isolation is associated with less cultural diversity, and that the latter is associated with higher trade openness, share of migrants, and log of income per capita.

The research mentioned so far provides clues on differences in particular values or beliefs, such as trust, violence, gender roles, or cultural diversity. Other research looks at the emergence of more systematic cultural differences across countries. A very interesting paper by Greif and Tabellini (2017) looks at the difference between China and Europe in terms of cultural values and institutions. In ancient China, the basic organization of collectivities and urban concentrations was based on the clan, i.e., extended kinship relations, whereas in premodern Europe, the cities, whose members were not based on any particular kinship group, played an important role. European cities invested in legal infrastructure, taxed citizens, and provided public goods like safety and defense, justice, education, and poor relief. In China, the same functions were performed by the clan elders. Greif and Tabellini argue that this different organization of society led to important cultural divergence. In particular, the clan-based organization of cities led to the development of norms of limited morality. Norms of cooperation were only valid toward members of the clan who were part of the community. In European cities, in contrast, norms of morality became universal as they applied to any citizen, independent of his kinship background. They build a model where a slight difference in the prevalence of limited morality over generalized morality will result in a bifurcation toward clan-based versus citizen-based urban environment. That in turn will lead to important cultural divergence. They document that kinship norms had been stronger in China compared to Europe. Obviously, one wonders how to explain this initial difference. Nevertheless, the analysis is quite compelling. While their emphasis is on the difference between limited and general morality, it is also consistent with the difference between collectivism and individualism. Indeed, collectivism emphasizes loyalty and conformity to the ingroup, be it the clan or the tribe, whereas individualism takes as its basis individuals as citizens with equal rights and responsibilities. Generalized morality is an attribute of individualism and limited morality is an attribute of collectivism. While it raises many questions, the Greif and Tabellini framework provides a historically compelling analysis of cultural divergence between China and Europe.

Somewhat related is the work by Gorodnichenko and Roland (2015, 2017). In their empirical analysis of the effects of individualism and collectivism on innovation and long-run growth, on one hand, and on democratization on the other hand, they propose instrumental variables for individualism and collectivism that may explain some of the cultural divergence. One such explanation is based on the work of Fincher et al. (2008), who show that stronger historical pathogen prevalence in certain regions of the world gave a definite advantage to the spread of collectivist values. The idea is that areas with high pathogen prevalence would lead to high mortality unless human collectivities developed rigid norms related to contact with strangers, sexual behavior, openness to experimentation, strict adherence to collective norms, etc. In other words, a stronger pathogen prevalence would have encouraged the emergence of collectivist values. A similar story can be told relative to the frequency of particular genes in populations (in particular, genes related to propensity to depression in the face of stressful events or related to the intensity of psychological suffering from social exclusion) which various studies have argued to favor the emergence and consolidation over time of a collectivist culture in order to protect individuals from the negative consequences of these particular genetic endowments. These ideas are interesting in the sense that they provide exogenous sources of variation for the emergence of individualist versus collectivist culture. Nevertheless, they can only be part of the story when it comes to explaining the determinants of cultural divergence.

Another hypothesis relative to the origin of collectivist culture is the rice production hypothesis developed by Talhelm et al. (2014). The idea is that areas where farmers grew rice crops required much more collaboration because rice-growing is very labor-intensive and necessitates careful irrigation. The study found on the basis of surveys of 1,162 Chinese students that those who came from rice-growing regions had more collectivist values and beliefs relative to students from regions where wheat was grown. The results are intriguing. This raises the question of why Northern China, which was the cradle of Chinese civilization, developed a collectivist culture.

Finally, another explanation of the cultural divergence between individualism and collectivism is proposed by Olsson and Paik (2015). They find that the length of time since the Neolithic transition from hunter-gatherer societies to agricultural societies is a good predictor of collectivism. Their theory is that the establishment of agricultural societies fosters collectivist values and behaviors. Agricultural production led to a higher population density, which necessitated strong norms of behavior, usually associated with autocratic rulers. Agricultural societies were often threatened by outside predators, which required a strong defense capacity. Therefore, early agricultural societies tended to develop collectivist norms. Individuals with more individualistic preferences would prefer to flee these societies and settle in the periphery to enjoy more freedom. The extension of agriculture led to the imposition of collectivist norms, which in turn led individualists to move out, and so on. As a result, the societies that became agricultural earlier are more collectivist than those that introduced agriculture later on. They find that regions that adopted agriculture earlier tend to value obedience more and feel less in control of their lives. Moreover, they have had little experience with democracy. This is an interesting theory, but the data all pertain to Europe and the Middle East, where the latter is more collectivist than the former. One would like to see what we find for the whole world, since the difference between Asia and Europe is the most important one, when it comes to individualism and collectivism. Moreover, since all countries with a sufficiently high GDP per capita have experienced the Neolithic transition thousands of years ago, one wonders why the difference in timing of the Neolithic transition would have such an impact.

The evidence so far on the origins of cultural diversity across the world is still only very partial. One needs to understand much better, in a comprehensive way, the sources of divergence between the most important cultural families on the planet. The answer will most likely be a combination between different factors: the random production of philosophies and the evolutionary survival of some depending on the local geographical environment, the institutional environment, the technological endowment, and possibly elements of genetic endowment. There really is a need for deep historical research combining archeology, anthropology, climate science, genetics, and history of religion and philosophy.

One path, maybe the most promising path, is to study the coevolution of institutions and culture in a historical perspective. A recent model by Bisin and Verdier (2016) encourages us to go in this direction. Recent empirical work in the context of history (Murrell and Schmidt 2011) and development (Lowes et al. 2017) has been done in that direction.

12.6. PATH-FINDING DIRECTIONS OF FUTURE RESEARCH

In this section, we draw conclusions based on the above survey on what should be pathfinding directions of future research. We try to be as exhaustive as possible and propose some prioritization at the end of the section.

12.6.1. A Finer Measurement of the Effects of Culture

There are many reasons why it is not easy to precisely measure the effects of culture. First, culture is a social phenomenon. It is not just the addition of individual preferences, network effects are important in the spreading of culture, and measuring network effects is always very tricky and difficult. Second, culture moves slowly. There are no sudden shocks that introduce new cultures or new cultural values overnight. Therefore, it is difficult to untangle the effects of culture from many other possible confounding variables.

This does not mean that one should abstain from doing work on culture. It is a subject that is too important to be ignored. More precise measurement will imply a stronger focus on subnational analysis, or comparisons between different sides of cultural borders facing similar economic and geographical circumstances. This should be a very useful direction of research. The haunting trade-off between internal and external validity will nevertheless always be there.

12.6.2. Use the Epidemiological Method Also Outside the United States

The epidemiological method is methodologically quite clean and should be used much more outside the United States. Many countries in the modern world are composed to a larger extent than one might assume of migrants from many countries of origin. This is clearly true for France, Germany, and England, for example. Studies using the epidemiological method would be very helpful in contexts other than the United States, if only to validate studies done for the United States. Even if the epidemiological method is methodologically very sound and innovative, it is limited to analyzing the persistence and spread of culture as well as the effect of culture on individual behavior and actions. It does not allow analysis of the effects of culture on aggregate variables implying collective actions since collectivities are composed of people with many different countries of ancestry.

12.6.3. More Comprehensive Measures of Culture

An important task is to better understand the link between different dimensions of culture and have as comprehensive a measure as possible of cultural differences across the world. Cultures are derived from different views of the world that usually form a relatively consistent whole. The most comprehensive measure that we have so far is the Hofstede individualism/collectivism index and the related Schwartz data. Even these measures do not cover the whole array of values associated with a culture. This measure is nevertheless more comprehensive than other measures in the literature that focus only on particular values or subsets of values. One of the reasons the individualism/collectivism index is very popular in other social sciences that have used it extensively is that the ranking of countries it produces is very robust. Other studies for which similar value surveys have been done for other professions (teachers, lawyers, flight attendants) yield similar rankings in terms of individualism and collectivism. Since these data are based on subjective surveys, the information provided by the rankings is the most important one, more important than the difference in scores between any two countries. As discussed above, the robustness in these rankings may mean that there are unmeasured values that are strongly correlated with the measured values, so that the rankings reflect a more comprehensive measure of cultural differences. That being said, efforts are still needed to come up with comprehensive measures.

One area where there is a gaping hole in the economics literature on culture is the lack of measurement of indigenous cultures in developing countries. Here, economists must learn from the data gathered by anthropologists. Mainstream development economics has tended to ignore the cultural background of communities in developing countries, focusing solely on importing technology and human capital. One should analyze the data gathered by anthropologists to identify and classify cultural families in developing countries, based on the views of the world represented by these cultures and the effects it may have on economic behavior of individuals and communities.

12.6.4. More Laboratory Experiments on Culture

More international laboratory experiments are needed to better understand the effects of culture. I am not at all a specialist of laboratory experiments and do not have much to say about it. It nevertheless makes it possible to test directly some hypotheses of the effects of culture on forms of economic behavior. The few laboratory experiments done using participants with different cultural backgrounds have provided interesting insights. As cross-cultural psychologists have performed a large number of experiments, especially in testing the differences between individualism and collectivism, there is no need to replicate their studies, but one must think of interesting scenarios that can be played out in the laboratory where cultural differences might yield differences in economic behavior and outcomes.

12.6.5. Does Globalization Lead to Cultural Convergence or to the Strengthening of Cultural Identities?

This is a very important question. Globalization leads not only to exchange of goods and services, but also to exchange of information and ideas. Like never before, people are exposed to the ways of thinking, habits, values, and beliefs of other people all across the world. Does this extraordinary availability of information lead to some process of cultural convergence, whereby people "pick and choose" among the cultural values on the global marketplace of ideas, in a similar way that they purchase commodities produced all across the globe? This is one hypothesis. The other hypothesis is that globalization may appear as a threat to the survival of local cultures. This perceived threat may then instead lead people to cling to their traditional values in a rigid way. If the latter hypothesis is true, then globalization may not be sustainable in the long run, as different communities may try to cut themselves off from the outside world, as was the case for China and Japan several centuries ago. To our knowledge, this question has not come up at all in the literature on culture and development. This is, however, a first-order question. It is relevant both internationally, but also within countries. From a normative perspective, cultural exchange can only enrich people as they learn from others, even if they decide to hang on to their own values. Cultural exchange is, however, a two-way street that requires tolerance and understanding on both sides of the exchange.

A related question, which is currently of first-order effect, is the impact of various policies of cultural integration and assimilation. In advanced economies that have been experiencing large inflows of migrants from poor countries, policies of integration vary strongly, from simple coexistence of communities (multiculturalism) to policies of forced assimilation (prohibition of the Islamic veil and insistence on strong adoption of secularism as in the French model of laïcité). We do not have a good understanding of the effect of these policies. Multiculturalism has been accused of undermining the cohesion of a country and being the recipe for future intercommunity conflict. On the other hand, policies of forced assimilation may lead to radicalization of minorities, preventing a peaceful integration of migrants and rejecting them to the margins of society. It is clear that we need research to understand what are the best policies for integrating migrants. Surely, the speed of inflow is a key policy variable, but there may be shocks like the large inflow of Syrian refugees in Europe since 2015 that cannot be prevented.

Analyzing this question ideally requires a dynamic general equilibrium approach where decisions to trade and to migrate respond to existing cultural values, which unleash economic forces that may affect the evolution of cultural values over time, leading either to forms of cultural and economic convergence or divergence.

12.6.6. Which Cultural Values Change Faster and Which Change Slower?

Skeptics of the idea of cultural inertia will tend to show counterexamples where a particular subset of cultural values changes fast: attitudes toward cigarettes, values on gender roles, for example. It is important to dig further in the direction started by Giavazzi et al. (2014) to better understand which cultural values tend to be more inert than others and why. This will also be very important to understand the dynamics of cultural change.

In addition, it is critical to make a difference between opinion surveys and measurements of cultural values. These are often confused. Opinion polls are quite volatile and change depending on the economic situation and other variables that change in the short run. Temporary changes in opinions in certain areas, or in voting intentions, are in no way representative of changes in values. Even though this difference makes sense, we have not yet developed methods to deal with this issue.

12.6.7. Understanding Better the Sources of Cultural Diversity

Understanding better the sources of cultural diversity is of crucial importance to better understanding the effects of culture. Cross-country studies on the effects of culture are often received with skepticism because our measures of culture are mostly recent and instrumental variables at the macroeconomic level are rarely completely clean, in terms of the exclusion restriction. The remnants of the Marxist intellectual tradition of seeing culture as determined by economic factors are still very present in the economics profession, albeit unconsciously. There is no doubt that culture has a lot of inertia, but if we understand better the historical origins of modern cultures, we will be in a situation to better understand its effects.

Understanding the roots of cultural diversity is, however, a huge nut to crack. Cultural evolution is tightly interwoven in the long-run history of countries. Investigating how different conditions led historically to different cultures requires a massive data-gathering approach combining political and economic history, geography, archeology, and anthropology.

12.6.8. Research Priorities

The biggest priority, in my view, is research on better understanding the sources of cultural diversity. This trumps all other questions as this will help shed light on the other path-finding research questions identified. It will help explain the singularities and commonalities between various cultures as well as their determinants. To put it in another way, it will help explain what are the fundamental pillars of different cultures and why they matter. It will also help explain cultural evolution and its determinants.

Next, I think that laboratory experiments to understand the effects of cross-cultural variation will be very important, certainly in terms of expected academic payoff. They should be combined with the epidemiological approach. Here, games with large numbers of players, one recent innovation in laboratory experiments, will help widen the usefulness of the epidemiological approach so as to understand the cultural effects on group behavior.

Finally, better understanding cultural coexistence in a globalized world, and in the context of large migration flows, is a key policy question of our time.

12.7. SOME POLICY CONCLUSIONS

In this section, I define some policy conclusions that can already be drawn from the vast research undertaken in the last decade on culture and economics.

12.7.1. Taking Culture as Given Instead of Pushing for Cultural Change

A first and very important conclusion is that taking culture on board means first of all to take into account the effects of different cultures when designing development policies. One should take cultures as given and see what are the best development policies given the prevailing culture. Particular policies or institutional reforms must be tailored to fit the existing cultural environment. This is how they work best.

The most important mistake one may tend to make when integrating culture in development policies is to try to change existing cultures so as to obtain one's desired policies. Pushing for cultural change can be dangerous and counterproductive. The well-documented inertia of culture explains the difficulty and multiple failures in transplanting institutions (see, e.g., Berkowitz et al. 2003; Francois and Zabojnik 2005). While some particular cultural values can change quite fast (within one generation), as a rule whole cultures do not change fast at all. Policies that promote cultural change can only deliver effects in the long run via elite education, the propagation of role models for young people to emulate, and a slow trickle-down process. Betting on fast cultural change to make policies work is a recipe for failure.

12.7.2. Institutional Change May Trigger Gradual Cultural Changes

Institutional change may under certain conditions lead to gradual changes in cultural norms, as shown by Aldashev et al. (2012). This is a subtle issue. Drastic institutional change, forced from above, that clashes with the existing culture will meet resistance and will likely fail. Nevertheless, it is possible that some institutional change, that acts like a nudge, may lead gradually to changes in behavior. These changes in behavior may then persist and be consolidated if they result in gradual cultural changes. These institutional changes are more likely to be successful and also to affect cultural values, because they do not represent a radical break with the incumbent culture, but push it in a direction in which particular groups of actors can recognize their interests and fight for changes in values. Laws that lead to empowerment of women in countries where they are suffering from discrimination can thus be a strong vehicle for cultural change. These laws serve to legitimize more equal gender values. They can thus be more effective than "soft" empowerment measures because the formal institutions give support to those people who want to push for different values, thus giving them a larger and lasting bargaining power.

In that context, media may play a role in the diffusion of cultural values and the possible promotion of cultural change (see the companion EDI survey by Eliana la Ferrara 2017).

12.7.3. The Need for Internationally Accepted Norms
of Respect of Cultural Diversity

The world is multicultural and will in all likelihood stay that way. Cultures may compete peacefully with each other, but it would be unrealistic to think that one culture will come to dominate others or that some cultures will drastically adapt to others. Instead of aggressively asserting one's own culture's superiority and rejecting others, it is important to develop bilateral norms of respect where both sides recognize mutual cultural differences, but agree to coexist peacefully, respecting each other's dignity and right to individual beliefs and values. The same is true within each country. Everybody's right to their own beliefs and values should be recognized as long as the actions derived from it do not conflict with local legal arrangements.

APPENDIX:

Detailed Discussion of the Economic Effects of Culture

This appendix discusses in greater detail the economic effects of culture as referenced in table 12.1.

12.A.1. Trust

Effects on Income Per Capita and Growth. In different studies, Knack and Keefer (1997) and Algan and Cahuc (2010) gave evidence that more trust leads to higher income per capita and growth, the former instrument trust with an ethnolinguistic variable. These days, we would question the validity of the exclusion restriction since ethnolinguistic variables may affect income per capita directly, or through other means than trust, for example through human capital or through other cultural variables. Algan and Cahuc (2010) use another strategy and estimate the evolution of trust in the home country of US citizens by exploiting the timing of arrivals of immigrants. They regress the evolution of income per capita on variation in trust, measured by the difference between the current level of trust in a country and a proxy for the past level of trust, measured by the inherited trust of US citizens whose ancestors came from that country in different time periods. This delivers a measure of the effect of trust on income per capita, which is significant.

Trade and Investment. Guiso et al. (2009) use bilateral measures of trust between European countries and find that, everything else equal, a lower level of bilateral trust leads to less trade and less foreign direct investment between countries. Trust between countries is affected by cultural distance, past history, and genetic distance. Unfortunately, these bilateral trust measures exist only for Europe, and we do not know if these results would be valid for the world as a whole. Giuliano et al. (2013) found that the effect of genetic distance on trade disappears once one correctly controls for measures of geographical distance.

Financial Market Development. Guiso et al. (2004) have found that higher trust is associated with stronger financial market development. They find that Italians who come from regions where trust is high (Northern regions) are more likely to use the financial system: bank accounts, checks, mortgage contracts, stock portfolios, and bank credit. An interesting aspect of their research is that these results hold when people move from a high trust to a low trust region and vice versa. It is not clear how these results carry over outside Italy, but one can make arguments for why they should. Cole et al. (2013) found in a randomized field experiment in India that farming households fail to take up rainfall insurance contracts, in part because of lack of trust: demand is somewhat higher when the insurance product is offered by someone they trust.

Organization of the Firm. The level of trust may also affect the organization of firms. If there is a greater atmosphere of trust between employees, then there will be more delegation of tasks and responsibilities to the lower levels and thus a more decentralized organizational form. Using firm data on Italy, Cingano and Pinotti (2012) construct measures of delegation for a representative sample of firms based on a survey done by the Bank of Italy, filtering out industry and regional effects. They find that regions with a higher level of trust have on average a higher level of decentralization and a larger firm size. They instrument trust by institutional variables from regions' historical past, like in Tabellini (2010). They find similar results for a sample of industries across 15 European countries, using the European Social Survey which contains trust survey data as well as data on the perception of employees of how much delegation authority they enjoy.

Labor Relations. Trust has also been found to affect labor relations. Algan and Cahuc (2009) found that a higher level of civic virtue was associated with a higher flexibility in labor markets as well as with a higher level of labor income insurance as protection for workers. Low civic virtue is instead associated with worker protection through rigid labor market regulations. Their theory is that if citizens have civic virtue, they will not abuse unemployment benefit systems. The government will therefore provide adequate unemployment insurance. If, on the other hand, there is a mentality of cheating and people do not seriously look for jobs when unemployed, then protection of workers will instead be better provided by regulations that protect jobs. They find that there is a significant relation between the level of unemployment insurance and labor market flexibility on one hand, and a measure of civic virtue on the other hand. The latter is derived from the World Values Survey that contains a question on whether people consider it justifiable to claim benefits from the government even when one is not entitled to them. They also find that evolution of civic virtue between 1980 and 2000 is positively related to changes in labor insurance. Finally, they instrument civic virtue in a country by the predicted civic virtue of US citizens based on their country of origin and can claim a causal effect from civic virtue on the form of labor market protection.

Institutions. There are a number of papers that analyze the impact of trust on the quality of institutions. This is an important topic, because institutions are known to have a major impact on growth and economic performance. Finding a causal effect of culture on institutions can thus shed light on the determinants of the quality of institutions. The effect of culture on institutions is a recurrent topic in this literature. Here, we treat exclusively with research on the effect of trust on institutions. We discuss further below the effect of other dimensions of culture. Tabellini (2008b) analyzed the effect of trust on the quality of institutions. He interprets trust as "generalized morality" as opposed to "limited morality." Generalized morality is characterized by norms of conduct that apply universally to all other citizens, independently of their family or social background. These norms of behavior are not personal, based on family or tribal relationships, but based on citizenship. Expectations of dealing with people in a culture of generalized morality lead in turn to norms of behavior where people can in general be trusted because they share this common set of values. Limited morality instead has strong ethical norms within the family, the tribe, or the clan, but people outside this ingroup are not to be trusted. This distinction reflects cultural values that are typical of Northern versus Southern Italy. The norms of limited morality in Southern Italy had been documented by the classical work of Banfield (1958) on "amoral familism": strong norms of morality within the family, opportunistic behavior with the rest of society. The argument is that in a society with norms of generalized morality, not only are people to behave in a more cooperative way, but politicians and public administrators behave more in the interest of the public and are expected to behave in a non-corrupt way. Tabellini found that a higher level of trust was associated with a better quality of institutions, measured by a composite of institutional measures used by Hall and Jones (1999). To measure a causal effect from trust to the quality of institutions, he uses two instrumental variables, both based on linguistic differences that have been argued to reflect cultural differences. The first difference is whether or not the use of pronouns is mandatory in sentences. This reflects a stronger distinction between individuals and others and a better recognition of the individual as a distinct entity. The second difference is whether or not there is a distinction between the second person of the singular and the second person of the plural, the *tu-vos* distinction as exists in Latin. When this distinction exists, it is supposed to reflect more hierarchical values in society. On that basis, Tabellini finds a significant causal effect from trust to the quality of institutions.

There are many different kinds of institutions and thus different angles of focus. Aghion et al. (2010) for example found a link between trust and regulation. In a society with low trust, there will be a high demand for regulation because people will not trust government officials not to be corrupt and thus demand limits on their behavior. As a consequence, one will find an association between a high level of regulation and corruption. In this theory, they are not directly related to each other but are related to the general level of trust in society. Empirically, they find an association between measures of trust from the World Values Survey and measures of regulation, be it regulation of entry or price regulation. Pinotti (2012) gets similar results showing that less trust increases the demand for regulation. He interprets this as beliefs about the strength of negative externalities affecting market regulation. He shows that there is no negative relation between the extent of regulation and measures of economic performance, once one controls for trust.

Aghion et al. (2011) also analyze the relation between trust on one hand and union density and minimum-wage regulation on the other. They find that if there is a low level of trust, this will lead to the setting of high minimum wages by the government because there is little trust that negotiation between employers and unions will lead to good results. High minimum wages in turn reduce incentives to become trade union members and discourage workers from engaging in collective negotiations.

Electoral Accountability: Putnam (1993) had already shown that lower levels of civil society development and social capital were associated with a lower quality of public good procurement in Italy. Nannicini et al. (2013) showed evidence, also based on Italy, showing that lower levels of trust were associated with lower levels of electoral accountability. They build a model where different regions have a varying proportion of civic and uncivic voters. Civic voters care about social welfare and are less tolerant of corrupt behavior by politicians. Uncivic voters, on the other hand, care more about how politicians will cater to their narrow personal interest. They show that higher levels of social capital, measured by the level of blood donations per capita but also by density of nongovernmental organizations in electoral districts, are associated with better politician behavior, measured by being the subject of criminal indictment (request by the judicial system to lift an elected representative's immunity), absenteeism in parliament, and number of bills submitted.

12.A.2. Individualism and Collectivism

Gorodnichenko and Roland, among others, have written a number of papers examining the economic effects of the differences between individualism and collectivism.

Innovation and Long-Run Growth. In Gorodnichenko and Roland (2011, 2017), empirical evidence is given suggesting a possible robust causal effect from individualism and collectivism to innovation and long-run growth. The theory is based on endogenous growth theory. It is assumed that in countries with an individualist culture, there is a social status reward for innovation as people strive to stand out from the crowd. It is also assumed that countries with a collectivist culture have an advantage in coordination of manufacturing activity. In an endogenous growth context, the latter has a static effect, raising income per capita, but the former has growth effects as it raises the innovation rate and thus gives a dynamic advantage. They confirm that countries with an individualist culture have higher income per capita, higher TFP growth and innovation rates, using different measures of innovation, and controlling for variables that are usually important in growth regressions (institutions, geography, human capital). As the relation between culture and growth can go both ways, they use different instrumental variables to establish a causal effect. A first instrumental variable is the frequency of certain genes in a population (the frequency of the S-allele in the serotonin transporter gene 5HTTLPR making people more prone to depression when confronted with stressful events). A second instrumental variable is the frequency of the G allele in polymorphism A118G in μ-opoid receptor gene creating a stronger psychological pain from social exclusion. A third instrumental variable is historical pathogen prevalence in a particular geographical area. According to recent advances in genetics and psychology, these genetic variables appear to *directly* affect personality traits. Chiao and Blizinsky (2010), Way and Lieberman (2010) and others argue that communities with a higher frequency of these two genes and with a higher pathogen prevalence developed social norms to adapt to this genetic and epidemiological environment. Since those variables are only available for a limited number of countries, another instrumental variable that is more widely available worldwide is a measure of genetic distance between the population in a given country and the population in the United Kingdom, which is the second most individualistic country in the world. Obviously, parents transmit their genes as well as their cultural values to their offspring. Populations that interbreed a lot should be genetically and culturally close because a similar parental transmission mechanism is at work in both cases. Therefore, measures of genetic distance can be seen as a proxy measure of differences in cultural values. Since there are no identified direct genetic causes for why some countries became wealthier than others, genetic distance can be argued to satisfy the exclusion restriction. In this case, they use genetic distance based on frequencies of blood types, which is available for the largest number of countries.

A potential drawback of genetic distance is that there could be channels other than individualism through which genetic distance can be indirectly related to long-run growth (e.g., another cultural dimension).

Democratization. Gorodnichenko and Roland (2015) build a simple model with the following trade-off: collectivist cultures, compared to individualistic cultures, have a higher probability of solving their collective action problem, but have less propensity to orient revolt toward changing the political system. The model predicts that collectivist cultures, in contrast to individualistic cultures, will be more reluctant to revolt against a "good" autocrat delivering strong economic development. Therefore, collectivist cultures are likely to end up in the long run with either a good autocracy or with democracy. Individualistic cultures on the other hand will in the long run end up only with democracy. Despite a lower probability of success of collective action, individualistic cultures will introduce democracy on average earlier than collectivist cultures. They bring empirical evidence that fit those predictions. As an instrumental variable for individualism and collectivism, they use historical pathogen prevalence, which, as discussed above, was shown by psychologists to foster a collectivist culture. Using this instrument, individualism is shown to have a positive effect on a country's average polity score over the period 1980–2010, controlling for measures of conflict, religion, income, institutions, inequality, education, and various measures of fractionalization. Similar results are obtained when the dependent variable is the number of years a country has been democratic. Individualism is also negatively associated with a transition from autocracy to autocracy and with revolt against autocracy. These results are somewhat at odds with modernization theory, the dominant theory of democratization in political science, which suggests that countries all become democratic as income rises (Lipset 1959), or that there are no reversals of democracy past a certain income level (Przeworski and Limongi 1997). They suggest that there is a clear cultural component in this process. Countries like China, where the culture is collectivist, may not become democratic for a very long time, even after income has reached high levels, and may follow the path of "efficient" autocracies like Singapore.

Institutions. Kyriacou (2016) does an exercise similar to Tabellini (2008b) and Licht et al. (2007), which we review below, analyzing the impact of individualism on the quality of institutions, as measured by ICRG indicators used frequently in the literature on institutions. This is not too surprising, as individualism is positively correlated with trust. Many of the features associated with generalized morality can be derived from individualism. Individuals need rights in order to express their individuality, and thus see themselves as citizens equal before the law. Interestingly, Kyriacou finds that the effect of individualism on GDP per capita disappears once one controls for the quality of institutions. This would mean that the effect of individualism on GDP per capita would work solely through its effect on the quality of institutions. This result differs from Gorodnichenko and Roland (2017). These differences are related to differences in the choice of instruments. Kyriacou instruments individualism by the prohibition of the pronoun drop, used also by Tabellini, and the quality of institutions by legal origins, instead of settler mortality. Klasing (2012) tests the effect of different measures of culture on the quality of institutions: trust, religion, Hofstede's cultural measures, as well as those of Schwartz discussed below. She instruments culture by a weighted average of cultural attitudes in neighboring countries. She finds that only individualism and power distance (the extent to which inequality in the distribution of power is tolerated, another Hofstede index) are strongly and statistically significant predictors of observed cross-country differences in institutional quality.

Outsourcing in International Trade. Cultural differences matter in international economics, as we saw above in the case of bilateral trust. Gorodnichenko et al. (2015) look at the effect of cultural distance on decisions of multinational firms to outsource their supplies from independent suppliers or from their own subsidiary in a foreign country. They construct a model showing that there is a basic trade-off at work: vertical integration leads to better coordination within the firm but entails frictions between managers in the different countries that are more costly when cultural differences are greater. They find that the share of intrafirm imports in the US declines with cultural distance at the firm level as well as at the industry level. They also find, using the Bureau Van Dijck Orbis data, that share ownership of parent companies in daughter companies decreases with cultural distance. The cultural distance they use is the Hofstede individualism-collectivism index. Other measures of cultural distance turn out to be less significant.

12.A.3. Autonomy/Embeddedness

Effect on Institutions. Licht et al. (2007) were the first to analyze the effect of culture on institutions. They used the Schwartz data for this purpose. Their idea is that in societies whose prevailing culture emphasizes the moral equality of individuals and legitimizes individuals' pursuit of their own preferences, one is likely to find greater compliance with formal legal rules, exercise of discretionary power undistorted by bribes, and feedback mechanisms of accountability. They were the first to use as instrumental variable the prohibition of the pronoun drop, a variable used also by Tabellini (2008) and Kyriacou (2016).

12.A.4. Luck Versus Effort

Redistribution. Alesina and Angeletos (2005) built a political economy model where belief in effort paying off leads to low taxation and high individual effort. A stronger belief in the role of luck relative to effort leads to political demand for redistribution, which in turn tends to dull incentives, thereby confirming beliefs that the role of effort in success is less important. They use the model to explain why Europe has a more developed welfare state than the United States.

12.A.5. Gender Roles

Effects on Labor Force Participation of Women. Fernandez et al. (2004), Fernandez (2007), and Fernandez and Fogli (2009) have examined the role of culture in determining the labor force participation of women in the United States. In Fernandez and Fogli (2009) for example, there is a consistent finding that households with ancestors in countries with lower participation rates of women in 1950 have a lower participation rate in the United States. They control for other variables, such as the level of education, which play a role in determining labor force participation of women. Note that the ancestry of the husband matters more than that of the wife.

Fertility Choices. Fernandez and Fogli (2006, 2009) do a similar exercise for fertility choices. They find that culture, as measured by fertility rates in the ancestors' country of origin, affects current fertility choices, even after controlling for other variables that have been found significant in the literature on fertility choices, such as for example the number of siblings a woman has.

Preference for Boys and the Sex Ratio. Since Amartya Sen (1990) alerted the world to the phenomenon of "missing women," i.e., an imbalanced sex ratio favoring males over females in a large number of countries, such as India and China, researchers have been investigating the consequences of unbalanced sex ratios in developing countries. One well-known example is China. Following the adoption of the "One child" policy, selective abortions have led to a high male-to-female sex ratio given the preference for boys. Edlund et al. (2013) for example found that the increase in the sex ratio has led to an increase in crime.

12.A.6. Family Values

Institutions of Regulation. Alesina et al. (2010) found that labor market regulations were stricter in societies with stronger family ties. The reason is that individuals are very reluctant to work far away from their families. This leads to support regulations that make labor markets more rigid and that limit labor mobility.

Female Labor Force Participation. Alesina and Giuliano (2007) found that in countries with stronger family ties, female labor force participation was lower as women tend to participate more in the economic activities of the household. This is still valid in the United States for second-generation immigrants, after controlling for individual characteristics such as age and education.

Extent of Public Pensions. The strength of family ties also affects the demand for public pensions. Galasso and Profeta (2018) have analyzed the link between both. The argument is that with weak family ties, pensions act as a safety net, since people can rely less on solidarity within the family. Instead, with strong family ties, there is less initial demand for public pensions, but when pension systems are introduced, the elderly are given generous replacement rates as substitutes for their children taking care of them. Again, exploiting data from the United States, they find that countries with looser family ties have a stronger preference for public pensions.

Marriage Decisions. Strong family ties create obligations to pool resources inside the extended family. Luke and Munshi (2006) found, in studying remittances in Kenya, that high-ability individuals who are obliged to send large sums to their families tend to delay marriage to escape these obligations before marriage.

12.A.7. Culture of Honor

Homicide. Pauline Grosjean (2014), following path-breaking work by psychologists Nisbett and Cohen (1996), showed that the higher homicide rate in the US South relative to the North could be traced back to the different origin of migrants in the nineteenth century. They were of Scottish-Irish origin and from families of herders. As explained in the main text, in societies where herding is an important part of economic activity (for example Sardinia, Albania), a culture of honor is more widespread. This culture of honor has persisted more than a hundred years after people migrated to the United States, resulting in more violent behavior to "defend one's honor" and thus higher homicide rates.

Coordination. The culture of honor can also be an impediment to efficient collaboration between people. Brooks et al. (2015) report on coordination games that they have been running in India, in Uttar Pradesh province, in 2005. They found that upper caste Indians had a harder time solving coordination problems, and that this was related to their culture of honor.

NOTES

I am grateful to participants at the Namur January 2016 conference, to Maitreesh Ghatak, and to two anonymous referees for comments received on the initial presentation and on the revised version.
1.   The most current version of the data is available at http://www.geert-hofstede.com/.
2.   See for example Hoppe's (1990) study among members of parliaments, labor and employer leaders, academics, and artists in 18 countries; Shane's (1995) study across 28 countries for international companies other than IBM; Merritt's (2000) study on commercial airline pilots in 19 countries; de Mooij's (2003) survey among consumers in 15 European countries; and van Nimwegen's (2002) research among employees of ABN-AMRO bank in 19 countries.

REFERENCES

Aghion, P., Y. Algan, and P. Cahuc. 2011. "Can Policy Affect Culture? Minimum Wage and the Quality of Labor Relations." *Journal of the European Economic Association* 9(1): 3–42.

Aghion, P., Y. Algan, P. Cahuc, and A. Shleifer. 2010. "Regulation and Distrust." *Quarterly Journal of Economics* 125(3): 1015–1049.

Aldashev, G., I. Chaara, J.-P. Platteau, and Z. Wahhaj. 2012. "Using the Law to Change the Custom." *Journal of Development Economics* 97(2): 182–200.

Alesina, A., Y. Algan, P. Cahuc, and P. Giuliano. 2010. "Family Values and the Regulation of Labor." *Journal of the European Economic Association* 13(4): 599–630.

Alesina, A. and G.-M. Angeletos. 2005. "Fairness and Redistribution." *American Economic Review* 95(4): 960–980.

Alesina, A. and P. Giuliano. 2007. "The Power of the Family." *Journal of Economic Growth* 15(2): 93–125.

———. 2011. "Family Ties and Political Participation." *Journal of the European Economic Association* 9(5): 817–839.

———. 2014. "Family Ties." In *Handbook of Economic Growth*, edited by P. Aghion and S. Durlauf, vol. 2A, 177–215. Amsterdam: North Holland.

———. 2015. "Culture and Institutions." *Journal of Economic Literature* 53(4): 898–944.

Alesina, A., P. Giuliano, and N. Nunn. 2013. "On the Origins of Gender Roles: Women and the Plough." *Quarterly Journal of Economics* 128(2): 469–530.

Algan, Y. and P. Cahuc. 2009. "Civic Virtue and Labor Market Institutions." *American Economic Journal: Macroeconomics* 1(1): 111–145.

———. 2010. "Inherited Trust and Growth." *American Economic Review* 100: 2060–2092.

———. 2014. "Trust, Growth and Happiness: New Evidence and Policy Implications." In *Handbook of Economic Growth*, edited by P. Aghion and S. Durlauf, vol. 2A. Amsterdam: North Holland.

Almond, D., H. Li, and S. Zhang. 2019. "Land Reform and Sex Selection in China." *Journal of Political Economy* 127(2): 560–585.

Arrow, K. 1972. "Gifts and Exchanges." *Philosophy and Public Affairs* 1(2): 343–362.

Ashraf, Q. and O. Galor. 2007. "Cultural Assimilation, Cultural Diffusion and the Origin of the Wealth of Nations." Working Paper, Brown University.

———. 2011. "Cultural Diversity, Geographical Isolation, and the Origin of the Wealth of Nations." NBER Working Paper No. 17640.

Banfield, E. 1958. *The Moral Basis of a Backward Society*. New York: Simon & Schuster.

Becker, S. O., K. Boeckh, C. Hainz, and L. Woessmann. 2016. "The Empire Is Dead, Long Live the Empire! Long Run Persistence of Trust and Corruption in the Bureaucracy." *Economic Journal* 126(590): 40–74.

Berkowitz, D., K. Pistor, and J.-F. Henry. 2003. "The Transplant Effect." *American Society of Corporate Law* 51(1): 163–203.

Besley, T. and M. Ghatak. 2016. "Market Incentives and the Evolution of Intrinsic Motivation." Working Paper, London School of Economics.

Bisin, A., E. Patacchini, and T. Verdier. 2016. "Bend It Like Beckham: Identity, Socialization, and Assimilation." *European Economic Review* 90(1): 146–164.

Bisin, A., G. Topa, and T. Verdier. 2004. "Religious Intermarriage and Socialization in the United States." *Journal of Political Economy* 112(3): 615–664.

Bisin, A. and T. Verdier. 2000. "'Beyond the Melting Pot': Cultural Transmission, Marriage, and the Evolution of Ethnic and Religious Traits." *Quarterly Journal of Economics* 115(3): 955–988.

———. 2001. "The Economics of Cultural Transmission and the Dynamics of Preferences." *Journal of Economic Theory* 97: 298–319.

———. 2004. "Work Ethic and Redistribution: A Cultural Transmission Model of the Welfare State." Working Paper, New York University.

———. 2016. "On the Joint Evolution of Culture and Institutions." Working Paper, New York University.

Bloom, N., R. Sadun, and J. Van Reenen. 2012. "The Organization of Firms Across Countries." *Quarterly Journal of Economics* 127(4): 1663–1705.

Bornthorst, F., A. Ichino, O. Kirchkamp, K. H. Schlag, and E. Winter. 2010. "Similarities and Differences When Building Trust: The Role of Cultures." *Experimental Economics* 1(3): 260–283.

Boyd, R., H. Gintis, S. Bowles, and P. Richerson. 2003. "The Evolution of Altruistic Punishment." *Proceedings of the National Academy of Sciences* 100(6): 3531–3535.

Boyd, R. and P. Richerson. 1985. *Culture and the Evolutionary Process.* Chicago: University of Chicago Press.

Brooks, B., K. Hoff, and P. Pandey. 2015. "Culture and the Efficiency of Coordination: Experiments with High- and Low-Caste Men in Rural India." Working Paper, World Bank.

Cassar, A., G. d'Adda, and P. Grosjean. 2013. "Institutional Quality, Culture, and Norms of Cooperation: Evidence from a Behavioral Field Experiment." *Australian School of Business Research Paper* No. 2013, Econ 10.

Chiao, J. Y. and K. D. Blizinsky. 2010. "Culture-Gene Coevolution Of Individualism-Collectivism and the Serotonin Transporter Gene." *Proceedings—Royal Society. Biological Sciences* 277(1681): 529–537.

Cingano, F. and P. Pinotti. 2012. "Trust, Firm Organization and the Structure of Production." Paola Baffi Center Research Paper.

Cole, S., X. Gine, J. Tobacman, R. Townsend, P. Topalova, and J. Vickery. 2013. "Barriers to Household Risk Management: Evidence from India." *American Economic Journal: Applied Economics* 5(1): 104–135.

De Mooij, M. 2003. "Convergence and Divergence in Consumer Behaviour: Implications for Global Advertising." *International Journal of Advertising* 22(2): 183–202.

Di Tella, R., S. Galiani, and E. Schargrodsky. 2007. "The Formation of Beliefs: Evidence from the Allocation of Land Titles to Squatters." *Quarterly Journal of Economics* 122(1): 209–241.

Doepke, M. and F. Zilibotti. 2008. "Occupational Choice and the Spirit of Capitalism." *Quarterly Journal of Economics* 123(2): 747–793.

Dohmen, T., A. Falk, D. Huffman, and U. Sunde. 2010. "Are Risk Aversion and Impatience Related to Cognitive Ability?" *American Economic Review* 100(3): 1238–1260.

Dohmen, T., A. Falk, D. Huffman, U. Sunde, J. Schupp, and G. Wagner. 2011. "Individual Risk Attitudes: Measurements, Determinants and Behavioral Consequences." *Journal of the European Economic Association* 9(3): 522–550.

Durante, R. 2010. "Risk, Cooperation, and the Economic Origins of Social Trust: An Empirical Investigation." http://www.rubendurante.net/trust.pdf.

Edlund, L., H. Li, J. Yi, and J. Zhang. 2013. "Sex Ratios and Crime: Evidence from China." *Review of Economics and Statistics* 95(5): 1520–1534.

Eugster, B., R. Lalive, A. Steinhauer, and J. Zweimuller. 2011. "The Demand for Social Insurance: Does Culture Matter?" *Economic Journal* 121(10): 413–448.

Farre, L. and F. Vella. 2013. "The Intergenerational Transmission of Gender Role Attitudes and Its Implications for Female Labor Force Participation." *Economica* 80(318): 219–247.

Fehr, E. 2010. "On the Economics of Biology and Trust." *Journal of the European Economic Association* 7(2–3): 235–266.

Fehr, E. and K. Schmidt. 2009. "A Theory of Fairness, Competition and Cooperation." *Quarterly Journal of Economics* 114(3): 817–868.

Fernandez, R. 2007. "John Marshall Lecture: Women, Work, and Culture." *Journal of the European Economic Association* 5(2–3): 305–332.

———. 2011. "Does Culture Matter?" In *Handbook of Social Economics, Vol. 1A*, edited by J. Benhabib, M. O. Jackson, and A. Bisin, 482–508. Amersterdam: North-Holland.

———. 2013. "Cultural Change as Learning: The Evolution of Female Labor Force Participation over a Century." *American Economic Review* 103(1): 472–500.

Fernandez, R. and A. Fogli. 2006. "Fertility: The Role of Culture and Family Experience." *Journal of the European Economic Association* 4(2–3): 552–561.

———. 2009. "Culture: An Empirical Investigation of Beliefs, Work and Fertility." *American Economic Journal: Macroeconomics* 1(1): 146–177.

Fernandez, R., A. Fogli, and C. Olivetti. 2004. "Mothers and Sons: Preference Formation and Female Labor Force Dynamics." *Quarterly Journal of Economics* 119(4): 1249–1299.

Fincher, C. L., R. Thornhill, D. R. Murray, and M. Schaller. 2008. "Pathogen Prevalence Predicts Human Cross-Cultural Variability in Individualism/Collectivism." *Proceedings—Royal Society. Biological Sciences* 275(1640): 1279–1285.

Fischer, D. H. 1989. *Albion's Seed: Four British Folkways in America.* Oxford: Oxford University Press.

Fisman, R. and E. Miguel. 2007. "Corruption, Norms and Legal Enforcement: Evidence from Diplomatic Parking Tickets." *Journal of Political Economy* 115(6): 1020–1048.

Fong, C. 2001. "Social Preferences, Self-Interest, and the Demand for Redistribution." *Journal of Public Economics* 82: 225–246.

Francois, P. and J. Zabojnik. 2005. "Trust, Social Capital, and Economic Development." *Journal of the European Economic Association* 3(1): 51–94.

Galasso, V. and P. Profeta. 2018. "When the State Mirrors the Family: The Design of Pension System." *Journal of the European Economic Association* 16(6): 1712–1763.

Giavazzi, F., I. Petkov, and F. Schiantarelli. 2014. "Culture: Persistence or Evolution." NBER Working Paper No. 20174.

Giuliano, P. 2007. "Living Arrangements in Western Europe: Does Cultural Origin Matter?" *Journal of the European Economic Association* 5(5): 927–952.

Giuliano, P. and A. Spilimbergo. 2009. "Growing Up in a Recession: Beliefs and the Macroeconomy." *Review of Economic Studies* 81(2): 787–817.

Giuliano, P., A. Spilimbergo, and G. Tonon. 2013. "Genetic Distance, Transportation Costs, and Trade." *Journal of Economic Geography* 14(2013): 179–198.

Glaeser, E. L., D. I. Laibson, J. A. Scheinkman, and C. L. Soutter. 2000. "Measuring Trust." *Quarterly Journal of Economics* 115(3): 811–846.

Gorodnichenko, Y., B. Kukharskyy, and G. Roland. 2015. "Culture and Global Sourcing." NBER Working Paper No. 21198.

Gorodnichenko, Y. and G. Roland. 2011. "Which Dimensions of Culture Matter for Long-Run Growth?" *American Economic Review. Papers and Proceedings* 101(3): 492–498.

———. 2015. "Culture, Institutions and Democratization." NBER Working Paper No 21117.

———. 2017. "Culture, Institutions and the Wealth of Nations." *Review of Economics and Statistics* 99(3): 402–416.

Greif, A. 1994. "Cultural Beliefs and the Organization of Society: A Historical and Theoretical Reflection on Collectivist and Individualist Societies." *Journal of Political Economy* 102(5): 912–950.

Greif, A. and G. Tabellini. 2017. "The Clan and the Corporation: Sustaining Cooperation in China and Europe." *Journal of Comparative Economics* 45(1): 1–35.

Grosfeld, I., A. Rodnyansky, and E. Zhuravskaya. 2013. "Persistent Antimarket Culture: A Legacy of the Pale of Settlement after the Holocaust." *American Economic Journal: Economic Policy* 2013 5(3): 189–226.

Grosfeld, I. and E. Zhuravskaya. 2015. "Cultural vs. Economic Legacies of Empires: Evidence from the Partition of Poland." *Journal of Comparative Economics* 43(1): 55–75.

Grosjean, P. 2011. "The Weight of History on European Cultural Integration: A Gravity Approach." *American Economic Review* 101: 504–508.

———. 2014. "A History of Violence: The Culture of Honor and Homicide in the US South." *Journal of the European Economic Association* 12(5): 1285–1316.

Guiso, L., P. Sapienza, and L. Zingales. 2004. "The Role of Social Capital in Financial Development." *American Economic Review* 94(3): 526–556.

———. 2006. "Does Culture Affect Economic Outcomes?" *Journal of Economic Perspectives* 20(2): 23–48.

———. 2009. "Cultural Biases in Economic Exchange." *Quarterly Journal of Economics* 124(3): 1095–1131.

Hall, R. E. and C. I. Jones. 1999. "Why Do Some Countries Produce So Much More Output Per Worker than Others?" *Quarterly Journal of Economics* 114(1): 83–116.

Hauk, E. and Maria Saez-Marti. 2001. "On the Cultural Transmission of Corruption." *Journal of Economic Theory* 107: 311–335.

Heine, S. J. 2007. *Cultural Psychology*. New York: Norton.

Henrich, J., R. Boyd, S. Bowles, C. F. Camerer, E. Fehr, and H. Gintis. 2001. "In Search of *Homo economicus*: Behavioral Experiments in 15 Small-Scale Societies." *American Economic Review* 91(2): 73–78.

Hiller, V. 2011. "Work Organization, Preference Dynamics and the Industrialization Process." *European Economic Review* 55(7): 1007–1025.

———. 2014. "Gender Inequality, Endogenous Cultural Norms, and Economic Development." *Scandinavian Journal of Economics* 116(2): 455–481.

Hofstede, G. 2001. *Culture's Consequences: Comparing Values, Behaviors, and Organizations Across Nations.* New York: Sage Publications.

Hoppe, M. H. 1990. "A Comparative Study of Country Elites: International Differences in Work-Related Values and Learning and Their Implications for Management Training and Development." PhD thesis, University of North Carolina at Chapel Hill.

Klasing, M. J. 2012. "Cultural Dimensions, Collective Values and Their Importance for Institutions." *Journal of Comparative Economics* 41(2): 447–467.

Knack, S. and P. Keefer. 1997. "Does Social Capital Have an Economic Payoff: A Cross-Country Investigation." *Quarterly Journal of Economics* 112(4): 1251–1288.

Kyriacou, A. 2016. "Individualism-Collectivism, Governance and Economic Development." *European Journal of Political Economy* 42C: 91–104.

La Ferrara, E. 2017. "Media and Development." EDI survey.

Licht, A. N., C. Goldschmidt, and S. H. Schwartz. 2003. "Culture Rules: The Foundations of the Rule of Law and Other Norms of Governance." *Journal of Comparative Economics* 35(4): 659–688.

Lindbeck, A. and S. Nyberg. 2006. "Raising Children to Work Hard: Altruism, Work Norms and Social Insurance." *Quarterly Journal of Economics* 121(4): 1473–1503.

Lipset, S. M. 1959. "Some Social Requisites of Democracy: Economic Development and Political Legitimacy." *American Political Science Review* 53: 69–105.

Ljunge, M. 2014. "Trust Issues: Evidence on the Intergenerational Trust Transmission Among Children of Immigrants." *Journal of Economic Behavior and Organization* 106: 175–196.

Lowes, S., N. Nunn, J. Robinson, and J. Weigel. 2017. "The Evolution of Culture and Institutions: Evidence from the Kuba Kingdom." *Econometrica* 85(4): 1065–1091.

Luke, N. and K. Munshi. 2006. "New Roles for Marriage in Urban Africa: Kinship Networks and the Labor Market in Kenya." *Review of Economics and Statistics* 88(2): 264–282.

Luttmer, E. and M. Singhal. 2011. "Culture, Context and the Taste for Redistribution." *American Economic Journal: Economic Policy* 3: 157–179.

Markus, H. and S. Kitayama. 1991. "Culture and the Self: Implications for Cognition, Emotion and Motivation." *Psychological Review* 98(2): 224–253.

Maystre, N., J. Oliver, M. Thoenig, and T. Verdier. 2013. "Product-based Cultural Change: Is the Village Global?" *Journal of International Economics* 92(2014): 212–230.

Merritt, A. 2000. "Culture in the Cockpit: Do Hofstede's Dimensions Replicate?" *Journal of Cross-Cultural Psychology* 31(3): 283–301.

Michau, J.-B. 2013. "Unemployment Insurance and Cultural Transmission: Theory and Application to European Unemployment." *Journal of the European Economic Association* 11: 1320–1347.

Miguel, E., S. M. Saiegh, and S. Satyanath. 2008. "National Cultures and Soccer Violence." NBER Working Paper No. 13968.

Munshi, K. and J. Myaux. 2006. "Social Norms and the Fertility Transition." *Journal of Development Economics* 80(1): 1–38.

Murrell, P. and M. Schmidt. 2011. "The Coevolution of Culture and Institutions in Seventeenth Century England." Working Paper, University of Maryland.

Nannicini, T., A. Stella, G. Tabellini, and U. Troiano. 2013. "Social Capital and Political Accountability." *American Economic Journal: Economic Policy* 5(2): 222–250.

Naylor, R. 1989. "Strikes, Free Riders, and Social Customs." *Quarterly Journal of Economics* 104: 771–785.

Nisbett, R. and D. Cohen. 1996. *Culture of Honor: The Psychology of Violence in the South*. Boulder, CO: Westview Press.

Nunn, N. and L. Wantchekon. 2011. "The Slave Trade and the Origins of Mistrust in Africa." *American Economic Review* 101(7): 3221–3252.

Olsson, O. and C. Paik. 2015. "Long-Run Cultural Divergence: Evidence from the Neolithic Revolution." Working Paper, University of Gothenburg.

Ostrom, E. 1990. *Governing the Commons. The Evolution of Institutions for Collective Action.* Cambridge: Cambridge University Press.

Pinotti, P. 2012. "Trust, Regulation and Market Failures." *Review of Economics and Statistics* 95: 650–658.

Przeworski, A. and F. Limongi. 1997. "Modernization: Theories and Facts." *World Politics* 49: 155–183.

Putnam, R. 1993. *Making Democracy Work: Civic Traditions in Modern Italy* (with Robert Leonardi and Rafaella Y. Nanetti). Princeton, NJ: Princeton University Press.

Putterman, L. and D. N. Weil. 2010. "Post-1500 Population Flows and the Long Run Determinants of Economic Growth and Inequalities." *Quarterly Journal of Economics* 125(4): 1627–1682.

Roland, G. 2004. "Understanding Institutional Change: Fast-Moving and Slow-Moving Institutions." *Studies in Comparative International Development* 38(4): 109–131.

———. 2016. "Individualist and Collectivist Culture and Their Economic Effects." In *Constraints and Driving Forces in Economic Systems. Studies in Honor of Janos Kornai,* edited by Rosta Miklos, 31–50. Cambridge: Cambridge Scholars Publishing.

Roth, A., V. Prasnikar, M. Okuno-Fujiwara, and S. Zamir. 1991. "Bargaining and Market Behavior in Jerusalem, Ljubljana, Pittsburgh and Tokyo." *American Economic Review* 81(5): 1068–1095.

Saleh, M. 2018. "On the Road to Heaven: Self-selection, Religion and Socio-Economic Status." *Journal of Economic History* 78(2): 394–434.

Sen, A. 1990. "More than 100 Million Women Are Missing." *New York Review of Books* 37(20): 12–20.

Shane, S. 1995. "Uncertainty Avoidance and the Preference for Innovation Championing Roles." *Journal of International Business Studies* 26(1): 47–68.

Tabellini, G. 2008a. "The Scope of Cooperation: Values and Incentives." *Quarterly Journal of Economics* 123(3): 863–904.

———. 2008b. "Presidential Address: Institutions and Culture." *Journal of European Economic Association* 6: 255–294.

———. 2010. "Culture and Institutions: Economic Development in the Regions of Europe." *Journal of the European Economic Association* 8(4): 677–716.

Talhelm, T., X. Zhang, S. Oishi, C. Shimin, D. Duan, X. Lan, and S. Kitayama. 2014. "Large-Scale Psychological Differences Within China Explained by Rice versus Wheat Agriculture." *Science* 344(6184): 603–608.

Van Nimwegen, T. 2002. "Global Banking, Global Values: The In-House Reception of the Corporate Values of ABN-AMRO." PhD dissertation, Nyenrode University Delft, Netherlands.

Voigtlander, N. and H.-J. Voth. 2014. Nazi Indoctrination and Anti-Semitic Beliefs in Germany." *Proceedings of the National Academy of Science (PNAS)* 112(26): 7931–7936.

Way, B. M. and M. D. Lieberman. 2010. "Is There a Genetic Contribution to Cultural Differences? Collectivism, Individualism and Genetic Markers of Social Sensitivity." *Social Cognitive & Affective Neuroscience* 5(2–3): 203–211.

13

THE DYNAMICS OF FAMILY SYSTEMS

Lessons from Past and Present Times

Catherine Guirkinger and Jean-Philippe Platteau

13.1. INTRODUCTION

Important synthesizing works have recently appeared that deal with the economics of the family or the household, typically an informal institution according to the definition used in chapter 1. One such work is the book *Economics of the Family* (Browning et al. 2014). Another is the extensive survey paper, "Household Formation and Marriage Markets in Rural Areas" (Fafchamps and Quisumbing 2007). In the same volume, we also find a chapter by Donald Cox and Marcel Fafchamps (2008) entitled "Extended Families and Kinship Networks: Economic Insights and Evolutionary Directions." A last piece worth mentioning is the contribution by Eliana La Ferrara, "Family and Kinship Ties in Development: An Economist's Perspective" (2011).

While the book by Browning et al. is very elaborate regarding theoretical frameworks on a variety of important family issues, its focus is on the developed countries. Specifically, it deals mainly with the intra-household allocation in simple households and the functioning of the marriage market in situations of high turnover. The paper by Cox and Fafchamps focuses largely on private inter-household transfers, their economic rationale, and their mode of operation. Using the evolutionary approach, they also provide fascinating insights into the very long-term processes that have helped establish some important family institutions, such as rules of "mate-guarding" and support for grandchildren. The paper by Fafchamps and Quisumbing, as well as the contribution by La Ferrara, deals explicitly with developing countries, particularly poor countries where market imperfections are pervasive. The former, as the title suggests, devotes a lot of attention to marriage issues, but it also deals extensively with the different functions of the family, such as the provision of start-up capital, assistance in job search, insurance and old-age support, collective production and consumption allowing for the exploitation of scale and scope economies, and the inculcation of social norms and values useful for success in life. The latter also considers these functions and, based on the work of Alesina and Giuliano (2015), it discusses the possible competition between the market and the family. Both papers stress the advantage of the family as an effective contract enforcer. As for the shortcomings of the family and its potential inefficiencies to individual members, they are mentioned, yet not really elaborated. Both contributions have also ignored the literature on family firms as well as the literature that enters into the details of the operation of family farms (which are exclusively regarded as the locus of scale economies in production). The same can be said for issues of endogeneity of household size and composition to economic conditions, which are essentially bypassed in La Ferrara and incompletely addressed in Fafchamps and Quisumbing.

This chapter does not aim so much at updating the aforecited contributions on the basis of the recent literature as at adopting a complementary perspective focused on some neglected roles of the family and its dynamics in the presence of changes in the economic environment. This means that attention will be directed to the response of family systems to changes in resource endowments, outside economic opportunities, the development of markets, and surrounding institutions. Two other original features of our investigation deserve to be emphasized. First, unlike what is generally done in economics, we extensively draw from scholarly works of social scientists, family historians in particular. This will allow us to assess the state of knowledge regarding the dynamics of family patterns in Europe during a long period stretching back to the early Middle Ages and even earlier.

Second, our foray is systematically based on a crucial distinction between two different notions of the family: the family conceived as a co-residential unit whose members produce and consume collectively, on the one hand, and the family conceived as a group of co-residential units tied through blood or adoption and sharing rights and obligations, on the other hand. While the former notion refers to what is generally called the household (the family *sensu stricto*), the latter may be taken to designate the family as such (the family *sensu lato*). This distinction is actually similar to that proposed by Fafchamps and Quisumbing (2007), for whom the term household designates a larger group of individuals living together (generally, or mostly, composed of family members), while the term family designates a group of individuals related by marriage and consanguinity. It is useful not only to delineate the issues that we want to examine, but also to better identify both the contributions and the limitations of the surveys of La Ferrara, Cox and Fafchamps, and Fafchamps and Quisumbing. Fafchamps and Quisumbing have essentially dealt with several dimensions of the household formation process, Cox and Fafchamps were concerned by certain aspects of the family as network. As for La Ferrara, she opted for a flexible approach that encompasses many different types of family defined as forms of blood relationship, running from very proximate (the nuclear family) to very distant ones (the clan of the kin group). A number of key roles are thus seen as being played by "families, kin and ethnic groups," other roles are probably the prerogative of small family units, whereas still others are characteristic of larger units.

In our discussion, a large place will be devoted to the mechanisms of transformation of the household because this is an area where recent theorizing has taken place and contributions by social scientists, historians in particular, provide novel insights. Furthermore, important aspects of the wider dimension of family systems have been well covered by the economics literature of the last decades. Not all of them, however, have received from the profession the attention that they deserve, and our attention will therefore be directed to the underestimated functions and potential problems associated with the family *sensu lato*. An interesting insight that will come out of our foray is that, in a dynamic perspective, increased efficiency of one dimension of family systems may go hand in hand with increased inefficiency of the other dimension. More specifically, the household may efficiently adapt to the economic environment while the family may retain a form that is increasingly inefficient.

The current review leaves fertility and marriage market considerations largely aside, not because we fail to recognize that these are fundamental aspects of family systems (a central function of family systems is to enable and regulate the reproduction of its members), but more pragmatically because an in-depth review of these questions would considerably increase the length of the current review. Moreover, as we have seen, these aspects are at the heart of Fafchamps and Quisumbing's review (2007). Nonetheless, when we deal with the impacts of formal law governing family systems, we refer largely to marriage and inheritance, since those are the main aspects of family systems that are regulated by laws.

The remainder of the chapter consists of three central parts. The first part examines the two dimensions of the family from a theoretical standpoint that includes the question of the social efficiency of family forms. The second part looks at the empirical evidence available, whether of the rigorous, quantitative type favored by economists (for whom the issue of causality has absolute priority), or of the more intuitive or qualitative type widely used by social scientists. In the third part, keeping in mind that prevailing family forms may be socially inefficient, attention is shifted to the possible role of legal rules in modifying certain characteristics of the family. This is done by reviewing a number of salient studies that have estimated the impact of certain family laws on behavior patterns that they were intended to change. Such an issue is of great relevance, as one of the central concerns of this Handbook is to look into interactions between formal and informal institutions (see chapter 1).

13.2. HOUSEHOLD AND FAMILY: THEORETICAL INSIGHTS

13.2.1. Transformation of the Household

Economists have so far proposed few theories of the transformation of the household as development proceeds or resource endowments change. Rather, recent attempts have focused on the situation of agricultural households, and most available theories concern either the shift from the collective farm to the mixed farm in which individual and collective fields coexist, or the breakup of the collective farms into individual units. A new framework has nevertheless been put forward that aims at explaining both phenomena simultaneously. In the discussion below, we review these theories successively because they rest on different analytical arguments. Thus, while one theory is framed in terms of a commitment problem on the part of the household head, another one is based on the idea that the household is the locus of joint consumption of a public good and diseconomies to joint production. Still another theory assumes the existence of a moral-hazard-in-team problem in collective production in the setting of a collective decision-making unit. Finally, in the most comprehensive theory, the same assumption of moral hazard is made but is now integrated in a principal-agent framework in which the principal is a patriarchal head bent on maximizing his own rent.

13.2.1.1. Theories of Partial Individualization of Family Farmland

Partial individualization of a household farm occurs when private plots are awarded to individual members of the household for their own private use and coexist with farm plots that are jointly cultivated by all members of the household. Partial individualization is an interesting issue because this form can be intuitively seen as an intermediate stage between the fully collective household farm and its breakup following land division of family land. Personal fieldwork in West Africa has revealed that household heads may be reluctant to award private plots to members because they allegedly fear that this could be a first step toward an inescapable breakup of the farm. A paper reviewed in the last subsection shows that the two forms of individualization respond to the same force, growing land scarcity, and it sheds light on the order of succession in which they may succeed each other. In this first subsection, we are interested in reviewing alternative explanations of the emergence of private plots as they come out of the scant literature devoted to the subject.

In order to explain the decision of the household head to allocate individual plots to family members, Fafchamps (2001) relies on the assumption that a serious commitment problem exists inside the family: the head is unwilling or unable to commit to reward the work of other family members on the family field after the harvest, and the latter are therefore tempted to relax their labor efforts or to divert them to other income-earning activities. To solve this commitment problem, the head decides to reward his wife and dependents by granting them access to individual plots of land and the right to freely dispose of the resulting produce. Such a commitment problem, however, can only exist if the short-term gain for the household head of deviating from cooperation (reneging on the promise to reward the workers for their effort on the collective field) exceeds the long-term flow of benefits ensuing from a smooth relationship between him and the working members. As Fafchamps himself admits, this condition is restrictive since the game played within the family is by definition of a long (and indeterminate) duration, and the discount rate of future benefits typically low (future cooperation among close relatives matters a lot). Moreover, even assuming that Fafchamps's hypothesis is valid, it remains unclear why there should be a tendency over time for collective farms to transform themselves into mixed farms, as seems to occur in reality.

Other authors have tried to explain the coexistence of collective fields and individual plots in agricultural farms, yet they explicitly refer to agricultural producer cooperatives or quasi-feudal setups rather than extended family farms. Regarding producer cooperatives, emphasis is typically put on the existence of scale economies for certain types of activities, or on the need for insurance and the role of income-pooling (Chayanov 1991; Putterman 1983, 1985, 1987, 1989; Putterman and DiGiorgio 1985; Carter 1987). Interestingly, the latter argument has been recently extended to the family context by Delpierre, Guirkinger, and Platteau (2015). Like in Carter (1987), the analysis focuses on a trade-off between efficiency and insurance considerations. The trade-off arises because working in common on a collective field and distributing the output equally among participant members insures them against idiosyncratic risks, but joint farming also entails efficiency losses owing to the moral-hazard-in-team problem (itself caused by the impossibility of measuring individual contributions and rewarding them accordingly). Unlike in Carter, however, it is assumed that joint production is not the only way to share risk, as family members may make voluntary transfers between themselves for the purpose of smoothing idiosyncratic variations in income. This assumption partly relaxes the classical efficiency-insurance trade-off. In spite of that generous assumption in favor of individualization, Delpierre et al. show that the optimum may correspond to the mixed farm regime, where a collective field subsists.[1]

There is a last theoretical argument that deserves to be mentioned here, even though it has been made in the context of landlord-tenant rather than intra-household relationships. Due to Sadoulet (1992), it is based on the idea that limited liability constraints and the demand for insurance are the critical considerations prompting the (feudal) owner of an estate to adopt a mixed farm structure, implying that tenants possess individual fields and work for free on the landlord's field.[2] When the landlord thus worries about the possibility that his tenants are unable to pay the entire amount of their land rents or shares because of a wealth constraint, awarding them a private plot under a labor exchange arrangement is the best way for him to extract surplus from the tenants. Sadoulet shows that the labor-service contract (the exchange of free labor for use on the landlord's field against free access to a private plot of land for personal use by the tenant) enables the landlord to impose an optimal level of insurance and, thus, efficient resource use on the tenant.

If in the above argument we replace the term landlord with the term head of a patriarchal household, and the term tenants by the term household members, we have a potential explanation for the coexistence of family and private plots inside an agricultural household. Note, however, that the validity of the explanation rests on the restrictive assumption that the landlord/head can costlessly monitor the efforts applied on his estate by the tenants/workers.

Before turning our attention to the next strand of theories, we must note that in all except the last formal settings, the institutional arrangement of the mixed farm is second-best optimal: given the existence of production uncertainty and informational, commitment, or limited liability problems, and on each model's own premises, there is no better solution available to the household head acting as the principal.

13.2.1.2. Theories of Household Splits or Farm Breakups
One of the key references here is Foster and Rosenzweig (2002). Because in their framework co-residence implies collective farming only, they do not allow for individual plots and limit their effort to understanding the reasons that could motivate the breakup of a family farm.

They use a collective household model and analyze the decision of family members to stay together or to split the household into independent units run by the sons of the original head. Gains from co-residence arise from consuming household public goods and enjoying information-sharing regarding farming techniques. Moreover, it is assumed that married daughters who join their husbands' households can make insurance transfers for the benefit of their fathers' households (direct transfers to their brothers' separate households are ruled out). Offsetting these gains, members have a direct preference for autarchic residence and may differ in their preference for the public good. There may also be diseconomies to joint production. Therefore, as pointed out by the authors (Foster and Rosenzweig 2002: 842), "whether households remain intact depends on the production technology, risk, the taste for privacy, individual preference heterogeneity and the household technology."

Three restrictions on behavior in joint households are imposed by the authors. First, decisions about joint residence in a given period must be made before the income shocks are realized. Second, intra-household allocations, conditional on residence and income realizations, must be ex ante Pareto efficient. Third, each claimant must receive an ex ante expected utility level at least equal to that achievable under separate residence. Household splits occur when this third condition is violated, meaning that individual members are better off in an independent household, given a set of predefined entitlement rules (e.g., inheritance laws). In the above framework, clearly, a potential source of conflict that may trigger separation lies in the heterogeneity of individual preferences for the public good, which much be consumed at equal levels by all claimants when co-resident.

One first important result of their analysis is that technical progress may increase the likelihood of splits. The mechanism proposed is the following. Technical change deepens within-household differences in autarchic incomes (due to differences in schooling) and leads to greater conflicts over the level of public good and thus to a higher likelihood of splits. Another important result is that divisions are more likely to occur upon the death of the household head who has a special role in holding the household together: because the head has above average preference for the public good, his death reduces total household surplus.

The roles of technological change and conflicts about joint consumption are addressed differently in other contributions to the literature. In order to explain the increasing incidence of individual farms, the two following trends have been singled out: (i) a growing disinterest of younger generations in the sort of public goods jointly produced and consumed on the collective farm, and (ii) technical change reflected in the rising importance of decreasing returns to scale as a result of the shift to more land-intensive agricultural techniques.

A recent attempt related to hypothesis (i) is found in Guirkinger, Platteau, and Goetghebuer (2015) who analyze the question of timing of land bequest (inter-vivos or post-mortem) in a context of rural-urban migration where parents wish to retain (some) children close to them. Unlike in Foster and Rosenzweig, their model is based on a principal-agent framework and not on a collective decision-making mechanism. Specifically, a household head decides (in the first period of the game) whether the family land that he owns will be shared among his sons upon his death or will be handed over as an inter-vivos gift (pre-mortem inheritance). His utility has an argument that reflects his preference for keeping sons around him whether in the joint household's framework or as heads of independent farms located in the native village. The utility of each son comprises an argument expressing the intensity of his desire for autonomy, whether as head of an independent farm or in migration. The problem involves a trade-off for the head insofar as his desire to keep his sons close to him may be at the expense of his own consumption (if the landholding is sufficiently small). If the head chooses to refuse pre-mortem gifts of land and the sons choose to remain in agriculture, the family remains integrated as a joint household until the death of the head and then splits between independent farms that reproduce the same life cycle. If, on the contrary, inter-vivos gifts are made, independent farms managed by (non-migrant) sons can be established when they are younger (for example, upon their marriage) since they do not have to wait until the death of their father to themselves head a household.

One important finding is that when land is very abundant, or the sons' reservation utility very low, no land is distributed pre-mortem by the father, and all sons work on the family farm. At the other extreme, when land is very scarce, or the sons' reservation utility is very high, there is again no pre-mortem bequest, and a fraction of the sons, possibly all of them, opt for migration. Pre-mortem division of land, whether or not combined with the migration of some sons, is a possible outcome for intermediate values of the family land endowment or the sons' reservation utility.[3] Note moreover that, because they can be combined with the migration of a varying number of sons, the two regimes, household collective production and pre-mortem division, do not necessarily succeed each other in a linear manner as land pressure increases.

Turning now to hypothesis (ii) on the role of technological change, we must mention the pioneering work of Boserup (1965), who attributes the rise of peasant farms to growing land scarcity and the consequent intensification of agricultural techniques. The underlying argument has enjoyed a wide resonance among development economists who have helped express it in the language of modern information theory (Binswanger and Rosenzweig 1986; Binswanger and McIntire 1987; Pingali, Bigot, and Binswanger 1987; Binswanger, McIntire, and Udry 1989; Hayami and Platteau 1998). It can be stated as follows. As land pressure increases, farmers are induced to shift to more intensive forms of land use, which implies that they adopt increasingly land-saving and labor-using techniques. An important characteristic of these techniques is that labor quality, which is costly to monitor, assumes growing importance. Given the incentive problems associated with care-intensive activities (sometimes labeled "management diseconomies of scale"), the small family or peasant farm in which a few coworkers (spouses and their children) are residual claimants appears as the most efficient farm structure.

A different framework to understand farm breakups has been advanced by Bardhan et al. (2014) and by Guirkinger and Platteau (2015). The explanation is centered on land scarcity, while technical progress of the land-augmenting type (rather than of the labor quality–using type) has the opposite effect of favoring farm consolidation. Since the second paper will be reviewed in the next subsection, we look only at the first one in the remainder of this subsection.

The farm household in the B-L-M-P model is a collective decision-making unit whose members have transferable utilities and jointly cultivate the whole land available, possibly with the help of hired labor. Because of a lack of perfect mutual observability of effort, or inability to enter into enforceable binding agreements concerning their respective efforts, and because income is shared equally, a moral-hazard-in-team problem arises in agricultural production. It is nonetheless mitigated by the imperfect altruism of household members. Land size critically determines labor allocation. Thus, land-poor households have surplus labor that they sell on the outside market. Also, members spend too little time on the family farm due to free-riding. In households that are not land-poor, members work full time on the family farm and there is no free-riding because imperfect altruism is sufficient to cancel the incentive to free ride on other members' efforts: the equilibrium maximizes income per member. While land-medium households are self-sufficient in terms of labor, land-rich households need to hire workers from the market. These workers are landless individuals coming from households whose landholdings are so small that they cannot cover fixed costs and the family farm is therefore not operated.

Allowing household members to exit (migrate) or households to split into smaller households leads the authors to define a stable distribution of farming households as one in which no household wants to shed members or subdivide. A farming household is considered stable if there is no inefficiency in the form of free-riding (incentive-compatibility condition) and each member earns at least the (reservation) wage paid on the labor market (participation condition). Because utilities are assumed to be transferable within each household, and exits and divisions can be accompanied by side transfers among members, exits and division take place only if the aggregate income of members of the original household increases as a result. It is thus noteworthy that the framework used imposes efficiency not only inside the household but also at the level of the agrarian structure, which encompasses the allocation of individuals between different farm households or the allocation of land between farming households of different sizes.

Assume that the equilibrium is disturbed by a shock in the form of an increase in the number of household members. In land-poor households, which exhibit a decreasing collective income in the number of members, incentives exist for exit or for division. This is not true in households defined as land-rich and land-medium where the total income is increasing in the number of members. Which of the two outcomes—exit or division—will happen in land-poor households depends on how tight the participation constraint is in the initial equilibrium. Indeed, since all members should earn at least as much as what they would earn on their own working full time on the labor market, there is a minimum landholding size below which members would no longer be willing to work on the family farm. Division may therefore be infeasible if the original household owns less than this minimum, implying that at the lower end of the land distribution, demographic growth will result in exits causing greater landlessness. The situation gets more complicated if a local land market is active: population growth in some households may now prompt land purchases rather than exit or division. The likelihood of buying land appears to be increasing in the number of members per unit of land, while the likelihood of selling land is decreasing in the same.

If, following technical progress, the shock takes on the form of a sudden increase in agricultural profitability, both the incentive compatibility and the participation constraints are relaxed. Exits and land divisions occurring because of demographic growth are slowed down as a result.

13.2.1.3. A Theory of Household Splits and Partial Individualization of Family Farmland
Guirkinger and Platteau (2015) have proposed a theory purported to account for the gradual individualization of agricultural households where individualization is understood as the growing incidence of both private plots within mixed farming units and splits of complex into nuclear households. Like Boserup, they put primary emphasis on the role of changing land/labor ratios yet, unlike her, they do not refer to technological change as the key mechanism through which the influence of land pressure is being felt. Moreover, like in the B-L-M-P model, their explanation does not rely on the diminishing value of joint consumption. Their observations in West Africa indicate that individualization of complex households in the form of private plots does not end the practice of common kitchens and collective meals. Finally, they do not need to allow for risk aversion to justify the existence of collective farms.

The analytical framework is a standard principal-agent model in which the principal is the household head, or the patriarch, and the agent is composed of the other male adult family members. The principal maximizes his income obtained from the collective field under the participation constraints of the agents. The problem is a two-stage game. In the first stage, the patriarch chooses the share of the collective output that he keeps for himself, the size of the individual plots allotted to members inside the joint family farm (this size can be set at zero), and the number of male adults who stay on the paternal farm. In the second stage, the members observe these choices and individually decide how much effort to apply to the collective field and how much to their individual plot. While making this choice, they act non-cooperatively because of the impossibility to enforce binding agreements regarding their respective efforts (on the collective field).

The central mechanism that operates in their framework relies on the existence of a strong patriarchal authority inside the extended household. It is because the household head acts as a selfish principal that a trade-off arises between efficiency and rent capture considerations.[4] When deciding whether to give private plots to members and how large they should be, the head weighs down two factors. For one thing, production is more efficient on private plots than on the collective field where cultivation is plagued by the moral-hazard-in-team problem. Since the head must ensure that family members agree to stay on the family farm while they have outside options available to them, awarding individual plots allows him to more easily satisfy their participation constraints. For another thing, because the head's income entirely comes from the produce obtained on the collective field owing to unenforceable transfers from the private plots, competition between the two types of plots for the allocation of work effort by the members is bound to cause a drop in the head's income. It is evident that, if transfers from private plots were enforceable by the head, he would earmark the whole family land for private use by individual members and maximize efficiency. It is clearly the non-enforceability of transfers from members to the head that cause efficiency losses.

There is another decision that the patriarch has to make, i.e., whether to maintain the family and the farm whole (with or without private plots) or to allow a split of the joint household and the concomitant division of the family land. The extent of the split itself is to be decided since the number of (male) members authorized to leave may vary. In the case of a pre-mortem split, the total labor force available for work on the collective field decreases, which harms the patriarch, yet it is no more incumbent on him to provide for the needs of the departed members, which favors him. Depending on the relative importance of the various effects at work, he may prefer a mixed regime with private plots to the collective regime, or he may choose to split the family.

How does the agricultural household evolve when land becomes more scarce, or when outside opportunities improve for the members? The general answer provided by the G-P model is that if a change occurs, it will be in the direction of increasing individualization. As land pressure increases (or as outside opportunities improve), the patriarch may decide to transform a collective farm into a mixed farm or into smaller independent units. The initial organizational form is always the collective farm, which is optimal when land is sufficiently abundant. Which individualized form will first succeed the collective one is a complex issue. The reason is that there actually exist many possibilities depending upon the number of (male) members authorized to leave and upon whether private plots are granted to the remaining members when some of them have left with a portion of the family land.

It should be evident from the above discussion that, unlike what is obtained in the B-L-M-P model, the patriarchal household is not socially efficient in the G-P model where there is no imperfect altruism: owing to the moral-hazard-in-team problem, the aggregate welfare of the members could be increased if the entire family land could be partitioned into private plots (through awarding of private plots and/or household split). If the head refuses to choose that option, it is because he is unable to enforce transfers from the private plots. However, a key result of the model is that, by forcing the head to increasingly individualize his farm, scarcity of land at the household level reduces social inefficiencies. Attractive exit opportunities reflected in abundant land on the local/regional level (for example) will yield the same effect—and vice-versa when land is abundant at the household level yet scarce on the wider level.

Finally, it must be mentioned that an important assumption underpinning the whole above framework is that adjustment to rising land pressure is easier to achieve through change in the household structure than through demographic change and fertility reduction, or through land (and labor) markets. While fertility reduction requires a long-term horizon, land markets are highly imperfect owing to large transaction costs or because the fear of losing land prevents the supply side of the market from being activated (Basu 1986; Boucher et al. 2008; Platteau 2000: chap. 4). In this setup, any change in land allocation is the outcome of a decision regarding the organization of the household. The simplifying framework of assumptions thus adopted appears as the price paid in order to make tractable a model that simultaneously explains household splits and the awarding of private plots to household members. By contrast, the B-L-M-P model allows for the operation of local labor and land markets, yet it leaves aside the possibility of mixed farms.

13.2.1.4. A Note on Technical Progress

As is evident from our review, the impact of technical progress on household size depends on its specific characteristics. If the main effect of agricultural technical change is to relax the constraint of land scarcity while being neutral with respect to other inputs' use, we expect land divisions to be slowed down whether we use as underlying framework the B-L-M-P or the G-P model. This prediction is apparently inverted when technical change in agriculture is defined in a Boserupean manner, that is, as requiring labor quality and work conscientiousness. When the Boserupean argument is combined with considerations of land scarcity, however, two effects are at work that run in opposite directions: as a result of technical progress, land productivity increases so that the land scarcity constraint is relaxed but, on the other hand, the rising importance of labor quality in a context of informational asymmetry calls for a reduction of the household group size. A priori, it is difficult to say which effect predominates.

The conclusion that technical change encourages rather than discourages household division may also be derived from the F-R model where the argument is based on consumption instead of productive efficiency considerations. Households are assumed to be heterogeneous in terms of the school levels and technical skills of their members and, as a consequence, technical change deepens within-household differences in autarchic incomes, thereby causing divergences in the individual preferences for the household public good. A recently proposed theory of household nuclearization also uses an argument based on the heterogeneity of the household in the presence of technical change, yet heterogeneity is defined vertically rather than horizontally (Pensieroso and Sommacal 2014). The idea is that the status of the elderly diminishes in an increasingly technical world because their inherited knowledge and wisdom were better adapted to an unchanging universe dominated by tradition.

With the help of a dynamic general equilibrium model, the authors show that, when technical progress is fast enough, the society experiences a shift in intergenerational living arrangements from co-residence to separate residence. Concomitantly, the social status of the elderly, as measured by the fraction of resources allocated to them compared to the one allocated to the younger generation, tends to deteriorate. The intergenerational allocation of resources is determined by the bargaining power of the young. Technically, the economy is populated by two generations of individuals living for two periods, and to derive conclusions about the respective role of economic and cultural factors in causing the above shift in living arrangements, the authors use an endogenous growth model. This implies that the amount of time that the young invest in schooling, which is endogenous, determines their relative human capital. The decisional setup of the household is a collective model of bargaining: co-residence between the two generations occurs only when the distribution of bargaining power is such that co-residence remains (weakly) attractive to both generations. Nuclearization is encouraged by the advantage of the young generation in terms of human capital and an exogenous taste of the young for independence. Living together enables sharing the cost of a public good. An increase in the relative bargaining power of the young generation decreases the desirability of co-residence for the old but increases it for the young. It is also shown that, when the shift in living arrangements is explained by changes in the direct taste for co-residence (that is, is explained culturally rather than economically), the economy experiences a reduction of the growth rate along a balanced growth path.[5]

13.2.2. Transformation of the Family

Economists have devoted considerable attention to the family conceived as a network linking households tied through consanguinous relations. They have analyzed a number of its key functions, particularly those enabled by trust or mutual compliance such as they exist between kinsfolk. From this type of analysis, it is possible to infer the conditions under which the effectiveness of the family may be eroded over time. The literature concerned is well-known and, therefore, we will only briefly mention its main strands and salient results. By contrast, more space will be devoted to functions of the family that economists have largely ignored.

13.2.2.1. Risk-Pooling as the Focal Function

A recurrent theme in the institutional economics literature is that intra-familial relationships follow the logic of a repeated game in which information circulates well. When reputation effects are strong and punishment strategies such as ostracization (based on the threat of exclusion from future exchange with members of the network) are allowed, kin-based networks may effectively enforce contracts. Such capacity is reinforced as a result of the fact that blood relations are not only long-lasting but also multifaceted, thereby permitting punishment to be meted out in what Aoki (2001) has called interlinked games. Foremost among these related games are social games that play an important role in all societies based on highly personalized relationships. Here is a critical advantage of (extended) families and communities when strong legal enforcement agencies are absent or when transactions are too small to justify the expenses involved in court actions. In contexts where markets are highly imperfect or altogether absent, provision of insurance and credit, and the exchange of goods and services through trading, can be achieved in the setup of personalized and continuous relationships epitomized by the family. Public goods can also be more easily produced within the same setup.

The theoretical literature directly or indirectly addressing the above issues is particularly abundant. The part dealing with private, reciprocal inter-household transfers, in particular, has been well covered in rather recent surveys published in three different volumes of the *Handbook in Economics* series (see, in particular, Kolm 2006; Platteau 2006; Cox and Fafchamps 2008; Fafchamps 2011). It is generally focused on risk-sharing, or on mechanisms that evoke risk-sharing: private transfers then appear as part of an informal insurance contract among self-interested people. While symmetric risk-pooling fosters horizontal relationships between members, asymmetric ones may give rise to patron-client ties (Fafchamps 1992; Platteau 1995a; Platteau 1995b).

A major result obtained by the pioneer model of Coate and Ravallion (1993) is that, when people are unable to make binding commitments, full sharing of risks is infeasible even in the absence of any problem of asymmetric information. Moreover, the authors are able to identify a number of factors that determine the extent to which informal risk-sharing arrangements diverge from first-best sharing corresponding to full income pooling. In particular, the amount of transfer gets nearer to the first-best amount when the discount rate is lower (that is, when participants are less impatient or when they think there is a higher probability that interactions among them will continue, or that the frequency of random shocks is higher), the degree of relative risk aversion is higher, and income differences between participants are smaller. The latter prediction may seem counterintuitive, and Besley (1995) has indeed argued that the agents' inability to commit is responsible for this result since they will be reluctant to pay high transfer amounts when income differences are large. The conclusion can be inverted by just assuming imperfect information. In Besley's words: "If individuals' incomes depend upon effort and luck, but effort is hard to observe, then under certain conditions, it will be reasonable to infer that very bad draws are due to bad luck and good ones due to good luck. The incentive consequences of helping individuals in the tails of the income distribution will thus not be as severe as helping out around the mean" (2168).

The theory becomes more complex when non-stationary strategies are posited, such as with the debt contract with occasional forgiveness defined by Ligon, Thomas, and Worrall (2001). History now matters in the sense that past transfers affect current transfers net of contemporaneous shocks. The key finding here is that, by allowing the distribution rule to be shifted in favor of the better-off household, the latter's incentive to renege on his promise by withholding his transfer when it does particularly well can be removed. As a consequence, the loss relative to the first-best risk-sharing contract is kept to a minimum. However, the arrangement is clearly not incentive-compatible when information is imperfect (income shocks are not observable). Claiming to have a bad shock is then an attractive strategy not only because a positive transfer can be currently received, but also because previous debts are forgotten, and consequently an opportunistic agent would make this claim each period (Ligon et al. 2001).

Foster and Rosenzweig (2001) have examined whether risk-pooling is more advantageous among altruistic compared to selfish agents in a framework where individuals cannot make binding commitments. In theory, the answer is rather straightforward: to the extent that agents entering into a risk-sharing arrangement care about each other's welfare, they should gain more from insurance than they would otherwise and the scope of risk-sharing contracts should be greater. Even the one-shot game can actually support some transfers if agents are altruists. In a repeated framework, too, altruistic agents are more likely to engage in a risk-pooling arrangement since their altruism has the effect of ameliorating the commitment constraint arising from the impossibility to legally enforce the contract. Adapting Thomas and Worrall's two-agent model to the case where each agent cares about the other, Foster and Rosenzweig have reached interesting conclusions. First and as expected, history matters, since a household that has recently received transfers is less likely to receive subsequent transfers than is a household that has recently provided transfers. Moreover, for a given degree of income correlation, reciprocal transfers exhibit not only a weaker negative dependence on past transfers but also a more positive relationship with own income shocks when transfer partners are altruistic than when they are selfish.[6] Second, the extent of risk-sharing is facilitated both by low levels of income correlation and high degrees of altruism between transfer partners. Finally, for each level of correlation, the surplus generated by the optimal implementable risk-sharing contract rises sharply with altruism and then levels off. Beyond a certain threshold, the surplus also declines, reflecting the fact that autarchy is no more a credible threat when the partners are sufficiently altruistic (Foster and Rosenzweig 2001: 390–394).

On the assumption that altruism is more likely among family than non-family members, Foster and Rosenzweig predict that the family will play a primary role in the provision of insurance (since a higher surplus is thereby generated for a given income correlation). However, the family cannot be expected to provide all the insurance because the number of potential family partners is small and income correlation among them is likely to be comparatively large. (Also, too much altruism may be problematic insofar as the threat to relegate the insurance partner to an autarchic position loses a great deal of its credibility when an agent cares a lot about his partner.) Note that this is a re-statement of the famous insurance dilemma obtained in the presence of asymmetric information rather than imperfect commitment (see Posner 1980 and Platteau 1991). Since information circulates better among kin than among non-kin, so that punishing deviance is more effective, insurance is more efficiently provided in a kin-based network. Yet, since the size of such a network is necessarily limited, risk diversification is constrained. Hence, because of the trade-off between contract enforcement and risk diversification considerations, a kin-based network is not necessarily a better insurance provider than a larger, more anonymous group.

Finally, Genicot and Ray (2003) have examined the question of the optimal size of risk-sharing networks in a framework of limited commitment (and perfect information) similar to that of Coate and Ravallion, except that they allow for coalitions or groups of households to leave the group and to continue to share risk among themselves (instead of considering solely individual incentives to leave a risk-sharing group). Introducing the possibility that subgroups of individuals may destabilize insurance arrangements among the larger group yields results that go against the simple intuition that a larger size implies a greater scope for risk-sharing. Indeed, the authors show that stable groups (from which no subgroup wishes to depart) have bounded size and that increasing the need for insurance may decrease group size. This is because when the need for insurance increases, smaller groups become stable.

13.2.2.2. Other Family Functions Seen Through the Economists' Lens

Reciprocity does not answer insurance or exchange needs only. It may also be activated for purposes of investment, as illustrated in the case of informal credit transactions in Ghana (La Ferrara 2003), or in the case of intergenerational transfers motivated by the financing of educational expenses in Cameroon (Baland et al. 2016). La Ferrara (2003) studies kinship band networks as capital market institutions. With the help of an overlapping generations repayment game with endogenous matching between lenders and borrowers, she argues that membership in a community where individuals are dynastically linked has three effects on informal credit transactions. First, the non-anonymity of the dynastic link allows to sanction the defaulters' offspring and induce compliance even in short-term interactions (social enforcement). For example, future lenders deny credit to the child of a defaulter, thus indirectly harming the parent in the event the child is born poor and cannot afford to support the parent ("indirect" punishment). Second, preferential agreements can arise in which kin members condition their behavior on the characteristics of a player's predecessor. Thus, in a context where there are more poor than rich individuals and, therefore, some poor individuals will not obtain a loan (with uniform random matching between lenders and borrowers), a rich person who anticipates that one of his children may be poor will preferentially lend money to the children of those who were rich in the previous period. This is because, if every lender obeys this rule (what the authors call "matching with reciprocity among lenders"), their own children will get a loan with probability 1. As for the third effect, it concerns the terms of the loans: the equilibrium interest rate is lower on "reciprocal" loans than on "market" loans because reciprocity alters the individuals' incentive compatibility constraints. Preferential agreements among some set of individuals make it less profitable for others to comply with the reciprocity norm, hence the necessity to improve the terms of the transaction for the latter.

Baland et al. (2016) also use an overlapping generation model, and in their framework, imperfect intergenerational altruism (altruism vis-à-vis siblings is precluded) is assumed to prevail. Transfers within extended families are theorized as a generalized system of reciprocal credit, mainly for education purposes. Specifically, when they are young adults, elder siblings support their younger siblings and finance their education. Younger siblings in turn reciprocate at a later stage by supporting the children of their elder siblings. Baland et al. identify the conditions under which, in the absence of saving and credit markets, the above arrangement increases the welfare of all participants. They also explore its consequences on incentives to work. The model predicts that younger siblings exert lower labor effort as young adults (than elder siblings) but work harder when they have to support the children of their elder siblings. In addition, younger siblings are predicted to have fewer children, who are themselves less educated than the children of their elder siblings.

Another kin-based institution that facilitates investment is labor-pooling, which may take many different forms such as rotating arrangements and labor gangs. While labor-pooling may serve an insurance purpose by helping a farmer who falls ill at a critical moment of the agricultural season or by rescuing a fisherman who is in trouble out at sea (Platteau 1997), for example, it often constitutes a credit rather than an insurance informal institution. The rotation schedule is then predictable and clearly established, such as is observed for agricultural and other works (the construction of a house, for example) that require a labor force exceeding the supply of a household. Whichever the precise purpose, extended families and kinship ties can help in ensuring that participants do not renege ex post (that is, after they have benefited from others' efforts) on their earlier commitments to provide labor to the group. In the same line, capital assets (agricultural implements, draught animals) may be shared according to a predetermined arrangement so that participants do not all need to own them. In this instance, however, it is generally the case that one household, that which owns the assets, is richer than the others, so that the framework of cooperation is based on asymmetric reciprocity and patronage. But if the asset is a natural resource under common property, and its limited size requires sharing access, the reciprocity arrangement is likely to be horizontal (Baland and Platteau, 1996: 197–209). The same holds true when relatives decide to pool resources together to form a partnership business venture.

Three last functions deserve to be mentioned: child-fostering, information-sharing, and physical security. To begin with, child-fostering may help households to send children to somewhat distant (secondary) schools thanks to the presence in the destination place of a kin-related household that agrees to provide lodging and boarding to the schoolchildren for the time needed (Akresh 2005). Hosting nieces and nephews, for example, may also be motivated by locational constraints related to employment rather than schooling and training. Migration networks may play a similar role of helping relatives to get integrated in an alien place by providing shelter, job access, and critical information (Munshi 2003, 2008), and they may potentially serve the function of a claim enforcement mechanism if they ensure proper discipline to the effect that migrants send regular remittances to the family in the village of origin (see Chort, Gubert, and Senne 2012, for a simple modeling of this role of the migration network).

The interesting thing about information-sharing is that it can sustain efficient cooperation within the framework of an informal economy, or it can buttress market development. The first possibility is especially evident when members of a kin-based network have the incentive to share information regarding a critical aspect of their productive activities. For example, with the context of Japanese coastal communities in mind, Platteau and Seki (2001) have shown formally that sharing information about detection of fish shoals, or sharing allocation of fishing spots whose yields are uncertain among members of a network that practices income-pooling, is Pareto-efficient. In this instance, income-pooling provides the necessary incentive for the effective enforcement of information-sharing arrangements. As for the second possibility, kin-based networks facilitate market exchange by conveying market-relevant information, such as information about jobs, business opportunities, prices, goods for sale, house rentals, and the quality of products and services (see, e.g., Fafchamps 2004), but also by circulating information about individual members' actions. In the latter instance, information-sharing networks increase market efficiency despite the fact that they do not directly

enforce contracts: their role consists of providing information that is relevant to reputation mechanisms (Cox and Fafchamps 2008: 3726).

Finally, because protection against physical insecurity involves important economies
of scale, groups such as families are well suited to fulfil this function. Thus, people may
collectively organize with relatives and kin against roving bandits and lawless armies
or militia. Kin ties are particularly helpful to provide shelter in the event of attacks or
distress (Cox and Fafchamps 2008: 3716). As has been well documented in the social science literature (see for example Bates 2001), protection includes deterrence strategies
whereby a clan or a kinship group threatens potential aggressors of one of their members with severe retaliation measures (an example of multilateral punishment).

13.2.2.3. The Role of Norms and Emotions

So far, the impression may have been gained that the advantage of the family rests essentially on two key attributes, good information and continuous interactions, both enabled by a moderate size of the group. We nevertheless know from game theory that
when these two conditions are observed, a multiplicity of equilibria remain possible in
repeated games, and there is therefore no certainty that cooperation will be established.
For instance, we may need for people to have enough trust in other members to decide
to cooperate in the first stage of the game (Gambetta 1988: 227–228). This is precisely
where families seem to have a decisive advantage over other kinds of groups because
they seem better able to inculcate from early childhood the sort of emotions, guilt and
shame, that are so useful for the effective enforcement of informal contracts (Platteau
2000: chap. 7). This mechanism has been formalized in well-known economic models of
cultural transmission pioneered by Bisin and Verdier (1998).

When young individuals are socialized by their parents, a process called "primary
socialization" by Berger and Luckmann (1967), the context is one of "an emotionally
charged identification of a child with his (her) significant others" (158).[7] Another step in
the socialization process, called "secondary socialization," takes place through inter-
changeable providers of specific knowledge acquired in schools, churches, factories, etc.
This form of socialization is nevertheless less powerful than primary socialization
because the world internalized in the latter is "so much more firmly entrenched in consciousness than worlds internalized in secondary socializations" (161–162). Yet its role is
crucial because it enables the individual to identify with a set of other individuals beyond the immediate sphere of relationships with the parents (the significant others). In
a kin-based society, these other individuals are members of the kinship group, and the
values inculcated belong to the "limited morality" type. The need to enforce informal
contracts or agreements does not extend beyond the sphere defined by family, clan, or
ethnic affiliation (Platteau 2000: chap. 7). Instruments of this secondary socialization not
only foster guilt and shame emotions when cheating other members of the reference
group, but also stimulate anger and the desire to punish, even at a positive cost, those
who exploit them. Anger is useful insofar as it helps to make the threat of retaliation
credible: "when a person is motivated by indignation, his act of punishment . . . will give
him the *pleasure of revenge*" (Elster 1998: 69; Axelrod 1986).

Note that cultural transmission need not be strictly applied to members with consanguinous ties, thus making possible the adoption of other members into the kin group.
We know from the anthropological literature that kinship ties can be socially created

through various methods that aim at inculcating feelings of identification and loyalty vis-à-vis the genetically defined core group. This is typically done by establishing surrogate family links, such as godparenthood ties, and by providing bonding experiences, such as initiation ceremonies and similar rituals (Baland and Platteau 1996: 195–197). The size of kinship groups is therefore not strictly predetermined or fixed.

Aside from negative emotions of guilt, shame, and anger, socialization is also strongly associated with the maturing of emotional predispositions to empathy; it nurtures altruistic attitudes. It is therefore not surprising that altruism has been found to be stronger among genetically related individuals (Cox and Fafchamps 2008: 3727). Since altruism may substitute for, or reinforce emotions of, guilt and shame, it promotes cooperation within the kin group and, in particular, it facilitates contract enforcement, as formally shown in the aforementioned paper by Foster and Rosenzweig (2001). In fact, even a bit of altruism is often sufficient to eliminate free-riding in prisoner's dilemma situations (Durlauf and Fafchamps 2005; Cox 1987). Kazianga and Wahhaj (2016) have recently explored the idea that altruism between family members varies with the strength of family ties and, more specifically, that altruism is stronger in small family units such as nuclear family households than in larger units. They show that, within the same geographic, economic, and social environments, households where members have stronger familial ties achieve near Pareto-efficient allocation of productive resources and Pareto-efficient allocation of consumption, while households with weaker familial ties do not.

Before Kazianga and Wahhaj, however, Alger and Weibull (2010) reached somewhat different conclusions about the impact of altruism. Unlike the former authors, they use the framework of evolutionary game theory, and they focus on the role of a particular household form (one with two siblings), assuming that it is the sole insurance provider for its members. The siblings are assumed to be mutually altruistic, and they choose their risk-reducing efforts, anticipating possible future transfers between them. Alger and Weibull find that altruism is actually a double-edged sword: if it enhances the extent to which individuals internalize the external effects of their actions (the empathy effect), it also increases free-riding in the productive activity (the free-rider effect). The latter effect follows from the fact that, knowing that they will be better helped in the event of a negative shock, siblings are prompted to relax their current efforts. The central result of the paper is that the empathy effect outweighs the free-rider effect at high levels of altruism, while the opposite is true at intermediate levels. In addition, they study how, for a given level of intra-household altruism, environmental factors affect the productive efforts applied by the members and also how evolutionary forces, whether genetic or sociocultural, may affect the level of sibling altruism in a society. They show that neither very weak nor very strong family ties are stable against evolutionary drift and that intermediate degrees of family altruism are locally evolutionarily stable in many environments. Furthermore, the harsher the environment, the weaker are the family ties.

13.2.2.4. The Missing Dimension and the Missing Functions
What the above discussion reveals is that, although economists have devoted considerable attention to the family as network, they have done so through a specific angle that privileges decentralized relations. The central role played by the concept of risk-pooling seems to have set a strong benchmark inviting a look at the family as a network based on close and repeated interactions between individuals typically well informed about

each other's doings. There are two problems or limitations associated with this otherwise useful approach. First, there is much empirical evidence that, to enforce contracts and solve collective action problems, the family often relies on an authority structure or a hierarchy rather than only on a purely decentralized network of inter-individual relationships.

Second, this decentralized approach to the family tends to rule out functions that are important but involve a collective mechanism of coordination. For example, protection against physical insecurity is assumed to be achieved through a mutual help mechanism based on reciprocity, while it can obviously be more effectively provided through a hierachical organization acting on behalf of the kinship group. To contend that members could put up the needed authority structure in a decentralized manner is not a satisfactory answer since we know that in many cases the authority has been in place for a long time and is transmitted dynastically or through non-participatory procedures.

A set of key roles of the family are not well accounted for in the tight framework of decentralized interactions: administrative, judiciary (conflict settlement), rule-setting (inheritance informal rules, for instance), political, and even military functions. The political function involves representation of the family's interests at the higher, supra-family level, which includes the central political level if it exists. The way the family is embedded in the political system and the role it is assigned are therefore important dimensions that need to be understood. Although it needs some adjusting, one strand of economic theory, the theory of decentralized development, can shed light on the desirability of having family or kinship groups perform the aforementioned functions. At the core of this theory lies a trade-off that appears pertinent for the issue at hand (see Bardhan 2002; Mookherjee 2015, for relevant surveys). Transposed to the family, it can be stated as follows: on the one hand, the family has an advantage over a centralized administrative and political body in that it possesses a lot of location-specific information and is also better able to enforce rules, monitor behavior, and verify actions, but, on the other hand, it is much more vulnerable to rent capture by a hard-to-monitor hierarchy. The problem of capture arises from the fact that men in power, elders from the main lineage, for example, may be in a position to make their own preferences prevail over those of ordinary people, and their weight in collective decision-making may distort collective regulation toward their interests at the cost of efficiency.

Although obtained in a specific setting that is obviously inappropriate in our context (in particular, the assumption of a two-party electoral competition with probabilistic voting behavior and lobbying by special interest groups that can make campaign contributions), one result deserves attention: decentralization increases elite capture in high-inequality localities and lowers it in low-inequality ones (Bardhan and Mookherjee 1999, 2000). When applied to the family, the intuition is rather straightforward: when family leaders concentrate a lot of wealth and they risk using it to promote their own interests, decentralization may not only perpetuate inequality but also impair efficiency. Instead of going through an electoral process, rent capture is the outcome of unequal bargaining strength, such as depicted in Banerjee et al. (2001) in their account of sugar cooperatives in Maharashtra.

In a more recent paper, Munshi and Rosenzweig (2016) have proposed an alternative theory in which the family equivalent (a caste or an ethnic group) draws the benefits of internal cooperation but evinces no concern for members of the other groups (families).

If the group gets elected to the position of community representative, it enjoys the prerogative of allocating two independent budgets: one devoted to the production of a local public good and the other intended for targeted welfare transfers. While the public good benefits everybody in the community, welfare transfers are privately appropriated by members of the group whose leader has been elected. It is possible that members of the smaller groups vote for the candidate of the bigger group if the disadvantage of being excluded from welfare benefits is outweighed by the gain of a more effectively provided public good. Underlying the rather complex mechanism at work in the theory is a positive relationship between the size of the group and the effectiveness in providing the public good. In their model, this positive correlation is the result of the selection of higher quality incumbents in the larger ethnic group. Alternatively, it could be imagined that this relationship is caused by the fact that bigger groups are better able to get funds from higher-level political authorities owing to a stronger bargaining position (say, because of the higher political weight that a larger group size represents).

13.2.2.5. Dynamics of the Family

The comparative statics derived from the analytical framework used by economists to understand the multiple roles of the family suggests that this institution should gradually lose its significance as the market develops and the state becomes better able to create legal enforcement institutions as well as to devise and implement social protection programs. This is because the family is essentially viewed as a substitute for markets, legal enforcement mechanisms, and state-devised social protection. In particular, the emergence and development of insurance, credit, capital, and labor markets is predicted to make the family less and less useful. It is true that some markets, especially the insurance market, may get established only slowly. However, even if the state does not compensate for this market failure, the expansion of new income-earning opportunities as a result of growing market integration and general development will allow households to diversify their risks, thus providing them with effective self-insurance possibilities.

If that scenario were true, we would expect a rather monotonous process of dissolution of the family with perhaps sudden and temporary reversals in times of economic crisis or war conditions. Things may not be so simple, though, if path dependence and lock-in mechanisms exist. The former possibility can be illustrated by reference to kin-based trading networks (Greif 1989, 1994, 2006a). Thanks to well-circulating information and repeated interactions, such networks provide an effective arrangement to enforce contracts, yet this advantage is obtained within the purview of a predetermined group the size of which is not necessarily optimal. And even assuming that it was optimal to begin with, it will cease being so as soon as market opportunities start to expand and the economic space gets larger. A similar point has been made by Kali (1999): once kin-based networks are seen as endogenous to the reliability of the legal system, the possibility exists that they are inefficient in general equilibrium even though they enhance efficiency in partial equilibrium. The reason is that they may exert a negative effect on the functioning of the anonymous market, say because they leave aside non-kin who remain undisciplined when engaged in anonymous market exchange. As a consequence, the payoff from market exchange is lowered. Kali finds that networks are economically inefficient unless they are relatively large. If they are rather small, they appear as a poor substitute for reliable institutional support that guarantees written contracts. Moreover, trade diversification possibilities and skill complementarities are not optimally exploited, thereby causing the loss of valuable income possibilities (La Ferrara 2002; Alesina and La Ferrara 2005). In a dynamic perspective, the efficiency costs associated with a given size of the family network are bound to increase as the market expands and new economic opportunities emerge.

The same idea of the rising inefficiency of kinship groups has been explored by Hoff and Sen (2005) although on the basis of a different argument. In their model, like in Kali, they assume that the population is divided into two groups. The first group is a single kin system whose members are denoted as K-individuals: they share concepts, beliefs, and commitment devices, and they exhibit physical markers, speech, or other behaviors that distinguish them from others. The second group is a set of independent individuals who are not bound by any kinship ties: they are denoted as I-individuals. Each K-individual is committed to abide by the following mutual assistance norm: if the individual gets a white-collar job in the modern sector, he has to help improve the well-being of one (or more) pre-identified member(s) of the kin group. If he violates this norm, he exits. The problem arises because employers, owing to the mutual assistance norm, find it more costly to hire K-individuals than I-individuals. Crucially, K-individuals cannot signal to the market that they no longer participate in the kin system, if they wish to do so. As a consequence, even though K-individuals would be better off leaving this system, they may choose to stay, resulting in a loss of efficiency. A key message from Hoff and Sen's analysis is that, following a logic well highlighted by Akerlof (1976), individuals, out of their own self-interest, may cling to a social system that is harmful to them. This implies that the initial group size may remain unchanged.

The foregoing discussion seems to suggest that the predetermined size of the kinship group is the cause of the increased inefficiency that accompanies market development. It can be argued, however, that the main problem lies not so much in the sub-optimal size of the kinship network as in the very logic of kinship ties. To see this, assume that instead of being predetermined, the size of the kinship group can be increased in response to a changing market environment thanks, say, to a member's adoption mechanism. A problem akin to the insurance dilemma then arises: as the size of the kinship group increases, information-sharing and internal monitoring become more difficult and, as a consequence, its contract enforcement capacity is impaired. A trade-off thus arises between the ability of the kinship group to exploit new economic opportunities and its ability to effectively enforce contracts. The best way to overcome this nasty dilemma may be to shift to a radically new set of institutions that support anonymous market exchange, such as family firms, corporations, and legal contract enforcement mechanisms. Over time, these institutions will prove their worth, but the returns may be uncertain and a fixed cost must be incurred to establish them. It can be reasonably surmised that, in such circumstances, the incentive to innovate is likely to be greater when the existing institution is blatantly inadequate with regard to the new opportunities. Thus, unlike the collectivist culture of Maghribi traders from North Africa who could rely on kin-based enforcement, the individualism of Genovese traders, constrained to operate on the basis of relatively inefficient bilateral reputation and punishment mechanisms, provided an impetus for the development and perfection of ultimately more successful third-party enforcement of claims (Greif 1989: 874–877; see also Bowles 1998: 95; Kennedy 1988: 143–146).

The above argument, it may be noted, can explain a reversal of fortune: because it is more strongly motivated or better able to make an institutional jump in the presence of a new economic environment or challenge, a society initially endowed with a rather weak institutional setup may overtake another society that surpassed it in the former situation. The conservatism of a society that was rather efficient in the past may originate in different sources: strong aversion to risk, myopic behavior, or ideological inertia reflected in the inability to move from one system of beliefs or expectations to another (see Kuran 2011, for an application of this idea to Islamic institutions in Middle Eastern countries). In particular, if the shift from collectivist to individualistic beliefs is difficult, the transformation of societies based on multilateral reputation mechanisms will be blocked, or their adaptation will be limited to a "patching up" solution.

Based on the idea of complementarities between moral systems and institutions, the explanation recently offered by Greif and Tabellini (2010, 2017) to account for the different long-term trajectories of China and Western Europe belongs to the above strand of thought. While premodern China was based on the clan, Western Europe relied on the city in the sense of a self-governing organization based on cross-kinship links. On the eve of the urban expansion in China and Europe circa 1000 CE, in particular, large kinship organizations were common in China but not in Europe (any more). The Chinese clan is a kinship-based hierarchical organization in which strong moral ties and reputation among clan members are especially important to sustain cooperation. In the cities of Medieval Europe, by contrast, cooperation is across kinship lines and external enforcement plays a relatively big role. These distinct institutional setups, which have given rise to distinct trajectories during the last millennium, are the outcome of different initial moral systems and kinship organizations. It is through complementarities and positive feedbacks between morality, institutions, and the implied pattern of cooperation that these initial conditions influenced subsequent evolution in the two regions.

Greif and Tabellini's theoretical investigation proceeds in two steps. In the first step, they use a static framework in which individuals with given values choose which organization to join (the clan vs. the city). The resulting equilibrium configuration depends on the initial distribution of values in society. In the second step, the perspective adopted is dynamic: the diffusion of values is seen as being shaped over time by the prevailing organizational forms, hence the existence of a joint dynamics of social organization (the relative size of the city vs. clan) and endogenous values. The authors derive the conditions under which two steady states are obtained, the one in which most of the population lives in the clan and the other in which most of it lives in the city. Moreover, they show that even small differences in the initial social and moral conditions in an otherwise identical economic and social environment lead to lasting and significant distinctions in both the distribution of values and the organization of society.

The dynamic equilibria can be intuitively described in the following manner. A society that starts out with a diffuse sense of loyalty to the clan will find it optimal to mainly rely on the clan to provide public goods, and only a small fraction of the population will be attracted to the city. In equilibrium (an equilibrium with segregation in the clan), all individuals of the clannish type remain in the clan while those who adhere to a code of generalized reciprocity—a predisposition to act honestly with any other individual in the wide society—are distributed both in the clan and in the city. There are two reasons why clan size is large and city size is small. First, the majority of the population has clan-centered values, and all of these individuals find it optimal to remain in the clan. Second, only some of the individuals with generalized morality have an incentive to stay in the city: being large, indeed, the clan is more attractive than the city (it can exploit economies of scale associated with public good provision). And since the clan can rely on many loyal individuals, it can work smoothly with no free-riding. This situation, which epitomizes China, persists over time because the moral people who are attracted to the clan are more likely to give rise to offspring endowed with clan-oriented values, compared to their brethern living in the city. The comparative advantage of the clan over the city is thereby reinforced. By analogous reasoning, the same argument can be easily repeated for the European situation: in this case, the society starts out with a widespread diffusion of values consistent with generalized morality, and the outcome will be an equilibrium with segregation in the city. Clearly, because the initial conditions differed, endogenous social institutions and morality evolved in different directions in China and Western Europe.

In an aforecited paper, Alger and Weibull (2010) provided another framework (an evolutionary game) that also makes the point that current differences in family ties may be due to differences traceable to the distant past. In their setting, family ties affect economic outcomes, and evolutionary forces shape these ties differently in different environments.

Going beyond simple comparative-static results, and allowing for dynamic processes of long-term development, we have highlighted the fact that legacies from a long time past may well survive into the present, even when various aspects of the environment have changed. A new and possibly complementary perspective opens up when we direct our attention to the administrative, judiciary, political, and military functions of the family. Indeed, as soon as the family is conceived as a political actor in its own right, we see another reason why large families or kinship groups may endure over long periods of time: family or clan leaders may use their political clout and their military power to oppose changes that may harm their interests by eroding the role of the clan. Heads may thus strive to maintain the strength of their lineage for fear that it might disappear, thereby undermining their own influence and prestige. They themselves, or other family functionaries belonging to their inner circle, may have everything to lose from the disappearance of the family even though ordinary or entrepreneurial members might benefit from new forms of organization. For example, a legal system would make the conflict-settlement functions of the kinship group redundant or simply illegal. In China, clan rules regularly discouraged litigation and favored arbitration provided by the clan authorities. This judiciary role of the clan leadership was actually supported by the state, which needed the cooperation of clan elders to buttress its own power (Greif and Tabellini 2010a: 3–4). Political economics considerations may thus explain why kinship groups may remain strong even though their role would better be taken over by new and better adapted institutions.

A final remark is in order. One may consider the family/clan as an alternative or a substitute for central political power, rather than as a component of a centralized polity. The idea is then that clans become the prominent unit of social organization whenever the central authority declines and, to the extent that history is characterized by successive periods of strong and weak central power, there is no monotonous process of nuclearization of the family. Thus, for example, it is when the residents of Genoa and Venice found themselves in a political vacuum as a result of the decreasing influence of the Byzantine Empire (for Venice) and the Holy Roman Empire (for Genoa) that these two cities began to be based on the political cooperation between the strongest clans. Members of these clans understood that the corporate family was better able than the nuclear household to defend their wealth and status through enhanced solidarity among the aristocratic classes (Herlihy 1969: 174–178; Greif and Laitin 2004: 640).

13.3. HOUSEHOLD AND FAMILIES: EMPIRICAL EVIDENCE

13.3.1. Transformation of the Household: Testing Economic Theories of Household Individualization

The three main theories discussed in section 13.2.1 have actually been tested empirically. We briefly review below the most salient findings obtained by their respective authors as well as some related findings that are pertinent for this review.

We begin with the theory of household splits proposed by Foster and Rosenzweig (2002). They estimate a rather sophisticated structural model using longitudinal farm household data from India over the period 1971–1982 (ARIS-RED dataset). A first result confirms an important modeling assumption: the probability of a household receiving a transfer in the event of an adverse shock significantly increases with the number of daughters-in-law residing in the household and the number of daughters of the head married in other households. A second result bears out the prediction that division is more likely among households experiencing a death of the head. A third result is that production technology exhibits modest static scale diseconomies. In the fourth result, obtained through simulation, lies the central message of their paper.

In the model, it is not a priori obvious how technical change affects the propensity for households to divide. What they find is a complex pattern arising from the differential effect of technical change for small and large farms. More precisely, increased agricultural technical change has a substantially stronger negative effect on division probabilities for the farm households in the top quartiles of the per-capita land endowment. In contrast, it slightly increases division propensity for the bottom two quartiles. To explain the differential impact of technical progress on household division, the authors argue that "increases in agricultural productivity growth raise income and therefore the demand for the household public good more in the land-rich households" (Foster and Rosenzweig 2002: 865). This has the effect of exacerbating autarchic income differentials for given schooling heterogeneity and thus enhancing disagreement in preferences for the household public good. On this count, division should be more likely among land-rich households. However, this is forgetting "the gains from human capital externalities associated with returns to information sharing that are enhanced when rates of technical change are high" (ibid.). This latter effect actually outweighs the former. For land-poor households, the effect of preference heterogeneity over the public goods is less important than for the land-rich households yet, on the other hand, the incidence of human capital externalities is also much less important. Overall, division of the household becomes more attractive.

Turning now to the theory proposed by Bardhan et al. (2014), the impacts of technical change and land pressure on household divisions (and also on labor mobility and land transactions) are analyzed both as the direct effects of population growth and as the indirect effects of land reforms in West Bengal (India) during the period 1967–2004. The two main predictions of the theory appear to be borne out by reduced-form analysis conducted on longitudinal data. First and foremost, population growth significantly raises division rates. Second, as a result of the increase in farm profitability induced by the reform, the probability of household division decreases for small farms (those below the land ceiling set by the land reform program). In contrast and unexpectedly, large farms responded to the reform by increasing their division rates. This is explained by the presumed motivation of large landowners to strategically divide their property in anticipation of potential future land reforms. It bears emphasizing that the indirect effects of the land reforms on household division have been found to be quantitatively negligible relative to the effect of population growth.

Last, we consider the theory of household division and private plots of Guirkinger and Platteau (2015). Owing to data limitations, they were able to test only the part of the theory that deals with the partial individualization in the form of private plots. The estimated model is a simple probit model in which the dependent variable is the probability to grant private plots to (male) members. In accordance with expectations, the household head is more likely to distribute private plots when the land-man ratio is lower and when the family is larger.[8] Regarding the latter, the implication of the theory must be borne in mind: when the size of the workforce on the collective field is larger, the scope of the moral-hazard-in-team problem increases, which enhances the relative attractiveness of private plots where no efficiency problem arises. The two key explanatory variables—land availability and size of family workforce—have been instrumented with the help of historical data. In this way, the potential endogeneity of current land availability and household size—residential choices, and therefore household size, are likely to be directly influenced by land allocation—is addressed.[9]

The second main result of the above study is much less expected. When the family is broken down into married men and other members, only the first category appears to have a significant influence on private plot allocation, and the effect is strongly significant. Moreover, the magnitude of the effect is far from negligible: thus, an increase of one unit in the number of married men increases the probability of individual plots by almost 10 percentage points. This suggests that the standard moral-hazard-in-team argument needs to be refined. As usually stated, this argument implies that the magnitude of the efficiency loss increases with the number of team members considered as equivalent units. Clearly, the assumption of an undifferentiated impact of group size is not applicable to the context of an extended or complex family.

Why is it that free-riding on other members' efforts in collective cultivation is observed when several married men work together and not when unmarried ones do? Two types of explanation are proposed by the authors. First, being strangers, daughters- or sisters-in-law tend to make the household more heterogeneous: they are not tied to the household by the same emotions and feelings of loyalty as their husbands. The weakening of solidarity may also arise from the behavior of the sons or nephews if, once they get married, they tend to identify with their nuclear family more than with the extended family. As a result, they may not feel as loyal as before to the large household unit, thereby fostering feelings of competition and rivalry. This mechanism is close to that suggested in an aforementioned paper by Kazianga and Wahhaj (2016) where stronger family ties are associated with more efficient allocation of production and consumption inside the household. Second, when the families of married men are of unequal size, the sharing rule is bound to look arbitrary to at least some couples. Thus, if the sharing rule provides for equal incomes to all married adults regardless of the size of their family, parents with more children feel discriminated against. On the contrary, if shares are proportional to family size, parents with fewer children feel exploited because they work partly for the benefit of larger conjugal units. Interestingly, these two weaknesses of complex households are also stressed in anthropological and historical literature (see, for example, Worobec 1995: 81 for pre-communist Russia).

In another paper, Guirkinger and Platteau, together with Goetghebuer, have tested their theory through a different angle, that is, they have compared land productivity levels between collective fields and private plots (Guirkinger et al. 2015). In other words, they have put to a quantitative test their assumption that effort is more efficiently applied to the latter than to the former. When a variety of possible confounding factors (including variations in land quality, intensity of use of modern inputs, and crop choices) are controlled for, private plots turn out to be more productive than collective plots, and there is strong evidence that productivity differentials can be attributed to substantial variations in labor effort applied to cultivation. A second finding deserves attention because it provides indirect support for the incentive-based mechanism behind the theory: the productivity advantage of private plots exists for care-intensive crops yet not for care-saving crops. Because of the minor role of labour quality in the production process of care-saving crops, these crops are less vulnerable or not at all vulnerable to the moral-hazard-in-team problem.

How then can we explain that, in another contribution also devoted to Burkina Faso, Kazianga and Wahhaj (2013) reached a conclusion opposite to the above? Comparing productivity of senior male plots (assumed to be collectively farmed) with junior male private plots and female private plots, they find that plots owned by the household head (common plots) are farmed more intensively and achieve higher yields than plots with similar characteristics owned by other household members. To account for this rather unexpected result, the authors emphasize the public character of the good produced on the family field: social norms exist that require the head to use all the proceeds of this field for the common good so that every member benefits from it. Moreover, junior partners are assumed to have a particularly strong preference for the public good thus generated and hence they are more willing to work on the collective field than on their private plots. A plausible explanation behind the difference between the two contrasting sets of findings is the following: households are more restricted in size and much more homogeneous in Burkina Faso (there are very few private plots controlled by siblings in their sample) than in the traditional, Bambara area of Mali where the study of Guirkinger et al. took place. Therefore, incentive problems on the collective field can be expected to be less serious in Burkina Faso than in Mali.

Last, it is useful to bring evidence that concerns the timing of land bequests and household divisions, using anthropological information collected in Russia. Extended households, wherever they existed, were placed under the authority of the head, or patriarch, who held absolute power over management of the household economy and the labor efforts of family members. This implied that he could encourage a son to take a job at a domestic industry, in which case he would have to "remit his wages, minus any expenses incurred while he was away on the job, to the household's coffers" (Worobec 1995 : 11). Household divisions typically took place at the death of the patriarch, often as a result of internal tensions. In the words of Christine Worobec: "if a son became household head upon his father's death, he could not command authority over his brothers as had his father, since all brothers were treated equally in the devolution of property. The other brothers were intent on being masters of their own households" (81). They preferred to break away from the stem household rather than submit to their elder brother's authority (Moon 1999: 171).

Pre-mortem divisions were also observed, however, and they often arose from suspicions of free-riding, for example, those caused by the unequal sizes of the different conjugal units forming the joint household.[10] But there were many other pretexts or reasons nurturing jealous feelings among siblings, and the relationships between daughters-in-law and mothers-in-law inside households were particularly vulnerable to such feelings (Moon 1999: 196). Let us now turn to the dynamics of pre-mortem household division. In the late nineteenth century, after the abolition of serfdom and other reforms, improved outside opportunities in the form of expanding opportunities for wage labor contributed to a surge in pre-mortem fissions and the growth in nuclear family households (Worobec 1995: 87, 115). Household divisions thus increased more rapidly in areas "where a substantial portion of the population derived its income from non-agricultural pursuits" (105), a phenomenon particularly noticeable in the central non-black earth region and elsewhere in the forest heartland (Moon 1999: 176).[11] The above situation, which is according to predictions of the theories of Guirkinger and Platteau (2014, 2015) regarding both household splits and the timing of land bequests, contrasts with that often observed in the Pre-Emancipation period in which communal elders, "who were heads of their own households, backed each other up in maintaining their authority over the younger generations," which implies in particular that younger peasants were discouraged from leaving their stem households (Moon 2006: 385). Still, pre-mortem household fissions occurred "in a substantial minority of cases" (Waldron 1997: 71).

It is noteworthy that the above empirical evidence concerns rural areas since the corresponding theories were constructed with this context in mind. However, some insights gained from these theories can well apply to more urban contexts. This is obviously the case with the comparative static effect of changes in outside options: in the G-P model, an improvement in these options has the effect of encouraging household division. The argument is of course reversible and the occurrence of an economic crisis is then expected to delay division or even lead to a re-consolidation of the household. Strong evidence supporting both scenarios is available. In the context of South Africa, Klasen and Woolard (2009) show that unemployment delays the setting up of an individual household by young adults, sometimes by decades, and may even lead to the dissolution of existing households. Matsudaira (2016) shows that changes in the living arrangement of young adults in the United States between 1960 and 2011 are largely explained by economic conditions. In particular, fewer jobs, low wages, and high rental costs all lead to increases in the numbers of men and women living with their parents. Relatedly, Kaplan (2012) and Cobb-Clark (2008) indicate that an important form of insurance against unemployment is the possibility for young adults (respectively in the United States and in Australia) to move back to their parents.

13.3.2. Transformation of the Household: Lessons from European History

13.3.2.1. Introduction

A good amount of empirical research effort has been devoted to the study of family patterns and their evolution across Europe during the last decades. The outcome of these efforts is potentially of great value since not only is the period covered very long (from the early Middle Ages to the eve of the Industrial Revolution) but also the different regions within the European territory have largely varying characteristics. This is especially so because conventional knowledge about the timing and the conditions of emergence of the nuclear household in Europe is seriously called into question. According to a widespread view that held sway until recently, the modernization of Europe went hand in hand with the individualization of (farming) households (and the concomitant development of private property rights): family households gradually evolved from rather collective to more individualized forms, that is, from complex, multi-generational, and early-marriage patterns to simple, nuclear, and late-marriage patterns. Institutional change is thus posited to be a monotonous process that gets started at some point marking the beginning of modern economic development.

Before the publication of of Alan Macfarlane's book, *The Origins of English Individualism* (1978), the overwhelmingly dominant view was that the appearance of the nuclear family came rather late, stretching over the centuries immediately preceding the Industrial Revolution, a period then revealingly identified as "early modern" by most historians of Europe. Macfarlane's work shook that approach to European modern history and contributed to spreading the alternative view that England was an exceptional case where nuclearization of households and the development of freehold or full-fledged private property rights occurred much earlier, in the late Middle Ages. The temptation was then strong to infer causality from the observed correlation between the pioneer role of England with respect to the individualization of the household (and the establishment of private property rights) and her leading role in industrialization.

More recent evidence is shattering the above picture in two main senses. First, the appearance of the nuclear form of the family and the farm can be dated back to even earlier periods than what is suggested in Macfarlane, and this phenomenon is not unique to England. Second, change in the family household has not been monotonous but has followed more complex patterns such as when individualized forms were succeeded by more collective forms that were in turn replaced by individualized forms. In the discussion below, we provide a rough sketch of these three canonical steps in the transformation of European households. Thereafter, we mention alternative paths of evolution and discuss some factors underlying the observed variations. Finally, we end our foray into European history by examining the role of some key rules that govern the functioning of households.

13.3.2.2. A Canonical Model, Phase 1: Early Nuclearization

Early nuclearization of households in Europe has been linked by some scholars to the emergence of independent small-scale family farms toward the end of the Roman Empire and the subsequent rise of women's age at marriage.

According to David Herlihy (1985) and Georges Duby (1973), as the slave economy of antiquity collapsed in the period of the late Roman Empire from the fourth century, and as the supply of slaves dried up with the stabilization or erosion of Rome's frontiers (the so-called problem of the *agri deserti*, or "abandoned fields"), big landlords dealt with the shortage of agricultural labor by shifting to a system based on incentives. They thus allowed some slaves to marry and to settle on the empty lands. Although these erstwhile slaves paid some form of rent to their lords and patrons (usually under the form of "labor rents" that in the worst cases represented several days of work per week), they could hold permanent rights over the lands they cleared and the houses they built, including the rights to retain the greater part of the produce and to pass them on to their heirs. Their bargaining strength was reinforced by the emergence of the institution of the roman colonate which was created for the purpose of encouraging resettlement on the basis of small-scale family farms. The "coloni" were free cultivators granted the right to benefit from the labor efforts spent in clearing and cultivating the land and, contrary to the erstwhile slaves on estate lands, they did not have to pay any compensation to a lord. In a desperate move to stop the economic decline of the empire, the Roman government went as far as settling even barbarian contingents upon the land, again on the basis of family farms endowed with permanent possession rights (Herlihy 1985: 59–61).

The mechanism through which the above circumstances promoted the nuclear family system is not clear, however. Thus, for Hartman, the nuclear pattern is correlated with the development of the late-marriage system. Manorial records, which began to be rather widespread from the mid-eighth century, reveal that "unlike the earlier Roman pattern of women marrying in their mid- to late teens and men in their late twenties, both sexes on the reorganised family farms married in their early to mid-twenties, with men only slightly older than women" (Hartman 2004: 87). The argument is that, as a result of the emergence of improved tenure rights—the ability to bequeath land to children in particular—the value of labor greatly increased for both men and women, and parents became quite eager to keep daughters as long as possible within the household. The marriage of women was thus delayed. Unfortunately, we are not told why the practice of postponing daughters' marriage explains the early dominance of the nuclear residential form (99). To make the argument consistent, Hartman should also have mentioned the ability of the parents to retain their sons after marriage within the household, which would go against the trend toward nuclearization. In sum, even though there is sparse but serious evidence that nuclear households did exist even before the tenth century, we still do not understand well how they emerged.

13.3.2.3. A Canonical Model, Phase 2: Complexification

In the parts of Europe where the feudal-seigneurial system became gradually implanted after the demise of the Roman Empire, family structures often evolved from simple to more complex living arrangements such as the joint or complex household. Newly married couples are then incorporated into the household to form an extended family structure led by a patriarch. He holds absolute power over management of the household economy and the labor input of family members within limitations set by the commune and the local community. In general, this situation lasts until his death, when authority is devolved to the most senior member of the family in the male line, either his eldest brother or his eldest son. At this point, other male family members had to decide whether to remain in the household or to split off from the household and leave it with their inheritance share.

The shift to more complex households occurred when household heads underwent strong pressures from newly asserting manorial lords who were eager to keep their land-holdings as large as possible for fiscal and other reasons that include labor mobilization. Hence their desire to control both the size and composition of their dependent households. In England and in central Europe, the same motivation led them to impose, or try to impose, single-heir devolution to maintain peasant holdings intact. In areas of strong manorial control, this strategy seems to have succeeded well (Berkner and Mendels 1978: 212; Brenner 1985: 295–296). To the extent that the adoption of unigeniture was often accompanied by changes in co-residential rules or practices, the effect was to complexify the household. The inheriting son could thus be required to remain on the parental farm throughout his whole life cycle, implying that he would take over the headship only upon the death of his parents. As a result, several conjugal units of different generations coexisted within the same household.

A similar process was also observed in Russia. Nuclear peasant families seem to have dominated until the seventeenth century when the re-enserfment of the peasants led the serf owners to work with the state authorities to impose more collective family forms, giving rise to the so-called second serfdom (Blum 1957, 1961; see also Brenner 1976, 1985). The motivation behind this institutional shift was to create large enough family units to allow easy collection of taxes and mobilization of serf labor services. Revealingly, the Ministry of State Domains allowed household divisions only when the original household was so large that the new units would have at least three male laborers each. Offenders who dared set up new households without first seeking the bailiff's permission were severely punished. In Russia, too, estate owners attempted to impose single-heir devolution, yet this rule was too antagonistic to prevailing customs to be acceptable by the peasantry. Thus, when during the pre-emancipation period, restrictive measures were adopted by the ruling class (serf owners and the Ministry of State Domains) with the purpose of establishing unigeniture in the countryside and thereby minimizing the risk of defaulting on military and tax obligations, they failed to produce tangible results because of the peasantry's strong attachment to the norm of equal inheritance (Worobec 1995: 84–87).

13.3.2.4. A Canonical Model, Phase 3: Re-Nuclearization

When the feudal-seigneurial system collapsed, farming households had the opportunity to become nuclear again. Interestingly, it seems that the incidence of the nuclear family pattern such as it could be observed in the early modern era coincided with the prior manorialized areas of the whole of Europe, not only of England (Hartman 2004: 86). An interesting question is whether the demise of the feudal system was caused by strictly political factors or was also aided by economic forces. In the latter instance, it can be argued that economics played an important role in the re-assertion of the nuclear household.

This is precisely the point made by a number of historians for whom the Black Plague (or the Black Death) and its long aftermath, stretching from 1347 to 1450, proved to be a critical period marked by an acute scarcity of labor relative to land. Western Europe then suffered a devastating and prolonged decline in population that radically changed the balance of power in favor of the peasantry. This had two distinct effects. First, since land was now easily accessible outside the confines of the manor or the village community, young adults could make a move of their own without waiting for their parents to award them land on the customary holding. In other words, the sudden rise of new exit opportunities conferred new bargaining strength upon the youth. Second, because they were eager to retain their customary serfs on the land or to persuade newcomers to take up vacant holdings, landlords were compelled to accede to the peasants' most important demands, namely the reduction of land rents and the forfeiture of labor services on the demesne. As a consequence, a far-reaching mutation of the relationship between manor and village took place. Not only did the distinction between servile and free tenants fade, but also a number of structural changes occurred in the layout and the operation of the village economy.[12] These changes had the effect of loosening the bond between manor and village, breaking up demesne agriculture, loosening the anchorage of the peasant family cycle in the transmission of customary holdings from fathers to sons, eroding the influence of manorial customs based on an intricate web of duties and conditional rights and protections, undermining the power of manor courts (to the benefit of Royal courts), and diminishing manorial autonomy (Seccombe 1992: 93–94, 133, 136–148; see also Herlihy 1985: 153–155).

The weakening or even disintegration of manorial rules was not confined to land rights and household composition and size. It also affected the regulatory framework for marriage, sparking the shift to late and non-universal marriage. As a result of that process, Seccombe speculates, the Malthusian explanation according to which land abundance should encourage rather than discourage early marriage and increase rather than decrease nuptiality does not hold. The idea is that in the feudal system, because they were eager to maximize the productive contribution of each tenant family to demesne agriculture, the lords were strongly reluctant to allow single people of either sex to take up tenancies while remaining unmarried, or to retain them without remarrying if widowed. In sum, the manorial lords had an economic incentive to hasten marriage and remarriage. This is precisely the situation that was profoundly disturbed by the mortality crisis of the Black Death: the lords were compelled to relinquish labor services and lease out demesne land, which undermined their incentive to exert pressure for early marriage and the quick remarriage of widows. Absent the meddling of the manorial lord in marital affairs, the local community tended to discourage early marriage by requiring that sufficiently large parcels be assembled before assenting to a match (Seccombe 1992: 148–156).

Voigtlander and Voth (2013) have also traced back the origin of late marriage in Europe to the Black Plague period. The detailed mechanism behind their explanation is depicted as follows:

> By killing between a third and half of the European population, it [the Black Plague] raised land-labor ratios. Land abundance favored the land-intensive sector—animal husbandry. Because plow agriculture requires physical strength, women have a comparative advantage in livestock farming. Hence, after the Black Death, female employment opportunities improved. Working in husbandry mainly took the form of farm service—a contract that required year-round labor services in exchange for money, room, and board. As a condition of employment, all servants had to remain celibate—pregnancy and marriage resulted in termination of employment. Because many more women began to work in the booming pastoral sector after 1350, mar-

riage ages increased. This lowered fertility in the aggregate. In a Malthusian world, there were second-round effects: lower fertility reduced population pressure, ensuring that per capita output never returned to pre-plague levels. (2228)

It is thus the opportunity cost of women's involvement in husbandry production rather than in grain production and "production" of children that is the key variable behind the marriage pattern for women. Changes in this pattern in response to variations in women's opportunity cost are explained within a particular decision-making framework where women are unconstrained maximizers of their own utility. An empirical test of the mechanism is provided that uses detailed data from England. Moreover, to account for the differential evolution of the marriage pattern between northwestern Europe, on the one hand, and Mediterranean and Eastern Europe, and even China, on the other hand, Voigtlander and Voth propose an explanation based on the relative importance of grain and husbandry in the prevailing agricultural system, and the specific characteristics of the husbandry technology. In the Mediterranean regions, large herds could not be sustained throughout the whole year without resorting to transhumance. As a result, so they argue, there was no regular demand for women's labor services. In Eastern Europe (and China), husbandry remained uncompetitive vis-à-vis grain production, therefore reducing the need for women's labor. Another finding of Voigtlander and Voth is that, within the late-marriage societies, the change in age at marriage of women was, but only partly, reversible. Indeed, as the comparative advantage of animal husbandry declined vis-à-vis grain production, demand for women's labor declined, thereby causing earlier marriages. The decline, however, was never so strong as to mark a return to the preceding system of early marriage.

In some regions, another force that contributed to the nuclearization of households has an effect analogous to an increase in local or regional availability of land: the expansion of off-farm income opportunities. This became a systematic trend only with the development of cottage industries. Marking the beginning of proto-industrialization, they were established only during the long sixteenth century when the population of Europe increased rapidly by premodern standards, and during the seventeenth century when they became increasingly based on specialized craftmanship (Medick 1981). The gradual rise of a labor market helped resolve a deep conflict between fathers and sons. Seccombe (1992) described the deadlock that this conflict created in the village economy in the following terms. Fathers in northwestern Europe were unwilling to retire and relinquish control of the family holding, yet at the same time they did not have sufficient authority to force their sons to marry inside the paternal household. In no position to force their father to retire early, neither could the sons accept remaining under his headship upon reaching adult age, and they therefore pushed away from the household in order to acquire more economic independence (187). It is apparently during the sixteenth and seventeenth centuries in northwestern and central Europe, when land pressure increased considerably, that the spread of service in husbandry was fastest. It seems that the resulting change in the power balance between fathers and sons gradually prompted the former to make pre-mortem gifts of land to the latter (103).

Even before that period, in some regions, local labor markets existed that allowed children from land-poor households to work on the farms of land-rich households, thereby helping to equalize land-labor ratios across farms. In some parts of England at least, the market for domestic service seems to have predated the Black Plague: according to one in-depth study of Essex, even before 1350, only a quarter of people passed their entire lives in the parish of their birth with the rest, who were primarily wage earners, regularly moving about (Poos 1991). In northwestern Europe—in pre-industrial England, Iceland, Denmark, western Germany, Flanders, the Netherlands, and Austria—it is in the early Modern Era corresponding to the late fourteenth and fifteenth centuries that the practice of domestic service for young single adults (from 15 to 30 years of age) seems to have become commonplace (Seccombe 1992: 197–198; Szołtysek 2015: 10).[13] Following a rather standard scenario, poor households delayed the marriages of their offspring and often sent them out as young adults to serve in another, richer household where their wages could be accumulated in a fund earmarked for their eventual marriage settlements (money to purchase land for young men and to constitute the dowry for young women).

It bears emphasizing that domestic workers were not attached or tied to their employers in any way. They worked on a contract basis, normally for one-year stints with the reciprocal option of renewal. While first placements were ususally arranged by parents (which explains why it was not rare to see servants working in families related to their own), subsequent hirings occurred on a face-to-face basis. The portion of the wage paid in cash was paid out in a lump sum at the end of the contract period. As for the portion paid in kind, it included boarding and lodging and frequently access to a garden plot and the right to raise a sheep or two. Servants typically came under the continuous paternal jurisdiction of their master and could not leave him with impunity until the contract period had elapsed. In the words of Seccombe (1992): "Service was not an alternative to the prolonged subordination of young adults to patriarchal authority, but an extension of familial discipline with a change of masters" (198). What needs to be emphasized, however, is that discipline was exerted only within a limited labor contract period. Micro-level evidence thus indicates that in England the majority of domestic servants actually moved after one year, while in Germany the average stay was one and a half years. In the interludes between two successive hirings, servants often returned home because they were unable to find work or their parents needed their assistance. Finally, it bears pointing out that most servants did not move far from home, the average distance between different postings not exceeding a few kilometers (198–199).

A picture of more radical change emerges from other accounts, though. In areas where manorialization survived after the Black Plague, it appears that the efforts of the landlords to restrict emigration did not succeed in preventing young women and men from displaying "astonishing mobility": many of them left the manor of their birth temporarily for service on another, or permanently for marriage, or even abandoned manorial security altogether for the freedom of nearby towns (Hartman 2004: 73).

In theory, not only labor but also land exchanges can correct land-labor imbalances across households. Evidence about active land sales markets in European history is nevertheless scant. Manorial court rolls indicate that there was an active market in freehold land in the Middle Ages but it was essentially limited to England, and the recorded transfers are typically lease arrangements, not sales (Seccombe 1992: 99). Moreover, when sales occurred, they were often subject to the limitation of reversionary rights, implying that there was a marked tendency for land "to revert into the possession of either the original family who had alienated it or their 'successor' in the land market" (Blanchard 1984: 242).

13.3.2.5. Variant Paths

Not all the parts of Europe have actually followed the above-sketched sequence. For example, in some areas of Europe (England, Holland, Denmark) nuclear households seem to have persisted throughout the whole period covered (Todd 2011: 399–407, 453–454). In other areas belonging to southern and eastern Europe, nuclear households became complexified and remain thus even to this date. In still other areas, the complex form was never really abandoned. To make matters even more complicated, variations could be observed inside regions not only with respect to household forms observed at a given point in time but also with respect to the transformation trajectory followed. In the discussion below, stress is again placed on the influence of micro-, meso-, or macro-political factors that were evidently at work in the transformation of household forms that we have just highlighted. The role of these factors testifies that assumptions of unfettered individual rationality of household members—for example, Voigtländer and Voth's assumption that women are unconstrained maximizers of their own utility—is questionable in the presence of strong family headship (e.g., a patriarch) and/or upper-level political authorities.

As predicted by the G-P theory of household transformation, and illustrated by aforementioned historical evidence, the expansion of off-farm income opportunities encourages household division or, at least, the awarding of private plots to tenants or family members. What needs to be added now is that these outcomes may fail to materialize if young adults, especially women, are prevented by their parents and the local lord from moving to other locations if needed. In many regions of Eastern and Mediterranean Europe (as in Mediterranean France and medieval Italy), the existence of an unbroken tradition of strong patriarchal control in the hands of the older generation, as well as deep-rooted taboos against, and fear of, premarital sex and all sorts of sexual misconduct, considerably slowed down the spread of service in husbandry (Seccombe 1992: 103, 119, 125; Herlihy 1985: 153–155; Le Roy Ladurie 1976: 62–63; Berkner and Mendels 1978; Szołtysek 2015: 16). The same patriarchy-enforced customs also prevented young men and especially women from seizing potential employment opportunities in the post-plague era, testifying again to the conditioning role of institutions. Based on a comparative study by Goldberg (1992), Hartman (2004: 77) thus notes that "in England the labour shortage produced by the huge increase in mortality from the plague prompted an influx of unmarried women into the town, a rise in marriage age, and an increase in the proportion of women never marrying." In Italy, on the contrary, "eligible young women remained at home, despite the jump in potential employment opportunities."

Households in many parts of Italy remained vertically integrated as a result not only of patriarchal norms but also, and relatedly, as a result of the control exerted by big landlords. Thus, as documented in a micro-study of a Tuscan village over the eighteenth and nineteenth centuries (Derosas et al. 2014), more than one-third of the households representing half the total population were complex. The heads of these complex households tended to be wealthy sharecroppers upon whom local landlords exerted a strong control to ensure that land fragmentation and household division did not occur: not only were adult members prevented from leaving the family group, but also their marriages were discouraged and delayed (Dribe et al. 2014: 95, 105, 107). In these instances, therefore, the practice of late marriage occurred within the framework of complex families.

The same influence of authority structures can be detected when intermediate forms of farm individualization are considered. Thus, the peasants' rights over the land were minimal in the huge estates run as demesne manors by ecclesiastical orders—separate peasant plots were essentially non-existent—while, at the other extreme, peasants' rights were most developed in the manors of absentee lords, which were often divided entirely into peasant plots (so that the lord's income consisted exclusively of rent in various forms) (Seccombe 1992: 78).[14]

Until recently, Russia and Eastern Europe have been typically considered as having followed a different institutional trajectory from Western Europe (see, for example, Pipes 1995, 1999). In terms of family structures, their situation is closer to southern Europe, and a common view is that the eastern regions have been ensnared into a sort of collectivist trap that was reinforced at the time of the "second serfdom." We have nonetheless fitted Russia into the nuclear-complex-nuclear scheme presented above, thereby departing from the conventional view. In fact, recent research justifies this choice and actually points to the danger of overemphasizing the differences between Russia and Eastern Europe, on the one hand, and Western Europe, on the other hand. Not only do the differences appear to be less dramatic than usually thought, but also variations inside the former regions seem to be quite significant. In the words of Markus Cerman (2012), author of a survey on this question: "The idea of a structural difference between Western and Eastern Europe should be treated with extreme caution, in particular with respect to possible medieval roots. Some of the general trends influencing the tenant economy in late medieval Western Europe—such as the fragmentation of lordship, the reduction of demesne farming, urbanization and changes in property rights and tenure—also occurred in East-Central and Eastern Europe" (57).

More specifically, there was no such thing as a monolithic "second serfdom" in Russia and in East-Central and Eastern Europe: a substantial portion of the Russian peasantry, for example, was not submitted to demesne lordship. As a consequence, the image of a dualism in the European agrarian structure is too simple and must be questioned (Waldron 1997; Moon 1999, 2006; Dennison 2011; Cerman 2012). Cerman also warns us that "contrary to previous accounts, secure property rights among the rural population were the rule rather than the exception in demesne lordship. What is uncontested is that hereditary property rights of tenant farms and smallholdings were practically universal in the late medieval period. The later existence of insecure property rights, caused by developments beginning in the sixteenth century, cannot be denied, but they were often confined regionally or to a specific period" (29). The idea of a systematic expropriation of tenant farmers as a result of the extension of demesne farming from the late fifteenth century onward is just a myth (58–61). The fact of the matter is that "the power of demesne lords was far from absolute and that there were legal and other ways for successful action and resistance by the rural population" which was better able to follow its own interests than had been previously assumed (39). Finally, explaining the rise of early modern demesne lordship as a consequence of the Black Plague and the resulting assertion of lords' power seems quite debatable (40–57).

13.3.2.6. The Household as the Locus of Multiple Rules: Static Considerations

A major finding coming out of the historical literature devoted to the European family is that the size and composition of household units are the result of a complex set of rules and economic constraints. These include: the marriage ages for men and women as well as the difference between them; the role of the family head in arranging marriages and rules governing marriage arrangements; the prevalence of celibacy, the co-residence rules, and the home-leaving pattern; inheritance rules; the strength of familial authority, family values, and the incidence of life-cycle domestic servants. It is evident that this multiplicity of variables would not pose much of a problem if they were well correlated. This is the presupposition underlying the well-known typology of families proposed by Frédéric Le Play, George Homans, John Hajnal, and Peter Laslett, in particular.

For Le Play (1871), the vertically extended family type, known as the "stem family," is inextricably associated with unigeniture in inheritance, whereas partible inheritance could give rise either to joint, horizontally extended households or to nuclear families. Organized to preserve the integrity of the ancestral farm, the stem family provides that it should pass from the family chief to a single heir, usually the oldest but sometimes the youngest son or a son designated by the father. Only the inheriting son was allowed to marry, an option that he was able to use before the parents' death or retirement. His siblings, by contrast, could stay on the farm only if they remained celibate. As a consequence, the stem family typically comprised three generations: the old parents, a single married son and his unmarried siblings, and the children of the young married couple. Where partible inheritance predominated, several brothers could decide to keep their common patrimony undivided, even after one or several of them had married. The resulting family type is the horizontally extended, joint household. Another solution, however, consisted of dividing the paternal farm upon the father's death, in which case partible inheritance would lead to a proliferation of small farms and nuclear families. Homans (1953) faithfully followed Le Play's typology when he attempted to classify the household structures found in England.

Hajnal (1982) and Laslett (1971) gave a lot of attention to the marriage system and, in so doing, they departed from the above characterization yet clung to a dichotomous typology. In multi-generational families or complex households, marriage occurred at an early age, especially for women, and it was universal. In nuclear family households, on the contrary, marriage was late, not only for men but also for women; the age difference at marriage between the two sexes was small; and marriage was far from universal. For Hajnal, the two systems could be geographically delineated in a clear manner: the nuclear, late-marriage family system was a unique characteristic of northwestern Europe, while the complex, early-marriage system was dominant to the east and south of a demarcation line running from St. Petersburg to Trieste, through central Europe. As for Laslett, although he proposed a geographical demarcation based on four rather than two zones, he retained Hajnal's view that western Europe (and England in particular) was unique in its emphasis on the nuclear family household. The distinction between two sharply contrasting family systems, and its apparent usefulness in mapping out the whole European continent, were so appealing that they "came to represent a kind of historical and sociological orthodoxy" (Szołtysek 2015: 7). Two scholars who later played a major role in pursuing the debate on the Hajnal-Laslett analytical scheme are Seccombe (1992) and Hartman (2004).

Recent research based on detailed micro-evidence has revealed not only that the geographical divide proposed by Hajnal (and even Laslett) was questionable, but also that the classification of family systems was much too simple. As a matter of fact, the various dimensions of a family system are not well correlated. For instance, in his study of the manor of Halesowen near Birmingham, Razi (1980) has shown that there was no clear relationship between the inheritance rule and family organization. Another example, as we already had the opportunity to illustrate, is the lack of systematic relationship between the age for marriage for girls and family organization (Hartman 2004). Moreover, simple families were common throughout substantial parts of early modern Europe outside its northwestern core. In the words of Mikolaj Szołtysek (2015): "A long but discontinuous belt of other territories in which nuclear families predominated was shown to have stretched from southern Italy and Iberia, through certain areas in both northern and southern German-speaking territories, to seventeenth-century Bohemia" (14). It has even become clearer that the pattern extends to the east and southeast of early modern Europe, in western Poland-Lithuania, in Wallachia (in present-day Romania), and western Ukraine, for example.

For Szołtysek, a serious problem that arises with Hajnal's demarcation line is the misplacement of areas located in the western parts of Eastern Europe: in these areas, important features of the family system (such as the size and composition of the households, nuptiality patterns, the recourse to domestic service, the timing of home-leaving and household formation) made them closer to the northwestern model than to the eastern and southern European ones. This failure is obviously easy to remedy through an appropriate redrawing of the map that would join Poland, Lithuania, Estonia, Latvia, Hungary, the Czech and Slovak lands, and Western Ukraine to northwestern Europe. Harder to handle, however, is the conclusion that the northwestern part of Europe may have been much less homogeneous than was previously believed, or that a considerable degree of interregional variation in familial organization prevailed within historical areas traditionally considered as having simple (and neo-local) household systems, such as in England, northern Europe, and central Europe (Wall et al. 1983; Wall et al. 2001). For example, joint or complex households could be found in many parts of historic Europe, including early medieval Germanic societies, fifteenth-century Tuscany and central Italy, early modern central France, some parts of the Alps, Finland, and the Balkans (Szołtysek 2015: 16; Todd 2011: 319–326; Viazzo and Albera 1990).

Admitting such complexity of the European family patterns should not, however, lead us to reject Hajnal's intuition altogether, as some social scientists have done (see, e.g., Todd 2011). Along some dimension, the difference between the adjusted northwestern zone and the southern and eastern zones is difficult to dismiss. This is especially true with respect to gender-based differences in the age at marriage, and to life-cycle domestic service.

13.3.2.7. The Household as the Locus of Multiple Rules: Dynamic Considerations

If we now adopt a dynamic perspective, a major lesson from the historical literature is that to go through the complex web of interrelationships involved in family systems, we need to have a clear idea of which dimensions are invariant, slow-moving, and fast-moving. Moreover, we have to allow for the fact that the answer to this question may vary depending upon the specific circumstances obtaining in particular locations and particular periods of time. Only then will we be able to sketch a theory that can under-pin efforts to interpret empirical data. We illustrate the importance of the context by referring to the role of nuptiality and inheritance rules.

We begin with the nuptiality pattern. If the age at marriage is a fast-moving dependent variable, a sort of Malthusian nuptiality adjustment mechanism is at work. By contrast, if it reflects a deeply rooted social norm, it is by definition a slow-moving variable, and other adjustment mechanisms will be set into motion, such as the inheritance rule. The former scenario in which age at marriage and the incidence of celibacy quickly adjust to changes in the economic environment has been persuasively shown to be at work in England during the seventeenth to nineteenth centuries (Wrigley and Schofield 1981). Another example is provided by Oris et al. (2014) in the context of rural communities in nineteenth-century eastern Belgium. In this instance, under conditions of growing land pressure, parents used their influence to delay and discourage marriages so as to maintain the farm holding intact. Age at marriage and celibacy consequently increased.[15] The possibility also existed, as illustrated in the same study, that children refuse to stay home and instead move to nearby cities with a view to seizing job opportunities. In this way they hoped to earn enough income to set up their own household either in the city or in the countryside if they chose to return to agriculture once they had purchased enough land. As for the second scenario, it is well illustrated by the absence of response to improving labor market opportunities in Mediterranean Europe in the post-plague period. This lack of response reflected a deep-rooted resistance against any delaying of marriage, especially for women, and provides a neat contrast with the situation prevailing in England, as pointed out earlier.

Inheritance rules provide another illustration of the different ways in which the dynamics of household structures may unfold. When dealing with inheritance, economists typically assume that the rule, whether of impartible or partible inheritance, is fixed and exogenously given. The implication is that adjustment of the household to changes in the economic environment takes place via other channels such as household size and composition, or the nuptiality pattern. In reality, however, inheritance rules may be flexible. Thus, evidence exists that, when land pressure increased beyond a certain point, the household head could choose to limit the fragmentation of the land by giving preference to one heir. In the words of Mary Hartman (2004), pressures of population growth on property "prompted serf families by the later Middle Ages to adopt a single-heir system throughout the manorialized region as a way of keeping their landed holdings viable as farming units" (74).

It is important to note that, in the above example, the adaptability of the inheritance rule is conditional upon the local sociopolitical structure. This confirms the strong correlation often observed between the incidence of primogeniture and the extent of (past) manorialization: areas that adopted primogeniture coincided "remarkably faithfully" with areas of widespread manorialization (Howell 1976: 117; Le Roy Ladurie 1976: 58; Berkner and Mendels 1978: 212). Impartible inheritance was actually born with feudalism and adopted mainly inside the high aristocracy.[16] This class, indeed, was eager to protect the indivisibility of seigneurial authority and strongly determined to perpetuate the name, power, and prestige of the family. The integrity of the land and mansion thus became the physical symbol of the unity and indivisibility of the political and military functions associated with the lord's estate, as well as of the sanctity of patriarchal relations. As has been hinted at earlier, the high nobles or overlords were also interested in imposing impartible inheritance on dependent households because imposing taxes and labor or other services on large, undivided farm units allowed them to minimize transaction costs and the risk of tax-defaulting (Berkner 1976: 77; Brenner 1976: 19; Hilton 1985: 125; Platteau and Baland 2001: 29–32). It is thus revealing that primogeniture was less dominant in France than in England, where the portion of the surface fully in the hands of the lords was much larger (Brenner 1985: 295–296). Also, in Lower Saxony (Germany), the area of Calenberg where impartible holdings were the rule had most of its land "under the strictest manorial control," whereas in the area of Göttingen, where manorial control was weak (only minimal manorial dues were paid), land used to be divided into smaller fragments with each passing generation (Berkner 1976: 80–82).

Under the influence of new outside economic opportunities, the inheritance rule could change in the opposite direction, from impartible to partible bequest. Seccombe (1992) thus notes that: "Even in impartible zones of stronger seigneurial pressure, the loss of viable arable land and the development of a second income source relaxed the impartible imperative . . . Once the livelihood of future generations was no longer dependent on arable acreage, the impartible rule was placed in abeyance." This was particularly the case "if common rights could be retained for all heirs no matter how minuscule their holdings" (183–184). Adaptation of the single-heir devolution rule was most often observed in areas where a scanty agrarian income could be supplemented by developing domestic industries and crafts, and this was particularly likely in the context of the development of cottage industries and proto-industrialization (Thompson 1976: 342; see also Habakkuk 1955: 10). According to one account of the life of villagers in the canton of Zürich during the seventeenth and eighteenth centuries:

> The earning possibilities generated by the putting-out industry of Zürich, however, created an entirely new situation. . . . the circumstances of inheritance rights were transformed . . . Previously fathers and sons avoided dividing fairly large and, even more, modest holdings, for they were concerned that each piece be able to nourish its holder. This fear vanished entirely with the diffusion of manufactures and cottage industry; and now the sons redivided the parcels received from their fathers, themselves the product perhaps of several divisions, because people are convinced that even a small field is enough to feed a diligent holder along with wife and children. (Braun 1978: 311)

It must be finally remarked that the dynamics of inheritance rules could be even more complex than what has just been suggested. This is because neither impartible nor partible inheritance was prevalent as a pure type (Seccombe 1992: 96). This was especially true for the ordinary peasants who tended to behave pragmatically and among whom written wills played a minor role due to the prevalence of pre-mortem inheritance and to the high proportion of them dying intestate. "While aristocrats generally adhered to principles such as primogeniture quite strictly, planning far in advance precisely how the steps of devolution would unfold, peasant heads could not afford to fulfil such codes to the letter" (100).[17] Even more important for our purpose is the fact that compensatory practices tended to predominate in areas of unigeniture and were generally based on the practice of inter-vivos gifts.[18]

For instance, in the medieval parish of Halesowen (England), where the prevailing custom was impartible inheritance, parents often bestowed some holdings on younger siblings, while earmarking the major portion for the principal heir. This allowed the non-inheriting sons and daughters to start a family on their own even though they had to supplement the income obtained from their inherited portions through work as hired hands. Moreover, even the principal heir often helped his younger brothers or sisters to acquire land, sometimes assigning them parts of his own patrimony (Razi 1980). Herlihy (1985) concludes as follows: "People, in sum, found ways around the customary rules. And, doubtless too, in regions of partible inheritance, parents might favour one offspring over the others. At all events, at Halesowen and surely elsewhere too, younger sons were not forced to remain celibate. The community was not divided into propertied household heads and their landless and celibate younger siblings. The requirement that younger siblings remain celibate, which the system of the stem family demanded, was simply too harsh to command full compliance" (138). Evidence supporting this conclusion is plentiful (Goody 1973; Berkner 1972, 1976; Le Roy Ladurie 1976; Berkner and Mendels 1978; Gaunt 1983; Dribe and Lundh 2005).

The practice of compensations allowed for much more flexibility than would have been possible if unigeniture was strictly enforced. Thus, in conditions of land scarcity, the size of the provision for the younger children was left to the discretion of the heir—such as was the case, for example, over most parts of Germany outside the Rhineland and Thuringia (Habakkuk 1955: 3).[19] He was then free to reduce the inheritance portions of his siblings in order to avoid de-capitalization of the family property. When the succession and the provision for the children were determined by the parents (for example, they were specified in detail in a settlement made on their marriage), though, the room of manœuvre for the privileged heir was much more restricted and economic consequences could be rather similar to those produced by a system of partible heritance. In the area of Cambridgeshire, which was nominally one of primogeniture, for example, fathers made provisions for their younger children in their wills in the form of fragments of land and of cash sums for younger sons and of dowries for daughters, as well as maintenance for the widow. Yet, all these provisions, which did not come out of accumulated savings of the testator, amounted "to a very considerable burden on the main holding and on the inheriting son," with the result that many holdings of 15 to 45 acres broke down in spite of the rule of primogeniture (Spufford 1976: 157).[20] In some places, however, parents willing to achieve some social justice between their children in conditions where compensations would have brought the family farm below viable size chose to establish a temporary co-ownership of the family land among siblings (for references, see Lundh and Kurosu 2014: 29).

13.3.2.8. East and West: A Comparative Perspective

Unfortunately, the richness of empirical material available on the history of the European families contrasts with the dearth of evidence accessible to the international research community regarding the dynamics of families in other parts of the world. An interesting but limited exception is the Eurasia Population and Family History Project launched in 1994 by historical demographers. It consists of a set of comparative micro-studies of Italy, Sweden, Belgium, Japan, and China. On the basis of these studies, the leading team has reached the conclusion that marriage patterns and family systems in Asia are substantially different from those observed in Europe. At the same time, important variations exist inside each region. In particular, the findings "verify the picture of early and universal marriage in Asia, especially for females, and of later marriages and larger proportions of people who never married in Europe" (Lundh and Kurosu 2014: 443). Furthermore, while in the European populations marriage was closely associated with reproduction—first births typically occurred immediately or soon after the wedding—in the Asian populations the time span was quite long between marriage and reproduction. This difference corresponds to the contrast between the widespread practice of arranged marriages in Asia and the large role of individual consent and choice in European marriages. While marriages are placed under the control of (extended) families in Asia, they tend to be the concern of the marriage candidates themselves in Europe, and this is true both psychologically and financially (456–457).

For the sake of comparison with Europe, the case of China is especially interesting. This is because, like most European countries, China has been subject to relentless land pressure for many centuries (Pomeranz 2000). What has prevailed in this populous Asian country is typically the complex household system. Thus, in late imperial China, a period for which documents are relatively abundant, "married couples lived in a large household together with the husband's parents, unmarried sisters, married brothers, and even cousins. Married brothers often continued to live together after their father's death, especially among propertied families and especially while their mother or grandfather was alive . . . individual couples did not have to accumulate material wealth by themselves to establish separate households. Rather, the material wealth for marriage was allocated by the household head. Therefore parents, in consultation with a wider network of kin, arranged marriages" (Chen et al. 2014: 395–396). While in elite families engagement could take place when sons and daughters were still children, lower status families had a shorter engagement period since they tended not to start the search for a partner until the children were older (396).

Finally, patrilineal inheritance was pervasive in late imperial China, implying that women had no property rights either as daughters or as wives. Upon their marriage, women became subordinate to their husbands. It is puzzling to note, however, that this situation was not observed before the fourteenth century. It is actually the Mongol invasion of China in the thirteenth century that seems to have precipitated a lasting transformation of marriage and property laws that deprived women of their property rights and reduced their legal and economic autonomy. As argued by Bettine Birge (2002), indigenous social forces actually combined with foreign invasion and cultural confrontation to bring laws more into line with the goals of the radical Confucian philosophers who wished to curtail women's financial and personal autonomy. As early as in the Sung dynasty (960–1279), these philosophers sought to reaffirm classical Confucian gender roles, questioning inheritance by daughters and instead encouraging agnatic adoption to carry on family lines. They also encouraged women to donate all or part of their dowry to their husband's household and, by the end of the dynasty, judges themselves toed that line and tried to prevent women from leaving marriages with their personal property (143–144). It therefore appears that in China, too, there has been no such thing as a monotonous transformation of family institutions, property rights, and gender roles: in early times, the rights of women were remarkably well established.

In general, evidence regarding recent trends in household living arrangements in developing countries is far from settled. Due to lack of systematic census samples from these countries before the mid-twentieth century, there is an ongoing debate between two views. According to the first, economic development is associated with a decline in family complexity and intergenerational co-residence, as attested by clear evidence from Japan, Korea, and Taiwan. Defenders of the second view, however, suggest that there have been no clear trends in co-residence in developing countries (for references, see Ruggles 2009: 250–251). In his own work, Ruggles (2009) compares the recent trends in the probability that elderly people stay with a child in developing countries (since 1950) to those detected in developed countries at comparable stages of economic growth. Controlling for the importance of agriculture in the economy and for demographic conditions, he concludes that the trends are similar. However, when the trends that are compared concern the importance of multi-generational families with two or more married children (that is, joint families), the trends appear to be different, with Europe and North America being much less likely to have this type of living arrangement (Ruggles 2010).

13.3.3. Transformation of the Family: Looking for the Big Picture in World and European History

Regarding the dynamics of the family, the economics profession has focused mainly on the way interpersonal transfers are affected by welfare state policies: this is usually referred to as the crowding-out effect, which we are going to consider in section 13.4. Economists also often point out that the displacement of the insurance function of the family may be the result of market development. Here, alternative mechanisms mainly consist of insurance markets and self-insurance possibilities through savings accumulation and better income diversification. The process may not necessarily lead to the complete disappearance of the kinship group but instead to its erosion and diminished effectiveness. This is evident if improvements in future income prospects benefit the best of the kinship group who are then prompted to exit, thereby making the rest of the group worse off (Platteau 1991; Fafchamps 1992). Beyond that rather narrow yet important concern, economists have contributed very little to the understanding of the issue of dynamic transformation of the family. The aforementioned paper by Alesina and Giuliano (2015) adduces evidence that market development displaces the family. Their analysis is based on reduced-form cross-country regressions, and to measure the importance of the family, they rely on subjective variables drawn from the World Value Survey. The mechanism proposed (but not strictly tested) to explain family displacement is the increasing opportunity cost of participation in familial activities that market development entails (a point earlier made by Hoff and Sen 2005: 183, for example). It is thus implicitly assumed that the multiple advantages provided by the family are not enhanced, or not enhanced too much, by market development. Using micro-level historical data, Aldashev and Guirkinger (2016) provide evidence of the decreasing importance of the family in regulating access to land and labor when Kazakh nomads sedentarized during Russian colonization in the early twentieth century. Specifically they show how the rules governing land and labor allocation at the supra-household level evolved toward greater decentralization. This process of individualization at the clan level is similar to the processes described in the section on the individualization of farming households (sections 13.2.1 and 13.3.1).

Compared to these limited contributions by economists, the works of historians and political scientists appear to be much more ambitious and of potentially greater significance. We shall see that recently a few economists have started to look at some aspects of the wider issues of family dynamics, where the family is considered as a network with multiple functions, not only economic but also political, administrative, military, and judiciary. One of the most fascinating questions that arise with regard to this dynamics can be stated as follows: why is it that, unlike many other regions in the world, Western Europe succeeded in suppressing the forces of kinship groups at an early stage of its history? Before we address this question, we illustrate very summarily the persistence of some form of clan-based organization in two important regions of the world, the Middle East and China. We then look at the experience of Western Europe and the dominant explanation for the early demise of clanism there.[21]

13.3.3.1. The Middle East and China

Islam was born in a region riddled with tribal warfare, and it is therefore not surprising that the Prophet and the succeeding caliphs were eager to build a state based on a unifying ideology. Because it emphasized universal human equality before God, the new faith was apparently well designed to transcend tribal affiliations and the associated loyalties. This theme has been recurrent in the history of Islam, and great hopes were repeatedly placed in the capacity of Islam's central concept of umma (the universal community of the Muslims) to put an end to internal splintering and social fragmentation. The achievements of Islam as a unifying ideology have proven quite dismal, however (see Platteau 2017). During the Umayyad period, tribal divisions and animosities precluded the formation of a strong centralized state. It did not take long before the new Muslim elite "realised that the tribal identification was too well rooted in Arabian society simply to be abolished by decree or swept aside by a few measures that tended to transcend the exclusiveness of the tribal bond. The success of the integration of the tribesmen into a state, then, depended as much upon their ability to use tribal ties for their own ends as it did upon their ability to override those ties" (Donner 1981: 258; also cited in Fukuyama 2012; 195–196). Thus, under the Abbasid rulers who succeeded the Umayyads, power continued to rest less in abstractions like the "state" than in the extended households of the leading figures of the military elites (Berkey 2003: 214).

To overcome tribal or kinship divisions, Abbasid rulers resorted to a system known as military slavery: they recruited slaves of foreign origin to form the core of their army and thus hoped to build up more reliable loyalty. Since they were kidnapped as children and then raised in artificial households, the slaves were expected to be intensely loyal to their master, the only person they could identify with. In the complete absence of kinship ties, their loyalty was owed to the caliph, presented as the superior embodiment of the state and the public interest. The success of military slavery in defeating the centrifugal forces of tribal fragmentation did not prove durable, however. In the Ghaznavid and Egyptian Mamluk cases (the Ghaznavid Empire was a Turkic successor state centered in Afghanistan), the decline of the state was essentially caused by the reappearance of kinship and patrimonialism within the Mamluk institution itself. In Egypt, this failure was compounded by the fact that the Mamluks escaped civilian control and turned the country into a military dictatorship (Hodgson 1974a: 39–57, 267–268, 415–422). As for the Ottomans, they were clearly more successful since, for nearly three centuries, they kept the military under firm civilian control while banishing patrimonialism and tribal-based cronyism from their state machinery. Yet, in Turkey too, patrimonialism eventually returned, and the hereditary principle was reasserted from the late seventeenth century onward, sealing the gradual decline of the empire (Fukuyama 2012: 201; Hodgson 1974b: 99–133). Furthermore, even during the era of stability and prosperity, the Ottoman state was much more successful in reducing the influence of tribal organizations in the Anatolian and Balkan heartland than in the Arab provinces, and particularly in the peripheral Bedouin communities (230).

Interestingly, the deleterous process of what Fukuyama labeled the "repatrimonialization" of the state—the successful efforts of kin groups to reinsert themselves into politics—was observed not only in the Middle East but also in China, as witnessed by the decay and eventual demise of the Han dynasty. There, too, state institutions had been created to overcome the limitations imposed by clan-based societies and make the individuals loyal to the state rather than to their specific kin group (Fukuyama 2012: chap. 9, and p. 229). In fact, the whole history of unified China can be seen as an endless struggle between the Confucian and the Legalist traditions, the former tradition serving to justify a family-based sociopolitical structure and the latter serving to advocate the establishment of a strong centralized state. Family and kinship were at the core of any Chinese patrimonial order that existed, and Confucianism is a philosophy that propounds a broad moral doctrine of the state modeled on the family. According to this doctrine, if a conflict of interest arises between duty to one's father and duty to the state, the former should always trump the latter: family obligations carry more legitimacy than political ones. By contrast, the Legalists saw Confucianism and its glorification of the family as a serious obstacle to the consolidation of political power. Their central concern was to make subjects obey a strong central authority even by inflicting the harshest punishments on them (119–121). In the succession of Chinese dynasties and during the chaotic transitory periods, impersonal dictatorial regimes inspired by the commandery/prefecture structure of the founding Qin monarchy, which the Legalists favored, alternated with attempts to restore a feudal order that entrusted subordinate kingdoms to old families, which Confucianists promoted (128–132).

In late imperial China (during the Sung dynasty), a period to which we referred in the previous section, the clans were obviously wielding significant administrative and judicial powers that the Chinese state delegated to them. They collected taxes from their members, were legally liable for their criminal conduct, and cooperated with the magistrates in the provision of public goods. This delegation was the outcome of a genuine cooperation between the state and the clans: the former deliberately reinforced intra-clan cohesion by adopting regulations such as linking rights to purchase land to membership in local clans, regulating geographical mobility, and rendering the lineage collectively responsible for crimes committed by individual members (see references in Greif and Tabellini 2017).

In the cases of both China and the Middle East, processes of reversion to patrimonial or clan-based rule (repatrimonialization) were possible because clans and tribes continued to exist outside the ambit of the central state and posed a continuous threat to its persistence, or because the official classes wanted to emulate this dominant type of social organization. In order to survive, central rulers had to tightly control clan heads and rely on their support (see Greif and Tabellini 2010, 2017, for a comparison between China and Western Europe). Observation of the present and recent past in Muslim lands confirms that tribal affiliations have remained omnipresent and practically untouched in many places, especially through the Arab Middle East. This is particularly evident in the cases of Afghanistan, Iraq, Lebanon, Libya, Syria, Yemen, Pakistan, and the Caucasus countries where Western powers and Russia learned the lesson through bitter experiences of failed interventionism. In Saudi Arabia, too, tribalism persisted to the present day. In this country, however, a single tribe, the Sauds, succeeded in appropriating power and establishing a strong monarchical rule resulting in political stability.

13.3.3.2. Western Europe

In light of the above evidence, it is remarkable that local communities and groups organized around tightly bonded kinship groups claiming descent from a common ancestor disappeared from Western Europe a long time ago, before the advent of feudalism. The question of how it is that, so early in its history, Western Europe succeeded in eliminating extended families and their communal logic even before the forces of the modern market and the industrialization set in is therefore of considerable importance. In the words of Fukuyama (2012):

> Rather than being the outcome of these great modernising shifts, change in the family was more likely a facilitative condition for modernisation to happen in the first place. . . . European society was, in other words, individualistic at a very early point, in the sense that individuals and not their families or kin groups could make important decisions about marriage, property, and other personal issues. Individualism in the family is the foundation of all other individualisms. Individualism did not wait for the emergence of a state declaring the legal rights of the individuals and using the weight of its coercive power to enforce those rights. Rather, states were formed on top of societies in which individuals already enjoyed substantial freedom from social obligations to kindreds. In Europe, *social development preceded political development*. (239, 231)

Fukuyama proposes an explanation based on the following four facts. First, an important step in the individualization process is the ability of individuals to dispose of their land and chattels as they see fit and without necessitating the approval of many kinsmen. Even more important is the emergence of women's rights to hold, bequeath, and dispose of property, which marks a rupture with agnatic societies where women achieve legal personhood only by virtue of their marriage and mothering of a male in the lineage. In this regard, it is a noteworthy feat that from at least the thirteenth century, English women could not only own land and chattels but they could also sue and be sued, and make wills and contracts without permission of a male guardian. Such rights are inconceivable in a patrilineal society in which property is under the control of the lineage (Fukuyama 2012: 233).

Second, as demonstrated by Marc Bloch (1962), large agnatic lineages tracing descent to a single ancestor had practically disappeared from Western Europe by the twelfth century: "The Roman *gens* had owed the exceptional firmness of its pattern to the absolute primacy of descent in the male line. Nothing like this was known in the feudal epoch" (137). Because Europeans in the Middle Ages did not trace their descent unilineally through the father, the boundaries between lineage segments could not be maintained, and "the group was too unstable to serve as the basis of the whole social structure" (138). One of the origins of this instability is the system in which the ties of relationship through women were nearly as important as those of paternal consanguinity, as witnessed by the fact that there was no fixed rule regarding name-giving: children took their names either from the father or the mother (137). As a consequence, there was often no feeling of belonging to one family to the exclusion of the other, and blood feuds became confusing enterprises.

The central message is that in Europe, feudalism did not break large kin networks as is sometimes believed. Instead, individualized families formed the basis on which feudalism was erected. As a matter of fact, it is because the protection of individuals against the security threats caused by the disintegration of the Carolingian Empire could no longer be properly guaranteed by kin networks that many people sought or accepted ties of personal dependence vis-à-vis strongmen. True, physical insecurity and the disruption of trade also pushed urban dwellers to retreat into self-sufficient villages which, combined with the collapse of larger political structures, did rekindle kinship groups to some extent. Yet, Europe's agnatic lineages had been too weakened previously to be a source of effective support for their members during these times of trouble, and an alternative had therefore become necessary.

Third, following an argument made by Jack Goody (1983), the transition to a new family system departing from the strongly agnatic or patrilineal pattern of the Mediterranean region can be attributed to the actions (and institutional interests) of the Catholic Church. Reforms initiated by Pope Gregory I (in the late sixth century), later strengthened by those of Gregory VII (in the eleventh century), had the effect of dramatically transforming the structure of the family and the nature of gender relations. They consisted of a number of prohibitions against practices, called "strategies of heirship" by Goody (1983: 42), that allowed kinship groups to maintain their control over property when it is transmitted across successive generations: marriages between close kin, levirate, adoption of children, concubinage, divorce, and remarriage. The Church also curtailed parents' ability to retain kinship ties through arranged marriages by requiring that the bride give her explicit consent to the union. To understand the importance of the "strategies of heirship," it must be remembered that in those times, the probability that a couple would produce a male heir surviving into adulthood and thus able to carry on the ancestral line was quite low. By severely restricting the avenues available to families for bequeathing land and property to descendants in the absence of a biological male heir, and by simultaneously encouraging voluntary donations to the Church, the Gregorian reforms created a situation in which this institution could benefit materially from a growing pool of Christians dying heirless. It is hard to imagine that these effects were unintended: "It does not seem accidental that the Church appears to have condemned the very practices that would have deprived it of property" (95).

Women occupied a pivotal position in the church's strategy because, once they were given the right to own property and dispose of it as they wished, they became a substantial source of potential donations, mainly as childless widows and spinsters. Thus, if a widow is not compelled to remarry, she can enter a nunnery, and her property would then escape the kinship group and accrue to the Church. By undermining the principle of unilineal descent, the awarding of property rights to women thus "spelled the death knell for agnatic lineages," and thereby ushered in a new family system in Western

Europe (Fukuyama 2012: 238). It is revealing in this regard that the kinship structures of the German, Norse, Magyar, and Slavic tribes dissolved within two or three generations of their conversion to Christianity, and that there is a large and significant negative correlation between the spread of Christianity (for at least 500 years) and the absence of clans and lineages (Korotayev 2003).[22] Fukuyama has characterized this massive change in a particularly vivid manner:

> Europe (and its colonial offshoots) was exceptional insofar as the transition out of complex kinship occurred first on a social and cultural level rather than on a political one. By changing marriage and inheritance rules, the church in a sense acted politically and for economic motives. But the church was not the sovereign ruler of the territories where it operated; rather, it was a social actor whose influence lay in its ability to set cultural rules. As a result, a far more individualistic European society was already in place during the Middle Ages, before the process of state building began, and centuries before the Reformation, Enlightenment, and Industrial Revolution. (239)

Goody's thesis seems to be supported by hard evidence. Thus, a recent study by Schulz (2017) has shown that countries with high cousin-marriage rates are more likely to be autocratic, and those with lower rates more likely to be democratic. Moreover, the Church's ban on kin marriages had a significant influence on political, economic, and demographic development: more comprehensive and longer-duration bans on consanguinity are associated with stronger state formation, higher population density, and more advanced urbanization. This is especially true of areas dominated by Western Christianity compared to those dominated by Eastern Christianity, where the ban of the Church on consanguinity was actually less comprehensive.

Fourth, feudalism, which substituted for weak kinship groups in times of trouble, resulted in the rise of an entrenched blood nobility that accumulated considerable wealth, military power, and legal prerogatives. That social institutions were based on feudalistic rather than kin relations proved to be critical for the subsequent political development of Europe. Indeed, although feudalism formalized a highly unequal and hierarchical society, it had the advantage of resting on contract obligations and broadening the understanding of legal personhood. It is no coincidence, therefore, that peasant revolts were framed in a language stressing breach of contract on the part of landlords. Moreover, once the rights of a feudal lord were legally established, they could not be constantly renegotiated in the way that authority within a lineage was (Fukuyama 2012: 240). In China, by contrast, local power holders never had the legal legitimacy that they earned in Western Europe, and they were never powerful enough to force a constitutional compromise on the monarch (132).

Also supporting the idea that the disappearance of clan-based organizations in Western Europe worked in favor of that region is an argument developed by Avner Greif (2006a, 2006b). According to him, the decline of large kinship groups during a period in which the state was also disintegrating, and the Church's secular authority was diminishing, created the need for a new solution to collective action problems. That solution turned out to consist of corporations, that is, voluntary, interest-based, self-governed, and intentionally created permanent associations possessing legal personality. Guilds, fraternities, universities, communes, and city-states are some of the corporations that have historically dominated Europe. They were to play a critical role in the long-term development of Western Europe. An illustration is provided in a recent paper by David de La Croix, Matthias Doepke, and Joel Mokyr (2016). The starting point is the following: it is mainly because it possessed superior institutions for the creation and dissemination of productive knowledge that Europe was able to pull ahead of other world regions at the time of the Industrial Revolution. Worth singling out are the apprenticeship institutions developed during the Middle Ages and based on the person-to-person transmission of tacit knowledge, the young learning as apprentices from the old (Mokyr 2002). Institutions such as the family, the guild, and the market organized who was going to learn from whom. The original contribution of de La Croix et al. lies in a formal argument according to which medieval European institutions such as guilds, and specific features such as journeymanship, offered Europe a decisive advantage over regions that relied on the transmission of knowledge within extended families or clans.

One of the reasons why guilds appeared in Europe is that the dominance of the nuclear family in this region created a need early on for organizations that cut across family lines. Moreover, because guilds had many antecedents that had a similar legal status, such as monasteries, universities, or independent cities, earlier institutional developments may have made the adoption of guilds in Europe much cheaper compared to clan-based societies. Other regions of the world had less to gain from adopting new institutions, since the clan-based system performed well for most purposes. China, for example, whose society was built on strong clan structures inherited from long ago, did not adopt the guild system presumably because the clan provided a number of advantages—mutual insurance, provision of public goods and intra-group cooperation, effective enforcement of contracts through kin-based "limited morality"—that would have made its abandonment quite costly (Platteau 2000 chap. 6–7; Greif and Tabellini 2010, 2017; Greif, Iyigun, and Sasson 2012; Greif and Iyigun 2013). The same argument probably also applies to India and the Islamic world (Kumar and Matsusaka 2009).

The conclusion drawn by Fukuyama (2012) emphasizes the unique nature of the Catholic Church which allowed it to play a central role in the economic and political development of Western Europe. Unlike in the world of Sunni Islam and in India where "religious authority never coalesced into a single, centralized bureaucratic institution outside the state," the Church "is intimately bound up with the development of the modern European state, and with the emergence of what we today call the rule of law" (241).

An unresolved problem with the preceding view of the historical role of Christianity, however, is the following: why is it that, until recently, some areas that are located in the heart of Western Europe and were part of the Roman Empire, such as Italy and southern France, have maintained comparatively large patriarchal families and the associated practices? In other words, it seems that the religious law was not equally enforced throughout Western Europe (as suggested by the aforementioned study of Schulz 2017), and the reasons underlying this variation have not been properly elucidated. Moreover, as Goody was well aware, the motives behind the Gregorian reforms were self-interested and their positive long-term effects were unintended and unanticipated. The defense of women's rights, for example, did not directly stem from Christian doctrine. Instead, it was opportunistically adopted as a means to fulfill a selfish objective of the Catholic Church acting as a collective agent. The immediate implication is that contingent circumstances may well have driven Gregorian reforms and that another centralized church adhering to the same religious tenets may have behaved differently. It is telling that the Eastern Orthodox Church did not undertake similar reforms, and that kin-based communities survived in most of the lands ruled by Byzantium (Fukuyama 2012: 241). Even today, it is striking that in countries like Albania, Kosovo, Serbia, Montenegro, Romania, and Bulgaria, large family units and kin-based networks continue to be an important source of cultural identity and yield a pervasive influence on the way the economy, the society, and the polity function.[23] And it is equally impressive that these networks have survived despite almost half a century of centralized communism. Precisely the same observation can be made with regard to the countries of Central Asia (Uzbekistan, Kazakhstan, Turkmenistan, Kirguizistan, Tajikistan) which were part of the Soviet Union. Unlike the Catholic Church, the Russian Orthodox Church proved to be a conservative institution unable to reform itself (Riasanovsky 1993; Obolonsky 2003).

The important and generally overlooked lesson from the foregoing discussion is that the family system may greatly impede the ability of a society to endow itself with an effective centralized state. Whether such a state is bent on improving the welfare of its people or pursuing the aim of self-aggrandizement is another matter, which proves that appropriate family structures are a necessary but not sufficient condition for long-term development. Since family patterns themselves embed deep-rooted cultural values, modernization typically requires or involves a cultural revolution. In Western Europe, it appears that in a rather inadvertent manner, the Catholic Church gave a strong helping hand to such a revolution.

13.4. TRANSFORMATION OF THE HOUSEHOLD AND THE FAMILY: PUBLIC INTERVENTIONS

Our historical accounts have provided examples of the crucial influence that the state may have in triggering changes of the household and of the family. In this section we take a contemporaneous perspective and discuss the transformations of the household and the family resulting from two types of public interventions: welfare policies that unintentionally affect the organization of households and families, on the one hand, and family laws explicitly aimed at changing the family, on the other. In order to put these public interventions in the proper perspective, we first need to highlight the motives that may prompt a state to initiate them. This implies that we carefully examine the main potential sources of inefficiency in households and families. Also, we should not lose sight of the fact that many public actions and laws are designed to correct inequalities and fight against institutional traits deemed to be unfair. Before embarking upon the discussion, a remark is in order. Because many family laws affect both the household and the family, in this section we look at those impacts simultaneously. For example, in matrilineal societies, a law enhancing the inheritance rights of direct descendants of the deceased may not only encourage household nuclearization but also reduce the power of the matri-clan. We will see that the same argument applies to welfare state policies.

13.4.1. Efficiency of the Household and the Family

The issue of the efficiency of intra-household resource allocation is at the heart of most contributions of economists to the understanding of the household. In classic empirical analysis of consumption data from developed countries, efficiency is very rarely rejected

(Browning et al. 2014), and this conclusion is reflected in the body of assumptions that underlay most theories of the household. The canonical model has thus become the collective model understood as a decision mechanism leading to Pareto-efficient outcomes. In an analytically convenient form, utilities are assumed to be transferable, in which case efficiency becomes equivalent to simply maximizing the aggregate welfare of the household members. As pointed out by Browning et al. (103), there are two situations in which the efficiency assumption fails to apply. The first is when existing social norms prescribe patterns of behavior that conflict with efficiency. In section 13.3.2, we saw that in patriarchal households (in southern Europe in particular), women may be prevented from pursuing off-farm labor opportunities. The second situation may arise because some decisions are taken only once (or a few times), thus giving rise to a commitment problem. In this case, the repeated-game argument does not apply, and any inability of household members to commit may obviously result in inefficient outcomes. This problem is serious as, for example, it is impossible to credibly commit not to divorce. This second situation raises concern about the relevance of the static efficiency assumption in collective models of household decisions.

This concern is all the more serious as empirical studies from developing countries, or studies based on experimental methods rather than on the analysis of consumption data, tend to reject efficiency in intra-household allocation. Following Udry (1996), who shows that labour allocation across family plots is not Pareto-efficient using micro-data from Burkina Faso, a series of papers have confirmed that productive efficiency is violated in large households cultivating both collective and individual plots (Goldstein and Udry 2008; Kazianga and Wahhaj 2013; Guirkinger et al. 2015; Kazianga and Wahhaj 2016). Another strand of the literature rejects intertemporal efficiency in consumption by showing that risk-sharing is not perfect within households (Dercon and Krishnan 2000; Duflo and Udry 2004; Goldstein 2004). Experiments offer another promising avenue to evaluate intra-household efficiency and the process of intra-household decision-making. A recent review of this literature by Alistair Munro (2015) concludes on the basis of evidence from more than 20 different countries that "evidence of joint payoff maximization between spouses is rather thin on the grounds" (36).

In the above discussion, it is clear that attention is limited to what happens inside the household. The issue of *inter*-household resource allocation is therefore ignored. This would not matter if markets were perfect or if a perfect state could substitute for imperfect markets. As we know, however, such an assumption is especially restrictive in the context of poor developing countries. As a consequence, the organization of the family (a household-linking network) becomes fundamental, and an analytical approach limited to the question of intra-household efficiency is unsatisfactory. For instance, splitting of a stem household may be seen as a response to imperfect land markets. The question of whether the branch household does or does not remain part of the family then becomes crucial since continued membership of the family may condition access to critical services (e.g., insurance, credit, asset-pooling, information, etc.). And if the family operates as a perfect "internal" market or as a perfect mini-state, first-best efficiency could be achieved. This is very unlikely, though, because the size of the family is typically predetermined and it may be infra-optimal for the efficient fulfillment of services (such as credit, insurance, etc.), and because the family is vulnerable to collective action problems.

Supporting evidence for family imperfections comes primarily from the literature dealing with informal insurance and with contract enforcement. Regarding insurance, all recent survey papers emphasize the following: while intra-family risk-sharing undoubtedly exists, it is only partial, not complete, and the poorest category of people tend to be excluded (Morduch 1999; Platteau 2006; Cox and Fafchamps 2008; Fafchamps 2011). These findings confirm the theory according to which informal insurance is plagued by incentive problems. Concrete examples of the existence of these incentive problems are found in recent contributions showing that people may resort to costly strategies to avoid their obligations vis-à-vis their families (Baland et al. 2011; Jakiela and Ozier 2015; Boltz, Marazyan, and Villar 2015). Insurance-oriented voluntary transfers are increasingly distinguished from asymmetric transfers that tax the successful individuals to dampen inequality. These taxes have obvious efficiency costs as they discourage investment and risk-taking, and it seems that these costs increase as market opportunities expand (Platteau 2014). As for contract enforcement, bear in mind the aforementioned works of Avner Greif, who emphasizes the fact that the size of the community (family), which typically has multiple functions, is not determined by the need for effective contract enforcement alone. It may therefore be suboptimal from that point of view, and it risks being increasingly so as market opportunities are expanding.

The problem of the inefficiency of the family is compounded when administrative, judiciary, political, and military functions are considered. Indeed, families may wield enough power to block political change at the upper level, thus preventing the rise of a strong state able to perform the tasks required for modernization. These tasks include the integration of the economic space, the building of communication and other infrastructures over the national territory, the creation of law and order institutions over a unified political space, as well as the generalization and systematization of the use of uniform measures and standards, all steps that have the effect of encouraging market integration and division of labor. In short, familial authorities may defend a political order that suits their own immediate interests at the price of dynamic efficiency losses.

In a context of absent or highly imperfect markets, and of imperfect families and central state, second-best efficiency is the best outcome that can be sought. Reflected in trade-offs that imply efficiency losses, it is well illustrated by most models reviewed in section 13.2.1. Consider first the model of Foster and Rosenzweig (2002). Although intra-household resource allocation is assumed to be optimal, an efficiency loss is unavoidable insofar as preference heterogeneity conflicts with scale economies. The former requires an organization of the household (its division in smaller units) that is potentially too small to optimally exploit scale economies (if they turn out to exist), and vice-versa. In theory, the above conflict could be avoided if household composition could be adjusted in such a way that members have homogeneous preferences. But this condition is not satisfied in reality. In another model, that of Delpierre, Guirkinger, and Platteau (2019), the potential trade-off is between productive inefficiency and risk-sharing. The former arises from a moral-hazard-in-team problem, while the latter takes the form of equal distribution of the farm collective output and private, voluntary transfers. Since the private transfers are also allowed in the event of splitting, the model implicitly assumes that a family subsists after splitting and fulfills an economic role. Because of that assumption, it may be the case that the above trade-off vanishes and the household splits (still the outcome is second-best efficient owing to commitment problems).

In the model of Guirkinger and Platteau (2015), the assumption of household-level efficiency is relaxed: asymmetric information between a patriarch acting as principal and household members acting as agents gives rise to two kinds of inefficiencies: one caused by the moral-hazard-in-team problem and the other arising from a share contract of labor remuneration. The decision to allocate private plots or to split the household depends on the way the trade-off between productive efficiency and the rent extracted by the principal is resolved in a context of imperfect markets.

Last, the model of Bardhan et al. (2014) is peculiar in that no trade-off persists at equilibrium. This is because the authors assume not only intra-household allocative efficiency but also the existence of perfect input markets. These markets allow households to achieve a size that precludes any productive efficiency loss. More precisely, they assume that there exists a collective action problem at the level of the household, yet this problem can be overcome through a recourse to the labor and land markets.

A last but important remark is in order. Public interventions are not only justified on the grounds of efficiency but also for the purpose of improving equity. At the level of the household, among inequities that call for mitigation, the one that has drawn most attention from social scientists is gender asymmetry. Note that in this case, equity costs are often accompanied by efficiency costs (as in the case of social norms barring women from outside employment). Another important type of intra-household inequality that also gives rise to inefficiencies lies in the asymmetry of power between the older and the younger generations. Thus, the existence of a strong patriarchal authority may have been justified when solving collective action problems was crucial for the subsistence of household members. Yet it becomes an obstacle to development when the young generation possesses modern skills and knowledge that the older generation lacks.[24] All these problems arise not only at the level of the household but also at the level of the family or the clan. In this connection, recall the aforementioned theory of Pensieroso and Sommacal (2014), according to which, when technical progress is fast enough, an efficient transition occurs from coresidence to non-coresidence and the social status of the elderly should deteriorate. If, however, the shift in living arrangements is explained by cultural factors, as reflected in the direct taste for co-residence, the economy experiences a reduction of the growth rate along a balanced growth path.

We are now ready to consider a variety of public actions designed to remedy a number of failures at the level of the household or the family. Before looking at them, we say a few words about public actions whose impacts on the household and the family were unintended, welfare state policies in particular.

13.4.2. Public Actions with Unintended Effects on the Household and the Family: Welfare Policies

One of the primary objectives of welfare state policies is to provide effective insurance to people. In order to correctly assess their effects, a question that naturally arises is to what extent welfare schemes substitute for family risk-sharing arrangements. This has been a topic of interest to economists since data on interpersonal transfers have been more widely available. More specifically, economists have tried to estimate the reduction in inter-household private transfers following an increase in public transfers. Cox and Fafchamps (2008) provide an excellent and very detailed review of this literature. They indicate that there is an "exceedingly wide" range of estimates of crowding-out in the literature, with a modal or medium transfer derivative suggesting that an increase in 1 dollar of public transfer decreases inter-household private transfers by about 20–25 cents. To explain the wide differences in the estimates of the crowding-out effect, they mention differences in data collection, in estimation strategies but in transfer motives as well. They also point out that "the current state of the art is not sufficiently developed to easily reconcile existing differences." The handful of more recent empirical papers who report the extent of substitution between public programs and inter-household transfers (Juarez 2009; Amuedo-Dorantes and Juarez 2015; Hidrobo et al. 2014; Edmonds and Shrestha 2014) confirm that the extent of crowding-out varies substantially across studies (from nearly 0 to almost 100%).

It is remarkable that the crowding-out literature focuses on inter-household transfers when co-residence living arrangements probably constitute the most important form of insurance and redistribution. Indeed, effects of social policies on household size and composition are typically overlooked in the evaluation of public interventions. An important exception is the recent paper by Hamoudi and Thomas (2014), who look at the effect of the expansion of the South African Old Age Pension program on living arrangements of beneficiaries. They show that beneficiaries of the program are more likely to co-reside with children or grandchildren who are disadvantaged in terms of human capital. The authors speculate that the underlying mechanism is as follows: pension recipients demand greater elderly care, and they seek co-residence with family members who are in a better position to care for them. Those tend to be less educated people whose opportunity cost of time is comparatively low. An important lesson from this study is that any impact evaluation of social programs that takes household composition as fixed is likely to yield biased results. The authors cite the case of PROGRESA (in Mexico) that conditions receipt of the transfer on continuously residing in the same household. As a consequence, this program reduces the incentive for an individual to leave the household or migrate out of the community in search of better prospects.

This literature suggests that insofar as states develop and take up the insurance and redistributive functions of families, the latter may reduce their involvement in those functions. Other things being equal, the expansion of social security programs is expected to reduce the role of the family and to enhance individual autonomy, particularly that of the younger generations.[25] Given the varied functions that families fulfill, however, the emergence of the welfare state does not imply that they will disappear. In addition, when the state fails in condition of economic crisis, the family has been shown to be an ultimate fall-back option for impoverished members (see subsections 13.2.2 and 13.4.1). Evidently, the family may more readily play this fallback role when it has subsisted and been kept alive because of its other functions, such as assistance in job search, provision of start-up capital, and support for uninsurable shocks.

13.4.3. Legal Actions Aimed at Changing the Household and the Family

Family laws immediately come to mind when one thinks of legal initiatives explicitly designed to transform the household and the family. Other laws nevertheless exist that may have an important effect on these institutions, although they are not directly concerned with matters of personal status. Laws setting minimum farm size belong to that category and, in this instance, the lawmaker's intent clearly is to prevent excessive subdivision of farmland. This type of regulation, if effectively enforced in areas where partible inheritance prevails, should prompt household heads to shift to more exclusive rules of bequest. The size and the composition of the household would be simultaneously modified in the event that excluded children decide to stay in the stem household. Assuming effective enforcement nevertheless appears to be quite unrealistic. In pregenocide Rwanda, for example, where land pressure was extremely high, a state decree provided that no agricultural land can be alienated or subdivided if its size is below two hectares. However, André and Platteau (1998) have argued that, although it was well known, the law was continuously violated by people eager to follow their erstwhile custom of partible inheritance. Similarly, we saw earlier that in tsarist Russia peasants strongly resisted top-down attempts to establish unigeniture. The twentieth-century world experience actually confirms that it is only in brutal authoritarian regimes that such kinds of laws are likely to be strictly applied.

Family laws, to which we now turn our attention, are mostly aimed at modifying inheritance rules, enhancing women's rights, promoting monogamy, and regulating marriage and divorce. Before examining their impact on family systems, it is useful to contrast the recent evolutions of family laws in the Western world and in developing countries. Radical changes have been made to family laws in the last century in many Western countries, including authorizing and then simplifying divorce procedures, changing the rules governing property rights within marriage and child custody, and changing inheritance rules (to the benefit of the surviving spouse). It is more difficult to summarize recent changes in family laws in the developing world as wide heterogeneity exists and degrees of enforcement may vary substantially. In their review of legal traditions in family laws in the "global South," Htun and Weldon (2012) distinguish four traditions that have undergone distinct changes in recent times: (i) Islamic family laws; (ii) multiple legal systems; (iii) civil law; and (iv) socialist and communist law. It is beyond the scope of this text to summarize the characteristics of each system, as described by these authors. We refer the interested reader to appendix I of this chapter, where the main trends of recent family reforms under the different systems are briefly outlined.

There are unfortunately very few studies that assess the impact of family laws in a reliable manner and in the context of developing countries (there are indeed many attempts to measure the impact of divorce laws in the United States). Existing studies are mainly concerned with changes in inheritance law, the 2005 reform of the Hindu Succession Act in India, in particular. Undertaken in some states, this reform grants the same rights to daughters and sons. Deininger et al. (2013) review the effect of the law on inheritance practices and educational outcomes. They conclude that the legal reform has improved the situation of the daughters on both counts. However, these results are challenged by Roy (2015), who convincingly shows that the reform did not increase the propensity of a daughter to inherit land, but instead increased the compensatory transfers to daughters in the form of dowries or increased education. Interestingly, social scientists have also pointed to this type of indirect and moderate effect. For example, as compensation for their de facto exclusion from land inheritance, women of Niger receive part of the crop harvested on the family land by their brothers under an arrangement known as *aro* (Cooper 1997: 78).

Four other studies by economists have shown how the above change in the Indian law has yielded even more subtle effects on other planes of women's life and well-being. Thus, Rosenblum (2015) suggests that it has had adverse effects on female child mortality.

Anderson and Genicot (2015) find that it decreased the difference between male and female suicide rates, but increased both female and male suicide rates. They rely on a model of intra-household conflict to explain their results: increased access to inheritance raises a woman's bargaining power with the consequence of engendering more conflicts over household resources. In the same vein, Bhalotra et al. (2016) have highlighted another perverse effect of the inheritance legal reform in the form of increased female foeticide. The apparent reason is that the reform raised the cost of having daughters, thereby exacerbating son preference. Finally, Mookerjee (2015) argues that women's bargaining power increased as a result of the reform, yet not at the expense of the husband but rather at the expense of the members of the extended family. Specifically, she finds that (i) the reform enhanced the propensity of young couples to reside in nuclear rather than in joint households (with the hubsband's parents), and (ii) even when they reside with the husband's parents, they are more likely to be involved in consumption decisions.

A few more recent studies have examined the impact of change in inheritance laws in other countries than India. La Ferrara and Milazzo (2017) examine the effects of a reform of inheritance law in Ghana that affects matrilineal groups but not patrilineal groups. They show that the law decreases investments in a son's education, and they interpret the result as indicating that parents were over-investing in education to substitute for land inheritance. Harari (2014) explores the effects of the change in statutory law that granted women equal inheritance rights in Kenya. Exploiting differences in pre-reform inheritance rights across religious groups, she finds that the pro-women inheritance reform increases their education, reduces the probability of female genital mutilation, delays marriage, and improves marriage outcomes. In short, the reform empowers women, even in a context of poor enforcement. Carranza (2012) exploits changes in Islamic inheritance law to explore the determinants of son preference in Indonesia. She shows that when the Koranic inheritance exclusion rule is strictly applied, whereby the brothers of a deceased man are inheriting his wealth unless the deceased has a surviving son, couples exhibit a strong preference for sons and practice sex-differential fertility stopping. Finally, Hallward-Driemeier and Gajigo (2013) look at the effects of a reform in family law in Ethiopia. They conclude that expanding wives' access to marital property and removing restrictions against their working outside the house raised women's outcomes in the labor market.

We evidently need more studies to confirm the above highlighted effects. This is because the existing studies encompass a very limited number of countries, the identification problems inherent in attempts to measure the impact of legal change are particularly serious, and the time frame used is excessively short. An interesting lesson that nonetheless emerges from the available studies is the following: any law aimed at modifying personal status and position within such a vital fabric as the family is bound to generate complex and indirect effects. It is therefore crucial to have an adequate model of the family to be able to accurately anticipate what these effects can be. This is not an easy task, however, as attested by the fierce debates around the effects of the introduction of unilateral divorce law in the United States. In fact, the predicted effects may vary a lot, and even be inverted, depending upon the specific setup of the model chosen (for a short review of the literature on the impact of this law, see appendix II to this chapter). In the context of developing countries where customs are typically pervasive and where families still have multiple functions, top-down changes that typically favor some categories of people are bound to generate antagonistic reactions. Since families are characterized by infinitely repeated and highly personalized relations, they are eager to avoid adversarial or confrontational relations among their members. It is not coincidental that informal justice systems are determined to save the faces of all the parties involved and that they use compensation as a key mechanism to settle conflicts. When changes are imposed from above, the tendency is either to ignore them or to mitigate them in a way that best preserves the tradition. This is evident when in patriarchal societies daughters do not receive land inheritance even when it is mandated by the law, but are granted material compensations to indemnify them (see above).

The question of the time frame deserves special attention in the context of family change. Precisely because of the aforementioned fact that changes in personal status are often delicate—they affect the immediate social order in which individuals are embedded in a deep manner—we do not expect them to take place in a short period of time. We have seen in section 13.3.3 that the Western European family is claimed to have been deeply transformed as a result of changes in the religious law that occurred early on (as early as the seventh century). The changes spanned over centuries yet we do not know precisely how long it took for the transformation to be completed and how gradual the process of change was. In the light of this evidence, empirical economic analysis of the impact of legal changes appears to be strangely short-sighted. To follow the reforms enacted by the Catholic Church in Europe, it appears that the impact may not even materialize over a very long period of time. This is attested by the situation observed in southern and eastern Europe. The differential impact between these regions and northwestern Europe suggests that initial family forms and/or the economic, demographic, and political environment in which they operated and later evolved differed between these two broad regions. The complexity resulting from the multi-dimensional nature of the household and the family, and the varying influence of social norms governing the behavior of members vis-à-vis each other, probably explain the observed intra-European differences in the responses provided to the same legal shock.

A theory is available that sheds useful light on the complex dynamics of family change following a legal shock (Aldashev et al. 2012a, 2012b; Platteau and Wahhaj 2014). Based on the idea of legal pluralism, it accounts not only for the less-than-perfect impact of a new family law but also for the gradual unfolding of its effects over time. According to this so-called magnet effect theory, there are two channels through which the impact of a legal change can make itself felt. First, there is the effect felt by the plaintiffs who go to the formal court to have a conflict around the implementation of the law settled. Formal judges are expected to apply the law, and its impact at this level is therefore perfect. Second, there is the effect felt by those plaintiffs who prefer to maintain their ties with their original community (extended family) and therefore ask the informal local mediator to resolve the conflict. The mediator or customary authority applies the custom, yet the custom is not an unchanging norm: it may actually evolve in the direction of the law (which thus acts as a magnet) because the informal judge does not want too many community members to opt out of his judicial domain, thereby reducing his prestige and authority. Overall, therefore, the effect of the law cannot be complete. On the other hand, however, it cannot be inferred from evidence of low recourse to the formal law that the latter has a zero or negligible impact.

Furthermore, the impact of the law may increase gradually over time for the following reason. When people choose to leave the ambit of their community, they can simultaneously avail themselves of increased outside opportunities, say, urban employment or self-employment opportunities. A sudden expansion of such opportunities has an effect analogous to the one of a legal reform that antagonizes the custom: in both instances, the welfare prospects of individuals discriminated against by the custom, say, the women, are being improved, enhancing their incentive to move from the informal to the formal (urban) sector. Now, if the outside opportunities continuously expand, two effects occur. On the one hand, more women leave their original locations in the countryside for cities where they enjoy the twin benefits of better employment prospects and more favorable judicial outcomes (in the event of a conflict). On the other hand, forward-looking informal judges or mediators, anticipating the adverse effects of this transformation for themselves, respond by relaxing the custom and pronouncing judgments that get gradually closer to the statutory law. The impact of the law thus becomes increasingly complete.

Suggestive evidence exists in support of the theory of "magnet effect." For example, the PNDC Law 111 (1981) whereby the Ghanaian government attempted to regulate practices of intestate succession in favor of the wives and children of a deceased man seems to have encouraged a partial shift of the inheritance custom in the direction of the Law among the Akan people traditionally governed by a matrilineal system (see Aldashev et al. 2012b; Platteau and Wahhaj 2014: 666–672). This theory may nevertheless fail to provide a correct representation of reality in all cases, or in some important cases at least. Its main merit, perhaps, is that it points the way toward the sort of analytical effort required to achieve a more comprehensive understanding of the impact of legal reforms of the family and the (concomitant) role of the economic environment. It also yields conclusions that lie in-between excessively negative and unduly optimistic assessments. "Laws are dead letters" is a statement often pronounced by law anthropologists, while among economists there is a tendency to expect quick and measurable effects of legal reforms if they can be effectively enforced.

13.5. CONCLUSION

The present review has chosen to focus on the transformation of family systems, and the whole progression of the arguments has been governed by the critical distinction between the household (a co-residence arrangement) and the family (a network linking people with consanguinous ties). Economists have studied both forms, but in each case they have adopted a partial standpoint. With few exceptions, households are viewed as collective agents that, thanks to transferable utilities, can achieve efficient resource allocation. This approach assumes away the effect of social norms, such as gender patterns, and their influence on the sharing rule. In addition, it precludes the analysis of all situations where decisions are made only once and thus give rise to commitment problems (who can commit not to divorce?).

As for families, they are mainly viewed as imperfect risk-sharing networks based on decentralized inter-individual relations. This implies not only that other critical functions of the family are ignored, in particular administrative, judiciary, and political functions, but also that the existence of authority structures is generally denied. This is an unsatisfactory situation: because families are vulnerable to a number of important imperfections which include rent capture and abuse of authorities, they cannot perfectly substitute for imperfect markets and state institutions. The question therefore arises: what is the second-best optimal mix of state, markets, and families? The problem is actually more tricky than what an analysis based on the assumption of independent state, market, and family institutions might suggest. As a matter of fact, insofar as families exert political influence, they are liable to block or retard the development of well-functioning markets and a strong and effective central state. Thus, familial authorities may negatively react to an encroachment of their customary prerogatives that results from new state policies and legal reforms. Their resistance often takes the form of efforts to impede or mitigate the enforcement of such reforms. Likewise, they may distort the emerging markets through nepotistic and other discriminatory practices.

Clearly, we need an approach that not only adopts a general equilibrium perspective featuring the state, the market, and the families, but also allows for feedback and other dynamic mechanisms. Economists need to study how families relate to the wider society and to the polity, in a broader perspective than that adopted by the crowding-out literature. Moreover, households themselves must be analyzed as parts of a family since the family sets the rules that determine the size and the composition of the households as well as their internal mode of operation (gender roles, marriage arrangements, etc.).

The dynamic aspects stressed above have to do with the interactions between the state, the markets, and the families. Yet, the process of transformation of the households and the families themselves has also been under-studied by economists. The contributions of other social scientists, family historians especially, have been much more significant, and this explains why they have received a great deal of attention throughout this chapter. They have revealed that adaptation of household patterns and family systems to evolving economic, demographic, and technological circumstances is conditional upon prevailing social norms, political conditions, and authority systems. Inside Europe, inter-regional variations in such conditions have given rise to different paths of evolution of living arrangements: in the northwestern part of Europe, individualization of the household has been observed since the times of the decay of the Roman Empire, while in the southern and eastern parts, the process has been much more unequal and unstable.

Two other highly instructive lessons from our foray into history are important to point out. First, the path of transformation of both the households and the families is not generally monotonous as is explicitly assumed in the modernization theory and implicitly assumed in many economic approaches to long-term economic growth. For example, nuclear households may have been collectivized (that is, transformed into joint or complex households) before being re-nuclearized. Second, it is remarkable that in northwestern Europe the influence of families as kinship groups has been apparently undermined by events and religious legal reforms dating back to as early as the seventh century. In contrast, families have remained quite powerful in many other parts of Europe, including in Mediterranean Europe (despite belonging to an area affected by the same legal reforms) and the Balkans, and the same diagnosis applies to Africa, the Middle East (with the notable exception of Iran), and Asia. It is again striking that transformation trajectories have not been monotonous. In the Middle East and China, in particular, periods of assertion of a strong centralized state have alternated with periods of repatrimonialization during which kinship groups returned to the front stage of the society and polity.

Dynamic processes of change in family institutions are therefore highly heterogeneous and complex. In spite of commendable attempts by social scientists, we are still a long way from a reasonably good understanding of the mechanisms underlying these diverse and nonlinear paths of transformation. Through their analytical lens, economists should do much more to shed new light on the issues involved. Not only are such issues far from trivial but they also involve high stakes as reflected, for example, in the large efficiency and equity costs resulting from the persistence of clan-ism in many contemporary developing countries.

Finally, we cannot end this chapter without emphasizing the fact that most works of economists have centered on agricultural households and rural family networks. This focus implies that the issue of land division has received primary attention. Since intergenerational and extended households also seem to prevail in the urban areas of many developing countries, there is a clear research gap here. This gap needs to be remedied because conclusions about agricultural or rural households cannot be straightforwardly applied to their urban counterparts: traditional land-sharing arrangements, for example, cannot be found in city surroundings, even in peri-urban areas. How family firms differ from family farms and how they foster capital accumulation and growth in nonfood sectors, manufacturing in particular, are thus issues of utmost relevance that have been largely ignored.

Appendix I:

Changes in Family Laws in the Developing World

i. Islamic family laws (for example, in Egypt, Indonesia, Iran, Morocco, Pakistan, or Saudi Arabia) have typically changed relatively little since their recent codification throughout the twentieth century. Most common adjustments were: an increase in the minimum legal age at marriage, restrictive conditions on polygamous marriages, and an expansion in women's rights to divorce. An important exception is Morocco, where a major change in the family law "virtually overnight [. . .] eliminated most of the disadvantage suffered by women." Countries where Islamic family laws prevail sometimes go through periods of regression from the point of view of women's rights. In Iran for example, the age at marriage was decreased to 9 years old for girls and 15 years for boys after the Islamic revolution. In Indonesia, the law of 1991 removed equal inheritance rights for women and the need for their consent in regard of marriage.

ii. Multiple legal systems are characterized by the formal coexistence of customary, religious, and civil/common law. Most former British colonies are ruled by multiple legal systems in the area of family laws (for example, Bangladesh, India, Kenya, Nigeria, Malaysia, South Africa), partly as a result of the principle of non-interference in the personal laws adopted in British colonies. Legal pluralism typically leads to complex law systems that are particularly hard to implement. Also, reforms often concern one body of law but not another. Thus, in India, the reform of the Hindu Succession Act granted inheritance rights to women in 2005, while no such change occurred in the Muslim personal law of the same country.

iii. Civil law is the most widely used system in the world, including in Latin America, China, Korea, Japan, or Ivory Coast. Family law in most civil law countries has undergone profound transformations in the last century. Married women's property rights and civil capacity were reinforced, and the clause of obedience to husbands was revoked. Finally, divorce became an option. Some countries legalized divorce in the late nineteenth century, others in the twentieth, and some in the twenty-first (Chile).

iv. Finally, socialist or communist law from civil laws have often played a key role as a vehicle of change in family matters. Thus, the Soviet decree on marriage and divorce of 1917 and the Family Code of 1918 stood in sharp contrast with the religious principles previously guiding family law. The main changes concerned divorce (made much easier) and the equality between parents. Communist states in the South (North Korea, China, North Vietnam, South Yemen, Cuba) adopted similar family laws and insisted on the free choice of the spouse (in China in particular).

APPENDIX II:

The Complex Effects of Changes in Divorce Law
in the United States

Theoretically, most discussions on the expected impacts of a simplification of divorce procedures take Coase's theorem as a benchmark (Mechoulan 2005). This theorem suggests that if a change in the law does not affect the gains from marriage, then it should not change divorce rates (the initial distribution of legal entitlements does not matter as long as they are tradable). The idea is that the law may be bypassed through ex ante contracting between spouses intent on maximizing gains from marriage and defining property division in case of divorce. This result rests on strong assumptions regarding intra-household decision-making: full information at time of marriage, no transaction costs, enforceable pre-nuptial and transferable utilities between spouses. Mechoulan (2005) notes that none of these assumptions are defensible with regard to the issue of marital dissolution. Under more reasonable models of intra-household behavior, predictions about the impacts of divorce laws are more complex and critically depend on modeling choices (regarding intra-household bargaining, household production, and the transferability of utilities, in particular). Wickelgren (2009) or Browning et al. (2014) explore specific cases in detail. An important insight emerging from these studies is that modeling assumptions crucially affect not only the predictions about divorce and marriage rates but also the expected welfare implications of the legal change.

Beyond the question of the adequate model of intra-household bargaining, a general equilibrium perspective suggests that a change in the law has additional effects on the selection into marriage and on the composition of the marriage pool. Matouschek and Rasul (2008) describe these selection effects under various theories of marriage.[26]

Turning to the empirical literature, there have been fierce debates on the impacts of the no-fault divorce reforms in the United States on divorce rates. Friedberg (1998) concluded that "the change in the law raised divorce rates significantly, strongly and permanently." Yet Wolfers (2006) argues (using the same data) that the divorce rate increased for one decade but that the effect reversed in the following decade. The recent work of Gonzalez-Val and Marcén (2012) suggests that these studies have confounded the effect of the no-fault divorce reform and the simultaneous changes in child custody rules. They conclude that the divorce reform has led to a long term increase in divorce rates after all.[27]

NOTES

1. This is because commitment problems plague voluntary transfers. A trade-off therefore subsists between inefficient joint production where income-pooling de facto obtains and efficient individual production where commitment problems prevail.

2. Such a system has been widely observed, for example in the post-Carolingian manors of medieval Europe, in American plantations using slave labor, in Russian boyar estates using serf labor (Van Zanden 2009: 56, fn. 13; Blum 1961; Kolchin 1987), in feudal Japanese farms during the Tokugawa era (Smith 1959), or among estate landlords of Latin America, such as those employing inquilino laborers in Chile after the middle of the eighteenth century (Bauer 1975; de Janvry 1981).

3. The production function used is subject to increasing returns to scale, an assumption that gives an undue advantage to collective production and therefore artificially restricts the possibilities of pre-mortem division.

4. Note that the trade-off would persist, albeit in a mitigated manner, if the household head is assumed to be imperfectly altruistic.

5. It bears emphasizing that the public good is excluded from the utility functions in the dynamic analysis. Therefore, the only rationale for co-residence is a greater availability of resources: young people choose co-residence if by doing so they get more resources for themselves.

6. When levels of altruism are so high as to correspond to those in which full risk-sharing is achieved, there is simply no history dependence.

7. In primary socialization, the child does not comprehend his significant others as institutional functionaries, but as mediators of the only conceivable reality: in other words, he (she) internalizes the world of his (her) parents not as one of many possible worlds, not as the world appertaining to a specific institutional context, but as *the* world *tout court* (Berger and Luckmann 1967: 154).

8. This result continues to hold if what is explained is not the presence or absence of private plots but the share of the family land that is earmarked for individual cultivation.

9. More precisely, endogeneity would be present if sons are inclined to leave the family farm when no individual plots are awarded by their father. The absence of individual plots would then appear, spuriously, to arise from small families and land abundance.

10. Thus, "a brother resented having to work twice as hard, or so he believed, because one of his brothers had twice as many children" (Worobec 1995: 81).

11. The tendency for households to split in such conditions was accentuated by the fact that wage-earning members sometimes resented having to pay toward the upkeep of their fathers' households. If so, they tried to keep all or part of the money for themselves, rather than hand it over to the head, which could lead to severe conflicts and determine them to demand partition "so that they could become the masters of their own households" (Moon 1999: 176, 196).

12. In particular, peasants started regrouping their fields in contiguous parcels near their farmsteads, some customary holdings were converted into leasehold thereby activating a land market, labor hiring became the dominant contractual relationship, tenants were increasingly mobile both within and across villages with the consequence that family continuity through inheritance was under threat, and the leasing out of demesne land to tenants by absentee landlords became increasingly frequent.

13. Note that this definition of early modern history departs from the conventional definition that extends from the sixteenth to the eighteenth century.

14. The crucial difference between freeholders (a minority of peasants in the Middle Ages) and villeins (common peasants or villagers) is that the former paid their rents in money or kind, and were therefore exempt from the labor services which the latter were compelled to supply to their lord (Seccombe 1992: 88). It is therefore more justifiable to analyze villeins than freeholders as agents possessing private plots inside a collective hierarchical structure to which they must provide labor services.

15. In a rural sample, marriage was so late that only 40% of the unmarried people under the age of 25 lived with both a father and a mother who were still alive (Neven 2003: 245, cited from Oris et al. 2014: 272).

16. All the old legal traditions—Roman, Lombard, Germanic, and Frankish—envisioned that land should be partible among heirs, and it is revealing that there were no powerful overlords in the corresponding territories. With the spread of feudal tenure in the post-Carolingian Age, more varied inheritance rules began to prevail that affected real property and the organization of families. It is only in a second phase of evolution starting roughly in 1300 and continuing well into

the Modern Age that landed noble families more commonly adopted the rule of unigeniture, typically primogeniture. Before that date, fiefs tended to be both heritable and partible. It is also striking that the new practice, and the dynastic lineage intimately connected with the rise of feudal principalities, were not universally followed by the nobility, being much more widespread among the high feudal nobility (the territorial princes and the great barons) than among the rear and petty vassals and the knights who were often granted the right to partition their fiefs (Herlihy 1985: 88–95).

17. For example, even in the case of primogeniture, whereas nobles selected an heir on the basis of strictly predetermined criteria (typically, birth order), among the peasantry the "hearth heir" custom allowed a father to choose a successor on his merits (competence and commitment to the family farm). Following this flexible principle, peasants were inclined to give a preference to a son who had remained loyally at home over another who had migrated and whose return was uncertain.

18. The origin of pre-mortem inheritance, it is speculated, lay in the seigneurial drive to replace the elderly, elderly widows in particular, with young and vigorous males. In this process, impatient heirs eager to move into full tenancy were tactical allies of local lords (Seccombe 1992: 101).

19. As a matter of course, the objectives of compensating non-heirs (including daughters in the form of dowries) and retaining the family holding intact were easily met when the family was rich enough to provide them with non-land assets or cash sufficient to form a good starting capital (Howell 1976: 139, 153–155).

20. In Chippenham, in particular, the granting to younger sons of small portions of land which were not in themselves adequate for support "merely weakened the main holding" in the sense that it could not be maintained intact and could even be brought close to ruin. This is because it had to support the burden of compensations which could not be provided without eroding the farm's capital. On the other hand, the small bequests of land to the younger sons often ended up in the hands of rural moneylenders-cum-landowners (enterprising yeomen who built up their holdings by acquiring mortgages while they were still farming) because they were not viable economic concerns and could not weather bad harvests or other adverse shocks. The same effects frequently obtained when, instead of receiving portions of the family land, the younger sons received a cash sum "to start them off in life" (Spufford 1976: 161–166; see also Thompson 1976: 346; Schofield 1989; and Todd 1990: 38, 44).

21. This part is heavily inspired from Platteau (2017: chap. 10, sec. 3).

22. Even among the Germanic tribes, by as early as the eighth century, the term "family" denoted one's immediate family, and it did not take long for the tribes to become institutionally irrelevant. In England, court rolls testify that in the thirteenth century even cousins were as likely to be in the presence of non-kin as with each other (Greif 2006b: 309).

23. In rural Montenegro, for example, villages may carry the names of the founding ancestor family and be mainly inhabited by offspring households. They then vote cohesively for a member of their clan regardless of ideological preferences based on party programs and policy orientations (personal observation of Jean-Philippe Platteau 2012).

24. The increase in life expectancy complicates this problem.

25. However, if state benefits are more specifically targeted to the older age categories, household size may actually increase because the incentives to stay together are enhanced for both younger and older members.

26. Specifically, they show how a decrease in divorce costs has opposite effects on divorce rates whether ones considers that (a) marriage provides some exogenous benefit to the couple, (b) marriage serves as a commitment device, or (c) marriage serves as a signaling device.

27. Other impacts of the divorce law reform have been analyzed by economists, including studies on fertility (Alesina and Giuliano 2007; Drewianka 2008); female labor supply (Gray 1998; Genadek et al. 2007; Stevenson 2008); domestic violence and suicide (Dee 2003; Stevenson and Wolfers 2006).

REFERENCES

Akerlof, G. 1976. "The Economics of Caste and of the Rat Race and Other Woeful Tales." *Quarterly Journal of Economics* 90: 599–617.

Akresh, I. R. 2005. "Risk, Network Quality, and Family Structure: Child Fostering Decisions in Burkina Faso." Discussion Paper No. 902, Economic Growth Center, Yale University.

Aldashev, G., I. Chaara, J-P. Platteau, and Z. Wahhaj. 2012a. "Using the Law to Change the Custom." *Journal of Development Economics* 97(1): 182–200.

———. 2012b. "Formal Law as a Magnet to Reform the Custom." *Economic Development and Cultural Change* 60(4): 795–828.

Aldashev, G., and C. Guirkinger. 2016. Colonization and Changing Social Structure: Kazakhstan 1896–1910. *ECARES Working Papers.*

Alesina, A., and P. Giuliano. 2015. "Culture and Institutions." *Journal of Economic Literature* 53(4): 898–944.

Alesina, A., and E. La Ferrara. 2005. "Ethnic Diversity and Economic Performance." *Journal of Economic Literature* 43(3): 762–800.

Alger, I., and J. W. Weibull. 2010. "Kinship, Incentives, and Evolution." *American Economic Review* 100(4): 1725–1758.

Amuedo-Dorantes, C., and L. Juarez. 2015. "Old-Age Government Transfers and the Crowding Out of Private Gifts: The 70 and Above Program for the Rural Elderly in Mexico." *Southern Economic Journal* 81(3): 782–802.

Anderson, S., and G. Genicot. 2015. "Suicide and Property Rights in India." *Journal of Development Economics* 114: 64–78.

André, C., and J.-P. Platteau. 1998. "Land Relations Under Unbearable Stress: Rwanda Caught in the Malthusian Trap." *Journal of Economic Behavior and Organization* 34(1): 1–47.

Aoki, M. 2001. *Toward a Comparative Institutional Analysis.* Cambridge, MA: MIT Press.

Axelrod, R. 1986. "An Evolutionary Approach to Norms." *American Political Science Review* 80(4): 1095–1111; reprinted in R. Axelrod, 1997, *The Complexity of Cooperation—Agent-Based Models of Competition and Collaboration,* 44–68. Princeton, NJ: Princeton University Press.

Baland, J. M., I. Bonjean, C. Guirkinger, and R. Ziparo. 2016. "Family Pressures and Investment Incentives in Cameroon." *Journal of Development Economics* 123: 38–56.

Baland, J. M., C. Guirkinger, and C. Mali. 2011. "Pretending to Be Poor: Borrowing to Escape Forced Solidarity in Cameroon." *Economic Development and Cultural Change* 60(1): 1–16.

Baland, J. M., and J.-P. Platteau. 1996. *Halting Degradation of Natural Resources—Is There a Role for Rural Communities?* Oxford: Oxford University Press.

Banerjee, A., D. Mookherjee, K. Munshi, and D. Ray. 2001. "Inequality, Control Rights and Rent-Seeking: Sugar Cooperatives in Maharashtra." *Journal of Political Economy* 109(1): 138–190.

Bardhan, P. 2002. "Decentralization of Governance and Development." *Journal of Economic Perspectives* 16(4): 185–205.

Bardhan, P., M. Luca, D. Mookherjee, and F. Pino. 2014. "Evolution of Land Distribution in West Bengal 1967–2004: Role of Land Reform and Demographic Changes." *Journal of Development Economics* 110: 171–190.

Bardhan, P., and D. Mookherjee. 1999. "Relative Capture of Local and Central Governments: An Essay in the Political Economy of Decentralization." Working Paper. Boston University, Department of Economics.

———. 2000. "Capture and Governance at Local and National Levels." *American Economic Review—Papers and Proceedings* 90(2): 135–139.

Basu, K. 1986. "The Market for Land: An Analysis of Interim Transactions." *Journal of Development Economics* 20(1): 163–177.

Bates, R. H. 2001. *Prosperity and Violence: The Political Economy of Development.* New York: Norton.

Bauer, A. J. 1975. *Chilean Rural Society from the Spanish Conquest to 1930.* Cambridge: Cambridge University Press.

Berger, P., and T. Luckmann. 1967. *The Social Construction of Reality.* Harmondsworth: Penguin Books.

Berkey, J. P. 2003. *The Formation of Islam—Religion and Society in the Near East, 600–1800.* Cambridge: Cambridge University Press.

Berkner, L. K. 1972. "The Stem Family and the Developmental Cycle of the Peasant Household: An Eighteenth-Century Austrian Example." *American Historical Review* 77(2): 398–418.

———. 1976. "Inheritance, Land Tenure and Peasant Family Structure: A German Regional Comparison." In *Family and Inheritance—Rural Society in Western Europe, 1200–1800,* edited by J. Goody, J. Thirsk, and E. P. Thompson, 71–95. Cambridge: Cambridge University Press.

Berkner, L. K., and F. F. Mendels. 1978. "Inheritance Systems, Family Structure, and Demographic Patterns in Western Europe, 1700–1900." In *Historical Studies of Changing Fertility,* edited by C. Tilly, 209–223. Princeton, NJ: Princeton University Press.

Besley, T. 1995. "Savings, Credit and Insurance." In *Handbook of Development Economics—Vol. 3A,* edited by J. Behrman and T. N. Srinivasan, 2123–2207. Amsterdam: Elsevier and North-Holland.

Bhalotra, S., R. Brulé, and S. Roy. 2016. "Women's Inheritance Rights Reform and the Preference for Sons in India." Mimeo, New York University Abu Dhabi.

Binswanger, H., and J. McIntire. 1987. "Behavioral and Material Determinants of Production Relations in Land-Abundant Tropical Agriculture." *Economic Development and Cultural Change* 36(1): 73–99.

Binswanger, H., J. McIntire, and C. Udry. 1989. "Production Relations in Semi-Arid African Agriculture." In *The Economic Theory of Agrarian Institutions*, edited by P. Bardhan, 122–144. Oxford: Clarendon Press.

Binswanger, H., and M. Rosenzweig. 1986. "Behavioral and Material Determinants of Production Relations in Agriculture." *Journal of Development Studies* 22(3): 503–539.

Birge, B. 2002. *Women, Property, and Confucian Reaction in Sung and Yuan China*. Cambridge: Cambridge University Press.

Bisin, A., and T. Verdier. 1998. "On the Cultural Transmission of Preferences for Social Status." *Journal of Public Economics* 70(1): 75–97.

———. 2010. "The Economics of Cultural Transmission and Socialization." In *Handbook of Social Economics*, edited by J. Benhabib, A. Bisin, and M. Jackson. Amsterdam: Elsevier and North-Holland.

Blanchard, I. 1984. "Industrial Employment and the Rural Land Market, 1380–1520." In *Land, Kinship and Life-Cycle*, edited by R. M. Smith. Cambridge: Cambridge University Press.

Bloch, M. 1962. *Feudal Society, I: The Growth of Ties of Dependence*, second edition. London and New York: Routledge and Kegan Paul.

Blum, J. 1957. "The Rise of Serfdom in Eastern Europe." *American Historical Review* 63: 807–836.

———. 1961. *Lord and Peasant in Russia From the Ninth to the Nineteenth Century*. Princeton, NJ: Princeton University Press.

Boltz, M., K. Marazyan, and P. Villar. 2015. Preference for Hidden Income and Redistribution to Kin and Neighbors: A Lab-in-the-field Experiment in Senegal Mimeo.

Boserup, E. 1965. *Conditions of Agricultural Growth*. Chicago: Aldine.

Boucher S., M. Carter, and C. Guirkinger. 2008. "Risk Rationing and Activity Choice in Moral Hazard Constrained Credit Market." *American Journal of Agricultural Economics* 90(2).

Bowles, S. 1998. "Endogenous Preferences: The Cultural Consequences of Markets and Other Economic Institutions." *Journal of Economic Literature* 36(1): 75–111.

Braun, R. 1978. "Early Industrialization and Demographic Change in the Canton of Zürich." In *Historical Studies of Changing Fertility*, edited by C. Tilly, 289–334. Princeton, NJ: Princeton University Press.

Brenner, R. 1976. "Agrarian Class Structure and Economic Development in Pre-Industrial Europe." *Past and Present* 70 (February), reprinted in *The Brenner Debate—Agrarian Class Structure and Economic Development in Pre-Industrial Europe*, edited by T. H. Aston and C.H.E. Philpin, 10–63. Cambridge: Cambridge University Press, 1985.

———. 1985. "The Agrarian Roots of European Capitalism." In *The Brenner Debate—Agrarian Class Structure and Economic Development in Pre-Industrial Europe*, edited by T. H. Aston and C.H.E. Philpin, 213–327. Cambridge: Cambridge University Press.

Browning, Martin, Pierre-André Chiappori, and Yoram Weiss. 2014. *Economics of the Family*. Cambridge: Cambridge University Press.

Brulé, R., and N. Gaikwad. 2016. "Culture, Capital and the Gender Gap in Political Economy Preferences: Evidence from Meghalaya's Tribes." Mimeo, New York University, Abu Dhabi.

Caeyers, B., and S. Dercon. 2011. "Political Connections and Social Networks in Targeted Transfer Programmes: Evidence from Rural Ethiopia." *Economic Development and Cultural Change* 60(4): 639–675.

Carranza, E. 2012. "Islamic Inheritance Law, Son Preference and Fertility Behavior of Muslim Couples in Indonesia." *World Bank Policy Research Working Paper* (5972).

Carter, M. 1987. "Risk Sharing and Incentives in the Decollectivization of Agriculture." *Oxford Economic Papers* 39: 577–595.

Cerman, M. 2012. *Villagers and Lords in Eastern Europe, 1300–1800*. Basingstoke: Palgrave Macmillan.

Chayanov, A. 1991. *The Theory of Peasant Cooperatives*. London and New York: I.B. Tauris.

Chen, S., C. Campbell, and J. Lee. 2014. "Categorical Inequality and Gender Difference: Marriage and Remarriage in Notheast China, 1749–1913." In *Similarity in Difference: Marriage in Europe and Asia, 1700–1900*, edited by C. Lundh and S. Kurosu, 393–436. Cambridge, MA and London: MIT Press.

Chort, I., F. Gubert, and J. N. Senne. 2012. "Migrant Networks as a Basis for Social Control: Remittance Incentives among Senegalese in France and Italy." *Regional Science and Urban Economics* 42(5): 858–874.

Chu, C. Y. 1991. "Primogeniture." *Journal of Political Economy* 99(1): 78–99.

Coate, S., and M. Ravallion. 1993. "Reciprocity Without Commitment: Characterization and Performance of Informal Insurance Arrangements." *Journal of Development Economics* 40(1): 1–24.

Cobb-Clark, D. A. 2008. "Leaving Home: What Economics Has to Say about the Living Arrangements of Young Australians." *Australian Economic Review* 41(2): 123–229.

Cooper, B. M. 1997. *Marriage in Maradi. Gender and Culture in a Hausa Society in Niger, 1900–1989*. Oxford: James Currey.

Cox, D. 1987. "Motives for Private Income Transfers." *Journal of Political Economy* 95: 508–546.

Cox, D., and M. Fafchamps. 2008. "Extended Family and Kinship Networks: Economic Insights and Evolutionary Directions." *Handbook of Development Economics*, Vol. 4, 3711–3784. Elsevier North-Holland.

Dee, Thomas S. 2003. "Until Death Do You Part: The Effects of Unilateral Divorce on Spousal Homicides." *Economic Inquiry* 41(1): 163–182.

Deininger, K., A. Goyal, and H. Nagarajan. 2013. "Women's Inheritance Rights and Intergenerational Transmission of Resources in India." *Journal of Human Resources* 48(1): 114–141.

De Janvry, A. 1981. *The Agrarian Question and Reformism in Latin America*. Baltimore and London Johns Hopkins University Press.

De La Croix, D., M. Doepke, and J. Mokyr. 2016. "Clans, Guilds, and Markets: Apprenticeship Institutions and Growth in the Pre-Industrial Economy." Unpublished manuscript, Northwestern University and Catholic University of Louvain.

Delpierre, M., C. Guirkinger, and J.-P. Platteau. 2019. "Risk as an Impediment to Individualization of Land Tenure? The Role of Collective Fields in Extended Agricultural Households." *Economic Development and Cultural Change* (forthcoming).

Dennison, T. 2011. *The Institutional Framework of Russian Serfdom*. Cambridge: Cambridge University Press.

Dercon, S., T. Bold, J. De Weerdt, and A. Pankhurst. 2006. "Group-Based Funeral Insurance in Ethiopia and Tanzania." *World Development* 34(4): 685–703.

Dercon S., and P. Krishnan. 2000. "In Sickness and in Health: Risk Sharing Within Households in Rural Ethiopia." *Journal of Political Economy* 108(4): 688–727.

Derosas, R., M. Breschi, A. Fornasin, M. Manfredini, and C. Munno. 2014. "Between Constraints and Coercion: Marriage and Social Reproduction in Northern and Central Italy in the Eighteenth and Nineteenth Centuries." In *Similarity in Difference: Marriage in Europe and Asia, 1700–1900*, edited by C. Lundh and S. Kurosu, 295–348. Cambridge, MA: MIT Press.

Donner, F. M. 1981. *The Early Islamic Conquests*. Princeton, NJ: Princeton University Press.

Drewianka, S. 2008. "Divorce Law and Family Formation." *Journal of Population Economics* 21(2): 485–503.

Dribe, M., and C. Lundh. 2005. "Gender Aspects on Inheritance Strategies and Land Transmission in Rural Scania, Sweden, in 1720–1840." *History of the Family* 10(3): 293–308.

Dribe, M., M. Manfredini, and M. Oris. 2014. "The Roads to Reproduction: Comparing Life-Course Trajectories in Preindustrial Eurasia." In *Similarity in Difference: Marriage in Europe and Asia, 1700–1900*, edited by C. Lundh and S. Kurosu, 89–120. Cambridge, MA: MIT Press.

Duby, G. 1973. *Hommes et structures du Moyen Age*. Paris and La Haye: Mouton.

Duflo, E., and C. Udry. 2004. *Intrahousehold Resource Allocation in Cote d'Ivoire: Social Norms, Separate Accounts and Consumption Choices*. National Bureau of Economic Research.

Durlauf, S. N., and M. Fafchamps. 2005. "Social Capital." In *Handbook of Economic Growth*, edited by S. N. Durlauf and P. Aghion. Amsterdam: Elsevier and North-Holland.

Edmonds, E. V., and M. Shrestha. 2014. "You Get What You Pay For: Schooling Incentives and Child Labor." *Journal of Development Economics* 111: 196–211.

Elster, J. 1998. "Emotions and Economic Theory." *Journal of Economic Literature* 36(1): 47–74.

Fafchamps, M. 1992. "Solidarity Networks in Preindustrial Societies: Rational Peasants with a Moral Economy." *Economic Development and Cultural Change* 41(1): 147–174.

———. 2001. "Intrahousehold Access to Land and Sources of Inefficiency: Theory and Concepts." In *Access to Land, Rural Poverty and Public Action*, edited by A. de Janvry et al. Oxford: Oxford University Press.

———. 2004. *Market Institutions in Sub-Saharan Africa*. Cambridge, MA: MIT Press

———. 2011. "Risk Sharing Between Households." In *Handbook of Social Economics*, vol. 1, chap. 24, edited by J. Benhabib et al., 1255–1279. Elsevier North Holland.

Fafchamps, M., and A. R. Quisumbing. 2007. "Household Formation and Marriage Markets in Rural Areas." *Handbook of Development Economics*, vol. 4, chap. 51, 3187–3247. Elsevier North-Holland.

Faith, R. 1966. "Peasant Families and Inheritance Customs in Medieval England." *Agricultural History Review* 14: 77–95.

Foster, A. D., and M. R. Rosenzweig. 2001. "Imperfect Commitment, Altruism, and the Family: Evidence from Transfer Behavior in Low-Income Rural Areas." *Review of Economics and Statistics* 83(3): 389–407.

———. 2002. "Household Division and Rural Economic Growth." *Review of Economic Studies* 69: 839–869.

Friedberg, L. 1998. "Did Unilateral Divorce Raise Divorce Rates? Evidence from Panel Data." *American Economic Review* 88(3): 608–627.

Fukuyama, F. 1992. *The End of History and the Last Man*. New York: Free Press.

———. 2012. *The Origins of Political Order: From Prehuman Times to the French Revolution*. London: Profile Books.

Gambetta, D. 1988. "Can We Trust Trust?" In *Trust-Making and Breaking Cooperative Relations*, edited by D. Gambetta, 213–237. Oxford: Basil Blackwell.

Gaunt, D. 1983. "The Property and Kin Relationships of Retired Farmers in Northern and Central Europe." In *Family Forms in Historic Europe*, edited by R. Wall et al., 249–279. Cambridge: Cambridge University Press.

Gedzi, V. 2009. *Principles and Practices of Dispute Resolution: Ewe and Akan Procedures on Females' Inheritance and Property Rights*. Maastricht: Shaker.

Genadek, Katie R., Wendy A. Stock, and Christiana Stoddard. 2007. "No-Fault Divorce Laws and the Labor Supply of Women With and Without Children." *Journal of Human Resources* 42(1): 247–274.

Genicot, G., and D. Ray. 2003. "Group Formation in Risk-Sharing Arrangements." *Review of Economic Studies* 70.1: 87–113.

Goldberg, P.J.P. 1992. *Women, Work and Life Cycle in a Medieval Economy: Women in York and Yorkshire c. 1300–1520*. Oxford: Oxford University Press.

Goldstein, M. 2004. *Intrahousehold Efficiency and Individual Insurance in Ghana*. London School of Economics and Political Science, LSE Library.

Goldstein, M., and C. Udry. 2008. "The Profits of Power: Land Rights and Agricultural Investment in Ghana." *Journal of Political Economy* 116(6): 981–1022.

González-Val, R., and M. Marcén. 2012. "Unilateral Divorce versus Child Custody and Child Support in the US." *Journal of Economic Behavior and Organization* 81(2): 613–643.

Goody, J. 1973. "Strategies of Heirship." *Comparative Studies in Society and History* 15(1): 3–20.

———. 1983. *The Development of the Family and Marriage in Europe*. Cambridge: Cambridge University Press.

Gray, Jeffrey S. 1998. "Divorce-Law Changes, Household Bargaining, and Married Women's Labor Supply." *American Economic Review* 88(3): 628–642.

Greif, A. 1989. "Reputation and Coalitions in Medieval Trade: Evidence on the Maghribi Traders." *Journal of Economic History* 49(4): 857–882.

———. 1994. "Cultural Beliefs and the Organization of Society: A Historical and Theoretical Reflection on Collectivist and Individualist Societies." *Journal of Political Economy* 102(5): 912–950.

———. 2006a. *Institutions and the Path to the Modern Economy—Lessons from Medieval Trade*. Cambridge: Cambridge University Press.

———. 2006b. "Family Structure, Institutions, and Growth: The Origins and Implications of Western Corporations." *American Economic Review—Papers and Proceedings* 96: 308–312.

Greif, A., and M. Iyigun. 2013. "Social Organizations, Violence, and Modern Growth." *American Economic Review* 103(3): 534–538.

Greif, A., M. Iyigun, and D. Sasson. 2012. "Social Institutions and Economic Growth: Why England and Not China Became the First Modern Economy." Unpublished Working Paper, University of Colorado.

Greif, A., and D. D. Laitin. 2004. "A Theory of Endogenous Institutional Change." *American Political Science Review* 98(4): 633–652.

Greif, A., and G. Tabellini. 2010. "Cultural and Institutional Bifurcation: China and Europe Compared." *American Economic Review—Papers and Proceedings* 100(2): 1–10.

———. 2017. "The Clan and the Corporation: Sustaining Cooperation in China and Europe." *Journal of Comparative Economics* 45(1).

Greif, A., and S. Tadelis. 2010. "A Theory of Moral Persistence: Crypto-Morality and Political Legitimacy." *Journal of Comparative Economics* 38(3): 229–244.

Guirkinger, C., and J.-P. Platteau. 2014. "The Effect of Land Scarcity on Farm Structure: Empirical Evidence from Mali." *Economic Development and Cultural Change* 62(2): 195–238.

———. 2015. "Transformation of the Family under Rising Land Pressure: A Theoretical Essay." *Journal of Comparative Economics* 43, no. 1 (February): 112–137.

Guirkinger, C., J.-P. Platteau, and T. Goetghebuer. 2015. "Productive Inefficiency in Extended Agricultural Households: Evidence from Mali." *Journal of Development Economics* 116: 17–27.

Habakkuk, H. J. 1955. "Family Structure and Economic Change in Nineteenth Century Europe." *Journal of Economic History* 15(1): 1–12.

Hajnal, J. 1982. "Two Kinds of Pre-industrial Household Systems." *Population and Development Review* 8(3): 449–494.

Hallward-Driemeier, M., and O. Gajigo. 2013. "Strengthening Economic Rights and Women's Occupational Choice: The Impact of Reforming Ethiopia's Family Law." *World Bank Policy Research Working Paper* 6695.

Hamoudi, A., and D. Thomas. 2014. "Endogenous Coresidence and Program Incidence: South Africa's Old Age Pension." *Journal of Development Economics* 109: 30–37.

Harari, M. 2014. Women's Inheritance Rights and Bargaining Power: Evidence from Kenya. Mimeo.

Hartman, M. S. 2004. *The Household and the Making of History—A Subversive View of the Western Past*. Cambridge: Cambridge University Press.

Hayami, Y., and J.-P. Platteau. 1998. "Resource Endowments and Agricultural Development: Africa versus Asia." In *The Institutional Foundations of East Asian Economic Development*, edited by M. Aoki and Y. Hayami, 357–410. London: Macmillan.

Herlihy, D. 1969. "Family Solidarity in Medieval Italian History." In *Economy, Society, and Government in Medieval Italy: Essays in Memory of Robert L. Reynolds*, edited by D. Herlihy et al., 173–184. Kent, OH: Kent State University Press.

———. 1985. *Medieval Households*. Cambridge, MA: Harvard University Press.

Hidrobo, M., J. Hoddinott, A. Peterman, A. Margolies, and V. Moreira. 2014. "Cash, Food, or Vouchers? Evidence from a Randomized Experiment in Northern Ecuador." *Journal of Development Economics* 107: 144–156.

Hilton, R. H. 1985. "A Crisis of Feudalism." In *The Brenner Debate—Agrarian Class Structure and Economic Development in Pre-Industrial Europe*, edited by T. H. Aston and C.H.E. Philpin, 119–137. Cambridge: Cambridge University Press.

Hodgson, M.G.S. 1974a. *The Venture of Islam—Conscience and History in a World Civilization, Vol. 2: The Expansion of Islam in the Middle Periods*. Chicago and London: University of Chicago Press.

———. 1974b. *The Venture of Islam—Conscience and History in a World Civilization, Vol. 3: The Gunpowder Empires and Modern Times*. Chicago and London: University of Chicago Press.

Hoff, K., and A. Sen. 2005. "The Extended Family System and Market Interactions." In *The Social Economics of Poverty: On Identities, Communities, Groups, and Networks*, edited by C. B. Barrett, 171–187. London and New York: Routledge.

Homans, G. C. 1953. "The Rural Sociology of Medieval England." *Past and Present* 4(1): 32–43.

Howell, C. 1976. "Peasant Inheritance Customs in the Midlands, 1280–1700." In *Family and Inheritance—Rural Society in Western Europe, 1200–1800*, edited by J. Goody et al., 112–155. Cambridge: Cambridge University Press.

Htun, M., and S. L. Weldon. 2012. "The Civic Origins of Progressive Policy Change: Combating Violence against Women in Global Perspective, 1975–2005." *American Political Science Review* 106(3): 548–569.

Jakiela, P., and O. Ozier. 2015. "Does Africa Need a Rotten Kin Theorem? Experimental Evidence from Village Economies." *Review of Economic Studies* 83(1): 231–268.

Juarez, L. 2009. "Crowding Out of Private Support to the Elderly: Evidence from a Demogrant in Mexico." *Journal of Public Economics* 93(3): 454–463.

Kali, R. 1999. "Endogenous Business Networks." *Journal of Law, Economics, and Organization* 15(3): 615–636.

Kaplan, G. 2012. "Inequality and the Life Cycle." *Quantitative Economics* 3(3): 471–525.

Kazianga, H., and Z. Wahhaj. 2013. "Gender, Social Norms, and Household Production in Burkina Faso." *Economic Development and Cultural Change* 61(3): 539–576.

———. 2016. "Intra-Household Resource Allocation and Familial Ties." School of Economics Discussion Papers, KDPE 1601, University of Kent.

Kennedy, P. 1988. *African Capitalism—The Struggle for Ascendency*. Cambridge: Cambridge University Press.

King, E. 1973. *Peterborough Abbey 1086–1310*. Cambridge: Cambridge University Press.

Klasen, S., and I. Woolard. 2009. "Surviving Unemployment without State Support: Unemployment and Household Formation in South Africa." *Journal of African Economies* 18(1): 1–51.

Kolchin, Peter (Ed.). 1987. *Unfree Labor—American Slavery and Russian Serfdom*. Cambridge, MA and London: Belknap Press of Harvard University Press.

Kolm, S. C. 2006. "Reciprocity: Its Scope, Rationales, and Consequences." In *Handbook of the Economics of Giving, Altruism and Reciprocity*, Vol. 1, Chap. 6, edited by S. C. Kolm and J. M. Ythier, 371–541. North-Holland and Elsevier.

Korotayev, A. V. 2003. "Unilineal Descent Organization and Deep Christianization: A Cross-Cultural Comparison." *Cross-Cultural Research* 37(1): 133–157.

Kumar, K. B., and J. G. Matsusaka. 2009. "From Families to Formal Contracts: An Approach to Development." *Journal of Development Economics* 90(1): 106–119.

Kuran, T. 2011. *The Long Divergence—How Islamic Law Held Back the Middle East*. Princeton, NJ: Princeton University Press.

La Ferrara, E. 2002. "Self-Help Groups and Income Generation in the Informal Settlements of Nairobi." *Journal of African Economies* 11(1): 61–89.

———. 2003. "Kin Groups and Reciprocity: A Model of Credit Transactions in Ghana." *American Economic Review* 93(5): 1730–1751.

———. 2007. "Descent Rules and Strategic Transfers—Evidence from Matrilineal Groups in Ghana." *Journal of Development Economics* 83(2): 280–301.

———. 2011. "Family and Kinship Ties in Development: An Economist's Perspective." In *Culture, Institutions, and Development: New Insights Into an Old Debate*, edited by J.-P. Platteau and R. Peccoud. London: Routledge.

La Ferrara, E., and A. Milazzo. 2017. "Customary Norms, Inheritance, and Human Capital: Evidence from a Reform of the Matrilineal System in Ghana. *American Economic Journal: Applied Economics* 9(4): 166–185.

Laslett, J. 1971. *The World We Have Lost*. London: Methuen.

Laslett, P. 1972. "Introduction: The History of the Family." In *Household and Family in Past Time*, edited by P. Laslett. Cambridge: Cambridge University Press.

Le Play. 1871. *L'organisation de la famille*. Paris: Téqui.

Le Roy Ladurie, E. 1976. "Family Structures and Inheritance Customs in Sixteenth-Century France." In *Family and Inheritance—Rural Society in Western Europe, 1200–1800*, edited by J. Goody et al. Cambridge: Cambridge University Press.

Ligon, E., J. P. Thomas, and T. Worrall. 2001. "Informal Insurance Arrangements with Limited Commitment: Theory and Evidence in Village Economies." *Review of Economic Studies* 69: 209–244.

Lundh, C., and S. Kurosu. 2014. *Similarity in Difference: Marriage in Europe and Asia, 1700–1900*. Cambridge, MA and London: MIT Press.

Macfarlane, A. 1978. *The Origins of English Individualism—The Family, Property and Social Transition*. Oxford: Basil Blackwell.

Matouschek, N., and I. Rasul. 2008. "The Economics of the Marriage Contract: Theories and Evidence." *Journal of Law and Economics* 51: 59–110.

Matsudaira, J. 2016. "Economic Conditions and the Living Arrangements of Young Adults: 1960 to 2011." *Journal of Population Economics* 29(1): 167–195.

Mechoulan, S. 2005. "Economic Theory's Stance on No-Fault Divorce." *Review of Economics of the Household* 3(3): 337–359.

Medick, H. 1981. "The Proto-Industrial Family Economy." In *Industrialization before Industrialization*, edited by P. Kriedte et al. Cambridge: Cambridge University Press.

Mokyr, J. 2002. *The Gift of Athena—Historical Origins of the Knowledge Economy*. Princeton, NJ: Princeton University Press.

Mookerjee, S. 2015. "Gender-Neutral Inheritance Laws, Family Structure, and Women's Social Status in India." Mimeo.

Mookherjee, D. 2015. "Political Decentralization." *Annual Review of Economics* 7: 231–249.

Moon, D. 1999. *The Russian Peasantry, 1600–1930—The World the Peasants Made*. London and New York: Longman.

———. 2006. "Peasants and Agriculture." In *The Cambridge History of Russia, Vol. II: Imperial Russia, 1689–1917*, edited by D. Lieven, 369–393. Cambridge: Cambridge University Press.

Morduch, J. 1999. "Between the State And The Market: Can Informal Insurance Patch the Safety Net?" *World Bank Research Observer* 14.2: 187–207.

Munro, A. 2015. Intra-household Experiments: A Survey and Some Methodological Observations. *GRIPS Discussion Papers*, 15.

Munshi, K. 2003. "Networks in a Modern Economy: Mexican Migrants in the US Labor Market." *Quarterly Journal of Economics* 118: 549–599.

———. 2008. "Information Networks in Dynamic Agrarian Economies." *Handbook of Development Economics*, Vol. 4, 3086–3113. Elsevier North-Holland.

Munshi, K., and M. Rosenzweig. 2016. "Networks and Misallocation: Insurance, Migration, and the Rural-Urban Wage Gap." *American Economic Review* 106(1): 46–98.

Neven, M. 2003. *Individus et familles. Les dynamiques d'une société rurale en transition. Le Pays de Herve durant la seconde moitié du 19ème siècle*. Genève: Droz.

Obolonsky, A.V. 2003. *The Drama of Russian Political History: System Against Individuality*. Austin: Texas A & M University Press.

Oris, M., G. Alter, and P. Servais. 2014. "Prudence as Obstinate Resistance to Pressure: Marriage in Nineteenth-Century Rural Eastern Belgium." In *Similarity in Difference: Marriage in Europe and Asia, 1700–1900*, edited by C. Lundh and K. Satomi. Cambridge, MA: MIT Press.

Parish, W. L., and M. Schwartz. 1972. "Household Complexity in Nineteenth Century France." *American Sociological Review* 37 (April): 154–173.

Pensieroso, L., and A. Sommacal. 2014. "Economic Development and Family Structure: From Pater Familias To The Nuclear Family." *European Economic Review* 71: 80–100.

Pingali, P., Y. Bigot, and H. P. Binswanger. 1987. *Agricultural Mechanization and the Evolution of Farming Systems in Sub-Saharan Africa*. Baltimore and London: Johns Hopkins University Press.

Pipes, R. 1995. *Russia under the Old Regime*. London: Penguin Books.

———. 1999. *Property and Freedom*. New York: Alfred A. Knopf.

Platteau, J.-P. 1991. "Traditional Systems of Social Security and Hunger Insurance: Past Achievements and Modern Challenges." In *Social Security in Developing Countries*, edited by E. Ahmad et al., 112–170. Oxford: Clarendon Press.

———. 1995a. "A Framework for the Analysis of Evolving Patron-Client Ties in Agrarian Economies." *World Development* 23(5): 767–786.

———. 1995b. "An Indian Model of Aristocratic Patronage." *Oxford Economic Papers* 47(4): 636–662.

———. 1997. "Mutual Insurance as an Elusive Concept in Traditional Rural Societies." *Journal of Development Studies* 33(6): 764–796.

———. 2000. *Institutions, Social Norms, and Economic Development*. London: Routledge.

———. 2006. "Solidarity Norms and Institutions in Agrarian Societies: Static and Dynamic Considerations." In *Handbook on Gift-Giving, Reciprocity and Altruism*, vol. 1, edited by S. Kolm, J. Mercier-Ythier, and G. Varet, 819–886. Amsterdam: North-Holland and Elsevier.

———. 2014. "Redistributive Pressures in Sub-Saharan Africa: Causes, Consequences, and Coping Strategies." In *African Development in Historical Perspective*, edited by E. Akyeampong, R. Bates, N. Nunn, and J. Robinson, 153–207. Cambridge: Cambridge University Press.

———. 2017. *Islam Instrumentalized: Religion and Politics in Historical Perspective*. Cambridge: Cambridge University Press.

Platteau, J.-P., and J. M. Baland. 2001. "Impartible Inheritance Versus Equal Division: A Comparative Perspective Centered on Europe and Sub-Saharan Africa." In *Access to Land, Rural Poverty, and Public Action*, edited by de Janvry et al., 27–67. Oxford: Oxford University Press.

Platteau, J.-P., and E. Seki. 2001. "Coordination and Pooling Arrangements in Japanese Coastal Fisheries." In *Community and Market in Economic Development*, edited by M. Aoki and Y. Hayami, 344–402. Oxford: Clarendon Press.

———. 2007. "Heterogeneity, Social Esteem and the Feasibility of Collective Action." *Journal of Development Economics* 83(2): 302–325.

Platteau, J.-P., and Z. Wahhaj. 2014. "Interactions Between Modern Law and Custom." In *Handbook of the Economics of Art and Culture*, vol. 2, chap. 22, edited by V. Ginsburgh and D. Throsby, 633–678. Elsevier and North-Holland.

Pomeranz, K. 2000. *The Great Divergence—China, Europe, and the Making of the Modern World Economy*. Princeton, NJ: Princeton University Press.

Poos, L. R. 1985. "The Rural Population of Essex in the Later Middle Ages." *Economic History Review* 38(4): 515–530.

———. 1991. *A Rural Society After the Black Death: Essex 1350–1525*. Cambridge: Cambridge University Press.

Posner, R. 1980. "A Theory of Primitive Society, with Special Reference to Law." *Journal of Law and Economics* 23: 1–53.

Putterman, L. 1983. "A Modified Collective Agriculture in Rural Growth-with-Equity: Reconsidering the Private, Unimodal Solution." *World Development* 11(2): 77–100.

———. 1985. "Extrinsic Versus Intrinsic Problems of Agricultural Cooperation: Antiincentivism in Tanzania and China." *Journal of Development Studies* 21: 175–204.

———. 1987. "The Incentive Problem and the Demise of Team Farming in China." *Journal of Development Economics* 26: 103–127.

———. 1989. "Agricultural Producer Co-operatives." In *The Economic Theory of Agrarian Institutions*, edited by P. Bardhan, 319–339. Oxford: Clarendon Press.

Putterman, L., and M. Digiorgio. 1985. "Choice and Efficiency in a Model of Democratic Semicollective Agriculture." *Oxford Economic Papers* 37: 1–21.

Razi, Z. 1980. *Life, Marriage and Death in a Medieval Parish: Economy, Society and Demography in Halesowen, 1270–1400*. Cambridge: Cambridge University Press.

Riasanovsky, N. V. 1993. *A History of Russia*, 5th edition. New York and Oxford: Oxford University Press.

Rosenblum, D. 2015. "Unintended Consequences of Women's Inheritance Rights on Female Mortality in India." *Economic Development and Cultural Change* 63(2): 223–248.

Roy, S. 2015. "Empowering Women? Inheritance Rights, Female Education and Dowry Payments in India." *Journal of Development Economics* 114: 233–251.

Ruggles, S. 2009. "Reconsidering the Northwest European Family System: Living Arrangements of the Aged in Comparative Historical Perspective." *Population and Development Review* 35(2): 249–273.

———. 2010. "Stem Families and Joint Families in Comparative Historical Perspective." *Population and Development Review* 36(3): 563–577.

Sadoulet, E. 1992. "Labor-service Tenancy Contracts in a Latin American Context." *American Economic Review* 82: 1031–1042.

Schofield, R. 1989. "Family Structure, Demographic Behavior, and Economic Growth." In *Famine, Disease and the Social Order in Early Modern Society*, edited by J. Walter and R. Schofield, 279–304. Cambridge: Cambridge University Press.

Schulz, J. F. 2017. "The Churches' Bans on Consanguinity, Kin-Networks and Democracy." Mimeo, Yale University.

Seccombe, W. 1992. *A Millenium of Family Change—Feudalism to Capitalism in Northwestern Europe*. London and New York: Verso.

Smith, T. C. 1959. *The Agrarian Origins of Modern Japan*. Stanford, CA: Stanford University Press.

Spufford, M. 1976. "Peasant Inheritance Customs and Land Distribution in Cambridgeshire from the Sixteenth to the Eighteenth Centuries." In *Family and Inheritance—Rural Society in Western Europe, 1200–1800*, edited by J. Goody et al., 156–176. Cambridge: Cambridge University Press.

Stevenson, Betsey. 2008. "Divorce Law and Women's Labor Supply." *Journal of Empirical Legal Studies* 5(4): 853–873.

Stevenson, Betsey, and Justin Wolfers. 2006. "Bargaining in the Shadow of the Law: Divorce Laws and Family Distress." *Quarterly Journal of Economics* 121(1): 267–288.

Szołtysek, M. 2015. "Households and Family Systems." In *The Oxford Handbook of Early Modern European History, 1350–1750, Volume I: Peoples and Place*, 313.

Thompson, E. P. 1976. "The Grid of Inheritance: A Comment." In *Family and Inheritance—Rural Society in Western Europe, 1200–1800*, edited by J. Goody et al., 328–360. Cambridge: Cambridge University Press.

Todd, E. 1990. *L'invention de l'Europe*. Paris: Editions du Seuil.

———. 2011. *L'origine des Systèmes Familiaux, Tome 1 : l'Eurasie*. Paris: Gallimard.

Udry, C. 1996. "Gender, Agricultural Production, and the Theory of the Household." *Journal of Political Economy* 104(5): 1010–1046.

Van Zanden, J. 2009. *The Long Road to the Industrial Revolution—The European Economy in a Global Perspective, 1000–1800*. Leiden and Boston: Brill.

Viazzo, P. P., and D. Albera. 1990. "The Peasant Family in Northern Italy, 1750–1930: A Reassessment." *Journal of Family History* 15(4): 461–482.

Voigtländer, N., and H. J. Voth. 2013. "How the West 'Invented' Fertility Restriction." *American Economic Review* 103(6): 2227–2264.

Waldron, P. 1997. *The End of Imperial Russia, 1855–1917*. London: Macmillan Press.

Wall, R., M. Cerman, T. Hareven, and J. Ehmer (Eds.). 2001. *Family History Revisited: Comparative Perspectives*. Newark: University of Delaware Press.

Wall, R., J. Robin, and P. Laslett (Eds.). 1983. *Family Forms in Historic Europe*. Cambridge: Cambridge University Press.

Wickelgren, A. L. 2009. "Why Divorce Laws Matter: Incentives for Noncontractible Marital Investments under Unilateral and Consent Divorce." *Journal of Law, Economics, and Organization* 25(1): 80–106.

Wolfers, J. 2006. "Did Unilateral Divorce Laws Raise Divorce Rates? A Reconciliation and New Results." *American Economic Review* 96(5): 1802–1820.

Worobec, C. 1995. *Peasant Russia—Family and Community in the Post-Emancipation Period*. Dekalb: Northern Illinois University Press.

Wrigley, E. A., and R. Schofield. 1981. *The Population History of England, 1541–1871: A Reconstruction*. London: Edward Arnold.

14

GENDER INSTITUTIONS AND ECONOMIC DEVELOPMENT

Stephan Klasen

14.1. INTRODUCTION

Institutions pertaining to gender relations are an important element in the overall institutional landscape of a society. Such institutions are often informal and include norms and expectations regarding appropriate behavior of males and females in different age groups and social circumstances (e.g., single, married, widowed, divorced). The institutions regulating gendered behavior can sometimes be formalized in laws that, for example, set gender-specific rules regulating gender roles in the household, marriage, inheritance, the economy, and in politics. To the extent that such formalized gender-specific rules have existed, they tended to particularly constrain women's options (World Bank 2001), such as requiring permission of a senior male to travel, work, and marry; denying them the right to vote; or treating the two genders unequally in marriage and divorce, inheritance, or access to property and factors of production (Hallward-Driemeier et al. 2013a). As discussed below, in recent decades such formalized gender gaps have been reduced substantially across the world, although some gaps still exist (Hallward-Driemeier et al. 2013a).

In addition to these gender gaps in *formal* institutions, gender gaps in *informal* institutions powerfully affect the economic and social roles of males and females. These informal institutions are particularly deep-seated and durable and are often couched as central elements of the cultural and/or religious identity of a society. Since they also touch private lives and, among other things, also govern the way societies organize reproduction (and thus their long-term survival), they are quite durable and not easily changed by policy interventions. At the same time they are, of course, affected by wider economic and social trends. Similar to gender differentials in existing formal laws, most of these informal institutions have also tended to place greater constraints on female private and public activities such as restricting their economic opportunities or their involvement in public life while relegating much of the reproductive and care activities to them (OECD 2015).

These gender gaps in formal and informal institutions are not only a question of equity, but can powerfully affect the economic performance and social well-being of societies in several ways: First, institutions shaping reproduction are affecting economic development through the well-known impacts of demographic change on economic performance (e.g., Bloom and Williamson 1998). Second, as shown below, women's economic opportunities have a powerful effect on overall economic performance. Last, women's reproductive and care activities are critical for the well-being of societies, even though this is not adequately captured in conventional national income accounting (OECD 1995; UNDP 1995).

In recent decades, these issues of gender inequality have received a great deal of attention in international development policy. Gender advocacy groups focused particularly on equity issues, while development agencies were additionally concerned with the instrumental effects of gender gaps on economic development (e.g., World Bank 2001, 2011; King, Klasen, and Porter 2009). This was spurred by a literature that showed that gender gaps, particularly in education but also employment, were indeed associated with lower economic growth (e.g., Klasen 2002; Klasen and Lamanna 2009; Esteve-Volart 2009); similarly a literature developed that showed that cash in the hands of women had greater development impacts, particularly related to spending on health and education of children, than did funds in the hands of men (Thomas 1990, 1997; Pitt and Kandker 1998; World Bank 2001); last, several studies found that women's greater political participation led to a range of positive development outcomes, including more public goods and less corruption (e.g., Chattopadhyay and Duflo 2004; Branisa et al. 2013). This literature will be briefly reviewed below.

As a result of concerns for gender equity and the impact of women on overall economic development, many initiatives to address gender gaps were launched. They included rights-based approaches to development, most notably CEDAW (the Convention on the Elimination of Discrimination against Women) which has been signed and ratified by nearly all countries of the world (though many countries expressed reservations with respect to certain articles; see Cho 2014). In addition, many national and international policy initiatives focused on reducing particular gender gaps, with specific emphasis on reducing gender gaps in education. While some initiatives were directly targeting gender gaps (e.g., Bangladesh's secondary school stipend program that is only available to girls), others combined addressing gender gaps with other policy objectives. For example, Mexico's Progresa/Oportunidades Program gave a larger conditional cash transfer for the education of girls than boys and always transferred the funds to the mothers in the belief that the money would be better spent than in the hands of fathers (e.g., Behrmann, Parker, and Todd 2008). Similarly, many microcredit programs target women for the same reason (see Pitt and Khandker 1998; King, Klasen, and Porter 2009). Last, girls and women benefited disproportionately from particular policy initiatives not directly related to gender. For example, a push toward universal schooling automatically benefited girls more than boys if there were existing gender gaps in schooling before. Or particular types of growth strategies benefited women more as they relied heavily on labor-intensive exports in typically female-dominated sectors such as textiles, garments, toys, electronics, or other light manufacturing (Seguino 2000a).

As I will demonstrate below, there has been remarkable progress in reducing some gender gaps, most notably in education and in rights in recent decades, with some regional heterogeneity in the pace of progress. At the same time, there is great heterogeneity by region and dimension in other types of gender gaps. For example, gender gaps in labor force participation have closed much more slowly in general, with little progress at all in some regions (Gaddis and Klasen 2014; Klasen and Pieters 2015). Occupational and sectoral segregation by gender remains as large as ever (Borrowman and Klasen 2017), and gender gaps in time use have been falling very slowly and unevenly. Gender gaps in mortality have fallen but remained large in some parts (most notably China and India), and rates of female genital mutilation (FGM) and domestic violence seem to have changed very little (World Bank 2014).

This leads to a range of open research and policy issues that deserve greater attention as the links between gender, institutions, and economic development are being investigated. First, what explains the differential rate of progress by dimension and by region? Is this a result of policy, initial conditions, or other developments? As part of this larger question, it is important to understand why the huge progress in reducing gender gaps in schooling has not translated (yet?) in commensurate reductions in gaps in other dimensions of gender inequality, especially women's economic participation, pay gaps, time use, and gendered norms. Similarly, are there (targeted or general) policy interventions or secular changes that can affect more deep-rooted gender norms? Second, while there has been relatively little regress in the reduction of gender gaps in most places, there appears to be mounting resistance and backlash in some regions against the closing of gender gaps in rights, economic participation, and even education. It is not clear whether these are isolated incidents or more general trends.

This chapter addresses these issues in turn. It is organized as follows: the next section first clarifies the nature of gender relations as a key social institution and examines gender gaps in social institutions across the world. The third section then reviews the theoretical and empirical literature on the impact of gender gaps on economic performance. The fourth section examines trends in gender gaps over time, while section 14.5 then speculates about various factors that might have caused this heterogeneous performance. The last section concludes with open research and policy issues.

14.2. GENDER INEQUALITY IN SOCIAL INSTITUTION AND WOMEN'S ECONOMIC ROLES

Since the household is the basic economic and social institution organizing production, employment, and reproduction, gender relations within the household clearly are a central social institution governing these production and reproduction issues. And since the way production and reproduction are organized is affecting the long-term development of societies, it is critical to understand how gender roles are affecting the way production and reproduction are organized. To be sure, while women's care work and household production are critical for the long-term survival of societies, they are not included in conventional measures of economic performance, including gross national income (which does not include non-marketed services by households, e.g., UNDP 1995; OECD 1995; Waring 1988). So its impact is felt only indirectly, but this can still have powerful effects on (conventionally measured) economic performance.

Now consider how gender issues affect the way reproduction is organized and the implications this has for economic development. A key element here is the drivers of the quantity and "quality" of children. This will depend, for example, on norms governing marriage ages, the existence and acceptance of polygamy, patrilocality, and associated son preference, the acceptance of divorce and independent living for single and divorced women, the locus of control over fertility decisions, and the amount of time invested by mothers and fathers in raising their children. There have been large regional differences in these norms governing fertility behavior that have persisted over long periods of time (e.g., Jones 1984; Hajnal 1982); for example, most Western and Northern European countries have long been characterized by late and not universal marriage, setting up of a new household by the couple, and the economic and social acceptance of single women and men (usually living with their married siblings or in service); in contrast, marriage ages have been very low, marriage universal, and women's control over marriage and reproductive decisions very limited in many South Asian, Middle Eastern, and some African settings, although great difference existed in the precise organization of marriages and organization of reproduction (see also the chapter by Guirkinger and Platteau in this volume). These latter regimes were more favorable to high fertility rates and a strong emphasis on women to focus on reproduction. This fertility dynamics has had an important effect on the long-term economic performance of countries, particularly by affecting the timing of the demographic transition (e.g., Galor and Weil 2000). The gender dynamics underlying this has been found to be a key driver of this economic performance (e.g., Lagerlöf 2003). And, of course, the stability and strength of these social institutions governing families and fertility will then play a role in how policy can affect, for example, fertility and early marriage.[1]

The norms and institutions governing women's reproductive roles (as well as other care and home production activities) circumscribe the opportunities women have to be involved in production (i.e., the part picked up by GNI, such as producing goods or services for/in the market or producing goods for self-consumption in the household). Mainly this is mediated via the time constraint. If women are burdened with care and home production, related also to high fertility, their ability to be involved in production is seriously constrained to activities that can be combined with these domestic responsibilities such as self-employment in agriculture (as is common in Sub-Saharan Africa). Of course, the time constraint is not the only constraint to women's productive activities; in addition, social norms governing the acceptability of women's involvement in productive activities as well as their access to education and to means of production can be additional powerful constraints (e.g., OECD 2015; World Bank 2011; Klasen and Pieters 2015). For example, there is a strong, robust, and well-documented linkage between female education and fertility, with better-educated women having fewer children (e.g., Murthi, Guio, and Drèze 1995; Summers 1994). At the same time, other economic and social institutions can also affect this relationship between female education and fertility. As shown in figure 14.1, the linkage is stronger in South Asia and the Middle East than in Sub-Saharan Africa (particularly West and East Africa) where fertility levels are higher and are less affected by female education.

In turn, as discussed in detail below, women's involvement in production will have a direct and important impact on economic performance (e.g., Teignier and Cuberes 2015; Klasen and Lamanna 2009), so that the social institutions circumscribing women's productive activities are a first-order issue of how institutions can affect economic performance.

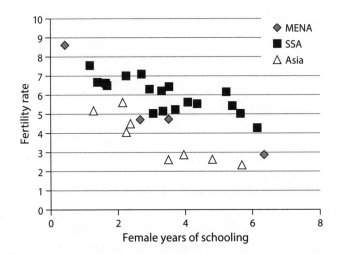

FIGURE 14.1. Female years of schooling and the total fertility rate. *Note*: The figure plots total years of schooling of women aged 15+ and the total fertility rate in 15 countries in Sub-Saharan Africa (SSA), the Middle East, and North Africa (MENA), and South and South-Eastern Asia (Asia) in 1990 and 2010. *Source*: Barro and Lee (2013) and World Development Indicators.

At the same time, one needs to recognize that, from a normative point of view, the welfare consequences or different arrangements governing production and reproduction are not necessarily obvious. It may be the case that a certain social arrangement that strongly limits women's productive roles is detrimental for economic performance and for gender equity, but may be consistent with expressed gendered preferences and existing norms accepted by men and women (see Klasen 2016). The case for institutional change to promote gender equity and economic performance may then not be as straightforward. One argument could be Sen's distinction between well-being and agency, suggesting that there would be a case for institutional change if it furthers "objectively" measured well-being, even if women as agents are not in favor of such changes (Sen 1990). A second can be the poltiticization and public discussion of such unequal gendered institutions as a prelude to promoting institutional change; in many countries, such discussions are taking place. Third, it can often be the case that women view existing institutional arrangements as excessively constraining, even if they do not question unequal gender roles overall. Last, norms and values governing gender roles do change over time and may thus change the normative assessment of unequal gender institutions. For example, the acceptability of domestic violence is receding over time in developing countries (see World Bank 2014) and so are stated preferences for males to be given preference in education or the labor market when jobs are scarce (World Bank 2011).

To conclude, gender differentials in social institutions are critical for economic performance and gender equity, even if the case for institutional change has to be weighed carefully from a normative perspective. It is now important to study how social institutions affecting gender vary across space and time, a subject to which I now turn.

In principle, it is challenging to "measure" the extent of gender inequality in social institutions, since many informal institutions and norms cannot be easily quantified, let alone compared and aggregated. At the same time, databases now exist that have

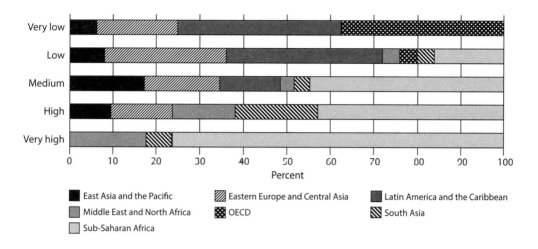

FIGURE 14.2. Gender inequality in social institutions. *Source*: OECD (2015).

attempted to quantify central institutional features that deal with gender. Two of them, the Cingarella-Richardsen (CIRI) database, as well as the World Bank's Women and the Law Database (Cingarella, Richardson, and Clay 2014; Hallward-Driemeier et al. 2013a) provide expert judgments on gender inequality in rights in various domains, thus focusing more on formal institutions governing gender relations. They have the advantage of a clear focus and provide comparable data over many years.[2] A broader database is the OECD's Gender and Social Institutions Database and the Social Institutions and Gender Index built on it (Branisa et al. 2014; OECD 2015). For our purposes, this broader approach is particularly useful as it considers gender inequality in formal and informal social institutions pertaining to five central domains: family code, civil liberties, physical integrity, son preference, and access to assets and resources. Within each of those domains, gender inequality in particular indicators is measured. For example, within the domain family code, gender inequality in the legal age and the prevalence of early marriage, gender inequality in rights regarding own children and inheritance are measured. This information is available in three (not fully comparable) cross-sections covering roughly the periods 2000, 2005, and 2010 (OECD 2015). Figure 14.2, based on the 2014 version of the SIGI, shows that there are considerable regional differences in gender inequality in social institutions. In particular, a large share of countries from the Middle East and North Africa, South Asia, and Sub-Saharan Africa have high or very high (average) gender inequality in social institutions. Interestingly, however, there is substantial variation within regions, with all three regions also containing countries where gender inequality in social institutions is very low.

Figure 14.3 shows that the type of gender inequality in social institutions also differs between the three regions. While in the Middle East and North Africa, discriminatory family code, restricted civil liberties, and resource access are a particular problem, in South Asia, discriminatory family code, son bias, and restricted resource access are the most serious inequalities. In Sub-Saharan Africa, restricted physical integrity, discriminatory family code, and restricted resource access are the most pressing issues. So both intensity and type of inequality differ by region. And, as already apparent from figure 14.2,

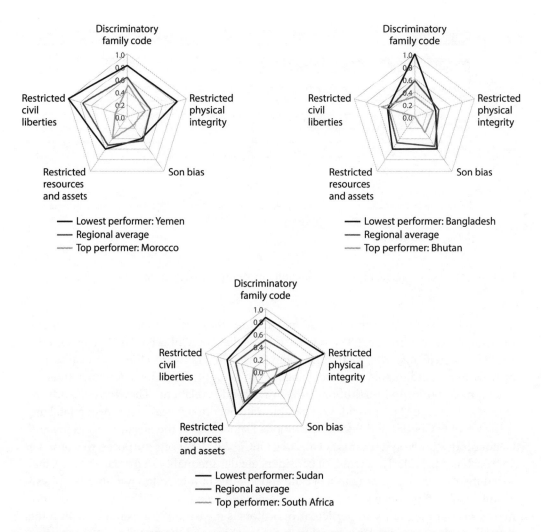

FIGURE 14.3. Gender inequality in social institutions by region (Middle East, South Asia, and Sub-Saharan Africa).

the diversity within regions is substantial, suggesting that these issues are not only related to religious and cultural issues of particular regions.

There is a literature that has demonstrated that these inequalities in social institutions are also associated with other gendered development outcomes, including female education levels, fertility levels, child mortality and, interestingly, the level of corruption (Branisa et al. 2013; and Klasen 2018a). These are of course directly relevant for women's well-being but indirectly affect overall economic performance. And indeed there is also evidence that gender gaps in these institutions are also directly associated with lower economic growth (Ferrant and Kolev 2016). We will revisit these impacts in more detail in the next section.

At the same time, it is important to point out that gender inequality in social institutions has a more complex relationship with women's economic roles, in particular their participation in production. While gender inequality in social institutions goes hand-in-hand with reduced economic opportunities for women in the Middle East and South Asia, Sub-Saharan Africa is the great outlier here, where gender inequality in social institutions is substantial, while women's labor force participation rates are nevertheless quite high. This is related to women's high participation rates in subsistence agriculture, which appears to be related to long-standing differences in the nature of African agriculture and the role women play in it (Boserup 1970; Klasen 2018b).[3]

In fact, when studying women's economic roles, long-standing regional differences in economic opportunities and conditions appear to play a role, and a recent literature has investigated these historical drivers of gender roles more closely, where social institutions such as norms play a mediating role. Inspired by the work of Boserup (1970), Alesina, Giuliano, and Nunn (2013) test the hypothesis that suitability of plow agriculture was inimical to women's economic roles as it required greater male strength to operate them. Hansen, Jensen, and Skovsgaard (2014) suggest instead that a longer time since the Neolithic revolution caused women's more restricted roles, with fertility levels and crop type being key transmission channels. Similarly, Hazarika, Jha, and Sarangi (2015) argue that historical resource scarcity, as well as low land availability, circumscribed women's economic roles. Last, Santos-Silva et al. (2017) argue that access to cool water and year-round water availability is associated with greater gender equity in education, health, and employment today, with decentralized family-oriented agriculture and, due to better health conditions, late and more autonomous and egalitarian marriages being key transmission channels (see also the chapter by Guirkinger and Platteau in this volume). Even to the extent that these underlying geographic or agronomic causes are no longer relevant today, norms regarding gender equality and women's economic roles have strong persistence and are being re-created and transmitted in successive generations and even persist when migrating. As shown by the work of Fernandez and Fogli (2009) and Fernandez (2011), one can identify distinct gendered patterns of behavior regarding women's economic and social roles among immigrant communities in the United States that are related to social norms in their countries of origin.

To conclude this section, social institutions relating to gender set parameters for the interplay between production and reproduction and particularly affect women's economic and social opportunities and constraints. There is great regional heterogeneity in these social institutions regarding gender, also by dimension considered. These social institutions affect women's economic and social roles, their fertility, and education levels. And they are the outcome of long-standing historical developments with considerable persistence. We now need to investigate more closely how these gender gaps affect economic performance, to which we now turn.

14.3. GENDER GAPS AND ECONOMIC PERFORMANCE

A number of theoretical and empirical studies have examined the impact of gender inequality on economic performance, particularly focusing on the impact of gender inequality in education, employment, and earnings on aggregate economic performance. I will briefly summarize the most important insights here.[4]

There are three arguments that suggest that particular gender gaps could actually promote economic performance. The first goes back to Becker (1981), essentially arguing that there are (static) efficiency gains to a sexual division of labor where each gender specializes in the tasks where they have a comparative advantage, which Becker sees for women in home production (due to the complementarity of child-bearing and child-rearing). Whatever the merits of the argument, it is likely to become less relevant as fertility declines and household production becomes less time-consuming. A second argument was recently made by Tertilt and Doepke (2014) who argue that higher women's earnings or transfers might actually reduce growth, as it might reduce investment in physical capital or land (though this would not hold if human capital was relatively more important). A third argument relates to the role of pay gaps, in association with low gender gaps in education and earnings (see below). As suggested by Seguino (2000a), high gender pay gaps might become a competitive advantage for countries, particularly in export-oriented manufacturing (and associated FDI to develop the sector). We will return to this argument below.

On the other hand, there are a substantial number of papers arguing the reverse, i.e., that gender gaps reduce economic performance. Regarding gender inequality in education, the theoretical literature suggests as a first argument that such gender inequality reduces the average amount of human capital in a society and thus harms economic performance. It does so by artificially restricting the pool of talent from which to draw for education and thereby excluding highly qualified girls (and taking less qualified boys instead, e.g., Dollar and Gatti 1999; Teignier and Cuberes 2015). Moreover, if there are declining marginal returns to education, restricting the education of girls to lower levels while taking the education of boys to higher levels means that the marginal return to educating girls is higher than that of boys and thus would boost overall economic performance; this effect would be exacerbated if males and females are imperfect substitutes (World Bank 2001; Knowles et al. 2002).

A second argument relates to externalities of female education. Promoting female education is known to reduce fertility levels, reduce child mortality levels, and promote the education of the next generation. Each factor in turn has a positive impact on economic growth (World Bank 2001; King, Klasen, and Porter 2009). The strong linkage of female education to fertility was already discussed above, showing also that there are regional differences in its influence (see figure 14.1). Some models emphasize that there is a potential of vicious cycles with larger gender gaps in education or pay reproducing themselves across generations leading to low-income poverty traps (e.g., Galor and Weil 1996; Lagerlöf 2003). But there is also an important timing issue involved here. Reducing gender gaps in education will lead to reduced fertility levels which will, after some 20 years, lead to a favorable demographic constellation which Bloom and Williamson (1998) refer to as a "demographic gift." For a period of several decades, the working-age population will grow much faster than overall population, thus lowering dependency rates with positive repercussions for per capita economic growth.[5]

A third argument relates to international competitiveness and complements the argument made by Seguino (2000a) above. Many East Asian countries have been able to be competitive on world markets through the use of female-intensive export-oriented manufacturing industries, a strategy that is now finding followers in South Asia (particularly Bangladesh) and individual countries across the developing world (e.g., Seguino, 2000a, 2000b). In order for such competitive export industries to emerge and grow, women need to be educated, and there must be no barrier to their employment in such sectors. Gender inequality in education and employment would reduce the ability of countries to capitalize on these opportunities (World Bank 2001; Busse and Spielmann 2006).

Regarding gender gaps in employment, there are a number of closely related arguments. First, there is a similar argument that it imposes a distortion on the economy, as do gender gaps in education. It artificially reduces the pool of talent from which employers can draw, thereby reducing the average ability of the workforce (e.g., Esteve-Volart 2009; Teignier and Cuberes 2015). Such distortions would not only affect employees, but similar arguments could be made for the self-employed in agricultural and non-agricultural sectors where unequal access to critical inputs, technologies, and resources would reduce the average productivity of these ventures, thereby reducing economic growth (see Blackden et al. 2007). As self-employment (including in agriculture) is included in our empirical assessment, these arguments might have some empirical relevance in accounting for the results.

A second, closely related argument suggests that gender inequality in employment can reduce economic growth via demographic effects. A model by Cavalcanti and Tavares (2007) suggests that gender inequality in employment would be associated with higher fertility levels which in turn reduce economic growth.

Third, the results by Seguino (2000a, 2000b) on the impact of gender gaps in pay on international competitiveness imply that gender gaps in employment access would also reduce economic growth as it would deprive countries the use of (relatively cheap) female labor as a competitive advantage in an export-oriented growth strategy.

A fourth argument relates to the importance of female employment and earnings for their bargaining power within families and makes the converse claim to Tertilt and Doepke (2014) discussed above. There is a sizable literature that demonstrates that female employment and earnings increase their bargaining power in the home (e.g., Sen 1990; Thomas 1997; Haddad, Hoddinott, and Alderman 1997; World Bank 2001; Klasen and Wink 2003; King, Klasen, and Porter 2009). This not only benefits the women concerned, but their greater bargaining power can have a range of growth-enhancing effects. These could include higher savings as women and men differ in their savings behavior (e.g., Seguino and Floro 2003), more productive investments and use and repayment of credit (see Stotsky 2006), and higher investments in the health and education of their children, thus promoting human capital of the next generation and therefore economic growth (e.g., Thomas 1997; World Bank 2001).

A fifth argument relates to governance. There is a growing but still rather speculative and suggestive literature that has collected evidence that women workers, on average, appear to be less prone to corruption and nepotism than men (World Bank 2001; Swamy et al. 2001; Branisa et al. 2013).[6] If these findings prove to be robust, greater female employment might be beneficial for economic performance in this sense as well.[7]

There is a related theoretical literature that examines the impact of gender discrimination in pay on economic performance. Here the theoretical literature is quite divided. On the one hand, studies by Galor and Weil (1996) and Cavalcanti and Tavares (2007) suggest that large gender pay gaps will reduce economic growth. Such gender pay gaps reduce female employment, which in turn increases fertility and lowers economic growth through these participation and demographic effects. In contrast, Blecker and Seguino (2002) highlight a different mechanism, leading to contrasting results. They suggest that high gender pay gaps and associated low female wages increase the competitiveness of export-oriented industrializing economies and thus boost the growth performance of these countries. The most important difference of this study, in contrast to the models considered above, is that it is focusing more on short-term demand-induced growth effects, while the other models are long-term growth models where growth is driven by supply constraints. Clearly, both effects can be relevant, depending on the time horizon considered.

It is important to point out that it is theoretically not easy to separate the effects between gender gaps in education, employment, and pay. In fact, in most of the models considered above, gender gaps in one dimension tend to lead to gender gaps in other dimensions, with the causality running in both directions.[8] For example, gender gaps in education might automatically lead to gender gaps in employment, particularly in the formal sector, where employers will prefer educated workers and will not consider applications of uneducated women. Conversely, if there are large barriers to female employment or gender gaps in pay, rational parents (and girls) might decide that education of girls is not as lucrative, which might therefore lead to lower demands for female education and resulting gender gaps in education.[9] Thus, gender gaps in education and employment are closely related to each other.[10]

They are not measuring the same thing, however, and thus are important to investigate separately. For one, it might be the case that the two issues are largely driven by institutional factors that govern education and employment access and do not therefore greatly depend on each other. For example, one might think of an education policy that strives to achieve universal education and thus reduces gender gaps, while there continue to be significant barriers to employment for females in the labor market. This might be particularly relevant to the situation in the Middle East and North Africa, but most recently also for South Asia, where education gaps have narrowed but employment gaps remain wide (see Gaddis and Klasen 2014; Klasen and Pieters 2015). Moreover, the externalities of female education and female employment are not all the same. For example, female education is likely to lead to lower fertility and child mortality of the offspring, while the effect of female employment on this is likely to be much smaller and more indirect (working mainly through greater female bargaining power; and there may also be opposite effects, including that the absence of women in the home might in some cases negatively impact the quality of child care). Conversely, the governance externality applies solely to female employment, not to female education.

There is also some literature examining the impact of gender gaps in political empowerment on economic outcomes. That literature is mainly focused on the impact female politicians, due to their different preferences to men, can have on the provision of public goods with repercussions on development outcomes (e.g., Duflo 2012).

Given these many, and partly conflicting, arguments, it essentially becomes an empirical question to investigate these effects. A particularly large literature has developed that examines the impact of gender gaps in education on economic performance. Most of that literature relies on cross-country cross-section and panel regressions, while some studies have used subnational data or time series techniques for single countries. An early study by Barro and Lee (1994) pointed to a negative effect of female education on growth (while male education had a positive effect). Further scrutiny of these results showed that they were related to the use of initial-year schooling variables (in a pure cross-section), the failure to control for unmeasured regional effects, and multicollinearity among the education variables (see Lorgelly and Owen 1999; Klasen 2002).

Most subsequent studies point to a negative effect of gender gaps. For example, King and Hill (1993) as well as Knowles et al. (2002) use a Solow-growth framework and find that gender gaps in education significantly reduce the level of GDP. Dollar and Gatti (1999), Forbes (2000), Yamarik and Ghosh (2003), Appiah and McMahon (2002), and Klasen (2002) investigate the impact of gender gaps on economic growth, and all find that gender gaps in education have a negative impact on subsequent economic growth. By now some 55 studies have investigated the impact of gender gaps on economic growth (or levels of GDP per capita), 35 of which use cross-country data, and the others relying on subnational and single-country time series data. Of course, the quality of the econometric approach differs and ranges from simple correlation analyses with few covariates to fixed effects panel models with a large set of control variables and IV techniques to control for endogeneity. As discussed in a systematic review and meta-analysis of these studies by Minasyan et al. (2018), studies using male and female education as separate covariates show a larger effect of female than male education on growth, except when an arguably problematic regression specification popularized by Barro is used. A meta-regression analysis of studies using the female-male ratio in education shows that, on average, it is positively associated with economic growth, including in most of the studies with the greatest econometric rigor. Based on this assessment, the balance of evidence clearly favors the view that gender inequality in education appears to lead to lower economic growth.

There are many fewer empirical studies on the impact of gender gaps in employment and pay on economic growth. A recent study by Teignier and Cuberes (2015) is based on calibrating a macro-model to data from different regions showing that gender gaps in labor force participation can lead to particularly large growth penalties in the Middle East and North Africa, as well as South Asia. There are few econometric studies that are largely related to data and econometric issues discussed above. Klasen (1999) found that increases in female labor force participation and formal sector employment were associated with higher growth in a cross-country context. Differences in female participation and employment are estimated to have accounted for another 0.3 percentage points in the growth difference between the MENA region and East Asia and the Pacific (EAP). But these findings have to be treated with caution as they may suffer from reverse causality. In particular, it might be the case that high growth draws women into the labor force (rather than increasing female participation promoting economic growth).[11] There are no easy ways to correct for this econometrically as there are unlikely to be valid instruments that can be used. Also, there are questions about the international comparability of data on labor force participation and formal sector employment rates (see Gaddis and Klasen 2014). To the extent that the problems of comparability affect levels but not trends over time, these problems might be avoided in a fixed-effects panel setting. Last, there is the question of collinearity between gender gaps in education and employment which can lead to misleading conclusions. In regressions that only consider the effect of gender gaps in education, they might implicitly also measure the impacts of gender gaps in employment, particularly if the two are highly correlated. So the robust effect discussed above of educational gender gaps may be partly mediated by affecting gender gaps in employment.

At the same time, such a high correlation between education and employment gaps might also make it difficult to separately identify the effects when both are included in a regression (due to the multicollinearity problem). Also, it will be difficult to assess which of the two is the causal driver of the other, given the close and plausible theoretical and empirical linkage.

Klasen and Lamanna (2009) study the impact of initial gender gaps in education and labor force participation on subsequent growth using a cross-country fixed-effects panel framework. They find that both gender gaps in education and labor force participation negatively affect growth, although the results are not always significant when both variables are included, presumably due to multicollinearity. In reduced samples that focus on particular regions, however, the results are significant and estimate growth costs of gender gaps that are particularly sizable in South Asia and the Middle East. In the Middle East, the employment gaps are more important for growth than the education gaps, while in South Asia the reverse is the case. In this sense as well as in the estimated magnitudes, they are highly consistent with Teignier and Cuberes (2015).

At the subnational level, Berta Esteve-Volart has found significant negative effects of gender gaps in employment and managerial positions on economic growth of India's states using panel data and controlling for endogeneity by using instrumental variables (Esteve-Volart 2009).

Some papers by Seguino (2000a, 2000b) support the contention that the combination of low gender gaps in education and employment with large gender gaps in pay (and resulting low female wages) were a contributing factor to the growth experience of export-oriented middle-income countries. Supporting this empirical claim is a paper by Busse and Spielmann (2006) which finds for a sample of 23 developing countries that a combination of low gender gaps in education and employment and large gender gaps in pay helped promote exports. Unfortunately, the analysis is based on a small sample of semi-industrialized countries, and the measures of gender wage gaps are rather crude; in fact, Schober and Winter-Ebmer (2011) show that the results disappear or even reverse if arguably more robust measures of gender wage gaps are used, so that these findings cannot be considered robust at this stage.[12]

The literature has also examined the impact of other gaps on economic outcomes. In particular, papers by Chatthopadyay and Duflo (2004), Bhalotra and Clots-Figueras (2014), and Duflo (2012), have found evidence that women's political empowerment promotes the provision of public goods, better human capital, and lower child mortality. These outcomes are, of course, valuable in and of themselves, but also have an indirect impact on growth. While some of these effects have turned out to be sizable, Duflo (2012) argues that they only have a relatively limited impact on overall economic development. This conclusion is challenged by King, Klasen, and Porter (2009), who produce simulation results that women's political empowerment can have sizable development impacts through its effect on income growth as well as mortality reduction.

There is also a sizeable literature that has examined the impact of unearned incomes, credit, or targeted transfers for women on household expenditures, health, and education outcomes. The overwhelming finding of many studies is that the effect of such monies brought in by women has a larger impact on household expenditures, health, and education outcomes than those brought by men (e.g., Pitt and Khandker 1998; Pitt, Khandker, and Cartwright 2006; Thomas 1990, 1997; World Bank 2001, 2011). Simulations by

King, Klasen, and Porter (2009) show that the effect of such interventions to increase women's incomes on economic performance as well as reduced mortality can be sizeable.

While all this literature has studied the impact of educational and economic gender gaps on overall economic performance, these gaps are, as discussed above, related to deeper institutional and legal gender gaps. In fact, papers by Branisa et al. (2013, 2014) and Yoon and Klasen (2018) have shown that social institutions related to gender are indeed important drivers of female education, fertility, and child mortality. Similarly, Hallward-Driemeier et al. (2013b) provide evidence that reducing legal gender gaps is associated with higher rates of female education, employment, as well as higher marriage ages, although the effects appear to be smaller in poorer countries.

An emerging literature has also examined whether these gender gaps in social institutions as well as gender gaps in laws also can be linked to worse economic performance. Ferrant and Kolev (2016) show that higher gender inequality in social institutions is associated with worse growth outcomes, over and above the effect this has on educational and labor force gaps.

In sum, there is considerable theoretical support for the notion that gender gaps in education and employment are likely to reduce economic performance (while the literature on the effect of gender gaps in pay is more divided). The empirical results also point rather robustly to negative effects of gender gaps in education, but there is less evidence on gender gaps in employment, although most existing studies suggest the effects are negative as well. Last, there is evidence that reducing gender gaps in political participation, laws, social institutions as well as increasing resources to women can promote income, health, and education outcomes (see also Klasen 2018a).

It is important to point out that showing the inefficiency of (most) of these gender gaps does not imply that there will be automatic processes (facilitated by markets or political economy) that will reduce these inefficiencies. As discussed extensively in the literature (e.g., Hill and King 1995; King, Klasen, and Porter 2009; Duflo 2012), inefficient arrangements can persist and reproduce themselves. Mechanisms that ensure persistent inefficient arrangements include externalities that drive a wedge between private and socially optimal behavior (e.g., it may be socially valuable for parents to educate daughters as much as sons, but in settings where the daughter leaves the household upon marriage while the son stays, the private incentive is to prefer the education of sons), or there may be self-reproducing norms that maintain such gaps, or questions of power and control might militate against reducing some gaps. As a result, it is important to understand what drives changes in gender gaps as these are not passing phenomena that self-correct. Before examining drivers of change, we need to first understand how these different gaps have developed over time, to which we turn now.

14.4. HETEROGENEOUS TRENDS IN GENDER GAPS IN DEVELOPING COUNTRIES

When examining the world in 1960, gender gaps in many social, economic, and political dimensions were ubiquitous and not confined to developing countries. Since then, many gaps have been sharply reduced in the developed world (especially regarding rights, education, political participation, and economic participation). In developing countries, gender gaps have also generally moved only in one direction (becoming smaller), yet the pace of change has been much more heterogeneous by region, but even more so by dimension. In fact, as I will show below, there appear to be three velocities of reducing gaps: fast in the case of education and rights, moderate in the case of economic and po-litical participation as well as health, and slow to very slow in the case of occupational and sectoral segregation and issues of violence within households (including domestic violence and female genital mutilation). In this section I will document these trends by region. While the change has been in one direction so far, it is not guaranteed that this will continue in the future. In particular, there are possibilities of backlash against the closing of some of these gaps, a subject to which I will return at the end of the next section.

The fastest pace of reduction in gaps has been in the fields of (formal) rights and edu-cation. Focusing first on education, figure 14.4 shows the dramatic narrowing of gender gaps in educational enrollments at primary, secondary, and tertiary levels.

As can be seen, gender gaps in gross primary enrollment rates have nearly entirely disappeared. Small gaps remain in Sub-Saharan Africa and the Middle East, but if the trend continues they are likely to have mostly disappeared by now. In secondary enroll-ments, the gender gaps have also shrunk dramatically. Again, Sub-Saharan Africa is lag-ging behind, presumably due to the somewhat slower pace of educational expansion there in recent years compared to other regions. Maybe most surprising is that, with the exception of South Asia and Sub-Saharan Africa, gender gaps in tertiary gross enroll-ment rates now favor females, in some regions with a sizable margin. Educational achievement indicators, such as total years of schooling, show similar progress, with an expected delay (Barro and Lee 2013; see also Abu-Ghaida and Klasen 2004). It is also no-ticeable that the elimination of gender gaps in educational enrollments have led in short order to the elimination in gender gaps in educational achievement, such as test scores. Figure 14.5 in fact shows that girls regularly outperform boys in literacy skills, and while they lag boys in mathematics, the difference is much smaller and not universal. Thus it appears that "all" that was missing to ensure gender equality in educational outcomes was to ensure that girls and women got equal chances to go to school. Once they get the chance to participate and stay in school, gender gaps in outcomes disappear.[13] In short, gender gaps in education are about to close everywhere, and, in some places, gender gaps hurting males are emerging.[14]

Similarly, there has been rapid progress in closing gender gaps in rights. As depicted in figure 14.6, progress is universal, across all regions and dimensions, but some inter-esting heterogeneities are noteworthy. Nearly all constitutions now include an equality principle, and an increasing share mention gender explicitly in that principle. Nearly all countries grant property rights to unmarried women, while many more (but far from all) extend these rights to married women. And in fewer countries, women are restricted in their independent legal capacity. As a result, the formal legal restrictions women face have been falling substantially across all regions, but progress has been slowest in Sub-Saharan Africa. This pertains to formal statutory law. In many countries, however, cus-tomary law continues to be recognized, particularly in areas relating to the family, so that the reality of women's rights may look worse in societies where customary law plays an important role (Hallward-Driemeier et al. 2013a, 2013b).

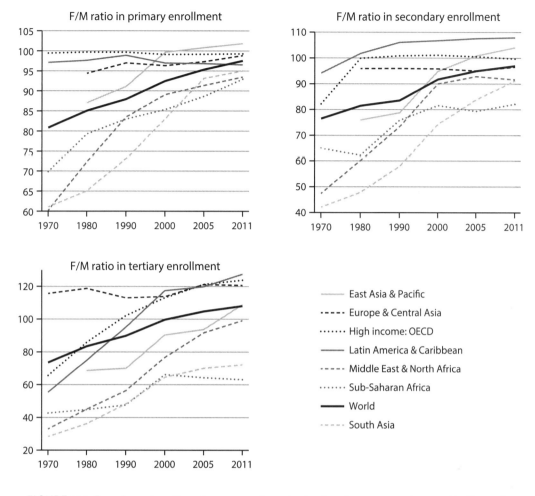

FIGURE 14.4. Female-male ratios of gross enrollment rates in primary, secondary, and tertiary education, by region. *Source*: World Development Indicators.

Progress has been substantially slower in the case of health, labor force participation, political participation, and time use. Gender gaps in health have been referred to in the literature as the so-called missing women issue (Sen 1989; Klasen 1994). This referred to the lower than expected sex ratios (males/females) in some parts of the developing world, most notably South Asia, China, the Middle East, and North Africa. As many studies have shown, this shortage of females is linked to excess female mortality, both pre- and post-birth (e.g., Banister and Coale 1994; Klasen and Wink 2002, 2003). As shown in detail in Klasen and Wink (2002, 2003) and Kahlert (2014), gender bias in mortality has been falling in the regions most affected by it. But progress has been quite slow in some regions, including India, and in fact, has worsened in some, including China from 1990 to 2000, as shown in table 14.1. There has also been at least a temporary worsening of gender bias in mortality associated with HIV/AIDS where (young) women in Sub-Saharan Africa have suffered disproportionately (see the example of Botswana in figure 14.7).[15]

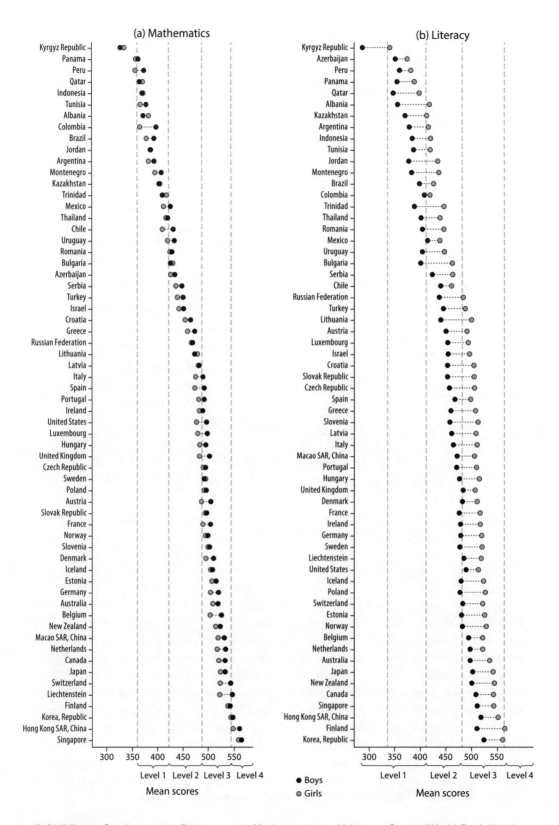

FIGURE 14.5. Gender gaps in Pisa scores in Mathematics and Literacy. *Source*: World Bank (2011).

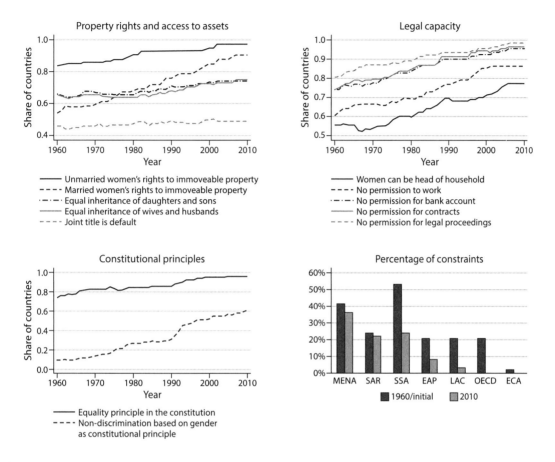

FIGURE 14.6. Gender gaps in rights, trends, and regional differences. *Source*: Hallward-Driemeier et al. (2013a, 2013b).

Similarly, gender gaps in labor force participation have also narrowed in many regions, but rather slowly and again with great regional heterogeneity, as shown in figure 14.8 (see also Klasen 2018b). Several points are noteworthy here. First, as already discussed above, female labor force participation has been high in East Asia, Sub-Saharan Africa, Eastern Europe, and Central Asia, as well as OECD countries, while it has been much lower in Latin America, South Asia, and the Middle East (in that order); this is closely related to the "deep drivers" debate I mentioned above. Second, while there has been a rapid expansion of female economic participation in Latin America and OECD countries, the pace of expansion in the Middle East and South Asia has been much slower, despite their lower initial levels. In fact, in India, there has been no increase at all in female labor force participation rates in urban areas, and in rural areas, participation has fallen (Klasen and Pieters 2015). And this is despite the fact that educational gender gaps have been declining rapidly in those regions, as has fertility, both of which should promote greater female economic participation.

This is also closely related to very slow progress in reducing gender gaps in time spent in household production. Even in places where women have entered the labor force in large numbers, there has been no commensurate reallocation of time use on childcare,

Table 14.1. Missing Women in 1990 and 2000

	(1) Number of Women	(2) Expected Sex Ratio	Around 2000			Around 1990	
			(3) Expected Number of Women	(4) 'Missing' Women	(5) Share Missing	(6) 'Missing Women'	(7) Share Missing
China	612.3	1.001	653.2	40.9	6.7%	34.6	6.3%
Taiwan	10.8	1.002	11.3	0.5	4.7%	0.7	7.3%
South Korea	22.2	1.000	22.4	0.2	0.7%	-0.0	-0.1%
India	495.7	0.993	534.8	39.1	7.9%	38.4	9.4%
Pakistan	62.7	1.003	67.6	4.9	7.8%	4.3	10.8%
Bangladesh	63.4	0.996	66.1	2.7	4.2%	3.8	8.9%
Nepal	11.6	0.992	11.7	0.1	0.5%	0.6	7.7%
Sri Lanka	8.6	1.006	8.6	0.0	0.0%	0.3	3.4%
West Asia	92.0	1.002	95.8	3.8	4.2%	3.9	7.1%
Of which: Turkey	27.9	1.003	28.5	0.7	2.4%	0.8	3.2%
Syria	6.7	1.016	6.9	0.2	3.1%	0.4	5.0%
Afghanistan	11.1	0.964	12.1	1.0	9.3%	0.6	9.7%
Iran	29.5	0.996	30.6	1.1	3.7%	1.1	4.5%
Egypt	29.0	1.003	30.3	1.3	4.5%	1.2	5.1%
Algeria	14.5	1.005	14.7	0.2	1.2%	0.3	2.7%
Tunisia	4.3	1.000	4.4	0.1	2.1%	0.2	4.5%
Sub-Saharan Africa	307.0	0.970	312.5	5.5	1.8%	4.9	1.9%
World	1774.8			101.3	5.7%	94.7	6.5%

Source: Klasen and Wink (2002, 2003).

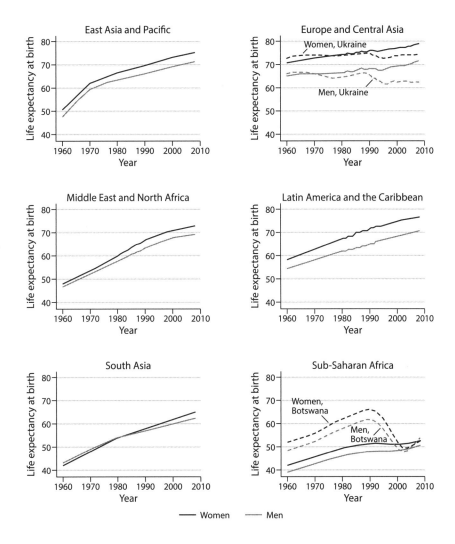

FIGURE 14.7. Gender gaps in life expectancy. *Source*: World Bank (2011).

other care, and housework activities to which women continue to devote substantially more time than men (World Bank 2011).

Last, gender gaps in political participation have also fallen only slightly and remain very large in many parts of the developing world, as shown in figure 14.9 for the case of female parliamentary representation. Noteworthy is that the trends in all regions (with the exception of East Asia and the Pacific, which is heavily dominated by China) have been rather uniform and steadily increasing. Of particular interest is the development in transition countries. During socialist times, parliaments had little say and female representation was high. In the transition process, freely elected parliaments have become more powerful and the female share initially fell strongly (see also Klasen 1993).

There is a last category of gender gaps where it appears that there has been no progress whatsoever over the past 40–50 years, although the database for such an assessment is not strong. Two gender gaps related to labor are the unexplained gender wage

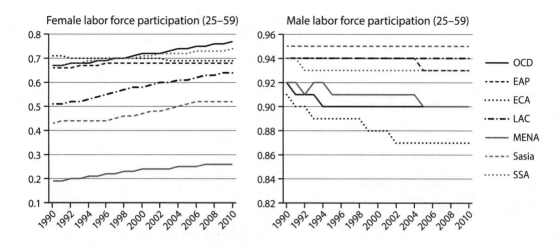

FIGURE 14.8. Gender gaps in labor force participation by region. *Source*: ILO (2011).

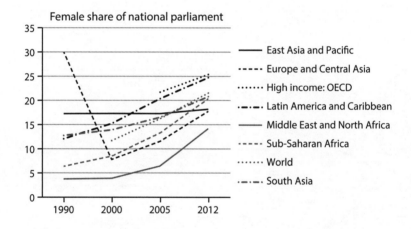

FIGURE 14.9. Female representation in national parliaments. *Source*: World Development Indicators.

gap and occupational and sectoral segregation by gender. While the decline in human capital differences has led to a smaller overall gender wage gap and, in an increasing number of countries, to the complete elimination of the explained gender wage gap, the unexplained portion, which is closely related to occupational and sectoral differences among genders as well as pay discrimination and other unmeasured gender differentials, has remained largely unchanged, as shown in figure 14.10 from Weichselbäumer and Winter-Ebmer (2005). Given this, it is not surprising that occupational and sectoral segregation has also not changed over time and, interestingly, does not appear to change as countries get richer and more women join the labor force (World Bank 2011; Borrowman and Klasen 2017). It thus appears that as females enter the labor market, they often do so in proportion to the existing female shares in particular sectors and occupations, rather than by breaking into more male-dominated sectors and occupations. As a result, some sectors become heavily female-dominated (including personal services, education,

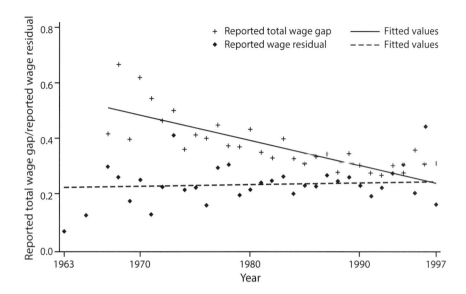

FIGURE 14.10. Explained and residual gender gap over time. *Source*: Weichselbäumer and Winter-Ebmer (2005).

health, and public sector) while others remain largely male-dominated (including construction, mining, and parts of manufacturing, IT services, etc.).

Other gendered issues which appear not to change very much relate to particular forms of violence against women, including domestic violence and female genital mutilation. While the data on those forms of violence against women is patchy and often not comparable across space and time, it appears that the incidence of both problems has not fallen over time (e.g., World Bank 2014), although a recent report by the World Bank suggests that the *acceptance* of domestic violence among women is falling slightly in developing countries (World Bank 2014).

This descriptive discussion suggests a bewildering diversity of trends in gender gaps along different dimensions. While there are few gender gaps that have actually gotten worse over time, the pace of improvement ranges from none to very fast by dimension, with substantial differences in speed across regions. In particular, while we have witnessed breathtaking progress in reducing gender gaps in education, there has been much less progress in other dimensions. This is surprising insofar as one would have expected that closing of this particularly important gap would contribute to eventually closing other gaps, but this has happened at most in part. It is therefore now important to make sense of these divergent trends by theorizing about the drivers of falling gender gaps across dimensions in developing countries. Much of this will be highly speculative, pointing to the urgent need to investigate the drivers of this differential performance more closely.

14.5. THEORIZING ABOUT DRIVERS OF CHANGE

Before considering different factors affecting gender gaps, a strong presumption ought to be that trends in gender gaps should be closely correlated, either because one gap promotes another, or because the same secular trends affect both gaps simultaneously. For example, it is hard to see how one can close the gender gap in formal sector pay without closing the gender gap in education and sectoral segregation. Similarly, a secular change that draws women into the labor force will raise their returns to schooling and should therefore reduce the gender gap in education as well. Or an anti-discrimination policy could affect several gaps at the same time. But as the descriptive section above showed, this has not happened to the extent expected, with gender gaps moving at different speeds in different dimensions and regions. Thus, we will now theorize about drivers of change for each of these gaps, noting the potential linkage between them.

In this, rather speculative, section, I will try to spell out some hypotheses that might account for the very heterogeneous nature of progress across dimensions of gender gaps, as well as across regions. While it surely is the case that there are unique factors that affect the development of a particular gender gap in a particular region, I will start with some broader hypotheses that might affect the pace of change.

A first group of factors that might affect the pace of change I would call structural economic factors. One of them is economic growth and development itself, which might have an immediate impact on a particular gender gap through several mechanisms. First, it may increase the resource base of households that reduce the need for rationing of scarce household resources on sons where son preference is prevalent, for example in the case of education and health. Second, such growth also tends to increase public resources that can be devoted to improving and lowering the private costs of education and health and improving access for all. As countries move toward universal access, the previously left-out girls and women can benefit disproportionately. Third, economic growth can increase the demand for greater female education and employment by raising labor demand for women, a point already made by Engels in 1884 (Engels 1884). It can also increase the demand for female education to improve their ability to participate in the economy or to increase the education of their children. Fourth, growth is often associated with rapid pace of technological change that can, among other things, lower the relative importance of physical strength relative to cognitive abilities and thus reduce the salience of the male advantage in physical strength (Galor and Weil 1996). Last, growth can be accompanied by structural change toward manufacturing and services, which can lead to disproportionate demand for female labor. To be sure, growth is unlikely to address all gender gaps. These effects are likely to be particularly relevant for gender gaps in education, health, and labor force participation, but less so in the case of time use, occupational segregation, political representation, and the like. Nor will all types of growth have the same effects. For example, growth based on resource extraction will not generate many of the effects discussed above.

A second structural economic factor is globalization. In particular, falling trade barriers and increasing trade have increased competition and sometimes put pressure on wages in previously protected and often male-dominated sectors. This has also led to a greater demand for flexibility and thus put pressure on previously stable and long-term male breadwinner employment models. As argued by Standing (1999), women can be the relative beneficiaries of this trend as they are more willing to work under flexible and worse-paid work arrangements (see also Braunstein 2012; Kis-Katos and Sparrow 2015; Gaddis and Pieters 2016). This would increase the demand for female education and labor force participation, particularly in those countries that are actively participating in global value chains and export manufactured goods and services.

A second group of factors I would call the scope for policy to affect gaps. Some gaps can be addressed relatively easily by a policy intervention, while other gaps are much harder to change. For example, the scope for changing laws that treat the two sexes unequally is high (if the political will is there). Such initiatives can then also be supported by international processes such as the ratification of conventions that demand equal treatment (including the CEDAW convention). Similarly, gender gaps in schooling can be reduced relatively easily through supply-side (e.g., building schools, equipping them better) as well as demand-side interventions (e.g., subsidies, conditional cash transfers), or even compulsory schooling mandates (when the conditions actually allow its enforcement). Increasing the share of women in parliaments can be done relatively easily in systems of proportional representation by mandating a share of party lists to be reserved for female candidates. In contrast, other gaps are much harder to influence directly by policy. Occupational choice can only be affected marginally through policy interventions (e.g., using role models, mentoring, etc.), and the scope for policy to affect time use in household production is also comparatively small. In fact, despite many efforts, particularly in developed countries, the success in equally sharing the care burden for children and elderly has been limited (Gehringer and Klasen 2017).

A third closely related group of factors relates to the policy attention a particular gap received in national and international policy debates. And here, clear differences exist. Gender gaps in rights have received considerable attention and are a great focus of the CEDAW convention, signed and ratified (with reservations) by nearly all countries of the world. In addition, a strong national and international advocacy community has supported ratification, implementation, and turning into national law of gender equality in rights. Similarly, gender gaps in education received great attention in national and international policy debates, both from people in the education field, as well as those from the gender field. Removing gender gaps in education were the key targets of the third MDG on gender equity, and there was strong donor support for addressing gender gaps. In contrast, policy attention was less in the fields of labor force participation, even less in occupational and sectoral segregation, and gender inequality in social institutions. Issues such as domestic violence or FGM have not generally enjoyed such a broad-based discussion and policy attention (although of course there are people working on all of these issues).

A fourth group of factors relates to the strength of gender norms in a particular dimension: the stronger the norms in a dimension, the harder it is to change gender gaps as it will also shape preferences of all parties concerned. The strength of gender norms of course differs by dimension across regions, and these norms are themselves affected by other factors. For example, women's employment outside of the home (including unaccompanied travel to and from work) is perfectly normal in some places and seen as deeply problematic in others, and this might differ by social status and change over the development process (Klasen 2018b). But one hypothesis regarding the gender norms across dimensions could be that gender norms tend to be stronger in areas that relate to regulating life in households and families. As a result, it is particularly difficult to change gender gaps that directly challenge gender norms within the household, including for example widespread norms allocating the primary care burden for children (and elderly) to women. So for example, it is then relatively easier to push for female education which does not, in principle, question this norm. But it would be harder to allow women to work outside of the home or to reshape time use within the home.[16]

A fifth group of factors relates to the roles of crises and shocks. Severe economic crises, wars, and other shocks can powerfully affect gender relations. They can pose opportunities and threats. One the one hand, they can question long-established norms, for example regarding the appropriate sexual division of labor. There is a literature that has demonstrated that wartime absence of men gave a push to increasing female labor force participation rates (e.g., Akbulut et al. 2011; Kreibaum and Klasen 2015), and postwar settlements offer opportunities to rewrite constitutions. At the same time, wars and crises can of course also be times to roll back changes, a subject to which I return briefly below.

Sixth, it may matter whether addressing the gender gap in question is perceived to be a zero-sum game or a win-win situation for both sexes. At the one extreme, increasing female representation in parliaments will necessarily reduce male representation. At the other extreme, increasing education for girls can be seen largely as a win-win situation. It will help girls and women, but also produce more educated wives and mothers, from which males will benefit in many ways. And, as discussed above, it has positive economic effects for all. Addressing many other gender gaps are in-between these extremes. Greater female employment, for example, can be seen to come at the expense of male employment, but it also provides additional household incomes which can be particularly critical if households are poor or incomes are uncertain.

Last, it is also important to discuss the roles and interests of men in sustaining or reducing gender gaps. Beyond the question of win-win versus zero-sum situations, it is important to point out that men may have divided interests, as argued by Doepke and Tertilt (2009) and Fernandez (2014). In particular, while they may want to do little to reduce gender gaps affecting women of their generation (including their spouses) as they benefit from the privileges they enjoy, they may be altruistic toward their daughters and will be more willing to accept and even support lower gender gaps in the next generation. The relative importance they place on enjoying privileges themselves versus ensuring high well-being for their daughters can then determine how much they will support or resist the reduction of gender gaps.[17]

With these hypotheses in mind, one can now speculate about the drivers of differential progress across dimensions of gender gaps (and, to a lesser extent, across regions). To be sure, this is really more the definition of a research agenda than actual findings.

Starting with the rapid closing of educational gender gaps, it appears that a range of favorable circumstances have come together. Economic growth enabled an expansion of education, bringing girls into the system. In addition, it turns out that a range of demand- and supply-side policies are quite effective at getting girls to school (e.g., World Bank 2001), there was a great policy attention on the issue in national and international circles, it is not strongly challenging existing gender norms about gender roles and sexual division of labor, gender norms have shifted substantially toward equal opportunities in education (see World Bank 2011), and (maybe also influenced by the studies mentioned above) promoting female education was seen as a win-win situation that promotes gender equity and overall economic development. It is then also not surprising that the largest gender schooling gaps remain in remote areas in very poor countries with relatively little growth, where the progress toward closing the gaps was commensurately slower.

Also, conflicts and crisis situations could also slow down progress or reverse gains, although not as much as one might have feared (e.g., Khan and Seltzer 2015).

Turning to gender gaps in rights, progress is likely to have been spurred by the relative ease through which such changes can be effected and the substantial policy attention devoted to it, also related to CEDAW and related UN conferences (see World Bank 2011; Hallward-Driemeier et al. 2013b). In addition, as shown by Hallward-Driemeier et al. (2013b), crises and dramatic political change has helped, particularly if it involved writing a new constitution which then tended to be much more gender-balanced in rights than previous versions. Similarly, as shown by World Bank (2011), popular support for equal rights, including among men, is quite high and rising. At the same time, of course, one has to be cautious when interpreting these changes. There might have been rapid progress in equality of rights on paper with few changes on the ground.[18]

Turning to the more slow-moving reductions in gender gaps, let me first discuss gender gaps in health. Here progress was facilitated by economic growth and rising household incomes that reduced the need to ration scarce household resources (e.g., Klasen and Wink 2003). Policy attention was quite substantial in the countries affected by it, but the levers for policy action are not as straight-forward, as effective action depends on effective primary healthcare services for all at little or no costs to the users (see World Bank 2003). In some countries, most notably China, policy action actually worsened gender bias in mortality as an unintended consequence of the strict one-child policy in a situation of remaining strong son preference (Klasen and Wink 2003). In addition, technological change limited progress in reducing the "missing women" problem as it facilitated, through the spread of ultrasound technologies, prenatal sex selection and associated sex-selective abortions, particularly in China and India (Banister and Coale 1994; Klasen and Wink 2003).

The factors affecting trends in labor force participation are also more varied than in the case of education (see also Klasen 2018b). First, the relationship between economic growth and female labor force participation is more complicated than commonly presumed. While there is some literature that claims that the relationship between incomes and labor force participation follows a U-shape, there is no strong empirical support for this claim (Gaddis and Klasen 2014). Instead, large country-differences in labor force participation, likely related to the deep drivers discussed above, are more important for the level of labor force participation than income levels are. At the country level, the relationship is also more complicated, as higher incomes might induce some poorer women to get out of (undesirable) employment while drawing more educated women into the labor force (e.g., Klasen and Pieters 2015). Different patterns of structural change are also likely to affect women's economic opportunities (Klasen 2018b). Policy clearly can play a role in boosting female participation. In particular, policies to improve the compatibility of female employment with having and raising children (e.g., through provision of affordable child care), or tax policies that encourage female participation have been found to affect female labor force participation (e.g., Klasen and Minasyan 2017; Gehringer and Klasen 2017). But nearly all of this evidence is from rich countries, and it is less clear whether it is easily transferable to developing countries where childcare arrangements are quite different and tax policies have limited reach. Thus, the lack of easily implementable policies may be one reason for the sluggish progress here.

On the other hand, there is some evidence that globalization and the opening up of economies has, *relative* to men, improved female labor force participation and lowered gender gaps (Kis-Katos and Sparrow 2015; Kis-Katos et al. 2018; Gaddis and Pieters 2017), supporting the notion that the working arrangements that come alongside greater international competition tend to relatively favor females who are more willing work under these arrangements (Standing 1999; Braunstein 2012). At the same time, trade liberalization has led to *absolute* gains to female participation in only a few countries and to losses in more countries (Kan and Klasen 2018). And, perversely, economic crises tend to boost female labor force participation as female labor force participation tends to be strongly countercyclical in developing countries (Bhalotra and Umaña-Aponte 2010).

Last, female labor force participation can more easily be seen as a zero-sum game, and pose more direct challenges to existing norms and beliefs about the appropriate gender roles and the associated desired sexual division of labor; it may particularly also challenge more deep-seated notions about the division of labor in the home. This can be considered particularly problematic when female earnings are not seen as strictly "necessary" to escape poverty. It is not surprising that norms about who should get jobs when they are scarce have only improved little and still show much greater support for a male preference than in the case of education (World Bank 2011).

As a result, it is not so surprising that the changes in gender gaps in labor force participation have generally been slower and more uneven across regions. For example, it is possible that progress in the Middle East has been slow due to slow growth and little structural change as well as strongly persistent norms regarding female employment, while in places such as India, higher growth and strong norms combine to reduce women's labor force participation at the low end of the education distribution (Klasen and Pieters 2015; Klasen 2018b).

Turning to gender gaps in political participation, progress has been helped by the relative ease with which such change can be enacted and the considerable policy attention it has received, including widely noted quota policies in many developing countries. Quotas are particularly easy to implement in systems of proportional representation, while first-past-the-post systems actually need to resort to reserving certain seats for women to be effective. Since gender gaps in political participation are still wide, and in many countries husbands or other male family members exercise influence over female elected leaders, it is unclear how far reductions in gaps go before they generate rising resistance due to their zero-sum nature.

It is also not surprising that progress in reallocating domestic care work has been very slow. There has been relatively little policy attention on this issue, it is hard for policy to influence this significantly, and it goes to the heart of gender norms that are particularly resistant to change as they focus on women's roles in reproduction and within the home.

Finally, among the areas with very little change, it is also not so surprising that progress has been largely absent in the case of occupational and sectoral segregation. While growth may draw women into the labor force, there are few structural forces that would generate a more even distribution across sectors. Policy attention in developing countries has been low, and experiences from industrialized countries also show that it is hard for policy to have a serious impact. And the occupational and sectoral segregation is intimately linked with gender norms about an appropriate sexual division of labor. It is therefore to be expected that these roles and norms will reproduce themselves across generations, as upbringing, parental roles, as well as education are likely to reinforce these norms over time.

The continued high prevalence of domestic violence and the (regionally concentrated) prevalence of FGM can partly be related to the fact that there are no structural processes that would work to reduce them. Indeed, they might persist also as an indication of how conflictual some of the changes in gender gaps have been, and that these conflicts unload themselves in domestic violence. For example, there is a literature that shows that greater female employment, higher earnings than their spouse, and unemployment of the husband can lead to higher incidence of domestic violence (although the empirics is not entirely clear at this stage; see Lenze and Klasen 2017; World Bank 2014; Anderson and Genicot 2015).

These are just some speculations about the differential nature of progress in closing gender gaps across regions. Many of these claims have not been tested empirically, and testing these hypotheses would be of central importance for research and policy.

Before concluding this section, it is important to discuss the question of backlash. So far, the entire discussion has operated on the premise that there is only one direction for gender gaps: to become smaller. All the discussion was focused on differential speeds by dimension and region. But this view might be too sanguine. Instead, it is possible that there could be a serious backlash to some reduction in gender gaps, leading them to widen again. It appears that backlash can become an issue in several circumstances. First, resistance to reduced gender gaps can build up as part of anti-Western agitation. Promoting women's rights and their involvement in the economy can be seen as an assault on traditional values and norms, leading to resistance as part of a wider resistance to the West. Extreme manifestations of this are the fight against female education by the Taliban in Afghanistan and Pakistan (Khan and Seltzer 2015), Islamic State, or by Boko Haram in Nigeria. Second, political transitions from governments with a strong ideological stance in favor of gender equality can lead to a backlash once these governments are ousted. In transition countries this has been visible during the transition process where women suffered from much higher unemployment, reduced labor force participation, and sharply declining female representation in parliaments (e.g., Klasen 1993); similar developments are now evident in some Middle Eastern countries affected by the Arab Spring rebellion. Third, the threat of backlash can be particularly strong in conflict and war situations where rule of law is replaced by rule of the strongest (usually men), and this often leads to excesses of violence against women (such as mass rapes, enslavement, and the like). But a backlash can also develop more gradually as a resistance to increasing gains made by women. For example, as women increased their education and labor force participation in the United States, it was accompanied by claims that this was ultimately against their best interests, as argued by Faludi (1991).[19] Similarly, the rise of white male-dominated right-wing movements in many advanced countries can also be seen as a reaction to the gains made by women (and non-white or minority groups). Thus it is not clear yet whether gender gaps are invariably on their way out and only the speed with which they disappear will differ. There is significant resistance to the reduction in some gaps, and it is unclear whether such backlashes will be more than isolated incidences of pushback. This is another area for further investigation.

14.6. CONCLUSIONS AND A RESEARCH AGENDA

This chapter has shown that gender relations are a central institutional feature of societies. They particularly provide opportunities and constraints for women's productive and reproductive roles. As I have shown in the survey, the way these institutions work out matters not only for gender equity but for overall economic development. The survey has also revealed that gender gaps in key economic, social, and political variables have changed at vastly different speeds. While there has been massive progress in eliminating gender gaps in education (and formal rights), the progress in reducing other gaps has been much smaller. I have tried to spell out some hypotheses for why these differential trends might exist. But we know surprisingly little about the drivers of these changes and to what extent policy can have an impact. Thus, a forward-looking research agenda should at least tackle the following questions:

1. To what extent have the different forces (development, structural change, globalization, scope for policy action, policy attention, strength of norms, perceptions of win-win versus zero-sum, crises, and role of men) empirically affected the development of gender gaps across dimensions and across countries?
2. What is the respective importance of these groups of factors? In particular, how important are structural changes, and how important have policy interventions and policy attention been?
3. What drives the differential impact of policy (including policies by developing countries but also by donors and international organizations) on the different gender gaps? What are examples where policy has made a difference in closing slow-moving gaps faster? What is the role of overall macro- and structural policies versus targeted interventions in addressing gender gaps?
4. How strong are the linkages between different gender gaps? For example, how long can/will low gaps in education co-exist with large gaps in employment? What are the mechanisms that drive these linkages and what are the temporal dynamics? And how important is closing gender gaps in politics for closing other gender gaps? Or would it be better to tackle other gender gaps in order to make the largest progress?
5. How do gender norms develop, how do they differ between men and women, and how much do they respond to changing economic conditions, structural forces, and policies?
6. How serious is the threat of backlash and what are the conditions for reversals to happen? Are these reversals durable or temporary?
7. What are the welfare effects of pushing for reductions in particular gender gaps? To the extent that they reflect norms and preferences, what is the case for policy intervention? Are there gaps where the welfare case for addressing them is not clear?
8. Which gaps can be successfully addressed by different players, including governments, NGOs and civil society, and international actors?

There is no doubt that much remains to be understood in the relationship between institutions, gender, and economic development. But one thing appears clear: the very fast progress that the world has seen in reducing gender gaps in education is unlikely to translate into similar developments in other dimensions. As a result, tackling remaining gender gaps will likely become increasingly difficult, and this is an area that deserves urgent attention for research and policy.

NOTES

I would like to thank Francois Bourguignon, Jean-Philippe Platteau, Markus Goldstein, Jean-Marie Baland, two referees, and participants at seminars in New York, Namur, and Paris for helpful comments on earlier versions of this chapter. Funding from DFID through the EDI project as well as support from IDRC-DFID and the Hewlett Foundation as part of the GROW (Growth and Economic Opportunities for Women) project is gratefully acknowledged.

1. The recently concluded SDGs have, for example, called for the elimination of child marriage, which of course is closely related to these social institutions.
2. The two databases differ substantially in approach. While the CIRI database is broader in its coverage of women's political, economic, and social rights, it is based on expert judgment that provides a summary assessment of rights in a particular domain. The World Bank's Women and the Law Database focuses more narrowly on codified law and quantifies the number of unequal treatments or restrictions in particular domains.
3. There is an interesting and plausible correlation between women's economic roles, son preference, and marriage payments. For example, in South Asia, women have low participation rates, dowries are common, and son preference in high, while in Sub-Saharan Africa, women's participation is high, son preference low, and bride wealth is common. But there is also an outlier here which is China, where son preference is high, despite women's relatively strong economic roles. For a discussion, see Klasen and Wink (2002, 2003).
4. See, for example, Klasen (2002, 2006, 2018a) and Stotsky (2006) for more detailed reviews.
5. See Bloom and Williamson (1998) and Klasen (2002) for a full exposition of these arguments.
6. The underlying causes of these differences in behavior may well be related to different socialization of girls and boys, or that women as outsiders may also not be part of networks that are often conducive to corruption.
7. See a related discussion in King, Klasen, and Porter (2009) about the growth and welfare effects of women as policymakers.
8. The one exception is again the two short-term structuralist models of Blecker and Seguino (2002), where large gender gaps in pay, implicitly combined with no gender gaps in education and employment, can deliver the income-enhancing effects.
9. On these issues, see discussions in King and Hill (1993), Alderman et al. (1995, 1996), and World Bank (2001).
10. Also, it is not obvious which factor is the prime cause of gender gaps that one should then include in a reduced-form estimation.
11. But note that, as discussed below, economic growth has not generally pulled women into the labor force. See discussion below and Gaddis and Klasen (2014). So reverse causality might be less serious than presumed.
12. In the case of these papers, the focus on semi-industrialized, export-oriented countries was intended. But this can not therefore address the question whether there is a more general relationship between pay gaps and growth in developing countries that do not belong to this small group.
13. This is not very surprising. For example, Alderman et al. (1995, 1996) suggested as much in their analysis of cognitive skills gaps in Pakistan: once supply and demand for education were equalized across gender, the cognitive skills gap favoring boys disappeared or even reversed.
14. This is a statement about averages. There are still places where gender gaps in education persist, including remote rural areas in South Asia and Sub-Saharan Africa.
15. There has been some suggestion, motivated by a paper of Anderson and Ray (2010) as well as World Bank (2011), that the annual death toll from excess female mortality is much larger than the previous literature has suggested and is also more prevalent among adults and in Sub-Saharan Africa. But the results are not credible as they are based on an implausible reference standard for defining what constitutes excess female mortality. See Klasen and Vollmer (2013) for a discussion.
16. There is, of course, also the question of whether there are systematic differences in preferences by gender that exist beyond norms and socialization. It may be the case, for example, that there are differences in preferences toward care work (not only in the home but also in outside

employment) that partly account for persistent sectoral segregation by gender as well as unequal time use in the home. For a discussion, see Klasen (2016).

17. This is how Doepke and Tertilt (2009) explain why women in the United States, for example, were granted equal economic rights before they had any political rights, including the right to vote. Men found equal economic rights for their daughters important enough to tolerate granting economic rights to women of their generation.

18. On the ability of laws and social engineering to overcome women-hurting customs, see also Platteau, Camilotti, and Auriol (2017).

19. In her book *Backlash* she argued that women were being dissuaded from joining the labor force and pursuing higher education by false claims that this would reduce their ability to find husbands, have healthy children, or be happy. See Faludi (1991) for details.

REFERENCES

Abu-Ghaida, Dina and Stephan Klasen. 2004. "The Costs of Missing the Millennium Development Goal on Gender Equity." *World Development* 32(7): 1075–1107.

Akbulut-Yuksel, M., M. Khamis, and M. Yuksel. 2011. "Rubble Women: The Long-Term Effects of Postwar Reconstruction on Female Labor Market Outcomes." IZA Discussion Paper No. 6148.

Alderman, H., J. Behrman, S. Khan, D. Ross, and R. Sabot. 1995. "Public Schooling Expenditures in Rural Pakistan: Efficiently Targeting Girls and a Lagging Region." In *Public Spending and the Poor: Theory and Evidence*, edited by D. van de Walle and K. Nead. Baltimore, MD: Johns Hopkins University Press.

Alderman H., J. Behrman, D. Ross, and R. Sabot. 1996. "Decomposing the Gender Gap in Cognitive Skills in a Poor Rural Economy." *Journal of Human Resources* 31: 229–254.

Alesina, A., P. Giuliano, and N. Nunn. 2013. "On the Origins of Gender Roles: Women and the Plough." *Quarterly Journal of Economics* 128(2): 469–530.

Anderson, S. and G. Genicot. 2015. "Suicide and Property Rights in India." *Journal of Development Economics* 114: 64–78.

Anderson, S. and D. Ray. 2010. "Missing Women." *Age and Disease* 77(4): 1262–1300.

Appiah, Elizabeth and Walter McMahon. 2002. "The Social Outcomes of Education and Feedbacks on Growth in Africa." *Journal of Development Studies* 38: 27–68.

Banister, J. and A. Coale. 1994. "Five Decades of Missing Females in China." *Demography* 31(3): 459–479.

Barro, Robert and Jong-Wha Lee. 1994. "Sources of Economic Growth." *Carnegie-Rochester Conference Series on Public Policy* 40: 1–46.

———. 2013. "A New Data Set of Educational Attainment in the World, 1950–2010." *Journal of Development Economics* 104: 184–198.

Becker G. 1981. *A Treatise on the Family.* Chicago: University of Chicago Press.

Behrmann, J., S. Parker, and P. Todd. 2009. "Medium-term Impacts of the Oportunidades Conditional Cash Transfer Program on Rural Youth in Mexico." In *Poverty, Inequality, and Policy in Latin America*, edited by S. Klasen and F. Nowak-Lehmann. Cambridge, MA: MIT Press.

Bhalotra, A. and I. Clots-Figueras. 2014. "Health and the Political Agency of Women." *American Economic Journal: Economic Policy* 6(2): 164–197.

Bhalotra, S. and M. Umaña-Aponte. 2010. "The Dynamics of Women's Labor Supply in Developing Countries." IZA Discussion Paper Series, No. 4879.

Blackden, Mark, Sudharshan Canagarajah, Stephan Klasen, and David Lawson. 2007. "Gender and Growth in Africa: Evidence and Issues." In *Advancing Development: Core Themes in Global Development*, edited by George Mavrotas and Anthony Shorrocks. WIDER, Helsinki, Finland and UNU-WIDER Research Paper No. 2006/37.

Blecker, Robert and Stephanie Seguino. 2002. "Macroeconomic Effect of Reducing Gender Wage Inequality in an Export-Oriented, Semi-Industrialized Economy." *Review of Development Economics* 6(1): 103–119.

Bloom, David and Jeffrey Williamson. 1998. "Demographic Transition and Economic Miracles in Emerging Asia." *World Bank Economic Review* 12(3): 419–455.

Borrowman, M. and S. Klasen. 2017. "Drivers of Gendered Occupational and Sectoral Segregation in Developing Countries." Courant Research Centre: Poverty, Equity and Growth—Discussion Paper No. 222, University of Göttingen.

Boserup, E. 1970. *Women's Role in Economic Development.* Chicago: University of Chicago Press.

Branisa, B., S. Klasen, and M. Ziegler. 2013. "Gender Inequality in Social Institutions and Gendered Development Outcomes." *World Development* 45: 252–268.

Branisa, B., S. Klasen, M. Ziegler, J. Jütting, and D. Drechsler. 2014. "The Institutional Basis of Gender Inequality: The Social Institutions and Gender Index (SIGI)." *Feminist Economics* 20(2): 29–64.

Braunstein, E. 2012. "Neoliberal Development Macroeconomics." UNRISD Research Paper 2012–1.

Busse, Matthias and Christian Spielmann. 2006. "Gender Inequality and Trade." *Review of International Economics* 14(3): 362–379.

Cavalcanti, T. V. and J. Tavares. 2007. "The Output Costs of Gender Discrimination: A Model-Based Macroeconomic Estimate." Mimeo, University of Lisbon.

Chattopadhyay R. and E. Duflo. 2004. "Women as Policy Makers: Evidence from a Nationwide Randomized Experiment in India." *Econometrica* 72: 1409–1443.

Cho, Seo-Young. 2014. "International Women's Convention, Democracy and Gender Equality." *Social Science Quarterly* 95(3): 719–739.

Cingarella, David L., David L. Richardson, and K. Chad Clay. 2014. "The CIRI Human Rights Dataset." http://www.humanrightsdara.com. Version 2014.04.14.

Doepke, M. and M. Tertilt. 2009. "Women's Liberation: What's In It for Men?" *Quarterly Journal of Economics* 124: 1541–91.

Dollar, David and Roberta Gatti. 1999. "Gender Inequality, Income and Growth: Are Good Times Good for Women?" World Bank Policy Research Report Working Paper No. 1.

Duflo, E. 2012. "Women Empowerment and Economic Development." *Journal of Economic Literature* 50(4): 1051–1079.

Engels, F. 1884. *Origins of the Family, Private Property, and the State*. Zurich.

Esteve-Volart, B. 2009. "Gender Discrimination and Growth: Theory and Evidence from India." Mimeo, University of York, Canada.

Faludi, S. 1991. *Backlash: The undeclared war on American women*. New York: Crown.

Fernandez, R. 2011. "Does Culture Matter?" In *Handbook of Social Economics* Vol. 1A, edited by J. Benhabib et al. Amsterdam: North Holland.

———. 2014. "Women's Rights and Development." *Journal of Economic Growth* 19(1): 37–80.

Fernandez, R. and A. Fogli. 2009. "Culture: An Empirical Investigation of Beliefs, Work, and Fertility." *American Economic Journal: Macroeconomics* 1: 146–177.

Ferrant, G. and A. Kolev. 2016. "Does Gender Discrimination in Social Institutions Matter for Long-Term Growth?" OECD Development Centre Working Paper No. 330. Paris: OECD.

Forbes, Kristin. 2000. "A Reassessment of the Relationship between Inequality and Growth." *American Economic Review* 90: 869–887.

Gaddis, I. and S. Klasen. 2014. "Economic Development, Structural Change, and Women's Labor Force Participation Rate: A Re-Examination of the Feminization U-Hypothesis." *Journal of Population Economics* 27: 639–681.

Gaddis, I. and J. Pieters. 2017. "The Gendered Labor Market Impacts of Trade Liberalization: Evidence from Brazil." *Journal of Human Resource* 52(2): 457–490.

Galor, O. and D. Weil. 1996. "The Gender Gap, Fertility, and Growth." *American Economic Review* 86: 374–387.

———. 2000. "Population, Technology and Growth." *American Economic Review* 90(4): 806–828.

Gehringer, A. and S. Klasen. 2017. "Labor Force Participation of Women in the EU: What Role Do Family Policies Play?" *LABOUR* 31(1): 15–42.

Haddad, L., J. Hoddinott, and H. Alderman. 1997. *Intrahousehold Resource Allocation In Developing Countries*. Baltimore, MD: Johns Hopkins University Press.

Hajnal, J. 1982. "Two Kinds of Pre-industrial Household Systems." *Population and Development Review* 8(3): 449–494.

Hallward-Driemeier, M., T. Hasan, and A. B. Rusu. 2013a. "Women's Legal Rights over 50 Years: Progress, Stagnation or Regression?" World Bank Policy Research Working Paper No. 6616. Washington, DC: World Bank.

———. 2013b. "Women's Legal Rights over 50 Years: What Is the Impact of Reform?" World Bank Policy Research Working Paper No. 6617. Washington, DC: World Bank.

Hansen, Casper Worm, Peter Sandholt Jensen, and Christian Volmar Skovsgaard. 2014. "Modern Gender Roles and Agricultural History: The Neolithic Inheritance." *Journal of Economic Growth* 20(4): 365–404.

Hazarika, Gautam, Chandan Kumar Jha, and Sudipta Sarangi. 2015. "The Role of Historical Resource Scarcity in Modern Gender Inequality." Unpublished Working Paper.

Hill, Anne and Elisabeth King. 1995. "Women's Education and Economic Well-being." *Feminist Economics* 1(2): 1–26.

ILO. 2011. *ILO Estimates and Projections of the Economically Active Population: 1990–2020*, 6th edition. International Labour Organization, Geneva. http://laborsta.ilo.org/.

Jones, E. L. 1984. *The European Miracle*. New York: Oxford University Press.

Kahlert, M. 2014. "Missing Women in the 2000s." Mimeo, University of Göttingen.

Kan, S. and S. Klasen. 2018. "Macroeconomics and Gender: Recent Research on Economic Growth and Women's Economic Empowerment." Ottawa: IDRC.

Khan, S. and A. Seltzer. 2015. "The Impact of Fundamentalist Terrorism on School Enrolment: Evidence from North-Western Pakistan, 2004–09." Mimeo, UCL.

King, Elizabeth and Anne Hill. 1993. *Women's Education in Developing Countries: Barriers, Benefits, and Policies*. Baltimore, MD: Johns Hopkins University Press.

King, E., S. Klasen, and M. Porter. 2009. "Women and Development." In *Global Crises, Global Solutions*, 2nd edition, edited by B. Lomborg. Cambridge: Cambridge University Press.

Kis-Katos, K. and R. Sparrow. 2015. "Poverty, Labour Markets and Trade Liberalization in Indonesia." *Journal of Development Economics* 117: 94–106.

Kis-Katos, K., J. Pieters, and R. Sparrow. 2018. "Globalization and Social Change: Gender-Specific Effects of Trade Liberalization in Indonesia." *IMF Economic Review* 66(4): 763–793.

Klasen, S. 1993. "Human Development and Women's Lives in a Restructured Eastern Bloc." In *The Economics of Transformation: Theory and Practise in the New Market Economies*, edited by A. Schipke and A. Taylor. New York: Springer.

———. 1994. "Missing Women Reconsidered." *World Development* 22(7): 1061–1071.

———. 1999. "Does Gender Inequality Reduce Growth and Development?" World Bank Policy Research Report Working Paper No. 7.

———. 2002. "Low Schooling for Girls, Slower Growth for All? Cross-Country Evidence on the Effect of Gender Inequality in Education on Economic Development." *World Bank Economic Review* 16(3): 345–373.

———. 2006. "Gender and Pro-Poor Growth." In *Pro-Poor Growth: Evidence and Policies*, edited by L. Menkoff. Berlin: Dunker & Humblot.

———. 2016. "Measuring Gender Inequality Using the Capability Approach: Issues and Challenges." Mimeo, University of Göttingen.

———. 2018a. "The Impact of Gender Inequality on Economic Performance in Developing Countries." *Annual Review of Resource Economics* 10, DOI: 10.1146/annurev-resource-100517-023429.

———. 2018b. "What Explains Uneven Female Labor Force Participation Levels and Trends in Developing Countries?" Courant Research Center Discussion Paper No. 246, University of Göttingen.

Klasen, S. and F. Lamanna. 2009. "The Impact of Gender Inequality in Education and Employment on Economic Growth: New Evidence for a Panel of Countries." *Feminist Economics* 15(3): 91–132.

Klasen, S. and A. Minasyan. 2017. "Gender Inequality and Growth in Europe." *Intereconomics* 52(1): 17–23.

Klasen, S. and J. Pieters. 2015. "What Explains the Stagnation of Female Labor Force Participation in Urban India?" *World Bank Economic Review* 29(3): 449–478.

Klasen, S. and S. Vollmer. 2013. "Missing Women: Age and Disease: A Correction." Courant Research Center Discussion Paper No. 133, University of Göttingen.

Klasen, S. and C. Wink. 2002. "A Turning Point in Gender Bias in Mortality? An Update on the Number of Missing Women." *Population and Development Review* 28(2): 285–312.

———. 2003. "Missing Women: Revisiting the Debate." *Feminist Economics* 9: 263–299.

Knowles, Stephen, Paula Lorgelly, and Dorian Owen. 2002. "Are Educational Gender Gaps a Brake on Economic Development? Some Cross-Country Empirical Evidence." *Oxford Economic Papers* 54: 118–149.

Kreibaum, M. and S. Klasen. 2015. "Missing Men: Differential Effects of Wars and Socialism on Female Labor-Force Participation in Vietnam." Courant Research Center Discussion Paper No. 181, University of Göttingen.

Lagerlöf, N. 2003. "Gender Equality and Long-Run Growth." *Journal of Economic Growth* 8(4): 403–426.

Lenze, J. and S. Klasen. 2017. "The Impact of Women's Labour Force Participation on Domestic Violence in Jordan." *Feminist Economics* 23(1): 1–29.

Lorgelly, Paula and Dorian Owen. 1999. "The Effect of Female and Male Schooling on Economic Growth in the Barro-Lee Model." *Empirical Economics*, 24, August.

Minasyan, A., J. Zenker, S. Klasen, and S. Vollmer. 2018. "The Impact of Gender Inequality in Education on Economic Growth: A Systematic Review and Meta-Regression Analysis." Mimeo. Courant Research Center Discussion Paper No. 255, University of Göttingen.

Murthi, Mamta, Anne-Catherine Guio, and Jean Drèze. 1995. "Mortality, Fertility, and Gender Bias in India: A District-Level Analysis." *Population and Development Review* 21(4): 745–782.

OECD. 1995. *Household Production in OECD Countries.* Paris: OECD.

———. 2015. *Social Institutions and Gender Index Synthesis Report.* Paris: OECD.

Pitt, M. and S. Khandker. 1998. "The Impact of Group-based Credit Programs on Poor Households in Bangladesh." *Journal of Political Economy* 106: 958–996.

Pitt, M., S. Khandker, and J. Cartwright. 2006. "Enmpowering Women with Micro Finance: Evidence from Bangladesh." *Economic Development and Cultural Change* 54(4): 791–831.

Platteau, J.-P., E. Camiloti, and E. Auriol. 2017. "Eradicating Women-Hurting Customs: What Role for Social Engineering?" Paper presented at WIDER Gender and Development Meeting, February.

Santos-Silva, M., A. Alexander, S. Klasen, and C. Welzel. 2017. "The Roots of Female Emancipation: From Perennial Cool Water Via Pre-Industrial Late Marriages to Postindustrial Gender Equality." Courant Research Centre: Poverty, Equity and Growth—Discussion Paper No 241 University of Göttingen.

Schober, T. and R. Winter-Ebmer. 2011. "Gender Wage Inequality and Economic Growth: Is There Really a Puzzle? A Comment." *World Development* 39(8): 1476–1484.

Seguino, S. 2000a. "Gender Inequality and Economic Growth: A Cross-Country Analysis." *World Development* 28: 1211–1230.

———. 2000b. "Accounting for Gender in Asian Economic Growth." *Feminist Economics, Taylow and Francis Journals* 6(3): 27–58.

Seguino, Stephanie and Maria Sagrario Floro. 2003. "Does Gender Have Any Effect on Aggregate Saving?" *International Review of Applied Economics* 17(2): 147–166.

Sen, A. 1989. "Women's Survival as a Development Problem." *Bulletin of the American Academy of Arts and Sciences* 43(2): 14–29.

———. 1990. "Gender and Cooperative Conflict." In *Persistent Inequalities—Women and World Development*, edited by Irene Tinker, 123–149. New York: Oxford University Press.

Standing, G. 1999. "Global Feminization Through Flexible Labor: A Theme Revisited." *World Development* 27(3): 583–602.

Stotsky, Janet. 2006. "Gender and Its Relevance to Macroeconomic Policy: A Survey." IMF Working Paper, WP/06/233.

Summers, L. 1994. *Investing in All the People.* Washington, DC: World Bank.

Swamy, Anand, Omar Azfar, Stephen Knack, and Young Lee. 2001. "Gender and Corruption." *Journal of Development Economics* 64(1): 25–55.

Teignier, M. and D. Cuberes. 2015. "Aggregate Costs of Gender Gaps in the Labor Market: A Quantitative Exercise." *Journal of Human Capital* 10 (1): 1–32.

Tertilt, M. and M. Doepke. 2014. "Does Female Empowerment Promote Economic Development?" NBER Working Paper No. 19888.

Thomas, D. 1990. "Intrahousehold Resource Allocation: An Inferential Approach." *Journal of Human Resources* 25(4): 635–664.

Thomas, Duncan. 1997. "Incomes, Expenditures and Health Outcomes: Evidence on Intrahousehold Resource Allocation." In *Intrahousehold Resource Allocation in Developing Countries*, edited by L. Haddad et al. Baltimore, MD: Johns Hopkins University Press.

UNDP. 1995. *Human Development Report.* New York: Oxford University Press.

Waring, M. 1988. *If Women Counted.* New York: Harper & Row.

Weichselbäumer, D., and R. Winter-Ebmer. 2005. "A Meta-Analysis of the International Gender Wage Gap." *Journal of Economic Surveys* 19(3): 479–511.

World Bank. 2001. *Engendering Development.* Washington, DC: World Bank.

———. 2003. *World Development Report 2004: Making Services Work for Poor People.* Washington, DC: World Bank.

———. 2011. *World Development Report 2012: Gender equality and Development.* Washington, DC: World Bank.

———. 2014. *Voice and Agency. Empowering Women and Girls for Shared Prosperity.* Washington, DC: World Bank.

Yamarik, S. and S. Ghosh. 2003. "Is Female Education Productive? A Reassessment." Mimeo, Tufts University, Medford, MA.

Yoon, J. and S. Klasen. 2018. "An Application of Partial Least Squares to the Construction of the Social Institutions and Gender Index (SIGI) and the Corruption Perception Index (CPI)." *Social Indicators Research* 138: 61–88. DOI 10.1007/s11205-017-1655-8.

PART 5

SECTORAL APPROACHES

15

FIRMS, WORKERS, AND LABOR MARKETS

Imran Rasul

15.1. INTRODUCTION

This chapter reviews evidence on some aspects related to labor markets in low-income countries. Our aim is to synthesize some key lessons from this literature, consolidating what is known about the key drivers of worker outcomes (including those of micro-entrepreneurs), firm behavior, and the interaction between firms and workers in labor markets as a whole. Throughout, we place emphasis on understanding the role of institutions and the state in determining these outcomes.

The concept of institutions we utilize is broad, ranging from the interventionist role of the state in labor markets, to underlying economic features of labor markets in low-income settings. Examples of the kinds of institutions we discuss relate to labor market regulations that firms face, licensing or customs requirements, the functioning of the judicial system, the entrenchment of private property rights, and the stability of the political environment. An example of an institutional feature we discuss relating to underlying economic characteristics of labor markets includes informational asymmetries between workers and firms.

Understanding the interlinkages between labor markets and such institutions is important from both a macroeconomic and microeconomic perspective. Labor markets play a central role in the economic development of countries. Most models of aggregate growth imply long-run output depends on the ability of workers and capital to be allocated to the sectors in which the returns to their labor are highest. There also exists a large class of models highlighting links between macro-intermediation, entrepreneurship, and growth that emphasizes improvements in financial intermediation spurs firm investment and income growth (Evans and Jovanovic 1989; Banerjee and Newman 1993; Galor and Zeira 1993; Buera et al. 2011).[1] From a microeconomic perspective, labor is the fundamental factor endowment that all the world's poor start their lives with: being able to optimally invest in the accumulation of human capital and to earn returns from such investments in the labor market are key to lifetime welfare.[2]

We draw on cross-country and within-country evidence, as well as novel evidence from ongoing studies. The cross-country evidence we draw on is derived from the World

Bank Enterprise Survey (WBES): this is a firm-level survey that covers a representative sample of registered private sector firms with five or more employees. The data were collected between 2006 and 2011. The WBES covers topics predominantly related to the business environment and the constraints faced by firms.[3] The within-country studies we draw on utilize a wide range of experimental and non-experimental research designs. We do not aim for our review to be exhaustive of all the relevant literature or topics: rather, we focus on a few key lessons that the body of work has established with regard to the functioning of labor markets and how this relates to institutions, and identify important gaps for future work to address.[4]

15.2. FIRMS

15.2.1. Firm Size Distribution

The firm size distribution in most low-income countries is positively skewed relative to the distribution in richer countries, such as the United States. Figure 15.1 draws together evidence on firm sizes from four developing countries: Uganda, India, Indonesia, and Mexico, and compares these to what is observed in the United States. The top panel of figure 15.1 shows that in the four developing countries, there are very few firms that employ more than 10 employees. The United States has a lower share of small firms (defined as those firms with between 2 and 5 employees) and a higher share of firms in all other size bin-categories (6–10, 11–20, 21–50, 51+ employees). The lower panel in figure 15.1 shows that as a result, in the United States the majority of workers are employed in firms with at least 51 employees; in the four low-income countries, the majority of workers are employed in firms with at most 20 employees.

These figures highlight that the firm size distribution is quite similar across low-income countries: the modal group are firms of size 0–9 full-time employees in all four countries. The WBES data only cover registered firms, and so do not shed much light on the informal economy. If such informal firms were included, we would expect the resulting firm size distribution to be even more skewed. The second feature to note is that the proportion of very large firms does vary across low-income countries. In Mexico, for example, almost as many workers are employed in firms of size 50+ as in firms of size 1–9. Hence, throughout our discussion, we will highlight the differences in institutional environment faced by small and large firms.

This skewed firm size distribution relative to more advanced economies has spurred much debate about the causes and consequences of the "missing middle," and whether institutional features of developing countries are responsible for this outcome. This is important if small and medium-size enterprises (SMEs) are truly the engines of economic growth, creating employment and adding value. If so, the relaxation of constraints on SMEs will, in the short run, lead to an expansion in the size of SMEs with concomitant impacts on employment, and potentially on productivity and profitability. In the long run, relaxing such constraints allows a better allocation of entrepreneurial talent, thus spurring economy-wide growth (Lucas 1978).[5]

The kinds of constraints relevant for SMEs fall into two broad groups. First, there is an established literature emphasizing that SMEs face more binding constraints, relative to large firms, related to input markets, where credit and labor market imperfections have

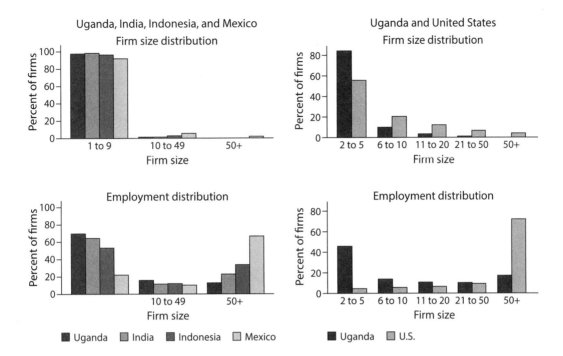

FIGURE 15.1. Firm size and employment distributions, by country. *Sources*: Census of Business Establishment—UBOS, and Hsieh and Olken (2014). Census of Business Establishment–UBOS and Business Dynamics Statistics—US Census Bureau.

been most studied. An older and parallel literature has emphasized that institutional constraints, such as state regulations, registration/licensing requirements, taxes, insecure property rights, and so on, can also play an important role in determining the firm size distribution (Harris and Todaro 1970; De Soto 1989; Tybout 2000).

With improvements in the availability and comparability of detailed firm level data across countries, researchers have been able to revisit the issue of the firm size distribution. Hsieh and Olken (2014) do so, using data from India, Indonesia, and Mexico. To understand whether there is a missing middle, they examine whether SMEs appear to operate at the efficient scale of production. Assuming a Cobb-Douglas production function, the marginal and average product of labor are proportional to each other. This insight avoids having to calculate the marginal product of labor directly, that would otherwise require estimating firm production functions directly. To operationalize the insight, they use the average revenue product of labor (ARP_L), defined as the value added per worker, as a proxy for the average product of labor. Figure 15.2 shows their graphs of how the ARP_L varies over firm size. Strikingly they find that for each country, the ARP_L is *unimodal* and *increasing* in firm size: this is contrary to the textbook view of constrained SMEs and will no doubt rightly spur further study that can help reconcile the macro and micro evidence on whether SMEs really are constrained and operating at an inefficient scale.

Figure 15.3 collates data from some prominent studies to show parts of the firm size distribution have been focused on in micro-studies of constraints to SME expansion:

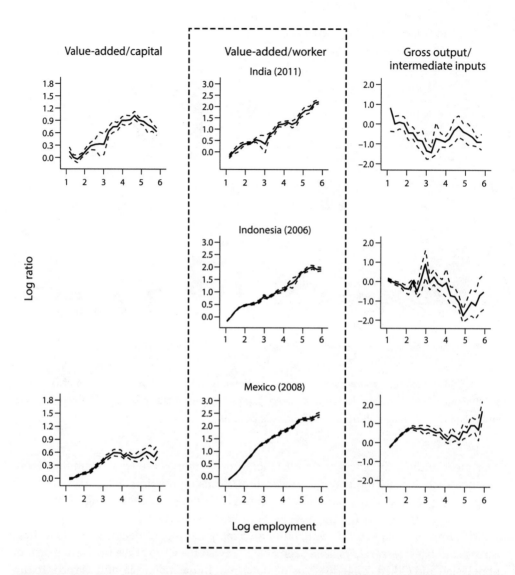

FIGURE 15.2. The Missing Missing Middle (average product and firm size). *Source*: Hsieh and Olken (2014).

there has been a slight concentration of studies of micro-entrepreneurs, those firms operating with zero or one employee. There remains a relative scarcity of studies focusing on firms of size 1–9 employees, that as figure 15.1 highlighted, remains the most important segment of the firm size distribution in low-income settings. The study of micro-entrepreneurs is of course important and we will return to the issue throughout, especially on what is known about the nature of self-selection into micro-entrepreneurship. More precisely, whether the low marginal productivity of these firms is indicative of individuals entering such activities primarily as a form of insurance against idiosyncratic income risk, or whether they really are a stepping stone toward creating larger firms.

Siba and Soderbom (2011) provide a detailed analysis of firm dynamics in Ethiopia. A motivating fact for their study is that 60% of firms entering the Ethiopian manufacturing

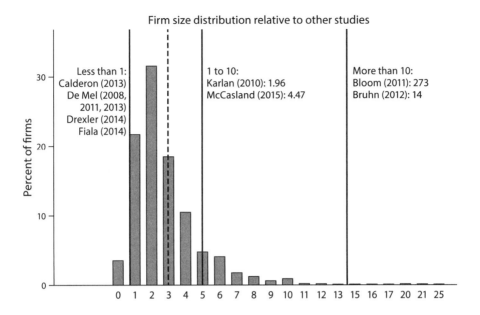

FIGURE 15.3. Firm size distribution in some cited studies. *Source*: Baseline Data.

sector exit within three years. Their study seeks to shed light on two questions: (i) why do young firms have such high exit rates?; (ii) how do productivity, prices, and demand evolve in the initial years following entry? Using detailed data on output prices, the authors are able to distinguish between price and productivity effects and thus shed some light on whether young firms are less productive or just face higher demand constraints/lower prices. The authors use data on a panel of Ethiopian manufacturing firms collected from 1996 to 2006 and including 1,000 firms with 10 or more employees. Their main findings are: (i) young and small firms are more likely to exit relative to established and larger firms: higher output demand has a positive impact on survival, but productivity has little impact on firm survival; (ii) market entrants have lower revenue-based productivity, driven mainly by higher demand constraints; they find little evidence of productivity differences between entrants and incumbents.

Gallipoli and Goyette (2015) provide insights on how institutions can distort the firm size distribution in a low-income setting. They study distortions arising from tax liabilities and credit constraints for firms in Uganda. They embed a key feature of the tax audit system in Uganda that leads to the probability of a firm being audited to increase sharply for firms with more than 30 employees, into an other standard model of firm growth based on Hopenhayn (1992). They also allow for credit market imperfections that arise due to imperfect enforceability of contracts. This results in lenders asking for collateral to guarantee loans, and so the lack of collateral prevents some entrepreneurs from borrowing their desired amount. The parameters of the model are in part calibrated and in part estimated by matching moments to firm level data. The model is used to compare the benchmark equilibrium to counterfactual scenarios assuming no tax distortions, perfect capital markets, and so on. Moving from the benchmark world to the first best would increase output per worker by between 52% and 94%. However, the vast majority of the efficiency loss is attributable to credit constraints rather than tax audits, although the way in which the tax audit system works is what drives the missing middle and skewed firm size distribution.

There remains enormous scope for future work to use similar structural approaches to estimating economy-wide distortions to the firm size distribution and firm productivity resulting from regulations, interventions, and other features of markets in low-income settings.[6]

15.2.2 The Desire of Firms to Expand

We present novel descriptive evidence on the desire to expand employment in SMEs as expressed by firm owners in Uganda. This evidence is based on an ongoing study that covers a nationally representative sample of SMEs operating in eight sectors in Uganda: motor-mechanics, plumbing, catering, tailoring, hairdressing, construction, and electrical wiring. This corresponds to a large share of all SMEs in Uganda. The sample covers firms with between 1 and 15 employees with the median firm size being 3 employees. The final sample is 2,300 firms, representative of SMEs in these eight sectors across urban Uganda. This represents a relatively large sample of firms compared to other publicly available datasets from Uganda. For example, the WBES Uganda sample from 2013 covers 546 firms.[7]

Panels a to c in figure 15.4 report firm owners' desire to expand based on baseline interviews in our ongoing study. The majority of SMEs report a desire to expand scale: 55% report wanting to increase by at least one worker (recall that the median firm starts with three employees), 30% report wanting to at least double their size, and 15% report already being at their ideal employment scale. This finding is robust across firm size, ages, and sectors. Panel d then provides evidence on the *actual* changes in firm size over the year prior to the survey. We observe that 45% of firms have no change in size, while 32% (20%) increase (decrease) employment.

Although much work remains to understand the desires and long-run ambitions of firm owners, and the dynamics of firm size, taken together this evidence suggests firms do want to expand size, and a significant fraction of them might face constraints to do so. We now turn to discuss what is known about these constraints.

15.2.3 Constraints Firms Face

The WBES is an important source of information on the cross-country differences in the constraints to expansion that firms report facing. The WBES allows us to build a descriptive evidence base for those across countries and across firms of different size: we classify firms as being small if they have between 5 and 19 employees, and as large if they have between 20 and 99 employees. Importantly, the WBES data highlight the importance of a wide range of constraints, not just those that have been mostly studied in the economics literature, and as such can provide a clear pathway toward the types of barrier that might have been hitherto relatively understudied.

Figures 15.5a and 15.5b highlight that across a range of low-income countries, there are multiple relevant constraints to expansion that firms report facing, and that the relative importance of these constraints differs across small and large firms in the same country. Given the focus of this chapter, we note that institutional constraints cover a range of factors, including taxes firms are liable for, licensing/customs requirements, the

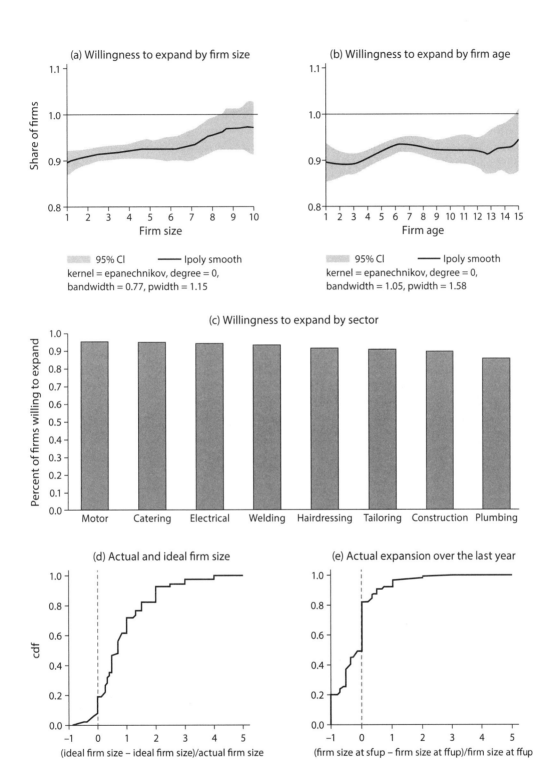

FIGURE 15.4. Firms desired and actual expansion. *Source*: Author's own ongoing work with various co-authors.

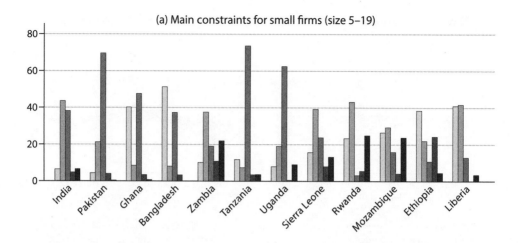

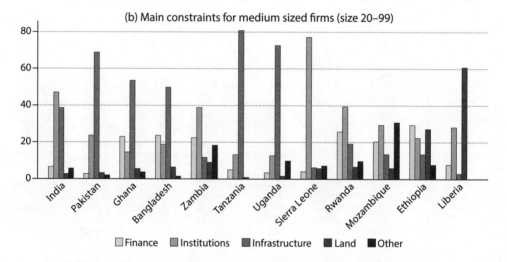

Countries are ordered from richest to poorest according to GDP per capita, PPP, in 2006.

FIGURE 15.5. (*a*) Main constraints for small firms (size 5–19). (*b*) Main constraints for medium-sized firms (size 20–99). *Source*: WBES.

prevalence of crime/reliability of courts, labor regulations, and corruption/stability. Among small firms, such institutional constraints are prominent in India, Zambia, Sierra Leone, Rwanda, Mozambique, and Liberia. In this set of countries, institutional constraints are more important for larger firms, as shown in figure 15.5b. The countries in figures 15.5a and 15.5b are ordered in descending order of GDP. This is done to highlight that there is no clear relationship between constraints and GDP per capita, and this applies to all the constraints shown, not just those related to institutions.[8]

Figure 15.6 unpacks institutional constraints into their various subcomponents, by country and firm size. This reveals that taxes are the dominant institutional constraint to expansion that small firms report facing across countries: as discussed later, poorly designed tax regimes might leave many smaller firms better off remaining unregistered

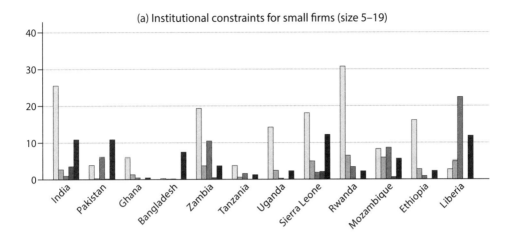

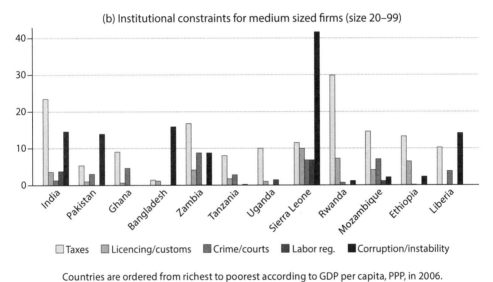

Countries are ordered from richest to poorest according to GDP per capita, PPP, in 2006.

FIGURE 15.6. (*a*) Institutional constraints for small firms (size 5–19). (*b*) Institutional constraints for medium-sized firms (size 20–99). *Source:* WBES.

in the informal sector. Among large firms, corruption and instability are relatively more frequently cited, and this is especially so in Bangladesh, Sierra Leone, and Liberia. To get a clearer sense of how the importance of different types of institutional constraint differ across small and large firms, figure 15.7 shows a scatter plot of these institutional constraint ranks. On the whole, each type of institutional constraint is similarly ranked across the firm size distribution in the same country.

For some of these institutional constraints, the evidence base on how firms respond to changes in them remains scarce and future work should be encouraged. A prominent study on labor regulation is Besley and Burgess (2004), who exploit differences in labor regulation across Indian states and over time to estimate their impact on firm performance. They find that more pro-worker regulations lower output, employment, and investment

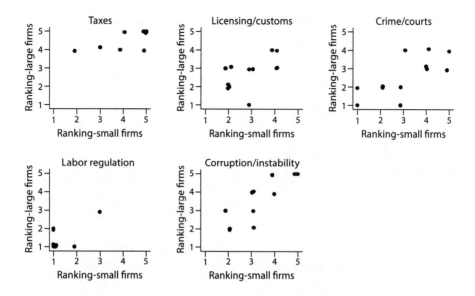

FIGURE 15.7. Ranking institutional constraints by firm size. *Notes*: Each observation represents the ranking by importance of a constraint within a country. Location of points has been perturbated to show overlapping observations. *Source*: WBES.

in the registered manufacturing sector and increase output in the informal sector. On corruption, Fisman and Svensson (2007), using self-reported bribery payments, find that corruption has a strong negative effect on firm growth in Uganda. Cai et al. (2011), using an alternative measure of bribery, also find that corruption had a strong negative effect on firm performance, but this effect is much weaker if firms are located in cities with low-quality government services, if they are subject to severe government expropriation, and if they do not have a strong relationship with clients and suppliers.

These papers provide a basis for future work and highlight the need for a parallel political economy literature to develop to understand what drives the initial formation of labor regulations, the development of the tax system, and anti-corruption policies in the first place.

We next return to the micro-evidence on constraints SMEs face using our data from ongoing work in Uganda. To underpin the validity of the information from this sample, figure 15.8 shows how the aggregate evidence related to the importance of labor and credit constraints obtained from our sample of firms relates to the same statistics as obtained in WBES sample of firms. We see that: (i) across countries in the WBES sample, Uganda ranks relatively highly in firm owners reporting both forms of constraint as limiting employment expansion; (ii) the percentage of firms' owners reporting each constraint (labor- or capital-related) is similar between the WBES Uganda sample and our study sample: in both, the majority of firms report such constraints as being relevant.

The top part of figure 15.9 then shows self-reported constraints to expansion from our sample of Ugandan SMEs: these are grouped into labor-related constraints, capital-related constraints, and other constraints (that includes the institutional environment as being a constraining factor). We see that all three dimensions of constraint are important for

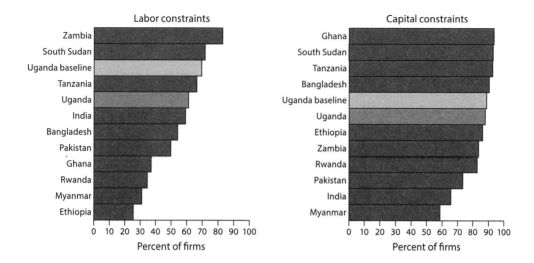

FIGURE 15.8. Labor- and capital-related constraints across LDCs. *Source*: WBES.

SMEs in Uganda in the eight sectors of study. More specifically, within labor constraints, the data suggest that search and matching frictions prevent firms from hiring suitable workers, where suitability can be defined as either the skills of workers, their willingness to work, their trustworthiness, or based on some other trait. We return below to examine studies trying to uncover more direct evidence on the nature and importance of such search and matching frictions. On credit-related constraints, both the availability of capital/machinery and sources of financing of purchasing such machines appear as constraints to SME expansion. Finally, we highlight that among our sample, constraints related to the institutional environment are cited as the single most frequent obstacle for SMEs expanding employment.

The lower panel in figure 15.9 complements this evidence by showing self-reported causes of stock-outs for firms, that again might be indicative of them being constrained in their operations along margins other than employment. As reported by SME owners, the incidence of stock-outs is related to the lack of working capital (that again highlights the importance of credit constraints), as well as poor management practices. The reliability of suppliers does not appear to be a key reason for stock-outs in this context, which might indicate that the fact that contracts are not perfectly enforceable is not in itself a major impediment on firms relative to input market constraints related to labor and capital. Along these lines, Macchiavello and Marjoria (2015) provide evidence on the nature and impacts of inter-firm contracts in the context of the Kenyan rose sector. While the volume of trade is reduced due to a lack of contractual enforcement, they show that seller's reputation and relational contracting are key to understanding firm outcomes. Macchiavello and Miquel-Florensa (2016) study similar contracting issues in the context of coffee production in Costa Rica, studying whether relational contracts or vertical integration are used to overcome inefficiencies due to contractual incompleteness. This work is opening up interesting avenues for research at the nexus of industrial organization and organizational economics that can help shed light on strategic firm interactions in low-income settings.

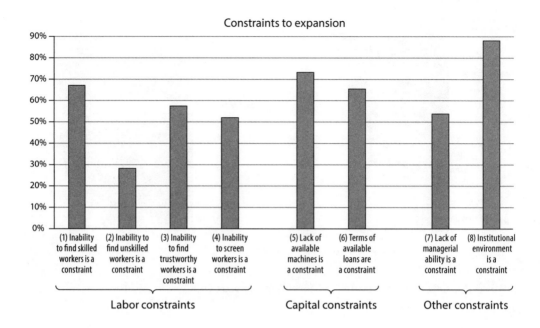

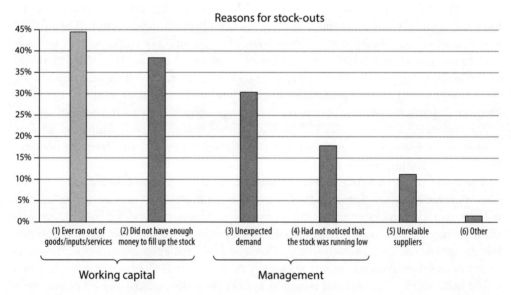

FIGURE 15.9. Perceived constraints. *Source*: Author's own ongoing work with various co-authors.

15.2.4 Evidence on Relaxing Constraints

Much of the literature has focused on constraints to small firm expansion arising from input markets, especially capital and labor markets. Here we review the evidence on the impacts of relaxing capital constraints, both on existing SMEs and on the creation of new micro-enterprises. We then review evidence related to wage subsidies, information asymmetries at the point of hiring labor, the provision of entrepreneurial skills, and evaluations of combined asset and skill transfers. The backdrop to much of this evidence is the missing middle debate: if firms already operate at the efficient scale, then attempting to relax constraints related to labor hires, say, will simply lead to full crowding-out of new hires, and no net change in total employment.[9] Finally, we note that although most of the literature has studied one constraint in isolation, there is increased recognition that firms typically face multiple constraints simultaneously and the most effective interventions might target more than one dimension at the same time (Karlan and Fischer 2015).

15.2.4.1 Capital

A growing body of evidence suggests firms in low-income countries are constrained in their access to finance (de Mel et al. 2008a; Banerjee and Duflo 2014). One way to establish the existence of capital constraints is to see if firms are characterized by high average returns to capital (Udry and Anagol 2006; de Mel et al. 2008a, 2011).

Banerjee and Duflo (2014) study whether relatively large firms in India are credit constrained by exploiting variation in access to directed credit. As a result of a policy reform in 1998, a group of Indian firms gained eligibility to a directed lending program. This group of firms lost eligibility in 2000 following another policy reform. The trends in sales and profits of these firms are compared to those of firms that were already eligible for the directed lending program before 1998 and remained eligible after 2000. They find that once firms become eligible, they expand their total borrowing and when they lose eligibility they reduce their total borrowing. Therefore, firms do not just use the directed credit to substitute other (more expensive) sources of credit. This implies that firms are in fact credit constrained. For these large firms, the authors estimate the marginal productivity of capital to be very high (around 89%), well above formal interest rates, thereby highlighting the degree to which large firms are credit constrained.

De Mel et al. (2008a) estimate returns to capital in micro-enterprises in Sri Lanka. They do so using a randomized control trial (RCT), providing capital grants to micro-entrepreneurs. The estimated average returns to capital are high, around 5% per month, and so on the order of 60% per year (so again well above market interest rates). However, there is significant variation in the returns to capital among their sample of micro-entrepreneurs: 60% of women and about 20% of men micro-entrepreneurs have returns below market interest rates. The study shows that returns are higher for more constrained entrepreneurs (those identified to have less access to liquidity to begin with). On the other hand, they find no evidence that individual traits of micro-entrepreneurs, such as the risk aversion or uncertainty faced, drive heterogeneous returns to capital. This indicates that imperfections in credit markets, rather than a lack of insurance, create a significant constraint to expansion for micro-entrepreneurs in their setting.

A number of studies have investigated whether the *form* in which capital is provided to micro-entrepreneurs matters for firm outcomes. Fafchamps et al. (2014) test whether cash grants and in-kind grants have the same impact on micro-enterprise growth in Ghana. A sample of male and female business owners with no paid employees was randomly divided into a control and two treatment groups: the first treatment group received an unconditional cash grant of $120; the second received an in-kind grant of $120 in equipment/inventory/materials, according to the owners' stated preferences. The findings revealed large average returns of in-kind grants, but among women, in-kind grants increased profits only for the enterprises that were more asset-rich to begin with. Cash grants had lower average returns, and actually had zero return for women micro-entrepreneurs.

For them, cash grants were used predominantly for consumption: this might well be the case if there are imperfect insurance markets, so the ability to smooth consumption in the face of idiosyncratic income risk is limited. The study is important because it clearly highlights that cash transfers alone may be insufficient to spur SME expansion, especially in the presence of related market imperfections, such as those in insurance markets.

On direct access to credit for existing micro-entrepreneurs, de Mel et al. (2011) provide non-experimental evidence on the matter, following from the findings in de Mel et al. (2008a) that estimated high returns to capital in micro-enterprises in Sri Lanka. De Mel et al. (2011) test for the role of information in improving access to credit, through an information intervention: 383 micro-enterprises were sent a letter informing them of a loan product already available on the market. In addition to providing information, the intervention also aimed to relax requirements on the loan application procedure, such as reducing the number of guarantors from two to one. All businesses operating in an area were offered the loan, with businesses operating in a neighboring area defined as the control group using a difference-in-difference research strategy. Just over 60% of entrepreneurs eligible for the treatment attended an initial meeting where information was provided. Of these, 41 entrepreneurs submitted an application and 38 (10% of the original sample) were eventually given a loan. There is evidence that the firms that did not apply for the loans were still credit constrained, with the main reason they did not apply for the loan being difficulty in meeting the application criteria rather than lack of demand for credit. Using the difference-in-difference research design, the study concludes the program raised loans in the area by 6–7% relative to the neighboring area that did not receive the intervention, and the estimated return to the loan is of the order of 5–6%. These are comparable to the average returns found by the authors in previous studies, such as de Mel et al. (2008a).

In terms of the relationship between credit and micro-enterprise start-ups, many evaluations of microfinance have now taken place, and the emerging view is that such interventions do not have strong impacts on the creation of new businesses (Karlan and Zinman 2011; Kaboski and Townsend 2011; Banerjee et al. 2015; Crepon et al. 2015; Karlan et al. 2015). On the other hand, the provision of unconditional cash transfers can induce successful transitions into micro-entrepreneurship. For example, Blattman et al. (2014) study a program in Uganda's conflict-affected north in which youths were invited to form groups and submit grant proposals for vocational training and business start-up. Funding was randomly assigned among screened and eligible groups. Treatment groups received unsupervised grants of $382 per member. They find that after four years, grant recipients invested in tools and materials and half practiced a skilled trade. Relative to the control group, the program increased business assets by 57%, work hours by 17%, and earnings by 38%. Many also formalize their enterprises and hire labor.[10]

Finally, there is a nascent literature on identifying entrepreneurs. Clearly, not everyone should be an entrepreneur so there are important selection and policy targeting issues to be understood: while subsistence entrepreneurship can be preferable to outside options in the labor market, such occupations often have limited potential for growth. There thus remains a pressing need to understand who becomes an entrepreneur, what are their motives for becoming self-employed, and how can potential entrepreneurs be targeted ex ante (Fafchamps and Woodruff 2014). Blattman and Dercon (2016) provide some important new evidence in this direction: they randomized entry-level applicants to five industrial firms in Ethiopia to one of three treatment arms: an industrial job offer; a control group; or an entrepreneurship program of $300 plus business training. Following individuals for a year, they determined that most applicants quit the industrial sector quickly, finding industrial jobs unpleasant and risky (but that they understood these risks ex ante, and used the time to search on the job). The entrepreneurship program stimulated self-employment, raised earnings by 33%, provided steady work hours, and halved the likelihood of taking an industrial job in future.

15.2.4.2 Labor

Wage subsidies are commonly used by governments to reduce unemployment or to sustain employment during downturns. There is some suggestion that by increasing labor market attachment for individuals, short-term wage subsidies may have long-term consequences on their labor market outcomes (Ham and Lalonde 1996; Bell et al. 1999). Some of the key motivations for giving micro-entrepreneurs wage subsidies in developing countries are that they may be uncertain about their own abilities to hire workers, uncertain whether they face enough demand to support an additional employee, or simply too credit constrained to invest in an additional employee. If any of the previous conditions hold, micro-entrepreneurs may decide not to hire an additional worker even if the marginal return from hiring would be positive.

Galasso et al. (2004) evaluate the *Proempleo Experiment* in Argentina, a program designed to assist the transition from workfare to regular work for individuals. The target population in this case included men and women enrolled in workfare programs. Program participants were randomly allocated to three groups: one group was given a voucher entitling any private sector employer to a wage subsidy; a second group was given the voucher and the offer to participate in a vocational training program. The third group was used as control. Being assigned the wage subsidy voucher had a positive impact on employment probability but not on income. However, take-up of the wage subsidy by firms was very low. A possible explanation for the low take-up is that program design firms had to register the new worker in order to be granted the subsidy. While the value of the subsidy exceeded the registration costs, the subsidy only lasted 18 months and so employers would have incurred substantial costs in order to retain the registered employee in the longer run. In addition, many potential employers were operating informally, so they could not register any worker at all. Still, some entrepreneurs decided to employ the workers with the voucher. The authors' interpretation of this finding is that either the voucher itself was viewed as a positive signal of employee quality by employers, or it gave stronger motivation to workers to look for a job. The extra impact of training over the wage subsidy were found to be very small.

De Mel et al. (2010) present evidence on the impacts of wage subsidies to micro-entrepreneurs using randomized experiment bases on Sri Lanka. Treated SMEs were offered a wage subsidy to employ a new worker. The wage subsidy was offered to 803 firms with fewer than two paid employees at baseline. The subsidy was fixed in monetary value and so did not vary across firms or regions, corresponding to approximately 50% of the average low-skill wage in the study area. The subsidy was offered for 6 months and phased out in months 7 and 8. They find that 22% of the firms offered the subsidy actually employed a new worker. Take-up was lower in Colombo, reflecting the fact that

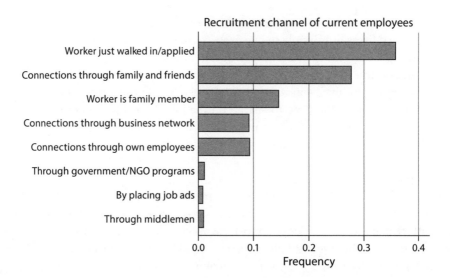

FIGURE 15.10. Worker recruitment channels. *Source*: Author's own ongoing work with various co-authors.

wages are higher in the capital city. There is some evidence that take-up was higher among larger SMEs with more assets to begin with, and that more skilled entrepreneurs were more likely to take up the subsidy. Interestingly, the recruitment of the new workers occurred mainly through social connections, rather than the placement of job advertisements or other intermediaries in the labor market. The authors find tremendous variation in the wage paid to the new workers. In fact, as the subsidy was independent of the wage paid to the new employee, a quarter of the firms taking up the subsidy effectively employed the new worker at zero cost. Eighty-six percent of the entrepreneurs expect to continue to employ the worker after the subsidy was removed, and the median firm expected to increase sales by 25% as a result of hiring the employee. This study shows that a short-run wage subsidy could have long-run impacts on firm growth. However, a puzzle raised by the results of this study is why only 22% of firms employed a new worker, especially when most of them could have done so at zero effective cost. Two possible explanations are: (i) there may be important information problems in local labor markets that a wage subsidy may not be able to overcome (as reflected in the use of social connections for new hires); (ii) there may be a lack of skilled workers in the local labor market.

Asymmetric information appears to be a fundamental feature of labor markets: firms and workers both have private information at the time they meet. This can lead to inefficient recruitment and a misallocation of workers to firms. In turn, such mismatches can have self-enforcing effects on workers' ex ante incentives to invest in skills or search behaviors. To provide some evidence on the potential for information asymmetries to play a role in low-income labor markets, we return to our ongoing study in Uganda, where firms were surveyed about their hiring practices. Figure 15.10 provides evidence on their recruitment channels: we see the majority of workers are hired through individuals approaching the firm (who are unknown to the firm beforehand). Middle men

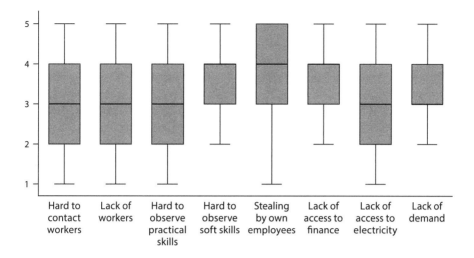

FIGURE 15.11. Perceived importance of labor market constraints. *Source*: Author's own ongoing work with various co-authors.

and job advertisements play a negligible role in hiring in this sample. Figure 15.11 then shows a box and whisker plot of the perceived importance firm owners have over various informational constraints related to worker hires. The standout concerns relate to information over the trustworthiness of workers and their soft skills: such constraints are reported to be as important as those related to access to credit. Figure 15.12 complements this with a report of the kinds of information that firm owners say they wish to have on employees at the point of recruitment: trustworthiness is the top characteristic, although other aspects, such as an individual's creativity, communication skills, and willingness to help others, all feature highly. Table 15.1 shows that there is a low correlation in such skills among workers we have interviewed in Ugandan labor markets, so that the same underlying trait is not simply being picked up in multiple different ways (indeed, a number of the correlations are close to zero or even negative).

Other papers have studied matching and job placement in the labor market. For example, Hardy and McCasland (2015) use a field experiment that randomly placed unemployed young individuals as apprentices with SMEs in Ghana. The intervention reduced search costs for firms and workers, but also allowed firms to better screen workers as workers' participation required them to incur non-monetary costs. They find firms that were offered apprentices, hired and retained them for at least six months, and apprenticeships are associated with monthly increases of around 7–10% in firm revenues and profits relative to the baseline. The findings suggest the presence of economically significant search costs in this context. Franklin (2015) presents evidence from an RCT that randomly assigned transport subsidies to unemployed youth in Addis Ababa. He finds that lowering transport costs increases the intensity of job search and increases the likelihood of finding good employment in the short run. Treated respondents also reallocate time away from labor supply in temporary work toward search activities. Abebe et al. (2016) present further evidence from the same setting that experimentally reducing job search costs (either by providing a transport subsidy or by certifying their skills

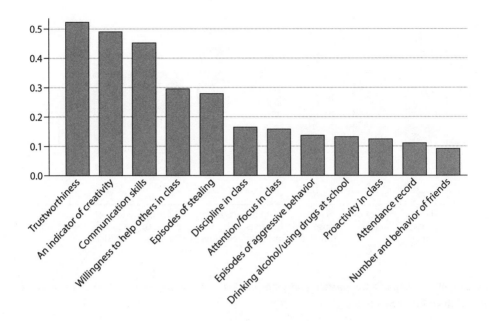

FIGURE 15.12. Information firm owners would like to observe on potential hires. *Source*: Author's own ongoing work with various co-authors.

Table 15.1. Correlation Among Non-Cognitive Skills

	Pairwise correlation coefficients				
	Creativity	Communication skills	Willingness to help others	Attendance	Trustworthiness
Creativity	1				
Communication skills	0.0824	1			
Willingness to help others	0.0989	0.6329	1		
Attendance	0.0727	0.6608	0.6583	1	
Trustworthiness	0.0472	−0.0346	−0.0615	0.0357	1

Source: Author's own ongoing work with various co-authors.

and teaching them how to make effective job applications). They find that both treatments significantly improve the quality of jobs obtained and that the impacts are concentrated among women and the least educated.

We return to the issue in the next section when discussing workers' non-cognitive skills: if there are returns to them in low-income labor markets, and whether such skills are observable by potential hiring firms.

15.2.4.3 Entrepreneurial Skills

On the provision of entrepreneurial skills, there is generally a view emerging that such programs have had disappointing impacts on firm performance. This is the case for most stand-alone short-term training programs targeted to existing micro-entrepreneurs. A meta-analysis of such interventions in McKenzie and Woodruff (2013) finds little impact of entrepreneurial training programs in SMEs (Field et al. 2010; Karlan and Valdivia 2011; Drexler et al. 2014; Fairlie et al. 2015; Bruhn et al. 2016). One exception to this is the study by Calderon et al. (2013) based on micro-enterprises in rural Mexico, who report that the key channel through which such entrepreneurial programs impact firm outcomes is through an altered product mix.

A separate strand of literature has studied the complementarity between capital and entrepreneurial skills. Recent evaluations of business training programs for aspiring entrepreneurs with and without capital grants provide evidence of such complementarity (McKenzie and Woodruff 2012). This is consistent with the fact that many evaluations of microfinance alone suggest it does not help create new businesses (Karlan and Zinman 2011; Kaboski and Townsend 2011; Banerjee, Duflo, Glennerster et al. 2015; Crepon et al. 2015) and with the disappointing performance of most stand-alone short-term training programs for existing micro-entrepreneurs as described above.

Beaman et al. (2014) examine a specific form of constraint related to the human capital of firm owners: the limited attention of entrepreneurs toward their business. The authors focus on a particular business decision—how much change to keep on the business premises to break large bills and ensure business transactions can occur. The authors study a sample of 508 micro-enterprises operating in markets in Kenya. Lack of change seems to be a common problem for these firms: at baseline the average firm loses 5–8% of profits due to lack of appropriate change. The authors carry out two interventions using a randomized experiment. The first is a "reminder" intervention: firms are visited weekly and asked questions on whether and how often they ran out of change in the past week and the value of sales lost as a result. Asking these questions was designed to make salient to entrepreneurs the problem of lack of change. Firms taking part in the study started receiving visits at different points in time, and this is used to identify the effect of such reminders. A second intervention was an "information" intervention. A random set of firms, after a few visits, were also told how much profit they had lost due to the lack of change. Comparing firms that received the information intervention to firms that did not receive the intervention (holding constant the total number of visits) reveals the impact of the information intervention. The authors find that the reminder intervention significantly reduced the number of times firms run out of change by 12%, while the information intervention reduced it by 20%. Profits increased by 12% in the information intervention (the effect of the reminder intervention was not statistically significant).

While training programs targeting micro-entrepreneurs have met with limited success, there is increased recognition that management practices in firms can account for a large share of cross-country productivity differences (Bloom and Van Reenen 2007; McKenzie and Woodruff 2015). Indeed, experimental impacts of managerial capital have been found for larger firms (Bloom et al. 2013). Contrary to the prevalence of institutional constraints highlighted in figure 15.6, the quality of management practices does exhibit a correlation with GDP per capita. Bruhn et al. (2016) present evidence from a randomized control trial with 432 SMEs in Mexico, showing that access to management consulting had positive effects on total factor productivity and return-on-assets. They find permanent increases in the number of employees and total wage bill five years post-intervention. While they document heterogeneity in the specific managerial practices that improved as a result of the consulting, the three most prominent areas were marketing, financial accounting, and long-term business planning. Following from the results reported in Calderon et al. (2013) as described above, improving managerial capital in SMEs is certainly worth studying further in future work. However, such interventions seem to have different impacts across contexts, so more needs to be done to understand what drives these differences: for example, Karlan et al. (2015) conducted a randomized control trial in urban Ghana in which 160 tailoring micro-enterprises received consulting advice, cash, both, or neither. They find that no treatment led to higher profits on average and that in the long run, micro-entrepreneurs reverted back to their prior business practices.

15.2.4.4 Asset Transfers

We have focused the discussion on entrepreneurs operating in the manufacturing or service sectors. However, in many low-income countries, the majority of the labor force remains engaged in agricultural work. Subsistence entrepreneurship, namely, livelihoods based around livestock businesses in the rural sector, remain of fundamental importance in driving income growth. Such activities are not well documented in cross-country datasets such as the WBES data. However, a recent body of evidence has emerged to understand whether subsistence entrepreneurship can be kick-started among ultra-poor households, many of whom typically do not qualify for microfinance programs due to their lack of assets (Banerjee et al. 2015; Bandiera et al. 2016). This evidence base suggests programs targeting the very poorest households with: (i) high valued asset transfers in the form of livestock, coupled with (ii) complementary training in using livestock as productive assets, are effective in kick-starting these households' engagement into basic entrepreneurship. In turn, this leads to such ultra-poor households becoming less reliant on more volatile income streams earned from participation in agricultural spot labor markets. In contrast, forms of basic entrepreneurship based around the sale of livestock produce and animal rearing lead to sustained increases in labor productivity, average incomes, and reduced income volatility, allowing consumption to be smoothed over time and asset accumulation to be undertaken. Overall, these interventions are found to be cost-effective with internal rates of return of between 10% and 20% across contexts.

Table 15.2 summarizes the impacts found in such studies, where three-year impacts are reported: these provide a relatively consistent picture of the types of effects that such asset-skills transfer programs have on subsistence entrepreneurship, across a range of economic and social outcomes. Bandiera et al. (2017) use a partial population experiment to also document the general equilibrium and distributional impacts of such large-scale asset-skills transfer programs on village economies. Banerjee et al. (2016) and Bandiera et al. (2017) provide evidence on the long-run impacts of such programs, some seven years after the injection of capital and skills is first provided. This shows sustained improvements in household outcomes, suggestive of the fact that such programs place households on a sustained trajectory out of poverty.[11]

There remain issues to be researched related to the optimal design of such asset-skill transfer programs: (i) what is the optimal package of transfers to make, in other words, what is the relative importance of constraints related to capital and those related to labor productivity?; (ii) how heterogeneous are the impacts of asset transfer programs across households, and given that such programs are costly, what does this heterogeneity of

Table 15.2. Comparison with Pilot Results from Six Countries

Standard Errors in Parentheses, Clustered by BRAC Branch Area

Panel A	(1) Total per capita consumption, standardized	(2) Food security index	(3) Asset index	(4) Financial inclusion index	(5) Total time spent working by main woman, standardized	(6) Total time spent working by both respondents pooled, standardized	(7) Incomes and revenues index
Treatment effect—four-year endline	0.314***	0.256***	0.327***	0.313***	0.122*	0.065	0.627***
	(0.034)	(0.079)	(0.029)	(0.040)	(0.065)	(0.047)	(0.074)
Treatment Effect in Banerjee et al. (2015)—three-year endline	*0.120**	*0.113***	*0.249***	*0.212***	*n/a*	*0.054***	*0.273***
	(0.024)	*(0.022)*	*(0.024)*	*(0.031)*		*(0.018)*	*(0.029)*

Panel B	(8) Physical health index	(9) Mental health index	(10) Political Awareness index	(11) Women's empower-ment index
Treatment effect—four-year endline	0.108***	0.077*	0.269***	0.077
	(0.027)	(0.043)	(0.091)	(0.056)
Treatment Effect in Banerjee et al. (2015)—three-year endline	*0.029*	*0.071***	*0.064***	*0.022*
	(0.020)	*(0.020)*	*(0.019)*	*(0.025)*

Source: Bandiera et al. (2017).

impact imply about the optimal targeting of such asset transfer programs?; (iii) as with the literature described earlier on capital injections to firms, a remaining set of issues to explore in future research relates to comparing the impacts of such asset transfer programs with offering the poorest households the equivalent unconditional cash transfer. Understanding from the policymakers' perspective the choice between in-kind asset transfers and training versus the provision of equivalent valued unconditional cash transfers gets to the heart of the design of social protection policies. Studying this comparison in the same setting and understanding how households choose to invest cash sheds light on the existence and nature of market constraints that cause capital and labor constraints to bind in the first place.

15.3. WORKERS

Raising the human capital of individuals and aiding them to become productive members of the labor force are key issues all policymakers in low-income countries face. The demographics of much of the developing world make the transitions between schooling and the labor force an especially important time to study. One billion people on the planet are aged between 15 and 24 and reside in a developing country, an increase of 17% since 1995, and there are great demands on policymakers to consider responses to this "youth bulge" (World Bank 2007, 2009). The central policy challenge is to provide skills and job opportunities to increasing numbers of young people. This phenomenon is most pronounced in Sub-Saharan Africa, where 60% of the population is younger than age 25 (World Bank 2009). Youths face severe economic challenges, as they account for most of the region's poor and unemployed: in Sub-Saharan Africa, 60% of the total unemployed are aged 15–24, and on average 72% of the youth population live on less than $2 per day.

We consider two branches of literature studying workers in low-income labor markets. These relate to the provision of vocational and on-the-job training (i.e., apprenticeships), the returns to and provision of non-cognitive skills.

15.3.1. Training

The WBES allows us to explore issues related to training provision in formal sector firms. Figure 15.13 shows the percentage of firms reporting to provide training to their workers, by country (ranked by GDP per capita in 2006). We see that a large percentage of firms provide training, and this is nearly always higher in larger firms. There are two primary competing models of firm investment in training. Becker's (1962) seminal work argues that firms operating in perfect markets always have an incentive to invest in firm-specific training, that is, in those skills that are useful only with the current firm. However, firms never have an incentive to invest in general training, that is, in such skills that are useful also in other firms: in perfect markets workers are paid their marginal product and thus they appropriate all the returns from general training. Thus, all observed firm-sponsored training should be in firm-specific skills.

Acemoglu and Pischke (1999) instead show that when the labor market is characterized by a compressed wage structure, that is, when frictions in the labor market imply that firms make higher profits from more skilled workers, firms have incentives to also invest in general training. Labor market frictions, such as unemployment, asymmetric information, or high search costs, reduce the outside option for skilled workers relatively

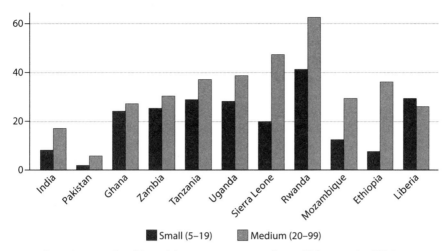

Small (5–19)   Medium (20–99)

Countries are ordered from richest to poorest according to GDP per capita, PPP, in 2006.

FIGURE 15.13. Provision of formal training. *Source*: WBES.

more than for unskilled workers. This creates a distortion in the wage structure. In consequence, firms are able to appropriate some of the returns from general training, and so find it profitable to invest in the general skills of their employees. Two immediate comparative static results of this theory are that we should observe more on-the-job training and higher tenure effects in labor markets with a more compressed wage structure. Hence, in countries with a more compressed wage structure, on-the-job training is an even more important source of human capital accumulation and skill creation.

There is a substantive empirical literature on why firms invest in the general skills of workers in Europe and the United States. Most of these studies suggest that informational asymmetries on the skills of workers justify firm-sponsored general training (Acemoglu and Pischke 1998, 1999; Autor 2001). While evaluations of labor market training programs in industrialized countries generally produce mixed results (Card, Kluve, and Weber 2010, 2015), such programs may have larger impacts in middle- and low-income countries, where the returns to skills are higher and where the skill level of the population is lower to begin with. On the consequences of training, the academic literature has evaluated several large-scale labor market programs in Latin America. Attanasio et al. (2011) and Card et al. (2011) are the two most prominent examples.

Attanasio et al. (2011) study the impact of a randomized training program on the employment outcomes of disadvantaged youth in Colombia. The program studied, Jovenes en Accion, was introduced between 2001 and 2005 and provided subsidized training to poor unemployed young people (age 18–25) belonging to the lowest socioeconomic strata of the population and residing in urban areas. Training consisted of three months of in-classroom training and three months of on-the-job training (i.e., an apprenticeship). On-the-job training was provided in the form of unpaid internships at legally registered firms. The program cost US$750 per recipient, operating in the seven largest cities of Colombia. Training was delivered in a number of occupational sectors chosen by the training institutions to meet labor market demand. Training institutions were asked to select a number of applicants greater than they could accommodate. An oversubscription design was then utilized so that applicants were randomly selected into a treatment group and a control group. The study uses a sample of 2,040 and 2,310 individuals in the treatment and control groups respectively. Two survey waves were conducted: a baseline in 2005 and a follow-up between August and October 2006. The issue of non-random attrition is documented to be a slight concern for men. The authors estimate the ITT impact of the offer of training. As the compliance rate is 97%, the identified effect is close to an average treatment effect for those volunteering for the program. They find that for women, employment increases significantly by 6.1 percentage points and paid employment increases by 7.1 percentage points. This is mirrored by a significant increase in the days per month and hours per week. Salary earnings increase by 22% of control women's earnings. They find no significant effects for men, except a higher probability of working in the formal sector. Overall, the program appears to have had strong effects for women.

Attanasio et al. (2015) go on to use administrative records to trace through the longer term impacts of the same intervention. They find that a decade later, the program had a positive and significant effect on the probability of working in the formal sector. Treated applicants contributed more months to social security and were more likely to work for a large firm. Earnings of treated applicants were 12% higher. Finally, they report the benefits of the program are higher than its costs, leading to an internal rate of return of at least 22%. This compares favorably with other development policy interventions.

Card et al. (2011) evaluate a similar training program for disadvantaged youth in the Dominican Republic. The program studied, *Juventud y Empleo*, provided three months of in-class training and two months of on-the-job training to low-income youth with less than a high school diploma, currently not working or attending school. The data come from a baseline survey and a follow-up. The authors find no impact of the training program on the likelihood of being employed at follow-up. They instead find a 10% effect on earnings. The program has no effect on hours but a 7–10% effect on wages.

Evidence on training programs outside of Latin America remain scarce but are beginning to emerge. Hicks et al. (2011) present preliminary evidence of the impact of the *Technical and Vocational Vouchers Program*, a vocational training voucher and information program for disadvantaged youth in Kenya. There were 526 applicants randomly assigned unrestricted vouchers (to be spent in either private or public vocational training centers); 529 were randomly assigned vouchers for public training centres; 1,108 youth served as control group. A random sample of applicants was also given detailed information about the returns from training: applicants were told about the large gaps in the typical earnings in male-dominated occupations such as auto mechanics relative to female-dominated occupations such as tailoring. The early results of the intervention are: (i) 74% of the individuals offered a voucher enrolled into a VTP: the main reasons for not enrolling were costs related to transportation or room and board, or factors related to maternity and child care; (ii) at baseline, applicants had optimistic expected returns from training: they believed the average returns to be 61% compared to an estimated Mincerian return of 37%. Also, they had imprecise information about the highest earning trades. The information intervention had an impact on the choice of women to enroll for male-dominated occupations.

Alfonsi et al. (2016) evaluate the two most common forms of training against each other: vocational training and on-the-job training, in a representative sample of urban labor markets in Uganda. Their core contribution is to separate out the returns to each element of training: (i) the type of training workers receive; (ii) the fact that workers are matched to firms and so increase their labor market experience per se. The experimental design assigns workers to two treatment groups: (T1) those offered placement of on-the-job training with interested firms; (T2) those offered the provision of six months of sector-specific vocational skills training. Comparing T1 and T2 reveals the differential returns of the two most common forms of training program utilized in developed and developing countries (on-the-job training vs. vocational training). The randomization exploits an oversubscription design, where individuals initially apply for the vocational training program. The evaluation is then based on tracking more than 1,700 workers from baseline through follow-up surveys after 24 and 36 months. The firms that workers are matched to in T3 and T4 are from a nationally representative sample of SMEs operating in the same sectors in which training was provided/sought on application.

The reduced form impacts comparing on-the-job and vocational training show that: (i) both forms of training have significant impacts on the extensive margin of finding wage employment (by around 25% relative to the control group); (ii) both treatments have significant impacts on hourly workers, hourly wages, and total earnings (by at least 30%). These results are shown to be robust to allowing for selective attrition using Lee bound estimates. Following Attanasio et al. (2011) they split the total earnings impacts into those arising from a change in composition of employed workers (extensive margin impacts) and those arising from pure productivity impacts. Their bounds estimates of the productivity impacts suggest both forms of training have positive productivity impacts, with vocational training having the larger impact on worker productivity. They verify the impacts on hourly earnings and productivity bounds by implementing a practical skills test to workers in all treatment groups: in line with the earlier evidence, this shows vocational training to significantly raise practical skills, both relative to the control group and relative to the workers that were assigned to on-the-job training. The final part of their analysis estimates a structural model of worker job search, where workers make two endogenous choices: (i) how much search effort to exert; (ii) their reservation wage. Using monthly data on labor market histories for workers, they use the experiment to identify the structural model and shed light on how training impacts these two endogenous outcomes through two mechanisms: (i) worker beliefs over the arrival of job offers; (ii) the distribution of offered wages. They use these structural estimates to conduct counterfactual policy analysis, and to estimate the lifetime benefits of training and matching routes into the labor market, and so estimate the internal rate of return of each treatment to be around 22%.

The evidence on training in low-income settings is continuing to grow: we have little evidence outside Latin America, and it remains to be well understood why so few individuals take up such programs despite their high returns, or how policy can encourage the efficient supply of such programs. In particular, it is important to establish how the suppliers of such training programs, be they governments, NGOs, or private entities, determine what skills to provide, the quality of provision, and to what extent workers are aware of the quality of training they receive.

15.3.2 Non-Cognitive and Life Skills

Evidence from the United States and Europe suggests that both non-cognitive abilities (such as motivation, perseverance, trustworthiness, and tenacity) and cognitive abilities (such as IQ) are important determinants of labor market outcomes [controlling for education, experience, and other practical skills]. Many studies suggest non-cognitive skills may be more important than cognitive abilities (Bowles and Gintis 2001; Heckman et al. 2006), especially in low-skilled occupations (Linqvist and Vestman 2011) in which employers tend to value docility, dependability, and persistence more than cognitive skills (Bowles and Gintis 2001). This area remains under researched in low-income settings.

An insight into the issue is provided in Bassi and Nansamba (2016), who study information frictions on the soft skills of workers during the hiring process in firms. They present results from a field experiment in which such worker skills are revealed to potential employers at the time of hiring. They find that in the control group where no new information is revealed, firm owners of higher cognitive ability are more likely to hire workers with higher skills. High ability owners react to the information revelation treatment by increasing hires among matched workers with a lower level of the skills being signaled. On the contrary, firm owners of lower ability do not react to the new information. The intervention is shown to have persistent effects, and also affects the outside options of workers, thus facilitating the reallocation of labor across jobs in the economy. Overall, the study highlights that there are positive returns to soft skills in this low-income labor market, and that such skills are difficult to observe for employers.

A body of work now exists to study life skills programs that have typically been targeted to adolescent girls in low-income contexts. For adolescent girls, economic concerns on acquiring labor market skills are compounded by health-related challenges such as early wedlock and pregnancy, exposure to STDs, and HIV infection. These economic and health issues are obviously interlinked: teen pregnancy and early marriage are likely to have a decisive impact on the ability of young girls to accumulate human capital, and thereby limit their future labor force participation (Field and Ambrus 2008). At the same time, a lack of future labor market opportunities can reduce the incentives for young girls to invest in their human capital and raise labor productivity (Jensen 2012), leading to early marriage and childbearing, and potentially increasing their dependency on older men (Dupas 2011).[12] Economic empowerment and control over the body thus interact in a powerful way during adolescence. Hence, interventions targeted toward adolescent girls might have higher returns than later timed interventions (Heckman and Mosso 2014).

Many policy interventions targeted to youth focus on: HIV education and related issues to reduce risky behaviors, or vocational training to improve labor market outcomes. There are relatively weak impacts of single-pronged interventions (Gallant and Maticka-Tyndale 2004; McCoy et al. 2010), and so an emerging literature has focused attention on multi-pronged interventions.

One example is Bandiera et al. (2015), who evaluate an intervention attempting to jump-start adolescent women's empowerment in Uganda. The intervention relaxes the human capital constraints that adolescent girls face by simultaneously providing them vocational training and information on sex, reproduction, and marriage. Relative to adolescents in control communities, after two years the intervention raises the likelihood that girls engage in income-generating activities by 72% (driven by increased self-employment) and raises their expenditure on private consumption goods by 38%. Teen pregnancy falls by 26%, and early entry into marriage/cohabitation falls by 58%. Strikingly, the share of girls reporting sex against their will drops from 14% to almost half that level, and aspired ages at marriage and childbearing both move forward. The findings suggest women's economic and social empowerment can be jump-started through the combined provision of hard and soft skills, in the form of vocational and life skills, and is not necessarily held back by binding constraints arising from social norms or low aspirations.

Duflo et al. (2014) study the coupling of soft-skill transfers with financial incentives. They evaluate a school-based HIV prevention program in Kenya coupled with subsidies to attend school, and present evidence highlighting the joint determination of schooling and pregnancy outcomes for adolescent girls. This shows the efficacy of providing adolescent girls information on how to reduce their exposure to pregnancy risks, and this becomes more efficient when reinforced by program components that simultaneously empower girls to lead economically independent lives.[13]

Finally, Blattman et al. (2017) report evidence from an RCT targeted toward criminally engaged men in Liberia, randomizing half to eight weeks of cognitive behavioral therapy (CBT) designed to foster self-regulation, patience, and a noncriminal identity. They also randomized participants into receiving $200 cash grants. They find that cash transfers alone and CBT alone initially reduced crime and violence, but effects dissipate over time. However, when cash followed therapy, crime and violence decreased dramatically for at least a year. They hypothesize that cash reinforced therapy's impacts by prolonging learning-by-doing, lifestyle changes, and enabling individuals to engage in self-investment. The study is important for highlighting links between non-cognitive skills and resources.

Just as with understanding constraints on firms, there is an open agenda on understanding the interlinkages of constraints individuals face in making investments in their human capital, that can help them successfully transition into the labor market. Understanding these complementarities or substitutabilities is needed to feed into the design of more cost-effective policies.

15.4. LABOR MARKETS

We now study marketwide issues that enable us to link back to the kinds of institutional constraint highlighted as relevant drags on firm expansion in the WBES data.

15.4.1. (In)Formality

A large share of SMEs in low-income countries are informal, and as documented in Freeman (2009), the informal sector increased its share of the workforce in the developing world in the past two decades. While informal firms tend to be small and unproductive, in aggregate they represent a substantial share of economic activity, nearly one-third on average across low-income countries and in some, such as Tanzania, Zambia, and Myanmar, well over half (Schneider et al. 2010). This has two important consequences. First, informality deprives the government of tax revenues and weakens the provision of public services. Second, informality can allow persistent dispersion in marginal production

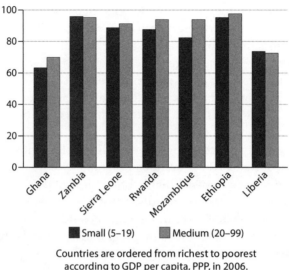

Small (5–19)   Medium (20–99)

Countries are ordered from richest to poorest
according to GDP per capita, PPP, in 2006.

FIGURE 15.14. Firms formally registered when started. *Source*: WBES.

costs, leading to an inefficient allocation of resources and hindering economic growth (La Porta and Shleifer 2008).

The WBES covers only firms that are formally registered. However, these data still allow us to explore some features of the informal sector. Firms are asked if they registered when they started business or after some time and whether they have informal competitors. As figures 15.14 and 15.15 show, these data suggest the majority of formally registered firms started out that way or registered soon after operations commenced.

Only a handful of countries make a concerted effort to identify and survey informal firms. Mexico's Economic Census (CE) is one such example. Comparing these data with the distribution of firms in the WBES sample for Mexico provides some indication of the gaps. Small firms, those with ten or fewer employees, are substantially more prevalent in the CE, representing over 90% of firms in manufacturing, retail, and services, in contrast to roughly 40% in the weighted WBES data for the same sectors. This is no surprise— the WBES targets registered firms with five or more employees. Busso et al. (2012) draw three conclusions from the Mexican data. First, informality and illegality are not equivalent. It is possible for both firms and workers to be informal and legal. This is because the Mexican labor regulation requires firms to register their salaried workers: those that are paid a fixed amount of money per unit of time. Non-salaried workers, paid in the form of a piece rate or anyway irrespective of the amount of time they work, don't have to be registered. Therefore, if a firm only employs nonsalaried workers and doesn't register any of them, it is considered informal and legal. Second, while informality is certainly correlated with size, it is not equivalent. There are many small and formal firms as well as large and informal firms. Third, informal firms do not necessarily perform poorly. Many are actually highly productive.

There is a body of empirical evidence studying aspects of entrepreneurs' decisions to formally register their businesses. De Soto's (1989) work has had a profound effect on

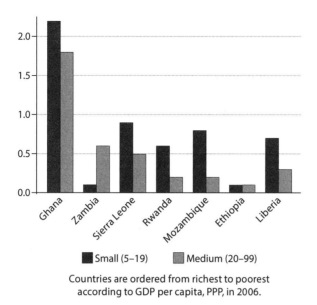

Small (5–19)   Medium (20–99)

Countries are ordered from richest to poorest
according to GDP per capita, PPP, in 2006.

FIGURE 15.15. Number of years firms operated without registration. *Source*: WBES.

how policymakers think about formalization, arguing that burdensome regulation prevents small firms from formalizing. Partly in response to these arguments, nearly three-quarters of the countries included in the World Bank and IFC's Doing Business surveys have adopted at least one reform designed to facilitate business registration.

Much of the work in this area has been done in Mexico, which has high-quality data on informal firms via its Economics Census and also has enacted significant reforms to the formalization process, including reducing the time to register a firm in some sectors from 30 to 2 days at the municipal level. These reforms induced modest increases in formalization (the fraction of registered businesses increased by 5%) but the mechanism through which even these small changes were affected remains uncertain. Bruhn (2011) finds that any increases appear to be due to new entry rather than the formalization of existing firms, while Kaplan et al. (2011) use different data and find the opposite result. Fanjzylber et al. (2011) find that increased formality is associated with higher productivity in small firms.

The SIMPLES program in Brazil has also attracted significant study. This reform simplified the tax system for micro- and small enterprises by combining six different taxes into one. It also reduced the overall tax burden and the red tape involved in the tax payment. Monteiro and Assunção (2012) provide evidence that the reform did affect registration behavior, showing an increase in formality for just those sectors affected by the reform. Fajnzylber et al. (2011) find that firms opening post-reform tend to be larger and more likely to have a permanent location. They interpret this finding as evidence that formalization improves performance, but as de Mel et al. (2013) point out, this could also result from selective firm entry.

A relatively new strand of the literature suggests that high levels of informality may stem from the modest ongoing benefits of formality rather than the high up-front cost of formalization. Emerging evidence from Sri Lanka and Peru suggests that while firms may overestimate the costs to formalization, the short-run gains are similarly muted (Alcázar et al. 2010; de Mel et al. 2013). Maloney (2004) suggests that smaller and less productive firms may get little benefit from formalization, so that informality may be a rational calculation of costs and benefits. McKenzie and Sakho (2010) demonstrate significant heterogeneity in response to firm registration in Bolivia. Even if formalization may bring benefits to some small firms, perhaps these benefits are not universal. Jaramillo (2013) studies a registration subsidy for micro-enterprises in Lima, Peru. He finds that the limited growth aspirations of these firms combined with the recurring costs and low perceived benefits of formalization yield very low demand for formalization.

De Mel et al. (2013) provide compelling evidence that reducing formalization costs alone may have a limited impact on registrations and provide further support for the hypothesis that a lack of meaningful ongoing benefits may be the key obstacle to increasing formalization. Their study builds on a randomized experiment testing different incentives for formality in Sri Lanka. Providing information about the registration process and reimbursing all direct costs was not enough to get firms to register. Even with powerful monetary incentives, up to an additional two months of the median profits for firms in their sample, only half of firms choose to register. Those that do report higher profits on average, but this result is driven by a few very successful firms.

Finally, a contrasting empirical approach is followed by Meghir et al. (2015), who develop and estimate an equilibrium wage-posting model with heterogeneous firms to explain the choice between formality and informality. Estimating the model on Brazilian labor force survey data they find that in equilibrium, firms of equal productivity located in different sectors and wages are characterized by compensating differentials. They show that tightening enforcement on firm registration does not increase unemployment. However, better enforcement does increase wages, output, and welfare because it allows an improved allocation of workers to higher productivity jobs, and increases competition in the formal labor market.

15.4.2 Other Issues: Infrastructure and Unions

The state plays a leading role in the provision of infrastructure, and this can have dramatic impacts on labor markets, by increasing interfirm linkages, connecting firms to markets, and by increasing the scope of search possibilities for workers. At the aggregate level, a large body of literature, starting with Aschauer (1989), has found a positive relation between infrastructure capital and TFP in the United States. Mitra et al. (2002) estimate this effect for the Indian manufacturing sector. They find that infrastructure endowments explain a large part of TFP differences across Indian states. Within this literature, another strand has focused on specific components of infrastructure and their impact on economic outcomes. The role of energy is sufficiently important to merit its own focus. Using firm-level data, Reinikka and Svensson (1999) show that the lack of reliable power supply in Uganda reduces private investment productivity by forcing firms to invest in generators and other low-productivity substitutes for reliable public provision of power. Allcott et al. (2016) study the impact of power shortages on firms' productivity in India. They find that although power cuts are perceived as very damaging by entrepreneurs, the effect is small.

On the impact of transportation links on firms, Banerjee et al. (2012) and Donaldson (2018) estimate the impact of railroads in China and India, respectively. The former find that in China, proximity to the transportation network had a small impact on the levels of GDP per capita but no effect on growth. In India, Donaldson (2018) finds railroads increased trade and income per capita. On the effects of other infrastructure on firms, Duflo and Pande (2007) find that irrigation dams in India increase agricultural productivity and reduce rural poverty in downstream districts, while having the opposite effect in the districts where dams are built.

Unions play an important role in determining outcomes in labor markets, yet are relatively understudied in the context of low-income countries. Freeman (2009) provides an excellent review of the literature on the impact of government regulations and union activity on labor outcomes, summarizing some of his findings as follows: (i) labor institutions vary greatly among developing countries, with unions and collective bargaining being less important in developing than in advanced countries, while government regulations are as important; (ii) many developing countries' compliance with minimum wage regulations produce spikes in wage distributions around the minimum in covered sectors; (iii) minimum wages often go on to impact informal sector wages, producing spikes in the wage distributions there as well; (iv) employment protection regulations and related laws shift output and employment to informal sectors and reduce gross labor mobility; (v) mandated benefits increase labor costs and reduce employment modestly, while the costs of others are shifted largely to labor; (vi) unions affect non-wage outcomes as well as wage outcomes.

Rios-Avila (2014) examines the impact of unions on productivity in the manufacturing sector across six Latin American countries. By estimating firm production functions using the WBES data, he finds that unions have positive, but mostly small, effects on productivity, but with some exceptions. In most cases, he finds the positive productivity effects barely offset higher union compensation, and that unions are negatively related to investment in capital and research and development. Given the heterogenous findings across countries, much still needs to be understood on the role of unions on firms, the distribution of wages, as well as the impacts on individual members.

15.5. DISCUSSION

We now bring together the earlier discussion to reiterate research areas where the role of institutions in relation to firms, workers, and labor markets is most in need of development.

On firms, an evidence base needs to be built across the entire firm size distribution, and to further open up the nature of institutional constraints faced by firms. For example, the functioning of land markets and firm performance, the link between infrastructure and firm TFP, and the impacts of labor regulations and corrupt behavior of officials on firms are all areas ripe for future study. We echo the appeal of Karlan and Fischer (2015) in suggesting the need to study the interplay between constraints rather than considering constraints on firms in isolation, and to have a more central focus on managerial practices in SMEs that seem to offer some promise as a cost-effective route by which to raise the productivity of small enterprises.[14]

Beyond constraints, many issues of the optimal targeting of policy remain: how do we identify firms with the highest growth potential, or channel resources toward those individuals with a comparative advantage in micro-entrepreneurship? The collective work on asset-skills transfers to the ultra-poor (Banerjee, Duflo, Goldberg et al. 2015; Bandiera et al. 2016) and on cash transfers to disadvantaged youth (Blattman et al. 2017) suggests that even those that start with low levels of human capital can become successful entrepreneurs.

On workers, a better understanding must be gleaned on the changing returns to cognitive and non-cognitive skills during the process of economic development. Much of this is being accelerated through trade linkages, which foster the development of new sectors in low-income countries. As with firms, there are analogous counterparts to understanding what constrains workers from acquiring the skills relevant for the labor market and the interplay between constraints. There are important supply-side issues to consider, most obviously in terms of understanding the market for training providers: what drives their quality, and can their incentives be designed to align their objectives with those of society?

On data and design issues, there are encouraging trends in the collection of both administrative datasets that allow worker outcomes to be tracked and matched employer-employee data in low-income contexts. These can play an enormous role in advancing understanding of how worker-firm matches occur and the dynamics of labor market transitions for workers. These new forms of data can also foster methodological advances. For example, they encourage the use of job search/worker-firm matching models, and this is best done through a combination of reduced form (experimental) and structural form modeling. Such structural job ladder models can be used to recover and explain wage distributions and potentially may also be used to understand consumption inequality. From a micro perspective, firm level studies must try to build into their design the possibility of measuring spillover effects of firm level interventions on other firms (local competitors, or upstream/downstream supply chains), and to further study the longer term impacts of interventions.[15]

All of this will be challenging but hugely insightful for policy.

NOTES

Presented at the Mid-year Conference of the Economic Development and Institutions (EDI) Project. I would like to thank the Project for providing helpful suggestions for the content of this chapter and for supporting this research. This chapter draws on research with numerous co-authors, as well as an IGC Evidence Paper jointly with Greg Fischer and Giulia Zane. Vittorio Bassi provided additional research assistance. All errors remain my own.

1. Another paper in this evidence review, Ayyagari et al. (2016) synthesizes the literature on firm financing, institutions, and growth in developing countries.
2. Banerjee and Duflo (2007) document how the poorest lack land and productive assets. In South Asia, it is well established that the rural landless poor mostly allocate their time toward forms of casual wage labor. According to the Indian NSS, 46% of the female rural workforce have agricultural wage employment as their main occupation, and 98% of agricultural wage employment is through casual employment typified by spot markets, not long-run contracts (Kaur 2014).
3. The sampling unit of the WBES is the "establishment": a physical location where business is carried out. As the survey describes, each sampling unit must "make its own financial decisions and have its own financial statements separate from those of the firm" and it must "have its own management and control over its payroll." The World Bank Enterprise Survey data are computed directly by the World Bank and made available on the website http://www.enterprisesurveys.org/.
4. For example, we note that there is substantial literature in trade investigating the impact of foreign competition, trade liberalization, or the interactions between domestic firms and multinationals on labor market outcomes in developed and developing countries. This is outside

the scope of the current chapter. Recent reviews of some aspects of this literature include Antras (2015), Foley and Manova (2015), and Bernard et al. (2017).

5. Teal (2016) shows that the number of jobs in Ghana's manufacturing sector expanded rapidly over the period from 1987 to 2003, almost entirely in small firms.

6. In a similar methodological spirit, Garicano et al. (2016) study the distortionary effects of Employment Protection Legislation (EPL) on the size and productivity distribution of firms in France. The study is motivated by the fact that EPL becomes particularly onerous for firms with more than 50 employees.

7. An alternative data source would be the Global Entrepreneurship Monitor Adult Population Survey (GEM) that took place over the period 2008–2010. These are individual-level surveys with a focus on entrepreneurial activity and aspirations. The GEM Uganda sample from 2010 covers 760 firms.

8. Countries are ranked according to their per capita GDP in 2006 based on purchasing power parity (PPP), using the World Bank's International Comparison Program database.

9. There are methodological challenges in all such work. For example, de Mel et al. (2009) provide evidence on how to best record micro-enterprise profits in low-income contexts. SMEs in developing countries generally do not keep financial records; firm owners may be reluctant to reveal earnings for fear that the information may be used for tax purposes (recall the importance of tax-related constraints reported in the WBES).

10. Fafchamps and Quinn (2016a) present evidence that giving US$1,000 cash transfers to winners of a business plan competition in Africa led to sizeable impacts on self-employment activity (relative to runners up in the competition).

11. Bauchet et al. (2015) evaluate a similar program in India but find little impact: the explanation is that in that context, households have good outside options in wage labor through the NREGA program, rather than taking up subsistence entrepreneurship through livestock rearing.

12. Baird et al. (2011) document that marriage and schooling are mutually exclusive activities in Malawi, and Ozier (2018) provides similar evidence from Kenya. In Bangladesh, Field and Ambrus (2008) show that each additional year that marriage is delayed is associated with 0.3 additional years of schooling and 6.5% higher literacy rates.

13. Relatedly, Baird et al. (2011) evaluate an intervention using only using financial incentives. They find a cash transfer of $10 per month conditional on school attendance for adolescent girls in Malawi led to significant declines in early marriage, teenage pregnancy, and self-reported sexual activity after a year. Baird et al. (2014) also report beneficial impacts on the economic and social empowerment of adolescent girls in Malawi who have dropped out of formal schooling from a cash transfer conditioned on school attendance.

14. An example of such an approach is Fiala (2014), who reports results from a field experiment targeting micro-entrepreneurs in Uganda to receive loans, cash grants, business skills training, or a combination of these programs. The results suggest that male-owned micro-enterprises can grow through finance when paired with training, but that the impacts on female entrepreneurs are muted for each intervention.

15. Fafchamps and Quinn (2018) provide an example of work in this direction, examining the diffusion of management practices in laboratory-induced social network ties between entrepreneurs. Outside of the lab, Fafchamps and Quinn (2016b) present evidence from a field experiment linking managers of manufacturing firms in Ethiopia, Tanzania, and Zambia. They find significant diffusion of business practices in terms of VAT registration and having a current bank account. This diffusion is a combination of diffusion of innovation and imitation.

REFERENCES

Abebe, G., S. Caria, M. Fafchamps, P. Falco, S. Franklin, and S. Quinn. 2016. "Curse of Anonymity or Tyranny of Distance? The Impacts of Job-Search Support in Urban Ethiopia." Mimeo, Oxford University.

Acemoglu, D. and J. S. Pischke. 1998. "Why Do Firms Train Workers? Theory and Evidence." *Quarterly Journal of Economics* 113: 79–119.

———. 1999. "The Structure of Wages and Investment in General Training." *Journal of Political Economy* 107: 539–572.

Alcázar, Lorena, Raúl Andrade, and Miguel Jaramillo. 2010. "Panel/Tracer Study on the Impact of Business Facilitation Processes on Enterprises and Identification of Priorities for Future Business

Enabling Environment Projects in Lima, Peru—Report 5: Impact Evaluation After the Third Round." Report to the International Finance Corporation, Mimeo.

Alfonsi, L., O. Bandiera, V. Bassi, R. Burgess, I. Rasul, M. Sulaiman, and A.Vitali. 2016. The Returns to Training in Low-income Labor Markets: Evidence from a Field Experiment and Structural Model. Mimeo, UCL.

Allcott, H., A. Collard-Wexler, and S. D. O'Connell. 2016. "How Do Input Shortages Affect Productivity? Evidence from Blackouts in India." *American Economic Review:* 587–624.

Antras, P. 2015. *Global Production: Firms, Contracts, and Trade Structure.* Princeton, NJ: Princeton University Press.

Aschauer, D. 1989. "Is Public Expenditure Productive?," *Journal of Monetary Economics* 23: 177–200.

Attanasio, O., A. Guarin, and C. Meghir. 2015. Long-Term Impacts of Vouchers for Vocational Training: Experimental Evidence for Colombia. Mimeo, UCL.

Attanasio, O. P., A. Kugler, and C. Meghir. 2011. "Subsidized Vocational Training for Disadvantaged Youth in Developing Countries: Evidence from a Randomized Trial." *American Economic Journal: Applied Economics* 3: 188–220.

Autor, D. 2001. "Why Do Temporary Help Firms Provide Free General Skills Training?" *Quarterly Journal of Economics* 116: 1409–1448.

Ayyagarim, A., A. Demirgüç-Kunt, and V. Maksimovic. 2016. Institutions, Firm Financing, and Growth. EDI Paper.

Baird, S. J., E. Chirwa, J. De Hoop, and B. Ozler. 2014. "Girl Power: Cash Transfers and Adolescent Welfare, Evidence from a Cluster-Randomized Experiment in Malawi." NBER Chapters, in *African Successes: Human Capital,* NBER.

Baird, S. J., C. T. Mcintosh, and B. Ozler. 2011. "Cash or Condition: Evidence from a Cash Transfer Experiment." *Quarterly Journal of Economics* 126: 1709–1753.

Bandiera, O., N. Buehren, R. Burgess, M. Goldstein, S. Gulesci, I. Rasul, and M. Sulaiman. 2015. Empowering Adolescent Girls: Evidence from a Randomized Control Trial in Uganda. Mimeo, UCL.

Bandiera, O., R. Burgess, N. Das, S. Gulesci, I. Rasul, and M. Sulaiman. 2017. "Labor Markets and Poverty in Village Economies." *Quarterly Journal of Economics* 132(May): 811–870.

Banerjee, A. V. and E. Duflo. 2007. "The Economic Lives of the Poor." *Journal of Economic Perspectives* 21: 141–168.

———. 2014. "Do Firms Want to Borrow More? Testing Credit Constraints Using a Directed Lending Program." *Review of Economic Studies* 81: 572–607.

Banerjee, A., E. Duflo, R. Glennerster, and C. Kinnan. 2015. "The Miracle of Microfinance? Evidence from a Randomized Evaluation." *American Economic Journal: Applied Economics* 7: 22–53.

Banerjee, A. V., E. Duflo, N. Goldberg, D. Karlan, R. Osei, W. Pariente, J. Shapiro, B. Thuysbaert, and C. Udry. 2015. "A Multi-faceted Program Causes Lasting Progress for the Very Poor: Evidence from Six Countries." *Science* 348: Issue 6236.

Banerjee, A. V., E. Duflo, and N. Qian. 2012. On the Road: Access to Transportation Infrastructure and Economic Growth in China. NBER Working Paper 17897.

Banerjee, A. V. and A. F. Newman. 1993. "Occupational Choice and the Process of Development." *Journal of Political Economy* 101: 274–298.

Bassi, V. and A. Nansamba. 2016. Information Frictions in the Labor Market: Evidence from a Field Experiment in Uganda. Mimeo, UCL.

Bauchet, Jonathan, Jonathan Morduch, and Shamika Ravi. 2015. "Failure vs Displacement: Why an Innovative Anti-Poverty Program Showed No Net Impact in South India." *Journal of Development Economics* 116 (September): 1–16.

Beaman, L., J. Magruder, and J. Robinson. 2014. "Minding Small Change: Limited Attention among Small Firms in Kenya." *Journal of Development Economics* 108: 69–86.

Becker, G. S. 1962. "Investment in Human Capital: A Theoretical Analysis." *Journal of Political Economy* 70: 9–49.

Bell, B., R. Blundell, and J. Van Reenen. 1999. "Getting the Unemployed Back to Work: The Role of Targeted Wage Subsidies." *International Tax and Public Finance* 6: 339–360.

Bernard, A., B. Jensen, S. Redding, and P. Schott. 2017. "Global Firms." *Journal of Economic Literature.*

Besley, T. and R. Burgess. 2004. "Can Labor Regulation Hinder Economic Performance? Evidence from India." *Quarterly Journal Of Economics* 119: 91–134.

Blattman, C. and S. Dercon. 2016. Occupational Choice in Early Industrializing Societies: Experimental Evidence on the Income and Health Effects of Industrial and Entrepreneurial Work. Mimeo, University of Chicago.

Blattman, C., N. Fiala, and S. Martinez. 2014. "Generating Skilled Self-employment in Developing Countries: Experimental Evidence from Uganda." *Quarterly Journal of Economics* 129: 697–752.

Blattman, C., J. Jamison, and M. Sheridan. 2017. "Reducing Crime and Violence: Experimental Evidence on Cognitive Behavioral Therapy in Liberia." *American Economic Review* 107(4): 1165–1206.

Bloom, N., B. Eifert, A. Mahajan, D. Mckenzie, and J. Roberts. 2013. "Does Management Matter: Evidence from India." *Quarterly Journal of Economics* 128: 1–51.

Bloom, N. and J. Van Reenen. 2007. "Measuring and Explaining Management Practices Across Firms and Countries." *Quarterly Journal of Economics* 122: 1351–1408.

Bowles, S. and H. Gintis. 2001. "Schooling in Capitalist America Revisited." *Sociology of Education* 75: 1–18.

Bruhn, M. 2011. "License to Sell: The Effect of Business Registration Reform on Entrepreneurial Activity in Mexico." *Review of Economics and Statistics* 93: 382–386.

Bruhn, M., D. Karlan, and A. Schoar. 2016. The Impact of Consulting Services on Small and Medium Enterprises: Evidence from a Randomized Trial in Mexico. Mimeo, Yale University.

Buera, F., J. P. Kaboski, and Y. Shin. 2011. "Finance and Development: A Tale of Two Sectors." *American Economic Review* 101: 800–820.

Busso, M., M. V. Fazio, and S. Levy Algazi. 2012. (In)Formal and (Un)Productive: The Productivity Costs of Excessive Informality in Mexico, Research Department Publications 4789, Inter-American Development Bank, Research Department.

Cai, H., H. Fang, and L. C. Xu. 2011. "Eat, Drink, Firms and Government: An Investigation of Corruption from Entertainment and Travel Costs of Chinese Firms." *Journal of Law and Economics* 54: 55–78.

Calderon, G., J. Cunha, and G. De Giorgi. 2013. Business Literacy and Development: Evidence from a Randomized Trial in Rural Mexico. Mimeo, Stanford University.

Card, D., P. Ibarran, F. Regalia, D. Rosas-Shady, and Y. Soares. 2011. "The Labor Market Impacts of Youth Training in the Dominican Republic." *Journal of Labor Economics* 29: 267–300.

Card, D., J. Kluve, and A. Weber. 2010. "Active Labour Market Policy Evaluations: A Meta Analysis." *Economic Journal* 120: F452–F477.

———. 2015. What Works? A Meta Analysis of Recent Active Labor Market Program Evaluations, IZA DP 9236.

Crepon, B., F. Devoto, E. Duflo, and W. Pariente. 2015. "Estimating the Impact of Microcredit on Those Who Take It Up: Evidence from a Randomized Experiment in Morocco." *American Economic Journal: Applied Economics*: 123–150.

De Mel, S., D. Mckenzie, and C. Woodruff. 2008a. "Returns to Capital in Microenterprises: Evidence from a Field Experiment." *Quarterly Journal Of Economics* 123: 1329–1372.

———. 2008b. "Mental Health Recovery and Economic Recovery after the Tsunami: High-Frequency Longitudinal Evidence from Sri Lankan Small Business Owners." *Social Science and Medicine* 66: 582–595.

———. 2009. "Measuring Microenterprise Profits: Must We Ask How the Sausage Is Made?" *Journal of Development Economics* 88: 19–31.

———. 2010. "Wage Subsidies for Microenterprises." *American Economic Review* 100: 614–618.

———. 2011. "Getting Credit to High-Return Microenterprises: The Results of an Information Intervention." *World Bank Economic Review* 25: 456–485.

———. 2013. "The Demand for, and Consequences of, Formalization among Informal Firms in Sri Lanka." *American Economic Journal: Applied Economics* 5: 122–150.

De Soto, H. 1989. *The Other Path: The Economic Answer to Terrorism.* New York: Harper & Row.

Donaldson, D. 2018. "Railroads of the Raj: Estimating the Impact of Transportation Infrastructure." *American Economic Review* 108(4–5): 899–934.

Drexler, A., G. Fischer, and A. Schoar. 2014. "Keeping It Simple: Financial Literacy and Rules of Thumb." *American Economic Journal: Applied Economics* 6: 1–31.

Duflo, E., P. Dupas, and M. Kremer. 2015. "Education, HIV and Early Fertility: Experimental Evidence from Kenya." *American Economic Review* 105(9): 2757–2797.

Duflo, E. and R. Pande. 2007. "Dams," *Quarterly Journal of Economics* 122: 601–646.

Dupas, P. 2011. "Do Teenagers Respond to HIV Risk Information? Evidence for a Field Experiment in Kenya." *American Economic Journal: Applied Economics* 3: 1–34.

Evans, D. S. and B. Jovanovic. 1989. "An Estimated Model of Entrepreneurial Choice Under Liquidity Constraints." *Journal of Political Economy* 97: 808–827.

Fafchamps, M., D. Mckenzie, S. R. Quinn, and C. Woodruff. 2014. "When Is Capital Enough to Get Female Microenterprises Growing? Evidence from a Randomized Experiment in Ghana." *Journal of Development Economics* 106: 211–226.

Fafchamps, M. and S. Quinn. 2016a. Aspire. Mimeo, Oxford University.

———. 2016b. Networks and Manufacturing Firms in Africa: Results from a Randomized Field Experiment. Mimeo, Oxford University.

———. 2018. "Networks and Manufacturing Firms in Africa: Results from a Randomized Field Experiment." *World Bank Economic Review* 32(3): 656–675.

Fafchamps, M. and C. Woodruff. 2014. Identifying Gazelles: Expert Panels vs. Surveys as a Means to Identify Firms with Rapid Growth Potential. Mimeo, Warwick University.

Fairlie, R., D. Karlan, and J. Zinman. 2015. "Behind the GATE Experiment: Evidence on Effects of and Rationales for Subsidized Entrepreneurship Training." *American Economic Journal: Economic Policy* 7: 125–161.

Fajnzylber, P., W. Maloney, and G. Montes-Rojas. 2011. "Does Formality Improve Micro-firm Performance? Evidence from the Brazilian SIMPLES Program." *Journal of Development Economics* 94: 262–276.

Fiala, N. 2014. Stimulating Microenterprise Growth: Results from a Loans, Grants and Training Experiment in Uganda. Mimeo, DIW Berlin.

Field, E. and A. Ambrus. 2008. "Early Marriage, Age of Menarche and Female Schooling Attainment in Bangladesh." *Journal of Political Economy* 116: 881–930.

Field, E., S. Jayachandran, and R. Pande. 2010. "Do Traditional Institutions Constrain Female Entrepreneurial Investment? A Field Experiment on Business Training in India." *American Economic Review Papers and Proceedings* 100: 125–129.

Fisman, R. and J. Svensson. 2007. "Are Corruption and Taxation Really Harmful to Growth? Firm Level Evidence." *Journal of Development Economics* 83: 63–75.

Foley, F. and K. Manova. 2015. "International Trade, Multinational Activity, and Corporate Finance." *Annual Review of Economics* 7: 119–146.

Franklin, S. 2015. Location, Search Costs and Youth Unemployment: A Randomized Trial of Transport Subsidies in Ethiopia, CSAE WPS/2015–11.

Freeman, R. B. 2009. Labor Regulations, Unions, and Social Protection in Developing Countries: Market Distortions or Efficient Institutions? NBER Working Paper 14789.

Galasso, E., M. Ravallion, and A. Salvia. 2004. "Assisting the Transition from Work-fare to Work: A Randomized Experiment." *Industrial and Labor Relations Review* 58: Article 6.

Gallant, M. and E. Maticka-Tyndale. 2004. "School-Based HIV Prevention Programs for African Youth." *Social Science and Medicine* 58: 1337–1351.

Gallipoli, G. and J. Goyette. 2015. "Distortions, Efficiency and the Size Distribution of Firms." *Journal of Macroeconomics* 45: 202–221.

Galor, O. and J. Zeira. 1993. "Income Distribution and Macroeconomics." *Review of Economic Studies* 60: 35–52.

Garicano, L., C. Lelarge, and J. Van Reenen. 2016. Size Distortions and the Productivity Distribution: Evidence from France. CEP Working Paper.

Ham, J. C. and R. J. Lalonde. 1996. "The Effect of Sample Selection and Initial Conditions in Duration Models: Evidence from Experimental Data on Training." *Econometrica* 64: 175–205.

Hardy, M. and J. McCasland. 2015. Are Small Firms Labor Constrained? Experimental Evidence from Ghana. Mimeo, UBC.

Harris, J. R. and M. P. Todaro. 1970. "Migration, Unemployment and Development: A Two-Sector Analysis." *American Economic Review* 60: 126–142.

Heckman, J. J. and S. Mosso. 2014. "The Economics of Human Development and Social Mobility." *Annual Review of Economics* 6: 689–733.

Heckman, J. J., J. Stixrud, and S. Urzua. 2006. "The Effects of Cognitive and Noncognitive Abilities on Labor Market Outcomes and Social Behavior." *Journal of Labor Economics* 24: 411–482.

Heckman, J. J. and E. Vytlacil. 2001. "Identifying the Role of Cognitive Ability in Explaining the Level of and Change in the Return to Schooling." *Review of Economics and Statistics* 83: 1–12.

Hicks, J. H., M. Kremer, I. Mbiti, and E. Miguel. 2011. "Vocational Education Voucher Delivery and Labor Market Returns: A Randomized Evaluation Among Kenyan Youth." Report for Spanish Impact Evaluation Fund (SIEF) Phase II.

Hopenhayn, H. 1992. "Entry, Exit, and Firm Dynamics in Long Run Equilibrium." *Econometrica* 60: 1127–1150.

Hsieh, C.-T. and B. Olken. 2014. "The Missing 'Missing Middle.'" *Journal of Economic Perspectives* 28: 89–108.

Jaramillo, M. 2013. Is There Demand for Formality Among Informal Firms? Evidence from Micro-firms in Downtown Lima, Avances de Investigación 0013, Grupo de Análisis para el Desarrollo (GRADE).

Jensen, R. 2012. "Do Labor Market Opportunities Affect Young Women's Work and Family Decisions? Experimental Evidence from India." *Quarterly Journal of Economics* 127: 753–792.

Kaboski, J. and R. M. Townsend. 2011. "A Structural Evaluation of a Large-Scale Quasi-Experimental Microfinance Initiative." *Econometrica* 79: 1357–406.

Kaplan, D., E. Piedra, and E. Seira. 2011. "Entry Regulation and Business Start-Ups: Evidence from Mexico." *Journal of Public Economics* 95: 1501–1515.

Karlan, D. and G. Fischer. 2015. "The Catch-22 of External Validity in the Context of Constraints to Firm Growth." *American Economic Review Papers and Proceedings* 105: 295–299.

Karlan, D., R. Knight, and C. Udry. 2015. "Consulting and Capital Experiments wth Micro and Small Tailoring Enterprises in Ghana." *Journal of Economic Behavior and Organization* 118: 281–302.

Karlan, D. and M. Valdivia. 2011. "Teaching Entrepreneurship: Impact of Business Training on Microfinance Clients and Institutions." *Review of Economics and Statistics* 93: 510–527.

Karlan, D. and J. Zinman. 2011. "Microcredit in Theory and Practice: Using Randomized Credit Scoring for Impact Evaluation." *Science* 332: 1278–1284.

Kaur, S. 2014. Nominal Wage Rigidity in Village Labor Markets. Mimeo, Columbia University.

Kingombe, C. 2011. Lessons for Developing Countries from Experience with Technical and Vocational Education and Training, Paper for the International Growth Center—Sierra Leone Country Programme.

La Porta, R. and A. Shleifer. 2008. "The Unofficial Economy and Economic Development." Brookings Papers on Economic Activity, Economic Studies Program, Brookings Institution 39: 275–363.

Lindqvist, E. and R. Vestman. 2011. "The Labor Market Returns to Cognitive and Noncognitive Ability: Evidence from the Swedish Enlistment." *American Economic Journal: Applied Economics* 3: 101–128.

Lucas, R. E. 1978. "On the Size Distribution of Business Firms." *Bell Journal of Economics* 9: 508–523.

Macchiavello, R. and P. Miquel-Florensa. 2016. Vertical Integration and Relational Contracts: Evidence from the Costa Rica Coffee Chain, with Pepita Miquel-Florensa. Mimeo, Warwick University.

Macchiavello, R. and A. Morjaria. 2015. "The Value of Relationships: Evidence from a Supply Shock to Kenya Rose Exports." *American Economic Review* 105(9): 2911–2956.

Maloney, W. F. 2004. "Informality Revisited." *World Development* 32: 1159–1178.

McCoy, S. L., R. A. Kangwende, and N. C. Padian. 2010. "Behavior Change Interventions to Prevent HIV Infection Among Women Living in Low and Middle Income Countries: A Systematic Review." *AIDS and Behavior* 14: 469–482.

McKenzie, D. and Y. S. Sakho. 2010. "Does It Pay Firms to Register for Taxes? The Impact of Formality on Firm Profitability." *Journal of Development Economics* 91: 15–24.

McKenzie, D. and C. Woodruff. 2012. "What Are We Learning from Business Training and Entrepreneurship Evaluations Around the Developing World?" *World Bank Research Observer*.

———. 2015. Business Practices in Small Firms in Developing Countries. Mimeo, University of Warwick.

Meghir, C., R. Narita, and J.-M. Robin. 2015. "Wages and Informality in Developing Countries." *American Economic Review* 105: 1509–1546.

Mitra, A., A. Varoudakis, and M. Veganzones-Varoudkis. 2002. "Productivity and Technical Efficiency in Indian States' Manufacturing: The Role of Infrastructure." *Economic Development and Cultural Change* 50: 395–426.

Monteiro, J. and J. Assunção. 2012. "Coming Out of the Shadows? Estimating the Impact of Bureaucracy Simplification and Tax Cut on Formality in Brazilian Microenterprises." *Journal of Development Economics* 99: 105–115.

Morduch, J., S. Ravi, and J. Bauchet. 2015. "Failure vs. Displacement: Why an Innovative Anti-Poverty Program Showed No Impact." *Journal of Development Economics* 116: 1–16.

Ozier, Owen. 2018. "The Impact of Secondary Schooling in Kenya: A Regression Discontinuity Analysis." *Journal of Human Resources* 53(1): 157–188.

Reinikka, R. and J. Svensson. 1999. How Inadequate Provision of Public Infrastructure and Services Affect Private Investment?, Policy Research Working Paper 2262. Washington, DC: World Bank.

Rios-Avila, F. 2014. Unions and Economic Performance in Developing Countries: Case Studies from Latin America. Mimeo, Levy Economics Institute of Bard College.

Schneider, F., A. Buehnand, and C. Montenegro. 2010. Shadow Economies All Over the World: New Estimates for 162 Countries from 1999 to 2007. Policy Research Working Paper Series 5356, Washington, DC: World Bank.

Siba, E. and M. Soderbom. 2011. The Performance of New Firms: Evidence from Ethiopia's Manufacturing Sector. Mimeo, University of Gothenburg.

Teal, F. 2016. What Constrains the Demand for Labour in Firms in Sub-Saharan Africa? Some Evidence from Ghana. Mimeo, Oxford University.

Tybout, J. R. 2000. "Manufacturing Firms in Developing Countries: How Well Do They Do, and Why?" *Journal of Economic Literature* 38: 11–44.

Udry, C. and S. Anagol. 2006. "The Return to Capital in Ghana." *American Economic Review Papers & Proceedings* 96: 388–393.

World Bank. 2007. *World Development Report 2007: Development and the Next Generation.* Washington DC: World Bank.

———. 2009. *Africa Development Indicators 2008/9: Youth and Employment in Africa.* Washington, DC: World Bank.

16

INSTITUTIONS, FIRM FINANCING, AND GROWTH

Meghana Ayyagari, Asli Demirgüç-Kunt, and Vojislav Maksimovic

16.1. INTRODUCTION

A large theoretical and empirical literature has established that financial development is a critical determinant of entrepreneurship, innovation, and growth. Yet, there is also evidence to suggest that this is not necessarily always the case for all types of financial activity and at all levels of development. Financial economists disagree on the role different types of financial systems—bank versus market based, informal versus formal—play in a country's development. Furthermore, access to finance and its determinants vary widely across firms and country-level institutions. Research that analyzes the role of different institutions on firm financing and their differential impact at the firm level is crucial in shaping policy prescriptions for developing countries.

In this chapter, we compile and assess the substantial body of work on the role of institutions on firm financing and growth in developing countries. We begin by setting the stage in section 16.2, with a description of the different institutional constraints facing firms in developing economies. An extensive body of work in this area included cross-country, industry-level, and firm-level empirical evidence showing that access to external finance has a positive effect on growth. We then discuss the literature in law and finance that focuses on the role of legal institutions and property rights protection in explaining international differences in financial development. The core argument in the law and finance theory holds that in countries where legal institutions protect investor rights, enforce private property rights, and support private contractual arrangements, investors are more willing to finance firms and financial markets flourish. In contrast, countries with weak legal institutions that do not protect investors and facilitate private contracting have weak financial systems, and firms are more financially constrained. Compounding the effects of weak legal institutions, firms and investors in these economies are also impeded by information barriers arising from poor accounting standards, lack of adequate information sharing through credit bureaus and public credit registries, corruption, and political favoritism.[1]

The chapter also makes clear that our understanding of the link between institutions and firm financing has evolved with the scope and quality of datasets available to researchers and the methodological advances in the empirical finance-and-growth literature. Thus, in section 16.3, we discuss and critique the empirical challenges in development finance research and the different empirical techniques aimed at teasing out a causal argument including cross-country regressions, instrumental variable approaches, panel data methods, and randomized control trials.

In section 16.4, we discuss how firm financing patterns and capital structure choices vary between developed and developing countries and the role played by institutions. We focus largely on the use of short-term versus long-term finance across countries. In this section, we also review the literature on financing constraints faced by firms—both accounting measures as well as firms' perceptions of financing constraints—and their impact on firm growth.

The relative advantages and disadvantages of different financial systems for economic growth is a long-debated issue in economics. In section 16.5 we survey the literature on the prevalence of different financial systems across the world and their relative merits. We begin with a review of the evidence on bank versus market-based systems and discuss research that shows that different financial structures may be better at promoting economic activity at different stages of a country's economic development. We also focus on the role informal finance plays and whether it can be a functional substitute to formal finance in developing countries. A critical examination of the evidence suggests that although informal finance is very prevalent in many economies, at the margin it seems to be bank finance that is associated with firm growth.

In section 16.6, we pay close attention to the role of firm size. We begin with a comparison of small versus large firms in growth, productivity, and job creation and how this might vary across developed versus developing countries. We note that firm size distributions in developing economies are dominated by micro and small firms, and we review the evidence on the missing middle in firm size distributions. While small firms are the biggest creators of employment in many of these countries, an examination of their financing patterns reveals that small firms are also the most constrained in access to external finance. We then review the findings about large firms in developing economies.

In section 16.7, we summarize the current knowledge on finance and growth over a firm's life cycle, focusing on new firms and factors that influence firm creation. We examine the role of institutions versus initial starting characteristics of firms in predicting growth and productivity over the life cycle. This allows us to examine the primacy of institutions over other factors at different stages of a firm's life. In section 16.8, we highlight areas that need additional research and conclude with policy implications of the existing body of theoretical and empirical evidence on institutions and firm financing for low-income countries.

16.2. FINANCE, INSTITUTIONS, AND GROWTH: A MICRO-LEVEL PERSPECTIVE

While a detailed review of the theoretical literature on the history of economic thought on financial development and growth is beyond the scope of this chapter, we summarize below the findings of this literature on why a financial system matters for economic growth. In particular, a financial system serves the following roles:

Monitoring: Diamond's (1984) model of delegated monitoring illustrates how financial intermediaries such as banks have an incentive to act as a delegated monitor and produce the information necessary for an efficient allocation of resources. Others focus on how debt contracts lower the cost of monitoring firm insiders and reduce free cash flow, thereby decreasing managerial slack (e.g., Townsend 1979; Gale and Hellwig 1985; and Aghion, Dewatripont, and Rey 1999). A large and influential literature since Jensen and Meckling (1976) has also highlighted the role played by stock markets in promoting corporate governance. Stock markets help align managerial incentives with those of owners through the market for corporate control (Scharfstein 1988 and Stein 1988) and by linking managerial compensation to stock performance (Diamond and Verrecchia 1982).

Information Production and Capital Allocation. Early finance literature since Schumpeter (1912) has stressed the role played by finance in identifying the best ideas and allocating capital to entrepreneurs with the best chances of undertaking innovative activity (e.g., Goldsmith 1969; McKinnon 1973; and Shaw 1973). From Goldsmith (1969): finance "accelerates economic growth and improves economic performance to the extent that it facilitates the migration of funds to the best user, i.e., to the place in the economic system where the funds will yield the highest social return." This is possible because financial intermediaries such as banks reduce the costs of acquiring and processing information which improves the ex ante assessment of investment opportunities leading to better resource allocation and thus accelerating economic growth (e.g., Boyd and Prescott 1986; Greenwood and Jovanovic 1990). Other literature has stressed the role played by liquid stock markets in information production (Grossman and Stiglitz 1980; Kyle 1984; Merton 1987).[2]

Risk-Sharing. One of the most important functions of the financial system is risk-sharing. Several papers have shown how financial markets make it easier for people to diversify the risk associated with individual projects, firms, or industries (e.g., Greenwood and Jovanovic 1990; Obstfeld 1994; Devereux and Smith 1994). While these studies focus on the cross-sectional diversification of risk, Allen and Gale (1997) focus on intertemporal smoothing of risks that cannot be diversified at a given point in time, such as macroeconomic shocks. Allen and Gale (1997) show that financial intermediaries facilitate this type of risk-sharing by building reserves when the returns on the banks' assets are high and running them down when they are low.

Transaction Costs Reduction: Greenwood and Smith (1996) model the link between transaction costs, specialization, and innovation and show that financial systems that lower transaction costs facilitate greater specialization, technological innovation, and growth.

Savings Mobilization. Financial systems facilitate the pooling of savings of individuals and disparate investors, allowing them to exploit economies of scale and overcome investment indivisibilities. The development of financial intermediaries has long been argued to elicit increased savings (Cameron 1967; McKinnon 1973; Pagano 1993). In the model by Acemoglu and Zilibotti (1997), an increase in the volume of intermediation is associated with greater mobilization of savings, allowing agents to hold a diversified portfolio of risky projects that fosters better resource allocation toward higher return activities.

16.2.1. Empirical Evidence on Finance and Growth

An extensive literature has focused on establishing the empirical linkages between finance and growth. Modern cross-country growth regressions work began with King and Levine (1993) who, using data on 80 countries over the 1960–1989 period, reported a strong positive association between financial development and real per capita GDP growth and the rate of physical capital accumulation. Levine and Zervos (1998) showed that stock market liquidity is also a predictor of long-run economic growth and that stock markets provide different services from banks. Figure 16.1 illustrates the commonly used measures of financial system size and shows a positive correlation between the development of financial systems and level of income.

Following this early work, several papers focused on establishing whether the relationship between financial development and growth was causal. Studies focused on panel data, such as Levine, Loayza, and Beck (2000) and Beck, Levine, and Loayza (2000), use a panel GMM estimator to exploit the time series variation in the data and overcome the unobserved country-specific heterogeneity in pure cross-country data regressions. Others such as Levine, Loayza, and Beck (2000) and Beck, Demirgüç-Kunt, and Levine (2003) use legal origin from La Porta et al. (1998) as an instrumental variable to address exogenous variation in financial development and find that, correcting for endogeneity, there is a link between finance and growth. We review this literature in greater detail in section 16.2.2.

A second approach to addressing causality has been to use data at the industry and firm level. In a path-breaking paper, Rajan and Zingales (1998) use a cross-industry cross-country approach based on the assumption that more efficient market intermediaries help overcome market frictions. Thus, they argue that industries that rely more heavily on external finance should benefit disproportionately more from greater financial development than industries that are not naturally heavy users of external finance. They first use the extent to which industries in the United States depend on external finance to develop an industry index of external finance, based on the assumption that since US financial markets are developed, sophisticated, have fewer market imperfections, and are relatively open, they should allow US firms to achieve their desired financial structure. Thus, assuming that there are technological reasons why some industries depend more on external finance than others, the RZ index offers an exogenous way to identify the extent of external dependence of an industry anywhere in the world. The methodology does not require that the US markets are perfect but rather that market imperfections in the United States do not distort the ranking of industries in terms of their technological dependence on external financing. Next they use a difference-in-difference approach, where they use variation across industries in their dependence on external

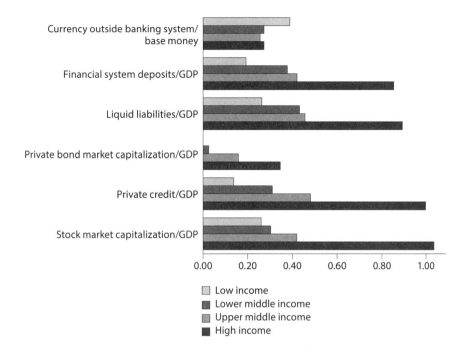

FIGURE 16.1. Financial system size and income. *Source*: Beck, Demirgüç-Kunt, and Levine (2009).

finance and variation across countries in their level of financial development to assess the impact of finance on industry growth.[3] Wurgler (2000) also uses industry-level data and to show that countries with higher levels of financial development are better able than countries with lower levels at increasing (decreasing) investment in growing (declining) industries.

Demirgüç-Kunt and Maksimovic (1998) adopt a more micro-level approach by using a financial planning model that allows them to calculate how fast firms could be expected to grow without external finance but instead only with retained earnings and cash from operations. They first show that the extent to which firms are able to grow faster than this internally financed growth rate is a function of the dependence of a firm's growth on external finance as measured by the proportions of increases in total assets financed by long-term debt and newly issued shares. They then also establish that the proportion of firms that grow at rates exceeding the non–externally financed rate is positively associated with stock market liquidity, banking system size, and the perceived efficiency of the legal system.

Other approaches have been to use regional analysis within a country. Guiso, Sapienza, and Zingales (2004) examine differences in financial development across regions in Italy, particularly on small firms and entrepreneurship, and find that local financial development matters for economic success. Individual country case studies investigating the impact of structural banking reforms in the United States, France, and other countries also find that a more efficient banking sector following deregulation is associated with higher income growth (Jayaratne and Strahan 1996); increased survival; and better performance of more efficient firms (Black and Strahan 2002; Cetorelli and Strahan 2006;

Bertrand, Schoar, and Thesmar 2007; Kerr and Nanda 2009). Rice and Strahan (2010) find that bank deregulation reduces firms' cost of borrowing, but does not affect the amount borrowed by small firms.

Taken as a whole, the bulk of existing research has shown that countries with better functioning banks and markets grow faster even after accounting for endogeneity. The work on the channels through which finance should affect growth has been more limited. Levine, Loayza, and Beck (2000) show that financial sector development helps economic growth through more efficient resource allocation rather than through increases in the scale of investment or savings mobilization. Bekaert, Harvey, and Lundblad (2001, 2005) focus on financial liberalization and in a cross-country setting show that liberalization boosts economic growth by improving the allocation of resources and the investment rate.

Other studies have focused on establishing a link between finance and innovation. In a cross-country setting, Hsu, Tian, and Xu (2014) show that financial market development affects technological innovation using data on 32 developed and emerging countries. Using patent data on large, publicly traded US corporations, Atanassov (2015) shows that arm's-length financing such as public debt and equity is associated with greater innovation and higher-quality innovation than relationship-based banking. While these studies have focused on large, publicly traded firms, Ayyagari, Demirgüç-Kunt, and Maksimovic (2011) use Enterprise Surveys (from the World Bank) across 47 developing economies and find that the externally financed proportion of a firm's investment expenditures is positively related to firm innovation, controlling for investment opportunities. The highlight in their paper is that they define innovation broadly to include not only core innovation activities, such as introducing new product lines and new technology, but also sourcing decisions that affect the overall organization of firms' activities, and other types of activities that promote knowledge transfers, such as signing joint ventures with foreign partners and obtaining new licensing agreements, all of which reflect overall firm dynamism.

The evidence on bank deregulation and innovation is more mixed. Amore, Schneider, and Žaldokas (2013) find that interstate deregulation leads to greater firm innovation, while intrastate deregulation does not. Similarly, Chava et al. (2013) find that intra-state banking deregulation decreases the level and risk of innovation by young private firms, whereas interstate banking deregulation increases the level and risk of innovation of young, private firms. Cornaggia, Mao, Tian, and Wolfe (2015) argue that banking competition enables small, innovative firms to secure financing instead of being acquired by public corporations, which reduces the portion of state-level innovation attributable to public corporations headquartered in deregulating states.

Studies such as Klapper, Laeven, and Rajan (2006) identify an entrepreneurship channel through which finance affects growth. They use data on more than 3 million firms across Europe across the Amadeus database and find that facilitating easier access to external finance via accounting standards and property rights protection is positively related to the number of start-ups. This is based on the idea that since new entrants need to raise capital to implement their idea, financial systems that can selectively finance the most promising entrepreneurs should be associated with higher entrepreneurship rates and growth. Kerr and Nanda (2009, 2010) also find that US banking reform leads to increased entry of small firms and reduces average entry size.

16.2.2. Legal Traditions and Property Rights

The finding that financial development has a causal impact on growth raises the critical question of why is it that some countries have well-developed financing systems whereas others do not. In a series of papers on the Law and Finance view, La Porta, Lopez-de-Silanes, Shleifer, and Vishny (1997, 1998, henceforth LLSV) advance the idea that in countries where legal systems support private contractual agreements, enforce property rights, and protect the rights of shareholders and creditors, investors are more willing to finance firms leading to more developed stock markets and banking systems. This view follows naturally from corporate finance theory that stresses that a firm is a nexus of contracts (Jensen and Meckling 1976) and laws, and the degree to which courts enforce these laws shapes the types of contracts used to address agency problems. This literature also recognizes that countries' laws are typically transplanted from a few legal traditions—English common law, French Civil law, German Civil law, and Scandinavian Civil Law—through imitation, conquest, or imperialism.

While the LLSV papers are mostly cross-country studies, there is significant microeconomic-based work relating investor protection laws and corporate financing decisions of firms. Demirgüç-Kunt and Maksimovic (1998) show that countries with better investor rights have better functioning financial systems that fund faster growing firms. Other studies link stronger investor protection laws to higher corporate valuations (e.g., Claessens et al. 2002; LLSV 2002; and Caprio et al. 2003), ownership concentration and private benefits of corporate control (e.g., Claessens et al. 2000; LLS 1999; Zingales 1995; Dyck and Zingales 2004), and corporate governance ratings (Doidge, Karolyi, and Stulz 2007).

The Law and Finance view, however, is not without its skeptics. Some researchers emphasize the political roots of legal institutions and argue that politics determines the degree of investor protection laws and hence the development of financial markets (see Rajan and Zingales 2003; Haber, Maurer, and Razo 2003; Pagano and Volpin 2001; and Roe 1994). Scholars highlighting culture (e.g. Stulz and Williamson 2003) highlight the role of religion in shaping creditor rights while Guiso et al. (2004) highlight the role of social capital in shaping financial systems. Most significantly, the geography/endowment view put forth by Diamond (1997), Engerman and Sokoloff (1997, 2002), and Acemoglu, Johnson, and Robinson (2001, 2002) emphasize the critical role of differences in geography and disease environment that have shaped institutional development. Others, including Easterly and Levine (1997), Tavares and Wacziarg (2001), and Alesina et al. (2003) argue that the extent of ethnic fractionalization in a country has a negative effect on economic growth and quality of government.

Berkowitz, Pistor, and Richard (2003) also show that the way in which the law was initially transplanted is a more important determinant of effective legal institutions than the supply of law from a particular legal family. So the transplanting process—whether countries had developed formal legal orders internally, whether they adapted the transplanted law to local conditions and had a population familiar with the basic legal principles of the transplanted law—is much more important than the particular legal family for developing strong legal institutions

Ayyagari, Demirgüç-Kunt, and Maksimovic (2008, 2013) run an empirical horse race between the various theories to test which institutional theory best explains the variation in property rights protection as perceived by firms and find maximum support for ethnic fractionalization. Using the World Business Environment Survey, which surveys firms across 62 developing countries on their perceptions of how well protected their property rights are in practice, they also show that the dominance of the Law and Finance view in explaining property rights variation depends critically on sample selection, specifically with the inclusion of former Socialist economies, which arguably have more in common than just legal tradition.

Overall there has been an active debate in the literature on the role of legal institutions in shaping financial development with several alternate theories being put forward. In addition, some studies have questioned the fundamental premise that stronger creditor rights are always linked to greater financial development and access to finance. Using the passage of a secured transactions law which strengthened creditor rights in India as a natural experiment, Vig (2013) shows that there is a threshold level of creditor rights beyond which strengthening creditor rights leads to reduction in the quantity of secured debt. Acharya, Amihud, and Litov (2011) also show that stronger creditor rights in bankruptcy induces firms to engage in reduced risk-taking which in turn decreases value. Thus, the differential impact of stronger creditor rights on different types of firms is an active area of research.

16.2.3. Information Quality and Availability

A firm's information environment plays a critical role in financing (both access to credit and cost of capital) and corporate governance, thus impacting overall firm value. There are two main sources of this information—first is the credit information sharing schemes that reduce asymmetric information between lenders and borrowers. These schemes allow lenders to disseminate to other lenders knowledge of borrowers' payment history, total debt exposure, and overall creditworthiness, either through a privately held credit bureau or publicly regulated credit registry, thus bridging the information divide between lenders and borrowers.[4]

The information sharing that occurs through credit bureaus and registries is particularly relevant for small firms in developing countries. Seminal work by Stiglitz and Weiss (1981) shows that asymmetric information prevents efficient allocation of lending such that demand for credit exceeds supply, driving a wedge between lending and borrowing rates, also resulting in credit rationing. Theoretical studies emphasize the different channels through which information sharing can potentially impact firm financing— reduced adverse selection and increase in the volume and efficiency of lending (Pagano and Jappelli 1993), reputation effects leading to higher repayment of loans and lower default rates (Klein 1992), and increased borrower disciplines and reduced moral hazard (Vercammen 1995; Padilla and Pagano 1997, 2000).

There has been a large empirical literature documenting the positive impact of credit sharing schemes. In cross-country work, Jappelli and Pagano (2002) and Djankov, McLiesh, and Shleifer (2007) collect data on the existence and operation of credit bureaus around the world and find that bank lending is higher and credit risk is lower in countries where lenders share information. Galindo and Miller (2001) use firm-level data, albeit in a cross-section setting, and find that scope and quality of credit information schemes are correlated with lower financing constraints. Brown, Jappelli, and Pagano (2009) use firm-level panel data that allow them to control for unobserved firm heterogeneity for 24 countries in 2002 from Eastern Europe and the Former Soviet Union and show that greater information sharing is associated with improved availability and lower cost of credit to firms, especially for more opaque firms and for firms in countries with weak legal environments.

These findings are not causal so while the above studies suggest that banks lend more to firms in countries with information sharing systems than in countries without these systems, they do not suggest that the implementation of an information sharing scheme caused banks to lend more to firms. More recent work has paid closer attention to causality concerns using a difference-in-difference setting and/or matching methods

Love, Martinez Peria, and Singh (2016) find that introducing collateral registries for movable assets increases firms' access to bank finance, especially for smaller firms. Ayyagari et al. (2016) use the introduction of credit bureaus as an exogenous shock to the supply of credit in more than 4 million firms in 29 developing countries and find that the resulting access to finance results in higher employment growth, especially among micro, small, and medium enterprises.

Another strand of the literature has used natural or randomized experiments to examine the implementation of credit information systems that showed variation either in the firms covered under the information system or in the use of information by lenders. The findings can be attributed to be causal under the assumption that the counterfactual is valid (i.e., the treatment and comparison groups are indeed comparable in terms of their observable and unobservable).

For instance, Hertzberg, Liberti, and Paravisini (2011) use the expansion of the Public Credit Registry in Argentina in 1998 as a natural experiment to show coordination between lenders to new information. Prior to 1998, the registry only covered borrowers with total debt above $200,000, and this threshold was eliminated in 1998, leading to the disclosure of information about additional borrowers, for which credit assessments were previously only known privately. The reform was announced in April 1998 and implemented in July of that year. Hertzberg, Liberti, and Paravisini study the difference in lenders' behavior between the time prior to the announcement and the period between announcement and implementation for borrowers below the threshold and on whom the lender has negative information. While the announcement generates no new information for this sample of borrowers, the fact that the information is now public leads the lender to reduce lending because the lender realizes that other lenders would reduce credit once the information is public. They do not find a decrease in debt for firms that were slightly above the threshold (for whom the information was always available) and for those who borrow from only one lender (for whom there is no coordination problem). Their results are demonstrated in figure 16.2.

Other studies that examine the effects of the introduction of a new credit registry in different countries include Liberti, Seru, and Vig (2016) in Argentina; Luoto, McIntosh, and Wydick (2007) and de Janvry, McIntosh, and Sadoulet (2010) in Guatemala; Behr and Sonnekalb (2012) in Albania; and Cheng and Degryse (2010) in China. While these studies are able to provide clean identification, they have limited generalizability since they are focused on single countries or identify a very local effect (for instance, the Hertzberg paper tells us about lender behavior for borrowers around the $200,000 threshold).

A parallel literature has focused on information sharing in capital markets. Merton's (1987) investor recognition hypothesis describes how firm value is increasing in the

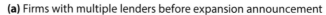

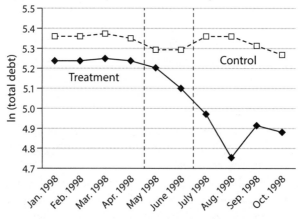

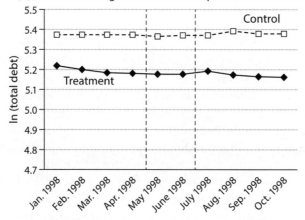

FIGURE 16.2. (*a*) Firms with multiple lenders before expansion announcement. (*b*) Firms with a single lender before expansion announcement. *Source*: Hertzberg, Liberti, and Paravisini (2011).

degree of investor recognition of the firm. Investors buy and hold only those securities about which they have enough information. Greater transparency and better quality of firm-specific information also makes for more efficient contracting between management and investors and makes it easier for firms to identify good investment opportunities. One strand of this literature has used the quality of accounting standards in a country as a measure of information quality, at least on the large public firms. LLSV (1998, 1999) compile an index of accounting standards across countries and find that the quality of accounting standards varies by legal origins. They show that countries with an English legal tradition have better accounting standards than French or German Civil Law countries. Leuz, Nanda, and Wysocki (2003) also establish a link between a country's legal and institutional environment and the quality of accounting earnings reported to investors. Others have shown that cross-country differences in accounting standards also explain differences in financial development (e.g., Levine, Loayza, and Beck 2000), and volume of mergers and acquisitions (Rossi and Volpin 2004).

A second stream of literature has focused on different measures of firm-level information quality. Several papers have used the number of analysts following the firm and the accuracy of analyst forecasts as a measure of the information environment of the firm (see Healy, Hutton, and Palepu 1999; Gebhardt, Lee, and Swaminathan 2001; Lang, Lins, and Miller 2003). The literature on cross-listings in the United States considers the extensive information disclosure associated with meeting disclosure requirements mandated by the SEC and the listing exchange and shows that it leads to improved analyst coverage, more accurate earnings forecasts, and higher valuations (e.g., Baker, Nosfinger, and Weaver 2002; Lang, Lins, and Miller 2003; Bailey, Karolyi, and Salva 2006).[5] Mitton (2002) shows that higher disclosure quality as proxied by a cross-listing and having a Big Six international accounting firm as an auditor was associated with a better stock price performance during the East Asian crisis. Other studies such as Durnev and Kim (2005) find that firm-level governance and disclosure is positively related to a firm's growth opportunities and need for external financing.

16.2.4. Government Intervention, Corruption, and Political Ties

In this section we examine the implications of government ownership in financial markets. In particular, we examine three specific issues: state ownership of banks and directed lending programs, political elitism where the government in power favors certain firms that they are politically associated with, and public rent-seeking by government officials.

A large literature has examined the implications of government ownership in financial markets. Several papers have shown that not only is government ownership of banks pervasive around the world, especially in countries with poor institutions, but also is associated with poorer financial development, growth, and productivity (e.g., Barth et al. 2009; La Porta et al. 2002). Dinc (2005) also uses a cross-country setting to show that government-owned banks increase their lending in election years relative to private banks in 22 emerging markets. Other studies use a more detailed single-country approach to analyze the consequences of government lending. Using loan-level data from Pakistan, Khwaja, and Mian (2005) find that government banks differentially favor politically connected firms by providing greater access to credit—firms that are politically connected borrow 45% more but also have 50% higher default rates. Sapienza (2004) also finds that Italian public banks charge lower interest rates than private banks, and the stronger the political party in the area where the firm is borrowing, the lower the interest rates charged. Cole (2009) studies agricultural lending by government banks in India and finds that government-owned bank lending tracks the electoral cycle with agricultural credit increasing by 5–10 percentage points in an election year. Carvalho (2014) studies Brazilian manufacturing plants and finds that in exchange for government bank loans, firms expand employment and investment in politically attractive regions.

A second stream of literature on political connections shows that firms actively establish political connections and that political connections increase firm value (e.g., Fisman 2001; Johnson and Mitton 2003; Goldman, Rocholl, and So 2009). The typical channels through which political contributions are found to be beneficial are preferential access to credit (Dinc 2005; Khwaja and Mian 2005) and receipt of government bailout funds during periods of financial distress (e.g., Duchin and Sosyura 2012; Faccio, Masulis, and McConnell 2006).

Other studies argue that political connections are detrimental to firm value. Fan, Wong, and Zhang (2007) analyze the post-IPO performance of newly privatized SOEs in China and find that Chinese firms with politically connected CEOs underperform those without politically connected CEOs in terms of stock returns, earnings growth, sales growth, and return on sales. A parallel literature on privatization provides direct evidence on how the politicization of firm investment may prove detrimental to a firm's public shareholders. Dinc and Gupta (2011) find that political patronage plays a significant role in the privatization decisions of Indian firms. They find that privatization is delayed if the main operations of a firm are located in more competitive electoral districts and no government-owned firm located in the home state of the politician in charge is ever privatized. Other studies have examined the role of politics on investment. In a cross-country setting, Julio and Yook (2012) find that political uncertainty surrounding elections leads to a drop in investments and investment sensitivity to stock prices during election years. Alok and Ayyagari (2015) document a political investment cycle in the corporate investment decisions of state-owned firms in India. They show that state-owned firms announce more capital investment projects in election years, especially "visible" investment projects like in infrastructure. They also show that these projects have negative announcement returns and crowd out private sector investment. Ru (2018) also finds that increased credit to SOEs in China crowds out private firm activities in the same industry. Together, these studies point to the value-destroying nature of government interference in firm investment.

Finally, one of the most commonly studied aspects of government intervention in economies, especially in developing countries, is public rent-seeking by government officials. Corruption is commonly defined as the "misuse of public office for private gain" (Svensson 2005) or more specifically as the "sale by government officials of government property for personal gain" (Shleifer and Vishny 1993). In their seminal paper on corruption, Shleifer and Vishny (1993) show that corruption is costly to investment and economic development because of two main reasons: First, with a weak central government that cannot prevent individual government agencies from soliciting complementary bribes, the cumulative burden of bribes increases, thus hindering investment and growth. Second, the secrecy of corruption leads to investment distortions from high-value projects to those that offer greater opportunities for hidden corruption. The solution, they argue, is to have better accounting systems (e.g., in the collection of taxes and custom duties) that prevent agents from stealing from the government, and economic and political competition that can reduce the level of corruption and its adverse effects. Murphy, Shleifer, and Vishny (1993) argue that public rent-seeking by government officials is particularly harmful for innovation since innovators are more vulnerable than established firms because they have a high (and inelastic) demand for government-supplied goods such as permits and licenses. Other theoretical frameworks of corruption and government intervention include Banerjee (1997), Bliss and Di Tella (1997), and Ades and Di Tella (1999).

Several cross-country and country-specific studies have established that corruption negatively affects financial development, growth, and trade and investment prospects (e.g., Mauro 1995, 1997; Wei 2000; Fisman and Svensson 2007). Ayyagari, Demirgüç-Kunt, and Maksimovic (2010) use data on bribe payments across 25,000 firms in 57 countries and show that corruption acts like a tax on innovating firms—innovating firms pay more bribes to government officials than non-innovating firms, though there is no evidence that they receive better services than firms that do not bribe. Banerjee, Mullainathan, and Hanna (2012) highlight gaps in the theoretical and empirical literature on corruption and recommend moving away from a crime and punishment approach to understanding the nature of the particular economic decision or the task in which the bureaucrat is participating.

16.3. EMPIRICAL CHALLENGES IN DEVELOPMENT FINANCE RESEARCH

In recent years, much work has identified challenges to the study of the effect of institutions in empirical finance that turn out to be more severe than the earlier literature had recognized. Some of these challenges arise from data issues and others from the emphasis, required for policy prescriptions, on rigorously characterizing causal relations, rather than on assuming causality in statistical relations. This section briefly highlights the principal concerns and discusses some alternative approaches that have been adopted.

In development economics, the conventional wisdom has been that natural experiments and randomized control trials (RCTs) represent credible bases for causal inference, thus facilitating evidence-based policy prescriptions. RCTs and natural experiments have high internal validity provided that the required randomization and exogeneity conditions, respectively, are satisfied. Both techniques are also relatively easy to understand and compelling. Their use in the study of the impact of financial institutions on growth has been more limited, but growing over time. For instance, they have most often been used to study small-scale enterprises and issues such as financial literacy as in the case of Cole, Sampson, and Zia (2010). Other studies have used natural experiments to study the impact of credit rights on firm debt and asset growth (Vig 2013) and how collateral values affect firm investment (Gan 2007), to name a few. Bruhn and Love (2014) use a natural experiment to investigate how opening new bank branches in Mexico affects labor market activity and poverty.

However, as discussed by Rodrik (2008), for a large range of issues involving first-order policy questions, RCTs are not feasible. Bulte et al. (2014) also argue that these experiments are not double-blind and hence subjects can knowingly alter their behavior, giving rise to a pseudo-placebo effect. In the context of an agricultural development intervention in Tanzania, where farmers were given modern and traditional seed varieties, they showed that farmers in the double-blind experiment altered their behavior, and that these pseudo-placebo effects may be large and can explain the entire treatment effect on the treated, as conventionally measured.

In many other cases, the RCT and quasi-experimental approaches require policymakers to extrapolate conclusions about policies from a very specific instance and specific institutional arrangements. This is difficult to do well. In practice, attempts to do this often amount to informal matching on observables between the sample and the countries of interest. However, attempts to generalize in this manner obviate the principal advantage of RCTs, that in-sample they are not dependent on matching on observables but also randomize over unobserved characteristics (Cartwright 2007). As a result of these difficulties in implementation of RCTs and natural experiments, the practical choices are often between a more limited study using quasi-experimental techniques and a cross-country study using more descriptive techniques, augmented with instrumental variable approach as feasible.

A widely adopted approach along these lines to studying the effect of institutions is based on Rajan and Zingales's (1998) analysis of how financial development affects the growth rate of industries across the world, as discussed in section 16.2.1. Other studies use instrumental variable approaches. To be valid, instruments have to be exogenous, be highly correlated with the policy variable of interest (high first-stage R-square), and at the same time not have a direct effect on the dependent variable of interest or an indirect effect through some other channel than the policy variable (exclusion restriction). Several ingenious solutions have been proposed. Acemoglu, Johnson, and Robinson (2001), for example, use mortality rates of early European settlers in colonies as an instrument for the quality of the legal systems in those countries today.[6] How plausible one finds such instruments in cross-country studies is a matter of judgment.

As Deaton (2010) points out, both RCTs and econometric techniques depending on IVs work best when the entities studied are relatively homogeneous. When the subpopulations are sufficiently different that they react differently to a specific instrument, the use of an arbitrary IV estimator may not provide a good estimate of the mean effect in the population of a change in the explanatory variables. To clarify matters, consider an example in which the researcher is attempting to estimate the effect of the number of banking relationships a firm has on its growth, where the firms decide whether or not to attempt to apply to a new bank for a loan. Since banking relationships are endogenous, one might want to instrument for the decision to apply. However, if firms are heterogeneous and different types of firms decide to apply to a new bank in response to different instruments, each instrumental estimate of the effect of banking relationships on growth will differ. Under conditions derived in Imbens and Angrist (1994), the estimates will each yield a local average treatment estimator (LATE).[7] These will in general be different and depend on the specific instrument used. Deaton (2010) argues that, as a result, to be useful in addressing policy questions or testing theory, a formal model is often needed to clarify the interpretation of the instrumental variable estimates.

16.4. INSTITUTIONS AND FIRM FINANCING

We focus on how differences in institutions between developing and developed countries affect two aspects of financing of firms: the provision of long-term finance and financial constraints, two areas important for firm growth. Long-term financing facilitates investment in long-term assets—property, plant, and equipment—and permits firms to engage in long-term projects. In the absence of long-term financing, firms have to rely on short-term debt and are thus subject to rollover risk and interest rate risk. To the extent that these firms are financially constrained, they will be unable to invest optimally, and will thereby realize lower growth rates.

A large literature has focused on the limited use of long-term finance in developing economies relative to developed ones and on the role played by institutions and the providers of long-term finance—banks and capital markets. Using a sample of publicly traded firms in 30 countries between 1980 and 1991, Demirgüç-Kunt and Maksimovic

(1999) show that firms in developed countries had more long-term debt, after controlling for firm size. This difference, however, is mediated by the institutions in each country. Thus, they show that in countries with effective legal systems, large firms in countries use more long-term debt compared to short-term debt, while small firms do not respond in the same way to the effectiveness of the legal system. They also note that the size of the banking sector is associated with more long-term debt and less short-long term debt for small firms. Large firms are unaffected. By contrast, stock market activity is positively associated with debt levels of large firms but not small firms. Thus, overall, institutions affect large and small public firms differentially—an effective legal system and an active stock market are associated with the provision of long-term debt to large firms, whereas a large banking system is associated with more long-term financing of smaller firms.

These results are consistent with the notion that the financing of smaller firms requires the existence of financial intermediaries that can closely monitor firms and provide funds as appropriate. Larger firms can obtain financing and monitoring in public markets. The types of institutions required for each purpose are somewhat different.

There have been a number of studies trying to determine which factors affect the use of debt and equity financing in developing countries, and how well these factors correspond to those found to affect financing in developed countries. For listed firms, Booth, Aivazian, Demirgüç-Kunt, and Maksimovic (2001) find that while similar factors such as profitability and asset tangibility affect debt ratios in both developed and developing countries, there are also systematic differences in the way these ratios are affected by institutional factors such as capital market development, GDP growth, and inflation. Other studies have emphasized the importance of a strong legal and institutional framework for the supply of long-term debt that may include strong creditor rights (Giannetti 2003; Bae and Goyal 2009), good contract enforcement (Qian and Strahan 2007), existence of information sharing mechanisms such as credit bureaus (Ayyagari et al. 2016), and an adequate collateral framework (Love, Martinez-Peria, and Singh 2016). Fan, Titman, and Twite (2012) find that a country's legal and tax system, the level of corruption, and the preferences of capital suppliers explain a significant portion of the variation in leverage and debt maturity ratios across countries. Specifically they find that firms in more corrupt countries and with weaker laws use more short-term debt whereas firms in countries with strong bankruptcy codes and deposit insurance use more long-term debt.

A separate strand of the literature analyzes the financing of foreign-owned firms in developing countries. Desai, Foley, and Hines (2005) look at foreign affiliates of US corporations and find that multinational affiliates use less external debt in countries with underdeveloped capital markets and weak creditor rights. To overcome capital market imperfections in these markets, they are more likely to source funds internally by borrowing from parent companies.

Overall, the body of evidence suggests that institutional factors such as legal institutions, the level of banking, and stock market development are important determinants of firms' leverage choices and choices of short-term versus long-term debt. Much of this literature has focused on publicly listed firms, which are large and perhaps unrepresentative of the financing needs of smaller firms, especially in developing countries. More recently, however, the World Bank Enterprise Surveys, which are a series of cross-country firm surveys conducted by the World Bank, have greatly expanded the information available about financing patterns of especially small and medium firms across countries.

These surveys include micro-, small, and medium enterprises and contain a large set of questions on the business environment in which the firm operates, the proportion of investment and working capital that is financed externally, and also the source of external financing (i.e., debt, equity, suppliers' credit, leasing, and other sources such as development banks, moneylenders, public sector, or other informal sources). The more recent surveys also contain sampling weights that allow us to draw inferences about the population of firms in each country.

While several studies have used these surveys, their rich potential has not been sufficiently exposed. As an example, the data from the Enterprise Surveys, conducted from 2006 to 2010, show that a large proportion of firms, especially small and medium firms, do not have any bank loans. The firm survey results suggest that this reflects both firms being refused bank loans as well as a lack of demand for bank loans either because of other financing sources or lack of good projects to finance. Some of the common reasons why firms claim that they are excluded from bank finance include high interest rates, collateral requirements, a perception on the part of firms that bank lending officers are often corrupt, and difficulties firms have in completing paperwork.

Beck, Demirgüç-Kunt, and Maksimovic (2008) use the World Business Environment Survey (WBES), a precursor to the Enterprise Surveys, to look at the financing of small firms. They find a strong relation between institutions and the form of external financing. Firms in countries with poor institutions use less bank debt and equity financing, and other financing sources such as trade credit, leasing, factoring, or fixed-asset lending do not substitute for the lower access to bank finance for small firms in developing countries.

Financial constraints arise when firms are unable to invest in positive net present value projects because they are unable to obtain funds from external investors. In developed countries, financial constraints are hypothesized to arise because of adverse selection in the market for external capital and moral hazard, which arises from the agency conflicts between investors and the firms' insiders. Such constraints are likely to be even more severe in contexts where legal institutions are underdeveloped.

A dominant strand of this literature has developed methodologies to detect constraints indirectly using investment-cash flow sensitivities developed by Fazzari, Hubbard, and Petersen (1988, 2000),[8] or the propensity of firms to save cash out of incremental cash flow (e.g., Almeida, Campello, and Weisbach 2004). The implications of these studies for financing constraints of firms in developing countries are unclear since they are largely based on listed firms in developed economies.

Beck, Demirgüç-Kunt, and Maksimovic (2005) use survey data to provide the first direct evidence of whether firms in developing countries perceive themselves to be financially constrained and whether reported financing constraints are related to firm growth. They use a size-stratified survey of more than 4,000 firms in 54 countries, where firms reported on a scale of 1 (no obstacle) to 4 (major obstacle) the extent to which financing, legal, and corruption problems presented obstacles to the operation and growth of their businesses. Table 16.1, adapted from their paper, shows that all three obstacles have a negative and significant impact on firm growth when entered individually. When entered together, the effect of the corruption obstacle is subsumed by the other two. They also show that the smallest firms are consistently the most adversely affected by all obstacles. Financial and institutional development attenuates the relation between firm

Table 16.1. Impact of Obstacles on Firm Growth

	Dependent Variable: Firm growth over the past three years			
	1	2	3	4
Financing Obstacle	−0.031***			−0.023***
	(0.009)			(0.009)
Legal Obstacle		−0.029***		−0.023***
		(0.009)		(0.011)
Corruption			−0.021***	0.007
			(0.009)	(0.011)
Number of firms	4204	3968	3991	3800
Number of countries	54	54	54	54
R-square within	0.01	0.01	0.01	0.02
R-square between	0.28	0.27	0.25	0.26
R-square overall	0.02	0.03	0.02	0.02

Note: *, **, and *** represent significance at 10%, 5%, and 1% levels respectively. Other regressors: Dummy for government ownership, Dummy for foreign ownership, Exporter dummy, Dummy that indicates if the firm receives subsidies from national or local authorities, Number of competitors, Industry dummies, Log GDP, Growth rate of GDP/Capita, GDP/Capita, Inflation.
Source: Beck, Demirgüç-Kunt, and Maksimovic (2005, table IV).

growth and reported financial, legal, and corruption obstacles. Small firms benefit the most from developments in financial and legal institutions.

Firms in developing countries report a large list of institutional obstacles that affect their day-to-day operations and growth. Given this large list, it is unclear whether finance is a binding constraint to growth compared to other reported obstacles. Ayyagari, Demirgüç-Kunt, and Maksimovic (2008) attempt to address this question using survey data on the different obstacles to growth that firms report—access to finance, inadequate security and enforcement of property rights, poor provision of infrastructure, inefficient regulation and taxation, corruption, and macroeconomic instability. They find that, in fact, financing obstacles are of primary importance in limiting firm growth. Their methodology allows for each of the obstacles reported by firms in the survey to either affect firm growth directly, only indirectly through their influence on other factors, or to have no effect. Using regressions as well as Directed Acyclic Graph (DAG) methodology, they find that access to finance emerges consistently as the most robust obstacle-constraining firm growth. And of the many specific financing obstacles firms identify, only the cost of borrowing is directly associated with firm growth. But the cost of borrowing is itself affected by imperfections in financial markets such as difficulties with posting collateral, limited access to long-term financing, and firms that face high interest rates also perceive that the banks to which they have access are corrupt, underfunded, and require excessive paperwork.

Together, the studies reviewed in this section suggest that access to financing is one of the most constraining obstacles to growth for firms in developing countries and that it is, in turn, closely related to the firms' institutional environment.

16.5. FINANCIAL STRUCTURE AND ECONOMIC DEVELOPMENT

16.5.1. Banks versus Markets

A large body of literature has emphasized the importance of financial structure—the mixture of financial institutions and securities markets in an economy—for economic development. Economic theory argues that banks and markets provide different financial services and have unique advantages in solving different types of financial frictions. The advantages of banks include more efficient *information acquisition* due to their long-run lending relationships with firms (Gerschenkron 1962; Boot, Greenbaum, and Thakor 1993; Rajan and Zingales 1998), better *intertemporal risk-sharing* services (Allen and Gale 1997), superior *corporate governance* due to their ability to exert corporate control (e.g., Shleifer and Vishny 1994), and *savings mobilization* (e.g., Lamoreaux 1995). Well-developed stock markets on the other hand stimulate information production (e.g., Grossman and Stiglitz 1980; Kyle 1984), foster corporate governance by aligning interests of managers and owners via takeover threats and linking managerial compensation to stock prices (e.g., Diamond and Verrecchia 1982; Jensen and Murphy 1990; Scharfstein 1988; Stein 1988), encourage innovation and entrepreneurship, and are better at cross-sectional risk-sharing (e.g., Allen and Gale 1997). While much of the theoretical literature has framed this debate as banks versus markets, i.e., that banks and markets compete and develop at the expense of the other (Allen and Gale 1997, 2000; Boot and Thakor 1997; Dewatripont and Maskin 1995), other studies emphasize the complementarity between banks and markets (e.g., Allen and Gale 2000; Holmstrom and Tirole 1997; and Song and Thakor 2010).

The empirical literature, however, has found no evidence that one type of financial structure is better than another for access to finance or growth. Financial structure has not been shown to explain cross-country differences in financial development (e.g., Levine 2002) or differential growth rates of financially dependent industries across countries (e.g., Beck and Levine 2002). Demirgüç-Kunt and Maksimovic (2002) also reject the idea that firms' access to external financing is a function of the relative development of stock markets to banks.

Schmukler and Vesperoni (2001) argue that the difference between bank-based versus market-based systems is less important than the difference between emerging and developed economies for firms' financing choices—sources of financing, leverage ratios, and maturity structure.

This is not to say that financial structure does not matter. As discussed in section 16.4, there is some literature to show that maturity of firm financing is related to financial structure. Demirgüç-Kunt and Maksimovic (2002) suggest that a larger securities market is associated with better access of firms to long-term financing while banking development is more associated with availability of short-term financing. Allen et al. (2010) compare and contrast the predominantly bank-based systems in Germany and Japan with the market-based structures in the United States and United Kingdom and suggest that a variety of financial structures can lead to higher growth.

Other studies have suggested that different structures are optimal at different stages of development. For instance, while Demirgüç-Kunt and Levine (2001) do not find a link between financial structure and economic growth, they do provide some evidence that financial systems become more market-based as countries become richer. More recently, Demirgüç-Kunt, Feyen, and Levine (2011) show that different financial structures may be better at promoting economic activity at different stages of a country's economic development. In particular, they show that during the process of economic development, the relative demand for services provided by securities markets increases. They also show that deviations of actual financial structure from an economy's optimal financial structure negatively impacts overall economic development.

16.5.2. Formal vs. Informal Finance

A common feature of developing economies is the wide prevalence of informal financial systems in facilitating access to credit. Informal financing arrangements are very diverse, ranging from simple to complex, and they include loans made by moneylenders, traders, landlords, family, and friends, as well as loans from institutions such as rotating savings and credit associations (ROSCAs), savings and credit cooperatives (SACCOs), and other community-based financial organizations (see Besley 1995 for a survey of the different forms on informal financing mechanisms). Unlike formal financial intermediation, informal arrangements are typically based on business or personal relationships characterized by the use of self-enforcing contracts and social sanctions (e.g., Kandori 1992; Udry 1994; Straub 2005) and do not rely on the state to enforce contractual obligations (e.g., Ayyagari, Demirgüç-Kunt, and Maksimovic 2010).

A recent set of papers in the finance-growth literature has examined the role of informal finance in stimulating firm growth. On the one hand, Allen, Qian, and Qian (2005) argue that informal finance supports the growth of the private sector in developing economies like China. They present China as an important counter-example to the focus on formal institutions, since the private sector firms in China, despite facing weaker legal protections and poorer access to finance than firms in the state and listed sectors, are the fastest growing due to their reliance on alternative financing and governance mechanisms. On the other hand, Ayyagari, Demirgüç-Kunt, and Maksimovic (2010), and Cheng and Degryse (2010) show that informal financing plays a very limited role in firm growth in China. Ayyagari et al. (2010) show that while non-bank sources of financing are very prevalent, it is the formal financing channel, specifically bank finance, that is positively associated with higher growth and reinvestment.

This debate on formal versus informal finance has spawned a large literature trying to reconcile the mixed findings. Allen, Qian, and Xie (2018) argue that the type of informal financing is important. So mechanisms such as trade credit or loans from family and friends that rely on information advantages and monitoring mechanisms through social or business networks, support firm growth, whereas underground financing, such as moneylenders, is not associated with firm growth. Degryse, Lu, and Ongena (2016) find a complementary effect between formal finance and informal finance for small firm growth, but find a negative effect of informal finance on growth of large firms. They argue that the optimal choice for small firms may be co-funding due to the scalability of formal finance and informational advantages of informal finance.

Madestam (2014) formalizes the co-existence of informal and formal finance in a theoretical model where he shows that when there are credit market distortions, informal lenders' monitoring ability helps banks reduce agency costs by letting them channel formal credit through the informal sector.

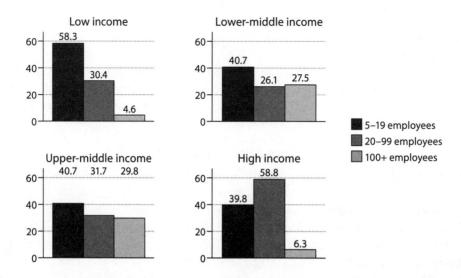

FIGURE 16.3. Job creation by size class across country income groups. *Source*: Ayyagari, Demirgüç-Kunt, and Maksimovic (2014).

Overall, the evidence suggests that while informal financing is very prevalent in China, it still offers a second-best solution since there is no evidence that informal financing is scalable and may even be detrimental to higher growth and productivity of firms.

16.6. FIRM SIZE AND FIRM SIZE DISTRIBUTIONS

In this section we survey the empirical evidence on how small and large firms differ in their growth, productivity, and job creation. We also discuss the unique challenges faced by small firms.

There is conflicting cross-country evidence on small firms' contribution to growth and jobs. Ayyagari, Demirgüç-Kunt, and Maksimovic (2014) construct a cross-country estimate of the contribution of small and medium enterprises to total employment, job creation, and growth. The estimates are calculated across 104 developing economies and show that small and medium enterprises (enterprises with less than 99 employees) not only employ nearly half the workforce in the average country but also generate the most new jobs (see figure 16.3) and have the highest growth rates. Other studies, such as Neumark, Wall, and Zhang (2011), among others, have found an inverse relationship between firm size and net growth rates in the United States, for example. However, Beck, Demirgüç-Kunt, and Levine (2005) show that while a large small and medium enterprise (SME) sector is a characteristic of successful economies, the relationship between the SME sector's share of formal manufacturing employment and growth is not causal. Using US Census data, Haltiwanger, Jarmin, and Miranda (2013) show that once we control for age, there is no systematic relationship between firm size and net growth rates.

A large number of studies show that small firms tend to be the most financially constrained (e.g., Demirgüç-Kunt and Maksimovic 1998; Rajan and Zingales 1998; Beck, Demirgüç-Kunt, and Maksimovic 2005; and Galindo and Micco 2005). Ayyagari, Demirgüç-Kunt, and Maksimovic (2008) use firm level survey data from the World Business

Environment Survey and find that not only do small firms report higher financing obstacles than large firms, they are also more severely affected. Beck, Demirgüç-Kunt, and Maksimovic (2005) find that the growth of smaller firms is hindered most by financing constraints, especially collateral requirements, bureaucracy, the need for special connections, and interest rate payments. Beck, Demirgüç-Kunt, and Maksimovic (2008) compare the financing patterns of small and large firms and find that small firms in developing countries use less external finance, especially bank finance. They also find that other sources of finance such as leasing, supplier finance, finance from development banks and other government sources do not fill the financing gap of small firms. De Mel, McKenzie, and Woodruff 2008; Udry and Anagol 2006; and Kremer, Lee, Robinson, and Rostapshova (2013) show that small firms have high marginal returns to the capital, as would be expected given that they are constrained in their ability to obtain additional capital. Beck et al. (2005, 2008) also suggest that on the margin, small firms benefit disproportionately as the financial systems develop. In a comprehensive study, Laeven (2003) finds that small firms' financing constraints decrease following financial liberalization episodes such as interest rate liberalization, elimination of credit controls, privatization, and bank entry, whereas those of large firms actually increase, reflecting the loss of political patronage and erosion of entrenched interests.

Banerjee and Duflo (2014), however, make the point that because small firms are a relatively small part of the overall capital stock in a country, the aggregate differences between developed and developing countries imply that even large firms in developing countries are credit constrained. They conjecture this by analyzing the directed lending program in India and show that large firms were severely constrained during 1998–2002 and unable to take advantage of growth opportunities.

16.6.1. Is There a Missing Middle in Firm Size Distributions in Developing Countries?

It is widely believed that in developing countries, firm size distributions are bimodal. Under this "missing middle" hypothesis, a few large firms and many very small and micro firms contribute to the bulk of employment and value added in the economy (e.g., Biggs and Oppenheim 1986; Tybout 2000; Krueger 2013). The literature has offered several explanations for the missing middle. One strand of this literature suggests that onerous regulation and bureaucracy associated with being formal that particularly disadvantages small sized firms (e.g., Rauch 1991) that would form the missing middle. In addition, weak demand and poor institutional infrastructure gives large-scale producers a comparative advantage over small, formal firms (e.g., Tybout 2000). The literature discussed above on credit constraints faced by small firms also suggests that small firms face difficulties in becoming middle-sized firms, particularly in low-income countries, giving rise to the missing middle.

A second strand of the literature favors a dual-economy model of large high-productivity firms and small low-productivity firms (e.g., Harris and Todaro 1970) and argues that large firms are subject to constraints and regulations that small firms avoid. Along these lines, in a particularly interesting paper, Dharmapala, Slemrod, and Wilson (2011) have argued that the missing middle may be the result of optimal tax policy where the government economizes on administrative costs by exempting small firms, but in turn intermediate-sized firms reduce their output to tax-exempt levels.

Empirical research on the size distribution of firms in developing countries has been limited by the absence of available census data, and most studies have had to rely on small survey samples. Thus, while there are several case studies analyzing the missing middle in a single country context such as Côte d'Ivoire (e.g., Sleuwaegen and Goedhuys 2002), there has been no systematic research/data on the prevalence of the missing middle across countries. More recently, however, Hseih and Olken (2014) obtain census micro-data from India, Indonesia, and Mexico and argue that there is no "missing middle" in the sense of a bimodal distribution in any of these three countries—mid-sized firms are missing, but large firms are missing too, and most firms are small in these developing countries. Thus, the resolution of the question of the missing middle awaits further research.

16.6.2. Size-Productivity Covariance

Several recent papers have argued that the large differences in productivity between rich and poor countries can be explained by different patterns of heterogeneity in firm-level productivity within developing and developed countries. This difference in patterns can in turn be attributed to the resource mis-allocation in developing countries. Specifically, Bartelsman, Haltiwanger, and Scarpetta (2013) show that the within-industry covariance between size and productivity is a robust measure of this mis-allocation and that this size/productivity relationship is stronger in the more advanced economies.[9]

The underlying logic of the covariance measure is as follows: In the absence of any distortions, the traditional models of firm size distribution (e.g., Lucas 1978; Melitz 2003) predict a positive correlation between size and productivity so that larger firms are more productive. However, distortions in developing countries affect both resource mis-allocation (too many resources are devoted to small unproductive firms) and selection processes (highly productive firms may exit and low-productivity firms may be allowed to operate) which lead to a great deal of variation in the size-productivity relation across countries. This variation is then captured by the cross-country variation in the covariance between size and productivity. Using Enterprise Survey data, Ayyagari, Demirgüç-Kunt, and Maksimovic (2015b) show that the covariance term is largely negative in developing countries. Thus, large firms are less productive than small firms, indicating allocative inefficiency. However, they also find that the resource mis-allocation seems to decrease with firm age, suggesting that on average the unproductive firms exit so older firms are more productive.

16.7. FIRM LIFE CYCLE

Recent research in finance has shown that firm life-cycle stages can predict many fundamental corporate finance policies.[10] However, much less is known about the factors that explain the evolution of firm size and productivity with age, and how it is affected by institutions.

The issue begins with the question of how new firms are started and how the individuals who start these firms select into entrepreneurship. There has been a great deal of work on this topic, and the challenge is to combine a rigorous statistical design with good micro-data. We use Bernstein, Colonnelli, Malacrino, and McQuade (2018) to illustrate this class of work.

Bernstein et al. (2018) aim to characterize the kind of individuals that start entrepreneurial firms when economic opportunities improve and to relate firm creation by these individuals to local institutions in developing countries, using Brazil as an example. The first step in such an analysis is to identify an exogenous shock to local opportunities across Brazil, followed by firm creation in response to this shock. To the extent that different regions in Brazil differ in their exposure to the shock and in their levels of development, the researchers can determine the role of institutions in a cross-sectional setting.

The specific shocks that Bernstein et al. (2018) study are the exposure of municipalities in Brazil to fluctuations in world commodity prices. Each municipality in Brazil has a different local agricultural endowment: different crops are suitable for different climatic conditions, soils, and topography. As a result, changes in world commodity prices affect different municipalities differently. These differences can be quantified by measuring agricultural endowments from prior crop usage and using these measures to estimate the impact of each year's changes in world prices of the crops on the revenues of the municipality.

Since world commodity prices are mostly unaffected by Brazilian agricultural output, these impacts are arguably exogenous to firm creation across municipalities. Moreover, these impacts shift the incomes of local farmers. These shifts create exogenous economic shocks for local firms in the non-tradeable sector (mostly in construction, retail, and wholesale industries), as well as financing opportunities for local firms in the tradeable sectors. The excess firm creation that occurs in response to these shocks can be analyzed and, most important, under certain conditions, can be interpreted as being caused by these shocks.

Brazil is particularly fortunate in having excellent and easily accessible data on firm formation and employee characteristics. The RAIS database (Relacao Anual de Informacoes Sociais) has individual level data on the universe of formal sector employees in Brazil. This includes information on the firm and the establishment that employs each worker, including tax identifiers, location, industry, and legal status. There is also extensive information on each employee, including payroll data, tenure, and hiring and termination dates, gender, nationality, age, education, hours worked, reasons for hiring and firing, and contract details and occupational category. Crucially, each employee can be tracked as he moves from job to job, and in particular, from an incumbent firm to a newly founded firm.

With these data in hand, Bernstein et al. (2018) find that the founders of firms created in response to local agricultural shocks are young individuals with above average skills. Further, these responsive individuals are younger and more skilled than the average entrepreneur in the population. Firm creation was higher in municipalities with better access to finance and more skilled human capital, showing that skill levels of the local population may have a significant impact on the entrepreneurial responsiveness of localities.

Bernstein et al. (2018) is notable because it shows how much can be achieved using a plausible source of exogenous economic shocks and an exceptionally rich data source at a country-wide level. Both of these conditions are not likely to be met in most empirical projects. At the same time, the paper shows how much remains elusive even when these conditions are met. For example, most of the firm creation in response to the agricultural

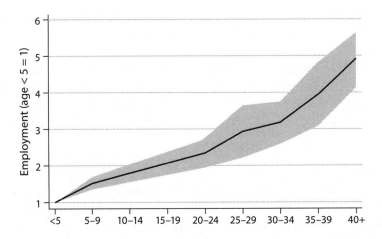

FIGURE 16.4. Firm employment by age—estimates in 120 developing countries. *Source*: Ayyagari, Demirgüç-Kunt, and Maksimovic (2015a).

shocks occurs in a very narrow range of industries—construction, retail, and wholesale firms. Firms in these industries are on average half the size of firms in the rest of the economy in Brazil, and it is unclear whether the findings generalize to other industries or other shocks. Fortunately, the data sources are sufficiently rich that further work, perhaps using different shocks, is likely to yield significant insight on these other sectors.

For established firms, Hsieh and Klenow (2014) compare growth trajectories over the long run (35+ years) in India and Mexico with those in the United States. They show that the growth trajectories of firms in India and Mexico are much flatter than in the United States, suggesting that financial and product market imperfections in developing countries are limiting the growth trajectories of firms. Ayyagari, Demirgüç-Kunt, and Maksimovic (2015a), however, argue that there is a great deal of heterogeneity in the mix of developing countries. Using Enterprise Survey data from the World Bank on formally registered firms, they show that, on average, older firms are substantially larger than younger firms in developing countries. Thus, as shown in figure 16.4, the average firm that is 40 years and older employs five times as many workers as the average firm under the age of 5 years, suggesting that the frictions may slow growth but may not restrict relative firm size over long horizons.

Using survey data from 120 developing countries, Ayyagari, Demirgüç-Kunt, and Maksimovic (2015b) use the institutional and firm characteristics at the time of the creation of the firm to predict the size, growth, and productivity of the firm over its life cycle. As shown in table 16.2, they argue that while the institutional factors examined in the literature (e.g., legal origin, endowments, ethnic fractionalization) predict firms' growth trajectories, firm-level characteristics are comparable and sometimes even superior to institutional factors in predicting firm size and growth, although not productivity. In particular, firm size at birth plays a key role in predicting variation in subsequent firm size, whereas country factors dominate in predicting variation in labor productivity across the life cycle.

Using better data from the Indian census of manufacturing firms, and in more careful analysis afforded by a single country setting (India), Ayyagari, Demirgüç-Kunt, and

Table 16.2. Firm Size and Life Cycle—Analysis of Variance

Age Groups	1 All	2 Young (<5)	3 Mid-Age (5–19)	4 Old (20–39)	5 Young (<5)	6 Mid-Age (5–19)	7 Old (20–39)
Country Characteristics							
Country dummies	0.092	0.125	0.089	0.092	0.187	0.105	0.059
Legal origin	0.008	0.018	0.017	0.014	0.056	0.04	0.015
Ethnic fractionalization	0.023	0.037	0.021	0.009	0.097	0.041	0.009
Latitude	0.004	0.018	0.009	0.01	0.035	0.01	0.001
Settler mortality	0.029	0.045	0.033	0.022	0.044	0.024	0.016
Legal origin, Latitude, Ethnic fractionalization	31.52%	36%	37.08%	23.91%	0.127	0.075	0.037
Legal origin, Latitude, Ethnic fractionalization, Settler mortality					67.91%	71.43%	62.71%
Firm-level Characteristics							
Age	0.068						
Sector dummies	0.046	0.051	0.041	0.026	0.069	0.033	0.017
Location (city size) dummies	0.005	0.002	0.002	0.01	0.014	0.009	0.008
Ownership dummies	0.039	0.05	0.044	0.026	0.084	0.052	0.038
Legal Organization dummies	0.101	0.05	0.086	0.154	0.097	0.104	0.148
Log(Size at birth)	0.357	0.522	0.373	0.272	0.577	0.429	0.273
All together	0.423	0.511	0.389	0.346	0.62	0.487	0.37
N	33982	6119	20144	5724	2234	8352	3896

Source: Ayyagari, Demirgüç-Kunt, and Maksimovic (2015b).

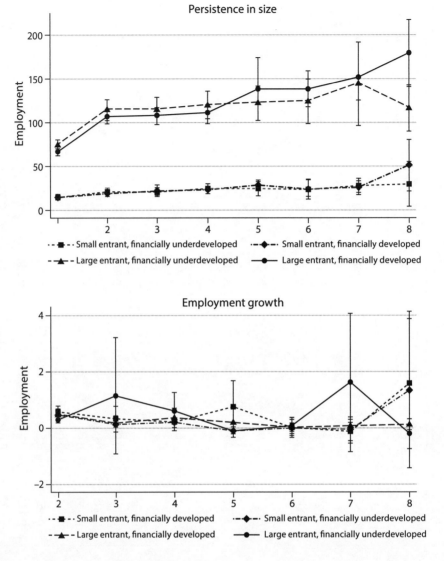

FIGURE 16.5. Persistence in initial size across different levels of financial development in India. *Source*: Ayyagari, Demirgüç-Kunt, and Maksimovic (2015a).

Maksimovic (2017) show that the founding conditions of a firm, specifically size of the start-up, are a strong predictor of persistence in firm size over the first 8 years of firm life cycle. Start-up size is in turn determined by local institutions. Thus, institutions matter for the selection of firms. The average entrant is smaller in states with greater financial development. However, greater financial development is also associated with higher firm entry rates. Subsequent to entry, however, and consistent with Gibrat's Law, during early life cycle, large and small entrants do not grow at different rates across states with different institutions or in industries with differing reliance on external finance. These results are illustrated in figure 16.5, taken from their paper. In the top panel, the difference between large entrants (or between small entrants) in states with good and bad institutions is not economically significant. The bottom panel shows that large and small entrants do not grow at different growth rates in states with good versus weak financial development.

16.8. GAPS IN EXISTING RESEARCH AND POLICY IMPLICATIONS FOR LOW-INCOME COUNTRIES

The review of evidence above points to two somewhat conflicting interpretations about the role of institutions in firm growth. First, there is ample evidence that specific institutional deficiencies and obstacles directly affect the growth of firms. This evidence is from the association between direct reports of constraints faced by firms and their performance (e.g., Beck, Demirgüç-Kunt, and Maksimovic 2005) and from natural experiments relating specific institutional changes to subsequent firm growth (e.g., Kerr and Nanda 2009). Second, there is also evidence that the firm's initial conditions are highly predictive of firm outcomes, and that surviving firms register similar growth trajectories over multi-year periods across a wide variation of institutional frameworks, once the initial characteristics of the firms at the time of entry are taken into account (e.g., Ayyagari, Demirgüç-Kunt, and Maksimovic 2015, 2016).

While the first strand of literature would seem to place more emphasis on the role of institutions than the second strand, this is in fact not the case. The second approach would place greater stress on the effect of institutions on the conditions of entry and entrepreneurship than on the growth trajectories of mature firms. Thus, it is quite clear that institutions have a major effect on both the quantity and quality of entry (e.g., Klapper, Laeven, and Rajan 2006; Ayyagari, Demirgüç-Kunt, and Maksimovic 2016; and Kerr and Nanda 2009).

A second issue that arises is that as the firm traverses its life cycle, its growth trajectory is potentially impacted by several different institutional regimes, and those regimes can affect the firm differently at different stages of its development. The effect of institutional regime switches may impact firm growth at the micro-level in a manner analogous to the effect of growth spurts on the whole economy at the macro-level. Thus, periods of growth during which corruption, say, is relatively unchecked may be interspersed by periods during which it is more carefully regulated. These episodes will affect firms directly, and the effect may be very different on young and old firms. However, to the extent that the episodes are temporary and irregular, their effect may substantially cancel out over time, thus partially masking the role of institutional variations, for example, government changes may affect large and small firms differentially.

In principle, the interaction of firm characteristics and institutions of firm growth can be addressed using panel-data methods. Thus, regressing firm outcomes on interactions of institutional changes with firm life-cycle stages will give estimates of the differential effect of the change on the outcomes for firms of different ages.

A problem arises due to the difficulties of finding rich firm-level data for a suitable cross-section of countries. Such data are available from the Census Offices of most developed countries and some developing countries. However, generating micro-data for a sufficient cross-section of countries with different institutions, especially if given the further requirement that there is sufficient fluidity of institutions within countries to obtain some degree of time-series identification, is very challenging. The task is made more difficult by attempts to find a suitable instrument or natural experiment that is plausibly likely to hold across a set of countries with different institutions undergoing changes in regime.

Consistent cross-country cross-sectional data for non-listed firms are difficult to obtain. Panel data covering a large number of developing countries are even more difficult to locate. A researcher might address this challenge in several ways.

First, on a descriptive level one might extend the Hsieh and Klenow (2014) methodology to attempt to measure the effect of institutions at different stages of the firm life cycle. Hsieh and Klenow take a cross-section of the Indian Manufacturing Census, which contains information of firm size (number of employees) and firm age. From that cross-section one can derive a size-age profile. Any attempt to compare such profiles directly across countries rests on the assumption that the institutions in each country remain constant over time. A natural extension would be to allow breaks in institutions within countries—allowing for different regimes due to the Indian industrial deregulation being one such example.

An obvious further step would be to allow for differential effects of institutions at different points of the firm's life cycle. Thus, for example, take the case of the sample of 10-year-old firms across a set of countries. Their life cycle can be decomposed into two five-year stages. The growth rate of the firm over its first five years will in principle be affected by the interaction of the firm's quality, as measured by its initial characteristics and the institutions in existence at this time, b_{ct} and c_{ct} respectively, where the subscript c indexes the country and the subscript t references the time period. Denote the effect of the interaction of the institutions and the country-level effects by $f(ct, c_{ct})$. We can obtain a similar expression for the second stage (b_{ct}, c_{ct}). Putting the two together, one can then model the firm's growth over its first ten years.

The variation in institutions across countries and changes in institutions over time within a country can identify the role of institutions on firm growth over its life cycle. The functions $f(bct, c_c t)$ and $g(bct, c_c t)$ can be modeled either as fixed effects in a variance decomposition exercise or using more formal nonparametric methods.

The indicator variable for each of the intervals could take value 0 if, say, capital investment in the firm's industry was regulated during the interval and 1 if the firm was not regulated. Furthermore, firms of different ages can be stacked together for added estimation efficiency.

Once specific institution-life-cycle strategies are identified, the second stage of the research can proceed with a more detailed analysis stressing the existence of casual relations. The central question here is whether or not the change in a specific institution might affect firms at a specific stage in their life cycle. For example, changes in WTO trading rules might affect firms of different size and firms in countries with different financial systems differently. The key for this analysis is the choice of instruments or of a natural experiment. Thus, one might not be able to forecast a specific test until the relevant instruments are found and the plausibility of the exclusion condition determined. As such, the specifics of this analysis are by nature more difficult to predict.

Taken together, the two stages can clarify whether the previous lack of evidence of long-term effects of institutions on firms is because such effects are small or because favorable regimes alternate over time with unfavorable regimes, creating a leveling effect. More broadly, the research can clarify the extent to which different institutions are complements or substitutes. Thus, it can provide policy guidance on which interventions are likely to positively affect firms at different stages in their life cycle.

Viewed in this way, such research would provide a cross-country parallel for the intensive quantitative and qualitative research program proposed by Professor Francois Bourguignon.

NOTES

1. We adopt a micro perspective and focus on firm-level studies throughout the review. For a macro perspective on the issues related to finance and growth, see Beck's chapter in this volume.
2. Morck, Yeung, and Yu (2000) provide tests of the information content of stock markets.
3. Fisman and Love (2007) critique the Rajan and Zingales (1998) methodology as not measuring the extent to which financial systems foster growth of inherently financially dependent industries but rather measuring whether financial intermediaries allow firms to respond to global shocks to growth opportunities. Notwithstanding, the methodology has found extensive use in finance. Beck (2002) uses the methodology to show that financial development influences the structure of trade balances; Cetorelli and Gambera (2001) use it to show that bank concentration promotes growth of industries that are heavy users of external finance; Claessens and Laeven (2003) build on Rajan-Zingales to examine the joint impact of financial development and property rights protection on access to finance; and Beck, Demirgüç-Kunt, Laeven, and Levine (2008) show that industries that are naturally composed of smaller firms grow faster in countries with better-developed financial systems.
4. Private credit bureaus operate on the principle of reciprocity, collecting and distributing the information supplied by its members, whereas public credit registries are managed by country central banks that mandate the reporting of data on borrowers. Some studies point to the differing impact of private versus public credit registries. For instance, Djankov, McLiesh, and Shleifer (2007) find that only public registries are associated with more private credit only in poorer countries.
5. Karolyi (2006) provides an excellent review of the cross-listings literature.
6. The argument being that when the mortality rate was high, the legal system was set up to extract resources from the indigenous population rather than to protect property rights. See Murray (2006) for an econometric critique of this approach.
7. See Imbens and Angrist (1994), and Heckman and Vytlacil (2007).
8. Several papers have challenged the usefulness of investment-cash flow sensitivities to measure financing constraints on both theoretical and empirical grounds. See Kaplan and Zingales (1997, 2000), and Erickson and Whited (2000).
9. See also Bartelsman, Haltiwanger, and Scarpetta (2004), Banerjee and Duflo (2014), Jeong and Townsend (2007), Restuccia and Rogerson (2008), Hsieh and Klenow (2009), Alfaro, Charlton, and Kanczuk (2009), and Midrigan and Yi Xu (2014).
10. See, for example, studies on dividends (Fama and French 2001; Grullon et al. 2002; DeAngelo, DeAngelo, and Stulz 2006; and Denis and Osobov 2008); financing (Berger and Udell, 1990); stock valuations (Pastor and Veronesi 2003); and acquisitions (Maksimovic and Philips 2008; Arikan and Stulz 2016). Hadlock and Pierce (2010) show that size and age are closely related and are good predictors of financing constraints.

REFERENCES

Acemoglu, D., and Johnson, S. 2005. "Unbundling Institutions." *Journal of Political Economy* 113(5): 949–995.

Acemoglu, D., Johnson, S., and Robinson, J. A. 2001. "The Colonial Origins of Comparative Development: An Empirical Investigation." *American Economic Review* 91: 1369–1401.

———. 2002. "Reversal of Fortunes: Geography and Institutions in the Making of the Modern World Income Distribution." *Quarterly Journal of Economics* 117(4): 1231–1294.

Acemoglu, D., and Zilibotti, F. 1997. "Was Prometheus Unbound by Chance? Risk, Diversification, and Growth." *Journal of Political Economy* 105: 709–775.

Acharya, V. V., Amihud, Y., and Litov, L. 2011. "Creditor Rights and Corporate Risk-taking." *Journal of Financial Economics* 102(1): 150–166.

Ades, A., and Di Tella, R. 1999. "Rents, Competition, and Corruption." *American Economic Review* 89(4): 982–993.

Agarwal, R., and Audretsch, D. B. 2001. "Does Entry Size Matter? The Impact of the Life Cycle and Technology on Firm Survival." *Journal of Industrial Economics* 49(1): 21–43.

Aghion, P., Dewatripont, M., and Rey, P. 1999. "Competition, Financial Discipline and Growth." *Review of Economic Studies* 66(4): 825–852.

Alesina, A., Devleeschauwer, A., Easterly, W., Kurlat, S., and Wacziarg, R. 2003. "Fractionalization." *Journal of Economic Growth* 8(20): 155–194.

Alfaro, L., Charlton, A., and Kanczuk, F. 2009. "Plant-Size Distribution and Cross-Country Income Differences." *NBER International Seminar on Macroeconomics* 5(1): 243–272.

Allen, F., Capie, F., Fohlin, C., Miyajima, H., Sylla, R., Yafeh, Y., and Wood, G. 2010. "How important historically were financial systems for growth in the UK, US, Germany, and Japan?" SSRN Working paper series.

Allen, F., and Gale, D. 1997. "Financial Markets, Intermediaries, and Intertemporal Smoothing." *Journal of Political Economy* 105: 523–546.

———. 2000. *Comparing Financial Systems*. Cambridge, MA: MIT Press.

Allen, F., Qian, J., Qian, M. 2005. "Law, Finance, and Economic Growth in China." *Journal of Financial Economics* 77(1): 57–116.

Allen, F., Qian, M., and Xie, J. 2018. "Understanding Informal Financing." *Journal of Financial Intermediation*. In press.

Almazan, A., De Motta, A. D., Titman, S., and Uysal, V. 2010. "Financial Structure, Acquisition Opportunities, and Firm Locations." *Journal of Finance* 65(2): 529–563.

Almeida, H., Campello, M., and Weisbach, M. S. 2004. "The Cash Flow Sensitivity of Cash." *Journal of Finance* 59(4): 1777–1804.

Alok, S., and Ayyagari, M. 2015. "Politics, State Ownership, and Corporate Investment." ISB Working paper series.

Amore, M. D., Schneider, C., and Žaldokas, A. 2013. "Credit Supply and Corporate Innovation." *Journal of Financial Economics* 109(3): 835–855.

Arikan, A. M., and Stulz, R. 2016. "Corporate Acquisitions, Diversification, and the Firm's Lifecycle." *Journal of Finance* 71(1): 139–194.

Asker, J., Farre-Mensa, J., and Ljungqvist, A. 2015. "Corporate Investment and Stock Market Listing: A Puzzle." *Review of Financial Studies* 28(2): 342–390.

Atanassov, J. 2015. "Arm's Length Financing and Innovation: Evidence from Publicly Traded Firms." *Management Science* 62(1): 128–155.

Ayyagari, M., Demirgüç-Kunt, A., and Maksimovic, V. 2008. "How Well Do Institutional Theories Explain Firms Perception of Property Rights." *Review of Financial Studies* 21(4): 1833–1871.

———. 2010. "Formal versus Informal Finance: Evidence from China." *Review of Financial Studies* 23(8): 3048–3097.

———. 2011. "Firm Innovation in Emerging Markets: The Role of Finance, Governance, and Competition." *Journal of Financial and Quantitative Analysis* 46(6): 1545–1580.

———. 2013. "What Determines Protection of Property Rights? An Analysis of Direct and Indirect Effects." *Journal of Financial Econometrics* 11(4): 610–649.

———. 2014. "Who Creates Jobs in Developing Countries?" *Small Business Economics* 43(1): 75–99.

———. 2015a. "Does Financial Development Matter for Firm Lifecycle? Evidence from India." SSRN Working paper series.

———. 2015b. "Are Large Firms Born or Made? Evidence from Developing Countries." SSRN Working paper series.

———. 2017. "What Determines Entrepreneurial Outcomes in Emerging Markets? The Role of Initial Conditions." *Review of Financial Studies* 30(7): 2478–2522.

Ayyagari, M., Juarros, P., Martinez-Peria, S., and Singh, S. 2016. "Access to Finance And Job Growth: Firm-Level Evidence Across Developing Countries." SSRN Working paper series.

Bae, K., and Goyal, V. K. 2009. "Creditor Rights, Enforcement, and Bank Loans." *Journal of Finance* 64(2): 823–860.

Bailey, W., Karolyi, G. A., and Salva, C. 2006. "The Economic Consequences of Increased Disclosure: Evidence from International Cross-Listings." *Journal of Financial Economics* 81(1): 175–213.

Baker, H. K., Nofsinger, J. R., and Weaver, D. G. 2002. "International Cross-Listing and Visibility." *Journal of Financial and Quantitative Analysis* 37(3): 495–521.

Banerjee, Abhijit V. 1997. "A Theory of Misgovernance." *Quarterly Journal of Economics* 112(4): 1289–1332.

Banerjee, A. V., and Duflo, E. 2014. "Do Firms Want to Borrow More? Testing Credit Constraints Using a Directed Lending Program." *Review of Economic Studies* 81(2): 572–607.

Banerjee, A., Mullainathan, S., and Hanna, R. 2012. "Corruption." NBER Working paper No. w17968. National Bureau of Economic Research.

Bardhan, P. 1997. "Corruption and Development: A Review of Issues." *Journal of Economic Literature* 35 (September): 1320–1346.

Bargeron, L. L., Schlingemann, F. P., Stulz, R. M., and Zutter, C. J. 2008. "Why Do Private Acquirers Pay So Little Compared to Public Acquirers?" *Journal of Financial Economics* 89(3): 375–390.

Bartelsman, E., Haltiwanger, J., and Scarpetta, S. 2004. "Microeconomic Evidence of Creative Destruction in Industrial and Developing Countries." World Bank, Policy Research Working Paper No. 3464, December.

———. 2013. "Cross-Country Differences in Productivity: The Role of Allocation and Selection." *American Economic Review* 103(1): 305–334.

Barth, J., Lin, C., Lin, P., and Song, F. 2009. "Corruption in Bank Lending to Firms: Cross-Country Micro Evidence on the Beneficial Role of Competition and Information Sharing." *Journal of Financial Economics* 91: 361–388.

Beck, T., Demirgüç-Kunt, A., Laeven, L., and Levine, R. 2008. "Finance, Firm Size, and Growth." *Journal of Money, Credit and Banking* 40(7): 1379–1405.

Beck, T., Demirgüç-Kunt, A., and Levine, R. 2003. "Law and Finance: Why Does Legal Origin Matter?" *Journal of Comparative Economics* 31(4): 653–675.

———. 2005. "SMEs, Growth, and Poverty: Cross-Country Evidence." *Journal of Economic Growth* 10(3): 199–229.

———. 2009. "Financial Institutions and Markets across Countries and over Time: Data and Analysis." World Bank Policy Research Working Paper 4943.

Beck, T., Demirgüç-Kunt, A., and Maksimovic, V. 2005. "Financial and Legal Constraints to Firm Growth: Does Firm Size Matter?" *Journal of Finance* 137–177.

———. 2008. "Financing Patterns Around the World: Are Small Firms Different?" *Journal of Financial Economics* 89(3): 467–487.

Beck, T., and Levine, R. 2002. "Industry Growth and Capital Allocation: Does Having a Market or Bank Based System Matter?" *Journal of Financial Economics* 64(2): 147–180.

Beck, T., Levine, R., and Loayza, N. 2000. "Finance and the Sources of Growth." *Journal of Financial Economics* 58: 261–300.

Beck, T., Lin, C., and Ma, Y. 2014. "Why Do Firms Evade Taxes? The Role of Information Sharing and Financial Sector Outreach." *Journal of Finance* 69(2): 763–817.

Behr, P., and Sonnekalb, S. 2012. "The Effect of Information Sharing Between Lenders on Access to Credit, Cost of Credit, and Loan Performance—Evidence from a Credit Registry Introduction." *Journal of Banking and Finance* 36(11): 3017–3032.

Bekaert, G., Harvey, C., and Lundblad, C. 2005. "Does Financial Liberalization Spur Growth?" *Journal of Financial Economics* 77(1): 3–55.

———. 2001. "Emerging Equity Markets and Economic Development?" *Journal of Development Economics* 66: 465–504.

Bena, J., and Ortiz-Molina, H. 2013. "Pyramidal Ownership and the Creation of New Firms." *Journal of Financial Economics* 108(3): 798–821.

Benmelech, E., and Frydman, C. 2015. "Military CEOs." *Journal of Financial Economics* 117: 43–59.

Bennedsen, M., Nielsen, K. M., Perez-Gonzalez, F., and Wolfenzon, D. 2007. "Inside the Family Firm: The Role of Families in Succession Decisions and Performance." *Quarterly Journal of Economics* 122: 647–691.

Berger, A. N., and Udell, F. U. 1990. "Collateral, Loan Quality, and Bank Risk." *Journal of Monetary Economics* 25: 21–42.

Berkowitz, D., Pistor, K., and Richard, J. F. 2003. "Economic Development, Legality, and the Transplant Effect." *European Economic Review* 47(1): 165–195.

Bernstein, S., Colonnelli, E., Malacrino, D., and McQuade, T. 2018. "Who Creates New Firms When Local Opportunities Arise?" IMF Working Paper Series.

Bertrand, M., and Schoar, A. 2003. "Managing with Style: The Effect of Managers on Firm Policies." *Quarterly Journal of Economics* 118: 1169–1208.

Bertrand, M., Schoar, A., and Thesmar, D. 2007. "Banking Deregulation and Industry Structure: Evidence from the French Banking Reforms of 1985." *Journal of Finance* 62(2): 597–628.

Besley, T. 1995. "Property Rights and Investment Incentives: Theory and Evidence from Ghana." *Journal of Political Economy* 103(5): 903–937.

Biggs, T., and Oppenheim, J. 1986. *What Drives the Size Distribution of Firms in Developing Countries?* Employment and Enterprise Policy Analysis Project.

Black, S., and Strahan, P. E. 2002. "Entrepreneurship and Bank Credit Availability." *Journal of Finance* 57: 2807–2833.

Bliss, Christopher, and Di Tella, Rafael. 1997. "Does Competition Kill Corruption." *Journal of Political Economy* 105(5): 1001–1023.

Bloom, Nicholas, and Van Reenen, John. 2007. "Measuring and Explaining Management Practices across Firms and Countries." *Quarterly Journal of Economics* 122(4): 1351–1408.

———. 2010. "Why Do Management Practices Differ Across Firms and Countries?" *Journal of Economic Perspectives* 24(1): 203–224.

Boot, A. W., Greenbaum, S. I., and Thakor, A. V. 1993. "Reputation and Discretion in Financial Contracting." *American Economic Review* 83: 1165–1183.

Boot, A. W., and Thakor, A. V. 1997. "Financial System Architecture." *Review of Financial Studies* 10(3): 693–733.

Booth, L., Aivazian, V., Demirgüç-Kunt, A., and Maksimovic, V. 2001. "Capital Structures in Developing Countries." *Journal of Finance* 56(1): 87–130.

Botero, J. C., Djankov, S., La Porta, R., Lopez-de-Silanes, F., and Shleifer, A. 2004. "The Regulation of Labor." *Quarterly Journal of Economics* 119(4): 1339–1382.

Boubakri, N., and Cosset, J. 1998. "The Financial And Operating Performance Of Newly Privatized Firms: Evidence From Developing Countries." *Journal of Finance* 53: 1081–1110.

Boyd, J. H., and Prescott, E. C. 1986. "Financial Intermediary-Coalitions." *Journal of Economics Theory* 38: 211–232.

Brav, A., Graham, J. R., Harvey, C., and Michaely, R. 2005. "Payout Policy in the 21st Century." *Journal of Financial Economics* 77(3): 483–527.

Brav, O. 2009. "Access to Capital, Capital Structure, and the Funding of the Firm." *Journal of Finance* 64(1): 263–308.

Brown, M., Jappelli, T., and Pagano, M. 2009. "Information Sharing and Credit: Firm-level Evidence from Transition Countries." *Journal of Financial Intermediation* 18(2): 151–172.

Bruhn, M., and Love, I. 2014. "The Real Impact of Improved Access to Finance: Evidence from Mexico." *Journal of Finance* 69(3): 1347–1376.

Bulte, E., Beekman, G., Falco, S. D., Pan, L., and Hella, J. 2014. "Behavioral Responses and the Impact of New Agricultural Technologies: Evidence from a Double-Blind Field Experiment in Tanzania." *American Journal of Agricultural Economics* 9(3): 813–830.

Cabral, L., and Mata, J. 2003. "On the Evolution of the Firm Size Distribution: Facts and Theory." *American Economic Review* 93(4): 1075–1090.

Cameron, R. 1967. "Scotland, 1750–1845." In *Banking in the Early Stages of Industrialization: A Study in Comparative Economic History,* edited by R. Cameron, et al., 60–99. New York: Oxford University Press.

Campello, M., Giambona, E., Graham, J. R., and Harvey, C. R. 2011. "Liquidity Management and Corporate Investment During a Financial Crisis." *Review of Financial Studies* 24(6): 1944–1979.

Caprio, G., Jr., Laeven, L., and Levine, R. 2003. "Governance and Bank Valuation." *Journal of Financial Intermediation* 16(4): 584–617.

Cartwright, N. 2007. "Are RCTs the Gold Standard?." *BioSocieties* 2(1): 11–20.

Carvalho, D. 2014. "The Real Effects of Government-Owned Banks: Evidence from an Emerging Market." *Journal of Finance* 69(2): 577–609.

Cetorelli, N. 2004. "Real Effects of Bank Competition." *Journal of Money, Credit, and Banking* 36: 543–558.

Cetorelli, N., and Gambera, M. 2001. "Banking Market Structure, Financial Dependence and Growth: International Evidence from Industry Data." *Journal of Finance* 56(2): 617–648.

Cetorelli, N., and Strahan, P. E. 2006. "Finance as a Barrier to Entry: Bank Competition and Industry Structure in Local U.S. Markets." *Journal of Finance* 61(1): 437–461.

Chava, S., Oettl, A., Subramanian, A., and Subramanian, K. V. 2013. "Banking Deregulation and Innovation." *Journal of Financial Economics* 109(3): 759–774.

Cheng, Xiaoqiang, and Degryse, Hans. 2010. Information Sharing and Credit Rationing: Evidence from the Introduction of a Public Credit Registry. Discussion Paper 2010-34S, Center for Economic Research, Tilburg University, Tilburg, the Netherlands.

Claessens, S., Daniela K., and Schmukler, S. L. 2002. "The Future Of Stock Markets In Emerging Economies." In *Brookings-Wharton Papers on Financial Services 2002,* edited by Robert E. Litan and Richard Herring, 167–212. Washington, DC: Brookings Institution.

Claessens, S., Djankov, S., and Lang, L.H.P. 2000. "The Separation of Ownership and Control in East Asian Corporations." *Journal of Financial Economics* 58(1–2): 81–112.

Claessens, S., and Laeven, L. 2003. "Financial Development, Property Rights, and Growth." *Journal of Finance* 58(6): 2401–2436.

Cole, S. 2009. "Financial Development, Bank Ownership, and Growth: Or, Does Quantity Imply Quality?" *Review of Economics and Statistics* 91: 33–51.

Cronqvist, H., Makhija, A., and Yonker, S. E. 2012. "Behavioral Consistency in Corporate Finance: CEO Personal and Corporate Leverage." *Journal of Financial Economics* 103(1): 20–40.

Cull, R., and Xu, L. C. 2005. "Institutions, Ownership, and Finance: The Determinants of Investment among Chinese Firms." *Journal of Financial Economics* 77: 117–146.

Davis, S., Haltiwanger, J., and Schuh, S. 1996. *Job Creation and Destruction.* Cambridge, MA: MIT Press.

DeAngelo, H., DeAngelo, L., and Stulz, R. 2006. "Dividend Policy and the Earned/Contributed Capital Mix: A Test of the Lifecycle Theory." *Journal of Financial Economics* 81(2): 227–254.

Deaton, A. 2010. "Instruments, Randomization, and Learning About Development." *Journal of Economic Literature* 48(2): 424–55.

Degryse, H., Lu, L., and Ongena, S. 2016. "Informal or Formal Financing? Evidence on the Co-Funding of Chinese Firms." *Journal of Financial Intermediation* 27: 31–50.

De Janvry, Alain, McIntosh, Craig, and Sadoulet, Elisabeth. 2010. "The Supply and Demand Side Impacts of Credit Market Information." *Journal of Development Economics* 93: 173–188.

De Mel, S., McKenzie, D., and Woodruff, C. 2008. "Returns to Capital in Microenterprises: Evidence from a Field Experiment." *Quarterly Journal of Economics* 123(4): 1329–1372.

Demirgüç-Kunt, A., Feyen, E., and Levine, R. 2011. *The Evolving Importance of Banks and Securities Markets.* World Bank.

Demirgüç-Kunt, A., and Levine, R. 2001. "Financial Structure and Economic Growth: Perspectives and Lessons." In *Financial Structure and Economic Growth: A Cross-Country Comparison of Banks, Markets, and Development*, 3–14. Cambridge, MA: MIT Press.

Demirgüç-Kunt, A., Love, I., and Maksimovic, V. 2006. "Business Environment and the Incorporation Decision." *Journal of Banking and Finance* 30(11): 2967–2993.

Demirgüç-Kunt, A., and Maksimovic, V. 1998. "Law, Finance, and Firm Growth." *Journal of Finance* 53(6): 2107–2137.

———. 1999. "Institutions, Financial Markets and Firm Debt Maturity." *Journal of Financial Economics* 54(3): 295–336.

———. 2002. "Funding Growth in Bank-Based and Market-Based Financial Systems: Evidence from Firm-Level Data." *Journal of Financial Economics* 65(3): 337–363.

Denis, D. J., and Osobov, I. 2008. "Why Do Firms Pay Dividends? International Evidence on the Determinants of Dividend Policy." *Journal of Financial Economics* 89(1): 62–82.

Desai, M. A., Foley, C. F., and Hines, J. R., Jr. 2004. "A Multinational Perspective on Capital Structure Choice and Internal Capital Markets." *Journal of Finance* 59(6): 2451–2487.

———. 2005. "Foreign Direct Investment and the Domestic Capital Stock." *American Economic Review* 95(2): 33–38.

Devereux, M. B., and Smith, G. W. 1994. "International Risk Sharing and Economic Growth." *International Economic Review* 35: 535–550.

Dewatripont, M., and Maskin, E. 1995. "Credit Efficiency in Centralized and Decentralized Economies." *Review of Economic Studies* 62: 541–555.

Dewenter, K. L., and Malatesta, P. H. 2001. "State-Owned and Privately Owned Firms: An Empirical Analysis of Profitability, Leverage, and Labor Intensity." *American Economic Review* 91: 320–334.

Dharmapala, D., Slemrod, J., and Wilson, J. D. 2011. "Tax Policy and the Missing Middle: Optimal Tax Remittance with Firm-Level Administrative Costs." *Journal of Public Economics* 95: 1036–1047.

Diamond, D. W. 1984. "Financial Intermediation and Delegated Monitoring." *Review of Economic Studies* 51: 393–414.

Diamond, D., and Verrecchia, R. E. 1982. "Optimal Managerial Contracts and Equilibrium Security Prices." *Journal of Finance* 37(2): 275–287.

Diamond, Jared. 1997. *Guns, Germs, and Steel: The Fate of Human Societies.* New York: Norton.

Dinc, S. 2005. "Politicians and Banks: Political Influences on Government-Owned Banks in Emerging Markets." *Journal of Financial Economics* 77(2): 453–479.

Dinc, S., and Gupta, N. 2011. "The Decision to Privatize: Finance and Politics." *Journal of Finance* 66(1): 241–269.

Djankov, S., La Porta, R., Lopez-de-Silanes, F., and Shleifer, A. 2002. "The Regulation of Entry." *Quarterly Journal of Economics* 117(1): 1–37.

———. 2003. "Courts." *Quarterly Journal of Economics* 118(2): 453–517.

Djankov, S., McLiesh, C., and Shleifer, A. 2007. "Private Credit in 129 Countries." *Journal of Financial Economics* 12(2): 77–99.

Doidge, C., Karolyi, A. G., and Stulz, R. 2007. "Why Do Countries Matter So Much For Corporate Governance?" *Journal of Financial Economics* 86: 1–39.

Duchin, R., and Sosyura, D. 2012. "The Politics of Government Investment." *Journal of Financial Economics* 106(1): 24–48.

Dunne, T., Roberts, M., and Samuelson, L. 1989. "The Growth and Failure of U.S. Manufacturing Firms." *Quarterly Journal of Economics* 104(4): 671–698.

Durnev, A., and Kim, E. H. 2005. "To Steal or Not to Steal: Firm Attributes, Legal Environment, and Valuation." *Journal of Finance* 60(3): 1461–1493.

Dyck, A., and Zingales, L. 2004. "Private Benefits of Control: An International Comparison." *Journal of Finance* 59(4): 537–600.

Easterly, W., and Levine, R. 1997. "Africa's Growth Tragedy: Policies and Ethnic Divisions." *Quarterly Journal of Economics* 112: 1203–1250.

Engerman, S., and Sokoloff, K. 1997. "Factor Endowments, Institutions, and Differential Paths of Growth Among New World Economies." In *How Latin America Fell Behind*, edited by S. H. Haber, 260–304. Stanford, CA: Stanford University Press.

———. 2002. "Factor Endowments, Inequality, and Paths of Development among New World Economies." *Economía* 3(1): 41–109.

Ericson, R., and Pakes, A. 1998. "Empirical Implications of Alternative Models of Firm Dynamics." *Journal of Economic Theory* 79(1): 1–45.

Erickson, T., and Whited, T. M. 2000. "Measurement Error and the Relationship between Investment and *q*." *Journal of Political Economy* 108(5): 1027–1057.

Evans, David S. 1987. "The Relationship between Firm Growth, Size, and Age: Estimates for 100 Manufacturing Industries." *Journal of Industrial Economics* 35(4): 567–581.

Faccio, Mara, Masulis, Ronald W., and McConnell, John J. 2006. "Political Connections and Corporate Bailouts." *Journal of Finance* 61: 2597–2635.

Fama, E. F., and French, K. R. 2001. "Disappearing Dividends: Changing Firm Characteristics or Lower Propensity to Pay?" *Journal of Financial Economics* 60(1): 3–43.

Fan, J. P., Titman, S., and Twite, G. 2012. "An International Comparison of Capital Structure and Debt Maturity Choices." *Journal of Financial and Quantitative Analysis* 47(1): 23–56.

Fan, J. P., Wong, T. J., and Zhang, T. 2007. "Politically Connected CEOs, Corporate Governance, and Post-IPO Performance of China's Newly Partially Privatized Firms." *Journal of Financial Economics* 84(2): 330–357.

Farre-Mensa, J. 2012. Comparing the Cash Policies of Public and Private Firms. Unpublished working paper, Harvard University.

Fazzari, S., Hubbard, R. G., and Petersen, B. 1988. "Investment, Financing Decisions, and Tax Policy." *American Economic Review* 78(2): 200–205.

———. 2000. "Investment-Cash Flow Sensitivities Are Useful: A Comment on Kaplan and Zingales." *Quarterly Journal of Economics* 115(2): 695–705.

Fisman, R. 2001. "Estimating the Value of Political Connections." *American Economic Review* 91, 1095–1102.

Fisman, R., and Love, I. 2007. "Financial Dependence and Growth Revisited." *Journal of the European Economic Association* 5(2–3): 470–479.

Fisman, R., and Svensson, J. 2007. "Are Corruption and Taxation Really Harmful to Growth? Firm Level Evidence." *Journal of Development Economics* 83(1): 63–75.

Foster, L., Haltiwanger, J. C., and Syverson, C. 2012. The Slow Growth of New Firms: Learning about Demand? National Bureau of Economic Research Working Papers No. 17853.

Gale, D., and Hellwig, M. 1985. "Incentive-Compatible Debt Contracts: The One-Period Problem." *Review of Economic Studies* 52(4): 647–663.

Galindo, A., and Micco, A. 2005. Bank Credit to Small and Medium-Sized Enterprises: The Role of Creditor Protection. IDB Working Paper No. 438.

Galindo, A., and Miller, M. 2001. Can Credit Registries Reduce Credit Constraints? Empirical Evidence on the Role of Credit Registries in Firm Investment Decisions. IDB-IIC 42nd Annual Meeting. Santiago, Chile.

Gan, J. 2007. "Collateral, Debt Capacity, and Corporate Investment. Evidence from a Natural Experiment." *Journal of Financial Economics* 85(3): 709–734.

Gao, H., Harford, J., and Li, K. 2013. "Determinants of Corporate Cash Policy: Insights from Private Firms." *Journal of Financial Economics* 109: 623–639.

Gebhardt, W. R., Lee, C. M., and Swaminathan, B. 2001. "Toward an Implied Cost of Capital." *Journal of Accounting Research* 39(1): 135–176.

Geroski, P. A. 1995. "What Do We Know About Entry?" *International Journal of Industrial Organization* 13(4): 421–440.

Gerschenkron, A. 1962. *Economic Backwardness in Historical Perspective—A Book of Essays*. Cambridge, MA: Harvard University Press.

Giannetti, M. 2003. "Do Better Institutions Mitigate Agency Problems? Evidence from Corporate Finance Choices." *Journal of Financial and Quantitative Analysis* 38(1): 185–212.

Glaeser, E., Kallal, H., Scheinkman, J., and Shleifer, A. 1992. "Growth in Cities." *Journal of Political Economy* 100: 1126–1152.

Goldman, Eitan, Rocholl, Jörg, and Jongil, So. 2009. "Do Politically Connected Boards Affect Firm Value." *Review of Financial Studies* 22: 2331–2360.

Goldsmith, R. W. 1969. *Financial Structure and Development*. New Haven, CT: Yale University Press.

Graham, J. R., and Harvey, C. R. 2001. "The Theory and Practice of Corporate Finance: Evidence from the Field." *Journal of Financial Economics* 60: 187–243.

Graham, J. R., Li, S., and Qiu, J. 2012. "Managerial Attributes and Executive Compensation." *Review of Financial Studies* 25(1): 144–186.

Greenwood, J., and Jovanovic, B. 1990. "Financial Development, Growth, and the Distribution of Income." *Journal of Political Economy* 98: 1076–1107.

Greenwood, J., and Smith, B. 1996. "Financial Markets in Development, and the Development of Financial Markets." *Journal of Economic Dynamics and Control* 21: 145–181.

Grossman, S. J., and Stiglitz, J. 1980. "On the Impossibility of Informationally Efficient Markets." *American Economic Review* 70: 393–408.

Grullon, G., Michaely, R., and Swaminathan, B. 2002. "Are Dividend Changes a Sign of Firm Maturity?" *Journal of Business* 75(3): 387–424.

Guiso, L., Sapienza, P., and Zingales, L. 2004. "The Role of Social Capital in Financial Development." *American Economic Review* 94: 526–556.

Gupta, N. 2005. "Partial Privatization and Firm Performance." *Journal of Finance* 60(2): 987–1015.

Haber, S. H., Maurer, N., and Razo, A. 2003. *The Politics of Property Rights: Political Instability, Credible Commitments, and Economic Growth in Mexico*. New York: Cambridge University Press.

Hadlock, C., and Pierce, J. R. 2010. "New Evidence on Measuring Financial Constraints: Moving Beyond the KZ Index." *Review of Financial Studies* 23(5): 1909–1940.

Haltiwanger, J., Jarmin, R. S., and Miranda, J. 2013. "Who Creates Jobs? Small Versus Large Versus Young." *Review of Economics and Statistics* 95(2): 347–361.

Harris, J. R., and Todaro, M. P. 1970. "Migration, Unemployment and Development: A Two-Sector Analysis." *American Economic Review* 60(1): 126–142.

Hayek, Friedrich. 1960. *The Constitution of Liberty*. Chicago: University of Chicago Press.

Healy, P. M., Hutton, A. P., and Palepu, K. G. 1999. "Stock Performance and Intermediation Changes Surrounding Sustained Increases in Disclosure." *Contemporary Accounting Research* 16(3): 485–520.

Heckman, J. J., and Vytlacil, E. J. 2007. "Econometric Evaluation of Social Programs, Part I: Causal Models, Structural Models and Econometric Policy Evaluation." *Handbook of Econometrics* 6: 4779–4874.

Hertzberg, A., Liberti, J. M., and Paravisini, D. 2011. "Public Information and Coordination: Evidence from a Credit Registry Expansion." *Journal of Finance* 66(2): 379–412.

Holmes, T. 1999. "Localization of Industry and Vertical Disintegration." *Review of Economics and Statistics* 81(2): 314–325.

Hsieh, C. T., and Klenow, P. 2009. "Misallocation and Manufacturing TFP in China and India." *Quarterly Journal of Economics* 124: 1403–1448.

———. 2014. "The Lifecycle of Firms in India and Mexico." *Quarterly Journal of Economics* 129(3): 1035–1084.

Hsieh, C. T., and Olken, B. A. 2014. "The Missing 'Missing Middle.'" *Journal of Economic Perspectives* 28(3): 89–108.

Hsu, P., Tian, X., and Xu, Y. 2014. "Financial Development and Innovation: Cross-Country Evidence." *Journal of Financial Economics* 112(1): 116–135.

Imbens, G. W., and Angrist, J. D. 1994. "Identification and Estimation of Local Average Treatment Effects." *Econometrica* 62(2): 467–475.

Jappelli, T., and Pagano, M. 2002. "Information Sharing, Lending and Defaults: Cross-Country Evidence." *Journal of Banking and Finance* 2017–2045.

———. 2003. "Public Credit Information: A European Perspective." In *Credit Reporting Systems and the International Economy*, edited by Margaret J. Miller, 81–114. Cambridge, MA: MIT Press.

Jayaratne, J., and Strahan, P. E. 1996. "The Finance-Growth Nexus: Evidence from Bank Branch Deregulation." *Quarterly Journal of Economics* 111(3): 639–670.

Jensen, M. C., and Meckling, W. H. 1976. "Theory of the Firm: Managerial Behavior, Agency Costs, and Ownership Structure." *Journal of Financial Economics* 3(4): 305–360.

Jensen, M., and Murphy, K. 1990. "Performance Pay and Top Management Incentives." *Journal of Political Economy* 98: 225–263.

Jeong, H., and Townsend, R. M. 2007. "Sources of TFP Growth: Occupational Choice and Financial Deepening." *Economic Theory* 32(1): 179–221.

John, K., Knyazeva, A., and Knyazeva, D. 2011. "Does Geography Matter? Firm Location and Corporate Payout Policy." *Journal of Financial Economics* 101(3): 533–551.

Johnson, Simon, and Mitton, Todd. 2003. "Cronyism and Capital Controls: Evidence from Malaysia." *Journal of Financial Economics* 67: 351–382.

Jovanovic, B. 1982. "Selection and Evolution in Industry." *Econometrica* 50: 649–670.

Julio, B., and Yook, Y. 2012. "Political Uncertainty and Corporate Investment Cycles." *Journal of Finance* 67(1): 45–83.

Kandori, M. 1992. "Social Norms and Community Enforcement." *Review of Economic Studies* 59(1): 63–80.

Kang, J., and Kim, J. 2008. "The Geography of Block Acquisitions." *Journal of Finance* 63(6): 2817–2858.

Kaplan, S., Klebanov, M. M., and Sorensen, M. 2012. "Which CEO Characteristics and Abilities Matter?" *Journal of Finance* 67: 973–1007.

Kaplan, S. N., and Zingales, L. 1997. "Do Investment-Cash Flow Sensitivities Provide Useful Measures of Financing Constraints?" *Quarterly Journal of Economics* 112(1): 169–215.

———. 2000. "Investment-Cash Flow Sensitivities Are not Valid Measures of Financing Constraints." *Quarterly Journal of Economics* 115(2): 707–712.

Karolyi, G. A. 2006. "The World of Cross-Listings and Cross-Listings of the World: Challenging Conventional Wisdom." *Review of Finance* 10(1): 99–152.

Kerr, W., and Nanda, R. 2009. "Democratizing Entry: Banking Deregulations, Financing Constraints, and Entrepreneurship." *Journal of Financial Economics* 94(1): 124–149.

———. 2010. "Banking Deregulations, Financing Constraints and Firm Entry Size." *Journal of the European Economic Association* 8(2–3): 582–592.

Khanna, T., and Rivkin, J. 2001. "Estimating the Performance Effects of Business Groups in Emerging Markets." *Strategic Management Journal* 22(1): 45–74.

Khwaja, A. I., and Mian, A. 2005. "Do Lenders Favor Politically Connected Firms? Rent Provision in an Emerging Financial Market." *Quarterly Journal of Economics* 120(4): 1371–1411.

King, R. G., and Levine, R. 1993. "Finance and Growth: Schumpeter Might Be Right." *Quarterly Journal of Economics* 108: 717–738.

Klapper, L., Laeven, L., and Rajan, R. 2006. "Entry Regulation as a Barrier to Entrepreneurship." *Journal of Financial Economics* 82: 591–629.

Klein, Daniel B. 1992. "Promise Keeping in the Great Society: A Model of Credit Information Sharing." *Economics and Politics* 4: 117–136.

Klepper, S. 2001. "Employee Startups in High-Tech Industries." *Industrial & Corporate Change* 10(3): 639–667.

Kögel, Tomas. 2005. "Youth Dependency and Total Factor Productivity." *Journal of Development Economics* 76: 147–173.

Kremer, M., Lee, J., Robinson, J., and Rostapshova, O. 2013. "Behavioral Biases and Firm Behavior: Evidence from Kenyan Retail Shops." *American Economic Review* 103(3): 362–368.

Krueger, Anne O. 2013. "The Missing Middle." In *Economic Reform in India: Challenges, Prospects, and Lessons*, edited by Nicholas C. Hope, Anjini Kochar, Roger Noll, and T. N. Srinivasan, chap. 9. Cambridge University Press.

Kyle, A. S. 1984. "Market Structure, Information, Futures Markets, and Price Formation." In *International Agricultural Trade: Advanced Readings in Price Formation, Market Structure, and Price Instability*, edited by G. G. Storey, A. Schmitz, and A. H. Sarris. Boulder, CO: Westview.

LaPorta, R., and Lopez-de-Silanes, F. 1999. "Benefits of Privatization—Evidence from Mexico." *Quarterly Journal of Economics* 114: 1193–1242.

La Porta, R., Lopez-de-Silanes, F., and Shleifer, A. 1999. "Corporate Ownership around the World." *Journal of Finance* 54(2): 471–517.

———. 2002. "Government Ownership of Banks." *Journal of Finance* 57: 265–301.

La Porta, R., Lopez-de-Silanes, F., Shleifer, A., and Vishny, R. W. 1997. "Legal Determinants of External Finance." *Journal of Finance* 52(3): 1131–1150.

———. 1998. "Law and Finance." *Journal of Political Economy* 106: 1113–1155.

———. 2002. "Investor Protection and Firm Valuation." *Journal of Finance* 57(3): 1147–1170.

La Porta, R., and Shleifer, A. 2008. "The Unofficial Economy and Economic Development." *Brookings Papers in Economic Activity*, 275–352.

Laeven, L. 2003. "Does Financial Liberalization Reduce Financing Constraints?" *Financial Management* 1: 5–34.

Lamoreaux, Naomi. 1995. *Insider Lending: Banks, Personal Connections, and Economic Development in Industrial New England*. New York: Cambridge University Press.

Lang, M., Lins, K., and Miller, D. P. 2003. "ADRs, Analysts and Accuracy: Does Cross-Listing in the U.S. Improve a Firm's Information Environment and Increase Market Value?" *Journal of Accounting Research* 41(2): 317–345.

Leuz, C., Nanda, D., and Wysocki, P. D. 2003. "Earnings Management and Investor Protection: An International Comparison." *Journal of Financial Economics* 69(3): 505–527.

Levine, R. 2002. "Bank-Based or Market-Based Financial Systems: Which Is Better?." *Journal of Financial Intermediation* 11(4): 398–428.

Levine, R., Loayza, N., and Beck, T. 2000. "Financial Intermediation and Growth: Causality and Causes." *Journal of Monetary Economics* 46: 31–77.

Levine, R., and Zervos, S. 1998. "Stock Markets, Banks, and Economic Growth." *American Economic Review* 88: 537–558.

Liberti, J. M., Seru, A., and Vig, V. 2016. Information, Credit, and Organization. Working Paper, Northwestern University.

Lins, K. V., Servaes, H., and Tufano, P. 2010. "What Drives Corporate Liquidity? An International Survey of Cash Holdings and Lines of Credit." *Journal of Financial Economics* 98(1): 160–176.

Loughran, T., and Schultz, P. 2005. "Liquidity: Urban versus Rural Firms." *Journal of Financial Economics* 78(2): 341–374.

Love, I., Martinez-Peria, S., and Singh, S. 2016. "Collateral Registries for Movable Assets: Does Their Introduction Spur Firms' Access to Bank Finance?" *Journal of Financial Services Research* 49(1): 1–37.

Lucas, R. E. 1978. "On the Size Distribution of Business Firms." *Bell Journal of Economics* 9: 508–523.

Luoto, J., McIntosh, C., and Wydick, B. 2007. "Credit Information Systems in Less-Developed Countries: Recent History and a Test." *Economic Development and Cultural Change* 55: 313–334.

Madestam, A. 2014. "Informal Finance: A Theory of Moneylenders." *Journal of Development Economics* 107: 157–174.

Maksimovic, V., and Phillips, G. 2008. "The Industry Life Cycle, Acquisitions and Investment: Does Firm Organization Matter? *Journal of Finance* 63(2): 673–708.

Maksimovic, V., Phillips, G., and Yang, L. 2013. "Private and Public Merger Waves." *Journal of Finance* 68(5): 2177–2217.

Malmendier, U., and Nagel, S. 2011. "Depression Babies: Do Macroeconomic Experiences Affect Risk-Taking?" *Quarterly Journal of Economics* 126(1): 373–416.

Malmendier, U., Tate, G., and Yan, J. 2011. "Overconfidence and Early-life Experiences: The Effect of Managerial Traits on Corporate Financial Policies." *Journal of Finance* 66: 1687–1733.

Marshall, A. 1890. *Principles of Economics*. London: Macmillan.

Masters, William, and Margaret McMillan. 2001. "Climate and Scale in Economic Growth." *Journal of Economic Literature* 6: 167–186.

Mauro, Paolo. 1995. "Corruption and Growth." *Quarterly Journal of Economics* 110(3): 681–712.

———. 1997. "The Effects of Corruption on Growth, Investment, and Government Expenditure: A Cross Country Analysis." In *Corruption in the Global Economy*, ELUOT, Kimberly A. (Ed.). Washington, DC: Institute for International Economics, 83.107.

McGahan, A. M., and Porter, M. E. 1997. "How Much Does Industry Matter, Really?" *Strategic Management Journal* 18: 15–30.

———. 2002. "What Do We Know About Variance in Accounting Profitability?" *Management Science* 48(7): 834–851.

McKinnon, R. I. 1973. *Money and Capital in Economic Development*. Washington, DC: Brookings Institution.

Megginson, W. L., and Netter, J. 2001. "From State to Market: A Survey of Empirical Studies on Privatization." *Journal of Economic Literature* 39: 321–389.

Melitz, M. 2003. "The Impact of Trade on Intra-Industry Reallocations and Aggregate Industry Productivity." *Econometrica* 71(6): 1695–1725.

Merryman, John Henry. 1985. *The Civil Law Tradition: An Introduction to the Legal Systems of Western Europe and Latin America*. Stanford, CA: Stanford University Press.

Merton, R. C. 1987. "A Simple Model of Capital Market Equilibrium with Incomplete Information." *Journal of Finance* 42: 483–510.

Michaely, R., and Roberts, M. R. 2012. "Corporate Dividend Policies: Lessons from Private Firms." *Review of Financial Studies* 25(3): 711–746.

Midrigan, V., and Xu, D. Y. 2014. "Finance and Misallocation: Evidence from Plant-Level Data." *American Economic Review* 104(2): 422–458.

Mitton, T. 2002. "A Cross-Firm Analysis of the Impact of Corporate Governance on the East Asian Financial Crisis." *Journal of Financial Economics* 64(2): 215–241.

Morck, R., Yeung, B., and Yu, W. 2000. "The Information Content of Stock Markets: Why Do Emerging Markets Have Synchronous Stock Price Movements?" *Journal of Financial Economics* 58(1–2): 215–260.

Murphy, Kevin M., Shleifer, Andrei, and Vishny, Robert. 1993. "Why Is Rent-Seeking Costly to Growth?" *American Economic Review* 82(2): 409–414.

Murray, M. P. 2006. "The Bad, the Weak, and the Ugly: Avoiding the Pitfalls of Instrumental Variables Estimation." SSRN Working Paper Series No. 843185.

Neumark, D., Wall, B., and Zhang, J. 2011. "Do Small Businesses Create More jobs? New Evidence for the United States from the National Establishment Time Series." *Review of Economics and Statistics* 93(1): 16–29.

Obstfeld, M. 1994. "Risk-Taking, Global Diversification, and Growth." *American Economic Review* 84: 1310–1329.

Olley, S. G., and Pakes, A. 1996. "The Dynamics of Productivity in the Telecommunications Equipment Industry." *Econometrica* 64(6): 1263–1297.

Ono, Y. 2003. "Outsourcing Business Services and the Role of Central Administrative Offices." *Journal of Urban Economics* 53(3): 377–395.

Padilla, A. Jorge, and Pagano, Marco. 1997. "Endogenous Communication among Lenders and Entrepreneurial Incentives." *Review of Financial Studies* 10: 205–36.

———. 2000. "Sharing Default Information as a Borrower Discipline Device." *European Economic Review* 44: 1951–1980.

Pagano, M. 1993. "Financial Markets and Growth: An Overview." *European Economic Review* 37(2–3): 613–622.

Pagano, Marco, and Jappelli, Tullio. 1993. "Information Sharing in Credit Markets." *Journal of Finance* 48(5): 1693–1718.

Pagano, M., and Volpin, P. 2001. "The Political Economy of Finance." *Oxford Review of Economic Policy* 17: 502–519.

Pagano, P., and Schivardi, F. 2003. "Firm Size Distribution and Growth." *Scandinavian Journal of Economics* 105(2): 255–274.

Pastor, L., and Veronesi, P. 2003. "Stock Valuation and Learning about Profitability." *Journal of Finance* 58(5): 1749–1790.

Perez-Gonzalez, F. 2006. "Inherited Control and Firm Performance." *American Economic Review* 96: 1559–1588.

Qian, J., and Strahan, P. E. 2007. "How Laws and Institutions Shape Financial Contracts: The Case of Bank Loans." *Journal of Finance* 62(6): 2803–2834.

Rajan, R., and Zingales, L. 1998. "Financial Dependence and Growth." *American Economic Review* 88(3): 559–586.

———. 2003. *Saving Capitalism from the Capitalists.* New York: Random House.

Rauch, J. E. 1991. "Modelling the Informal Sector Informally." *Journal of Development Economics* 35: 33–47.

Restuccia, D., and Rogerson, R. 2008. "Policy Distortions and Aggregate Productivity with Heterogeneous Establishments." *Review of Economic Dynamics* 11(4): 707–720.

Rice, T., and Strahan, P. E. 2010. "Does Credit Competition Affect Small-Firm Finance?" *Journal of Finance* 65(3): 861–889.

Rodrik, D. 2008. The New Development Economics: We Shall Experiment, But How Shall We Learn? HKS Working Paper No. RWP08-055.

Roe, M. 1994. *Strong Managers, Weak Owners: The Political Roots of American Corporate Finance.* Princeton, NJ: Princeton University Press.

Rossi, S., and Volpin, P. F. 2004. "Cross-Country Determinants of Mergers and Acquisitions." *Journal of Financial Economics* 74(2): 277–304.

Ru, H. 2018. "Government Credit, a Double-Edged Sword: Evidence from the China Development Bank." *Journal of Finance* 73(1): 275–316.

Rumelt, R. 1991. "How Much Does Industry Matter?" *Strategic Management Journal* 12(3): 167–185.

Sapienza, P. 2004. "The Effects of Government Ownership on Bank Lending." *Journal of Financial Economics* 72(2): 357–384.

Scharfstein, D. 1988. "The Disciplinary Role of Takeovers." *Review of Economic Studies* 55(2): 185–199.

Schmalensee, R. 1985. "Do Markets Differ Much?" *American Economic Review* 75(3): 341–351.

Schmukler, S., and Vesperoni, E. 2001. "Firms' Financing Choices In Bank-Based And Market-Based Economies." In *Financial Structure and Economic Growth: A Cross-Country Comparison of Banks, Markets, and Development*, p. 347.

Schumpeter, J. A. 1912. *The Theory of Economic Development*. Cambridge, MA: Harvard University Press.

Shaw, Edward S. 1973. *Financial Deepening in Economic Development*. New York: Oxford University Press.

Sheen, A. 2009. "Do Public and Private Firms Behave Differently? An Examination of Investment in the Chemical Industry." Working Paper, UCLA.

Shleifer, A. 1998. "State versus Private Ownership." *Journal of Economic Perspectives* 12(4): 133–150.

Shleifer, A., and Vishny, R. W. 1993. "Corruption." *Quarterly Journal of Economics* 108(3): 599–617.

———. 1994. "Politicians and Firms." *Quarterly Journal of Economics* 109(4): 995–1025.

———. 1997. "A Survey of Corporate Governance." *Journal of Finance* 52(2): 737–783.

Sleuwaegen, L., and Goedhuys, M. 2002. "Growth of Firms in Developing Countries, Evidence from Cote d'Ivoire." *Journal of Development Economics* 68: 117–135.

Song, F., and Thakor, A. V. 2010. "Financial System Architecture and the Co-evolution of Banks and Capital Markets." *Economic Journal* 120: 1021–1055.

Stein, J. 1988. "Takeover Threats and Managerial Myopia." *Journal of Political Economy* 96(1): 61–80.

Stiglitz, Joseph, and Weiss, Andrew. 1981. "Credit Rationing in Markets with Imperfect Information." *American Economic Review* 71: 393–410.

Straub, S. 2005. "Informal Sector: The Credit Market Channel." *Journal of Development Economics* 78: 299–321.

Stulz, R. M., and Williamson, R. 2003. "Culture, Openness, and Finance." *Journal of Financial Economics* 70(3): 313–349.

Sutton, J. 1997. "Gibrat's Legacy." *Journal of Economic Literature* 35: 40–59.

Svensson, J. 2005. "Eight Questions about Corruption." *Journal of Economic Perspectives* 19(3): 19–42.

Tavares, J., and Wacziarg, R. 2001. "How Democracy Affects Growth." *European Economic Review* 45(8): 1341–1378.

Townsend, Robert M. 1979. "Optimal Contracts And Competitive Markets with Costly State Verification." *Journal of Economic Theory* 21(2): 265–293.

Tybout, James. 2000. "Manufacturing Firms in Developing Countries: How Well Do They Do, and Why?" *Journal of Economic Literature* 37: 11–44.

Udry, C. 1994. "Risk and Insurance in a Rural Credit Market: An Empirical Investigation in Northern Nigeria." *Review of Economic Studies* 61(3): 495–526.

Udry, C., and Anagol, S. 2006. "The Return to Capital in Ghana." *American Economic Review* 96(2): 388–393.

Uysal, V., Kedia, S., and Panchapagesan, V. 2008. "Geography and Acquirer Returns." *Journal of Financial Intermediation* 17(2): 256–275.

Vercammen, James A. 1995. "Credit Bureau Policy and Sustainable Reputation Effects in Credit Markets." *Economica* 62: 461–478.

Vig, V. 2013. "Access to Collateral and Corporate Debt Structure: Evidence from a Natural Experiment." *Journal of Finance* 68(3): 881–928.

Wei, Shang-Jin. 2000. "How Taxing Is Corruption on International Investors?" *Review of Economics and Statistics* 82(1): 1–11.

Wurgler, Jeffrey. 2000. "Financial Markets and the Allocation of Capital." *Journal of Financial Economics* 58: 187–214.

Zingales, Luigi. 1995. "The Value of the Voting Right: A Study of the Milan Stock Exchange." *Review of Financial Studies* 7: 125–148.

17

INSTITUTIONS FOR INFRASTRUCTURE IN DEVELOPING COUNTRIES

What we know . . . and the lot we still need to know

Antonio Estache

17.1. INTRODUCTION

This chapter discusses the theory and analytical empirical evidence on the effectiveness of efforts to match, on the one hand, infrastructure policy and projects designs, and on the other hand, institutional context, constraints, and needs, in order to achieve desired policy outcomes. The institutions we focus on cover the main formal legal and regulatory dimensions that constrain or at least influence formally or informally the behavior and the interactions of producers, consumers, and financing sources in the sector to match the definition suggested by Baland et al. (2018) in the introduction to this volume. But we also cover as needed, and again, as suggested by Baland et al. (2018), more informal institutional actors such as NGOs or even at times religious actors, when these are relevant to understanding the evolution of infrastructure outcomes. In infrastructure policy, these outcomes are typically defined in terms of access to services, the quality of these services, and their affordability to users and taxpayers.

For the purpose of this chapter, infrastructure is defined as all activities related to water, electricity, sanitation, public transport, and telecommunications services. From an operational perspective, these services are often still best provided by large networked systems characterized by large economies of scale and scope to try to minimize average production costs. The investment projects tend to be lumpy and demand significant lead times in construction. A new road or a new power generator demands large investment commitments and does not get built in a few months but may take a few years instead. This has fiscal and political implications. Both can be influenced by the institutional context of the sector.

Technology has been changing, and it is allowing in sectors such as water and energy the possibility of relying on smaller investment. These changes are also leading to institutional changes in the overall organization of the sector (e.g., Nepal et al. 2018 for energy and WHO 2010 for water). Conceptually, however, the need to recover the cost, to maintain the assets properly, and to ensure the recovery of the investment costs continues to be at the core of the mandates assigned to all the institutions associated with the sector.

Most subsectors also demand a long-term budgetary commitment to maintenance of the assets.[1] Potholes on roads, falling bridges, and regular power outages are visible indicators of poor maintenance and of poor budgetary practice. But under-maintenance can also reveal an underestimation of demand in the design of the projects. More generally, maintenance underperformance reveals institutional arrangements unable to ensure that the investments are of the right size, at the right price and quality, at the right location, and at the right fiscal level. The issues can arise at the subnational, national, or supranational level.[2]

When structured public decision processes fail to deliver the cost-efficient solutions, often, in poor countries, the basic technologies adopted end up being ad hoc and location-specific without necessarily being socially, or even financially, optimal. Process failures lead to institutional and technological Darwinism. Less capital-intensive production alternatives are adopted, and more local implementation and monitoring mechanisms get put in place. These mechanisms define the production differentiation needed to meet local initial conditions and preferences, ranging from technological choices matching skills to contractual arrangements matching local and national legal traditions and local cultural norms. Usually, these mechanisms are subject to more subtle incentives structures largely ignored in "macro" efforts to improve performance in the sector conducted in the last 30 years.

These macro efforts tend to push for standardized approaches under the assumption that, to achieve performance goals faster and to access the latest production and management technologies, it makes sense to import institutional designs from developed countries into developing countries and to adapt them as needed. The idea has often been that the local populations would adjust to any change in their interactions with providers because it would be in their best interest to do so. It did not work out that way.

For now, progress in the delivery of infrastructure resulting from multiple waves of institutional reforms continues to be slow, but the evidence also shows that sticking to the old "pre-reform" model would not have made much of a difference, in terms of access notably. Indeed, for those sticking to the old "business as usual" public enterprise approach or those trying alternative options by choice or by force (because they could not try out the private option, not because private operators were not interested), the achievements have been just as modest. Under most institutional models, success stories have been partial and/or local rather than national. Few can easily be adapted to other contexts on a large scale.

Simply put, close to 30 years of trials and (often) errors, access, and quality progress have been slow and gaps are, simply, still huge. A glance at infrastructure statistics available for 2018 on the website of any international development agency shows that about 0.84 billion individuals (roughly 1 in 8) in the world still lack access to safe water, 2.1 billion lack safely managed drinking water, 4.5 billion lack access to safely managed sanitation, 892 million still practice open defecation, and an estimated 3.6 billion people live in areas that are potentially water-scarce at least one month per year. More than 80% of sewage in developing countries is untreated. Around 1.1 billion people don't have access to electricity, and a third of the developing countries go through at least 20 hours of power outages per month. Almost 3 billion still cook with polluting fuels (kerosene, wood, charcoal, or dung). And close to 1 billion do not have direct access to an all-season road. With the increased urbanization, mobility is also increasingly rationed in cities when investment does not follow since, for 1,000 new inhabitants, roughly, an added 350 extra daily trips are generated.

The de facto limited access to basic infrastructure is not a minor issue either, since it hurts human well-being (Lipscomb et al. 2013; McRae 2015; Torero 2015;or Ashraf et al. 2017). But it is not only about access, infrastructure is also broadly seen as essential to growth and competitiveness (Calderon and Serven 2014 and Alby et al. 2013). It matters to regional integration (Kuroda et al. 2007). It matters to job creation (Dinkelman 2011) or to food security (Blimpo et al. 2013).

The sector's enormous social and hence political importance imposes its own set of constraints on institutional options. Residential demand is strong and low-income users are willing to pay up to 30% of their income for these services. Their residential consumption is characterized by low long-term demand elasticities to both price and income. But many users are also quite emotionally sensitive to price increases, even when they are the only alternative to subsidies for a given service level. In the water sector, for instance, households tend to be unwilling to pay tariffs that cover costs, even if they are willing to pay up to 5% of their income on the water and sanitation services (often more in fact).

Its strong social relevance, added to its role in facilitating growth and in defining the level and types of environmental externalities, makes it hard to understand why infrastructure is underfinanced. And yet it is. Most estimates of the foreseeable annual infrastructure expenditure gap (including the costs of greening the sector) are in the US$1.5–2 trillion range. At the country level, this is about 3–10% of GDP depending on the country's development level. The poorer is the country, the higher is the gap. For some African countries, infrastructure investment and matching maintenance expenditures needed to support the growth rates demanded by efforts to erase poverty are as high as 15% of GDP. In many upper-middle-income countries, these needs drop to around 4–6% of GDP, which is still quite significant. Rationing resulting from this macroeconomic infrastructure expenditure gap hits the poor the most. And the gap also forces many firms to invest in costly alternatives or give up on potentially competitive activities. The slower the progress in improving access to reliable infrastructure, the slower poverty reduction is. Time matters and delays hurt.

For now, on average, only 50%, at most, of the expenditure needs find financing in developing countries. From this, roughly 80% is from public sources (including international and bilateral donors) and 20% from private sources, on average also but with a very large variance. The poorest countries do not get any private financing, while BRICS get a much larger than average share. Only 45% of developing countries get some significant form of private sector participation and about 25% face a similar situation in their electricity sector.

The infrastructure challenge is actually probably bigger than these figures suggest. It is likely that the gap estimations are lower bound because they assume that the projects are selected to minimize their costs throughout the project cycles. The assumption is a strong one, since the scope for costs cuts from procurement improvements and productivity gains are quite significant in most countries.[3] Poor project selection, poor maintenance, and poor ability to improve access overall are all linked to institutional choices. And the financing gap gives an idea of the cost of getting policies and institution wrong.

As the rest of the chapter argues, a mismatch between policy and financing decisions on the one hand, and institutional weaknesses or preferences on the other, helps explain the sector's financing problem. Since the mid-1990s, the most "popular" institutional and policy decisions to increase financing have often been anchored in a conviction that limiting and refocusing the role of the public sector would be enough to: (i) open the flows of private money to the sector, and (ii) provide the right maintenance incentives for the normally long life assets.[4]

Implicitly, the idea was that public money would no longer be needed or only be needed for the few activities the private sector would not be interested in. *"Get the investment climate right by implementing the right institutional reforms and the rest will follow"* has been, and continues to be, a common message that also applies to infrastructure. In many cases, *"right"* has been taken to simply mean *"less"* rather than *"better"* government intervention. In other words, since the instruments to achieve the policy goals have largely been pre-set, the remaining thing to do is to adapt the institutions to these choices. This ignores a possible two-way causality between institutions and policy.

A common (explicit or implicit) argument in favor of this approach is that, since it worked for telecoms, it should also work for other infrastructures. But this is misleading. The telecom's success is largely driven by an exceptional continuous technological transformation since the 1980s which has cut costs (and hence eased cost recovery) in a way that no other subsector has been able to replicate. Institutions are essentially only needed to make sure the rents are shared. For now, all stakeholders (users, taxpayers, workers, investors, and providers) are better off than they were in the 1980s in telecoms.

In the other subsectors, the distribution of payoffs is less predictable, as illustrated by a recent survey of 25 years of electricity reform experiences by Jamasb et al. (2017). Even in relatively well-prepared reform cases, many of the institutional changes were incomplete and failed to deliver on promises to some of the stakeholders (e.g., job creation or gross of tax average service price cuts). Often, the failure was rooted in the adoption of over-standardized institutional changes across subsectors and across countries. This is despite the fact that these were constrained by very different broader non–sector specific capacity, governance, and political constraints. Mexico's constraints are not Mali's constraints, and yet the initial broad reform approaches were similar because the international community underestimated how serious the differences were in many dimensions. We now know they are important, but we did not know then. This was also true in the case of transition economies. The similarity of approaches across the region was based on the assumption that markets orientation would automatically lead to the adoption of market-oriented institutions (von Hirshhausen and Waelde 2001).

What many casual analysts of the sector had in mind (and still have in mind) when they thought about institutional reforms in infrastructure was: (i) deregulation, (ii) privatization broadly defined and corporatization of the residual public enterprises, and (iii) the creation of autonomous independent regulatory agencies (i.e., autonomous from their ministries and independent from political interference). But institutions cover more players in practice and these are often ignored. An increased role for consumer associations, cooperatives, NGOs, and other civil society actors should also be part of the institutional toolkit. In addition, procurement, market design, market coordination, and planning are all essential components of this toolkit to produce the institutional adjustments needed to improve governance in this traditionally highly corrupt sector. And for urban infrastructure, ignoring the relevance of the design of decentralization to allow subnational and local governments to decide for themselves among the options for local public services would be a major omission. And, as pointed out by Collier and Venables (2016), within designing these policies is the need to manage the urban fragmentation of urban authority. In many countries, this results from incomplete or incoherent approaches to decentralization.

The recent policy literature also points to a variety of omitted institutional dimensions much harder to target through policy. Yet, they should be controlled for in the design of policy and in the choice of instruments. These include the legal tradition, the colonization history, ethnic heterogeneity, religion, culture, and other traditional norms, including those that define informal institutions, for instance. In the context of infrastructure, many of these dimensions have often been better studied by non-economists than by economists. For instance, anthropologists have quite effectively documented how these factors impact infrastructure and how they can help or slow institutional reforms because of some of their non-economic implications. (e.g., Larkin 2013). They see infrastructure as enabling the circulation of "political" power control as much as the circulation of people or goods.

Finally, both evidence and theory now emphasize the role of politics in the sector, with the benefits of insights granted by experience (i.e., usually mistakes). The initial reason is the incompatibility between the long-term commitments to be made to long-lived assets that require maintenance and the short political life cycles. Many of the ex ante cost benefit analyses for these projects imply long-term commitments to maintain the assets properly. These commitments are routinely violated when fiscal constraints become binding or resource allocation priorities change. Unsurprisingly, ex post evaluations then find the returns on the project to be lower than anticipated simply because service levels are poor, or because rehabilitation costs needed to address under-maintenance explode. Part of this is linked to a second bias politics often introduced: white elephants. To get approval for projects with high political payoffs but uncertain economic value, strategic underestimation of costs ex ante and overestimation of demand is quite common. It happens because there is little political accountability for political interference or lasting bureaucratic weakness.

This chapter focuses on the recent evidence from economic research. This is a limitation, as some key constraints identified by non-economists are only mentioned rather than discussed. This means also that some effects may be underestimated, such as the relevance of changes in power structures driven by changes in ownership or space management. Another weakness is linked to the fact that the test of time has not been friendly to a lot of the empirical evidence on the impact of institutional restructuring of infrastructure over the last 30 years. While the purely theoretical research is still quite useful in guiding analysis, much of the empirical evidence has established correlations rather than causality. This reduces the robustness and some of the relevance of this evidence.

With these limitations in mind, the chapter is organized as follows. Section 17.2 reviews some important concepts on infrastructure and some technical and political dimensions relevant to the institutional challenges and options. Section 17.3 summarizes the theories dealing with the sector's institutions. Section 17.4 surveys the empirical evidence on the impact of institutions. Section 17.5 discusses what policy could learn from academia to draw the sort of checklists needed to conduct proper institutional diagnostics. Section 17.6 discusses core knowledge gaps to inspire a research agenda. Section 17.7 concludes.

17.2. SOME TECHNICAL BACKGROUND

This section provides the unfamiliar reader with some basic concepts and a brief reminder of the main institutional changes that have been observed in the sector in the last 30 years. It briefly reviews most of the institutional dimensions that are typically covered as part of project preparation or policy development in the sector, including planning, procurement, regulation, and the assignment of responsibilities across government levels and government agencies. Its main purpose is to highlight the changes in the relative importance assigned to the various dimensions over time.

In public policy, the concept of infrastructure covers: (i) the physical constructions and components of the utilities and transport networks of an economy (e.g., energy generators and transmission lines, airport runways and terminals, sewage collection networks, telecommunications wires), and (ii) the services they provide. Utilities cover energy, water, sanitation, and telecommunications, while transport covers airports, bridges, ports, rails, roads, buses, subway and tram networks, and waterways.[5] The investments, also known in the regulatory literature as capital expenditures or *Capex*, are needed to ensure the delivery of the services. Over time, the accumulation of Capex adds up to large infrastructure assets that need to be operated and maintained to deliver the services properly. The operation and maintenance expenditures are known as operational expenditures or *Opex* in the regulatory literature.

Very roughly, the Capex are needed to ensure access to a service and to deal with technological concerns such as minimization of climate change effects or optimization of the use of labor in the development and/or delivery of the services. The Opex drive the marginal cost of increasing usage and service quality (e.g., the more a road is used, the more it needs to be maintained). Opex also end up impacting the average service price when the costs are to be recovered to reduce or avoid subsidy requirements.

This is not anecdotal in a development context since the higher the average price expected by investors interested in recovering their commitments, the more challenging it is to ensure affordability under the most popular forms of price discrimination adopted by operators and regulators (without subsidies). In practice, the main challenge is linked to the recovery of the connection charges rather than the usage charges. When set too high, it limits actual access to services provided by large utilities in the sector (e.g., water may be available but if some consumers can't afford it, they, de facto, have no access). But to recover costs and risks, it often has to be set higher than what many users are willing or able to pay, if there are no subsidies.

This average price is also linked to institutional capacity through cost and demand forecast mistakes. The investments in the sector are usually not only lumpy but also characterized by a high degree of investment specificity (i.e., sunk investments). When a road expansion costs US$50 million, a 5% mistake (from a wrong traffic forecast or procurement process) does not have minor consequences for the users or taxpayers.

Mistakes can actually also be a proxy of the size of the potential rents stakeholders fight for in the context of a project or a policy reform. They tend to be large and repeated, which illustrates the size of the rent for firms and/or politicians if mistakes are intentional and possible because of weak institutional capacity.[6] This is why getting institutions right from the procurement stage to the regulation stage is essential. The infrastructure industries typically demand significant government supervision and eventually a commitment to deliver residual needs.

The record makes some institutional sources of performance failure predictable. Procurement design and implementation, unclear property rights (i.e., ownership confusion), imperfect contract designs, monitoring and enforcement weaknesses, and captured or incoherent regulation have all hurt since the early 1990s (Clifton et al. 2014). However, the gap between what can be learned from failures and what policymakers decide is still large. Who should do what in the public sector (which public agency or ministry at which government level with which policy tool?) and what should be left to the market (which market?) or to private operators with market power is an unfinished debate, with policy implications still tainted by ideology (dressed up as best practice).[7] Missing from these diagnostics, as discussed later, is the basic question emerging from the diversity of sources of market, government, and institutional failures: *"under what circumstances to achieve which objective should which institutional and policy instrument choice be made?"* (Estache and Wren-Lewis 2009).

Answering this question requires, first, a good handle on the characteristics of the market, in the specific sector, of the specific country, region, or community trying to improve performance, as hinted earlier. The size of the sector and the sense of entitlement to the services, combined with the difficulty of monitoring providers with market power that are better informed than the authorities on their costs and on their customer, all matter to the institutional choices. The less transparent the market is: (i) the more—international or national—politics interfere with otherwise technical decisions (think of procurement); (ii) the more complex the scope to replace weak, easy to capture, institutions by alternative institutions capable of ensuring efficient, fair, and financially/fiscally sustainable infrastructures. In the Acemoglu-Robinson (2012; Acemoglu and Johnson 2005) view of the world, unless the mechanisms that maintain extractive institutions are better understood, it will be hard to create inclusive institutions.[8] This is why answering the question also requires a good diagnostic of the main institutional characteristics of the sector with an emphasis on the potential political and administrative/bureaucratic weaknesses.

With the benefits of insights of almost 30 years of experience now, we know that the challenge is particularly complex when governments suffer from a weaker technical or political capacity to engage in negotiation with some of the large international players who dominate some significant parts of the sector in parts of the developing world. This is not anecdotal or just conceptual (Clifton et al. 2016). There are few potential providers in key infrastructure services and, in addition, these are quite regionally specialized (e.g., French firms tend to be more present in Francophone Africa and Spanish firms are very present in Latin America, while American and British firms are very present in Asia and the Middle East). The combination is an easy recipe for abuses and conflicts in sectors in which high profit margins linked to poor regulation imply high average tariffs or high subsidies. For instance, in April 2016, the French government launched an investigation of a major French transport player in Africa (Bollore). Similar investigations of key international infrastructure players have been conducted by Germany, Norway, or Sweden.

The monitoring and supervision functions have been particularly sensitive issues, symptomatic of governance challenges. Since the efforts to rely more on the private sector through competition *in and for* the markets launched in the 1990s, it has been central to the case made to ensure the regulators' independence from political intervention. Historically, one of the main purposes of this decision was to reduce the risk of de facto partial expropriations resulting from politically motivated or corrupt interferences with contractual commitments made by governments to private investors and operators. We now have enough evidence to assess the extent to which the decisions paid off. As discussed later, the record is quite mixed but it is quite sensitive to the initial conditions that lead to this institutional restructuring as options for new reforms are being considered.

The efforts to try to attract private financing and know-how have also resulted from other institutional changes aiming at liberalizing key aspects of central public management. Key functions, traditionally implemented by the public sector, have been passed on to the private partners. Passing on procurement responsibilities for the key investments and services as well as the due diligence typically associated with many large projects to ensure proper consultation with all the stakeholders has not been problem-free. For instance, allowing the private operator to run key parts of the procurement process to minimize corruption risks can also open the door to poorly supervised transfer pricing techniques between the private service provider and some of its spinoffs turned into service or good providers. More generally, the evidence collected in recent years suggests a mismatch between the institutional constraints and the institutional development needs and the limited margin for adaptation of the procurement design largely imposed by international organizations as a condition for their willingness to finance the sector.

Some traditional functions have been de-emphasized but they are part of the institutional drivers to be considered. An example is the downsizing of public sector indicative planning capacity within each subsector. It has largely been the result of a justified concern for past government failures linked to weak governance leading to white elephants in the sector. Unfortunately, as discussed later in the chapter, it also largely ignores some of the costs of not planning at all. This includes misspecifications of objectives and lack of clarity on the strategy to be adopted to implement the vision. In increasingly demanding policy environments, policies need to aim at multiple objectives (population coverage, competitiveness, environmental concerns, fiscal concerns, social concerns). Too often, these objectives end up implicitly being defined by the available sources of financing rather than by efforts to manage the multiple goals.

The blurred vision and the lack of planning are particularly damaging in infrastructure because of the long life of the assets. Most project evaluations conducted by donors assume that the public and private discount rates are the same, but they are not. Most omit the cost of raising public funds as well (Auriol and Warlters 2012). Many projects ignore the coordination of investments decisions within sectors. Think of the management of the growing concern for water scarcity (e.g., Taher et al. 2016) or of the diversification of the possible sources of energy with efforts to favor renewables. With the desire to ensure increased autonomy to private operators in investment and operational choices, in many countries (developed and developing), the planning role has lost its effective significance, with important consequences. In developing countries, it has often resulted in cream-skimming driving the optimal sequencing of investment and other system im-provements. In developed countries, the failure to coordinate; in the electricity sector, transmission investment decisions with the greening of generation nicely illustrates one of the consequences of this institutional change.

The hope is that this section convinced the reader of the multiplicity of dimensions to deal with, in the design of policy and projects in this sector. This multiplicity can be quite overwhelming in practice and explains why getting it right often requires a bit of luck as much as skill. It also should convince the reader that research can help, but it is un-likely to be able to tackle this multiplicity of dimensions easily, as discussed in the next section. Worse yet, focusing on too narrow a characterization of institution can result in misleading or counterproductive policy advice if it ignores the interactions with the other institutional characteristics of a sector (e.g., Polemis 2016).

17.3. THE PLACE OF INSTITUTIONS IN POLICY-ORIENTED RESEARCH ON INFRASTRUCTURE

The mainstreaming of the concern for institutions is relatively recent in the "technical/ analytical" academic infrastructure development literature. Getting a sense of the his-torical evolution is useful because it shows how different schools of thought have focused on different parts of the multiplicity of dimensions and produced a very broad and het-erogeneous volume of results. It also shows that they have relied on approaches that are complementary rather than substitutes, with a bias of all approaches in favor of a num-ber of narrow high-profile policy issues.

Institutions are a relatively recent focus of mainstream infrastructure research. They only began to have a recurring profile in the early 1990s. Until then, they did not appear much on radar screens except when arguing that public enterprises were failing and that performance or management contracts were the solution (Gomez-Ibanez 2007). Between the 1950s and 1980s, a lot of policy-oriented research focused on pricing, project evalua-tion, and more specific technical issues published by the aid (and theory) community (e.g., Hirshman 1958 for one of the earliest systematic discussions of the specific role of infrastructure in development, and Jimenez 1995 for a stock-taking survey).

The next wave, from the mid-1990s, focused on the infrastructure-GDP empirical link. This was catalyzed by the 1994 World Bank Annual Report on infrastructure as it ex-tended Aschauer's work (1989) on the importance of infrastructure in the United States to poorer countries (e.g., Canning, Fay, and Perotti 1994; Ferreira 1996). This also launched an interest in infrastructure as an impediment to growth convergence *within* countries (e.g., Demurger 2001 for China). It is during this research phase that institutions began to become recognized as being empirically relevant, with Esfahani and Ramirez's (2003) evidence on the infrastructure-growth-institutions nexus convergence from large pan-els of countries. But the modeling of incentives was too general to be able to get to sector-specific recommendations since it was relying on very aggregate approximations of in-stitutions at the national level rather than sector-specific characterizations.

The real interest of academic economists in infrastructure specificities started in the late 1980s–early 1990s, as a reaction to the early evidence of the effects of the British priva-tization wave of the 1980s and as follow-up to Argentina's and Chile's equivalent ex-periments. Development economists started to focus on this institutional change as a way to improve upon the incentive effects of performance or management contracts. In the privatization debates of the 1990s, the analysis of the role of institutions complemented the broader conceptual concern for the developing countries' specificities to be picked up in regulatory designs. This included the horizontal as much as the vertical unbundling of the various dimensions of the infrastructure business (procuring, financing, delivering, regulating). The extent to which regulators should be independent and accountable is easy to analyze in this framework. So is the nature of the financing of the various activities.

Much of our current understanding can still be credited to the late Jean-Jacques Laffont and several of his co-authors (e.g., Laffont and Meleu 2001; Laffont and Martimort 1998, 1999). Laffont, like many at that time, discussed the relevance of the privatization debates for developing countries but also addressed the relevance of market structures, risks, financing options, and their interactions with regulatory design. With his co-authors, he also looked at the internal organization of institutions (e.g., the accountability incentive built into the delegation of functions within and across ministries and agencies). He synthesized most of the conceptual and supporting empirical literature in his last book (*Regulation and Development* 2005), which may still be the best synthetic diagnostic of the incentive issues and their institutional implications for developing countries.

The "*Laffont view*" of development infrastructure, essentially anchored in agency models and incomplete contract theory, has been, and continues to be, influential in both academic and policy work when information asymmetries dominate and multiple agency problems characterize complex institutions. It emphasizes the incentive issues and is quite detailed on the distortion of incentives by regulation and institutions at a high cost to performance in terms of access, quality, and/or affordability. It has also been quite good at showing how the optimal design of regulation and various types of institutional constraints interact. It points to limited accountability, credibility, commitment, and technical and fiscal capacity as institutional constraints that can be determinants of performance outcomes under various regulatory designs.

Since it starts from a modeling of the sector-specific institutional weaknesses as well as country-wide weaknesses as constraints, it is essentially a second-best approach on the optimal choice of regulation. Some of the analysis conducted within this view also shows how some constraints can be alleviated and thereby change the optimal design of regulation and financing of the sector. More generally, the approach shows that when the full set of constraints typical of developing countries are considered, drastic approaches such as full privatization or the creation of autonomous regulatory agencies can be counterproductive. Reform packages, which deal in much more targeted institutional changes, have better chances of enjoying sustainable success and establishing the credibility of reformers.[9]

But this is not the only theoretical approach, nor the first to look at institutions in infrastructure. There are at least seven other approaches relevant to the institutional debates on infrastructure in developing countries. Clearly, this classification is subjective, but it may be useful to highlight similarities and differences as well as the value added of more recent perspectives as complements to the earlier perspectives.[10]

The Other Views on Institutions in Infrastructure. The sector's institutional policy issues have also been analyzed with other tools. Besides the Laffont view, there are at least seven other options on how to address institutional issues in infrastructure relevant to policy discussions in developing and emerging economies.

1. "Spiller or transaction costs cum politics" view advocated by Spiller and his followers.
2. The broadly "legalistic" view documented today by Shleifer and some of his colleagues at Harvard.
3. The "public choice" view with a lot of overlapping with the public administration perspective on the sector.
4. The "anthropological" view voiced today under different disguises by Bardhan, Platteau, or Wade.
5. The "dynamic political," more historical, view argued by Acemoglu, Robinson, or Rodrik.
6. The emerging "behavioral" view of institutional design.
7. The "empiricist view" which is made of a large number of papers with little theory but lots of interesting and generally useful data.

The "Spiller view" has strongly influenced our collective understanding of the extent to which institutions, in particular political institutions, impacted and constrained Latin American infrastructure reforms (Savedoff and Spiller 1999; Spiller 2013; Guasch and Spiller 1999; Spiller and Tommasi 2005). Spiller started working on the limits of government in the sector at around the same time Laffont began to extend his joint work with Tirole to policy diagnostics in developing countries.

Spiller's perspective has also been particularly influential in assessing the optimal organization of the production structure as a way to minimize transaction costs (bundling vs. unbundling). Although the first steps should probably be credited to Williamson (1979) and to some extent Coase (1992), Spiller is actually quite close to Laffont's view, both in terms of concerns and to some extent in the modeling of the sources of institutional failures, although Spiller and his followers tend to focus on the impact on private investments in the sector and on the importance of the lack of public sector commitment. Although it is not as concerned with optimal regulation as Laffont's view, the Spiller view is just as interested in the relevance of rents and of their sources. And, similar to Laffont's school of thoughts, Spiller's argues that the desirable institutional mechanisms will be different across countries and match institutional initial capacity.

Its main impact may have been the emphasis of the need to identify incentive and transactions costs issues associated with government opportunism (essentially the ability of governments to change the rules of the game and extract quasi rents from investors) and third-party opportunism (essentially the questioning by NGOs, civil society, etc.). Politics should thus be central to regulatory assessments because it defines the governance of public-private interactions. The approach is closely related to arguments made by political scientists such as Henisz and his co-authors, Bergara et al. (1998), Henisz (2002), Henisz and Zelner (2006). Their main message is that political stability makes infrastructure investment easier, and instability slows or biases investment in the sector.

A closely related school of thought working on the institutions in network industries is linked to the Florence School of Regulation (which to a large extent could just as well have been labeled the Sorbonne School since so many of the Florence voices were initially anchored in Paris). Its members are also anchored into the transactions costs view of the world, which can also be read as a view that points to the failure to internalize the coordination costs associated with the development of governance as suggested by Dixit (2009). However, they tend to have broader views on the issues and are quite effective at discussing the hybrid organizational outcomes of transactions cost in regulated industries (e.g., Brousseau and Glachant 2008; Finger and Künneke 2011; Menard 2011; Glachant et al. 2013; and Saussier 2015). They also have a stronger focus on the technical implementation details of the regulation of these sectors than Spiller and his co-authors. Some of them are particularly good at unbundling the characteristics of contracts and highlighting their relevance for performance (e.g. Chong et al. 2015 and Saussier 2015). Although most of their research is on OECD countries, many of their insights have broader implications. Their main conclusions are: (i) one size does not fit all when it comes to regulation and contract design; (ii) details matter at all stages of the production process; (iii) coordination is particularly challenging in hybrid institutional models. They are not unexpected and they validate earlier results, but the fact that they reach them from another angle is reassuring.

The Legalistic View or "Shleifer" View. The law, its origin, and its implementation also matter. The relevance of the legal system to the performance of the economy has a long record which may have started with the early Coase papers (e.g., Coase 1992). The global empirical comparative evaluation of legal approaches owes to the early research championed by Shleifer and his co-authors (e.g., Djankov, Glaeser, Laporta, Lopez-de-Silanes). Their point is that legal biases have an impact on economic outcomes because they influence and often shape laws, legal processes, and dispute resolution in case of conflicts. The main distinction they make is between the (French) civil law tradition and the (English) common law tradition. Their evidence has been extensively used in infrastructure discussions as it raised the concern that civil law increases the riskiness of investment as compared to common law. They blame the outcome on excess formalism under civil as compared to common law (which increases transaction costs, fueling Spiller's perspective). It results in slower judicial proceedings, lower consistency, and poorer fairness in decisions, as well as more corruption. The idea has now been turned into a legal origins theory which is leading to a questioning of some of the original conclusions, as discussed in the next section.

The Broad Public Choice View. Just as in the case of the Laffont and Spiller views, incentives tend to matter in the public choice view, but its focus is mostly on politics and on the state internal organization. Political and bureaucratic biases and failures, common in infrastructure, have long been the concern of public choice theory in its various perspectives. They have also been central in the public administration literature. Politics, rent-seeking, capture risks, internal organization of government are all part of the bread and butter of this view of infrastructure. Many of its insights have influenced some of the other theories. They have often also been essential to force reformers to think through essential process dimensions. This is particularly true in the analysis of regulatory capture and of the resulting failure of the sector to minimize the risks of massive inefficiencies and cost overruns. Most of the widely quoted evidence on infrastructure cost overruns has actually been produced by the public administration literature in its efforts to detail the bureaucratic failures identified by the public choice researchers (e.g., Flyvbjerg 2009, 2014 for recent overviews).

Another important contribution of this literature is to show that the specific dynamics of political parties matter. Partisan theory and pork-barrel politics, in particular, argue that the relative importance of infrastructure may be used strategically to favor or penalize regions, cities, or other parties. This explains why the level and/or quality of infrastructure at the country level or across regions can be impacted by changes in political majorities (e.g., Costa-i-Font et al. 2003 for Mexico).

The overall pragmatic lesson of this research directly relevant to the efforts to improve infrastructure performance may simply be that the importance of political institutions, rules, and practice is easy to underestimate. It also points to the fact that many of the institutional challenges of the sector are not in the sector. This, in turn, implies that first best solutions for the sector may be naïve and unsustainable if and when they ignore these higher level constraints.

The Anthropological or "Ostrom" View. To economists, Ostrom may be the face of this non-economic view of the sector. With her followers, she has provided insights not initially dealt with in the economic literature, in particular in the context of rural infrastructures. With her co-authors, she also validated the importance of the internal governance of institutions already suggested in Laffont's concerns for the multiplicity of principals and agents in organizational designs, as well as the concerns for the optimal organization of production argued in Spiller's visions. She was also among the first to point out to economic audiences that incentives for the delivery of key infrastructure services can be influenced by social norms and culture. Since then, the role of culture, norms, and other values has enjoyed quite a broad recognition among economists (e.g., Alesina et al. 1999, 2003,; Alesina and Giulano 2015; Bardhan 2000; Bardhan and Ray 2006; Platteau 2000; Wade 2003). As discussed later, these dimensions are currently revisited, and often validated, by behavioral economists relying on lab and field (quasi-)experiments (e.g., Torero and some of his colleagues at IFPRI).

But there is more to the impact anthropologists are having on institutions such as processes. The ethnographic interest in infrastructure—from public toilets to municipal water systems to roads—is relevant to the management of consultation, for instance in the preparation of projects. The design of consultations and of the matching processes explain the growing feeling of entitlement in interactions with providers, public or private, but also with all the actors associated with the infrastructure production process. Harvey and Knox (2015, 2012) focus on highway-building in South America to show how large public infrastructural project implementations are driven by the degree and speed of state formation, by social relations, and politics. They show how local populations are concerned with the key choices, including routing, and with the distribution of benefits. This is where institutional strengthening starts when bottom-up approaches are deemed necessary, but this is not something economic policy tends to internalize enough. The main message of this approach is that processes matter to institutional-building.

The "Acemoglu-Robinson-Rodrik (ARR) View." It is somewhat of a stretch to already include this political/historical perspective in the theories relevant to understanding the institutional perspective on infrastructure, since it has not yet really been tested for the sector. But it is important because it validates the importance of politics for the sector already identified by the Laffont and Spiller views when they look at capture risks in the sector. Laffont (2000) and Laffont and Tirole (1991), for instance, already discussed how rules shape incentives, including in regulation, through political processes.[11] What the ARR view may add is a longer term historical perspective on the relevance of politics, including the fact that the colonial past matters as well and more so than simply through the legal tradition. Acemoglu and Robinson (2012) as well as Rodrik (2000, 2007) help focus on the issue, even if none of their papers/books actually looks at infrastructure institutions per se.

Their plea for a more systematic assessment of the role of politics and political economy in explaining lasting market failures rings a bell in infrastructure. This is, indeed, a sector in which competition is easily limited or biased. Gomez-Ibanez (2006), for instance, had already been very effective at showing how the infrastructure reforms of the 1990s and early 2000s were all characterized by relatively easily identifiable winners and losers in a political sense. This is consistent with a more political diagnostic argued by ARR.

One of the interests in applying Acemoglu-Robinson (2012) to infrastructure is to take a view on the ranking of stakeholders in terms of their political (bargaining) power. The anecdotal evidence would suggest that for developing countries, the winners may have been foreign operators, the banks financing their investments, and incumbent politicians when procurement and regulatory processes had been in place.[12] Users and taxpayers would be short-term winners when growth in access rates, improvements in efficiency, or cuts in subsidies requirements were delivered by the reform. However, renegotiations leading to higher user fees or increased subsidies would imply longer term losses for at least some of these players. These losses are the outcome of their lack of power in sector-specific property rights enforcements. They also reflect the capture of regulators who are supposed to control excesses by power-holders keen on maximizing rents. In their terminology, infrastructure performance has continued to be influenced by extractive institutions. And reforms ("the privatization cum competition revolution" as they could have called it) have failed to turn them into inclusive institutions able to rely on competition to minimize the scope for rents. These reforms seem to have transformed the old extractive institutions into new extractive institutions. Is it because the reforms were narrow based rather than broad based, as Acemoglu and Robinson (2012) argue?

To be fair, the heterogeneity of the subsectors outcomes suggests that telecoms and part of the power sector (generation) have been able to benefit from increased competition to increase the number of local players while most of the activities that had to rely on competition for the market have not been very successful at this. It would be potentially useful to analyze with the tools of this theory why the foreign actors in this game have been able to replicate their ability to join the extractive group in a wider variety of countries. For instance, large water deals tend to be operated by a small number of French, German, and American companies present on most of the bids organized by international organizations (Estache and Iimi 2011). It would also be interesting to look with this analytical perspective into the reasons why the infrastructure reforms and policies have not always had the same impact on performance in infrastructure. And, it would be useful to look at the extent to which the fact that different types of colonization policies created different sets of institutions can help explain the differences in impact of these infrastructure reforms in Francophone and Anglophone Africa.

The Emerging Behavioral View. This approach focuses on different forms of non-pecuniary motivation, also known as intrinsic motivation. The need to account for sources of non-rationality (e.g., anchoring, framing, endowment, present, hindsight, self-serving, loss aversion, status quo, attribution biases) in the behavior of infrastructure consumers, investors, and operators in developing countries is now an increasing concern for regulators in the definition of rules and processes. It is also increasingly becoming policy-relevant in some debates, showing the relevance of consumption and production alternatives. Moreover, it provides a better sense of the scope for nudging consumers and producers into social welfare–enhancing behavior (World Bank 2015).

One of the main early contributions of the applied research in the field is evidence on the relevance of institutions on the incidence of social context and environment for key policy decisions. As pointed out by Ceriani et al. (2009), Clifton et al. (2011) for European consumers for instance, preference heterogeneity matters to the optimal choice of public service provision and regulation. Similar evidence has been provided for the water sector in developing countries, for instance in the context of the willingness to pay for water storage systems (Price et al. 2016). This emphasizes the demand side of the market as a driver of the choice of institutions, including key processes in an environment in which the production and financing side tends to dominate the institutional choices. Social, cultural, or other sources of differences all contribute to demand heterogeneity and this matters to public services just as much as it matters to many consumption goods. These sources thus need to be diagnosed as well.

The behavioral research evidence on social dimensions also shows that fairness matters to optimal consumption and production decisions (Kahneman et al. 1986). This confirms similar conclusions reached by anthropologists Larkin (2013) or Harvey and Knox (2015). It adds that, to be fair, processes matter and are easy to underemphasize or underestimate in practice when implementing policies. This had also been identified in the Laffont view in any multiple principals, multiple agents settings (which are the norm in regulated industries, e.g., Laffont and Martimort 1998, 1999). Frey et al. (2003) point to the importance of "procedural utility" in environments in which we care not only about outcomes but also about the procedures leading to those outcomes. Ultimately, much of this is making a strong case to empower consumers, as suggested by Clifton et al. (2011). In environments in which ethnic, tribal, religious, or other historical drivers of social interactions matter, this observation is particularly relevant, and yet largely ignored in the design of infrastructure policies.

This view thus argues for an explicit assessment of the extent to which all consumers and producers enjoy equivalent opportunities to make the most of reforms. This links back to the inclusive-exclusive dichotomization proposed by Acemoglu and Robinson (2012), to the diagnostic case made by Rodrik (2010), or by the winners and losers perspective emphasized by Gomez-Ibanez (2006) for infrastructure diagnostics. As pointed out by Clifton et al. (2011) in the case of consumers, social, cultural, and economic environments all matter and yet tend to be ignored in the design of policy. This is increasingly well documented in the context of research on energy poverty in the UK for instance. The most vulnerable tend to be at a disadvantage in their ability to make the most of increased competition and the matching increased volume of information on options, for instance (George et al. 2011). In sum, this perspective on institutional design suggests that empowerment, as implemented by default, may be biased and typically regressive from the consumers' viewpoint, as discussed later.

All of this shows that the assessment of non-pecuniary motivations is just as important in understanding the incentives to account for when trying to influence producers, consumers, and financiers of the sector. They also impact selection and organization design. There is, as yet, no unified approach for studying these issues, and our knowledge is quite fragmentary. However, examining these issues is now a part of the mainstream agenda in economics.

The Empiricists' View. This last view regroups the research that concentrates on running regressions, most of the time on panels, to test whether the creation of a specific reform (e.g., the creation of a separate regulatory agency, the opening of a market to private operators) makes a difference. These are usually modeled as binary variables (yes vs. no) and the outcomes are measured in one or more of few performance indicators for which long enough time series are available. Typically, the quantity variables focus on access rates and network size. The quality variables tend to be approximated by technical measures (e.g., service interruption, safety incidents, maintenance costs). There are many papers focusing on various types of efficiency measures (e.g., allocative, technical, technological) but many of these actually measure labor productivity as a proxy because little reliable data exist on capital and other inputs to do better.

The first generation of papers suffered from major endogeneity issues (i.e., the omitted or mis-measurement of variables identified by some of the theories). Many of the papers ignored cream-skimming issues in the design of policies when relying on biased samples, erroneously assumed to be random. This is often what allowed a focus on the positive impacts of policies such as privatization. It ignored the "collateral damage" not picked up in the sample. For instance, looking at the impact of reform in a city is not the same as looking at the impact of that reform for a region in which rural areas are losing financing or access to scale and scope economies. Finally, it tends to ignore the many interactions between the various characterizations of infrastructure institutions. This is quite problematic, since the two dimensions may be complemented in some settings and substituted in others.[13] This is why estimates of the academic assessment of the relevance of institutions is often seen by practitioners as at best biased, at worst irrelevant.

Despite the limitations due to biased representations of the pure economic trade-offs between efficiency, equity, and/or financial viability of a policy, many of the contributions tend to be quite useful. The correlations they document may not be directly useful in policy evaluations but help identify additional research interests to settle the debates. Much of the empirical research in this field has been produced by international organizations staff or financed by them because of their privileged access to the required data— by the way, why are these data so often not public? And as data and techniques improve, the level of uncertainty on the predictability of reform effects seems to be increasing. This implies that we may have been overconfident on outcomes from institutional reforms until not too long ago. One of the main lessons of the most recent papers is that initial conditions matter a lot more than the early empirical papers assumed. And this is hard to pick up well in multi-country, multi-year data panels. This, in turn, makes the argument for relying on case studies to complement or validate the stories emerging from the treatment of panels.

This is at least in part why looking at case studies through impact evaluations has become popular but, at least in the context of infrastructure, it has its own set of problems.

The first is that most of the research related to infrastructure focuses on the water and sanitation sector. In the 2015 3i database of impact evaluations, infrastructure only claims 258 of them, which is about 6% of the total, half for water and sanitation and about a quarter for ICT (Information and Communication Technology). There are only ten covering the transport sector. The second is that most of these evaluations are about targeting and tools, not about institutional designs.

The interest in behavioral approaches is now leading to new evaluations to cover characteristics such as norms, culture, and similar dimensions linked to institutional constraints and opportunities. But we are only at the beginning of the use of this new approach. A lot more is needed to test and validate some of the institutional characteristics the various theoretical reviews have identified as relevant in principle.

Summing Up. The preceding overview of academic contributions leads to a list of dimensions that should be expected to be of some relevance in diagnostics of institutional quality of the sector. This list is the first column in table 17.1, which is also an attempt to give some credit to the various theories and their empirical support, for their contribution to this list in the context of infrastructure.[14]

Three observations stand out. First, not a single theory covers every dimension, not even the empiricist approach, even if many empirical papers are not married to a single view of institutions in infrastructure and use all of them as an input in the choice of explanatory variables when assessing sector performance. The second is that almost all theories have a view on the relevance of ownership, de- and re-regulation, politics, and the internal organization of institutions (e.g., bureaucratic organizations, board nomination and composition, etc.) or of the state (i.e., decentralization and inter-ministry and inter-agency coordination). This suggests that these items, covered in common country diagnostics, are indeed necessary. The third is that most of the gaps in coverage concern the relevance of processes, accountability, staff skills, non-pecuniary norms, and history. Most, if not all, of these dimensions tend to be influenced by country characteristics rather than by sector-specific characteristics. Ignoring legal and cultural processes and norms as drivers of incentives is essentially ignoring internal governance issues, and underestimating the administrative and financing feasibility of institutional changes. And yet the evidence suggests that this is part of the make or break of institutional reforms as they define the equivalent of the growth diagnostic bottlenecks.

What the table does not show is that too much of the evidence and theoretical analysis is often stuck in ceteris paribus assumptions. This comes out more often in case studies (e.g., Gomez-Ibanez 2006) and country-specific diagnostics. Ignoring what is hidden in that assumption is what makes it so difficult to come with a predictable sign on the effects of reforms on key performance indicators, as discussed in the next section.

17.4. ON THE EMPIRICAL EVIDENCE OF THE RELEVANCE OF INSTITUTIONS IN INFRASTRUCTURE

Many casual observers of policy debates in the sector may believe that the main academic research on institutional options in the sector are about deregulation, privatization, and the creation of independent regulatory agencies since it has been a key concern for most of the theoretical and dogmatic debate on the sector. The outcome of the review of the

Table 17.1. Overview of the Main Institutional Dimensions Picked Up by the Various Theoretical Visions

	Laffont (Agency)	Spiller (Transaction costs)	Shleifer (Legal)	Public Choice	Ostrom (Anthrop.)	Behavioral	ARR (History)	Empiricists
Primary focus								
Ownership	X	X	X	X	X	X	X	X
De- and re-regulation	X	X	X	X			X	X
Accountable regulatory autonomy	X	X		X	X			X
Contract and regulatory design	X	X			X	X		X
Politics	X	X	X	X	X	X	X	X
Other focuses								
Enforcement	X	X	X	X	X			
Internal governance of agencies and of government	X	X		X	X	X	X	X
Processes	X	X	X					
Technical skills and staffing	X			X	X	X		
Monitoring organization	X			X	X			X
Financing of institutions	X	X		X	X	X		X
Legal norms	X	X	X	X			X	X
Non-pecuniary norms	X				X	X	X	X
History			X		X		X	

research conducted in the last 10 years or so suggests otherwise. What emerges instead is a sense that many empirical researchers have been able to synthesize at least part of the various theoretical approaches. It feels as if each research team had come up with its own set of relevant institutional dimensions. The outcome is an impressive heterogeneity of partial sets of institutional characteristics credited with being performance drivers in infrastructure. The following is an (heroic?) attempt at reporting the main dimensions covered and the main lessons learned on each dimension.

Market Structure and Deregulation. The early 1990s research and policy discussions documented the potential payoff of unbundling the vertically integrated historical operators of the sector. Unbundling was an opportunity to increase competition, and where competition in the market was limited, it was also an opportunity to introduce competition for the market at a time when auction theory was becoming a popular tool among policymakers in OECD countries. Competition in the market and for the market both implied the need to open the business to private providers. The reviews of experiences suggest that competition tended to be good most of the time as it opened the sector to new technologies and new sources of financing (e.g., Vagliasindi and Besant-Jones 2013; Nepal and Jasmab 2015; Nepal, Sen, and Jasmab 2018; Jasmab et al. 2017; or Sen et al. 2018 for recent overviews for the energy sector; Berg et al. 2011, 2012 or Bertomeu-Sanchez et al. 2018 for the water and sanitation sector in general; or Mande Bafua 2015 in the African water context and Bel et al. 2015; Beuran et al. 2015; Soomro and Zhang 2011; Percoco 2014; or Raballand et al. 2010 for the transport sector).

The enthusiasm for competition for the market has been toned down somewhat, however, as a result of more careful monitoring of a few variables. The first is the accumulation of experiences in which the risk perceptions may have been underestimated by market designers. In environments in which the ability to pay is limited and the financing costly, competition can be excessive if it fuels the risks perception levels, in particular when alternative financing options from donors are available. Higher risks imply a higher cost of capital which in turn implies a higher average tariff. This is usually a politically difficult outcome in general, and more so in poor countries.[15] One option is to limit competition to ensure some minimum market size to the operators or to reduce the degree of unbundling. This is what happened in Cameroon, for instance, where after a first failed attempt at relying on competition in the market by unbundling the electricity sector, the country decided to try again with a vertically integrated firm. The next attempt managed to attract foreign operators and, most important, foreign investors. A second limitation of market restructuring is linked to cherry-picking by operators. Even when required to deliver full coverage of population, many private operators tend to leave high-cost customers for last in their investment plans. This explains why progress has been much lower in rural or peri-urban areas than in other areas. Finally, as suggested by Vagliasindi and Besant-Jones (2013) for the energy sector, there is evidence of a threshold system size and per capita income level below which unbundling of the power supply chain is not expected to be worthwhile. In other words, unbundling may be a bad idea sometimes.

Over time, both academics and policy advisors realized that there was a real case for relying on alternative small-scale suppliers such as cooperatives or alternative local technologies providers. Torero (2015), for instance, shows that in rural areas where most of the so-far non-electrified population live, because demand is very low, it makes sense to limit electrification through grid extension programs and to consider off-grid dissemination programs. In other recent research (at least in the context of infrastructure), the scope for community- or NGO-managed supply has started to enjoy supporting conceptual and empirical evidence (e.g., Bennett and Iossa 2010). This research shows that there are many conditions under which supply by not-for-profit providers can lead to greater investment and hence coverage than poorly regulated private provision focusing on profit.

The main point to retain may be that alternative institutional arrangements (e.g., small scale operators, NGOs, and so on) should be seen systematically as relevant options of sector design and planning. They are often pragmatic options to diversify risks and may speed up access. This is particularly important when large size investments are too slow to be able to speed up access rates.[16] But for institutional option menus to account for the various constraints, detailed regulatory dimensions such as service obligations and limitations to service exclusivity need to be addressed. Competition from alternative providers has to be considered, just as the complementarity between these providers and classical providers may be useful. In practice, developing this menu of options is quite feasible and, depending on the specific constraints and concerns, it is usually possible to come up with hybrid solutions in which large-scale producers are instructed to work with small-scale providers or less formal providers to ensure timely delivery of services. Some of the Spanish (Union Fenosa) or American (AES) electricity companies have been quite effective at these mixed institutional solutions to ensure improved rural coverage in Latin America. But this requires a willingness not to rely on pre-packaged market design solutions.

The role and design of procurement is a subtle but essential complement to this discussion of deregulation and regulation. Competition for the market is one of the key sources of competition in the infrastructure sector, and in developing countries, it is largely dominated by rules defined by the international organizations. These rules are widely seen as being constraining for many of the payoffs expected from better auction designs aiming at developing more effectively local players in the development, delivery, and operations of infrastructure (see for instance Engineers against Poverty 2006 for an operational perspective and Estache and Iimi 2011 for estimates of the cost of constraining procurement and the payoffs to various potential changes in practice in developing countries). For example, encouraging (local and foreign) fringe bidders to actively participate in the bidding process, while maintaining the quality of the projects, can cut costs (and hence average tariffs) significantly.

Today, some of these potential players are excluded from common procurement practice. They eventually participate in service delivery through subcontracting, but this simply increases the profit margin of the bids' winners, without benefiting the users or taxpayers. Similarly, the division of large contracts into smaller contracts or contract lots is an important policy choice for auctioneers to cut costs. Deciding how far to go on this requires a much better (yet feasible) understanding of cost drivers (scale and scope) than is currently accounted for in standard procurement practices.

The evidence shows that, in general, there is a trade-off between competition in auctions and size of contracts. Larger projects could benefit from scale and scope economies, but large contracts may undermine competition. Bidder entry is actually endogenous because it is determined by the auctioneer's bundling and unbundling strategy. If ease of auction justifies water treatment plant and distribution networks bundling in a single lot package, it comes at a price if it raises public procurement costs of infrastructure because of a lack of competition.

The evidence also shows that developing countries have a limited capacity to properly negotiate the allocation of risks in infrastructure. Blanc-Brude and Makovsek (2014) have been able to put together a unique dataset that reveals that project sponsors almost completely avoid construction risk when comprehensive risk transfer can be achieved through credible contracts. This is probably good news if the goal is to increase the prospects of private participation, but it also implies that someone else is assuming the risk. Typically, the users or the taxpayers do when procurement contracts are not negotiated to ensure a reasonable risk allocation.

Given the importance of activities that are going to continue to be subject to these procurement practices, any effort to do better in the sector needs to factor procurement reform into its agenda, with or without international organizations. The desire of many countries to continue to work with unsolicited proposals illustrates the underestimation of the potential payoffs to better procurement practice. This is what Takano (2017) recently showed for urban projects in Lima (Peru). Analyzing how the design and performance of procurement approaches adapted to enable PPPs, he finds that they eased rent-seeking behavior in subnational contexts. The outcome in his case study is that the expected payoffs did not materialize as a result of a number of design flaws.

The bottom line is that failing to take procurement design in infrastructure seriously has a high cost to most countries. Estache and Iimi (2011) estimate that a better use of auction design options would cut total infrastructure development procurement costs in the developing world by at least 8–10%. Just to put the relevance of this matter in context, it may be worth emphasizing that this affects at least 80% of the expenditure of the sector. This represents more than 10–15% of GDP in the poorest countries and about 6–8% in the middle-income developing countries.

Public vs. Private. The public and the private sector are complementary, and the degree of complementarity depends on a number of market-specific characteristics typically linked to demand, supply, and financing risk factors. This is why there is a continuum of options available on the scope for public-private partnerships (PPPs) which can unbundle to various degrees finance, construction, and operation into separate long-term contracts with private firms and focus on the sharing of risks between the investors, the users, and the taxpayers.[17]

The debate on the case for increasing the private sector role in infrastructure may be one of the oldest. It has been divisive, characterized by often excessively polarizing views rather than pragmatic ones. It is still not settled because, as is often the case, conclusions are the results of incomplete assessments. In their meta-analysis of the water and solid waste sectors in mostly OECD countries, Bel et al. (2010) offer a useful illustration of the difficulty of arguing that privatization leads to lower costs on average. They show that the conclusion does not hold up when they control for sample size, publication bias (papers obtaining significant cost savings are more likely to be published), timing bias (cost differences are less likely in more recent studies), service characteristics, and geographic area. Most of these factors are just as likely to be relevant in the assessment of privatization in developing countries.

A lot of research on PPPs in developing countries also recognizes the importance of the risk allocation between the partners. This is an essential component at the deal level. It is also important when considering the total risk level taken on with the government since it can add up to a significant fiscal risk. And there are many other dimensions that are likely to be relevant but that have not yet been picked up in diagnostics of institutional reform needs.

The discussion on institutional design options has been biased by (at least) five weaknesses in the evidence produced. First, a lot of the literature has been tainted by *selection biases* in the subsectors used to represent infrastructure. This matters because focusing on the most successful sector (telecoms) leads to overestimation of the potential of a policy while focusing on the least successful (water) may lead to underestimation of this potential. As mentioned earlier, the telecoms sector may have been the most common illustration for the claim of superiority of the private sector even if it is not representative of the typical infrastructure market structure. In telecoms, the private sector has indeed been quite effective at improving efficiency and access to services but largely because of technological innovation combined with reasonably effective competition policies. The same cannot be said of the other subsectors.

The evidence suggests that the switch to the private sector is often, even if not always, a good strategy to improve efficiency in the short run, much less so in the long run when regulation is weak. In practice, in the short run, it usually functions like shock therapy because it breaks historical political, business, tribal, family, or labor privileges inherited from long-term interactions full of inertia.[18] The evidence also shows that it is often the result of improvements in labor productivity, one of the main criticisms of the International Labor Organization (1998, 2003) for instance because it is happening in labor-abundant countries with underemployment issues.[19] A 1990s referendum in Uruguay suggested that, in that country, consumers preferred to pay 30% more for their water to maintain the overstaffing of the sector.

A second, somewhat related bias is the common practice of restructuring markets to make them more attractive to the private investors. This repackaging is designed to allow "cream-skimming" or "cherry-picking." While this approach is often successful at attracting private financing and operations, it ignores the residual negative fiscal consequences, since the public sector can no longer rely on intra-sectoral cross subsidies (Estache and Wren-Lewis 2009). Yet, historically, these cross-subsidies have been particularly important to be able to finance progress in high cost and rural areas, for instance. This is not picked up by most of the empirical modeling of reforms even though it has been highlighted by the conceptual research (e.g., Laffont 2005). Most empirical papers simply look at whether the private sector enters or not, but ignore the fiscal consequences and the rationing it implies in the ability of the public sector to finance sector-specific and other expenditures. This is a common mistake in the modeling of the effects of water privatization, for instance, when urban needs are unbundled from rural needs as was done in various Argentinean provinces. Privatization can look good when it can focus on the low-cost, low-risk business segments but not so good if the full picture is taken into account.

A third common bias is the fact that the complementarity between PPP options and regulation as well as other more specific characteristics (e.g., market size, market design, governance quality) are not systematically picked up. When researchers do account for it, they show that poor regulation with PPP can be counterproductive (e.g., Mande 2015 for the water privatization experience in Africa, or Vagliasindi and Besant-Jones 2013 for electricity in general). Indeed, where regulation has been weak (which is the norm in developing countries), access improvements associated with privatization have been slower than expected or sometimes not statistically different from those achieved with public provision. When the importance of regulation and competition is poorly approximated or ignored in the interpretation of the results on privatization, it tends to overestimate the PPP payoffs. Laffont (2005) documented this early when they emphasized the importance of government and regulatory commitment capacity for the effectiveness of reforms. And it has been more recently extended in the context of an assessment of the importance of regulatory credibility by Iossa and Martimort (2015).

The fourth bias results from a lack of precise data on the relevant institutional characteristics. The difficulty of measuring institutions emphasized by Glaeser et al. (2004) and Woodruff (2006) for instance is just as common in infrastructure as in other policy areas. Standard databases measure institutional quality in infrastructure such as risk of expropriation, government effectiveness, and constraints on policy design. But these can be "outcomes" of broader institutional and political dimensions rather than sector-specific institutional characteristics driving performance. Many studies fail to account for the fact that there is a continuum in the PPPs, since most model the presence of the private sector as a binary event and many more ignore the relevance of informal institutions that make contracts enforceable or not. The problem with this bias is that it is not clear whether it underestimates or overestimates the role of the private sector.

A final bias is the omission of the relevance of politics in the process that leads to the decision to increase the scope for private sector involvement in public service. This has been a recurrent theme in the analysis of regulated public services (e.g., Laffont 2000 or Spiller 1990). Ignoring the fact that politics plays a role that can be both positive (when it leads to pragmatic decisions accounting for complex contexts) or negative (when it is associated with capture, e.g., Sheely 2015, or clientelism, e.g., Wantcheckon and Vicente 2009) is at best naïve. When considered in some detail, the evidence on its impact is usually quite revealing of the diversity of its impacts. For instance, Blimpo et al. (2013) find support for the argument that political factors affect the location of roads after controlling for the economic importance of the areas, as well as many other factors. Politically marginalized areas have significantly fewer roads, and this affects basic needs such as food security. In sum, ignoring politics can lead to a mis-estimation of the impact of the role of private participations (see also Bel et al. 2015 for a series of OECD case studies of local public services). This is not new (Bergara et al. 1998; Henisz 2002) but it has taken some time to trickle down to mainstream economic assessments of PPPs and regulation.

Many of the biases in econometric results could be fixed by unbundling some institutional proxies to refine the dimensions accounted. This is exactly what more recent studies try to do (e.g., Vagliasindi 2013). But it is not straightforward. The most recent studies have done a better job at taking this into account, but it is hard to be as complete as necessary. Vagliasindi and Besant-Jones (2013) show for the energy sector that the market size and design matter to the impact of the introduction of the private sector. When the systems are too small, they find that an increased private participation can be counterproductive. But they also suggest that other variables may be important.

Ultimately, the evidence suggests that the combination of deregulation, re-regulation, and privatization has often delivered cost reductions (and other efficiency gains) but: (i) it has never been a guaranteed success, (ii) it has often been counterproductive in terms of performance, (iii) it has often benefited more operators, investors, and taxpayers than users, and (iv) one size does not fit all. Most of these are the outcome of political choices or incompetence. When they are choices, there is not much that can be done besides making sure the voters understand. But when they are the result of incompetence, there is scope for intervention. We know now that in the water sector, and to a lesser extent in the transport sector, ownership switches have had a hard time delivering as much as expected under most of the contract types that have been tried. This is so much so that, between 2000 and 2016, many toll roads have been renationalized, water companies are now increasingly relying on management contracts, and many small private ports and airports are not doing any better than their public counterparts. Under all scenarios, it should also be clear to all interested parties that getting it wrong also has equity consequences. The evidence on the social costs of poorly regulated privatizations in many of the poorer countries is quite strong (e.g., Trillas and Gianandrea 2007 and Calderon and Serven 2014).[20] And this is something that can be managed better.

In sum, privatization without sound regulation has not been a success story and is increasingly being rejected by policymakers unconvinced of their ability to regulate properly. With sound, transparent, and focused regulation, it can turn into a powerful and useful instrument in the interest of users, taxpayers, and investors happy with a return matching their costs of capital for the long run, rather than excessively focused on rents and high short-term dividends.

With or Without Separate Regulatory Agencies. The debate on regulatory agencies started with the debate on privatization (see Gomez-Ibanez 2006 and Castaneda et al. 2014 for complementary discussions). In addition to PPPs and a matching adequate regulation, a common institutional reform is the assignment of the regulatory function to a separate autonomous institution. By unbundling and isolating regulation from other government interventions, the reformers expect to send a signal to potential investors demonstrating their commitment to minimize the risks of political interference in the management of the sector.[21]

Under this approach, the newly created agencies take over from the ministries the main regulatory functions (e.g., contract enforcement, tariff, cost and/or quality monitoring, fining). In developing countries in particular, their margin for discretionary decisions is often limited because most of the regulatory rules are usually specified in a contract and sometimes in a matching sector law. The re-politicization of regulation in that context often results from the incompleteness of the contract. This incompleteness in turn is often the result of their excessive standardization. Contracts are too often transferred from one country to another with as much adaptation as seen fit, but this process often leaves gaps and sometimes incoherence. The process saves time and money but implies costs when conflicts arise. And these conflicts are common.

Guasch et al. (2014) remind us that 68% of the PPP contracts are renegotiated within a year (87% for water contracts and 78% for transport contracts vs. 41% for electricity contracts). The monetary costs of these renegotiations are often linked to the need to mobilize experts. This boils down to outsourcing institutional capacity. The non-monetary costs are linked to the risk of political interference in regulation from all donors, including foreign governments supporting the interests of the operators exposed in conflicts. The French and Spanish governments were quite active during the 2001 Argentinean crisis, for instance, and they had already been active in project-specific conflicts. The French government has traditionally been quite interactive with African governments when French firms were at risk, and this has trickled down to all regulatory conflicts.

The real issue with respect to autonomous regulatory agencies is, thus, the extent to which they are really independent from political interference. The odds of being independent from political interference are higher when they can rely on their own sources of funding (i.e., regulatory fees), when they are accountable to the parliament rather than to the ministries, or when the commissioners are named to minimize the risk of capture by politicians or by operators. The evidence available suggests that increasing the financial autonomy of regulators increases the odds of a good performance of the sector for a given level of accountability (e.g., Cambini and Franzi 2014). And increasing accountability further improves performance. Reducing political interventions minimizes the risk of capture of efficiency gains achieved in the sector.

Another omission is linked to the lip service often paid to technical or human capital limitations (Estache and Wren-Lewis 2009). The technical limitations result from the adoption of the Western idea of independent agencies by countries without the matching accounting and process tradition that allows the supervision of the regulated firms. Regulatory and cost accounting continue as sources of tension between regulated firms who want to maintain as much as possible of the information asymmetry they enjoy from the lack of accounting tradition. And for regulators keen on reducing the information asymmetry, two issues often arise. The first is that it takes time to build up the financial, accounting, and technical tools needed to assess the performance of the operators. As long as the institutions do not have the right tools, their ability and credibility are limited. In practice, this issue is often solved by outsourcing regulatory work (O'Rourke 2003). There is indeed a solid consulting industry helping countries set tariffs, measuring efficiency, or implementing the most technical dimensions of regulation (both in developed and developing countries). The second issue is that enthusiasm about their desire to increase performance transparency may result in a temptation to micro-manage. And this is just as much of an issue, in particular when the operational and financial expertise is limited in the regulatory agency.

The concern for corruption, capture, or collusion is another margin in deciding on the desirability of an autonomous agency as well as on the specific form of regulation to adopt. This is quite a well-documented concern when considering the design of institutions and their rules (Dal Bó and Rossi 2007; Auriol and Blanc 2009; Auriol and Straub 2011; Seim and Soreide 2009; Rose-Ackerman and Soreide 2011; Soreide and Williams 2014; Estache 2014; and OECD 2015). It is also a serious concern when considering the acceptability of institutional reforms. For Latin America, Martimort and Straub (2009) show that the degree of corruption that prevails in a society responds to changes in the ownership structure of major public service providers. In cases in which privatization opens the door to new corruption (say through opaque procurement processes or regulatory decisions), public dissatisfaction may increase to the point of rejection, even though the reforms can be credited with positive effects on access.

Despite these limitations, most countries today have adopted some form of autonomous regulatory agency. Most count now on an energy regulator that is no longer a unit of a ministry for the energy sector. For the Sub-Saharan African electricity sector, Imam et al. (2018) find that the creation of independent regulators combined with privatization efforts has managed to offset the negative effects of corruption on the technical efficiency of the sector and the efforts to increase access to electricity. Similarly, for the Latin American electricity sector, Wren-Lewis (2015) also finds that greater corruption is associated with lower firm labor productivity, but this association is reduced when an independent regulatory agency is present.

There are fewer water-specific regulators, although there are many multi-sector regulators that cover both water and energy and in many of those cases, introducing a regulator did not do much (Berg 2013). Some countries have also created transport regulators, but when intermodal competition is strong enough, competition agencies tend to monitor what is happening in the sector. There are, however, units in charge of the supervision of toll roads, airport, rail, or port concessions in countries opened to private operators or running public operators on a commercial basis.

The debate on the ability of current institutional designs is quite intense in transport these days in view of the growing evidence of the mismanagement of traffic and safety across subsectors in both facilities and services around the world. In their book on PPPs, Engel, Fisher, and Galetovic (2014) recommend unbundling institutions in transport to match the various stages of transport service production process. They argue that one of the problems of the sector is that all the stages of PPP contracts are governed by agencies inside the same ministry (typically, the Public Works or Transport Ministry). They suggest that this centralized institutional arrangement should be replaced by at least three agencies as independent from government as possible: one to select the project (this is about procurement), another to enforce the contract (this includes monitoring), and a panel of experts to adjudicate controversies in renegotiations (this is about dealing with the consequences of incompleteness in contracts).

In general, the econometric evidence suggests that these regulatory agencies have a positive impact on access at least (Andres et al. 2013; Cubbin and Stern 2006; Guasch et al. 2012; Gassner and Pushak 2014; Vagliasindi 2013; or Mande Bafua 2015). More generally, the mere existence of an autonomous regulator is correlated with improvements in the overall performance of the sector in particular. The impact is stronger when combined with the possibility of entry by private operators to compete for the temporary right to operate a firm or a sector. Note that the modeling of the importance of agencies is usually done as a binary variable (agency yes/no), and it should be clear by now that this is quite imperfect, since there exists a wide range of possibilities in terms of the degree of financial, legal, and political autonomy that an agency can enjoy. This is a recurring theme that has been hard to tackle in practice (e.g., Trillas and Montoya 2009; Trillas 2010; or Eberhard 2007).

In concluding this quick overview of the role of agencies, it is important to add that the existence of an agency is not a necessary condition for performance improvements.

Independent regulation is often a useful option, but the credibility and legitimacy of regulation depend just as much on the tools and the transparency of the use of the tools and of the decisions. Hybrid models that combine traditional visions with more modern approaches can be better to match the local country context, including in terms of governance and capacity. Improvements in regulated sectors can be achieved *without* creating a new agency when the business to supervise is specific or narrow enough.

In some cases, as for single railway deals in West Africa, small units within the Ministries of Transport have done just as well as any agency would have done, since the main content of the job is to supervise compliance with a fairly detailed contract. In other cases, as in the restructuring of the Romanian Water sector, the local institutional weaknesses have been compensated by the nomination of a panel of external foreign experts conducting scheduled regulatory audits. In addition to these options typically managed by the authorities, there are other options that give a voice to consumers, organized or not. Public hearings or consultations are now part of the institutional toolkit of many regulators.

When concerns for independence are serious, NGOs can have a significant monitoring and voice role, although the challenge is to define the limit between a monitoring/ watchdog role and the advocacy/activist role that some of these organizations also aim at. These not-for-profit organizations can have a role as watchdogs (Aldashev et al. 2015). The punishment inflicted by the NGO if the misbehavior of the firm is detected can take the form of active interference with the production process (organizing worker revolts or destroying some parts of the firm's production lines), which implies that the firm has to spend resources in order to continue to produce normally. This is somewhat different from the channel of influence of Baron and Diermeier (2007), where NGO conducts boycotts or reputation-damaging activism. For the sake of simplicity, we assume that the NGO campaign against the misbehaving firm has a sufficiently strong effect to serve as a credible threat for the firm (Baron 2010).

The implicit, quite rational, philosophy in these alternative solutions is to outsource key institutional responsibilities around clear contractual and "monitorable" specifications of commitments made by all parties. This achieves the expected accountability in environments in which it is going to be hard to achieve independence. It minimizes the risks of negative consequences associated with excessive discretionary powers in an environment in which these powers are not needed and local capacity to exercise them without interference is limited (e.g., Bitran et al. 2013 and Guasch et al. 2014). As Moszoro et al. (2016) put it, the idea is to find a way to minimize the transaction costs associated with regulation. And often, the simplest accountable system is the best one because it is also the most pragmatic solution in complex institutional environments.

With More or Less Decentralization and Other Local Participation Mechanisms. The unbundling of policy design, mandates, expenditure responsibilities, and regulatory functions to increase local responsibilities and accountability is an additional instrument, and there is evidence that it can pay off. For instance, Kis-Katos and Sjahrir (2014) find that, when expenditure decentralization in Indonesia created two new layers of subnational governments, investments in public infrastructures in districts with little initial infrastructure increased. Pal and Wahhaj (2012) had already shown that this decentralization had led to an increase in the share of spending on physical infrastructure, as well as a convergence in spending across communities with different types of local institutions. This payoff is often credited to the increased accountability of government from a closer leverage of citizens on their politicians (Bardhan and Mookerjee 2006).

This is also related to the growing literature on community-based monitoring and on the payoffs from increased empowering of local communities over their service providers (see Mansuri and Rao 2013 for a recent survey). This is largely about the payoffs to empowerment when interactions with politicians and operators take place on a repeated basis. In that perspective, empowerment makes it easy for consumers and voters to use access to new information.

Empowerment through better access to information in the sector in which projects costs are often quite large is particularly effective to minimize local elite capture. This is also true in democratic environments and is typically anchored in national audits (notably as part of anti-corruption programs) targeting the risks of local elite capture. For Brazil, Ferraz, and Finan (2008, 2011) show that providing information improved outcomes. Moreover, increasing the odds of audits reduced the rents captured by local officials. For Bolivia, Yanez-Pagans and Machicado-Salas (2014) showed that the central role of grassroots organizations in increasing access to information allows reductions in bureaucratic delays within the allocation of small infrastructure projects.

Thinking of decentralization broadly defined as an additional institutional instrument is thus a realistic option, but as in all of the institutional reforms reviewed so far, it does not guarantee success. For instance, Olken (2007, 2010) finds that grassroots participation in monitoring of a village road construction program in Indonesia had little average impact but that monitoring by an external agency makes a difference (i.e., independent audits equivalent to those done by an independent regulator helps). Casey et al. (2012) find similar results, looking at an infrastructure project in Sierra Leone involving both relatively large grants and the application of processes to enhance local empowerment and participatory governance in the planning and implementation phases. Bobonis et al. (2017), working with local election data in North-East Brazil, show that economic clientelism in the context of residential water cisterns in drought-prone areas is stronger the more vulnerable voters are.

There are many explanations for the dispersion of outcomes from this institutional approach. For instance, it can depend on the homogeneity of populations. A strong ethnic diversity at the local level worsens public good provision. This is because this diversity makes social sanctions become more difficult to enforce across different ethnic groups (e.g., Miguel and Gugerty 2005; Cassan and Vandewalle 2017). Ethnic, gender, or social heterogeneity may also favor ethnically or socially biased targeting (e.g., Chattopadhyay and Duflo 2004). This research field suggests, for instance, that in India, lower-caste areas receive more local public infrastructures when the village leaders are lower-caste politicians. There is also a risk of local elite capture of local public goods associated with decentralization. And in this context, Alatas et al. (2013) document an Indonesian case study in which they find that local officials seemed to capture some transfers in villages where transfers are large relative to private consumption, although the rent produced is less than 1% of the welfare produced by the social programs. This is linked to the relevance of the design of intergovernmental transfers for the performance of the sector, e.g., Frank and Martinez-Vazquez (2014) or Goel and Saunoris (2016).

The economic incentives built in transfer design are well understood in general and in particular with respect to the operation and financing of infrastructure services. The relevance of the importance of political incentives emphasized by several of the theories discussed in section 17.2 also impacts the effectiveness of decentralization of infrastructure mandates when these mandates are shared across government levels rather than assigned to a single government level. This is quite common in the water sector, for instance, where provision can be local but sanitation, because of the spillover effects, has to be coordinated at the regional or national level. For instance, Estache et al. (2016) show for Brazil, where sanitation supervision is split between the state and the municipal governments, that water treatment efforts are sensitive to political alignment across government levels. When elections led to misalignments of political affiliations of authorities across government levels, they also caused a deterioration of water treatment. The main point here is that in democratic systems, the implementation of shared mandates forces a pragmatic look at the desire to increase local participation in all stages of the production chain of a public service in environments in which political misalignments are recurring outcomes of democratic processes. Delegating to maximize local involvement may end up being counterproductive simply because politics matter to efforts to collaborate.

Before concluding the discussion of decentralization, it is important to also point out that there are many very practical technical details that can easily be a source of trouble in infrastructure decentralization. For instance, urban planning rules that differ across municipalities can make it difficult to deploy telecom infrastructure (ducts, trenches, or antennas). There are many more instances in which local governments can block activities decided by national agencies. This can be solved in theory by minimizing the delegation of activities with spillovers. But this ignores that local permits requirements for any type of construction work essentially give a veto right on any project, including those assigned to higher government levels.

In sum, an increased role for local actors in the institutional design of infrastructure policymaking, design, implementation, and monitoring is certainly yet another good idea. But as for all institutional options, it would be a mistake to ignore its limitations. And there are many such limitations, including in particular the increased complexity linked to local politics in environments in which they interact with an ethnic context, uncoordinated elections, shortened decision cycles, and political diversity. Any of these characteristics can create intergovernmental tensions leading to the sector's mismanagement.

Civil Law vs. Common Law. The implications of the differences between the two main approaches to law have long ruled the advice on how to improve the investment climate (and hence the scope for improvements in the access to private financing of increases in access rates to infrastructure services). Recently, however, the empirical foundation of this policy vision has been questioned. The main criticism stems from the excessive dichotomization in the modeling of the legal institutions. Guerriero (2011a, 2011b) has recently produced infrastructure-specific evidence documenting the relevance of the endogeneity of the legal system in environments with weak political institutions. He shows that it impacts the trade-offs between the flexibility of judges (or regulators) in common law and the rigidity of decisions under civil law. It turns out that in very uncertain environments with weak governance, civil law may lead to more efficient outcomes. The same can be concluded if preferences are homogeneous rather than heterogeneous.

Clearly, the jury is still out on the actual relevance of the legal tradition for outcomes simply because there seems to be much less inertia in the practice of law than suggested by the early diagnostics. The debate is, however, essential to developing countries having to assess the optimal choice of contract and regulatory design in infrastructure. For now, we know that PPPs have resulted in hybrid legal environments in which incomplete contracts (e.g., *contrats d'affermage*) inspired by civil law traditions are assigned to regulators with mandates and power inspired by common law tradition (e.g., *concession contracts*), rather than to a higher tribunal (e.g., Conseil d'Etat in France or the Tribunal de Cuentas in Spain).

A lot of anecdotal evidence suggests that the combination is risky. In too many cases, PPP contracts signed in Africa, Asia, Latin America, or Eastern Europe during the transition were simple adaptations of American, British, French, German, or Spanish contracts, with at least some incompatibility with local legal practice and enforcement willingness and capacity. For instance, the large number of contract renegotiations or cancellations in Latin America or Africa can be partially blamed on an imperfect reconciliation of the legal approach of investors with strong bargaining power and the local legal approaches (e.g., the common vs. civil law practice). They are linked to the difficulty of ensuring a robust matching between the new types of contracts and local preferences and capacities (e.g., Albalate et al. 2015). Too many of the matching efforts are based on extrapolated data because there is no systematic assessment that accounts for the endogeneity of the legal norms in infrastructure. They are sensitive to predictable characteristics on preferences for technologies and to the nature and intensity of governance and political uncertainty. If this turns out to be relevant empirically in developing countries, it questions the systematic push for a growing role for common law as suggested by Guerriero (2016).

Accounting for Norms, Processes, and Non-Pecuniary Motives or Not. In retrospect, one of the most underestimated damaging dimensions of institutional reforms in infrastructure may have been the decision to import institutional arrangements from OECD countries without much consideration for the role of local cultural norms, preferences, and capacities. Bardhan (2004) made an equivalent point quite forcefully over a decade ago to an African audience. The same speech could have been made in any region of the developing world on almost any sector.

The bias is common and not neutral to outcomes as often argued by behavioral economists in particular (World Bank 2015). It may indeed drive many of the small failures in process which resulted in lower than expected effectiveness of reform. For instance, it may explain why many well-intended consultations of users to decide on projects, programs, or policies often lead nowhere. Process matters in much more subtle ways than the formal interactions modeled on OECD practices.

On a more positive note, a growing pool of academic evidence discussed below is documenting how and how much ethnic, religious, accounting, financial, legal, or other equivalent preferences matter to maintenance efforts, to willingness to pay for basic public services or to technology choices. This research also shows that accounting systematically for these dimensions may improve performance.

Most research has focused on water because of the relevance of norms on the way common pool resources are shared, used, and operated. So far, this literature has revealed insights with much broader implications for the other infrastructure sectors and for the design of institutions designed to make the most of the resources used in any sector. Guiteras et al. (2015) study the behavior of households living within compounds in slums of Dhaka, Bangladesh, to document how non-pecuniary incentives could help improve sanitary conditions. They find that behavior change messages designed to elicit disgust and shame can promote treating drinking water and hand washing with soap in low-income urban housing compounds more effectively than classic public health messages talking about germs. Shaming works in many cultures. How the shaming takes place matters, though. It works better if the community cares enough to sanction norm-breakers by rewarding someone who sanctions a norm-breaker with social approval and lowering the status of those failing to sanction norm-breakers.

Waddington et al. (2009) survey the factors influencing sustained adoption of safe water, hygiene, and sanitation (WASH) technologies. The conclusion opened research doors. Few have assessed the determinants of long-term, sustained WASH practice. Hulland et al. (2015) complement this survey by focusing on the few studies that looked at individual psychosocial factors, such as perceived benefit and self-efficacy, as well as interpersonal factors like social norms. They seem to strongly affect continued WASH behaviors. Age and gender are also strong determinants of good behavior. The broader lesson is that policy should account for this dimension more systematically. Demand management is an important complement to the focus on the technical dimensions (supply side). Project supervision should invest in longer-term behavior maintenance. It seems that we are only in the early stages of the potential offered by behavioral economics to build on basic human characteristics to improve policy, and it may be easier than anticipated in many cases. Ahtiainen et al. (2015), for instance, show that individual and perceptions-based status quo alternatives can relatively easily be documented in choice experiments for readily observable and familiar goods such as water quality.

More generally, one of the broadest lessons so far is that the users' heterogeneity (in language, culture, norms, social cohesion, social status) should matter more to the design of policies and the choices of technologies. There is a significant scope to improve our collective understanding of this work in all subsectors, as argued for the longest time by many authors (Bates 1974, 2000; Ostrom 1994; or Platteau 2000).

Heterogeneity can also explain how norms differences make it easier to accept or reject specific institutional arrangements as shown by Athias and Wicht (2014). They look at differences in preferences for public versus private provision of public services by French- and German-speaking Swiss citizens. They find it is harder to convince the Francophones to go for private provision. Ethnic heterogeneity such as differences in language or caste among irrigators impact cooperative behavior more generally.

The relevance of ethnic politics as a potential problem for the supply and distortion of public goods allocation in many developing countries has become a recurring concern in development economics and has tended to focus on the fact that ethnicity leads to benefit insiders at the expense of outsiders in public resource allocation quite generally (Miguel and Gugerty 2005; Anderson et al. 2015; Burgess et al. 2015). It is also a major concern in the management of infrastructure needs in post-conflict situations (Anand 2005; Azam 2010; Mardirosian 2010).[22] In a recent paper, Munshi and Rosenzweig (2016) propose a model with direct implications for infrastructure. The inclusive dimensions of ethnicity favor collaboration, which can be positive for public good delivery because every ethnic group wants to be represented as well as possible in multi-ethnic settings. However, there is also an exclusionary dimension that hurts the sector because it results in efforts to capture public resources rather than to optimize resource allocation. They test their model on India to show that the exclusionary effect dominates.

The concern for the challenges of designing infrastructure in an environment in which ethnicity matters is not new. Earlier, La Porta et al. (1999) and Alesina et al. (2003) had also established a negative correlation between ethnic fragmentation and infrastructure quality, among other indicators. Experimental and behavioral research is also pointing in similar directions in their assessment of trust, norms, and altruism. The implication of this heterogeneity for the creation of institutions may be that it increases the transactions costs of putting them in place as well as the risks of failures.

But the research on norms defined broadly is now increasingly diversified, both in theory and in sector coverage. Aldashev et al. (2012a, 2012b) provide infrastructure-relevant insights on the interactions between laws and norms, and on the extent to which new laws can ease norm changes. However, they also show how inherited norms can lead to the poor implementation of new laws. Stimulating social interactions can improve policy effectiveness across sectors. Tanguy and Torero (2015) find that in Ethiopia, in a household decision to connect to a new electrical grid, the "keeping up with neighbors" mechanism can be just as important as social learning of the benefits of electricity or direct externalities of one's connection on others' well-being. Aker and Mbiti (2010) reach an equivalent conclusion for mobile phone proliferation in Africa.

There is also research on norms and privatization that can be translated into infrastructure-related concerns as suggested by Baland and Francois (2005). They point to some of the limits of privatization in the context of commons that are quite closely related to the literature on access pricing and rules for shared facilities such as rail tracks or transmission lines. All solutions are indeed arbitrary to some extent. The challenge is to match this bias with local preferences rather than imposed (often imported) preferences.

Religion is an easily underestimated dimension of preferences in the sector increasingly recognized as a performance driver (Aldashev and Platteau 2014). In recent research it has emerged as an explanation for underinvestment in infrastructure. Pal and Wahhaj (2012) provide evidence for Indonesia of heterogeneity in preferences for public goods across communities linked to religious practice. They find greater spending on schools and health centers in communities that observe traditional *adat* laws (which promote an ethic of mutual cooperation).[23] They also find lower spending on roads, public transport, communications, etc., in communities concerned with giving outside options to their members to avoid the risks of deterioration in intra-community cooperation. Similar conclusions are obtained by Estache and Fourati (2017) from an analysis of the access to power of a religious party committed to improve access to public services in Tunisia after the end of a long dictatorship. They show that there is indeed a relationship between access to infrastructure services and support for religious parties when infrastructure gaps exist. Infrastructure brought more votes to the religious party than to other parties because of the religious foundation of the commitment to invest in infrastructure to give access to those who lack it.

What this line of research shows is that resistance to change just like support for change has motives (e.g., the desire to preserve the indigenous identity or the better credibility of the commitment because of a religious association) seldom factored into policy design. But it fails to show that the extent to which those aiming at preserving an identity or at focusing political preferences on narrow concerns may be ignoring some key dimensions. For instance, in the Indonesian cases, the religious preferences are leading to a management of the complementarity between social goods which preserve the identity (linked to health and education) and the infrastructure goods. These examples are only the tip of an iceberg of policy issues demanding more detailed research.

Finally, there is also growing evidence that the early theoretical insights on the relevance of processes provided by several of the views summarized earlier apply across norms and across institutional reforms. For instance, Yanez-Pagans and Machicado-Salas (2014), as mentioned earlier, document how bureaucratic delay within the allocation of small infrastructure projects in Bolivia influences outcomes. But they also show, through a randomized field experiment, how monitoring tools designed to promote transparency and accountability through access to information by grassroots organizations can improve public service delivery outcomes.

Summing Up. A lot of evidence has thus been collected over the last 30 years or so, and there is a lot we have learned collectively from this. We have identified many institutional characteristics that matter as discussed above. In addition, we now also have a fairly predictable set of performance indicators for which we have some proxies that can be used to assess some of the main impact of changes (at least on average). These indicators include access rates, affordability, average costs, operations and maintenance efforts, service and technical quality, net fiscal cost, various financial indicators.

Table 17.2 summarizes my reading of this evidence. Keep in mind that I focus on the average sign that emerges by the various studies that have tested the impact of a specific institutional change on a specific performance indicator. Unless I missed out on major results, this qualitative meta-analysis of impacts of key institutional characteristics on key performance indicators calls for humility. There is little we can easily predict when it comes to the effects of institutional changes.

The first observation to stand out is that very little is predictable from past experiences. Neither privatization nor deregulation have proven to be bullet-proof sector organization reforms for all sectors. Independent regulation seems to deliver good technical outcomes but probably at a cost that has implications for affordability and may scare off some investors who are keener on capturing regulators than on proper contract enforcement. Decentralization is just as uncertain an option, in particular when mandates are shared across government levels when politics are misaligned.

Unfortunately, the accumulated evidence reviewed here suggests that the correlation between performance and implementation characteristics such as contract commitment and enforcement strength, credibility, civil servant and regulators skills, governance, and norms is mostly unpredictable. The only indicator systematically benefiting from improvements in these institutional characteristics is the investment level. And there, political interference or legal and local norms can actually impact either way. There could

Table 17.2. Prediction of Correlation Between the Main Institutional Characteristics and Key Performance Indicators

Institutional dimensions	Performance indicators						
	Access/ Investment	Affordable	O&M	Quality matching	Technology matching	Production cost	Long term fiscal cost
Privatization/ outsourcing	?	–	?	+	+/?	Worse/?	Worse/?
Deregulation	+/?	?	?	?	+/?	Worse/?	Worse/?
Independent regulation	+/?	?	Better	+	+	+/?	?
Decentralized	?	?	?	+	+	?	?
Shared Mandates	?	?	?	?	?	?	?

be a presumption of improved quality and technology matching with local preferences when local norms are accounted for, but the evidence is still too rare to be able to argue the case more convincingly.

Moreover, most of these results are obtained from partial equilibrium models and we have no idea how the interactions between institutional changes reinforce or weaken, on average, the most common policy solutions to sector financing and management problems. As mentioned earlier, there are too many interactions and too much endogeneity to be accounted for to be able to come up with general statements of the desirability of specific reforms. But all of these insights should be useful when going through a sector-specific diagnostic in a specific country to assess the possibility of unexpected effects.

17.5. SO WHERE DOES POLICY GO FROM HERE?

A positive or optimistic interpretation of the results summarized in table 17.2 is that research has produced a lot of insights on how institutional options can impact infrastructure performance and which performance indicators to focus on. The optimism probably needs to be tempered because many insights cannot yet be turned into a coherent framework to provide analytical guidance for sector diagnostics similar to the growth diagnostics suggested by Hausmann et al. (2005). They could be used to produce a robust checklist focusing on institutional weaknesses similar to those used by credit rating agencies to assess countries or firms, for instance, but this has not yet been done in a coherent way. Yet this is probably the minimum that one could expect from this research when poor performance calls for institutional action to support or drive policy. And it is all the more important when the initial weakness of institutions may also be important to the optimal policy tool choice (e.g., Ashraf at al. 2016).

So far, the donor community has been quite helpful in pushing for partial performance diagnostics that focus on outcomes. In the last 10 years or so, the international development agencies have provided extremely useful partial regional diagnostics of the sector (e.g., the African Infrastructure Country Diagnostics (AICD) or equivalent ones for all the other developing regions). They have also developed sector-specific indicators data-bases which have already been used quite extensively by academics to enhance policy analysis (e.g., the International Benchmarking Network for Water and Sanitation Utilities, or IBNET).

Thanks to these efforts, we now have a better sense of the technical and to some extent the economic, financial, and social performance of the sector. This also helps to appreciate the role of key regulatory policies (e.g., tariff design, rate of return estimations, asset valuation, etc.) in explaining this performance thanks to basic correlations. PPIAF, a multi-donor agency hosted by the World Bank, has also financed many studies that have largely contributed to the empiricist approach, and this has proven to be useful as well.[24]

But in most cases the focus is on outcomes, not on the details of policy and institutional choices. Outcomes can motivate the reform decisions and choices, but they don't characterize them. The institutional characterizations available widely from benchmarking exercises are too basic to be useful in practice in the context of an assessment of bottlenecks to performance enhancements. As mentioned earlier, having an independent regulator or not, or privatizing or not, may simply be irrelevant if other governance and institutional issues are not tackled first. Worse yet, it is often hard to predict if they will help or hurt without a more thorough appreciation of a wide range of details which include norms and politics, for instance.[25] The sequencing of reforms matters in this sector as in any other. But this has not really been sufficiently studied in infrastructure.

This bias against looking into the institutional details identified by research is not really unexpected since, as discussed earlier, politics matter in a tremendous way in defining institutional performance, and most of the international development agencies avoid politics (at least formally). There is a realistic concern that they could be blamed for interfering with sovereignty if they were to take a formal position on the impact of politics in the sector performance.

This constraint should not be too limitative. It has not been an issue for growth diagnostics (Hausmann et al. 2005). It can simply be seen as another potential bottleneck and internalized in the efforts to match the institutional design options with desired expected performance outcome based on evidence available on what works and what doesn't. Without getting into politics, Ostrom's research has usually been quite good at looking into these details for local water projects. More recently, Vagliasindi (2008, 2012, 2013) has been able to get into highly relevant institutional details and produce new insights for the power sector. Any sector infrastructure institutional diagnostic would want to be able to produce the same level of details at the country level and then use it to link it to the scope for performance improvement.[26]

Building on the partial checklists and evidence available, it is thus realistic to adapt the macro growth diagnostics to more detailed sector diagnostics. At that level, they should be able to identify and address the many interactions between various institutional dimensions that more technical empirical work has not been able to address. These diagnostics would also make it easier to match desired outcomes with institutional and policy options. A reasonable bet is that this assessment would lead to packages of reforms rather than specific reforms that account for all relevant characteristics, including interactions between institutions, and will be significantly less standardized than some of today's policy decisions continue to be.

To increase the transparency of these characteristics in a more encompassing perspective, table 17.3 summarizes the information discussed earlier. It focuses on the most relevant from an operational perspective. It is a very rough attempt at using the information available on the relevance of institutions to conduct a preliminary institutional diagnostic of the sector. Each column is a policy area to be covered by the diagnostic. The items below the heading in each column list the specific characteristics that would have to be covered by the specific policy area.

There are clear gaps. For instance, an explicit "politics" column could have been added. It would force the evaluators to go through a checklist of political constraints on the development and improvement of infrastructure management. But as it is, it will force the evaluator to identify political bottlenecks within each of the more standard concerns of policy design in the sector. Ideally, this would be matched with the timing of the various requirements over the regulatory life cycle and with an assessment of the potential bottlenecks.

Ultimately what this exercise delivers is the equivalent of a general equilibrium perspective on the role of institutions in a sector. It highlights the multiplicity of local incentives, but begs for an assessment of the interactions between these local incentives. These interactions help better understand the endogeneity of institutions argued by so many theoretical authors in a very operational and concrete way within a sector. But our conceptual knowledge of the interactions mechanisms and of the joint relevance of the initial sector and country conditions are not yet well understood. And this is where additional theory has to help.

17.6. AND WHERE COULD RESEARCH GO FROM HERE TO HELP POLICY?

There are at least four broad research areas that would help the policy effectiveness of academic work on infrastructure based on the implicit gaps revealed by this survey of what we know on the relevance of institutions for infrastructure performance (in terms of access and coverage rates, pricing and affordability, efficiency, technical and service matching with willingness and ability to pay, cost recovery, and financial and fiscal viability). These have to do with:

1. Theory
2. Cross-country empirics
3. Randomized controlled trials and other impact evaluations
4. Data

On Theory. The theoretical coverage of the institutional dimensions of the sector is already impressive, although somewhat atomized across theories. The sum of it all is useful, but incomplete. There are four more research areas that help fill the gap on the importance of institutions for policy effectiveness in this sector.

The first gap is a general positive theory that figures out a way of picking up many of the interactions of the various institutional dimensions. The ceteris paribus assumption is really costly in this sector. It misses out on interactions and yet it has justified the focus on single policies in a field in which policy packages make a lot more sense because of these interactions. Too much of the empirical evidence would suggest that the theory on

Table 17.3. A minimal checklist of variables to be included in a country infrastructure sector diagnostic

Sector vision	Market structure	Ownership structure	Financing structure	Regulatory structure	Pricing	Quality
Global Strategy, incl. coherence across government levels and across regions	Degree of unbundling	Public vs. private vs. outsourcing vs. NGOs . . .	Financing needs assessment	Allocation of mandates across national and subnational agencies and ministries and compatibility with local mandates and preferences	Level and structure	Match of technical options with willingness and ability to pay
Investment plan	Choice of competition	Mandate allocation	Public vs. private vs. non-commercial private With vs. without guarantees	Degree of independence and accountability, including composition of the board, salaries, decision and voting rules, transparency of votes, and revolving door issues	Relevance of ethnic divisions, cultural or religious norms in willingness to pay	Degree and forms of customer orientation as indicator of service quality
Financing plan	Formal vs. informal provision	Risk allocation as a function of financing sources	Local vs. foreign	Incentive basis of regulatory design process to assess it including its impact on incentives to accelerate or delay investments	User fees, subsidies, and cross subsidies	Coherence across policy area (e.g., technical & service vs. environmental quality)

Formal and informal legal support	Urban vs. rural	Relevance of ethnic divisions, cultural or religious norms in willingness to share ownership and matching responsibilities	Risk-level assessment and allocation across stakeholders	Staffing (including outsourcing) Tooling (financial modelling, efficiency analysis, audits, . . .) and financing (budget allocation vs. regulatory fee) Fining rules and allocation of fine revenue	Other forms of local financing such as microfinance or other solidarity-based options
Procurement rules for public & private	Degree of decentralization		Leveraging	Contract dependence and coherence	
	Extent of shared mandates and assessment of political alignment		Cost of capital and process for its update	Accounting requirement, required processes, and technical data access	
	Employment		Asset valuation, and process incl. its impact on investments speed	Organization of consultation processes	

the sector should also account for interactions with institutional constraints that are not sector-specific. The evidence shows that the general initial conditions in a country, a region, or a city can explain differences in outcomes associated with the same sector-specific institution.

The second gap may be the lack of attention paid to the dynamics of the sector and to the interactions between institutional dimensions. Infrastructure investment is central to improvements in access rates and to countries' ability to deal with climate change and other environmental concerns. Moreover, the institutional matching game is a moving target so a lot of the empirical can only validate a snapshot, not the adequacy of this snapshot on the path to adjusting institutional and other conditions. The right institutional context is, indeed, probably an adjusting institutional context that can follow several paths, depending on the interactions within the sector and with other segments of the economy. The matching is a dynamic challenge. And yet a lot of the theory used to justify institutional choices is anchored in partial static models. This is partially because it is quite difficult to get to simple first-best policy recommendations in a world in which time inconsistency linked to policy uncertainty and asymmetric information appear jointly. The only thing we know for now is that the fear of regulatory hold up on irreversible investments (i.e., arbitrary cut ex post on promised return on that investment) may lead to under-investment . . . ceteris paribus.

The third gap may be the underestimation of the interactions between institutional choices in infrastructure and financing options. Regulation theory has not been very effective at linking finance and optimal regulation choices to begin with, but when it has made an effort to do so, it has ignored how this choice could bias institutional dimensions.[27] Are institutions in the sector captured because of financial constraints, or is the weakness of institutions the driver of the optimal financing solution? The modeling of optimal regulatory choices is too basic to allow an identification of the main relevant trade-offs. It also ignores the possibility of a two-way causality between infrastructure institutions and financing options. Policy deserves a better effort to consider more explicitly the relevance of finance for the design of incentives in the sector, accounting for institutional strength and weaknesses.

The final direction in which theory could improve its current contributions is with respect to the relevance of politics. Politics is everywhere in this sector, and academics have been good at picking it up. But it has not really been internalized as operationally as needed to sort out the matching challenge in a politically sensitive context. This line of research would merge the traditional optimal regulation theory with insights from the political economy of reform in a dynamic perspective. This would account for the details of the full project cycle of the investment decisions in infrastructure, including the key earlier stages in the decision-making process (including for instance the role of planning and procurement limitations). It would also look into the ways in which the margin for political capture can reduce or offset the concern for holdup. Lim and Yuru-kuglu (2015) provide a dynamic model that looks into this possibility for US electric companies.

On Cross-Country Empirics. On the empirical front that can be useful to policymaking, there are a few low-hanging fruits (although time-consuming) that should be picked by the academic community. The first is the need to close surprising knowledge gaps on what we learned from the dispersion of results on the impact of institutions over countries/regions and over time. A meta-analysis such as the one conducted by Bel et al. (2010) on the impact of reforms on public services for OECD countries has not been conducted for developing countries in any sector. Most of the surveys available tend to be like this one: a qualitative interpretation of the dominating factors. These are quite useful already, and the 3i NGO has been very effective at making these sorts of overviews available to wide audiences. But they leave too much margin to subjectivity in deciding what matters and what does not. This can be avoided for papers following roughly comparable approaches to the analysis of a problem through a meta-analysis.

Note that it would also be useful to have a few surveys or meta-analysis of price and income elasticity per income classes and user types, accounting for various dimensions such as initial economic, social, and institutional conditions. These are the sort of surveys that help turn qualitative discussions on reforms into quantitative ones. This is potentially just as important as having information on capital or labor supply to taxes. Yet it is much harder to come by.

A second empirical piece with a quick potential payoff would be a more systematic tracking of the degree of concentration of international players capable of influencing procurement of infrastructure markets. As mentioned earlier, there is a lot of anecdotal evidence showing that market concentration is penalizing the development of formal local players in the sector. There is equivalent evidence of excessive operators' profitability as a major political issue in view of the wide diversity of feelings about the potential role of the private sector. There seems to be a good reason to document this more precisely. This concentration was a documented issue before the global crisis (Benitez and Estache 2005). It would make sense to assess whether the crisis has increased the bargaining power of large players in the sector or not. And quite frankly, it would also make sense to have a look at the extent to which aid money is captured by the big players in the sector simply because procurement rules have too often been biased in favor of large historical players in the sector.

A final potential area of research with lots of externalities would be a creative think piece on how to deal with the endogeneity of institutions. The multi-directional causalities that case studies and anecdotal evidence point to are an econometric nightmare. Few of us have taken the time to think them through. Yet, this would certainly improve the quality of empirical work on the role of institutions in the sector.

Randomized Controlled Trials and Other Impact Evaluations. This is where there is scope for more creativity.[28] There are already a large number of experiments being produced on the water and sanitation component of infrastructure. There is much less work on the scope for nudging accounting for norms, culture, and other behavioral biases for electricity and transport. In transport, for instance, assessing the extent to which these biases often built in institutional characteristics can help promote modal switches, safety, speed control, reductions in fraud in the use of public transport—all important research topics with strong potential payoffs in developing countries. Of particular interest in this context is the relevance of the heterogeneity of preferences and perceptions of the value of services. This will have implications for the effectiveness of traditional policies but also for the scope to improve the financing of a highly subsidized sector.

The approach is also quite useful to look at the role of informal and local solutions as well as the role of NGOs, cooperatives, and other community-anchored arrangements in water and energy. This would be particularly useful when considering the possible relevance of institutional designs and market organizations in minimizing the risks of quantity-quality trade-offs in environments in which budget constraints are quite binding. It is also relevant to assess the opportunity alternative modes of organization and provision cater to the sense of urgency which is seldom reflected in the discount rate used for most project assessments. Time matters in a way not reflected in the standard 8–12% discount rate used by the donor's community in assessing its projects. This is just as true for infrastructure in general as it is for climate change–related projects. Randomized trials should help demonstrate this more systematically.

We also need to have a better sense of how fairness is perceived in the context of all infrastructure activities with common goods dimensions. Extending Ostrom to look into the roles of religious and ethnic solidarity to all local infrastructure is a potential field of interest to the sector as well. An equivalent assessment of the reasons why supranational projects are not as popular as rationality anchored in scale economies would suggest is another, somewhat related research field.

Finally, this tool is also potentially quite useful to assess the extent to which local norms can turn incomplete contracts into complete contracts without having to rely on formal regulators. Local arbitrations are quite common and may be much less costly than imported institutions, at least for local public goods.

Each of these suggestions should be framed in an effort to learn to improve the optimal matching of institutions, instrument choices, and performance goals. It is a way to validate some of the intuitions generated by cross-country empiricisms. It is also a way to document more effectively the institutional sources of potential trade-offs between the different performance indicators.

On Data. Data gaps on infrastructure are a recurring theme that the international community has not yet managed to close to any decent level of satisfaction to either academics or policymakers.[29] As mentioned earlier, regional benchmarking exercises have been conducted and there are a few international sector-specific datasets. But most of these data suffer from three major issues.

First, they are biased toward information relevant to engineering supervision, not to financial, fiscal, social, or institutional supervision. Second, the data are often missing, incomplete, or too aggregated to be able to deliver solid basic diagnostics without some creative econometric or other statistics treatment. Better and more detailed data will also allow more robust tests of the interactions. The next time a regional or sectoral diagnostic is conducted by the international community, it would make sense to add a questionnaire producing standardized information on many of the variables identified here and summarized in table 17.3. Third, a lot of the data are a de facto private good controlled by donors with limited access to the international community (WB, Regional DB, OECD, IMF, and all bilaterals + PPIAF + IEA). In some cases, the agencies actually sell the data even if the data have already, de facto, been paid by the international community. Just as for academic publications, when there is no reason to claim a confidentiality clause, the data collected should be a public good. Infrastructure data are no different from national accounts, public finance, health, or education data, which are all of easier access.

An additional data issue to address to improve the quality of project-specific data available from the major development agencies is implicit in Kilby (2000, 2015), where he demonstrates quite a bit of creativity in processing the data on the quality of project preparation to assess its impact on project outcomes for international organizations. For now, he argues, it is possible for project outcome assessments to inform the evaluation of preparation (or other aspects of donor performance) which points to a major endogeneity issue. The more general data issue is that the monitoring systems in place are a problem that deserves a more detailed look. Kilby (2000) circumvents the feedback between performance and supervision by examining the link between supervision over a given year and the subsequent annual change in an intermediate measure of project performance.

17.7. CONCLUDING COMMENTS

Notwithstanding the many limitations identified in this chapter, the accumulated evidence provides some robust policy, research, and dissemination messages.

The first is, unsurprisingly, that *institutions do indeed matter in the sector, both formal and informal ones.* They matter probably much more in developing countries than in developed countries because access gaps are strongly correlated with weak institutions and not just financing constraints. The institutional challenges are also more complex in poorer countries because many of the ad hoc solutions adopted to compensate for the lack of more modern approaches are often location specific rather than national or regional. These pragmatic solutions developed to ensure a reasonable sector performance include options anchored in cultural, religious, and other equivalent preferences, as well an increase of the role of NGOs and other similar organizations created to give a voice to civil society. Complexity is not only part of the problem as sometimes claimed by "one size fits all" reformers, it can also be part of the solution to performance enhancement efforts.

Second, *there is no magical solution that suits all situations, and initial conditions matter much more than pre-packaged approaches acknowledge.* These initial conditions drive not only the optimal timing and sequencing of change but also the specific institutional choice that makes sense at that time. The sector diagnostics suggestion to focus on the identification of the main bottlenecks to target policies and institutional changes can be useful to design and rank options with a dynamic view of progress for the sector. There has to be a matching of institutional constraints with policy, financing, and regulatory options which has not really taken place systematically enough in this sector.

Third, in cases of lasting undesirable rigidities—i.e., when complexity is a problem rather than a solution—*change for the sake of change is sometimes useful*, i.e., a shock therapy. This is particularly relevant if change is designed to deal with bottlenecks to minimize the risks of further long-term change (most notably to break "captured" institutions). This is a pragmatic perspective often used in practice to buy time. Time may indeed be the most underrated dimension of efforts to improve sectors and institutions in a sustainable way. To work for the long run, the short-term shock therapy needs to be coordinated with the vision of the sector. This has proven to be a problem in an industry that has largely dropped serious planning from its toolkit. The therapy also must account for an assessment of the long-term dynamics of the political economy of the sector. And this can be quite challenging, as the winners and losers of the changes tend to evolve throughout policy and project cycles. This is what time consistency of a policy means in practice in the politically charged infrastructure sector but is often omitted by shock therapists.

Fourth, *the margin for policymakers and their advisors to use theory to improve performance is significant*. This is particularly obvious in the fact that current often outdated procurement and project management practices have not been able to stop or even slow the continuous flow of new corruption, capture, and collusion cases at a time when procurement theory has enjoyed an explosion of policy-relevant creativity. Similar conclusions could be reached on the use of regulatory tools (e.g., efficiency measurement under data incompleteness, asset valuation techniques, etc.). Implementation details and accountability for these details matter to the performance of the sector, to the size of the rents linked to the sector, and to the distribution of this rent between users, foreign and local investors, taxpayers and . . . politicians. They matter at all stages of the project or policy cycle if the basic information asymmetry problem is to be solved. In this sector with so many limitations to competitive presses, procurement and regulation theory have made the case for the adoption of cost accounting systems designed to improve the monitoring of the residual non-competitive segments of the sector. This case has largely been ignored in the developing world in interactions between governments and large-scale operators.[30]

Fifth, *the margin for academics to get a better sense of the realities of the sector is also still quite large*. This is largely what defines the research agenda discussed earlier. There is, indeed, a lot we still don't know about how institutions can be improved to make the sector work better, including with respect to the interactions between formal and informal institutions in the slow transitions toward more cost-effective solutions to increase affordable and reliable access to these services. The research agenda is not small and is much needed to close some significant knowledge gaps identified in this chapter. This includes an explicit assessment of the role of institutions as a function of context (i.e., infrastructure has a different role in poor, post-conflict, middle-income countries). Ideally, it should make room for interdisciplinary learning as already argued by authors such as Bardhan, Ostrom, or Platteau. In this context, we can learn a lot from the cases in which changes were counterproductive or resulted in excessive rents captured by operators and sometimes shared with dishonest politicians. The policy focus tends to be on best practice, but bad practice can teach at least as much.

Sixth, despite the many knowledge limitations and gaps, *we know enough to be able to start conducting pilot institutional diagnostics of the sector in a somewhat structured way more effectively than less than 10 years ago*. From a research perspective, these diagnostics are also useful because they will highlight the black holes on policy-relevant dimensions deserving better analytical assessments, some probably omitted by this survey. But it is not enough to close the knowledge gaps. It is worth emphasizing, to conclude, that any effort to close these gaps should: (i) be anchored in a commitment of the main aid agencies to coordinate their efforts to collect decent data on the sector on a regular basis; and, just as important (ii) ensure the sharing of the data with all the stakeholders rather than simply sharing the results of the analytical data treatment. This could be achieved with a closer collaboration between these agencies and the academic world, which would allow early academic inputs in the process and allow some scope for a larger number of independent analytical perspectives on the lessons to be drawn from the data.

Without an effort along those lines, it will be hard to improve our collective assessment of the matches between institutional constraints, options, and outcomes. We will be stuck with the very useful but incomplete sporadic large-scale efforts covering multiple countries, at a fairly aggregate level, and with digestions (like this one) of many partial, not necessarily comparable, case studies. This is useful, but the scope to do so much better is significant. Why not try it?

NOTES

This is a background paper prepared for the Economic Development and Institutions (EDI) Initiative Research Program financed by the Department for International Development. I am grateful to G. Aldashev, L. Athias, E. Auriol, J. M. Baland, G. Bel, F. Bourguignon, O. d'Aoust, J.-P. Platteau, G. Raballand, Richard Schlirf, T. Serebrisky, and J. Tzegaegbe for useful discussion during the preparation of this chapter, and to S. Bertomeu Sanchez, D. Camos, A. Colombo, R. Foucart, A. González Fanfalon, J. Pereyra, and F. Trillas for detailed comments and discussions. Any omission, mistake, or misinterpretation of theory or facts is, however, exclusively my responsibility.

1. It is easy to forget that social rates of return are computed under the assumption that maintenance will take place over the lifetime of the assets, not just randomly subject to political decisions to allocate resources to budget or not.
2. The degree of complexity is not linear in the level of government. For instance, supranationality complicates the optimal design of regulation but not always predictably (Auriol and Biancini 2015).
3. Infrastructure productivity gains could cut financing needs by $1 trillion/year (McKinsey 2013). Flyvbjerg (2014) reminds us that, over a 70-year period, for a sample of 258 transportation infrastructure projects in 20 countries spread over five continents, road projects averaged cost overruns of 20.4%; bridges and tunnels averaged cost overruns of 33.8%; and rail projects averaged a 44.7% cost overrun.
4. See Rodrik and Mukand (2016) for a broader discussion of ideology in policy marketing.
5. Housing and irrigation facilities are sometimes also included in the concept, but they will be (largely) ignored in this chapter.
6. And the potential size of this rent explains why there is a bias in favor of large projects.
7. Rodrik (2010) makes this case for a much broader range of policies.
8. Inclusive economic institutions create incentives and opportunities for the majority of the population, and inclusive political institutions are those allowing broad participation and imposing limits and accountability on politicians. In contrast, extractive economic institutions create incentives and opportunities for a few and extractive political institutions concentrate political and economic power in the hands of a few, without accountability.
9. For recent discussions and examples relevant to debates in developing countries, see Auriol and Picard (2009, 2013); Iossa and Martimort (2015, 2016); and Estache and Wren-Lewis (2009).
10. Trillas has a useful perspective on the institutional debates on network industries on his blog. See http://realprogressinenglish.blogspot.fr/2016/05/second-best-and-new-institutional.html.
11. Roughly, their view is that the degree to which politicians care more about the service provider profit or the consumers depends on whether their constituency is dominated by pro-shareholder or pro-consumer voters. The details of regulation are then designed to hold public officials accountable to the dominating group rather than to society at large.
12. Various authors have documented the growing concentration of market power in international markets by former national monopolies. See, for instance, Bonardi (2004), Chari and Gupta (2008), or Clifton et al. (2011).
13. A typical example is the debate on the extent to which contracts are regulatory instruments needed by regulatory agencies or whether contracts and agencies are substitutes.
14. I am well aware that this table is a very personal interpretation of the contributions of each theory. Some readers are likely to disagree with my attributions, but its main purpose is to highlight the perceptions of a dedicated follower of research and practice unable to review every single paper, book, or fact.
15. Vagliasindi and Besant-Jones (2013), in the most exhaustive quantitative diagnostic of reforms in the electricity sector so far find that, between 1999 and 2009, a higher private sector participation share significantly raises the level of tariffs to be able to attract private participation in distribution.

16. A common argument to prefer large-scale operators is their decreasing average costs and their low marginal costs. This is fine in a static view of the world. When time becomes pressing, the rate of time preference matters and so does the discount rate. For villages having to wait for 10 years to gain access to the services offered by a large utility, it is not necessarily the case that the cost-benefit analysis will favor the large-scale lowest cost but slow operator over the small-scale, higher cost but fast operator.

17. Saussier (2015) is an impressive collection of surveys of each of the key dimensions on PPP. The current version of the book is in French, but a translation in English is due soon. An additional extremely useful source is the PPIAF-sponsored website Body of Knowledge which is essentially an encyclopedia, updated on a regular basis; available at http://regulationbodyofknowledge.org/.

18. The privatization of the Argentinean transmission electricity company raised a number of conceptual issues since transmission is the natural regulator of the sector, but it had been captured by complex political interests, and its privatization was a way of cleaning its board from interference with the proper operational decisions on investment and maintenance.

19. The fact that many of the studies assessing the improvements in efficiency are linked to privatization or tend to focus on labor productivity as a proxy for efficiency is quite revealing.

20. Note that these conclusions are quite robust to the contract type used to privatize since they have been observed under concessions contracts, asset ownership switches, or more general targeted contracts (e.g., build-operate-transfer (BOT) and equivalent).

21. Bardhan (2009) looks at the decentralization of public services with similar concern for both autonomy and accountability.

22. The importance of infrastructure in a post-conflict context deserves a detailed survey in itself. In this context, the reconstruction of infrastructure institutions is part of a much broader reconstruction effort. There is an ongoing effort to document the issues and the options sponsored by PPIAF and led by the Public Utility Research Center of the University of Florida, which will provide a useful complement to this survey. Until this becomes available, Anand (2005) offers a very thorough review of the issues.

23. *Adat* is the traditional law of the indigenous peoples of Malaysia and Indonesia among other countries in East Asia. It governs all aspects of personal conduct from birth to death and serves as a conflict resolution instrument. It is over 500 years old but it has been significantly transformed by the adoption of Islamic codes and of European legal systems.

24. One of the problems with these multi-country diagnostics is that most of the data collection efforts financed by these institutions benefit mostly the donor agencies coordinating the data collection. Besides the usual data on access and output which is public for all organizations, the data produced for more detailed policy papers are essentially a private good which cannot be accessed by the academic community, even if financed with public money. The notable exceptions are the AICD diagnostic, the PPIAF privatization database, and the World Bank water and sanitation performance indicator databases which have made all the data (in addition to the reports) available on dedicated websites (e.g., http://www.ib-net.org/). A simple test will make my point clearer. The reader may want to find the data on the proxies used to assess whether a country has an independent regulator or not, a variable that has been used in almost all studies in the last 10 years. It is not public.

25. For some countries, with financing from the Spanish and French development agencies, the World Bank delivered more thorough infrastructure diagnostics linking policy to outcomes to policy choices and to some extent to institutional choices (i.e., the World Bank REDIs, or Recent Economic Developments in Infrastructure, available on the World Bank website). But this effort was short-lived and when the funding disappeared, so did the country-specific diagnostics.

26. Ideally, the impact on performance of the composition of the regulatory authority (i.e., lawyers vs. engineers vs. financial analysts vs. economists vs. accountants) or the hierarchical structure (i.e., board of commissioners vs. presidential structure) should also be documented.

27. The main exception is a reasonably solid literature on the impact on the cost of capital of regulated industries of the regulatory regime (Alexander et al. 2000; Jenkinson 2006; and a matching literature on the relevance of regulation for the choice of leveraging (e.g., Spiegel 1994 and Moore et al. 2014).

28. For up-to-date inventories of infrastructure-related experiments, see 3ie or PPIAF (http://www.ppiaf.org/page/ppiaf-impact-stories).

29. Berg (2013a) makes the point for the water sector in quite a systematic way.

30. The theory also has other, more detailed concrete implications. For instance, without professionally dedicated teams equipped to plan, evaluate ex ante projects, organize the procurement process, and supervise or regulate as needed, and that can be audited by truly independent third parties, many policies and projects are less likely to be effective.

REFERENCES

Acemoglu, D. and S. Johnson. 2005. "Unbundling Institutions." *Journal of Political Economy* 113(5): 949–995.

Acemoglu, D. and J. A. Robinson. 2012. *Why Nations Fail: The Origins of Power, Prosperity, and Poverty.* New York: Crown.

———. 2013. "Economics versus Politics: Pitfalls of Policy Advice." *Journal of Economic Perspectives,* American Economic Association, Spring, 27(2): 173–192.

Ahtiainen, H., E. Pouta, and J. Artell. 2015. "Modelling Asymmetric Preferences for Water Quality in Choice Experiments with Individual-Specific Status Quo Alternatives." *Water Resources and Economics* 12 (October): 1–13.

Aker, J. C. and I. M. Mbiti. 2010. "Mobile Phones and Economic Development in Africa." *Journal of Economic Perspectives* 24(3): 207–232.

Alatas, V., A. Banerjee, A. G. Chandrasekhar, R. Hanna, B. Olken, R. Purnamasari, and M. Wai-Poi. 2013. "Does Elite Capture Matter? Local Elites and Targeted Welfare Programs in Indonesia." *NBER Working Paper* No. 18798.

Albalate, D., G. Bel, and R. Geddes. 2015. "The Determinants of Contractual Choice for Private Involvement in Infrastructure Projects." *Public Money & Management* 35(1), January: 87–94.

Alby, P., Dethier, J. J., and Straub, S. 2013. "Firms Operating Under Electricity Constraints in Developing Countries." *World Bank Economic Review* (January): 109–132.

Aldashev, G., I. Chaara, J.-P. Platteau, and W. Zaki. 2012a. "Using the Law to Change the Custom." *Journal of Development Economics* 97(2): 182–200.

Aldashev, G., I. Chaara, J.-P. Platteau, and W. Zaki. 2012b. "Formal Law as a Magnet to Reform Custom." *Economic Development and Cultural Change* 60(4): 795–828.

Aldashev, G., M. Limardi, and T. Verdier. 2015. "Watchdogs of the Invisible Hands: NGO Monitoring and Industry Equilibrium." *Journal of Development Economics* 116(1): 28–42.

Aldashev, G. and J.-P. Platteau. 2014. "Religion, Culture, and Development." In *Handbook of the Economics of Art and Culture,* vol. 2, edited by V. Ginsburgh and D. Throsby, 587–631. Amsterdam: North Holland.

Alesina, A. and P. Giuliano. 2015. "Culture and Institutions." *Journal of Economic Literature* 53(4), December: 898–944.

Alesina, A., A. Devleschauwer, W. Easterly, S. Kurlat, and R. Wacziarg. 2003. "Fractionalization." *Journal of Economic Growth* 8: 155–194.

Alesina, A., R. Baqir, and W. Easterly. 1999. Public Goods and Ethnic Divisions. *Quarterly Journal of Economics* 114: 1243–1284.

Alexander, I., A. Estache, and A. Oliveri. 2000. "A Few Things Transport Regulators Should Know About Risk and the Cost of Capital." *Utilities Policy* 9: 1–13.

Anand, P. B. 2005. "Getting Infrastructure Priorities Right in Post-Conflict Reconstruction." Research Paper 2005/042. Helsinki: UNU-WIDER.

Anderson, S., P. François, and A. Kotwal. 2015. "Clientelism in Indian Villages." *American Economic Review* 105(6): 1780–1816.

Andres, L., J. Schwarz, and J. L. Guasch. 2013. *Uncovering the Drivers of Utility Performance: Lessons from Latin America.* World Bank.

Aschauer, D. 1989. "Is Public Expenditure Productive?" *Journal of Monetary Economics* 23(2): 177–200.

Ashraf, N., E. Glaeser, A. Holland, and B. M. Steinberg. 2017. "Water, Health and Wealth." *NBER Working Paper* No. 23807.

Ashraf, N., E. L. Glaeser, and G.A.M. Ponzetto. 2016. "Infrastructure, Incentives and Institutions." *NBER Working Paper* No. 21910.

Athias, L. and P. Wicht. 2014. "Cultural Biases in Public Service Delivery: Evidence from a Regression Discontinuity Approach." *MPRA Paper 60639,* University Library of Munich, Germany.

Auriol, E. and S. Biancini. 2015. "Powering Up Developing Countries through Integration." *World Bank Economic Review* 116, September: 105–121.

Auriol, E. and Blanc, A. 2009. "Capture and Corruption in Public Utilities: The Cases of Water and Electricity in Sub-Saharan Africa." *Utilities Policy* 17(2): 203–216, June.

Auriol, E. and P. Picard. 2009. "Infrastructure and Public Utilities Privatization in Developing Countries." *World Bank Economic Review* 23(1): 77–100.

———. 2013. "A Theory of BOT Concession Contracts." *Journal of Economic Behavior & Organization,* Elsevier, 89: 187–209.

Auriol, E. and S. Straub. 2011. "Privatization of Rent-Generating Industries and Corruption." In *International Handbook on the Economics of Corruption,* Vol. 2, chap. 7, edited by S. Rose-Ackerman and T. Soreide. Cheltenham: Edward Elgar.

Auriol, E. and M. Warlters. 2012. "The Marginal Cost of Public Funds and Tax Reform in Africa." *Journal of Development Economics* 97(1): 58–72, January.

Azam, J.-P. 2010. "A State Is Born: Transport Infrastructure and Democracy in Somaliland." Toulouse School of Economics, *TSE Working Paper* no. 10–229.

Baland, J.-M., F. Bourguignon, J.-P. Platteau, and T. Verdier. 2018. "Economic Development and Institutions: An Introduction," in this volume.

Baland, J.-M. and P. François. 2005. "Commons as Insurance and the Welfare Impact of Privatization." *Journal of Public Economics* 89(2–3): 211–231, February.

Baland, J.-M. and J.-P. Platteau. 1999. "The Ambiguous Impact of Inequality on Local Resource Management." *World Development* 27: 773–788.

Banerjee, A. and L. Iyer. 2005. "History, Institutions and Economic Performance: The Legacy of Colonial Land Tenure Systems in India." *American Economic Review* 95(4), September.

Bardhan, P. K. 2000. "Irrigation and Cooperation: An Empirical Analysis of 48 Irrigation Communities in South India." *Economic Development and Cultural Change* 48: 847–865.

Bardhan, P. 2004. "Governance Issues in Delivery of Public Services." *Journal of African Economies* 13(1): i167–i182, July.

———. 2009. "Governance Dilemmas in Service Delivery." In *Does Decentralization Enhance Service Delivery and Poverty Reduction?*, chap. 3, edited by E. Ahmad and G. Brosio. Cheltenham: Edward Elgar.

Bardhan, P. and D. Mookherjee. 2006. "Decentralisation and Accountability in Infrastructure Delivery in Developing Countries." *Economic Journal* 116 (508): 101–127.

Bardhan, P. and I. Ray. 2006. "Symposium on Anthropologists' Views on Common Resources: Methodological Approaches to the Question of the Commons." *Economic Development and Cultural Change* 54(3): 655–676, April.

Baron, D. 2001. "Private Politics, Corporate Social Responsibility, and Integrated Strategy." *Journal of Economic Management and Strategy* 10: 7–45.

———. 2010. "Morally Motivated Self-Regulation." *American Economic Review* 100: 1299–1329.

Baron, D. and D. Diermeier. 2007. "Strategic Activism and Nonmarket Strategy." *Journal of Economic Management and Strategy* 16: 599–634.

Bates, R. H. 2000. "Ethnicity and Development in Africa: A Reappraisal." *American Economic Review* 90(2). *Papers and Proceedings of the One Hundred Twelfth Annual Meeting of the American Economic Association* (May): 131–134.

———. 1974. "Ethnic Competition and Modernization in Contemporary Africa." *Comparative Political Studies* 6(4): 457–484.

Bel, G., T. Brown, and R. Cunha, ed. 2015. *Public-Private Partnerships: Infrastructure, Transportation and Local Services.* New York: Routledge.

Bel, G., X. Fageda, and M. E. Warnerd. 2010. "Is Private Production of Public Service Cheaper Than Public Production? A Meta-Regression Analysis of Solid Waste and Water Services." *Journal of Policy Analysis and Management* 29(3): 553–577.

Benitez, D. and A. Estache. 2005. "How Concentrated Are Global Infrastructure Markets?" *Review of Network Economics* 4(3): 1–23.

Bennett, J. and E. Iossa. 2010. "Contracting Out Public Service Provision to Not-For-Profit Firms." *Oxford Economic Papers* 62(4): 784–802.

Berg, Sanford V. 2013a. "Advances in Benchmarking to Improve Water Utility Operations: A Review of Six IWA Books." *Water Policy* 15: 325–333.

———. 2013b. "Best Practices in Regulating State-Owned and Municipal Water Utilities," ECLAC best practice note, May, available at http://www.eclac.org/publicaciones/xml/1/49891/Bestpracticesinregulating.pdf

Berg, S., and R. Cunha Marques. 2011. "Quantitative Studies of Water and Sanitation Utilities: A Literature Survey." *Water Policy* 135: 591–606.

Berg, S., L. Jiang, and C. Lin. 2012. "Regulation and Corporate Corruption: New Evidence from the Telecom Sector." *Journal of Comparative Economics* 40: 22–43.

Bergara, D., W. Henisz, and P. Spiller. 1998. "Political Institutions and Electric Utility Investment: A Cross-Nation Analysis." *California Management Review* 40: 18–35.

Bertomeu-Sanchez, S., D. Camos, and A. Estache. 2018. "Do Private Water Utility Operators Care about Regulatory Agencies in Developing Countries?" *Utilities Policy* 50(C): 153–163.

Besley, T. and R. Burgess. 2002. "The Political Economy of Government Responsiveness: Theory and Evidence from India." *Quarterly Journal of Economics* 117(4): 1415–1451.

Besley, T. and M. Ghatak. 2007. "Retailing Public Goods: The Economics of Corporate Social Responsibility." *Journal of Public Economics* 91: 1645–1663.

———. 2014. "Solving Agency Problems: Intrinsic Motivation, Incentives, and Productivity." Background paper for the World Development Report 2015.

Beuran, M., M. Gachassin, and Gaël Raballand. 2015. "Are There Myths on Road Impact and Transport in Sub-Saharan Africa?" *Development Policy Review*, Overseas Development Institute 33(5): 673–700.

Bitran E., S. Nieto-Parra, and J. S. Robledo. 2013. "Opening the Black Box of Contract Renegotiations: An Analysis of Road Concessions in Chile, Colombia and Peru." OECD Development Centre Working Papers 317.

Blanc-Brude, F. and D. Makovsek. 2014. "How Much Construction Risk Do Sponsors Take in Project Finance?" EDHEC-Risk Institute Publications.

Blimpo, M. P., R. Harding, and L. Wantchekon. 2013. "Public Investment in Rural Infrastructure: Some Political Economy Considerations." *Journal of African Economies*: ii57–ii83.

Bobonis, G. J., P. Gertler, M. Gonzalez-Navarro, and S. Nichter. 2017. "Vulnerability and Clientelism." *NBER Working Paper* No. 23589, July.

Bonardi, J. P. 2004. "Global and Political Strategies in Deregulated Industries: The Asymmetric Behaviors of Former Monopolies." *Strategic Management Journal* 25(2): 101–120.

Brousseau, E. and J. M. Glachant, ed. 2008. *New Institutional Economics. A Guidebook*. Cambridge University Press.

Burgess, R., R. Jedwab, E. Miguel, A. Morjaria, and G. Padro i Miquel. 2015. "The Value of Democracy: Evidence from Road Building in Kenya." *American Economic Review* 105(6): 1817–1851.

Cadot, O., L. H. Röller, and A. Stephan. 2006. "Contribution to Productivity or Pork Barrel? The Two Faces of Infrastructure Investment." *Journal of Public Economics* 90: 1133–1153.

Calderon, C. and L. Serven. 2014. "Infrastructure, Growth, and Inequality: An Overview." Policy Research Working Paper Series 7034, World Bank.

Cambini, C. and D. Franzi. 2014. "Independent Regulatory Agencies and Rules Harmonization for the Electricity Sector and Renewables in the Mediterranean Region." *Energy Policy* 60: 179–191.

Cambini, C., L. Rondi, and S. De Masi. 2015. "Incentive Compensation in Energy Firms: Does Regulation Matter?" *Corporate Governance: An International Review* 23(4): 378–395.

Canning, D., M. Fay, and R. Perotti. 1994. "Infrastructure and Growth." In *International Differences in Growth Rates*, edited by M. Bsaldassarri, M. Paganetto, and E. S. Phelps, 285–310. New York: St. Martins Press.

Carvalho, P., R. Marques, R. Cunha, and S. Berg. 2012. "A Meta-Regression Analysis of Benchmarking Studies On Water Utilities Market Structure." *Utilities Policy*, Elsevier, 21(C): 40–49.

Casey, K., R. Glennerster, and E. Miguel. 2012. "Reshaping Institutions: Evidence on Aid Impacts Using a Pre-Analysis Plan." *Quarterly Journal of Economics* 127(4): 1755–1812.

Cassan, G. and L. Vandewalle. 2017. "Identities and Public Policies: Unintended Effects of Political Reservations for Women in India." IHEID Working Papers 18-2017, Economics Section, The Graduate Institute of International Studies.

Castaneda, A., M. A. Jamison, and M. Phillips. 2014. "Considerations for the Design and Transformation of Regulatory Systems." University of Florida, Department of Economics, PURC Working Paper.

Ceriani, L., R. Doronzo, and M. Florio. 2009. "Privatization, Unbundling, and Liberalization of Network Industries: A Discussion of the Dominant Policy Paradigm in the EU." Departmental Working Papers 2009-09, Department of Economics, Management and Quantitative Methods at Università degli Studi di Milano.

Chari, A. and N. Gupta. 2008. "Incumbents and Protectionism: The Political Economy of Foreign Entry Liberalization." *Journal of Financial Economics* 88(3): 633–656.

Chattopadhyay, R. and E. Duflo. 2004. "Women as Policy Makers: Evidence from a Randomized Policy Experiment in India." *Econometrica* 72: 1409–1443.

Chong, E., S. Saussier, and B. Silverman. 2015. "Water under the Bridge: City Size, Bargaining Power, Price and Franchise Renewals in the Provision of Water." *Journal of Law, Economics, and Organization* 31(1): 3–39.

Chowdhury, S., F. Yamauchi, and R. Dewina. 2009. Governance Decentralization and Local Infrastructure Provision in Indonesia. *IFPRI Discussion Paper 00902.*

Cingolani, L., K. Thomsson, and D. de Crombrugghe. 2015. "Minding Weber More Than Ever? The Impacts of State Capacity and Bureaucratic Autonomy on Development Goals." *World Development* 72 (August): 191–207.

Clifton, J. 2000. "On The Political Consequences of Privatisation: The Case of Teléfonos de México." *Bulletin of Latin American Studies* 19: 63–79.

Clifton, J., F. Comín, and D. Díaz-Fuentes. 2011. "From National Monopoly to Multinational Corporation: How Regulation Shaped the Road Towards Telecommunications Internationalisation." *Business History* 53(5): 761–781, August.

Clifton, J., F. Díaz-Fuentes, and P. Lanthier. 2014. "Editorial: Utility Policy and Development since Bretton Woods: The Role of Multinationals, Governments and International Financial Institutions."
Utilities Policy.

Clifton, J., D. Díaz-Fuentes, and M. Warner. 2016. "The Loss of Public Values When Public Utilities
Go Abroad." *Utilities Policy* 40 (June): 134–143.

Coase, R. 1992. "The Institutional Structure of Production." *American Economic Review* 82(4): 713–719.

Collier, P. and A. J. Venables. 2016. "Urban Infrastructure for Development." *Oxford Review of Economic
Policy,* Oxford University Press, vol. 32(3): 391–409.

Costa-i-Font, J., E. Rodriguez-Oreggia, and D. Lunapla. 2003. "Political Competition and Pork-Barrel
Politics in the Allocation of Public Investment in Mexico." *Public Choice* 116: 185–204.

Cubbin, J. and J. Stern. 2006. "The Impact of Regulatory Governance and Privatization on Electricity
Industry Capacity in Developing Countries." *World Bank Economic Review* 20(1): 115–41.

Dal Bó, E. and M. A. Rossi. 2007. "Corruption and Inefficiency: Theory and Evidence from Electric
Utilities." *Journal of Public Economics* 91(5–6): 939–962.

Dayton-Johnson, J. 2000. "Choosing Rules to Govern the Commons: A Model with Evidence from Mexico." *Journal of Economic Behavior and Organization* 42: 19–41.

Demurger, S. 2001. "Infrastructure Development and Economic Growth: An Explanation for Regional
Disparities in China?" *Journal of Comparative Economics* 29(1): 95–117.

Desrieux C., E. Chong, and S. Saussier. 2013. "Putting All One's Eggs in One Basket: Relational Contracts and the Management of Local Water Public Services." *Journal of Economic Behavior and Organization* 89: 167–186.

Dinkelman, T. 2011. "The Effects of Rural Electrification on Employment: New Evidence from South
Africa." *American Economic Review* 101(7): 3078–3108.

Dixit, A. 2009. "Governance Institutions and Economic Activity." *American Economic Review* 99(1): 5–24.

Djankov, S., R. LaPorta, F. Lopez-de-Silanes, and A. Shleifer. 2003. "Courts." *Quarterly Journal of Economics* 118(2): 453–517.

Eberhard, A. 2007. *Matching Regulatory Design to Country Circumstances: The Potential of Hybrid and Transitional Models.* Washington, DC: World Bank.

Engel, E., R. Fisher, and A. Galetovic. 2014. *The Economics of Public-Private Partnerships: A Basic Guide.*
Cambridge University Press.

Engineers Against Poverty. 2006. Modifying Infrastructure Procurement to Enhance Social Development. London.

Esfahani, H. S. and M. T. Ramirez. 2003. "Institutions, Infrastructure and Economic Growth." *Journal
of Development Economics* 70(2): 443–477, April.

Estache, A. 2014. "Infrastructure and Corruption: A Brief Survey." ECARES Working Papers 2014-37,
Universite Libre de Bruxelles.

Estache, A. and M. Fourati. 2017. "Infrastructure Provision, Politics and Religion: Insights from Tunisia's New Democracy." ECARES Working Papers 2017–24, Universite Libre de Bruxelles.

Estache, A., G. Garsous, and R. Seroa da Motta. 2016. "Shared Mandates, Moral Hazard and Political
(Mis)alignment in a Decentralized Economy." *World Development* 83 (July): 98–110.

Estache, A. and A. Iimi. 2011. *The Economics of Infrastructure Procurement: Theory and Evidence.* London:
CEPR.

Estache, A., T. Serebrisky, and L. Wren-Lewis. 2015. "Financing Infrastructure in Developing
Countries." *Oxford Review of Economic Policy* 31(3–4): 279–304.

Estache, A. and L. Wren-Lewis. 2009. "Toward a Theory of Regulation for Developing Countries:
Following Jean-Jacques Laffont's Lead." *Journal of Economic Literature* 47: 729–770.

Faguet, J. P. 2004. "Does Decentralisation Increase Government Responsiveness to Local Needs?
Evidence from Bolivia." *Journal of Public Economics* 88(3–4): 867–893.

Faguet, J. P. and C. Poschl (eds). 2015. *Is Decentralization Good for Development?* Oxford: Oxford
University Press.

Ferraz, C. and F. Finan. 2008. "Exposing Corrupt Politicians: The Effects of Brazil's Publicly Released
Audits on Electoral Outcomes." *Quarterly Journal of Economics* 123(2): 703–745.

———. 2011. "Electoral Accountability and Corruption: Evidence from the Audits of Local Governments." *American Economic Review* 101(4): 1274–1311.

Ferreira, P. C. 1996. "Investimento em Infra-estrutura no Brasil: Fatos Estilizados e Relacoes de Longo
Prazo." *Pesquisa e Planejamento Economico* 26: 231–252.

Finger M. and R. Künneke. 2011. *International Handbook of Network Industries. The Liberalization of Infrastructures.* Cheltenham: Edward Elgar.

Flyvbjerg, B. 2009. "Survival of the Unfittest: Why the Worst Infrastructure Gets Built, and What We Can Do About It." *Oxford Review of Economic Policy* 25(3): 344–367.

———. 2014. "What You Should Know About Megaprojects and Why: An Overview." *Project Management Journal* April/May: 6–19.

Foster, V., S. Witte, S. G. Banerjee, and A. Moreno. 2017. "Charting the Diffusion of Power Sector Reforms Across the Developing World." World Bank, Policy Research Working Paper 8235.

Frank, J. and J. Martinez-Vazquez. 2014. "Decentralization and Infrastructure: From Gaps to Solutions." International Center for Public Policy Working Paper Series, at AYSPS, GSU paper1405, Georgia State University.

Frey, F. S., M. Benz, and A. Stutzer. 2003. "Introducing Procedural Utility: Not Only What, But Also How Matters." Working Paper 2003–2 Center for Research in Economics, Management and the Arts, Basel.

Galilea, P. and F. Medda. 2010. "Does the Political and Economic Context Influence the Success of a Transport Project? An Analysis of Transport Public-Private Partnerships." *Research in Transportation Economics* 30: 102–109.

Gassner, K., A. Popov, and N. Pushak. 2009. "Does Private Sector Participation Improve Performance in Electricity and Water Distribution." World Bank, PPIAF, *Trends and Policy Option* 6.

Gassner, K. and N. Pushak. 2014. "30 Years of British Utility Regulation: Developing Country Experience and Outlook." *Utilities Policy* 31(C): 44–51.

George, M., C. Graham, and L. Lennard. 2011. *Too Many Hurdles: Information and Advice Barriers in the Energy Market.* Centre for Consumers and Essential Services, Leicester.

Glachant, J. M., H. Khalfallah, Y. Perez, V. Rious, and M. Saguan. 2013. "Implementing Incentive Regulation Through an Alignment with Resource Bounded Regulators." *Competition and Regulation in Network Industries* 14(3): 265–290.

Glaeser, E. L., R. LaPorta, F. López-de-Silanes, and A. Shleifer. 2004. "Do Institutions Cause Growth?" *Journal of Economic Growth* 9(3): 271–303.

Goel, R. K. and J. W. Saunoris. 2016. "Forms of Government Decentralization and Institutional Quality: Evidence from a Large Sample of Nation." March, *ADBI Working Paper* 562.

Gomez-Ibanez, J. A. 2006. *Regulating Infrastructure: Monopoly, Contracts, and Discretion.* Cambridge, MA: Harvard University Press.

———. 2007. "Alternatives to Infrastructure Privatization Revisited: Public Enterprise Reform from the 1960s to the 1980s." World Bank Working Paper No. 4391, November.

Guasch, J. L. 2004. *Granting and Renegotiating Concession Contracts: Doing It Right.* Washington, DC: World Bank.

Guasch, J. L., D. Benitez, I. Portabales, and L. Flor. 2014. "The Renegotiation of PPP Contracts: An Overview of Its Recent Evolution in Latin America." *International Transport Forum*, Discussion Paper No. 2014–18.

Guasch, J. L., J. J. Laffont, and S. Straub. 2008. "Renegotiation of Concession Contracts in Latin America." *International Journal of Industrial Organization* 26(2): 421–442.

Guasch, J. L. and P. Spiller. 1999. *Managing the Regulatory Process: Design, Concepts, Issues, and the Latin American and Caribbean Story.* World Bank Directions in Development Series.

Guerriero, C. 2011a. "Accountability in Government and Regulatory Policies: Theory and Evidence." *Journal of Comparative Economics* 39(2011): 453–469.

———. 2011b. "Legal Traditions and Economic Performances: Theory and Evidence." In *Encyclopedia of Law and Economics*, 2nd ed., Vol. 7, edited by Bouckaert, Boudewijn, and Gerrit De Geest, ch. 9, 144–163. Cheltenham: Edward Elgar.

Guerriero, Carmine. 2016. "Endogenous Legal Traditions and Economic Outcomes." *Journal of Comparative Economics* 44(2): 416–433.

Guiteras, R., K. Jannat, D. Levine, and T. Polley. 2015. *Testing Disgust and Shame-Based Safe Water and Handwashing Promotion in Dhaka, Bangladesh,* 3ie Grantee Final Report. New Delhi: International Initiative for Impact Evaluation.

Harvey, P. and H. Knox. 2012. "The Enchantments of Infrastructure." *Mobilities* 7(4): 521–536.

———. 2015. *Roads: An Anthropology of Infrastructure and Expertise.* Ithaca, NY: Cornell University Press.

Hausmann, R. 2008. "In Search of the Chains that Hold Brazil Back." CID Working Paper No. 180, Center for International Development, Harvard University, Cambridge.

Hausmann, R., D. Rodrik, and A. Velasco. 2005. "Growth Diagnostics." In *The Washington Consensus Reconsidered: Towards a New Global Governance*, edited by N. Serra and J. E. Stiglitz, 324–355. Oxford, UK: Oxford University Press.

Henisz, W. 2002. "The Institutional Environment for Infrastructure Investment." *Industrial and Corporate Change* 11(2): 355–389.

Henisz, W. and B. Zelner. 2006. "Interest Groups, Veto Points and Electricity Infrastructure Deployment." *International Organization* 60(1): 263–286.

Hirschman, A. 1958. *Strategy of Economic Development*. New Haven, CT: Yale University Press.

Hulland, K., N. Martin, R. Dreibelbis, J. De Bruicker Valliant, and P. Winch. 2015. "What Factors Affect Sustained Adoption of Safe Water, Hygiene and Sanitation Technologies?" 3ie *Systematic Review* Summary 2.

Imam, M., T. Jamasb, and M. Llorca. 2018. "Power Sector Reform and Corruption: Evidence from Electricity Industry in Sub-Saharan Africa." Cambridge Working Papers in Economics 1801, Faculty of Economics, University of Cambridge.

International Labor Organization. 1998. Lessons from Privatization. Labour Issues in Developing and Transitional Countries, Geneva.

———. 2003. Challenges and Opportunities Facing Public Utilities, Geneva.

Iossa, E. and D. Martimort. 2015. "The Simple Microeconomics of Public-Private Partnerships." *Journal of Public Economic Theory*, Special Issue on Public-Private Partnerships 17(1): 4–48.

———. 2016. "Corruption in PPPs, Incentives and Contract Incompleteness." *International Journal of Industrial Organization* 44(C): 85–100.

Iversen, V., R. Palmer-Jones, and K. Sen. 2013. "On the Colonial Origins of Agricultural Development in India: A Re-Examination of Banerjee and Iyer, History, Institutions and Economic Performance." *Journal of Development Studies* 49(12): 1631–1646.

Jasmab, T., R. Nepal, and G. R. Timilsina. 2017. "A Quarter Century Effort Yet to Come of Age: A Survey of Electricity Sector Reform in Developing Countries." *Energy Journal* 38(3): 195–234.

Jasmab, T., R. Nepal, G. R. Timilsina, and M. Toman. 2014. "Energy Sector Reform, Economic Efficiency and Poverty Reduction." Discussion Papers Series 529, School of Economics, University of Queensland, Australia.

Jenkinson, T. J. 2006. "Regulation and the Cost of Capital." In *International Handbook on Economic Regulation*, edited by Michael Crew and David Parker, 146–165. Cheltenham: Edward Elgar.

Jimenez, E. 1995. "Human and Physical Infrastructure: Public Investment and Pricing Policies in Developing Countries." In *Handbook of Development Economics, Volume 3B*, chap. 43, 2773–2843. Amsterdam: North Holland.

Kahneman, D., J. L. Knetsch, and R. H. Thaler. 1986. "Fairness as a Constraint on Profit Seeking: Entitlements in the Market." *American Economic Review* 76(4).

Kilby, C. 2000. "Supervision and Performance: The Case of World Bank Projects." *Journal of Development Economics* 62(1): 233–259.

———. 2015. "Assessing the Impact of World Bank Preparation on Project Outcomes." *Journal of Development Economics*, Elsevier, 115(C): 111–123.

Kis-Katos, K. and B. S. Sjahrir. 2014. "The Impact of Fiscal and Political Decentralization on Local Public Investments in Indonesia." *IZA Discussion Papers* 7884, Institute for the Study of Labor (IZA).

Knox, H. and P. Harvey. 2011. "Anticipating Harm: Regulation and Irregularity on a Road Construction Project in the Peruvian Andes." *Theory, Culture and Society* 28(6): 142–163.

Kuroda, H., M. Kawai, and R. Nangia. 2007. "Infrastructures et coopération régionale." *Revue d'économie du développement* 15(4): 91–124. doi:10.3917/edd.214.0091.

Laffont, J. J. 2000. *Incentives and Political Economy*. Oxford University Press.

———. 2005. *Regulation and Development*. Cambridge University Press.

Laffont, J. J. and D. Martimort. 1998. "Transaction Costs, Institutional Design and the Separation of Powers." *European Economic Review*, Elsevier, 42(3–5): 673–684, May.

———. 1999. "Separation of Regulators Against Collusive Behavior." *RAND Journal of Economics* 30(2): 232–262, Summer.

Laffont, J. J. and Mathieu Meleu. 2001. "Separation of Powers and Development." *Journal of Development Economics*, Elsevier, 64(1): 129–145, February.

Laffont, J. J. and J. Tirole. 1990. "The Politics of Government Decision Making: Regulatory Institutions." *Journal of Law, Economics and Organization* 6(1): 1–31, Spring.

———. 1991. "The Politics of Government Decision-Making: A Theory of Regulatory Capture." *Quarterly Journal of Economics* 106(4): 1089–127, November.

LaPorta, R., F. López-de-Silanes, C. Pop-Eleches, and A. Shleifer. 2004. "Judicial Checks and Balances." *Journal of Political Economy* 112(2): 445–420.

La Porta, R., F. López-de-Silanes, and A. Shleifer. 2008. "The Economic Consequences of Legal Origins." *Journal of Economic Literature* 46: 285–332.

La Porta R., F. López-de-Silanes, A. Shleifer, and R. Vishny. 1999. "The Quality of Government." *Journal of Law, Economics and Organization* 15(1): 222–279, March.

Larkin, B. 2013. "The Politics and Poetics of Infrastructure." *Annual Review of Anthropology* 42: 327–343.

Levy, B. and P. Spiller. 1994. "The Institutional Foundations of Regulatory Commitment: A Comparative Analysis of Telecommunications Regulation." *Journal of Law, Economics and Organization* 10: 201–246.

Lim, C. and A. Yurukuglu. 2015. "Dynamic Natural Monopoly Regulation: Time Inconsistency, Moral Hazard, and Political Environments." Graduate School of Business, Stanford University, mimeo, November.

Lipscomb, M., A. M. Mobarak, and T. Barham. 2013. "Development Effects of Electrification: Evidence from Topographic Placement of Hydropower Plants in Brazil." *American Economic Journal: Applied Economics* 5(2): 200–231.

Mande Bafua, P. 2015. "Efficiency of Urban Water Supply in Sub-Saharan Africa: Do Organization and Regulation Matter?" *Utilities Policy* 37: 13–22.

Mansuri, G. and V. Rao. 2013. *Localizing Development: Does Participation Work?* Washington, DC: World Bank.

Mardirosian, R. C. 2010. Infrastructure Development in the Shadow of Conflict: Aligning Incentives and Attracting Investment. Working Paper 57, Collaboratory for Research on Global Projects, Stanford University, May.

Martimort, D. 1999. "The Life Cycle of Regulatory Agencies: Dynamic Capture and Transaction Costs." *Review of Economic Studies* 66(4): 929–947, October.

Martimort, D. and S. Straub. 2009. "Infrastructure Privatization and Changes in Corruption Patterns: The Roots of Public Discontent." *Journal of Development Economics* 90(1): 69–84, September.

Maskin, E. and J. Tirole. 2004. "The Politician and the Judge: Accountability in Government." *American Economic Review* 94: 1034–1054.

McKenzie, D. and D. Mookherjee. 2003. "The Distributive Impact of Privatization in Latin America: Evidence from Four Countries." *Economia, Journal of the Latin American and Caribbean Economic Association*: 161–234.

McKinsey Global Institute Report. 2013. *Infrastructure Productivity: How to Save $1 Trillion a Year.* Available at mckinsey.com.

McRae, S. 2015. "Infrastructure Quality and the Subsidy Trap." *American Economic Review* 105(1): 35–66.

Meenakshi, J. V., A. Banerji, A. Mukherji, and A. Gupta. 2013. "Does Marginal Cost Pricing of Electricity Affect the Groundwater Pumping Behaviour of Farmers? Evidence from India." *3ie Impact Evaluation Report 4.*

Menard, C. 2011. "Hybrid Modes of Organization: Alliances, Joint Ventures, Networks, and Other 'Strange' Animals." In *Handbook of Organizational Economics*, edited by R. Gibbons and J. Roberts. Princeton, NJ: Princeton University Press.

Menard, C. and A. Peeroo. 2011. "Liberalization in the Water Sector: Three Leading Models." In *Handbook of Liberalization*, edited by M. Finger and R. W. Kunneke. Cheltenham: Edward Elgar.

Miguel, E. and M. K. Gugerty. 2005. "Ethnic Diversity, Social Sanctions, and Public Goods in Kenya." *Journal of Public Economics* 89(1112): 2325–2368.

Moore, A., S. Straub, and J. J. Dethier. 2014. "Regulation, Renegotiation and Capital Structure: Theory and Evidence from Latin American Transport Concessions." *Journal of Regulatory Economics*, Springer, 45(2): 209–232.

Moszoro, M., P. T. Spiller, and S. Stolorz. 2016. "Rigidity of Public Contracts." *Journal of Empirical Legal Studies* 13(3): 396–427.

Mukherji, A., B. Das, N. Majumdar, N. C. Nayak, R. R. Sethi, B. R. Sharma, and P. S. Banerjee. 2009. "Metering of Agricultural Power Supply in West Bengal: Who Gains and Who Loses?" *Energy Policy* 37(12): 5530–5539.

Munshi, K. and M. Mark Rosenzweig. 2016. "Insiders and Outsiders: Local Ethnic Politics and Public Good Provision." Cambridge University, mimeo, March.

Nepal, R., and T. Jasmab. 2015. "Caught between Theory and Practice: Government, Market, and Regulatory Failure in Electricity Sector Reforms." *Economic Analysis and Policy* 46: 16–24.

Nepal, R., A. Sen, and T. Jasmab. 2018. "Small Systems, Big Targets: Power Sector Reforms and Renewable Energy in Small Systems" *Energy Policy* 116, May: 119–129.

North, D. C. 1990. *Institutions, Institutional Change and Economic Performance.* Cambridge: Cambridge University Press.

Null, C., J. Garcia Hombrados, M. Kremer, R. Meeks, E. Miguel, and A. Peterson Zwane. 2012. "Willingness to Pay for Cleaner Water in Less Developed Countries: Systematic Review of Experimental Evidence." *Systematic Review* 006, May.

OECD. 2015. Consequences of Corruption at the Sector Level and Implications for Economic Growth and Development. Paris, France.

Olken, B. A. 2007. "Monitoring Corruption: Evidence from a Field Experiment in Indonesia." *Journal of Political Economy* 115: 200–249.

———. 2010. "Direct Democracy and Local Public Goods: Evidence from a Field Experiment in Indonesia." *American Political Science Review* 104(2): 243–267.

O'Rourke, D. 2003. "Outsourcing Regulation: Analyzing Non-Governmental Systems of Labor Standards and Monitoring." *Policy Studies Journal* 31: 1–29.

Ostrom, E. 2005. *Understanding Institutional Diversity*. Princeton, NJ: Princeton University Press.

———. 2010. "Beyond Markets and States: Polycentric Governance of Complex Economic Systems." *American Economic Review* 100(3): 641–672, June.

Ostrom, Elinor. 1990. *Governing the Commons: The Evolution of Institutions for Collective Action*. Cambridge and New York: Cambridge University Press.

Pal, S. 2009. Norms, Culture and Local Infrastructure: Evidence from Indonesia, Brunel University, *CEDI Working Paper* No. 09–08.

Pal, S. and Z. Wahhaj. 2012. Fiscal Decentralisation, Local Institutions and Public Goods Provision: Evidence from Indonesia. University of Kent, School of Economics Discussion Papers, KDPE 1216.

Parker, D., C. Kirkpatrick, and C. Figueira-Theodorakopoulou. 2008. "Infrastructure Regulation and Poverty Reduction in Developing Countries: A Review of the Evidence and a Research Agenda." *Quarterly Review of Economics and Finance* 48(2): 177–188.

Pérard, E. 2008. "Private Sector Participation and Regulatory Reform in Water Supply: The Southern Mediterranean Experience." OECD Development Centre Working Paper No. 26.

Percoco, M. 2014. "Quality of Institutions and Private Participation in Transport Infrastructure Investment: Evidence From Developing Countries." *Transportation Research Part A: Policy and Practice* 70(C): 50–58.

Platteau, J. P. 2000. *Institutions, Social Norms and Economic Development*. London: Harwood Academic.

———. 2008. "Religion, Politics, and Development: Lessons from the Lands of Islam." *Journal of Economic Behavior & Organization*, Elsevier, 68(2): 329–351.

———. 2009. "Institutional Obstacles to African Economic Development: State, Ethnicity, and Custom." *Journal of Economic Behavior & Organization* 71(3): 669–689.

Platteau, J. P. and A. Abraham. 2002. "Participatory Development in the Presence of Endogenous Community Imperfections." *Journal of Development Studies*, Taylor & Francis Journals, 39(2): 104–136.

Polemis, M. L. 2016. "New Evidence on the Impact of Structural Reforms on Electricity Sector Performance." *Energy Policy* 92: 420–431.

Price, J. I., J. Janmaat, F. Sugden, and L. Bharatim. 2016. "Water Storage Systems and Preference Heterogeneity in Water-Scarce Environments: A Choice Experiment in Nepal's Koshi River Basin." *Water Resources and Economics* 13 (January): 6–18.

Raballand, G., P. Patricia Macchi, and C. Petracco. 2010. "Rural Road Investment Efficiency: Lessons from Burkina Faso, Cameroon, and Uganda." *Directions in Development*, World Bank Publications.

Rodrik, D. 2000. "Institutions for High-Quality Growth: What They Are and How to Acquire Them." *Studies in Comparative International Development* 35(3): 3–31.

———. 2007. *One Economics, Many Recipes: Globalization, Institutions, and Economic Growth*. Princeton, NJ: Princeton University Press.

———. 2010. "Diagnostics Before Prescription." *Journal of Economic Perspectives* 24(3): 33–44, Summer.

Rodrik, D. and S. Mukand. 2016. "Ideas versus Interests: A Unified Political Economy Framework." Mimeo, available at http://drodrik.scholar.harvard.edu/files/dani-rodrik/files/ideasinterestsapr10sm_dr.pdf?m=1460386309.

Rose-Ackerman, S. and T. Soreide (eds.). 2011. *International Handbook on the Economics of Corruption*, Vol. Two. Cheltenham: Edward Elgar.

Saussier, S. (ed). 2015. *Économie des partenariats public-privé: Développements théoriques et empiriques*. Louvain-la-Neuve: De Boeck

Saussier, S., C. Staropoli, and A. Yvrande-Billon. 2009. "Public–Private Agreements, Institutions, and Competition: When Economic Theory Meets Facts." *Review of Industrial Organization* 35(1): 1–18.

Savedoff, W. and P. Spiller (eds.). 1999. "Spilled Water: Institutional Commitment in the Provision of Water Services in Latin America." Inter-American Development Bank, Washington, DC.

Seabright, P. 2000. "Skill versus Judgement and the Architecture of Organisations." *European Economic Review* 44(4–6): 856–868, May.

Seim, L. T. and T. Soreide. 2009. "Bureaucratic Complexity and Impacts of Corruption in Utilities." *Utilities Policy* 17(2): 176–184.

Sen, A., R. R. Nepal, and T. Jamasb. 2018. "Have Model, Will Reform? Assessing the Outcomes of Electricity Reforms in Non-OECD Asia." *Energy Journal* 39(4): 181–209.

Sheely, R. 2015. "Mobilization, Participatory Planning Institutions, and Elite Capture." *World Development* 67: 221–266, March.

Shleifer, A. and E. L. Glaeser. 2001. "A Reason for Quantity Regulation." *American Economic Review Papers and Proceedings* 91(2): 431–435.

Soomro, M. and X. Zhang. 2011. "An Analytical Review on Transportation Public-Private Partnerships Failures." *International Journal of Sustainable Construction Engineering & Technology* 2–2: 62–80.

Soreide, T. and A. Williams (eds.). 2014. *Corruption, Grabbing and Development: Real World Challenges.* Cheltenham: Edward Elgar.

Spiegel, Y. 1994. "The Capital Structure and Investment of Regulated Firms Under Alternative Regulatory Regimes." *Journal of Regulatory Economics* 6(3): 297–319.

Spiller, P. 1990. "Politicians, Interest Groups, and Regulators: A Multiple-Principals Agency Theory of Regulation, or 'Let Them Be Bribed.'" *Journal of Law and Economics* 33(1): 65–101, April.

———. 2013. "Transaction Cost Regulation." *Journal of Economic Behavior & Organization* 89: 232–242.

Spiller, P. and M. Tommasi. 2005. "The Institutions of Regulation." In *Handbook of New Institutional Economics,* edited by C. Menard and M. Shirley.

Taher, M. H., A. Dinar, and J. Albiac. 2016. "Cooperative Water Management and Ecosystem Protection Under Scarcity and Drought in Arid and Semiarid Regions. *Water Resources and Economics* 13: 60–74.

Takano, G. 2017. "Public-Private Partnerships as Rent-Seeking Opportunities: A Case Study on ann Unsolicited Proposal in Lima, Peru." *Utilities Policy,* Elsevier, vol. 48(C): 184–194.

Tanguy, B. and M. Torero. 2015. "Social Interaction Effects and Connection to Electricity: Experimental Evidence from Rural Ethiopia." *Economic Development and Cultural Change* 63(3): 459–484.

Torero, M. 2015. "The Impact of Rural Electrification. " *AFD Research Paper Series,* No. 2015–16, May.

Trillas, F. 2010. "Independent Regulators: Theory, Evidence and Reform Proposals." *IESE Business School* Working Paper No. 860.

Trillas, F. and S. Gianandrea. 2007. "Regulatory Reform, Development And Distributive Concerns." IESE Research Papers D/665, IESE Business School.

Trillas, F. and M. A. Montoya. 2009. "The Measurement of Regulator Independence in Practice: Latin America and the Caribbean." *International Journal of Public Policy* 4(1/2): 113–134.

Vagliasindi, M. 2008. "The Effectiveness of Boards of Directors of State Owned Enterprises in Developing Countries." World Bank Policy Research Working Papers, March.

———. 2012. "The Role of Regulatory Governance in Driving PPPs in Electricity Transmission and Distribution in Developing Countries: A Cross-Country Analysis." Policy Research Working Paper 6121, World Bank, Washington, DC

———. 2013. *Revisiting Public-Private Partnerships in the Power Sector.* Washington, DC: World Bank.

Vagliasindi, M. and J. Besant-Jones. 2013. *Power Market Structure: Revisiting Policy Options.* Directions in Development. Washington, DC: World Bank.

von Hirschhausen, C. and T. Waelde. 2001. "The End of Transition: An Institutional Interpretation of Energy Sector Reform in Eastern Europe and CIS." *Economic Policy in Transitional Economies* 11(1): 93–110.

Waddington, H., B. Snilstveit, H. White, and L. Fewtrell. 2009. "Water, Sanitation and Hygiene Interventions to Combat Childhood Diarrhoea in Developing Countries." Synthetic Review No. 001. New Delhi, India: International Initiative for Impact Evaluation (3ie).

Wade, R. H. 2003. *Governing the Market: Economic Theory and the Role of Government in East Asian Industrialization.* Princeton, NJ: Princeton University Press.

Wantchekon, L. and P. Vicente. 2009. "Clientism and Vote Buying: Lessons from Field Experiments in West Africa." *Oxford Review of Economic Policy* 25.2: 292–305.

WHO. 2010. "Think Big Start Small Scale Up: A Road Map to Support Country-Level Implantation of Water Safety Plans." Geneva: World Health Organization. http://www.who.int/water_sanitation _health/publications/thinkbigstartsmall/en/.

Williamson, O. E. 1999. "Public and Private Bureaucracies: A Transaction Cost Economics Perspectives." *Journal of Law Economics and Organization:* 306–342.

———. 2000. "The New Institutional Economics: Taking Stock, Looking Ahead." *Journal of Economic Literature* 38(3): 595–613, September.

Wilson, J. Q. 1989. *Bureaucracy: What Government Agencies Do and Why They Do It.* Basic Books.

Woodruff, C. 2006. "Measuring Institutions." In *International Handbook on the Economics of Corruption,* edited by Rose-Ackerman, chap. 3. Cheltenham: Edward Elgar.

World Bank. 1994. *World Development Report 1994: Infrastructure for Development.* Washington, DC.

———. 2015. *World Development Report—Mind, Society, and Behavior.* Washington, DC.

World Economic Forum. 2012. Financing Green Growth in a Resource-constrained World: Partnerships for Triggering Private Finance at Scale.

Wren-Lewis, L. 2015. "Do Infrastructure Reforms Reduce the Effect of Corruption? Theory and Evidence from Latin America and the Caribbean." *World Bank Economic Review* World Bank Group 29(2): 353–384.

Yanez-Pagans, M. and G. Machicado-Salas. 2014. "Bureaucratic Delay, Local-Level Monitoring, and Delivery of Small Infrastructure Projects: Evidence from a Field Experiment in Bolivia." *World Development* 59(C): 394–407.

18

EDUCATION, INSTITUTIONS, AND DEVELOPMENT

Tessa Bold and Jakob Svensson

18.1. INTRODUCTION

An educated workforce is necessary for long-run economic growth and a high standard of living. Increasing the human capital of the poor may also be one of the most effective ways to reduce absolute poverty and increase economic mobility.

Over the last 25 years, school enrollment, at all levels, has increased universally, and most children in developing countries now complete primary school. For example, the primary enrollment rate in South Asia and Sub-Saharan Africa was 51 and 61, respectively in 1970 and was in both cases over 100 in 2010 (see table 18.1). However, enrolling in school does not guarantee that children acquire the human capital they are expected to. In fact, a growing literature has documented that a large share of children in low-income countries learn little and complete their primary education lacking even basic reading, writing, and arithmetic skills. For example, across grade 6 students in 15 Southern and Eastern African countries tested as part of the SACMEQ assessment in 2007, less than 50% got beyond the level of "reading for meaning" and less than 40% got beyond "basic numeracy." Among sixth grade students tested in 10 Francophone countries in Western and Central Africa in 2015 as part of the PASEC assessment, less than 45% surpassed the "sufficient" competency level in reading or mathematics (Hungi et al. 2010). Test results from (rural) India in 2013 show, for example, that 38% of children in third grade in public schools could not read simple words, and less than 27% could master double-digit subtraction (ASER 2013). Thus, in many low-income countries, the increase in school enrollment has not resulted in a general increase in human capital.

In response to these poor learning outcomes, in the last decade there has been a push, both by economists and education researchers, to identify ways to improve the quality of education. To date, there are more than 150 high-quality impact studies from developing countries on various ways to raise test scores. A handful of systematic reviews have also synthesized and drawn conclusions, based on these studies, about the best ways to improve education quality. However, to date, there is no clear consensus among

Table 18.1. Primary enrollment rates

	Primary enrollment 1970	Primary enrollment 2010	Primary completion rate 2010
OECD	104	103	99
East Asia & Pacific	95	112	99
East Europe & Central Asia	105	103	98
Latin America & Caribbean	102	107	98
Middle East & North Africa	77	105	98
South Asia	51	110	92
Sub-Saharan Africa	61	109	68

Source: World Bank Development Indicators.

researchers about what are the most effective ways to increase the quality of primary education.

The starting point in this review is different. While the systematic reviews are important, there are also clear limitations of what one can learn from them—given variation in context, variation in the details of the design, and the fact that most interventions, by design, include various components. Maybe even more problematic, given (a) the decentralized way research is organized, and rightly so; (b) the interdependence of various factors determining learning outcomes; and (c) the lack of systematic evidence of what teachers actually do and know, it is difficult to assess whether the interventions that have been assessed experimentally really are the interventions one ought to focus on. For these reasons, this review begins with recent work by Bold et al. (2017a), which uses data from nationally representative surveys from seven Sub-Saharan African countries, representing close to 40% of the region's total population, to assess what primary school teachers in Sub-Saharan Africa know and do. This assessment provides an empirical context through which the growing experimental and quasi-experimental literature on education in low-income countries can be interpreted and understood. It also points to important gaps in our knowledge, with implications for future research and policy.

Questions about government implementation and scaling up are also largely missing from the existing reviews. That is, the reviews draw heavily from studies that mainly examine demand and supply factors at the individual or school level, often with well-functioning NGOs and/or the research team playing an important role in implementing, monitoring, and supervising the intervention. While these studies are crucial for identifying potentially scalable cost-effective interventions, and for estimating key mechanisms at play, when moving from impact estimates to policy guidance it is crucial to also take into account various implementation constraints. We focus on two such implementation constraints here.

First, many interventions implemented at the school level hinge on the existence of a third party that can monitor and enforce the program—typically a higher authority. As discussed in this Handbook (Baland, Bourguignon, Platteau, and Verdier, this volume), such an enforcement mechanism can be seen as a defining feature of formal institutions. Enforcement, in turn, requires the possibility of sanctions. In many low-income countries, however, those (public) agencies/actors assigned to enforce education programs are often weak and possibly corrupt. We label these type of constraints "local rent-seeking constraint" and discuss attempts to study them as well as ways to relax them. We also briefly discuss the role of voice versus exit. Specifically, in settings in which public institutions do not work well, an argument could be made to facilitate low-income families' exit options; i.e., enroll their children in private schools.

Second, national scale-up may induce political economy reactions from groups whose rents are threatened by the new policy. We label these as national rent-seeking constraints and again discuss attempts to study them and speculate on ways to relax them. Importantly, we argue and show that an experimental approach can also be used to study both of these implementation constraints.

Overall, our focus here is on primary education in low-income countries, with a specific focus on Sub-Saharan Africa.

We proceed by first providing a brief review of the recent reviews of the experimental and quasi-experimental literature on the quality of education. We then briefly discuss recent evidence of student learning. Thereafter we summarize the main findings in Bold et al. (2017a) on what teachers know and do; i.e., we provide an empirical context through which the literature on improving learning outcomes could be interpreted. The stylized facts we present, we argue, suggest that teacher effort, knowledge, and skills are crucial binding constraints in low-income countries, and especially so in Sub-Saharan Africa, and we therefore briefly discuss the available evidence on attempts to address them. We thereafter turn to the issues of scaling up and the politics of education and discuss two implementation constraints (local and national rent-seeking constraints). We end by outlining research questions and areas that need more work.

18.2. A SHORT REVIEW OF THE REVIEWS

There is no shortage of reviews about the best ways to raise student test scores. In fact, over the last few years at least eight such reviews have been published. Kremer, Brannen, and Glennerster (2013)—a narrative review of a set of randomized controlled trials (RCTs)—argue that interventions that match teaching to student learning levels, contract teachers, and interventions improving access to schooling are the most effective. Krishnaratne, White, and Carpenter (2013)—a meta-analysis of 69 RCT and quasi-experimental studies—argue that the most compelling evidence of what works is computer-assisted learning tools, a result closely in line with McEwan's (2015) meta-analysis of 77 RCT studies. Murnane and Ganimian (2016), on the other hand, in a narrative review drawing on 115 RCT and quasi-experimental studies, conclude that the strongest evidence (unconditionally) of impact comes from studies providing information about school quality and returns to schooling. Conn (2017)—a meta-analysis based on 56 studies conducted in Sub-Saharan Africa—finds that pedagogical interventions (changes in instructional techniques) have the highest effect size on achievement outcomes. Glewwe and Muralidharan (2016)—employing a voting counting approach based on 118 studies (of which 80 are RCTs)—conclude that teaching at the right level (remedial programs) and teacher performance and accountability interventions are the most promising.[1]

Overall, the reviews show that there is by now a substantial number of high-quality, micro-based studies on the effects of various demand and supply interventions. Several of these interventions have been implemented in different contexts, and with slight variations in the design, but still yielded similar impact estimates. Still, based on the reviews, no clear consensus exists, based on the micro estimates only, about the most effective ways to increase student learning.

18.3. THE QUALITY OF PRIMARY EDUCATION—WITH A FOCUS ON SUB-SAHARAN AFRICA

What do we really know about quality (learning) in primary education in Sub-Saharan Africa? In the last decade, the International Association for the Evaluation of Educational Achievement (IEA) and OECD testing programs have expanded dramatically, with more than 100 participating countries in at least one of these assessments in 2012 (Hanusheck and Woessmann 2015). Low-income countries, and countries in Sub-Saharan Africa in particular, are still largely not included in these international assessments. For example, only one Sub-Saharan African country (Botswana) participated in the last IEA mathematics tests at the primary level, and only three countries (Botswana, Ghana, and South Africa) participated at the secondary level.[2] As illustrated in table 18.2, test results at the secondary level for these three countries suggest *average* test scores below the lowest *5th percentile* score in the United States. But even those low scores are likely biased upward since in all three countries, a significant share of students performed worse than chance (based on multiple choice items), implying that the tests are unable to provide a reliable measurement of average student achievement (TIMSS 2011).

There exist a number of regional testing programs in Africa, including SACMEQ (tests students in 15 Southern and Eastern African countries), PASEC (tests students in Francophone countries in Western and Central Africa), and Uwezo (tests children in Kenya, Tanzania, and Uganda). The results from these assessments also paint a bleak picture. As mentioned in the introduction, of the grade 6 students tested as part of the SACMEQ assessment in 2007, less than 50% got beyond the level of "reading for meaning" and less than 40% got beyond "basic numeracy." Among sixth grade students tested in 10 Francophone countries in Western and Central Africa in 2015 as part of the PASEC assessment, less than 45% surpass the "sufficient" competency level in reading or mathematics (Hungi et al. 2010).

Table 18.2. International test scores, mathematics

Country	Region	Mean Score	Grade assessed	Lowest 5th percentile	Percentage of students performing below chance
Ghana	Lower middle income	331	8th		33
South Africa	Lower middle income	352	9th		32
Botswana	Upper middle income	397	9th		19
USA	High income, OECD	509	8th	308	3

Source: TIMMS 2011.

Bold et al. (2017b) present evidence from the Service Delivery Indicator program, which to date have collected data from nationally representative surveys of primary schools from seven Sub-Saharan African countries, representing close to 40% of the region's total population. Fourth grade students in sampled schools were assessed in basic reading, writing, and arithmetic skills, the "three Rs," based on a review of primary curriculum materials from 13 African countries.

After three completed years of primary public schooling, almost half of the students assessed could not read a simple word; 70% of the students could not read all the words in a basic sentence. And only one in seven students could read a simple paragraph and infer meaning from it.[3]

In mathematics, two out of ten students could not recognize numbers, and five out of ten students could not order numbers between 0 and 100; 20% could not do single-digit addition, and three in four could not do single-digit subtraction. Just over half of the students assessed managed double-digit addition, and less than a third mastered double-digit subtraction—tasks that, according to the official curriculum, students should master at the end of grade 3.

Using the raw test scores to determine the grade level of proficiency of students—a test score measure they label as "effective human capital years acquired," they estimate that, on average, Sub-Saharan African students have about 1.6 years of quality-adjusted human capital after three and half years of studies.

While a significant share of children in primary schools in Sub-Saharan Africa do not learn much in school, Sub-Saharan Africa is unfortunately not a specific case. Test results from (rural) India in 2013 show, for example, that 38% of children in third grade in public schools could not read simple words, and less than 27% could master double-digit subtraction (ASER 2013).

The reasons behind this policy failure are multifaceted. However, evidence from recent research on education in developing countries, showing that traditional educational inputs have little impact on test scores but increasing teacher effort and pedagogy do, suggest that teacher behavior and teacher ability play a crucial role. We turn to this next.

18.4. WHAT DO TEACHERS KNOW AND DO?

Bold et al. (2017a), using data collected through direct observations, unannounced visits, and tests, provide quantitative answers to three questions: How much time do teachers actually spend teaching? Do teachers have the relevant knowledge to teach both basic and higher-order language and mathematics skills? Do teachers have the pedagogical knowledge and skills to transfer what they know to students in an effective way?

On the first question, Bold et al. (2017a) show that students receive about two and a half hours of teaching a day—or less than half the scheduled time—largely because teachers, even when in school, do not teach. Absence from school (about 2 out of 10 teachers on average) turns out to be about as common as being present in the school but absent from class, implying that only 6 out of 10 teachers—on a regular day—are actually teaching. Absenteeism rates also appear to be remarkably stable over time in countries. Chaudhury et al. (2006) estimated a school absence rate of 27% in Uganda in 2002–2003. Bold et al. (2017a) find that 30% of teachers are absent from school, using data collected in 2013.

For teachers to be effective, they must have the knowledge necessary for good teaching. In particular, they must know the subject they teach (subject content knowledge), how to translate this knowledge into meaningful teaching (general and pedagogy content knowledge), and how children learn (knowledge of the context of learning). Subject content knowledge was assessed by given synthetic pieces of children's work in the language of instruction (English/French/Portuguese) and in mathematics based (mainly) on the curriculum the teacher was teaching. Bold et al. (2017a) present results for two outcome measures: whether teachers master their students' curriculum in language and whether they have minimum subject (in language and mathematics) content knowledge.[4]

Bold et al. (2017a) show, even using the very low bar of mastering their students' curriculum, that 40% of primary school teachers are not as knowledgeable as their students should be.[5] Looking at the score for "minimum knowledge," only one in ten language teachers in Sub-Saharan Africa passes the bar.[6] Moreover, subject knowledge among language teachers is also uniformly low across the seven countries. To illustrate what these findings mean, it is informative to disaggregate the scores by task. Bold et al. (2017a) show, for example, that one in five teachers could not spell a simple word (like "traffic" for example).

In mathematics, minimum subject content knowledge was defined as being able to accurately correct children's work in such aspects of numeracy as manipulating numbers using basic operations and solving simple math story problems. This requirement amounts to scoring correctly on 80% of the questions on the lower primary portion of the mathematics test. Bold et al. (2017a) show that less than two-thirds of the mathematics teachers have minimum knowledge according to this definition. Again, the disaggregated scores give an informative sense of teachers' knowledge: 23 percent of mathematics teachers could not subtract double digits and 30% could not multiply double digits. When it comes to understanding and solving a simple math story problem, about half of the teachers managed to do so. Bold et al. (2017a) further show that when looking at more advanced tasks, such as interpreting information in a Venn diagram and/or a graph, only a minority of mathematics teachers, and in some countries almost none, could master them.

Knowing one's subject and curriculum is a necessary, but not sufficient, condition for good teaching. Teachers must also know how to translate their subject knowledge into effective pedagogy. Bold et al. (2017a) provide information on two scores—teachers' knowledge of pedagogy and the context of learning—and in both cases the results are depressing. Only 10% of teachers reached the threshold for having minimum general pedagogy knowledge and essentially no teachers were knowledgeable about the context of learning.[7]

Combining their measures of teacher effort, knowledge, and skills, Bold et al. (2017a) estimate that very few primary public school students in the seven countries they surveyed attend schools where teachers spend a significant share of the scheduled time teaching a subject they master to teach.

A growing literature has documented large impacts for students, both in the short and longer run, of being taught by high-quality teachers. For example, Chetty, Friedman, and Rockoff (2014) estimate, using data for more than one million US children, that replacing a teacher whose measured quality is in the bottom 5% with an average teacher would increase the present value of students' lifetime income by approximately $250,000 per classroom. Similarly, the results presented in Bau and Das (2017), using data from the province of Punjab, Pakistan, strongly suggest that teacher quality matters as much or more for students in low-income countries. In Bold et al. (2017b) the authors exploit the Service Delivery Indicator data to estimate the effect of teacher content knowledge on student performance. As mentioned above, they find that after four years of schooling, the majority of students fail to master tasks covered in the second-year curriculum. They further show that this result, exploiting within-student within-teacher variation, adjusting for the cumulative process of knowledge acquisition, imperfect persistence in learning between grades, and measurement error, can partly be explained by the fact that many teachers struggle with tasks that their students should master in lower primary. Their estimates imply that had all students been taught by teachers deemed to master the lower secondary curriculum—a minimum official criterion in the countries in the sample—students would have acquired on average 1.5 more years of curriculum-adjusted human capital after four years.

We next turn to the growing experimental literature in education to review what we know about effective ways to raise teacher effort, knowledge, and skills.

18.5. TEACHER EFFORT, KNOWLEDGE, AND SKILLS: WHAT'S THE EVIDENCE?

18.5.1. Teacher Effort

On teacher effort, knowledge, and skills, economists have, by far, so far, focused on interventions aimed at incentivizing teachers to exert higher effort. Following Glewwe and Muralidharan (2016), we can group these interventions into four sets: (a) Performance pay; i.e., linking payments to attendance or test score; (b) Community monitoring; i.e., bottom-up approaches intended to increase monitoring by parents and the local community; (c) Strengthening existing institutions, such as school committees or PTAs that play a monitoring and disciplining role; (d) Contract teachers; i.e., linking tenure to performance.

18.5.1.1. Performance Pay

The results from studies assessing performance pay is overall positive. Duflo, Hanna, and Ryan (2012) assess an intervention in which teacher attendance in informal schools in Rajasthan, India, was monitored using cameras and teachers were paid as a function of the number of valid days of attendance. They document a large reduction in teacher absence rates (from 42% to 21%), and a smaller but significant increase in student test scores.

Muralidharan and Sundararaman (2011) evaluate a bonus payment program to teachers (in India) based on the average improvement of their students' test scores. They do not observe any reduction in teacher absence from school (and do not measure absenteeism from classrooms conditional on being in school). However, they too document a significant increase in student test scores, including in subjects that were not "incentivized."

Glewwe, Ilias, and Kremer (2010), on the other hand, who also evaluate a bonus payment program (in Kenya), but where bonuses were paid to schools based on best performance, show that students scored higher on the exams linked to teacher incentives but
not on other exams. That is, consistent with Holmström and Milgrom's (1991) multitasking model, teachers appeared to have reallocated effort from uncompensated, but
potentially important, activities toward compensated activities ("teaching to the test").

18.5.1.2. Community Monitoring
The results from studies evaluating community monitoring as a way to strengthen local
accountability relationships are mixed. Banerjee et al. (2010) study different approaches
to enhance community involvement in primary schools in Uttar Pradesh, India. They
find no impact on community participation, teacher effort, or learning outcomes.

Pandey, Goyal, and Sundararaman (2009) evaluate an information campaign to improve parental participation in village education committees (in India). They find positive impacts on various process measures but, in general, mixed evidence on learning
outcomes.

18.5.1.3. Strengthening Local Institutions
A related set of interventions focus on strengthening already existing local institutions,
with the objective of getting these locally grounded institutions to become more active
as monitors of local service provision.

Pradhan et al. (2014) assess a series of interventions with the focus to enhance community participation in school management (in Indonesia). In one of their intervention
arms, which involved democratic elections of school committee members and linking
the school committee to the village council through facilitated meetings, they document
an increase in language test scores, but no effects in mathematics.

Lassibille et al. (2010) and Glewwe and Maiga (2011) evaluate the AGEMAD program
in Madagascar—a large-scale program aimed at strengthening school management at
the district, subdistrict, school, and teacher levels. Neither study found an impact on student test score.

On the other hand, Duflo, Dupas, and Kremer's (2015) study of a contract teacher program in which, in one treatment arm, school-based management (SBM) training was
provided to the PTA committee and, importantly, the decision whether to renew the contract teachers' contracts was delegated to the PTA, showed better performance of contract teachers and significant improvements in student achievement.

18.5.1.4. Contract Teachers
Another set of studies focus on providing incentives to teachers (specifically newly hired
teachers) by making tenure decisions conditional on performance.

Duflo, Dupas, and Kremer (2015) design their experiment (in Kenya) in a way that separates out the direct effect of incentives from the effect of class size reduction; i.e., students can benefit from two effects of hiring a new contract teacher with a contract where
tenure is conditional on performance. First, provided the incentives bind, students taught
by the contract teachers may benefit from a teacher exerting higher effort. Second, as the
number of teachers teaching increases in response to the hire, students may benefit from
a lower student-teacher ratio. The authors find that holding class size constant, students

taught by contract teachers scored higher on tests than those taught by civil service teachers, even though the contract teachers are paid much lower salaries.

Bold et al. (2018) replicate the Duflo et al. (2015) study across different parts of Kenya. They find positive and significant effects of the contract teacher program, across diverse baseline conditions, when the contract teacher program was administered by an international NGO.

Muralidharan and Sundararaman (2013) assess the impact of an extra contract teacher in government-run schools (in India). They show that contract teachers were less likely to be absent from school than civil service teachers, and students in schools with an extra contract teacher performed significantly better in both math and language tests, respectively.

18.5.1.5. Sum-up: Teacher Effort

There is strong evidence that teacher effort can be raised, leading to improved learning outcomes, by linking payments or tenure to performance. Details in the design of the incentive program appear to matter, however. Softer incentives, through strengthening and encouraging existing local institutions or the community more generally to become more active as monitors of teachers, appear to be less effective. However, while incentivizing effort results in higher effort exerted by the teacher, and increased test score of students, it is important to stress that incentivizing effort alone likely will not be enough to substantially increase student learning outcomes, given teachers' limited knowledge and skills as briefly presented above. That is, there is an obvious upper bar on the effect of exerting more effort to teach when one cannot master the subject one teaches. This is in fact indirectly evident from the studies themselves: Given the large gaps in student knowledge, the estimated effect sizes are relatively small.

18.5.2. Teacher Knowledge

While there are by now numerous studies on ways to elicit more effort from teachers, the evidence on cost-effective ways to increase content knowledge of teachers, and the impact thereof, are largely missing. In fact, there is no high-quality study on the impact on student learning of raising the content knowledge of teachers, and research on this topic is urgently called for. This is especially true given the effect sizes documented in Bold et al. (2017b).

18.5.3 Teacher Skills

A smaller number of studies have evaluated intervention that at least broadly could be interpreted as dealing with primary school pedagogy. One can divide these studies into three groups:[8] (i) Remedial education programs, where new instructors are trained to provide basic education to children lagging behind; (ii) Tracking of students, where students with similar observable skills are grouped together in order to make it easier for teachers to more effectively match the difficulty level they teach to the level of their students; (iii) Literary programs, in which new or existing teachers are trained to provide a pre-specified literary program.

Before reviewing the evidence on these three types of interventions, it is important to note that all of these interventions involve more changes at the school or student level than changing the pedagogy. Of course, in itself this should not be viewed as a shortcoming. In fact, there are very strong reasons to believe there are important com-plementarities between school inputs, teacher effort, knowledge, and skills, and research-ers have so far paid too little attention to trying to quantify and understand these complementarities. Even so, the results from the evaluations discussed below do raise the question of exactly what combination of changes is driving the findings.

18.5.3.1. Remedial Education Programs

A smaller set of randomized trials has assessed the impact of remedial education pro-grams, all finding positive, and typically large, effects on student learning. Banerjee et al. (2007) evaluate a remedial education program in the Indian cities of Mumbai and Vadodara, where an informal teacher taught children lagging behind two hours per day. They show that the program resulted in improved students' test scores in both math and English and argue that the effect was driven by the fact that students being pulled out of the classroom (to receive remedial education) were taught at a level corresponding to their current proficiency.

Banerjee et al. (2010) assess a remedial instruction program, also in India, where read-ing camps were run by trained youth volunteers. The program resulted in a significant and relatively large increase in literacy.

Lakshminarayana et al. (2013) evaluate a remedial education program in a set of vil-lages in Andhra Pradesh in which volunteers provided two hours of remedial instruc-tion per day after normal school hours. They too document large and significant increases on language test scores.

18.5.3.2. Tracking

While a number of studies have evaluated different versions of remedial education pro-grams, much less is known about the impact of tracking students. Duflo, Dupas, and Kremer's (2011) is an exception. They assess an intervention in Kenya in which students were tracked and streamed based on initial test score. The intervention resulted in in-creased student test scores that remained (at least) one year after the program ended.

18.5.3.3. Literary Programs

The impact of various literacy programs has been assessed in several studies, with some-what varying results. Abeberese, Kumler, and Linden (2014) evaluate the short-run im-pact of a reading program for grade 4 students in the Philippines where teachers were trained and provided with age-appropriate reading materials—materials that were in-tended to be incorporated into their teaching. The program had significant but relatively small effects on reading scores after four months.

Lucas et al. (2014) assess a reading instruction intervention implemented in a set of schools in both Kenya and Uganda. The program involved several components, includ-ing training of teachers, regular support to teachers, and provision of new material. The evaluation showed that the reading intervention resulted in significant positive effects in Uganda, but smaller and less precise effects in Kenya.

Piper and Korda (2011) evaluate a literacy instruction program in Liberia. As in Lucas et al. (2014), the intervention involved several components. Specifically, in the full treat-ment group, reading levels were assessed; teachers were trained how to continually assess student performance; teachers were provided frequent school-based pedagogic support, resource materials, and books; and, in addition, parents and communities were informed of student performance. After 18 months, and starting from a low level, the program dramatically accelerated children's learning.

18.5.3.4. Sum-up: Teacher Skills (Pedagogy)

There is strong evidence that very basic pedagogical interventions, including providing simple teaching at the right level, i.e., remedial education programs, and providing teachers with hands-on, focused training on how to teach scripted lessons effectively, improve student outcomes starting from very low levels.

However, it is important to note that these programs, just like some of the successful computer-assisted learning programs, are to some extent programs intended to "automate" the teacher (to follow rather simple tasks). Given the low level of knowledge and skills of teachers, as discussed in section 18.4, such interventions may at least in the short run be an effective method to raise learning outcomes, especially at early grades and for lower-order learning. But it is also clear that there are obvious limits to what these kinds of program can achieve. More generally, there is still scant evidence on how to effectively improve general pedagogy at primary school in low-income countries. For example, we know little about how to effectively teach teachers how to teach "higher-order" tasks. We know little of how to improve pedagogy along the dimensions uncovered in the SDI, including having clearly structured lessons; having an appropriate mix of basic and higher-order tasks; being able to write lesson plans; and being able to assess students' progress and give feedback.

18.6. FROM EXPERIMENTAL STUDIES TO SCALABLE POLICIES

In the best-case scenario, with high levels of governmental capacity and commitment, the evidence reviewed above could have a direct bearing on policy design and policy reform in the education sector. Such reforms would likely involve reform of the curriculum (including defining learning standards in core subjects for every grade level and curricula well-aligned with the learning standards); introduce a process for assessing student mastery of the standards; develop teacher training programs that attract talented students and prepare them to teach the curriculum effectively; and put in place effective incentives schemes that ensures high effort and continued upgrading of knowledge and skills.

However, in most low-income settings, the problems identified at the school level—low efforts, capacity, skills—characterize the whole service delivery chain, making the transition from the identification of cost-effective interventions to evidence-based policymaking a complicated one.

Assembling information on the cost-effectiveness of various potential reforms/interventions provides a crucial first step in a strategy to develop an evidence-based policy program, but in general, and especially in countries characterized by weak institutions and a capacity-constrained public sector, that evidence only is not enough to guide policy. Thus, while many of these studies differ starkly from so-called proof-of-concept studies in medicine and public health, where the participants' behavior is partly controlled, they still provide estimates of effectiveness that may significantly depart from what can be achieved when going to scale and/or when moving to government implementation.

When identifying, choosing, and designing programs to be scaled-up, and especially when the scaled-up version involves government implementation, it is important to have an understanding of the whole delivery chain; from the institutional constraints that affect central government policy decisions, through the incentive constraints that influence different layers of government agencies and officials implementing a given policy, to the actions and incentives of teachers and students (and parents).

One way to conceptualize the problem is to think of implementation design as identifying the most cost-effective interventions subject to two rent-seeking constraints. First, local actors—be they teachers, local public officials, or supervisors—may try to extract rent from the program which, if they are successful, lowers the program's impact. Second, large-scale implementation may provoke political economy reactions because rents of powerful insiders are threatened. Such an endogenous policy response—a "seesaw effect" to use the terminology of Acemoglu (2010)—may counteract and even reverse the objectives of reform. We can think of the first implementation constraint as a "local rent-seeking constraint" and the second as a "national rent-seeking constraint." We turn to a discussion of the research on them next.

18.6.1. Local Rent-Seeking Constraints

Social service delivery in many developed countries grew out of a system of locally governed institutions. Importantly, these locally governed institutions, some of them now formalized into the local institutional framework that is intended to ensure high quality and adequate services, still play an important role. In many low-income countries, on the other hand, the adoption of centralized state control over service delivery at independence, coupled with a weak central state, have resulted in a system characterized by centralized, but weak, state control and often low-capacity, locally governed institutions for education provision. The education system is characterized by extensive leakage and inefficiencies, where parents have little influence on how schools are managed. Any intervention intended to be sustainably run in such an institutional environment needs to be carefully designed to take these institutional constraints into account.

The research on how community participation and civil society organizations could be strengthened and the impact thereof take its starting point in this institutional failure to deliver high-quality services. In short, as beneficiaries (parents) ought to have intrinsic motivations to ensure that children learn in school, local control is viewed as a way to overcome the "monitoring the monitor problem." The focus on civil society and community participation is also important since, historically, civil society has played an important role in the advancement of institutional/political reforms in many countries. Moreover, community participation interventions, primarily meant to (informally) influence norms and collective actions and thereby local decision-making, can be viewed as an attempt to enhance common interests, albeit starting at a small scale, and the strength of common interest in society, together with the structure of political institutions, has recently been highlighted in the macro-political literature as key underlying determinants for policy decisions in sectors like education and health (see for instance Besley and Persson 2011).

In policy discussions, and at an abstract level, service delivery is often discussed as a principal-agent problem where the government is the principal that sets policy and delegates implementation and monitoring to various lower-level public actors. Implicit in this approach is that lower-level public actors will mechanically execute what they are asked to do (and do so in a way that benefits the intended beneficiaries). This, however, contrast starkly with the way in which policy implementation is carried out in practice. In practice, policy implementation and monitoring are delegated to agents that themselves are not monitored, resulting in a broken accountability link (the who's monitoring the monitors problem).

The micro-political research on service delivery, again at an abstract level, basically turn the incentive problem upside-down, viewing individual citizens as the principals and service delivery actors as agents. As the principal's ability to control the agents is typically constrained by the local institutions in place, the core objective of this research program is to identify ways to relax such constraints.

The canonical contract problem requires the principal to write sufficiently detailed contracts ex ante and the ability to measure and verify performance ex post, and such types of contracts may simply be unfeasible in many settings. Thus, a complementary approach, again at an abstract level, is the incomplete contract approach, where the issue is how to optimally assign decision rights to different actors, including individual citizens or communities, to influence bargaining strengths and thus influence incentives.

We next turn to discuss two incentive contract approaches to deal with local rent-seeking constraints: Local control and private provision.

18.6.1.1. Local Control

There is a growing literature on local accountability (local control, beneficiary control, community monitoring) with what appears, at first sight, to include, at best, mixed findings. However, a closer investigation of the interventions that have been designed and evaluated suggests that a pattern is emerging. Specifically, interventions that yield users decision rights (formal or informal) or assist in the process of agreeing on contract-specifying actions, and, importantly, address underlying informational asymmetries by either provision of relevant and actionable information or provision of tools for beneficiaries to acquire such information, do seem to result in improved service delivery performance and improved outcomes. On the contrary, interventions focusing on enhancing participation where service delivery problems are vented and discussed, and/or provide information that is not directly informative or actionable, do not appear to result in systematic changes in service delivery performance.

Specifically, Björkman and Svensson (2009) and Björkman, de Walque, and Svensson (2017) analyze the impact of various ways to strengthen local accountability in primary health care in Uganda. Björkman and Svensson (2009) designed an intervention (*information & participation intervention*) that combined traditional tools to enhance community participation with the dissemination of report card information on staff performance. The intervention can, again at a somewhat abstract level, be viewed as the facilitation of a contract problem; i.e., the community's (the principal's) problem of eliciting effort from the service provider (the agent). In fact, a core component of the intervention was the design of a joint contract specifying actions that need to be taken and by whom and when. In such a contract, the final outcome depends on the principal's ability to identify tasks that both map into better health service and can be influenced by the health workers' actions. It also depends on the principal's ability to observe actions and the compensation scheme.[9] When applying the framework to community monitoring, one must also take into account the fact that there are multiple principals (the users) who may disagree about both objectives and the mapping between actions and outcomes. The participatory component of the intervention was intended to facilitate the process of reaching an agreement. Providing information on performance was also intended to enhance that process but was primarily intended to assist the principal in identifying and observing actionable tasks over time.

Björkman and Svensson (2009) show that a year after the intervention began, treatment communities were more involved in monitoring the provider, and health workers appeared to exert greater effort to serve the community. They further document large increases in utilization and improved health outcomes, including reduced child mortality, that compare favorably to some of the more successful community-based intervention trials reported in the medical literature.

Björkman, de Walque, and Svensson (2017) assess the longer-run impact of the community-driven local accountability studied in Björkman and Svensson (2009). They also examine the role of information in these kinds of community-driven accountability programs. To that end, an additional intervention (*participation intervention*), which replicated the participatory components of the original intervention but did not provide communities with baseline information on performance, was designed, evaluated, and compared to the information & participation intervention.

Björkman et al. (2017) present two key findings. First, the large treatment effects on staff performance and health outcomes identified in the short run (in the information & participation intervention) remain more than four years after the initial intervention despite minimal follow-up. Second, the impact of the cheaper participation intervention differed markedly from the impact of the information & participation intervention—both in the short and longer run. In fact, without information, the process of stimulating participation and engagement had little impact on the staff's behavior, health outcomes, or the quality of healthcare.

To investigate why the provision of information appeared to have played such a key role, the authors use data from the implementation phases of the two interventions. A core component of both experiments was the agreement of a joint action plan, or contract, outlining the community's and the providers' agreement on what needs to be done, and by whom, in order to improve healthcare delivery. They show that while the process of reaching an agreement looks similar on some observable measures in the two treatment groups—for example, similar number of community members participated in the community meetings and, on average, the two groups identified the same number of actions to be addressed—the types of issues identified differ significantly. Specifically, and as illustrated in figure 18.1, in the participation group the health provider and the community identified issues that primarily required third-party actions; e.g., more financial and in-kind support from upper-level authorities and NGOs. In the information & participation group, by contrast, the participants focused almost exclusively on local problems, which either the health workers or the users could address themselves, including absenteeism, opening hours, waiting time, and patient-clinician interactions. These results are consistent with the hypothesis that lack of information on performance makes it more difficult to identify and challenge (mis)behavior by the provider, and hence constrains the community's ability to hold providers to account. That is, with access to information, users are better able to distinguish between the actions of health workers and

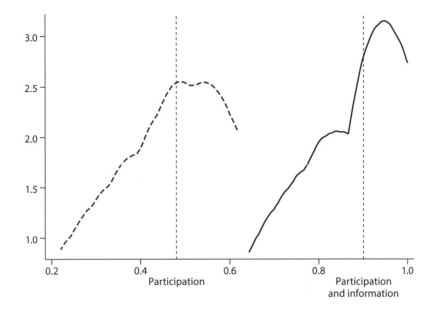

FIGURE 18.1. Share of location actions in action plan. *Source*: Björkman, de Walque, and Svensson (2017).

factors beyond their control and, as a result, turn their focus to issues that they can manage and work on locally.

The study by Duflo et al. (2015), while different in several dimensions, reinforces the conclusion above.[10] Specifically, Duflo et al. (2015) evaluate a contract teachers program in Kenya where one of their treatment arms included School-Based Management (SBM) training of the PTA committee. Committee members were given specific training on how to monitor and assess teachers' effort and performance, and a set of parents were asked to perform attendance checks on the teachers on a regular basis. A formal subcommittee of parents was formed to evaluate the contract teacher and deliver a performance report at the end of the year. The PTA was also given influence over the decision whether to retain the contract teacher or not. While this intervention did not directly provide quantitative information on performance, it provided detailed training to the community on how to measure it throughout the year and how to combine the information in a performance report that could be shared with others. Thus, in short, the intervention assigned decision rights to parents and provided them with tools to collect performance information. Duflo et al. (2015) show that SBM training for PTA committees with formal decision rights reduced teachers' absenteeism and increased student test scores.

More generally, the study also highlights two additional important results. First, in the presence of weak institutions, increases in resources, as was the case here, may be undermined by the behavioral response of existing providers. This in essence is the local rent-seeking constraints. Second, and importantly, the solution to this problem is not some general decentralization reform, as devolving control of various educational aspects to districts, absent complementary governance reforms, may allow local agents of the state to use devolution to capture rents.

18.6.1.2. Private Provision: Voice vs. Exit

Decision rights could be delegated to a group of beneficiaries as in Duflo et al. (2015). But it could also be delegated to individuals. One example of that is to provide parents with a choice of which service provider, or school more specifically, to send their children to. If funding follows the student, parents' bargaining rights are then strengthened and in principle this might provide incentives for public schools to improve service provision. More generally, in settings in which public institutions do not work well, and reforms of the system are difficult to implement, and even if public funds do not follow students, a strong argument could be made to facilitate low-income families' exit options; for example by providing vouchers to low-income households that would allow them to enroll their children in private schools.

There has been a rapid growth of private schools in low-income countries in recent years, although public spending on education in many low-income countries has increased. Baum et al. (2014), for example, estimate that private schools account for approximately 20% of total primary school enrollment in low-income countries. There are several reasons for this private sector expansion. For example, many have argued that the huge growth in enrollment, largely as a result of removals of user fees in public schools, has further diluted the quality of public education, resulting in increased demand, especially from better off households.

The main criticism of private schooling is that it causes increased economic stratification and reduces pressure of public schools to supply quality education. Whether that is true or not is likely to depend on how the actual subsidization of privately provided education is organized. Moreover, if the idea is to subsidize poor households' ability to send their children to private schools, the concern that it will increase economic stratification is likely muted.

Of course, private schooling per se does not necessarily mean that the quality is high. However, one could at least make a credible argument that private schools should be more accountable and responsive to parents. Moreover, the Service Delivery Indicators data we discuss in section 18.4, while providing evidence of substantial shortcomings with respect to effort, knowledge, and skills also among primary teachers in private schools, still show that in all these dimensions, teachers in private schools outperform teachers in public schools (Bold et al. 2017c).

In the end, whether scarce funds should be spent on facilitating poor households' exit options or not is primarily an empirical question, one for which to date we have very little high-quality evidence.

In fact, there is only one randomized control study on the impact of vouchers in primary education. Specifically, Muralidharan and Sundararaman (2015) evaluate a voucher program to assess the *individual impacts* of school choice. They find no difference between the test scores of voucher beneficiaries (or more precisely their children) in language (native language of Andhra Pradesh) and mathematics, but private schools spend significantly less instructional time on local language and math and more on English and other subjects (Hindi).

Clearly, more research is needed here. The impact of voucher programs is likely to be context-specific and depend on the quality of accessible and affordable private schools. General equilibrium effects, and especially whether, and if so to what extent, students in public sector schools are adversely affected if vouchers for private schools are provided to a significant segment of the student population, are issues we know little about. Overall, and connecting back to the proof-of-principle discussion that began this section, whether the voucher program is done as a small separate activity or as part of an overall reform of the education sector (where funds follow students) will obviously matter greatly for the impacts one would tend to observe.

18.6.2. National Rent-Seeking Constraints

Large-scale policy implementation may provoke political economy reactions because rents of powerful insiders are threatened. Such a "seesaw effect" may undermine the very objective of the reform, and failure to anticipate it, and adjust policy accordingly, may severely impact what in the end will be implemented.

National rent-seeking constraints, and the seesaw effect in particular, are illustrated in the work of Bold et al. (2018). This paper takes one of the criticisms of the RCT literature head on; i.e., the issue of external validity in policy analysis, and importantly, it does so without relaxing the emphasis on identification.

The study takes as its starting point one of the more extensively tested school-level interventions to raise student learning in primary schools: the provision of contract teachers. Compared to a civil servant teacher who is given immediate tenure and faces few pecuniary incentives to exert high effort as salaries and promotions are largely determined by seniority, a contract teacher is thought to improve learning through two channels: a selection effect, as better performing contract teachers may have a better chance to be transferred into a better paid civil servant position, and an incentive effect, as poorly performing contract teachers may be fired or at least not re-hired.

One of the two main questions addressed in Bold et al. (2018) is whether successful NGO pilots can be replicated by governments. To answer that question they set up a randomized controlled trial to compare the impact of the contract teacher program run by the Kenyan government with one under the coordination of an international NGO. The experimental evaluation was implemented as part of the pilot phase of a nationwide program that was intended to employ 18,000 contract teachers in 2010. The pilot was designed to test the Ministry of Education's ability to implement a fairly close variant of the NGO project described above (Duflo et al. 2015) and to replicate the results across diverse conditions, spanning urban slums in Nairobi and nomadic communities in the remote Northeastern province.

As part of the government's contract teacher pilot, schools were chosen from across all eight Kenyan provinces and randomly assigned to three arms: a control group, a group receiving a contract teacher as part of the government program, and a group receiving a contract teacher under the coordination of the local affiliate of an international NGO, World Vision Kenya. The timing, salary levels, recruitment procedures, and all other experimental protocols were held constant across the government and NGO arms of the evaluation.

The results of the evaluation are striking. Similar to earlier studies, the authors found a positive effect on student learning overall. However, the effect is entirely due to the increase in test scores in the randomly assigned subgroup of treatment schools where the program was administered by the international NGO. They find a significant, positive, and relatively large effect on test scores in schools randomly assigned to NGO implementation and zero effect in schools receiving contract teachers from the Ministry of Education.

Two crucial insights emerge from this work. First, the study confirms the hypothesis that interventions, and especially interventions that are likely to threaten the rents of insiders (in this case unionized teachers), cannot be adequately described without attention to the broader institutional setting. Second, the work illustrates how, through an experimental approach, one can identify important bureaucratic and political constraints facing, in this case, the Kenyan Ministry of Education's ability to scale up interventions that have been shown to work. That is, an experimental approach can also be used to study and assess constraints to scaling up.

So why did the program fail when implemented by the government? The evidence strongly suggests that the stark contrast in success between government implementation and NGO implementation can be traced back to the "seesaw effect" identified by Acemoglu (2010) and the "implementer bias" highlighted by Heckman (1991). Specifically, the government's ambitious plan to employ 18,000 contract teachers nationwide posed a significant threat to the Kenyan National Union of Teachers. In response, the teachers' union waged an intense political and legal battle against the contract teacher program, including a lawsuit which delayed implementation by over a year; street protests in central Nairobi; and the threat of a national strike. The political battle eventually altered the program in two key respects. First, primary responsibility for employing contract teachers (both during the pilot and the full scale-up) was shifted away from its natural home within the government. Second, after a prolonged political battle, the Ministry of Education acquiesced to union demands to absorb the contract teachers into civil service employment at the end of their contracts, thus effectively removing the very incentives the contract teacher reform was intended to create. While this change did not take place until after the trial ended, the political actions by the teacher labor union during the trial likely influenced the contract teachers' expectations of the link between performance and tenure in the government arm, and thus their willingness to exert effort.

18.7. EXPERIMENTAL APPROACH TO SCALING-UP

For several reasons, the recent experimental research in education has focused attention on demand and supply factors at the school and individual levels. Research on effective ways to take these findings, and the implementation constraints highlighted above, to formalize effective and scalable policies, are, with few exceptions (see below), largely missing. An interesting exception is the recent work by Banerjee et al. (2017).

Bold et al. (2018) show how an experimental approach can be used to assess and identify political constraints that have bearing on the government's ability to scale-up interventions shown to be effective. Banerjee et al. (2017) go one important step further. Specifically, they study the design of a scalable remedial education program in India.

The starting point for their work is a set of proof-of-principle studies in India, reviewed in section 18.5, showing that learning camps that are held outside of normal school hours where trained instructors use learning-appropriate remedial materials are highly effective in raising test scores (Banerjee et al. 2007, 2010).

Based on these findings, two large experiments were launched in government schools in two districts in India. In this scaled-up version of the program, regular teachers were trained, new materials were provided, and volunteer teachers who could assist with re-medial education were made available to schools. Unlike the proof-of-principle studies guiding the scaled-up version, and similar to Bold et al. (2018), the authors found no ef-fect in the government-operated program, since teachers de facto did not change their behavior.

The research team did not stop there, however. Instead, they used the lessons from the failure to identify key constraints, worked with the bureaucracy and developed a vari-ant of the proof-of-principle intervention, making the revised intervention an integral part of the curriculum. This new version was implemented (as RCTs) in two districts, showing promising effects, and the positive findings of the revised intervention in the end led to successful statewide rollout, with 23,000 schools, 60,000 teachers, and 1.4 mil-lion children.

18.8. RESEARCH QUESTIONS OR AREAS THAT NEED FURTHER STUDY

Our review of the literature highlights important avenues for future research. The most general, but likely also the most important one given the evidence, is that research on increasing the quality of primary education should be high on the agenda. It is hard to think of an area with larger potential impact on both short-run well-being and longer-run economic performance than improving the quality of education for those who can-not afford to buy high-quality education in private markets. High-quality public educa-tion may also be one of the most effective ways to raise the welfare of the poorer segment of the population and enhance economic mobility.

In policy discussions about education in low-income countries, however, there has re-cently been a shift toward secondary and tertiary education. While access to and qual-ity of higher education is clearly crucial, and has become more important over time, the notion that significant progress in primary school enrollment in developing regions should imply a shift in focus toward higher education, at the expense of primary educa-tion, is a worrisome one, given that a large share of children in low-income countries learn little and complete their primary education lacking even basic reading, writing, and arithmetic skills.

The second, slightly less general recommendation for future research, again based on the evidence, is that there must be more focus on teachers' effort, knowledge, and skills. It is hard to think of any policy reform in education that would have dramatic effects on learning outcomes, assuming teachers should still play an important role, if teachers only teach half of the scheduled time and a large share of them cannot even master their stu-dents' curriculum. There is also growing quasi-experimental research, so far primarily from the United States, documenting the great values for students (in both the short and long run) of having high-quality teachers (Chetty, Friedman, and Rockoff 2014). More specifically, while there is a growing evidence on promising interventions linking payments or tenure to performance, and some evidence on interventions that could be viewed as automating teachers to perform rather simple tasks, we know little about cost-effective ways to teach teachers how to teach "higher-order" tasks or how to improve general pedagogy. There are also no high-quality studies on how to cost-effectively raise teachers' content knowledge or more general skills to teach.

Our review has also highlighted a general question that still remains under-researched. Namely, how do we go from evidence gained from what can largely be viewed as proof-of-principle studies to scaled-up programs? We argue that this calls for research along two lines: one dealing with what we labeled a local rent-seeking constraint—and here we argue for identifying and experimenting with interventions inspired by the incomplete contract approach; i.e., by assigning decision rights to the users and overcoming informational constraints. There is growing evidence here on various ways to achieve this, but research that explicitly deals with how interventions will work without relying on either monitoring and support from researchers or monitoring and support from other public actors that in many cases lack the incentive to effectively provide monitoring and supervision ought to be high on the agenda.

We also have highlighted the role of information. We argue that devolving authority to the actual users; i.e., strengthening beneficiary control, is in principle an effective way to deal with the monitoring-the-monitors problem and various local rent-seeking constraints. However, lacking information to properly act on, devolution of authority may not be enough to constrain rent-seeking behavior by various public actors, including the providers themselves. Providing users with actionable information, or ways to collect such information, appears to be crucial in order to mitigate the capture of rents. Here, though, more research is called for. The cost of collecting, assembling, and disseminating information may be high, so an especially promising line of research is to experiment with advances in ICT to bring the cost down and increase users' understanding of the information and willingness to act on it.

The macro-political economy literature also highlights the crucial relationship between information dissemination and accountability (of politicians). Thus, systematically collecting "informative performance data"—the Service Delivery Indicators (SDI) is one example of this—and properly disseminating it can be an important complementary strategy to boost the incentives for effective reforms in education, both at the local and national levels. Such information can be used by users and local communities to help identify problems and search for solutions.

More generally, experimenting with interventions that are explicitly designed in a way that takes implementation constraints—such as a weak public sector—into account (if/when going to scale) is important. This is true even though those constraints may not be particularly important when running the project on a small scale. An example of that is Bold and Svensson (2016). Their design calls for evaluating an incentive program in primary education in which financial rewards, conditional on test score performance, are paid out in the form of a chance to win, i.e., taking part in a lottery.[11] From an implementation point of view, lottery incentives, compared to an incentive program that offered each school a certain payment conditional on performance, have one major advantage. Specifically, under certain conditions, while the chance to win offers incentives for all, only the winner's performance needs to be assessed and only the winner needs to be paid.

We have also argued and provided examples of how RCTs can be used to measure and identify constraints to government scale-up and how a research program relying on a series of RCTs, each building on each other, can be used to identify scalable proof-of-principle interventions. Both approaches, and especially the latter, are promising ways forward if the aim is to identify evidence-based policies for educational reforms in low-income countries.

Finally, when public institutions do not work well, an argument could be made to facilitate low-income families' exit options; i.e., to subsidize the enrollment of their children in private schools. The encouragement and support of privately provided education is often criticized for leading to increased economic stratification and reduced pressure of public schools to supply quality education. However, increased economic stratification is not likely to be a problem when subsidizing private education of the poor. There is to date little high-quality evidence of voucher programs, and to our knowledge none from Sub-Saharan Africa. Again, this seems to us an important area for future research.

NOTES

We are grateful for comments from participants at the EDI workshops in Namur and Paris. If readers have specific queries, you may reach us at (i) IIES, Stockholm University, tessa.bold@iies.su.se; (ii) IIES, Stockholm University, jakob.svensson@iies.su.se.

1. Evans and Popova (2016) provide a review of these reviews to assess which findings are consistent, and which divergent, across these studies.
2. The Trends in International Mathematics and Science Study (TIMSS) by the IEA test grade 4 (primary) and grade 8 (secondary) students on common elements of primary and secondary school curricula. In Botswana, grade 6 students were assessed, as it was deemed too difficult for fourth grade students to take the TIMSS fourth grade assessment. Similarly, in Botswana and South Africa, ninth grade students were assessed with the TIMSS eighth grade assessment. No Sub-Saharan African country participated in the testing program run by OECD (Programme for International Student Assessment, PISA).
3. Depending on the country, the language was English, French, or Portuguese.
4. In contrast to other approaches where teachers sit for exams, this method of assessment aimed to assess teachers in a way that was consistent with their normal activities—namely, grading students' work—and to value them as professionals and not undermine their self-esteem. See Bold et al. (2017a) for details.
5. There is wide variation across countries in this score. See Bold et al. (2017a) for details.
6. Having knowledge equivalent to the fourth grade curriculum is of course not sufficient to teach language in lower primary, because language teaching is monolithic. Bold et al. (2017a) define minimum subject content knowledge for language teachers if the teacher can confidently correct children's work in such aspects of literacy as reading comprehension, vocabulary, and formal correctness (grammar, spelling, syntax, and punctuation), all of which are competencies a teacher in lower primary would routinely be required to have. To this end, the language test contained (in addition to the spelling and grammar exercises), Cloze passages to assess vocabulary and reading comprehension, and a letter written to a friend describing their school, which the teacher had to mark and correct. Minimum knowledge in language measured as marking at least 80% of the items on the language test correctly.
7. For details, see Bold et al. (2017a). They also examine to what extent teachers apply what they know in the classroom.
8. There are also a number of recent evaluations of so-called computer-assisted learning programs. We do not review them here, as the programs differ too much in design and implementation details to be categorized as a family of similar interventions.
9. The compensation scheme; i.e., the ability to reward and punish the agent, was not explicitly addressed in these types of programs. Instead the community had to rely on informal forms of social recognition and/or social opprobrium. Within reasonable bounds, it is possible that non-financial rewards (social recognition) may be just as effective at eliciting effort as financial incentives.
10. Additional support for the conclusion that delegating formal (as in Duflo et al. 2015) or informal (as in Björkman and Svensson 2009) decision rights to users and addressing underlying informational asymmetries are key in successfully influencing service delivery performance is provided in Barr et al. (2014). They study different ways to provide SMC members with tools to monitor teacher performance. In line with the findings in Björkman and Svensson (2009), they show that the provision of tools for assembling performance information, combined with an explicit

participatory component, resulted in reduction in teacher absenteeism and increased student test scores.

11. For an evaluation of a lottery incentive program for HIV prevention, see Björkman-Nykvist et al. (2015).

REFERENCES

Abeberese, A. B., T. J. Kumler, and L. L. Linden. 2014. "Improving Reading Skills by Encouraging Children to Read in School: A Randomized Evaluation of the Sa Aklat Sisikat Reading Program in the Philippines." *Journal of Human Resources* 49(3): 611–633.

Acemoglu, D. 2010. "Theory, General Equilibrium, and Political Economy in Development Economics." *Journal of Economic Perspectives* 24(3): 17–32.

ASER. 2013. *Annual Status of Education Report 2013*. ASER Center, New Delhi.

Banerjee, A., R. Banerji, J. Berry, E. Duflo, S. Mukherji, M. Shotland, and M. Walton. 2017. "From Proof of Concept to Scalable Policies: Challenges and Solutions, with an Application." *Journal of Economic Perspectives* 31(4): 73–102.

Banerjee, A., S. Cole, E. Duflo, and L. Linden. 2007. "Remedying Education: Evidence from Two Randomized Experiments in India." *Quarterly Journal of Economics*: 1235–1264.

Banerjee, A., R. Banerji, E. Duflo, R. Glennerster, and S. Khemani. 2010. "Pitfalls of Participatory Programs: Evidence from a Randomized Evaluation in Education in India." *American Economic Journal: Economic Policy* 2(1): 1–30.

Barr, Abigail, Frederick Mugisha, Pieter Serneels, and Andrew Zeitlin. 2014. "Information and Collective Action in Community-Based Monitoring of Schools: Field and Lab Experimental Evidence from Uganda." Unpublished.

Bau, N., and J. Das. 2017. "The Misallocation of Pay and Productivity in the Public Sector: Evidence from the Labor Market for Teachers." Policy Research Working Paper No. 8050. World Bank, Washington, DC.

Baum, D., L. Lewis, O. Lusk-Stover, and H. Patrinos. 2014. "What Matters Most for Engaging the Private Sector in Education: A Framework Paper." Systems Approach for Better Education Results (SABER) Working Paper Series No. 8. World Bank.

Besley, T. and T. Persson. 2011. *Pillars of Prosperity: The Political Economics of Development Clusters*. Princeton, NJ: Princeton University Press.

Björkman-Nykvist, M., D. de Walque, and J. Svensson. 2017. "Experimental Evidence on the Long-Run Impact of Community Based Monitoring." *American Economic Journal: Applied* 9(1): 33–69.

Björkman, M. and J. Svensson. 2009. "Power to the People: Evidence from a Randomized Field Experiment of a Community-Based Monitoring Project in Uganda." *Quarterly Journal of Economics* 124(2): 735–769.

Bold, Tessa, Deon Filmer, Gayle Martin, Ezequiel Molina, Brian Stacy, Christophe Rockmore, Jakob Svensson, and Waly Wane. 2017a. "Enrollment Without Learning: Teacher Effort, Knowledge, and Skill in Primary Schools in Africa." *Journal of Economic Perspectives* 31(4): 185–204.

Bold, T., D. Filmer, E. Molina, and J. Svensson. 2017b. "The Lost Human Capital: Teacher Knowledge and Student Achievement in Africa." Working Paper, IIES.

Bold, Tessa, Deon Filmer, Gayle Martin, Ezequiel Molina, Christophe Rockmore, Brian Stacy, Jakob Svensson, and Waly Wane. 2017c. "What Do Teachers Know and Do? Does It Matter? Evidence from Primary Schools in Africa." Policy Research Working Paper No. 7956, World Bank, Washington, DC.

Bold, T., M. Kimenyi, G. Mwabu, A. Ng'ang'a, and J. Sandefur. 2018. "Experimental Evidence on Scaling Up Education Reforms in Kenya." *Journal of Public Economics* 168: 1–20.

Bold, Tessa and Jakob Svensson. 2016. "Lotteries for Teachers: Experimenting with Incentives with Low Implementation Costs—A Design Note." Working Paper, IIES.

Chaudhury, N., J. Hammer, M. Kremer, K. Muralidharan, and H. Rogers. 2006. "Missing in Action: Teacher and Health Worker Absence in Developing Countries." *Journal of Economic Perspectives* 20(1): 91–116.

Chetty, R., J. N. Friedman, and J. E. Rockoff. 2014. "Measuring the Impacts of Teachers II: Teacher Value-Added and Student Outcomes in Adulthood." *American Economic Review* 104(9): 2593–2632.

Conn, K. 2017. "Identifying Effective Education Interventions in Sub-Saharan Africa: A Meta-analysis of Rigorous Impact Evaluations." *Review of Educational Research* 87 (5): 863–898.

Duflo, E., P. Dupas, and M. Kremer. 2011. "Peer Effects, Teacher Incentives, and the Impact of Tracking: Evidence from a Randomized Evaluation in Kenya." *American Economic Review* 101: 1739–1774.

———. 2015. "School Governance, Teacher Incentives, and Pupil-Teacher Ratios: Experimental Evidence from Kenyan Primary Schools." *Journal of Public Economics* 123: 92–110.

Duflo, E., R. Hanna, and S. P. Ryan. 2012. "Incentives Work: Getting Teachers to Come to School." *American Economic Review* 102(4): 1241–1278.

Evans, D. and A. Popova. 2016. "What Really Works to Improve Learning in Developing Countries: An Analysis of Divergent Findings in Systematic Reviews." *World Bank Researcher Observer* 31: 242–270.

Glewwe, P., N. Ilias, and M. Kremer. 2010. "Teacher Incentives." *American Economic Journal: Applied Economics*, 205–227.

Glewwe, P. and E.W.H. Maiga. 2011. "The Impacts of School Management Reforms in Madagascar: Do the Impacts Vary by Teacher Type?" *Journal of Development Effectiveness* 3(4): 435–469.

Glewwe, P. and K. Muralidharan. 2016. "Improving Education Outcomes in Developing Countries: Evidence, Knowledge Gaps, and Policy Implications." In *Handbook of the Economics of Education*, 653–743. Amsterdam: Elsevier North-Holland.

Hanushek, E. A. and L. Woessmann. 2015. *The Knowledge Capital of Nations: Education and the Economics of Growth*. Cambridge, MA: MIT Press.

Heckman, J. 1991. "Randomization and Social Policy Evaluation." NBER Technical Working Paper No. 107.

Holmstrom, B. and P. Milgrom. 1991. "Multi-Task Principal-Agent Analysis: Incentive Contracts, Asset Ownership, and Job Design." *Journal of Law, Economics, and Organization* 7: 24–52.

Hungi, N., D. Makuwa, K. Ross, M. Saito, S. Dolata, and F. V. Cappelle. 2010. "SACMEQIII Project Result: Pupil Achievement Levels in Reading and Mathematics." Working Document Number 1. Paris: SACMEQ.

Kremer, M., C. Brannen, and R. Glennerster. 2013. "The Challenge of Education and Learning in the Developing World." *Science* 340: 297–300.

Krishnaratne, S., H. White, and E. Carpenter. 2013. "Quality Education for All Children? What Works in Education in Developing Countries." International Initiative for Impact Evaluation (3ie) Working Paper 20. New Delhi.

Lakshminarayana, R., A. Eble, P. Bhakta, C. Frost, P. Boone, D. Elbourne, and V. Mann. 2013. "The Support to Rural India's Public Education System (STRIPES): A Cluster Randomised Controlled Trial of Supplementary Teaching, Learning Material and Material Support." *PloS one* 8(7): e65775.

Lassibille, G., J-P. Tan, C. Jesse, and T. Nguyen. 2010. "Managing for Results in Primary Education in Madagascar: Evaluating the Impact of Selected Workflow Interventions." *World Bank Economic Review* 24(2): 303–329.

Lucas, A. M., P. J. McEwan, M. Ngware, and M. Oketch. 2014. "Improving Early Grade Literacy in East Africa: Experimental Evidence from Kenya and Uganda." *Journal of Policy Analysis and Management* 33(4): 950–976.

McEwan, P. 2015. "Improving Learning in Primary Schools in Developing Countries: A Meta-Analysis of Randomized Experiments." *Review of Educational Research* 85(3): 353–394.

Muralidharan, K. and V. Sundararaman. 2011. "Teacher Performance Pay: Experimental Evidence from India." *Journal of Political Economy* 119(1): 39–77.

———. 2013. "Contract Teachers: Experimental Evidence from India." NBER Working Paper No. 19440.

———. 2015. "The Aggregate Effect of School Choice: Evidence from a Two-Stage Experiment in India." *Quarterly Journal of Economics* 130(3): 1011–1066.

Murnane, R. and A. Ganimian. 2016. "Improving Educational Outcomes in Developing Countries: Lessons from Rigorous Evaluations." *Review of Educational Research* 86(3): 719–755.

Pandey, P., S. Goyal, and V. Sundararaman. 2009. "Community Participation in Public Schools: Impact of Information Campaigns in Three Indian States." *Education Economics* 17(3): 355–375.

Piper, B. and M. Korda. 2011. "EGRA Plus: Liberia: Program Evaluation Report." Report prepared for USAID/Liberia.

Pradhan, M., D. Suryadarma, A. Beatty, M. Wong, A. Gaduh, A. Alisjahbana, and R. P. Artha. 2014. "Improving Educational Quality through Enhancing Community Participation: Results from a Randomized Field Experiment in Indonesia." *American Economic Journal: Applied Economics* 6(2): 105–126.

TIMSS. 2011. *TIMSS 2011 Assessment*. International Association for the Evaluation of Educational Achievement (IEA). TIMSS & PIRLS International Study Center, Lynch School of Education, Boston College.

19

MEDIA AS A TOOL FOR INSTITUTIONAL CHANGE IN DEVELOPMENT

Eliana La Ferrara

19.1. INTRODUCTION

One of the most striking phenomena that have affected developing countries in recent years is the rapid spread of mass media and information and communications technologies (ICT), from radio to television to mobile phones. Data from the Demographic and Health Surveys for Sub-Saharan Africa, for example, show that between 1990 and 2010, TV ownership rates in many countries increased by a factor of four or more. In addition to having profound effects on social and economic variables (see, e.g., DellaVigna and La Ferrara 2015; La Ferrara 2016), this generates new opportunities for using the media as a vehicle for institutional change. The goal of this chapter is to assess what we know about the effectiveness of the media in playing such a role, and what gaps in knowledge need to be filled.

For the purpose of the present analysis, institutions will be defined as rules and structures that formally or informally constrain the behavior of individuals in society, aggregate preferences, and coordinate beliefs. As such, the impact of the media on institutions will include both impact on formal political institutions (electoral accountability, policy choice, etc.) and the effect on social norms (e.g., mediated by change in individual preferences and values).

I develop the argument in two parts. In the first part I analyze the political economy of the media in developing contexts. I start by covering the literature on media as a tool for accountability: by providing information on candidates ex ante, and on politicians' performance ex post, an independent media can allow the system of checks and balances embedded in a democracy to work, ensure that electoral threat incentivizes governments, and ultimately improve the functioning of institutions. I then analyze how the content of the media is determined, focusing in particular on media bias. The issue of media bias is particularly salient in weak institutional contexts, where the media may be captured by powerful interests or by the ruling elite. After briefly reviewing the theory of media bias, I discuss how to operationalize the concept in light of recent advances in the measurement of media bias across different outlets. I then survey the existing evidence on media bias, including capture by politicians as well as by other groups, and the evidence on the impact of biased media on individual behavior, including effects on voting, conflict, etc.

In the second part of the chapter I stress a different angle that has been relatively less explored, at least in the economics literature: the media can be used to change citizens' preferences and values, as an intermediate step to changing institutions. In fact, "manipulating" institutions in the short run may not have long-term effects if individuals do not change their way of thinking, what they demand of their peers, their families, and their policymakers. While changing values is intrinsically a complex process, often marked by historical transitions, recent research suggests that the rapid spread of mass media in developing countries can be a powerful tool to change poor people's preferences.

I start by reviewing the psychological basis for the role that mass media (and in particular television) can play in changing attitudes and behavior. I then summarize the existing empirical studies, with a focus on rigorously identified ones. These comprise studies on the effects of commercial media on socioeconomic outcomes, such as fertility preferences, gender norms, social capital, and trust. Finally, I discuss policy implications, with special reference to educational entertainment (edutainment) solutions. This includes an analysis of the potential for these types of programs as a tool for conveying information on government and institutional features of society, as well as for shaping individual beliefs and expectations.

Before turning to the analysis, a methodological premise is in order. If one were to examine the correlation between the extent of information that citizens derive from the media (e.g., whether they read the newspaper, how many news channels they watch and for how long, etc.) and their political views or institutional outcomes in the locations where these individuals live, this would not allow us to draw a causal link from media to preferences or institutions. The reason is that there may be unobserved factors that affect both individuals' propensity to read or watch the news and the outcomes of interest (omitted variable bias). Also, there may be feedback mechanisms whereby citizens' political preferences or engagement induce changes in the supply of information and in media behavior in general (reverse causation).

To address these endogeneity problems, the existing literature has relied on three types of variation. The first is variation in access to media (and indirectly media consumption) generated by exogenous factors, e.g., staggered entry of media across locations or geographical features that affect signal reception. The second is variation in media content (or coverage) generated by programming strategies that are orthogonal to the outcome of interest, e.g., by the overlap of media markets and electoral districts. The third and last type of variation is directly generated by the researcher through experiments, e.g., randomized controlled trials. Depending on the context and the phenomenon under study, these strategies have generated empirical evidence that can shed light on how access to media and media content can shape political preferences and ultimately the functioning of institutions.

19.2. MEDIA, ACCOUNTABILITY, AND POLITICAL CHANGE

Voters need information about policies and who is responsible for them, in order to reward high-performing politicians and punish low-performing ones. Information collection and transmission is an activity with high fixed costs and relatively low marginal costs, and for this reason it is efficient for the media—as opposed to individuals—to collect and distribute information, thus lowering frictions. The extent to which the media succeed in this task depends on factors such as the degree of media competition, the size of the market, the demand for advertising, and delivery costs.

19.2.1. The Accountability Channel

Information provision is the main channel through which media affects political accountability: this information can be provided to the public before elections (e.g., information on candidates' platforms) as well as after a politician's performance is realized (e.g., compliance with electoral promises). Political information should increase voters' responsiveness to the performance of politicians, and in turn impact on policy choice.

19.2.1.1. Theoretical Framework

The literature on media coverage and accountability, carefully summarized by Strömberg (2015), features different models of the above-mentioned process, where the differences are mainly related to the type of information that the media provide. In Strömberg (2004a) the media carry information on who proposes and is responsible for a given policy; in Besley and Burgess (2001) and Besley and Prat (2006) the information concerns the incumbent's type with respect to altruism and to quality, respectively.

Strömberg (2015) embeds various contributions from the literature into a comprehensive model of the effects of media coverage on different outcomes. His model includes three types of actors: voters, politicians, and the media itself. Each of them defends their own interests, respectively: utility from policy, re-election with political rents, and profits from audience. An increase in the share of media consumers as well as higher media coverage of politics induces an increase in the share of informed voters, in the responsiveness of voters to perceived competence, in the expected competence of political actors, in spending levels and in the responsiveness of spending to need, and a decrease in political rents.

Another component of the model pertains to the market provision of news. Here the provision of public news is increasing in market size. Politically, this implies that larger countries and larger political jurisdictions within countries will have higher-quality political reporting, thus leading to better-informed voters and better political selection and incentives. Also, news provision becomes less expensive the lower is the cost of delivering news. Third, the higher the private value of news, the higher their provision. While the private value is exogenous in this model, in Strömberg (2004a) it is made endogenous, and it is higher for policies for which the variance in needs is larger. The model in Strömberg (2004a) predicts also that politicians attempt to distort policies in order to manage publicity in their favor: spending will be devoted to newsworthy projects financed from cuts to minor activities, which typically do not attract the attention of media.

Finally, in a world where a politician has many tasks and duties to pay attention to, information may induce distortion in incentives. Voters' level of information is not necessarily increasing in the importance of a task: the media may choose to inform voters about tasks that are not the most important from a social point of view. The politician, internalizing the higher level of information about the tasks covered by the media, may decide to devote more effort to them and thus induce a deviation from the welfare-maximizing outcome. This problem, which is an application of Holmström and Milgrom's (1991) "multitasking problem," is analyzed in Strömberg (2004a, 2004b).

19.2.1.2. Empirical Evidence

The existing empirical evidence seems to corroborate the mechanism of influence highlighted above: informed voters are more likely to participate in elections and to select politicians based on their platform; informed voters punish or reward politicians for their actions; and politicians change the policies they implement in response. I now briefly summarize this evidence.

Informed Citizens Vote More and Differently

Participating in elections is the main vehicle that citizens have to hold their politicians accountable. A first-order question is thus whether the media affect voter turnout, e.g., by providing information that induces voters to go to the polls to voice their opinion, or by increasing people's interest in politics more generally.

In an influential study, Strömberg (2004a) studies how radio penetration across US counties during 1920–1940 affected electoral outcomes and public spending. In order to circumvent the endogeneity of radio ownership, the author exploits variation in the quality of radio signals generated by geographic characteristics such as ground conductivity and share of woodland, etc. He finds that people living in municipalities with more radio ownership had higher voter turnout. This was especially true in rural areas, where newspaper circulation was lower and radio constituted a primary vehicle for learning about politics.

A different conclusion is reached by Gentzkow (2006), who focuses on television instead of radio and finds that turnout decreases instead of increasing in response to TV penetration. This different conclusion can be rationalized by considering the relative informational content of the media that is crowded out. In Strömberg (2004a), radio was not crowding out widely available sources of political information, especially in rural areas. In the case of television, instead, newspaper readership was affected, and because television programs were less rich in political content compared to newspapers, this may have reduced citizens' propensity to vote. Banerjee et al. (2011) find encouraging results for the case of India. In a random sample of slums in a large Indian city, residents received free newspapers containing report cards with information on the performance and qualifications of the incumbent legislator and on the qualifications of the two main opponents. In particular, the report cards contained the following performance measure for the incumbent: legislative activity, committee attendance, and spending of discretionary jurisdiction development funds; and it contained information on wealth, education, and past criminal record for both incumbent and challengers. Compared to the control group, treated slums were found to have a higher turnout, lower vote-buying, and higher vote share for incumbents that had performed well and were relatively qualified.

Not only information ex post on politicians' performance matters, but also ex ante information on their policy platforms. In an original policy experiment in Benin,

Fujiwara and Wantchekon (2013) worked with policy experts to develop programmatic platforms for the candidates and subsequently persuaded political candidates to run with these platforms (as opposed to the usual clientelistic messages) in a random subset of villages. The "experimental" campaigns involved town hall meetings and discussions, during which villagers could learn about the policy positions of the candidates. The authors found that in treated villages, voters were less likely to report vote-buying, but were as likely to turn out to vote as in control villages. This is noteworthy because it is often argued that in poor countries vote-buying is used to mobilize turnout. While on average no effect was found on vote shares of the "experimental candidate" (i.e., the candidate who was running with the programmatic platform and town hall meetings), heterogeneous effects emerged. In treated villages the vote share of the "dominant" candidate (i.e., the candidate who got the most votes) decreased compared to control villages. Because dominant candidates were likely better able to engage in clientelistic practices, this result suggests that information on programmatic platforms can benefit challengers and reduce the advantages of clientelistic schemes adopted by incumbents.

In a related experiment, Bidwell, Casey, and Glennerster (2015) study the effects of debates among candidates. In principle, these debates can serve multiple functions. First, they can convey information about the characteristics (e.g., competence) of the candidates and about their specific policy positions. Second, they can serve as a commitment device: to the extent that these debates are a public record of electoral promises, they may enhance the ex post accountability of elected officials. The authors set up a randomized controlled trial of public screenings of debates among candidates for the 2012 parliamentary elections in rural areas of Sierra Leone. They found that voters from villages that received the screenings were significantly more knowledgeable about candidates (they knew which candidates had been MPs) and were more likely to identify the candidate's top spending priorities. Interestingly, "policy alignment" also improved, as measured by a match between the policy position of a voter and that of the candidate they report having voted for. Voters in treated villages were also more likely to switch across ethnic-party lines and to vote for the candidate who had performed better in the debate.

Informed Voters Hold Politicians Accountable
Other studies have focused not so much on turnout, but on vote choices for specific candidates or parties in response to information about misuse of funds and irregular conduct. In their seminal paper on corruption in Brazil, Ferraz and Finan (2008) exploited a program of random audits of municipal governments and found that voters responded to the outcome of the audit by casting their vote in the next election. In particular, the reaction was mediated by the media, and specifically by exposure to radio in the municipality. Voters in municipalities that had a local radio station decreased their support for mayors who were more corrupt than average and increased their support for mayors who were less corrupt than average.

In a similar way, Larreguy, Marshall, and Snyder (2015) studied the impact of municipal audit reports in Mexico and the role played by the media. They compare corrupt mayors whose behavior is exposed during the year before the election to corrupt mayors whose behavior is exposed after the election. They also rely on within-municipality variation in the electoral districts covered by radio and TV stations: the underlying idea is that if the media station is located within the municipality, its coverage deals more with the relevant audit reports. The authors find that voters punish mayors with worse performance, but they do so only in the districts that have local media.

Overall, the above evidence suggests that access to information, through newspapers, radio, or other means, allows voters to exercise a credible threat vis-à-vis their representatives. How do politicians react in response?

Politicians Choose Policies in Response to Informed Voters

A first piece of evidence shows that when politicians know that they are being "monitored" by citizens, they increase their effort. Snyder and Strömberg (2010) analyze data on US congressmen during 1982–2004 where ideology and effort are measured by roll-call voting, committee assignments, and witness appearances. They find that in US districts where media coverage of politics is higher, congressmen are less ideologically extreme, they vote more frequently against their party leaders, they are more likely to stand as witness before congressional hearings, and more likely to serve on committees that can directly benefit their constituencies.[1] The authors separately identify the effect of selection and of incentives: moderation is found to stem from selection, whereas the increase in witness appearance is driven by incentives.

Other evidence has shown a direct link from media penetration to policy choice. Besley and Burgess (2002) study the distribution of food and calamity relief in a panel of Indian states between 1958 and 1992. They find that, controlling for local food production and flood damage, states with higher newspaper circulation receive more food subsidies and calamity relief spending, respectively.[2] They also find that media consumption affects the responsiveness of policy to need: the coefficient on the interaction term between newspaper circulation and proxies for need is positive and significant. In other words, spending is more linked to actual need in localities where newspaper circulation was higher. This effect is driven by newspapers in local languages, as opposed to English or Hindi, corroborating the interpretation that people's access to local information was the key driver of politicians' response.

In his study of the impact of radio in the United States, Strömberg (2004a) finds that counties with higher radio ownership rates received more unemployment relief funds through the New Deal's program. This effect was particularly pronounced in rural areas that had less access to alternative sources of information, and where radio accounted for about 20% more public spending than in urban counties.

In their study of electoral debates in Sierra Leone, Bidwell et al. (2015) find that communities that had (randomly) received the debate screenings saw an increase in campaign spending by candidates, more visits, and more gifts by the candidates. Ex post accountability also seems to have worked: once elected, MPs who had participated in the debates spent more than twice as much on verifiable development expenditures for their constituencies.

Naturally, the accountability channel of voters' information may not always work in a benign way. In particular, it may distort funds or policies away from communities that are particularly needy yet have poor access to information (hence constitute less of an electoral threat). Reinikka and Svensson (2005) provide direct evidence of such a mechanism, as they find that schools that were located closer to newspaper outlets received more government funds; the bias in this case penalized more remote and isolated localities.

While the availability of media outlets is crucial to create accountability, it may not per se be enough. What issues are covered in the media? If the press or other media are not reporting—or not reporting objectively—on political issues, this may have severe consequences, even in well-functioning democracies. The next step is thus to understand what determines media coverage and media bias.

19.2.2. Media Coverage and Bias

Understanding how media coverage impacts political institutions and policy choices is a non-trivial task. In fact, more severe problems are more likely to both receive policy attention and attract media coverage. Moreover, a reverse causality problem may arise since political agendas can drive policy but also influence media coverage.

An early attempt to circumvent these obstacles was made by Eisensee and Strömberg (2007), who analyzed the effect of media coverage of natural disasters on foreign aid allocation. The authors exploit the occurrence of newsworthy events (e.g., sport events) in the same days of a disaster as a source of exogenous variation in media coverage. They find that disasters that are covered less by the media receive less attention from US policymakers, in the form of less emergency relief spending.

In a different setting, Snyder and Strömberg (2010) examine how the incentives to cover local politics in the United States depend on the "congruence" of the media and of the political audience.

The main idea is the following. Boundaries of media markets are typically determined by the "economic geography" of a locality, while the boundaries of US congressional districts generally depend on the "political geography" of an area. When the overlap ("congruence") between these two is significant, the media are more likely to cover local political news: they know that by doing so they will not "alienate" a large fraction of their audience, because most of the people buying the local newspaper or watching the local TV vote in the same district and are therefore interested in coverage of the same news. On the other hand, media in districts that have low "congruence" will be less likely to cover local politics because their audience for such news is limited. Applying this approach to 161 US newspapers over the period 1991–2002, Snyder and Strömberg (2010) show that higher congruence resulted in a greater number of news stories that contained the name of a representative from the district and the word "Congress."

This approach, which is applicable outside the United States to the extent that media markets are separated from electoral districts but at the same time there is some overlap, is very effective at predicting whether local political news will be covered in the media. But how are they covered? Which news items are selected to be transmitted to the general public? In the above contributions, coverage choices were driven by market forces, not so much by political strategy. However, the process of filtering and summarizing information necessarily entails discretionary choices, which may not be politically neutral. When this happens in a systematic way, and one outlet repeatedly favors one viewpoint over others, the media outlet is said to be "biased." Gentzkow, Shapiro, and Stone (2015) offer a formal definition of bias according to which media bias occurs when there are systematic differences across outlets in mapping facts into news reports, and these differences sway the target audience to the right or to the left. Media bias is especially relevant in weak institutional settings, where interest groups or elites have the power to bias media outlets in their favor and therefore to induce people's behavior to diverge from their own best interest.

19.2.2.1 Measuring Bias

A substantial literature has grown upon researchers' attempts to identify, classify, and analyze the ideological positions of media outlets. Media bias can come in many different shades: in favor of a particular political party, the incumbent, an industry, or a group of companies, etc. While the possibility of such a bias is not hard to conceptualize, it is challenging to measure it: claiming partiality per se entails a reference to another term, which can be non-trivial to define (a "neutral" outlet? the average preference of voters?). In some cases, the most straightforward object of measurement is the variation among media outlets, i.e., a notion of relative bias.

Two main approaches have been used to measure media bias. The first can be labeled as the *comparison approach* and consists in comparing media outlets with political or non-political actors whose ideological position is known. The second, which we can label as agenda approach, focuses on the amount of coverage devoted to different policy issues (agenda setting) or on the way in which issues are covered (framing and priming). I now briefly describe the main contributions in the two approaches.

The Comparison Approach

The comparison approach owes much to a subfield of automated analysis, the "author identification" or "stylometry." As the name suggests, the purpose of such a technique is to identify the author of a text by comparing the frequency of some characteristic words and trying to retrieve a similar mixture in other texts whose authorship is known.

Groseclose and Milyo (2005) assess the magnitude of bias via the similarities between the think tanks quoted by media and those cited by congressmen. They first assign to each think tank a score for their relative ideological bias, based on the propensity of lined-up politicians to positively quote some think tanks and negatively cite others. In a second step, the authors check how often newspapers back up the ideas of different think tanks. Finally, they attribute the same ideological bias to congressmen and journals that repeatedly cite the same think tank. The advantage of this approach is that it does not require classifying a given think tank as left or right: it is enough to consider which congressmen cite it. Groseclose and Milyo's results suggest that all but two of the sampled newspapers are located to the left of the average member of Congress.

Gentzkow and Shapiro (2010) build on the above idea but analyze a larger sample of newspapers and analyze the language used by newspapers. In particular, they assess the magnitude of media bias, exploiting the similarities between media language and congressmen's words. The authors identify the words and expressions whose frequency in use is most different between Democrats and Republicans: for example, Republicans would use the phrase "death tax" when Democrats would use "estate tax," etc. Then, they measured how often those phrases are included in articles of 433 newspapers from 2005. With this method, they find that partisanship (or "slant") of news outlets is positively correlated with the targeted audience's ideological leaning: newspapers expressing a more conservative viewpoint sold more copies in ZIP codes where the individuals were more prone to donate to Republican candidates, and vice versa for the liberal journals and districts. The work by Gentzkow and Shapiro (2010) therefore constitutes an example of media bias generated by demand-side factors (e.g., consumers' taste).

In a different vein, Puglisi and Snyder (2015) measure bias by analyzing ballot propositions. Their reasoning goes as follows: all interest groups take a position on propositions,

and citizens vote these pieces of law; therefore, within each state different groups (parties, interest groups, but also voters) can be arranged on a scale, given the expression of
their opinion. The authors find that newspapers are distributed about evenly around
each state's median voter, and that they tend to be centrist also with respect to interest
groups. They also find that newspapers appear to be more liberal than voters on many
social and cultural issues (e.g., gay marriage), while being more conservative than voters on economic subject matters (e.g., minimum wage).[3]

The Agenda Approach

The agenda approach rests on the idea that the choice of covering an issue, and the amount
of coverage devoted to it, affects viewers' or readers' tendency to judge politicians on
the basis of the issues covered. Larcinese, Puglisi, and Snyder (2011) apply this idea to the
coverage of economic topics in US newspapers between 1996 and 2005, and study the
variation in coverage of bad economic news as a function of the political affiliation of
the incumbent president. Their intuition is the following: when an outlet endorses a
candidate, it will highlight his achievements and attempt to hide his mistakes. Newspapers endorsing Republicans will attempt to weaken the popularity of a Democratic incumbent and thus cover the news concerning failures of the economic policy during that
presidency. Symmetrically, pro-Republican newspapers would give more coverage to the
president's successes when he is a Republican. By employing this method, the authors
find a considerable variation in the bias across their sample of newspapers; they also find
a significant correlation for the issue of unemployment between the explicit bias of newspapers and the implicit endorsement detected with the above-mentioned technique.

Puglisi and Snyder (2011) adopt a similar framework in analyzing the coverage of 32
political scandals that occurred in the United States between 1997 and 2007. They find
that newspapers endorsing Democratic candidates were likely to cover scandals impli-
cating Democrats, while providing extensive coverage of Republicans' scandals. The
same mechanism, with inverted parties, was found to hold true for newspapers with pro-
Republican bias. These results were robust to controlling for a number of factors such as
partisan readership.

One aspect that is evident from the above list of contributions is that the literature on
measuring media bias has almost exclusively focused on the United States. This seems a
serious shortcoming if we want to implement serious empirical studies of media bias in
developing countries. While some of the methodologies may in principle be applied to
low-income countries' settings, there may be other specificities that need to be taken into
account. The ability of politicians or interest groups to directly control the media, for example, may be highly sensitive to the level of institutional development of the country.
The phenomenon of "media capture" is revealing in this respect.

19.2.3. Media Capture

Media capture is a condition in which politicians or other interest groups manage to control (partially or totally) the content of media outlets. In order to document media capture and its effects, it is not sufficient to show media bias, since the latter can also be
driven by demand-side factors (e.g., outlets adjust to the tastes of their audience). I start
by examining the available evidence on media capture and the factors that favor it, and
then move to discussing the effects of media capture on individual behavior.

19.2.3.1. How Media Capture Occurs, and Why

Governments can realize media capture through different channels, ranging from direct ownership to provision of funding, regulation, and so on. An example of direct payments (through bribes) is presented in McMillan and Zoido (2004). They studied Fujimori's Peru, where Vladimir Montesinos (the head of the secret police) kept track of all the bribes paid by the government. The authors show that directors of TV channels were offered up to 100 times more money than politicians or judges: in exchange the bribed media outlets allowed Montesinos to review the daily news before broadcasting, and they agreed to only convey information he had explicitly given consent to. The fact that buying the media was worth so much can be rationalized through the hold-up problem: it is enough for a single TV channel or newspaper to leak information that the whole regime will suffer from it. Indeed, a typical priority of rulers after a coup d'etat is to gain control of the media. Political influence over the media is systematic, and more common in autocracies. In their study of 97 countries, Djankov et al. (2003) find that 29% of the press and 64% of television are owned by the State.

A different example of direct provision of funds by the government (through government-sponsored advertising) is described in Di Tella and Franceschelli (2011): the authors study the frequency of reporting on corruption stories in newspapers that receive funding from the government. The setting of their research is 1990s–2000s Argentina, where the authors find that newspapers that were more dependent on government advertising were less likely to report on government corruption.

Media regulation is another channel in the hands of government for controlling media content. Stanig (2015) shows that defamation regulations are crucial determinants of news reporting for corruption stories in Mexico. Local newspapers reported less corruption in Mexico in 2001 in states whose defamation regulation was stricter. Similar findings were reported in Starr (2004), who provides a cross-country historical overview of media development, regulation, and capture.

Interestingly, some heterogeneity is attained in media content even in countries whose governments have full control of press and media in general. For instance, Qin et al. (2014) show that the set of issues appearing in Chinese newspapers depends on the strength of the link between the outlets and the Communist party. They find that the most controlled outlets were more likely to write about low-level corruption as compared to commercial media; these results support the idea by Egorov et el. (2009) that autocratic governments exploit mass media to monitor their lower-level public officials.

Gentzkow and Shapiro (2008) show that, even in countries with relatively high freedom of media, governments influence outlets via regulations or restricted access to information. Qian and Yanagizawa-Drott (2017) show that during the Cold War some interests in US foreign policy managed to shape the coverage of human rights violation in newspapers.

However, governments are not the only actors who can manipulate media: media owners, advertisers, journalists, private companies, and single politicians also have the incentives to distort information and coverage. For instance when in 1979 Mother Jones, a leading independent news organization, published a critical article on the addictive effects of cigarettes, tobacco companies reacted by withdrawing their advertising from the journal. Reuter and Zitzewitz (2006) highlight that all but one of the sampled financial magazines are biased toward advertisers in their recommendations for mutual funds investments.

Media capture in recent years is taking new forms, due to the advancements in technology and the broader reach of information: governments cannot perfectly control all pieces of information (think of all existing blogs, sites, etc.); they do, however, engage in selective removal of content. This is especially the case in China, as described in King et al. (2013): the authors attempt to disentangle the reasons leading to the deletion of certain content. They do so by photographing the Chinese blogosphere every 20 minutes and ex post identifying deleted content. Their results suggest that the government tends to delete appeals for coordination and forms of collective action, even more than explicit criticism against Communism or against the incumbent regime. These results are also confirmed in King et al. (2014).

Other work has explored the factors favoring media capture, distinguishing between "demand for capture" and "supply of capture," where the former includes the incentives of interest groups to control the media, whereas the latter entails the willingness of media outlets to adjust their content. More generally, Djankov et al. (2003) maintain that the lack of political competition and direct government ownership are crucial factors driving media capture by government. However, the ability of outlets to raise independent revenues can safeguard the media from capture, as suggested by Petrova (2011), who presents empirical evidence that in the nineteenth century the increase in advertising made US newspapers more independent.

19.2.3.2. Effects of Media Capture

While there is a generally shared notion that media capture is undesirable, pinning down its negative effects in a credible way is challenging. The main difficulty lies in the fact that individuals' decisions on which media product they want to consume is endogenous. In a perfectly Bayesian setting, captured media would not exert any impact, since consumers would detect the bias and discount information accordingly. However, there are reasons to doubt that full discounting takes place in reality: a signal of this can be the fact that countries with the highest media censorship are not always those where people have less trust in media. In fact, the Global Trust Barometer suggests that Chinese people are the most likely to trust their media (Enikolopov and Petrova 2015).

Several empirical studies document the effect that captured media can exert on individual behavior. Yanagizawa-Drott (2014) studies the impact on violence: exploiting geographical variation in the reach of the radio signal of RTLM (a Rwandan transmitter inciting violence against the Tutsi minority), he finds that the radio was responsible for 10% of anti-Tutsi actions that occurred during genocide in 1994.

Other work shows that the media have an effect also when they are targeting foreigners. For instance, DellaVigna et al. (2014) study the case of a Serbian radio whose content was managed by the Serbian government but whose signal reached Croatia so that many Croatians listened to this radio, even though its programs were explicitly hostile to their ethnicity. The authors find that exposure to this radio increased adherence to the extreme Croatian nationalist party. Participants in lab experiments also revealed a more marked anti-Serbian sentiment after listening to 10 minutes of radio.

In the range of possible relevant effects exerted by captured media, changes in voting behavior can be especially important. A number of studies have attempted to determine whether controlled media can affect political attitudes and decision-making. Gerber et al. (2009) ran a randomized control trial prior to the 2005 gubernatorial elections in

Virginia: two treatment groups received a free subscription, each to a different newspaper, and a third group constituted the control. The newspapers assigned were the *Washington Post* (relatively liberal) and the *Washington Times* (relatively conservative). The authors find that readers of the *Post* were 8 percentage points more likely to vote for Democrats in 2005 elections, whereas readers of the *Times* preferred the Democratic candidate by only 4 percentage points.

DellaVigna and Kaplan (2007) exploited the staggered introduction of the Fox News channel across cable markets in the United States and estimated its impact on voting behavior during the 1996 and 2000 presidential elections. They find that in localities where Fox News started to broadcast before 2000, Republicans registered a gain between 0.4 and 0.7 percentage points compared to localities where the same channel was introduced later.

The effect of media capture on voting and political outcomes is particularly worrisome, as it reduces the effectiveness of the system of checks and balances required for the well functioning of democratic institutions. For example, Brunetti and Weder (2003) show that the political longevity of the prime minister or the president across countries is positively correlated with the share of media outlets owned by the government. This is a source of concern if such longevity is not driven by satisfactory performance in delivering public goods and services. So what mechanisms exist to mitigate the negative effects of media capture? The two main mechanisms available are rationality or discounting on behalf of the citizens, and increased competition.

Discounting

As predicted by the theory, there is evidence that the public is able to discount information when they expect the source to be biased. Chiang and Knight (2011) study the impact that newspaper endorsements exert on readers' voting behavior and find that "unexpected endorsements" have an effect, whereas expected ones are discounted by readers. In other words: when a Democratic-leaning journal endorses the Republican candidate (unexpected), this has an impact on votes, whereas the support by pro-Democratic outlets toward Democrats (expected) has negligible effects.

Bai et al. (2014) study how people update their beliefs on air pollution in China after receiving information from the government or receiving it from independent sources. They find that people do not fully discount government-biased information, while they have problems in interpreting conflicting indications from independent sources. This is plausibly related to what was mentioned above, i.e., that Chinese people tend to trust their media.

Adena et al. (2015) take into account the beliefs of audiences and study the effects of propaganda in settings where people hold very different beliefs ex ante. They observe that the impact of radio propaganda in Nazi Germany strongly depended on the ex ante beliefs of the audience: although in general exposition to radio increased denunciation of Jews and anti-Semitic violence, in historically tolerant localities the effect was even opposite.

Competition

An important tool to counteract media capture is competition among media outlets. Theoretically, when the bias originates from the supply side, e.g., in the bias of those who produce information (media editors, journalists, etc.), then higher competition can lead to lower bias. But stronger competition may have opposite effects if newspapers fear to lose readers and decide to cover certain issues using an attention-grabbing extreme tone. Empirical evidence on the benefits of competition in reducing media bias is provided by Fonseca-Galvis et al. (2016), who find that partisan newspapers devoted more coverage to scandals involving their preferred party in localities where there was at least one newspaper affiliated with the opposing party.

In addition, competition gives to the audiences the option to switch from one media outlet to another. Durante and Knight (2012) show that Italian viewers responded to changes in TV channels by switching to other news sources: when Berlusconi was the prime minister, the news content in public TV channels shifted to the right. As a consequence, public television attracted relatively more right-wing voters, and left-wing viewers turned to other channels. Also, while the right-wing viewers increased their trust in media, left-wing viewers saw it decrease.

A separate but related question is whether, in a context where most media outlets are captured, an independent one can make a difference. Enikolopov, Petrova, and Zhuravskaya (2011) test the effects of an independent TV channel on votes cast for Vladimir Putin in 1999. They exploit geographical variation in the access to this independent TV channel and show that such exposure increased the vote share of opposition parties by 6.3 percentage points, while decreasing the votes pro-Putin by 8.9 percentage points.

Despite the above evidence, it is not always true that in captured contexts independent outlets are successful in improving accountability. Malesky, Schuler, and Tran (2012) study the effect of increasing information on legislative performance of the politicians in Vietnam. They find that information provision did not improve the performance of delegates, but deputies of regions with higher Internet diffusion began avoiding initiatives that could shed a negative light on regime leaders. At the same time, increased availability of information on some politicians made them less likely to be reappointed by the regime.

19.2.4. Open Questions

The above discussion on media coverage and media bias makes clear that a large share of the evidence that we have available on these topics comes from high-income countries. When thinking about the possibility of translating that evidence to low-income settings, a number of questions emerge.

What are the incentives to provide accurate information in low-income settings? Is the mitigating force of information discounting equally at play? The fact that individuals rationally anticipate that information is biased in a certain direction requires some degree of awareness of the bias and of the manipulation of information, and if there are no other sources of knowledge than the official ones, this awareness may be difficult to achieve.

How do the incentives to provide accurate information work in settings where advertising is not the driving force? Commercial television and the printed press in advanced democracies typically get most of their revenues from advertising. While this may create bias toward certain businesses (e.g., Reuter and Zitzewitz 2006), it does impose a constraint that the content provided must be appealing enough that viewers or readers want to "consume" this content. In settings where news outlets are financed by the government or by a few powerful interest groups, what incentives remain to provide reliable information?

More generally, a systematic understanding of media ownership patterns in low-income countries and of how ownership patterns affect media content in these settings is needed. Very little rigorous empirical evidence exists on this front.

Also, the theoretical framework linking media content and accountability has been largely developed for democracies. We know a lot less about how these mechanisms work in autocracies—something that is highly relevant for a number of developing countries.

An important gap in the literature relates to the possibility of using new media (e.g., social networks and online platforms) to improve accountability. Enikolopov, Makarin, and Petrova (2016) test if social media can help reduce collective action problems by studying the penetration of VK, the Russian equivalent of Facebook, across cities. They show that VK penetration increased protest activities in 2011 and that this was not due to the network spreading information that was critical of the incumbent government (if anything, network penetration increased support for the government), but rather to the reduced costs of coordination that the network allowed. More work is needed to understand the potential of social media for political accountability.

Providing credible answers to the above questions is crucial and has important policy implications, ranging from regulation to legal reform. In terms of regulation, platform-specific regulation may involve limits on ownership by single companies/platforms and limits on cross-platform ownership. Also, competition policy cannot be limited to ensuring low concentration (as measured by a low Herfindahl index): there is a specific need for media plurality, i.e., it is crucial that different viewpoints and ideologies are represented, not just that market shares do not exceed certain values. The role of direct provision of news content is also a sensitive one. While there exist excellent examples of public service broadcasting (e.g., the BBC), the risk of capture and propaganda in settings with bad governance is high.

19.3. MEDIA AND SOCIAL CHANGE

The above discussion has analyzed under what circumstances the media contributes to accountability and to the well functioning of political institutions. But what makes citizens demand accountable governments? One of the greatest puzzles in the political economy of development is why voters keep electing politicians that do not deliver good policies. Even if a country had the right legal and political infrastructure in place, if citizens maintain low expectations about their leaders or if they do not deem institutional change as possible, changing the rules of the game will not be enough. It is therefore crucial to understand the formation of citizens' beliefs and preferences, and how the media contributes to shaping beliefs and preferences.

Mass media have the potential to induce important changes in people's preferences and beliefs by providing information on the economics environment and available opportunities and by influencing aspirations through role modeling.[4] Evidence on this point has been offered focusing on outcomes that are particularly related to social norms (e.g., gender norms) and for which the presence of "new" content on TV or radio may offer alternative models and lead to changes in social norms.

For example, La Ferrara, Chong, and Duryea (2012) study the effect of Brazilian soap operas (*novelas*) on fertility patterns from the mid-1960s to the mid-1990s. While population control was not a goal of the producers of these *novelas*, reasons related to the development of the plot implied that for many years the main female characters in these soap operas had very few children, if any. The authors exploit the staggered entry of Rede Globo, the main novela producer in the country, across municipalities to test if locations exposed to these programs see a reduction in fertility. They find a significant reduction in fertility, equivalent to the one that would be achieved through an increase of 1.6 years in women's education. The effect is stronger for families of low socioeconomic status and for women closer in age to the main *novela* character in any given year, consistent with greater identification with such characters. Chong and La Ferrara (2009) confirm that these commercial TV programs were capable of inducing changes in other social norms, as municipalities exposed to Rede Globo saw an increase in divorce and separation rates compared to other municipalities.

Jensen and Oster (2009) study a different setting, India, and explore how the introduction of cable TV across rural villages exposed the local population to values and behavior typical of Western societies. They find that after the introduction of cable TV, villagers were less likely to tolerate domestic violence, they expressed less son preference, and reported greater autonomy in decision-making for women.

While the above media content was not designed to change individual attitudes in a certain direction (the change in behavior and norms was a by-product of a commercial strategy), there is scope for explicitly designing media content in order to achieve the desired social and behavioral change. This is what the so-called educational entertainment does.

19.3.1. Educational Entertainment

Educational entertainment (EE, or *edutainment*) is "the process of purposely designing and implementing a media message to both entertain and educate, in order to increase audience members' knowledge about an issue, create favorable attitudes, shift social norms, and change the overt behavior of individuals and communities" (Singhal and Rogers 2004: 5). Underlying this notion are some pillars from social psychology that can be attributed to the work of Albert Bandura.

The first is Bandura's (1976) *social learning theory*. This theory postulates that individuals learn not only through their own experience, but also through the experience of others, so that media programs constitute an opportunity to learn from characters' successes and failures without personally incurring the costs. The second building block is the concept of *self-efficacy*, that is, the "beliefs in one's capabilities to organize and execute the courses of action required to produce given attainments" (Bandura 1997: 3). Here the idea is that the media can offer role models who successfully pursue certain goals, make those goals seem attainable, and induce the viewers to act to pursue those objectives. Role modeling, identification, and exemplification are thus crucial features of edutainment productions, since the early days of Miguel Sabido's (1981) edutainment soap operas.

While these ideas have been popular among practitioners for many years, only recently have they been rigorously evaluated from an empirical point of view. These evaluations point to two main roles that edutainment productions can perform.

First, edutainment seems effective in providing information. For example, Berg and Zia (2013) introduced a plot on over-borrowing and financial education into a mainstream soap opera in South Africa and found significant improvements in financial knowledge of viewers who were (exogenously) incentivized to watch this soap. Ravallion et al. (2015) study the National Rural Employment Guarantee Scheme (NREGS) in Bihar, India. In order to increase the take-up of the program among poor rural households, the authors produced a short movie telling the story of a migrant who is able to stay in his village, close to his family, thanks to the availability of work through the public works scheme. The movie shows how the scheme works and provides some pieces of information related to eligibility, contractual conditions, etc. Evaluating this movie through a randomized controlled trial, Ravallion et al. find that knowledge of NREGS and perceptions about its usefulness were significantly improved, while actual usage of the program was not. On a different topic (health instead of public policy), Banerjee, Barnhardt, and Duflo (2015) show that a short movie is more effective in increasing consumption of double-fortified salt (used against anemia) than a traditional information campaign done through flyers.

A second objective for edutainment productions, after information provision, is that of changing people's preferences in a way that is conducive to positive behavior, through role modeling. This function is particularly relevant when thinking of institutional change, as it may be hypothesized that the persistence of dysfunctional institutions or norms may be linked to "aspiration failures" (e.g., Genicot and Ray 2015; Dalton, Ghosal, and Mani 2016). Two recent studies suggest that edutainment can be successful in raising the aspirations of the poor. Bernard et al. (2014) show that short documentaries telling success stories of young Ethiopians improved viewers' aspirations and locus of control, also leading parents to invest more in their children's education. Bjorvatn et al. (2015) evaluate an edutainment show in Tanzania aimed at fostering entrepreneurship among high school students. They find positive effects both on aspirations and on actual decisions to start a business, although this is at the expense of academic achievement (as the program did not trace a link from schooling to entrepreneurial success).

Particularly relevant for institutional change are the contributions of Paluck (2009) and Paluck and Green (2009). These authors study post-genocide reconciliation in Rwanda, and in particular assess whether a radio soap opera containing messages on the importance of independent judgment and on the origins of violence is able to change beliefs about the source of violence and norms of trust and cooperation. The authors find a positive effect on "prescriptive" social norms (i.e., norms prescribing how people should behave) but no impact on "descriptive" social norms (i.e., how people actually behave). The lack of an effect on the latter variable points to the importance of coordinating beliefs when using edutainment to change deeply rooted norms.

Trujillo and Paluck (2011) experiment with using a Mexican soap opera to change political attitudes of the Latino population in relation to perceived threats from immigration legislation. During the 2010 US Census there was concern among Latino communities for the possibility that immigration officials would use the Census to target immigration raids. This led some members of the Latino population to boycott the Census. Trujillo and Paluck's study is set in Arizona, Texas, and New Jersey, where the authors randomly assigned Latino study participants to watch scenes that encouraged participation in the Census. They found improved attitudes toward the US government among treated individuals, as well as support for the Census (as proxied by wearing Census stickers). However, they did not find improved attitudes in Arizona, where the recent passage of the immigration bill SB 1070 led the local Latinos to perceive a direct threat from the US government. These findings point to a potential (albeit limited) role for edutainment in changing civic attitudes and trust in government.

19.3.1.1. Caveats

While overall the existing evidence leaves room for optimism regarding the possibility of using mass media to transmit information and affect preferences and beliefs in a way that is conducive to institutional development, some caveats are in order. The first relates to time use. When people spend time in front of the television or listening to the radio, they allocate that time away from other activities. The net effect of the exposure thus depends on the activities that are "crowded out" by media consumption. In a famous book, Putnam (2000) argues that the spread of television in the United States has increased people's isolation and decreased social capital. Olken (2009) tests this hypothesis in Indonesia, relying on variation in the number of TV channels available across different villages. This in turn depends on variation in the quality of the signal, which is a function of topography and other terrain characteristics. His results suggest that an increase in the number of available TV channels leads to fewer social groups and less participation in group meetings, especially for non-religious groups such as rotating savings and credit associations. It is thus important to assess the appropriateness of different strategies to use mass media for institutional change, privileging the ones that do not discourage social interaction.

A second important caveat relates to ethical aspects. When using mass media for public policy, there is a risk that content may be strategically manipulated for propaganda purposes. This is especially worrisome from the point of view of institutional change because such manipulation is generally more likely in weak institutional settings. A well-known case in point is that of North Korea, where Kim Jong-il heavily used entertainment movies to promote his image as a leader and discredit Western countries (Fischer 2015). While content manipulation is an intrinsic risk for all media outlets (see the discussion above on media capture and bias), it appears in a new light in the case of edutainment because the possibility to justify state intervention in programming on the grounds of educational goals may provide an easy excuse for opportunistic distortion of information. When viewers are aware of content manipulation and have a choice among many outlets, the possibility to switch to less distorted outlets constitutes a safeguard, but in countries with limited supply of media outlets or where very few independent sources exist, this mechanism is not in place.

19.3.2. Open Questions and Concluding Remarks

A large part of the existing evidence on the effect of edutainment relates to educational or family outcomes, and only a small number of studies directly targeted political attitudes or civic norms. An important gap in the literature is thus to understand if and how entertainment media can be used to foster "civic values" and build awareness about political and institutional participation.

Another important issue is the interplay between media content and deeply rooted social norms. Is it possible for entertainment programs to change preferences and beliefs to the point that they induce a shift in deeply rooted social norms? Here the issue of coordination and of social effects becomes central. While viewers may be able to identify a desirable behavior as transmitted by positive role model in the program, they may not act correspondingly if they do not anticipate other people to do the same. For example, if an edutainment program warns against corruption and discourages viewers from paying bribes to obtain public services, viewers may still decide to pay bribes if they expect everyone else to do it and they do not want to be cut out of public service provision. In ongoing work, Banerjee, La Ferrara, and Orozco (2015) address similar issues in evaluating the impact of a TV series produced by MTV in Nigeria to reduce risky sexual behavior and domestic violence. Their experimental design creates exogenous variation in the beliefs about other people's behavior, thus allowing viewers to understand the interplay between edutainment content and social effects.

A third question that is important for the edutainment agenda in dealing with institutional change relates to the optimal degree of challenging the status quo in promoting new norms. A message that is too mild may not induce the desired change, but a message that is too far away from the existing norm may discourage behavioral change if the new behavior is perceived as too threatening. Little, if any, evidence exists on this point.

Finally, in an increasingly globalized world, it is too limiting to think of media content as being only locally generated. People are exposed to information and values that come from different countries and very different cultures. Whether this leads to institutional convergence or not is an open question for future research.

Overall, the existing evidence suggests that mass media have the potential to convey political information but also values and models that can lead to behavioral change in developing countries. Contextualizing this behavioral change in the case of different institutions is something that has not been done systematically, and that promises to yield important payoffs. Also, with the rapid spread of new social media that partly substitute for traditional ones, an opportunity opens up to reach new segments of the population (Singhal 2013). How to accomplish this goal is something that future policy interventions and research should determine.

NOTES

I thank seminar participants at the EDI Conferences in Namur and Paris for helpful comments. Giulia Caprini provided excellent research assistance.

1. See below for a description of the identification strategy used to isolate the exogenous component of news content.
2. In order to address the endogeneity problem, the authors use an instrumental variables approach, instrumenting newspaper circulation with variables that represent ownership by parties, private associations, etc. The underlying rationale is that in states where newspapers are owned by the parties, for example, voters will anticipate that the content is likely to be biased and will have a lower demand for newspapers.
3. Yet another example is given by Ho and Quinn (2008), who analyzed the editorials in 25 US newspapers covering about 495 Supreme Court cases between 1994 and 2004. For each journal, they observed whether it supported the minority or majority position for all the different cases. By making use of the actual votes cast by the Supreme Court justices on the same cases, the authors managed to profile the relative partisanship of journals and justices. As for the newspapers, they find a majority of centrists relative to the distribution estimated for justices.
4. See DellaVigna and La Ferrara (2015) and La Ferrara (2016) for a review of contributions on these topics.

REFERENCES

Adena, M., Enikolopov, R., Petrova, M., Santarosa, V., and Zhuravskaya, E. 2015. "Radio and the Rise of the Nazis in Prewar Germany." *Quarterly Journal of Economics* 130(4): 1885–1939.

Bai, J., Golosov, M., Qian, N., and Kai, Y. 2014. "Understanding the Influence of Government Controlled Media: Evidence from Air Pollution in China." Mimeo.

Bandura, A. 1976. *Social Learning Theory.* Englewood Cliffs, NJ: Prentice-Hall.

———. 1997. *Self-efficacy: The Exercise of Control.* New York: Freeman.

Banerjee, A., Barnhardt, S., and Duflo, E. 2015. "Movies, Margins and Marketing: Encouraging the Adoption of Iron-Fortified Salt." In D. Wise (ed.), *Insights in the Economics of Aging*, NBER.

Banerjee, A., Kumar, S., Pande, R., and Su, F. 2011. "Do Informed Voters Make Better Choices? Experimental Evidence from Urban India." Mimeo, Harvard University.

Banerjee, A., La Ferrara, E., and Orozco, V. 2015. "Changing Norms and Behavior of Young People in Nigeria: An Evaluation of Entertainment TV." Mimeo, Bocconi University.

Berg, G., and Zia, B. 2013. "Harnessing Emotional Connections to Improve Financial Decisions: Evaluating the Impact of Financial Education in Mainstream Media." World Bank Policy Research Working Paper No. 6407.

Bernard, T., Dercon, S., Orkin, K., and Taffesse, A. S. 2014. "The Future in Mind: Aspirations and Forward-Looking Behaviour in Rural Ethiopia." CSAE Working Paper WPS/2014–16.

Besley, T., and Burgess, R. 2001. "Political Agency, Government Responsiveness and the Role of the Media." *European Economic Review* 45: 629–640.

———. 2002. "The Political Economy of Government Responsiveness: Theory and Evidence from India." *Quarterly Journal of Economics* 117(4): 1415–1451.

Besley, T., and Prat, A. 2006. "Handcuffs for the Grabbing Hand? The Role of the Media in Political Accountability." *American Economic Review* 96(3): 720–736.

Bidwell, K., Casey, K., and Glennerster, R. 2015. "Debates: The Impact of Voter Knowledge Initiatives in Sierra Leone." Mimeo, Innovations for Poverty Action.

Bjorvatn, K., Cappelen, A., Helgesson Sekeiz, L., Sorensen, E., and Tungodden, B. 2015. "Teaching through Television: Experimental Evidence on Entrepreneurship Education in Tanzania." Mimeo, NHH Norwegian School of Economics.

Brunetti, A., and Weder, B. 2003. "A Free Press Is Bad News for Corruption." *Journal of Public Economics* 7–8: 1801–1824.

Cheung, M. 2012. "Edutainment Radio, Women's Status and Primary School Participation: Evidence from Cambodia." Stockholm University, Working Paper.

Chiang, C. F., and Knight, B. 2011. "Media Bias and Influence: Evidence from Newspaper Endorsements." *Review of Economic Studies* 78(3): 795–820.

Chong, A., and La Ferrara, E. 2009. "Television and Divorce: Evidence from Brazilian Novelas." *Journal of the European Economic Association: Papers 8 Proceedings* 7(2–3): 458–468.

Dalton, P., Ghosal, S., and Mani, A. 2016. "Poverty and Aspirations Failure." *Economic Journal* 126(590): 165–188.

DellaVigna, S., Enikolopov, R., Mironova, V., Petrova, M., and Zhuravskaya, E. 2014. "Cross-border Media and Nationalism: Evidence from Serbian Radio in Croatia." *American Economic Journal: Applied Economics* 6(3): 103–132.

DellaVigna, S., and Gentzkow, M. 2010. "Persuasion: Empirical Evidence." *Annual Review of Economics* 2: 643–669.

DellaVigna, S., and Kaplan, E. D. 2007. "The Fox News Effect: Media Bias and Voting." *Quarterly Journal of Economics* 122(3): 1187–1234.

DellaVigna, S., and La Ferrara, E. 2015. "Economic and Social Impacts of the Media." In *Handbook of Media Economics*, vol. 1B, edited by S. Anderson, D. Stromberg, and J. Waldfogel. Amsterdam: North-Holland.

Di Tella, R., and Franceschelli, I. 2011. "Government Advertising and Media Coverage of Corruption Scandals." *American Economic Journal: Applied Economics* 3(4): 119–151.

Djankov, S., McLiesh, C., Nenova, T., and Shleifer, A. 2003. "Who Owns the Media?" *Journal of Law and Economics* 46(2): 2.

Durante, R., and Knight, B. 2012. "Partisan Control, Media Bias, and Viewer Responses: Evidence from Berlusconi's Italy." *Journal of the European Economic Association* 10(3): 451–481.

Egorov, G., Guriev, S., and Sonin, K. 2009. "Why Resource-Poor Dictators Allow Freer Media: A Theory and Evidence from Panel Data." *American Political Science Review* 103(4): 645–668.

Eisensee, T., and Strömberg, D. 2007. "News Droughts, News Floods, and U.S. Disaster Relief." *Quarterly Journal of Economics* 122(2): 693–728.

Enikolopov, R., Makarin, A., and Petrova, M. 2016. "Social Media and Protest Participation: Evidence from Russia." Mimeo.

Enikolopov, R., and Petrova. M. 2015. "Media Capture: Empirical Evidence." In *Handbook of Media Economics*, vol. 1B, edited by S. Anderson, D. Stromberg, and J. Waldfogel. Amsterdam: North-Holland.

Enikolopov, R., Petrova, M., and Zhuravskaya, E. 2011. "Media and Political Persuasion: Evidence from Russia." *American Economic Review* 111(7): 3253–3285.

Farré, L., and Fasani, F. 2013. "Media Exposure and Internal Migration—Evidence from Indonesia." *Journal of Development Economics* 102(C): 48–61.

Ferraz, C., and Finan, F. 2008. "Exposing Corrupt Politicians: The Effect of Brazil's Publicly Released Audits on Electoral Outcomes." *Quarterly Journal of Economics* 123(2): 703–745.

Fischer, P. 2015. *A Kim Jong-Il Production: The Extraordinary True Story of a Kid-napped Filmmaker, His Star Actress, and a Young Dictator's Rise to Power*. Flatiron Books.

Fonseca-Galvis, A., Snyder, J. M., and Song, B. K. 2016. "Newspaper Market Structure and Behavior: Partisan Coverage of Political Scandals in the US from 1870 to 1910." *Journal of Politics* 78(2): 368–381.

Fujiwara, T., and Wantchekon, L. 2013. "Can Informed Public Deliberation Overcome Clientelism? Experimental Evidence from Benin." *American Economic Journal: Applied Economics* 5(4): 241–255.

Genicot, G., and Ray, D. 2015. "Aspirations and Inequality." Mimeo, Georgetown University and NYU.

Gentzkow, M. 2006. "Television and Voter Turnout." *Quarterly Journal of Economics* 121(3): 931–972.

Gentzkow, M., and Shapiro, J. M. 2008. "Competition and Truth in the Market for News." *Journal of Economic Perspectives*, 133–154.

———. 2010. "What Drives Media Slant? Evidence from US Daily Newspapers." *Econometrica* 78(1): 35–71.

Gentzkow, M., Shapiro, J., and Stone, D. 2015. "Media Bias in the Marketplace: Theory." In *Handbook of Media Economics*, vol. 1B, edited by S. Anderson, D. Stromberg, and J. Waldfogel. Amsterdam: North-Holland.

Gerber, A. S., Karlan, D. S., and Bergan, D. 2009. "Does the Media Matter? A Field Experiment Measuring the Effect of Newspapers on Voting Behavior and Political Opinions." *American Economic Journal: Applied Economics* 1(2): 35–52.

Groseclose, T., and Milyo, J. 2005. "A Measure of Media Bias." *Quarterly Journal of Economics* 120: 1191–1237.

Ho, D. E., and Quinn, K. M. 2008. "Assessing Political Positions of the Media." *Quarterly Journal of Political Science* 3(4): 353–377.

Holmström, B., and Milgrom, P. 1991. "Multi-task Principal Agent Analyses: Incentive Contracts, Asset Ownership, and Job Design." *Journal of Law, Economics and Organization* 1991(7): 24–52.

Hufford, G. 2002. The ITS Irregular Terrain Model, Version 1.2.2: The Algorithm. Institute for Telecommunication Sciences, National Telecommunications and Information Administration. http://www.its.bldrdoc.gov/media/50674/itm.pdf.

Jensen, R., and Oster, E. 2009. "The Power of TV: Cable Television and Women's Status in India." *Quarterly Journal of Economics* 124(3): 1057–1094.

Keefer, P., and Khemani, S. 2011. "Mass Media and Public Services: The Effects of Radio Access on Public Education in Benin." Policy Research Working Paper Series 5559, World Bank.

King, G., Pan, J., and Roberts, M. E. 2013. "How Censorship in China Allows Government Criticism But Silences Collective Expression." *American Political Science Review* 107(02): 326–343.

———. 2014. "Reverse-Engineering Censorship in China: Randomized Experimentation and Participant Observation." *Science* 345 (6199): 1–10.

La Ferrara, E. 2016. "Mass Media and Social Change: Can We Use Television to Fight Poverty?" *Journal of the European Economic Association*, August.

La Ferrara, E., Chong, A., and Duryea, S. 2012. "Soap Operas and Fertility: Evidence from Brazil." *American Economic Journal: Applied Economics* 4(4): 1–31.

Larcinese, V., Puglisi, R., and Snyder, J. 2011. "Partisan Bias in Economic News: Evidence on the Agenda-Setting Behavior of US Newspapers." *Journal of Public Economics* 95(9–10): 1178–1189.

Malesky, E., Schuler, P., and Tran, A. 2012. "The Adverse Effects of Sunshine: A Field Experiment on Legislative Transparency in an Authoritarian Assembly." *American Political Science Review* 106(04): 762–786.

McMillan, J., and Zoido, P. 2004. "How to Subvert Democracy: Montesinos in Peru." *Journal of Economic Perspectives* 18(4): 69.

Moyer-Guse, E. 2008. "Toward a Theory of Entertainment Persuasion: Explaining the Persuasive Effects of Entertainment-Education Messages." *Communication Theory* 18(3): 407–425.

Olken, B. 2009. "Do TV and Radio Destroy Social Capital? Evidence from Indonesian Villages." *American Economic Journal: Applied Economics* 1(4): 1–33.

Paluck, E. L. 2009. "Reducing Intergroup Prejudice and Conflict Using the Media: A Field Experiment in Rwanda." *Journal of Personality and Social Psychology* 96: 574–587.

Paluck, E. L., and Green, D. P. (2009). "Deference, Dissent, and Dispute Resolution: A Field Experiment on a Mass Media Intervention in Rwanda." *American Political Science Review* 103(4): 622–644.

Pechmann, C., and Stewart, D. 1988. "A Critical Review of Wearin and Wearout." *Current Issues and Research in Advertising* 11: 285–330.

Petrova, M. 2011. "Newspapers and Parties: How Advertising Revenues Created an Independent Press." *American Political Science Review* 105(04): 790–808.

Puglisi, R., and Snyder, J. 2011. "Newspaper Coverage of Political Scandals." *Journal of Politics* 73(3): 931–950.

———. 2015. "The Balanced US Press." *Journal of the European Economic Association* 13(2): 240–264.

Putnam, R. 2000. *Bowling Alone: The Collapse and Revival of American Community*. New York: Simon & Schuster.

Qian, N., and Yanagizawa-Drott, D. 2017. "Government Distortion in Independently Owned Media: Evidence from US Cold War News Coverage of Human Rights." *Journal of the European Economic Association* 15(2): 463–499.

Qin, B., Wu, Y., and Strömberg, D. 2014. "The Determinants of Media Capture in China." Mimeo.

Ravallion, M., van de Walle, D., Dutta, P., and Murgai, R. 2015. "Empowering Poor People through Public Information? Lessons from a Movie in Rural India." *Journal of Public Economics* 132: 13–22.

Reinikka, R., and Svensson, J. 2005. "Fighting Corruption to Improve Schooling: Evidence from a Newspaper Campaign in Uganda." *Journal of the European Economic Association* 3: 259–267.

Reuter, J., and Zitzewitz, E. 2006. "Do Ads Influence Editors? Advertising and Bias in the Financial Media." *Quarterly Journal of Economics* (1): 197–227.

Sabido, M. 1981. "Towards the Social Use of Soap Operas." Mexico City: Institute for Communication Research.

Singhal, A. 2013. "Fairy Tale to Digital Games: The Rising Tide of Edutainment Education." *Critical Arts: South-North Cultural and Media Studies* 27(1): 1–8.

Singhal, A., and Rogers, E. 2004. "The Status of Entertainment Education Worldwide." In *Entertainment-Education and Social Change*, edited by A. Singhal, M. Cody, E. Rogers, and M. Sabido, ch 1. New York: Routledge.

Snyder, J., and Strömberg, D. 2010. "Press Coverage and Political Accountability." *Journal of Political Economy* 118(2): 355–408.

Stanig, P. 2015. "Regulation of Speech and Media Coverage of Corruption: An Empirical Analysis of the Mexican Press." *American Journal of Political Science* 59(1): 175–193.

Starr, P. 2004. "The Creation of the Media." *Political Origins of Modern Communications*. New York: Basic Books.

Strömberg, D. 2004a. "Radio's Impact on Public Spending." *Quarterly Journal of Economics* 119(1): 189–221.

———. 2004b. "Mass Media Competition, Political Competition and Public Policy." *Review of Economic Studies* 71(1): 265–284.

———. 2015. "Media Coverage and Political Accountability: Theory and Evidence." In *Handbook of Media Economics*, vol. 1B, edited by S. Anderson, D. Stromberg, and J. Waldfogel. Amsterdam: North-Holland.

Trujillo, M., and Paluck, E. L. 2011. "The Devil Knows Best: Experimental Effects of a Televised Soap Opera on Latino Trust in Government and Support for the 2010 Census." *Analysis of Social Issues and Public Policy* 12(1). DOI: 10.1111/j.1530-2415.2011.01249.x.

Yanagizawa-Drott, D. 2014. "Propaganda and Conflict: Evidence from the Rwandan Genocide." *Quarterly Journal of Economics* 129(4): 1947–1994.

20

INSTITUTIONS, THE ENVIRONMENT, AND DEVELOPMENT

E. Somanathan

20.1. INTRODUCTION

Environmental problems may be classified by the scale of the relevant externalities. Some externalities are primarily local, for example, those concerning the management of resources like forests, pastures and inland fisheries, or local air and water pollution. Others are mainly regional or national, like river and air pollution, that is carried over longer distances. Still others, like ozone depletion and climate change, are global. Institutions that can address issues at these different scales may be quite different in their genesis and structure. For example, community management that may work well for local commons under some circumstances is ineffective at larger scales, where state institutions are required.

This chapter examines the evolution and performance of institutions that address environmental issues in developing countries at various scales.

20.2. COMMUNITY MANAGEMENT

There is a large literature examining small-scale common property resources like pastures, village forests, and local fisheries. The institutions that sometimes succeed in protecting these resources have been much studied (Ostrom 1990; Baland and Platteau 1996). There is even an International Association for the Study of the Commons with annual conferences and a journal.

20.2.1. Theoretical Literature

Economic theory has conceptualized the problem of the commons in simple terms as a game played by n persons, each of whom gets a benefit from harvesting a resource and imposes a cost on the others when she does so. Due to the externality, the Nash equilibrium of this static game is inefficient, with harvest levels that are too high relative to a Pareto-optimum (Gordon 1954; Dasgupta and Heal 1979). The conclusion, most famously expressed by a biologist, Garrett Hardin, in his 1968 paper in *Science*, was that commons should either be privatized or regulated by the state. With the publication of Elinor Ostrom's book *Governing the Commons* in 1990, a work that was instrumental in her being awarded a Nobel Prize, it became clear that commons in the real world were often successfully governed by their users, and that Hardin's "tragedy" was by no means inevitable. In commons such as forests, pastures, and some local fisheries, institutions to regulate extraction have evolved and many are successful in restraining excessive extraction. These institutions are often predicated on social norms and sanctions that ultimately depend on the ability of a community to sanction offenders.

Cooperation in the commons, once its frequency became clear, was first explained by economists in terms of dynamic games. Provided individuals do not discount the future too heavily, a subgame-perfect equilibrium in which players harvest the common resource at socially optimal levels exists. Such an equilibrium is sustained by the threat that if any individual harvests more than the equilibrium level, then others would do so too in subsequent periods. The notion of subgame perfection captures the idea that such threats are credible in the sense that they are in the interest of the individual to actually carry out should the eventuality arise. The main insight that this approach offers is that cooperation is highly dependent on continued interaction. Communities with too much mobility or anonymity are unlikely to succeed in cooperation. One problem with this approach is that actually observed cooperation everywhere relies on explicit or implicit punishments for over-extraction, not on over-extraction as a punishment.

Alternative approaches that rely on explicit punishments for over-extraction or other non-cooperation have appealed to evolutionary game theory (Sethi and Somanathan 1996) or evolved preferences for reciprocity (ibid.). The latter model allows the examination of how heterogeneities in returns from exploiting the commons, and in the power to inflict punishment, affect the prospects for cooperation. Asymmetries of power can actually promote cooperation in certain cases, by enabling punishment by the powerful that is strong enough to deter opportunism. This is consistent with many examples of cooperation that rely on leadership by local elites who also gain a disproportionate share of the benefits from cooperation.

20.2.2. Forest Management as an Example

The restraining force of social sanctions has eroded the world over for a variety of reasons—a rise in the return to harvesting with technical progress, a rise in resource prices when isolated communities are connected to external markets, a fall in the effectiveness of social sanctions with an increase in mobility, and in many cases, expropriation of common pool resources by states. This has destabilized social norms of restraint in harvesting (Jodha 1986; Sethi and Somanathan 1996).

In some cases, states have responded to these difficulties by providing backing for community institutions, formalizing them and giving them the ability to raise taxes and levy fines. This has been the case, for example, in Uttarakhand in India in the colonial period (Somanathan 1991) and in Nepal (Kanel 2008). In other cases, as in most of India, the state has been much more reluctant to cede powers to local bodies, despite an official rhetoric that favors this. This has a long history. The colonization of Asia and Africa by European countries in the nineteenth century led to more or less successful attempts by conquering powers to seize control of forests from local populations. These led to nationalization and the creation of forest bureaucracies to administer forest resources so that the production of timber and other products could be sustained. The Indian Forest departments are the exemplar of this process, but more or less similar structures were created in French colonial Africa as well (Baland and Platteau 1996). The Indian Forest departments were created to administer most forest lands in the country and are in the control of state governments. Since Indian states are mostly of the size of large European countries, this is a highly centralized system that, even today, allows for very little local control.

Post-colonial states inherited these bureaucratic institutions and the resulting control of increasingly valuable natural assets as transport and labor availability increased. Not surprisingly, the incentive for local commons management was reduced and social norms governing resource use disrupted. For example, in the Indian central Himalaya, the system of traditional control of village forests by a council of elders was considerably weakened to the extent that one official wrote that "the oak is melting away in Kumaun like an iceberg on the equator" (Somanathan 1991).

In response to the obvious problems created by nationalization, there was a wave of decentralization of forest management across the developing world in the 1980s and 1990s, often encouraged by foreign donors. Participatory management became a buzzword. It has been estimated that more than a quarter of forests in the developing world are under indigenous or community management (Larson, Dahal, et al. 2012). However, Larson et al.'s paper also reveals that in many countries in Latin America, Africa, and Asia, there is a tussle between state officials and local people over control of forests. This can be expected to lead to degradation and under-investment due to the uncertainty generated in property rights. Of course, this applies to forests that are close to habitation. More remote forests may be managed by the state more effectively.

A systematic review of statistical studies of the effects of community management of forests in less developed countries found only 42 studies, with more than two-thirds of these from Asia (Bowler et al. 2011). The authors' meta-analysis found that tree density and basal area were on average greater in community-managed forests than in forests under other or no management. There were too few studies to statistically analyze effects on species diversity or welfare outcomes. More informally, on the basis of case studies in the literature, Baland and Platteau (1996) concluded that the evidence suggested that centralized management did not lead to better outcomes. A study in India found that local management of forests cost an order of magnitude less than state management and delivered forest conservation that was at least as good (Somanathan, Prabhakar, and Mehta 2009). This suggests another potential advantage of local management—it is likely to be less expensive than centralized management that relies on bureaucracies that have high labor costs.

Of course, there is a presumption that devolving powers to local bodies would lead to better outcomes for local communities. There is, however, the possibility that the dominance of local elites could result in the poor becoming worse off. There seems to be no clear evidence of this. While it may be the case that the poor get fewer benefits from community forests than the non-poor (Adhikari 2005), it is not known how this compares to what happens when there is no devolution. An investigation of the impact of the Nepal community forestry program on poorer households was inconclusive (Datta 2011). In any case, it is to be expected that there would be considerable heterogeneity on this score, and it is unlikely that any general conclusions could be drawn.

Even though devolution may not always lead to better welfare outcomes, and the evidence concerning its effects is far from complete, the present state of our understanding does suggest that in many circumstances, devolution would improve both efficiency and equity. The crucial question, therefore, is: *What leads states to devolve authority over natural resource management to local communities and authorities or households?* This is a question that is clearly related to broader questions concerning the nature of states.

Richer countries and more democratic countries tend to decentralize more (Arzaghi and Henderson 2005), but there is considerable variation. Moreover, it is not clear if the decentralization measure used in Arzaghi and Henderson (2005), which lumps provincial and local governments together, is a good measure of local autonomy. India and China, in different ways, do not fit this pattern. While India is quite democratic, and has strong provincial governments, local governments are very weak. In China, on the other hand, there is considerable autonomy given to local governments, perhaps because the authoritarian nature of the state limits political competition between levels of government. The relative autonomy of local governments means that centralization of authority over a particular sector, such as forests, is limited.

So far, we have treated common resources as exogenously given. But some of them could be privatized. This is the direction of tenure reforms in China's forestry sector. About 60% of China's forest area is collective, or village-controlled forest, with the remaining being state-owned (Yin, Yao, and Huo 2013). Tenurial reforms have taken place in collective forests. When the household responsibility system was introduced in 1978 for agricultural land, it was followed within a few years by similar reforms in forest land. But in the case of forests, the reforms varied by province and were subject to constraints and partial reversals. The village authorities maintained controls over harvesting and thinning, timber was subject to heavy taxes, and the timber market in southern China was controlled, with farmers obliged to sell timber to the state at low prices. The situation in the north was different because there was little forest of value, and the state was less concerned about ecological destruction. As a result, forest sector reforms went much further toward de facto privatization and free timber markets in the north.

There was a second wave of reforms in several provinces starting around 2003 which liberalized timber markets and reduced restrictions on households harvesting and thinning. This was followed by a large increase in timber harvests, a significant increase in the share of forestry in rural household incomes, and a large increase in afforestation. While not all these can be attributed to the tenure reforms—with increases in timber demand and prices playing an important role—the increase in afforestation in particular is a sign that fears of unsustainable harvesting without replanting induced by greater freedom to individual households may be unjustified (Xu 2010).

This history and the contrast with other regions is a reminder of the fact that institutions to manage natural resources are heavily shaped by the larger institutional environment and cannot be analyzed in isolation. Paradoxically, it may well be the absence of private property in China that is favorable to effective privatization—it may be easier to distribute new de facto property rights on a more or less equal basis when there are no prior hierarchies in wealth and property ownership.

Perhaps the most interesting question for future research is what it is about governmental structure that makes it more likely that devolution of property rights over forests to local communities or households will take place. The two cases in the developing world where this has proceeded furthest appear to be China and Nepal, which have, or had, very different state structures at the time of their major forestry reforms.

The Nepalese case and its contrast with India is instructive because it suggests the importance of institutional inertia in determining the prospects for decentralization. During the century until 1950, Nepal was under the rule of hereditary prime ministers called the Ranas. In the Rana period, forests in each village were managed by the headman who controlled harvesting and extraction. The replacement of Rana rule by a democratic government led to nationalization of the forests in 1957, motivated by a desire to undercut the power of the headmen, who were a mainstay of Rana rule. However, there was no bureaucracy or effective control of forests to replace the headmen, and this, together with population growth, led to rapid deforestation and degradation. The government did form a Forest Department, modeled after the Indian one, but it was much smaller and did not have the resources to exert actual control over forests. By the late 1980s, it had become clear that nationalization was a failure, and the government, influenced by foreign donors, opted for legislation to establish community forest management (Mahat, Griffin, and Shepherd 1986). This process began in the early 1990s and community forests now cover 29% of the forest area. Another 19% are under various kinds of community and state co-management, while perhaps another 30% are private forests (Rai et al. 2017). Thus, the only forests that are actually administered by the government are a few national parks and wildlife sanctuaries and remote forests in the mountains that are mostly inaccessible. In India, on the other hand, the vast majority of forests are administered and controlled by government bureaucracies, except in a few states. Although in both countries there was a shift in stated official policy toward decentralization at around the same time, implementation proceeded rapidly and comprehensively in Nepal, but made little progress in India. To a large extent, this is very likely because the existence of a powerful bureaucracy in India that was loath to relinquish control and rents (shared with state-level politicians) prevented decentralization, while its absence in Nepal facilitated it.

This discussion has been about forests. It should be noted that it does not generalize to fugitive resources like fisheries, wildlife, or groundwater. In those cases, it is much harder for local harvesters to discern the effect of their harvesting behavior on the stock, and this makes it much harder for them to self-regulate. While case studies of successful community management of forests are legion, success stories are notably absent in the case of fugitive resources. State regulation seems to be indispensable in these cases.

20.3. NATIONAL AND SUBNATIONAL ISSUES AND STATE INSTITUTIONS

Moving to slightly larger scales, even in small towns and cities, community-enforced norms of behavior are clearly insufficient for many environmental problems. The provision of clean water and sewage disposal are critical to avoid pollution by human waste leading to infectious disease. Yet these public goods are missing or very incomplete in most cities in low-income countries. This is the case with solid waste management and disposal as well. The provision of these public goods requires considerable physical investment in infrastructure, and this requires a state's power to tax. Accordingly, an understanding of these environmental problems is one of the principal issues of development economics—why public goods are underprovided in low-income countries.

Another set of issues that manifest themselves at municipal scales are those of air and water pollution and congestion. These issues span multiple scales, however, and especially for the pollution issues, the locus of regulatory action is often at a higher level, that of the provincial or national government.

A natural starting point to examine how state institutions shape environmental regulation, and the determinants of their performance, is to look at cross-national data on environmental regulation. Unfortunately, these data are very sparse. There appears to be only one cross-country dataset on the stringency of environmental regulation, and it is based on a single survey of governments conducted by the UN in 1990. Two different sets of researchers then coded the responses for some of the countries in the survey, so that an Environmental Policy Stringency index (EPS) is available for 54 countries (Pellegrini 2011). As we would expect, Pellegrini finds that the EPS is increasing in income and education measures. Surprisingly, though, it is decreasing in urbanization, at least when other controls are included. Obviously, these results must be interpreted with caution, given the non-random selection of countries and the likelihood of important omitted variables.

It is clear that a priority for future research is to collect much more comprehensive cross-country data on environmental regulation so that we may get at least a basic quantitative understanding of institutional performance in this domain. Such panel data would permit us to systematically examine the role of bureaucratic institutions, political factors, education, awareness, and other factors that influence the stringency of regulation.

In the absence of more data, we must turn to case studies.

I shall first take up the issue of the provision of clean water because it illustrates quite well some of the important themes and questions that appear for other environmental issues. It is obvious that the provision of a safe water supply is strongly increasing in per capita income, as seen in figure 20.1. This is unsurprising because we expect the demand for environmental quality and protection from health risks to be normal goods.

Figure 20.1 also shows that among poorer countries, there is considerable variation in the provision of water from "improved sources." It should be understood that this is not the same thing as provision of a water supply that is protected from fecal and other contamination. Clearly, there are other determinants of the supply of clean water.

Some of this may be demand-driven. Analyses of survey data from urban India show that, controlling for wealth and other demographics, the more educated and those more exposed to news media are willing to pay more to reduce their exposure to unsafe water, as measured by in-home water purification expenditures (Jalan, Somanathan, and Chaudhuri 2009). A randomized controlled trial that provided information to households in a suburb of Delhi about their water quality also revealed that households who learned that their water was potentially contaminated were willing to spend more to purify it (Jalan and Somanathan 2008).

Nevertheless, unlike per capita income, the level of awareness about environmental health risks is a factor that can be influenced by state institutions, even in the short run.

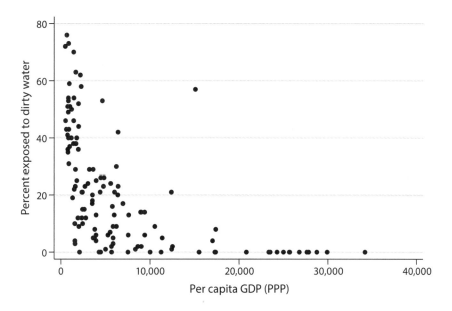

FIGURE 20.1. Percentage of population exposed to water from unimproved sources. *Data Source*: World Development Indicators.

The existence of regulatory institutions to control environmental pollution results in environmental monitoring. If the results are communicated to the public, this raises awareness of health risks. In this way, the supply of environmental quality can have a feedback effect on the demand. The creation of regulatory institutions can thus have an important effect on the provision of environmental quality in the long run, even after the initial stimulus for their creation has disappeared.

An example of such a positive feedback cycle in a different domain is the conservation of tigers in India. Initial efforts at tiger conservation began with the creation of Tiger Reserves in the early 1970s. These were triggered by the concerns of elite domestic and foreign conservationists that tigers were endangered. The prime minister was sympathetic and, being in a dominant political position, was able to pass a wildlife conservation act. Of course, the prime minister changed, and high-level political support for tiger conservation could well have gone with her. However, the tiger reserves soon became popular destinations for middle-class tourism, so much so that the extinction of tigers from a single reserve in the early 2000s triggered a media outcry that forced the government to create a Tiger Task Force that included critics of the government (Somanathan 2010).

Returning to water supply, a much better measure of safe water supply than that in the World Bank database is whether there is 24-hour provision of piped water (Kumpel and Nelson 2015). Continuous, as opposed to intermittent, water supply guarantees that pipes are pressurized, and, therefore, not subject to contamination from leaks. Second, when provision is intermittent, households and other establishments are obliged to store water on the premises. This water is very likely to be contaminated during storage and handling. A study of an intervention to provide 24-hour water to a few neighborhoods in Hubli, an Indian city in the state of Karnataka, found that nearly 32% of water samples were contaminated with *E. coli* in samples from areas with intermittent supply, while only 0.7% were contaminated in areas with continuous supply (Kumpel and Nelson 2013).

It may be thought that low-income countries would simply not have a demand for continuous piped water. The case of the Phnom Penh Water Supply Authority (PPWSA) provides a counterexample (Araral 2008; Biswas and Tortajada 2010). This was completely dysfunctional after the civil war ended in Cambodia and the capital was gradually repopulated in the 1980s. In the early 1990s, Cambodia had one of the highest infant mortality rates in the world. In 1992, the PPWSA had only five engineers. Most of the staff were not even capable of reading meters. Most of the city got no water even if it was connected to the piped system. In 1993, unaccounted for water exceeded 70%. According to Biswas and Tortajada (2010):

> Not only were the staff demoralized, but they had good reason to be demoralized, being, as they were, faced with poor governance, below subsistence pay, lack of discipline, an absence of any incentives, and pervasive corruption. Lethargy, poor working practices and a "could not care less" attitude to consumers were the norm. Therefore, the work culture had to be radically changed by enforcing strict disciplines in a sensitive, fair and transparent manner. This was a difficult task since the rest of the public sector employees in Cambodia were in a similar situation and behaved in a very similar manner. In fact, most public sector companies still continue to behave in a somewhat similar way at present.

In 1993, a study by Tokyo Engineering & Nihon Suido consultants was commissioned by the Japan International Cooperation Agency at the request of Cambodia. In consultation with the PPWSA they developed a Master Plan that became a blueprint for the building of the system. From 1993 to 2000, the authority performed pipe replacement and brought a drinkable water supply to the city center. Revenue for the necessary additional expenditures had to be raised somehow. An important source of such revenue was the reduction in leakage and the improvement in billing, as seen in the rapid decline in unaccounted-for-water in figure 20.2.

Improving the collection of existing tariffs was not, however, sufficient. "One of the most difficult components of this strategy to implement was to increase the tariff of water so that all costs could be recovered without generating any social and political unrest. This was done by ensuring that its customers first witnessed and appreciated a much better quality of reliable service before the tariffs were increased." The PPWSA got grants from the Japan International Cooperation Agency of $25 million in 1995 and $21 million in 1997. These were presumably crucial for improving service before raising tariffs. The PPWSA also received subsequent loans from the Asian Development Bank and the World Bank. The combination of improved collection and higher tariffs enabled the authority to cover its costs.

Before increasing tariffs, the authority conducted a survey of consumers to ascertain the various sources of water, what they paid for each, and whether they would be willing to pay more for water from the utility if service improved. The survey revealed, as is commonly the case in cities with an unreliable formal water supply, that consumers were paying private vendors far higher prices than the utility's existing tariff. Tariffs were raised in 1994, in 1997, and again in 2001.

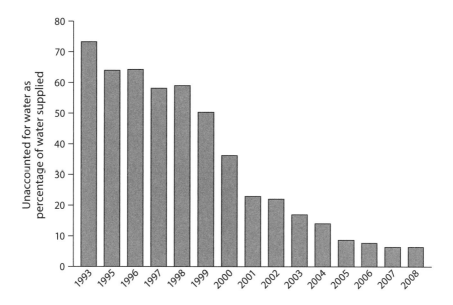

FIGURE 20.2. Unaccounted-for-water, Phnom Penh. *Source*: Biswas and Tortajada (2010) from records of the Phnom Penh Water Supply Authority.

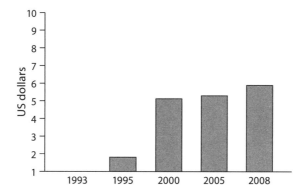

FIGURE 20.3. Average monthly household water bill. *Source*: Biswas and Tortajada (2010) from records of the Phnom Penh Water Supply Authority.

The Phnom Penh experience suggests that the absence of a potable and reliable water supply in many countries in Asia (McIntosh 2003) and Africa (Schwartz 2008) may be an institutional failure rather than simply a consequence of a low demand for high-quality service stemming from low incomes. If there are other successes in low-income countries, then the hypothesis that it is institutional failure, and not low income, per se, that is the cause of unsafe and unreliable water supplies would be strengthened. As seen in figure 20.4, there are, in fact, other examples of successful provision of 24-hour provision (McIntosh 2003, 2014).

Since the data are not a random sample of cities, nothing can be said about general relationships. But they do show that in addition to Phnom Penh (which appears twice),

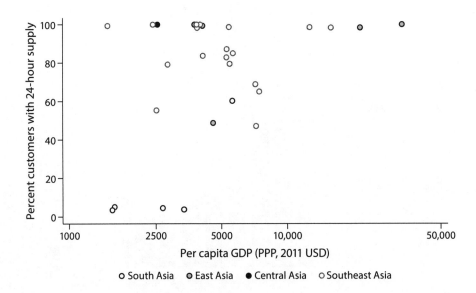

FIGURE 20.4. 24-hr water supply (% covered), Asian Cities, 2001 and 2007. *Source*: McIntosh (2003, 2014) for water supply. WDI databases of the World Bank for country GDP.

Tashkent, Chengdu, Shanghai, and three Vietnamese cities—Binh Duong, Hai Phong, and Ho Chi Minh City—all achieved complete 24-hour coverage in countries in which the per capita GDP was then below $5,000 (in 2011 PPP dollars). Near-complete coverage was also achieved in East Manila in 2007 when the Philippines had a per capita GDP of $5,200. Several Indonesian and Philippine cities achieved incomplete coverage, while all South Asian cities with the exception of Colombo had near-zero coverage. Even today, no Indian city has achieved a 24-hour water supply for a significant fraction of customers even though India's per capita GDP now exceeds $5,400.

As discussed above, part of the explanation for the failures in South Asia and Africa may be a lack of demand for high-quality supplies stemming from low education levels and awareness of health risks.

However, this is unlikely to be the whole explanation. When water supplies are intermittent, households incur considerable costs to cope with the resulting situation. These include purchasing water from private vendors, storing and pumping water, and in-home purification to cope with the health risks. A study in Kathmandu found that these costs were, on average, twice the water bill paid to the utility, while a contingent valuation exercise found the willingness to pay for reliable water to be still higher (Pattanayak et al. 2005).

Finally, another reason for under-provision of a safe water supply could be that it is blocked by politically powerful interests. It is useful to make a distinction between this political-economy explanation and one based on institutional or government failure. If institutional failure is the primary cause, a better understanding of policies that might help in getting out of a low-level equilibrium trap is important. If it is vested interests, then examining institutions will not be of any practical importance until the politics changes. Urban water supply is an issue that does not involve polluters who will lose from government action, so that the political economy explanations are likely to be less important. To be sure, this too, cannot be said with certainty since the private provision of water supply by tankers has become a sizeable business in some cities, and it may be that action to improve the public supply is blocked by these interests.

Nevertheless, the Phnom Penh case study does suggest the presence of a low-level equilibrium trap in many low-income cities—citizens are not willing to pay the higher tariffs needed to finance improvements because their experience does not inspire confidence that the increased payments will deliver improvements. This suggests a possible way out—the utility could improve the water supply in small geographic areas, then raise tariffs in these areas, and then expand the geographic scope of the process.

Whether there is a low-level equilibrium trap is an important question for research. More systematic studies of how much more consumers are willing to pay for better service are needed. There are valuation studies that measure coping costs and/or stated preference methods that address this question (such as the one by Pattanayak et al. 2005 mentioned above). A greater use of hedonic studies may also be helpful. A hedonic study in Bhutan that uses data from two rounds of the Bhutan Living Standards Survey finds that houses that are connected to piped water supply and sewage systems pay a substantial rental premium over those that are not, controlling for other measured characteristics including locality fixed effects (Dendup and Tshering 2018). Since households can be expected to sort themselves into connected and unconnected houses according to their willingness to pay for services, the existence of a positive rental premium implies that there is scope to raise tariffs and use the revenue to expand coverage. What is needed is more such studies that address the issue of service quality, rather than simply measuring whether households are connected to the system.

The case study shows that while finances and physical investment are an important part of the story, an equally important part is the change in work culture and incentives within the utility that are tied up with service quality. An important aspect of the story is that the government published a decree in 1996 that corporatized the PPWSA and gave it autonomy along with a structure of checks and balances (Biswas and Tortajada 2010; McIntosh 2014). Such institutional changes may have long-lasting effects because they change the locus of decision-making. Taking action, an energy- and time-consuming process for high-level administrators, is delegated to those who specialize in the particular issues.

Water supply is just an example of many environmental and development issues where such a low-level equilibrium trap may exist. Household air pollution is one of the most serious environmental issues in developing countries due to the use of solid fuels for cooking. It is listed as being the fourth-largest risk factor in the global burden of disease and the single largest risk factor in the disease burden in South Asia (Lim et al. 2012). One of the important routes to reducing it is to substitute electricity for solid fuels, but this requires a reliable electricity supply. In many low-income countries, a low-quality supply is a strong deterrent to the adoption of electricity for cooking, despite the appearance of inexpensive electric induction stoves and cookers of various kinds in developing countries in the last few years. Subsidized electric power leads to frequent blackouts, which in turn reduce the willingness to pay the higher tariffs needed to finance more reliable supplies.

Traffic congestion is a problem worldwide and is especially acute in the cities of developing countries with inadequate public transport, poor roads, and poor traffic management. Yet reducing it requires congestion charges that the public is unwilling to pay given the poor quality of transport infrastructure.

These sorts of problems are related to an inability to finance services of a reasonable quality, but, as noted earlier, they are not solely a financial issue; rather they are intimately related to the quality of institutions. Subsidized electric power, for example, may be accompanied by un-metered but rationed electricity provided to specific sectors like agriculture. Non-commercial allocation leads to a culture of theft and rent-seeking, while chronically loss-making public-sector utilities are unable to maintain staff morale and human capital. Blackouts that begin for financial reasons may persist due to a lack of qualified personnel (Ruet 2005). Similar considerations apply to traffic management and public transport.

When it comes to the regulation of industrial pollutants, it is clear that public awareness is essential to stimulate the formation of regulatory institutions that are capable of regulation. Historically, such formation has often begun with dramatic incidents, such as the presence of deformed animals highlighted in the bestselling book *Silent Spring* (Carson 1962) that stimulated pollution legislation in the developed world. Background pollution levels, even though they may be high, are often invisible to the public. Once the institutions were created and financed, monitoring became a part of their role. To the extent that the results of monitoring were communicated to the public, this increased awareness and maintained a public demand for continued environmental improvements.

While a similar dynamic has been seen in developing countries, lower levels of education and income lead to lower public demand. There may also be less accountability as suggested by Pellegrini's results reported earlier. Where the functioning of regulatory institutions is less transparent, the monitoring they do may not be publicly available, thus cutting one of the links in the virtuous cycle. Thus, for these issues, the availability of information and the extent to which it results in regulatory responses is an important area for research.

Distributional issues are also likely to be important in determining which environmental problems are addressed. For example, it may be the case that water pollution is not addressed as much as air pollution because the rich can protect themselves from water pollution with home water purification but are much less able to avoid air pollution. This needs to be researched.

20.4. GLOBAL ENVIRONMENTAL ISSUES AND INTERNATIONAL INSTITUTIONS

Finally, there are the international environmental issues that affect economic development. Climate change is, of course, the most prominent, but there are others that are pertinent for development, especially in some countries—ocean fisheries, for example. There is an enormous game-theoretic literature that seeks to understand the provision of treaties—these are the principal institution in the international context—to solve the common-pool problem.

The main approach has been to assume that country governments in these negotiations attempt to maximize national welfare. Here, country welfare is defined as the total benefit to a country from abatement of emissions of greenhouse gases and other climate forcers minus the total costs of abatement to that country. Most of the literature adopts the approach initiated by Carraro and Siniscalco (1993) and Barrett (1994). The analysis falls into the area known as the non-cooperative foundations of cooperative game theory. It is assumed that countries will adhere to a treaty once signed, but will sign only those treaties that leave them better off than not signing. The papers then characterize the set of treaties and associated pollution and welfare outcomes that may obtain under these assumptions (Carraro and Siniscalco 1993; Scott Barrett 1994). In the case of climate change, the results are generally pessimistic—the only feasible treaties are those that require the signatories to do very little, or those with very few signatories. In either case, little is accomplished.

This, however, is not the case with the problem of halting the damage to the ozone layer in the stratosphere arising from ozone-depleting chemicals such as halo-carbons. There are important differences between the two cases, and it has been argued that this is why the outcomes of negotiations predicted by the theory are different. In his book, *Environment and Statecraft*, Scott Barrett argues that the differences in actual outcomes align with the differences predicted by the theory (Barrett 2005). In the 1980s, when the Montreal Protocol was being negotiated, a single country, the United States, accounted for about 50% of the production and consumption of chloro-fluoro-carbons or CFCs, the largest category of ozone-depleting chemicals. In contrast, when the Kyoto Protocol was being negotiated in the late 1990s, the largest greenhouse gas emitter, at that time, the United States, accounted for only about 20% of global emissions.

The damage from a thinned ozone layer manifested itself directly in an increased rate of skin cancers, so that it was straightforward to calculate the damages in terms of increased death rates within the United States. Using an official estimate of the value of a statistical life, this was converted into a dollar figure that was two orders of magnitude higher than the abatement cost to the United States (Barrett 2005). This was an official estimate by the US Environmental Protection Agency. Thus, for the United States, and in all probability, for most industrial countries, the benefits from even a unilateral rapid phase-out of CFCs exceeded the costs by a wide margin. There was, however, no consensus on the economic damages from global warming and climate change. Even the global benefits of abatement, while positive, were small and did not justify significant abatement, according to the most widely cited author from the 1990s (Nordhaus and Boyer 2000). The social cost of carbon estimated by Nordhaus was less than $10/tCO2. Other authors concluded the opposite with a social cost of carbon being hundreds of dollars per ton of carbon dioxide (Cline 1992). However, Nordhaus got most of the attention.

High net benefits and asymmetrically situated countries are both predicted to be favorable conditions for an effective treaty—one that achieves substantial global abatement. Asymmetry helps because it reduces the number of participants needed for effective global action. The Montreal Protocol achieved near universal participation and near complete abatement. But in the case of climate change, where there was much less asymmetry, it was not so clear that the benefits of abatement exceeded the costs. The agreement that was negotiated at the end of the 1990s, the Kyoto Protocol, targeted only 5% of global emissions. It is for these reasons that Barrett concludes that the theory has some explanatory power.

Nevertheless, as we shall now see, the model of states as unitary decision-makers maximizing a national social welfare function is only of limited help in understanding the progress of climate negotiations, or of other issues like the depletion of ocean fisheries.

A better understanding of international environmental agreements will have to consider how within-country politics affects environmental issues with international dimensions.

Before coming to climate change, let us first re-consider the Montreal Protocol of 1987 that restricted the production of ozone-depleting substances. In the mid-1970s, shortly after the prediction by chemists that CFCs would damage the ozone layer, the United States unilaterally restricted the production and sale of CFCs in aerosol cans. This reduced the profitability of investments in CFCs for US firms and made it attractive to conduct R&D to find substitutes. In 1975, Dupont Chemicals, the market leader in the United States, had strongly argued against restricting CFCs, claiming that the costs of doing so would be huge. After this lobbying failed to prevent action, and the market for CFCs shrank, Dupont discovered inexpensive substitutes that it could profit from selling. It then reversed its previous stance and urged the US government to negotiate an effective agreement. This enabled US leadership in the negotiations with industry support (DeSombre 2000). It is clear that a proper understanding of why the Montreal Protocol was successful therefore requires an understanding of US domestic regulation and lobbying.

With regard to climate change, there are large un-internalized externalities from fossil fuel combustion in the form of local air pollution. For example, in the United States, despite air pollution regulation, excess deaths caused by air pollution from coal-fired power plants are still at a high level. When these deaths were valued at the official value of a statistical life, it was found that the external cost of the plants *exceeded* their value-added (Muller, Mendelsohn, and Nordhaus 2011). The US government's estimates of domestic health damages from US emissions are more than three times its estimates of the global climate-related damages from the emissions (EPA 2014, table ES-7).

This situation is not confined to the United States. An IMF study asked what the optimal carbon price would be for each of the 20 highest emitters of energy-related greenhouse gases if they acted to internalize remaining *local* air pollution and road congestion externalities by taxing carbon dioxide emissions. That is, the price-setting would ignore the climate externality. It found that the emission-weighted average locally optimal carbon price was $58/ton of CO_2 (Parry, Veung, and Heine 2015). The current official US Environmental Protection Agency estimate of the optimal carbon price based on global climate damages is much lower: it is $36/tCO2. There was also considerable variation in nationally efficient carbon prices—$63/tCO2 in China, $36/tCO2 in the United States, $93/tCO2 in Poland, and in the hundreds for Saudi Arabia and Iran. Only Brazil had a negative price of –23$/tCO2, due to high petroleum taxation and a power sector that did not rely on coal.

If governments were acting to maximize national welfare as conventionally defined, then countries would not have such high un-internalized externalities. Greenhouse gas emissions would be considerably lower. For example, the US Energy Information Administration projected that if a carbon price of $30/tCO2 had been imposed in 2013, then greenhouse gas emissions from the US electric power sector would have declined by 40% within four years (Energy Information Administration 2013).[1] Renewable technologies would have been deployed far more, creating new lobbies that would affect domestic policies and international agreements. The research agenda, therefore, has to incorporate a more sophisticated model of the interaction of domestic and international players in framing climate policies, as well as policies on other international environmental issues. It is necessary to model a two-level game—between domestic actors within countries with divergent interests regarding emissions and the effect that this has on negotiating strategies.

20.5. DISCUSSION

We have seen that there are a number of issues that need further research—for example—what drives devolution, the measurement of environmental regulation and performance, the role of awareness in the demand for environmental regulation, and incorporating domestic politics in the modeling of international negotiations. There are a few general points that should be added to this.

First, the case studies described here suggest that there is a strong institutional inertia. Institutions are not easily established, and once they are, they often persist and have long-run effects, although, of course, they also evolve and change. This suggests that more research is needed on the formation of regulatory institutions. Second, there is an aspect of devolution that may be very important but has not been discussed. This is that the devolution of power to local authorities may lead to more *experimentation*—in the presence of suitable incentives to local authorities. The case of Chinese economic reforms is perhaps the most well-known example of this phenomenon, but it has also been seen with regard to joint forest management in India, for example. However, environmental performance does not appear to have benefited from decentralized governance in China. This is due to the nature of incentives provided to local officials by the central government.

The lack of real devolution of power to local authorities in South Asia may also be responsible for the remarkably uniform record of failure to provide municipal public services like reliable piped water. This may, in turn, be related to the nature of hierarchies in South Asian governments inherited from British colonial rule—power flows through line departments so that there is no local government head with substantial authority.

NOTE

1. This would be driven largely by older coal plants being shut down and replaced by gas and renewables instead of being upgraded to comply with new pollution regulations.

REFERENCES

Adhikari, Bhim. 2005. "Poverty, Property Rights and Collective Action: Understanding the Distributive Aspects of Common Property Resource Management." *Environment and Development Economics* 10(01): 7–31.

Araral, Eduardo. 2008. "Public Provision for Urban Water: Getting Prices and Governance Right." *Governance: An International Journal of Policy, Administration, and Institutions* 21(4): 527–549.

Arzaghi, Mohammad, and J. Vernon Henderson. 2005. "Why Countries Are Fiscally Decentralizing." *Journal of Public Economics* 89(7): 1157–1189.

Baland, Jean-Marie, and Jean-Philippe Platteau. 1996. *Halting Degradation of Natural Resources: Is There a Role for Rural Communities?* Oxford: FAO and Oxford University Press.

Barrett, S. 2005. *Environment and Statecraft: The Strategy of Environmental Treaty-Making*. New York: Oxford University Press.

Barrett, Scott. 1994. "Self-Enforcing International Environmental Agreements." *Oxford Economic Papers*, 878–894.

Biswas, Asit K., and Cecilia Tortajada. 2010. "Water Supply of Phnom Penh: An Example of Good Governance." *Water Resources Development* 26(2): 157–172.

Bowler, Diana E., Lisette M. Buyung-Ali, John R. Healey, Julia PG Jones, Teri M. Knight, and Andrew S. Pullin. 2011. "Does Community Forest Management Provide Global Environmental Benefits and Improve Local Welfare?" *Frontiers in Ecology and the Environment* 10(1): 29–36.

Carraro, Carlo, and Domenico Siniscalco. 1993. "Strategies for the International Protection of the Environment." *Journal of Public Economics* 52(3): 309–328.

Carson, Rachel. 1962. *Silent Spring*. Boston: Houghton Mifflin.

Cline, William R. 1992. *The Economics of Global Warming*. Washington, DC: Institute for International Economics.

Dasgupta, P. S., and G. M. Heal. 1979. *Economic Theory and Exhaustible Resources*. Cambridge: Cambridge University Press. Available online at https://ideas.repec.org/b/cup/cbooks/9780521297615.html.

Datta, Ashokankur. 2011. "Essays in the Economics of Environmental Policy." Unpublished PhD thesis, Indian Statistical Institute.

DeSombre, Elizabeth R. 2000. "The Experience of the Montreal Protocol: Particularly Remarkable, and Remarkably Particular." *UCLA Journal of Environmental Law and Policy* 19(1): 49–81.

Dendup, Ngawang, and Kuenzang Tshering. "Demand for Piped Drinking Water and a Formal Sewer System in Bhutan." *Environmental Economics and Policy Studies* 20.3 (2018): 681–703.

Energy Information Administration. 2013. "Further Sensitivity Analysis of Hypothetical Policies to Limit Energy-Related Carbon Dioxide Emissions." https://www.eia.gov/forecasts/aeo/supplement /co2/.

EPA. 2014. *Regulatory Impact Analysis for the Proposed Carbon Pollution Guidelines for Existing Power Plants and Emission Standards for Modified and Reconstructed Power Plants*. June.

Gordon, H. Scott. 1954. "The Economic Theory of a Common-Property Resource: The Fishery." *Journal of Political Economy* 62(2): 124–142.

Jalan, Jyotsna, and E. Somanathan. 2008. "The Importance of Being Informed: Experimental Evidence on Demand for Environmental Quality." *Journal of Development Economics* 87(1): 14–28.

Jalan, Jyotsna, E. Somanathan, and Saraswata Chaudhuri. 2009. "Awareness and the Demand for Environmental Quality: Survey Evidence on Drinking Water in Urban India." *Environment and Development Economics* 14(06): 665–92. doi:10.1017/S1355770X08005020.

Jodha, Narpat S. 1986. "Common Property Resources and Rural Poor in Dry Regions of India." *Economic and Political Weekly*, 1169–1181.

Kanel, Keshav Raj. 2008. "So Far So Good: Next Steps in Community Forestry." In *Promise, Trust, and Evolution: Managing the Commons of South Asia*. Oxford: Oxford University Press.

Kumpel, Emily, and Kara L. Nelson. 2013. "Comparing Microbial Water Quality in an Intermittent and Continuous Piped Water Supply." *Water Research* 47(14): 5176–5188.

———. 2015. "Intermittent Water Supply: Prevalence, Practice, and Microbial Water Quality." *Environmental Science & Technology*. Available online at http://pubs.acs.org/doi/abs/10.1021/acs.est .5b03973.

Larson, Anne M., Ganga Ram Dahal, and others. 2012. "Forest Tenure Reform: New Resource Rights for Forest-Based Communities?" *Conservation and Society* 10(2): 77.

Lim, Stephen S., Theo Vos, Abraham D. Flaxman, Goodarz Danaei, Kenji Shibuya, Heather Adair-Rohani, Mohammad A. AlMazroa, et al. 2012. "A Comparative Risk Assessment of Burden of Disease and Injury Attributable to 67 Risk Factors and Risk Factor Clusters in 21 Regions, 1990–2010: A Systematic Analysis for the Global Burden of Disease Study 2010." *Lancet* 380 (9859): 2224–2260. doi:10.1016/S0140–6736(12)61766–8.

Mahat, Tej Bahadur Singh, David M. Griffin, and K. R. Shepherd. 1986. "Human Impact on Some Forests of the Middle Hills of Nepal 1. Forestry in the Context of the Traditional Resources of the State." *Mountain Research and Development*, 223–232.

McIntosh, Arthur C. 2003. "Asian Water Supplies Reaching the Urban Poor." Available online at https://openaccess.adb.org/handle/11540/264.

———. 2014. "Urban Water Supply and Sanitation in Southeast Asia: A Guide to Good Practice." https://openaccess.adb.org/handle/11540/2501.

Muller, Nicholas Z., Robert Mendelsohn, and William Nordhaus. 2011. "Environmental Accounting for Pollution in the United States Economy." *American Economic Review* 101(5): 1649–1675.

Nordhaus, W. D., and J Boyer. 2000. *Warming the World: Economic Models of Global Warming*. Cambridge, MA: MIT Press.

Ostrom, Elinor. 1990. *Governing the Commons: The Evolution of Institutions for Collective Action*. Cambridge: Cambridge University Press.

Parry, Ian, Chandara Veung, and Dirk Heine. 2015. "How Much Carbon Pricing Is in Countries' Own Interests? The Critical Role of Co-Benefits." *Climate Change Economics* 6(04): 1550019.

Pattanayak, Subhrendu K., Jui-Chen Yang, Dale Whittington, and K. C. Bal Kumar. 2005. "Coping with Unreliable Public Water Supplies: Averting Expenditures by Households in Kathmandu, Nepal." *Water Resources Research* 41(2). Available online at http://onlinelibrary.wiley.com/doi/10.1029/2003WR002443/full.

Pellegrini, Lorenzo. 2011. *Corruption, Development, and the Environment.* Dordrecht, Heidelberg, London, New York: Springer.

Rai, R. K., M. Nepal, B. S. Karky, E. Somanathan, N. Timalsina, M. S. Khadayat, and N. Bhattarai. 2017. "Costs and Benefits of Reducing Deforestation and Forest Degradation in Nepal." *ICIMOD Working Paper* 2017/5.

Ruet, Joel. 2005. *Privatising Power Cuts? Ownership and Reform of State Electricity Boards in India.* New Delhi: Academic Foundation.

Schwartz, Klaas. 2008. "The New Public Management: The Future for Reforms in the African Water Supply and Sanitation Sector?" *Utilities Policy* 16(1): 49–58.

Sethi, Rajiv, and E. Somanathan. 1996. "The Evolution of Social Norms in Common Property Resource Use." *American Economic Review* 86: 766–788.

———. 2006. "A Simple Model of Collective Action." *Economic Development and Cultural Change* 54: 725–747.

Somanathan, E. 1991. "Deforestation, Property Rights and Incentives in Central Himalaya." *Economic and Political Weekly* 26(4): PE37–46.

———. 2010. "Effects of Information on Environmental Quality in Developing Countries." *Review of Environmental Economics and Policy* 4(2): 275–292.

Somanathan, E., R. Prabhakar, and B. S. Mehta. 2009. "Decentralization for Cost-Effective Conservation." *Proceedings of the National Academy of Sciences* 106(11): 4143–4147.

Xu, J. T. 2010. "Collective Forest Tenure Reform in China: What Has Been Achieved So Far." In *World Bank Conference on Land Governance.* Washington, DC: World Bank. Available online at http://policydialogue.org/files/events/XuJintao_collective_forest_tenure_reform_china.pdf.

Yin, Runsheng, Shunbo Yao, and Xuexi Huo. 2013. "China's Forest Tenure Reform and Institutional Change in the New Century: What Has Been Implemented and What Remains to Be Pursued?" *Land Use Policy* 30(1): 825–833.

INDEX

Page numbers in *italics* refer to figures.